ANNUAL REVIEW OF PSYCHOLOGY

VOLUME 55, 2004

SUSAN T. FISKE, *Editor*
Princeton University

DANIEL L. SCHACTER, *Associate Editor*
Harvard University

CAROLYN ZAHN-WAXLER, *Associate Editor*
National Institute of Mental Health

www.annualreviews.org   science@annualreviews.org   650-493-4400

ANNUAL REVIEWS
4139 El Camino Way • P.O. Box 10139 • Palo Alto, California 94303-0139

ANNUAL REVIEWS
Palo Alto, California, USA

International Standard Serial Number: 0066-4308
International Standard Book Number: 0-8243-0255-9
Library of Congress Catalog Card Number: 50-13143

TYPESET BY TECHBOOKS, FAIRFAX, VA
PRINTED AND BOUND BY MALLOY INCORPORATED, ANN ARBOR, MI

PREFACE

If you are reading this preface, you are probably holding the book, and not a mouse, in your hand. But you could be holding a mouse. Having accessed the Annual Reviews home page, http://www.AnnualReviews.org, and selected the Psychology series, you would be one step closer to this preface. Of course, we don't really expect people to search the Web for this preface. Far more interesting opportunities await your cursor on our Web site. Let us mention three, and close with yet a fourth, digital advances, all part of launching the *Annual Review of Psychology* into the twenty-first century and making it easier for you to keep up with the field's latest trends.

Annual Reviews chapters are now available soon after they are accepted for publication as Reviews in Advance on our Web site. Simply go to the series home page (http://psych.annualreviews.org) and click on the RIA link. As the Web site notes, these are "full-length reviews published online immediately after full editing and revision... The date of each chapter's online release is posted on our Web site and is the official date of publication. Reviews can thus appear online up to 7 months before they appear in print." This means that neither authors nor readers need wait for the rest of the volume to be assembled, printed, and shipped.

To keep you still closer to actual release dates, by registering on the Annual Reviews Web site, you can request email notification for the *Annual Review of Psychology*. This allows you to create a favorites list down to the article level and to customize email alerts to receive specific notifications about topics you are tracking.

What's more, the Annual Reviews search engine is fast, convenient, and efficient. Entering search terms allows subscribers to search the full text of all articles in all 55 back volumes of *Annual Review of Psychology*, or even *all* back volumes of *all* series (be careful what you wish for). It is easy to refine your search at any stage. Plus, you can enter those criteria into your email notification profile, to search onward into the future. If you want, you can also see the 20 most downloaded and 20 most highly cited *Annual Review of Psychology* chapters, to see what everyone else is reading.

Finally, each print volume now has the possibility of digital add-ons, either color plates (e.g., neuroimaging) or Web site posting of dynamic images. For example, readers of this bound volume are referred to the Supplemental Materials links in several places in the Derrington, Allen, and Delicato chapter on visual analysis and motion detection. This supplemental material consists of animated graphics and illustrations. The graphics that will be bound in the print volume for this chapter are not trivial; they consist of one color figure and four grayscale figures, but the supplemental materials expand our flexibility. Altogether, we've made the *Annual Review of Psychology* far more than the paper resource it used to be. Come explore, by clicking as well as by flipping.

Susan T. Fiske, Princeton
Daniel L. Schacter, Cambridge
Carolyn Zahn-Waxler, Madison

Annual Review of Psychology
Volume 55, 2004

CONTENTS

Errata

An online log of corrections to *Annual Review of Psychology* chapters
may be found at http://psych.annualreviews.org/errata.shtml

RELATED ARTICLES

From the *Annual Review of Public Health*, Volume 24, 2003

Classification of Race and Ethnicity: Implications for Public Health,
Vickie M. Mays, Ninez A. Ponce, Donna L. Washington, and Susan D. Cochran

Will a Healthy Lifestyle Help Prevent Alzheimer's Disease?, Sandra K. Pope,
Valorie M. Shue, and Cornelia Beck

Violence Prevention and Control Through Environmental Modifications,
Julie Samia Mair and Michael Mair

*Methodologic Advances and Ongoing Challenges in Designing
Community-Based Health Promotion Programs*, Beti Thompson,
Gloria Coronado, Shedra A. Snipes, and Klaus Puschel

*Supporting Informed Consumer Health Care Decisions: Data Presentation
Approaches that Facilitate the Use of Information in Choice*,
Judith H. Hibbard and Ellen Peters

From the *Annual Review of Sociology*, Volume 29, 2003

Beyond Rational Choice Theory, Raymond Boudon

Teenage Childbearing as a Public Issue and Private Concern,
Frank F. Furstenberg Jr.

The Urban Street Gang After 1970, Brenda C. Coughlin and
Sudhir Alladi Venkatesh

The Science of Asking Questions, Nora Cate Schaeffer and Stanley Presser

Transitions from Prison to Community: Understanding Individual Pathways,
Christy A. Visher and Jeremy Travis

The Sociology of the Self, Peter L. Callero

Skills Mismatch in the Labor Market, Michael J. Handel

The Dynamics of Racial Residential Segregation, Camille Zubrinsky Charles

The African American "Great Migration" and Beyond, Stewart E. Tolnay

The Potential Relevances of Biology to Social Inquiry, Jeremy Freese,
Jui-Chung Allen Li, and Lisa D. Wade

Relationships in Adolescence, Peggy C. Giordano

Day Labor Work, Abel Valenzuela, Jr.

*Still "Not Quite as Good as Having Your Own"? Toward a Sociology
of Adoption*, Allen P. Fisher

The Lopsided Continent: Inequality in Latin America, Kelly Hoffman and
Miguel Angel Centeno

Covert Political Conflict in Organizations: Challenges from Below,
Calvin Morrill, Mayer N. Zald, and Hayagreeva Rao

Walter Mischel

Annu. Rev. Psychol. 2004. 55:1–22
doi: 10.1146/annurev.psych.55.042902.130709
Copyright © 2004 by Annual Reviews. All rights reserved
First published online as a Review in Advance on November 10, 2003

Toward an Integrative Science of the Person

Walter Mischel

*Department of Psychology, Columbia University, New York, New York 10027;
email: wm@psych.columbia.edu*

Key Words   personality, social cognitive theory, personality processes, personality
dynamics, role of situation, personality paradox, personality signatures

■ **Abstract**   To build a science of the person, the most basic question was, and
remains, how can one identify and understand the psychological invariance that distinctively characterizes an individual and that underlies the variations in the thoughts,
feelings, and actions that occur across contexts and over time? This question proved
particularly difficult because of the discrepancies that soon emerged between the expressions of consistency that were expected and those that were found. The resulting
dilemma became known as the classic "personality paradox": How can we reconcile
our intuitions—and theories—about the invariance and stability of personality with
the equally compelling empirical evidence for the variability of the person's behavior
across diverse situations? Which is right: the intuitions or the research findings? In this
chapter I review and discuss some of the advances made to answer this question since
it was posed. These findings have allowed a resolution of the paradox, and provide the
outlines for a conception of the underlying structure and dynamics of personality that
seems to better account for the data.

CONTENTS

0066-4308/04/0204-0001$14.00   **1**

INTRODUCTION

In this essay, I discuss advances made in the long search to identify and understand the invariance that characterizes personality, focusing on the consistencies that are being found in unexpected places that violate earlier assumptions that previously had guided the field. The consistencies are seen in the stable patterns of cross-situational variability, rather than constancy, which characterize the individual when behavior is examined in relation to the situations in which it occurs. These distinctive patterns of person-situation interactions, in turn, hint at the organization of the underlying system that generates them. I consider the outlines of that system, its implications for the conceptualization of personality structure, processing dynamics, and assessment, and the role of the situation in the organization and expressions of personality. This effort draws on findings on mind, brain, and behavior coming from advances in the larger science that are still waiting to be integrated into the theory and assessment of the individual as an organized, dynamic, agentic system functioning in the social world—an often-forgotten aim that motivated the study of personality in the first place.

FINDING THE INVARIANCE—IN THE VARIABILITY

My entry into the search for the basic coherence of personality began four decades ago when I reviewed the state of the field at that time in the 1968 monograph, *Personality and Assessment* (Mischel 1968). The conclusions to which it led were upsetting because I proposed that for many years researchers had been looking in the wrong places, guided by untenable assumptions, and therefore could not find the expected results.

Beginning with Hartshorne & May's (1928) studies of conscientiousness in schoolchildren, research had been driven by the assumption that the invariance of personality would be reflected in the stable rank-ordering of individuals in their behavior on any given dimension (e.g., conscientiousness, sociability, dependency), assessed with the cross-situational consistency coefficient. The assumption was rooted in a conceptualization of individual differences in social behaviors as direct reflections of behavioral dispositions, or traits. Dispositions and their behavioral expressions were assumed by definition to correspond directly, so that the more a person has a trait of conscientiousness, for example, the more conscientious the person's behavior was expected to be over many different kinds of situations, relative to other people. Given that assumption, the persistent findings that the individual's behavior and rank order position on virtually any psychological dimension tends to vary considerably across diverse situations, typically yielding low correlations, distressed the field and changed its agenda for years.

To illustrate, in one landmark attempt, Theodore Newcomb (1929) studied extraversion-introversion in 51 boys in 21 situations in a summer camp. He laboriously collected daily records of distinctly remembered incidents such as "How much of the time did he talk at table?" "What percent of the time did he work or play alone?" Newcomb was shocked to find that the average correlation coefficient based on daily behavior records across the situations was about 0.14. The results yielded a normal distribution with the modal point at zero—and ultimately led him to switch his career to become a social psychologist studying the culture of Bennington College.

For the next 50 or more years many other researchers followed in Newcomb's tracks, only to find similar results, creating a crisis in the paradigm (e.g., D. Fiske unpublished manuscript; Krahe 1990; Magnusson & Endler 1977; Mischel 1968, 1973; Mischel & Peake 1982; Moskowitz 1982, 1994; Nisbett & Ross 1980; Peterson 1968; Ross & Nisbett 1991; Vernon 1964). The finding that the same individual will show substantial variation as the situations vary has become a widely accepted truism—and to researchers who closely track any aspect of a person's experience, such as the salience of particular types of thoughts, feelings, and actions across diverse situations and over time, perhaps it should never have been surprising in the first place. Still controversial, however, and fundamental for the conception of personality, is how such data on the variability of behavior across contexts should be interpreted. Here researchers face two alternatives that lead in very different directions, and these two paths continue to be pursued and still define much of the research agenda in the field.

Eliminating Context by Aggregation Across Situations

One interpretation of the data was that they reflect the noise and error of measurement, and that was the most widely accepted response to the 1968 monograph (Mischel 1968). It acknowledges the importance of situations and the low correlations in the individual's behavior found from situation to situation (Epstein 1979). It is then customary to aggregate the individual's behavior on a given dimension (e.g., "conscientiousness," "sociability") over many different situations to estimate an overall "true score" (as discussed in Epstein 1979, 1980; Mischel & Peake 1982; Pervin 1994). These correlations document that people differ significantly on virtually any dimension, showing stable overall individual differences: on the whole, some people are more sociable than others, some are more open-minded, some are more punctual, and so on. Such aggregate information is useful for many goals, and its strengths as well as its limits have been extensively described elsewhere (e.g., Mischel & Shoda 1998, Mischel et al. 2004).

Removing the situation by aggregation follows directly from the core assumption that guided the predominant theoretical view of personality in psychology. In that classic view, the basic qualities of the person are assumed to be independent of, and unconnected with, situations: Causal powers then are attributed either to one or to the other. Given that assumption, to find the stable basic characteristics of the person requires taking out the variability introduced by different situations, rather than focusing on it. From that perspective, a personality psychologist who took seriously the variability of the person's behavior across situations, and argued for the need to incorporate the situation into the conception and assessment of invariance, was easily seen as trying to bury personality as a field and construct. And that is how *Personality and Assessment* (Mischel 1968) was often read: Most personality psychologists saw it as an assault to undo the field, trivializing "the power of the person" and the importance of personality, and inflating the significance of the situation as an influence on personality.

This zero-sum conception of the relationship between personality and situation, in which to the degree that the person was important in causal explanations of behavior, the situation was not, and vice versa, led to the "person versus situation" debate. It fueled a period of prolonged controversy throughout the 1970s and early 1980s, with heated but futile battles about which one accounts for the bigger variance. For many years these turf wars widened the split between subdisciplines, narrowly defined, in which personality psychologists continued to look for consistencies in the situation-free person while social psychology became devoted to demonstrating the power of the situation (Nisbett & Ross 1980, Ross & Nisbett 1991). In my view, advocates on either side of the person versus situation debate missed the point, not unlike the equally futile nature versus nurture dichotomy that for so long also obscured the need for fine-grained analyses of interactions rather than battles between reified unidirectional causal entities. In time, the need to consider both person and situation was recognized. However, systematic attention remained deflected from studying their interactions within which the understanding of both might be illuminated, with some notable exceptions (e.g., Fleeson 2001; Magnusson & Endler 1977; Moskowitz 1982, 1994; Vansteelandt & Van Mechelen 1998).

Incorporating the Situation into the Search for Coherence

The alternative view of the variability of behavior and the aggregation route began with the conviction that the search for the invariance of personality needed to also incorporate findings from the cognitive revolution which already 30 years ago had begun to transform the understanding of how the human minds works. With that goal, in 1973 I proposed a set of social cognitive person variables that, rather than drawing on trait terms from the lexicon, were based on psychological constructs important in basic social, cognitive, and motivational processes (Mischel 1973). These include how the person construes (encodes, appraises) situations (including people and the self) and the beliefs, expectancies, goals, and self-regulatory competencies that became activated within the individual in the continuous stream of interactions with situations.

This approach outlined the underlying psychological processes that might lead people to interpret the meanings of situations in their characteristic ways, and that could link their resulting specific, distinctive patterns of behavior to particular types of conditions and situations in potentially predictable ways. The focus thus shifted away from broad situation-free trait descriptors with adjectives (e.g., conscientious, sociable) to more situation-qualified characterizations of persons in contexts, making dispositions situationally hedged, conditional, and interactive with the situations in which they were expressed. A main message was then—as it still is 30 years later—that the term "personality psychology" need not be preempted for the study of differences between individuals in their global trait descriptions on trait adjective ratings; it fits equally well for the study of the distinctiveness and stability that characterize the individual's social cognitive and emotional processes as they play out in the social world.

In this social cognitive view of personality, if different situations acquire different meanings for the same individual, as they surely do, the kinds of appraisals, expectations and beliefs, affects, goals, and behavioral scripts that are likely to become activated in relation to particular situations will vary. Therefore, there is no theoretical reason to expect the individual to display similar behavior in relation to different psychological situations unless they are functionally equivalent in meaning. On the contrary, adaptive behavior should be enhanced by discriminative facility—the ability to make fine-grained distinctions among situations—and undermined by broad response tendencies insensitive to context and the different consequences produced by even subtle differences in behavior when situations differ in their nuance (Cantor & Kihlstrom 1987; Cheng 2001, 2003; Chiu et al. 1995; Mendoza-Denton et al. 2001; Mischel 1973). In short, the route to finding the invariance in personality requires taking account of the situation and its meaning for the individual, and may be seen in the stable interactions and interplay between them (e.g., Cervone & Shoda 1999, Higgins 1990, Kunda 1999, Magnusson & Endler 1977, Mischel 1973, Mischel & Shoda 1995).

Personality Coherence in the Pattern of Variability

To move from this interpretation to its empirical demonstration was the essential next step. Direct investigations of the role of situations and behavioral variability in the search for personality coherence have been scarce, again with few exceptions (e.g., Mischel & Peake 1982, Mischel & Shoda 1995, Shoda et al. 1994). One of these, a large field study at a midwestern college in the United States, provided some hints toward the resolution of the personality paradox. In this study, behavior relevant to "college conscientiousness" and friendliness was observed in vivo over multiple situations and occasions (Mischel & Peake 1982). To assure their personal meaningfulness for the participants, undergraduates from the college supplied the specific behaviors and contexts relevant to the traits in pretesting. Conscientiousness was sampled in various situations such as in the classroom, in the dormitory, and in the library, and the assessments occurred over repeated occasions in the course of the semester.

The data again were consistent with the earlier findings of researchers like Newcomb but also yielded a new lead toward the possible resolution of the paradox. Two facts emerged. On the one hand, just as Newcomb did, we also found that behaviors were highly variable across different situations. An individual might be higher than most people in a trait in some situations but also distinctively lower than most in other situations. On the other hand, individuals also showed temporal stability in their behavior *within* particular situations that were highly similar and formed a type, or "functional equivalence class," of situations. It was noteworthy that their perceptions of their own trait consistency were strongly related to that temporal stability, and unrelated to the variability of their behavior from one type of situation to another.

These findings suggested that the pattern of variability from one type of situation to another might not be entirely random. Specifically, if behaviors are stable within each type of situation but varied from one type to another, the pattern of the latter variation should be stable and characteristic for each individual. A person may be less agreeable than others in one type of situation, but more agreeable than others in another type, and the data suggested such difference between situations may indeed be stable, and could express something important about how the individual experiences the situations. Thus, it might be worth attending to the patterns of variability in the search for the invariance of the person. We recognized that much of the observed variation across situations is random fluctuation. But we expected that within the noise there also would be stable patterns that might provide a route for glimpsing the structure and organization of the underlying system that generates them (Mischel & Shoda 1995; Shoda & LeeTiernan 2002; Shoda et al. 1994, 2002). We decided to pursue those patterns next.

Although conspicuously absent in most personality psychology, such patterns are portrayed in virtually every character study in literature, revealing as they unfold the protagonists' underlying motivations and character structures, and making them come alive. As a simple example, suppose two people display the same overall average level of a type of behavior, such as aggression, but vary in their pattern of *where* it is displayed (Shoda et al. 1989, 1993b). Suppose that one is highly aggressive with individuals over whom he has power, but is exceptionally friendly and nonaggressive with those who have power over him, whereas the other person shows the opposite pattern. Even if on average their aggressiveness score is the same, if their distinctive patterns remain stable when observed repeatedly, they cannot be dismissed as chance fluctuations or errors of measurement. And they begin to provide clues about differences in their motivations, goals, and other characteristics, which would be lost if one only aggregates their behavior across these different situations. Although attention to patterns like this helps to define the dynamics that motivate complex behavior patterns (e.g., Kunda 1999), they are obscured when the context is aggregated out in the search for the invariance of personality.

Looking for Coherence in the Variability: Empirical Evidence from Directly Observed Behavior Patterns

There are good reasons why systematic studies to determine if these patterns are stable and meaningful aspects of personality invariance were slow to be done. They call both for a change in the core assumptions that traditionally guided the search and, at the empirical level, for a massive data archive of in vivo behavior observations to trace the individual's behavior across multiple situations and over time. Such data are not only extremely costly and time-consuming to obtain but also require techniques for voluminous data gathering and analysis that were not available in earlier years in pioneering studies like those by Hartshorne & May and Newcomb.

To search for the order that might underlie the variability of a person's behavior across diverse situations ideally required a naturalistic site in which such observations could be almost continuously obtained over a prolonged period of time, under well-controlled field conditions. In Newcomb's classic study, a summer camp for children provided such a setting, and more than half a century later, equipped now with video cameras and computers, we conducted a follow up, again in a summer camp. In this residential camp setting and treatment program for children with a variety of behavior problems, particularly aggression and self-regulation, it was possible to directly observe the participants over many hours and weeks. Diverse measures were obtained across multiple situations and repeated occasions, under conditions that assured high reliability among well-trained observers (e.g., Mischel et al. 2002; Shoda et al. 1993a,b, 1994).

Consistent with the earlier work that led to the articulation of the personality paradox in the first place, we found again, and by now quite unsurprisingly, that individual differences (rank order positions) in behavior with regard to such dimensions as physical and verbal aggression were relatively inconsistent across different types of psychological situations (e.g., "when teased or provoked by peers" versus "when warned by adults" or "when approached positively by peers"). As expected, aggressive behavior in one type of situation did not strongly predict the individual's behavior in a different type of situation.

The role of the situation in the search for personality invariance has often been misunderstood as little more than the recognition that of course situations make a difference and they do so by changing the expected normative levels of behavior. It is self-evident that people will become more aggressive in situations in which they are provoked or teased than when they are approached positively or praised. But the novel finding of theoretical importance was that the person's rank order in relation to others *changes* systematically and predictably in different situations. The same individual who is one of the least aggressive when teased may be well known for his characteristically high level of anger and irritation when flattered and praised. Thus, individuals are characterized by distinctive and stable patterns of behavior variability across situations.

Behavioral Signatures of Personality

The findings made clear that individuals who had similar average levels of a type of behavior (e.g., their overall aggression) nevertheless differed predictably in the types of situations in which their aggressiveness occurs. A child characterized by a pattern of becoming exceptionally aggressive when peers approach him to play, but less aggressive than most other children when chastised by an adult for misbehaving, is different from one who shows the opposite pattern, even if both have similar overall levels of total aggressive behavior. Collectively, the results showed that when closely observed, individuals are characterized by stable, distinctive, and highly meaningful patterns of variability in their actions, thoughts, and feelings across different types of situations. These *if . . . then . . .* situation-behavior relationships provide a kind of "behavioral signature of personality" that identifies the individual and maps on to the impressions formed by observers about what they are like (Shoda et al. 1993a, 1994). Although the camp findings provide perhaps the strongest evidence for the stability of *if . . . then . . .* behavioral signatures, data from other studies (e.g., Vansteelandt & Van Mechelen 1998) are beginning to indicate that such reliable patterns of behavior variability characterize individuals distinctively as a rule, rather than an exception (e.g., Andersen & Chen 2002, Cervone & Shoda 1999, Morf & Rhodewalt 2001, Shoda & LeeTiernan 2002).

It is a type of stability that contradicts earlier assumptions about the consistency and structure of dispositions and their behavioral expressions. In the classical psychometric conception of behavioral dispositions, the individual's "true score" on the behavioral dimension, relative to normative levels in each situation, should remain constant. Because the deviations from the true score observed in each situation are assumed to reflect measurement noise or random fluctuation, if the data are standardized and rescaled relative to the typical level of behaviors expected in each situation, the "shape" of the profile should be random over multiple times and observations. But the stable *if . . . then . . .* patterns that were found directly contradict this classic assumption, and reveal a second type of within-person consistency that needs to be assessed and explained in the search for personality invariance. The two types of variability coexist as two aspects of the expressions of coherence, seen in the elevation (Type 1), and shape (Type 2), of behavioral signatures. Each is important and informative: The need is for a theory of personality that accounts for and predicts both of them.

SEARCHING FOR THE UNDERLYING ORGANIZATION

In sum, two types of behavioral consistency have been demonstrated and an adequate conception of personality invariance has to begin by being able to predict and account for both at least at a theoretical level. Type 1 consistency has been abundantly shown by the aggregation strategy, and has proven to be of much value, especially for the description of broad individual differences on trait ratings of what individuals "are like on the whole." Type 2 consistency is seen in the intraindividual patterns of variability—the behavioral signatures of personality described above, which show a distinctive pattern of *if . . . then . . .* relationships. Although an account that predicts these two aspects of behavioral consistency must be the sine qua non for a comprehensive theory of personality, much more is also required. A framework for conceptualizing the invariance that distinctively characterizes the individual and the processes that underlie it needs to also take into account the wealth of relevant findings coming from diverse areas of science and philosophy of mind. The search for the structure and organization of personality, indeed for its "architecture" (Cervone 2003), need not be restricted to models based on the lexicon and the language of traits, nor to common-sense typologies that date back to the ancient Greeks.

Framework for a Dynamic Personality System

Gordon Allport (1937) launched the field of personality psychology to investigate how the individual person functions and is organized. He wanted to go beyond studies confined to the "operations of a hypothetical 'average' mind" (p. 61). If an argument for such a within-person focus is still needed, it is that social behavior and human experience is a function not just of the component information-processing mechanisms in general. It also depends on the contents of the memory and motivated meaning system that guide the person's interpretations of situations and thus the person-situation interactions that are played out within the social world.

This recognition led to the study of person-situation interaction from the start. As Cronbach (1957) put it: "[I]f for each environment there is a best organism, for every organism there is a best environment" (p. 679). In the same vein, Kurt Lewin in his field theory observed that: "[G]eneral laws and individual differences are merely two aspects of one problem; they are mutually dependent on each other and the study of the one cannot proceed without the study of the other (Lewin 1946, p. 794)." Since then, it has been increasingly recognized that in the social sciences higher-order interactions, not main effects, tend to be the rule when the data are closely examined (Shweder 1999). In the early 1950s, George Kelly (1955), already anticipating the cognitive revolution, focused his psychology of personal constructs on the elaboration, analysis, and potential modification of the meaning systems that guide experience and action at the individual level. The challenge now is how to capture both the processes within the individual and the relevant individual differences between individuals, in light of what has been learned about basic psychological processes.

Discoveries about mind, brain, and behavior that have vitalized psychological science in the last few decades are providing insights into such directly personality-relevant processes as memory, attention control, and executive functions including planning and conflict-monitoring, emotion and self-regulation, meta-cognition, and unconscious, automatic processing—to name a few (e.g., Cervone & Mischel 2002, Mischel et al. 2004). As the understanding of the subsystems and part-processes that collectively constitute the person's mental and emotional architecture grows, it seems propitious to revisit the ambitious and still largely unmet goals that motivated the study of personality in the first place. That requires a focus on how the component processes within the individual operate, as it were, "in concert," and play out in interactions with situations. It calls for a comprehensive framework that draws on diverse disciplines to integrate how relevant part-processes operate together as an organized whole system within the individual functioning in the social world.

In cognitive science, the development of models of the mind, inspired by work on neural networks that deal with knowledge and memory, appear promising for a meta-system of the individual's distinctive mental and emotional processes operating in concert at the molar level (e.g., Anderson & Lebiere 1998). They seem promising in part because they avoid many of the problems that made earlier computer-based information-processing models inappropriate for dealing with the human mind. They do not require a central control plan, they do not assume that information is first stored and then retrieved (rather than contextually reconstructed), and they do not assume serial processing. On the positive side, they do seem able to deal with the concurrent operation of multiple processes at varying levels of awareness. They do deal with the interactions among diverse mental and emotional representations with each other and in response to stimulus features from the situations that are encountered and generated by the system.

In these systems, concepts are not stored as discrete units, but rather are represented by different patterns of activation across many units. Consequently, concepts or memories represented by different patterns of activation across many units are not retrieved intact from storage, but instead are reconstructed each time there is activation in the system, and the reconstruction depends in part on the context in which it occurs. Any reconstruction will be imperfect and influenced by the person's other knowledge and the particular context and circumstances (Mischel & Morf 2003). And because the whole system is connected and each unit can be involved in the representation of many different concepts, whenever one part is activated, other parts are affected also and possibly changed. For example, various beliefs are linked to each other, forming a meaning system in which one belief supports another to make sense of the world. Further, components of a belief system are connected to affective reactions, goals, and potential behavioral strategies within the larger organized system, functioning as a coherent organic whole.

A major advantage of these systems is that they are able to generate exceedingly complex behavior patterns as a function of the network of relationships among the units within them. They allow parsimonious analyses of personality processes and their behavioral expressions without having to strip away their complexities and contextualized, interactive nature. Especially relevant for a processing approach to personality, such models can account for a system that is predisposed in distinctive ways by its biological (e.g., temperament, genetic predispositions) and psychosocial-developmental history. The patterns of thoughts, feelings, and behavior that are generated are constrained and guided by the existing network in nonrandom, at least partially predictable ways, that are seen in the behavioral signatures that characterize the individual (Mischel & Shoda 1995, Shoda & Mischel 2000). More than a promissory note, these models seem to produce coherent and adaptive, meaningful patterns of behaviors that reflect the dynamic interplay among multiple processes (Kashima & Kerekes 1994, Kunda & Thagard

1996, Read & Miller 1998, Shoda & Mischel 1998, Smith & DeCoster 1998), and that allow a systematic account of self-regulation and proactive, goal-directed, agentic behavior (Mischel & Morf 2003).

THE CAPS MODEL   The Cognitive-Affective Processing System, or CAPS (Mischel & Shoda 1995, Shoda & Mischel 1998), was developed as an exemplar of this kind of framework intended to predict the two types of behavioral consistency discovered in personality research. According to this model, the personality system contains mental representations whose activation leads to the behavioral consistencies that characterize the person. These representations consist of diverse cognitive-affective units or CAUs, which include the person's construal and representations of the self, people, and situations, enduring goals, expectations-beliefs, and feeling states, as well as memories of people and past events. For a given person, some of these representations are more available and highly accessible, while others are less accessible or available (Higgins 1996).

What determines the adaptive responses of such a system to different situations and generates the two types of behavioral consistency? The answer we thought calls for a system in which the CAUs are not isolated, but rather are interconnected and organized, guided by a stable network of cognitions and affects characteristic for that individual (Mischel & Shoda 1995). It is assumed that individuals differ stably in this network of interconnections or associations. Individual differences in this model reflect differences both in the chronic accessibility of CAUs and in the distinctive organization of interrelationships among them within each individual. As the person experiences situations that contain different psychological features, different CAUs and their characteristic interrelationships become activated in relation to these features. Consequently, the activation of CAUs changes from one time to another and from one situation to another. The change occurs not only within the individual psychologically but also in what is expressed and enacted interpersonally so that, for example, the "self" activated in relation to mother when visiting the family for the holidays is different from the one salient in relation to one's partner on the drive home (e.g., Andersen & Chen 2002, Zayas et al. 2002). Although cognitions and affects that are activated at a given time change, *how* they change, that is, the sequence and pattern of their activation, remains stable, reflecting the stable structure of the organization within the system (Mischel & Shoda 1995, Shoda & Mischel 1998). The result is a distinctive pattern of *if . . . then . . .* relations, or behavioral signatures, manifested as the individual moves across different situations.

Computer simulations have demonstrated that this type of system generates both Type 1 and Type 2 behavioral consistency: It generates unique and stable profiles of variability, reflected in *if . . . then . . .* behavioral signatures, as well as mean differences in the average levels of these profiles (Shoda & Mischel 1998, 2000; Shoda et al. 2002). The CAPS conceptualization of personality as a stable and distinctive network of knowledge representations explicitly predicts, and can account for, the seeming inconsistencies in people's behaviors across situations that have so long been perplexing in the pursuit of the consistency of personality. It makes variability of behavior across situations an essential reflection of the stable personality system and indeed its distinctive signature.

RESOLUTION OF THE PERSONALITY PARADOX: LINKING THE INTUITION OF CONSIS-TENCY TO THE STABILITY OF BEHAVIORAL SIGNATURES   If behavioral signatures are meaningful reflections of personality invariance, they also should be linked to perceptions and intuitions about one's own consistency. To test this expectation, the relationship between the stability of *if . . . then . . .* signatures that character-ize an individual in a particular domain of behavior and the self-perception of consistency was closely examined empirically. The results spoke directly to the personality paradox, and allowed a fresh look at the behavioral roots for the per-ception of personality consistency.

With that goal, the data used in the study of conscientiousness and sociability in college students (Mischel & Peake 1982) were reexamined to test the hypo-thesis that the students' perceptions of their consistency would be predicted by the intraindividual stability of their behavior signatures. In fact, those who perceived themselves as consistent with regard to the trait did not show greater overall cross-situational consistency in their behavior than those who did not, as measured by their rank-order positions across different trait-relevant situations. In contrast, as expected, their perceptions of trait consistency were linked closely to the stability of their behavioral signatures for the trait-relevant behaviors. For individuals who perceived themselves as consistent in conscientiousness, the average *if . . . then . . .* signature stability correlation was near 0.5, whereas it was trivial for those who saw themselves as inconsistent (Mischel & Shoda 1995). This suggests that when asked about their behavioral consistency, people may base their impressions on the inferred motivations, beliefs, values, and other mental qualities that account for and explain those behaviors. If so, the impression of consistency should be linked to the stability of the behavioral signatures that reflect the underlying mental system.

In fact, a growing body of research suggests that intuitive perceivers seem to be more sophisticated personality theorists than most experiments in person percep-tion have allowed them to be. They spontaneously use contextual information in subtle ways (Trope 1986), and their impressions of people are linked to the *if . . . then . . .* behavioral signatures of the perceived, interpreted as indicators of their underlying motivations and meanings (e.g., L.K. Kammrath, R. Mendoza-Denton, & W. Mischel, manuscript in preparation; Shoda et al. 1993a). To explain the re-sponses of significant others in their lives, peoples' intuitive lay theories include beliefs about their *if . . . then . . .* psychological states—"*If* Bill wants to create a good impression, *then* he acts friendly" (Chen 2003). They make inferences about the underlying stable personality system that generates and explains observed be-havioral signatures when they are given the data to do so, and the motivation for expending the effort (Chen-Idson & Mischel 2001, Shoda et al. 1989). Collectively, the findings suggest that *if . . . then . . .* relations are basic units in lay conceptions of personality (Chen 2003), and are used to infer the underlying mental states and personality characteristics that account for them.

In sum, presumably the impressions of others, as well as of the self, are linked to the observed or inferred stability of their behavioral signatures that serve as diagnostic indicators of the underlying system that generates them. But to reveal these lay theories of personality requires that perceivers have the opportunity to observe the behaviors of the perceived across diverse situations. In most experiments on person perception and impression formation, such information is absent. When people do have the chance to observe behavioral signatures, rather than discounting the situation as classic attribution theory expects, they use them instead to infer the underlying motivations and characteristics of the perceived (e.g., Cantor et al. 1982, Chen-Idson & Mischel 2001, Wright & Mischel 1988, Vonk 1998). Furthermore, stable patterns of variations lead to a greater, rather than diminished, sense of personality coherence (Plaks et al. 2003).

In retrospect, the intuition of consistency turns out to be neither paradoxical nor illusory: It is linked to behavioral consistency but not the sort for which the field was searching for so many years, and it was found by incorporating the situation into the search for invariance rather than by removing it. The personality paradox is resolved, or rather dissolves, when the assumptions about the nature, locus, and expressions of personality consistency are revised to better fit the data and state of the science.

A Next Challenge: Organization and Dynamics of Personality Systems?

If personality is conceptualized as a dynamic cognitive-affective processing system, new questions and research challenges quickly arise about its structure, organization, and processing dynamics. What characterizes the patterns of activation among the cognitive-affective units that distinguish particular individuals and types and that underlie their behavioral signatures? How do the person's distinctive meaning and motivational systems, and the action patterns to which they lead, interact with the psychological features of situations in which they become activated? What are the executive and cognitive attentional control mechanisms and strategies that enable the individual to self-regulate adaptively and engage in proactive sustained goal pursuit?

CAPS was cast as a meta-theory of the person as an organized, coherent system, designed to facilitate and invite questions about how the specifics of its multiple constituent components and subsystems and processes interact and exert their influences (e.g., Cervone 2003). These components do not operate in isolation, nor do they have equal weights, but are organized hierarchically in terms of their importance for the functioning and maintenance of the priorities and goals of the system as a whole. The nature and organization of the goal hierarchies and self-regulatory strategies in goal pursuit that characterize the system are being explored by research into the behavioral signatures and processing dynamics of different personality types, such as the narcissistic type and the anxious rejection-sensitivity type.

PERSONALITY TYPES: DISTINCTIVE PROCESSING DYNAMICS AND BEHAVIORAL SIGNA-
TURES   In this framework, a personality type consists of people who share a common organization of relations among mediating units in the processing of certain situational features. The types are defined in terms of characteristic social cognitive and affective processing dynamics that generate characteristic *if . . . then . . .* patterns of thoughts, feelings, and behavior visible in distinctive types of situations. To illustrate, the rejection-sensitivity type (Downey et al. 2000, Feldman & Downey 1994) describes individuals who have intense anxieties about interpersonal rejection and abandonment that become evident if they encounter in their intimate relationships what could be construed as uncaring behavior (e.g., partner is attentive to someone else). They scan interpersonal situations for possible cues about rejection, and appraise them in terms of their potential rejection threats, anxiously expecting to find them and vigilantly ready to see them. Then they tend to become excessively concerned about whether or not they are loved, and their own ruminations further trigger a cascade of feelings of anger, resentment, and rage as their fears of abandonment escalate. In response, they may activate coercive and controlling behaviors, often blaming them on the partner's actions, creating a self-fulfilling prophecy in which fears of abandonment become validated by the rejections that they in part generate for themselves. Nevertheless, on the whole, they may not be more likely than others to express anger, disapproval, and coercive behaviors, and under some conditions can be exceptionally caring and thoughtful to their partners.

Rejection-sensitive people appraise interpersonal situations, especially in intimate relationships, anxiously to see how likely they are to be rejected and hurt, magnifying the potential threats and ready to overreact to them. In contrast, narcissists seem to see the same situations as challenges for eagerly showing off how good they are, affirming and bolstering their grandiose self-concepts by outdoing the other person. Likewise, they easily create posthoc interpretations of experiences that ingeniously amplify the positive feedback to them while discounting the negative to a greater degree than most people. These examples are part of a pattern of distinctive mechanisms that characterize their efforts at self-affirmation (Morf & Rhodewalt 2001). Once the outlines of such personality signatures become clear, the route opens to exploring the psychological processes and the social and biological histories that underlie them, and the mechanisms through which they are maintained or open to change.

Personality assessment in a CAPS framework leads to the construction of typologies based on distinctive processing dynamics and personality signatures that are linked to the types of situations in which they are likely to be expressed. A goal of such a typology is to enable specific predictions about how people of a particular type, that is, people who have similar processing dynamics, are likely to think, feel, and behave in certain kinds of situations. This ambition, articulated years ago (e.g.,

Bem 1983), is now beginning to be actively pursued (e.g., Mendoza-Denton et al. 2002, Shoda 2003, Vansteelandt & Van Mechelen 1998). It provides a route to explore systematically the processing dynamics of selected types, their psychosocial and biological histories, current functioning, and potential future outcomes. It also raises questions about possible therapeutic interventions and self-generated efforts to modify the system's dynamics constructively when desired and possible.

IDENTIFYING THE ACTIVE INGREDIENTS OF SITUATIONS   The development of typologies of processing dynamics and structures requires not only incorporating situations into the study of persons but also going beyond their surface features or nominal characteristics (such as in the hallway, in classroom) to capture their psychologically active ingredients (Shoda et al. 1994). These are the features of the situation that have significant meaning for a given individual or type, and that are related to the experienced psychological situation—the thoughts and affects and goals that become activated within the personality system. The key for achieving generalizability is to identify psychological features of situations that play a functional role in the generation of behaviors, and that are contained in a wide range of nominal situations (Shoda et al. 1994, Wright & Mischel 1988). The aim in this type of analysis is to capture those features that are encoded by perceivers in characteristic ways and that activate other relevant social cognitive person variables (e.g., expectancies and goals) in the mediating process (Wright & Mischel 1988).

To the degree that particular sets of such active ingredients or psychological features for an individual (or for a personality type) are imbedded in diverse nominal situations (e.g., at woodworking in camp, on the playground at school, at mealtime at home), it becomes possible to predict behavior across those seemingly different situations and contexts, allowing much broader predictability even for quite specific behavioral manifestations (Mischel & Shoda 1995, 1998; Shoda et al. 1994). The importance of finding these features and elaborating their meaning for the individual has long been recognized (e.g., Kelly 1955). The encouraging development is that new methods are becoming available to facilitate analyses of active ingredients of situations (e.g., Shoda & LeeTiernan 2002, LeeTiernan 2002). These innovations make it possible to go beyond the single case to identify types of individuals for whom particular sets of features have common meanings and activate similar processing dynamics (Ayduk et al. 1999, Cervone & Shoda 1999, Shoda 2003, Wright & Mischel 1987).

WHEN THE "SITUATION" IS ANOTHER PERSON   The CAPS analysis provides not only a model of the person but also of situations when they consist of other people. In a close relationship, one person's behavioral output becomes the other person's situational input, and vice versa, forming a dyadic system. To the degree that each partner's personality is characterized by a stable *if . . . then . . .* behavioral signature, it becomes possible to model the interactions between them, and to predict the "personality" of the interpersonal system they form, characterized by its own distinctive relationship signature and dynamics.

Intuitively, a long-term interpersonal relationship is sometimes said to have its own personality that becomes more than simply an average of the personalities within it; witness the unlikely combinations that may work best because their "chemistry" is right. The CAPS analysis allows one to model these emergent qualities of relationships, and their links to the personalities of the individuals as their interpersonal systems evolve. In a CAPS demonstration study, each individual was modeled by a stable and distinct *if . . . then . . .* pattern or "behavioral signature," where "if" is the psychological features present in a situation, and "then" is the cognitions and affects that become activated by them (Shoda et al. 2002). This conceptualization of an individual makes it possible to explicitly model the process by which the "personality" of relationships emerges out of the interactions among individuals. Computer simulations using a parallel constraint satisfaction network illustrated how each interpersonal system formed by a combination of two individuals generates predictable and distinctive behaviors and patterns of interactions. The model and the computer simulation predicts that the cognitive and affective states that an individual experiences in a given relationship are an emergent property of that interpersonal system, not a simple combination or average of the personalities of the individuals.

Such predictions illustrate another direction for this type of processing analysis. They lead to empirical studies of the emergent qualities of interpersonal relationships that ultimately may allow *specific* predictions about the cognitions, affects, and behaviors of an individual in a given relationship, based on information about the partner. In a loose analogy, the possibility is not unlike that of chemistry, in which the "behaviors" of substance A in reaction to substance B are predicted by knowing the molecular structures of both. Understanding and empirically assessing each individual's cognitive-affective system may be a step toward being able to predict the "chemistry" of interpersonal systems, as well as that of the individual in interaction with the important situations of life. A great deal has been learned about situations, making it possible to construct a taxonomy of them, as illustrated by Harold Kelley and colleagues (2003) in their *Atlas of Interpersonal Situations*. An interesting next step may be to link those interpersonal situations to the psychological chemistry of their participants.

Just as the personality of interpersonal systems can be understood as an emergent quality, the *if . . . then . . .* behavioral signature that characterizes an individual itself is an emergent quality, arising from interactions among the components of the person's cognitive-affective processing system. This points to still another line of empirical studies to assess the distinctive network of associations among the components, now with the benefit of modern social cognitive techniques (e.g., priming, Implicit Association Test) to permit subtler assessments that go well beyond self-reports. Theoretically, some of the *if . . . then . . .* behavioral signature expected to be generated by an individual can then be predicted, for example by using a computer simulation of that person's network, based on the empirically derived assessment of the network connection patterns (Shoda et al. 2002).

ROLE OF SELF-REGULATION AND SELF-REGULATORY COMPETENCIES   An organized, coherent system does not imply the absence of internal conflicts. Conflicting goals and seemingly inconsistent behavior tendencies observable in different contexts and domains may be understood in terms of the concurrent operation of different goals and different motives functioning at different levels of the system, jointly exerting their influences in self-regulation. That raises questions about the kinds of problematic organization that produce fragmentation, compartmentalization, debilitating anxiety, and other potentially negative outcomes and self-defeating behavior patterns. Conversely, it leads to questions about the cognitive, attention, and brain processes essential for adaptive self-regulation in the face of strong temptations and immediate "hot" situational triggers that elicit impulsive, automatic responses that threaten the individual's pursuit of more important distal goals (e.g., LeDoux 1996, Metcalfe & Mischel 1999, Ochsner et al. 2002, Posner & Rothbart 2000).

Self-regulatory mechanisms and competencies are central for understanding human agency and self-directed change, as well as the coherence and stability of the individual. First, these competencies and cognitive "cooling" strategies allow people to overcome diverse momentary "hot" situational pressures in their proactive pursuit of long-term goals and life projects. They enable coping behaviors that can have long-term adaptive and protective effects. For example, self-regulatory competencies can buffer individuals against the otherwise negative consequences of their dispositional vulnerabilities, such as chronic anxious rejection sensitivity. People high in this sensitivity are at risk to develop low self-esteem and to become either aggressive or depressed when dealing with interpersonal situations that activate their rejection concerns. However, that pattern may not have to be their destiny. Highly rejection-sensitive people who also are high in self-regulatory competencies did not develop the expected negative outcomes associated with rejection sensitivity (Ayduk et al. 2002). Second, the cognitive and attention control competencies and executive mechanisms that enable self-regulation are relatively stable, and have implications for important developmental continuities and outcomes over much of the life course. For example, the number of seconds preschoolers are able to wait for a larger treat later, rather than settle for a smaller one immediately, significantly predicts long-term outcomes that range from their SAT scores and ratings of their adaptive social and cognitive functioning in adolescence to effective goal pursuit, positive self-concepts, well-being, and less cocaine drug use in adulthood (Ayduk et al. 2000, Mischel et al. 1989). The effortful control strategies tapped in the preschool delay-of-gratification task have meaningful correlates visible earlier in life. These are seen in the toddler's attention deployment strategies when dealing with brief maternal separation in the strange situation (Sethi et al. 2000), and may have roots even earlier in infancy and temperament (Derryberry 2002).

The mechanisms that underlie effective self-regulation have been speculated about ever since Adam and Eve failed to use them, and people began to struggle with their self-defeating vulnerabilities. The convergence of research into the diverse processes—from the biological and neural to the cognitive and social—that collectively enable adaptive self-regulation, promises to make the core mechanisms and necessary skills less mysterious and more open to change (e.g., Baumeister & Vohs 2004). That also increases the hope that ultimately people do not have to be the victims of either their predispositions or their biographies. A challenge for future research, drawing on what is being learned about the mechanisms that enable self-regulation, is to identify the interventions that can enhance the potential for human agency.

CONCLUSION: *PERSONALITY AND ASSESSMENT* (1968) IN RETROSPECT

Not very long ago a student burst into my office to tell me that on a state licensing examination in psychology the correct response to the question, "Which psychologist does not believe in personality?" was Mischel. With that test item still in mind, I looked back at the conclusions of *Personality and Assessment*:

> "Global traits and states are excessively crude, gross units to encompass adequately the extraordinary complexity and subtlety of the discriminations that people constantly make . . .. The traditional trait-state conceptualizations of personality, while often paying lip service to [peoples'] complexity and to the uniqueness of each person, in fact lead to a grossly oversimplified view that misses both the richness and the uniqueness of individual lives . . . [and their] extraordinary adaptiveness and capacities for discrimination, awareness, and self-regulation" (Mischel 1968, p. 301).

I would not change those conclusions today, and if descriptions of people in terms of broad traits and states using situation-free adjectives define "personality," the test makers need not reconsider their item.

In 1968, the limitations of traditional approaches were becoming evident, but the alternatives were just beginning to emerge. Since then, the study of personality has expanded vigorously into an increasingly interdisciplinary science, renewing the hopes with which personality psychology was founded (Cervone & Mischel 2002). The field was intended to ask the deepest questions about human nature, and to become the meta-discipline—the hub—for integrating the basic findings and general principles revealed by work at different levels of analysis within the larger science as they speak to the coherence and organization of the individual. The aim was to build on whatever was relevant, from the biological to the psychosocial and cultural, to capture the unique patterning and organization of the functioning, distinctive "whole person" (Allport 1937, 1961). The young psychological science within which personality psychology began was limited by the dominance of behaviorism on the one side, and early psychoanalytic theory on the other. In contrast, current efforts to return to the field's original aims can build on the explosion of discoveries that have transformed psychological science in the last few decades. If so, perhaps the original hopes for the study of personality, in which the individual is the organizing principle (Magnusson 2000) may still be realized.

The main message of my 1968 monograph was that the situation has to be incorporated into the conception and assessment of personality. In the years since, contexts and psychological situations have come to play a central role in attempts to understand mental processes and social behavior (Kagan 2003), even in their most complex forms. In a discussion of linguistic ability, George Miller (1999, p. 1) noted, "The ability to exploit context in order to determine meaning and resolve potential ambiguities" allows one to identify the intended meanings of words. That also seems to be true for how we can come to understand a person.

The *Annual Review of Psychology* is online at http://psych.annualreviews.org

LITERATURE CITED

Allport GW. 1937. *Personality: A Psychological Interpretation*. New York: Holt, Rinehart & Winston

Allport GW. 1961. *Pattern and Growth in Personality*. New York: Holt, Rinehart & Winston

Andersen SM, Chen S. 2002. The relational self: an interpersonal social-cognitive theory. *Psychol. Rev.* 109:619–45

Anderson JR, Lebiere C. 1998. *The Atomic Components of Thought*. Mahwah, NJ: Erlbaum

Ayduk O, Downey G, Testa A, Yen Y, Shoda Y. 1999. Does rejection sensitivity elicit hostility in rejection-sensitive women? *Soc. Cogn.* 17:245–71

Ayduk O, Mendoza-Denton R, Mischel W, Downey G, Peake PK, Rodriguez M. 2000. Regulating the interpersonal self: strategic self-regulation for coping with rejection sensitivity. *J. Personal. Soc. Psychol.* 79:776–92

Ayduk O, Mischel W, Downey G. 2002. Attentional mechanisms linking rejection to hostile reactivity: the role of "hot" vs. "cool" focus. *Psychol. Sci.* 13:443–48

Baumeister RF, Vohs KD, eds. 2004. *Handbook of Self-Regulation Research*. New York: Guilford

Bem DJ. 1983. Constructing a theory of triple typology: some (second) thoughts on nomothetic and idiographic approaches to personality. *J. Personal.* 51:566–77

Cantor N, Kihlstrom JF. 1987. *Personality and Social Intelligence*. Englewood Cliffs, NJ: Erlbaum

Cantor N, Mischel W, Schwartz J. 1982. A prototype analysis of psychological situations. *Cogn. Psychol.* 14:45–77

Cervone D. 2003. The architecture of personality. *Psychol. Rev.* In press

Cervone D, Mischel W. 2002. Personality science. In *Advances in Personality Science*, ed. D Cervone, W Mischel, pp. 1–26. New York: Guilford

Cervone D, Shoda Y. 1999. Social cognitive theories and the coherence of personality. In *The Coherence of Personality: Social-Cognitive Bases of Consistency, Variability, and Organization*, ed. D Cervone, Y Shoda, pp. 155–81. New York: Guilford

Chen S. 2003. Psychological state theories about significant others: Implications for the content and structure of significant-other representations. *Personal. Soc. Psychol. Bull.* In press

Chen-Idson L, Mischel W. 2001. The personality of familiar and significant people: the lay perceiver as a social cognitive theorist. *J. Personal. Soc. Psychol.* 80:585–96

Cheng C. 2001. Assessing coping flexibility in real-life and laboratory settings: a multimethod approach. *J. Personal. Soc. Psychol.* 80:814–33

Cheng C. 2003. Cognitive and motivational

processes underlying coping flexibility: a dual-process model. *J. Personal. Soc. Psychol.* 84:425–38

Chiu C, Hong Y, Mischel W, Shoda Y. 1995. Discriminative facility in social competence: conditional versus dispositional encoding and monitoring-blunting of information. *Soc. Cogn.* 13:49–70

Cronbach LJ. 1957. The two disciplines of scientific psychology. *Am. Psychol.* 12:671–84

Derryberry D. 2002. Attention and voluntary self-control. *Self Identity* 1:105–11

Downey G, Feldman S, Ayduk O. 2000. Rejection sensitivity and male violence in romantic relationships. *Pers. Relat.* 7:45–61

Epstein S. 1979. The stability of behavior: I. on predicting most of the people much of the time. *J. Personal. Soc. Psychol.* 37:1097–126

Epstein S. 1980. The stability of behavior: II. implications for psychological research. *Am. Psychol.* 35:790–806

Feldman SI, Downey G. 1994. Rejection sensitivity as a mediator of the impact of childhood exposure to family violence on adult attachment behavior. *Dev. Psychopathol.* 6:231–47

Fleeson W. 2001. Toward a structure- and process-integrated view of personality: traits as density distribution of states. *J. Personal. Soc. Psychol.* 80:1011–27

Hartshorne H, May A. 1928. *Studies in the Nature of Character: Studies in Deceit.* New York: Macmillan

Higgins ET. 1990. Personality, social psychology, and person-situation relations: standards and knowledge activation as a common language. In *Handbook of Personality: Theory and Research*, ed. LA Pervin, pp. 301–38. New York: Guilford

Higgins ET. 1996. Ideals, oughts, & regulatory focus: affect and motivation from distinct pains and pleasures. In *The Psychology of Action: Linking Cognition and Motivation to Behavior*, ed. PM Gollwitzer, JA Bargh, pp. 91–114. New York: Guilford

Kagan J. 2003. Biology, context, and developmental inquiry. *Annu. Rev. Psychol.* 54:1–23

Kashima Y, Kerekes ARZ. 1994. A distributed memory model of averaging phenomena in personal impression formation. *J. Exp. Soc. Psychol.* 30:407–55

Kelley HH, Holmes JG, Kerr NL, Reis HT, Rusbult CE, Van Lange PAM. 2003. *An Atlas of Interpersonal Situations.* New York: Cambridge Univ. Press

Kelly GA. 1955. *The Psychology of Personal Constructs.* New York: Norton

Krahe B. 1990. *Situation Cognition and Coherence in Personality: An Individual-Centered Approach.* Cambridge, UK: Cambridge Univ. Press

Kunda Z. 1999. *Social Cognition: Making Sense of People.* Cambridge, MA: MIT Press

Kunda Z, Thagard P. 1996. Forming impressions from stereotypes, traits, and behaviors: a parallel-constraint-satisfaction theory. *Psychol. Rev.* 103:284–308

LeDoux J. 1996. *The Emotional Brain.* New York: Simon & Schuster

LeeTiernan S. 2002. *Modeling and predicting stable response variation across situations.* Unpublished doc. diss. thesis. Univ. Wash., Seattle

Lewin K. 1946. Behavior and development as a function of the total situation. In *Manual of Child Psychology*, ed. L Carmichael, pp. 791–802. New York: Wiley

Magnusson D. 2000. The individual as the organizing principle in psychological inquiry. In *Developmental Sciences and the Holistic Approach*, ed. LR Bergman, RB Cairns, LG Nilsson, L Nystedt, pp. 33–47. Mahwah, NJ: Erlbaum

Magnusson D, Endler NS. 1977. Interactional psychology: present status and future prospects. In *Personality at the Crossroads: Current Issues in Interactional Psychology*, ed. D Magnusson, NS Endler, pp. 3–31. Hillsdale, NJ: Erlbaum

Mendoza-Denton R, Ayduk O, Mischel W, Shoda Y, Testa A. 2001. Person × situation interactionism in self-encoding (*I am ... when ...*): implications for affect regulation and social information processing. *J. Personal. Soc. Psychol.* 80:533–44

Mendoza-Denton R, Downey G, Purdie VJ, Davis A, Pietrzak J. 2002. Sensitivity to status-based rejection: implications for African-American students' college experience. *J. Personal. Soc. Psychol.* 83:896–918

Metcalfe J, Mischel W. 1999. A hot/cool system analysis of delay of gratification: dynamics of willpower. *Psychol. Rev.* 106:3–19

Miller GA. 1999. On knowing a word. *Annu. Rev. Psychol.* 50:1–19

Mischel W. 1968. *Personality and Assessment.* New York: Wiley

Mischel W. 1973. Toward a cognitive social learning reconceptualization of personality. *Psychol. Rev.* 80:252–83

Mischel W, Morf CC. 2003. The self as a psycho-social dynamic processing system: a meta-perspective on a century of the self in psychology. In *Handbook of Self and Identity*, ed. M Leary, J Tangney, pp. 15–43. New York: Guilford

Mischel W, Peake PK. 1982. In search of consistency: measure for measure. In *Consistency in Social Behavior: The Ontario Symposium*, ed. MP Zanna, ET Higgins, CP Herman, pp. 187–207. Hillsdale, NJ: Erlbaum

Mischel W, Shoda Y. 1995. A cognitive-affective system theory of personality: reconceptualizing situations, dispositions, dynamics, and invariance in personality structure. *Psychol. Rev.* 102:246–68

Mischel W, Shoda Y. 1998. Reconciling processing dynamics and personality dispositions. *Annu. Rev. Psychol.* 49:229–58

Mischel W, Shoda Y, Mendoza-Denton R. 2002. Situation-behavior profiles as a locus of consistency in personality. *Curr. Dir. Psychol. Sci.* 11:50–54

Mischel W, Shoda Y, Rodriguez M. 1989. Delay of gratification in children. *Science* 244:933–38

Mischel W, Shoda Y, Smith RE. 2004. *Introduction to Personality: Toward an Integration.* New York: Wiley

Morf CC, Rhodewalt F. 2001. Expanding the dynamic self-regulatory processing model of narcissism: research directions for the future. *Psychol. Inq.* 12:243–51

Moskowitz DS. 1982. Coherence and cross-situational generality in personality: a new

analysis of old problems. *J. Personal. Soc. Psychol.* 43:754–68

Moskowitz DS. 1994. Cross-situational generality and the interpersonal circumplex. *J. Personal. Soc. Psychol.* 66:921–33

Newcombe TM. 1929. *Consistency of Certain Extrovert-Introvert Behavior Patterns in 51 Problem Boys.* New York: Columbia Univ., Teachers College, Bur. Publ.

Nisbett RE, Ross LD. 1980. *Human Inference: Strategies and Shortcomings of Social Judgment.* Englewood Cliffs, NJ: Prentice Hall

Ochsner KN, Bunge SA, Gross JJ, Gabrieli JD. 2002. Rethinking feelings: an FMRI study of the cognitive regulation of emotion. *J. Cogn. Neurosci.* 14:1215–29

Pervin LA. 1994. A critical analysis of trait theory. *Psychol. Inq.* 5:103–13

Peterson DR. 1968. *The Clinical Study of Social Behavior.* New York: Appleton

Plaks JE, Shafer JL, Shoda Y. 2003. Perceiving individuals and groups as coherent: How do perceivers make sense of variable behavior? *Soc. Cogn.* In press

Posner MI, Rothbart MK. 2000. Developing mechanisms of self-regulation. *Dev. Psychopathol.* 12:427–41

Read SJ, Miller LC. 1998. On the dynamic construction of meaning: an interactive activation and competition model of social perception. In *Connectionist Models of Social Reasoning and Social Behavior*, ed. SJ Read, LC Miller, pp. 27–68. Mahwah, NJ: Erlbaum

Ross L, Nisbett RE. 1991. *The Person and the Situation: Perspectives of Social Psychology.* New York: McGraw-Hill

Sethi A, Mischel W, Aber L, Shoda Y, Rodriguez M. 2000. The role of strategic attention deployment in development of self-regulation: predicting preschoolers' delay of gratification from mother-toddler interactions. *Dev. Psychol.* 36:767–77

Shoda Y. 2003. Individual differences in social psychology: Understanding situations to understand people, understanding people to understand situations. In *Handbook of Methods in Psychology*, ed. C Sansone, C Morf, A Panter. Thousand Oaks, CA: Sage. In press

Shoda Y, LeeTiernan SJ. 2002. What remains invariant? Finding order within a person's thoughts, feelings, and behaviors across situations. See Cervone & Mischel 2002, pp. 241–70

Shoda Y, LeeTiernan SJ, Mischel W. 2002. Personality as a dynamical system: emergence of stability and consistency in intra- and interpersonal interactions. *Personal. Soc. Psychol. Rev.* 6:316–25

Shoda Y, Mischel W. 1998. Personality as a stable cognitive-affective activation network: characteristic patterns of behavior variation emerge from a stable personality structure. See Read & Miller 1998, pp. 175–208

Shoda Y, Mischel W. 2000. Reconciling contextualism with the core assumptions of personality psychology. *Eur. J. Personal.* 14:407–28

Shoda Y, Mischel W, Wright JC. 1989. Intuitive interactionism in person perception: effects of situation-behavior relations on dispositional judgments. *J. Personal. Soc. Psychol.* 56:41–53

Shoda Y, Mischel W, Wright JC. 1993a. Links between personality judgments and contextualized behavior patterns: situation-behavior profiles of personality prototypes. *Soc. Cogn.* 4:399–429

Shoda Y, Mischel W, Wright JC. 1993b. The role of situational demands and cognitive competencies in behavior organization and personality coherence. *J. Personal. Soc. Psychol.* 65:1023–35

Shoda Y, Mischel W, Wright JC. 1994. Intra-individual stability in the organization and patterning of behavior: incorporating psychological situations into the ideographic analysis of personality. *J. Personal. Soc. Psychol.* 67:674–87

Shweder RA. 1999. Humans really are different. *Science* 283:798–99

Smith ER, DeCoster J. 1998. Person perception and stereotyping: simulation using distributed representations in a recurrent connectionist network. See Read & Miller 1998, pp. 111–40

Trope Y. 1986. Identification and inferential processes in dispositional attribution. *Psychol. Rev.* 93:239–57

Vansteelandt K, Van Mechelen I. 1998. Individual differences in situation-behavior profiles: a triple typology model. *J. Personal. Soc. Psychol.* 75:751–65

Vernon PE. 1964. *Personality Assessment: A Critical Survey.* New York: Wiley

Vonk R. 1998. The slime effect: suspicion and dislike of likeable behavior toward superiors. *J. Personal. Soc. Psychol.* 74:849–64

Wright JC, Mischel W. 1987. A conditional approach to dispositional constructs: the local predictability of social behavior. *J. Personal. Soc. Psychol.* 53:1159–77

Wright JC, Mischel W. 1988. Conditional hedges and the intuitive psychology of traits. *J. Personal. Soc. Psychol.* 55:454–69

Zayas V, Shoda Y, Ayduk O. 2002. Personality in context: an interpersonal systems perspective. *J. Personal.* 70:851–98

Annu. Rev. Psychol. 2004. 55:23–50
doi: 10.1146/annurev.psych.55.090902.141907
First published online as a Review in Advance on October 20, 2003

ON BUILDING A BRIDGE BETWEEN BRAIN AND BEHAVIOR

Jeffrey D. Schall

*Center for Integrative & Cognitive Neuroscience, Vanderbilt Vision Research Center,
Department of Psychology, Vanderbilt University, Nashville, Tennessee 37203;
email: jeffrey.d.schall@vanderbilt.edu*

Key Words   linking proposition, linking hypothesis, stop signal, countermanding, response preparation, intention, eye field, reaction time, response time, saccade

■ **Abstract**   Cognitive neuroscience is motivated by the precept that a discoverable correspondence exists between mental states and brain states. This precept seems to be supported by remarkable observations and conclusions derived from event-related potentials and functional imaging with humans and neurophysiology with behaving monkeys. This review evaluates specific conceptual and technical limits of claims of correspondence between neural events, overt behavior, and hypothesized covert processes examined using data on the neural control of saccadic eye movements.

CONTENTS

0066-4308/04/0204-0023$14.00

INTRODUCTION

Many authors write with conviction that the correspondence of the mental with the neural is so secure that an ultimate theory of mental phenomena will reduce to neural terms (e.g., Churchland 1986, Crick 1994). Others argue that mental states depend on but are not reducible to the physical states of the brain (e.g., Davidson 1970, Fodor 1981, Pylyshyn 1984). Determining whether the mental reduces to or emerges from the neural cannot be accomplished without correctly describing the mapping between the two.

Inferring Mechanism from Behavior

Before the development of methods to monitor brain states during behavior, physiological mechanisms could be inferred only from behavioral testing. Nevertheless, in the nineteenth century investigators began to articulate the correspondence between mental and physical processes. For example, Mach wrote, "To every psychical there corresponds a physical, and conversely. Like psychical processes correspond to like physical, unlike to unlike. . . . Particulars of the physical correspond to all the particulars of the psychic" (Boring 1942). Even philosophers who advocate a nonreductionist position acknowledge a mapping between mental and physical processes—"Although the position I describe denies there are psychophysical laws, it is consistent with the view that mental characteristics are in some sense dependent, or supervenient, on physical characteristics. Such supervenience might be taken to mean that there cannot be two events alike in all physical respects but differing in some mental respects, or that an object cannot alter in some mental respect without altering in some physical respect" (Davidson 1970). Such a position can be translated into an effective research strategy according to the proposition that ". . .whenever two stimuli cause physically indistinguishable signals to be sent from the sense organs to the brain, the sensations produced by these stimuli, as reported by the subject in words, symbols or actions, must also be indistinguishable" (Brindley 1970). Application of this principle in sensory detection or discrimination experiments permits testing hypotheses about physiological processes.

Another approach to understanding the mechanisms responsible for behavior has been through mathematically precise models of cognitive processes tested against detailed measurements of performance (e.g., Townsend & Ashby 1983; Luce 1986, 1995). Unfortunately, cognitive psychology abounds with alternative models with mutually exclusive architectures or algorithms, many of which are difficult or impossible to distinguish through behavioral testing. For example, choice behavior can be accounted for by sequential sampling models in which a single accumulator represents the relative evidence for two alternatives (e.g., Ratcliff & Rouder 1998). An alternative to a random walk of a single accumulator between alternatives is a race among multiple accumulators representing each alternative (e.g., Bundesen 1990, Logan 2002). In fact, models with single or multiple accumulators can account for common sets of data (Van Zandt & Ratcliff 1995,

Van Zandt et al. 2000), highlighting the limitations of arriving at secure inferences about mechanism based only on behavior (e.g., Uttal 1997). The theoretical issue has been articulated most definitely in the theory of finite automata (Moore 1956). It has been proven that given any computer with a finite number of inputs, outputs, and internal states and any experiment that determines the mapping of outputs to inputs, there exist other computers that are experimentally distinguishable from the original computer for which the original experiment would have given the same results. In other words, different architectures and algorithms can produce the same output from a given input.

Inferring Function from Neuronal Properties

The propositions quoted above were regarded initially as axiomatic, but the development of diverse means of monitoring neurophysiological processes directly or indirectly during behavior has afforded the unprecedented opportunity to investigate directly how mental processes relate to neural processes. Over the past decade numerous publications have carried titles like "Neural Correlate of X" where X is some cognitive capacity or behavior. For example, by monitoring the activity of neurons in macaque monkeys performing various tasks, this author has had opportunities to investigate neural correlates of visual perception (Logothetis & Schall 1989, Thompson & Schall 2000), attention and decision making (Thompson et al. 1996, Bichot & Schall 1999, Sato et al. 2001, Murthy et al. 2001; Sato & Schall 2003), response preparation (Hanes & Schall 1996, Hanes et al. 1998), and self-monitoring (Stuphorn et al. 2000, Schall et al. 2002). But what does "neural correlate" mean?

First, such attributions depend on whether the monkeys in these studies were perceiving, attending, deciding, preparing, and monitoring while the neural activity was recorded. A true mapping of neural and mental must be immediate; a mental state can only be supervenient on a neural state in the instant of occurrence. Now, neural states can be measured instantaneously through physiological methods. But, being subjective, mental states are not directly accessible for objective study, they can only be inferred from an overt response produced after the mental state has proceeded or even concluded. Measures of response time or accuracy can support the inference that some mental state occurred (Garner et al. 1956), but the mental state was *not monitored as it occurred*. Under such conditions a hypothesized link between neural state and mental state cannot be direct.

Second, to study neural correlates of some cognitive state, that state and the conditions for invoking and measuring it must be specified. Although obvious, many reports in the literature lay claim to a neural correlate of some cognitive state but present no converging behavioral measure of that state. Consider the confusion in the literature on neural correlates of cognitive factors influencing saccade production (Sparks 1999). Modulation of the activity of neurons in the superior colliculus has been ascribed to spatial attention (Goldberg & Wurtz 1972, Kustov & Robinson 1996), motor memory (Mays & Sparks 1980), response selection (Glimcher & Sparks 1992), response preparation (Dorris & Munoz 1998, Dorris et al. 1997), motor set (Basso & Wurtz 1998), and target selection (Horwitz & Newsome 1999, McPeek & Keller 2002). This diversity of terminology probably exceeds the diversity of relevant cognitive processes. Therefore, an effective taxonomy of cognitive processes is needed that specifies the training and testing conditions necessary to invoke and manipulate the different cognitive processes. Fortunately, experimental psychologists have devised various means of probing stimulus encoding, attention, memory, response preparation, and error monitoring.

Third, neural activity associated with processes like stimulus encoding, attention, memory, and response preparation varies with history and context (e.g., Dorris & Munoz 1998, Bichot & Schall 2002). Thus, did a particular change in discharge rate occur because the stimulus was stronger or the subject was more attentive or was more prepared to respond or a different effector was to be used or because the payoff was better? A nomohistorical barrier prevents interpretation of raw brain states because each neuron is part of a brain that is part of an organism embedded in an environment at a particular point in history (Clark 1999).

It seems obvious that an understanding of mechanism requires a description of inner workings, and much research in basic neuroscience is motivated by the belief that function will be revealed through an accurate description of the properties of the brain. While form and function are deeply related in nervous systems (e.g., Leventhal & Schall 1983), descriptions of structural and physiological characteristics have not provided explanations of functions performed. This has been articulated most forcefully from the engineering perspective that distinguishes a functional level of explanation from distinct algorithms and physical instantiations (Marr 1982, Robinson 1992).

Thus, we face a conundrum. The same computation can be performed with different algorithms (e.g., single or multiple accumulators), so it is necessary to observe inner workings to understand the mechanism. However, the properties of the inner workings do not directly reveal function. How can we proceed? It seems that some kind of synthetic bootstrap is necessary.

LINKING PROPOSITIONS

The relationship between mental and physical descriptions can be articulated through linking propositions that specify the nature of the mapping between particular cognitive states and neural states (Brindley 1970, Teller 1984, Teller & Pugh 1983). Different kinds of linking propositions can be distinguished: identity, similarity, mutual exclusivity, simplicity, and analogy (the interested reader is directed to Teller 1984). A complete linking proposition encompasses a set of logical relations. The initial proposition states that identical neural states map onto identical cognitive states. The contrapositive of the initial proposition states that nonidentical cognitive states correspond to nonidentical neural states. These two statements are equivalent logically. The converse proposition states: identical cognitive states map onto identical neural states, and the contrapositive of the converse states: nonidentical neural states entail nonidentical cognitive states. These two statements are logically equivalent. However, given the complexity in mapping mental and neural properties, the truth of the converse statement is not implied by or contingent on the truth of the initial proposition.

Testing Linking Propositions

The empirical evaluation of linking propositions raises several fundamental issues. First, what is meant by "identical"? Obviously, it must mean "statistically indistinguishable." Also, identity cannot refer to constancy within an individual over time; you cannot step twice in the same river. However, experimental psychology presumes rough identity across subjects because (absent clinical or other exceptions) common brain areas serve common functions across individuals. What about identity across species? Do brain structures that are homologous across species have common functional states producing common behaviors and cognitive states? It seems we must grant this at least for nonhuman primates. If not, then how can neurophysiological data from macaque monkeys be related meaningfully to human cognition? Extending such homologous identity to rodents or invertebrates seems less secure.

Second, at what behavioral and neural scale must the comparison be judged? Surely common mental states cannot require common states of each receptor and ion channel in the nervous system. If this were so, then we could not think the same thought twice. But, if the exemplar-based view of cognition is correct, then perhaps we never do (e.g., Barsalou et al. 1998). Also, if a molecular scale description is necessary, then we are faced with an effectively insurmountable challenge. Another of Moore's (1956) theorems proves that the number of steps needed to learn about the internal structure of a computing machine is at least the same order of magnitude as the number of states of the machine. Indeed, the ability to write the systems of equations describing the dynamics of a simple single cell does not confer the ability to solve those equations in a realistic period (Tomita 2001). The computational challenge of simulating neural networks large enough to be relevant for explaining behavior at a membrane scale in real time seems effectively insurmountable with current computational devices.

Fortunately, a molecular-scale description of a brain state may not be necessary. Cogent arguments have been made that the discharges of neurons constitute the most appropriate level of analysis of the computational function of the brain (Barlow 1995). However, it is well known that the discharges of neurons are typically quite variable for reasons that remain unclear (e.g., Softky & Koch 1993, Shadlen & Newsome 1998). Perhaps the copious variation in neural states may be irrelevant for evaluating meaningful linking propositions. Perhaps the states of brain corresponding to perceptions, thoughts, intentions, and emotions are fewer. Ultimately, it seems most likely that a useful identity between cognitive and neural processes resides at the level of some ensemble of neurons (and glia?) comprising an anatomically interconnected network. Analyses of the reliability of the relationship between discharge rate and overt behavior indicate that the ensemble sufficient to account for performance can be as small as 10–100 neurons (Shadlen et al. 1996, Bichot et al. 2001). However, to produce an overt response, orders of magnitude more neurons are necessary (e.g., Newsome & Paré 1988, Schiller & Chou 2000, Schiller & Lee 1994). It seems that neurons selected at random from a pool can be an effective proxy for that pool because a degree of correlation exists in the activity of neurons within the pool. This suggests that in explaining behavior, the particular state of a particular neuron may not be necessary to specify. In other words, the variability observed in the activity of single neurons may overestimate the variability of the state embodied by the pool of neurons.

Finally, we must understand that the mapping of a linking proposition holds only for certain neurons, referred to as the bridge locus (Teller 1984, Teller & Pugh 1983). This is the population of neurons that comprise the most immediate substrate for the behavior and cognitive process. How can such neurons be identified? Positive evidence of a correspondence between the activity of neurons and the presence of a particular cognitive process is a good start, but the logic of exclusion is ultimately necessary (Platt 1964). All neurons that do not bear a predictable relationship with the behavior or cognitive state cannot be part of the bridge locus. In other words, the bridge locus is the set of neurons for which the linking proposition is not rejected.

Anatomical characteristics provide necessary, converging evidence. The first fact of neuroanatomy is that the brain is comprised of different types of neurons with a variety of morphological and ultrastructural characteristics, entertaining different connections. Localization of function has been at the heart of psychology and neuroscience since Bell and Magendie distinguished the sensory and motor roots of the spinal cord and Müller popularized the labeled lines of sensory processing (Boring 1942). Distinctions between functional types of neurons become much more complex further removed from the sensory or motor periphery; however, even in sensorimotor structures, proper testing can reveal neurons with different relations to covert processes and overt responses (e.g., Hanes et al. 1998, Horwitz & Newsome 1999, McPeek & Keller 2002, Sato & Schall 2003).

Connectivity is crucial converging evidence for admitting or excluding certain neurons from a bridge locus. Do the axons of the neurons in question convey spikes to the appropriate parts of the brain to instantiate the hypothesized process? For example, if a neuron does not innervate downstream motor structures, it seems extravagant to claim that activity of this neuron instantiates response preparation. Likewise, if a neuron innervates visual areas of the cortex, then it is incoherent to claim that the activity does not influence visual processing in some way. Thus, a bridge locus is a population of neurons interconnected in particular ways possibly across anatomically distinct parts of the brain with inputs suitable to convey the necessary signals and outputs appropriate to exert the necessary influence.

LINKING PROPOSITIONS ABOUT
SACCADE PRODUCTION

A wealth of information and insight informs the evaluation of specific linking propositions concerning sensation and perception (e.g., Parker & Newsome 1998, Romo & Salinas 2003), but additional insights may be gained by exploring the linking propositions for the preparation and production of movements. We will focus on saccadic eye movements, the rapid shifts of gaze used to explore scenes, because so much is known about the mechanics of the movement and the neural signals responsible (e.g., Wurtz & Goldberg 1989, Carpenter 1991).

Saccades are produced by a pulse of force that rapidly rotates the eyes followed by a step of force appropriate to resist the elastic forces of the orbit and maintain eccentric gaze. This pattern of force is exerted on the eyes by muscles innervated by neurons in the brainstem (Scudder et al. 2002, Sparks 2002) (Figure 1). Burst neurons innervate the extraocular motoneurons to provide the high-frequency burst of spikes necessary to produce saccadic eye movements. Different burst neurons innervating different motor neurons that innervate different muscles discharge for saccades in different directions. The burst neurons are subject to potent monosynaptic inhibition from omnipause neurons. Omnipause neurons discharge tonically during fixation. Immediately prior to initiation of a saccade in any direction, omnipause neurons cease discharging, releasing the inhibition on the appropriate pools of burst neurons to produce the burst in the motor neurons necessary to shift gaze in the desired direction. Upon completion of the saccade, omnipause neurons reactivate to reinstate inhibition on the burst neurons. Tonic neurons with activity proportional to the angle of the eyes in the orbit are also present in the brainstem. These tonic neurons innervate motor neurons and are innervated by burst neurons. The activation from tonic neurons results in a measure of innervation of the motor neurons necessary to maintain eccentric fixation against the centripetal elastic forces of the orbit.

The neural events preceding activation of the brainstem saccade generator occur in a circuit distributed through particular areas of the frontal lobe (Schall 1997), the basal ganglia (Hikosaka et al. 2000), cerebellum (Thier et al. 2002, Lefevre et al. 1998), and superior colliculus (Munoz & Schall 2003, Munoz et al. 2000). This circuit conveys to the brainstem saccade generator where and when to shift gaze. The superior colliculus is organized in a topographic map of saccade direction and amplitude. The frontal eye field has a rougher map of saccade amplitude, and the frontal eye field and superior colliculus are connected topographically. Thus, the direction and amplitude of the saccade produced is dictated by the location in the map of the active population of neurons. However, neurons in the frontal eye field and superior colliculus have broad movement fields, so many neurons contribute to any saccade. The activity of the pool of neurons is combined as a vector average to produce the particular saccade. The neurons in the superior colliculus that generate saccades are under tonic inhibition from neurons in the rostral end of the superior colliculus and in the basal ganglia that are active during fixation.

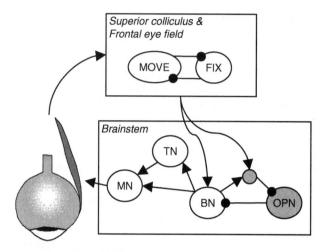

Figure 1   Simplified circuitry responsible for preparing and executing saccades. The extraocular muscles are innervated by motor neurons (MN) that produce a high-frequency burst of action potentials during saccades driven by burst neurons (BN). Tonic neurons (TN) integrate the burst to produce motor neuron activity necessary to maintain eccentric gaze. Burst neurons are under inhibitory control of omnipause neurons (OPN). The saccade generator in the brainstem receives signals for where and when to shift gaze from a circuit including the superior colliculus and frontal eye field, which consists of gaze-shifting movement neurons (MOVE) and gaze-holding fixation neurons (FIX). Movement and fixation neurons are also in reciprocal inhibitory relationship. Arrow ends signify excitatory connections and circle ends signify inhibitory connections.

Thus, another level of reciprocal inhibition outside the brainstem controls saccade production.

Influential models of this circuit formulate admirably specific propositions linking the mechanics and dynamics of saccadic eye movements, the properties of these neurons, and the control signals presumed necessary to produce saccades (e.g., Robinson 1975, Tweed & Vilis 1985, Scudder 1988, Lefevre et al. 1998; but see Robinson 1992). The discharge rate of burst neurons corresponds to eye velocity (at least for saccades less than 20 degrees). Tonic neurons are referred to as the neural integrator according to the hypothesis that they integrate the velocity signal of the burst neurons to signal eye position. Saccade termination is hypothesized to be controlled through a local feedback circuit that is driven by the error between the current eye position (or displacement) and the desired eye position (or displacement). According to these models, the discharge rate of the burst neurons corresponds to this dynamic motor error signal that creates the velocity signal to move the eyes.

Compelling evidence supports the hypothesis of a feedback control circuit. First, transient activation of the omnipause neurons while a saccade is in flight results in reduced eye velocity, even to nearly zero; however, when the omnipause neurons are returned to their normal state, the saccade continues to completion, as if the error signal had not yet been expended (e.g., Kaneko 1996). Second, reversible inactivation of the burst neurons in the brainstem results in markedly slower saccades but the duration is increased proportionally to expend the error (Barton et al. 2003). The scope and power of these models should be admired. However, it is sobering to realize that fundamental questions remain unanswered (Sparks 2002). Some limitations are technical. For example, a comprehensive account of the relation of motor neuron activity to movements of the eye requires knowledge of the characteristics of the particular muscle fibers innervated by a given motor neuron, but at present it is not possible to monitor and selectively influence selected populations of cells simultaneously. Conceptual limitations also impede understanding. For example, the unfulfilled search for the mechanism that compares current with desired eye position (or displacement) suggests that perhaps current models make incorrect assumptions or lack essential overlooked features (e.g., Steinman 1986, Brooks 2001).

Evidence for Covert Response Preparation

Stimuli can be presented and overt responses measured. However, to explain orderly relationships between responses and stimuli, it is now regarded as useful if not necessary to hypothesize certain covert processes mediating the encoding, selection, and categorization of stimuli and preparation of responses. For example, the time of an overt response to a given stimulus is variable and unpredictable (Luce 1986). Within that unpredictability, though, certain trends have been observed. For example, when given a warning ("ready") before an imperative trigger signal ("go"), subjects respond earlier and more reliably than when no warning is given (Niemi & Näätänen 1981). But, this occurs only if the passage of time allows a sense of expectation (Näätänen 1971). Reaction time can also be influenced by repetition of stimuli or responses (e.g., Dorris et al. 1999, Carpenter 2001, Bichot & Schall 2002) or by success in previous trials (Rabbitt 2002). To explain this variation, one can hypothesize a process that transpires after a warning signal and is influenced by events in preceding trials to influence the readiness to initiate a movement. Such a covert process may be called response preparation. Further evidence for response preparation is the fact that partially prepared responses can be withheld if an imperative "stop" signal occurs (e.g., Osman et al. 1986, 1990). This ability can be explained by hypothesizing another covert process that prevents movements (Logan & Cowan 1984). Before continuing, it is important to be clear what is and is not meant by response preparation.

Response Preparation and Intention

Science travels on its terminology. Formulating effective linking propositions requires characterization of covert processes that is accurate, operational, and not extravagant. However, as indicated above, such is not always the case. For example, some authors have identified *intention* with neural modulation in the parietal lobe of macaque monkeys preceding a movement (Snyder et al. 2000). Can neurophysiology reach this far?

The term intention is complex (e.g., Aune 1967). The disposition to perform some act is a central feature of an intention, but intention cannot be identified entirely with response preparation. A statement of intention must also answer, "Why was that done?" Of course, one answer can be the causal path through neurons to muscles, but this is incomplete. A satisfactory explanation must address the reasons for the action based on preferences, goals, and beliefs. In other words, to judge whether a movement was intended, one must refer to the agent's beliefs about which action must be performed under what circumstances to bring about the desired object of the intention. A consequence of this is that intentions may not be realized, but success can be judged only with reference to the description of the goal and the conditions under which it could be achieved (e.g., Heckhausen & Beckmann 1990). Furthermore, a particular movement may be intentional under one description but not under another. For example, an eye may wink or blink.

These concepts about intention have been formulated in the domain of human interactions. We cannot take for granted that they apply to animals used in neuroscience experiments. If animals cannot be said to have intentions, then information gained by invasive neurophysiology experiments cannot be related to intention. Fortunately, behavioral research describing communication and deception, for example, indicates that the attribution of intention to monkeys seems justified (e.g., Tomasello & Call 1997, Hauser et al. 2002). Certainly, abundant evidence confirms that response preparation can be studied in macaque monkeys.

Bridge Locus for Response Preparation

To discover the mechanism of response preparation, neural activity must be monitored when response preparation occurs. Therefore, subjects must perform a task that creates a state of readiness and an overt measure of that readiness. A prepared movement should be distinguished by some improvement in performance. Specific criteria for identifying a bridge locus for response preparation have been articulated (Riehle & Requin 1993). First, the neuronal discharge rate must change during a warning period before the movement. Second, the magnitude of neural modulation must be proportional to the likelihood of a movement being directed into the response field of a neuron. Third, the magnitude of neural modulation must be predictive of the probability of responding and of reaction time.

These criteria can be tested in tasks with instructional warning signals preceding imperative trigger signals. Early work described "preparatory set cells" in premotor cortex based on the observation that the neurons discharged following instructions and changed discharge rate if instructions changed (e.g., Wise & Mauritz 1985). But this attribution can be questioned because no relation was reported between neural activity and a measure of performance such as reaction time. In fact, reaction time was not affected by the waiting period; therefore, the state of preparation is not clear. Subsequent reports provided more directly concomitant neural and performance data (Riehle & Requin 1993, Riehle et al. 1994). A cue provided complete, partial, or no information about the direction and extent of a wrist movement that was executed following an imperative trigger signal. Neural activity in primary motor and in premotor cortex was correlated with the changes in reaction time depending on the amount of information conveyed by the cue. The greater the activity, the shorter the reaction time, especially when the direction of the movement was cued. These data meet the aforementioned criteria. Similar data have been obtained in the superior colliculus of monkeys performing a saccade task with varying probabilities of target appearance at one of two locations (Dorris & Munoz 1998).

In general, neurons in the frontal eye field, basal ganglia, and the superior colliculus exhibit modulated discharge rates during a warning period that correlate with the variation of reaction time (reviewed by Munoz & Schall 2003). Often preparation results in undesirable, premature movements; sprinters know this. Preparation serves nothing if movements are initiated at the least measure of activation. Toward this end, the motor system seems designed to prevent preparation from producing too many premature movements. For example, omnipause neurons are not modulated at all during periods of saccade preparation (Everling et al. 1998). The maintenance of the inhibition of the omnipause neurons on the burst neurons prevents premature saccades.

Control of Saccade Initiation

A task known as countermanding provides another avenue for identifying neurons constituting the bridge locus of response preparation. This task was developed to investigate the control of thought and action (reviewed by Logan 1994). A subject's ability to control the production of movements is probed in a reaction time task by infrequently presenting an imperative stop signal. The subject is rewarded for withholding the movement if the stop signal occurs. Performance in the countermanding task is probabilistic. In a given trial, one can predict only to an extent whether a subject will cancel the partially prepared movement. The probability of inhibiting a movement decreases as the delay between the go signal and the stop signal increases. This unpredictability arises because reaction time is fundamentally stochastic. Obviously, movements generated with shorter reaction times can occur in spite of the stop signal if they are initiated before the stop signal influences the system. Likewise, movements that would occur after longer reaction times can be canceled if a stop signal occurs because enough time is available for the process elicited by a stop signal to interrupt response preparation.

Three measures of performance can be obtained—reaction time on trials with no stop signal, reaction time of trials that escape inhibition, and the probability of inhibiting the movement. These overt measures can be accounted for remarkably well by a very simple model consisting of two processes, a GO process and a STOP process, in a race with independent, random finish times (Logan & Cowan 1984; see also Lisberger et al. 1975, Becker & Jürgens 1979). The GO process initiates the movement after presentation of the target. When no stop signal is given, only the GO process is active, so the distribution of reaction times in these trials is the distribution of finish times of the GO process. If the stop signal is presented after the target, then while the GO process proceeds, the STOP process may be invoked. If the STOP process finishes before the GO process, then the partially prepared movement is canceled. Alternatively, if the GO process finishes before the STOP process, then the movement occurs. Analysis of the overt behavior in terms of this race model affords an estimate of the duration of the covert STOP process, referred to as the stop-signal reaction time (SSRT); this is the interval required to cancel the movement that was being prepared.

A saccade version of this paradigm was developed for testing with macaque monkeys (Hanes & Schall 1995). Reinforcement was given following a saccade to a peripheral target that appeared when the fixation spot disappeared unless a stop signal was presented. The stop signal was reappearance of the fixation spot. If the stop signal appeared, reinforcement was contingent on withholding the saccade. The average SSRT for monkeys performing the saccade countermanding task is around 100 ms (Hanes & Schall 1995, Hanes et al. 1998). Performance of human subjects in the saccade countermanding task matches that of monkeys, although with slightly longer SSRT (Hanes & Carpenter 1999, Cabel et al. 2000, Logan & Irwin 2000, Asrress & Carpenter 2001, Colonius et al. 2001).

Relation of Neural Activity to Response Time

To understand how partially prepared saccades are canceled, first we must know how they are initiated. Current data show that saccades are initiated when the discharge rate of certain neurons in the superior colliculus and frontal eye field reaches a particular level, and this level does not vary with reaction time (Sparks 1978, Hanes & Schall 1996, Dorris et al. 1997) (Figure 2). The same relationship holds for activation in primary motor cortex before forelimb movements measured at the level of single neurons (Lecas et al. 1986) or at the level of an event-related scalp potential called the lateralized readiness potential (Gratton et al. 1988).

This relationship between discharge rate and reaction time holds for only a subset of the neurons encountered in these structures. The activity of neurons that have exclusively visual responses exhibits no relation to the time of saccade initiation (Brown et al. 2001). The neurons with activity that relates to saccade initiation time are specifically those that are modulated exclusively or particularly before saccades, even when no visual stimulus is present. Other research indicates that the axons of such saccade-related movement neurons project from the superior colliculus to the brainstem saccade generator (e.g., Raybourn & Keller 1977) and from frontal eye field to the superior colliculus and brainstem saccade generator (Segraves 1992, Segraves & Goldberg 1987, Sommer & Wurtz 2000). Consequently, electrical stimulation at the sites where saccade-related movement neurons are recorded elicits saccades with very low current levels while more current is needed to elicit saccades from sites where visually responsive neurons are encountered (e.g., Robinson 1972, Bruce et al. 1985).

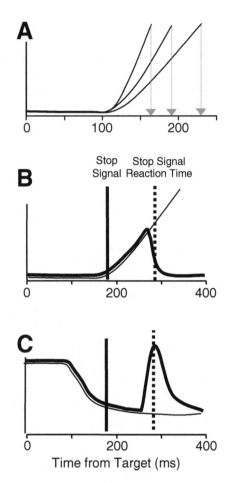

Figure 2 Stylized pattern of neural activity controlling the initiation of saccades. (A) Saccades are initiated when the discharge rate of movement neurons reaches a threshold level. The variability in reaction time originates in variability of the time taken for the neural activity to reach the threshold. (B) Comparison of activity of movement neurons in the superior colliculus and frontal eye field occurring during countermanding trials with no stop signal (thin) or trials with a stop signal in which the saccade was canceled (thick). Thick vertical line marks stop signal presentation. Dashed vertical line marks stop signal reaction time. When saccades are canceled, movement neuron activity that was increasing toward the threshold decreases rapidly, within the stop signal reaction time. (C) Comparison of fixation neuron activity during countermanding trials with no stop signal (thin) or trials with a stop signal in which the saccade was canceled (thick). When saccades are canceled, fixation neuron activity that was suppressed increases rapidly, within the stop signal reaction time.

Many models have been developed to explain the variability of reaction time under various conditions. Common sequential sampling models suppose that in response to a stimulus, some signal accumulates until it reaches a threshold, thereby triggering a response to the stimulus. One version supposes that the variability in reaction time arises from randomness in the level of the trigger threshold (e.g., Grice et al. 1982). Another version assumes that the threshold is constant and the variability in reaction time arises from randomness in the rate of growth of the accumulator (e.g., Carpenter & Williams 1995, Ratcliff & Rouder 1998). In fact, this is another instance in which different architectures cannot be distinguished by overt behavior (Dzhafarov 1993). The neurophysiological data indicate that the variability in saccade reaction time arises from variation in the rate of growth of the movement-related activity toward the trigger threshold (Figure 2). This observation of inner workings has been interpreted as evidence for the fixed-threshold, variable-growth architecture and against the variable-threshold, fixed-growth architecture (Hanes & Schall 1996).

Of course, this observation is relevant for distinguishing the alternative model architectures only if the population of neurons for which the observation holds is the bridge locus of the accumulator. This cannot be taken for granted. The accumulator conceived of in sequential sampling models is commonly regarded as the growth of evidence about alternative stimuli. Such models incorporate an additional sensory and motor transduction and transmission delay, but this is regarded as a fixed interval (e.g., Ratcliff & Rouder 1998, Usher & McClelland 2001). Recent neurophysiological studies have interpreted a slowly increasing neural activation as just such an accumulation of evidence (Gold & Shadlen 2000, Roitman & Shadlen 2002, Cook & Manusell 2002, Krauzlis & Dill 2002). This interpretation is strengthened by the possible correspondence between this neural signal and the ratio of the likelihood of the alternatives, which is an optimal decision variable (Gold & Shadlen 2001). However, none of these models or neural studies explains how satisfaction of a criterion of evidence can initiate a movement of the body.

As reviewed above, the original physiological evidence that movements were initiated when neural activity reached a threshold was obtained from neural signals that should be identified with response preparation (Gratton et al. 1988, Hanes & Schall 1996). Therefore, if the original models were about the form of the accumulation of evidence, then the pattern of movement-related activity seems irrelevant, unless one wishes to identify accumulating evidence with response preparation. However, such an identification is clearly incorrect. The distinction between accumulating evidence and preparing a response can be made explicit when an arbitrary mapping of response onto stimulus is introduced. For example, recent studies have demonstrated that arbitrary stimulus-response mapping (e.g., prosaccade versus antisaccade responses) changes the influence of electrical stimulation of frontal eye field (Gold & Shadlen 2003) and introduces measurable delays in the time taken to encode stimulus properties, select targets for saccades, and initiate movements (Sato & Schall 2003). The joint observations of variability in the time taken to accumulate evidence and variability in the time taken to prepare a response coupled with the fact that arbitrary movements can be produced in response to a given stimulus seem to require a theoretical framework comprised of distinct, successive stages of processing (Sternberg 2001, Schall 2003).

The hypothesis that stimulus-guided behavior is the outcome of distinct, successive stages of processing entails unavoidable methodological and conceptual problems. For example, how can the finish times of successive stochastic stages be distinguished within the distribution of random reaction times? Also, are the transformations within and transmissions between stages continuous or discrete (e.g., Coles et al. 1985, Miller 1988)? Neurophysiological data from behaving monkeys can address these questions by measuring the duration of intermediate stages of processing through the evolution of neural activity in the frontal eye field of monkeys performing visual search (Thompson et al. 1996, Sato & Schall 2003, Sato et al. 2001). Also, it has been possible to show that the processes of saccade preparation assessed through the activation of saccade-related movement neurons is influenced by the properties of visual stimuli, which is evidence in support of the continuous flow between stages (Bichot et al. 2001). However, both of these observations are interpretable only insofar as the neural events that are measured map onto the relevant cognitive processes. Indeed, the fact that such conclusions hinge on this mapping highlights the necessary role of explicit linking propositions in reasoning about the relation between neural processes and the supervening functional processes.

Relation of Neural Activity to Movement Cancellation

The countermanding paradigm provides two criteria for determining whether a neuron comprises the bridge locus for saccade production. First, obviously, activation must be different when movements are produced versus not produced. Second, critically, the difference in activation when movements are canceled must occur within the SSRT, that is, within the time that the movement was canceled. Certain but not all neurons in the frontal eye field and superior colliculus meet these criteria (Hanes et al. 1998, Paré & Hanes 2003) (Figure 2). Neurons with saccade-related activity, which began to increase toward the trigger threshold, failed to reach the threshold activation level when saccades were canceled. Instead, when partially prepared saccades were canceled, the saccade-related activity decreased rapidly after the stop signal was presented. Moreover, the saccade-related activity associated with canceling as compared to executing the saccade became different just before the SSRT elapsed. A complementary pattern of neural activity was observed in fixation neurons. If eye movements were canceled, fixation neurons that had decreased firing generated a rapid increase of discharge rate before the SSRT. Notably, neurons with exclusively visual responses modulate not at all or too late when saccades are canceled. According to the logic of the countermanding paradigm, the activity of movement and fixation but not visual neurons in frontal eye field and superior colliculus is logically sufficient to specify whether or not a saccade will be produced and therefore comprise the bridge locus of saccade preparation. The same conclusions can be drawn from the variation of the magnitude of the lateralized readiness potential in humans performing manual movements in a stop-signal task (De Jong et al. 1990, 1995; van Boxtel et al. 2001).

Alternative Propositions Mapping GO and STOP onto Neural Processes

The GO and STOP processes are defined at a functional level by the race model. How do they map onto brain processes? This seems deceptively simple to articulate, but we will proceed deliberately by considering three propositions: (*a*) GO and STOP map onto different cortical areas or subcortical structures, (*b*) GO and STOP map onto distinct kinds of neurons, and (*c*) GO and STOP map onto particular periods of activation of particular pools of neurons.

Consider the proposition that GO and STOP map onto distinct structures. Some reports have identified certain parts of the frontal lobe with response inhibition (e.g., Aron et al. 2003). However, as reviewed above, certain neurons are active in a manner sufficient to instantiate the GO and STOP processes, but others within the same structure decidedly do not. The heterogeneity of neurons in frontal eye field and superior colliculus compels rejection of the proposition that GO and STOP map onto distinct cortical areas or subcortical structures. Generalizing this conclusion to other parts of the brain and other tasks highlights the severe limits of inferences about mechanism possible from noninvasive measurements such as event-related potentials or functional brain imaging (Uttal 2001, Friston 2002).

Next, consider the proposition that GO and STOP map onto distinct kinds of neurons. In the context of saccade production, it seems sensible to identify the GO process with gaze-shifting (movement) neurons and the STOP process with gaze-holding (fixation) neurons. This simple interpretation is challenged, though, by the observation that when the GO process leads to a saccade, movement neurons exhibit increased discharge rate but *at the same time* fixation neurons exhibit decreased discharge rate (e.g., Dorris & Munoz 1998, Dorris et al. 1997) (Figure 2). Likewise, when saccades are canceled, fixation neurons exhibit a rapid increase in discharge rate while at effectively the same time movement neurons exhibit a rapid decrease in discharge rate (Hanes et al. 1998, Paré & Hanes 2003). As reviewed above, this coordinated pattern of activation probably comes about through reciprocal inhibition between fixation cells and movement neurons within and across structures. The concurrent modulation of the movement and fixation neurons associated with gaze shifting and gaze holding suggests rejection of the proposition that GO and STOP map exclusively onto distinct kinds of neurons.

Consequently, by exclusion the GO and STOP processes map onto periods of activation of particular sets of interconnected neurons in a distributed network. GO can map onto the coordinated increase of movement cell activity and decrease of fixation cell activity. STOP can map onto the neural events that occur in canceled trials—the concomitant rapid increase of fixation cell activity and decrease of movement cell activity. Current evidence indicates that this reciprocal activation of movement and fixation neurons occurs through mutual inhibition (e.g., Munoz & Wurtz 1993b, Munoz & Istvan 1998, Quaia et al. 1999).

The proposition that the GO and STOP processes map onto common pools of interacting neurons poses a potential paradox—how can two processes racing with independent finish times emerge from a network of interacting units? Perhaps the formulation of a race between GO and STOP is flawed. Some reports have presented evidence inconsistent with the predictions of the race model (Colonius et al. 2001). However, this evidence amounts to the performance of rare, exceptional subjects. Moreover, an alternative account has not been formulated.

On the other hand, several lines of evidence are consistent with predictions of the race model. First, if the presence of the stop signal slowed the process of generating the movement, then the trials that are produced in spite of the stop signal should have slower reaction time. However, the reaction times of movements that escape inhibition correspond to the reaction times in trials with no stop signal with values less than the SSRT (Logan & Cowan 1984; Osman et al. 1986, 1990; Band et al. 2003). Second, if the presence of the stop signal interfered with the process of generating the movement, then saccade amplitude or velocity should be reduced. However, saccade amplitude and velocity are not different during noncanceled trials and trials with no stop signal (Hanes & Schall 1995). Third, if the response to the stop signal affected response preparation, then the neural processes leading to noncanceled movements should be different from those leading to movements when no stop signal occurs. However, neither the lateralized readiness potential (De Jong et al. 1990, van Boxtel et al. 2001) nor the activity of movement and fixation neurons in frontal eye field and superior colliculus (Hanes et al. 1998, Paré & Hanes 2003) are different between noncanceled trials and trials with no stop signal. Finally, weak violation of the finish time independence premise is not fatal; it only means that the estimate of the SSRT will vary as a function of stop-signal delay (De Jong et al. 1990, Band et al. 2003). Therefore, according to its effectiveness and elegance, we have no basis to reject the validity of the race formulation, so we must contend with the challenge of reconciling performance described by a race model produced by a mechanism comprised of interacting units.

The reconciliation hinges on a deeper understanding of the constitution of the GO and STOP processes. The Logan & Cowan (1984) race model assumes stochastic independence of the finish times of GO and STOP processes. The model says nothing about the means by which the process reaches the finish times. The model is also mute about what happens after either process finishes, beyond requiring that the completion of the STOP process interrupts the GO process and vice versa. The model is not explicit about how this interaction occurs or about how the GO and STOP processes are reset. The key to understanding how independent finish times can arise from interacting elements is to realize that SSRT measures the *end of the STOP process*, but the interval from presentation of the stop signal to successful interruption of response preparation must be occupied by at least two processes, one that encodes the stop signal and a subsequent one that interrupts response preparation to cancel the movement. Only the latter process should be identified with a STOP process that directly influences response preparation. The more potent this terminal STOP process, then the briefer the interaction with the GO process and thus the more independent appear the finish times of GO and STOP.

Realizing that a complete response to the stop signal includes encoding, mapping and enacting provides insight into quantitative differences in SSRT observed across studies. Previous studies using acoustic stop signals and manual movements yielded SSRT values of around 200 msec (Logan 1994) while use of a fixation spot at a stop signal for saccades yields SSRT values around 100 msec (Hanes & Schall 1995). The difference in SSRT between the saccade and manual versions of the countermanding task probably derives from the fact that a visual stimulus flashing in the fovea directly activates the gaze-holding fixation system (Munoz & Wurtz 1993a), but more time is needed to interpret an acoustic stimulus as a signal to stop a limb movement.

Realizing that a complete response to the stop signal includes encoding, mapping, and enacting also provides a critical perspective on the validity of some of the arguments in support of the independence premise. It has been argued that the lack of a difference in the lateralized readiness potential (De Jong et al. 1990, van Boxtel et al. 2001) or the activity of movement and fixation neurons in frontal eye field and superior colliculus (Hanes et al. 1998, Paré & Hanes 2003) between noncanceled trials and trials with no stop signal is evidence in support of the independence premise. However, this reasoning is flawed on two counts. First, it confuses dynamics with finish times. Second, presence of the stop signal does not guarantee that the STOP process was active. In fact, fixation cells in frontal eye field and superior colliculus are not activated on noncanceled trials of the saccade countermanding task. If this modulation of gaze-holding fixation cells instantiates the STOP process, then the STOP process was not activated on noncanceled trials in this task. Therefore, this test of independence is invalid because the STOP process was not activated. In fact, the absence of modulation of fixation and movement neurons in noncanceled trials has been used to interpret the possible role of activity of neurons in the medial frontal lobe in monitoring errors and response conflict (Stuphorn et al. 2000, Ito et al. 2003).

EVALUATING LINKING PROPOSITIONS FOR THE PRODUCTION OF SACCADES

Three decades of research on the neural basis of saccade production has produced a wealth of information that should provide a basis to evaluate the family of relations linking neural events with the preparation and execution of saccades.

Do Identical Neural States Map onto Identical Saccades?

The foregoing discussion indicates that "identical neural state" means "statistically indistinguishable state of a particular population of neurons with connections appropriate to mediate the hypothesized function." What does "identical saccade" mean? Saccades can be identical according to endpoint, amplitude, and velocity, although saccades exhibit a stereotyped relation between amplitude and velocity (Becker 1989).

Much evidence supports this proposition for saccade execution. A very high correlation exists between saccade metrics and dynamics and the discharge rate of individual oculomotor, burst, and tonic neurons, but there is definite variability in the activity of single neurons associated with saccades of a given direction and amplitude (e.g., Sylvestre & Cullen 1999). However, it seems clear that the innervation that moves and holds the eyes is the result of a population of neurons with less collective variability. Differences in the pattern and degree of burst, tonic, and motor neuron discharge translate immediately into different muscle contractions and so to different eye movements.

Microstimulation of a given site in superior colliculus or frontal eye field evokes saccades of a particular direction and amplitude, and the variation in the endpoint of the saccade evoked by electrical stimulation is less than that for visually guided saccades (Bruce et al. 1985, van Opstal et al. 1990). Likewise, when saccades of different directions and amplitudes are made, the spatial distribution of activation in the superior colliculus and frontal eye field shifts accordingly. While the endpoints of repetitive saccades exhibit some scatter, the quantitative characteristics of this scatter suggest that it originates in random variation of activation within the motor map of superior colliculus (van Opstal & van Gisbergen 1989).

The identity between the timing of neural discharge and the initiation of a saccade entails certain complexities. First, the original analyses measured the threshold as the mean discharge rate across the sets of trials with particular reaction times. Obviously, the functional threshold cannot be the average because on all trials with activity less than the average, no saccade should be produced, and it is not clear how the nervous system could calculate the average. Moreover, the activity of any single neuron may be sufficient to predict reaction time with reasonable reliability (Hanes et al. 1998), but the collective activity of many neurons is necessary to produce saccades (e.g., Schiller & Chou 2000). A more reasonable hypothesis is that the threshold is some minimum value of activation across a pool of neurons. The value of this minimum and the size of this pool can be estimated from data collected in the countermanding task which afford a more quantitative statement of this proposition—the probability of generating a saccade given that a stop signal occurred is equal to the probability that the activity of the relevant neurons reaches the threshold. Current evidence indicates that a pool of around 10 movement neurons in frontal eye field provide activity of sufficient reliability to instantiate such a threshold (Brown et al. 2001).

However, exceptions to the hypothesis of a fixed threshold for evoking saccades have been observed. First, the magnitude of activity of movements cells in superior colliculus and frontal eye field before antisaccades is systematically less than that before prosaccades (Everling & Munoz 2000). However, this difference may be related to differences in the metrics and dynamics of antisaccades. Second, another experiment recorded neural activity in one frontal eye field while electrically stimulating the contralateral frontal eye field to evoke saccades (Schlag et al. 1998). Stimulation of the contralateral frontal eye field could produce an identical burst of action potentials in certain frontal eye field neurons whether or not a saccade was evoked. Further research is needed to determine the generality of these exceptions.

Despite these qualifications, it seems clear that indistinguishable neural states do map onto indistinguishable saccade metrics, dynamics, and initiation time.

Do Identical Saccades Map onto Identical Neural States?

Several lines of evidence demonstrate that the same saccade can originate from markedly different brain states. For example, a saccade of a given vector can be evoked by electrical stimulation of a particular site in the superior colliculus or frontal eye field. But the same saccade can be evoked by simultaneous stimulation of two different sites such that the resulting saccade is the vector average of the pair of respective saccades (Robinson 1972). Likewise, a recent study has shown that a given saccade can occur under one circumstance following the activation of a pool of neurons in the superior colliculus responding to a single stimulus and under another circumstance following the activation of two pools of neurons responding to two stimuli presented simultaneously (Edelman & Keller 1998). This dissociation has been referred to as a motomere (Sparks 1999), in parallel with perceptual metemeres that are physically distinct stimuli that evoke indistinguishable perceptual reports (e.g., Ratcliff & Sirovich 1978). The existence of perceptual metemeres presents at once an opportunity and a barrier to describing how perceptual reports relate to neural states because they demonstrate a many-to-one mapping of brain states onto perception.

The fact that physically different stimuli cannot be distinguished perceptually means that somewhere between the receptors and the bridge locus information was lost. The existence of motomere equivalence classes has somewhat different implications. First, given that saccades are produced ultimately by a network in the brainstem, the pattern of activation in this network must bear a much more direct correspondence to the saccade that is produced. Consequently, ambiguity inherent in the pattern of activation in the superior colliculus and frontal eye field must be resolved in the brainstem to produce one particular saccade.

Second, evidence for many-to-one mapping of brain states onto movements has important implications for the neural basis of intentional actions. If the mapping of neural activity onto movement were one-to-one, then the causal basis of movements would be clear—a particular action follows necessarily from a given brain state as reliably as a reflex. While such an automatic causal process seems an adequate account of certain kinds of movements (e.g., blinks), it cannot provide a satisfactory account of other kinds of movements (e.g., winks). Intended movements are owned ("I did") while unintended movements are not ("It happened"). In other words, we can distinguish the *cause of* from the *reason for* movements (Davidson 1963).

In fact, some have argued that a many-to-one mapping of neural activity onto cognition and behavior provides room for intentional reasons within neural causes (Juarrero 1999). If a given saccade can be the realization of different brain states, then according to the argument, the dependence of the behavior on an intention holds in virtue of the content of the representation of the intention and not its neural realization as such (van Gulick 1993, Dretske 1998, Kim 1998). The relevant content answers, "Why did you do that?" Thus, the argument goes, a movement can be called an intentional action if and only if it originates from a cognitive state with meaningful content, and this content defines the cognitive state's causal influence.

We can apply this argument to saccades. The same saccade can be the outcome of two (or more) distinguishable patterns of neural activity instantiating two (or more) distinguishable representations. The representation of a single focus of activation in the superior colliculus leading to a saccade of a particular vector can be distinguished from the representation of two foci of activation leading to the same saccade through averaging. However, the two mappings of neural representations onto saccades do not have equal status. Averaging saccades are maladaptive, for they direct gaze to neither stimulus; they are errors that must be corrected to achieve the goal of vision. According to this analysis, averaging saccades would be regarded as unintentional errors. If asked, subjects would typically report that they did not intend to shift gaze into the space between two stimuli. In contrast, an accurate saccade to one of the two stimuli would achieve the goal of vision and would more likely be owned as intentional.

This analysis depends on whether the brain can represent the consequences of actions. Does the brain know what it means to do? Recent research has shown that the medial frontal lobe registers errors and success (e.g., Botvinick et al. 2001, Blakemore et al. 2002, Schall et al. 2002). For example, in monkeys performing the countermanding saccade task neurons signaling errors were observed in the supplementary eye field (Stuphorn et al. 2000) and anterior cingulate cortex (Ito et al. 2003). Many of these neurons responded as well to omission of earned reinforcement. Such signals can be used to adjust behavior and provide the basis for distinguishing "I did" from "It happened."

SUMMARY AND CONCLUSIONS

The current literature in cognitive neuroscience includes many claims identifying certain neural events (usually activation of neurons in some part of the brain) with particular cognitive capacities (often multifaceted such as decision making, memory, or even social cooperation). This review has examined the conceptual and technical complexity of formulating and evaluating such claims in the domain of saccadic eye movements. Much is at stake in this endeavor in view of the ethical and legal ramifications of determining the nature of the mapping between mental states and brain states (Farah 2002, Moreno 2003). But, if the relationship between neural events and control of gaze is so difficult to elucidate, what hope have we of understanding the mechanisms of more elaborate cognitive processes? Despite fantastic technical developments, lingering methodological and conceptual limitations hinder progress in understanding how mental processes (wrapped up in folk psychology) reduce to or emerge from neural processes. Will we understand how "I do" even though I don't, like we understand how the "sun rises" even though it doesn't?

ACKNOWLEDGMENTS

I thank B. Atkinson, G. Fox, E. Gotcher, and C. Wiley for assistance in manuscript preparation and R. Blake, M. Chun, P. Churchland, K. Cullen, D. Noelle, T. Palmeri, S. Shorter-Jacobi, and V. Stuphorn for helpful discussion. Support was provided by NEI, NICHD, NIMH, NSF, and the McKnight Endowment Fund for Neuroscience.

The *Annual Review of Psychology* is online at http://psych.annualreviews.org

LITERATURE CITED

Aron AR, Fletcher PC, Bullmore ET, Sahakian BJ, Robbins TW. 2003. Stop-signal inhibition disrupted by damage to right inferior frontal gyrus in humans. *Nat. Neurosci.* 6:115–16

Asrress KN, Carpenter RHS. 2001. Saccadic countermanding: a comparison of central and peripheral stop signals. *Vis. Res.* 41:2645–51

Aune B. 1967. Intention. In *The Encyclopedia of Philosophy*, Vol. 4, ed. P Edwards. New York: Macmillan

Band GP, Van der Molen MW, Logan GD. 2003. Horse-race model simulations of the stop-signal procedure. *Acta Psychol.* 112:105–42

Barlow HB. 1995. The neuron doctrine in perception. In *The Cognitive Neurosciences*, ed. MS Gazzaniga, pp. 415–35. Cambridge, MA: MIT Press

Barsalou LW, Huttenlocher J, Lamberts K. 1998. Basing categorization on individuals and events. *Cogn. Psychol.* 36:203–72

Barton EJ, Nelson JS, Gandhi NJ, Sparks DL. 2003. Effects of partical lidocaine inactivation of the paramedian pontine reticular formatin on saccades of macaques. *J. Neurophysiol.* (Feb. 12, 2003). 10.1152/jn.01041.2002 [epub ahead of print]

Basso MA, Wurtz RH. 1998. Modulation of neuronal activity in superior colliculus by changes in target probability. *J. Neurosci.* 18:7519–34

Becker W. 1989. Saccades. In *The Neurobiology of Saccadic Eye Movements*, ed. RH Wurtz, ME Goldberg, pp. 13–98. New York: Elsevier

Becker W, Jürgens R. 1979. An analysis of the saccadic system by means of double step stimuli. *Vis. Res.* 19:967–83

Bichot NP, Rao SC, Schall JD. 2001. Continuous processing in macaque frontal cortex during visual search. *Neuropsychologia* 39:972–82

Bichot NP, Schall JD. 1999. Effects of similarity and history on neural mechanisms of visual selection. *Nat. Neurosci.* 2:549–54

Bichot NP, Schall JD. 2002. Priming in macaque frontal cortex during popout visual search: feature-based facilitation and location-based inhibition of return. *J. Neurosci.* 22:4675–85

Blakemore SJ, Wolpert DM, Frith CD. 2002. Abnormalities in the awareness of action. *Trends Cogn. Sci.* 6:237–42

Boring E. 1942. *Sensation and Perception in the History of Experimental Psychology*. New York: Appleton-Century

Botvinick MM, Braver TS, Barch DM, Carter CS, Cohen JD. 2001. Conflict monitoring and cognitive control. *Psychol. Rev.* 108:624–52

Brindley GS. 1970. *Physiology of Retina and Visual Pathways.* Baltimore: Williams & Wilkins. 2nd ed.

Brooks R. 2001. The relationship between matter and life. *Nature* 409: 409–11

Brown JW, Stuphorn V, Schall JD. 2001. Reliability of macaque FEF but not SEF movement neurons predicting saccade initiation. *Soc. Neurosci. Abstr.* 27:575.9

Bruce CJ, Goldberg ME, Bushnell C, Stanton GB. 1985. Primate frontal eye fields. II. Physiological and anatomical correlates of electrically evoked eye movements. *J. Neurophysiol.* 54:714–34

Bundesen C. 1990. A theory of visual attention. *Psychol. Rev.* 97:523–47

Cabel DWJ, Armstrong IT, Reingold E, Munoz DP. 2000. Control of saccade initiation in a countermanding task using visual and auditory stop signals. *Exp. Brain Res.* 133:431–41

Carpenter RHS. 1991. *Eye Movements.* Volume 8. *Vision and Visual Dysfunction.* Boston: CRC

Carpenter RHS. 2001. Express saccades: Is bimodality a result of the order of stimulus presentation? *Vis. Res.* 41:1145–51

Carpenter RHS, Williams MLL. 1995. Neural computation of log likelihood in the control of saccadic eye movements. *Nature* 377:59–62

Churchland PS. 1986. *Neurophilosophy: Toward a Unified Science of the Mind-Brain.* Cambridge, MA: MIT Press

Clark A. 1999. An embodied cognitive science? *Trends Cogn. Sci.* 3:345–51

Coles MG, Gratton G, Bashore TR, Eriksen CW, Donchin E. 1985. A psychophysiological investigation of the continuous flow model of human information processing. *J. Exp. Psychol. Hum. Percept. Perform.* 11:529–53

Colonius H, Ozyurt J, Arndt PA. 2001. Countermanding saccades with auditory stop signals: testing the race model. *Vis. Res.* 41:1951–68

Cook EP, Maunsell JH. 2002. Dynamics of neuronal responses in macaque MT and VIP during motion detection. *Nat. Neurosci.* 5:985–94

Crick F. 1994. *The Astonishing Hypothesis.* New York: Scribner's

Davidson D. 1963. Actions, reasons and causes. *J. Philos.* 60:685–700

Davidson D. 1970. Mental events. In *Essays on Actions and Events*, pp. 207–27. Oxford, UK: Clarendon. Reprinted 2001

De Jong R, Coles MG, Logan GD. 1995. Strategies and mechanisms in nonselective and selective inhibitory motor control. *J. Exp. Psychol. Hum. Percept. Perform.* 21:498–511

De Jong R, Coles MG, Logan GD, Gratton G. 1990. In search of the point of no return: the control of response processes. *J. Exp. Psychol. Hum. Percept. Perform.* 16:164–82

Dorris MC, Munoz DP. 1998. Saccadic probability influences motor preparation signals and time to saccadic initiation. *J. Neurosci.* 18:7015–26

Dorris MC, Paré M, Munoz DP. 1997. Neuronal activity in monkey superior colliculus related to the initiation of saccadic eye movements. *J. Neurosci.* 17:8566–79

Dorris MC, Taylor TL, Klein RM, Munoz DP. 1999. Influence of previous visual stimulus or saccade on saccadic reaction times in monkey. *J. Neurophysiol.* 81:2429–36

Dretske F. 1988. *Explaining Behavior; Reasons in a World of Causes.* Cambridge, MA: MIT Press

Dretske F. 1998. Minds, machines, and money: what really explains behavior. In *Human Action, Deliberation and Causation: Philosophical Studies Series*, ed. J Bransen, SE Cuypers, 77:157–73. Dordrecht, Netherlands/Norwell, MA: Kluwer Acad.

Dzhafarov EN. 1993. Grice-representability of response time distribution families. *Psychometrika* 58:281–314

Edelman JA, Keller EL. 1998. Dependence on target configuration of express saccade-related activity in the primate superior colliculus. *J. Neurophysiol.* 80:1407–26

Everling S, Munoz DP. 2000. Neuronal correlates for preparatory set associated with prosaccades and anti-saccades in the primate frontal eye field. *J. Neurosci.* 20:387–400

Everling S, Pare M, Dorris MC, Munoz DP. 1998. Comparison of the discharge characteristics of brain stem omnipause neurons and superior colliculus fixation neurons in monkey: implications for control of fixation and saccade behavior. *J. Neurophysiol.* 79:511–28

Farah MJ. 2002. Emerging ethical issues in neuroscience. *Nat. Neurosci.* 5:1123–29

Fodor J. 1981. *Representations.* Cambridge, MA: MIT Press

Friston K. 2002. Beyond phrenology: What can neuroimaging tell us about distributed circuitry? *Annu. Rev. Neurosci.* 25:221–50

Garner WR, Hake HW, Eriksen CW. 1956. Operationism and the concept of perception. *Psychol. Rev.* 63:149–59

Glimcher PW, Sparks DL. 1992. Movement selection in advance of action in the superior colliculus. *Nature* 355:542–45

Gold JI, Shadlen MN. 2000. Representation of a perceptual decision in developing oculomotor commands. *Nature* 404:390–94

Gold JI, Shadlen MN. 2001. Neural computations that underlie decisions about sensory stimuli. *Trends Cogn. Sci.* 5:10–16

Gold JI, Shadlen MN. 2003. The influence of behavioral context on the representation of a perceptual decision in developing oculomotor commands. *J. Neurosci.* 23:632–51

Goldberg ME, Wurtz RH. 1972. Activity of superior colliculus in behaving monkey. II. Effect of attention on neuronal responses. *J. Neurophysiol.* 35:560–74

Gratton G, Coles MGH, Sirevaag EJ, Eriksen CW, Donchin E. 1988. Pre- and poststimulus activation of response channels: a psychophysiological analysis. *J. Exp. Psychol. Hum. Percept. Perform.* 14:331–44

Grice GR, Nullmeyer R, Spiker VA. 1982. Human reaction time: toward a general theory. *J. Exp. Psychol. Gen.* 111:135–53

Hanes DP, Carpenter RHS. 1999. Countermanding saccades in humans: evidence for a race-to-threshold process. *Vis. Res.* 39:2777–91

Hanes DP, Patterson WF, Schall JD. 1998. The role of frontal eye field in countermanding saccades: visual, movement and fixation activity. *J. Neurophysiol.* 79:817–34

Hanes DP, Schall JD. 1995. Countermanding saccades in macaque. *Vis. Neurosci.* 12:929–37

Hanes DP, Schall JD. 1996. Neural control of voluntary movement initiation. *Science* 274:427–30

Hauser MD, Chomsky N, Fitch WT. 2002. The faculty of language: What is it, who has it, and how did it evolve? *Science* 298:1569–79

Heckhausen H, Beckmann J. 1990. Intentional action and action slips. *Psychol. Rev.* 97:36–48

Hikosaka O, Takikawa Y, Kawagoe R. 2000. Role of the basal ganglia in the control of purposive saccadic eye movements. *Physiol. Rev.* 80:953–78

Horwitz GD, Newsome WT. 1999. Separate signals for target selection and movement specification in the superior colliculus. *Science* 284:1158–61

Ito S, Stuphorn V, Brown JW, Schall JD. 2003. Performance monitoring by anterior cingulate cortex: comparison not conflict during countermanding. *Science.* In press

Juarrero A. 1999. *Dynamics in Action: Intentional Behavior as a Complex System.* Cambridge, MA: MIT Press

Kaneko CRS. 1996. Effect of ibotenic acid lesions of the omnipause neurons on saccadic eye movements in rhesus macaques. *J. Neurophysiol.* 75:2229–42

Kim J. 1998. *Mind in a Physical World: An Essay on the Mind-Body Problem and Mental Causation.* Cambridge, MA: MIT Press

Krauzlis R, Dill N. 2002. Neural correlates of target choice for pursuit and saccades in the primate superior colliculus. *Neuron* 35:355–63

Kustov AA, Robinson DL. 1996. Shared neural control of attentional shifts and eye movements. *Nature* 384:74–77

Lecas J-C, Requin J, Anger C, Vitton N.

1986. Changes in neuronal activity of the monkey precentral cortex during preparation for movement. *J. Neurophysiol.* 56:1680–702

Lefevre P, Quaia C, Optican LM. 1998. Distributed model of control of saccades by superior colliculus and cerebellum. *Neural Netw.* 11:1175–90

Leventhal AG, Schall JD. 1983. Structural basis of orientation sensitivity in cat retinal ganglion cells. *J. Comp. Neurol.* 220:465–75

Lisberger SG, Fuchs AF, King WM, Evinger LC. 1975. Effect of mean reaction time on saccadic responses to two-step stimuli with horizontal and vertical components. *Vis. Res.* 15:1021–25

Logan GD. 1994. On the ability to inhibit thought and action: A user's guide to the stop signal paradigm. In *Inhibitory Processes in Attention, Memory and Language*, ed. D Dagenbach, TH Carr, pp. 189–239. San Diego, CA: Academic

Logan GD. 2002. An instance theory of attention and memory. *Psychol. Rev.* 109:376–400

Logan GD, Cowan WB. 1984. On the ability to inhibit thought and action: a theory of an act of control. *Psychol. Rev.* 91:295–327

Logan GD, Irwin DE. 2000. Don't look! Don't touch! Inhibitory control of eye and hand movements. *Psychon. Bull. Rev.* 7:107–12

Logothetis NK, Schall JD. 1989. Neuronal correlates of subjective visual perception. *Science* 245:761–63

Luce RD. 1986. *Response Times: Their Role in Inferring Elementary Mental Organization.* Oxford, UK: Oxford Univ. Press

Luce RD. 1995. Four tensions concerning mathematical modeling in psychology. *Annu. Rev. Psychol.* 46:1–26

Marr D. 1982. *Vision: A Computational Investigation into the Human Representation and Processing of Visual Information.* San Francisco: Freeman

Mays LE, Sparks DL. 1980. Saccades are spatially, not retinocentrically, coded. *Science* 208:1163–65

McPeek RM, Keller EL. 2002. Saccade target selection in the superior colliculus during a visual search task. *J. Neurophysiol.* 88:2019–34

Miller JO. 1988. Discrete and continuous models of human information processing; theoretical distinctions and empirical results. *Acta Psychol.* 67:191–257

Moore EF. 1956. Gedanken-experiments on sequential machines. In *Automata Studies,* ed. CE Shannon, J McCarthy, pp. 129–53. Princeton, NJ: Princeton Univ. Press

Moreno JD. 2003. Neuroethics: an agenda for neuroscience and society. *Nat. Rev. Neurosci.* 4:149–53

Munoz DP, Dorris MC, Pare M, Everling S. 2000. On your mark, get set: brainstem circuitry underlying saccadic initiation. *Can. J. Physiol. Pharmacol.* 78:934–44

Munoz DP, Istvan PJ. 1998. Lateral inhibitory interactions in the intermediate layers of the monkey superior colliculus. *J. Neurophysiol.* 79:1193–209

Munoz DP, Schall JD. 2003. Concurrent distributed control of saccades. In *The Oculomotor System: New Approaches for Studying Sensorimotor Integration,* ed. WC Hall, AK Moschovakis. Boca Raton, FL: CRC Press. In press

Munoz DP, Wurtz RH. 1993a. Fixation cells in monkey superior colliculus. I. Characteristics of cell discharge. *J. Neurophysiol.* 70:559–75

Munoz DP, Wurtz RH. 1993b. Fixation cells in monkey superior colliculus. II. Reversible activation and deactivation. *J. Neurophysiol.* 70:576–89

Murthy A, Thompson KG, Schall JD. 2001. Dynamic dissociation of visual selection from saccade programming in FEF. *J. Neurophysiol.* 86:2634–37

Näätänen R. 1971. Non-aging foreperiods and simple reaction time. *Acta Psychol.* 35:316–27

Newsome WT, Paré EB. 1988. A selective impairment of motion perception following lesions of the middle temporal visual area (MT). *J. Neurosci.* 8:2201–11

Niemi P, Näätänen R. 1981. Foreperiod and

simple reaction time. *Psychol. Bull.* 89:133–62

Osman A, Kornblum S, Meyer DE. 1986. The point of no return in choice reaction time: controlled and ballistic stages of response preparation. *J. Exp. Psychol. Hum. Percept. Perform.* 12:243–58

Osman A, Kornblum S, Meyer DE. 1990. Does motor programming necessitate response execution? *J. Exp. Psychol. Hum. Percept. Perform.* 16:183–98

Paré M, Hanes DP. 2003. Controlled movement processing: superior colliculus activity associated with countermanded saccades. *J. Neurosci.* 23:6480–89

Parker AJ, Newsome WT. 1998. Sense and the single neuron: probing the physiology of perception. *Annu. Rev. Neurosci.* 21:227–77

Platt JR. 1964. Strong inference. *Science* 146:347–53

Pylyshyn Z. 1984. *Computation and Cognition.* Cambridge, MA: MIT Press

Quaia C, Lefevre P, Optican LM. 1999. Model of the control of saccades by superior colliculus and cerebellum. *J. Neurophysiol.* 82:999–1018

Rabbitt P. 2002. Consciousness is slower than you think. *Q. J. Exp. Psychol. A* 55:1081–92

Ratcliff R, Rouder JN. 1998. Modeling response times for two-choice decisions. *Psychol. Sci.* 9:347–56

Ratcliff F, Sirovich L. 1978. Equivalence classes of visual stimuli. *Vis. Res.* 18:845–51

Raybourn MS, Keller EL. 1977. Colliculoreticular organization in primate oculomotor system. *J. Neurophysiol.* 40:861–78

Riehle A, MacKay WA, Requin J. 1994. Are extent and force independent movement parameters? Preparation- and movement-related neuronal activity in the monkey cortex. *Exp. Brain Res.* 99:56–74

Riehle A, Requin J. 1993. The predictive value for performance speed of preparatory changes in neuronal activity of the monkey motor and premotor cortex. *Behav. Brain Res.* 53:35–49

Robinson DA. 1972. Eye movements evoked by collicular stimulation in the alert monkey. *Vis. Res.* 12:1795–808

Robinson DA. 1975. Oculomotor control signals. In *Basic Mechanisms of Ocular Motility and Their Clinical Implications,* ed. P Bach-y-Rita, G Lennerstrand, pp. 337–74. Oxford, UK: Pergamon

Robinson DA. 1992. Implications of neural networks for how we think about brain-function. *Behav. Brain Sci.* 15:644–55

Roitman JD, Shadlen MN. 2002. Response of neurons in the lateral intraparietal area (LIP) during a combined visual discrimination reaction time task. *J. Neurosci.* 22:9475–89

Romo R, Salinas E. 2003. Flutter discrimination: neural codes, perception, memory and decision making. *Nat. Rev. Neurosci.* 4:203–18

Sato T, Murthy A, Thompson KG, Schall JD. 2001. Search efficiency but not response interference affects visual selection in frontal eye field. *Neuron* 30:583–91

Sato T, Schall JD. 2003. Effects of stimulus-response compatibility on neural selection in frontal eye field. *Neuron.* 38:637–48

Schall JD. 1997. Visuomotor areas of the frontal lobe. In *Cerebral Cortex.* Volume 12. *Extrastriate Cortex of Primates,* ed. K Rockland, A Peters, J Kaas, pp. 527–638. New York: Plenum

Schall JD. 2003. Neural correlates of decision processes: neural and mental chronometry. *Curr. Opin. Neurobiol.* 13:182–86

Schall JD, Stuphorn V, Brown J. 2002. Monitoring and control of gaze by the frontal lobes. *Neuron* 36:309–22

Schiller PH, Chou I. 2000. The effects of anterior arcuate and dorsomedial frontal cortex lesions on visually guided eye movements in the rhesus monkey: 1. Single and sequential targets. *Vis. Res.* 40:1609–26

Schiller PH, Lee K. 1994. The effects of lateral geniculate nucleus, area V4, and middle temporal (MT) lesions on visually guided eye movements. *Vis. Neurosci.* 11:229–41

Schlag J, Dassonville P, Schlag-Rey M. 1998.

Interaction of the two frontal eye fields before saccade onset. *J. Neurophysiol.* 79:64–72

Scudder CA. 1988. A new local feedback model of the saccadic burst generator. *J. Neurophysiol.* 59:1455–75

Scudder CA, Kaneko CRS, Fuchs AF. 2002. The brainstem burst generator for saccadic eye movements: a modern synthesis. *Exp. Brain Res.* 142:439–62

Segraves MA. 1992. Activity of monkey frontal eye field neurons projecting to oculomotor regions of the pons. *J. Neurophysiol.* 68:1967–85

Segraves MA, Goldberg ME. 1987. Functional properties of corticotectal neurons in the monkey's frontal eye fields. *J. Neurophysiol.* 58:1387–419

Shadlen MN, Britten KH, Newsome WT, Movshon JA. 1996. A computational analysis of the relationship between neuronal and behavioral responses to visual motion. *J. Neurosci.* 16:1486–510

Shadlen MN, Newsome WT. 1998. The variable discharge of cortical neurons: implications for connectivity, computation, and information coding. *J. Neurosci.* 18:3870–96

Snyder LH, Batista AP, Andersen RA. 2000. Intention-related activity in the posterior parietal cortex: a review. *Vis. Res.* 40:1433–41

Softky WR, Koch C. 1993. The highly irregular firing of cortical cells is inconsistent with temporal integration of random EPSPs. *J. Neurosci.* 13:334–50

Sommer MA, Wurtz RH. 2000. Composition and topographic organization of signals sent from the frontal eye field to the superior colliculus. *J. Neurophysiol.* 83:1979–2001

Sparks DL. 1978. Functional properties of neurons in the monkey superior colliculus: coupling of neuronal activity and saccade onset. *Brain Res.* 156:x1–16

Sparks DL. 1999. Conceptual issues related to the role of the superior colliculus in the control of gaze. *Curr. Opin. Neurobiol.* 9:698–707

Sparks DL. 2002. The brainstem control of saccadic eye movements. *Nat. Rev. Neurosci.* 3:952–64

Steinman RM. 1986. The need for an eclectic, rather than systems, approach to the study of the primate oculomotor system. *Vis. Res.* 26:101–12

Sternberg S. 2001. Separate modifiability, mental modules, and the use of pure and composite measure to reveal them. *Acta Psychol.* 106:147–246

Stuphorn V, Taylor TL, Schall JD. 2000. Performance monitoring by the supplementary eye field. *Nature* 408:857–60

Sylvestre PA, Cullen KE. 1999. Quantitative analysis of abducens neuron discharge dynamics during saccadic and slow eye movements. *J. Neurophysiol.* 82:2612–32

Teller DY. 1984. Linking propositions. *Vis. Res.* 24:1233–46

Teller DY, Pugh E. 1983. Linking propositions in color vision. In *Colour Vision: Physiology and Psychophysics*, ed. JD Mollon, LT Sharpe. London: Academic

Thier P, Dicke PW, Haas R, Thielert CD, Catz N. 2002. The role of the oculomotor vermis in the control of saccadic eye movements. *Ann. NY Acad. Sci.* 978:50–62

Thompson KG, Hanes DP, Bichot NP, Schall JD. 1996. Perceptual and motor processing stages identified in the activity of macaque FEF neurons during visual search. *J. Neurophysiol.* 76:4040–55

Thompson KG, Schall JD. 2000. Antecedents and correlates of visual detection and awareness in macaque prefrontal cortex. *Vis. Res.* 40:1523–38

Tomasello M, Call J. 1997. *Primate Cognition.* New York: Oxford Univ. Press

Tomita M. 2001. Whole-cell simulation: a grand challenge of the 21st century. *Trends Biotechnol.* 19:205–10

Townsend JT, Ashby FG. 1983. *The Stochastic Modeling of Elementary Psychological Processes.* New York/London: Cambridge Univ. Press

Tweed D, Villis T. 1985. A two dimensional model for saccade generation. *Biol. Cybern.* 52:219–27

Usher M, McClelland JL. 2001. The time course of perceptual choice: the leaky, competing accumulator model. *Psychol. Rev.* 108:550–92

Uttal WR. 1997. Do theoretical bridges exist between perceptual experience and neurophysiology? *Perspect. Biol. Med.* 40:280–302

Uttal WR. 2001. *The New Phrenology: The Limits of Localizing Cognitive Processes in the Brain.* Cambridge, MA: MIT Press

Van Boxtel GJ, Van der Molen MW, Jennings JR, Brunia CH. 2001. A psychophysiological analysis of inhibitory motor control in the stop-signal paradigm. *Biol. Psychol.* 58:229–62

Van Gulick R. 1993. Who's in charge here? And who's doing all the work? In *Mental Causation*, ed. J Heil, A Mele, pp. 230–56. London: Oxford Univ. Press

Van Opstal AJ, Van Gisbergen JA. 1989. Scatter in the metrics of saccades and properties of the collicular motor map. *Vis. Res.* 29:1183–96

Van Opstal AJ, Van Gisbergen JA, Smit AC. 1990. Comparison of saccades evoked by visual stimulation and collicular electrical stimulation in the alert monkey. *Exp. Brain Res.* 79:299–312

Van Zandt T, Ratcliff R. 1995. Statistical mimicking of reaction time data: single-process models, parameter variability and mixtures. *Psychon. Bull. Rev.* 2:20–54

Van Zandt T, Colonius H, Proctor RW. 2000. A comparison of two response time models applied to perceptual matching. *Psychon. Bull. Rev.* 7:208–56

Wise SP, Mauritz KH. 1985. Set-related neuronal activity in the premotor cortex of rhesus monkeys: effects of changes in motor set. *Proc. R. Soc. London Ser. B* 223:331–54

Wurtz RH, Goldberg ME. 1989. *The Neurobiology of Saccadic Eye Movements.* New York: Elsevier

Annu. Rev. Psychol. 2004. 55:51–86
doi: 10.1146/annurev.psych.55.090902.142050
Copyright © 2004 by Annual Reviews. All rights reserved
First published online as a Review in Advance on October 6, 2003

THE NEUROBIOLOGY OF CONSOLIDATIONS, OR, HOW STABLE IS THE ENGRAM?

Yadin Dudai

*Department of Neurobiology, The Weizmann Institute of Science, Rehovot 76100, Israel;
email: yadin.dudai@weizmann.ac.il*

Key Words   memory, consolidation, persistence, retrieval, reconsolidation

■ **Abstract**   Consolidation is the progressive postacquisition stabilization of long-term memory. The term is commonly used to refer to two types of processes: synaptic consolidation, which is accomplished within the first minutes to hours after learning and occurs in all memory systems studied so far; and system consolidation, which takes much longer, and in which memories that are initially dependent upon the hippocampus undergo reorganization and may become hippocampal-independent. The textbook account of consolidation is that for any item in memory, consolidation starts and ends just once. Recently, a heated debate has been revitalized on whether this is indeed the case, or, alternatively, whether memories become labile and must undergo some form of renewed consolidation every time they are activated. This debate focuses attention on fundamental issues concerning the nature of the memory trace, its maturation, persistence, retrievability, and modifiability.

CONTENTS

INTRODUCTION

In the domain of memory research and theory, consolidation (Latin for "to make firm"), or memory consolidation, refers to the progressive postacquisition stabilization of long-term memory, as well as to the memory phase(s) during which such presumed stabilization takes place (Dudai 2002a). It has long been suggested that fresh memories need time to stabilize, and that often, such traces are prone to interference by distracting stimuli, injuries, or toxins, which, however, lose their effectiveness with the passage of time. The first documented reference to memory consolidation is in the writings of Quintillian, the noted Roman teacher of rhetoric, who turns his readers' attention to the "curious fact . . . that the interval of a single night will greatly increase the strength of the memory," and raises the possibility that " . . . the power of recollection . . . undergoes a process of ripening and maturing during the time which intervenes" (Quintillian first century A.D.). That such posttraining, time-dependent maturation process takes place was therefore probably known in the Middle Ages to orators and mnemonists who were well versed in the writings and mnemonotechniques of their Roman predecessors. The idea resurfaced again occasionally in different versions before the birth of experimental psychology (e.g., Hartley 1810).

The term "consolidation" is attributed to Muller & Pilzecker, who rediscovered, in a series of studies carried out in Gottingen between 1892 and 1900, that memory takes time to fixate, or undergo *Konsolidierung* (Muller & Pilzecker 1900). Their evidence was based on systematic search for the laws that govern the acquisition and retrieval of verbal material, á la Ebbinghaus (1885). Muller & Pilzecker found that correct recall of the target material improved during the first few minutes after training, and that if presented during the first minutes after training, intervening new stimuli tend to impair recall of the target material (a phenomenon they termed "retroactive inhibition"). They suggested that this reflects a posttraining interval during which associations consolidate in memory. Interestingly, as aptly noted by Lechner et al. (1999), though the Muller & Pilzecker study is frequently cited and referred to as the beginning of the modern era in the prolific field of memory consolidation, it has never been translated in full from German, and non-German readers must rely on abstracts and extracts (Lechner et al. 1999,

McDougall 1901). In spite of several reports of failure to replicate the aforementioned Muller & Pilzecker's findings (e.g., McGeoch 1933, reviewed and analyzed in Wixted 2004), their conclusion, that the trace is still uncompleted when training is over, has been overall well consolidated in the collective memory of memory research.

Shortly before Muller & Pilzecker introduced the term, the process of consolidation was also proposed based on clinical data. In "global," organic amnesia, memory of the recent past is commonly affected more than memory of the distant past; this observation is epitomized in Ribot's Law, or the Law of Regression: "Progressive destruction advances progressively from the unstable to the stable" (Ribot 1882). The idea was further elaborated a few years later by Burnham, who in a signal paper on amnesia integrated findings from experimental psychology and neurology, while at the same time emphasizing the dynamic nature of postexperience memory maturation: "There must be time for the processes of organization and assimilation (of memory) to take place. There must be time for nature to do her part. ... Hurry defeats its own end" (Burnham 1903). It is noteworthy that Burnham's "time" actually refers to two different types of consolidation kinetics: fast, such as unveiled by the studies of Muller & Pilzecker, and slow, such as unveiled by the observations of residual premorbid memory in global amnesics. This temporal dichotomy suggests at the outset that the generic term "consolidation" conceals different types of processes and mechanisms. This is reflected in the title of this chapter and is further discussed below.

The quest for the neurobiological foundations of both slow and fast consolidation gained real momentum only in the second half of the last century. Quantitative, systematic studies of retrograde amnesia started to appear in the 1960s and 1970s (e.g., Sanders & Warrington 1971). These were accompanied by the development of animal models of human amnesia and attempts to identify brain substrates critical for slow consolidation (reviewed in Squire et al. 2001). In parallel, neuropharmacology, first systemic and later targeted to selected brain areas, began to unravel molecular candidates for the cellular machinery that subserves fast consolidation (Dudai & Morris 2000; McGaugh 1966, 2000). Cellular preparations and advanced molecular biology and neurogenetics have together revolutionized the field in the past two decades (Dudai 2002a, Milner et al. 1998). For the first time since Quintillian noted it, Ribot conceptualized it, and Muller & Pilzecker named it, we are now in a position to discuss the processes and mechanisms of consolidation at multiple levels of brain organization, from the molecular to the behavioral. Furthermore, the time is now ripe to reevaluate the status of the consolidation hypothesis: How valid is it? And what are the implications concerning the stability and retrievability of engrams and the nature of memory? In this review, I first discuss two main types of neuronal processes to which the term "consolidation" currently refers; then review data that have recently stirred anew a heated debate concerning the nature of the consolidated trace, and discuss their possible interpretation; and finally focus on selected issues that bear on our understanding of the nature of the engram and its persistence.

ON THE TERMINOLOGY OF CONSOLIDATION

The term "consolidation" is currently used in the neuroscience literature to refer to two types of processes, or a family of processes (Dudai 1996, Dudai & Morris 2000; Figure 1). One type is accomplished within the first minutes to hours after the encoding has occurred or practice ended. Ample evidence indicates that this relatively fast type of process takes place in local nodes in the neuronal

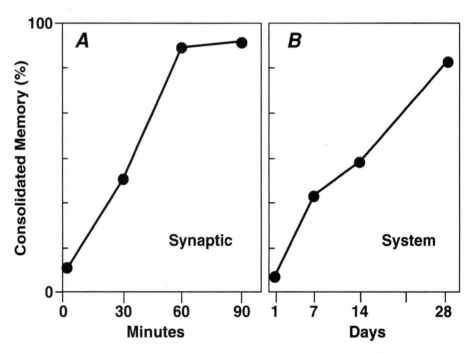

Figure 1 Types of consolidation. (*A*) The time course of *synaptic* (cellular, local) consolidation, determined by measuring the sensitivity of memory to the inhibition of protein synthesis. Consolidated memory is defined as treatment-resistant long-term memory. The data are from experiments on shuttle-box learning in the goldfish (Agranoff et al. 1966). The protein synthesis inhibitor was administered to separate groups of fish at the indicated time points after training. The sensitivity of memory to protein synthesis inhibition was over by about one hour. A consolidation process that depends on protein synthesis during and immediately after training is a universal property of the nervous system. (*B*) The time course of *system* consolidation, determined by measuring the sensitivity of long-term memory to hippocampal damage. The data are from experiments on contextual fear conditioning in the rat (Kim & Fanselow 1992). The lesion was inflicted to separate groups at the indicated time points after training. The dependence of long-term memory on the hippocampus in this case was over by about one month. System consolidation, lasting weeks or longer, during which the memory becomes independent of the hippocampus, is observed in declarative memory. (Figure adapted from Dudai 2002a.)

circuit(s) that encode(s) the experience-dependent internal representation, i.e., the memory. Much attention has been devoted to processes and mechanisms of fast consolidation in synapses; therefore the phenomenon is commonly termed "synaptic consolidation." But it is now evident that this type of consolidation depends on cross talk between synapses and their cell body and nucleus (Dudai & Morris 2000, and see below). The terms "cellular" or "local consolidation" are therefore also appropriate. "Synaptic consolidation" will be preferred in the current discussion, because it focuses on a major site of use-dependent modification in neuronal circuits, and fits the prevailing dogma that synaptic plasticity underlies learning and memory.

Another type of consolidation process(es) takes weeks, months, or even years to be accomplished. It is believed to involve reorganization over time of the brain circuits, or the systems, that encode the memory, and in the course of this the trace may spread to new locations in the brain while at the same time relinquishing its dependence on parts of the circuits that have subserved its acquisition. This type of process is termed "system consolidation." The term "reorganization" has been proposed, but brain reorganization may occur under conditions other than memory consolidation, such as development, housekeeping, and homeostasis, and response to injury—though similar neural mechanisms might be involved. Moreover, shifting levels of analysis, reorganization applies to synaptic consolidation as well, involving remodeling of synaptic connectivity. "Slow consolidation" is sometimes used to refer to system consolidation, but is questionable because there might be cases in which system consolidation is accomplished within a time frame not so different from that of synaptic consolidation. "Early" and "late" consolidation is also occasionally used, which is fine as far as no implicit assumption is being made about when the process starts. And last, the terms "short-term" and "long-term" consolidation are also used to refer to synaptic and system consolidation, respectively, but this should be better avoided because these terms may connote short or long persistence of the trace, which is a different issue.

GENERIC CRITERIA FOR CONSOLIDATION

Because the assumption that some form or another of consolidation does take place has already attained the status of tenet in the neurobiology of memory (admittedly, with lingering opposition, as noted below), it is prudent to review the criteria for demonstrating that consolidation has indeed taken place in a given system or preparation. By definition, consolidation is progressive postacquisition stabilization of memory. Hence to demonstrate consolidation, a limited time window of susceptibility of long-term memory to an amnesic agent must be proven, following cessation of experience or training. This agent should be devoid of significant effects on sensorimotor faculties required to execute the task, as well as on acquisition per se and on short-term memory, and should not induce state-dependent memory in the protocol used. Monotonous effectiveness of a blocking agent over time suggests that this agent impairs the maintenance, retrieval, or expression of memory, not its consolidation. The aforementioned criterion is necessary and sufficient. Studies that report consolidation merely on the basis of time-dependent postacquisition changes in brain activity use a correlative approach that might supplement the aforementioned criterion, but by themselves do not prove that consolidation has taken place, as the observed changes might not necessarily be causally related to the stabilization or functional reorganization of memory.

SYNAPTIC CONSOLIDATION

Synaptic consolidation is universal; it has been described in all the species, preparations, and memory tasks investigated to date, so far as the task results in long-term memory. Long-term memory, in the context of discussion of synaptic consolidation, is conventionally defined as memory that lasts more than 24 hours, except in the study of long-term potentiation, a popular model of learning-related synaptic plasticity, in which even one hour is considered long. Listed below are selected common themes that emerge from the experimental data on synaptic consolidation (Dudai & Morris 2000):

a. Within a short time after training, new memories become resistant to interferences, or agents, which otherwise are capable of truncating the formation of long-term memory. These types of interferences or blockers include behavioral distractors, drugs, seizures, and anatomical lesions. The time window of susceptibility depends on the task and type of interference or blocker, and ranges from seconds to minutes (e.g., electroconvulsive shock in conditioning, Duncan 1949, McGaugh 1966), to hours (distractor tasks in motor skills, Shadmehr & Holocomb 1997; macromolecular synthesis inhibition in many types of tasks, see below).

b. The stabilization process is not a step-function, but rather various drugs or mutations can be used to dissect it into what appears to be intermediate phases in consolidation (e.g., DeZazzo & Tully 1995, Ghirardi et al. 1995, Grecksch & Matthies 1980, Rosenzweig et al. 1993, Winder et al. 1998). The time course of at least some of these phases is not a given, and could be altered by experimental manipulations, which may mimic in vivo stimuli and processes (Frey & Morris 1997). It is also unclear whether phases of consolidation must take place in a prescribed order for the consolidation to complete successfully.

c. The application of RNA or protein synthesis inhibitors during or immediately after training blocks the formation of long-term memory (Agranoff & Klinger 1964, Davis & Squire 1984, Freeman et al. 1995, Montarolo et al. 1986, Rosenblum et al. 1993). At least in the behaving animal, massive reduction in protein synthesis ($>90\%$) is required to achieve the effect. Usually, a similar transient reduction in macromolecular synthesis does not significantly affect perception, short-term memory, or either the retention or the retrieval of long-term memory once it has been established, with the single (important) exception of application of these inhibitors immediately after retrieval, which is discussed below.

d. Intracellular signal transduction cascades[1], and particularly the cyclic adenosine monophosphate (cAMP) response element (CRE)-mediated modulation of gene expression by such cascades, are thought to play an important role in the consolidation of short- into long-term memory. This has been established in neuronal models of plasticity as well as in behaving animals (e.g., Deisseroth et al. 1996, Frank & Greenberg 1994, Kaang et al. 1993, Lamprecht et al. 1997, Yin et al. 1994). A prominent example is the cAMP cascade, which involves activation of a cAMP-dependent kinase[2], which phosphorylates and activates isoforms of cAMP-response element binding proteins (CREBs). The balance between activator and repressor forms of CREBs may be critical in triggering long-term cellular information storage (Bourtchuladze et al. 1994, Yin et al. 1994). CREB modulates the expression of CRE-regulated genes, including a number of immediate-early genes (IEGs), such as transcription factors that, in turn, regulate the expression of late response genes[3]. Other IEGs include cell adhesion molecules, and enzymes that control the degradation of intracellular or extracellular proteins.

e. Processes of neuronal protein synthesis that correlate with and are required for consolidation are now known to be multiphasic, involving the concerted recruitment of synaptic and cell-wide mechanisms (Huber et al. 2000, Martin et al. 1997, Steward et al. 1998). It appears that the activated synapse is somehow "tagged," possibly by posttranslational modification of synaptic protein(s), or by reorganization of such proteins (Dudai 1989, Frey & Morris 1997, Katz & Halstad 1950, Martin et al. 1997). This results in a new local synaptic configuration, which itself might attract new proteins from the cell. In addition, proteins synthesized in the synapse itself may strengthen the tagging of this synapse, and/or serve as retrograde messages, which travel to the cell body and inform the nucleus about the change (e.g., Casadio et al. 1999). There is also modulation of gene expression in the nucleus, and production of new messenger RNAs (mRNAs) and proteins, which are funneled into the tagged synapse. Overall, the process is hence assumed to

---

[1]Intracellular signal transduction cascades are molecular pathways that decode extracellular signals, such as neurotransmitters or hormones, and convert the information into cellular response. These cascades commonly involve the operation of "second messengers," small molecules that transmit information from one macromolecular complex to another within the cell. cAMP is such a "second messenger."

[2]A protein kinase is a ubiquitous type of enzyme that modifies proteins and regulates their function by catalyzing the addition of a phosphoryl group, a process called phosphorylation.

[3]Immediate early genes (IEGs) are genes whose products are induced rapidly and transiently in cells, such as nerve cells, in response to extracellular stimulation, via the operation of intracellular signal transduction cascades. Late response genes are genes whose products are induced in response to extracellular stimulation with a delay of a few hours.

involve coordination between the activated synapse and the nucleus, which possibly optimize exploitation of the metabolic resources of the neuron and the specificity of the long-term change (Dudai & Morris 2000).

f. The long-term changes in the synapse involve trafficking of new receptor molecules and possibly other proteins into the synaptic membrane, and alteration in the association of receptors with cellular cytoskeleton and signal transduction cascades (e.g., El-Husseini et al. 2002, Shi et al. 1999). In addition, there is evidence that long-term synaptic plasticity and long-term memory are correlated with morphological changes in synapses (e.g., Bailey & Kandel 1993, Weiler et al. 1995).

THE STANDARD MODEL OF SYNAPTIC CONSOLIDATION

The above and additional findings served as the basis for the formulation of the standard model of synaptic consolidation (Figure 2). This model posits that memory traces can exist in at least two forms: short-term and labile, and long-term and

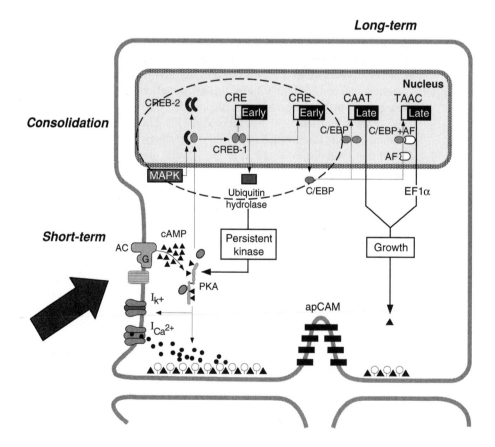

stable (Hebb 1949; as noted above, it is now recognized that intermediate forms exist as well). The short-term trace may decay, or mature into a long-term form, or, alternatively, the short- and the long-term forms may develop in parallel. The physiological conditions that give rise to the long-term form are not yet fully identified but may involve suprathreshold neurotransmitter signal, or, probably more prevalent, coincidence of two or more inputs, including neuromodulatory ones.[4] These signals initiate or promote synaptic consolidation. This involves posttranslational modification of synaptic proteins, activation of transcription factors, modulation

---

[4]In which case diffused neuromodulatory systems, hormones, and the amygdalar complex play a decisive role; they probably play a role in system consolidation as well (McGaugh 2002).

←

Figure 2 The standard model of synaptic consolidation. Information (left arrow) triggers intracellular signal transduction cascades, leading to modification of synaptic proteins and subsequently to alteration of synaptic excitability and of the amount of neurotransmitter(s) released onto target nerve cells. According to this dominant model, the same or interconnected intracellular signal transduction cascades can also activate transcription factors, leading to modulation of gene expression (first early genes, early, later late genes, late; see also the section on Synaptic Consolidation in the text). This culminates in long-term modification of synaptic proteins and in synaptic remodeling and growth. The activation, expression, and function of certain transcription factors and early genes is an essential part of the cascade of events, which occurs during a limited time window during and immediately after training, and can be disrupted by several types of agents, including inhibitors of protein synthesis. This time window is assumed to correspond to synaptic consolidation (a selection of the molecular species involved are schematically depicted by the elliptic broken line). The process, however, involves not only the synapse but also the cell body and nucleus. The scheme is highly simplified and depicts only a few presynaptic processes. AC, adenylate cyclase, an enzyme that generates the intracellular messenger cAMP; AF, activation factor, regulates transcription; apCAM, a cell adhesion molecule, takes part in synaptic remodeling; CAAT, a nucleotide sequence that regulates transcription; cAMP, cyclic adenosine monophosphate, a ubiquitous intracellular messenger; CRE, cAMP response element, regulates gene expression; C/EBP, enhancer binding protein, another protein that regulates gene expression; CREB, CRE binding protein; EF1α, elongation factor 1α, required for protein synthesis; I_{K+}, potassium channel, controls synaptic excitability; I_{Ca2+}, calcium channel, controls synaptic excitability, signal transduction cascades, and neurotransmitter release; kinase, an enzyme that modifies proteins by phosphorylating them; MAPK, mitogen activated protein kinase, a family of kinases that respond (indirectly) to extracellular stimuli; ubiquitin hydrolase, an enzyme that takes part in degradation of proteins. The figure is based on studies of simple learning in defensive responses in the mollusk *Aplysia* (e.g., Milner et al. 1998), but is considered to apply to other systems as well.

of gene expression at synapses and cell body, reorganization of synaptic proteins including membrane receptors and cytoskeletal elements, all together culminating in synaptic remodeling, which is assumed to make the trace stable. All this is fitted into a conceptual framework that depicts the cellular manifestation of memory consolidation as a growth or developmental process. In both development and use-dependent plasticity, gene expression is regulated by extracellular signals, and in both cases, similar ubiquitous intracellular signaling cascades, such as the cAMP and the mitogen-activated protein kinase (MAPK) cascades, are recruited, and cellular remodeling and growth occur. A caveat is, however, appropriate: It is not yet proven that in real life, synaptic remodeling and growth indeed encode the new memory and embodies its persistence over time. Alternatively, it could subserve homeostasis or expansion of computational space for new anticipated needs of the activated circuit (Dudai 2002a).

SYSTEM CONSOLIDATION

The evidence for system consolidation stems from both human and animal studies. Here is a selection of the major findings:

a. Many human "global" amnesics, as noted above, display temporally graded retrograde amnesia for declarative memory, i.e., remote memory is spared relative to more recent memory (Burnham 1903, Ribot 1882, Russell & Nathan 1946, Squire & Alvarez 1995). Other cases, however, display dense ungraded retrograde amnesia extending over many decades. Whereas the temporally graded retrograde amnesia is most often associated with damage to the medial temporal lobe, including the hippocampal formation and associated cortici, flat extensive retrograde amnesia usually also involves damage to neocortex in the lateral and anterior temporal lobe (Squire et al. 2001). Furthermore, amnesic patients with medial temporal lobe lesions can still recollect remote autobiographical events in great detail (Bayley et al. 2003). All this is commonly taken to imply that the medial temporal lobe, including the hippocampal formation and associated cortici, is required for intact long-term declarative memory, but its role is limited in time, and storage is ultimately relegated to the neocortex.

b. The memory of "global" amnesics for nondeclarative information is often spared, sometimes to a remarkable degree. This indicates that the mediotemporal lobe is not required for the consolidation (or other memory faculties) of skills and other forms of nondeclarative memory (e.g., Brooks & Baddeley 1976, Cohen 1984, Corkin 2002, Knowlton et al. 1996, Milner et al. 1968). Even when postmorbid facts are acquired, this seems to be done in a nondeclarative manner (Bayley & Squire 2002).

c. The immediate recall of dense amnesics, such as patient H.M. (Corkin 2002, Scoville & Milner 1957), is in the normal range. Taken together with the retention of old memories, this implies that the deficit in amnesia is not in acquisition, short-term memory, or overall storage capabilities, but rather in either consolidation or retrieval. The temporally graded amnesia is taken as evidence that the deficit is in consolidation (but see below).

d. Selective lesions to the hippocampal formation or entorhinal cortex in laboratory animals, including mice, rats, rabbits, and monkeys, produce postlesion temporally graded amnesia, extending weeks, in several types of memory tasks (Cho et al. 1993, Clark et al. 2002, Kim & Fanselow 1992, Kim et al. 1995, Kubie et al. 1999, Winocur 1990, Zola-Morgan & Squire 1990). This is congruent with the aforementioned human amnesia data and with the notion that the hippocampal formation and related structures have a temporally limited role in long-term memory.

e. Some studies of functional brain imaging unveil postacquisition temporally graded activity in mediotemporal structures in the human brain (Haist et al. 2001), and in the hippocampal formation in mice (Bontempi et al. 1999), which suggests that time-dependent reorganization of brain circuitry is involved in the formation of long-term memory.

THE STANDARD MODEL OF SYSTEM CONSOLIDATION

The above findings served as the basis for the formulation of the standard model of system consolidation (Figure 3). This model posits that long-term memories that depend in their encoding on the hippocampal formation and related structures in the mediotemporal lobe and the telencephalon are initially registered, probably in different formats, in both the hippocampal formation and the relevant neocortex. The stabilization of these internal representations is assumed to involve synaptic consolidation, which is achieved within minutes to hours. In parallel, or as a consequence, a process of system consolidation is initiated, characterized by much slower temporal kinetics. In this process the trace reorganizes over a period of weeks or more, shifting the burden of retention to the neocortex, so that ultimately the neocortex can independently maintain the specific internal representation and actualize it in retrieval. It is not yet known what triggers system consolidation, but the most parsimonious account is that over time, upon recurrent activation of the hippocampal trace either in explicit recall or in implicit processing (e.g., sleep), the hippocampal formation and related structures send synaptic messages to neocortical neurons, and these messages trigger synaptic consolidation locally.

DOES SYSTEM CONSOLIDATION OCCUR ONLY IN DECLARATIVE SYSTEMS?

The textbook account of system consolidation is that it applies to hippocampal-dependent memory only, whereas in nondeclarative systems, which do not depend on the hippocampal formation and related structures, consolidation is restricted to the same circuits that have encoded the information on-line. That nondeclarative memories do not undergo system consolidation should not, however, be taken as

Initial Storage

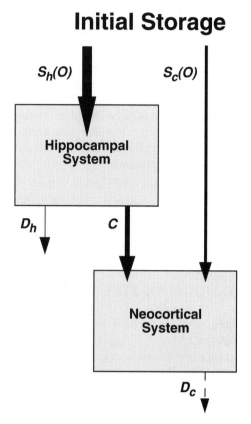

Figure 3   The standard model of system consolidation is depicted in a flowchart. Initial storage, i.e., encoding and registration of the perceived information (Dudai 2002a), occurs in both the hippocampal system and the neocortical system. $S_h(0)$ and $S_c(0)$ represent the strength of the initial hippocampal and neocortical traces, respectively. These traces are expected to differ, with the hippocampal one probably representing a compressed version of the internal representation. The hippocampal representation later becomes active either in explicit recall, or in implicit processes such as sleep. This gives rise to reinstatement of the corresponding neocortical memory, resulting in incremental adjustment of neocortical connections, probably involving local, synaptic consolidation. In parallel, memory also decays, faster in the hippocampus (D_h) than in the cortex (D_c). The net result is that memories initially dependent on the hippocampus gradually become independent of it. In reality this happens over weeks or longer. The hippocampal system can hence be viewed not only as a memory store but also as a teacher of the neocortical system. This process (C, rate of consolidation) is proposed to allow the hippocampal system to rapidly learn new information without disrupting old memory stored in the neocortex, while at the same time allowing gradual integration of the new information into the older, structured information. Adapted from McClelland et al. (1995).

an established given. There are actually two questions here: (*a*) Is there a process of slow circuit reorganization in nondeclarative systems that continues after the initial wave of synaptic consolidation has been accomplished, and in which parts of the circuit become dispensable for retention or retrieval, and (*b*) Is there spread of the trace to new circuits that did not subserve encoding? Motor skill learning provides a suitable system to investigate these questions. Multiple brain areas subserve this type of task, including among others the primary motor cortex, other neocortical areas, the cerebellar cortex and deep nuclei, and the striatum (Doyon et al. 1997, Karni et al. 1998, Kleim et al. 2002, Nudo et al. 1996, Ungerleider et al. 2002). It has been reported that within six hours after completion of practice in a visuomotor pursuit task, the brain engages new regions to perform the task, as visualized by positron emission tomography imaging; specifically, this involved a shift from prefrontal cortex to posterioparietal cortex and cerebellar structures (Shadmehr & Holocomb 1997). Brain reorganization of task-related activity has also been demonstrated by fMRI in the brain of subjects acquiring skilled sequential finger movement (Karni et al. 1998, Ungerleider et al. 2002). Here changes in the primary motor cortex (M1) were detected very early in learning, in parallel with rapid changes of activity in the cerebellum, striatum, and other motor-related cortici, which was followed by slowly evolving reorganization of M1 over weeks (Ungerleider et al. 2002). A model has been suggested on the basis of these studies, which proposes that early in learning there is transfer of experience-dependent changes from the cerebellar cortex to the dentate nuclei of the cerebellum, and then later from a cerebellar-cortical to a striatal-cortical network (Doyon et al. 2002). The protocol used, however, involved incremental learning; therefore the observed changes could not be attributed to consolidation per se, but rather might be due to extended practice. In another study, repetitive transcranial magnetic stimulation of M1, but not other brain areas, was reported to disrupt the retention of the behavioral improvement on skilled finger-movement tasks if it was applied within about six hours of training (Muellbacher et al. 2002). Basal motor behavior, task performance, motor learning by subsequent practice, or recall of the newly acquired motor skill were not affected. This was taken to indicate that M1 is involved in the consolidation of motor skill within a few hours of practice.

It is also noteworthy that the evidence for the requirement for sleep, particularly dream sleep, in memory consolidation (and see System Consolidation section above) is particularly prominent in nondeclarative tasks, which suggests that consolidation lasts for several hours (Jenkins & Dallenbach 1924, Maquet et al. 2003, Pennartz et al. 2002, Stickgold et al. 2001).[5] Yet a few hours, whether asleep (ibid.)

---

[5] Again this is a place to pay tribute to Quintillian (first century A.D.) and Hartley (1810), harbingers of the study of the relationship between sleep and memory. Of particular interest is the view of Hartley: "The wildness of dreams seems to be of singular use to us, by interrupting and breaking the course of our associations. For, if we were always awake, some accidental associations would be so much cemented by continuance, as that nothing could afterwards disjoin them; which would be madness." This is echoed in a more recent hypothesis on the relevance of dream sleep to consolidation (Crick & Mitchison 1983).

or awake (Brashers-Krug et al. 1996), is still within the accepted time window of synaptic consolidation. At the time of writing, no evidence is available for more prolonged consolidation of skill. Nor is there evidence that the slow reorganization of the brain areas, which is suggested by the evolving patterns of brain activity over days and weeks in certain skill acquisition protocols, is a signature of the representation of a specific item in memory, let alone indication that this representation invades new circuits, that part of the original circuits become dispensable for recall, or that it is at all consolidation and not transition among acquisition strategies. The resolution of these issues could benefit from selective lesion experiments in laboratory animals, similar to the approach used in investigation of the consolidation of declarative memory in the mediotemporal lobe.

WHY CONSOLIDATE?

Why do memories consolidate in the first place? One could envisage a situation in which newly encoded memories stabilize instantaneously (this is what some opponents of the consolidation theory propose; see Reservations Concerning the Consolidation Theory section below), or that memories never really stabilize at all (and this is what some orthodox proponents of reconsolidation hypothesis might claim; see Reconsolidation section below). This question could be applied to both synaptic and system consolidation, and in each case, it could be discussed at different levels of analysis. Two levels of analyses, following the type-of-level analysis by Marr (1982), are the most pertinent to the current discussion: the level of the computational theory, i.e., what is the goal of the system and what is the logic of the strategy by which the computations are carried out; and the level of hardware implementation, i.e., how are the algorithms that execute the computations implemented in the biological hardware? One generic possibility at the level of computational theory, which applies to both synaptic and system consolidation, is that instant stabilization of every encoded internal representation is bound to waste brain computational space on useless items and hence rapidly reduce processing and storage capacity. Another possible explanation is that in the poststimulus time window of consolidation the newly acquired information is particularly malleable and readily associates with other inputs, of either on-line or off-line sources, so that information is bound together in a more useful manner and meaningful narratives are more easily formed. Again, this type of potential explanation has been suggested for both synaptic and system consolidation. In the former, it has been linked to the finding that activated synapses are tagged for a short postactivation period and during this tagging period could be stabilized in response to concurrent activity in other synapses on the same neuron (Frey & Morris 1997), permitting generalization and binding at the synaptic level within the circuit (Dudai & Morris 2000; for a harbinger of this notion see Landauer 1969, itself a sequel to the idea that consolidation is a period of reinforcement; Thorndike 1933; see also White 1989). But the more popular version of this type of explanation was applied to system consolidation in the corticohippocampal system, and is supported by modeling (McClelland & Goddard 1996, McClelland et al. 1995; Figure 3). Briefly, the suggestion is that new episodes are stored in the hippocampal formation, which recurrently replays them over time to the neocortical system, interleaving them with other encoded experiences. This process allows the cortex, according to the model, to gradually discover the structure in ensembles of experiences, leading to categorization and generalization of cortical memories, which is clearly advantageous for cognitive function. Furthermore, according to this model, having these complementary learning systems in the hippocampus and neocortex allows the brain to rapidly learn new on-line events without disrupting the structure of off-line information, and then to integrate these new events properly with previously stored experiences. This type of processing might be particularly suitable for declarative memories, considering that a proposed primitive of such memories is their flexibility, transitivity, and generalizability (Cohen et al. 1997, Eichenbaum 1997). Actually, in this respect, it is the hen-and-egg type of issue: Did the system evolve this way to promote the aforementioned primitives of declarative memory, or did these primitives of declarative memory emerge as by-products of system evolution, which had a different, yet unknown selective pressure?

Which brings us to an utterly different type of putative explanation for consolidation. The explanations proposed so far assume that the system works in a particular way because this is adaptive, more generally, because natural selection is an optimizing agent. These explanations are dubbed adaptionist or Panglossian[6] (Gould & Lewontin 1979). But it is also possible that the system is the way it is because of accumulative, built-in operational constraints, irrespective of the assumed adaptivity, or alternatively that the system is still far from optimization. Hence the possibility should also be entertained that consolidation is a spin-off of the constraints imposed on biological memory by the design and maintenance of biological systems, rather than by functional properties selected in evolution. This possibility might apply particularly to synaptic consolidation, where the standard dogma depicts processes that are engaged to overcome the brief life span of proteins due to their molecular turnover, itself a mechanistic constraint of biological material, which might be advantageous in development or housekeeping but not necessarily in memory systems.

RESERVATIONS CONCERNING THE CONSOLIDATION THEORY[7]

Almost from its outset the consolidation theory was not without its share of criticism and skepticism. These are commonly brought up in the context of discussions of system consolidation but are relevant to synaptic consolidation as well. They

---

[6]Dr. Pangloss, the mentor of Voltaire's Candide, was an incurable optimist, justifying every disaster under the sun by the a priori assumption that everything is always for a good cause.
[7]The term "consolidation theory" is in common use in the literature. It is not really a theory in terms of abstract laws and their interrelationships, but rather a hypothesis or a generalization, as currently is any other "theory" in biology. The term is used here to refer to both synaptic and system consolidation, although each of these processes could be considered independently.

stem from findings obtained in the study of experimentally induced amnesia in laboratory animals and of cases of human amnesia. There are two levels of criticism. One questions the mere concept of consolidation. The other doubts whether the standard models are valid.

a. *Spontaneous recovery.* Over the years there were multiple reports in the animal literature that memory could recover spontaneously after amnestic treatment (e.g., Lewis et al. 1968, Miller et al. 1974). This was taken to imply that consolidation blockers do not prevent the formation of a long-term trace but rather block its expression.

b. *Reminder effects.* Similarly, a substantial number of studies have reported that in laboratory animals the retrograde amnesia produced by agents regarded as consolidation blockers could be reversed by reexposure to the conditioned stimulus (CS) alone (reattempted retrieval, reminder), to the unconditioned stimulus (US) alone (reinstatement), to stimulating drugs, or even to the amnestic agent[8] (Bradley & Galal 1988, DeVietti & Hopfer 1974, Gordon & Mowrer 1980, Hinderliter et al. 1975, Mactutus et al. 1982, Miller & Springer 1972, Quartermain et al. 1970). This implies that the consolidation blockers used under the conditions described do not block the formation of a long-term trace, but rather cause a deficit which can later be remedied, so that the latent trace resurfaces; or, in other words, that the deficit caused is not in long-term storage but rather in retrieval. Several related possibilities have been proposed considering the nature of the retrieval deficits, including that the amnestic treatment induces a specific internal state, resulting in state-dependent learning, so that the original memory cannot be retrieved unless the original state is reinstated; or that the amnestic agent provides cues that must be reprovided to allow retrieval to proceed (for a recent recount of this type of interpretation, see Miller & Matzel 2000, Millin et al. 2001).

c. *Memory in amnesic patients.* More than 30 years ago, Warrington & Weiskrantz (1970) reported that amnesic patients could remember verbal material if tested in a protocol that provides partial information about the target. Hence the performance of these patients was similar to nonamnesic controls when fragmented target words were presented for identification in the test (1–11 minutes posttraining), but not when the patients were requested to recall these words or recognize them in a mixed list of new and old words. The authors therefore suggested that it is inappropriate to characterize the amnesic syndrome as being a failure of registration or consolidation of information, but rather, it is a retrieval deficit: Given the appropriate retrieval cues, the memory becomes available. This proposal, which later came to evoke recurrent debates in the amnesia literature, is in line with the aforementioned

---

[8]Although the various manipulations differ with regard to the part of the internal representation they are expected to trigger, it is convenient to term them all as "reminders," and their effects as "reminder effects."

reminder effects observed in animal studies. Another type of opposition to the "standard" model of system consolidation refers specifically to the notion that in this process, episodic memory becomes gradually independent of the hippocampal formation. Here the main arguments are that (*a*) In many amnesic patients the retrograde amnesia is not temporally graded; (*b*) When temporally graded retrograde amnesia is detected, it is task dependent; (*c*) In some cases the so-called temporally graded retrograde amnesia covers decades, so that for all practical purposes the hippocampal formation appears to be involved in the memory throughout life (Moscovitch & Nadel 1998, Nadel & Moscovitch 1997); and (*d*) Some functional neuroimaging studies show equivalent activation of the hippocampal formation in healthy volunteers in recollection of events up to 20 years ago (Ryan et al. 2001; but see Haist et al. 2001 for different conclusions concerning the activation of medial temporal lobe structure in remote memory, particularly the entorhinal cortex). This observation is congruent with the idea that damage to the hippocampal formation causes retrieval deficits. Taking these types of findings into account, Nadel & Moscovitch (1997) have proposed an alternative to the standard model of system consolidation, in which the hippocampal formation is involved in some types of memory (episodic, spatial) for as long as these memories endure. In their model, the entire hippocampal-neocortical system encodes the trace in a distributed manner, but over time, repetitive reactivation of the trace results in hippocampal-dependent formation of multiple, related traces that facilitate the retrieval of an episode using a variety of cues, so that more extensive lesions are required to delete more remote memories. Note, however, that some version of system consolidation is still postulated in this model, because memory reorganization is assumed; only the idea that the role of the hippocampus is time-limited is rejected.

SELECTED RESPONSES TO THE RESERVATIONS

It could be claimed that spontaneous recovery occurs because the blockade of the consolidation process was incomplete and the process, or parts of it, ultimately escape inhibition. Further, many studies fail to find spontaneous recovery of amnesia, and although a negative result, it is a consistent one. The observation that the hippocampal formation lights up in functional neuroimaging of episodic retrieval, including of very remote memories, is itself not proof that this region is obligatory for retrieval. And as to retrieval accounts of amnesia in general, the question could be raised: What is it that is consolidated when a memory becomes long-term, and shouldn't the internal representations of states, cues, or hypothetical indices for retrieval be considered an integral part of the engram, and hence shouldn't their encoding consolidate as well? If one accepts this broader view of consolidation, namely that consolidation is not only stabilization of the persistent trace but also its maturation into a form suitable for future retrieval, then the retrieval type of explanation does not really contradict the consolidation theory. And as to the residual memory capabilities of human amnesics: The priming data used to support the retrieval deficit hypothesis are accounted for by the fact that "global" amnesics are damaged only in declarative, not in nondeclarative, memory systems such as the one that supports repetition priming (Schacter 1987, Squire 1987). Last, in general, in evaluating the status of the consolidation theory, one should also consider the rich literature that describes in remarkable detail molecular and cellular processes and mechanisms that correlate with synaptic consolidation, and whose blockade blocks long-term memory. Indeed, much more evidence is still needed to establish whether these processes and mechanisms embody the new long-term internal representation, or are only auxiliary to its formation (Dudai 2002a, Martin et al. 2000); yet the molecular and cellular data, combined with the pharmacological data and corroborated by some morphological evidence, strongly reinforce the now-classical notion that the trace is indeed transformed from a short-term, more labile form, into a long-term, more stable form, either in serial or parallel processes, and that this transformation is not instantaneous but requires postexperience time (Hebb 1949). Having said all this, even orthodox believers in the consolidation theory should still keep at the back of their minds the fact that a body of literature questions their faith. Pieces of puzzling data still call for explanation. Therefore, to assume that the current textbook models of consolidation are faithful to reality is a bit naive.

DO MEMORIES RECONSOLIDATE?

The standard model(s) of consolidation are conventionally taken to imply that for any memorized item, consolidation starts and ends just once. But currently, a hotly debated issue in memory research in general and in consolidation research in particular is whether this assumption is valid. Note that even if it is not, this does not annul the mere concept of a consolidation phase—it just modifies it to mean that the stability is under certain conditions ephemeral. The debate is not at all new, but has been resurrected in recent years. In 1968, Misanin et al. reported that electroconvulsive shock (ECS), a known amnestic agent, leads to memory loss if administered immediately after retrieval, 24 hours posttraining, of a seemingly consolidated, long-term conditioned passive-avoidance memory. Similarly, Schneider & Sherman (1968) reported that in a passive-avoidance task, rats became amnesic if ECS was administered immediately after noncontingent presentation of the US (i.e., a reinstatement trial) even if this was done six hours after CS–US conditioning, at which time the memory was known to become resistant to ECS. These reports were followed by additional reports of such apparent reconsolidation in other tasks or using other amnestic agents (e.g., Judge & Quartermain 1982, Lewis & Bergman 1973, Lewis et al. 1972). Controls were presented to show that this was specific to the activated memory, and not reinstatement of a general internal state. The basic idea that emerged from these experiments was that it is not the time since encoding that determines the susceptibility of a trace to interventions, but rather the functional state of the trace: An active (retrieved) trace can be truncated, but also augmented (Sara 2000); an inactive (stored) trace is immune to such manipulations (Lewis 1979). Others could not, however, replicate the reconsolidation phenomenon (Dawson & McGaugh 1969). Still others reported that the blocking of recall was transient only (Mactutus et al. 1979). Besides supplying the opposition of the consolidation theory with additional ammunition to criticize the idea that in consolidation memories are permanently stabilized, the reconsolidation reports should have provoked much attention and should have been followed by intense attempts to clarify the picture once and for all because of the obvious theoretical and clinical implications. This did not happen. There were multiple reasons for this decay of active interest, in addition to the aforementioned inconsistencies in the findings among different laboratories. First, the reconsolidation idea was not easy to reconcile with the zeitgeist. And second, the neurobiology of memory went cellular and molecular, and systemic interventions were not thought to be as fashionable as before; a similar trend was noted at about the same time in the study of synaptic consolidation in experimental animals (Dudai 2002a).

A new phase in the life of the reconsolidation hypothesis started a few years ago. Following additional papers on the topic (e.g., Bucherelli & Tassoni 1992, Przybyslawski & Sara 1997, Przybyslawski et al. 1999, Roullet & Sara 1998, Sekiguchi et al. 1997), Sara (2000) reviewed the field in detail, arguing more or less that reconsolidation is not a myth and should not be neglected. At about the same time, Nader et al. (2000) reported the phenomenon in fear conditioning, targeting directly a brain circuit assumed to subserve this memory. They trained rats on elemental, Pavlovian fear conditioning to associate a tone with foot shock. A common measure of the conditioned response in this paradigm is the immediate freezing to the tone. The consolidation of this type of memory can be blocked by microinfusion of the protein synthesis inhibitor anisomycin into the lateral and basal nuclei of the amygdala (LBA) immediately after training. Nader et al. reported that the consolidated fear memory can return to a labile state, in which local microinfusion of anisomycin into the LBA immediately after the retrieval of the fear memory, but not six hours afterward, produces amnesia on subsequent tests. This happened regardless of whether retrieval was 1 or 14 days after conditioning. The same treatment with anisomycin in the absence of memory reactivation left memory intact. Their conclusion was that consolidated fear memory, when reactivated, returns to a labile state that requires de novo protein synthesis for new consolidation, i.e., reconsolidation. In their paper Nader et al. (2000) did not provide evidence that the amnestic effect is long-term, rather than a transient drug effect. Later, however, the same group determined that the deficit lasts for at least three weeks (K. Nader, personal communication).

The Nader et al. (2000) report became highly visible and additional studies soon followed. Taubenfeld et al. (2001) reported that anisomycin impairs memory on an inhibitory avoidance task if injected systemically immediately after retrieval of a consolidated memory. Interestingly, whereas consolidation of this task depends on hippocampal protein synthesis, direct infusion of anisomycin into the hippocampus after retrieval had no effect on memory. Microinfusion of oligodeoxynucleotides antisense to the transcription factor β(C/EBPβ) into the hippocampus impaired memory only after acquisition but not after retrieval, which led the authors to propose that the consolidation of new but not reactivated memory requires this transcription factor, and also that brain areas other than the hippocampus (amygdala?) are involved in postretrieval consolidation. Kida et al. (2002) used transgenic mice with an inducible and reversible suppressor of the transcription factor CREB (see Synaptic Consolidation, above), and found that CREB is crucial for the consolidation of long-term contextual fear conditioning as well as for the stability of retrieved consolidated memory, but not for the encoding, retention, or retrieval of such memory. Using local microinfusions of anisomycin, Debiec et al. (2002) reported that de novo protein synthesis in the hippocampus is required for both the consolidation and the reconsolidation of contextual fear conditioning. Again, reactivation of the trace was essential for the effect to take place, and the amnesic deficit persisted after several weeks. Reconsolidation has since been observed in object recognition in rats, where mitogen-activated protein kinase (MAPK; see Figure 2) was identified as critical for the process, similar to its role in consolidation of a new memory (Kelly et al. 2003). Data construed as reconsolidation, dependent on protein synthesis and NMDA-type of glutamatergic receptors, were also reported in the crab *Chasmagnathus* in contextual fear conditioning (Pedreira et al. 2002). It is highly likely that between the time of writing of this review and its publication, numerous laboratories will report additional reconsolidation studies in various systems.

Whereas Nader et al. (2000) and Debiec et al. (2002) reported that reactivation-induced reconsolidation of fear conditioning can be obtained weeks after training, Milekic & Alberini (2002), using the inhibitory avoidance task, reported a temporal gradient of sensitivity to protein synthesis inhibition (achieved in this case by systemic rather than local administration of anisomycin). Susceptibility to disruption of the reactivated memory was very high at 2 days posttraining, was significant but lower at 7 days, but disappeared at 14 days. This implies that in this task and protocol, memories do become stabilized and immune to the effects of consolidation blocker after a period that is longer than that of synaptic consolidation, but much shorter than the life span of the memory.

Still other studies of the postretrieval effect of a consolidation blocker did not unveil lability of the original trace. Rats conditioned to associate a taste with delayed toxicosis (conditioned taste aversion, CTA) reject the conditioned taste for months afterwards. Microinfusion of anisomycin into the insular cortex, which contains the taste cortex, immediately before or after conditioning, prevents the consolidation of CTA. Once formed, CTA memory can be extinguished by presenting the taste in the absence of malaise. If immediately before or after the retrieval of taste aversion in an extinction protocol, anisomycin is microinfused into the insular cortex, extinction is blocked, whereas the original trace is spared (Berman & Dudai 2001, Berman et al. 2003). Similarly, microinfusion of anisomycin into the basolateral nucleus of the amygdala immediately after retrieval resulted in inhibition of CTA extinction rather than in diminution of the original association (Bahar et al. 2003). Vianna et al. (2001) reported that retrieval of memory of fear-associated inhibitory avoidance initiates extinction, which is blocked by protein synthesis inhibition in the hippocampus, again sparing the original trace. These studies are compatible with the idea that extinction is relearning rather than unlearning, and that the resulting memory, like any other long-term memory, undergoes protein synthesis–dependent synaptic consolidation. The original trace, however, does not seem to become labile in retrieval in these protocols.

There might be an explanation for these differences. In the study of Nader et al. (2000) on fear conditioning, the training and retrieval protocols do not lead to significant extinction upon retrieval, and the original trace is reported to enter a protein synthesis-dependent labile state; in the studies of Berman & Dudai (2001) and Vianna et al. (2001), the training and retrieval protocol results in significant extinction, and the original trace does not seem to enter a protein synthesis–dependent labile state. One possibility is, therefore, that the differences in the postretrieval lability of the trace are related to the retrieval protocol used (Dudai 2002b) and specifically to the interbalance or competition between the original trace (of the CS–US association, conventionally termed the excitatory trace) and the new trace (the CS–no US, conventionally termed the inhibitory trace) (Nader 2003). Eisenberg et al. (2003) recently found evidence that among competitive associations, the association that retains or gains behavioral control after the retrieval session, is the one that becomes sensitive anew to disruption by certain treatments that also block consolidation. Hence, if in CTA in the rat, the training is made intensive and the memory more robust and resistant to extinction, microinfusion of anisomycin into the insular cortex immediately after retrieval impairs performance guided by the original trace. In contrast, if the training allows extinction, the same treatment blocks the newly developing CS–no US association, as previously described by Berman & Dudai (2001). Similarly, if in shock avoidance in the *Medaka* fish, an anesthetic is administered in retrieval early in extinction training, when extinction has not yet developed, the original association is inhibited; if, however, the same treatment is applied in a later retrieval session, the new trace—of the CS–no US association—is impaired. The impairment, however, does not reflect erasure of the trace: In both cases reinstatement could later be detected by readministration of the unpaired US (M. Eisenberg, T. Kobilo, & Y. Dudai, in preparation). It thus seems that the stability of a memory item upon its retrieval is inversely correlated with the trace dominance (i.e., its control of behavior at that point in time), but loss of stability does not result in irreversible corruption of the entire trace. This observation notwithstanding, the stability~f(1/dominance) rule might account for some of the discrepancies in the reconsolidation data so far.

DIFFERENCES BETWEEN SYNAPTIC CONSOLIDATION AND POSTULATED RECONSOLIDATION

Scrutiny of the reconsolidation or attempted-reconsolidation data indicates that postretrieval consolidation does not recapitulate faithfully the consolidation of a new trace. First, the sensitivity of the two processes to consolidation blockers seems to be different. Both increased and decreased sensitivity have been reported. Deeper cooling was required to block consolidation compared to reconsolidation in shock avoidance in the rat, which suggests that reconsolidation is more vulnerable to disruption (Mactutus et al. 1982). However, a dose of anisomycin similar to the dose used to block the original consolidation had no effect on presumed reconsolidation in a shock-avoidance task (Taubenfeld 2001), but doubling that dose had an effect in fear conditioning (Debiec et al. 2002), which suggests that reconsolidation is less vulnerable to disruption. Admittedly, these dose differences also raise the possibility that the anisomycin acts on different targets in each case. At the time of writing, no dose-response measurement of protein synthesis inhibition at the target was reported in any of the new attempted-reconsolidation studies except in the aforementioned CTA studies, and the mechanism of anisomycin action is hence inferred from other systems. Like many other drugs, this drug has multiple cellular targets (Kyriakis et al. 1994). Another difference is in the time course. The onset of amnesia was more rapid in cooling-sensitive reconsolidation of the shock-avoidance task (Mactutus et al. 1982), and the time window of anisomycin sensitivity was shorter in reconsolidation (Judge & Quartermain 1982; see also the brief time window of postretrieval consolidation in Berman & Dudai 2001). Furthermore, in CTA, the molecular processes of the original and the postretrieval consolidation processes, though sharing components, are not identical (Berman & Dudai 2001). This is also in line with the report of Taubenfeld et al. (2001), mentioned above, that the consolidation of new but not reactivated memory requires the transcription factor C/EBPβ.

A critical question concerning the reconsolidation studies is whether the detected amnesia is stable, or, alternatively, only a reflection of a transient latency of the trace, induced by the postretrieval treatment. The postretrieval-induced amnesia was shown to be stable in fear conditioning (Nader et al., personal communication). However, in earlier studies of reconsolidation in the rat (e.g., Mactutus et al. 1979), using cooling as the consolidation blocker, or in recent studies in the chick, using inhibition of macromolecular synthesis (Anokhin et al. 2002), the recall deficit obtained after retrieval was temporary. In CTA in the rat and in fear conditioning in *Medaka*, the blocked conditioned behavior did not recover spontaneously, but, as mentioned above, could be reinstated by the unpaired US (M. Eisenberg, T. Kobilo, & Y. Dudai, in preparation). Transiency of amnesia was also reported in part of the earlier reconsolidation literature, but it is noteworthy that the same groups also reported reversibility of the amnesia obtained following inhibition of the original consolidation (e.g., Mactutus et al. 1982; see also Radyushkin & Anokhin 1999).

THE POSSIBILITY OF SYSTEM RECONSOLIDATION

The evidence cited above (see also Nader 2003, Sara 2000) could be construed as indicating that upon reactivation in retrieval, traces undergo a consolidation process, which might be different in its temporal and molecular characteristics from the original consolidation, but still depends on de novo protein synthesis. The time window of this process (minutes to hours) and the dependence on protein synthesis implicate synaptic types of processes. Is there also evidence for system reconsolidation?

Because contextual fear conditioning is hippocampus dependent, it is a suitable system to put this question to a test. Debiec et al. (2002) did just that. In this system, like in other hippocampal-dependent memory tasks, the trace becomes practically independent of hippocampal function after a few weeks, i.e., it undergoes system consolidation. Debiec et al. showed that postactivation intrahippocampal microinfusion of anisomycin caused subsequent amnesia for the contextual fear memory, even when the reactivation was delayed for 45 days after training, when the memory is already hippocampal independent. This was taken to imply that reactivation of a hippocampus-independent memory caused the trace to again become hippocampus dependent. Further, Debiec et al. prepared rats with either sham or electrolytic lesions of the hippocampus 45 days after conditioning. Two other groups were treated identically except that immediately prior to surgery they received a reactivation (i.e., CS-induced retrieval) session. The hippocampal lesions (but not neocortical lesions) caused amnesia only in the animals that had received a reactivation session, and this amnesia did not show spontaneous recovery over a month. However, in contrast to system consolidation, which requires weeks to complete, the proposed system reconsolidation lasted for only two days.

The data of Milekic & Alberini (2002), mentioned above, showing a temporal gradient of sensitivity to protein synthesis inhibition in the hippocampal-dependent inhibitory avoidance task, are incongruent with the notion that memories can reconsolidate long after system consolidation has been completed. A caveat, however, is appropriate here. The Milekic & Alberini study involves another type of memory and another intervention protocol (systemic administration of the blocker versus target-directed). Furthermore, because the sensitivity of consolidation and reconsolidation to inhibition of protein synthesis may vary (see above), it is possible that the temporally graded requirement for protein synthesis following memory reactivation might be altered by increasing the dose of the inhibitor, or by targeting it to brain circuits outside the hippocampus, such as the amygdala.

All in all, at the time of writing, there is indication for system reconsolidation in one system and protocol; the phenomenon, and its generality, await further analysis.

ON THE MULTIPLE VERSIONS
OF THE RECONSOLIDATION HYPOTHESIS

The reconsolidation hypothesis assumes consolidation upon activation of the trace in retrieval (Lewis 1979; Figure 4).[9] Ample evidence from behavioral and neurobiological analysis indicates that retrieval could involve reconstruction of the

---

[9]For the sake of brevity and argument, the possibility of latent recurrent activation in maintenance or reorganization of the trace (e.g., McClelland et al. 1995; see also the section on System Reconsolidation) is not discussed. However, should such activation happen and reconsolidation apply, an interesting question arises concerning the ongoing potential frailty of at least some types of long-term memory traces.

A

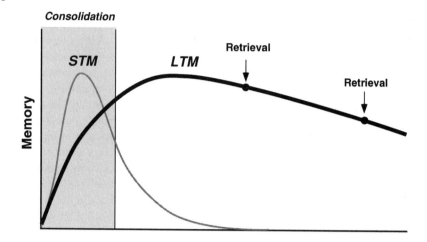

B

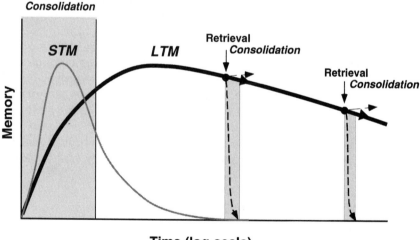

Time (log scale)

Figure 4   Two views of consolidation. (*A*) The standard models of consolidation are conventionally taken to imply that for any memorized item, consolidation starts and ends just once. (*B*) The revised model claims that consolidation can occur multiple times in the life of a memory item, specifically, after its activation in retrieval. The soft, trivial version of this hypothesis refers to the consolidation of new elements that are integrated into the old memory after its retrieval. The stronger versions refer to the possibility that the old memory reconsolidates after its activation and may become modified in the process.

trace, including its amalgamation with new information obtained in the retrieval situations (Bartlett 1932, Dudai 2002a, Schacter et al. 1998, Tulving 1983). This explains why in fact there are three versions to the reconsolidation hypothesis: a weak one, and two stronger ones. The "soft" or "weak" version states that upon retrieval the trace is updated but only the new parts of the modified trace undergo consolidation. This version is trivial, because it refers to consolidation of a new trace rather than to genuine reconsolidation of the old one. It will not be further discussed here. The "intermediate" version of the reconsolidation hypothesis claims that upon retrieval the activated trace becomes labile and modifiable, and has to undergo some new process of stabilization. Given the appropriate interference, parts of the trace that were encoded and consolidated in the original experience might become corrupted in the process, either permanently or transiently. This susceptibility to corruption might be the price paid for modifiability. In real life, consolidation blockers are not frequent—we don't usually swallow anisomycin upon recalling our past—so the price might not be too high. In any case, according to this version of the hypothesis, a core of the original trace remains immune to the new wave of consolidation because it is too mature, or is retained in multiple copies, and/or is richly associated with other traces. This version is the one most comfortable to accommodate with the current data and theory. The "strong" version of the reconsolidation hypothesis is, as its name implies, the most radical one. It also assumes, like the intermediate version, that consolidation does not occur just once in the life of the trace, but further posits that the entire trace, including its original parts, becomes labile and potentially disruptable upon activation in retrieval, and could therefore be utterly erased by consolidation blockers. This hypothetical version, which promotes genuine overall reconsolidation of the original consolidated trace, is the major focus of the renewed debate in the neuroscience of memory.

RESERVATIONS CONCERNING THE STRONGER VERSIONS OF THE RECONSOLIDATION HYPOTHESIS

Briefly, the following arguments are or could be raised. They apply to some degree to both the intermediate and the strong hypotheses but in practice focus specifically on the strong hypothesis, which is more provocative. These arguments are based on data cited above, and only the bottom line will be provided in each case.

   a. *Apparent inconsistencies in the findings.* These have been sampled above. Most importantly, in some systems, and under certain protocols, the original trace becomes labile to interference upon its activation, in others it's not. In some studies, reconsolidation was observed long after the memory has consolidated, in others, only for a limited period after synaptic consolidation. In some studies, in both the initial and the current wave of research on reconsolidation, the amnesia produced by the postactivation consolidation blocker was transient, or could be overcome by reinstatement; in others, it persisted throughout the period studied.

b. *The need for more data.* At the time of writing, several notable studies have already been published on reconsolidation, but the body of research as a whole is still relatively modest, some would claim too modest to reach firm conclusions on the boundary conditions and generality of the phenomenon. Particularly noteworthy are two issues. First, laboratories that currently investigate reconsolidation use different systems and protocols. Second, several types of controls, which are highly desirable, are still missing in some studies. Hence the possibility could be raised that after the retrieval experience, a new trace is formed that takes control over behavior, similar to the situation in experimental extinction, in which case reconsolidation effects might actually represent accelerated extinction. This is not a very appealing explanation, because anisomycin blocks consolidation after learning, so why should it accelerate memory after relearning, i.e., experimental extinction? Still, the possibility should be checked. Extinction is characterized by the possibility of spontaneous recovery, saving, reinstatement, and renewal (Dudai 2002a), all of which are amenable to experimental analysis. Such experiments could be useful in probing the possibility that the old trace is only reverted to a latent state.

c. *Lady Macbeth's argument.* Using the original formulation, it goes like this: "What's done cannot be undone." Suppose formation of the engram involves induction of functional and morphological changes in a finite number of synapses at time $t = i$; it is counterintuitive, so goes the argument, to assume that after a long time, a new experience could retrace the former changes and undo them so that the state of these same synapses at time $t = j$ returns to its values at $t = i$. It is in contradiction with what we currently know about the massive turnover of synapses in the mammalian brain and the intricate dynamics of intracellular signal cascades. This argument is discussed below.

d. *Reconsolidation is against the zeitgeist.* This is not really a valid argument, and has nothing to do with how experimental science should be conducted; rather, it is within the domain of the pragmatics and sociology of science. But it does occasionally pop up in discussions, so it should be spelled out.

SELECTED RESPONSES TO THE RESERVATIONS

It is noteworthy that arguments similar to those raised against the stronger versions of the reconsolidation hypothesis were raised several decades ago against the consolidation theory. Prominent among them is the possibility that the amnesia produced is reversible. In many experiments performed in the past 50 years no reversibility of amnesia produced by consolidation blockade has been reported, and those few cases in which reversibility was observed were either explained (e.g., by dissociation of memory systems) or essentially neglected. It remains to be seen how many laboratories will report irreversibility of amnesia following postreactivation consolidation blockade, in order to determine the majority vote and seek explanations for the exceptions. As to discrepancies in the sensitivity of the original trace to postreactivation interference, as noted above, the shifting identity of the behaviorally dominant trace after retrieval might explain at least some of these. Also, because at the time of writing no lab has yet replicated exactly the same protocol of any other lab in this field, the term "inconsistencies" should be taken with a pinch of salt. And the possibility that a new trace—which somehow blocks the expression of the original trace—is formed in reactivation must still be scrutinized. Of all the criticism briefly cited above, it is the "what's done cannot be undone" that deserves special attention, because it is less dependent on additional experimental data than the other arguments.

ON THE DISTINCTION BETWEEN RECONSOLIDATION AND DECONSOLIDATION

What the proponents of the reversibility argument probably mean is not that an acquired behavior cannot be undone, but rather that reconsolidation is impossible because the hardware modifications that have led to the encoding of the trace and to its persistence over time are unlikely to be undone. Regardless of whether the stronger versions of the reconsolidation hypothesis are factually valid or not, a fallacy is hidden in the above argument. Its resolution requires a clear delineation of levels of function and analysis, and a distinction between reconsolidation and deconsolidation. This argument assumes deconsolidation: that the state of the system at time $t = j$, after reconsolidation has taken place, is restored to the state of the system at $t = i$, before consolidation had been completed. As noted above, it is not only counterintuitive that the nervous system will be able to retrace its long-ago changes for every item in memory and undo them almost instantaneously, it is also unfeasible to expect, based on what we do know about the life of synapses (e.g., Trachtenberg et al. 2002). It is questionable whether many synapses that had been modified in the original consolidation survive to the time of retrieval months or years later. Reconsolidation, if it occurs, cannot be based on deconsolidation at the synaptic hardware level.

Memories, i.e., experience-dependent internal representations (Dudai 1989), are expected to be encoded in the spatiotemporal states of neuronal circuits or populations. Such states are unlikely to correspond to singular configurations of sets of unique individual synapses; at least in the vertebrate brain, it is highly probable that practically equivalent behavioral states could be replicated by the spatiotemporal activity patterns of distributed systems in which individual synapses are interchangeable or could be gracefully degraded. It makes, therefore, more sense to consider the notion of reconsolidation as referring to functional-state reversal rather than hardware-state reversal. The illusion of the need for hardware-state reversal stems from being entrapped, usually implicitly, in metaphors that portray the structure of items in memory, once formed, as stagnant (Dudai 2002a, Roediger 1980). Stagnation should not be confounded with stability and stability with persistence. We know that physical systems, neural networks included, could endure for long in semistable energy minima and still show much dynamics and flux (Amit 1989). There is nothing inherent in the concept of reconsolidation that contradicts the logic of such systems. Reconsolidation could hence involve undoing the acquired ability to actualize or reconstruct a certain spatiotemporal neuronal state without undoing the old connections that have created this acquired state in the first place. This still involves synaptic plasticity, i.e., alteration of synaptic weights, and even instances of their reversal—but these synapses should not necessarily be expected to be the original synapses, let alone these same synapses retracing their molecular history.[10] Even if the strong version of the reconsolidation hypothesis is proven valid and survives the independent replications and careful controls that its critics, rightly so, demand, the only thing that it will contradict will be the view that consolidation is a singular event in the life of a memory item.

EPILOGUE

The study of consolidation is of great importance in memory research because it bears on cardinal theoretical and practical issues. To start with the latter, it could cast light on the etiology and treatment of amnesia, on pathologies that involve obsessive recollection, on posttraumatic stress disorder, acquired phobia, and additional affective and cognitive disorders. Consider, for example, the possibility that a specific traumatic memory could be erased upon retrieval; this might lead to a treatment for posttraumatic stress disorder, which is a devastating pathology. Furthermore, understanding consolidation might culminate in methods to improve various types of memory, including the acquisition and reacquisition of skill, a process of significant economic value. On the theoretical side, studies of consolidations contribute to our understanding the nature of the trace, its maturation, its persistence, and its retrievability and expression.

The question of what it is that physically persists in long-term memory is fundamental, yet is only infrequently discussed explicitly in the neurobiological literature (Dudai 2002b). It is futile to try to understand consolidation or the possibility of reconsolidation without addressing the issue of persistence. It is noteworthy,

---

[10]There is a suggestion that synaptic changes may be undone after a long delay, in memory extinction in *Drosophila* (Schwaerzel et al. 2002). In its most parsimonious interpretation, this idea requires the same synapse to survive throughout the life of the memory. It is unlikely to happen in extinction in mammals, which is considered relearning rather than unlearning.

toward that end, to recapitulate some points that were briefly noted, or only alluded to, in this discussion:

- The long-term trace probably persists in a dormant, inactive, representational state until reactivated in retrieval—or possibly also, in a behaviorally opaque manner, in the course of reorganization or maintenance of memory systems. The activation of the trace implies re-creation or reconstruction of a certain spatiotemporal pattern of neuronal activity. The distinction between inactive and active states of the trace deserves more attention than it has so far received since Lewis (1979) explicitly formulated it.

- To persist in a functionally useful manner, the trace must possess not only the ability to re-express the specific internal representation, but also "retrieval handles" that permit activation by some but not other representations. Each act of retrieval might involve the use and use-dependent modification of only part of the set of retrieval handles of that particular representation. The role of consolidation, particularly synaptic consolidation, in establishing and remodeling persistent retrieval handles is mostly a *terra incognita* whose exploration might promote the understanding of postacquisition and postretrieval consolidation.

- At least in the mammalian cortex, the trace is unlikely to persist over prolonged periods by being dependent on the same set of individual synapses that had subserved its encoding. Spatiotemporal patterns of neural population activity, which have a similar mental and behavioral meaning, might be reactivated or reconstructed by nonidentical synaptic ensembles.

- In biological memory systems, persistence should not, therefore, be confounded with structural stability, and stability with stagnation.

- Moreover, modifications in synapses and nerve cells should not be simply equated with modifications in memory. Those are different levels of organization and function, where one level (cellular) is assumed to subserve, by virtue of its plasticity, the other (behavioral), but the translation rules that govern this interaction are not yet known. Further, it is premature to determine whether identified functional or morphological changes in synapses, which are correlated with, and obligatory for, the processes of learning and consolidation, are indeed causally related to the encoding and persistence of memory per se, as opposed to auxiliary processes that are required for the formation of the trace but do not embody it.

- Overall, therefore, consolidation should not be portrayed as freezing of a structural state of the synapse, let alone reconsolidation, if it does exist in its stronger versions, as reversal to the prefrozen physical state. The system is too dynamic to allow such reversal; moreover, it most likely does not require it for replicating or annulling behaviorally meaningful states.

Scientific paradigms might be more static and resistant to change than brains. The current exciting debates in the field of memory consolidation are bound to culminate in models that will be more faithful to reality. In the meantime, these debates shake the zeitgeist a bit, which can do only good. They also turn our attention to the possibility that when it applies to memory, consolidated memory included, the Greeks got it right again: Everything flows, *Panta Rei*.

ACKNOWLEDGMENTS

I am grateful to Josh Berke, Howard Eichenbaum, Joe Manns, and Karim Nader for valuable discussions. This review was written while I was on sabbatical leave at the Center for Memory and Brain, Boston University. I thank the members and the administration of the Center for their warm and effective hospitality and for the intellectually stimulating environment. The work in my laboratory on consolidation and postretrieval consolidation is supported by the Human Frontiers Science Program, The Volkswagen Foundation, The Minerva Foundation, The Israeli Science Foundation, and the Dominique Center for Brain Research.

The *Annual Review of Psychology* is online at http://psych.annualreviews.org

LITERATURE CITED

Agranoff BW, David RE, Brink JJ. 1966. Chemical studies on memory fixation in goldfish. *Brain Res.* 1:303–9

Agranoff BW, Klinger PD. 1964. Puromycin effect on memory fixation in the goldfish. *Science* 146:952–53

Amit DJ. 1989. *Modeling Brain Function. The World of Attractor Neural Networks*. New York: Cambridge Univ. Press

Anokhin KV, Tiunova AA, Rose SPR. 2002. Reminder effect—reconsolidation or retrieval deficit? Pharmacological dissection with protein synthesis inhibitors following reminder for a passive-avoidance task in young chick. *Eur. J. Neurosci.* 15:1759–65

Bahar A, Samuel A, Hazvi S, Dudai Y. 2003. The amygdalar circuit that acquires taste aversion memory differs from the circuit that extinguishes it. *Eur. J. Neurosci.* 17:1–4

Bailey CH, Kandel ER. 1993. Structural changes accompanying memory storage. *Annu. Rev. Physiol.* 55:397–426

Bartlett FC. 1932. *Remembering. A Study in Experimental and Social Psychology*. London: Cambridge Univ. Press

Bayley PJ, Hopkins RO, Squire LR. 2003. Successful recollection of remote autobiographical memories by amnesic patients with medial temporal lobe lesions. *Neuron* 38:135–44

Bayley PJ, Squire LR. 2002. Medial temporal lobe amnesia: gradual acquisition of factual information by nondeclarative memory. *J. Neurosci.* 22:5741–48

Berman DE, Dudai Y. 2001. Memory extinction, learning anew, and learning the new: dissociations in the molecular machinery of learning in cortex. *Science* 291:2417–19

Berman DE, Hazvi S, Stehberg J, Bahar A, Dudai Y. 2003. Conflicting processes in the extinction of conditioned taste aversion: behavioral and molecular aspects of latency, apparent stagnation, and spontaneous recovery. *Learn. Mem.* 10:16–25

Bontempi B, Laurent-Demir C, Destrade C, Jaffard R. 1999. Time-dependent reorganization of brain circuitry underlying long-term memory storage. *Nature* 400:671–75

Bourtchuladze R, Frenguelli B, Blendy J, Cioffi D, Schutz G, Silva AJ. 1994. Deficient long-term memory in mice with a targeted mutation in the cAMP-responsive element-binding protein. *Cell* 79:59–68

Bradley PM, Galal KM. 1988. State-dependent recall can be induced by protein synthesis inhibition: behavioral and morphological observations. *Brain Res.* 468:243–51

Brashers-Krug T, Shadmehr R, Bizzi E. 1996. Consolidation in human motor memory. *Nature* 382:252–55

Brooks ND, Baddeley AD. 1976. What can amnesic patients learn? *Neuropsychologia* 14:111–22

Bucherelli C, Tassoni G. 1992. Engram activation reinstates the susceptibility of consolidated memory traces to retrograde-amnesia by functional blockade of parabrachial nuclei. *Behav. Brain Res.* 51:61–65

Burnham WH. 1903. Retroactive amnesia: illustrative cases and a tentative explanation. *Am. J. Psychol.* 14:382–96

Casadio A, Martin K, Giusetto M, Zhu H, Chen M, et al. 1999. A transient, neuron-wide form of CREB-mediated long-term facilitation can be stabilized at specific synapses by local protein synthesis. *Cell* 99:221–37

Cho YH, Beracochea D, Jaffard R. 1993. Extended temporal gradient for the retrograde and anterograde amnesia produced by ibotenate entorhinal cortex lesions in mice. *J. Neurosci.* 13:1759–66

Clark RE, Broadbent NJ, Zola SM, Squire LR. 2002. Anterograde amnesia and temporally graded retrograde amnesia for a nonspatial memory task after lesions of hippocampus and subiculum. *J. Neurosci.* 22:4663–69

Cohen NJ. 1984. Preserved learning capacity in amnesia: evidence for multiple memory systems. In *Neuropsychology of Memory,* ed. LR Squire, N Butters, pp. 83–103. New York: Guilford

Cohen NJ, Poldrack RA, Eichenbaum H. 1997. Memory for items and memory for relations in the procedural/declarative memory framework. *Memory* 5:131–78

Corkin S. 2002. What's new with the amnesic patient H.M.? *Nat. Rev. Neurosci.* 3:153–60

Crick F, Mitchison G. 1983. The function of dream sleep. *Nature* 304:111–14

Davis HP, Squire LR. 1984. Protein synthesis and memory: a review. *Psychol. Bull.* 96:518–59

Dawson RG, McGaugh JL. 1969. Electroconvulsive shock effect on a reactivated memory: further examination. *Science* 166:525–27

Debiec J, LeDoux JE, Nader K. 2002. Cellular and systems reconsolidation in the hippocampus. *Neuron* 36:527–38

Deisseroth K, Bito H, Tsien RW. 1996. Signaling from synapse to nucleus: postsynaptic CREB phosphorylation during multiple forms of hippocampal synaptic plasticity. *Neuron* 16:89–101

DeVietti TL, Hopfer TM. 1974. Reinstatement of memory in rats: dependence upon two forms of retrieval deficit following electroconvulsive shock. *J. Comp. Physiol. Psychol.* 86:1090–99

DeZazzo J, Tully T. 1995. Dissection of memory formation: from behavioral pharmacology to molecular genetics. *Trends Neurosci.* 18:212–18

Doyon J, Guardeau D, Laforce RJ, Castonguay M, Bedard PJ, Bouchard JP. 1997. Role of striatum, cerebellum, and frontal lobes in the learning of a visuomotor sequence. *Brain Cogn.* 34:218–45

Doyon J, Song AW, Karni A, Lalonde F, Adams MM, Ungerleider LG. 2002. Experience-dependent changes in cerebellar contributions to motor sequence learning. *Proc. Natl. Acad. Sci. USA* 99:1017–22

Dudai Y. 1989. *The Neurobiology of Memory. Concepts, Findings, Trends.* Oxford: Oxford Univ. Press

Dudai Y. 1996. Consolidation: fragility on the road to the engram. *Neuron* 17:367–70

Dudai Y. 2002a. *Memory from A to Z. Keywords, Concepts and Beyond.* Oxford: Oxford Univ. Press

Dudai Y. 2002b. Molecular bases of long-term memories: a question of persistence. *Curr. Opin. Neurobiol.* 12:211–16

Dudai Y, Morris RGM. 2000. To consolidate or not to consolidate: What are the questions? In *Brain, Perception, Memory. Advances in*

Cognitive Sciences, ed. JJ Bulhuis, pp. 149–62. Oxford: Oxford Univ. Press

Duncan CP. 1949. The retroactive effect of electroconvulsive shock. *J. Comp. Physiol. Psychol.* 42:32–44

Ebbinghaus H. 1885/1964. *Memory: A Contribution to Experimental Psychology.* New York: Teachers College/Columbia Univ.

Eichenbaum H. 1997. Declarative memory: insights from cognitive neurobiology. *Annu. Rev. Psychol.* 48:547–72

Eisenberg M, Kobilo T, Berman DE, Dudai Y. 2003. Stability of retrieved memory: inverse correlation with trace dominance. *Science* 301:1102–4

El-Husseini Ael-D, Schnell E, Dakoji S, Sweeney N, Zhou Q, Prange O, et al. 2002. Synaptic strength regulated by palmitate cycling on PSD-95. *Cell* 108:849–63

Frank DA, Greenberg ME. 1994. CREB: a mediator of long-term memory from mollusks to mammals. *Cell* 79:5–8

Freeman FM, Rose SPR, Scholey AB. 1995. Two time windows of anisomycin-induced amnesia for passive avoidance training in the day-old chick. *Neurobiol. Learn. Mem.* 63:291–95

Frey U, Morris RGM. 1997. Synaptic tagging and long-term potentiation. *Nature* 385:533–36

Ghirardi M, Montarolo PG, Kandel ER. 1995. A novel intermediate stage in the transition between short- and long-term facilitation in the sensory to motor neuron synapse of *Aplysia Neuron* 14:413–20

Gordon WC, Mowrer RR. 1980. The use of an extinction trial as a reminder treatment following ECS. *Anim. Learn. Behav.* 8:363–67

Gould SJ, Lewontin RC. 1979. The spandrels of San Marco and the Panglossian paradigm: a critique of the adaptionist programme. *Proc. R. Soc. London Ser. B* 205:581–88

Greeksch G, Matthies H. 1980. Two sensitive periods for the amnesic effect of anisomycin. *Pharmacol. Biochem. Behav.* 12:663–65

Haist F, Gore JB, Mao H. 2001. Consolidation of human memory over decades revealed by functional magnetic resonance imaging. *Nat. Neurosci.* 4:1139–45

Hartley D. 1810. *Observations on Man, His Fame, His Duty and His Expectations.* London: Wilkie & Robinson

Hebb DO. 1949. *The Organization of Behavior: A Neuropsychological Theory.* New York: Wiley

Hinderliter CF, Webster T, Riccio DC. 1975. Amnesia induced by hypothermia as a function of treatment-test interval and recooling in rats. *Anim. Learn. Behav.* 3:257–63

Huber KM, Kayser MS, Bear MF. 2000. Role for rapid dendritic protein synthesis in hippocampal mGluR-dependent long-term depression. *Science* 288:1254–56

Jenkins JG, Dallenbach KM. 1924. Oblivience during sleep and waking. *Am. J. Psychol.* 35:605–12

Judge ME, Quartermain D. 1982. Characteristics of retrograde amnesia following reactivation of memory in mice. *Physiol. Behav.* 28:585–90

Kaang B-K, Kandel ER, Grant SGN. 1993. Activation of cAMP-responsive genes by stimuli that produce long-term facilitation in *Aplysia* sensory neurons. *Neuron* 10:427–35

Karni A, Meyer G, Rey-Hipolito C, Jezzard P, Adams MM, et al. 1998. The acquisition of skilled motor performance: fast and slow experience-driven changes in primary motor cortex. *Proc. Natl. Acad. Sci. USA* 95:861–68

Katz JJ, Halstad WC. 1950. Protein organization and mental function. *Comp. Psychol. Monogr.* 20:1–38

Kelly A, Laroche S, Davis S. 2003. Activation of mitogen-activated protein kinase/extracellular signal-regulated kinase in hippocampal circuitry is required for consolidation and reconsolidation of recognition memory. *J. Neurosci.* 23:5354–60

Kida S, Josselyn SA, Pena de Ortiz S, Kogan JH, Chevere I, et al. 2002. CREB required for the stability of new and reactivated fear memories. *Nat. Neurosci.* 5:348–55

Kim JJ, Clark RE, Thompson RF. 1995. Hippocampectomy impairs the memory of recently, but not remotely, acquired trace eyeblink conditioned response. *Behav. Neurosci.* 109:195–203

Kim JJ, Fabselow MS. 1992. Modality-specific retrograde amnesia of fear. *Science* 256:675–77

Kleim JA, Barbay S, Cooper NR, Hogg TM, Reidel CN, et al. 2002. Motor learning-dependent synaptogenesis is localized to functionally reorganized motor cortex. *Neurobiol. Learn. Mem.* 77:63–77

Knowlton BJ, Mangels JA, Squire LR. 1996. A neostriatal habit learning system in humans. *Science* 273:1399–402

Kubie JL, Suhterland RJ, Miller RU. 1999. Hippocampal lesions produce a temporally graded retrograde amnesia on a dry version of the Morris swimming task. *Psychobiology* 27:313–30

Kyriakis JM, Banerjee P, Nikolakai E, Dai T, Rubie EA, et al. 1994. The stress-activated protein kinase subfamily of c-Jun kinases. *Nature* 369:156–60

Lamprecht R, Hazvi S, Dudai Y. 1997. cAMP response element-binding protein in the amygdala is required for long- but not short-term conditioned taste aversion memory. *J. Neurosci.* 17:8443–50

Landauer TK. 1969. Reinforcement as consolidation. *Psychol. Rev.* 76:82–96

Lechner HA, Squire LR, Byrne JH. 1999. 100 years of consolidation—remembering Muller and Pilzecker. *Learn. Mem.* 6:77–87

Lewis D, Bergman NJ, Mahan J. 1972. Cue-dependent amnesia in rats. *J. Comp. Physiol. Psychol.* 81:243–47

Lewis DJ. 1979. Psychobiology of active and inactive memory. *Psychol. Bull.* 86:1054–83

Lewis DJ, Bergman NJ. 1973. Source of cues for cue-dependent amnesia in rats. *J. Comp. Physiol. Psychol.* 85:421–26

Lewis DJ, Misanin JR, Miller RR. 1968. The recovery of memory following amnestic treatment. *Nature* 220:704–5

Mactutus CF, Ferek JM, George CA, Riccio DC. 1982. Hypothermia-induced amnesia for newly acquired and old reactivated memories: commonalities and distinctions. *Physiol. Psychol.* 10:79–95

Mactutus CF, Riccio DC, Ferek JM. 1979. Retrograde amnesia for old (reactivated) memory: some anomalous characteristics. *Science* 204:1319–20

Maquet P, Schwartz S, Passingham R, Frith C. 2003. Sleep-related consolidation of a visuomotor skill: brain mechanisms as assessed by functional magnetic resonance imaging. *J. Neurosci.* 23:1432–40

Marr D. 1982. *Vision.* San Francisco: Freeman

Martin KC, Casadio A, Zhu HX, Rose JC, YP E, et al. 1997. Synapse-specific, long-term facilitation of *Aplysia* sensory to motor synapses: a function for local protein synthesis in memory storage. *Cell* 91:927–38

Martin SJ, Grimwood PD, Morris RGM. 2000. Synaptic plasticity and memory: an evaluation of the hypothesis. *Annu. Rev. Neurosci.* 23:649–711

McClelland JL, Goddard NH. 1996. Considerations arising from complementary learning systems perspective on hippocampus and neocortex. *Hippocampus* 6:654–65

McClelland JL, McNaughton BL, O'Reilly RC. 1995. Why there are complementary learning systems in the hippocampus and neocortex: insights from the successes and failures of connectionist models of learning and memory. *Psychol. Rev.* 102:419–57

McDougall W. 1901. Experimentelle Beitrage zur Lehre vom Gedächtniss. *Mind* 10:388–94

McGaugh JL. 1966. Time-dependent processes in memory storage. *Science* 153:1351–58

McGaugh JL. 2000. Memory—a century of consolidation. *Science* 287:248–51

McGaugh JL. 2002. Memory consolidation and the amygdala: a systems perspective. *Trends Neurosci.* 25:456–61

McGeoch JA. 1933. Studies in retroactive inhibition: II. Relationships between temporal point of interpolation, length of interval, and amount of retroactive inhibition. *J. Gen. Psychol.* 9:44–57

Milekic MH, Alberini CM. 2002. Temporally graded requirement for protein synthesis following memory reactivation. *Neuron* 36:521–25

Miller RR, Matzel LD. 2000. Memory involves far more than "consolidation." *Nat. Rev. Neurosci.* 1:214–16

Miller RR, Ott CA, Berk AM, Springer AD. 1974. Appetitive memory restoration after electroconvulsive shock in the rat. *J. Comp. Physiol. Psychol.* 87:717–23

Miller RR, Springer AD. 1972. Induced recovery of memory in rats following electroconvulsive shock. *Physiol. Behav.* 8:645–51

Millin PM, Moody EW, Riccio DC. 2001. Interpretations of retrograde amnesia: old problems redux. *Nat. Rev. Neurosci.* 2:68–70

Milner B, Corkin S, Teiber HL. 1968. Further analysis of the hippocampal amnesic syndrome: 14 years follow-up study of H.M. *Neuropsychologia* 6:251–34

Milner B, Squire LR, Kandel ER. 1998. Cognitive neuroscience and the study of memory. *Neuron* 20:445–68

Misanin JR, Miller RR, Lewis DJ. 1968. Retrograde amnesia produced by electroconvulsive shock after reactivation of consolidated memory trace. *Science* 160:554–55

Montarolo PG, Goelet P, Castellucci VF, Morgan J, Kandel ER, Schacher S. 1986. A critical period for macromolecular synthesis in long-term heterosynaptic facilitation in *Aplysia. Science* 234:1249–54

Moscovitch M, Nadel L. 1998. Consolidation and the hippocampal complex revisited: in defense of the multiple-trace model. *Curr. Opin. Neurobiol.* 8:297–300

Muellbacher W, Zlemann U, Wissel J, Dang N, Kofler M, et al. 2002. Early consolidation in human primary motor cortex. *Nature* 415:640–44

Muller GE, Pilzecker A. 1900. Experimentelle Beitrage zur Lehre von Gedächtnis. *Z. Psychol.* 1:1–300

Nadel L, Moscovitch M. 1997. Memory consolidation, retrograde amnesia, and the hippocampal complex. *Curr. Opin. Neurobiol.* 7:217–27

Nader K. 2003. Memory traces unbound. *Trends Neurosci.* 26:65–72

Nader K, Schafe GE, LeDoux JE. 2000. Fear memories require protein synthesis in the amygdala for reconsolidation after retrieval. *Nature* 406:722–26

Nudo RJ, Milliken GW, Jenkins WM, Merzenich MM. 1996. Use-dependent alterations of movement representations in primary motor cortex of adult squirrel monkeys. *J. Neurosci.* 16:785–807

Pedreira ME, Perez-Cuesta LM, Maldonado H. 2002. Reactivation and reconsolidation of long-term memory in the crab Chasmagnathus: protein synthesis requirement and mediation by NMDA-type glutamatergic receptors. *J. Neurosci.* 22:8305–11

Pennartz CMA, Uylings HBM, Barnes CA, McNaughton BL. 2002. Memory reactivation and consolidation during sleep: from cellular mechanisms to human performance. *Prog. Brain Res.* 138:143–66

Przybyslawski J, Roullet P, Sara SJ. 1999. Attenuation of emotional and nonemotional memories after their reactivation: role of beta adrenergic receptors. *J. Neurosci.* 19:6623–28

Przybyslawski J, Sara SJ. 1997. Reconsolidation of memory after its reactivation. *Behav. Brain Res.* 84:241–46

Quartermain D, McEwen BS, Azmitia EC. 1970. Amnesia produced by electroconvulsive shock or cycloheximide: conditions for recovery. *Science* 169:683–86

Quintillian. 1C AD/1921. *Institutio Oratoria.* London: Loeb Classical Libr.

Radyushkin KA, Anokhin KV. 1999. Recovery of memory in chicks after disruption during learning: the reversibility of amnesia induced by protein synthesis inhibitors. *Neurosci. Behav. Physiol.* 29:31–36

Ribot TA. 1882/1977. *Diseases of Memory.* Washington, DC: Univ. Publ. Am.

Roediger HL III. 1980. Memory metaphors in cognitive psychology. *Mem. Cogn.* 8:231–46

Rosenblum K, Meiri N, Dudai Y. 1993. Taste memory: the role of protein synthesis in gustatory cortex. *Behav. Neural. Biol.* 59:49–56

Rosenzweig MR, Bennett EL, Colombo PJ,

Lee DW, Serrano PA. 1993. Short-term, intermediate-term, and long-term memories. *Behav. Brain Res.* 57:193–98

Roullet P, Sara S. 1998. Consolidation of memory after its reactivation: involvement of beta noradrenergic receptors in the late phase. *Neural Plast.* 6:63–68

Russel WR, Nathan PW. 1946. Traumatic amnesia. *Brain* 69:280–300

Ryan L, Nadel L, Keil K, Putnam K, Schnyer D, et al. 2001. Hippocampal complex and retrieval of recent and very remote autobiographical memories: evidence from functional magnetic resonance imaging in neurologically intact people. *Hippocampus* 11:707–14

Sanders HI, Warrington EK. 1971. Memory for remote events in amnesic patients. *Brain* 94:661–68

Sara SJ. 2000. Retrieval and reconsolidation: toward a neurobiology of remembering. *Learn. Mem.* 7:73–84

Schacter DL. 1987. Implicit memory: history and current status. *J. Exp. Psychol.: Learn. Mem. Cogn.* 13:501–18

Schacter DL, Norman KA, Koustaal W. 1998. The cognitive neuroscience of constructive memory. *Annu. Rev. Psychol.* 49:289–319

Schneider AM, Sherman W. 1968. Amnesia: a function of the temporal relation of footshock to electroconvulsive shock. *Science* 159:219–21

Schwaerzel M, Heisneberg M, Zars T. 2002. Extinction antagonizes olfactory memory at the subcellular level. *Neuron* 35:951–60

Scoville WB, Milner B. 1957. Loss of recent memory after bilateral hippocampal lesions. *J. Neurol. Neurosurg. Psychiat.* 20:11–21

Sekiguchi T, Yamada A, Suzuki H. 1997. Reactivation-dependent changes in memory states in the terrestrial slug *Limax flavus*. *Learn. Mem.* 4:356–64

Shadmehr R, Holocomb HH. 1997. Neural correlates of motor memory consolidation. *Science* 277:821–25

Shi S-H, Hayashi Y, Petralia RS, Zaman SH, Wenthold RJ, et al. 1999. Rapid spine delivery and redistribution of AMPA receptors after synaptic NMDA receptor activation. *Science* 284:1811–16

Squire LR. 1987. *Memory and Brain.* New York: Oxford Univ. Press

Squire LR, Alvarez P. 1995. Retrograde amnesia and memory consolidation: a neurobiological perspective. *Curr. Biol.* 5:169–77

Squire LR, Clark RE, Knowlton BJ. 2001. Retrograde amnesia. *Hippocampus* 11:50–55

Steward O, Wallace CS, Lyford GL, Worley PF. 1998. Synaptic activation causes the mRNA for the IEG Arc to localize selectively near activated postsynaptic sites on dendrites. *Neuron* 21:741–51

Stickgold R, Hobson JA, Fosse R, Fosse M. 2001. Sleep, learning, and dreams: off-line memory reprocessing. *Science* 294:1052–57

Taubenfeld SM, Milekic MH, Monti B, Alberini CM. 2001. The consolidation of new but not reactivated memory requires hippocampal C/EBPβ. *Nat. Neurosci.* 4:813–18

Thorndike EL. 1933. A proof of the law of effect. *Science* 77:173–75

Trachtenberg JT, Chen BE, Knott GW, Feng G, Sanes JR, et al. 2002. Long-term in vivo imaging of experience-dependent synaptic plasticity in adult cortex. *Nature* 420:788–94

Tulving E. 1983. *Elements of Episodic Memory.* Oxford: Oxford Univ. Press

Ungerleider LG, Doyon J, Karni A. 2002. Imaging brain plasticity during motor skill learning. *Neurobiol. Learn. Mem.* 78:553–64

Vianna MRM, Szapiro G, McGaugh JL, Medina JH, Izquierdo I. 2001. Retrieval of memory for fear-motivated training initiates extinction requiring protein synthesis in the rat hippocampus. *Proc. Natl. Acad. Sci. USA* 98:12251–54

Warrington EK, Weiskrantz L. 1970. Amnesic syndrome: consolidation or retrieval? *Nature* 228:628–30

Weiler IJ, Hawrylak N, Greenough WT. 1995. Morphogenesis in memory formation: synaptic and cellular mechanisms. *Behav. Brain Res.* 66:1–6

White NM. 1989. Reward or reinforcement: What's the difference? *Neurosci. Biobehav. Rev.* 13:181–86

Winder DG, Mansuy IM, Osman M, Moallem TM, Kandel ER. 1998. Genetic and pharmacological evidence for a novel, intermediate phase of long-term potentiation suppressed by calcineurin. *Cell* 92:25–37

Winocur G. 1990. Anterograde and retrograde amnesia in rats with dorsal hippocampal or dorsomedial lesions. *Behav. Brain Res.* 38:145–54

Wixted J. 2004. The psychology and neuroscience of forgetting. *Annu. Rev. Psychol.* 55:235–69

Yin JCP, Wallach JS, Del Vecchio M, Wilder EL, Zhou H, et al. 1994. Induction of a dominant negative CREB transgene specifically blocks long-term memory in *Drosophila*. *Cell* 79:49–58

Zola-Morgan SM, Squire LR. 1990. The primate hippocampal formation: evidence for a time-limited role in memory storage. *Science* 250:288–90

Annu. Rev. Psychol. 2004. 55:87–124
doi: 10.1146/annurev.psych.55.090902.142044
First published online as a Review in Advance on October 27, 2003

UNDERSTANDING OTHER MINDS:
Linking Developmental Psychology and Functional Neuroimaging

R. Saxe, S. Carey, and N. Kanwisher

*Department of Brain and Cognitive Sciences, MIT, Cambridge, Massachusetts 02139;
email: saxe@mit.edu, scarey@wjh.harvard.edu, ngk@mit.edu*

Key Words   theory of mind, mentalizing, social cognition, cognitive neuroscience

■ **Abstract**   Evidence from developmental psychology suggests that understanding other minds constitutes a special domain of cognition with at least two components: an early-developing system for reasoning about goals, perceptions, and emotions, and a later-developing system for representing the contents of beliefs. Neuroimaging reinforces and elaborates upon this view by providing evidence that (*a*) domain-specific brain regions exist for representing belief contents, (*b*) these regions are apparently distinct from other regions engaged in reasoning about goals and actions (suggesting that the two developmental stages reflect the emergence of two distinct systems, rather than the elaboration of a single system), and (*c*) these regions are distinct from brain regions engaged in inhibitory control and in syntactic processing. The clear neural distinction between these processes is evidence that belief attribution is not dependent on either inhibitory control or syntax, but is subserved by a specialized neural system for theory of mind.

CONTENTS

0066-4308/04/0204-0087$14.00

INTRODUCTION

Unlike behaviorists, normal adults attribute to one another (and to themselves) unobservable internal mental states, such as goals, thoughts, and feelings, and use these to explain and predict behavior. This human capacity for reasoning about the mental causes of action is called a theory of mind. In the past 25 years, theory of mind has become a major topic of research, initially in developmental psychology and subsequently in other fields including social psychology, philosophy, and ethology.

Most recently, a new method for theory of mind research has joined the pack: functional brain imaging [especially functional magnetic resonance imaging (fMRI)]. The blood oxygenation level dependent (BOLD) signal measured by fMRI gives scientists unprecedented access to the hemodynamic changes (and indirectly to the neural activity) in the brain that are associated with psychological processes. fMRI may have by now exceeded all other techniques in psychology in terms of expense, growth rate, and public visibility. But many have wondered how much this new technology has actually contributed to the study of human cognition, and when—if ever—a finding from functional neuroimaging has constrained a cognitive theory.

In this review, we take the human theory of mind as a case study of real theoretical exchange between studies (and scientists) using functional neuroimaging and those using the more well-established techniques of developmental psychology. As such, this review will necessarily be selective. For more complete coverage of related research, we refer the reader to the many excellent recent reviews in the fields of cognitive neuroscience (e.g., Adolphs 2001, 2002, 2003; Allison et al. 2000; Blakemore & Decety 2001; Decety & Grezes 1999; Frith 2001; Frith & Frith 2000, 2003; Gallagher & Frith 2003; Gallese 2003; Greene & Haidt 2002; Grezes & Decety 2001; Puce & Perrett 2003; Siegal & Varley 2002) and developmental psychology (e.g., Baldwin & Baird 2001; Bartsch 2002; Csibra 2003; Flavell 1999; Johnson 2000, 2003; Meltzoff & Decety 2003; Wellman & Lagattuta 2000; Wellman et al. 2001).

This review is divided into two main sections, following the substantial evidence for at least two distinct stages in the development of theory of mind (see Figure 1a). The first half of the review deals with belief attribution. At approximately age 3 or 4 children begin to attribute representational epistemic mental states—thoughts, beliefs, and knowledge—to themselves and others. The second half of the review considers the earlier-developing mentalistic reasoning that occurs before age 3. Toddlers do reason about the mind and human behavior, but they do so with a more limited repertoire of mental state concepts, including desires, perceptions, and emotions. Within each section of the review, we first summarize theoretical questions and findings emerging from developmental psychology, and then consider potential and actual contributions made by functional neuroimaging to answering these questions.

Functional neuroimaging is particularly well suited to resolve questions of whether two tasks or processes engage common or distinct mechanisms. For instance, it has been suggested that the development of a concept of belief depends critically on the ability to represent sentence-complement syntax (e.g., de Villiers 2000). However, this dependence could arise either because children cannot learn about beliefs until they can understand the language adults use to talk about the mind, or it could arise because belief attribution is truly dependent on the cognitive and neural mechanisms for parsing sentence complement syntax (even in adulthood). Functional neuroimaging allows us to ask whether these two tasks recruit the same or different regions of the brain.[1] If different brain regions are involved in belief attribution and syntax, then it is less likely that a single functional mechanism is responsible for both. While this use of neuroimaging is potentially powerful in answering fundamental questions about cognition, it is subject to several pitfalls and ambiguities that are discussed briefly in the next section.

FUNCTIONAL NEUROIMAGING: STANDARDS OF EVIDENCE AND INFERENCE

If we are to accept a finding that two different tasks activate the same brain region as evidence that common psychological mechanisms are engaged in the two tasks, then we must consider two questions. First, what counts as the same brain region, and what kind of data can support a claim of common or distinct activations? Second, what is the relationship between brain regions and psychological mechanisms?

The location of an activation in the brain is often specified by general region (e.g., the occipital pole, or the temporo-parietal junction), or by the gyrus or sulcus where the activation is found (e.g., the fusiform gyrus, or the intraparietal sulcus). These descriptors can be useful, but are not very precise, as each one spans ten

---

[1]All of the functional imaging discussed in this paper used human adult subjects. In some cases, the adult results alone are sufficient to constrain theories, as this review illustrates. However, other questions and hypotheses could be tested only in the brains of infants and children themselves. For instance, are the brain regions involved in response conflict and in belief attribution independent in young children just beginning to attribute beliefs, as they are in adults? fMRI in children and infants is possible (e.g., Born et al. 1998, Burgund et al. 2002, Casey et al. 2001, Dehaene-Lambertz et al. 2002), but is not widespread. In particular, there are no published fMRI studies yet of children between 10 and 48 months old, the critical age range for theory of mind development, and no fMRI studies of theory of mind in any pediatric population.

or more square centimeters of cortex. Such large regions are likely to encompass many functionally distinct areas, as seen, for example, in extrastriate cortex where areas such as the visual motion area MT (Tootell et al. 1995) or the fusiform face area (Kanwisher et al. 1997, McCarthy et al. 1997) are typically one or two square centimeters in size. Thus, even if two tasks produce activations within the same general region of the brain, their activations may not overlap at all. (Imagine concluding that the brain does not contain distinct motor representations of hands and feet because both hand and foot movements are coordinated by primary motor cortex.) A further problem is that because individual brains differ from each other physically, there is no theory-neutral way to precisely specify what counts as the "same place" in two different brains.

These problems can be avoided in analyses of individual subjects. The strongest evidence for engagement of the same brain region by two different tasks arises

(a)

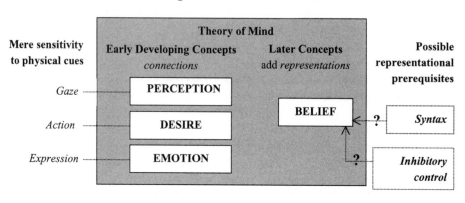

Attributing mental states to other minds

(b)

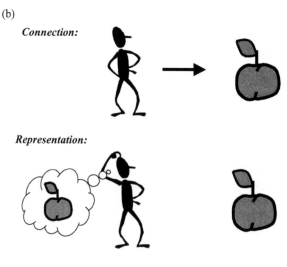

when the very same voxels in the same subject's brain (preferably from the same scanning session) are significantly activated by each of two different tasks. While some neuroimaging studies meet this high standard, many do not.

A related approach is to first functionally define a region of interest (ROI) individually within each subject based on a particular task comparison (or localizer scan), then pool over the voxels in that ROI to ask whether a second task activates the same ROI. This approach avoids the problem of having to register different brains, while making possible statistical analyses over multiple subjects' ROIs. However, in choosing a localizer to define an ROI the researcher is making an ontological assumption that this localizer contrast picks out a meaningful functional unit in the brain (i.e., a natural kind). Like other ontological assumptions

---

Figure 1   Schematic representation of the two principle stages in the development of theory of mind, and the central theoretical questions discussed in this review. (*a*, *left*) Toddlers reason about other minds with a limited repertoire of mental state concepts, including desire/goal, perception, and emotion. For both developmental psychology and neuroimaging, it is critical to distinguish attribution of desires, perceptions, and emotions (the "rich" or "mentalistic" interpretation) from mere behavioral sensitivity to the associated physical cues (including human body motions, gaze direction and emotional expressions—the "lean" interpretation). Two important characteristics of mentalistic attribution are reference (mental states are about objects or situations) and coherence (different mental state attributions interact causally and systematically). It is an open question, addressed in this review, whether these three mental state concepts are attributed using one common mechanism or multiple distinct mechanisms. (*a*, *right*) Starting at approximately age 3 or 4 children include a concept of belief in their reasoning about other minds. A central debate in developmental psychology concerns whether this later development reflects true conceptual change in the child's theory of mind, or simply the maturation of other capacities that are necessary for reasoning about beliefs. Two prominent candidate capacities are syntax and inhibitory control. Evidence reviewed here suggests that representing others' beliefs does not recruit the same brain mechanisms as either syntax or inhibitory control. (*b*) What then is the nature of the conceptual change between a toddler's theory of mind, and the later theory that incorporates attributions of belief? One possibility is that the toddler lacks the notion of a representational mental state, and instead conceives of mental relations between people and the world as direct connections. We can think of a connection as something like gravity or resonance to affordances in the environment, leaving no possibility for error or misperception. Thus goals, perceptions, and emotions may at first be understood as referential (about an object or situation) but not as representational (requiring an independent representation of the object or situation in the mind of the actor). The terms "connection" versus "representation" were used to characterize this developmental change by Flavell (1988), but a similar distinction is included in the theories of Perner (1993) and Wellman (e.g., Bartsch & Wellman 1995). The figure is adapted with permission from Bartsch & Wellman (1995).

in science, the utility of a particular functionally defined ROI is determined by the consistency of the data that emerge from it and the richness of the theoretical progress those data support.

Most common in the neuroimaging literature are group analyses, in which brain images from a dozen or more individuals are aligned (as best as possible) into a common space, and statistical analyses are then conducted across subjects. This method enables one to test whether an activation pattern is consistent across subjects, and it can sometimes provide greater statistical power than individual-subject analyses. However, it comes at the cost of blurring of activation maps due to the necessarily imperfect registration across physically different brains. Individuals vary not only in their physical anatomy but also in their functional anatomy, producing yet more blurring in group-averaged data. Thus, activations that may be completely nonoverlapping within each individual could be highly overlapping when the same data are averaged across subjects. This problem is exacerbated when comparing activations across subject groups or across studies.

Thus, although group-analyzed data can be informative, any claim that two tasks activate the same place in the brain are most convincing when they are based on analyses within individual subjects or within individually defined ROIs. The least convincing evidence for common mechanisms comes when each of two tasks produces an activation somewhere within the same large anatomical region (e.g., the temporo-parietal junction or superior temporal sulcus).

The opposite inference, that distinct cortical regions are engaged by two different tasks, is subject to a different and surprisingly common error. Researchers often argue that two tasks engage distinct mechanisms because task A activates region X significantly (compared to a control condition), whereas task B does not. Such arguments are not valid on their own: a difference in significances is not a significant difference. To argue for differential activation of region X by task A and task B, it is necessary to directly compare the activation for the two tasks.

Even with the proper statistical evidence, difficult theoretical issues remain. Psychological theories concern psychological processes whereas neuroimaging data can only test the activation of cortical voxels. What is the relationship between the two? A typical voxel in a neuroimaging study contains hundreds of thousands of neurons, so the common activation of a voxel by two different tasks could arise even if completely distinct neural populations within that voxel are engaged by the two tasks. Thus caution is required when we infer common mechanisms from common activations. That said, if a whole cluster of adjacent voxels shows activation for each of two different tasks but not for many others, it is a reasonable guess that even if distinct neural populations are involved, they are likely to be functionally related.

Caution is also required when making the opposite kind of inference. If each of two tasks activates a distinct and nonoverlapping cortical region, it is clear that different physical brain hardware is engaged by the two tasks, but this need not imply that qualitatively different psychological processes are involved in the two tasks. Consider a stimulus falling in the upper visual field versus the lower visual field: distinct and nonoverlapping regions within primary visual cortex would be activated, but the kind of processing that goes on in each is presumably very similar. Deciding whether dissociations at the cortical level correspond to qualitative differences in processing at the psychological level is a difficult judgment call that requires consideration of the wider theoretical context (e.g., does it make sense computationally that different processes may be engaged by these two tasks?) and the available empirical evidence (e.g., what other tasks activate these two regions?).

Armed with these cautionary notes about the use of neuroimaging data to resolve psychological questions, we turn now to a review of the literature on the development of theory of mind.

DEVELOPMENTAL PSYCHOLOGY: BELIEF ATTRIBUTION

An understanding of other people's thoughts and beliefs plays a central role in adult reasoning about the causes of other people's behavior (e.g., "she spilled the coffee because she thought the cup was empty," "he's going home because he thinks he left his keys there") (Malle 2001), but not, of course, in reasoning about the causes of mechanical events like clockwork or the tides. Given the centrality of beliefs in adult explanations of actions, we might expect that as soon as children begin to explain their own and others' actions, they would use this powerful notion of belief to do so. On the contrary, it is now well established that children do not begin to use beliefs to explain actions until relatively late in development, at age 3 or 4.

The most common test of children's ability to explain an action with reference to the actor's belief is the "false belief" task (Wimmer & Perner 1983; for reviews of this literature see Flavell 1999, Wellman & Lagattuta 2000, Wellman et al. 2001). In the standard version of this task (the "object transfer" problem), the child is told a story in which a character's belief about the location of a target object becomes false when the object is moved without the character's knowledge. In Wimmer & Perner's original version, for instance, Maxi's mother moves the chocolate from the green to the blue cupboard while Maxi is outside playing. The children are then variously asked to report the content of the character's belief ("Where does Maxi *think* the chocolate is?"), to predict the character's action ("Where will Maxi *look* for the chocolate?"), or sometimes to explain the completed action ("Why did Maxi look for the chocolate in the *green* cupboard?"). The critical feature of a false belief task is that the correct answers to all three of these questions—even the ones that do not specifically query a belief content—require the child to pay attention to Maxi's belief, and not to the actual location of the chocolate (Dennett 1978, Premack & Woodruff 1978). Dozens of versions of the false belief problem have now been used, and while the precise age of success varies between children and between task versions (Wellman et al. 2001), in general children younger than 3 or 4 do not correctly solve false belief problems, but older children do.

The contentious issue is not when success on false belief problems emerges but what such success reflects. One possibility is that children 3 or 4 years old undergo real change in the concepts they use to reason about other minds, acquiring a previously absent representational concept of belief (Flavell 1999, Perner 1993, Wellman et al. 2001), and producing a consequent improvement on false belief tasks.

A second possibility is that the concept of belief is already intact in young children but is masked in the false belief paradigm by immaturity in other capacities that are necessary for good performance on the task. Two such candidate capacities are inhibitory control and some aspects of syntactic knowledge (especially complement syntax), both of which are correlated with false belief task performance (Astington & Jenkins 1995, 1999; Carlson & Moses 2001; de Villiers & Pyers 2002; Watson et al. 2001). In the next two sections we will review the evidence for an association between the development of reasoning about beliefs and inhibitory control or syntax. We will focus in particular on evidence for (and against) false belief task performance as a measure of a newly acquired representational concept of belief, as opposed to simple unmasking by maturation of these other capacities.

Inhibitory Control and Belief Attribution

To answer a false belief question correctly, a child must be able to juggle two competing representations of reality (the actual state of affairs and the reality represented in the protagonist's head) and to inhibit an incorrect but compelling answer (the true location of the object). In variants of the false belief task, the demand for inhibitory control predicts children's performance. For instance, the current location of the target object may be made less salient and thus easier to inhibit: instead of being moved to the green cupboard, Maxi's chocolate is eaten, or the actual location of the chocolate is unknown to the child (described in Wellman et al. 2001; see also Zaitchik 1991). Children of all ages perform better on these versions of the task (Wellman et al. 2001). Conversely, when the inhibitory demands are increased by changing the protagonist's motivation to a negative desire (i.e., the protagonist's desire is not to find, but to *avoid* the target object), 4- and even 6-year-olds consistently fail to answer correctly (Leslie 2000, Leslie & Polizzi 1998). Finally, the inhibitory demands of false belief tasks are not restricted to reasoning about beliefs. Four-year-olds have more difficulty with logically equivalent problems about nonmental false representations (e.g., false photographs or maps; Leslie & Thaiss 1992, Zaitchik 1990), and with juggling two different verbal labels of a single object (Apperly & Robinson 2002).

Nevertheless the interpretation that false belief performance is limited by immature inhibitory control remains controversial (e.g., Perner et al. 1999). Wellman et al. (2001) note that the improvement in three-year-olds' performance on false belief tasks with salience manipulations reflects only a change from below-chance to chance performance, and therefore does not implicate an operational concept of belief (but see Moses 2001). They argue that the correlation between inhibitory control and false belief performance need not reflect masking of a preexisting competence. Instead, inhibitory control could facilitate knowledge acquisition and conceptual change in the domain of other minds, since a child who can disengage from the prepotent representation of reality may be more able to focus on and learn about mental representations (Moses 2001, Wellman et al. 2001).

In all, the role of executive function or inhibitory control in reasoning about beliefs remains open to investigation (see also Perner & Lang 2000). Is inhibitory control recruited during successful false belief task performance? Is it recruited even more generally during all reasoning about beliefs? Is the locus of such inhibition predominantly peripheral (resolving response conflict) or cognitive (inhibiting prepotent representations)? Alternatively, if executive function contributes only to children's early learning about the mind, then we would not expect the same brain regions to be recruited when adults engage in belief attribution and inhibitory control. Below, we examine whether neuroimaging of healthy human adults can help resolve some of these questions.

Language and Belief Attribution

A striking demonstration of the role of language in false belief task performance comes from studies of deaf children. Deaf children of hearing parents (i.e., non-native signers) are impaired on sign language versions of false belief tasks (de Villiers & de Villiers 2000a, Peterson & Siegal 1995). This deficit persists even on nonverbal (i.e., pictorial) versions of the false belief task (de Villiers & de Villiers 2000a, Woolfe et al. 2002). Deaf children of native signers show no impairment. Conversely, the quantity and quality of family talk about mental causes to which a normally developing toddler is exposed is correlated with performance on false belief tasks two years later (e.g., Cutting & Dunn 1999).

The causal relationship between developing competences in language and "theory of mind" has been controversial, though. Some models propose that linguistic competence is a necessary precursor of theory of mind (e.g., de Villiers 2000) while others suggest that theory of mind is a necessary precursor of language development (e.g., Baron-Cohen et al. 1985, Bloom 2000, Happe 1992). One possibility is that early-developing components of theory of mind (discussed in detail below) are necessary for some aspects of language acquisition (e.g., establishing the referents of newly heard words), whereas other aspects of language acquisition such as the syntax of complementation and the semantics of opacity are in turn necessary for the late-developing concept of belief (Malle 2003). The relationship between belief attribution and language is addressed here.

The specific attribute of language commonly implicated in representing another person's beliefs is the syntax and semantics of sentential complements. de Villiers (e.g., 2000; de Villiers & de Villiers 2000a,b) has proposed that "language is the only representational system that could" support the concept of (false) beliefs, because language is "propositional, and can therefore capture falsity and embeddedness of propositions." Mental state verbs share with verbs of communication a particular syntactic structure of referentially opaque embedded complements (the truth value of the sentence is independent of the truth value of the complement, as in "John thinks that *it is raining*"). Children's production and comprehension of this syntactic structure precedes and strongly predicts performance on both standard and nonverbal versions of the false belief task (de Villiers 2000; de Villiers & de Villiers 2000a,b; but see Bartsch & Wellman 1995, Ruffman et al. 2003).

However, linguistic skills may correlate with reasoning about beliefs simply because language enables a child to learn about (or to learn to talk about) the mind. Conversational experience (including comprehension of embedded sentence complements) contributes to children's developing knowledge about the mind, because first-person verbal report is our dominant source of information about subjective states occurring inside someone else's head (Harris 1989, Nelson 1996). Thus, sophisticated syntax may support the development of a concept of belief, but may not be recruited during reasoning with that concept.

What then is the role of language in adult reasoning about beliefs? If constructing the syntax of embedded propositional structures is necessary for all reasoning about (false) beliefs, then the same neural structures should be recruited by tasks that tap these two processes. This prediction is addressed below.

Beyond False Belief

In all, the extensive literature on false belief task performance in normally developing children has produced a consistent pattern of results and many competing interpretations. Wellman et al. (2001) thus conclude their meta-analysis of this literature with a plea that researchers move on to seek new and converging evidence for competing theories of the developing concept of belief. In fact, Bloom & German (2000) specify two reasons that researchers should abandon the false belief task as the benchmark of mature belief attribution. First, there is more to success on the false belief task than a concept of belief, as illustrated by the preceding review. Second, they point out, there is more to a concept of belief than passing the false belief task. In fact, theory of mind reasoning would not work if we did not attribute to others mostly true beliefs [and mostly rational actions (Dennett 1996)]. For all of these reasons, the false belief task is at best a limited tool for measuring the developing concept of belief.

So, is there evidence for the distinct emergence of a concept of belief, beyond the false belief task? The best such evidence is Bartsch & Wellman's (1995) investigation of children's spontaneous talk about beliefs. Bartsch & Wellman distinguish mere conversational turns of phrase ("know what?") from genuine psychological references, often identified by the children's use of contrastives: sentences using "think" or "know" that contrast expectations and outcomes, fiction and reality, or differences between individuals. The first genuine references to thoughts and beliefs appear around the third birthday, significantly later than genuine psychological reference to desires and emotions, but about half a year before children spontaneously explain actions in terms of beliefs (Bartsch & Wellman 1995), or pass false belief tasks (e.g., Wellman et al. 2001).

Evidence from both experimental tasks and spontaneous speech thus converge on a change in children's reasoning about beliefs that occurs in the third or fourth year. Is this development reflected in a specialized neural substrate for reasoning about beliefs? If so, what is the relationship between this neural substrate and brain regions subserving inhibitory control? Language? These questions could be addressed using functional neuroimaging.

NEUROIMAGING: BELIEF ATTRIBUTION

The first question for neuroimaging is, Can we find regions of the adult human brain that show activity specifically when subjects are required to attribute beliefs to another person? Of the neuroimaging studies that attempt to address this question directly, four have followed developmental psychology in using false belief problems (verbal and nonverbal) as the definitive belief attribution task (Fletcher et al. 1995, Gallagher et al. 2000, Saxe & Kanwisher 2003, Vogeley et al. 2001). One study gave subjects simple descriptions of events involving people, and instructed subjects to "try to understand their motivations, feelings and actions" (Ferstl & von Cramon 2002). Goel et al. (1995) used an original task: Subjects were asked to judge whether Christopher Columbus could have identified the function of a pictured object. Across these studies, when subjects reason about false beliefs or Columbus's knowledge or ignorance, blood flow increases in a consistent pattern of brain regions: medial prefrontal cortex (BA9), temporal poles bilaterally (BA38), anterior superior temporal sulcus (BA22), and bilateral temporo-parietal junction extending into posterior superior temporal sulcus (BA39/40/22).

Could any or all of these brain regions be a specialized neural substrate for reasoning about beliefs? The reasons to be cautious with results from the false belief task in developmental psychology apply equally to neuroimaging results. First, there is more to solving the false belief task than a concept of belief, and second, there is more to a concept of belief than passing the false belief task (Bloom & German 2000). In addition, "activity" in the standard subtraction methodology of neuroimaging is only as meaningful or specific as the subtracted control condition. Therefore, we propose two basic criteria for a brain region involved in the attribution of beliefs: generality and specificity. First, the candidate region must show increased activity to any stimuli that invite the attribution of beliefs, both true and false. Second, the response must be specific to belief attribution. That is, the candidate region must not show a high response to the presence of a person per se, or during reasoning about nonmental (false) representations. Another important question is whether brain regions involved in belief attribution may be distinct from those that represent other mental state concepts, such as emotion and goal, which emerge earlier in development. This third question is addressed in the "Neuroimaging: Desires, Perceptions, and Emotions" section below.

Few neuroimaging studies have directly tested the neural activity associated with attributing true beliefs. However, a number of studies have included a control condition in which the protagonist's action is not based on false belief or ignorance, but on true beliefs and perceptions of the situation (Fletcher et al. 1995,

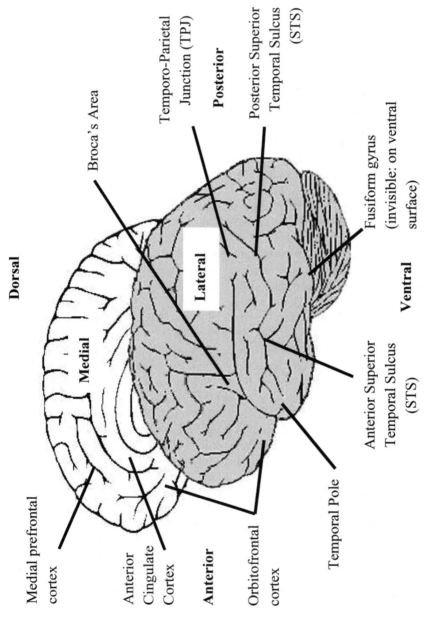

Figure 2 Schematic representation of brain regions associated with the attribution of mental states: beliefs, desires, perceptions, and/or emotions.

Gallagher et al. 2000, Saxe & Kanwisher 2003). This condition may therefore have invited belief attribution, even if reasoning about mental states was not required for successful performance. Consistent with this idea, the same brain regions that showed increased response during false belief stories generalized their activity to the stories that involved true beliefs (Fletcher et al. 1995, Gallagher et al. 2000).[2] Particularly strong confirmation comes from individual-subject and ROI analyses, showing that the very same voxels in individual subjects are activated for true and false belief attribution (as described in the "Functional Neuroimaging" section above; Saxe & Kanwisher 2003). Thus, the temporo-parietal junction, superior temporal sulcus, and medial prefrontal cortex may all generalize to show a strong activation for both true and false belief attribution.

A candidate region specialized for belief attribution must also be shown to be specific: that is, it must not show a high response during logically similar control conditions that do not require belief attributions. One logical element of reasoning about belief and action is the need to infer invisible causal mechanisms. A second logical ingredient, more specific to false belief stories, which must be included in a control, is the notion of a false representation. Saxe & Kanwisher (2003) therefore had subjects read stories from two control conditions. "Mechanical inference" stories required subjects to infer the operation of an invisible mechanical force (e.g., rusting, evaporation). "False photograph" control stories were modeled on the false photograph paradigm used by developmental psychologists (Leslie & Thaiss 1992, Zaitchik 1990). The false photograph stories can be closely matched to the original false belief stories. In a typical false photograph scenario, a photograph is taken of the scene (e.g., the chocolate in the green cupboard). After the target object has been moved (e.g., to the blue cupboard), the subject must reason about the contrasting states of affairs in the world and in the photograph, analogous to reasoning about a false belief. None of the brain regions that produced a strong response to false belief stories showed a high response to either of these logical control conditions, consistent with the hypothesis that these regions respond specifically during attribution of beliefs, not to any false representation or hidden cause.

Finally, any brain region specialized for representing beliefs must not respond to just the simple presence of a person present in the stimulus. Most studies have

---

[2]The only brain region that did not show this pattern was medial frontal cortex, which showed a significantly increased response only during false belief stories and not during stories about actions based on true beliefs (compared with jumbled sentence controls; Fletcher et al. 1995, Gallagher et al. 2000). A number of authors (Gallagher & Frith 2003, Gallagher et al. 2000) have concluded that medial frontal cortex is the only cortical region uniquely involved in "theory of mind." But, as we and others (e.g., Bloom & German 2000, Scholl & Leslie 2001) have argued, selective involvement in the false belief task per se is not equivalent to selective involvement in "theory of mind." The medial prefrontal cortex may nevertheless be involved in belief attribution. Saxe & Kanwisher (2003) found that medial prefrontal cortex activity did generalize to vignettes that did not require false belief attribution, and activity in this region has also been reported when subjects are simply instructed to try to understand a character's motivations (Ferstl & von Cramon 2002).

included a person in a control condition (Fletcher et al. 1995, Gallagher et al. 2000). Even when subjects were forced to attend to the details of a physical description of a person, the responses of the temporo-parietal junction regions bilaterally and the right anterior superior temporal sulcus were no higher than a control condition using physical description of nonhuman objects (Saxe & Kanwisher 2003). Recruitment of these regions requires thinking about a person's beliefs, not just a person's appearance.

Thus a number of brain regions, including bilateral regions of the temporo-parietal junction, posterior and anterior superior temporal cortex, and temporal pole appear to fulfill at least the basic criteria for the neural substrates of attributing beliefs: generality to both true and false belief attribution, and specificity to belief attribution rather than either (*a*) any reasoning about people or (*b*) reasoning about nonmental false representations or hidden causes in general.

Neuroimaging: Belief Attribution and Inhibitory Control

Given the characteristic pattern of brain activation associated with belief attribution, we can begin to address the theoretical questions raised in the first half of this section. First we consider whether brain regions associated with inhibitory control are recruited during (false) belief attribution.

Executive (or inhibitory) control has multiple distinct components, each of which could contribute to false belief attribution, including monitoring and detecting the conflict between competing representations or responses, selecting the correct response, and inhibiting the incorrect (possibly prepotent) response. A recent series of elegant neuroimaging studies have attempted to distinguish the neural correlates of these components (e.g., Botvinick et al. 1999, Braver et al. 2001, Garavan et al. 2002, Konishi et al. 1999, Milham et al. 2001, Sylvester et al. 2003).

Across a range of tasks, including the Eriksen flanker task[3] (Botvinick et al. 1999, Eriksen & Eriksen 1974), the Stroop task[4] (Milham et al. 2001, Stroop 1938),

---

[3]In the Eriksen flanker task, subjects make a response determined by the target object in the center of the array. On either side of the target, distractor objects are presented. Distractor objects may be associated with no response (neutral), the same response as the target (congruent), or a different response from the target (incongruent). Botvinick et al. (1999) found that the response of the anterior cingulate cortex was highest on incongruent trials that followed congruent trials, when the selective attention of subjects was relatively relaxed, thus provoking strong response conflict.

[4]In the Stroop task (Stroop 1938) subjects are required to name the ink color of a word. Response conflict increases when the word is the name of a different color (e.g., the subject sees the word "blue" printed in red ink, and must respond "red."). Milham et al. (2001) reported that anterior cingulate cortex activity was maximized when the word named a color in the response set (i.e., a possible ink color, with an assigned response), compared with trials in which the word named a color not in the response set. This finding is consistent with the idea that anterior cingulate cortex activity is an index of response conflict.

and the Go/No-Go task (Braver et al. 2001), response conflict is strongly correlated with activity in anterior cingulate cortex (ACC). Braver et al. (2001) found that a region of ACC is activated for any low-frequency response condition, whether it requires a response ("target detection") or the suppression of a response ("no-go" trials). This ACC activation is significantly posterior to the paracingulate region of activity associated with false belief problems (e.g., Gallagher et al. 2000). Brain regions consistently associated with response inhibition also include dorsolateral prefrontal cortex (BA 46/9) and superior parietal lobe (BA7; e.g., Braver et al. 2001, Sylvester et al. 2003). Selecting the appropriate response is associated with additional activity in bilateral frontal eye fields and intraparietal sulcus (Jiang & Kanwisher 2003). None of these brain regions are among those associated with reasoning about beliefs.

Thus belief attribution—even of false beliefs—appears to rely on distinct neural systems from those responsible for response conflict, selection, and inhibitory control. Consistent with this conclusion, the stories that describe a nonmental false representation—the false photograph stories—require inhibitory control similar to false belief stories, but do not elicit responses in regions associated with belief attribution (Saxe & Kanwisher 2003). At least for adults, then, false belief attribution may not depend on inhibitory control during task performance. This is consistent with Wellman et al.'s (2001) interpretation of the developmental correlation between inhibitory control and theory of mind: namely, that inhibitory control may help children learn about the mind.

An interesting exception is the target detection paradigm. When subjects are required to respond to a low-frequency, unpredictable, or unexpected target, brain activity increases in the temporo-parietal junction (Braver et al. 2001, Corbetta et al. 2002, Downar et al. 2002, Shulman et al. 2002), in a region near that activated by false belief tasks. Again, however, no study has directly compared these two paradigms within a single experiment. Are there distinct but neighboring subregions of the temporo-parietal junction involved in belief attribution and target detection? Or is there a functional relationship between these two tasks? This issue remains open for future work.

Neuroimaging: Belief Attribution and Language

As described above, de Villiers (2000) has advanced a specific, and testable, hypothesis about the relationship between language and belief attribution: that language is "the only representational system that could" support the concept of a false belief, because it allows the syntactic construction of embedded sentence complements. If so, then we would predict that both belief attribution and sentence-level syntax recruit the same neural structures. Do they?

Studies that vary the syntactic complexity of sentences often find brain activation in and around Broca's area in left inferior frontal cortex (Caplan 2001). The location of this region of activation is inconsistent across studies, but is not in close proximity to any of the regions implicated above in belief attribution. However, two other regions are also associated with syntax in some studies: left anterior superior temporal sulcus, near the temporal pole (Ferstl & von Cramon 2002, Friederici 2001, Vandenberghe et al. 2002), and posterior regions of the superior temporal sulcus, near Wernicke's area (Caplan 2001, Ferstl & von Cramon 2002, Just et al. 1996, Roder et al. 2002).

How do the regions of superior temporal sulcus that are involved in syntax compare to the regions of superior temporal sulcus implicated in belief attribution? One study has included versions of the two tasks within a single experiment. Ferstl & von Cramon (2002) scanned subjects while they read sentence pairs in one of two conditions. First, in the logic condition, subjects read two sentences describing a mechanical causal sequence, and were asked to judge whether the sequence was coherent.[5] In the second half of the experiment, subjects read sentences describing an event involving people, and were asked to try to "understand their feelings, motivations and actions." The controls for both conditions were sentences in pseudolanguage. Compared to this control, the "logic" and the "theory of mind" conditions elicited increased brain activity in strikingly similar regions of posterior and anterior superior temporal sulcus and temporo-parietal junction. Does this mean that syntax and belief attribution recruit similar regions of the posterior superior temporal sulcus (pSTS)? Unfortunately, it is not clear that Ferstl & von Cramon have isolated the parts of superior temporal sulcus responsible for syntax.[6] In their pseudolanguage control condition, half of the sentences contained familiar syntax, with pseudowords in place of content nouns. Sentences like this, with the syntax but not the content of real sentences, activate the syntax-related region of superior temporal gyrus almost as strongly as normal sentences (Roder et al. 2002). Moreover, the focus of activity associated with syntax in group analyses is typically located 2 or 3 cm anterior to the focus of activity associated with belief attribution).

---

[5]In their paper, Ferstl & von Cramon (2002) focused on the effect of coherence. In the "logic" condition, the response of the region of medial prefrontal cortex associated with false belief attribution increased significantly only when the pair of sentences was judged to be coherently connected. This may be important because a number of the early studies of false belief tasks (e.g., Fletcher et al. 1995, Gallagher et al. 2000) used random unlinked sentences as their baseline control condition. Ferstl & von Cramon concluded that the medial frontal cortex is responsible generally for "the maintenance of nonautomatic cognitive processes."

[6]It is a serious challenge to explain what did account for the activation of belief attribution–related regions of superior temporal sulcus in the "logic" condition of Ferstl & von Cramon (2002). Frith & Frith (2003) speculate that some of the stimuli may have invited attribution of beliefs and human actions in spite of the absence of people in the explicit descriptions. However, this seems unlikely: The "logic" stimuli were similar to the "mechanical inference" control stories used by Saxe & Kanwisher (2003) that did not elicit any response in the temporo-parietal junction or superior temporal sulcus regions. A different possibility is that the "coherence" instructions used by Ferstl & von Cramon in the "logic" condition encouraged subjects to consider the intentions of the author of the passage.

The relationship between the neural correlates of syntax and of belief attribution remains open to investigation, but the strong conclusion that syntax and belief attribution recruit the same brain regions seems unlikely. Neuropsychological evidence provides an additional hint that these two functions may be independent, at least in adulthood. Siegal and colleagues (Varley & Siegal 2000, Varley et al. 2001) have shown that two dense aphasics with dramatically impaired syntactic processing following strokes, nevertheless can attribute beliefs and even pass a nonverbal false belief task.

Belief Attribution: Conclusions

Developmental psychology and neuroimaging studies provide converging evidence for an anatomically and functionally distinct system for belief attribution in normally developing human children and adults. Children begin to use a novel representational concept of belief around age 3, and by age 4 this concept is robust enough to support successful performance on false belief tasks. The attribution of beliefs also seems to be associated with distinct brain regions, including the medial prefrontal cortex and temporo-parietal junction. One theoretical question about the emergence of belief attribution is the extent to which it depends only on maturation of other capacities. False belief task performance is correlated with both inhibitory control and syntax development. However, we have shown that these capacities recruit different regions of the brain, suggesting that distinct mechanisms are involved in belief attribution, inhibitory control, and syntax. The developmental correlation may therefore reflect the facilitation of knowledge development about the mind for children with mature inhibitory control or linguistic skills.

The most striking dissociation in the development of theory of mind, though, is that between the late development of the concept of belief, described above, and the much earlier development of attribution of other mental states, including desires, perceptions, and emotions (e.g., Bartsch & Wellman 1995). Henry Wellman has characterized this difference as a transition from "desire psychology" to "belief-desire psychology" (e.g., Bartsch & Wellman 1995). Many models of theory of mind include a similar distinction, although the precise characterizations and developmental time courses differ (e.g., Baron-Cohen 1997, Leslie 2000, Tager-Flusberg & Sullivan 2000). In the next section, we will investigate whether a similar distinction is instantiated in the brain regions recruited by theory of mind reasoning.

DEVELOPMENTAL PSYCHOLOGY: DESIRES, PERCEPTIONS, EMOTIONS

Passing the false belief task is sufficient but not necessary evidence of having a theory of mind. According to the criteria originally set out by Premack & Woodruff (1978), young preschoolers and even infants possess a full theory of mind because they can impute unobservable mental states to themselves and others, and use these mental states as a coherent framework to make predictions about behavior. The central notion in this earlier theory of mind seems to be a concept of desire or goal, but it also includes concepts of perception (or attention) and emotion. In this section, we discuss each of these concepts and consider whether they are processed and represented in one common system or in multiple distinct systems. In each case, we discriminate between two alternative accounts of the children's competence. According to the mentalistic (rich) interpretation, young children attribute mental states to others in order to predict and explain behavior. According to the lean interpretation, children have simply developed (or possess innately) sensitivities to certain physical cues, like changing eye gaze or a smile, without making any mental state attributions (Povinelli 2001). The evidence in this section that children do indeed make coherent, causally interrelated mental state attributions of desires/goals, perceptions, and emotions will help to establish the criteria for the neuroimaging studies that are examined in the "Neuroimaging: Desires, Perceptions, and Emotions" section below.

Desires/Goals

Children make genuine psychological references to desires in their spontaneous speech by their second birthday; references to beliefs appear 6 to 12 months later (Bartsch & Wellman 1995). In the lab, 2-year-old children respond appropriately to another person's desires, even when they differ from the child's own preferences [e.g., giving an adult experimenter more of the snack that she preferred (broccoli) rather than the one the child liked better (crackers) (Repacholi & Gopnik 1997; see also Rieffe et al. 2001)]. Fifteen-month-old children can distinguish between the intended goal of an action and its accidental consequences, selectively imitating the goal (Carpenter et al. 1998a, Meltzoff 1995). Furthermore, young children's attribution of goals is not restricted to human actors, but includes nonhuman agents capable of contingent interactions (Gergely & Csibra 1997, Johnson et al. 2001; but see Legerstee & Barillas 2003).

Strikingly, the concept of a goal seems to be available to preverbal infants. Five- to eight-month-old infants who have habituated to a reach-and-grasp motion by a human hand look longer when the object of the motion changes than when the physical path of the motion changes (Woodward 1998). That is, these infants appear to impute an unobservable mental state to the agent (a desire or goal to have the target object), and use this attribution to make a prediction about future behavior (that the agent will continue to reach for the same object and not, for instance, toward the same location in space).

What is the nature of this early concept of desire/goal? Although the concepts of desire, goal, and intention play distinct roles in adult speech and reasoning (e.g., Malle & Knobe 2001), Astington (2001b) has argued plausibly that toddlers have instead an undifferentiated notion of a volitional state (or "conation") tied to an action or an object. Critically, the toddler does not attribute knowledge or beliefs about the apple to Anne ("Anne thinks there is an apple"), but simply uses her own knowledge of the world ("There is an apple") plus a volitional connection from Anne to the apple (approximately "Anne wants the apple") (Figure 1*b*) to predict Anne's action (Bartsch & Wellman 1995, Wellman & Cross 2001).[7] An undifferentiated concept of volition is in principle sufficient to support everything from the 5-month-old's simple goal-directed interpretation of reaching (Woodward 1998) to the 24-month-old's understanding that different people can have different preferences (Repacholi & Gopnik 1997). However, it remains an open question whether the concept of desire/goal is essentially unchanged in the first two years of life and merely becomes more robust, or whether there is real conceptual change from a representation of a goal of hand actions in particular to a more general notion of desire.

Thus young children can attribute desires and goals long before they attribute beliefs. However, an important criterion of a theory of mind is that different mental state attributions interact in a coherent causal framework in order to allow explanations and predictions of action. In the next two subsections, we present evidence for such interactions between the early concepts of desire/goal, perception, and emotion.

PERCEPTIONS   Like the concept of desires/goals, a preliminary concept of perception (i.e., another person's ability to see or look at something) is available to children long before belief attribution. Verbs for seeing are in children's productive vocabulary by 26 months (Bretherton & Beeghly 1982), and children spontaneously produce embedded-clause syntax with "see" six months earlier than with "think" (Bartsch & Wellman 1995). The earliest sensitivity to others' eyes is evident before infants are 3 months old, expressed by a preference for faces with open eyes (Bakti et al. 2000) and by orientation toward the direction of gaze of a previously viewed face (Hood et al. 1998). However, early (and later) behavioral sensitivity to another's gaze is open to both rich and lean interpretations. According to the rich interpretation, infants (or young children) understand seeing as a mental state, providing the actor with selective visual access to (and possibly knowledge about) the world. According to a lean interpretation, on the other hand, gaze following does not demonstrate any mentalistic understanding (see Povinelli 2001); rather, the tendency of infants to follow gaze could depend on a learned association between the direction of adult gaze and interesting events in the world or on a hard-wired reflex (e.g., Corkum & Moore 1995).

---

[7]This characterization helps to resolve the puzzle of how the concept of desire could precede, and be independent of, the concept of belief. In some frameworks (e.g., Searle 1983) the concepts of desire and belief are logically identical, each composed of a proposition ("It will rain tomorrow") and an attitude (either "I want" or "I think"). However, according to this interpretation, young children do not have such a representational concept of desire. Rather, they may conceive of a desire as a direct connection between a person and a real object. If so, a toddler could understand desires without necessarily understanding representations.

When do children possess a genuinely psychological concept of perception? By early in their second year, children's concept of perception shows two hallmarks of being incorporated in their theory of mind: perception is understood to be referential, and to interact coherently with other attributed mental states, including goals and emotions. (We discuss this second point in the section on emotion understanding.)

A referential concept of perception specifies that gaze is directed *at* something; i.e., that looking is a relationship between a person and an object. A series of recent studies show that by 12 to 14 months, infants interpret others' gaze as referential (Brooks & Meltzoff 2002, Caron et al. 2002; but see Doherty & Anderson 1999). Brooks et al. (described in Caron et al. 2002) adapted Woodward's paradigm from goal-directed actions to measure referential understanding of perception. Fourteen-month-old infants were habituated to an adult with either open or closed eyes, who turned toward one of two objects. When the position of the objects was switched at test, the infants looked longer if the adult now looked to the old location (new object) than if the adult looked to the new location (old object), but only if the adult's eyes were open during habituation, suggesting that the infants understood that looking, but not head-turning, is object-directed. Gaze following is also not restricted to human gaze. Johnson et al. (1998) found that 12-month-old infants would follow the "gaze" of a faceless unfamiliar object after only 60 seconds of contingent interaction between the baby and the object, a finding that suggests gaze following at this age is not merely a conditioned response.

Infants use their mentalistic understanding of gaze in word learning. Dare Baldwin (1993) gave 14- and 18-month-old infants one object to play with, while another object was put into a bucket in front of the experimenter. When the infant was looking at the object she was playing with, the experimenter looked into the bucket, and introduced a novel noun: "It's a blicket!" This introduces a perfect perceptual association between the novel word and the object in the infant's hand. Instead of learning this association, the infants looked up to see where the experimenter was looking. The 1-year-olds then associated the new word "blicket" with the object that the experimenter was looking at, and not the one in their hand.

While the early concept of perception is referential, it is probably not representational. As with goals, young children may conceive of another person's perception as a direct connection between the person and the real object in the world (without positing any internal mental representation, Figure 1). This distinction helps to explain the long delay from the (referential) understanding that perception is object-directed, around 14 months, to the (representational) notion that perception can be inaccurate or only partial and so can lead to misperceptions, which is still developing in children 4 and 5 years old (e.g., Gopnik & Astington 1988, Lalonde & Chandler 2002).

EMOTIONS   Newborn infants already show sensitivity to, and synchrony with, others' emotions: they cry when other infants cry, and show some discrimination of happy versus sad expressions (Field & Walden 1982). By 6 months, infants undeniably discriminate facial expressions (Caron et al. 1988, Nelson 1987), and by their first birthday, infants use parental emotional expressions, for example of fear, to guide their own actions in novel situations ("social referencing," Feinman 1992). But the discrimination of emotional expressions is open to a lean, nonmentalistic interpretation. For instance, the physical configuration of emotional expressions may constitute (either learned or innate) intrinsic rewards or punishments to the perceiver (e.g., Blair 2003). When, then, do the emotions of others become incorporated in infants' emerging theory of mind? As mentioned above, one hallmark of such incorporation is the ability to form coherent combinations of attributed mental states, which emerges around age 14 months.

By 14 months, infants can combine information about a person's gaze and emotion both to infer the person's goal and to direct the infant's own actions. Phillips et al. (2002) habituated infants to an event in which an adult looked and smiled at one of two available objects, and then was shown holding the same object. At test, the adult looked and smiled either at the same (old) object or at the other (new) object, and then was shown holding the new object. Infants looked longer when the adult took the new object after gazing at the old object, which suggests that infants used gaze and emotion cues to infer the actor's subsequent goal.[8] Infants can also use emotional expressions to infer a previous goal. In a study by Tomasello et al. (1996), an adult used a nonword to announce an intention to find an object. The adult first picked up one object with obvious disappointment and rejected it, and then picked up a second object with glee (all nonverbally). Sixteen-month-old infants learned that the novel word referred to the object of the positive emotion, which suggests that infants know that happiness results from goal fulfillment. Finally Moses et al. (2001) adapted Baldwin's (1993) word learning paradigm to show that infants use the gaze direction of an adult to determine the referent of an emotional message. When an adult made a negative emotional noise, 12- and 18-month-olds looked up from the novel object in their hand to determine the gaze direction of the adult. Infants subsequently avoided only the object that had been the focus of the adult's gaze.

The causal relation between attributions of emotions and desires is also apparent once children begin to speak. Around 24 months, children begin to spontaneously talk about the causes of their own emotions (Bretherton et al. 1986, Wellman et al. 1995), especially the relationship between frustrated desires and negative mental states (Dunn & Brown 2001, Lagattuta & Wellman 2001). In the lab, 2-year-olds who were told about a boy who wanted a puppy and got one choose a happy face to show how the boy would feel, but the same children choose a sad face if the boy had wanted a bunny (Wellman & Woolley 1990).

---

[8]In an elegant control, the authors showed that if the contingency was reversed during habituation (i.e., the adult looked at one object, and then was shown with the other one), infants were not able to generalize this pattern to the test trials. Thus, infants were not simply learning a pattern of contingencies during the experiment.

Of course, as with concepts of perception and desire, children's understanding of emotions continues to develop after age 2. Complex social emotions, like pride, embarrassment, and guilt begin to be correctly attributed between the ages of 5 and 14 (e.g., Berti et al. 2000). But the framework for attributing basic emotions and their causal relations with desires and perception appears to be already intact in the second year of life.

COMMON OR DISTINCT MECHANISMS?   In all, in their second and third year, toddlers reason productively and coherently about action, using basic concepts of (and causal relations between) three kinds of mental states: desires or goals, perceptions, and emotions. This early theory of mind seems to emerge significantly earlier than the reasoning about beliefs described in the first half of this review.

An open question concerns the extent to which attributions of desires, perceptions, and emotions rely on distinct or common functional or anatomical substrates. For instance, Alan Leslie (1994), in his hierarchical model of theory of mind development, lumps perceptions and goals together as actional properties represented by a stage he calls the Theory of Mind Module 1. Actional properties are those that let an agent "act in pursuit of goals, react to the environment and interact with each other." Consistent with this proposal, in a longitudinal study of 9- to 15-month-olds, Carpenter et al. (1998b) found that the emergence of attentional engagement and gaze following (attribution of perception) and imitation of novel actions (goal attribution) were positively correlated with each other, and uncorrelated with concurrent nonsocial developments such as object permanence. The authors conclude that a mentalistic understanding of gaze and action are "two instances of the same underlying phenomenon." Simon Baron-Cohen (1994, 1997), on the other hand, has divided this domain into two distinct components. The "Intentionality Detector" represents behavior in terms of goals, while the "Eye Direction Detector" detects eyes and represents the direction as the agent "seeing." Neither model explicitly includes a mechanism for emotion attribution.

Neuroimaging: Desires, Perceptions, and Emotions

The above review suggests three central questions that could be addressed using neuroimaging. First, reasoning about beliefs develops later than, and may depend upon (e.g., Pellicano & Rhodes 2003), an earlier theory of mind that includes attribution of desires, perceptions, and emotion. Does the later emerging competence colonize the same neural systems that underpin earlier reasoning? If so, we would predict that attributions of desires, for instance, would recruit the same brain regions identified above as involved in belief attribution. If, on the other hand, reasoning about beliefs draws on distinct systems or abilities, then desire attribution should not produce activity in regions associated with belief attribution, and may recruit a distinct set of brain regions.

Second, the models of early theory of mind proposed by Leslie (1994) and Baron-Cohen (1994, 1997) disagree about whether attributions of perception and goals are the province of one common or two distinct modules. A preliminary approach to resolving this controversy is to ask whether these functions recruit the same or different brain regions in adults.

Finally, what is the relationship between the attribution of emotions and of other mental states?

NEUROIMAGING: ATTRIBUTING DESIRES AND GOALS   In functional neuroimaging studies, the attribution of desires, goals, and intentions to another person has been investigated in three basic paradigms. Studies of the first kind invite mental state attribution to a fictional character using vignettes, cartoons, or animations similar to the stimuli used in studies of belief attribution (Brunet et al. 2000; Castelli et al. 2000, 2002; Fletcher et al. 1995; Gallagher et al. 2000; Saxe & Kanwisher 2003; Schultz et al. 2003). In a second, related set of studies, subjects engage in a simple game, purportedly either with an unseen agent (presumably inviting goal attributions) or with a computer (discouraging goal attributions) (Gallagher et al. 2002, McCabe et al. 2001). Finally, in the third kind of study, subjects watch and interpret a video of a simple goal-directed action by a human actor (Chaminade et al. 2002; Decety et al. 2002; Koski et al. 2002; Zacks et al. 2001; R. Saxe, D.K. Xiao, G. Kovacs, D. Perrett, & N. Kanwisher, submitted). Below we consider the three sets of studies sequentially. Unfortunately, few of these studies also included a task designed to elicit belief attribution, and to our knowledge only one study to date explicitly aimed to contrast brain regions involved in the attribution of different kinds of mental states (R. Saxe, D.K. Xiao, G. Kovacs, D. Perrett, & N. Kanwisher, submitted).

Vignettes, cartoons, and animations that depict or suggest a character's goals, intentions, or desires are typically correlated with moderately increased activity (compared to scrambled or nonsocial controls) in the brain regions associated with belief attributions, including medial prefrontal cortex and posterior superior temporal sulcus (Brunet et al. 2000, Buccino et al. 2001, Castelli et al. 2000, Gallagher et al. 2000, Saxe & Kanwisher 2003, Schultz et al. 2003). For instance, stories describing a character's desires elicited significantly more activity in these regions than physical descriptions of a person, but significantly less than stories describing false beliefs (Saxe & Kanwisher 2003). The most important weakness of this evidence is that none of the stimuli in these studies were designed to exclude belief attribution. The intermediate activity in all of these studies may reflect weak but consistent activation of these regions during desire/goal attribution, but it may equally reflect subjects' occasional spontaneous belief attribution in response to these stimuli. Future studies are needed in which vignettes about different mental states are explicitly contrasted.

Games provide an appealing paradigm for investigations of goal attribution because they allow the stimuli to be exactly matched during goal-attribution and no-goal conditions. Two PET studies using this logic found increased activity in regions of medial prefrontal cortex when the opponent was (purportedly) a human, compared with computer-opponent trials (Gallagher et al. 2002, McCabe et al.

2001). This contrast is too broad to isolate goal attribution in particular, though. Differences in brain activity could reflect belief attribution as above, or just the felt presence of a human opponent [see description in Gallagher et al. 2002; Saxe & Kanwisher (2003) reported that a region of medial prefrontal cortex responded more to any story containing a person, including physical descriptions, than to nonhuman control stories]. To date, no studies have directly compared belief and goal attribution within the context of a game.

Many studies have investigated the neural correlates of observing human body movements. Here we concentrate on the subset of these studies that explicitly address the perception of intentional or goal-directed action. One context in which representation of goal-directed action has been investigated is imitation (Chaminade et al. 2002, Decety et al. 2002, Koski et al. 2002). For example, Koski et al. (2002) asked subjects to imitate simple index finger movements, viewed either with or without target dots (the target dots presumably made the finger movement appear goal-directed). The presence of the goal produced increased activation in lateral inferior frontal cortex bilaterally (Broca's area, also observed by Buccino et al. 2001 for object-directed versus mimed movements of hands and mouths). Furthermore, transient disruption of Broca's area by transcranial magnetic stimulation (TMS) interfered with imitation, but not with cued execution, of goal-directed finger movements (Heiser et al. 2003). Broca's area is not one of the regions associated with belief attribution, which provides preliminary evidence that at least very simple goals may be attributed using different brain regions from those involved in reasoning about beliefs.

Finally, two studies have investigated brain regions associated with the segmentation or interpretation of whole body actions. Zacks et al. (2001) looked for activity correlated with event boundaries in, or transitions between subgoals of, a complex goal-directed action (e.g., cleaning the kitchen). Saxe et al. (R. Saxe, D.K. Xiao, G. Kovacs, D. Perrett, & N. Kanwisher, submitted) varied the structure of a simple intentional action (walking across a room) by directing the actor to unexpectedly pause for a few seconds behind a large bookcase, perhaps requiring subjects to reformulate their interpretation of the action (the occlusion manipulation allowed the two conditions to be matched for average visual information, including biological motion). Both studies report activity related to action segmentation in right posterior superior temporal sulcus. Saxe et al. (R. Saxe, D.K. Xiao, G. Kovacs, D. Perrett, & N. Kanwisher, submitted) further established that this activation was specific to intentional actions, because the same pattern was not observed for passively occluded people, and generalized to other stimuli, because the same region showed a high response to two-dimensional animations portraying goal-directed actions compared with rapid rigid rotation. Activity in the same vicinity was also reported by Decety et al. (2002) when subjects viewed another person's hands performing an action similar to the action the subjects were concurrently executing, compared with viewing their own hands performing that action.

Is the region of posterior superior temporal sulcus that is involved in the analysis of intentional action the same as the nearby region associated with the attribution of beliefs? Saxe et al. (R. Saxe, D.K. Xiao, G. Kovacs, D. Perrett, & N. Kanwisher, submitted) argue that these two regions are distinct. The regions showing increased activity during false belief stories (dubbed the temporo-parietal junction region) and during the paused walking action (dubbed the pSTS visual analysis of action) did not overlap anatomically in individual subjects, and showed strikingly different functional profiles in ROI analyses.

The evidence is inconclusive as to whether interpreting the goal or intention of an observed action draws on distinct brain regions from those involved in assigning beliefs to the actor. Evidence for distinct brain regions for attributing goals comes from studies using videos of simple actions (e.g., Heiser et al. 2003; Koski et al. 2002; R. Saxe, D.K. Xiao, G. Kovacs, D. Perrett, & N. Kanwisher, submitted). Weaker evidence for common regions recruited during both belief and desire attributions comes from studies using vignettes, cartoons, animations, and games, although all of these studies have tended to confound attributions of beliefs and desires (Brunet et al. 2000; Castelli et al. 2000, 2002; Fletcher et al. 1995; Gallagher et al. 2000, 2002; McCabe et al. 2001; Saxe & Kanwisher 2003). One possible resolution is that the brain contains distinct representations of goals (restricted to simple, visible motor actions), similar to the notion of goal available to 5- to 8-month-olds, and desires (applicable more generally), available after the first birthday. This speculation awaits testing in future work.

To summarize, brain regions involved in representing goal-directed action (including pSTS and Broca's area) are distinct from the brain regions associated with belief attribution (including the temporo-parietal junction and medial prefrontal cortex). Thus brain activation patterns are consistent with developmental psychology in suggesting distinct mechanisms for attributing goals and beliefs. As summarized above, an understanding of goal-directed action is available to even very young infants, while belief attribution does not emerge until three years later. The critical, and unresolved, question remains the place of desires in this scheme. Young toddlers talk about desires long before they talk about beliefs (Bartsch & Wellman 1995), and seem to conceive of desire and goals similarly, as direct volitional connections to the world (Astington 2001a,b), which suggests that desire attribution should be similar to goal attribution and distinct from belief attribution. For adults, on the other hand, belief and desire attribution may be simply inseparable. In neuroimaging studies using vignettes, cartoons, animations, and games, attributions of desires and beliefs seem to elicit activity in the same set of regions [although beliefs and desires were always confounded in the stimuli (Brunet et al. 2000; Castelli et al. 2000, 2002; Fletcher et al. 1995; Gallagher et al. 2000, 2002; McCabe et al. 2001; Saxe & Kanwisher 2003)]. Alternatively, desires may be reanalyzed as representational as part of the conceptual transition to a representational treatment of belief. In adult folk theory, we desire a particular apple under a particular description, e.g., representing it as food that tastes good. Further work is necessary to determine whether the correct division of "natural kinds" in the adult brain places desires with goals or with beliefs.

NEUROIMAGING: ATTRIBUTING PERCEPTION   In developmental psychology, a controversy remains over whether the attribution of goals and of perceptions relies on a single system (e.g., Leslie 1994), or two distinct systems (e.g., Baron-Cohen 1997). One way to address this question is to ask whether attributions of goals and of perception recruit the same or distinct brain regions in adults.

Activity in the right pSTS is associated with perception of the gaze of a face: The response in this region is higher for moving eyes than for a moving checkerboard (Puce et al. 1998) or for a change in facial identity (Haxby et al. 2002), for open (direct or averted) eyes than for closed eyes (Wicker et al. 1998), and when subjects attend to the gaze rather than the identity of faces (Hoffman & Haxby 2000). However, as described above for the developmental studies, a sensitivity to gaze is not sufficient to indicate the attribution of perception. Perception is referential, gaze-directed toward something. In an elegant recent study, Pelphrey et al. (2003) showed that the response of the right pSTS to moving eyes is modulated by interaction with a target—a small checkerboard to the right or the left of the character's face. When the character quickly moved his eyes away from the target (incongruent) instead of toward the target (congruent), the response of the pSTS was sustained for many seconds longer. Pelphrey et al. (2003) suggest that on incongruent trials "the observer's expectation is violated and activity in the STS region is prolonged—perhaps related to a reformulation of an expectation."

What is the relationship between regions of the pSTS[9] associated with perception of gaze changes and of other intentional actions? To our knowledge, no single study has combined target-directed hand or body actions and gaze changes. Puce et al. (1998) reported that eye and mouth movements (with no goal) elicited activity in the same part of pSTS, but other studies using hand and body actions appeared to produce activity more lateral and anterior in the STS. On the other hand, centers of activity reported by Pelphrey et al. (2003) for unexpected gaze change and by Saxe et al. (R. Saxe, D.K. Xiao, G. Kovacs, D. Perrett, & N. Kanwisher, submitted) for unexpected action changes are anatomically and conceptually similar. A further suggestion of combined neural representation comes from the discovery of neurones in the anterior superior temporal sulcus of macaque monkeys that show increased response to target-directed hand actions only when the actor's gaze is directed toward the action (Jellema et al. 2000). Neuroimaging work along these lines may help to determine whether attributions of referential gaze and goal-directed actions rely on common or distinct brain regions, consistent with Carpenter et al's (1998b) conclusion described above that these two behaviors reflect "the same underlying phenomenon."

---

[9]Eye gaze—especially averted gaze—was also associated with activity in medial prefrontal cortex, compared with eyes looking down or closed (Calder et al. 2002). These authors point out the anatomical similarity between this activation and the region of medial prefrontal cortex associated with false belief task performance (e.g., Gallagher et al. 2000), and suggest that gaze information may recruit activity across the whole network of brain regions associated with theory of mind.

NEUROIMAGING: ATTRIBUTING EMOTIONS   Investigations of emotion have tended to proceed separately from investigations of theory of mind (but see Terwogt & Stegge 1998). Nevertheless, emotions can be attributed to others and are causally interrelated with other mental state attributions: fulfilled goals cause happiness, the object of fear can be identified by gaze direction, etc.

An overview of the neural systems associated with the perception, experience, and function of emotion is available from many recent reviews (Adolphs 2002, 2003; Blair 2003; Canli & Amin 2002; Cardinal et al. 2002; Hamann 2003; Haxby et al. 2000, 2002; LeDoux 2000; Morris 2002; Preston & de Waal 2002). Facial emotional expressions (usually compared with neutral faces) are associated with activity in a number of different brain regions, including extrastriate cortex, right parietal cortex, right fusiform gyrus, orbitofrontal cortices, amygdala, insula, and basal ganglia (Adolphs 2002).

For the purposes of this paper, we address the narrower question of brain regions recruited during the attribution of emotion to another person and the integration of emotions in a theory of mind. Thus we distinguish neural responses to facial expressions that reflect emotion attribution, from those that reflect, for example, threat detection (e.g., Adolphs & Tranel 2000), the intrinsic reward value of a facial expression (e.g., Blair 2003), resolution of environmental ambiguity (e.g., Whalen 1999), or the initiation of behavioral withdrawal (e.g., Anderson et al. 2000)—all of which may be independently correlated with the perception of facial expressions. We may also distinguish the attribution of an emotion ("she is feeling sad") from simple emotional contagion ("this makes me feel sad"), although is it controversial whether these are indeed distinct.

One way to look for brain regions involved in the attribution of emotion may be to use descriptions of personal emotional experiences. Along these lines, Decety & Chaminade (2003) asked subjects to watch videos in which actors recounted experiences (in the first person) that were either sad or neutral in content. The actors' facial and emotional expressions were also manipulated to be happy, sad or neutral. The sad narrative content, irrespective of emotional expression, led to increased neural activity in regions associated with negative emotions (e.g., the amygdala) and in regions associated with belief attribution (e.g., the temporal pole). Interestingly, attribution of emotion was also associated with activity in left lateral inferior frontal cortex (near Broca's area), which was associated with the representation of goals in the imitation paradigm (Koski et al. 2002). Two distinct functional patterns were observed. In the anterior part of this region (the pars orbitalis) the neural response was high during stories with sad negative content, regardless of the actor's expression. However, the more dorsal part (the pars opercularis) showed a high response to emotional expression (happy or sad) independent of narrative content. This pattern of results is suggestive of a dissociation between perception of facial emotion and understanding of emotional content in speech. The relationship between representations of goals and of emotions in lateral inferior cortex requires further investigation.

A second way to identify the neural correlates of emotion attribution may be to look for interactions between attributions of emotions and of other mental states.

Wicker et al. (2003) investigated whether specific brain regions are sensitive to the interaction between emotional expression and gaze (specifically, direct versus averted gaze). They reported that the response of a single region in the right anterior superior temporal gyrus was highest during emotional expressions directed at the subject, compared with direct neutral gaze, and the interaction with averted gaze was significant. However, these results are somewhat hard to interpret, since this region has not been previously associated either with the perception of gaze, or with the attribution of emotion. It is not possible to compare the brain regions recruited during attribution of perception and emotion in this study because all conditions included the same gaze shift. Again, this provides no clear evidence that either common or distinct brain regions are involved in the attribution of emotion and perception.

Finally, we might ask whether brain regions identified previously in this review as associated with the attribution of beliefs, goals, or perception are also associated with perception of facial emotion. One such candidate region is the posterior STS.[10] Regions of posterior STS have been associated with representations of action (Decety et al. 2002; R. Saxe, D.K. Xiao, G. Kovacs, D. Perrett, & N. Kanwisher, submitted) and of perception (Pelphrey et al. 2003). Both of these studies found increased activity in the right posterior STS when subjects' expectations about human behavior were violated. Decety & Chaminade (2003) found that a nearby region produced a high response when an actor recounted a negative personal experience using positive emotional facial and vocal expression. Such incongruence between narrative content and affect may constitute a violation of expectations about behavior in the emotional domain. (For further evidence of an association between posterior STS and emotion attribution, see Narumoto et al. 2001). Future work should aim to determine whether these regions of the STS reflect a common neural mechanism for the attribution of goals, perceptions,

---

[10]Another region worth considering in this context is the right fusiform gyrus. A number of studies have reported modulation of the right fusiform gyrus by facial emotional expression (greater response to emotional than neutral faces, e.g., Vuilleumier et al. 2002, Halgren et al. 2000). Geday et al. (2003) found that posterior right fusiform gyrus activity was greater for pictures of emotional complex social scenes than for neutral counterparts. These stimuli were specifically designed to be oriented away from the observer, in order to limit the possibility of direct threat or reward to the subject. Geday et al. therefore claim that their task selectively recruited regions involved in attributing emotions to others. The right fusiform gyrus has also been implicated when subjects view animations of social interactions designed to elicit mental state attributions (e.g., seduction, bullying: Castelli et al. 2000, Schultz et al. 2003). However, it is unclear whether fusiform gyrus activity associated with the animations reflects attributions of other mental states like desires or perceptions, or simply of emotions, since these were confounded in both studies. Further research is needed to determine the relationship between regions of the fusiform gyrus involved in the attribution of emotions and the subregion of the fusiform gyrus (cf. Schultz et al. 2003) known as the fusiform face area (Kanwisher et al. 1997), which shows a greater response for faces than all other familiar object classes.

and emotions, or whether neighboring but distinct subregions are independently responsible for each of these functions.

The question of the relationship between the attribution of emotion and other components of theory of mind remains unanswered. More work is needed on both psychological and anatomical commonalities between these two critical components of understanding others.

SUMMARY: DESIRES, PERCEPTIONS, AND EMOTIONS   Evidence from developmental psychology unequivocally supports distinct psychological mechanisms for attributing desires/goals, perceptions, and emotions to others (the early-developing theory of mind) from those mechanisms responsible for attributing beliefs. The results of the neuroimaging studies reviewed above suggest a similar division between brain regions. Videos of simple goal-directed action elicit activity in a region of posterior STS that is distinct from the nearby temporo-parietal junction region associated with belief attribution (Decety et al. 2002; R. Saxe, D.K. Xiao, G. Kovacs, D. Perrett, & N. Kanwisher, submitted). A similar region of posterior STS has also been implicated in attributing perception (Pelphrey et al. 2003) and even possibly emotion (Decety & Chaminade 2003, Narumoto et al. 2001). Future studies are necessary to determine whether this might indeed reflect a single underlying mechanism for representing all of the so-called actional properties of people that let them act in pursuit of goals, react to the environment, and interact with each other (Leslie 1994).

CONCLUSIONS

Substantial behavioral evidence indicates that understanding other minds follows a characteristic developmental trajectory, beginning with the early appearance (in the first 2 years of life) of a system for reasoning about other people's goals, perceptions, and emotions, and the later development (around 4 years of age) of a system for representing the contents of other people's beliefs. Here we asked whether neuroimaging research in adults has contributed or can contribute to theoretical debates about theory of mind that have arisen from the developmental literature. We argue that in several instances, the neuroimaging literature already provides important constraints on these debates.

First, neuroimaging has identified brain regions that are selectively engaged when people reason about the contents of other people's beliefs. This finding strengthens arguments that theory of mind constitutes a special domain of cognition, with its own domain-specific processing machinery. Second, the brain regions associated with belief attribution appear to be distinct from other regions engaged when people reason about other people's goals, which suggests that the two stages of development result from the appearance of two distinct mechanisms, rather than from the gradual enrichment of a single mechanism. Third, the brain regions associated with belief attribution appear to be distinct from those engaged in inhibitory control and from those engaged in syntactic processing. This finding argues against the hypothesis that these other functions are necessarily engaged when attributing beliefs. Instead, the neuroimaging data suggest that the reported correlations between the development of theory of mind and both inhibitory control and syntactic processing may reflect the requirement of these systems for learning about beliefs.

While these contributions from neuroimaging are substantial, they leave many other important questions unresolved. First, if we can engage reasoning about desires without engaging reasoning about beliefs, will we still see activation of brain regions associated with belief attribution, which would suggest the existence of common mechanisms, or will we fail to engage the same regions, consistent with a real dissociation between reasoning about beliefs and desires? Second, are the early-developing abilities to understand other people's goals, perceptions, and actions based on a single system, or several distinct systems? Third, when strict individual-subjects analyses are applied as described in the "Functional Neuroimaging: Standards of Evidence and Inference" section, are distinct but neighboring subregions of the temporo-parietal junction involved in belief attribution and target detection? If instead these tasks engage overlapping regions, what common process might explain that overlap? Finally, we are hopeful that neuroimaging can also address other important aspects of understanding other minds that we have not had space to address here, such as the perception and neural representation of agency (Csibra 2003; Farrer & Frith 2002; Farrer et al. 2003; Johnson 2000, 2003; Ruby & Decety 2001; Tremoulet & Feldman 2000), the relationship between action perception and action planning (Rizzolatti et al. 2001, Wolpert et al. 2003), the related problem of whether theory of mind is implemented as a pseudoscientific theory or as a simulation (Bartsch 2002, Gallese & Goldman 1998, Nichols et al. 1996, Stich & Nichols 1998), the relationship between moral cognition and emotion (Greene & Haidt 2003, Moll et al. 2002), and the relationship between attribution of enduring traits (like personality) and transient states of a person (like emotions and goals, e.g., Winston et al. 2002; A.S. Heberlein, R. Adolphs, D. Tranel, & H. Damasio, submitted).

In sum, we are optimistic that neuroimaging data can help to answer fundamental questions emerging from developmental psychology about our system for reasoning about other people. These contributions are clearest for questions about the basic architecture of the system for understanding other minds: What are its fundamental components? However, as argued in detail in the "Functional Neuroimaging: Standards of Evidence and Inference" section, neuroimaging can make a real contribution toward answering these questions only if we uphold strict standards concerning the way the data are analyzed and the kinds of inferences we draw from them.

ACKNOWLEDGMENTS

This work was funded by grant NIHM 66,696. We are grateful to Yuhong Jiang, Chris Baker, and Andrea Heberlein for comments and suggestions.

The *Annual Review of Psychology* is online at http://psych.annualreviews.org

LITERATURE CITED

Adolphs R. 2001. The neurobiology of social cognition. *Curr. Opin. Neurobiol.* 11:231–39

Adolphs R. 2002. Neural systems for recognizing emotion. *Curr. Opin. Neurobiol.* 12:169–77

Adolphs R. 2003. Cognitive neuroscience of human social behaviour. *Nat. Rev. Neurosci.* 4:165–78

Adolphs R, Tranel D. 2000. Emotion recognition and the human amygdala. In *The Amygdala: A Functional Analysis*, ed. JP Aggleton, pp. 587–630. London/New York: Oxford Univ. Press

Allison T, Puce A, McCarthy G. 2000. Social perception from visual cues: role of the STS region. *Trends Cogn. Sci.* 4:267–78

Anderson AK, Spencer DD, Fulbright RK, Phelps EA. 2000. Contribution of the anteromedialtemporal lobes to the evaluation of facial emotion. *Neuropsychology* 14:526–36

Apperly IA, Robinson EJ. 2002. Five year olds' handling of reference and description in the domains of language and mental representation. *J. Exp. Child Psychol.* 83:53–75

Astington JW. 2001a. The future of theory-of-mind research: understanding motivational states, the role of language, and real-world consequences. *Child Dev.* 72:685–87

Astington JW. 2001b. The paradox of intention: assessing children's metarepresentational understanding. See Malle et al. 2001, pp. 85–103

Astington JW, Jenkins JM. 1995. Theory of mind development and social understanding. *Cogn. Emot.* 9:151–65

Astington JW, Jenkins JM. 1999. A longitudinal study of the relation between language and theory of mind development. *Dev. Psychol.* 35:1311–20

Bakti A, Baron-Cohen S, Wheelwright A, Connellan J, Ahluwalia J. 2000. Is there an innate gaze module? Evidence from human neonates. *Infant Behav. Dev.* 23:223–29

Baldwin DA. 1993. Infants' ability to consult the speaker for clues to word reference. *J. Child Lang.* 20:395–418

Baldwin DA, Baird JA. 2001. Discerning intentions in dynamic human action. *Trends Cogn. Sci.* 5:171–78

Baron-Cohen S. 1994. How to build a baby that can read minds: cognitive mechanisms in mindreading. *Cah. Psychol. Cogn. Curr. Psychol. Cogn.* 13:513–52

Baron-Cohen S. 1997. *Mindblindness: An Essay on Autism and Theory of Mind*. Cambridge, MA: MIT Press. 171 pp.

Baron-Cohen S, Leslie A, Frith U. 1985. Does the autistic child have a theory of mind? *Cognition* 21:37–46

Baron-Cohen S, Tager-Flusberg H, Cohen DJ, eds. 2000. *Understanding Other Minds*. London/New York: Oxford Univ. Press

Bartsch K. 2002. The role of experience in children's developing folk epistemology: review and analysis from the theory-theory perspective. *New Ideas Psychol.* 20:145–61

Bartsch K, Wellman HM. 1995. *Children Talk About the Mind*. London/New York: Oxford Univ. Press

Berti AE, Garattoni C, Venturini B. 2000. The understanding of sadness, guilt, and shame in 5-, 7-, and 9-year-old children. *Genet. Soc. Gen. Psychol. Monogr.* 126: 293–318

Blair RJ. 2003. Facial expressions, their communicatory functions and neuro-cognitive substrates. *Philos. Trans. R. Soc. London Ser. B* 358:561–72

Blakemore SJ, Decety J. 2001. From the perception of action to the understanding of intention. *Nat. Rev. Neurosci.* 2:561–67

Bloom P. 2000. *How Children Learn the Meanings of Words*. Cambridge, MA: MIT Press. 300 pp.

Bloom P, German TP. 2000. Two reasons to abandon the false belief task as a test of theory of mind. *Cognition* 77:B25–31

Born P, Leth H, Miranda MJ, Rostrup E, Stensgaard A, et al. 1998. Visual activation in infants and young children studied by functional magnetic resonance imaging. *Pediatr. Res.* 44:578–83

Botvinick M, Nystrom LE, Fissell K, Carter CS, Cohen JD. 1999. Conflict monitoring versus selection-for-action in anterior cingulate cortex. *Nature* 402:179–81

Braver TS, Barch DM, Gray JR, Molfese DL, Snyder A. 2001. Anterior cingulate cortex and response conflict: effects of frequency, inhibition and errors. *Cereb. Cortex* 11:825–36

Bretherton I, Beeghly M. 1982. Talking about internal states: the acquisition of an explicit theory of mind. *Dev. Psychol.* 18:906–21

Bretherton I, Fritz J, Zahn-Waxler C, Ridgeway D. 1986. Learning to talk about emotion: a functionalist perspective. *Child Dev.* 57:529–48

Brooks R, Meltzoff AN. 2002. The importance of eyes: how infants interpret adult looking behavior. *Dev. Psychol.* 38:958–66

Brunet E, Sarfati Y, Hardy-Bayle MC, Decety J. 2000. A PET investigation of the attribution of intentions with a nonverbal task. *NeuroImage* 11:157–66

Buccino G, Binkofski F, Fink GR, Fadiga L, Fogassi L, et al. 2001. Action observation activates premotor and parietal areas in a somatotopic manner: an fMRI study. *Eur. J. Neurosci.* 13:400–4

Burgund ED, Kang HC, Kelly JE, Buckner RL, Snyder AZ, et al. 2002. The feasibility of a common stereotactic space for children and adults in fMRI studies of development. *NeuroImage* 17:184–200

Calder AJ, Lawrence AD, Keane J, Scott SK, Owen AM, et al. 2002. Reading the mind from eye gaze. *Neuropsychologia* 40:1129–38

Canli T, Amin Z. 2002. Neuroimaging of emotion and personality: scientific evidence and ethical considerations. *Brain Cogn.* 50:414–31

Caplan D. 2001. Functional neuroimaging studies of syntactic processing. *J. Psycholinguist. Res.* 30:297–320

Cardinal RN, Parkinson JA, Hall J, Everitt BJ.

2002. Emotion and motivation: the role of the amygdala, ventral striatum, and prefrontal cortex. *Neurosci. Biobehav. Rev.* 26:321–52

Carlson SM, Moses LJ. 2001. Individual differences in inhibitory control and children's theory of mind. *Child Dev.* 72:1032–53

Caron AJ, Butler S, Brooks R. 2002. Gaze following at 12 and 14 months: Do the eyes matter? *Br. J. Dev. Psychol.* 20:225–39

Caron AJ, Caron RF, MacLean DJ. 1988. Infant discrimination of naturalistic emotional expressions: the role of face and voice. *Child Dev.* 59:604–16

Carpenter M, Akhtar N, Tomasello M. 1998a. Fourteen through 18-month-old infants differentially imitate intentional and accidental actions. *Infant Behav. Dev.* 21:315–30

Carpenter M, Nagell K, Tomasello M. 1998b. Social cognition, joint attention, and communicative competence from 9 to 15 months of age. *Monogr. Soc. Res. Child Dev.* 63:1–143

Carruthers P, Smith PK, eds. 1996. *Theories of Theories of Mind*. New York/London: Cambridge Univ. Press. 390 pp.

Casey BJ, Thomas KM, McCandliss B. 2001. Applications of magnetic resonance imaging to the study of development. In *Handbook of Developmental Cognitive Neuroscience*, ed. CA Nelson, M Luciana, pp. 137–48. Cambridge, MA: MIT Press

Castelli F, Frith C, Happe F, Frith U. 2002. Autism, Asperger syndrome and brain mechanisms for the attribution of mental states to animated shapes. *Brain* 125:1839–49

Castelli F, Happe F, Frith U, Frith C. 2000. Movement and mind: a functional imaging study of perception and interpretation of complex intentional movement patterns. *NeuroImage* 12:314–25

Chaminade T, Meltzoff AN, Decety J. 2002. Does the end justify the means? A PET exploration of the mechanisms involved in human imitation. *NeuroImage* 15:318–28

Corbetta M, Kincade JM, Shulman GL. 2002. Neural systems for visual orienting and their relationships to spatial working memory. *J. Cogn. Neurosci.* 14:508–23

Corkum J, Moore C. 1995. Development of

joint visual attention in infants. In *Joint Attention: Its Origin and Role In Development*, ed. C Moore, PJ Dunham, pp. 61–85. Hillsdale, NJ: Erlbaum

Csibra G. 2003. Teleological and referential understanding of action in infancy. *Philos. Trans. R. Soc. London Ser. B* 358:447–58

Cutting AL, Dunn J. 1999. Theory of mind, emotion understanding, language and family background: individual differences and interrelations. *Child Dev.* 57:529–48

Decety J, Chaminade T. 2003. Neural correlates of feeling sympathy. *Neuropsychologia* 41:127–38

Decety J, Chaminade T, Grezes J, Meltzoff AN. 2002. A PET exploration of the neural mechanisms involved in reciprocal imitation. *NeuroImage* 15:265–72

Decety J, Grezes J. 1999. Neural mechanisms subserving the perception of human actions. *Trends Cogn. Sci.* 3:172–78

Dehaene-Lambertz G, Dehaene S, Hertz-Pannier L. 2002. Functional neuroimaging of speech perception in infants. *Science* 298:2013–15

Dennet D. 1996. *Kinds of Minds: Towards an Understanding of Consciousness.* New York/San Francisco: HarperCollins. 184 pp.

Dennett D. 1978. Beliefs about beliefs. *Behav. Brain Sci.* 1:568–70

de Villiers J. 2000. Language and theory of mind: What are the developmental relationships? See Baron-Cohen et al. 2000, pp. 83–123

de Villiers J, de Villiers PA. 2000a. Linguistic determinism and false belief. In *Children's Reasoning and the Mind*, ed. P Mitchell, K Riggs. Hove, Engl: Psychology Press

de Villiers J, de Villiers PA. 2000b. Linguistic determinism and the understanding of false beliefs. See Mitchell & Riggs 2000, pp. 191–228

de Villiers J, Pyers JE. 2002. Complements to cognition: a longitudinal study of the relationship between complex syntax and false-belief-understanding. *Cogn. Dev.* 17:1037–60

Doherty MJ, Anderson JR. 1999. A new look at

gaze: preschool children's understanding of eye direction. *Cogn. Dev.* 14:549–71

Downar J, Crawley AP, Mikulis DJ, Davis KD. 2002. A cortical network sensitive to stimulus salience in a neutral behavioral context across multiple sensory modalities. *J. Neurophysiol.* 87:615–20

Dunn J, Brown J. 2001. Emotion, pragmatics and developments in emotion understanding in the preschool year. In *Jerome Bruner: Language, Culture, Self*, ed. D Bakhurst, S Shanker, pp. 88–103. Thousand Oaks, CA: Sage

Eriksen BA, Eriksen CW. 1974. Effects of noise letters upon the identification of a target letter in a nonsearch task. *Percept. Psychophys.* 16:143–49

Farrer C, Franck N, Georgieff N, Frith CD, Decety J, Jeannerod M. 2003. Modulating the experience of agency: a positron emission tomography study. *NeuroImage* 18:324–33

Farrer C, Frith CD. 2002. Experiencing oneself vs another person as being the cause of an action: the neural correlates of the experience of agency. *NeuroImage* 15:596–603

Feinman S, ed. 1992. *Social Referencing and the Social Construction of Reality in Infancy.* New York: Plenum. 424 pp.

Ferstl EC, von Cramon DY. 2002. What does the frontomedian cortex contribute to language processing: coherence or theory of mind? *NeuroImage* 17:1599–612

Field TM, Walden TA. 1982. Production and perception of facial expressions in infancy and early childhood. *Adv. Child Dev. Behav.* 16:169–211

Flavell JH. 1988. The development of children's knowledge about the mind: from cognitive connections to mental representations. In *Developing Theories of Mind*, eds. JW Astington, PL Harris, DR Olson, pp. 244–67. New York/London: Cambridge Univ. Press

Flavell JH. 1999. Cognitive development: children's knowledge about the mind. *Annu. Rev. Psychol.* 50:21–45

Fletcher PC, Happe F, Frith U, Baker SC, Dolan RJ, et al. 1995. Other minds in the brain: a functional imaging study of "theory of mind" in story comprehension. *Cognition* 57:109–28

Friederici AD. 2001. Syntactic, prosodic, and semantic processes in the brain: evidence from event-related neuroimaging. *J. Psycholinguist. Res.* 30: 237–50

Frith CD, Frith U. 2000. The physiological basis of theory of mind: functional neuroimaging studies. See Baron-Cohen et al. 2000, pp. 335–56

Frith U. 2001. Mind blindness and the brain in autism. *Neuron* 32:969–79

Frith U, Frith CD. 2003. Development and neurophysiology of mentalizing. *Philos. Trans. R. Soc. London Ser. B* 358:459–73

Gallagher HL, Frith CD. 2003. Functional imaging of "theory of mind." *Trends Cogn. Sci.* 7:77–83

Gallagher HL, Happe F, Brunswick N, Fletcher PC, Frith U, Frith CD. 2000. Reading the mind in cartoons and stories: an fMRI study of "theory of mind" in verbal and nonverbal tasks. *Neuropsychologia* 38:11–21

Gallagher HL, Jack AI, Roepstorff A, Frith CD. 2002. Imaging the intentional stance in a competitive game. *NeuroImage* 16:814–21

Gallese V. 2003. The manifold nature of interpersonal relations: the quest for a common mechanism. *Philos. Trans. R. Soc. London Ser. B* 358:517–28

Gallese V, Goldman A. 1998. Mirror neurons and the simulation theory of mind-reading. *Trends Cogn. Sci.* 2:493–501

Garavan H, Ross TJ, Murphy K, Roche RA, Stein EA. 2002. Dissociable executive functions in the dynamic control of behavior: inhibition, error detection, and correction. *NeuroImage* 17:1820–29

Geday J, Gjedde A, Boldsen AS, Kupers R. 2003. Emotional valence modulates activity in the posterior fusiform gyrus and inferior medial prefrontal cortex in social perception. *NeuroImage* 18:675–84

Gergely G, Csibra G. 1997. Teleological reasoning in infancy: the infant's naive theory of rational action. A reply to Premack and Premack. *Cognition* 63:227–33

Goel V, Grafman J, Sadato N, Hallett M. 1995. Modeling other minds. *NeuroReport* 6:1741–46

Gopnik A, Astington JW. 1988. Children's understanding of representational change and its relation to the understanding of false belief and the appearance-reality distinction. *Child Dev.* 59:26–37

Greene J, Haidt J. 2002. How (and where) does moral judgment work? *Trends Cogn. Sci.* 6:517–23

Grezes J, Decety J. 2001. Functional anatomy of execution, mental simulation, observation, and verb generation of actions: a meta-analysis. *Hum. Brain Mapp.* 12:1–19

Halgren E, Raij T, Marinkovic K, Jousmaki V, Hari R. 2000. Cognitive response profile of the human fusiform face area as determined by MEG. *Cereb. Cortex* 10:69–81

Hamann S. 2003. Nosing in on the emotional brain. *Nat. Neurosci.* 6:106–8

Happe F. 1992. Communicative competence and theory of mind in autism: a test of relevance theory. *Cognition* 48:101–19

Harris PL. 1989. *Children and Emotion: The Development of Psychological Understanding.* Cambridge, MA: Basil Blackwell. 243 pp.

Haxby JV, Hoffman EA, Gobbini MI. 2000. The distributed human neural system for face perception. *Trends Cogn. Sci.* 4:223–33

Haxby JV, Hoffman EA, Gobbini MI. 2002. Human neural systems for face recognition and social communication. *Biol. Psychiatry* 51:59–67

Heiser M, Iacoboni M, Maeda F, Marcus J, Mazziotta JC. 2003. The essential role of Broca's area in imitation. *Eur. J. Neurosci.* 17:1123–28

Hoffman EA, Haxby JV. 2000. Distinct representations of eye gaze and identity in the distributed human neural system for face perception. *Nat. Neurosci.* 3:80–84

Hood BM, Willen JD, Driver J. 1998. Adult's eyes trigger shifts of visual attention in human infants. *Psychol. Sci.* 9:131–34

Jellema T, Baker CI, Wicker B, Perrett DI.

2000. Neural representation for the perception of the intentionality of actions. *Brain Cogn.* 44:280–302

Jiang Y, Kanwisher N. 2003. Common neural substrates for response selection across modalities and mapping paradigms. *J. Cogn. Neurosci.* In press

Johnson SC. 2000. The recognition of mentalistic agents in infancy. *Trends Cogn. Sci.* 4:22–28

Johnson SC. 2003. Detecting agents. *Philos. Trans. R. Soc. London Ser. B* 358:517–28

Johnson SC, Booth A, O'Hearn K. 2001. Inferring the goals of a non-human agent. *Cogn. Dev.* 16:637–56

Johnson SC, Slaughter V, Carey S. 1998. Whose gaze will infants follow? Features that elicit gaze-following in 12-month-olds. *Dev. Sci.* 1:233–38

Just MA, Carpenter PA, Keller TA, Eddy WF, Thulborn KR. 1996. Brain activation modulated by sentence comprehension. *Science* 274:114–16

Kanwisher N, McDermott J, Chun MM. 1997. The fusiform face area: a module in human extrastriate cortex specialized for face perception. *J. Neurosci.* 17:4302–11

Konishi S, Nakajima K, Uchida I, Kikyo H, Kameyama M, Miyashita Y. 1999. Common inhibitory mechanism in human inferior prefrontal cortex revealed by event-related functional MRI. *Brain* 122:981–91

Koski L, Wohlschlager A, Bekkering H, Woods RP, Dubeau MC, et al. 2002. Modulation of motor and premotor activity during imitation of target-directed actions. *Cereb. Cortex* 12:847–55

Lagattuta KH, Wellman HM. 2001. Thinking about the past: early knowledge about links between prior experience, thinking, and emotion. *Child Dev.* 72:82–102

Lalonde CE, Chandler MJ. 2002. Children's understanding of interpretation. *New Ideas Psychol.* 20:163–98

LeDoux JE. 2000. Emotion circuits in the brain. *Annu. Rev. Neurosci.* 23:155–84

Legerstee M, Barillas Y. 2003. Sharing attention and pointing to objects at 12 months: Is the intentional stance implied? *Cogn. Dev.* 18:91–110

Leslie A. 1994. A theory of ToMM, ToBy, and Agency: core architecture and domain specificity. In *Mapping the Mind: Domain Specificity in Cognition and Culture*, ed. L Hirschfeld, S Gelman, pp. 119–48. New York/London: Cambridge Univ. Press

Leslie A. 2000. "Theory of Mind" as a mechanism of selective attention. In *The New Cognitive Neurosciences*, ed. M Gazzaniga, pp. 1235–47. Cambridge, MA: MIT Press

Leslie A, Polizzi P. 1998. Inhibitory processing in the false belief task: two conjectures. *Dev. Sci.* 1:247–53

Leslie A, Thaiss L. 1992. Domain specificity in conceptual development. *Cognition* 43:225–51

Malle BF. 2001. Folk explanations of intentional action. See Malle et al. 2001, pp. 265–86

Malle BF. 2003. The relation between language and theory of mind in development and evolution. In *The Evolution of Language from Pre-Language*, ed. T Givon, BF Malle. Amsterdam/Erdenheim, PA: Benjamins. In press

Malle BF, Knobe J. 2001. The distinction between desire and intention: a folk-conceptual analysis. See Malle et al. 2001, pp. 45–67

Malle BF, Moses LJ, Baldwin DA, eds. 2001. *Intentions and Intentionality: Foundations of Social Cognition.* Cambridge, MA: MIT Press

McCabe K, Houser D, Ryan L, Smith V, Trouard T. 2001. A functional imaging study of cooperation in two-person reciprocal exchange. *Proc. Natl. Acad. Sci. USA* 98:11832–35

McCarthy G, Puce A, Gore JC, Allison T. 1997. Face-specific processing in the human fusiform gyrus. *J. Cogn. Neurosci.* 9:605–10

Meltzoff AN. 1995. Understanding the intentions of others: re-enactment of intended acts by 18-month-old children. *Dev. Psychol.* 31:838–50

Meltzoff AN, Decety J. 2003. What imitation tells us about social cognition: a rapprochement between developmental psychology and cognitive neuroscience. *Philos. Trans. R. Soc. London Ser. B* 358:491–500

Milham MP, Banich MT, Webb A, Barad V, Cohen NJ, et al. 2001. The relative involvement of anterior cingulate and prefrontal cortex in attentional control depends on nature of conflict. *Brain Res. Cogn. Brain Res.* 12:467–73

Mitchell P, Riggs KJ, eds. 2000. *Children's Reasoning and the Mind.* Hove, Engl.: Psychology Press/Taylor & Francis

Moll J, de Oliveira-Souza R, Eslinger PJ, Bramati IE, Mourao-Miranda J, et al. 2002. The neural correlates of moral sensitivity: a functional magnetic resonance imaging investigation of basic and moral emotions. *J. Neurosci.* 22:2730–36

Morris JS. 2002. How do you feel? *Trends Cogn. Sci.* 6:317–19

Moses LJ. 2001. Executive accounts of theory-of-mind development. *Child Dev.* 72:688–90

Moses LJ, Baldwin DA, Rosicky JG, Tidball G. 2001. Evidence for referential understanding in the emotions domain at twelve and eighteen months. *Child Dev.* 72:718–35

Narumoto J, Okada T, Sadato N, Fukui K, Yonekura Y. 2001. Attention to emotion modulates fMRI activity in human right superior temporal sulcus. *Brain Res. Cogn. Brain Res.* 12:225–31

Nelson CA. 1987. The recognition of facial expressions in the first two years of life: mechanisms of development. *Child Dev.* 58:889–909

Nelson K. 1996. *Language in Cognitive Development: Emergence of the Mediated Mind.* New York/London: Cambridge Univ. Press. 432 pp.

Nichols S, Stich S, Leslie A, Klein D. 1996. Varieties of off-line simulation. In *Theories of Theories of Mind,* eds. P Carruthers, PK Smith, pp. 39–74. New York/London: Cambridge Univ. Press

Pellicano E, Rhodes G. 2003. The role of eye-gaze in understanding other minds. *Br. J. Dev. Psychol.* 21:33–43

Pelphrey KA, Singerman JD, Allison T, McCarthy G. 2003. Brain activation evoked by perception of gaze shifts: the influence of context. *Neuropsychologia* 41:156–70

Perner J. 1993. *Understanding the Representational Mind.* Cambridge, MA: MIT Press

Perner J, Lang B. 2000. Theory of mind and executive function: Is there a developmental relationship? See Baron-Cohen et al. 2000, pp. 150–81

Perner J, Stummer S, Lang B. 1999. Executive functions and theory of mind: cognitive complexity or functional dependence? In *Developing Theories of Intention: Social Understanding and Self-Control,* ed. PD Zelazo, JW Astington, pp. 133–52. Mahwah, NJ: Erlbaum

Peterson CC, Siegal M. 1995. Deafness, conversation and theory of mind. *J. Child Psychol. Psychiatry* 36:459–74

Phillips AT, Wellman HM, Spelke ES. 2002. Infants' ability to connect gaze and emotional expression to intentional action. *Cognition* 85:53–78

Povinelli DJ. 2001. On the possibilities of detecting intentions prior to understanding them. See Malle et al. 2001, pp. 225–48

Premack D, Woodruff G. 1978. Does the chimpanzee have a theory of mind? *Behav. Brain Sci.* 1:515–26

Preston SD, de Waal FBM. 2002. Empathy: its ultimate and proximate bases. *Behav. Brain Sci.* 25:1–72

Puce A, Allison T, Bentin S, Gore JC, McCarthy G. 1998. Temporal cortex activation in humans viewing eye and mouth movements. *J. Neurosci.* 18:2188–99

Puce A, Perrett D. 2003. Electrophysiology and brain imaging of biological motion. *Philos. Trans. R. Soc. London Ser. B* 358:435–45

Repacholi BM, Gopnik A. 1997. Early reasoning about desires: evidence from 14- and 18-month-olds. *Dev. Psychol.* 33:12–21

Rieffe C, Terwogt MM, Koops W, Stegge H, Oomen A. 2001. Preschooler's appreciation of uncommon desires and subsequent emotions. *Br. J. Dev. Psychol.* 19:259–74

Rizzolatti G, Fogassi L, Gallese V. 2001. Neurophysiological mechanisms underlying the understanding and imitation of action. *Nat. Rev. Neurosci.* 2:661–70

Roder B, Stock O, Neville H, Bien S, Rosler F. 2002. Brain activation modulated by the comprehension of normal and pseudo-word sentences of different processing demands: a functional magnetic resonance imaging study. *NeuroImage* 15:1003–14

Ruby P, Decety J. 2001. Effect of subjective perspective taking during simulation of action: a PET investigation of agency. *Nat. Neurosci.* 4:546–50

Ruffman T, Slade L, Rowlandson K, Rumsey C, Garnham A. 2003. How language relates to belief, desire and emotion understanding. *Cogn. Dev.* 113:1–20

Saxe R, Kanwisher N. 2003. People thinking about thinking people: fMRI investigations of theory of mind. *NeuroImage.* In press

Scholl BJ, Leslie AM. 2001. Minds, modules, and meta-analysis. Commentary on "Meta-analysis of theory-of-mind development: the truth about false belief." *Child Dev.* 72:696–701

Schultz RT, Grelotti DJ, Klin A, Kleinman J, Van der Gaag C, et al. 2003. The role of the fusiform face area in social cognition: implications for the pathobiology of autism. *Philos. Trans. R. Soc. London Ser. B* 358:415–27

Searle JR. 1983. *Intentionality: An Essay in the Philosophy of Mind.* New York/London: Cambridge Univ. Press

Shulman GL, d'Avossa G, Tansy AP, Corbetta M. 2002. Two attentional processes in the parietal lobe. *Cereb. Cortex* 12:1124–31

Siegal M, Varley R. 2002. Neural systems involved in "theory of mind." *Nat. Rev. Neurosci.* 3:463–71

Stich S, Nichols S. 1998. Theory theory to the max. *Mind Lang.* 13:421–49

Stroop JR. 1938. Factors affecting speed in serial verbal reactions. *Psychol. Monogr.* 50:38–48

Sylvester CY, Wager TD, Lacey SC, Hernandez L, Nichols TE, et al. 2003. Switching attention and resolving interference: fMRI measures of executive functions. *Neuropsychologia* 41:357–70

Tager-Flusberg H, Sullivan K. 2000. A componential view of theory of mind: evidence from Williams syndrome. *Cognition* 76:59–90

Terwogt MM, Stegge H. 1998. Children's perspective on the emotion process. In *The Social Child,* ed. A Campbell, S Muncer, pp. 249–69. Hove, Engl.: Psychology Press/Erlbaum

Tomasello M, Strosberg R, Akhtar N. 1996. Eighteen-month-old children learn words in nonostensive contexts. *J. Child Lang.* 23:157–76

Tootell RB, Reppas JB, Kwong KK, Malach R, Born RT, et al. 1995. Functional analysis of human MT and related visual cortical areas using magnetic resonance imaging. *J. Neurosci.* 15:3215–30

Tremoulet PD, Feldman J. 2000. Perception of animacy from the motion of a single dot. *Perception* 29:943–51

Vandenberghe R, Nobre AC, Price CJ. 2002. The response of left temporal cortex to sentences. *J. Cogn. Neurosci.* 14:550–60

Varley R, Siegal M. 2000. Evidence for cognition without grammar from causal reasoning and "theory of mind" in an agrammatic aphasic patient. *Curr. Biol.* 10:723–26

Varley R, Siegal M, Want SC. 2001. Severe impairment in grammar does not preclude theory of mind. *Neurocase* 7:489–93

Vogeley K, Bussfeld P, Newen A, Herrmann S, Happe F, et al. 2001. Mind reading: neural mechanisms of theory of mind and self-perspective. *NeuroImage* 14:170–81

Vuilleumier P, Armony JL, Clarke K, Husain M, Driver J, Dolan RJ. 2002. Neural response to emotional faces with and without awareness: event-related fMRI in a parietal patient with visual extinction and spatial neglect. *Neuropsychologia* 40:2156–66

Watson AC, Painter KM, Bornstein MH. 2001. Longitudinal relations between 2-year-olds' language and 4-year-olds' theory of mind. *J. Cogn. Dev.* 2:449–57

Wellman HM, Cross D. 2001. Theory of mind and conceptual change. *Child Dev.* 72:702–7

Wellman HM, Cross D, Watson J. 2001.

Meta-analysis of theory-of-mind development: the truth about false belief. *Child Dev.* 72:655–84

Wellman HM, Harris PL, Banerjee M, Sinclair A. 1995. Early understanding of emotion: evidence from natural language. *Cogn. Emot.* 9:117–49

Wellman HM, Lagattuta KH. 2000. Developing understandings of mind. See Baron-Cohen et al. 2000, pp. 21–49

Wellman HM, Woolley JD. 1990. From simple desires to ordinary beliefs: the early development of everyday psychology. *Cognition* 35:245–75

Whalen PJ. 1999. Fear, vigilance and ambiguity: initial neuroimaging studies of the human amygdala. *Curr. Dir. Psychol. Sci.* 7:177–87

Wicker B, Michel F, Henaff MA, Decety J. 1998. Brain regions involved in the perception of gaze: a PET study. *NeuroImage* 8:221–27

Wicker B, Perrett DI, Baron-Cohen S, Decety J. 2003. Being the target of another's emotion: a PET study. *Neuropsychologia* 41:139–46

Wimmer H, Perner J. 1983. Beliefs about beliefs: representation and constraining function of wrong beliefs in young children's understanding of deception. *Cognition* 13:103–28

Winston JS, Strange BA, O'Doherty J, Dolan RJ. 2002. Automatic and intentional brain responses during evaluation of trustworthiness of faces. *Nat. Neurosci.* 5:277–83

Wolpert DM, Doya K, Kawato M. 2003. A unifying computational framework for motor control and social interaction. *Philos. Trans. R. Soc. London Ser. B* 358:593–602

Woodward AL. 1998. Infants selectively encode the goal object of an actor's reach. *Cognition* 69:1–34

Woolfe T, Want SC, Siegal M. 2002. Signposts to development: theory of mind in deaf children. *Child Dev.* 73:718–78

Zacks JM, Braver TS, Sheridan MA, Donaldson DI, Snyder AZ, et al. 2001. Human brain activity time-locked to perceptual event boundaries. *Nat. Neurosci.* 4:651–55

Zaitchik D. 1990. When representations conflict with reality: the preschooler's problem with false beliefs and "false" photographs. *Cognition* 35:41–68

Zaitchik D. 1991. Is only seeing really believing? Sources of the true belief in the false belief task. *Cogn. Dev.* 6:91–103

Annu. Rev. Psychol. 2004. 55:125–48
doi: 10.1146/annurev.psych.55.090902.141545
First published online as a Review in Advance on September 29, 2003

HYPOCRETIN (OREXIN): Role in Normal Behavior and Neuropathology*

Jerome M. Siegel

Veterans Affairs Greater Los Angeles Healthcare System-Sepulveda, and Department of Psychiatry and Biobehavioral Sciences, Center for Sleep Research, University of California, Los Angeles, North Hills, California 91343; email: jsiegel@ucla.edu

Key Words REM sleep, hypothalamus, narcolepsy, cataplexy, feeding, motor, alertness

■ **Abstract** The hypocretins (Hcrts, also known as orexins) are two peptides, both synthesized by a small group of neurons, most of which are in the lateral hypothalamic and perifornical regions of the hypothalamus. The hypothalamic Hcrt system directly and strongly innervates and potently excites noradrenergic, dopaminergic, serotonergic, histaminergic, and cholinergic neurons. Hcrt also has a major role in modulating the release of glutamate and other amino acid transmitters. Behavioral investigations have revealed that Hcrt is released at high levels in active waking and rapid eye movement (REM) sleep and at minimal levels in non-REM sleep. Hcrt release in waking is increased markedly during periods of increased motor activity relative to levels in quiet, alert waking. Evidence for a role for Hcrt in food intake regulation is inconsistent. I hypothesize that Hcrt's major role is to facilitate motor activity tonically and phasically in association with motivated behaviors and to coordinate this facilitation with the activation of attentional and sensory systems. Degeneration of Hcrt neurons or genetic mutations that prevent the normal synthesis of Hcrt or of its receptors causes human and animal narcolepsy. Narcolepsy is characterized by an impaired ability to maintain alertness for long periods and by sudden losses of muscle tone (cataplexy). Administration of Hcrt can reverse symptoms of narcolepsy in animals, may be effective in treating human narcolepsy, and may affect a broad range of motivated behaviors.

CONTENTS

---

*The U.S. Government has the right to retain a nonexclusive, royalty-free license in and to any copyright covering this paper.

THE DISCOVERY OF HYPOCRETIN (OREXIN)

The discovery of hypocretin (Hcrt) and of its clinical and biological significance is a landmark in recent neuroscience. In fewer than three years, the discovery led to the unraveling of the cause of narcolepsy, which had been a mystery since the identification of the disorder more than 120 years ago. We now know that most explanations prior to 2000, including the ideas that narcolepsy was a psychosomatic illness, was caused by excessive masturbation, was a form of schizophrenia (Douglass et al. 1993, Passouant 1976), or was a symptom of a subtle neurochemical imbalance were far off the mark. Now, five years after the identification of Hcrt, we know that the peptide has a major role in behavioral control through its regulation of aminergic, cholinergic, and amino acid transmitter systems in relation to sleep and waking behaviors. The Hcrt story is notable as an example of how basic research can lead to completely unanticipated insights into human disease.

In the late 1990s, Gregor Sutcliffe's group in San Diego was interested in identifying peptides that were linked to the control of food intake and the regulation of weight (De Lecea et al. 1998). With the epidemic of obesity in the United States and to a lesser extent in other wealthy nations, a better understanding of the weight regulatory system would be of enormous public health importance. It has long been known that the hypothalamus is the brain region most critical for appetite control. Lesions of the medial hypothalamus in rats and other animals lead to remarkable obesity, and lesions of the lateral hypothalamus produce profound anorexia (Levitt & Teitelbaum 1975). If peptides that are synthesized only in the hypothalamus could be found, they might be useful in appetite control. It would furthermore be reasonable to hope that receptors for peptides produced in this region would be ideal targets for pharmacological manipulation.

Sutcliffe's group used the technique of subtractive RNA hybridization to detect mRNAs synthesized in the hypothalamus, but not in the cerebellum. They reasoned that the cerebellum is not known to be strongly involved in food intake regulation. Therefore, a comparison of hypothalamic and cerebellar mRNAs might reveal peptides having functions related to appetite control.

They discovered a hypothalamus-specific mRNA that encodes a substance they named preprohypocretin, the precursor of two peptides that they named hypocretin-1 and hypocretin-2, from their hypothalamic location and their structural similarities to the gut hormone secretin. They mapped the locations of the peptides and concluded that they were restricted to neuronal cell bodies in the hypothalamus and their projections. Both peptides are found in the same neurons. The work was led by Luis De Lecea and Thomas Kilduff (De Lecea et al. 1998).

At about the same time that Sutcliffe's group was looking for hypothalamic peptides, Yanagisawa's group in Texas was looking for ligands for a number of orphan receptors. "Orphan receptors" are encoded by cDNA sequences that resemble those of known receptors, in this case G protein–coupled receptors; the first step to discovering the function of such receptors is to identify their ligands. They screened ligands for a receptor that they eventually named orexin receptor-1. They found two peptides in hypothalamic extracts, orexin-A and orexin-B, that strongly activated cell lines carrying this orphan receptor. Noting that orexin-B had a much weaker effect than orexin-A, they hypothesized that a second receptor existed for these peptides. A search of the genomic database led to the identification of a second receptor (orexin receptor-2) encoded by a gene with substantial sequence similarity to that of the orexin receptor-1 gene. It was found that orexin receptor-1 responded relatively selectively to orexin-A, whereas orexin receptor-2 responded to both orexin-A and orexin-B. No additional receptors for orexin have so far been identified.

Aware of the hypothalamic role in food intake regulation, they administered the peptides to rats by injection into the lateral ventricle, so that the peptides would circulate throughout the ventricular system within the brain. They found that eating was increased and because of this finding named the peptides "orexins," from the Greek word for appetite. The paper, whose lead author was Takeshi Sakurai, appeared less than a month after the paper from de Lecea et al. (Sakurai et al. 1998). Soon after the papers appeared, it became apparent that Hcrt-1 and -2 were identical to orexin-A and -B. In the current review we will use the term hypocretin (Hcrt) for the peptides (Hcrt-1 = orexin-A, Hcrt-2 = orexin-B).

As we will see, it is doubtful that the discovered peptides are critically important in appetite regulation. However, there is little doubt that the Hcrt peptides are vitally important in behavioral regulation, and that the integrity of the Hcrt system has important implications for proper neurological functioning.

STRUCTURE OF THE PEPTIDES

Hcrt-1 is a peptide that consists of 33 amino acids. The peptide bends back upon itself and is held in this position by disulfide bonds. Hcrt-2 is a 28 amino acid peptide that exists as a linear chain without any disulfide bonds (Sakurai et al. 1998). Both peptides are generated from preprohypocretin.

ANATOMY OF THE HCRT SYSTEM

Hcrt cell somas in the brain are concentrated in the hypothalamus. Although many papers have described them as being restricted to the "lateral hypothalamus," this description is not entirely accurate. The fornix is usually considered the dividing line between lateral and medial hypothalamus. Many Hcrt cells are located medial to the fornix. This is true in rats and is also apparent in humans, where a dense cluster of Hcrt cells is located in the dorsomedial hypothalamic nucleus, medial to the fornix (Figure 1, see color insert) (Thannickal et al. 2000). In addition to the hypothalamic grouping of cells staining for both Hcrt-1 and -2, it has been reported that small groups of neurons containing Hcrt-2, but not Hcrt-1, exist in the lateral division of the central nucleus of the amygdala, in the anterior lateral subnucleus of the bed nucleus of the stria terminalis immediately adjacent to the internal capsule, and in an area just ventral to the lateral ventricle (Ciriello et al. 2003), as well as in olfactory neurons (Caillol et al. 2003). Prior anatomical studies of the Hcrt system had not observed Hcrt cells in these areas (Nambu et al. 1999, Peyron et al. 1998).

Although most Hcrt somas are in the hypothalamus, these cells project axons widely throughout the brain. Heavily innervated regions include the locus coeruleus and raphe nuclei of the brainstem, the cholinergic neurons of the brainstem and forebrain, the histaminergic cells of the posterior hypothalamus and other hypothalamic nuclei (Figure 2, see color insert). Less densely innervated regions include the dorsal and ventral horns of the spinal cord, brainstem motor nuclei, limbic regions of the brainstem, and the neocortex (Fung et al. 2001, Nambu et al. 1999, Peyron et al. 1998, van den Pol 1999).

Brain Hcrt receptors are distributed throughout the innervated regions, but the distributions of mRNAs for Hcrt receptor-1 and -2 are strikingly different. Receptor-1 is the predominant receptor type in cingulate cortex, anterior olfactory nucleus, prefrontal and infralimbic cortex, bed nucleus of stria terminalis, anterior hypothalamus, and locus coeruleus. Receptor-2 is the predominant type in the medial septal nucleus, nucleus of the diagonal band, hippocampal CA3 field, arcuate nucleus of the hypothalamus, lateral hypothalamus, and tuberomammillary nucleus. Both receptors are present in substantial numbers in other regions (Marcus et al. 2001, Trivedi et al. 1998).

Most Hcrt cells in the hypothalamus also contain the peptide dynorphin (Chou et al. 2001). However, the vast majority of dynorphin containing neurons is located outside the hypothalamus. Neuronal activity-regulated pentraxin (Narp), a secreted neuronal protein implicated in regulating synapse formation and produced by an "immediate early gene" (one of a group of genes that is rapidly expressed in neurons when their metabolic activity is increased), is found in virtually all Hcrt cells. Narp is not present in non-Hcrt hypothalamic cells, although it is present in some non-Hcrt cells of the hippocampal mossy fiber pathway, projections of the habenula to the interpeduncular nucleus, and neurons of the vestibular system (Reti et al. 2002). It is likely that Narp is involved in the signaling functions of Hcrt neurons. Some evidence suggests that Hcrt cells may also contain glutamate as a cotransmitter (Abrahamson & Moore 2001); however, this work needs to be confirmed with studies of the distribution of a specific glutamate reuptake transporter, since glutamate is used in cellular metabolism and its presence alone does not prove that it is being used as a transmitter. Hcrt also has an important role in regulating amino acid release from non-Hcrt-containing cells, as will be discussed below.

Hcrt neurons exist outside the brain. Some neurons in the intestines and in the pancreas display Hcrt- and Hcrt receptor-like immunoreactivity, as do

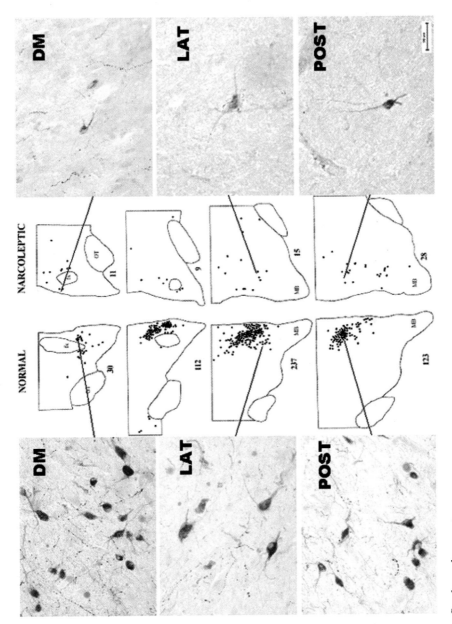

See legend on next page

Figure 1   Distribution of Hcrt-labeled cells in normal and narcoleptic humans. (*Left*) Normal human brain has approximately 70,000 Hcrt cells located in the hypothalamus, both medial and lateral to the fornix. (*Right*) Narcoleptic human brain has an 85%–95% loss of Hcrt cells. Normal Hcrt cell morphology is visible in surviving Hcrt cells in narcoleptics. DM, dorsomedial; LAT, lateral; POST, posterior hypothalamic nuclei. Calibration 50 μm. (Redrawn from Thannickal et al. 2000)

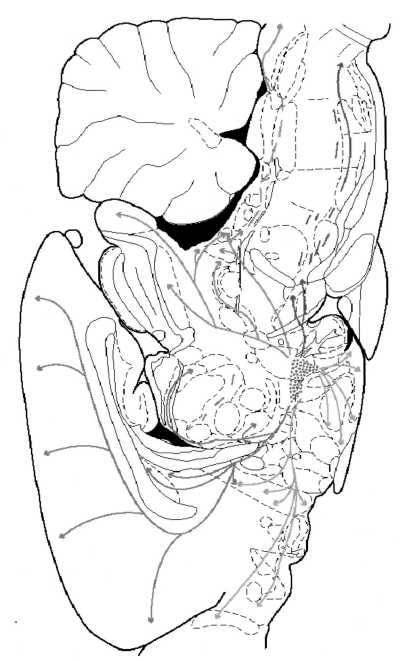

Figure 2 Locations of Hcrt cells in the hypothalamus in the rat and their ascending and descending projections. Some descending Hcrt axons terminate in the dorsal and ventral horns of the spinal cord. (From Peyron et al. 1998)

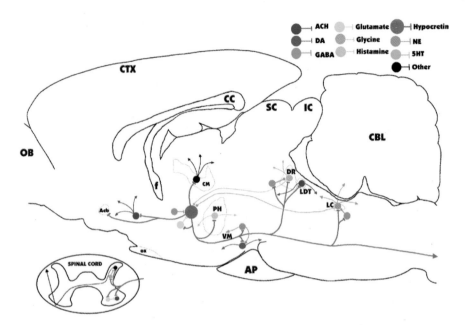

Figure 3 Major identified synaptic interactions of Hcrt neurons. Lines terminated by perpendicular lines denote excitation; circular terminations indicate inhibition. ACH, acetylcholine; DA, dopamine; NE, norepinephrine; 5HT, serotonin; OB, olfactory bulb; Acb, nucleus accumbens; f, fornix; OX, optic chiasm; CM, centromedian nucleus of the thalamus; PH, posterior hypothalamus; VM, ventral midbrain; AP, anterior pituitary; SC, superior colliculus; IC, inferior colliculus; DR, dorsal raphe; LDT, laterodorsal tegmental and pedunculopontine; LC, locus coeruleus; CBL, cerebellum.

vagal and spinal primary afferent neurons (Kirchgessner 2002). Hcrt mRNA has been reported in the testis (Johren et al. 2001). Hcrt receptors have been reported in the adrenal glands, particularly in male rats (Johren et al. 2001). Receptors have also been identified in the pituitary and median eminence (Date et al. 2000).

SYNAPTIC MECHANISMS UNDERLYING HCRT ACTION

Hypocretin's regulation of the release of other neurotransmitters appears to underlie many of its effects. These effects can be most readily investigated in brain slices maintained in a bath into which transmitter agonists and antagonists and chemicals that block action potentials can be applied. The disadvantage of this in vitro approach is that levels of transmitter agonists and other conditions in the living animal will undoubtedly differ from those created in vitro. Thus, a combination of in vitro studies and investigations of intact animals is essential for gaining a full understanding of how the peptides act.

Hcrt neurons have widely projecting axons innervating all the monoaminergic brain systems. Serotonergic and noradrenergic systems have descending connections strongly linked to movement and muscle tone control (Jacobs 1991, Kiyashchenko et al. 2001, Lai et al. 2001, Wu et al. 1999), as well as ascending projections to forebrain regions involved in sensory integration (Aston-Jones et al. 1994, Jacobs 1987). Histamine neurons are strongly involved in forebrain alerting (Lin et al. 1989). Dopamine neurons are involved in both alerting and reward (Dehaene & Changeux 2000, Rye & Jankovic 2002).

Hcrt cells also strongly innervate the major cholinergic cells in the brainstem (Burlet et al. 2002) and basal forebrain (Eggermann et al. 2003). These cells are known to play a central role in the cortical EEG activation that characterizes waking (Jones 2000). Therefore, the Hcrt system can serve to coordinate the activity of these arousal systems with motor activity.

Hcrt is excitatory at many of its projection sites. This is true for neurons of the noradrenergic locus coeruleus (Bourgin et al. 2000, Hagan et al. 1999, Horvath et al. 1999, Ivanov & Aston-Jones 2000, van den Pol et al. 2002), serotonergic dorsal raphe (Liu et al. 2002), histaminergic tuberomammillary (Bayer et al. 2001), cholinergic brainstem (Burlet et al. 2002), and cholinergic basal forebrain nuclei (Eggermann et al. 2003). Hcrt directly excites many dopaminergic neurons in the midbrain ventral tegmental region (Korotkova et al. 2003). Hcrt excites GABAergic neurons in the pars reticulata of the substantia nigra (Korotkova et al. 2003), neurons adjacent to the dopaminergic neurons supplying forebrain and brainstem regions. GABAergic neurons projecting from the septal nucleus to the hippocampus are also excited by Hcrt (Wu et al. 2002a). An important clue to its arousing actions is the report that Hcrt excites neurons of the nonspecific centromedian thalamic nucleus, which is known to be involved in generalized cortical arousal, but does not excite neurons of the specific thalamic sensory relays, which relay sensory information to the cortex. This centromedian excitation is mediated by type 2 Hcrt receptors (Bayer et al. 2002). Hcrt also increases sympathetic outflow from the medulla (Dun et al. 2000).

Cells in lamina 1 and 2 of the dorsal horn of the spinal cord, involved in the processing of somatosensory information, are excited by Hcrt, but most are also *indirectly* inhibited by Hcrt via glycine released by adjacent Hcrt responsive cells (Grudt et al. 2002). Similarly, other cells are affected both directly and indirectly by Hcrt. For example, serotonergic cells simultaneously receive direct Hcrt excitation and indirect GABAergic inhibition (Liu et al. 2002), and a similar pattern may occur with locus coeruleus cells (Kiyashchenko et al. 2002). Hcrt application onto vagal motoneurons has been reported both to depolarize (excite) these cells and simultaneously to inhibit them by increasing the number of inhibitory postsynaptic potentials.

This pattern of direct excitation accompanied by indirect inhibition or excitation suggests that the net effect of Hcrt in this situation is largely dependent on the inputs into the cells mediating the indirect effects. For example if Hcrt is directly exciting a postsynaptic cell and simultaneously exciting a GABAergic cell that inhibits the same postsynaptic cell, the inhibitory effect of Hcrt will be greatly enhanced if other excitatory inputs into the GABAergic cell are active. Conversely, the inhibitory effects will be blocked if the GABAergic cell is itself inhibited. In this manner, the indirect pathways utilized by Hcrt provide great flexibility for regulation of the effects of Hcrt. Like an electronic amplifier, this kind of circuit can amplify relatively weak inputs to produce a larger effect in postsynaptic cells.

Some critical sleep-related cell groups are not activated either directly or indirectly by Hcrt. For example, GABAergic sleep active neurons do not respond to Hcrt in the slice preparation (Eggermann et al. 2003). These neurons are thought to have a role in triggering sleep. Hcrt administration to the nucleus accumbens enhances inhibitory GABAergic currents but does not affect glycine action and it decreases NMDA glutamate receptor-induced currents (Martin et al. 2002). The nucleus accumbens is heavily innervated by dopaminergic cells and has a high density of Hcrt receptor-2.

Surprisingly, Hcrt neurons do not respond directly to Hcrt in vitro. Typically, neurons are inhibited when they are exposed to the transmitter they release, presumably as a means of feedback control. Li et al. (2002) showed that application of Hcrt to hypothalamic slices produced excitation of Hcrt cells. However, this effect was an indirect one. Blockade of action potentials within the slice with tetrodotoxin prevented the response, as did blockade of glutamatergic transmission. It was concluded that Hcrt excites the population of Hcrt neurons indirectly by increasing the activity of glutamatergic neurons adjacent to Hcrt neurons. This study also showed that norepinephrine and serotonin potently inhibit Hcrt neurons. Thus, one can identify an inhibitory feedback circuit onto Hcrt neurons mediated by serotonin and norepinephrine: Hcrt neurons directly excite norepinephrine and serotonin neurons and these neurons in turn project back onto Hcrt neurons, producing direct inhibition that counters the self excitation mediated by local glutamatergic neurons. Acetylcholine and histamine have little effect on Hcrt neurons; however, according to the study by Li et al. Hcrt has potent excitatory effects on histamine and acetylcholine-containing cells. Figure 3 (see color insert) summarizes some of the main synaptic connections described or hypothesized for Hcrt cells (Kiyashchenko et al. 2002; Li et al. 2002; Nitz & Siegel 1997a,b).

The synaptic effects documented in in vitro work can explain aspects of the pathology associated with Hcrt cell or receptor loss, as occurs in narcolepsy. The potent excitation of histamine cells by Hcrt (Eriksson et al. 2001, Yamanaka et al. 2002), largely mediated by Hcrt receptor-2, may be one element in the arousing effect of Hcrt administration (Hagan et al. 1999, Ivanov & Aston-Jones 2000). The sleepiness seen in Hcrt receptor-2 mutant narcoleptic dogs (Siegel 1999), the reduced levels of histamine in these canine and in human narcoleptics (Nishino et al. 2001, 2002), and the soporific effects of antihistamines (Welch et al. 2003) support this conclusion, as does the major role of histamine in mediating the arousing effects of Hcrt infusion into the lateral ventricles (Huang et al. 2001). Histamine blockers attenuate the Hcrt-induced increase in waking, but even high doses do not completely block the arousing response (Yamanaka et al. 2002), however, which suggests that other systems might also be involved. Indeed, the noradrenergic, cholinergic, and dopaminergic systems are also strongly excited by Hcrt, and it is likely that it is this coordinated activation, rather than the release of histamine alone, that is mediating Hcrt's arousing effects (Figure 3, see color insert). Locomotion induced by injection of Hcrt into the lateral ventricle was blocked by dopamine D_2 receptor antagonists (Nakamura et al. 2000, Sakurai et al. 1998), demonstrating that dopaminergic pathways play an important role in behavioral arousal due to Hcrt administration.

HCRT AND AMINO ACIDS

Van den Pol et al. (1998) and Follwell & Ferguson (2002) presented evidence from work in hypothalamic brain slices that Hcrt administration causes glutamate release, and under some conditions GABA release as well. John et al. (2001, 2003) measured changes in central glutamate release after intravenous administration of Hcrt in anesthetized rats. Intravenous administration caused a sustained (>50 min) and marked ($>60\%$) increase in glutamate release in the amygdala, a region with a moderate concentration of Hcrt receptors, but no such change in the cerebellar cortex, a region without substantial numbers of Hcrt receptors (Figure 4) (John et al. 2001, 2003). This release is calcium dependent, which indicates that the glutamate is released from synaptic vesicles (John et al. 2003). Similar increases in glutamate release have been seen in unanesthetized animals following systemic Hcrt administration (Kodama & Kimura 2002). Intravenous infusion of Hcrt increases behavioral activity and decreases REM sleep (John et al. 2000), effects also seen with central administration. Therefore, the intravenous effects are likely to be mediated, in part, by Hcrt-induced glutamate release.

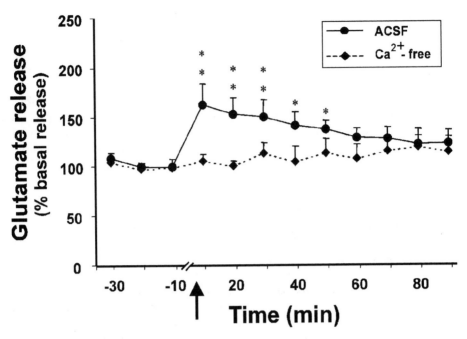

Figure 4 Effect of intravenous injection of Hcrt on central glutamate release in the amygdala, a Hcrt-innervated region. Intravenous Hcrt injection produces a marked, calcium-dependent increase in glutamate release. No such increase occurs in the cerebellar cortex, a region without substantial Hcrt innervation. This demonstrates that Hcrt effectively crosses the blood-brain barrier and produces a marked release of glutamate in Hcrt-innervated regions. (From John et al. 2003)

Hcrt neurons innervate motoneuron pools (Fung et al. 2001). When Hcrt was microinjected into the trigeminal motor nucleus, ipsilateral masseter muscle tone increased in a dose-dependent manner. Hcrt application into the hypoglossal motor nucleus also increased genioglossus muscle activity. However, pretreatment with D-AP5, an N-methyl-D-aspartic acid (NMDA) glutamate receptor antagonist, abolished the excitatory response of Hcrt application onto both groups of motoneurons (Figure 5) (Peever et al. 2003). These studies demonstrate that Hcrt's effects on these motoneurons are mediated by the release of glutamate, the most ubiquitous excitatory brain neurotransmitter.

HCRT'S ROLE IN NARCOLEPSY AND OTHER DISORDERS

After identifying the Hcrt peptides in rats, Yanagisawa's group created *prepro-hypocretin* knockout mice in which the peptides were not generated. Careful observation of the behavior of these animals revealed unusual, abrupt onset periods of inactivity. After ruling out various causes, they concluded that they had

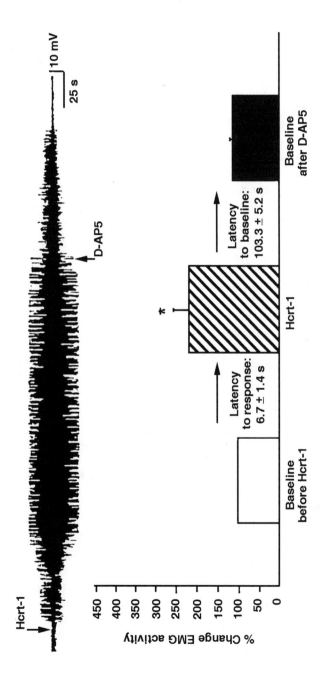

Figure 5   Interactions of Hcrt with glutamate after microinjection of Hcrt into motor nuclei. Hcrt microinjections potently excited trigeminal motoneurons, but this effect was completely blocked by the glutamate NMDA receptor antagonist AP-5. Glutamate is a major mediator of Hcrt effects in motor nuclei and in other regions of the brain. (From Peever et al. 2003)

created narcoleptic mice that were experiencing either attacks of sleep or cataplexy (Chemelli et al. 1999). At the same time, Lin et al. (1999) were investigating the genetics of canine narcolepsy. A genetic form of canine narcolepsy had been described in Doberman pinschers and Labrador retrievers (Baker & Dement 1985), and these dogs were bred and studied (Mitler et al. 1976; Siegel et al. 1991, 1999). Lin et al. found that this form of canine narcolepsy was caused by a mutation in the gene for Hcrt receptor-2.

Narcolepsy is a chronic disorder characterized by two types of symptoms (Siegel 1999, 2000a). The most debilitating symptom is usually chronic, overwhelming sleepiness. A narcoleptic person goes through the day as sleepy as a nonnarcoleptic person who has not slept for two or more days. The result is sleep in inappropriate and embarrassing situations and an inability to perform up to the individual's intellectual capacity due to the difficulty of sustaining alertness. Excessive daytime sleepiness also occurs in sleep apnea and other disorders and therefore is not by itself diagnostic of narcolepsy. A second symptom experienced by most narcoleptics is loss of muscle tone during waking, as is seen in cataplexy or sleep paralysis. Cataplexy is most commonly triggered by the patient's laughter, but can also be triggered by other sudden onset emotions such as anger, embarrassment, or by athletic exertion, or it may have no identified cause. During cataplexy, although unable to move to a greater or lesser extent, the patient is alert, aware of the environment, and understands and remembers what is going on. A similar loss of muscle tone called sleep paralysis frequently occurs at sleep onset or offset in narcoleptics, with awareness of the environment maintained during periods of motor paralysis lasting from seconds to minutes. Many narcoleptics also have hypnagogic hallucinations, often frightening hallucinations that incorporate elements of the environment. Narcoleptics have a very short sleep latency and tend to transition quickly from waking into REM sleep. Normal individuals who have been sleep deprived or nonnarcoleptics with other forms of sleep pathology can have equally short sleep latencies, but unlike narcoleptics they generally pass through an initial non-REM sleep period that lasts at least 5 minutes, at sleep onset. The hypnagogic hallucinations, cataplexy, sleep paralysis, and short REM sleep latency of narcoleptics have been explained as an "escape" of REM sleep components into the waking state, since in REM sleep, the skeletal motoneurons are inhibited and hallucinatory mentation is the norm. Narcolepsy is not uncommon, affecting more than 1 in 2000 individuals, an incidence approximately one half to one third that of multiple sclerosis and about one fourth that of Parkinson's disease.

The discoveries that mutations in the *preprohypocretin* or Hcrt receptor genes can cause narcolepsy in animals suggested that human narcolepsy might be caused by a similar pathology of the Hcrt system. However, human narcolepsy is clearly not genetically determined in the way that canine genetic narcolepsy is. Most human narcoleptics do not have parents or siblings with diagnosed narcolepsy, and most pairs of identical twins in which narcolepsy has been identified in at least one twin are discordant for the disease (Aldrich 1998, Guilleminault & Anognos 2000, Hublin et al. 1994). However, Honda and colleagues (Honda et al. 1984) showed that 85% to 95% of human narcoleptics share a particular human leucocytic antigen (HLA) genotype that is found in about 25% of the overall population. Subsequent work determined that this HLA type is DQB1*0602 (Olerup et al. 1990). The proteins encoded by genes in the HLA region are involved in presenting antigens to the immune system, and many autoimmune disorders are linked to one or more HLA haplotypes. Because of the strong HLA linkage present in narcolepsy, it was suspected that this disorder might also be an autoimmune disease. In narcoleptic dogs, we have seen degenerative changes in forebrain limbic regions, including many of the major projection regions of Hcrt neurons, which suggests that a degenerative process contributes to canine genetic narcolepsy (Siegel et al. 1999). However, no evidence of abnormal immune function had been detected in human narcoleptics and no target for immunological attack had been identified at the time we began our studies. Could the Hcrt neurons be targeted in narcoleptic humans?

Because narcolepsy is never a direct cause of death, brain tissue from human narcoleptics is rarely saved for investigation. Thannickal et al. (2000) had acquired several brains of human narcoleptics from Dr. Michael Aldrich and other sources, but they had been in fixative for 4 to 12 years. Thannickal et al. (2000) first tested immunohistochemical staining techniques on control tissue that had been in fix for equally long periods, and discovered that Hcrt neurons could not be stained in this "overfixed" tissue by conventional means, although they could easily be stained in freshly fixed human brains. Using antigen retrieval techniques, the overfixed tissue was stained, and it was discovered that narcoleptics had lost 85% to 95% of their Hcrt neurons (Figure 1). Surviving Hcrt cells were found in all narcoleptics, which suggests that residual Hcrt function may modulate symptoms and that strategies to maximize the impact of surviving Hcrt cells could be useful in therapies for narcolepsy. A further finding was glial proliferation (gliosis) in brain regions that normally contain Hcrt cells and in regions to which Hcrt neurons projected. Glial cells proliferate during inflammatory reactions, which suggests that such a reaction may have accompanied cell loss. A paper by Peyron et al. published at the same time also reported Hcrt depletion in narcolepsy (Peyron et al. 2000). Significant differences between the two papers were Peyron et al.'s report of no gliosis, no surviving Hcrt cells in narcoleptics, and much lower numbers of Hcrt cells in normal humans (20,000 versus the 70,000 calculated by Thannickal et al.). These discrepancies remain to be resolved, but they may be due to differences in the sensitivities of the Hcrt identification and glial staining techniques used. In work done subsequent to their initial publication, Thannickal et al. stained relatively fresh narcoleptic and normal tissue, and continued to see surviving Hcrt cells in all narcoleptic brains, a consistent pattern of gliosis in narcoleptics, and a count of 60,000 to 80,000 Hcrt neurons in normal human brains (Thannickal et al. 2000, 2003).

An examination of the pattern of gliosis in narcoleptics revealed that it is not confined to regions normally containing Hcrt cell somas, but rather is present throughout the projection fields of Hcrt axons. The density of gliosis is most strongly correlated with the density of Hcrt receptor-2, rather than the density of Hcrt receptor-1 or the density of Hcrt cell somas. This finding suggests that an inflammatory process accompanies Hcrt cell loss and that this process is intensified in regions with Hcrt receptor-2, perhaps with retrograde loss of the cell somas. The identity of an antigen, if any, against which an autoimmune response might be triggered in human narcolepsy remains unknown (Thannickal et al. 2003).

Further confirmation that Hcrt cell loss is sufficient to cause narcolepsy came from work with mice and rats. Hara and colleagues (Hara et al. 2001) created a transgenic mouse that carried a cytotoxic "ataxin-3" gene fragment driven by a functional *preprohypocretin* promoter. These animals lost all identifiable Hcrt cells postnatally and developed symptoms of narcolepsy in parallel with cell loss. Gerashchenko et al. (2001) injected Hcrt linked to the toxin saporin into Hcrt cell regions. The toxin caused the death of Hcrt cells and adjacent cells containing the Hcrt receptor. It also caused symptoms of sleepiness resembling narcolepsy, but not cataplexy.

The combination of direct excitatory and indirect inhibitory effects seen in dorsal raphe, locus coeruleus, and other regions (Figure 3) may underlie the dynamic aspects of the deficits caused by Hcrt cell loss. Narcolepsy is characterized by an instability of motor control and sleep-waking states. Narcoleptics inappropriately switch from having normal muscle tone to being partially or completely atonic when strong emotions are triggered. Conversely, their normal suppression of muscle tone in REM sleep tends to be interrupted by periods without muscle tone suppression (termed REM sleep behavior disorder) (Schenck & Mahowald 1992). Their waking rapidly switches into sleep, but they are unable to sleep for long periods because their non-REM sleep is frequently interrupted by waking (Guilleminault & Anognos 2000; Siegel 1999, 2000a,b; Thannickal et al. 2000). I hypothesize that the simultaneous inhibition and excitation mediated by Hcrt cells stabilizes control of the membranes of postsynaptic sleep- and motor-controlling neurons, in a way that would be impossible with only excitation or inhibition. "Push-pull" control produces stability. This is analogous to holding a large object with two hands rather than one. The loss of this mechanism with Hcrt cell death creates instability. Such instability in muscle tone and arousal control systems leads to the instability of motor and sleep-wake state control that characterizes narcolepsy.

The link between Hcrt and narcolepsy led to research into the possible role of Hcrt in other neurological disorders. A quick way of detecting Hcrt abnormalities is by measuring Hcrt levels in the cerebrospinal fluid; these levels were found to be undetectably low in human narcolepsy (Nishino et al. 2000). This abnormality seems relatively specific to narcolepsy, or to damage to the hypothalamic region in which the Hcrt cells are located. No obvious Hcrt abnormality was found in Alzheimer's disease (Thannickal et al. 2000), despite the massive brain degeneration seen in this disorder, or in Parkinson's disease (Ripley et al. 2001). Hcrt levels in schizophrenics did not differ from those in controls (Nishino et al. 2002). Levels in some cases of Guillain-Barré syndrome, a syndrome in which the hypothalamus can be damaged, were abnormally low (Ripley et al. 2001), as they are in myotonic dystrophy (Martinez-Rodriguez et al. 2003). In restless legs syndrome, whose sufferers cannot tolerate long periods of quiescence and must move to relieve uncomfortable sensations in their legs, Hcrt levels are elevated (Allen et al. 2002).

NORMAL BEHAVIORAL ROLE OF HCRT

The demonstrated link between the Hcrt system and the sleep disorder narcolepsy suggests that the release of Hcrt varies with sleep-waking state, but what is the nature of this variation? The direct excitatory connections with norepinephrine, serotonin, and histamine neurons suggest that Hcrt may drive these neurons and have the same sleep cycle discharge pattern shown by these cells groups. These three cell groups are all maximally active in active waking, decrease discharge in quiet waking, decrease discharge further in slow wave sleep, and are completely inactive in REM sleep (Siegel 2000b). On the other hand, Hcrt cells also strongly innervate and excite forebrain and brainstem cholinergic cells. These cholinergic cells are maximally active in waking, decrease discharge in quiet waking and non-REM sleep, but increase discharge in REM sleep to rates equal to or exceeding those in active waking (Siegel 2000b). Finally, dopaminergic cells are also strongly driven by Hcrt and have little or no change in activity over the sleep cycle (Shouse et al. 2000, Miller et al. 1983). Thus, the pattern of Hcrt release over the sleep cycle cannot easily be predicted by the activity of Hcrt target cell populations, all of which receive a variety of non-Hcrt inputs as well.

An initial recording study found cells in the Hcrt cell region of the rat hypothalamus with a variety of sleep cycle discharge patterns. Some were active in waking and off in REM sleep, others were active in both waking and REM sleep, and still others showed no significant change in discharge across the sleep cycle (Alam et al. 2002). However, this study did not determine which, if any, of these neuronal types contained Hcrt. The anatomical clustering of Hcrt cells, their generally similar and widespread projections, and their physiological uniformity (Li et al. 2002) suggest that the Hcrt cell population, like other widely projecting cell groups (Siegel 2000b), might show a relatively uniform pattern of sleep cycle discharge. But what is their discharge profile?

This question was addressed by Kiyashchenko et al. (2002) by using in vivo microdialysis in conjunction with the development of an extremely sensitive assay that allowed measurement of Hcrt in the 10 μl fluid samples that could be collected within 5-minute sleep periods (Kiyashchenko et al. 2002). The results are shown in Figure 6. It was discovered that Hcrt levels were at approximately equal levels in active waking and REM sleep and were greatly reduced in non-REM sleep and quiet waking. Furthermore, Hcrt levels were significantly and substantially higher in active waking than in alert, quiet waking.

The roles of movement, sleep, and feeding variables in Hcrt release were compared (Wu et al. 2002b). The name "orexin" refers to the hypothesized role of Hcrt in inducing food consumption. Much of the behavioral Hcrt literature has dealt with the effects of Hcrt infusion on feeding. However, the infusion of very large amounts of Hcrt into the lateral hypothalamus, the hypothalamic region known to

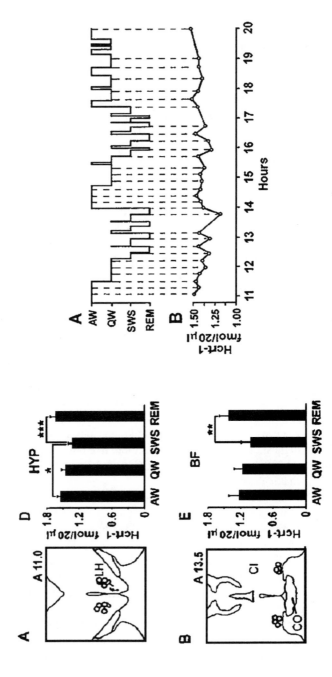

Figure 6   Sleep cycle release of Hcrt. (*Left*) Hcrt release is maximal in active waking and REM sleep, states with high levels of activity in central motor systems, and is significantly lower in non-REM sleep. Regions that were sampled are indicated in the drawing. CI, internal capsule; HYP, lateral hypothalamus; BF, basal forebrain. (*Right*) Time course of Hcrt release in successive 5-minute Hcrt samples across the sleep cycle. Maximal values are seen in waking and REM sleep. (From Kiyashchenko et al. 2002)

be involved in feeding, might induce changes in appetite by exciting lateral hypothalamic cells that would not normally be exposed to such high levels of Hcrt. In a similar manner, injection of Hcrt into the brain's ventricles might cause an abnormal pattern of excitation that would increase food intake, even if Hcrt normally had little role in food intake regulation. Therefore, we attempted to determine the effects of food deprivation and food intake on Hcrt *release* in normal dogs, thus taking advantage of the relative ease in larger animals of extracting sufficient quantities of cerebrospinal fluid for accurate Hcrt assay. It was found that food deprivation for as long as 48 hours did not increase Hcrt levels (Figure 7, *top*). Feeding at the end of this period also did not produce any change in Hcrt levels.

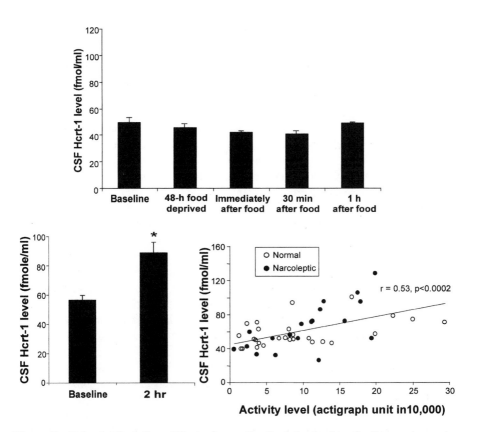

Figure 7   Behavioral studies of Hcrt release after food deprivation, feeding, and exercise. (*Top*) Effect of 48-hour food deprivation, feeding, and exercise on Hcrt release in normal dogs. In contrast to the changes in other putative feeding-related peptides, food deprivation does not increase Hcrt levels in cerebrospinal fluid. Feeding after deprivation also does not alter Hcrt levels. (*Bottom left*) Two-hour period of exercise produces marked increase in Hcrt levels. (*Bottom right*) Strong positive correlation between motor activity during exercise as measured by actigraph and levels of Hcrt in cerebrospinal fluid. (From Wu et al. 2002b)

This lack of variation in release in relation to feeding and food deprivation contrasts with the changes shown by other peptides implicated in feeding (reviewed in Wu et al. 2002b).

The hypothesis that an essential, underlying correlate of Hcrt release is motor activity can explain the reported effects of Hcrt system manipulation on food intake. Although injection of high levels of Hcrt directly into the hypothalamus has been reported to induce food consumption in some studies, other studies have reported that although 24-hour infusion increased feeding during the normally inactive daytime period, it had no effect on overall food consumption (Kotz et al. 2002, Yamanaka et al. 1999). The effects of Hcrt administration on food consumption are weak compared to those of neuropeptide Y, an established feeding-related peptide (Edwards et al. 1999, Ida et al. 1999). Hcrt infusion produces increased motor activity, even in the absence of food intake (Ida et al. 1999; John et al. 2000, 2003; Yamanaka et al. 2003) but, as discussed above, food intake or food deprivation in the absence of increased movement does not produce any increase in Hcrt level (Wu et al. 2002b). Hcrt may also increase overall metabolic rate to support motor activity (Lubkin & Stricker-Krongrad 1998). Increased body temperature is a well-known correlate of increased motor activity.

Hcrt knockout animals, which do not produce the Hcrt peptides, are not emaciated, contrary to what would be predicted by the Hcrt-feeding hypothesis. Although they eat somewhat less, their weight is normal. This is consistent with the idea that they are moving less and hence consuming less energy. Ataxin mutant animals, which lose their Hcrt cells postnatally, eat *less* than normal mice but become extremely obese (Hara et al. 2001). Likewise, human narcoleptics, who have lost their Hcrt cells, eat less than control groups yet have a significantly higher body mass index (Schuld et al. 2000). The increased body weight of human narcoleptics and ataxin mutants may be due to the loss of the Hcrt cells themselves, as compared to the loss of the ability of these cells to generate the peptides in Hcrt "knockout" animals. Alternatively, the differences between the ataxin mutant and Hcrt knockout animals may be a consequence of the differing genetic backgrounds of the animals. The relatively small weight elevation seen in human narcoleptics may be attributable to a reduction in motor activity consequent to the loss of Hcrt activation of motor systems.

We next deprived dogs of sleep for 24 hours by walking them when they became inactive. This produced a near doubling of Hcrt levels in their cerebrospinal fluid. Because this deprivation technique induced greater levels of physical activity, we also studied the effect of activity alone. We found that as little as 2 hours of active waking produced a doubling of Hcrt levels relative to levels in the same dogs during quiet waking periods (Figure 7, *lower left*). The levels of Hcrt seen in individual dogs were highly correlated with their levels of motor activity as measured with activity monitors (Figure 7, *lower right*). A similar conclusion was reached in a study in which immunoreactivity for Fos (a protein generated by an "immediate early" gene) was used as a measure of Hcrt cell activity (Torterolo et al. 2003).

One likely mediator of the effects of Hcrt on muscle tone is the locus coeruleus. Hcrt neurons strongly innervate the locus coeruleus (Nambu et al. 1999, Peyron

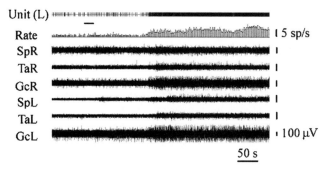

Figure 8   Effect of Hcrt microinjection adjacent to the locus coeruleus. This figure shows that Hcrt microinjection into the locus coeruleus raises muscle tone ipsilateral to the injection. The loss of this excitatory effect of Hcrt contributes to cataplexy, the sudden loss of muscle tone experienced by most narcoleptics. Locus coeruleus activity ceases during cataplexy (Wu et al. 1999). SpR, SpL: electromyogram (EMG) of muscle splenius (right and left side); TaR, TaL: EMG of tibialis anterior muscle (right and left side); GcR, GcL: EMG of gastrocnemius muscle (right and left side). (From Kiyashchenko et al. 2001)

et al. 1998). Brainstem-induced muscle tone suppression is linked to a cessation of norepinephrine release (Lai et al. 2001). Cessation of activity in noradrenergic cells of the locus coeruleus precedes and accompanies cataplexy in narcoleptic dogs (Wu et al. 1999). Microinjection of Hcrt into the locus coeruleus and certain other brain regions increases muscle tone (Figure 8) (Kiyashchenko et al. 2001, Lai et al. 2001, Mileykovskiy et al. 2002). These findings fit with anatomical studies that have identified the noradrenergic locus coeruleus as the largest extrahypothalamic projection of the Hcrt system (Peyron et al. 1998) and with our behavioral studies. The loss of this and other motor facilitatory Hcrt projections in narcoleptics can explain the loss of muscle tone in cataplexy and sleep paralysis. Sudden, strong emotions can produce muscle weakness in normal individuals. We get "weak in the knees" when we hear bad news. We "double over with laughter" when we hear or tell a good joke. But normal individuals do not fall to the ground at these times. Presumably, this is because, along with the weakness induced by circuits activated during these emotions, there is a counteracting activation of systems that excite motor systems. Hcrt is one of these systems. In its absence, as in narcolepsy, these same emotions can result in a complete loss of muscle tone for periods of seconds to minutes.

CONCLUSIONS

We have found that a major correlate of Hcrt release in waking is motor activity. The high level of release of Hcrt in REM sleep can also be seen as a correlate of motor activation, because REM sleep is a state in which central motor systems are highly active (Siegel 1979, Siegel & Tomaszewski 1983, Siegel et al. 1983), even though the expression of this internal motor activity is blocked at the motoneuron level (Chase & Morales 2000, Kodama et al. 2003, Lai et al. 2001, Wu et al. 1999).

When animals are motorically active, they must be alert in order to execute movements properly, carry out consummatory acts, and integrate sensory inputs. Thus, an activation of sensory and related forebrain cognitive systems is necessary during periods of activity.

Our finding that Hcrt levels in alert, immobile waking are not significantly higher than the levels seen in non-REM sleep argues against a major role for Hcrt in nonmotor-associated attentional processes in animals. Given the explanatory power of the motor activity hypothesis, it becomes incumbent upon those who hypothesize a relation to physiological changes independent of motor activity to quantify or control for the motor activity elicited by their experimental manipulations.

Current data do not indicate the precise nature of the role of Hcrt in motor activity. However, clues to the likely dynamics of Hcrt release can be derived from the symptoms seen in hypocretin-deficient or hypocretin-receptor mutant animals and humans (i.e., narcoleptics). As pointed out above, narcoleptics have two main symptoms, excessive sleepiness and cataplexy. The excessive sleepiness is a tonic symptom, expressed throughout the day, whereas cataplexy is expressed episodically.

A tonic role of Hcrt is hypothesized to be the activation of monoaminergic, cholinergic, and amino acid neurotransmitter systems during periods of maintained muscle tone. The release of Hcrt at these times is hypothesized to occur continuously, through the spontaneous discharge of these cells. In REM sleep, the tonic effects of Hcrt on nonadrenergic and serotonergic cell groups are blocked by indirect Hcrt facilitation of GABA release onto these same cells (Kiyashchenko et al. 2002). In waking, the tonic activity of Hcrt cells extends the duration of waking periods, blocking the onset of sleep.

Phasic release of Hcrt is hypothesized to counter the effects of emotion on muscle tone. Sudden strong emotions of certain types may produce a disfacilitation of motoneurons as a result of the inactivation of monoaminergic and other brainstem cell groups with descending projections to motoneurons. This disfacilitation could be combined with active inhibition mediated by glycine and GABA release onto motoneurons.

In the normal animal, this disfacilitation/inhibition could be countered by a burst of Hcrt activity, facilitating the activity of motoneurons and thereby maintaining muscle tone. Even in normal animals, sudden, very strong emotions will still reveal a motor inhibition, as in the weakness produced by strong laughter or anger. However, the counteracting effect of Hcrt would prevent any complete loss of muscle tone.

Cataplexy does not occur with equal frequency during all types of movements. Rather, it accompanies particular kinds of emotionally charged behaviors. In narcoleptic dogs, the consummatory behavior required to consume desirable, novel food triggers cataplexy, while consumption of the food that is ordinarily available does not. Vigorous play with the narcoleptic dog, for example by pulling on a towel the dog is holding in its mouth, throwing a toy to the dog, and other such pleasurable, motorically engaging activities, will also trigger cataplexy. In contrast, startling the animal or bringing it into an unfamiliar room will not trigger cataplexy, although the situation is highly alerting. In humans, as mentioned above, laughter, anger, or other sudden-onset emotions are the typical triggers of cataplexy. On the other hand, high levels of attention or even pain that is highly alerting are not typical triggers. These observations suggest that Hcrt release is linked to the sudden onset of certain kinds of emotions whose precise quality undoubtedly varies among species just as it does to a much lesser extent among patients with narcolepsy.

In summary, it is hypothesized that Hcrt cells maintain some tonic discharge during periods of waking motor activity. This discharge would be phasically increased during the sorts of sudden, strong emotions that trigger cataplexy and this release would both act to maintain muscle tone phasically and contribute to the tonic maintenance of alertness. The targets of Hcrt release, as indicated in Figure 3 (see color insert), are systems related to motor facilitation and systems related to forebrain alerting. Thus, Hcrt release would act to coordinate motor activity and arousal.

This extrapolation from the phenomena of excessive sleepiness and cataplexy in narcoleptic animals to the normal function of Hcrt release needs to be tested in normal animals. This can best be done by characterizing the activity pattern of identified Hcrt neurons during a range of behaviors.

Our work in dogs, in which Hcrt administration has been shown to reverse the deficits of narcolepsy (John et al. 2000), offers hope that Hcrt administration will be an effective treatment for this disorder. Manipulation of the Hcrt system may also be useful in other behavioral disorders.

ACKNOWLEDGMENTS

Supported by the Medical Research Service of the Department of Veterans Affairs, NS14610, NS64109, MH64109, and HL060246.

The *Annual Review of Psychology* is online at http://psych.annualreviews.org

LITERATURE CITED

Abrahamson EE, Moore RY. 2001. The posterior hypothalamic area: chemoarchitecture and afferent connections. *Brain Res.* 889:1–22

Alam MN, Gong H, Alam T, Jaganath R, McGinty D, Szymusiak R. 2002. Sleep-waking discharge patterns of neurons recorded in the rat perifornical lateral hypothalamic area. *J. Physiol.* 538:619–31

Aldrich MS. 1998. Diagnostic aspects of narcolepsy. *Neurology* 50:S2–7

Allen RP, Mignot E, Ripley B, Nishino S,

Earley CJ. 2002. Increased CSF hypocretin-1 (orexin-A) in restless legs syndrome. *Neurology* 59:639–41

Aston-Jones G, Rajkowski J, Kubiak P, Alexinsky T. 1994. Locus coeruleus neurons in monkey are selectively activated by attended cues in a vigilance task. *J. Neurosci.* 14:4467–80

Baker TL, Dement WC. 1985. Canine narcolepsy-cataplexy syndrome: evidence for an inherited monoaminergic-cholinergic imbalance. In *Brain Mechanisms of Sleep*, ed. DJ McGinty, R Drucker-Colin, A Morrison, PL Parmeggiani, pp. 199–234. New York: Raven

Bayer L, Eggermann E, Saint-Mleux B, Machard D, Jones BE, et al. 2002. Selective action of orexin (hypocretin) on nonspecific thalamocortical projection neurons. *J. Neurosci.* 22:7835–39

Bayer L, Eggermann E, Serafin M, Saint-Mleux B, Machard D, et al. 2001. Orexins (hypocretins) directly excite tuberomammillary neurons. *Eur. J. Neurosci.* 14:1571–75

Bourgin P, Huitron-Resendiz S, Spier AD, Fabre V, Morte B, et al. 2000. Hypocretin-1 modulates rapid eye movement sleep through activation of locus coeruleus neurons. *J. Neurosci.* 20:7760–65

Burlet S, Tyler CJ, Leonard CS. 2002. Direct and indirect excitation of laterodorsal tegmental neurons by hypocretin/orexin peptides: implications for wakefulness and narcolepsy. *J. Neurosci.* 22:2862–72

Caillol M, Aioun J, Baly C, Persuy MA, Salesse R. 2003. Localization of orexins and their receptors in the rat olfactory system: possible modulation of olfactory perception by a neuropeptide synthetized centrally or locally. *Brain Res.* 960:48–61

Chase MH, Morales FR. 2000. Control of motoneurons during sleep. See Kryger et al. 2000, pp. 155–68

Chemelli RM, Willie JT, Sinton C, Elmquist J, Scammell T, et al. 1999. Narcolepsy in *orexin* knockout mice: molecular genetics of sleep regulation. *Cell* 98:437–51

Chou TC, Lee CE, Lu J, Elmquist JK, Hara J,

et al. 2001. Orexin (hypocretin) neurons contain dynorphin. *J. Neurosci.* 21:RC168

Ciriello J, Rosas-Arellano MP, Solano-Flores LP, de Oliveira CV. 2003. Identification of neurons containing orexin-B (hypocretin-2) immunoreactivity in limbic structures. *Brain Res.* 967:123–31

Date Y, Mondal MS, Matsukura S, Ueta Y, Yamashita H, et al. 2000. Distribution of orexin/hypocretin in the rat median eminence and pituitary. *Brain Res. Mol. Brain Res.* 76:1–6

Dehaene S, Changeux JP. 2000. Reward-dependent learning in neuronal networks for planning and decision making. *Prog. Brain Res.* 126:217–29

De Lecea L, Kilduff T, Peyron C, Gao XB, Foye PE, et al. 1998. The hypocretins: hypothalamus-specific peptides with neuroexcitatory activity. *Proc. Natl. Acad. Sci. USA* 95:322–27

Douglass AB, Shipley JE, Haines RF, Scholten RC. 1993. Schizophrenia, narcolepsy, and HLA-DR15, DQ6. *Biol. Psychiatry* 34:773–80

Dun NJ, Le Dun S, Chen CT, Hwang LL, Kwok EH, Chang JK. 2000. Orexins: a role in medullary sympathetic outflow. *Regul. Pept.* 96:65–70

Edwards CM, Abusnana S, Sunter D, Murphy KG, Ghatei MA, Bloom SR. 1999. The effect of the orexins on food intake: comparison with neuropeptide Y, melanin-concentrating hormone and galanin. *J. Endocrinol.* 160:R7–12

Eggermann E, Serafin M, Bayer L, Machard D, Saint-Mleux B, et al. 2003. Orexins/hypocretins excite basal forebrain cholinergic neurones. *Neuroscience* 108:177–81

Eriksson KS, Sergeeva O, Brown RE, Haas HL. 2001. Orexin/hypocretin excites the histaminergic neurons of the tuberomammillary nucleus. *J. Neurosci.* 21:9273–79

Follwell MJ, Ferguson AV. 2002. Cellular mechanisms of orexin actions on paraventricular nucleus neurones in rat hypothalamus. *J. Physiol.* 545:855–67

Fung SJ, Yamuy J, Sampogna S, Morales FR,

Chase MH. 2001. Hypocretin (orexin) input to trigeminal and hypoglossal motoneurons in the cat: a double-labeling immunohistochemical study. *Brain Res.* 903:257–62

Gerashchenko D, Kohls MD, Greco M, Waleh NS, Salin-Pascual R, et al. 2001. Hypocretin-2-saporin lesions of the lateral hypothalamus produce narcoleptic-like sleep behavior in the rat. *J. Neurosci.* 21:7273–83

Grudt TJ, van den Pol AN, Perl ER. 2002. Hypocretin-2 (orexin-B) modulation of superficial dorsal horn activity in rat. *J. Physiol.* 538:517–25

Guilleminault C, Anognos A. 2000. Narcolepsy. See Kryger et al. 2000, pp. 676–86

Hagan JJ, Leslie RA, Patel S, Evans ML, Wattam TA, et al. 1999. Orexin A activates locus coeruleus cell firing and increases arousal in the rat. *Proc. Natl. Acad. Sci. USA* 96:10911–16

Hara J, Beuckmann CT, Nambu T, Willie JT, Chemelli RM, et al. 2001. Genetic ablation of orexin neurons in mice results in narcolepsy, hypophagia, and obesity. *Neuron* 30:345–54

Honda Y, Doi Y, Juji T, Satake M. 1984. Narcolepsy and HLA: positive DR2 as a prerequisite for the development of narcolepsy. *Folia Psychiatr. Neurol Jpn.* 38:360

Horvath TL, Peyron C, Diano S, Ivanov A, Aston-Jones G, et al. 1999. Hypocretin (orexin) activation and synaptic innervation of the locus coeruleus noradrenergic system. *J. Comp. Neurol.* 415:145–59

Huang ZL, Qu WM, Li WD, Mochizuki T, Eguchi N, et al. 2001. Arousal effect of orexin A depends on activation of the histaminergic system. *Proc. Natl. Acad. Sci. USA* 98:9965–70

Hublin C, Kaprio J, Partinen M, Koskenvuo M, Heikkila K, et al. 1994. The prevalence of narcolepsy: an epidemiological study of the Finnish twin cohort. *Ann. Neurol.* 35:709–16

Ida T, Nakahara K, Katayama T, Murakami N, Nakazato M. 1999. Effect of lateral cerebroventricular injection of the appetite-stimulating neuropeptide, orexin and neuropeptide Y, on the various behavioral activities of rats. *Brain Res.* 821:526–29

Ivanov A, Aston-Jones G. 2000. Hypocretin/orexin depolarizes and decreases potassium conductance in locus coeruleus neurons. *NeuroReport* 11:1755–58

Jacobs BL. 1987. Brain monoaminergic unit activity in behaving animals. In *Progress in Psychobiology and Physiological Psychology*, ed. AN Epstein, AR Morrison, pp. 171–206. New York: Academic

Jacobs BL. 1991. Serotonin and behavior: emphasis on motor control. *J. Clin. Psychiatry* 52(Suppl.):17–23

John J, Wu MF, Kodama T, Siegel JM. 2003. Intravenously administered hypocretin-1 alters brain amino acid release: an *in vivo* microdialysis study in rats. *J. Physiol.* 548.2:557–62

John J, Wu MF, Kodama T, Siegel JM. 2001. Hypocretin-1 (orexin-A) produced changes in glutamate and GABA release: an *in vivo* microdialysis study. *Sleep* 24:A20

John J, Wu MF, Siegel JM. 2000. Systemic administration of hypocretin-1 reduces cataplexy and normalizes sleep and waking durations in narcoleptic dogs. *Sleep Res.* 3:23–28. http://www.sro.org/2000/John/23/

Johren O, Neidert SJ, Kummer M, Dendorfer A, Dominiak P. 2001. Prepro-orexin and orexin receptor mRNAs are differentially expressed in peripheral tissues of male and female rats. *Endocrinology* 142:3324–31

Jones BE. 2000. Basic mechanisms of sleep-wake states. See Kryger et al. 2000, pp. 134–54

Kirchgessner AL. 2002. Orexins in the brain-gut axis. *Endocr. Rev.* 23:1–15

Kiyashchenko LI, Mileykovskiy BY, Lai YY, Siegel JM. 2001. Increased and decreased muscle tone with orexin (hypocretin) microinjections in the locus coeruleus and pontine inhibitory area. *J. Neurophysiol.* 85:2008–16

Kiyashchenko LI, Mileykovskiy BY, Maidment N, Lam HA, Wu MF, et al. 2002. Release of hypocretin (orexin) during waking and sleep states. *J. Neurosci.* 22:5282–86

Kodama T, Kimura M. 2002. Arousal effects of orexin-A correlate with GLU release from the locus coeruleus in rats. *Peptides* 23:1673–81

Kodama T, Lai YY, Siegel JM. 2003. Changes in inhibitory amino acid release linked to pontine-induced atonia: an in vivo microdialysis study. *J. Neurosci.* 23:1548–54

Korotkova TM, Sergeeva OA, Eriksson KS, Haas HL, Brown RE. 2003. Excitation of ventral tegmental area dopaminergic and nondopaminergic neurons by orexins/hypocretins. *J. Neurosci.* 23:7–11

Kotz CM, Teske JA, Levine JA, Wang C. 2002. Feeding and activity induced by orexin A in the lateral hypothalamus in rats. *Regul. Pept.* 104:27–32

Kryger MH, Roth T, Dement WC, eds. 2000. *Principles and Practice of Sleep Medicine.* Philadelphia: Saunders

Lai YY, Kodama T, Siegel JM. 2001. Changes in monoamine release in the ventral horn and hypoglossal nucleus linked to pontine inhibition of muscle tone: an in vivo microdialysis study. *J. Neurosci.* 21:7384–91

Lai YY, Kodama T, Siegel JM. 2001. Changes in monoamine release in the ventral horn and hypoglossal nucleus linked to pontine inhibition of muscle tone: an in vivo microdialysis study. *J. Neurosci.* 21:7384–91

Levitt DR, Teitelbaum P. 1975. Somnolence, akinesia, and sensory activation of motivated behavior in the lateral hypothalamic syndrome. *Proc. Natl. Acad. Sci. USA* 72:2819–23

Li Y, Gao XB, Sakurai T, van den Pol AN. 2002. Hypocretin/orexin excites hypocretin neurons via a local glutamate neuron-A potential mechanism for orchestrating the hypothalamic arousal system. *Neuron* 36:1169–81

Lin JS, Sakai K, Vanni-Mercier G, Jouvet M. 1989. A critical role of the posterior hypothalamus in the mechanisms of wakefulness determined by microinjection of muscimol in freely moving cats. *Brain Res.* 479:225–40

Lin L, Faraco J, Li R, Kadotani H, Rogers W, et al. 1999. The REM sleep disorder canine narcolepsy is caused by a mutation in the hypocretin (orexin) receptor gene. *Cell* 98:365–76

Liu RJ, van den Pol AN, Aghajanian GK. 2002. Hypocretins (orexins) regulate serotonin neurons in the dorsal raphe nucleus by excitatory direct and inhibitory indirect actions. *J. Neurosci.* 22:9453–64

Lubkin M, Stricker-Krongrad A. 1998. Independent feeding and metabolic actions of orexins in mice. *Biochem. Biophys. Res. Commun.* 253:241–45

Marcus JN, Aschkenasi CJ, Lee CE, Chemelli RM, Saper CB, et al. 2001. Differential expression of orexin receptors 1 and 2 in the rat brain. *J. Comp. Neurol.* 435:6–25

Martin G, Fabre V, Siggins GR, De Lecea L. 2002. Interaction of the hypocretins with neurotransmitters in the nucleus accumbens. *Regul. Pept.* 104:111–17

Martinez-Rodriguez JE, Lin L, Iranzo A, Genis D, Marti MJ, et al. 2003. Decreased hypocretin-1 (orexin-A) levels in the cerebrospinal fluid of patients with myotonic dystrophy and excessive daytime sleepiness. *Sleep* 26:287–90

Mileykovskiy BY, Kiyashchenko LI, Siegel JM. 2002. Muscle tone facilitation and inhibition after orexin-a (hypocretin-1) microinjections into the medial medulla. *J. Neurophysiol.* 87:2480–89

Miller JD, Farber J, Gatz P, Roffwarg H, German DC. 1983. Activity of mesencephalic dopamine and non-dopamine neurons across stages of sleep and waking in the rat. *Brain Res.* 273:133–41

Mitler MM, Soave O, Dement WC. 1976. Narcolepsy in seven dogs. *J. Am. Vet. Med. Assoc.* 168:1036–38

Nakamura T, Uramura K, Nambu T, Yada T, Goto K, et al. 2000. Orexin-induced hyperlocomotion and stereotypy are mediated by the dopaminergic system. *Brain Res.* 873:181–87

Nambu T, Sakurai T, Mizukami K, Hosoya Y, Yanagisawa M, Goto K. 1999. Distribution of orexin neurons in the adult rat brain. *Brain Res.* 827:243–60

Nishino S, Fujiki N, Ripley B, Sakurai E, Kato

M, et al. 2001. Decreased brain histamine content in hypocretin/orexin receptor-2 mutated narcoleptic dogs. *Neurosci. Lett.* 3(3):125–28

Nishino S, Ripley B, Mignot E, Benson KL, Zarcone VP. 2002. CSF hypocretin-1 levels in schizophrenics and controls: relationship to sleep architecture. *Psychiatry Res.* 110:1–7

Nishino S, Ripley B, Overeem S, Lammers GJ, Mignot E. 2000. Hypocretin (orexin) deficiency in human narcolepsy. *Lancet* 355:39–41

Nishino SS, Sakurai E, Nevisimalova S, Vankova J, Yoshida Y, et al. 2002. CSF histamine content is decreased in hypocretin-deficient human narcolepsy. *Sleep* 25:A476

Nitz D, Siegel JM. 1997a. GABA release in the dorsal raphe nucleus: role in the control of REM sleep. *Am. J. Physiol. Regul. Integr. Comp. Physiol.* 273:R451–55

Nitz D, Siegel JM. 1997b. GABA release in the cat locus coeruleus as a function of the sleep/wake state. *Neuroscience* 78:795–801

Olerup O, Schaffer M, Hillert J, Sachs C. 1990. The narcolepsy-associated DRw15, DQw6, Dw2 haplotype has no unique HLA-DQA or -DQB restriction fragments and does not extend to the HLA-DP subregion. *Immunogenetics* 32:41–44

Passouant P. 1976. The history of narcolepsy. In *Narcolepsy*, ed. C Guilleminault, WC Dement, P Passouant, pp. 3–14. New York: Spectrum

Peever JH, Lai YY, Siegel JM. 2003. Excitatory effects of hypocretin-1 (orexin-A) in the trigeminal motor nucleus are reversed by NMDA antagonism. *J. Neurophysiol.* 89:2591–600

Peyron C, Faraco J, Rogers W, Ripley B, Overeem S, et al. 2000. A mutation in a case of early onset narcolepsy and a generalized absence of hypocretin peptides in human narcoleptic brains. *Nat. Med.* 6:991–97

Peyron C, Tighe DK, van den Pol AN, de Lecea L, Heller HC, et al. 1998. Neurons containing hypocretin (orexin) project to multiple neuronal systems. *J. Neurosci.* 18:9996–10015

Reti IM, Minor LB, Baraban JM. 2002. Prominent expression of Narp in central vestibular pathways: selective effect of labyrinth ablation. *Eur. J. Neurosci.* 16:1949–58

Ripley B, Overeem S, Fujiki N, Nevsimalova S, Uchino M, et al. 2001. CSF hypocretin/orexin levels in narcolepsy and other neurological conditions. *Neurology* 57:2253–58

Rye DB, Jankovic J. 2002. Emerging views of dopamine in modulating sleep/wake state from an unlikely source: PD. *Neurology* 58:341–46

Sakurai T, Amemiya A, Ishii M, Matsuzaki I, Chemelli RM, et al. 1998. Orexins and orexin receptors: a family of hypothalamic neuropeptides and G protein-coupled receptors that regulate feeding behavior. *Cell* 92:573–85

Schenck CH, Mahowald MW. 1992. Motor dyscontrol in narcolepsy: rapid-eye-movement (REM) sleep without atonia and REM sleep behavior disorder. *Ann. Neurol.* 32:3–10

Schuld A, Hebebrand J, Geller F, Pollmacher T. 2000. Increased body-mass index in patients with narcolepsy. *Lancet* 355:1274–75

Shouse MN, Staba RJ, Saquib SF, Farber PR. 2000. Monoamines and sleep: microdialysis findings in pons and amygdala. *Brain Res.* 860:181–89

Siegel JM. 1979. Behavioral functions of the reticular formation. *Brain Res. Rev.* 1:69–105

Siegel JM. 1999. Narcolepsy: a key role for hypocretins (orexins). *Cell* 98:409–12

Siegel JM. 2000a. Narcolepsy. *Sci. Am.* 282:76–81

Siegel JM. 2000b. Brainstem mechanisms generating REM sleep. See Kryger et al. 2000, pp. 112–33

Siegel JM, Nienhuis R, Fahringer H, Paul R, Shiromani P, et al. 1991. Neuronal activity in narcolepsy: identification of cataplexy related cells in the medial medulla. *Science* 262:1315–18

Siegel JM, Nienhuis R, Gulyani S, Ouyang S, Wu MF, et al. 1999. Neuronal degeneration in canine narcolepsy. *J. Neurosci.* 19:248–57

Siegel JM, Tomaszewski KS. 1983. Behavioral

organization of reticular formation: studies in the unrestrained cat. I. Cells related to axial, limb, eye, and other movements. *J. Neurophysiol.* 50:696–716

Siegel JM, Tomaszewski KS, Wheeler RL. 1983. Behavioral organization of reticular formation: studies in the unrestrained cat: II. Cells related to facial movements. *J. Neurophysiol.* 50:717–23

Thannickal TC, Moore RY, Nienhuis R, Ramanathan L, Gulyani S, et al. 2000. Reduced number of hypocretin neurons in human narcolepsy. *Neuron* 27:469–74

Thannickal TC, Siegel JM, Nienhuis R, Moore RY. 2003. Pattern of hypocretin (orexin) soma and axon loss, and gliosis, in human narcolepsy. *Brain Pathol.* 13:340–51

Torterolo P, Yamuy J, Sampogna S, Morales FR, Chase MH. 2003. Hypocretinergic neurons are primarily involved in activation of the somatomotor system. *Sleep* 26:25–28

Trivedi P, Yu H, MacNeil DJ, Van der Ploeg LH, Guan XM. 1998. Distribution of orexin receptor mRNA in the rat brain. *FEBS Lett.* 438:71–75

van den Pol AN. 1999. Hypothalamic hypocretin (orexin): robust innervation of the spinal cord. *J. Neurosci.* 19:3171–82

van den Pol AN, Gao XB, Obrietan K, Kilduff TS, Belousov AB. 1998. Presynaptic and postsynaptic actions and modulation of neuroendocrine neurons by a new hypothalamic peptide, hypocretin/orexin. *J. Neurosci.* 18:7962–71

van den Pol AN, Ghosh PK, Liu RJ, Li Y, Aghajanian GK, Gao XB. 2002. Hypocretin (orexin) enhances neuron activity and

cell synchrony in developing mouse GFP-expressing locus coeruleus. *J. Physiol.* 541:169–85

Welch MJ, Meltzer EO, Simons FE. 2003. H1-antihistamines and the central nervous system. *Clin. Allergy Immunol.* 17:337–88

Wu M, Zhang ZM, Leranth C, Xu CQ, van den Pol AN, Alreja M. 2002a. Hypocretin increases impulse flow in the septohippocampal GABAergic pathway: implications for arousal via a mechanism of hippocampal disinhibition. *J. Neurosci.* 22:7754–65

Wu MF, Gulyani S, Yao E, Mignot E, Phan B, Siegel JM. 1999. Locus coeruleus neurons: cessation of activity during cataplexy. *Neuroscience* 91:1389–99

Wu MF, John J, Maidment N, Lam HA, Siegel JM. 2002b. Hypocretin release in normal and narcoleptic dogs after food and sleep deprivation, eating, and movement. *Am. J. Physiol. Regul. Integr. Comp. Physiol.* 283:R1079–86

Yamanaka A, Beuckmann CT, Willie JT, Hara J, Tsujino N, et al. 2003. Hypothalamic orexin neurons regulate arousal according to energy balance in mice. *Neuron* 38:701–13

Yamanaka A, Sakurai T, Katsumoto T, Yanagisawa M, Goto K. 1999. Chronic intracerebroventricular administration of orexin-a to rats increases food intake in daytime, but has no effect on body weight. *Brain Res.* 849:248–52

Yamanaka A, Tsujino N, Funahashi H, Honda K, Guan JL, et al. 2002. Orexins activate histaminergic neurons via the orexin 2 receptor. *Biochem. Biophys. Res. Commun.* 290:1237–45

Annu. Rev. Psychol. 2004. 55:149–79
doi: 10.1146/annurev.psych.55.090902.142028
Copyright © 2004 by Annual Reviews. All rights reserved
First published online as a Review in Advance on September 15, 2003

SPEECH PERCEPTION

Randy L. Diehl
*Department of Psychology and Center for Perceptual Systems, University of Texas,
Austin, Texas 78712-0187; email: diehl@psy.utexas.edu*

Andrew J. Lotto
*Boys Town National Research Hospital, Omaha, Nebraska 68131;
email: lottoa@boystown.org*

Lori L. Holt
*Department of Psychology and Center for the Neural Basis of Cognition, Carnegie
Mellon University, Pittsburgh, Pennsylvania 15213; email: lholt@andrew.cmu.edu*

Key Words auditory pattern recognition, categorical perception, phonetic context
effects, perceptual learning, speech production

■ **Abstract** This chapter focuses on one of the first steps in comprehending spoken language: How do listeners extract the most fundamental linguistic elements—
consonants and vowels, or the distinctive features which compose them—from the
acoustic signal? We begin by describing three major theoretical perspectives on the
perception of speech. Then we review several lines of research that are relevant to
distinguishing these perspectives. The research topics surveyed include categorical
perception, phonetic context effects, learning of speech and related nonspeech categories, and the relation between speech perception and production. Finally, we describe
challenges facing each of the major theoretical perspectives on speech perception.

CONTENTS

0066-4308/04/0204-0149$14.00

INTRODUCTION

Over the past 50 years, researchers in speech perception have focused on the mapping between properties of the acoustic signal and linguistic elements such as phonemes and distinctive features. This mapping has turned out to be quite complex, and a complete explanation of how humans recognize consonants and vowels remains elusive. The search for an explanation has given rise to three main theoretical perspectives on speech perception that frame much of the empirical work. In this chapter, we briefly describe these perspectives and then review some of the research most relevant to evaluating them. We end by highlighting some of the main challenges facing each theoretical view.

MOTOR THEORY OF SPEECH PERCEPTION

Beginning in the early 1950s, Alvin Liberman, Franklin Cooper, Pierre Delattre, and other researchers at the Haskins Laboratories carried out a series of landmark studies on the perception of synthetic speech sounds (Delattre et al. 1951, 1952, 1955, 1964; Liberman 1957; Liberman et al. 1952, 1954, 1956). This work provided the foundation of what is known about acoustic cues for linguistic units such as phonemes and features and revealed that the mapping between speech signals and linguistic units is quite complex. In time, Liberman and his colleagues became convinced that perceived phonemes and features have a simpler (i.e., more nearly one-to-one) relationship to articulation than to acoustics, and this gave rise to the motor theory of speech perception.

The motor theory (MT) has undergone significant changes since its initial formulation (Liberman 1996), but every version has claimed that the objects of speech perception are articulatory events rather than acoustic or auditory events. More specifically, it was hypothesized that the articulatory events recovered by human listeners are neuromotor commands to the articulators (e.g., tongue, lips, and vocal folds)—also referred to as intended gestures—rather than more peripheral events such as actual articulatory movements or gestures (Liberman & Mattingly 1985, Liberman et al. 1967). This theoretical choice was guided by a belief that the objects of speech perception must be more-or-less invariant with respect to phonemes or feature sets and by a further belief that such a requirement was satisfied only by neuromotor commands. The process of speech production was characterized by Liberman et al. (1967) as a series of causal links between descriptive levels:

phonemes (or sets of distinctive features) → neuromotor commands → muscle contractions → vocal tract shapes → acoustic signals. Whereas phonemes (or feature sets) were assumed to stand approximately in one-to-one correspondence with neuromotor commands and with muscle contractions, the mapping between muscle contractions and vocal tract shapes was thought to be highly complex owing to the fact that adjacent vowels and consonants are coarticulated (i.e., produced with temporal and, to some extent, spatial overlap). Because the relation between vocal tract shapes and acoustic signals was assumed to be one-to-one, the complex mapping between phonemes and speech sounds was attributed mainly to the effects of coarticulation.

As an illustration of the complex mapping between phonemes and their acoustic realizations, Liberman et al. (1967) displayed spectrograms of synthetic two-formant patterns (shown in Figure 1) that are perceived by listeners as the syllables /di/ ("dee") and /du/ ("doo"). In these patterns, the steady-state formants correspond to the target values of the vowels /i/ and /u/, and the rapidly changing formant frequencies (formant transitions) at the onset of each syllable carry important information about the initial consonant. In particular, the rising first-formant (F1) transition of both syllables signals that the consonant is a voiced "stop" such as /b/, /d/, or /g/, whereas the rising second-formant (F2) transition of /di/ and the

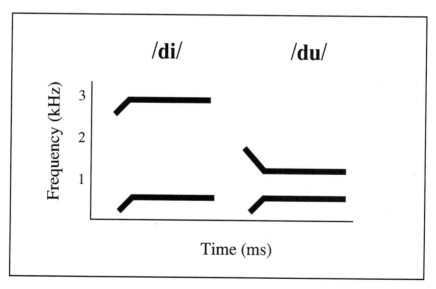

Figure 1 Formant patterns for simplified versions of /di/ and /du/. Note that the transition of the second formant (i.e., the one higher in frequency) differs dramatically for the two syllables. Nonetheless, the consonant in both cases is perceived as /d/. The first formant trajectory, which is equivalent in both syllables, is not informative about place of articulation and would be the same for /b/ and /g/ initial syllables. (Adapted from Delattre et al. 1952.)

falling F2 transition of /du/ provide critical information about place of articulation (i.e., that the consonant is /d/ rather than /b/ or /g/). That such different patterns of F2 transition could give rise to the same phonemic percept strongly suggested to the motor theorists that invariance must be sought at an articulatory rather than an acoustic level of description.

A second important claim of MT is that the human ability to perceive speech sounds cannot be ascribed to general mechanisms of audition and perceptual learning but instead depends on a specialized decoder or module that is speech-specific, unique to humans, and, in later versions of the theory (Liberman 1996, Liberman & Mattingly 1985), innately organized and part of the larger biological specialization for language. The speech decoder was hypothesized by Liberman et al. (1967) to operate by "somehow running the process [of speech production] backward" (p. 454). This claim was elaborated by Liberman & Mattingly (1985) as follows: "[T]he candidate signal descriptions are computed by an analogue of the production process—an internal, innately specified vocal-tract synthesizer...— that incorporates complete information about the anatomical and physiological characteristics of the vocal tract and also about the articulatory and acoustic consequences of linguistically significant gestures" (p. 26). Liberman and his colleagues argued that, among other theoretical advantages, MT is parsimonious inasmuch as the same mechanism is used for both speech production and speech perception.

DIRECT REALIST THEORY OF SPEECH PERCEPTION

Starting in the 1980s, an alternative to MT—referred to as the direct realist theory (DRT) of speech perception—was developed by Carol Fowler, also working at the Haskins Laboratories (Fowler 1981, 1984, 1986, 1989, 1994, 1996). Like MT, DRT claims that the objects of speech perception are articulatory rather than acoustic events. However, unlike MT, DRT asserts that the articulatory objects of perception are actual, phonetically structured, vocal tract movements, or gestures, and not events that are causally antecedent to these movements, such as neuromotor commands or intended gestures. DRT also contrasts sharply with MT in denying that specialized (i.e., speech-specific or human-specific) mechanisms play a role in speech perception. Instead, following the general theory of direct perception developed by James J. Gibson (1966, 1979), Fowler argues that speech perception can be broadly characterized in the same terms as, for example, visual perception of surface layout.

This view is elegantly summarized by Fowler (1996) in the following passage:

> Perceptual systems have a universal function. They constitute the sole means by which animals can know their niches. Moreover, they appear to serve this function in one way: They use structure in the media that has been lawfully caused by events in the environment as information for the events. Even though

it is the structure in media (light for vision, skin for touch, air for hearing) that sense organs transduce, it is not the structure in those media that animals perceive. Rather, essentially for their survival, they perceive the components of their niche that caused the structure. (p. 1732)

Thus, according to DRT, a talker's gestures (e.g., the closing and opening of the lips during the production of /pa/) structure the acoustic signal, which then serves as the informational medium for the listener to recover the gestures. The term "direct" in direct realism is meant to imply that perception is not mediated by processes of inference or hypothesis testing; rather, the information in the acoustic signal is assumed to be rich enough to specify (i.e., determine uniquely) the gestures that structure the signal. To perceive the gestures, it is sufficient for the listener simply to detect the relevant information. The term "realism" is intended to mean that perceivers recover actual (physical) properties of their niche, including, in the case of speech perception, phonetic segments that are realized as sets of physical gestures. This realist perspective contrasts with a mentalistic view that phonetic segments are "internally generated, the creature of some kind of perceptual-cognitive process" (Hammarberg 1976, p. 355; see also Repp 1981).

Just as MT was motivated in part by a particular view of speech production (especially, the claim that coarticulation of consonants and vowels results in a complex mapping between phonemes and vocal tract shapes and hence between phonemes and acoustic signals), DRT was seen as broadly compatible with an alternative view of speech production (Fowler 1980, 1981; Fowler & Smith 1986). According to this view, the temporal overlap of vowels and consonants does not result in a physical merging or assimilation of gestures; instead, the vowel and consonant gestures are coproduced. That is, they remain, to a considerable extent, separate and independent events analogous to, say, a singer's vocal production and any temporally overlapping musical accompaniment. Because coproduced gestures are assumed to structure the acoustic signal in independent (albeit temporally overlapping) ways, the listener should, on the assumptions of DRT, have no difficulty recovering those gestures and their temporal sequencing. Fowler & Smith (1986) likened the perception of coproduced segments to a kind of "vector analysis" in which complex stimulus events are appropriately factored into separate components. For example, in the context of a following nasal consonant (e.g., /n/), a vowel tends to be nasalized, an effect known as anticipatory coarticulation. However, listeners appear not to hear the vowel as nasalized, instead attributing the nasalization to the following consonant alone (Krakow et al. 1988).

Because MT and DRT both claim that the objects of speech perception are gestures (intended in the case of MT, actual in the case of DRT), advocates of the two theories cite some of the same empirical findings as supporting evidence. Thus, for example, the fact that /di/ and /du/ (see Figure 1) are perceived as having the same initial consonant (despite their disparate F2 transitions) is explained both by Liberman et al. (1967) and by Fowler (1996) in terms of an assumed commonality of gestures in the two cases.

GENERAL AUDITORY AND LEARNING APPROACHES
TO SPEECH PERCEPTION

In the mid 1970s, several new empirical findings posed a challenge to MT, the then-dominant account of human speech perception. Earlier work at Haskins Laboratories had found clear differences between perception of certain speech sounds and perception of nonspeech analogs of those speech stimuli (Liberman et al. 1961a,b; Mattingly et al. 1971). Because these results appeared to underscore the special nature of speech perception, they were interpreted as supporting MT (Liberman et al. 1967, 1972). However, Stevens & Klatt (1974), Miller et al. (1976), and Pisoni (1977) showed that in some instances perception of speech stimuli does parallel that of nonspeech stimuli provided they share critical temporal properties. The authors claimed that general auditory mechanisms were responsible for the observed similarities in perceptual performance. Even more surprising were demonstrations that nonhuman animals exhibit aspects of speech perceptual performance (Kuhl & Miller 1975, 1978) that were assumed by motor theorists to be unique to humans (Liberman et al. 1972). Some of these parallels between speech and nonspeech perception and between speech perception in humans and nonhumans are described later in more detail.

Stimulated by these and related findings, a number of speech investigators [e.g., Diehl 1987; Diehl & Kluender 1989a,b; Holt et al. 1998; Kingston & Diehl 1994, 1995; Kluender 1994; Kuhl 1986; Lotto 2000; Massaro & Oden 1980; Nearey 1990; Nearey & Hogan 1986; Ohala 1996; Pastore 1981; Sussman et al. 1998 (see Lane 1965 for an early critique of MT)] have explored alternatives to both MT and DRT, which will be referred to here as the general approach (GA). In contrast to MT, GA does not invoke special mechanisms or modules to explain speech perception. Rather, it assumes, as a working hypothesis, that speech sounds are perceived using the same mechanisms of audition and perceptual learning that have evolved in humans or human ancestors to handle other classes of environmental sounds. In contrast to MT and DRT, GA assumes that listeners' recovery of spoken messages from the acoustic signal (whether these messages are construed as distinctive features, phonemes, words, or some higher-level linguistic units) is neither equivalent to nor mediated by the perception of gestures.

Recall that the perceived equivalence of the consonant in /di/ and /du/ (despite varying acoustic patterns) was cited as supporting evidence for MT and DRT. A GA explanation for the perceptual equivalence would be based on the general ability of the perceiver to make use of multiple imperfect acoustic cues to categorize complex stimuli. In the same way that Brunswik (1956) proposed that object constancy in vision is the result of combining multiple attributes of varying ecological validity, the listener can maintain perceptual constancy in the face of structured variance in acoustics. For GA this constancy does not require the recovery of articulatory gestures or a special mode of perception. In support of this view, Kluender et al. (1987) demonstrated that birds could be trained to respond to natural /d/-initial

TABLE 1 Taxonomy of major theoretical approaches to speech perception

	Special mechanisms	**General mechanisms**
Gestural	Motor theory	Direct realism
Nongestural	Eclectic specializations	General approach

syllables versus /b/- and /g/-initial syllables. Despite the lack of any specialized mechanisms or experience producing speech, the birds were able to correctly respond to the same consonants in novel vowel contexts.

GA is labeled an approach rather than a theory because, as summarized in preceding paragraphs, it is quite abstract, defining itself mainly by its opposition to key claims of MT and DRT. At this level of abstraction, GA has too little content to be falsifiable. However, it does provide a general framework within which particular theoretical claims may be formulated and tested. Examples of such claims are reviewed in the following sections.

Table 1 presents a simplified taxonomy of the major theoretical approaches to speech perception based on the postulation of special versus general mechanisms and on the proposed objects of perception. The lower left quadrant corresponds to a possible claim that speech perception uses special mechanisms to recover a nongestural representation of linguistic elements. Although such a claim has not been developed into a coherent theory, there have been several proposals that specialized processes may work in concert with general perceptual mechanisms. For example, the ability of human infants to learn the phoneme categories of their native language has been attributed to specialized processes of categorization (Kuhl 1991, 1992, 1993) or to an attentional or learning bias for speech sounds (Jusczyk 1997). These are listed as "eclectic specializations" in the table.

CATEGORICAL PERCEPTION

An important early discovery at the Haskins Laboratories was an effect referred to as *categorical perception* (Liberman et al. 1957, 1961a,b). In a typical experiment, a series of synthetic consonant-vowel (CV) syllables varying in an acoustic parameter (e.g., the slope of the F2 transition) and ranging perceptually across several initial consonants (e.g., /bV/-/dV/-/gV/) were presented to listeners for phonemic labeling, or identification, and for discrimination of pairs of stimuli located near each other in the series. Two striking patterns were evident in the results. First, labeling functions exhibited abrupt boundaries between phoneme categories; second, discrimination accuracy was close to chance for stimulus pairs within a phoneme category but nearly perfect for stimulus pairs that straddled an identification boundary. These are the defining properties of categorical perception. They imply that in speech perception discriminability is closely related to the presence or absence of functional (i.e., phonemic) differences between sounds. Because categorical discrimination functions were not found for certain nonspeech analogs of the speech stimuli (Liberman et al. 1961a,b), the motor theorists cited categorical perception as a hallmark of perception in the "speech mode" (Liberman et al. 1967).

This section focuses mainly on perception of voice distinctions in syllable-initial stop consonants, for example, /ba/ versus /pa/, /da/ versus /ta/, and /ga/ versus /ka/. Linguists commonly describe /b/, /d/, and /g/ as having the distinctive feature +*voice* and /p/, /t/, and /k/ as having the distinctive feature −*voice*, where the former but not the latter are produced with voicing, or vocal fold vibration. In a cross-language study of initial stop consonants, Lisker & Abramson (1964) identified a key phonetic correlate of voice contrasts, e.g., voice onset time (VOT), the interval between the release of articulatory occlusion (e.g., the opening of the lips) and the onset of voicing. Cross-linguistically, initial stops tend to occur in one of three ranges of VOT values: long negative VOTs (voicing onset leads the articulatory release by 50 ms or more); short positive VOTs (voicing lags behind the release by no more than 20 ms); and long positive VOTs (voicing onset lags behind the release by more than 25 ms). From these three phonetic types, languages usually choose two to implement their voice contrasts. For example, Spanish uses long negative VOTs to realize +*voice* stops and short positive VOTs to realize −*voice* stops; whereas English uses short positive VOTs to implement +*voice* stops and long positive VOTs to implement −*voice* stops.

Lisker & Abramson (1970, Abramson & Lisker 1970) next examined VOT perception among native speakers of English, Spanish, and Thai. All three language groups showed clear evidence of categorical perception. However, the locations of phoneme boundaries and the associated peaks in discriminability varied among the groups, reflecting differences in the way each language realizes voice distinctions. These results suggested that categorical perception of VOT arises from language experience, with listeners becoming more sensitive to phonetic differences that play a functional role in their language and/or less sensitive to differences that do not.

Complicating this language learning explanation were results of experiments performed with human infants. Eimas et al. (1971) reported that infants from an English-speaking environment discriminate differences in VOT for stimulus pairs that straddle the English /ba/-/pa/ boundary but show no evidence of discriminating equivalent VOT differences when the stimuli are from the same English category. Consistent with later versions of MT, the authors interpreted these results as evidence of an innate linguistic mode of perception in humans. Further supporting this view, Lasky et al. (1975) found that infants raised in a Spanish-speaking environment can discriminate differences in VOT if the stimuli straddled either the Spanish or the English voice boundary but show no evidence of discrimination otherwise. The discriminability of the English voice contrast by Spanish-learning infants suggested that language experience is not a necessary condition for categorical discrimination of VOT stimuli (see also Aslin et al. 1981).

Recall that categorical perception was claimed by motor theorists to be a hallmark of the speech mode of perception (Liberman et al. 1967). However, later studies (Miller et al. 1976, Pisoni 1977) yielded convincing evidence of categorical perception for several types of nonspeech analogs of VOT stimuli. In naturally produced stop-vowel syllables, negative VOTs correspond to a low-frequency "voice bar" that precedes the articulatory release, whereas positive VOTs are associated with a sharp attenuation of F1 before voicing onset (see Figure 2A.) VOT can thus be abstractly described as the relative onset time of low- versus high-frequency signal components. Pisoni (1977) created nonspeech analogs of VOT stimuli that consisted of a lower and a higher frequency tone with onsets varying from −50-ms tone onset time (TOT) to +50-ms TOT, where negative values indicate prior onset of the lower-frequency tone (see Figure 2B). After training in labeling selected stimuli, adult listeners displayed abrupt identification boundaries near −20 ms and +20 ms TOT values (analogous to the Spanish and English VOT boundaries) as well as peaks in discriminability near those boundaries. Similar bimodal discrimination performance for TOT stimuli was observed for infants (Jusczyk et al. 1980). The close parallel between categorical perception of VOT and TOT stimuli was attributed by Pisoni (1977) to a psychophysical threshold for detecting the temporal order of stimulus components (Hirsh 1959, Hirsh & Sherrick 1961). By this account, onset asynchronies of less than approximately 20 ms are judged as simultaneous, while those greater than that are judged as ordered in time. This yields three natural categories of onset asynchrony that correspond well to the three phonetic voice categories commonly used among the world's languages. Thus, in the case of VOT, languages appear to locate phoneme contrasts to exploit natural auditory boundaries, thereby enhancing distinctiveness, intelligibility, and perhaps learnability.

The finding that categorical perception is not unique to speech sounds weakened one of the empirical arguments for MT. An even more serious challenge was raised by results of experiments with nonhuman animals. Liberman et al. (1972, p. 324) had written:

> Presumably, they [animals] lack the special processor necessary to decode the speech signal. If so, the perception of speech must be different from ours. They should not hear categorically, for instance, and they should not hear the [di]-[du] patterns...as two segment syllables which have the first segment in common.

As for the /di/-/du/ example, it was pointed out earlier that Kluender et al. (1987) trained Japanese quail to respond to /d/-initial tokens, but to refrain from responding to /b/- and /g/-initial tokens, in various vowel contexts. With respect to the claim that categorical perception is a uniquely human ability, Kuhl and her colleagues (Kuhl 1981; Kuhl & Miller 1975, 1978; Kuhl & Padden 1982) presented strong evidence of categorical perception of human speech sounds by chinchillas and macaque monkeys. For example, Kuhl & Miller (1978) trained chinchillas to respond differently to two endpoint stimuli of a synthetic VOT series (/da/, 0 ms

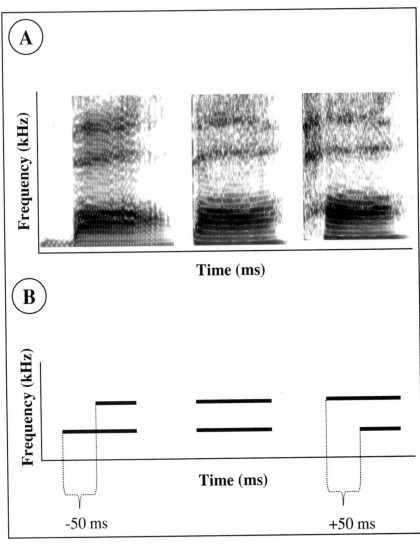

Figure 2   Spectrograms of (A) natural stop-vowel syllables with a voicing lead (negative VOT), short voicing lag (approximately 0 VOT), and long voicing lag (positive VOT) stop consonants. VOT is measured from the articulatory release (onset of formant transitions) to the onset of voicing, represented as low-frequency energy; and (B) corresponding TOT stimuli. These consist of two sine-wave segments that vary in relative onset time. (Adapted from Pisoni 1977.)

VOT; and /ta/, 80 ms VOT) and then tested the animals with stimuli at intermediate values. Their identification performance corresponded almost exactly to that of adult English-speaking listeners. Further generalization tests with labial (/ba/-/pa/) and velar (/ga/-/ka/) VOT stimuli, as well as tests of VOT discriminability (Kuhl 1981), also showed close agreement with the performance of English speakers.

Several neural correlates of categorical perception of VOT have been reported. Recording from a population of auditory nerve fibers in chinchilla, Sinex et al. (1991) found that cross-neuron variability in discharge patterns was reliably smaller for VOT stimuli near the English voice boundary than for stimuli located within either category. In a magnetoencephalographic study of the human primary auditory cortex, Simos et al. (1998) found that VOT stimulus pairs straddling the English voice boundary yielded differences in the location and amplitude of the peak response for native English-speaking listeners, whereas stimulus pairs drawn from the same category did not.

Although this discussion has focused on perception of VOT, other speech dimensions that are perceived categorically by humans appear to be perceived categorically by nonhumans as well. Kuhl & Padden (1983) reported that macaques show enhanced discriminability at phoneme boundaries for the feature place of articulation (/b/-/d/-/g/), and Dooling et al. (1995) found that budgerigars and zebra finches show enhanced discriminability at the English /r/-/l/ boundary. In both studies, discrimination performance of the animals closely matched that of human listeners.

The results of comparing speech and nonspeech perception and speech perception in humans and nonhumans strongly indicate that general auditory mechanisms (common to human adults and infants, other mammals, and even birds) contribute to the categorical perception of speech sounds. Evidently, however, language experience is also a significant factor in categorical perception. Lisker & Abramson (1970, Abramson & Lisker 1970) found cross-language differences in identification boundaries and discrimination peaks (see also Elman et al. 1977, Williams 1977). Although human infants exhibit heightened discriminability at both the Spanish and English voice boundaries, their language experience tends to maintain and perhaps enhance natural boundaries that coincide with phonemic boundaries and to downgrade natural boundaries that are linguistically nonfunctional (Werker & Tees 1984). In organizing their sound systems, languages exploit natural boundaries, but, within limits, they also modify them.

PHONETIC CONTEXT EFFECTS I: STIMULUS LENGTH EFFECT

The perceptual assessment of temporal cues for certain phoneme distinctions is known to depend on the duration of nearby regions of the acoustic signal (Diehl et al. 1980, Miller 1987, Summerfield 1981). For example, Miller & Liberman (1979) found that perception of the stop/glide distinction (e.g., /b/ versus /w/)

is influenced by the duration of the following vowel. Earlier research (Liberman et al. 1956) had demonstrated that the stop/glide distinction is reliably signaled by variation in the duration and slope of CV formant transitions, with shorter transitions specifying the stop category. The key result of Miller & Liberman (1979) was that a longer following vowel shifted the stop/glide boundary toward longer transition durations (i.e., more stops were perceived). Miller & Liberman explained this effect within the framework of MT: A longer vowel is evidence of a slower rate of articulation, and, to compensate perceptually, listeners accept a greater range of transition durations as compatible with the stop category.

Diehl & Walsh (1989) offered an alternative account of this stimulus length effect based on a putative general auditory factor referred to as durational contrast. According to this account, perceived length of an acoustic segment is affected contrastively by the duration of adjacent acoustic segments. Thus, a target segment will be judged as shorter next to a long segment than next to a short segment. Unlike the motor theoretic explanation of the stimulus length effect, the durational contrast hypothesis applies to both speech and nonspeech sounds.

To distinguish empirically between the two accounts, Diehl & Walsh compared labeling performance on several series of /ba/-/wa/ stimuli and on analogous non-speech stimuli. The latter consisted of single sine-wave stimuli that mimicked the F1 trajectories and amplitude rise times of the speech stimuli. Listeners were asked to categorize the nonspeech items as having either abrupt or gradual onsets. When the stop/glide distinction was signaled by changes in transition duration, there was a reliable stimulus length effect like that observed by Miller & Liberman. A very similar effect was found for the corresponding nonspeech stimuli. Changes in rise time had only a small effect on identification of either the speech or nonspeech stimuli. Indeed, for seven of eight comparisons (main effects and interactions) involving the factor speech versus nonspeech, there were no significant differences in labeling performance. (The one exception was that when the stop/glide distinction was cued by rise time, there was a reliable stimulus length effect, but no such effect occurred for the corresponding nonspeech stimuli.) On balance, the parallel results between the speech and nonspeech conditions supported the durational contrast account of the stimulus length effect. (For a critique of this conclusion from the perspective of DRT, see Fowler 1990, 1991, and for a reply see Diehl et al. 1991.)

PHONETIC CONTEXT EFFECTS II: COMPENSATION FOR COARTICULATION

As described earlier, phonemes are coarticulated in running speech. Consider the production of the CV syllables /da/ and /ga/ in English. In isolation, /d/ is typically produced with an occlusion anterior in the vocal tract as the tongue tip makes contact with the roof of the mouth. In contrast, /g/ is produced with a posterior occlusion created by the tongue body. However, the place of articulation for these CVs changes when they are produced in the context of a preceding /al/ or /ar/

syllable (e.g., /al da/). The anterior articulation of /l/ leads to /d/ and /g/ occlusions that are closer to the front of the mouth, whereas the more posterior production of /r/ shifts the /d/ and /g/ occlusions in the opposite direction.

Because the acoustics of speech sounds are a function of the position and movement of the articulators, coarticulation results in context-sensitive acoustics for phonetic segments. For example, /da/ and /ga/ are differentiated in part by the onset frequency of F3; as a result of its more anterior place of articulation, /da/ typically has a higher-frequency F3 onset than /ga/. When produced following /al/, CVs will have a higher F3 frequency onset, due to the shift in place of articulation, than when produced following /ar/. With this in mind, consider the cases of /al ga/ and /ar da/ in which an anterior and a posterior production are paired. The /al/ raises the F3 onset frequency of /g/, whereas the /ar/ lowers the F3 onset frequency of /d/. The result is that the acoustics of the CVs in these two disyllables are quite similar. A recognition system that simply matched the formant transitions of the consonant to templates for /da/ and /ga/ would have trouble identifying these ambiguous consonants.

How do human listeners contend with the context-sensitive acoustics of phonemes? To answer this question, Mann (1980) presented listeners with a series of synthesized CVs varying in F3 onset frequency from a good /da/ to a good /ga/. These target syllables were preceded by natural productions of the context syllables /al/ or /ar/ (with a 50-ms intersyllabic silent gap). Listeners' identifications of the target CVs shifted depending on the preceding context. More /ga/ responses were made following /al/ than following /ar/. These context-moderated perceptions are in the opposite direction of the effects of coarticulation. In production, /al/ contexts lead to more anterior or /da/-like productions. In perception, /al/ contexts lead to more /ga/ identifications. Perception appears to compensate for the effects of coarticulation. Coarticulatory effects on acoustics and apparent perceptual compensation have also been demonstrated for consonant contexts and vowel targets (Holt et al. 2000, Lindblom & Studdert-Kennedy 1967, Nearey 1989), vowel contexts and consonant targets (Holt 1999, Mann & Repp 1981), and vowel contexts with vowel targets (Fowler 1981).

Whereas context-sensitive acoustics are problematic for accounts of speech perception that rely on acoustic pattern recognition of phonemes, these results support predictions of theories that propose gestures as the objects of speech perception. The mapping between acoustics and perception is not transparent, but the mapping from intended gesture and perception is straightforward. Intended and perceived gestures are consistent even though the acoustics are variable. According to MT, the intended gesture is recovered by accessing tacit knowledge of the acoustic consequences of the candidate articulatory motor commands (Mann 1980). According to DRT, acoustics are parsed into responsible gestures as a result of the sensitivity of the perceiver to the dynamics of articulation. From this view, effects of coarticulation serve as information for the identity of the context segment as opposed to obfuscators of the identity of the target segment. Regardless of the mechanism, the factoring of the speech stream into gestures appears to occur independent of any linguistic representation. Mann (1986) demonstrated that the contexts /al/ and /ar/ can shift CV identification by Japanese speakers who cannot distinguish /r/ and /l/ (as both sounds are mapped to a single phoneme in Japanese). In addition, Fowler et al. (1990) found similar context-dependent shifts in responses of 4- to 5-month-old infants.

A GA account of perceptual compensation for coarticulation would rely on interactions between stimulus attributes in the auditory system or perceptual learning based on correlated features in the input. In support of a general auditory basis for these context effects, Lotto et al. (1997) demonstrated context-dependent responses to CVs in birds. Japanese quail were trained to peck a key when presented /da/ or /ga/. When ambiguous CV stimuli were presented following /al/ or /ar/, birds' responses shifted in the same manner as for humans. The extension of phonetic context effects to Japanese quail casts doubt on the necessity of specialized perceptual mechanisms. Lotto et al. (1997) suggested that the shifts in birds' responses were not due to the factoring of the signal into gestures but to general auditory interactions between the spectral components of the target and context. In particular, they proposed that the context effects are a result of spectral contrast. A redescription of the bird results in terms of acoustic components would be: Following a context with high-frequency F3 offset (/al/), more low-frequency F3 onset responses (/ga/) are obtained. Equivalently, following a context with low-frequency F3 offset (/ar/), more high-frequency F3 onset responses (/da/) are obtained. It should be noted that the proposed auditory contrast is between spectral patterns of higher versus lower energy in particular frequency regions, as opposed to changes in representations of frequency per se.

Evidence for spectral contrast has also been obtained with humans. Lotto & Kluender (1998) presented listeners with members of a /da/-/ga/ series preceded by nonspeech sounds that mimicked some of the important spectral content of the syllables /al/ and /ar/. The contexts were either tone glides modeling the offset transitions of F3 or steady-state tones set at F3 offset frequency. Despite a lack of articulatory or phonemic content, these contexts affected the identification of target CVs. Following high-frequency tones (based on /al/), more /ga/ identifications were obtained. The interaction of speech and nonspeech sounds runs counter to expectations of a modular approach to perception such as MT. Similar nonspeech context effects have been demonstrated for conditions that mimic consonant contexts with vowel targets (Holt et al. 2000) and vowel contexts with consonant targets (Holt 1999). Instead of proposing a special mechanism to handle the complexities of coarticulation, it may be that a general perceptual function allows (and even encourages) humans to coarticulate phonemes.

The spectral contrast account of phonetic context effects has been challenged by recent results of Fowler et al. (2000). They presented listeners with a /da/-/ga/ series preceded by a syllable that was perceptually ambiguous between /al/ and /ar/. The identity of this context was disambiguated by a synchronized video of a speaker producing /al da/ or /ar da/. The resulting identification of the target CV was a function of the visual input. Visual /al/ productions led to more /ga/ responses.

This result is consistent with gestural theories such as MT or DRT. The visual input provides information about the gestures involved in the context syllables and leads to appropriate compensation for coarticulation in perceiving the target. The results are inconsistent with an account that relies strictly on spectral contrast because there is no change in the acoustic makeup of the context in the two conditions. It should be noted that from the perspective of GA, it is quite reasonable to assume that humans learn correlations between visual and auditory input and that their perceptions are a result of a combination of these informational sources (Massaro 1987). That is, a generalist account does not require that all context effects be explained solely by spectral contrast or any purely auditory mechanism.

Despite the fact that visually moderated context effects would be consistent with all of the major theories of speech perception, the findings of Fowler et al. (2000) have recently been brought into question by new results. Stephens & Holt (2002) presented participants the ambiguous context and target CV sounds with aligned video /al/ and /ar/ and a blank screen during the CV. They failed to find a shift in CV identification as a function of context video. This raises the possibility that the effect reported by Fowler et al. was due to visual information associated with the target syllable rather than to the video aligned with the context. Although the videotaped speaker produced /da/ in both conditions, there were differences in the CV portion of the video for /al/ and /ar/ precursors. To examine the effect of these differences, Stephens & Holt (2002) presented the audio and video CV portions of the Fowler et al. stimuli with no auditory or visual context. The resulting identification functions resembled those originally obtained by Fowler et al. with boundary shifts as a function of whether the visual /da/ came from /al da/ or /ar da/. Thus, the identification shifts appear to be due to auditory and visual interactions during the target syllable and not due to visual moderation of the perceived context. These synchronized auditory-visual interactions are well known in speech perception as demonstrated by the McGurk effect (McGurk & McDonald 1976).

Whereas the results of Fowler et al. (2000) do not clearly indicate the existence of visually moderated context effects, there have been several demonstrations of lexically moderated context effects (Elman & McClelland 1988, Magnuson et al. 2003, Samuel & Pitt 2003). For example, Elman & McClelland (1988) presented context words that ended in an ambiguous fricative consonant. This consonant was disambiguated by lexical identity, being perceived as "s" in "copious_" and as "sh" in "Engli_." Despite the lack of acoustic change in this final consonant, identification of succeeding target consonants was shifted as a function of lexical context, from a /d/ following "English" to a /g/ following "copious." This result is difficult to reconcile with current accounts of phonetic context effects because the acoustic (and presumed corresponding gestural) characteristics of the precursor context stimuli are nearly identical across conditions. What remains unresolved is the type of representation on which lexicality asserts its effects. Cognitive models typically propose that lexical effects influence phonemic representations, but they could just as well be influencing gestural or auditory representations (or both).

The problem with phoneme representations here is that context effects have been demonstrated for listeners without the requisite linguistic representations (birds, infants, and Japanese listeners with /l/ and /r/ contexts). To fully account for all the results, future cognitive models of speech will need to incorporate richer auditory and/or gestural representations.

LEARNING SPEECH AND NONSPEECH CATEGORIES

So far, we have presented empirical and theoretical work concerning topics such as categorical perception and context effects that are relevant to the perception of the sounds of any language. However, one of the most important issues in speech perception is how listeners come to perceive sounds in a manner that is particular to their native language. In order to communicate proficiently, a listener must discriminate acoustic variance in the speech signal that is linguistically relevant and to generalize across variance that is irrelevant. Of course, what counts as relevant and irrelevant depends on the phoneme inventory of the specific language.

Before six months of age, infants have a well-documented ability to discriminate many (possibly most) of the sounds that are used contrastively in languages (e.g., Eilers 1977, Eimas 1974, Eimas et al. 1971, Miller & Eimas 1983). This includes the ability to tell apart sounds that are not phonemically distinctive in the infant's language environment (Best et al. 1988, Werker et al. 1981). Before the end of the first year of life, infants start to become perceptually "tuned" to their native language. That is, they respond to speech sounds in a language-specific manner; discriminating acoustic differences between phoneme categories of their language but no longer distinguishing sounds within those categories (Pegg & Werker 1997, Werker & Tees 1984). This change occurs before the development of a substantial lexicon.

In accord with MT, it has been suggested that these early speech perception abilities are indicative of "finely tuned linguistically relevant perceptual abilities" (Miller & Eimas 1983, p. 135) or even an "innately given, universal set of phonetic categories" (Eimas 1991, p.111). These proposals are analogous to the concept of a language acquisition device (LAD) offered by Chomsky (1965) for acquisition of syntax. Presumably, as with LAD, development would consist of retaining those phoneme contrasts that are used in the native language environment and discarding those that are not.

Most recent proposals on speech acquisition have tended to focus on the role of general perceptual learning rather than on innate knowledge and specialized perceptual mechanisms. It is hypothesized that infants acquire phoneme categories through the use of distributional properties of sounds in the language environment along with correlations between attributes of those sounds. This does not require specialized mechanisms, although speech may be a particularly salient signal for infants, and learning processes may be biased to pick up just the kind of information that is important for speech categories (Jusczyk 1993, 1997).

From the perspective of GA, the initial discriminative abilities of infants are a result of their well-developed auditory system, which provides sufficient temporal and frequency resolution (Werner & Bargones 1992). In addition, it seems reasonable to assume that languages tend to use contrasts that are readily distinguishable by language learners. Kuhl (1993) has proposed that much of the initial auditory space of the human infant (and other mammals) is segregated by natural boundaries that underlie many of the speech discrimination results.

Exposure to regularities within a natural language is proposed to lead to a reorganization of perception in terms of phoneme categories or equivalence classes. The information for these categories is present in the statistical properties of the input distributions. For many theorists, these categories provide mappings from acoustics to linguistic elements such as phonemes (e.g., Jusczyk 1993, 1997; Kluender et al. 1998; Kuhl 1993; Lotto 2000). From a DRT perspective, Best (1993, 1995) has offered the Perceptual Assimilation Model (PAM), according to which the initial discriminative abilities of infants are due to the direct recovery of the individual simple articulations that produce the sounds. With exposure to a language, infants begin to group coordinated gestures that are related to the phonemes of the language into equivalence classes.

Despite general agreement that perceptual learning depends on the distributional properties of stimuli, few attempts have been made to explore the actual mechanisms for auditory categorization of complex stimuli such as speech. One exception is a proposal by Kuhl (1991, 1993, 2000) that experience with speech sounds leads to the creation of category prototypes or high-density representations of exemplars that act as "perceptual magnets" that warp the perceptual space. However, the initial findings and subsequent predictions of the magnet model have not been supported (Frieda et al. 1999, Lively & Pisoni 1997, Lotto et al. 1998, Sussman & Lauckner-Morano 1995).

One difficulty of studying speech category learning in infants is a lack of control over the quality and quantity of language experience. In fact, there exists little information about typical speech input distributions for infants. In order to study general learning processes with known input distributions, Kluender et al. (1998) trained birds (starlings) to identify variants of the vowel in "heed" versus the vowel in "hid." The birds readily learned to peck a button when they heard one vowel category and to refrain for the complementary vowel category, and their responses generalized to novel variants of the vowels. Remarkably, the birds' peck rates were highest for those variants that human adult listeners judged as the best members of the vowel category. The correlation between bird responses and human "goodness" judgments was high across categories ($r = 0.99$) and within categories (average $r = 0.71$).

The bird and human data revealed two salient patterns. The first was a higher rate of responding (or higher goodness ratings) for stimuli located relatively far from the category boundary. The second was an increase in response near the centroid of the stimulus distribution used for training. This was the area of highest stimulus density during training, and the response pattern resembles a classic prototype effect (e.g., Rosch 1978). This pattern indicates that the birds picked up information about the structure of the input distribution even though it was not necessary to perform the task. (Use of a linear boundary between the two categories would be sufficient for perfect performance.) Thus, perceptual systems may be quite sensitive to input distributions of experienced auditory stimuli, and this information may affect later categorization. In support of this conclusion, Maye et al. (2002) reported that the shape of previously experienced distributions could alter responses of human infants to speech sounds. They presented infants with either a bimodal distribution (resembling two categories) or unimodal distribution (resembling a single category) of VOT stimuli. In a subsequent discrimination task, infants with bimodal experience discriminated endpoints of the series (as if they belonged to separate categories) whereas infants with unimodal experience showed poorer discrimination. Taken together with the animal work and experiments on the categorization of nonspeech sounds (Guenther et al. 1999, Lotto 2000), these results are part of a growing literature on the ability of listeners to extract information about the statistics of input distributions. These studies likely will play a substantial role in our understanding of phoneme acquisition.

In summary, from the perspective of GA, the data on infant speech perception can be explained by an interaction between the operating characteristics of the auditory system and processes of perceptual learning. This audition-learning interaction is exemplified in a recent study by Holt et al. (2003). They took advantage of the natural boundaries that have been demonstrated for temporal processing to examine the formation of nonspeech categories. Participants were presented TOT stimuli similar to those used by Pisoni (1977; see Figure 2) and asked to label them as belonging to the experimenter-defined categories A or B, with the correct answer indicated by feedback. For half the participants, the category distributions were separated by the natural TOT boundary of +20 ms. For the other participants, the distributions were separated by a TOT boundary of +40 ms. For this condition, the natural boundary fell within the A category.

Two findings were noteworthy. The first was that participants whose experimenter-defined boundary was consistent with the natural boundary learned the categories much more readily. They required fewer than half as many trials to reach a criterion of 90% correct than subjects with experimenter-defined boundaries that were inconsistent with the natural boundary. That is, because the auditory system provided an initial parsing of the distributions, listeners had little difficulty learning the proper labels for each stimulus. Similarly, separating those categories by a natural boundary may facilitate the task of learning the voice categories of a language. The fact that languages tend to use these natural boundaries may be due to an advantage of learnability.

The second finding of Holt et al. (2003) was that participants assigned to the unnatural boundary condition did eventually learn to categorize the stimuli with high accuracy (greater than 90%). That is, the natural temporal order boundary is not essential to the categorization of TOT stimuli and, by extension, VOT stimuli. Learning processes are flexible enough to overcome some natural auditory biases. The results of learning can be seen in the discrimination responses of adult speakers of Spanish, who show a much larger peak at the Spanish voice boundary than at the English voice boundary (Williams 1977). The results demonstrate the potential for perceptual learning studies to explain patterns of speech category acquisition.

RELATION BETWEEN SPEECH PRODUCTION AND PERCEPTION

Both MT and DRT assume that there exists a very close relationship between speech production and perception: Talkers produce gestures and listeners perceive them (or, in the case of MT, they perceive the intended gestures). Accordingly, regularities of speech production (e.g., context dependencies in the realization of successive phonemes) should be highly correlated with listeners' perceptual judgments. A wealth of data assures us that such a correlation exists, and on this point there is no serious disagreement among theorists (Diehl & Kluender 1987, Fowler 1986, Liberman 1996). However, GA differs from MT and DRT on how the correlation is to be explained.

GA offers two general accounts of the correlation between speech production and perception, which are, simply stated: Production follows perception, and perception follows production. The first of these is meant to subsume cases in which the need for auditory distinctiveness of phonemes shapes production. For example, as described earlier, languages tend to locate +voice and −voice phonemes so that they are separated by natural auditory boundaries along the VOT dimension. More generally, the sound systems of languages tend to satisfy a principle of dispersion, whereby interphoneme distances are maximized within the available phonetic space to promote intelligibility of utterances even under unfavorable listening conditions. In simulation experiments, the dispersion principle has been shown to predict the structure of common vowel inventories quite accurately, especially when realistic auditory models are used to define a measure of auditory distance (Diehl et al. 2003, Liljencrants & Lindblom 1972).

How is the dispersion principle implemented by talkers? A general answer to this question is provided by the auditory enhancement hypothesis (Diehl & Kluender 1989a,b; Diehl et al. 2001; Kingston & Diehl 1994, 1995), which states that the gestural correlates of individual phonemes are selected to yield mutually enhancing auditory effects. Consider, for example, the vowel /u/, which occurs in most of the world's languages (Maddieson 1984). The acoustic property that distinguishes /u/ from all other vowels is a low-frequency F2. When talkers are required to speak clearly (for example, in the presence of background noise), they typically produce /u/ by retracting and raising the tongue body, enlarging the pharynx by moving the tongue root forward, raising the velum (and thus blocking airflow from the mouth through the nasal cavities), lowering the larynx, protruding the lips, and constricting the lip orifice. Every one of these gestures independently contributes to lowering the frequency of F2; together they create a maximally distinctive /u/, that is, one that is acoustically (and hence auditorily) most distant from other vowels (Diehl & Kluender 1989a,b). The dispersion principle and the auditory enhancement hypothesis are the main content of the claim that production follows perception.

The other claim of GA is that perception follows production. According to GA, listeners do not recover gestures, but they do perceive the acoustic consequences of gestures. Any regularities of speech production (e.g., context dependencies) will be reflected in the acoustic signal, and, through general mechanisms of perceptual learning, listeners come to make use of the acoustic correlates of these production regularities in judging the phonemic content of speech signals.

An implication of this discussion is that, by itself, the high correlation between speech production and perception is uninformative with respect to the debate between MT, DRT, and GA. All three predict that such a correlation must exist. Distinguishing them empirically requires other kinds of data including (but not restricted to) speech and nonspeech comparisons or human and animal comparisons. To illustrate this point, we consider the McGurk effect (McGurk & MacDonald 1976), where visual speechreading information may actually override inconsistent auditory information in determining the identification of a phoneme. In normal speech communication, visual and auditory cues are consistent, and listeners use both in making phoneme judgments. Both motor theorists (Liberman & Mattingly 1985) and direct realists (Fowler 1986, 1996) have claimed that the McGurk effect and, more generally, the use of auditory and visual information in speech perception, support a gestural account of perception. As Fowler (1996) puts it, "[L]isteners perceive gestures, and some gestures are specified optically as well as acoustically" (p. 1733). However, from the perspective of GA both acoustic and visual cues map perceptually onto phonemes, and the link between these cues can be attributed to perceptual learning. It is worth noting that biologically plausible computational models have demonstrated unsupervised learning of cross-modal categories (e.g., de Sa & Ballard 1998). Thus, a GA account appears to be no less compatible with results such as the McGurk effect than a gestural account.

Appealing to results outside the realm of normal speech perception may break this theoretical impasse. Diehl & Kluender (1989a) noted that a GA account explains not only the integration of auditory and visual information for phonemes but other forms of cue integration as well. For example, when certain acoustic properties of speech are artificially transduced into vibrotactile patterns on the skin, perceivers can learn to use this information along with correlated auditory and visual cues to identify phonemes (see, e.g., Sparks et al. 1978). Because the vibrotactile patterns cannot meaningfully be said to specify gestures, neither MT nor DRT appear to be able to accommodate the result without invoking assumptions similar to those of GA.

In a different attempt to distinguish between gestural and GA accounts of the McGurk effect, Fowler & Dekle (1991) asked listeners to identify a series of synthetic syllables ranging from /ba/ to /ga/ while concurrently viewing a printed version of either syllable. The authors reasoned that literate perceivers have extensive experience seeing printed words and hearing the words spoken, and therefore if simple association learning is responsible for the McGurk effect, then an analogous result should be observed in their experiment. In fact, the printed syllables had no effect on identification of the synthetic syllables, and Fowler & Dekle concluded that this result was incompatible with an associationist account of the McGurk effect.

A problem with this conclusion is that GA does not view the process of perceptual learning as equivalent to simple associative learning per se. To learn the auditory, visual, or even vibrotactile correlates of a phoneme is to learn what kinds of stimulus properties serve as information (i.e., as perceptual cues) for that phoneme. The relation between a perceptual cue and the object/event that is signaled by the cue is correctly referred to as an association, but it is a very specific kind of association. It is quite unlike, for example, the links between semantic associates (e.g., doctor:nurse, dog:cat, and oak:maple), between objects and their names (dog: "dog"), or between phonemes and their orthographic representations (/b/:"B"). Concerning the latter kind of association, no amount of experience reading aloud is likely to establish an informational relationship between letters and phonemes such that "B" signals that /b/ is now occurring.

In a different analog of the McGurk & MacDonald (1976) experiment, Fowler & Dekle (1991) had listeners identify synthetic /ba/-/ga/ stimuli while concurrently touching the mouth of a talker producing the syllables /ba/ or /ga/. No visual information about the talker was available to the participants. As with the visual version of the McGurk & MacDonald experiment, this haptic version yielded reliable evidence of cross-modal effects on phoneme judgments. According to Fowler & Dekle, these results support a gestural account of speech perception (with both optical and haptic information specifying the gestures), while ruling out a perceptual learning account on the grounds that participants would not have had previous experience perceiving speech haptically.

Below we discuss reasons for denying the claim of DRT that humans use acoustic information to perceive gestures. However, no one would deny that at least some gestures (e.g., lip closing and opening) are visually accessible or that such visual information typically plays a useful role in speech perception. Nor is it surprising that humans can tell whether a talker is closing and opening the lips (as in the production of /ba/) merely by touching the talker's lips. Haptic speech perception may be unusual, but humans have abundant haptic experience with shapes and surface contours in general, ensuring likely success for this special case. GA would certainly not discount the use of gestural information to recognize phonemes in those cases where gestures are perceptually accessible.

As mentioned earlier, GA is not a theory as such but rather a general framework within which particular theoretical claims are formulated and tested. These claims may include competing explanations for the same phenomenon, as in the following example. A well-known correlate of the voice distinction is variation in fundamental frequency (f0): vowels immediately following +voice consonants tend to have lower f0 values than vowels following −voice consonants. Correspondingly, a lower f0 tends to shift the perceived voice boundary toward higher values of VOT (i.e., more stimuli are judged as +voice). Diehl (1991, Diehl & Molis 1995) claimed that f0 is controlled by talkers as part of a strategy of auditory enhancement of the voice distinction: Voicing during the consonant and a low f0 and F1 near the consonant all contribute to the low frequency periodicity that, by hypothesis, is a main distinctive acoustic correlate of +voice consonants. In this view, f0 affects voice perception for auditory reasons (e.g., integration of low frequency energy) and not because f0 is a learned cue for the voice distinction. However, such a perceptual learning account is clearly compatible with GA. To test the two competing claims, Holt et al. (2001) trained Japanese quail to respond to one of three series of VOT stimuli: one in which VOT and f0 varied in the natural way (shorter VOT, lower f0), one in which the pattern was reversed (shorter VOT, higher f0), and one in which the relation between VOT and f0 was random. For birds trained in the random condition, there was no effect of f0 on responses to novel VOT stimuli, while for the other two groups, responses followed the learned pattern of stimulus covariation. These findings strongly support the perceptual learning account, and appear to rule out the auditory (low-frequency integration) account, of the influence of f0 on VOT perception.

CONCLUDING REMARKS: CHALLENGES TO MT, DRT, AND GA

In this concluding section, we describe what we think are the main challenges to each of the three main theoretical perspectives on speech perception.

Motor Theory

We argue above that a high correlation between measures of speech production and perception is by itself uninformative theoretically because all major perspectives predict such a correlation. Accordingly, the empirical case for MT must ultimately rest on demonstrations of patterns of performance that are specific to speech perception by humans. During the last four decades, motor theorists have described a variety of empirical phenomena that they believed satisfied the condition of speech- and/or human-specificity (Liberman 1996, Liberman et al. 1967, Liberman & Mattingly 1985). In preceding sections, we examined some of these phenomena, including categorical perception and several phonetic context effects, and concluded that they were not, in fact, unique to speech or to human listeners.

Another phenomenon claimed to be diagnostic of perception in the speech mode is duplex perception. When all of a synthetic /da/ or /ga/ syllable except for the F2 transition (which specifies place of articulation) is presented to one ear of a listener and the F2 transition alone is presented in proper temporal alignment to the other ear, the listener experiences two percepts: a nonspeech "chirp" (corresponding to the F2 transition alone) and a full /da/ or /ga/ syllable. Thus, the same acoustic property is perceived in two very different ways, reflecting, according to Liberman & Mattingly (1985), the operation of both a speech and a nonspeech module that use the same input signal to create representations of distinct sound sources. However, Fowler & Rosenblum (1991) demonstrated an analog of duplex perception for the sound of a slamming door, with the high-frequency portion of the signal presented to one ear and the rest of the signal presented to the other ear. Because it is unlikely that humans have evolved specialized modules for slamming doors, Fowler & Rosenblum concluded that duplex perception does not provide clear evidence for MT.

A main challenge for motor theorists, therefore, is to offer more compelling evidence of genuine speech- and human-specific perceptual performance.

Direct Realist Theory

A core assumption of DRT is that perceivers recover the actual environmental events that structure informational media such as light or sound. Plainly, some environmental properties are perceptually accessible. Among them are the visually and haptically accessible layout of surfaces in the environment and the auditorily accessible location of sound sources. However, certain other environmental properties that structure light or sound are not similarly accessible. For example, organisms that are limited to two or three types of cone photopigments cannot unambiguously recover the spectral distribution of reflected light because every pattern of cone responses is compatible with an infinite set of hypothetical surface reflectances. In order for any environmental property to be perceptually recoverable in principle, there must be information available to the perceiver that uniquely specifies that property. This essential condition is met in the case of visual perception of surface layout [assuming some general constraints such as rigidity (Ullman 1984)] and in the case of auditory perception of sound location (Grantham 1995), but the condition is not met in the case of visual detection of surface reflectance.

The question of interest here is, Do acoustic signals uniquely specify the properties of sound sources such as the vocal tract? The answer appears to be no. Even if one restricts the discussion to anatomically possible vocal tract shapes, there are many different ways to produce a given speech signal. For example, approximately the same formant pattern can be achieved either by rounding the lips, lowering the larynx, or doing a little of both (Riordan 1977). Also, one can produce the distinctively low-frequency F3 of the American English vowel contained in the word "her" by making vocal tract constrictions at the lips, midpalate, or the midpharynx, or at some combination of these places (Ohala 1985, Lindau 1985). Additional evidence that different gestures can yield similar acoustic patterns is presented in Ladefoged et al. (1972), Nearey (1980), and Johnson et al. (1993).

Acoustic ambiguity of source specification also holds outside the domain of speech. For example, in a paper titled "One Cannot Hear the Shape of a Drum," Gordon et al. (1992) proved mathematically that quite different drum shapes can produce identical acoustic signals. Also, the same resonant sound can be initiated by air pressure sources generated by piston-like compression, bellows-like compression, or by a heat-induced pressure increase in a fixed container. Examples of such source ambiguity appear to be pervasive.

In attempting to solve the "inverse problem" (i.e., mapping speech signals onto vocal tract shapes that produced them), speech-processing engineers have found it necessary to assume various facts such as length or certain other characteristics of the vocal tract (Atal & Hanauer 1971, McGowan 1994). Without such assumptions, the inverse problem appears to be intractable. In principle, this is not a problem for MT, which assumes that the speech module reflects the coevolution in humans of both production and perception. In this view, the human perceiver of speech sounds has implicit knowledge of the speech production apparatus, which presumably can be applied to solve the inverse problem. However, DRT does not have this recourse. According to Fowler (1989), nonhuman listeners can perceive human speech gestures just as humans can (which is why parallels between human and nonhuman perceptual performance are not viewed as surprising from the perspective of DRT). Clearly, Japanese quail and macaque monkeys do not have the implicit knowledge of the human vocal tract that might constrain the solution to the inverse problem.

Thus, a major challenge for DRT is to offer a credible solution to the inverse problem that does not rely on prior knowledge of the human vocal tract.

General Approach

We have described GA as a general framework within which specific hypotheses are formulated and tested. Some of these hypotheses (e.g., threshold of temporal ordering, dispersion and auditory enhancement, spectral and durational contrast, and covariance learning) were discussed in light of relevant findings, and the overall approach seems promising. Nevertheless, the challenges facing GA are daunting. They fall into two general categories, reflecting the dual emphasis of GA on auditory processing and perceptual learning. Our knowledge of mammalian auditory processing is large and growing, but detailed and accurate models are still largely restricted to the auditory periphery. Some of the hypotheses described within the GA framework (e.g., durational contrast) are not independently justified on the basis of known mechanisms of auditory processing and are therefore rather ad hoc. Related to this, there are not yet principled grounds for precisely predicting the conditions under which such hypotheses apply. For example, evidence for durational contrast has been reliably found in some conditions (Diehl & Walsh 1989) but not in others (Fowler 1992). We need to know a great deal more about auditory processing, especially beyond the auditory nerve, to properly constrain our models of speech perception. Particular attention must be focused on the role of neural plasticity at higher levels of the auditory pathway.

Current knowledge about how humans learn speech categories is even more limited. As reviewed earlier, we are beginning to understand how listeners respond to various statistical properties of stimuli when experimenters control the input distributions. However, we lack comprehensive measurements of the statistical properties of natural speech sounds in the listener's environment. Without such measurements, it is impossible to formulate models of natural language learning with good predictive power.

Therefore, a major challenge for GA is to develop hypotheses based on far more accurate information about the auditory representation of speech and the statistical properties of natural speech.

ACKNOWLEDGMENTS

Preparation of this chapter was supported by NIH Grant R01 DC00427–14 to RLD and NIH Grant R01 DC04674–02 to AJL and LLH. We thank Sarah Sullivan for her help in preparing the manuscript.

The *Annual Review of Psychology* is online at http://psych.annualreviews.org

LITERATURE CITED

Abramson AS, Lisker L. 1970. Discriminability along the voicing continuum: cross language tests. In *Proc. Int. Congr. Phonet. Sci., 6th, Prague, 1967*, pp. 569–73. Prague: Academia

Aslin RN, Pisoni DB, Hennessy BL, Perey AJ. 1981. Discrimination of voice onset time by human infants: new findings and implications for the effects of early experience. *Child Dev.* 52:1135–45

Atal BS, Hanauer SL. 1971. Speech analysis and synthesis by linear prediction of the speech wave. *J. Acoust. Soc. Am.* 50:637–55

Best CT. 1993. Emergence of language-specific constraints in perception of non-native speech: a window on early phonological development. In *Developmental Neurocognition: Speech and Face Processing in the First Year of Life*, ed. B de Boysson-Bardies, S de Schonen, P Jusczyk, P MacNeilage, J Morton, pp. 289–304. Norwell, MA: Kluwer Acad.

Best CT. 1995. A direct realist view of cross-language speech perception. In *Speech Perception and Linguistic Experience: Issues in Cross-Language Research*, ed. W Strange, pp. 171–206. Baltimore, MD: New York Press

Best CT, McRoberts GW, Sithole NM. 1988. Examination of perceptual reorganization for nonnative speech contrasts: Zulu click discrimination by English-speaking adults and infants. *J. Exp. Psychol.: Hum. Percept. Perform.* 14:345–60

Brunswik E. 1956. *Perception and the Representative Design of Psychological Experiments.* Berkeley: Univ. Calif. Press

Chomsky N. 1965. *Aspects of the Theory of Syntax.* Cambridge, MA: MIT Press

Delattre PC, Liberman AM, Cooper FS. 1951. Voyelles synthétiques à deux formants et voyelles cardinales. *Le Maître Phon.* 96:30–37

Delattre PC, Liberman AM, Cooper FS. 1955. Acoustic loci and transitional cues for consonants. *J. Acoust. Soc. Am.* 27:769–73

Delattre PC, Liberman AM, Cooper FS. 1964. Formant transitions and loci as acoustic correlates of place of articulation in American fricatives. *Stud. Linguist.* 18:104–21

Delattre PC, Liberman AM, Cooper FS, Gerstman LJ. 1952. An experimental study of the acoustic determinants of vowel color. *Word* 8:195–210

de Sa VR, Ballard DH. 1998. Category learning through multimodal sensing. *Neurol. Comput.* 10:1097–117

Diehl RL. 1987. Auditory constraints on speech perception. In *The Psychophysics of Speech*

Perception, ed. MEH Schouten, 39:210–19. Dordrecht: Martimus-Nihboff

Diehl RL. 1991. The role of phonetics within the study of language. *Phonetica* 48:120–34

Diehl RL, Kluender KR. 1987. On the categorization of speech sounds. In *Categorical Perception*, ed. S Harnad, pp. 226–53. London: Cambridge Univ. Press

Diehl RL, Kluender KR. 1989a. On the objects of speech perception. *Ecol. Psychol.* 2:121–44

Diehl RL, Kluender KR. 1989b. Reply to commentators. *Ecol. Psychol.* 1:195–225

Diehl RL, Lindblom B, Creeger CP. 2003. Increasing realism of auditory representations yields further insights into vowel phonetics. In *Proc. Int. Congr. Phon. Sci., 15th, Barcelona.* 2:1381–84. Adelaide: Causal Publications

Diehl RL, Molis MR. 1995. Effects of fundamental frequency on medial [voice] judgments. *Phonetica* 52:188–95

Diehl RL, Molis MR, Castleman WA. 2001. Adaptive design of sound systems: some auditory considerations. In *The Role of Perceptual Phenomena in Phonological Theory*, ed. K Johnson, E Hume, pp. 123–39. San Diego: Academic

Diehl RL, Souther AF, Convis CL. 1980. Conditions on rate normalization in speech perception. *Percept. Psychophys.* 27:435–43

Diehl RL, Walsh MA. 1989. An auditory basis for the stimulus-length effect in the perception of stops and glides. *J. Acoust. Soc. Am.* 85:2154–64

Diehl RL, Walsh MA, Kluender KR. 1991. On the interpretability of speech/nonspeech comparisons: a reply to Fowler. *J. Acoust. Soc. Am.* 89:2905–9

Dooling RJ, Best CT, Brown SD. 1995. Discrimination of synthetic full-formant and sinewave /ra-la/ continua by budgerigars (*Melopsittacus undulatus*) and zebra finches (*Taeniopygia guttata*). *J. Acoust. Soc. Am.* 97:1839–46

Eilers RE. 1977. Context-sensitive perception of naturally produced stop and fricative consonants by infants. *J. Acoust. Soc. Am.* 61:1321–36

Eimas PD. 1974. Auditory and linguistic processing of cues for place of articulation by infants. *Percept. Psychophys.* 16:513–21

Eimas PD. 1991. Comment: some effects of language acquisition on speech perception. In *Modularity and the Motor Theory of Speech Perception*, ed. IG Mattingly, M Studdert-Kennedy, pp. 111–16. Hillsdale, NJ: Erlbaum

Eimas PD, Siqueland ER, Jusczyk P, Vigorito J. 1971. Speech perception in infants. *Science* 171:303–6

Elman JL, Diehl RL, Buchwald SE. 1977. Perceptual switching in bilinguals. *J. Acoust. Soc. Am.* 62:971–74

Elman JL, McClelland JL. 1988. Cognitive penetration of the mechanisms of perception: compensation for coarticulation of lexically restored phonemes. *J. Mem. Lang.* 27:143–65

Fowler CA. 1980. Coarticulation and theories of extrinsic timing. *J. Phon.* 8:113–33

Fowler CA. 1981. Production and perception of coarticulation among stressed and unstressed vowels. *J. Speech Hear. Res.* 24:127–39

Fowler CA. 1984. Segmentation of coarticulated speech in perception. *Percept. Psychophys.* 36:359–68

Fowler CA. 1986. An event approach to the study of speech perception from a direct-realist perspective. *J. Phon.* 14:3–28

Fowler CA. 1989. Real objects of speech perception: a commentary on Diehl and Kluender. *Ecol. Psychol.* 1:145–60

Fowler CA. 1990. Sound-producing sources as objects of perception: rate normalization and nonspeech perception. *J. Acoust. Soc. Am.* 88:1236–49

Fowler CA. 1991. Auditory perception is not special: We see the world, we feel the world, we hear the world. *J. Acoust. Soc. Am.* 89:2910–15

Fowler CA. 1992. Vowel duration and closure duration in voiced and unvoiced stops: There are no contrast effects here. *J. Phon.* 20:143–65

Fowler CA. 1994. Speech perception: direct

realist theory. In *The Encyclopedia of Language and Linguistics*, ed. RE Asher, pp. 4199–203. Oxford: Pergamon

Fowler CA. 1996. Listeners do hear sounds, not tongues. *J. Acoust. Soc. Am.* 99:1730–41

Fowler CA, Best CT, McRoberts GW. 1990. Young infants' perception of liquid coarticulatory influences on following stop consonants. *Percept. Psychophys.* 48:559–70

Fowler CA, Brown JM, Mann VA. 2000. Contrast effects do not underlie effects of preceding liquids on stop-consonant identification by humans. *J. Exp. Psychol.: Hum. Percept. Perform.* 26:877–88

Fowler CA, Dekle D. 1991. Listening with eye and hand: crossmodal contributions to speech perception. *J. Exp. Psychol.: Hum. Percept. Perform.* 17:816–28

Fowler CA, Rosenblum LD. 1991. The perception of phonetic gestures. In *Modularity and the Motor Theory of Speech Perception*, ed. IG Mattingly, M Studdert-Kennedy, pp. 33–59. Hillsdale NJ: Erlbaum

Fowler CA, Smith MR. 1986. Speech perception as "vector analysis": an approach to the problems of invariance and segmentation. In *Invariance and Variability in Speech Processes*, ed. JS Perkell, DH Klatt, pp. 123–39. Hillsdale, NJ: Erlbaum

Frieda EM, Walley AC, Flege JE, Sloane ME. 1999. Adults' perception of native and nonnative vowels: implications for the perceptual magnet effect. *Percept. Psychophys.* 61:561–77

Gibson JJ. 1966. *The Senses Considered as Perceptual Systems*. Boston: Houghton Mifflin

Gibson JJ. 1979. *The Ecological Approach to Visual Perception*. Boston: Houghton Mifflin

Gordon C, Webb DL, Wolpert S. 1992. One cannot hear the shape of a drum. *Bull. Am. Math. Soc.* 27:134–38

Grantham DW. 1995. Spatial hearing and related phenomena. In *Hearing*, ed. B Moore, pp. 297–345. San Diego, CA: Academic

Guenther FH, Husain FT, Cohen MA, Shinn-Cunningham BG. 1999. Effects of categorization and discrimination training on auditory perceptual space. *J. Acoust. Soc. Am.* 106:2900–12

Hammarberg R. 1976. The metaphysics of coarticulation. *J. Phon.* 4:353–63

Hirsh IJ. 1959. Auditory perception of temporal order. *J. Acoust. Soc. Am.* 31:759–67

Hirsh IJ, Sherrick CE. 1961. Perceived order in different sense modalities. *J. Exp. Psychol.* 62:423–32

Holt LL. 1999. *Auditory constraints on speech perception: an examination of spectral contrast*. PhD thesis. Univ. Wis. 132 pp.

Holt LL, Lotto AJ, Diehl RL. 2003. Perceptual discontinuities and categorization: Implications for speech perception. *J. Acoust. Soc. Am.* 113:2255

Holt LL, Lotto AJ, Kluender KR. 1998. Incorporating principles of general learning in theories of language acquisition. In *Chicago Linguistic Society: The Panels*, ed. M Gruber, CD Higgins, KS Olson, T Wysocki, 34:253–68. Chicago, IL: Chicago Linguist. Soc.

Holt LL, Lotto AJ, Kluender KR. 2000. Neighboring spectral content influences vowel identification. *J. Acoust. Soc. Am.* 108:710–22

Holt LL, Lotto AJ, Kluender KR. 2001. Influence of fundamental frequency on stop-consonant voicing perception: a case of learned covariation or auditory enhancement? *J. Acoust. Soc. Am.* 109:764–74

Johnson K, Flemming E, Wright R. 1993. The hyperspace effect: phonetic targets are hyperarticulated. *Language* 69:505–28

Jusczyk PW. 1993. From general to language-specific capacities: the WRAPSA model of how speech perception develops. *J. Phon.* 21:3–28

Jusczyk PW. 1997. *The Discovery of Spoken Language*. Cambridge, MA: MIT Press

Jusczyk PW, Pisoni DB, Walley A, Murray J. 1980. Discrimination of relative onset time of two-component tones by infants. *J. Acoust. Soc. Am.* 67:262–70

Kingston J, Diehl RL. 1994. Phonetic knowledge. *Language* 70:419–54

Kingston J, Diehl RL. 1995. Intermediate properties in the perception of distinctive feature values. In *Phonology and Phonetics: Papers in Laboratory Phonology*, ed. B Connell, A Arvaniti, 4:7–27. London: Cambridge Univ. Press

Kluender KR. 1994. Speech perception as a tractable problem in cognitive science. In *Handbook of Psycholinguistics*, ed. MA Gernsbacher, pp. 173–217. San Diego, CA: Academic

Kluender KR, Diehl RL, Killeen PR. 1987. Japanese quail can learn phonetic categories. *Science* 237:1195–97

Kluender KR, Lotto AJ, Holt LL, Bloedel SL. 1998. Role of experience for language-specific functional mappings of vowel sounds. *J. Acoust. Soc. Am.* 104:3568–82

Krakow RA, Beddor PS, Goldstein LM, Fowler CA. 1988. Coarticulatory influences on the perceived height of nasal vowels. *J. Acoust. Soc. Am.* 83:1146–58

Kuhl PK. 1981. Discrimination of speech by nonhuman animals: basic auditory sensitivities conducive to the perception of speech-sound categories. *J. Acoust. Soc. Am.* 95:340–49

Kuhl PK. 1986. Theoretical contributions of tests on animals to the special mechanisms debate in speech. *J. Exp. Biol.* 45:233–65

Kuhl PK. 1991. Human adults and human infants show a "perceptual magnet effect" for the prototypes of speech categories, monkeys do not. *Percept. Psychophys.* 50:93–107

Kuhl PK. 1992. Speech prototypes: studies on the nature, function, ontogeny and phylogeny of the "centers" of speech categories. In *Speech Perception, Production and Linguistic Structure*, ed. Y Tohkura, E Vatikiotis-Bateson, Y Sagisaka, pp. 239–64. Tokyo, Jpn: Ohmsha

Kuhl PK. 1993. Innate predispositions and the effects of experience in speech perception: the native language magnet theory. In *Developmental Neurocognition: Speech and Face Processing in the First Year of Life*, ed. B de Boysson-Bardies, S de Schonen, P Jusczyk, P MacNeilage, J Morton, pp. 259–74. Dordrecht, Netherlands: Kluwer Acad.

Kuhl PK. 2000. Language, mind, and the brain: Experience alters perception. In *The New Cognitive Neurosciences*, ed. MS Gazzaniga, pp. 99–115. Cambridge, MA: MIT Press

Kuhl PK, Miller JD. 1975. Speech perception by the chinchilla: voiced-voiceless distinction in alveolar plosive consonants. *Science* 190:69–72

Kuhl PK, Miller JD. 1978. Speech perception by the chinchilla: identification functions for synthetic VOT stimuli. *J. Acoust. Soc. Am.* 63:905–17

Kuhl PK, Padden DM. 1982. Enhanced discriminability at the phonetic boundaries for the voicing feature in macaques. *Percept. Psychophys.* 32:542–50

Kuhl PK, Padden DM. 1983. Enhanced discriminability at the phonetic boundaries for the place feature in macaques. *J. Acoust. Soc. Am.* 73:1003–10

Ladefoged P, DeClerk J, Lindau M, Papcun G. 1972. An auditory-motor theory of speech production. *UCLA Work. Pap. Phon.* 22:48–75

Lane H. 1965. The motor theory of speech perception: a critical review. *Psychol. Rev.* 72:275–309

Lasky RE, Syrdal-Lasky A, Klein RE. 1975. VOT discrimination by four to six and a half month old infants from Spanish environments. *J. Exp. Child Psychol.* 20:215–25

Liberman AM. 1957. Some results of research on speech perception. *J. Acoust. Soc. Am.* 29:117–23

Liberman AM. 1996. Introduction: some assumptions about speech and how they changed. In *Speech: A Special Code*. Cambridge, MA: MIT Press

Liberman AM, Cooper FS, Shankweiler DP, Studdert-Kennedy M. 1967. Perception of the speech code. *Psychol. Rev.* 74:431–61

Liberman AM, Delattre P, Cooper FS. 1952. The role of selected stimulus-variables in the perception of the unvoiced stop consonants. *Am. J. Psychol.* 65:497–516

Liberman AM, Delattre PC, Cooper FS, Gerstman LJ. 1954. The role of consonant-vowel transitions in the stop and nasal consonants. *Psychol. Monogr.* 68:1–13

Liberman AM, Delattre PC, Gerstman LJ, Cooper FS. 1956. Tempo of frequency change as a cue for distinguishing classes of speech sounds. *J. Exp. Psychol.* 52:127–37

Liberman AM, Harris K, Eimas P, Lisker L, Bastian J. 1961a. An effect of learning on speech perception: the discrimination of durations of silence with and without phonemic significance. *Lang. Speech* 4:175–95

Liberman AM, Harris KS, Hoffman HS, Griffith BC. 1957. The discrimination of speech sounds within and across phoneme boundaries. *J. Exp. Psychol.* 54:358–68

Liberman AM, Harris KS, Kinney JA, Lane H. 1961b. The discrimination of relative onset-time of the components of certain speech and nonspeech patterns. *J. Exp. Psychol.* 61:379–88

Liberman AM, Mattingly IG. 1985. The motor theory of speech perception revised. *Cognition* 21:1–36

Liberman AM, Mattingly IG, Turvey MT. 1972. Language codes and memory codes. In *Coding Processes in Human Memory*, ed. AW Melton, E Martin, pp. 307–34. Washington, DC: Winston

Liljencrants J, Lindblom B. 1972. Numerical simulation of vowel quality systems: the role of perceptual contrast. *Language* 48:839–62

Lindau M. 1985. The story of /r/. In *Phonetic Linguistics*, ed. V Fromkin, pp. 157–68. Orlando, FL: Academic

Lindblom BEF, Studdert-Kennedy M. 1967. On the role of formant transitions in vowel recognition. *J. Acoust. Soc. Am.* 42:830–43

Lisker L, Abramson AS. 1964. A cross-language study of voicing in initial stops: acoustical measurements. *Word* 20:384–422

Lisker L, Abramson AS. 1970. The voicing dimension: some experiments in comparative phonetics. In *Proc. Int. Congr. Phon. Sci., 6th, Prague, 1967*, pp. 563–67. Prague: Academia

Lively SE, Pisoni DB. 1997. On prototypes and phonetic categories: a critical assessment of the perceptual magnet effect in speech perception. *J. Exp. Psychol.: Hum. Percept. Perform.* 23:1665–79

Lotto AJ. 2000. Language acquisition as complex category formation. *Phonetica* 57:189–96

Lotto AJ, Kluender KR. 1998. General contrast effects of speech perception: effect of preceding liquid on stop consonant identification. *Percept. Psychophys.* 60:602–19

Lotto AJ, Kluender KR, Holt LL. 1997. Perceptual compensation for coarticulation by Japanese quail (*Coturnix coturnix japonica*). *J. Acoust. Soc. Am.* 102:1134–40

Lotto AJ, Kluender KR, Holt LL. 1998. The perceptual magnet effect depolarized. *J. Acoust. Soc. Am.* 103:3648–55

Maddieson I. 1984. *Patterns of Sound*. London: Cambridge Univ. Press

Magnuson JS, McMurray B, Tanenhaus MK, Aslin RN. 2003. Lexical effects on compensation for coarticulation: the ghost of Christmash past. *Cogn. Sci.* 27:285–98

Mann VA. 1980. Influence of preceding liquid on stop-consonant perception. *Percept. Psychophys.* 28:407–12

Mann VA. 1986. Distinguishing universal and language-dependent levels of speech perception: evidence from Japanese listeners' perception of English "l" and "r". *Cognition* 24:169–96

Mann VA, Repp BH. 1981. Influence of preceding fricative on stop consonant perception. *J. Acoust. Soc. Am.* 69:548–58

Massaro DW. 1987. *Speech Perception by Ear and Eye: A Paradigm for Psychological Inquiry*. Hillsdale, NJ: Erlbaum

Massaro DW, Oden GC. 1980. Evaluation and integration of acoustic features in speech perception. *J. Acoust. Soc. Am.* 67:996–1013

Mattingly IG, Liberman AM, Syrdal AK, Halwes T. 1971. Discrimination in speech and nonspeech modes. *Cogn. Psychol.* 2:131–57

Maye J, Werker JF, Gerken L. 2002. Infant sensitivity to distributional information can affect phonetic discrimination. *Cognition* 82:B101–11

McGowan RS. 1994. Recovering articulatory

movement from formant frequency trajectories using task dynamics and a genetic algorithm: preliminary results. *Speech Commun.* 14:19–49

McGurk H, MacDonald J. 1976. Hearing lips and seeing voices. *Nature* 264:746–47

Miller JD, Wier CC, Pastore RE, Kelly WJ, Dooling RJ. 1976. Discrimination and labeling of noise-buzz sequences with varying noise-lead times: an example of categorical perception. *J. Acoust. Soc. Am.* 60:410–17

Miller JL. 1987. Rate-dependent processing in speech perception. In *Progress in the Psychology of Language*, ed. A Ellis, pp. 119–57. Hillsdale, NJ: Erlbaum

Miller JL, Eimas PD. 1983. Studies on the categorization of speech by infants. *Cognition* 12:135–65

Miller JL, Liberman AM. 1979. Some effects of later-occurring information on the perception of stop consonant and semivowel. *Percept. Psychophys.* 25:457–65

Nearey TM. 1980. On the physical interpretation of vowel quality: cinefluorographic and acoustic evidence. *J. Phon.* 8:213–41

Nearey TM. 1989. Static, dynamic, and relational properties in vowel perception. *J. Acoust. Soc. Am.* 85:2088–113

Nearey TM. 1990. The segment as a unit of speech perception. *J. Phon.* 18:347–73

Nearey TM, Hogan J. 1986. Phonological contrast in experimental phonetics: relating distributions of production data to perceptual categorization curves. In *Experimental Phonology*, ed. JJ Ohala, J Jaeger, pp. 141–61. New York: Academic

Ohala JJ. 1985. Around flat. In *Phonetic Linguistics: Essays in Honor of Peter Ladefoged*, ed. VA Fromkin, pp. 223–41. Orlando, FL: Academic

Ohala JJ. 1996. Speech perception is hearing sounds, not tongues. *J. Acoust. Soc. Am.* 99: 1718–25

Pastore RE. 1981. Possible psychoacoustic factors in speech perception. In *Perspectives on the Study of Speech*, ed. PD Eimas, JL Miller, pp. 165–205. Hillsdale, NJ: Erlbaum

Pegg JE, Werker JF. 1997. Adult and infant perception of two English phones. *J. Acoust. Soc. Am.* 102:3742–53

Pisoni DB. 1977. Identification and discrimination of the relative onset time of two component tones: implications for voicing perception in stops. *J. Acoust. Soc. Am.* 61:1352–61

Repp BH. 1981. On levels of description in speech research. *J. Acoust. Soc. Am.* 69: 1462–64

Riordan CJ. 1977. Control of vocal-tract length in speech. *J. Acoust. Soc. Am.* 62:998–1002

Rosch EH. 1978. Principles of categorization. In *Cognition and Categorization*, ed. E Rosch, B Lloyd, pp. 28–48. Hillsdale, NJ: Erlbaum

Samuel AG, Pitt MA. 2003. Lexical activation (and other factors) can mediate compensation for coarticulation. *J. Mem. Lang.* 48: 416–34

Simos PG, Diehl RL, Breier JI, Molis MR, Zouridakis G, Papanicolaou AC. 1998. MEG correlates of categorical perception of a voice onset time continuum in humans. *Cogn. Brain Res.* 7:215–19

Sinex DG, McDonald LP, Mott JB. 1991. Neural correlates of nonmonotonic temporal acuity for voice onset time. *J. Acoust. Soc. Am.* 90:2441–49

Sparks DW, Kuhl P, Edmonds AE, Gray GP. 1978. Investigating the MESA (Multipoint Electrotactile Speech Aid): the transmission of segmental features of speech. *J. Acoust. Soc. Am.* 63:246–57

Stephens JD, Holt LL. 2002. Are context effects in speech perception modulated by visual information? *43rd Annu. Meet. Psychon. Soc., Kansas City, MO.*

Stevens KN, Klatt DH. 1974. Role of formant transitions in the voiced-voiceless distinction for stops. *J. Acoust. Soc. Am.* 55:653–59

Summerfield Q. 1981. On articulatory rate and perceptual constancy in phonetic perception. *J. Exp. Psychol.: Hum. Percept. Perform.* 7:1074–95

Sussman HM, Fruchter D, Hilbert J, Sirosh J. 1998. Linear correlates in the speech signal: the orderly output constraint. *Behav. Brain Sci.* 21:241–99

Sussman JE, Lauckner -Morano VJ. 1995. Further tests of the "perceptual magnet effect" in the perception of [i]: identification and change-no-change discrimination. *J. Acoust. Soc. Am.* 97:539–52

Ullman S. 1984. Maximizing rigidity: the incremental recovery of 3-D structure from rigid and nonrigid motion. *Perception* 13:255–74

Werker JF, Gilbert JHV, Humphrey K, Tees RC. 1981. Developmental aspects of cross-language speech perception. *Child Dev.* 52:349–53

Werker JF, Tees RC. 1984. Cross-language speech perception: evidence for perceptual reorganization during the first year of life. *Infant Behav. Dev.* 7:49–63

Werner LA, Bargones JY. 1992. Psychoacoustic development of human infants. In *Advances in Infancy Research*, ed. C Rovee-Collier, L Lipsitt, 7:103–45. Norwood, NJ: Ablex

Williams L. 1977. The perception of stop consonant voicing by Spanish-English bilinguals. *Percept. Psychophys.* 21:289–97

Annu. Rev. Psychol. 2004. 55:181–205
doi: 10.1146/annurev.psych.55.090902.141903
First published online as a Review in Advance on October 27, 2003

VISUAL MECHANISMS OF MOTION ANALYSIS AND MOTION PERCEPTION

Andrew M. Derrington,[1] Harriet A. Allen,[2] and Louise S. Delicato[3]

[1]School of Psychology, University Park, Nottingham, United Kingdom;
email: Andrew.Derrington@nottingham.ac.uk
[2]The School of Psychology, University of Birmingham, Edgbaston, Birmingham B15 2TT;
email: allenha@psg-fs5.bham.ac.uk
[3]Center for Neurobiology and Behavior, Columbia University, New York,
New York 10032; email: ld2040@columbia.edu

Key Words first-order motion, second-order motion, third-order motion, feature tracking, psychophysics

■ **Abstract** Psychophysical experiments on feature tracking suggest that most of our sensitivity to chromatic motion and to second-order motion depends on feature tracking. There is no reason to suppose that the visual system contains motion sensors dedicated to the analysis of second-order motion. Current psychophysical and physiological data indicate that local motion sensors are selective for orientation and spatial frequency but they do not eliminate any of the three main models—the Reichardt detector, the motion-energy filter, and gradient-based sensors. Both psychophysical and physiological data suggest that both broadly oriented and narrowly oriented motion sensors are important in the early analysis of motion in two dimensions.

CONTENTS

0066-4308/04/0204-0181$14.00

INTRODUCTION: OVERVIEW OF MOTION PERCEPTION AND MOTION ANALYSIS

This review considers the early stages of the analysis of motion by the visual system. The operation of these stages is revealed by simple perceptual tasks—requiring an observer to detect a moving stimulus or to identify its direction of motion. When carried out with appropriate stimuli, and informed by the results of neurophysiological recordings, experiments like these allow us to establish the properties of the early motion sensors and to begin to understand the ways in which the signals produced by those sensors are combined to compute the motion of surfaces and rigid objects. These are the two aspects of motion analysis covered by this review.

The mechanisms of motion analysis considered here are fundamental to motion perception. However, it is important to distinguish between motion analysis—the processing of signals generated by the motion of image features across the retina—and the perception of motion. The distinction is important because motion can be perceived—that is, an observer can form the perceptual impression that an object is moving or has moved—in the absence of any retinal image motion. Moreover, retinal image motion can be used by the visual system in order to provide information about the shape of objects or their layout rather than about their motion. Most of the observations discussed in this review analyze the conditions under which motion is perceived in order to make inferences about the mechanisms of motion analysis, thus it is necessary at the outset to clarify the distinction between motion perception and motion analysis.

Motion Perception

Motion perception is the process by which we acquire perceptual knowledge about the motion of objects and surfaces in the image. It is important to note that such knowledge can be derived in at least two ways. It can be derived directly, from the analysis of retinal motion (by dedicated motion sensors), or indirectly, by inferring motion from changes in the retinal position of objects, or their features, over time. This latter process, which is known as feature tracking (Del Viva & Morrone 1998) or third-order motion analysis (Lu & Sperling 1995), is a very powerful and versatile way of carrying out motion-discrimination tasks. This makes it important to establish conditions under which motion-discrimination tasks depend on feature tracking and to ensure that experiments intended to elucidate the properties of dedicated motion sensors are designed in such a way that observers are unable to use feature tracking to carry out the experimental task.

A third way of deriving information about the motion of an object, which is outside the scope of this review, is by monitoring the head and eye movements necessary to keep the image of the object stable on the retina if the eyes track the object as it moves. In the experiments we consider the eyes are kept stationary, often by voluntary fixation on a stable reference point, and the stimulus moves across the retina.

Motion Analysis

Just as motion perception may or may not depend on the signals generated by the motion of image features in the retina, the analysis of retinal motion signals may or may not lead to the perception that an object is moving. Perhaps the most striking everyday phenomenon in which the motion of an object is analyzed without giving rise to the perception that the object is moving is vection, the visually induced sensation that it is the observer, rather than objects in the external world, that is moving. Vection commonly occurs when we sit looking out the window of a stationary train and the train at the next platform begins to move and we have the sensation that our train has begun to move. The visual motion signals generated by the motion of an external object give us the impression we ourselves are moving.

A related phenomenon to vection occurs when an observer really does move through a static environment. The observer's motion sweeps the stationary objects in the environment across the retina, generating an array of motion signals known as optic flow. Optic flow signals are scientifically interesting because they can be used to compute the layout of objects and surfaces in the environment and to derive important parameters for controlling the observer's movement, such as heading direction and the time to collision (Koenderink 1986). On a smaller scale, shapes can be segregated from their backgrounds using translational motion signals (Braddick 1974).

The diversity of the perceptual functions supported by motion analysis suggests that motion might be a fundamental image property, analogous to color, that is analyzed at every point in the visual field and the results of the analysis are used to derive other perceptual information. This would require that motion be sensed independently of other image properties at all locations in the image. Thus, we would require motion sensors to operate locally at all points in the image. In the next section we consider a variety of lines of evidence for the existence of such a system of local motion sensors in the human visual system.

Evidence for Dedicated Local Motion Sensors

As noted above, in principle, motion could be sensed by combining information about the locations occupied by objects at different times. However it is well established that a sensation of motion can be elicited by two small, very brief, light flashes even when they are so close together in space that the observer cannot distinguish two spatial locations (Foster et al. 1981, 1989). This is evidence that our sense of visual motion is primary, that visual motion is sensed directly by dedicated sensors and is not derived from analyses of the locations of objects at different times.

Further evidence that the sense of visual motion need not be dependent on analyses of spatial position comes from the motion aftereffect, an everyday perceptual phenomenon with a very long history. It was mentioned by Aristotle more than two millennia ago, was rediscovered in the nineteenth century as the "waterfall illusion" (Addams 1834), and more recently has been systematically characterized (see below). The basic characteristic of the motion aftereffect is that when an area of the visual field receives prolonged stimulation by something moving continuously in a particular direction (Aristotle mentions a swiftly flowing river as an adapting stimulus; Addams mentions a waterfall), stationary objects viewed immediately afterward in that part of the visual field appear to move in the opposite direction. The motion aftereffect is not caused by a change in the position of objects; it is restricted to motion. Thus, although objects affected by the motion aftereffect appear to be moving, they do not appear to move a distance consistent with their apparent motion, although there is a slight shift in perceived position (McGraw et al. 2002). This is further evidence that the perception of motion does not depend on a perception of changing location over time and suggests that the motion aftereffect reflects a change in the activity of a visual mechanism that signals motion.

In the next section we consider the properties of the first stage in motion sensing. In the remainder of this section we consider current views on the overall architecture of motion analysis in relation to motion perception.

Architecture of Visual Motion Perception

At least two distinct visual subsystems analyze retinal motion, and some authors believe there are three (Lu & Sperling 1995). They are:

1. The feature-tracking motion system. This system is poorly defined but in principle it can track any kind of feature or object (Ullman 1979). Its sensitivity to displacement may be limited by the resolution with which the location of features can be encoded. Its operation may be dependent on our ability to attend to the features being tracked.

2. The "first-order" or "short-range" motion-filtering system (Braddick 1974). This is believed to be the substrate of our direct sense of motion. It has a first stage that consists of local, orientation-selective motion sensors (Adelson & Bergen 1985, van Santen & Sperling 1985, Watson & Ahumada 1985). Each sensor responds to motion of luminance-defined features in a particular direction. Thus, the location, speed, and direction of motion of a moving object is encoded in the visual system by the identity of the sensors that respond to it. In principle there are enough sensors to identify motion in every direction at every point in the visual field. The sensors are often characterized as filters selective for orientation, location, spatial frequency, temporal frequency, and direction of motion. Their likely neural substrate is the system of direction-selective neurons in area 17 of visual cortex. The orientation-selectivity of the first-stage motion sensors means that at each location in the visual field there must be a set of sensors to cover the full range of orientations and that the responses of the sensors selective for different orientations must be combined in a second stage in order to resolve the direction of motion in two dimensions (Adelson & Movshon 1982). In principle, it is possible for motion sensors to respond to motion that covers distances that would be too small to be detected as differences in spatial location.

3. The "second-order" motion system (Lu & Sperling 1995), a system based on sensors that respond to the motion of patterns defined by spatial modulation of local contrast (see Figure 1) or of other image properties.

The main disagreements about the architecture of motion perception center on the substrate of our sensitivity to the motion of contrast envelopes like that shown in Figure 1. Nobody doubts our ability to track objects and features, although there is no generally agreed model of how we do it (Del Viva & Morrone 1998). Similarly, the existence of the first-order motion system, based on sensors that respond mainly to the motion of luminance patterns, is not disputed, although there is disagreement about the detailed mode of operation of the motion filters and about the way that their outputs are combined to resolve the direction of 2-D motion. However, some authors argue that human sensitivity to the motion of spatial modulations of contrast can best be accounted for by a combination of feature tracking and a limited sensitivity of the first-order system to second-order

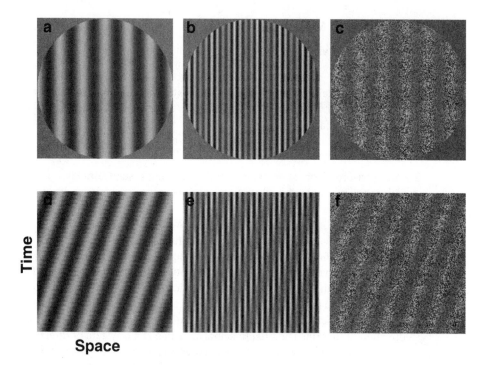

Space

Figure 1   Snapshots of contrast and luminance patterns (*upper panels*) and space-time plots of their motion (*lower panels*). To see examples of the moving stimuli, follow the Supplemental Material link from the Annual Reviews home page at http://www.annualreviews.org. (*a*) A sinusoidal grating—a luminance pattern widely used for studying linear filtering processes. (*b*) A typical second-order stimulus, a contrast-modulated, high spatial frequency grating. It is the product of a stationary high spatial frequency luminance grating (the "carrier"), which remains stationary, and a moving sinusoidal modulation (the "envelope"), which causes the contrast of the carrier to vary across its surface. In this case the envelope is the sum of a dc term and a sinusoid. (*c*) A contrast-modulated dynamic random dot pattern. The envelope is identical to that in (*b*) but the carrier is a random dot pattern. (*d*) A space-time plot of (*a*). The vertical axis is time. The plot shows a single slice across the display over time. The luminance profile moves rightward in small steps. The reciprocal of the gradient (displacement/time) gives the speed of motion. (*e*) Space-time plot of (*b*). Note that the speed is the same as in (*d*) and that the high spatial frequency grating does not move—its bars run vertically upward. It is the contrast modulation (the envelope) that moves. (*f*) Space-time plot of (*c*). Note that the envelope motion is like (*e*) but that the dot pattern changes on every frame.

patterns (Seiffert & Cavanagh 1998), whereas others believe that there is a second motion-filtering system with high sensitivity to texture patterns (Lu & Sperling 1995). The ability to measure performance in motion-detection tasks that exclude feature tracking is central to resolving this dispute, so the next section considers feature tracking. Then we consider first-order motion sensors.

FEATURE TRACKING

Expected Differences Between Feature Tracking and Direct Motion Sensing

Because there is a variety of possible approaches both to feature tracking and to motion sensing, it is difficult to specify exactly what are the differences in performance between feature-tracking mechanisms and motion-sensing mechanisms. However, six different experimental approaches, each based on a hypothetical difference in operation between feature tracking and motion sensing, have been used either to isolate or to exclude feature-tracking mechanisms.

1. In principle a feature tracker has to locate features before it can track them. Thus, we might expect that feature trackers would fail with very brief or very high temporal frequency stimuli because there might not be time to locate the features before they move (Derrington et al. 1992).

2. Feature trackers operate in two stages. First they extract and locate features, then they analyze whether their locations have changed. In theory the two stages could be separated, by displaying a moving stimulus intermittently with blank intervals in the moving display, without affecting the operation of the tracker. These manipulations would be expected to disrupt the operation of motion sensors based on filtering because these operate continuously and would integrate the blanks with the moving stimulus (Georgeson & Shackleton 1989, Smith 1994).

3. Because feature trackers operate on the locations of identified features, we would expect them to have a minimum distance threshold that is relatively constant and approximately matches the precision with which the locations of features can be discriminated (Seiffert & Cavanagh 1998).

4. It should be possible to manipulate the features in a display so that feature movement is reduced or reversed while leaving the motion filter signal relatively unaffected (Hammett et al. 1993, Smith 1994).

5. Motion sensors can be fatigued, which should produce perceptual aftereffects. A feature tracker might be expected not to show aftereffects (Anstis & Moulden 1970, Mather 1980).

6. A feature-tracking mechanism might be more demanding of resources. We might expect it to be impossible for a tracking system to monitor multiple motions in different parts of the visual field concurrently. Multiple motion monitoring should not be a problem for motion sensors because they operate in parallel across the whole visual field (Allen & Derrington 2000, Ashida et al. 2001).

In the following sections we consider the ways that each of these approaches has been used to address the question of how moving contrast or texture modulations are processed.

Brief Stimuli and High Temporal Frequencies

A mechanism that tracks features must first identify and register the location of features before it can track them. This suggests that motion perception based on this type of mechanism would fail if the pattern is only presented very briefly or if it moves with very high temporal frequency (Cropper & Derrington 1994).

By this logic, experiments with brief stimuli suggest that, close to threshold at least, the motion of color and contrast modulations is detected by feature tracking. Human observers are able to discriminate moving luminance patterns even at presentation durations of 15 milliseconds or less, whereas they are unable to discriminate the motion of contrast envelopes at durations below about 200 milliseconds (Cropper & Derrington 1994, Derrington et al. 1993). The increase in stimulus duration required to sense the motion of color or contrast patterns is more than an order of magnitude, which strongly suggests that a radically different mechanism is involved. At higher (chromatic) contrasts it becomes possible to discriminate the motion of color patterns at short durations, which suggests that some motion sensors are color-sensitive (Cropper & Derrington 1994, 1996).

The effect of varying temporal frequency supports a similar conclusion. Figure 2 shows that the ability to discriminate the direction of motion of moving contrast envelopes peaks below 1 Hz and falls off rapidly at approximately 3 Hz, whereas sensitivity to moving luminance patterns is highest between 1 and 10 Hz (Derrington & Badcock 1985b, Derrington & Cox 1998, Holliday & Anderson 1994). Complex patterns that contain a contrast envelope moving in the opposite direction to the local luminance profile are seen to move in the direction of the contrast envelope at low temporal frequencies and in the direction of the luminance profile at high temporal frequencies (Derrington & Ukkonen 1999, Derrington et al. 1992). At higher contrasts, resolution improves significantly and it becomes possible to discriminate the direction of motion of contrast envelopes at frequencies up to 12–15 Hz (Lu & Sperling 1995, Ukkonen & Derrington 2000).

In sum, the simplest explanation of the effects of varying temporal frequency and stimulus duration is that, at low contrasts, the motion of chromatic patterns and contrast envelopes is analyzed by feature tracking, and at higher contrasts chromatic motion and contrast-envelope motion are analyzed by motion sensors.

Intermittent Stimuli and Blank Intervals

Several patterns have been designed to stimulate motion sensors that signal one direction of motion but whose most salient features actually move in the opposite direction. This conflict can be engineered by using periodic patterns that have different kinds of features with different periodicities, and by moving the patterns in jumps; see Figure 3 for an example. Typically, when these patterns are presented stepping continuously, people report that they seem to move in the direction predicted by the motion sensors. If, however, the frames of the motion sequence are separated by gaps during which a blank screen is presented, the perceived

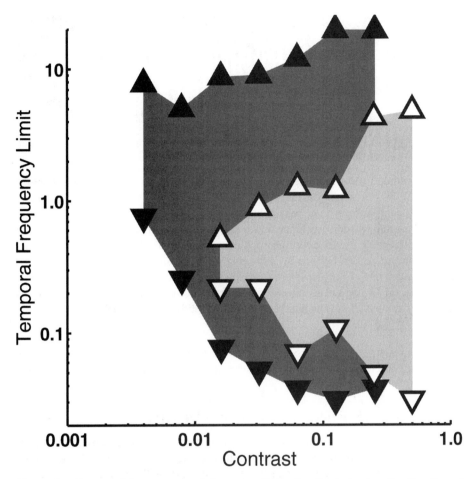

Figure 2   Upper and lower temporal frequency limits for discriminating the direction of motion of a first-order stimulus (grating) and a second-order stimulus (the contrast envelope of a beat pattern) at different contrasts. Except at the very highest contrasts second-order motion has a higher low-temporal frequency limit—it must move faster to be discriminable. At all contrasts the second-order motion has a much lower high-temporal frequency limit. The range of temporal frequencies and contrasts for which second-order motion can be discriminated (light shading) is much smaller than the corresponding range for second-order motion.

direction of motion changes to be the same as the direction of motion of the features (Georgeson & Harris 1990, Hammett 1993).

These findings are consistent with the idea that motion perception can arise both from the activation of motion sensors and from tracking features. However, inserting gaps into a moving pattern actually changes the stimulus in complex ways and some motion sensor models predict both the sensor and the feature-tracking directions described above with the appropriate abrupt onset and offset

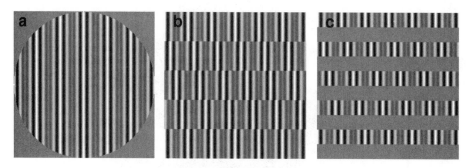

Figure 3   Stimuli and space-time (S-T) plots of the presentation modes used by Hammett et al. (1993). To see examples of the moving stimuli, follow the Supplemental Material link from the Annual Reviews home page at http://www.annualreviews.org. (*a*) The stimulus, a beat pattern made by adding gratings with a spatial frequency ratio of 3:4. (*b*) S-T plot of stimulus motion that causes both rightward motion visible to motion sensors (the carrier jumps rightward, as can be seen by inspecting the detail in the high-contrast areas) and leftward motion of features (the contrast envelope jumps leftward). Both motions are visible to observers. (*c*) Adding a blank interval to each frame makes it impossible to see the motion signaled by the sensors but the motion of the peaks is still clearly detectable.

and presence of blank screens (Johnston & Clifford 1995). Consequently, it may be difficult to interpret results obtained with intermittent motion stimuli containing blank intervals.

Performance in Relation to Displacement Detection

A mechanism that identifies and tracks features must be limited by the ability of the visual system to resolve those features. Thus, we would expect the minimum displacement that can be tracked to remain approximately constant over the range of speeds or temporal frequencies at which the mechanism operates effectively and perhaps to increase at higher temporal frequencies. This is not what happens when observers track the motion of a sinusoidally oscillating random dot pattern. Over a substantial range of temporal frequencies the displacement threshold falls in proportion to the frequency (Nakayama & Tyler 1981). Figure 4 shows an example of S-T plots of two equally detectable oscillations—the frequency differs by an order of magnitude and so does the displacement threshold. However, if the threshold is expressed as a velocity, it remains constant. The two oscillations presented in Figure 4 have the same peak velocity. This suggests that a motion sensor limited by velocity detects the motion of this luminance pattern.

When a similar experiment is done using contrast modulations, threshold displacements remain approximately constant, rising slightly with increasing temporal frequency (Seiffert & Cavanagh 1998). Similar results are obtained when the stimulus is an oscillating color modulation (Seiffert & Cavanagh 1999). However, at high contrasts both color patterns and contrast envelopes show a displacement

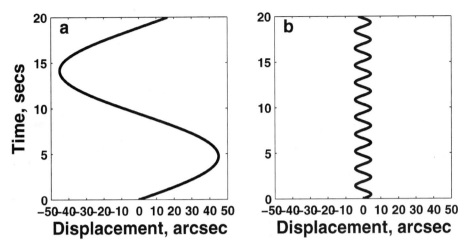

Figure 4   Space-time (S-T) plots of the trajectory of moving luminance patterns at the point at which their motion is just detectable (Nakayama & Tyler 1981). The two profiles have the same peak velocity but the maximum displacements differ by a factor of 10.

threshold that decreases with temporal frequency, just like the thresholds for a luminance pattern (Seiffert & Cavanagh 1999). This set of results is also consistent with the hypothesis that at low contrasts the motion of contrast envelopes and chromatic patterns is analyzed by feature tracking whereas at high contrasts it is analyzed by a motion sensor.

Manipulating Features

Adding a static, high-contrast static pattern, especially if it is an exact replica (a pedestal) to a moving pattern, should interfere with a mechanism that tracks features because it will cause the features to oscillate back and forth instead of moving consistently (see Figure 5) and may also cause spurious feature matches. Adding a static pattern to a moving pattern should not affect the output of a motion filter like that proposed for the first-order pathway because the pedestal has a different temporal frequency from that passed by the filter and so, provided its contrast is not very high, should not affect the output of the filter (Lu & Sperling 1995). In a variety of experiments pedestals impair motion discrimination using low-contrast chromatic patterns and contrast envelopes but not luminance patterns or high-contrast chromatic patterns and envelopes.

Smith (1994) found that moving contrast-modulation envelopes are masked by static contrast modulations, although Lu & Sperling (1995), found that a pedestal did not impair discrimination of the motion of the sinusoidal envelope of a high-contrast noise pattern or a luminance grating, although pedestals did block motion discrimination of patterns based on more complex perceptual attributes, such as stereoscopic depth. However, Ukkonen & Derrington (2000) found that adding

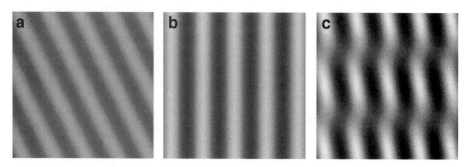

Figure 5   Space-time (S-T) plots of (*a*) a moving grating, (*b*) a pedestal, and (*c*) their sum. To see examples of the moving stimuli, follow the Supplemental Material link from the Annual Reviews home page at http://www.annualreviews.org.

a pedestal to a moving contrast modulation envelope increased the modulation depth required to discriminate the direction of motion if the mean contrast was low, but not if it was high. Moreover, Derrington & Ukkonen (1999) showed that when observers discriminate the motion of a complex pattern whose contrast envelope moves in the opposite direction to its luminance profile, a pedestal impairs perception of the contrast envelope but not the luminance profile. Lu et al. (1999) found that moving low-contrast color patterns failed the pedestal test.

Taken together, the results of pedestal experiments are consistent with the idea that the motion of luminance patterns, high-contrast color patterns, and contrast envelopes in patterns with high contrast is detected by motion sensors and that at low contrast, motion both of contrast envelopes and of color patterns is analyzed by feature tracking.

Aftereffects

The motion aftereffect has frequently been taken as evidence for the existence of a direction-selective motion detector. Adaptation to a moving luminance-defined pattern results in aftereffects, such as reducing the perceived speed of objects moving in the same direction as the adapting pattern and inducing static objects to appear to move in the reverse direction (e.g., Anstis 1980, Derrington & Badcock 1985b). There may also be direction-selective changes in sensitivity to subsequently viewed test patterns (e.g., Tolhurst & Heeger 1997, Turano 1991). Most motion aftereffect experiments are based on subjective judgments and thus are susceptible to a variety of nonvisual influences. Nevertheless, they suggest that contrast envelopes do not activate motion sensors.

Several different experiments have shown that color patterns will elicit a motion aftereffect although typically it is elicited with high-contrast stimuli and is weaker than the aftereffect seen with comparable luminance gratings (Cavanagh & Favreau 1985, Derrington & Badcock 1985a, Mullen & Baker 1985). These studies used relatively high contrasts and showed that color and luminance patterns will induce motion aftereffects in each other. This suggests that a subset of luminance-sensitive motion sensors also have color sensitivity.

In the case of moving contrast modulations the evidence regarding aftereffects is much more confusing. Some studies have found that moving contrast modulations induce little, if any, motion aftereffect with static (Anstis 1980, Derrington & Badcock 1985b) or moving (Cropper & Hammett 1997) test patterns. Other studies have found that moving contrast modulations do seem to induce aftereffects but only when the subsequently viewed test pattern is moving (Ledgeway 1994, Ledgeway & Smith 1997, Nishida & Sato 1995). One suggestion is that motion aftereffects with moving test patterns reflect the adaptation of higher-level mechanisms (Nishida & Sato 1995) that are susceptible to voluntary attention control (Nishida & Ashida 2000). This strengthens our reluctance to draw conclusions about the properties of low-level motion sensors on the basis of aftereffects. Even so, the results on aftereffects suggest that motion sensors are not sensitive to contrast envelopes but have some sensitivity to chromatic patterns.

Multiple Motions

Motion sensors tile the whole visual field and there is no reason to suppose that the analysis of motion at one location in the visual field should be made more or less difficult by the presence or absence of motion in another part of the visual field. We would expect, for example, that selecting or identifying one stimulus from many that are simultaneously present on the basis of its motion would be no more difficult, and not substantially slower, than selecting a stimulus on the basis of its color. On the other hand, if an object or feature must be consciously selected in order to be tracked then we would expect observers to require very long stimulus durations in order to perform tasks that require multiple moving stimuli to be monitored.

Experimental results are very clear indeed. Tasks that require multiple motion judgments on moving luminance stimuli are effortless and rapid whereas identical tasks with moving contrast envelopes as stimuli are extremely slow. When the moving stimuli are contrast envelopes the task is much more difficult; observers take much longer, sometimes several seconds to find a stimulus that moves inconsistently.

Allen & Derrington (2000) required subjects to discriminate between two displays. One display contained four patches of grating, all moving outward, away from the center. The other display contained four identical patches except that one of them was moving inward, toward the center. When the stimulus patches were luminance gratings, observers were able to perform the task with a stimulus duration of less than 200 milliseconds. When the stimuli were beat patterns in which the contrast envelope moved, observers were unable to perform the task unless they were allowed to scrutinize the moving stimuli for several seconds.

Similar results are obtained when observers are required to search a display containing multiple moving patches looking for the patch that is moving in a different direction. When the patterns that move are contrast envelopes of moderate contrast then search is very slow and depends strongly on the number of items in the stimulus but when the stimuli are luminance patches or the contrast is very high search is very rapid (Allen & Derrington 2000, Ashida et al. 2001). Searches for an odd-man-out among moving contrast envelopes are time-consuming even when the motion defines a surface (Dosher et al. 1989) or a shape with three-dimensional form (Ziegler & Hess 1999).

Interim Conclusions

The main conclusions from experiments relating to feature tracking can be summarized as follows.

- Experiments with brief, or high temporal frequency, stimuli suggest that both color patterns and contrast patterns gain access to motion sensors at high contrasts but not at low contrasts.
- Experiments with blank intervals confirm that feature tracking can occur with blank intervals in the display.
- Measurements of displacement limits suggest that it is only at high contrasts that motion sensors analyze the motion of chromatic stimuli and contrast patterns.
- Pedestal experiments confirm that at low contrasts feature trackers analyze the motion of both chromatic patterns and contrast envelopes and that at high contrasts motion sensors analyze contrast envelopes.
- Motion aftereffect measurements suggest that motion sensors analyze high-contrast color patterns but not contrast patterns.
- Experiments in which subjects make multiple motion judgments suggest quite strongly both that feature tracking is a process that occurs under conscious control and that feature tracking is the only way we have to analyze the motion of contrast envelopes in low-contrast displays.

Although the conclusions from the different experimental approaches are not all equally clear, the results are all consistent with the view that the motion of contrast envelopes and color patterns depends on feature tracking except when colors are well above threshold or mean contrast is high. Thus, our first significant conclusion is as follows: *It seems very unlikely that the visual system contains arrays of motion sensors dedicated to the analysis of contrast envelopes or color patterns.*

In the next section we consider the properties of standard motion sensors.

MOTION SENSORS

This section of the review has two subsections. First, we discuss candidate models of the motion sensor. Second, we discuss how oriented motion signals, which are inherently one-dimensional, are likely to be used to analyze motion in two dimensions.

Models of the Motion Sensor

The key property of the motion sensor is selectivity for the direction of motion of a luminance pattern. The sensor responds selectively to motion in one direction along a given axis. There are three main approaches to modeling motion sensors.

First, the ancestor of many current models of the motion sensor was inspired by analysis of the optomotor response in the beetle (Reichardt 1961). It derives a motion signal by spatiotemporal correlation of luminance signals from neighboring points in the image. Correlation extracts a motion signal because if a luminance pattern moves along the axis connecting the two points then the signal at one point will be a time-shifted version of the signal at the other (see Figure 6). The correlation approach has been used to account for aspects of human motion perception and to explain the physiological properties of direction-selective neurones.

The second approach to modeling motion sensors is to derive receptive fields selective for orientation in space-time (Adelson & Bergen 1985, Watson & Ahumada 1985). Oriented spatiotemporal receptive fields sense motion because, as

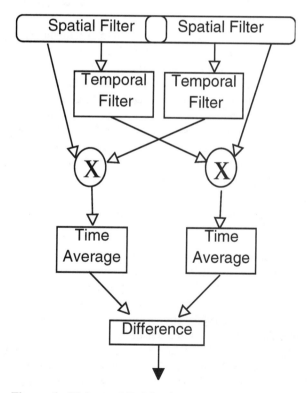

Figure 6   Elaborated Reichardt detector. See text for description.

Figure 1 shows, the gradient in a space-time plot indicates the speed and direction of motion.

A third approach to designing a motion sensor is to take the ratio of the temporal and spatial gradients of luminance in the moving image (Fennema & Thompson 1979, Johnston et al. 1992). The gradient motion sensor works because the temporal gradient is generated by the product of the spatial gradient and the velocity, so the ratio of the two gradients gives the velocity directly.

In the following sections we introduce examples of the different detectors that have been derived from these approaches and discuss their similarities. In each case we start by considering the motion detector as a device designed to respond selectively to one of the representations of motion shown in Figure 1.

Correlation—The Reichardt Detector

A motion sensor based on the principle of correlation exploits the fact that two receptive fields at different points on the trajectory of a moving image receive time-shifted versions of the same temporal signal. The time shift between the two profiles is simply the time it takes to move the distance between the two points at which the profile is measured. It is the distance between the two points divided by the velocity of the image motion.

A correlation-based motion sensor used to explain human psychophysical data consists of two stages, shown in Figure 6 (van Santen & Sperling 1984, 1985). The first stage correlates signals from two neighboring receptive fields (spatial filters) by multiplying the signal from one of them by a delayed version of the signal from its neighbor. The delay arises in a temporal filter and the first stage's output is maximal if the delay matches the time taken for the image to move the distance between the two input receptive fields. Each first stage has a symmetrical partner which time-shifts the signal from the second input receptive field instead of the first, in order to sense motion in the opposite direction. The second stage of the detector simply subtracts the signals of the two first stages.

Spatiotemporally Oriented Receptive Fields—The Linear Motion Sensor

Motion is represented as orientation in a space-time plot (Figure 1*d,e,f*). Thus, a sensor (or receptive field) with a sensitivity profile that is oriented in space-time will be selective for motion. Such a sensor can be constructed by adding or subtracting the outputs of sensors with different spatial and temporal profiles (Watson & Ahumada 1985). The construction of such a sensor is shown in Figure 7.

Figure 7*a* shows plots of the sensitivity profiles of pairs of spatial (S1, S2) and temporal (T1, T2) profiles that can be combined to produce an oriented motion sensor (Adelson & Bergen 1985). Multiplying the spatial and temporal profiles produces four possible sensors with spatiotemporal profiles that are not oriented, but that can be added or subtracted to produce oriented spatiotemporal profiles. Figure 7*b* shows two of the combinations (S1.T1 and S2.T2) that can be added to

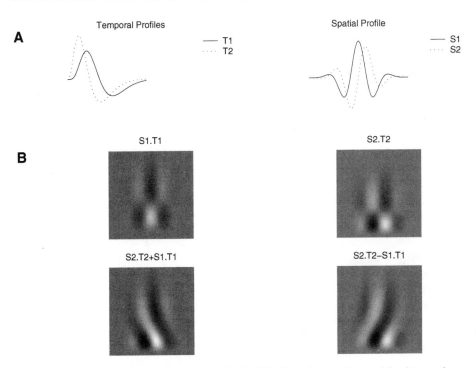

Figure 7 (*a*) Spatial (S1, S2) and temporal (T1, T2) filters that can be combined to produce
(*b*) a linear motion sensor. The first stage of the linear motion sensor consists of spatiotemporal
filters, each of which is the product of one of the two spatial filters and one of the two temporal filters. Space-time plots of the spatiotemporal sensitivity profiles of the two filters are
shown in the upper part of (*b*), labeled S1.T1 and S2.T2. These two filters are not selective for
direction—they are both left-right symmetric. However, their sum (S1.T1 + S2.T2) is selective for rightward motion and their difference (S2.T2 − S1.T1) is selective for leftward motion.

produce a sensor selective for a rightward moving edge or subtracted to produce
a sensor selective for a leftward moving edge. The other two combinations of the
same spatial and temporal filters would produce sensors selective for bars moving
rightward and leftward.

Motion-Energy Filtering

Linear motion sensors can be combined to produce a motion-energy filter, which is
produced by squaring and summing the outputs of edge-selective and bar-selective
linear motion sensors (Adelson & Bergen 1985). A final stage, in which the responses of the two symmetrical stages tuned to opposite directions of motion are
subtracted to give an output whose sign signals the direction of motion, can be
added to the motion-energy filter. The effect of this final stage is that, with appropriate choices for the spatial and temporal filters, it renders the motion-energy

filter formally equivalent to the elaborated Reichardt detector shown in Figure 6 (van Santen & Sperling 1985).

The motion energy filter gives no direct information about velocity. The filter's output depends on contrast, spatial frequency, and temporal frequency. For any given stimulus there is an optimal velocity, but the optimal velocity depends on the stimulus. However, the effects of stimulus differences can be discounted by comparing the responses of sensors selective for different stimulus properties. Adelson & Bergen (1985) suggest that in order to estimate velocity at a given spatial frequency the output of the motion energy filter could be divided by the output of a contrast energy filter tuned to zero temporal frequency.

Spatiotemporal Gradients

The spatial variations in luminance in a moving image give rise to temporal variations at different points in space when the image moves. If we make the assumption that all the temporal variation in a space-time image is caused by movement, it becomes possible to use the relation between spatial and temporal variations at any position to infer the nature of the motion exactly. As the gradient moves, the luminance at any point rises at a rate that is proportional to the product of steepness of the spatial gradient at that point and the velocity

$$V_x \cdot L/\cdot x = - \cdot L/\cdot t, \tag{1}$$

where V_x is the velocity along an axis x in the image, L is luminance at any point in the image, x is distance along the axis x in the image and t is time. The velocity is given by dividing the temporal derivative by the spatial derivative

$$V_x = (\cdot L/\cdot t)/(\cdot L/\cdot x). \tag{2}$$

This approach has been used successfully to derive local velocity signals from a sequence of television images and to segment the image on the basis of the different velocities present (Fennema & Thompson 1979). However, the gradient approach does suffer from the problem that the expression for the velocity is a fraction with the slope of the luminance profile as its denominator. This has the unfortunate consequence that the velocity computation will be very noisy when the luminance gradient is small or zero, that is, in parts of the image where the luminance is spatially uniform.

There are several possible solutions to this problem. The simplest, which was adopted by Fennema and Thompson and has been incorporated into a specific biological model of motion detection (Marr & Ullman 1981), is only to make the motion calculation locations where the spatial luminance gradient has already been identified as being sufficiently steep to produce a reliable result. An alternative is to include higher spatial derivatives in the velocity calculation, which has a stabilizing effect because it is rare for all the derivatives to be zero simultaneously (Johnston et al. 1992). Gradient-based motion sensors are also sensitive to the motion of contrast-envelopes (Benton 2002).

Similarity Between the Gradient Approach and Motion-Energy Filtering

Although, on the face of it, the computation of velocity as the ratio of the local temporal and spatial luminance derivatives in an image seems very different from the filtering approach, in fact there are ways of expressing the two approaches that bring them together. When the differentiation that calculates the spatial and temporal gradients is combined with filtering, as it generally is in any biologically plausible motion-detecting model, it is possible to express the two approaches in very similar ways (Bruce et al. 1996).

There are two reasons for this. First, differentiating an image and then filtering it with a linear filter gives exactly the same result as differentiating the filter and then using it to filter the original image. Second, differentiating a filter introduces differences similar to those that exist between the different spatial filters and the different temporal filters in Figure 7a. Differentiation also changes the amplitude spectrum of the filter, making it fall off more steeply at low frequencies. One consequence of this is that combining a low-pass or mildly band-pass blurring function, such as might be produced by retinal processing, with differentiation produces a band-pass filter which becomes narrower with subsequent differentiation operations. The consequence is that the same operation can be described either as filtering or as measuring the gradient—or the higher derivatives—of the spatial or temporal luminance profile. Consequently, there has not yet been an experiment that unequivocally favors one model of the motion sensor over others. However, as we shall see in the next section, physiological experiments on motion-selective neurons in cat striate cortex do favor the motion energy detector.

Physiology

The fact that different schemes for generating direction selectivity can be rendered exactly equivalent to one another makes it difficult to conceive of psychophysical experiments that would reveal the principles of operation of direction-selective mechanisms. Part of the difficulty is that in a typical psychophysical experiment the observer makes a single, usually binary, decision based on a large number of mechanisms. There is no access to the outputs of individual mechanisms. However, in physiological experiments on the mammalian visual cortex it is possible to record the outputs of single cells that can be represented as direction-selective spatiotemporal frequency filters (Cooper & Robson 1968, Movshon et al. 1978a,b).

Emerson et al. (1992) have shown that the responses of direction-selective complex cells to pairs of bars flashed in different sequences in different parts of its receptive field can be used to distinguish between different models of the motion sensor. The pattern of these responses is consistent with what would be produced by the motion energy filter, but not the Reichardt detector.

Although the qualitative similarity between the responses of direction-selective cortical neurones and those of the motion-energy filter is encouraging, the number of cells that have been examined in detail is small. Moreover, the detailed experiments that distinguish between the different possible models of motion sensor have not been done in primates. Thus, at this stage it would be premature to exclude other model motion sensors, so our second substantive conclusion is this: *It is not possible to choose between models of the motion sensor on the basis of currently available psychophysical or physiological data.* In the next section we consider how orientation-selectivity constrains motion analysis in two dimensions.

PROPERTIES OF THE MOTION SENSOR

2-Dimensional Motion Analysis

There is both psychophysical and physiological evidence to suggest that motion sensors are selective for orientation (Anderson et al. 1991, Hubel & Wiesel 1968). An orientation-selective motion sensor can only record motion in a single dimension—along an axis orthogonal to the sensor's preferred orientation. Conversely, a stimulus that only contains features of a single orientation is one-dimensional and can only be seen to move in a direction orthogonal to its orientation. One-dimensional motion signals give ambiguous information about the motion of two-dimensional objects. A second stage of motion analysis is necessary in order to resolve the true direction of motion of a 2-D object or pattern, which, by definition, is an object that contains features of more than one orientation (Adelson & Movshon 1982, Fennema & Thompson 1979). The remainder of this section discusses how the 1-D motion signals from sensors tuned to different orientations are combined to produce an unambiguous 2-D motion signal.

Resolving Direction Ambiguities: The Global Intersection of Constraints

Arguably the simplest 2-D pattern with which to compare 1-D and 2-D motion analysis is the plaid pattern, made by summing two sinusoidal gratings of different orientations. Plaids have been extensively used in vision research since their introduction by Adelson & Movshon (1982). When the two component gratings are very different in contrast, spatial frequency, or temporal frequency, they are seen as separate patterns that slide over one another. However, when their spatial frequency, temporal frequency, and contrast are similar, the gratings cohere perceptually to form a rigidly moving pattern whose speed and direction of motion is determined from the speeds and directions of motion of the component gratings by the intersection of constraints.

Perhaps the clearest evidence that the visual system uses the perceived motions of component gratings to compute the motion of plaid patterns comes from experiments in which the perceived speed of one of the components of a plaid pattern is reduced either by presenting it with lower contrast (Stone et al. 1990) or by adapting to a moving grating of the same spatial frequency and orientation presented in the same retinal position (Derrington & Suero 1991). The reduction in

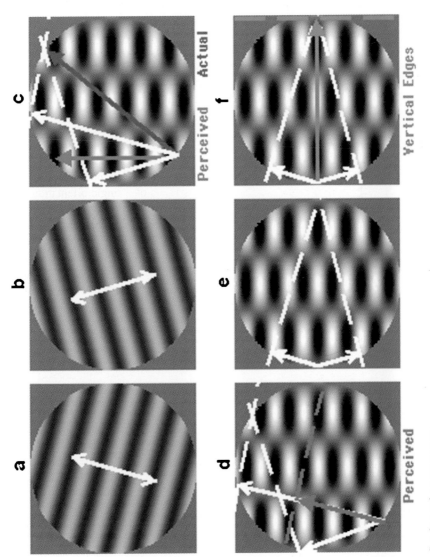

See legend on next page

Figure 8. Adding together the two sinusoidal gratings in panels *a* and *b* produces the plaid pattern shown in panels *c–f*. The true direction of motion of the plaid pattern—shown as a red arrow in the vector plot overlaid on the plaid in panel *c*—is given by the intersection of constraints (IOC). The IOC is the intersection of the two lines (shown dashed in *c*) drawn at right angles to, and through, the end points of the vectors representing the motion of the gratings. If presented for short durations or in peripheral vision, the plaid shown in *c* is perceived to move in a direction closer to the green arrow than the red arrow. Panel *d* shows that this misperception could be a consequence of a failure to register the difference in the speeds of the plaid's components before calculating the IOC. The motion of the plaid in panel *e* can be detected when the motion of its components is undetectable. Panel *f* shows that the motion of the vertical edges in the plaid (*blue arrow*) should be much more detectable than the motion of its components. For moving versions of the plaids, follow the Supplemental Material link from the Annual Reviews home page at http://www.annualreviews.org.

the perceived speed of the plaid's component changes the perceived axis of motion exactly as if the real speed of the component had been reduced.

Failures of Global and Local Intersections of Constraints

Although these studies are consistent with the idea that the visual system uses the motion of the component gratings to compute the motion of plaid patterns, two sets of experiments suggest that it is not the whole story. First, some types of plaid patterns appear to move in a different direction from that predicted by the components (Wilson et al. 1992). Second, plaid motion is visible when the motion of the components is invisible (Derrington & Badcock 1992, Derrington et al. 1992).

ERRORS IN THE PERCEIVED AXIS OF MOTION

When a plaid pattern consists of two gratings whose axes of motion make an acute angle and whose speeds are very different from one another, the axis of motion of the plaid falls outside the angle formed by the axes of the components. Such a plaid is known as a type II plaid (Ferrera & Wilson 1987). An example of the intersection of constraints (IOC) diagram for a type II plaid is shown in Figure 8c (see color insert). The axis of motion of type II plaids is systematically misperceived. It appears to be closer to the axes of motion of its components than it actually is (Ferrera & Wilson 1987). The misperception is more extreme for type II plaids presented for short durations or in peripheral vision. If they are presented for only 60 msecs, type II plaids appear to move approximately along the axis predicted by summing the 1-D vectors of their component gratings, and if they are presented in the periphery the perceived axis of motion may deviate by 40° from the true axis of motion (Yo & Wilson 1992).

Wilson et al. (1992) explain these misperceptions by proposing that the visual system uses a different algorithm to calculate 2-D velocity, that it sums the motion signals from the components instead of calculating the intersection of constraints. However, it is equally plausible to propose that the misperception arises from systematic errors in the 1-D velocities used to calculate the 2-D velocity. Figure 8d (see color insert) shows that underestimating the difference in speeds of the components would make the IOC calculation give a direction very close to what is perceived.

PLAID AND COMPONENT MOTION IDENTIFICATION THRESHOLDS

Subjects are able to discriminate correctly between leftward and rightward motion of a horizontally moving plaid pattern when it is moving so slowly that the motion of its component gratings is undetectable (Derrington & Badcock 1992). This could not happen if the visual system computed the motion of the plaid from the motions of its component gratings. In a more extensive study using vertical, horizontal, and oblique motion directions, Cox & Derrington (1994) found that when spatial frequency or contrast is high it is easier to discriminate the motion of the plaid than to discriminate the direction of motion of its component gratings.

These observations show that in analyzing the motion of plaid patterns the visual system must use something more than the motion signals from the component gratings. Derrington & Badcock (1992) suggested that there might be motion sensors with short receptive fields that would sense the motion of the local features in the plaid. Recent physiological work suggests that this is very likely to be the case. About 20% of the direction-sensitive neurons in marmoset striate cortex have short, broadly oriented receptive fields that respond more strongly to the local features rather than to the components in a plaid (Derrington et al. 2003, Tinsley et al. 2003). This means that an IOC calculation for a plaid would be based on 1-D vectors derived from broadly oriented sensors that sense local features. As Figure 8*f* (see color insert) shows, local features move faster than the components and so their motion should be detected at lower speeds. Thus, our final conclusion is that *2-dimensional motion analyses must use signals from localized broadly oriented motion sensors.*

CONCLUSIONS

We have three conclusions. First, there is no good reason to suppose that the visual system contains a system of dedicated sensors for second-order motion. Second, there is currently no way to choose between the three main candidates of motion sensor—the elaborated Reichardt detector, the motion-energy sensor, and gradient-based sensors. Third, analysis of 2-D motion depends on signals from local broadly oriented sensors as well as on signals from narrowly oriented sensors.

ACKNOWLEDGMENTS

Preparation of this manuscript was supported by grants from the Wellcome Trust and the Biotechnology and Biological Sciences Research Council.

The *Annual Review of Psychology* is online at http://psych.annualreviews.org

LITERATURE CITED

Addams R. 1834. An account of a peculiar optical phaenomenon seen after having looked at a moving body etc. *Lond. Edinb. Philos. Mag. J. Sci. 3rd Ser.* 5:373–74

Adelson EH, Bergen JR. 1985. Spatiotemporal energy models for the perception of motion. *J. Opt. Soc. Am. A* 2:284–99

Adelson EH, Movshon JA. 1982. Phenomenal coherence of moving visual patterns. *Nature* 300:523–25

Allen HA, Derrington AM. 2000. Slow discrimination of contrast-defined expansion patterns. *Vis. Res.* 40:735–44

Anderson SJ, Burr DC, Morrone MC. 1991. 2-dimensional spatial and spatial-frequency selectivity of motion-sensitive mechanisms in human vision. *J. Opt. Soc. Am. A* 8:1340–51

Anstis SM. 1980. The perception of apparent movement. *Phil. Trans. R. Soc. London Ser. B* 290:153–68

Anstis SM, Moulden BP. 1970. After effect of seen movement: evidence for peripheral and central components. *Q. J. Exp. Psychol.* 22:222–29

Ashida H, Seiffert AE, Osaka N. 2001. Inefficient visual search for second-order motion. *J. Opt. Soc. Am. A* 18:2255–66

Benton CP. 2002. Gradient-based analysis of non-Fourier motion. *Vis. Res.* 42:2869–77

Braddick O. 1974. A short-range process in apparent motion. *Vis. Res.* 14:519–27

Bruce V, Green PR, Georgeson MA. 1996. *Visual Perception, Physiology, Psychology, and Ecology.* Hove, UK: Psychology Press. 433 pp.

Cavanagh P, Favreau OE. 1985. Colour and luminance share a common motion pathway. *Vis. Res.* 25:1595–601

Cooper GF, Robson JG. 1968. *Successive transformations of spatial information in the visual system.* Presented at I.E.E./N.P.L. Conf. Pattern Recognit.

Cox MJ, Derrington AM. 1994. The analysis of motion of two-dimensional patterns: Do fourier components provide the first stage? *Vis. Res.* 34:59–72

Cropper SJ, Derrington AM. 1994. Motion of chromatic stimuli: first-order or second-order? *Vis. Res.* 34:49–58

Cropper SJ, Derrington AM. 1996. Rapid colour-specific detection of motion in human vision. *Nature* 379:72–74

Cropper SJ, Hammett ST. 1997. Adaptation to motion of a second-order pattern: The motion aftereffect is not a general result. *Vis. Res.* 37:2247–59

Del Viva MM, Morrone MC. 1998. Motion analysis by feature tracking. *Vis. Res.* 38:3633–53

Derrington AM, Badcock DR. 1985a. The low level motion system has both chromatic and luminance inputs. *Vis. Res.* 25:1879–84

Derrington AM, Badcock DR. 1985b. Separate detectors for simple and complex grating patterns? *Vis. Res.* 25:1869–78

Derrington AM, Badcock DR. 1992. Two-stage analysis of the motion of 2-dimensional patterns, what is the first stage? *Vis. Res.* 32:691–98

Derrington AM, Badcock DR, Henning GB. 1993. Discriminating the direction of second-order motion at short stimulus durations. *Vis. Res.* 33:1785–94

Derrington AM, Badcock DR, Holroyd SA. 1992. Analysis of the motion of 2-dimensional patterns: evidence for a second-order process. *Vis. Res.* 32:699–707

Derrington AM, Cox MJ. 1998. Temporal resolution of dichoptic and second-order motion mechanisms. *Vis. Res.* 38:3531–39

Derrington AM, Parker A, Webb BS, Tinsley CJ, Serrano Pedraza I. 2003. Broadly oriented motion detectors in marmoset V1 respond to local features in 2-D patterns. *J. Physiol.* 548P:O72

Derrington AM, Suero M. 1991. Motion of complex patterns is computed from the perceived motions of their components. *Vis. Res.* 31:139–49

Derrington AM, Ukkonen OI. 1999. Second-order motion discrimination by feature-tracking. *Vis. Res.* 39:1465–75

Dosher BA, Landy MS, Sperling G. 1989. Kinetic depth effect and optic flow I: 3d shape from Fourier motion. *Vis. Res.* 29:1789–813

Emerson RC, Adelson EH, Bergen JR. 1992. Directionally selective complex cells and the computation of motion energy in cat visual cortex. *Vis. Res.* 32:203–19

Fennema CL, Thompson WB. 1979. Velocity determination in scenes containing several moving objects. *Comput. Graph. Image Process.* 9:301–15

Ferrera VP, Wilson HR. 1987. Direction specific masking and the analysis of motion in two dimensions. *Vis. Res.* 27:1783–96

Foster DH, Gravano S, Tomoszek A. 1989. Acuity for fine-grain motion and for 2-dot spacing as a function of retinal eccentricity—differences in specialization of the central and peripheral retina. *Vis. Res.* 29:1017–31

Foster DH, Thorson J, McIlwain JT, Biedermanthorson M. 1981. The fine-grain movement illusion—a perceptual probe of neuronal connectivity in the human visual-system. *Vis. Res.* 21:1123–28

Georgeson MA, Harris M. 1990. The temporal range of motion sensing and motion perception. *Vis. Res.* 30:615–19

Georgeson MA, Shackleton TM. 1989. Monocular motion sensing, binocular motion perception. *Vis. Res.* 29:1511–23

Hammett ST, Ledgeway T, Smith AT. 1993. Transparent motion from feature-based and luminance-based processes. *Vis. Res.* 33:1119–22

Holliday IE, Anderson SJ. 1994. Different processes underlie the detection of second order motion at low and high temporal frequencies. *Proc. R. Soc. London Ser. B* 257:165–73

Hubel DH, Wiesel TN. 1968. Receptive fields and functional architecture of monkey striate cortex. *J. Physiol.* 195:215–43

Johnston A, Clifford CWG. 1995. A unified account of three apparent motion illusions. *Vis. Res.* 35:1109–23

Johnston A, McOwan PW, Buxton H. 1992. A computational model of the analysis of some first-order and second-order motion patterns by simple and complex cells. *Proc. R. Soc. London Ser. B* 250:297–306

Koenderink JJ. 1986. Optic flow. *Vis. Res.* 26: 161–80

Ledgeway T. 1994. Adaptation to second order motion results in a motion aftereffect for directionally ambiguous test stimuli. *Vis. Res.* 34:2879–89

Ledgeway T, Smith A. 1997. Changes in the perceived speed following adaption to first and second order motion. *Vis. Res.* 37:215–24

Lu Z, Lesmes LA, Sperling G. 1999. The mechanism of isoluminant chromatic motion perception. *Proc. Natl. Acad. Sci. USA* 96:8289–94

Lu Z, Sperling G. 1995. The functional architecture of human visual motion perception. *Vis. Res.* 35:2697–722

Marr D, Ullman S. 1981. Directional selectivity and its use in early visual processing. *Proc. R. Soc. London Ser. B* 211:151–80

Mather G. 1980. The movement aftereffect and a distribution-shift model for coding the direction of visual movement. *Perception* 9:379–92

McGraw PV, Whitaker D, Skillen J, Chung STL. 2002. Motion adaptation distorts perceived visual position. *Curr. Biol.* 12:2042–47

Movshon JA, Thompson ID, Tolhurst DJ. 1978a. Receptive field organization of complex cells in the cat's striate cortex. *J. Physiol.* 283:79–99

Movshon JA, Thompson ID, Tolhurst DJ. 1978b. Spatial summation in the receptive fields of simple cells in the cat's striate cortex. *J. Physiol.* 283:53–77

Mullen KT, Baker CL. 1985. A motion aftereffect from an isoluminant stimulus. *Vis. Res.* 25:685–88

Nakayama K, Tyler CW. 1981. Psychophysical isolation of movement sensitivity by removal of familiar position cues. *Vis. Res.* 21:427–33

Nishida S, Ashida H. 2000. A hierarchical structure of motion system revealed by interocular transfer of flicker motion aftereffects. *Vis. Res.* 40:265–78

Nishida S, Sato T. 1995. Motion aftereffect with flickering test pattern reveal higher stages of motion processing. *Vis. Res.* 35:477–90

Reichardt W. 1961. Autocorrelation, a principle for the evaluation of sensory information by the central nervous system. In *Sensory Communication*, ed. WA Rosenblith, pp. 303–17. New York: Wiley

Seiffert AE, Cavanagh P. 1998. Position displacement, not velocity, is the cue to motion detection of second-order stimuli. *Vis. Res.* 38:3569–82

Seiffert AE, Cavanagh P. 1999. Position-based motion perception for color and texture stimuli: effects of contrast and speed. *Vis. Res.* 39:4172–85

Smith AT. 1994. Correspondence-based and energy-based detection of second-order motion in human vision. *J. Opt. Soc. Am. A* 11:1940–48

Stone LS, Watson AB, Mulligan JB. 1990. Effect of contrast on the perceived direction of a moving plaid. *Vis. Res.* 30:1049–67

Tinsley CJ, Webb BS, Barraclough NE, Vincent CJ, Parker A, Derrington AM. 2003. The nature of V1 neural responses to 2D moving patterns depends upon receptive field structure in the marmoset monkey. *J. Neurophysiol.* 90:930–37

Tolhurst DJ, Heeger DJ. 1997. Contrast normalization and a linear model for the directional selectivity of simple cells. *Vis. Neurosci.* 14:19–25

Turano K. 1991. Evidence for a common motion mechanism of luminance and contrast-modulated patterns: selective adaptation. *Perception* 20:455–66

Ukkonen OI, Derrington AM. 2000. Motion of contrast-modulated gratings is analysed by different mechanisms at low and at high contrasts. *Vis. Res.* 40:3359–71

Ullman S. 1979. *The Interpretation of Visual Motion.* Cambridge, MA/London, Engl: MIT Press. 229 pp.

van Santen JPH, Sperling G. 1984. Temporal covariance model of human motion perception. *J. Opt. Soc. Am. A* 1:451–73

van Santen JPH, Sperling G. 1985. Elaborated Reichardt detectors. *J. Opt. Soc. Am. A* 2:300–21

Watson AB, Ahumada AJJ. 1985. Model of human visual-motion sensing. *J. Opt. Soc. Am. A* 2:322–42

Wilson HR, Ferrera VP, Yo C. 1992. A psychophysically motivated model for two-dimensional motion perception. *Vis. Neurosci.* 9:79–97

Yo C, Wilson HR. 1992. Perceived direction of moving two-dimensional patterns depends on duration, contrast and eccentricity. *Vis. Res.* 32:135–47

Ziegler LR, Hess RF. 1999. Stereoscopic depth but not shape perception from second-order stimuli. *Vis. Res.* 39:1491–507

Annu. Rev. Psychol. 2004. 55:207–34
doi: 10.1146/annurev.psych.55.090902.141415
Copyright © 2004 by Annual Reviews. All rights reserved
First published online as a Review in Advance on September 29, 2003

CUMULATIVE PROGRESS IN FORMAL THEORIES OF ATTENTION

Gordon D. Logan

Department of Psychology, Vanderbilt University, Nashville, Tennessee 37203;
email: gordon.logan@vanderbilt.edu

Key Words   signal detection, similarity, choice, attention, mathematical
psychology

■ **Abstract**   Formal theories of attention based on similarity-choice theory and
signal-detection theory are reviewed to document cumulative progress in theoretical understanding of attention from the 1950s to the present. Theories based on these
models have been developed to account for a wide variety of attentional phenomena, including attention to dimensions, attention to objects, and executive control. The review
describes the classical similarity-choice and signal-detection theories and relates them
to current theories of categorization, Garner tasks, visual search, cuing procedures,
task switching, and strategy choice.

CONTENTS

INTRODUCTION

Since the beginning of the cognitive revolution in the 1950s, attention has been a central topic in experimental psychology. In recent years, research on attention has been extended to neuroscience, in studies of humans and monkeys, and to clinical science, in studies of psychopathology. A cynic might argue that the history of research on attention has been a series of unrelated fashions and fads, focusing on different experimental paradigms. In the 1950s and 1960s, the focus was on selective listening. In the 1970s, it was automaticity and dual-task performance. In the 1980s, it was visual search, negative priming, and cuing. In the 1990s, it was the psychological refractory period and the attentional blink. Since the turn of the century, the focus has been on task switching. A cynic might argue that this constant shifting from topic to topic has led to little cumulative progress in our theoretical understanding of attentional phenomena. An optimist might argue that there has been substantial cumulative progress from the 1950s to the present at a deeper level of theory that integrates and explains the relations between the various empirical phenomena. I am an optimist and my purpose in writing this chapter is to document that cumulative progress by reviewing recent developments in formal theories of attention (for earlier reviews of formal theories of attention, see Bundesen 1996 and Swets 1984; for an earlier argument for cumulative progress in studies of attention, see Posner 1982).

The review will be organized around two "families" of theory that derive from seminal work in the 1950s. One class of theory adapts concepts from Shepard's work on similarity scaling and Luce's work on choice to problems of attention. The other class adapts concepts from Green's, Tanner's, and Swets's work on signal-detection theory to problems of attention. The two classes of theory are families in two senses. First, they represent successive generations of theory, with each new theory building on an ancestral theory by elaborating its assumptions or adding new assumptions and by extending its domain of applicability to new problems not addressed by the ancestor. Second, theories within each family share a common formal structure—similarity-choice theory or signal-detection theory— that is analogous to the genetic endowment shared by members of a family. These familial features—the successive elaboration of a powerful mathematical structure across several generations of theory—provide the basis for cumulative progress in understanding attention.

My goal in writing this review is to document cumulative progress and to show relations between formal theories of attention. In meeting this goal, I will ignore much of the recent progress in empirical studies of attention and much of the informal theorizing that accompanies it, hoping that other reviews, past and future, will cover these. My focus on similarity-choice theory and signal-detection theory necessarily excludes other work on formal models of attention, particularly connectionist models. The theories I do cover represent ideas that have been at the core of theoretical psychology since the beginning of the cognitive revolution, and I think it is worthwhile emphasizing their longstanding contributions to the field.

The review begins with a brief overview of similarity-choice theory and signal-detection theory that points out similarities and differences between them and describes conditions under which they are mathematically equivalent. The remainder of the review is organized around three main topics: (*a*) attention to dimensions, which includes subsections on categorization and the tasks introduced by Garner to study dimensional attention; (*b*) attention to objects, which includes subsections on visual search and cuing tasks; and (*c*) executive control of attention, which includes strategies and task switching.

SIMILARITY-CHOICE THEORY

Shepard-Luce Choice Rule

The initial work on similarity-choice theory was done by Shepard (1957) and Luce (1959, 1963). The main goal of similarity-choice theory was to predict choice probabilities from estimates of similarity and bias. According to the theory, the probability of choosing response *i* given stimulus *x* is given by the Shepard-Luce choice rule:

$$P(i|x) = \frac{\eta(x, i)\beta_i}{\sum\limits_{j \in R} \eta(x, j)\beta_j}, \tag{1}$$

where $\eta(x, i)$ is the similarity between object *x* and a representation of response category *i* and β_i is the subject's bias for giving response *i* in the choice situation. The probability of choosing response *i* for object *x* increases with the similarity between *x* and *i* and with the bias for *i*. The probability of choosing *i* given *x* decreases with the similarity between *x* and the other responses *j* in the response set *R*.

Classical similarity-choice theory assumes that objects and categories can be represented as points in multidimensional space and similarity is an exponential function of distance in that space (Shepard 1987). Thus,

$$\eta(x, i) = \exp[-s \cdot d_{xi}],$$

where *s* is a sensitivity parameter reflecting the steepness of the generalization gradient and d_{xi} is the distance between *x* and *i* in the multidimensional space:

$$d_{xi} = \left(\sum_{h=1}^{H} |u_{xh} - u_{ih}|^r \right)^{\frac{1}{r}}. \tag{2}$$

Distance between points is computed by calculating the distance between them along each of the H dimensions in the multidimensional space, raising the dimensional distances to the rth power, summing them over dimensions, and taking the rth root of the sum. The parameter r determines the distance metric. If $r = 1$, the distance metric is city-block; if $r = 2$, the distance metric is Euclidean.

Reaction Time and Response Selection

Similarity-choice theory predicts choice probabilities but not reaction times. Marley & Colonius (1992) and Bundesen (1993) showed that, under very general conditions, independent race models predict the same choice probabilities as the similarity-choice model. That is, for a given similarity-choice model, it is possible to construct an independent race model that gives exactly the same choice probabilities. Independent race models use time to choose among competing alternatives: The first alternative to finish is chosen. The equivalence of similarity-choice models and race models adds a temporal dimension to similarity-choice models and allows them to predict reaction time as well as response probability.

Bundesen (1990) interpreted his theory of visual attention as a race model, in which each categorization of each object raced against the other. He interpreted the elements of the choice equation [e.g., $\eta(x, i)\beta_i$] as rate parameters for exponential distributions. The finishing time for the winner of a race between exponential distributions is itself exponentially distributed with a rate parameter that is the sum of the rate parameters for the individual exponential distributions in the race. The mean finishing time for an exponential distribution is simply the reciprocal of the rate parameter. The mean finishing time for a race involving R categorizations of a single object is

$$FT = \frac{1}{\sum_{j \in R} \eta(x, j)\beta_j}, \tag{3}$$

which is 1 over the denominator of Equation 1. Equation 1 provides the choice probabilities and Equation 3 provides the time to make the choice.

The simple race model expressed in Equations 1 and 3 cannot deal with conflict situations, such as the Stroop (1935) task or the Eriksen & Eriksen (1974) flanker task, in which prepotent responses compete with the required response (Palmeri 1997). The race model predicts that conflict will create difficulty, but it places the effect of difficulty in the wrong dependent variable. The prepotent response likely will be chosen first, so conflict will appear in error rate. The finishing time of the first response determines reaction time, so conflict either will produce no cost in reaction time or it will speed up reaction time. The data show a different pattern: Conflict slows reaction time but has little effect on error rate.

To account for conflict situations, Logan (1996) and Nosofsky & Palmeri (1997a) added response selection processes to the basic similarity-choice model. The response selection processes accumulate evidence provided by the similarity-choice model. The race is run repeatedly and each categorization that comes out of the race is added to an accumulator for one response or another. In Logan's (1996) counter model, a response is selected when one of the accumulators reaches an absolute threshold (i.e., when it accumulates K categorizations). In Nosofsky & Palmeri's (1997a) exemplar-based random walk model, a response is selected when one of the accumulators reaches a relative threshold (i.e., when it accumulates K more categorizations than any other accumulator). The exemplar-based random walk model is particularly powerful. It is related formally to Ratcliff's (1978; Ratcliff et al. 1999) diffusion model, which is the most powerful model of reaction time available today. The diffusion model is a generalization of the random walk model, in which time and evidence are both continuous variables. It accounts for response probabilities and distributions of reaction times for correct and incorrect responses in terms of a small number of parameters. It provides estimates of the rate at which information accumulates (drift rate) but it does not explain why the rates take on different values in different conditions. An important contribution of the exemplar-based random walk model is to provide a theoretical account of variation in drift rate between conditions.

Cumulative Developments

Elements of similarity-choice theory have been used pervasively throughout cognitive psychology. The Shepard-Luce choice rule is used to predict choice probabilities in a variety of theories. Two major families of theory represent cumulative development, one addressing categorization and one addressing attention. The categorization family began with Medin & Schaffer's (1978) context model of classification, which used the Shepard-Luce choice rule to predict classification probabilities. Nosofsky's (1984, 1986, 1988) generalized context model extended Medin & Schaffer's model to include the similarity assumptions inherent in the choice rule. Kruschke (1992) added learning assumptions to Nosofsky's model, and Lamberts (2000) extended the assumptions about similarity to allow dynamic changes in similarity within the course of a single experimental trial. Nosofsky & Palmeri (1997a) combined Nosofsky's model with Logan's (1988) instance theory of automaticity to create the exemplar-based random walk model. The attention family began with Bundesen's (1987) fixed capacity independent race model, which Bundesen (1990) extended to the theory of visual attention. Logan (1996) added a perceptual front end to Bundesen's theory and Logan & Gordon (2001) extended that theory to dual-task performance and executive control. Logan (2002) combined the two families in a single instance theory of attention and memory that includes each of the ancestral theories as a special case.

SIGNAL-DETECTION THEORY

Sensitivity, Bias, and Similarity

Signal-detection theory was developed in the 1950s and 1960s by Tanner & Swets (1954) and Green & Swets (1966), among others. It had antecedents in Thurstone's (1927) work on comparative judgment. Whereas Thurstone was interested in developing psychophysical scales from comparative judgments, the main goal of signal-detection theory was to separate sensitivity from bias in a variety of perceptual discriminations. A key concept in signal-detection theory is the idea of internal noise: Variance in perceptual representations will cause similar stimuli to have overlapping representations. The classic signal-detection situation is a yes-no discrimination task, in which subjects must determine whether a stimulus—a signal—has been presented. The subject gets a single sample from the perceptual system and compares it to a decision criterion, deciding "yes" if the sample exceeds the criterion and "no" if it does not. The overlap of the distributions for signal (technically, signal plus noise) and no signal (noise) determines the subjects' sensitivity. The greater the overlap, the lower the sensitivity. The position of the decision criterion on the decision axis reflects the subject's response bias. A low criterion reflects a bias for saying "yes" and a high criterion reflects a bias for saying "no." The probability of a correct "yes" response—a hit—is proportional to the area of the signal-plus-noise distribution that exceeds the criterion, and the probability of an erroneous "yes" response—a false alarm—is proportional to the area of the noise distribution that exceeds the criterion.

Over the years, signal-detection theory has been used in many ways in many different applications. Often, it is used to generate dependent measures that separate sensitivity and bias (d' and β, respectively) without much theoretical commitment to the underlying processes. However, it has also become the core of several theories of memory, attention, and categorization, providing a language in which to articulate these more complex processes. Classical signal detection, applied to yes-no discrimination tasks, assumes univariate normal distributions with equal variance for signal-plus-noise and noise distributions, though other distributions and other assumptions about variance have been investigated thoroughly (e.g., Green & Swets 1966, Wickens 2002). Many of the applications to more complex processes assume normal distributions and several assume multivariate normal distributions. The general recognition theory of Ashby and his colleagues is a notable example (e.g., Ashby & Lee 1991, Ashby & Maddox 1993, Ashby & Perrin 1988, Ashby & Townsend 1986).

Signal-detection theory assumes that objects are represented as distributions in multidimensional space. As with similarity-choice theory, similarity can be interpreted as distance between objects in the multidimensional space. Distance is stochastic, however, because objects are represented as distributions, not points. Ashby & Perrin (1988) interpreted similarity in terms of overlap between distributions. Objects that are more similar are represented by distributions that overlap more; objects that are less similar are represented by distributions that overlap less. In the special case of multivariate normal distributions with equal variances and covariances, similarities calculated from overlap of distributions are equivalent to similarities calculated from distances between points (i.e., the means of the distributions; Ashby & Maddox 1993, Nosofsky 1992).

Reaction Time and Response Selection

Classical signal-detection approaches deal primarily with situations in which stimuli are weak or confusable, so accuracy is the primary dependent measure. In order to apply signal-detection theory to phenomena of attention, researchers often transform situations that are usually studied with reaction time methods into situations that can be studied with accuracy, by limiting exposure duration or masking the stimuli (e.g., Palmer 1994). Another approach is to assume that reaction time is proportional to the distance from the percept to the criterion. For example, Maddox & Ashby (1996) tested two assumptions about the relation between reaction time and distance, an exponential function

$$RT = \alpha \exp^{-\beta D} + c, \tag{4}$$

following Murdock (1985), and a power function

$$RT = \alpha D^{-\beta} + c, \tag{5}$$

where D is the distance between the percept and the decision boundary and α and β are constants and c is an intercept parameter. In their theory, response selection depends on the region the percept falls in (i.e., where it falls with respect to the decision boundaries) and reaction time depends on the distance from the percept to the decision boundary. This approach seems more descriptive than explanatory because no process interpretation is given for the relation between reaction time and distance. Recently, Ashby (2000) developed a stochastic version of general recognition theory that drives a multivariate diffusion process. This model is related to Ratcliff's (1978; Ratcliff et al. 1999) diffusion model and it provides a process interpretation of the relation between reaction time and distance from the percept to the boundary.

Cumulative Developments

Signal-detection theory may be even more pervasive than similarity-choice theory. It appears in many theories of perception, attention, memory, and categorization. There have been several different threads of cumulative development, but they have not yet been woven together in a single fabric, as Logan (2002) did with similarity-choice theory approaches to attention and categorization. The impressive cumulative developments from signal-detection theory include (*a*) the work of Sperling and his colleagues on focusing and switching attention (e.g., Reeves & Sperling 1986, Shih & Sperling 2002, Sperling & Reeves 1980, Sperling & Weichselgartner 1995); (*b*) the general recognition theory developed by Ashby and colleagues to account for identification and categorization (e.g., Ashby & Lee 1991, Ashby & Maddox 1993, Ashby & Perrin 1988, Ashby & Townsend 1986); (*c*) the work of Dosher & Lu on cuing and focusing attention (Dosher & Lu 2000a,b, Lu & Dosher 1998); and (*d*) the work of Palmer and colleagues on visual search (e.g., Eckstein et al. 2000; Palmer 1994, 1998; Palmer et al. 1993). It would be very interesting to see a formal integration of these different theories, but that must await future research.

ATTENTION TO DIMENSIONS: CATEGORIZATION

Attention researchers do not discuss categorization much, but the concept of attention to dimensions plays an important role in categorization research. Early rule-based theories of categorization assumed that subjects attended to dimensions relevant to categorization and ignored other dimensions (e.g., Bruner et al. 1956). In many experiments, the primary task was to discover which dimensions were relevant (Trabasso & Bower 1968). More recent similarity-based theories of categorization also consider attention to dimensions to be an important process in categorization, including similarity-choice theories and signal-detection theories.

Similarity-Choice Theory

Luce (1963) and others applied the choice rule to a variety of choice tasks that usually involved choosing a single response to a single stimulus (for a review, see Luce 1977). Nosofsky (1984, 1986, 1988) applied the choice rule to categorization, on the assumption that categories were represented as collections of instances. In Nosofsky's generalized context model, the probability of choosing category i for object x was directly related to the sum of the similarities between object x and the various instances of category i the subject had encountered, and inversely related to the sum of the similarities between object x and the various instances of the categories in the response set R. That is,

$$
P(i|x) = \frac{\sum_{m=1}^{N_i} \eta(x, i_m)\beta_i}{\sum_{j \in R} \sum_{m=1}^{N_j} \eta(x, j_m)\beta_j},
\tag{6}
$$

where N_i is the number of instances in category i.

An important contribution of the generalized context model was to relate choice probabilities in identification tasks to choice probabilities in categorization tasks. Shepard et al. (1961) applied Equations 1 and 2 to identification probabilities, extracted estimates of the similarities, and used them in Equations 1 and 6 to predict categorization probabilities. This attempt was a famous failure, which led Shepard et al. to conclude that the principles that governed identification were separate from the principles that governed categorization. Nosofsky (1984, 1986, 1988) noted that subjects might attend to the dimensions of the stimuli differently in identification and categorization. He rewrote Equation 2 to include a parameter, w_h, that represents the attention given to dimension h:

$$d_{xi} = \left(\sum_{h=1}^{H} w_h \left| u_{hx} - u_{hi} \right|^r \right)^{\frac{1}{r}}. \tag{7}$$

Nosofsky allowed the attention weight, w_h, to take on different values in identification and categorization and succeeded where Shepard et al. had failed: He was able to predict categorization probabilities from identification probabilities and vice versa. Categorization and identification could be explained by the same principles—those underlying similarity-choice theory.

Nosofsky (1984, 1986, 1988) assumed that subjects chose attention weights that optimized performance. Kruschke (1992) extended the generalized context model to include a connectionist model that learned attention weights. Consequently, Kruschke's model provides a better account of category learning than the generalized context model (Nosofsky et al. 1994, Nosofsky & Palmeri 1996).

The idea of dimensional attention weights is very powerful. Nosofsky et al. (1994) extended it to account for rule-based categorization. In their view, a rule amounts to exclusive attention to a single dimension. Johansen & Palmeri (2002) modeled the transition from rule-based categorization to instance-based categorization in terms of a shift from attending exclusively to one dimension to distributing attention across dimensions.

Nosofsky & Palmeri's (1997a) exemplar-based random walk model extends the generalized context model to account for reaction time phenomena as well as for choice probabilities. The random walk allows the exemplar-based random walk model to respond more deterministically than the generalized context model and provides a process interpretation for extensions to the generalized context model that allows it to respond deterministically. Moreover, the random walk process coupled with the idea that learning involves accumulating instances allows the exemplar-based random walk model to account for the effects of frequency of presentation on categorization performance. Nosofsky & Palmeri (1997b) showed that subjects responded faster to the more frequently presented of two stimuli that were equally distant from the decision bound (also see Verguts et al. 2003).

Signal-Detection Theory

General recognition theory accounts for categorization in terms of decision bounds that divide multidimensional space into regions corresponding to each category. A stimulus is classified according to the region in which it falls (e.g., Ashby & Lee 1991, Ashby & Maddox 1993). Ashby & Lee (1991) applied general recognition theory to similarity ratings and identification probabilities and then to the identification and categorization data of Nosofsky (1986). They found that general recognition theory fit Nosofsky's data better than the generalized context model. Moreover, general recognition theory fit the identification and categorization data without assuming a different distribution of attention weights in the two tasks. However, it did require different decision bounds and different assumptions about perceptual independence and perceptual separability. Maddox et al. (1998)

extended general recognition theory to account for reaction time distributions in perceptual categorization tasks. Recently, Maddox et al. (2002) extended general recognition theory to include a perceptual attention component that affects the variance of the multivariate distributions as well as a decisional attention component represented by decision bounds (cf. Bundesen 1990).

In the domain of categorization, general recognition theory competes fiercely with the generalized context model and the exemplar-based random walk model. Each theory provides an impressively exact account of an impressive amount of data. Indeed, the predictions of the two theories are often very similar to each other, despite fundamental differences in the underlying assumptions about the representations and processes used to perform the tasks. Ashby & Maddox (1993) and Nosofsky (1992) have shown conditions under which they are formally equivalent and make exactly the same predictions. It would be interesting to see the same effort extended to compare signal-detection and similarity-choice theories of other aspects of attention.

ATTENTION TO DIMENSIONS: GARNER TASKS

Attention to dimensions was investigated most thoroughly by Garner and his colleagues (see, e.g., Garner 1974). Prominent among their experiments is a filtering task that examines subjects' ability to disregard variation in irrelevant dimensions. For example, subjects may judge the height of rectangles while attempting to ignore their width. Two major phenomena must be explained: Garner interference and redundancy gains. Garner interference is measured by comparing a baseline task with a filtering task. In the baseline task, the relevant dimension varies but the irrelevant dimension is held constant (e.g., judging whether wide rectangles are tall or short). In the filtering task, the two dimensions vary independently (e.g., tall rectangles are wide and narrow; short rectangles are wide and narrow). If subjects are able to filter out variation in the irrelevant dimension, there should be no difference between baseline and filtering conditions—there will be no Garner interference. If subjects are not able to filter out variation in the irrelevant dimension, reaction time will be longer in the filtering task than in the baseline task—there will be Garner interference. Many studies have found that the presence or absence of Garner interference depends on the relation between the dimensions. If the dimensions are separable, like hue and height or brightness and width, then there is no Garner interference. If the dimensions are integral, like hue and brightness or height and width, then there is Garner interference.

Redundancy gain is observed by comparing correlated and orthogonal filtering tasks (Garner 1974). In a correlated task, both dimensions vary but their values are correlated (e.g., tall rectangles are wide; short rectangles are narrow), whereas in an orthogonal task, the two dimensions vary independently (e.g., tall rectangles are wide and narrow; so are short rectangles). A redundancy gain is observed if subjects are faster with the correlated task than with the orthogonal task. Again, whether redundancy gains are observed depends on the relation between the dimensions.

Separable dimensions usually show no redundancy gain; integral dimensions show strong redundancy gains.

Garner's research poses three key questions for formal theories to answer: What causes Garner interference? What causes redundancy gain? And what does it mean for dimensions to be separable or integral? Models based on similarity-choice theory and models based on signal-detection theory have answered these questions.

Similarity-Choice Theory

Nosofsky & Palmeri's (1997a) exemplar-based random walk model accounts for the difference between separable and integral dimensions in terms of the distance metric (i.e., the parameter r in Equations 2 and 7). If $r = 1$, the distance metric is city block and the dimensions are separable. Changing the distance on one dimension has no effect on the distance on the other dimension, so the dimensions can be processed independently without one intruding on the other. If $r = 2$, the distance metric is Euclidean and the dimensions are integral. Changing the distance on one dimension also changes the distance between the objects, so variation in the irrelevant dimension intrudes on judgments of the relevant dimension.

The exemplar-based random walk model accounts for Garner's results with separable dimensions in terms of attention weights. With separable dimensions, all of the attention weight can be given to the relevant dimension, so the irrelevant dimension has no influence. This distribution of attention weight stretches the relevant dimension and collapses the irrelevant dimension. Consequently, there is no difference between baseline and filtering tasks and no difference between orthogonal and correlated filtering tasks.

The exemplar-based random walk model accounts for Garner's results with integral dimensions in terms of differential repetition effects and differential confusions between stimuli. The baseline condition involves fewer stimuli than the filtering condition. In typical experiments, the baseline condition involves only two stimuli whereas the filtering condition involves four. Thus, stimuli and responses are more likely to repeat in the baseline condition, and repetition of stimuli and responses reduces reaction time (Nosofsky & Palmeri 1997a).

The different numbers of stimuli in the baseline and filtering tasks also creates differential confusions between stimuli. Consider a baseline condition in which subjects judge the height of narrow rectangles and a filtering condition in which they judge the height of wide and narrow rectangles. Imagine the subject is presented with a tall narrow rectangle. In the baseline condition, there is only one stimulus to be confused with the target—the short narrow rectangle. In the filtering condition, however, there are two stimuli to be confused with the target—the short narrow rectangle and the short wide rectangle. Consequently, the probability of choosing the target will be lower in the filtering condition and this will slow the random walk. The lower the choice probability, the slower the rate at which target categorizations accumulate. Moreover, the lower the choice probability, the more incorrect categorizations will accumulate in the other counter. The exemplar-based random walk model chooses a response when one counter has K more categorizations than any other, so the greater the number of categorizations in the incorrect counter, the greater the number of correct categorizations that must be accumulated. Nosofsky & Palmeri (1997a, 1997b) predict the data quantitatively.

The exemplar-based random walk model accounts for the difference between correlated and orthogonal filtering tasks in terms of differential repetition and differential distance between the alternatives. As with the baseline-filtering contrast, the contrast between correlated and orthogonal filtering tasks involves different numbers of stimuli. In a typical design, the correlated condition involves two stimuli whereas the orthogonal condition involves four. As with the baseline-filtering contrast, there are more opportunities for stimulus-response repetitions in the correlated condition than in the orthogonal condition, and this differential facilitation from repetition accounts for some of the difference in reaction time (Nosofsky & Palmeri 1997a).

The difference in distance between alternatives can be seen by imagining a set of four stimuli that vary on two dimensions arrayed as a square in multidimensional space. The orthogonal task requires subjects to discriminate the left two stimuli from the right two stimuli. The correlated task requires subjects to discriminate the bottom left stimulus from the top right stimulus. Imagine the bottom left stimulus has been presented. In the orthogonal task, the nearest (most confusable) alternative is the bottom right stimulus. In the correlated task, the nearest alternative is the top right stimulus. The bottom right stimulus is closer to the target than the top right stimulus, so choice probability will be lower, and reaction time will be longer. Nosofsky & Palmeri (1997a) predicted this difference quantitatively. Nosofsky & Palmeri (1997b) extended these predictions to reaction time distributions.

Signal-Detection Theory

In general recognition theory, the concepts of integrality and separability are closely tied to the concepts of perceptual and decisional independence (Ashby & Maddox 1994, Ashby & Townsend 1986). The theory distinguishes between perceptual separability and decisional separability. Consider a set of four stimuli produced by factorially combining two levels of two components, A and B. Perceptual separability holds if the perceptual effects of one stimulus component are independent of the perceptual effects of another. This can be assessed by comparing the marginal distributions of perceptual effects, $g_{AiB1}(x)$ and $g_{AiB2}(x)$, for level i of component A at levels 1 and 2 of component B. Perceptual separability holds if $g_{AiB1}(x) = g_{AiB2}(x)$ for $i = 1$ and 2. Perceptual separability is violated if $g_{AiB1}(x) \neq g_{AiB2}(x)$ for $i = 1$ and 2. Ashby & Maddox (1994) consider two cases in which perceptual separability can be violated: mean shift integrality and variance shift integrality. In mean shift integrality, the mean of the distribution of perceptual effects for one level of one component is different from the mean of the distribution of perceptual effects for the other level (i.e., the distributions have the same shape but the means are shifted relative to each other). In variance shift integrality, the means of the distributions are the same but the variances are different. Both mean-shift integrality and variance-shift integrality will produce violations of perceptual separability.

Decisional separability occurs if the decision about one component is unaffected by the perceptual effect of the other component. This occurs when the decision boundaries are parallel to the coordinate axes of the multidimensional space. Perceptual independence is assessed from the covariance between the distributions of perceptual effects in multidimensional space. Perceptual independence holds if the covariances are zero (for a complete discussion of independence, see Ashby & Townsend 1986).

The results in Garner's tasks are predicted from these assumptions about separability and integrality and from the idea that reaction time is proportional to the distance between the percept and the decision bound (Equations 4 and 5). If perceptual and decisional separability hold, then the percepts will be the same distance from the decision bound in the baseline and filtering tasks—there will be no Garner interference. If perceptual separability fails and decisional separability holds, then some percepts will be closer to the decision bound in the filtering condition than in the baseline condition, resulting in slower reaction times. In this way, general recognition theory predicts Garner interference with (perceptually) integral dimensions.

In orthogonal and correlated filtering tasks, the percepts will be the same distance from the decision bound if perceptual and decisional separability hold—there will be no redundancy gain. Maddox & Ashby (1996) noted that the optimal decision bounds were not orthogonal to the coordinate axes in the correlated filtering task (e.g., when the mean of one distribution is in the top left and the mean of the other is in the bottom right). With this configuration of distributions, the optimal decision bound is a diagonal line (going from the top right to the bottom left). This decision bound is optimal in the sense that it maximizes the distance between the percept and the decision bound, and that will speed reaction time. Consequently, Maddox & Ashby (1996) predicted redundancy gains with perceptually separable stimuli in the correlated filtering task, and they found them. In terms of their theory, they predicted that the correlated task would violate decisional separability.

ATTENTION TO OBJECTS: VISUAL SEARCH

Identification and categorization tasks represent a universe in which there is only one object. The real world and many attention tasks represent a universe in which there are several objects, and choosing an object to respond to is a significant problem. For the past 20 years, much research has been done on visual search tasks, in which subjects are faced with a display of many objects and must decide whether the display contains a target object. The main independent variable is display size—the number of objects in the display—and the main dependent variable is a measure of search efficiency—the extent to which reaction time or accuracy or both are affected by variation in the number of objects in the display. If search is efficient, reaction time and accuracy are largely unaffected by the number of objects in the display. If search is inefficient, reaction time and accuracy are strongly affected by the number of objects in the display. Much of the research has focused on factors that determine search efficiency and a number of alternative hypotheses have been proposed, some of which are informal and some of which are formal. Similarity-choice theory and signal-detection theory have been applied to these problems, suggesting their own hypotheses about the determinants of search efficiency.

Similarity-Choice Theory

The main contribution of Bundesen's (1990) theory of visual attention was an application of similarity-choice theory to the problem of object selection. His initial work focused primarily on partial report tasks (Sperling 1960), in which subjects are presented with several stimuli and are required to identify some of them. In partial report tasks, the objects to be identified typically share a property or set of properties that are independent of the properties relevant to identification. For example, subjects might be shown a display of red and black letters and asked to report the red ones. This kind of object selection was called stimulus set (Broadbent 1971), input selection (Treisman 1969), and filtering (Kahneman & Treisman 1984) in classical theories of attention.

In the theory of visual attention, objects are assigned attentional weights, and the probability of selecting an object increases with the attentional weight on the object. For a display of objects that are homogeneous (in the sense of Bundesen 1990, p. 524) the probability that object x is the first object selected is given:

$$P_\pi(x) = \frac{\sum_{k \in S} \eta(x, k)\pi_k}{\sum_{z \in D} \sum_{k \in S} \eta(z, k)\pi_k}, \tag{8}$$

where $\eta(x, k)$ is the extent to which object x has the property k in the stimulus set S (the set of target-defining properties), and D is the set of objects that are displayed on a given trial. The parameter π_k reflects the priority given to objects with property k. It has the same effect as the bias parameter in the Shepard-Luce choice rule but it is represented by a different symbol because it has a different function: π reflects the priority given to objects in the stimulus set, whereas β reflects the bias given to different categories in the response set. In the language of classical theories of attention, π reflects stimulus set or input selection, whereas β reflects response set (Broadbent 1971) or analyzer selection (Treisman 1969).

Changing priority changes the distribution of attention across the objects in the display. Objects whose properties are in the stimulus set S get more attention than objects whose properties are not in the stimulus set. By Equation 8, the $P_\pi(z)$ values sum to 1.0 across the display, so increasing the priority of one object necessarily decreases the priority of the others. This constraint limits the theory of visual attention's processing capacity (Bundesen 1990, Logan 2002).

Bundesen (1990) combined stimulus set and response set multiplicatively, in order to account for stimulus selection and response selection (for an explanation of the multiplicative combination, see Logan 2002). In the theory of visual attention, the probability of choosing object x and identifying it as a member of category i is given by:

$$P(x \cap i) = \frac{\eta(x, i)\beta_i P_\pi(x)}{\sum_{z \in D} \sum_{j \in R} \eta(z, j)\beta_j P_\pi(z)}. \tag{9}$$

Bundesen (1990) applied this equation to partial and whole report tasks and extended it to a variety of attention tasks, including efficient and inefficient visual search.

EFFICIENT AND INEFFICIENT SEARCH   The results from similarity-choice theories are generally consistent with more qualitative models (Treisman & Gelade 1980) or simulation models (Cave & Wolfe 1990, Wolfe 1994) that assume that efficient search is done in parallel and inefficient search is done in series. Bundesen (1990) modeled Treisman & Gelade's (1980) feature search task, in which a target differs from a set of homogeneous distractors in terms of a single feature (e.g., a red target among green distractors). If the target is not similar to the distractors, this task yields very efficient search. Bundesen modeled target-present responses as a race between alternatives. The distractors are not very similar to the target, so they intrude little on the race and reaction time is largely independent of the number of distractors. He modeled target-absent responses in terms of a deadline. The model responded "absent" if a target was not found by the time the deadline expired. However, Chun & Wolfe (1996) suggest that temporal deadlines may not be the best way to terminate search on target-absent trials. Logan (2002) extended the theory of visual attention to include the similarity assumptions of the generalized context model and the exemplar-based random walk model. He noted that subjects can vary attention weights (see Equation 7) in feature search tasks to increase the distance between the targets and the distractors in multidimensional similarity space, which increases choice probability and speeds reaction time.

Bricolo et al. (2002) provided serial and parallel models of inefficient search tasks, inspired by the theory of visual attention, that address changes in reaction time distributions as a function of the number of objects in the display (display size) and serial position effects on mean reaction time. The results of the display size experiment showed that the minimum of the reaction time distribution increased with display size for both target-present and target-absent responses but the increase was much larger for target-absent responses. This result was predicted by a serial self-terminating model and by a parallel self-terminating model with fixed capacity that is reallocated after each object is finished processing. The results of the serial position experiment showed an increase in reaction time with serial position, which could be predicted by a serial self-terminating model and by a parallel self-terminating model with fixed capacity that is not reallocated after each object is finished processing. The same serial model could account for both sets of results, but different parallel models were required for the two experiments, so Bricolo et al. (2002) favored the serial model.

Logan (2002) noted that subjects could not vary attention weights to optimize performance in many tasks that yield inefficient search. In conjunction search tasks, in which the target shares one feature with half of the distractors and another feature with the other half of the distractors, varying attention weight to move one of the distractors further away from the target moves the other distractor closer to the target, resulting in no net gain in discriminability. Logan (1996) provided decision rules for conjunction search tasks and noted that they predicted faster decisions for targets that differed from distractors on two features (triple conjunctions) than for targets that differed from distractors on one feature (double conjunctions; see Wolfe et al. 1989).

DISTANCE AND GROUPING BY PROXIMITY   A common finding in a variety of attention tasks is that performance is affected by the proximity of the objects. Nearby distractors impair target performance more than distant distractors (e.g., Eriksen & Eriksen 1974). Grouping by proximity is powerful and can have strong effects on performance. Targets that are grouped together with distractors are harder to find. Targets that are isolated from distractors are easier to find (e.g., Banks & Prinzmetal 1976). Bundesen's (1990) theory of visual attention cannot account for these effects. It assumes all objects in the display are processed in parallel and their processing rates are the same regardless of their spatial arrangement. Logan (1996) extended the theory of visual attention to account for the effects of proximity and grouping by proximity, adding Van Oeffelen & Vos's (1982, 1983) COntour DEtector (CODE) theory of perceptual grouping by proximity as a "front end" to produce the CODE theory of visual attention.

The CODE theory assumes that the representation of object location is not a point, but rather, is distributed over space (also see Ashby et al. 1996). The distributions representing nearby objects overlap substantially; distributions representing distant objects overlap very little. According to CODE, the distributions add together to produce a CODE surface that looks something like a mountain range. Grouping by proximity is determined by imposing a threshold on the CODE surface (i.e., drawing a plane of a certain height across the CODE surface) to create one or more above-threshold regions. The CODE theory claims that objects that fall within the same above-threshold region are part of the same perceptual group. CODE predicts subjects' grouping by proximity very well in textbook demonstrations (Van Oeffelen & Vos 1982, 1983) and reasonably well in random dot patterns (Compton & Logan 1993, 1999).

The CODE theory of visual attention assumes that the theory of visual attention samples information from the perceptual groups defined by above-threshold regions on the CODE surface. The probability that the theory of visual attention will sample a given object is equal to the proportion of the area or volume of the distribution of that object that falls within the sampled above-threshold region. Objects whose centers fall within the region are likely to be sampled because the central parts of their distributions fall within the above-threshold region. Objects whose centers fall outside the region (i.e., objects in different perceptual groups) will also be sampled with a probability equal to the proportion of their distribution that falls within the sampled above-threshold region, but that probability is lower because only the tails of the object intrude in the sampled above-threshold region. Moreover, the more distant the object, the smaller the proportion of its distribution will fall within the sampled above-threshold region, so the smaller the impact it will have on performance. Logan (1996) showed that these ideas accounted for distance and grouping by proximity effects in a variety of attention tasks, and Logan & Bundesen (1996) showed they accounted for distance and grouping effects in partial report tasks.

Signal-Detection Theory

Signal-detection approaches to search generally assume there are no perceptual capacity limitations on search and interpret search efficiency in terms of the impact of discriminability on a parallel decision process, inconsistent with feature integration theory (Treisman & Gelade 1980) and guided search (Cave & Wolfe 1990, Wolfe 1994, Wolfe et al. 1989), and consistent with parallel models (Duncan & Humphreys 1989, Heinke & Humphreys 2003, Humphreys & Müller 1993). Palmer and colleagues applied signal-detection theory to a variety of visual search tasks, including those that produce efficient and inefficient search (Eckstein et al. 2000; Palmer 1994, 1998; Palmer et al. 1993). In their models, a decision process takes a sample from each object in the display and decides "target present" if the largest sample exceeds a criterion and "target absent" if it does not exceed the criterion—that is, by applying a "max rule." Display size effects occur because of the max rule. On target-absent trials, the noise distribution is the distribution of the maximum of the values sampled from N distractors, and the mean of this distribution increases with N. On target-present trials, the signal-plus-noise distribution is the distribution of the maximum of $N - 1$ values sampled from the distractors and one value sampled from the target. The mean of this distribution also increases with N. The discriminability of these distributions of maxima depends on the discriminability of a single target from a single distractor—that is, on d'. The smaller the d' for a single discrimination, the greater the overlap between the noise and signal-plus-noise distributions of maxima, and the overlap increases as N increases. Thus, search tasks with hard discriminations produce large display size effects (inefficient search) and search tasks with easy discriminations produce small display size effects (efficient search). The same parallel decision process is used for easy and hard search. The difference in search efficiency is produced entirely by noise in the decision process.

Eckstein et al. (2000) extended the model to conjunction search tasks, in which targets and distractors vary on several dimensions. In their model, information from different dimensions is collapsed onto a single decision variable, which produces distributions of maxima for target-present and target-absent trials. If there are f relevant feature dimensions and the target differs from the distractors along r of them, then sensitivity for the conjunction discrimination, $d'_{r,f}$, is

$$d'_{r,f} = \frac{rd'_0}{\sqrt{f}},$$

where d'_0 is the sensitivity along each of the r dimensions, which is assumed to be equal for each dimension. This model produces a good quantitative description of the differences between feature, conjunction, and triple-conjunction conditions.

Geisler & Chou (1995) presented a signal-detection model of search performance in which sensitivity varied with eccentricity. They presented displays of single objects at known locations and measured subjects' ability to discriminate the target from the distractor. The known locations varied in eccentricity and discrimination performance decreased as eccentricity increased. Then they presented displays in which a target was or was not superimposed on a uniform texture made from the distractor pattern and in which target location was unknown. Performance on this task was completely predictable from the decline in discriminability with eccentricity, which suggests there were no capacity limits. This conclusion may be limited by presenting the distractors as a uniform field. The equivalence of performance when location is known and unknown may be another example of the general finding that search for a single target is not facilitated by knowledge of target location (Shiu & Pashler 1994).

These signal-detection approaches to visual search are impressive, but the situations they model are different in important ways from the situations in which visual search is usually studied. In all cases, the displays are presented briefly so that accuracy is the main dependent measure. The brief displays prevent sequential sampling from the display, either with covert attention or with overt eye movements. By contrast, typical search tasks present the display until the subject responds, allowing plenty of time for sequential sampling. Eye movements and covert shifts of attention may be important phenomena in visual search but these signal-detection approaches ignore them. Perhaps it should not be surprising that displays too brief to allow sequential sampling can be modeled with parallel processes. More importantly, it is not clear how the models applied to brief displays can be extended to account for reaction times with response-terminated displays. That is an important direction for future research.

ATTENTION TO OBJECTS: CUING PROCEDURES

Attention to objects is often studied by presenting subjects with displays of multiple objects and giving them cues that indicate the target's location or some other salient property. In some procedures, each object in the display is a potential target and the cue indicates which object to judge or report (e.g., Eriksen & Hoffman 1972, Sperling 1960). Consequently, subjects cannot respond to the target without first responding to the cue. In other procedures, the target differs from the distractors in some way and the cue merely indicates its position (e.g., Posner et al. 1980).

In these cases, subjects can respond to the target without first responding to the cue; nevertheless, the cue influences performance. Valid cues that indicate the correct location of the target facilitate performance, speeding reaction time and increasing accuracy. Invalid cues that indicate a location that does not contain the target impair performance, slowing reaction time and decreasing accuracy.

Similarity-Choice Theory

Bundesen (1987, 1990) applied his theory of visual attention to a variety of partial report tasks, including classical data from Sperling (1960). In his own experiments, he varied exposure duration and the number of targets and distractors. In all cases, the theory fit the data very well (also see Bundesen 2002, Logan & Bundesen 1996, Shibuya & Bundesen 1988). Recently, Duncan et al. (1999) used the theory of visual attention to analyze partial and whole report performance in neglect patients. In partial report, patients showed a bias against contralesional targets but a preserved bilateral ability to prioritize targets. In whole report, they showed a bilateral reduction in processing capacity, which suggests a bilateral component to neglect.

Bundesen (1990, 1998) applied the theory of visual attention to the cuing effects reported by Posner et al. (1980). The cue altered the priority (π in Equation 8) given to the cued location but had no effect on the bias (β in Equation 9) given to the target. Increasing priority increases the processing rate for the target on valid cue trials, speeding reaction time. Because the $P_\pi(z)$ values are constrained to sum to 1.0 across the display, increasing priority in an invalid location (on invalid cue trials) necessarily decreases processing rate for the target and slows reaction time.

Logan (2002) extended Bundesen's analysis, contrasting situations in which the cue was necessary to specify the target (e.g., Eriksen & Hoffman 1972, Sperling 1960) and situations in which the target could be specified independent of the cue (e.g., Posner et al. 1980). When the cue specifies the target, cuing can be accounted for entirely in terms of priority (π in Equation 8). However, when the target is specified independent of the cue and the cue merely indicates its location, both priority and bias (β in Equation 9) contribute to the cuing effect. Thus, from the perspective of the theory of visual attention, researchers interested in separating priority from bias should study situations in which cues specify the target and researchers interested in the interaction between priority and bias should study situations in which the cue merely indicates the target's location.

Signal-Detection Theory

Over the past 20 years, Sperling and colleagues have developed an episodic attention theory that accounts for performance in a variety of attention tasks (Reeves & Sperling 1986, Shih & Sperling 2002, Sperling & Reeves 1980, Sperling & Weichselgartner 1995). The most detailed applications of the theory have been to situations that involve rapid serial visual presentation (RSVP) to measure the reaction time of attention shifts, the discrete versus continuous nature of attention shifts, and the trajectory of attention through time and space. Sperling & Reeves (1980) measured reaction time by presenting two RSVP streams. When subjects detected a target in one of the streams, they were to shift attention to the other stream and report the first item they could. The lag between the target in one stream and the item reported in the other reflects the attention reaction time. Reeves & Sperling (1986) elaborated the procedure and the theory, requiring subjects to report as many items as they could from the second stream after detecting the target in the first. They found that subjects had good information about item identity (up to the limit of short-term memory) but poor information about the temporal order in which the items appeared. They modeled performance in terms of an attention gate that opened at the second stream some time after the target was detected in the first stream. The attention gate took the form of a gamma function (the convolution of two exponentials), and the strength of the tendency to report an item depended on the area it subtended under the gamma function. The values along the abscissa were determined by the presentation rate of the items, and the values along the ordinate were determined by the height of the gamma function. This attention gating model provided an excellent account of the data.

Sperling & Weichselgartner (1995) extended the attention gating theory to create the episodic theory of attention. In their theory, visual attention consists of a series of discrete attention episodes. Each episode is characterized by a three-dimensional distribution of attention that extends in time and space. A central contribution of this theory was to model attention shifts as discrete shifts from one spatial distribution to another, contrary to previous attempts to model attention shifts as continuous movements of a "spotlight" across space. Sperling & Weichselgartner (1995) fit their model to the data of several experiments that claimed to find evidence of spatially continuous shifts of attention. They found that their model accounted for the data very well without assuming a continuous shift.

Recently, Shih & Sperling (2002) extended the RSVP procedure and the model further to measure the trajectory of attention through time and space. Their RSVP procedure involves presenting successive displays of three rows of three items and cuing subjects to report items from one of the rows with a tone that varied in pitch (cf. Sperling 1960). They measured the trajectory of attention through time by noting which displays the reported letters came from and they measured the trajectory of attention through space by noting which rows the reported letters came from. They also tested their subjects on partial report tasks in which the delay of the cue and a poststimulus mask were varied and on whole report tasks in which mask delay was varied, using the same model to account for performance on these tasks and the RSVP task. They relate their theory to other procedures intended to measure shifts of spatial attention and to other models of visual spatial attention, such as Bundesen's (1990) theory of visual attention.

On the one hand, the RSVP procedure used in these experiments is quite different from most procedures used to measure cuing attention, so it is not immediately clear how the results from this procedure relate to results from the other procedures. Moreover, the model deals with accuracy of responding and it is not clear how it would deal with reaction time. On the other hand, Sperling and colleagues have taken great pains to apply their model to other procedures, formally in some cases and informally in others. The relations between the procedures can be seen through the model. Indeed, the main purpose of theories and models is to show the relations between disparate procedures.

Dosher & Lu (2000a,b; Lu & Dosher 1998) used a noisy perceptual template model to investigate the costs and benefits of valid and invalid cues, using external noise to distinguish among attention mechanisms. They added increasing amounts of external noise (white Gaussian random noise) to a visual stimulus and observed the effects on contrast thresholds. Typically, adding external noise has no effect on contrast threshold as long as external noise is smaller than the internal noise in the system. When external noise exceeds internal noise, contrast thresholds increase approximately linearly with the amount of noise, when plotted in log-log coordinates. Dosher & Lu distinguished three different attention mechanisms that affected these log-log plots in different ways: "Signal enhancement" shows an increased threshold for invalidly cued trials in the flat part of the log-log plot where external noise is smaller than internal noise. "External noise exclusion" shows an increased threshold for invalidly cued trials in the linear increasing part of the log-log plot where external noise is larger than internal noise. "Internal noise reduction" shows an increased threshold for invalidly cued trials throughout the log-log plot (i.e., in both the flat and the linearly increasing parts of the function). When there were only two locations, the pattern of performance was consistent with signal enhancement (Lu & Dosher 1998, Lu et al. 2000). When there were four or more locations, the pattern of performance was consistent with external noise exclusion (Dosher & Lu 2000a,b).

Again, the procedure required to assess the effects of adding external noise differs substantially from the usual procedures used to measure attention. It is not clear how models of near-threshold performance would extend to reaction times to stimuli that are exposed until the subject responds. These are important questions for future research.

EXECUTIVE CONTROL OF ATTENTION

Executive control is the process by which the mind programs itself. It is involved in understanding instructions, choosing among strategies, preparing and adopting a task set, monitoring performance, and disengaging task sets. It is an important and popular topic in cognitive science, neuroscience, clinical science, developmental science, and the study of individual differences. Optimization of performance is an important feature of executive control. Most theories assume optimality in one way or another but leave the task of optimization to an omnipotent homunculus that is outside the theory. A key idea in many studies of executive control is that an executive process programs subordinate processes. As influential as that idea is, it is empty without some specification of the subordinate process that says how it can be programmed. Formal theories of attention provide this specification and flesh out the idea.

Similarity-Choice Theory

Nosofsky (1984, 1986, 1988) assumed that attention weights were distributed across dimensions to optimize performance. Indeed, the best-fitting attention weights are often the ones that optimize performance. Kruschke (1992) replaced Nosofsky's homunculus with a connectionist module that learns to distribute attention weights across dimensions based on feedback during classification learning. It accounts for asymptotic categorization performance as well as the generalized context model and it provides a better account of classification learning (see, e.g., Nosofsky et al. 1994, Nosofsky & Palmeri 1996).

Logan & Gordon (2001) addressed the idea that an executive process programs a subordinate by proposing a theory of executive control in which Bundesen's (1990) theory of visual attention and Nosofsky & Palmeri's (1997a) exemplar-based random walk model were the subordinates. In the theory of visual attention and the exemplar-based random walk model, priority and bias parameters and the threshold for the random walk are determined by the homunculus, whereas the similarity parameters are determined by the quality of the stimulus information and the subject's experience with the members of the relevant categories. The theory of visual attention and the exemplar-based random walk model can be programmed—set to perform different tasks—by manipulating priority, bias, and threshold parameters. In Logan & Gordon's (2001) theory, a task set is a set of parameters that are sufficient to cause the theory of visual attention and the exemplar-based random walk model to perform particular tasks. Task sets are constructed by deriving parameters from propositional representations of the instructions in working memory. Task sets are enabled by transmitting the parameters from working memory to the place where the models reside in the processing system. Deriving the parameters in working memory is not sufficient to enable or change a task set. The task set must also be instantiated in the theory of visual attention and the exemplar-based random walk model. By analogy, having a program on disk is not sufficient to make it run. It must be loaded into core memory before it can be executed. Transmission of parameters takes time, and that time accounts for task-switching costs.

Logan & Gordon (2001) applied their theory to a dual-task situation called the psychological refractory period procedure, in which subjects must make separate responses to two stimuli that appear close together in time. In principle, the theory of visual attention and the exemplar-based random walk model could perform these two tasks in parallel or in series, but Logan and Gordon showed through simulations that performance was faster and more accurate if the models performed the tasks in series. They were able to account for task-switching costs and backward crosstalk from the second stimulus to the first with the model.

Logan & Bundesen (2003) extended the model to task-switching situations in which a cue indicating which task to perform is presented before each target stimulus. They developed formal models that assumed that the time-course functions reflect the cumulative distributions of finishing times for processes that encoded the cue and switched task sets (also see Sperling & Weichselgartner 1995). Reaction time is slow when cue encoding and set switching have not finished and fast when they have finished. Increasing the interval between the cue and the target increases the probability that cue encoding and set switching are finished. Consequently, reaction time decreases as cue-to-target interval increases. The mean cue-encoding time and set-switching time can be estimated by fitting these models to the time-course functions (also see Logan & Bundesen 1996).

Signal-Detection Theory

The idea of optimality has been a central tenet of signal-detection theory since the 1950s. It remains a central tenet in the general recognition theory (Ashby & Lee 1991, Ashby & Maddox 1993). Signal-detection theory was intended to describe normative decision making under uncertainty by an ideal observer (Geisler 1989, Green & Swets 1966). The β parameter in signal-detection theory, which reflects the placement of the criterion on the decision axis, incorporates the values of correct responses and errors as well as their probabilities. An ideal observer chooses a value of β that maximizes gains and minimizes losses (Green & Swets 1966).

Perhaps the most thorough signal-detection analysis of optimality in attention tasks was done by Sperling & Dosher (1986). They addressed single- and dual-task performance with accuracy and reaction time as dependent measures, examining tradeoffs between concurrent tasks and tradeoffs between speed and accuracy in single tasks. A key concept in their analysis is the idea of a performance-operating characteristic, which plots one measure of performance against another. In classical signal-detection theory, a receiver-operating characteristic plots the probability of hits against the probability of false alarms (Green & Swets 1966). In dual-task studies, an attention-operating characteristic plots performance on one task against performance on another (Sperling & Melchner 1978). Sperling & Dosher (1986) defined a strategy as a choice of a point on a performance-operating characteristic and they argued that choice of a strategy was determined by the expected utility that could be gained at that point.

CONCLUSIONS

In the spirit of competitive hypothesis testing that is so pervasive in psychology, it seems natural to ask, Which theory wins? That is a hard question to answer. It has been clear from the beginning that similarity-choice theory and signal-detection theory make very similar predictions (e.g., Broadbent 1971, Luce 1963). Recent analyses have shown that under some assumptions, the theories mimic each other exactly (Ashby & Maddox 1993, Nosofsky 1992). Moreover, the theories have been applied to so many different domains that it is hard to evaluate the outcome of a single battle in the context of such a large-scale war. Perhaps the theories should be evaluated in terms of other criteria, such as the explanations they provide for attentional phenomena and the assumptions they require to do so.

My personal impression is that similarity-choice theories provide better explanations. They provide processing interpretations of the phenomena that give insight into the underlying computations. Bundesen (1990) describes object selection in terms of competition instantiated as a race between perceptual objects. Nosofsky (1984, 1986, 1988) describes classification in terms of a competition instantiated as a race between memory traces. By contrast, signal-detection approaches seem more descriptive than explanatory. I find it hard to imagine the processes underlying a decision that an object falls within a region of similarity space (but see Ashby 2000). Perhaps my impression is due to differential familiarity—I have spent many more hours thinking about how to interpret attentional phenomena in terms of similarity-choice theory than in terms of signal-detection theory.

Similarity-choice theories and signal-detection theories differ fundamentally in their assumptions about noise. Similarity-choice theories assume no noise in perceptual representations; objects are represented as points in similarity space. Signal-detection theories assume noisy representations; objects are represented as distributions in similarity space. On the one hand, it seems reasonable to think of representations of category exemplars as relatively noise free. Subjects often examine exemplars at their leisure and have plenty of time to encode the nuances of the stimuli. It seems less reasonable to think that the representations are so noisy that their distributions overlap enough to cause frequent confusions. On the other hand, it seems reasonable to think of representations of brief stimuli as noisy. Indeed, it is hard to imagine how adding external noise to a weak stimulus would produce the bilinearity that Dosher & Lu (2000a,b) observe in log-log plots if the internal representation were not noisy. Similarity-choice theories may have a hard time dealing with results from that procedure. Perhaps this issue can be resolved by quantifying noise in neural representations of objects.

Similarity-choice theories and signal-detection theories both assume that objects can be represented as points or distributions in multidimensional similarity space. This representation is limited. It is not clear how structured objects can be represented as points or distributions. Moreover, the idea that similarity is proportional to distance in multidimensional space is problematic. Tversky spent much of his career challenging the metric assumptions of multidimensional similarity models (e.g., Tversky 1977, Tversky & Gati 1982, Tversky & Hutchinson 1986). Indeed, the similarity between structured objects may not be captured very well by a multidimensional similarity space. Medin et al. (1993) showed that relational measures of similarity may be more appropriate for such stimuli.

Ultimately, the most important question in evaluating similarity-choice and signal-detection theories may be this: What are the alternatives? No other theory of attention has a legacy as rich and as powerful as either of these theories. Their mathematical structure allows strong inferences and precise predictions. They make sense of diverse phenomena, bringing order to the fads and fashions that dominate empirical research on attention. Theories that adopt more complex assumptions about object representations are much more specialized, and consequently, lack the generality of similarity-choice and signal-detection approaches (e.g., Heinke & Humphreys 2003, Humphreys & Müller 1993). The theories reviewed here set a high standard for clarity, consistency, and longevity. They have allowed cumulative progress in our understanding of attention over the last 50 years and they promise to increase our cumulative understanding for many years to come. I am optimistic.

ACKNOWLEDGMENTS

This research was supported by grants BCS 0133202 and 0218507 from the National Science Foundation. I would like to thank Claus Bundesen and Tom Palmeri for valuable comments on the manuscript.

The *Annual Review of Psychology* is online at http://psych.annualreviews.org

LITERATURE CITED

Ashby FG. 2000. A stochastic version of general recognition theory. *J. Math. Psych.* 44:310–29

Ashby FG, Lee WW. 1991. Predicting similarity and categorization from identification. *J. Exp. Psychol.: Gen.* 120:150–72

Ashby FG, Maddox WT. 1993. Relations between prototype, exemplar, and decision bound models of categorization. *J. Math. Psych.* 37:372–400

Ashby FG, Maddox WT. 1994. A response time theory of separability and integrality in speeded classification. *J. Math. Psych.* 38:423–66

Ashby FG, Perrin NA. 1988. Toward a unified theory of similarity and recognition. *Psychol. Rev.* 95:124–50

Ashby FG, Prinzmetal W, Ivry R, Maddox WT. 1996. A formal theory of feature binding in object perception. *Psychol. Rev.* 103:165–92

Ashby FG, Townsend JT. 1986. Varieties of perceptual independence. *Psychol. Rev.* 93:154–79

Banks WP, Prinzmetal W. 1976. Configurational effects in visual information processing. *Percept. Psychophys.* 19:361–67

Bricolo E, Gianesini T, Fanini A, Bundesen C, Chelazzi L. 2002. Serial attention mechanisms in visual search: a direct behavioral demonstration. *J. Cogn. Neurosci.* 14:980–93

Broadbent DE. 1971. *Decision and Stress.* London: Academic

Bruner JS, Goodnow JJ, Austin GA. 1956. *A Study of Thinking.* New York: Wiley

Bundesen C. 1987. Visual attention: race models for selection from multielement displays. *Psychol. Res.* 49:113–21

Bundesen C. 1990. A theory of visual attention. *Psychol. Rev.* 97:523–47

Bundesen C. 1993. The relationship between independent race models and Luce's choice axiom. *J. Math. Psych.* 37:446–71

Bundesen C. 1996. Formal models of visual attention: a tutorial review. In *Converging Operations in the Study of Visual Selective Attention,* ed. AF Kramer, MGH Coles, GD Logan, pp. 1–44. Washington, DC: Amer. Psychol. Assoc.

Bundesen C. 1998. Visual selective attention: outlines of a choice model, a race model, and a computational theory. *Vis. Cogn.* 5:287–309

Bundesen C. 2002. A general theory of visual attention. In *Psychology at the Turn of the Millennium: Vol. 1. Cognitive, Biological, and Health Perspectives*, ed. L Bäckman, C von Hofsten, pp. 179–200. Hove, UK: Psychology Press

Cave KR, Wolfe JM. 1990. Modeling the role of parallel processing in visual search. *Cogn. Psychol.* 22:225–71

Chun MM, Wolfe JM. 1996. Just say no: How are visual searches terminated when there is no target present? *Cogn. Psychol.* 30:39–78

Compton BJ, Logan GD. 1993. Evaluating a computational model of perceptual grouping by proximity. *Percept. Psychophys.* 53:403–21

Compton BJ, Logan GD. 1999. Judgments of perceptual groups: reliability and sensitivity to stimulus transformation. *Percept. Psychophys.* 61:1320–35

Dosher BA, Lu Z-L. 2000a. Mechanisms of perceptual attention in precuing of location. *Vis. Res.* 40:1269–92

Dosher BA, Lu Z-L. 2000b. Noise exclusion in spatial attention. *Psychol. Sci.* 11:139–46

Duncan J, Bundesen C, Olson A, Humphreys G, Chavda S, Shibuya H. 1999. Systematic analysis of deficits in visual attention. *J. Exp. Psychol.: Gen.* 128:450–78

Duncan J, Humphreys GW. 1989. Visual search and stimulus similarity. *Psychol. Rev.* 96:433–58

Eckstein MP, Thomas JP, Palmer J, Shimozaki SS. 2000. A signal detection model predicts the effects of set size on visual search accuracy for feature, conjunction, triple conjunction, and disjunction displays. *Percept. Psychophys.* 62:425–51

Eriksen BA, Eriksen CW. 1974. Effects of noise letters upon the identification of a target letter in a nonsearch task. *Percept. Psychophys.* 16:143–49

Eriksen CW, Hoffman JE. 1972. Temporal and spatial characteristics of selective encoding from visual displays. *Percept. Psychophys.* 12:201–4

Garner WR. 1974. *The Processing of Information and Structure.* New York: Wiley

Geisler WS. 1989. Sequential ideal-observer analysis of visual discriminations. *Psychol. Rev.* 96:267–314

Geisler WS, Chou KL. 1995. Separation of low level and high level factors in complex tasks: visual search. *Psychol. Rev.* 102:356–78

Green DM, Swets JA. 1966. *Signal Detection Theory and Psychophysics.* New York: Krieger

Heinke D, Humphreys GW. 2003. Attention, spatial representation, and visual neglect: simulating emergent attention and spatial memory in the selective attention for identification model (SAIM). *Psychol. Rev.* 110:29–87

Humphreys GW, Müller HJ. 1993. SEarch via Recursive Rejection (SERR): a connectionist model of visual search. *Cogn. Psychol.* 25:43–110

Johansen MK, Palmeri TJ. 2002. Are there representational shifts during category learning? *Cogn. Psychol.* 45:482–553

Kahneman D, Treisman A. 1984. Changing views of attention and automaticity. In *Varieties of Attention*, ed. R Parasuraman, DR Davies, pp. 29–61. New York: Academic

Kruschke JK. 1992. ALCOVE: an exemplar-based connectionist model of category learning. *Psychol. Rev.* 99:22–44

Lamberts K. 2000. Information accumulation theory of categorization response times. *Psychol. Rev.* 107:227–60

Logan GD. 1988. Toward an instance theory of automatization. *Psychol. Rev.* 95:492–527

Logan GD. 1996. The CODE theory of visual attention: an integration of space-based and object-based attention. *Psychol. Rev.* 103:603–49

Logan GD. 2002. An instance theory of attention and memory. *Psychol. Rev.* 109:376–400

Logan GD, Bundesen C. 1996. Spatial effects in the partial report paradigm: a challenge for theories of visual-spatial attention. In *The Psychology of Learning and Motivation*, Vol. 35, ed. DL Medin, pp. 243–82. San Diego, CA: Academic

Logan GD, Bundesen C. 2003. Clever homunculus: Is there an endogenous act of control in the explicit task-cuing procedure? *J. Exp. Psychol.: Hum. Percept. Perform.* 29:575–99

Logan GD, Gordon RD. 2001. Executive control of visual attention in dual task situations. *Psychol. Rev.* 108:393–434

Lu Z-L, Dosher BA. 1998. External noise distinguishes attention mechanisms. *Vis. Res.* 38:1183–98

Lu Z-L, Lui CQ, Dosher BA. 2000. Attention mechanisms for multi-location first- and second-order motion perception. *Vis. Res.* 40:173–86

Luce RD. 1959. *Individual Choice Behavior.* New York: Wiley

Luce RD. 1963. Detection and recognition. In *Handbook of Mathematical Psychology*, ed. RD Luce, RR Bush, E Galanter, pp. 103–89. New York: Wiley

Luce RD. 1977. The choice axiom after twenty years. *J. Math. Psychol.* 15:215–33

Maddox WT, Ashby FG. 1996. Perceptual separability, decisional separability, and the identification-speeded classification relationship. *J. Exp. Psychol.: Hum. Percept. Perform.* 22:795–817

Maddox WT, Ashby FG, Gottlob LR. 1998. Response time distributions in multidimensional perceptual categorization. *Percept. Psychophys.* 60:620–37

Maddox WT, Ashby FG, Waldron EM. 2002. Multiple attention systems in perceptual categorization. *Mem. Cogn.* 30:325–39

Marley AAJ, Colonius H. 1992. The "horse race" random utility model for choice probabilities and reaction times, and its competing risks interpretation. *J. Math. Psychol.* 36:1–20

Medin DL, Goldstone RL, Gentner D. 1993. Respects for similarity. *Psychol. Rev.* 100:254–78

Medin DL, Schaffer MM. 1978. Context theory of classification. *Psychol. Rev.* 85:207–38

Murdock BB. 1985. An analysis of the strength-latency relationship. *Mem. Cogn.* 13:511–21

Nosofsky RM. 1984. Choice, similarity, and the context theory of classification. *J. Exp. Psychol.: Learn. Mem. Cogn.* 10:104–14

Nosofsky RM. 1986. Attention, similarity, and the identification-categorization relationship. *J. Exp. Psychol.: Gen.* 115:39–57

Nosofsky RM. 1988. Exemplar-based accounts of relations between classification, recognition, and typicality. *J. Exp. Psychol.: Learn. Mem. Cogn.* 14:700–8

Nosofsky RM. 1992. Similarity scaling and cognitive process models. *Annu. Rev. Psychol.* 43:25–53

Nosofsky RM, Gluck MA, Palmeri TJ, McKinley SC, Glauthier P. 1994. Comparing models of rule-based classification learning: a replication and extension of Shepard, Hovland, and Jenkins (1961). *Mem. Cogn.* 22:352–69

Nosofsky RM, Palmeri TJ. 1996. Learning to classify integral-dimension stimuli. *Psychon. Bull. Rev.* 3:222–26

Nosofsky RM, Palmeri TJ. 1997a. An exemplar-based random walk model of speeded classification. *Psychol. Rev.* 104:266–300

Nosofsky RM, Palmeri TJ. 1997b. Comparing exemplar-retrieval and decision-bound models of speeded perceptual classification. *Percept. Psychophys.* 59:1027–48

Nosofsky RM, Palmeri TJ, McKinley SC. 1994. Rule-plus-exception model of classification learning. *Psychol. Rev.* 101:53–79

Palmer J. 1994. Set-size effects in visual search: the effect of attention is independent of the stimulus for simple tasks. *Vis. Res.* 34:1703–21

Palmer J. 1998. Attentional effects in visual search: relating search accuracy and search time. In *Visual Attention*, ed. RD Wright, pp. 348–88. New York: Oxford Univ. Press

Palmer J, Ames CT, Lindsey DT. 1993. Measuring the effect of attention on simple visual search. *J. Exp. Psychol.: Hum. Percept. Perform.* 19:108–30

Palmeri TJ. 1997. Exemplar similarity and the development of automaticity. *J. Exp. Psychol.: Learn. Mem. Cogn.* 23:324–54

Posner MI. 1982. Cumulative development of attentional theory. *Am. Psychol.* 37:168–79

Posner MI, Snyder CRR, Davidson BJ. 1980. Attention and the detection of signals. *J. Exp. Psychol.: Gen.* 109:160–74

Ratcliff R. 1978. A theory of memory retrieval. *Psychol. Rev.* 85:59–108

Ratcliff R, van Zandt T, McKoon G. 1999.

Connectionist and diffusion models of reaction time. *Psychol. Rev.* 106:261–300

Reeves A, Sperling G. 1986. Attention gating in short-term visual memory. *Psychol. Rev.* 93:180–206

Shepard RN. 1957. Stimulus and response generalization: a stochastic model relating generalization to distance in psychological space. *Psychometrika* 22:325–45

Shepard RN. 1987. Toward a universal law of generalization for psychological space. *Science* 237:1317–23

Shepard RN, Hovland CI, Jenkins HM. 1961. Learning and memorization of classifications. *Psychol. Monogr.* 75:1–42

Shibuya H, Bundesen C. 1988. Visual selection from multielement displays: measuring and modeling the effects of exposure duration. *J. Exp. Psychol.: Hum. Percept. Perform.* 14:591–600

Shih S-I, Sperling G. 2002. Measuring and modeling the trajectory of visual spatial attention. *Psychol. Rev.* 109:260–305

Shiu L, Pashler H. 1994. Negligible effect of spatial precuing on identification of single digits. *J. Exp. Psychol.: Hum. Percept. Perform.* 20:1037–54

Sperling G. 1960. The information available in brief visual presentations. *Psychol. Monogr.* 74:(11, Whole No. 498)

Sperling G, Dosher BA. 1986. Strategy and optimization in human information processing. In *Handbook of Perception and Performance*, Vol. 1, ed. K Boff, L Kaufman, J Thomas, pp. 2-1– 2-65. New York: Wiley

Sperling G, Melchner MJ. 1978. The attention operating characteristic: some examples from visual search. *Science* 202:315–18

Sperling G, Reeves A. 1980. Measuring the reaction time of an unobservable response: a shift of visual attention. In *Attention and Performance VIII*, ed. RS Nickerson, pp. 347–60. New York: Academic

Sperling G, Weichselgartner E. 1995. Episodic theory of the dynamics of spatial attention. *Psychol. Rev.* 102:503–32

Stroop JR. 1935. Studies of interference in serial verbal reactions. *J. Exp. Psychol.* 18:643–62

Swets JA. 1984. Mathematical models of attention. In *Varieties of Attention*, ed. R Parasuraman, DR Davies, pp. 183–242. San Diego, CA: Academic

Tanner WP, Swets JA. 1954. A decision-making theory of visual detection. *Psychol. Rev.* 61:401–9

Thurstone LL. 1927. A law of comparative judgment. *Psychol. Rev.* 34:273–86

Trabasso TR, Bower GH. 1968. *Attention and Learning: Theory and Research.* New York: Wiley

Treisman A. 1969. Strategies and models of selective attention. *Psychol. Rev.* 76:282–99

Treisman A, Gelade G. 1980. A feature-integration theory of attention. *Cogn. Psychol.* 12:97–136

Tversky A. 1977. Features of similarity. *Psychol. Rev.* 84:327–52

Tversky A, Gati I. 1982. Similarity, separability, and the triangle inequality. *Psychol. Rev.* 89:123–54

Tversky A, Hutchinson JW. 1986. Nearest neighbor analysis of psychological spaces. *Psychol. Rev.* 93:3–22

Van Oeffelen MP, Vos PG. 1982. Configurational effects on the enumeration of dots: counting by groups. *Mem. Cogn.* 10:396–404

Van Oeffelen MP, Vos PG. 1983. An algorithm for pattern description on the level of relative proximity. *Pattern Recogn.* 16:341–48

Verguts T, Storms G, Tuerlinckx F. 2003. Decision-bound theory and the influence of familiarity. *Psychon. Bull. Rev.* 10:141–48

Wickens TD. 2002. *Elementary Signal Detection Theory.* New York: Oxford Univ. Press

Wolfe JM. 1994. Guided search 2.0: a revised model of visual search. *Psychonom. Bul. Rev.* 1:202–38

Wolfe JM, Cave KR, Franzel SL. 1989. Guided search: an alternative to the feature integration model for visual search. *J. Exp. Psychol.: Hum. Percept. Perform.* 15:419–33

Annu. Rev. Psychol. 2004. 55:235–69
doi: 10.1146/annurev.psych.55.090902.141555
First published online as a Review in Advance on November 3, 2003

THE PSYCHOLOGY AND NEUROSCIENCE OF FORGETTING

John T. Wixted

*Department of Psychology, University of California, San Diego, La Jolla,
California 92093-0109; email: jwixted@ucsd.edu*

Key Words   interference, consolidation, psychopharmacology, LTP, sleep

■ **Abstract**   Traditional theories of forgetting are wedded to the notion that cue-overload interference procedures (often involving the A-B, A-C list-learning paradigm) capture the most important elements of forgetting in everyday life. However, findings from a century of work in psychology, psychopharmacology, and neuroscience converge on the notion that such procedures may pertain mainly to forgetting in the laboratory and that everyday forgetting is attributable to an altogether different form of interference. According to this idea, recently formed memories that have not yet had a chance to consolidate are vulnerable to the interfering force of mental activity and memory formation (even if the interfering activity is not similar to the previously learned material). This account helps to explain why sleep, alcohol, and benzodiazepines all improve memory for a recently learned list, and it is consistent with recent work on the variables that affect the induction and maintenance of long-term potentiation in the hippocampus.

CONTENTS

0066-4308/04/0204-0001$14.00

INTRODUCTION

The question of why people forget what they once knew has been continuously investigated for more than a century, and standard accounts of what we have learned about this fundamental issue can be found in almost any general psychology textbook. Unfortunately, the story that those books tell has changed over the years from a theoretically coherent (but ultimately incorrect) interference-based account of forgetting to an atheoretical laundry list of factors that may or may not play a role. Once, the standard story was that the lion's share of forgetting is caused by interference and that the main culprit is interference from prior learning (i.e., proactive interference) rather than subsequent learning (i.e., retroactive interference). Theoretical mechanisms such as unlearning, spontaneous recovery, and response competition initially offered a compelling theoretical explanation for the interfering effects of prior learning, but this way of thinking unraveled in the face of disconfirming evidence more than 30 years ago (Tulving & Madigan 1970). Because no new theory emerged to take its place, authors now typically claim that retroactive and proactive interference may both be important and that forgetting probably also involves retrieval failure due to changed or otherwise inadequate retrieval cues. The notion that decay might play a role, which was once almost universally rejected, has also been resurrected to the status of a possible contributing factor. The tentative and atheoretical nature of the modern account of forgetting is somewhat disappointing after so many years of diligent effort. In the pages to follow, I review findings from psychology, psychopharmacology, and neuroscience in an effort to extract a more compelling theoretical message from the large body of research on forgetting that has accumulated over the years.

When grappling with fundamental questions about the nature of memory and retrieval, psychological theories have often been informed by progress in related fields. For example, theories concerned with the distinction between implicit and explicit memory have relied heavily on developments not only in psychology but also in neuropsychology and neuroscience (e.g., Gabrieli 1998, Schacter 1992). By contrast, theories of forgetting have rarely ventured beyond the traditional boundaries of experimental psychology. As a case in point, consider the notion that memory traces consolidate over time (an idea that will figure prominently in the account of forgetting that is presented below). According to this idea, memories become less fragile and, therefore, more resistant to interference as time passes. Consolidation theory is a standard account in neuroscience, but it is scarcely even mentioned in the psychology literature. To see that this is true, consider the numbers shown in Table 1. This table shows, for various journals, the number of articles that include "memory" as a keyword relative to the number of articles that include both "memory" and "consolidation" as keywords (according to PsychInfo). For six standard psychology journals, an average of 379 articles about memory appears for every one article that happens to mention both memory and consolidation. For six standard neuroscience journals, the corresponding number is 14. Evidently, Keppel (1984) accurately expressed the attitude that implicitly pervades the study

TABLE 1 Number of articles that list "memory" as a key word (A), number that list "memory" and "consolidation" as key words (B), and the ratio of those two values (A/B) for each of six cognitive and six neuroscience journals

Cognitive journal	A	B	A/B	Neuroscience journal	A	B	A/B
Journal of Verbal Learning & Verbal Behavior	546	1	546	*Journal of Neuroscience*	363	26	14
Journal of Memory & Language	262	1	262	*Neuroscience*	216	18	12
Journal of Experimental Psychology	3816	9	424	*Learning & Memory*	158	27	6
Journal of Experimental Psychology: Learning, Memory & Cognition	875	3	292	*Behavioral Neuroscience*	493	29	17
Cognitive Psychology	189	1	189	*Brain Research*	817	60	14
Memory & Cognition	1142	3	381	*Brain*	1691	70	24
Mean cognitive	**1137**	**3**	**379**	**Mean neuroscience**	**623**	**46**	**14**

of forgetting when he said, "For a cognitively oriented psychologist, I find little connection between the behavioral evidence obtained from human learning experiments on the one hand and neurophysiological theory on the other" (p. 157). What I hope to show here is that the situation has changed rather dramatically in that respect, and I begin with a more detailed consideration of what was once the standard theoretical account of forgetting.

THE (ONCE) STANDARD STORY OF FORGETTING

Is Forgetting Due to Interference or Decay?

The question of whether forgetting is due to interference or to natural decay commanded a great deal of attention early in the twentieth century. To answer this question, an ideal experiment to perform is one in which a learning phase is followed by a retention phase during which the subject's brain remains biologically active (allowing for natural decay processes to unfold) while his or her mind remains in a quiescent state (so that no new learning interferes with the prior learning). A classic study by Jenkins & Dallenbach (1924) approximated this ideal experiment by comparing memory for nonsense syllables when subjects slept through the retention interval compared to when they remained awake. Interference theory would predict less forgetting during sleep due to the absence of new learning, whereas decay theory would predict no difference between the two conditions. Because Jenkins & Dallenbach (1924) found that subjects recalled more items when they slept than when they remained awake, interference theory won the day and decay theory was essentially abandoned. Contributing to the demise of decay theory was McGeoch's (1932) oft-cited observation that the passage of time, per se, is not the cause of forgetting anymore than it is the cause of the physical deterioration associated with aging. Thus, a version of decay theory that attributes a causal role to the passage of time itself (a curious notion, to be sure) is conceptually flawed from the outset. A more reasonable decay theory might hold that forgetting is due to the deterioration of organic traces due to natural metabolic processes, but McGeogh (1932) was openly dubious about this possibility as well (though he obviously could not rule it out). His views were quite influential in the 1930s and 1940s, and they helped to cement the case in favor of interference theory.

The interference account of forgetting changed somewhat with the publication of a classic paper by Underwood in 1957. In that paper, Underwood considered the question of why it was that after subjects learned a list to a criterion of one perfect recall, the amount of forgetting that occurred over the next 24 hours varied greatly from study to study even though the studies in question involved similar stimulus materials (usually nonsense syllables) and similar subject populations (usually college students). Some studies reported that only 20% of the memorized items were forgotten after one day, whereas others reported that nearly 80% were forgotten. What Underwood discovered was that nearly all of the variability across studies could be explained by the number of prior lists the subjects had been asked to learn in the experimental setting. Studies in which subjects learned only a few prior lists reported much less forgetting than those in which subjects learned many prior lists. The inescapable conclusion was that forgetting was largely attributable to proactive interference (PI). Underwood (1957) went so far as to argue that retroactive interference (RI) is probably a minor cause of forgetting and that even the 20% of a memorized list that is forgotten over 24 hours when no prior lists are learned is more likely to be caused by proactive rather than retroactive interference. After all, subjects are more likely to have encountered similar interfering material at some point in their long past than in the 24 hours following their participation in a psychology experiment.

The realization that prior learning could profoundly affect the forgetting of subsequently learned material required a new theory, and interference theorists of the day developed one based on principles derived from the animal learning literature (Underwood & Postman 1960). Imagine that subjects learn a list of paired associates (the A-B list) and then later learn another list with the same stimulus terms but different response terms (the A-C list). When memory is later tested for the A-C list by presenting the A term as a retrieval cue and asking for the corresponding associate from the second list (i.e., C), performance will be worse than it would have been had the A-B list not been previously learned (i.e., PI will be observed). Moreover, the degree of proactive interference will be minimal shortly after the A-C list is learned but will increase as the retention interval following A-C learning increases. Theoretically, this occurs because while the subject is learning the A-C list, the B terms covertly come to mind. Because those terms are no longer correct, they are, in a sense, placed on an extinction schedule (i.e., recalling those items is not reinforced). Eventually, the A-B associations extinguish, which is to say that they are unlearned. It has been well documented in the animal learning literature that extinguished responses (e.g., extinguished bar presses in rats) eventually spontaneously recover, and that was assumed to be true of the A-B associations as well. When the A-B associations spontaneously recover at some point well after the A-C list is learned, they will compete with the retrieval of the C terms on a recall test (hence, PI).

Problems with the Standard Story of Forgetting

A major difficulty with the PI-based account of forgetting is that the Jenkins & Dallenbach (1924) sleep study appeared to establish the importance of RI in forgetting. If PI were responsible for most forgetting, why would sleep (which eliminates RI) have such a positive effect on retention? Underwood (1957) readily admitted that he had no explanation for this, and he simply hypothesized that the mechanisms responsible for PI may not be active during sleep. Although there was no obvious basis for this claim, it proved to be a testable hypothesis, and Ekstrand (1967) performed the relevant experiment. In this study, subjects first learned two lists, an A-B list of paired associates followed by an A-C list of paired associates. Half the subjects learned these lists late at night and then slept for eight hours, whereas the other half learned these lists in the morning and then remained awake for eight hours. The key finding was that memory for both lists was enhanced by sleep. That is, memory for the C items was enhanced following sleep even though memory for the supposedly proactively interfering B items was also enhanced. This led Ekstrand to conclude that the mechanisms of PI (which presumably involve competition between the B and C items) are, if anything, enhanced by sleep. As such, the beneficial effects of sleep are more likely to be due to a reduction in RI, which is what Jenkins & Dallenbach (1924) had originally assumed.

In a comprehensive overview of the interference literature, Postman (1971) noted that sleep studies point to "...retroactive interference produced by the subject's normal waking activities as a condition of forgetting" (p. 1123), but he went on to note that researchers who subsequently investigated the specific sources of interference did not capitalize on this observation. As Postman (1971) put it: "As it turned out, the systematic analysis of the latter problem focused on proactive rather than retroactive effects" (p. 1123). Unfortunately, that analysis ultimately suggested that PI might not account for much normal forgetting in spite of its large effects in the laboratory. Underwood & Postman (1960), for example, set out to show that a subject's preexperimental learning history could affect the rate of forgetting for lists learned in the laboratory. Their basic strategy involved comparing the rates of forgetting over a period of one week for a list of three-letter words (like *age*, *end*, *him*, and so on) versus a list of three-letter trigrams (like *ati*, *est*, *han*, and so on). The idea was that the words would have many more preexperimental associative connections to other words than the trigrams would. Those associations would, according to the standard theory of the day, need to be unlearned in order to form associations between the words on the list presented in the laboratory. No such unlearning would need to take place for the trigrams. Theoretically, the unlearned associations to the words would, in time, spontaneously recover and interfere with memory for the list of words. Thus, the rate of forgetting for words should exceed that for nonwords. Contrary to this prediction, the rates of forgetting were the same.

Conceivably, this failure to demonstrate the applicability of PI to real-life learning and forgetting was due to an inadequate theory. Indeed, as indicated above, the theory of unlearning followed by spontaneous recovery is no longer accepted, and if that theory is wrong, perhaps it does not follow that the rate of forgetting for words should exceed that for nonwords. More troubling for the notion that PI explains everyday forgetting, though, was a later study reported by Underwood & Ekstrand (1966, 1967). They showed that, in the laboratory, PI could be easily demonstrated if (as usual) the prior learning trials were massed. But if they were spaced over four days, which is the condition that presumably more closely reflects the way that extraexperimental learning has taken place, no PI was observed. If learning is typically distributed, these results suggest that PI may not be a major source of forgetting in everyday life. In a single sentence that appears without explanation in his earlier classic article, Underwood (1957) mentions that he included studies for consideration in his review only if the prior learning was massed. This curious (at the time) inclusion criterion makes sense in light of his later work suggesting that the effects of PI are not otherwise apparent.

As the work of Underwood and his colleagues began to cast doubt on the importance of PI in everyday forgetting, other studies continued to accumulate showing that the major assumptions of interference theory were simply untenable. Slamecka (1966), for example, showed that subjects do not unlearn previously acquired associations when learning new associations in the laboratory. By 1970, the field had clearly lost its patience with increasingly complicated interference theories of forgetting (e.g., Tulving & Madigan 1970), and little theoretical headway has been made since that time.

Summarizing the state of the art late in his career, Underwood (1983) said: "A relatively few years ago it seemed that a fairly comprehensive theoretical account of forgetting was close at hand, but that has slipped away. Some investigators have lost confidence in interference as a major cause forgetting, but none of the proposed replacements thus far has created a feeling that things are on a productive new track. But that will surely come" (p. 262). The productive new track that Underwood (1983) yearned for may be the track that interference theorists were on in the early part of the twentieth century. Indeed, the developments reviewed above suggest that the field may have made a wrong turn when it embraced PI as the primary cause of ordinary forgetting and when it adopted a cue-overload (A-B, A-C learning) approach to the study of the problem of forgetting. Quite possibly, the field was not very far off track even as late as 1951 when Carl Hovland, commenting on Jenkins & Dallenbach's (1924) classic sleep study, said "These experiments closely simulate the conditions of real life and indicate that intervening activity is a potent factor in producing forgetting" (p. 676). Note that the intervening activity that is eliminated by sleep does not necessarily involve activities that are captured by A-B, A-C list learning methods. Indeed, as Underwood (1957) pointed out when making his case for the effects of PI, most of the intervening activity would involve materials unrelated to the original list. Even so, beneficial effects of sleep on memory are observed.

One of Underwood's students, Geoffrey Keppel, argued that, on the whole, the results point to what he called nonspecific RI as the major cause of forgetting in everyday life (Keppel 1968). I believe that Keppel was on the right track in spite of the later doubts he expressed about the utility of consolidation theory. However, his arguments were made at the end of the heyday of interference theory, and few have paid much attention to his case. The rather dramatic claim that the A-B, A-C list learning methods favored by experimental psychologists since the 1930s fail to capture some of the most important elements of the story of forgetting has certainly not penetrated the field's collective consciousness even though it was also endorsed by Ekstrand (1972) and Wickelgren (1977). In what follows, I try to pick up the story where Keppel (1968) left off many years ago.

Starting Over

One way to progress beyond the tentative laundry list account of forgetting that came to replace the once standard interference-based story is to assemble the basic facts and look for a common message. In what follows, I assemble some of the relevant facts from psychology, psychopharmacology, and neuroscience. A common theme running through that review is based on one of the oldest relevant neuropsychological considerations, namely, the temporal gradient of retrograde amnesia. Clinical reports dating back more than 100 years have suggested that brain damage leading to anterograde amnesia (i.e., to the inability to lay down new memory records) is also associated with temporally graded retrograde amnesia (Ribot 1881/1882). That is, memories formed prior to brain damage are impaired, but the effect depends on the age of the memory trace at the time the damage occurs, with more recently formed memories suffering the most. This phenomenon is known as Ribot's Law, and the results of later experimental investigations of retrograde amnesia generally agreed with its stipulations (Brown 2002, Squire et al. 1975).

For almost 50 years it has been clear that the medial temporal lobes, which include the hippocampus and adjacent cortex, play a critical role in the formation of new memories. When patient H.M. had those areas surgically removed in an effort to control his epileptic seizures, it eventually became clear that his ability to form new memories was severely and permanently impaired (Scoville & Milner 1957). It is perhaps not surprising, therefore, that studies have found that temporally graded retrograde amnesia is particularly likely to be observed if the brain damage in question involves the hippocampal region (e.g., Manns et al. 2003). Although studies involving human patients are fraught with interpretative complications because they necessarily rely on retrospective methods, a recent review of 13 more precisely controlled prospective animal studies corroborates the existence of temporally graded retrograde amnesia and its association with hippocampal lesions (Squire et al. 2001).

The temporal gradient of retrograde amnesia provides compelling evidence that memories consolidate over time and that the hippocampal formation (consisting of the hippocampus, dentate gyrus, subiculum, and entorhinal cortex) plays an important role in that process. If the hippocampal formation is damaged before the consolidation process is complete, recently formed memories that are still undergoing the consolidation process will be impaired. The idea that memories consolidate, which is nowhere to be found in recent cognitive theories of memory and forgetting, happens to be the standard story in the neuroscience literature, and it is often referred to as such (e.g., Dudai 2004, McGaugh 2000) even by those who disagree with it (e.g., Nadel & Moscovitch 1997, 2001). The contrast between the views of cognitive psychologists and cognitive neuroscientists is so complete and so striking that, paradoxically, it is almost easy to overlook. But the numbers presented in Table 1 suggest that the contrast is real. Keppel (1984) once again stated explicitly what many cognitive psychologists seem to say implicitly with the theories they propose: "I am simply not convinced that the concepts of perseveration and consolidation 'buy' the cognitive psychologist any explanatory power, except perhaps as a metaphor and as a reasonable explanation of retrograde amnesia" (p. 157). But three distinct domains of research, one conducted over the course of the last century by experimental psychologists and two others conducted much more recently by psychopharmacologists and neuroscientists, converge on the notion that much of what we forget has fallen prey to the nonspecific effects of retroactive interference and that the effects of such interference differ depending on the degree to which the memory trace has consolidated.

PSYCHOLOGY

The Mathematical Form of Forgetting

A seemingly extraneous issue that may in fact be intimately related to the temporal gradient of retrograde amnesia is the mathematical form of forgetting. A forgetting function is a plot of the amount remembered, $R(t)$, as a function of time since learning, t. Almost everyone has an intuitive feel for what the forgetting function looks like. Everyone knows, for example, that the function will not increase with time but will instead decrease and that it will not be linear but will instead be curvilinear. But what is the mathematical form of this curvilinear function, and what does it imply about the nature of forgetting? If one had to hazard a guess as to the mathematical form of forgetting, a natural choice would be the exponential, $R(t) = ae^{-bt}$, where b and a are parameters analogous to the slope and intercept of a straight line. Many natural processes (e.g., radioactive decay) are exponential in form, and the exponential lends itself to simple mechanistic interpretations. One special property of the exponential is that it implies a constant proportional rate of decay. If a function drops by 50% in the first hour after learning (e.g., from 80% correct to 40% correct), the fact that it is exponential in form tells you that it will drop another 50% (i.e., from 40% correct to 20% correct) in the next hour. In fact, the function will drop by a factor of 0.5 every hour indefinitely. This constant proportional rate of decay characterizes what are sometimes called memoryless processes, which are processes with properties that don't depend at all on the prior state of the system.

What would a memoryless memory system be? That is, what would the implications be if memories decayed exponentially? The implication might be that memories do not consolidate. The original notion of consolidation held that the future vulnerability of a memory trace depends on how old that trace is—traces that have managed to survive for a time become less vulnerable to interference and thus decay less rapidly than younger traces (Müller & Pilzecker 1900). Thus, if memories consolidate, a forgetting function that drops by 50% in the first hour might drop by only 40% in the next hour (and by a lesser amount each hour after that). The absence of consolidation, by contrast, would be most easily reconciled with a constant proportional rate of decay (which, in turn, would imply exponential forgetting).

Ebbinghaus (1885/1913) reported long ago that forgetting functions are logarithmic in form, whereas Wickelgren (1974) argued that forgetting functions were better described by a power law, such as $R(t) = at^{-b}$. Wixted & Ebbesen (1991, 1997) showed that a variety of empirical forgetting functions are accurately characterized by both the power and logarithmic functions (with a slight edge going to the former) and very poorly described by the exponential. While the power law of forgetting is probably the leading contender (cf. Anderson & Schooler, 1991), White (2001) argued that a modified exponential, the exponential-power function, performs much better than the simple exponential and should be given serious consideration as well (cf. Rubin & Wenzel 1996). From this bewildering array of nonexponential possibilities, one important common denominator has emerged: All of the candidate forgetting functions are characterized by an ever *decreasing* proportional rate of decay, which is a property that forgetting functions might be expected to possess if memories consolidated (i.e., became more resistant to interference) the longer they survived. That forgetting functions possess this property is implied by Jost's (1897) second law, which holds that if two associations are of equal strength but of unequal age, the older association will decay less rapidly than the younger one. In fact, these considerations point to a heretofore unnoticed relationship between Ribot's Law (1881/1882) and Jost's Law. The temporal gradient of retrograde amnesia (i.e., Ribot's Law) implies that memories become more resistant to the effects of *brain damage* as they age. The power law of forgetting and Jost's Law imply (but do not prove) that memories may also become more resistant to the more ordinary effects of *retroactive interference* as they age. From this point of view, Ribot's Law and Jost's Law are simply two sides of the same coin.

Wickelgren (1974) once considered a consolidation-plus-RI explanation for the power law of forgetting, but he ultimately rejected it based on what may be an incorrect reading of the traditional interference literature. His possible misreading of that literature is not specific to him, and it may account for why psychologists have been so reluctant to embrace the notion that memories consolidate over time. The question of whether a temporal gradient of retroactive interference exists (the kind of gradient that is implied by the power law of forgetting) has been extensively investigated since the turn of the century, but it has never been thoroughly reviewed. What follows is an attempt to sort out that complicated literature.

Temporal Gradient of Retroactive Interference

EARLY STUDIES (1900–1933)   A number of studies have attempted to address the question of whether or not the magnitude of retroactive interference differs depending on the temporal point of interpolated learning (i.e., the point during the retention interval when the interference occurs). If memories do need time to consolidate, one might imagine that the effects of subsequent interfering learning would have temporal properties much like the effects of subsequent hippocampal damage. That is, RI should affect younger traces more than it affects older traces. If that is true, and if RI is a significant cause of forgetting, then it would provide a ready explanation as to why forgetting functions are not exponential in form but are instead characterized by an ever-decreasing proportional rate of decay.

The earliest study to address this question was performed by Müller & Pilzecker (1900). An English translation of Müller & Pilzecker's (1900) monograph is unfortunately not available, but Lechner et al. (1999) provide a summary of some of the more important studies performed by these German researchers. In one experiment, subjects studied six pairs of syllables (list A) and then studied a second list (list X) either 17 seconds or 6 minutes later. The results showed that the retention of list A was impaired on a cued recall test 1.5 hours later in the first condition only. Why would list X impair later memory for list A when learned immediately following list A but not when it was learned six minutes after that list? Müller & Pilzecker (1900) argued that physiological processes associated with list learning perseverate for a period of time after learning and that this perseveration serves to consolidate the memory trace. If list X is learned before the consolidation of memory for list A is complete, retroactive interference occurs.

Certain aspects of Müller & Pilzecker's (1900) preferred experimental design warrant close attention. Of particular importance is what the subjects were asked to do during those portions of the retention interval that did not involve studying interfering material. According to Lechner et al. (1999), in Müller & Pilzecker's early experiments, subjects were given reading material to help them suppress any tendency to rehearse the list during retention intervals. However, this practice was later abandoned as evidence for retroactive inhibition emerged, and subjects were merely instructed not to rehearse. It seems clear that Müller & Pilzecker came to believe that mental exertion itself is what interferes with the consolidation process:

> After all this, there is no alternative but to assume that after reading a list of syllables certain physiological processes ... continue with decreasing intensity for a period of time. These processes and their facilitating effects

on these associations are being weakened to a greater or lesser extent if the experimental subject experiences further mental exertion immediately after reading a list. (pp. 196–197) [translation by Lechner et al. (1999), pp. 81–82]

Thus, a test of the consolidation account amounted to imposing mental exertion at some point during a retention interval that was otherwise characterized by mental quietude. Note how different this idea is from the subsequent notion that came to dominate the interference literature, namely, that an A-B association is disrupted by the subsequent acquisition of an A-C association. The relevance of "cue-overload" effects like this to ordinary forgetting is what Keppel (1968), Ekstrand (1972), and Wickelgren (1977) all came to doubt. By contrast, the importance of mental exertion, which is the kind of RI that Müller & Pilzecker (1900) apparently had in mind, was never fully investigated. One of the main suggestions I make throughout this review is that interference from mental exertion (and its attendant memory formation) is much more relevant to everyday forgetting than interference due to the much more widely studied effects of cue overload.

These considerations help to reconcile the results of two later studies concerned with the temporal gradient of retroactive interference that are usually described as leading to opposite conclusions. One study, by Robinson (1920), presented subjects with a list of 10 three-digit numbers to recall after a 20-minute retention interval. At different points during the retention interval, subjects learned an interfering list of three-digit numbers. Some subjects learned the interfering list shortly after the original list, whereas other groups learned the interfering list later in the retention interval. No temporal gradient of RI was observed (i.e., the degree of RI was the same no matter where the interfering list was presented), which seems inconsistent with the results reported by Müller & Pilzecker (1900) and with a consolidation account in general. However, retention-interval activity during nonstudy periods in this experiment did not involve mental relaxation but instead involved reading newspaper articles from the *Chicago Tribune*. Thus, Robinson (1920) continued to use a procedure (namely, filling the retention interval with reading material) that had been determined by Müller & Pilzecker (1900) to be inappropriate. By design, mental exertion was in effect throughout the retention interval in Robinson's (1920) study, and this may explain why no temporal gradient of RI was observed.

Skaggs (1925) took Müller & Pilzecker's (1900) ideas more seriously and diligently attempted to achieve periods of mental quietude during the "off" times of the retention interval. In fact, Skaggs (1925) went further than Müller & Pilzecker (1900) in that he attempted to ensure that these quiet moments were even free of any rehearsal of the list material. Conceivably, in Müller & Pilzecker's (1900) experiment, interfering material presented a mere 17 seconds after learning might have been especially detrimental because it interfered with spontaneous rehearsal of the list, not because it interfered with an automatic physiological consolidation process. Skaggs (1925) attempted to address this issue and found that it was not easy. As he put it: ". . .it is extremely difficult to secure many 'ideal' rest intervals—ideal in the sense that the subject was mentally passive and indifferent and entirely away from the original learning material" (pp. 32–33). As such, Skaggs (1925) relied heavily on introspective reports to identify retention intervals characterized by mental quietude, and he came to believe that "Trained subjects are a necessity" (p. 58) because "As subjects become practiced they are better able to take an indifferent and passive attitude during the rest interval" (p. 59). Using practiced subjects, Skaggs (1925) found a temporal gradient of RI in many experiments involving stimulus materials as different as chess positions, words, nonsense syllables, and syllable pairs. In one experiment, for example, subjects learned nonsense syllables and then tried to recall them six minutes later. The interfering material consisted of unrelated mental exertion (namely, solving algebra problems) at different points in an otherwise quiet retention interval. The results generally supported Müller & Pilzecker's (1900) original observation of a temporal gradient of RI, though not all subjects showed the effect.

In other experiments, Skaggs (1925) also confirmed that similarity between the original and interfering material was an important variable, with greater similarity being associated with greater interference. However, no matter how dissimilar the intervening material was, substantial effects of RI were obtained. Conceivably, the interference mechanisms associated with the nonspecific effects of mental exertion differ from those associated with similarity, an argument that was actually made in eloquent fashion by Skaggs (1933) in a little-known comment that appeared in the *Journal of Comparative Psychology*. One process (mental exertion) may reflect an influence of intervening activity on the consolidation of recently formed memory traces. In his words:

> The writer has argued long for the view that there are two factors causing what is now called retroactive inhibitory effects. In one case, a strong mental-neural activity cuts in and disorganizes an on-going mental-neural process, a process of neural inertia. (p. 413)

The second inhibitory process (similarity) may reflect a retrieval phenomenon related to what nowadays might be regarded as cue overload effects. Skaggs (1933) referred to the second process as *reproductive inhibition*, which involved "...the establishment of wrong associative tendencies *which operate at the time of recall*" (p. 413, emphasis in original).

This very distinction was considered by Robinson (1920) in an interesting and thoughtful discussion section at the end of his monograph. However, he rejected the possibility that retroactive interference might involve two mechanisms (largely because he failed to find a temporal gradient of RI), and he clearly favored the idea that RI is always due to cue overload (or what he termed "a matter of transfer"). What I am suggesting here is the exact opposite, namely, that ordinary forgetting may not be a cue-overload phenomenon as much as it reflects the nonspecific effects of mental exertion and memory formation.

Why would mental exertion induce forgetting? One possibility, which is bolstered by the psychopharmacological research reviewed below, is that the resources available to consolidate recently formed memory traces are not unlimited. Mental exertion, such as reading newspaper articles, undoubtedly activates hippocampal circuits as memories associated with that exertion are formed. Even if the intervening study material is not related to the original learning in any obvious way, the new learning draws on a limited pool of resources that may have otherwise been available to consolidate the original learning. As a result, memory for the original material suffers. Note that this way of thinking fits with the findings reported by Jenkins & Dallenbach (1924), whose sleeping subjects presumably avoided mental exertion unrelated to the nonsense syllables that they had studied earlier (cf. Minami & Dallenbach 1946). It also fits with studies investigating the effects of alcohol and benzodiazepines on memory and with studies investigating the role of long-term potentiation in the formation of new memories. Before reviewing those literatures, however, I review additional research on the temporal gradient of retroactive interference that was conducted at a time when cue-overload procedures dominated the study of forgetting.

LATER STUDIES (1933–1974)   Quite a few studies performed after 1925 also investigated the question of whether or not a temporal gradient of RI exists. All of these studies relied on the use of similarity or cue overload (not mental exertion per se) to create RI during the retention interval. As such, those studies introduced issues that did not complicate the studies performed by Müller & Pilzecker (1900) and Skaggs (1925). In addition, none of the subsequent studies attempted to control the nature of mental activity that occurred during the off times of the retention interval. It actually would have been impossible to do so because these studies involved retention intervals on the order of days, not minutes. These nontrivial differences between the earlier and later studies might be expected to result in different outcomes. Then again, if the intervening cue-overload learning (e.g., intentionally memorizing a list of paired associates to a criterion of one perfect recall) was significantly more intense than the uncontrolled mental activity during the remainder of the retention interval, and if cue-overload effects do not have temporal properties that are opposite in direction to the effects due to mental exertion itself, then some evidence of the expected temporal gradient might be observed after all. Moreover, the later cue-overload studies have the advantage of investigating the temporal gradient over a much longer time period than the earlier studies did. Recent evidence suggests that memories consolidate over a much longer period of time than the few minutes envisioned by Müller & Pilzecker (1900), so it is worth knowing whether the temporal gradient of RI also extends over a time period that is longer than those employed by earlier researchers.

What did these later cue-overload studies find? Wickelgren (1977) summarized the relevant literature as follows:

> . . .studies of both recall and recognition of AB associations as a function of the delay between AB learning and subsequent AC interfering learning are virtually unanimous in rejecting the hypothesis that greater interference is obtained the shorter the delay between original learning and subsequent interference learning. (Wickelgren 1977, p. 385)

That is, according to Wickelgren, a temporal gradient of RI was not observed, and this is why he rejected the idea that the power law of forgetting arises because memories become less vulnerable to the effects of interference over time. Since this is, so far as I can determine, the standard reading of the relevant literature, it is perhaps not surprising that the field of psychology lost interest in the notion of consolidation. However, a closer look at these studies reveals that several contained a critical design flaw that requires that they be excluded from consideration. Moreover, most of the other studies actually found at least some evidence for a temporal gradient of retroactive interference even though they were not ideally suited to the question.

The flawed studies typically involved an A-B paired-associates learning phase followed by a test of cued recall sometime later (e.g., after a one-week retention interval). An interfering A-C list was learned either immediately after A-B learning or immediately before the recall test. Several studies using a design like this consistently failed to find any evidence that interference was greater when the A-C list was learned immediately after the A-B list was learned (Houston 1967, Howe 1969, McGeoch 1933, McGeoch & Nolen 1933), a result that appears to weigh against a consolidation account. However, whereas an A-C list that is learned shortly after the A-B list might interfere with A-B traces that are incompletely consolidated, an A-C list learned shortly before a recall test should impair retrieval of the A-B traces due to retrieval inhibition (e.g., Anderson et al.1994). That is, strengthening some items associated with a retrieval cue will, for a limited period of time, decrease the likelihood that other items associated with the cue will be recalled (MacLeod & Macrae 2001). Evidence that this is true can be seen in the results of some of the studies considered below. As such, a design like this compares two conditions that ought to be associated with reduced recall (for different reasons) relative to a condition involving an intermediate point of interpolated A-C learning. Skaggs (1933) explicitly warned against this kind of design when commenting on McGeoch & Nolen's (1933) study, but some of the later researchers seem not to have taken notice. In a cue-overload design, the use of more than two points of interpolated learning should reveal an inverted U pattern.

Several studies did include an intermediate point of interpolated learning, and these studies are more relevant to the question of interest. Sisson (1939) conducted one such study in which subjects first studied a ten-word list and then completed a free recall test 48 hours later. Different groups of subjects learned an interfering list of ten words (which were synonyms of the words in the original list) 0, 24, or 48 hours after the presentation of the first list (the latter occurring just prior to the recall test). Figure 1 reproduces the results of this study, and it is clear that a highly significant inverted U was obtained. One interpretation of this result (which is, of course, not the only interpretation) is that interfering material studied shortly after original learning permanently interfered with consolidation of the original list, whereas interfering material studied shortly before recall temporarily interfered with retrieval of the original list. The least interference occurred at the intermediate retention interval, perhaps because memories had been given a chance to consolidate and competition at retrieval was relatively

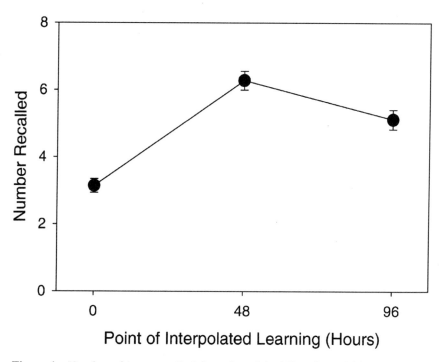

Figure 1   Number of items recalled from the original list after a 96-hour retention interval. An interfering list was learned immediately after the original list, 48 hours after the original list, or immediately prior to the retention test. The data are taken from Sisson (1939).

low due to the 24-hour gap between interfering learning and recall of the original list.

Postman & Alper (1946) conducted a more traditional verbal learning study in which subjects learned a list of ten paired associates (the A-B list) to a criterion of one perfect recall followed by a cued recall test 16 days later. Different groups of subjects learned an A-C interfering list at one of nine points during that retention interval (0, 1, 2, 4, 8, 12, 14, 15, or 16 days after A-B learning). A problem with this study is that there were only seven subjects per condition, so the data were predictably variable (and apparently uninterpretable). However, some indication of what was found can be gleaned by combining groups into short (0, 1, 2), medium (4, 8, 12), and long (14, 15, 16) conditions in order to create larger sample sizes. Figure 2 shows the results when the data are collapsed in that manner, and what emerges, once again, is the anticipated inverted U. This study obviously does not offer strong evidence in favor of the reality of that pattern, but the results certainly cannot be taken to weigh against the idea (even though they often are).

Archer & Underwood (1951) conducted another study involving an intermediate point of interpolated learning. In that study, subjects learned a list of ten paired associates (the A-B list) followed by a cued recall test 48 hours later. Different

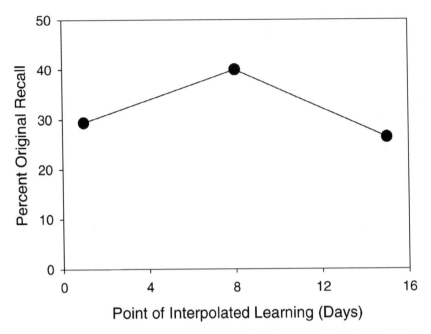

Figure 2 Percentage of items recalled from the original A-B list after a 16-day retention interval. Different groups of subjects learned an interfering A-C list at one of nine different points in the retention interval. The data have been averaged over sets of three adjacent groups to decrease the extreme variability that would otherwise be apparent. The data are taken from Postman & Alper (1946).

groups of subjects learned an A-C interfering list immediately following the A-B list, 24 hours after the A-B list, or 48 hours after the A-B list (just prior to the recall test). The degree of A-C learning was also varied across three levels, and this manipulation was crossed with the point of interpolated learning manipulation, yielding nine groups in all (three levels of A-C learning by three points of interpolated learning). The A-B list was learned to a criterion of one perfect recall, whereas the interfering A-C list was learned to a criterion of 60% correct (low), 100% correct (medium), or 100% correct plus five additional presentations of the A-C list (high). The question of interest was whether an inverted U pattern was observed. Such a pattern might not be expected in the low degree of A-C learning condition because that condition may not have entailed a degree of mental activity and memory formation much beyond what would have occurred anyway. The condition most likely to result in the expected inverted U is the high degree of A-C learning condition. Figure 3 shows the results of this experiment. No inverted U is evident in the low and medium conditions, but the inverted U pattern is clearly evident in the high degree of learning condition. Statistical power was quite low in that condition because there were only ten subjects per group. Still, a quadratic trend analysis performed (by me) on the data from this condition reveals a marginally significant effect, $F(1,74) = 2.83, p < 0.10$.

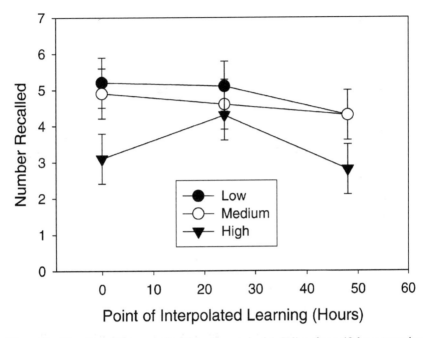

Figure 3   Number of items recalled from the original A-B list after a 48-hour retention interval. Different groups of subjects learned an interfering A-C list at one of three different points in the retention interval, and the degree of A-C learning was varied over three levels (for a total of nine groups in all). The data are taken from Archer & Underwood (1951).

Another study often cited as weighing against the notion of a temporal gradient of retroactive interference was performed by Newton & Wickens (1956). This study was essentially a replication of the medium degree of A-C learning condition from Archer & Underwood (1951), except that it involved twice as many subjects. Using a standard analysis of variance, they found no statistically significant effect of the temporal variable, but their results are reproduced in Figure 4. Once again, a clear inverted U is evident, and a higher-power quadratic trend analysis performed on these data (again, by me) yielded a significant result,[1] $F(1,54) = 5.91$, $p < 0.05$. Other findings reported by Newton & Wickens (1956), it should be acknowledged,

---

[1]Newton & Wickens (1956) did not provide the mean square error term for their Experiment 1, a value that is needed to perform a quadratic trend analysis. However, they did provide mean square error terms for their Experiments 2 and 3. The latter experiments were very similar to the first (same number of subjects, same number of lists, same number of learning trials, etc.) except they involved an A-B, C-D design instead of an A-B, A-C design. The mean square error terms for those two experiments were 3.52 and 3.25, respectively, and I used the average of those two values to perform the quadratic trend analysis for the data from Experiment 1.

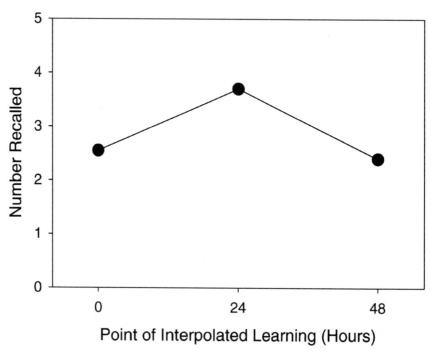

Figure 4   Number of items recalled from the original A-B list after a 48-hour retention interval. Different groups of subjects learned an interfering A-C list at one of three different points in the retention interval. The data are taken from Newton & Wickens (1956).

are hard to reconcile with any theory. In addition to the A-B, A-C study just described, they reported two studies involving an A-B, C-D design (with the C-D learning occurring at three points during the 48-hour retention interval). The results of those studies indicated that interference increased monotonically as the delay between A-B and C-D learning increased. This result is not predicted by a consolidation account or any other account based on interference theory, so its implications are hard to fathom.

The last two studies that investigated the temporal gradient of RI were published in 1974. Both involved cue-overload procedures and relatively short retention intervals. Wickelgren (1974) briefly described an experiment that he performed to address this issue. That experiment involved a continuous associative recognition procedure in which subjects were presented with a long series of paired-associate words to learn. Occasionally, a test pair was presented and subjects were asked to indicate whether the pair was intact (consisting of two words that had appeared together earlier in the series) or rearranged (consisting of two words that had appeared earlier in the series as part of different pairs). Because the entire retention interval between study and test was filled with the intentional learning of intervening word pairs, the temporal point of interpolated interference due to memory formation itself was not actually manipulated. Instead, memory formation was in effect throughout. What was manipulated was the temporal point of interpolated interference due to cue overload. Thus, if an A-B word pair had been studied earlier in the series, an interfering A-C pair was presented either early or late in the retention interval. Compared to a control condition, performance was impaired by the presentation of an A-C pair, but the degree of impairment was the same whether the A-C pair appeared early or late in the retention interval (i.e., no temporal gradient was observed).

Wickelgren's (1974) experiment involved a retention interval filled with the intentional formation of new memories, and memory formation itself may be the kind of interference that degrades previously encoded memories (more so for young, unconsolidated traces than for older, more consolidated traces). Cue overload effects are almost certainly a retrieval phenomenon, and consolidation theory does not speak to the question of whether cue overload effects vary depending on the temporal point of interpolated interference. Thus, from this perspective, Wickelgren's (1974) findings should not have been taken as evidence against the temporal gradient of RI.

Finally, a study performed by Landauer (1974) found clear evidence of a temporal gradient. Subjects in this experiment studied a continuous series of syllable-digit paired associates (such as CEM-2). Critical pairs (i.e., pairs that would be tested for memory at some later point) were followed by interfering items after varying delays, with filler items being easy, nonattention-demanding, nonconfusable word-digit pairs. Thus, the background task during the retention interval did not involve complete mental quietude, but the mental demands were reduced relative to the demands associated with learning the interfering material. A retention test conducted 20 minutes later revealed that memory for the critical items was worse when the difficult interfering items appeared shortly after the critical items compared to when the interfering items were delayed. In a second experiment, Landauer (1974) found a temporal gradient of RI even when more demanding material was presented throughout the retention interval. Given the results of Wickelgren's (1974) study and earlier research by Robinson (1920), who also used a filled retention interval, one might have expected to see the absence of a temporal gradient in this case, but one was found anyway.

SUMMARY   The main point of this section is that when interference consists of mental exertion imposed on an otherwise quiet retention interval, a temporal gradient of retroactive interference is reliably observed. Similar effects are observed when traditional A-B, A-C designs are used, but the additional complications introduced by the use of a cue-overload procedure have obscured that fact for many years. The results point to a theory of forgetting according to which the processes associated with the formation of new memories retroactively interfere with previously formed memories that are still undergoing the process of consolidation. The temporal gradient of RI can be hard to detect because, as Skaggs (1925) noted long ago, achieving mental quietude is not easy, and mental quietude may be essential to deactivate hippocampal circuits that, when active, interfere with the consolidation of prior memories.

For similar reasons, imaging studies that have attempted to detect hippocampal activation during a retrieval task have often failed (Martin 1999). What makes that activity hard to find, perhaps, is that the hippocampus may be active during retrieval tasks as well as during baseline comparison tasks that do not nominally involve encoding and retrieval. As Martin (1999) observed, much evidence is consistent with the idea that the medial temporal lobe ". . .is automatically engaged whenever an event is experienced" (p. 62). If the hippocampus is active both when the subject is given a retrieval task and when the subject is left to his her own devices, then detecting a contrast in activity between a test condition and baseline condition will be difficult indeed. The use of trained subjects may help to achieve the mental quietude necessary to reduce hippocampal activity, but the psychopharmacological methods reviewed below may do so in a more efficient way.

PSYCHOPHARMACOLOGY

The Curious Phenomenon of Retrograde Facilitation

As indicated above, damage to the medial temporal lobes induces anterograde amnesia (the inability to form new memories) as well as temporally graded retrograde amnesia (an impairment of recently formed memories). Anterograde amnesia can be induced by methods other than hippocampal damage, and some of these methods actually result in retrograde *facilitation*. That is, recently formed memories are retained better than they otherwise would have been even though new memories cannot easily be formed. A consideration of the conditions associated with this phenomenon reinforces the view that memories consolidate over time and that much of what we forget is lost because of retroactive interference arising from ordinary mental exertion and consequent memory formation acting on partially consolidated memory traces. The argument to be advanced below is that certain agents (such as alcohol and benzodiazepines) close the hippocampus to new input, thereby inducing anterograde amnesia, without compromising its ability to consolidate previously formed memories. Because new input is prevented, recently formed (and, therefore, incompletely consolidated) memories are protected from the retroactive interference that they would otherwise encounter. As such, these drugs act in the same way that sleep does even though the individual remains conscious. By contrast, hippocampal lesions both prevent new input (resulting in anterograde amnesia) and terminate the ongoing consolidation of recently formed memories (resulting in retrograde amnesia as well).

ALCOHOL   The anterograde amnesic effects of alcohol consumed prior to the learning of new material have been well established (Lister et al. 1987). The extreme version of this effect is alcoholic "blackout," which involves a complete loss of memory for events occurring while the individual was conscious but extremely intoxicated. It is generally accepted that blackouts are not the result of state-dependent learning but instead reflect a failure to encode or consolidate new information (Lisman 1974). In spite of its effects on the formation of new memories, alcohol intoxication generally does not affect one's ability to retrieve old memories (Birnbaum et al. 1978).

Whereas alcohol consumption induces a certain degree of anterograde amnesia for material studied under the influence of the drug, many studies have reported that it actually results in improved memory for material studied just prior to consumption (Bruce & Pihl 1997; Lamberty et al. 1990; Mann et al. 1984; Parker et al. 1980, 1981). This phenomenon is referred to as retrograde facilitation or retrograde enhancement, and its existence makes alcohol-induced amnesia quite unlike the amnesia produced by damage to the medial temporal lobes.

Theories advanced to explain this curious phenomenon include reduced retroactive interference versus a direct enhancement of the consolidation process. Efforts to differentiate these possibilities have proven to be inconclusive (e.g., Hewitt et al. 1996), so a choice between them will probably depend on the identification of the specific physiological mechanism responsible for the observed effects. As described in more detail below, recent evidence suggests one very plausible candidate, namely, the effects of alcohol on long-term potentiation. For the moment, though, it is worth pointing out that parsimony also favors the interference interpretation. That is, given the interference interpretation, the amnesic effects of alcohol can explain the retrograde facilitation of previously formed memories without having to postulate an additional effect of the drug on the consolidation process itself. By contrast, the idea that alcohol directly enhances the consolidation process seems less parsimonious and, in some ways, more problematic. Substances that enhance the consolidation process directly would be expected to result in both anterograde facilitation and retrograde facilitation, not anterograde *amnesia* and retrograde facilitation (which is what alcohol does). One such substance that is widely assumed to directly enhance the consolidation process is glucose, and, as might be expected, it does result in both anterograde and retrograde facilitation (Manning et al. 1992).

The simplest view, therefore, is that alcohol facilitates recently established memories precisely because it prevents the formation of new memories that would otherwise cause retroactive interference (Mueller et al. 1983). Although it has not been specifically shown, it stands to reason that drinking alcohol does not protect memories that are years old (and fully consolidated). Instead, it is the recently formed memories that differentially benefit because, theoretically, those are the ones most vulnerable to the effects of RI. This conclusion is the same one that emerged from a review of studies concerned with the temporal gradient of retroactive interference. Those studies were concerned with the effects of *introducing* RI, and they revealed that more recently formed memories are affected to a greater extent than older memories. The alcohol studies cited above are concerned with the effects of *subtracting* RI, and the parallel result obtains (namely, newly formed memories are enhanced to a greater extent than older memories).

BENZODIAZEPINES   Retrograde facilitation has also been observed with another class of amnesia-inducing drug, namely, benzodiazepines. The basic experimental paradigm is the same as that used with alcohol. Subjects typically study one list of words prior to drug administration and then study another list following drug administration. Memory for both lists is tested sometime later (usually while the subject is still under the influence of the drug), and performance is compared to that of a placebo control group. Typically, the drug group exhibits impaired recall for the list learned under the influence of the drug (thereby confirming its amnesia-inducing properties) and enhanced recall for the list learned prior to taking the drug (Coenen & Van Luijtelaar 1997, Fillmore et al. 2001, Hinrichs et al. 1984, Weingartner et al. 1995). Explanations for the retrograde enhancement effect once again include reduced interference, enhanced consolidation, or enhanced retrieval.

Coenen & Van Luijtelaar (1997) argued that the effects of benzodiazepines on memory were analogous to the beneficial effects of sleep reported by Jenkins & Dallenbach (1924). In both cases, information learned prior to sedation is remembered better than it otherwise would have been because retroactive interference is reduced due to the reduced rate of information uptake while sedated (or asleep). Note that this explanation is entirely in line with the idea that ordinary forgetting is a retroactive effect of subsequent memory formation that accompanies ordinary mental activity. If mental activity is reduced by sleep or if memory formation associated with mental activity is reduced by alcohol or a benzodiazepine drug, prior memories are protected from the effects of retroactive interference. And the memories that are protected are those that were recently formed and have not yet had a chance to consolidate.

Although reduced retroactive interference seems to be the most parsimonious account of retrograde facilitation (cf. Hinrichs et al. 1984), Weingartner et al. (1995) performed the only direct test of this hypothesis, and they arrived at a different conclusion. Their study is worth considering in some detail because it shows just how different the implications of a study can appear to be depending on whether one views them through the lens of traditional interference theory or in terms of the alternative nonspecific view of interference proposed here. Weingartner et al. (1995) presented subjects with a list of 12 words presented at a rate of one word per second ten minutes prior to the administration of triazolam (a benzodiazepine) or placebo. Ninety minutes after drug or placebo administration, a second, interfering, list of 12 words was presented at the slower rate of one word every five seconds. Twenty minutes later (nearly two hours after drug or placebo), a recognition test was administered that consisted of the 24 words from the two study lists as well as 12 new words. Memory for the predrug list was enhanced relative to the placebo control group (i.e., retrograde facilitation was observed), but, somewhat surprisingly, memory for the postdrug list was not significantly impaired (i.e., an amnesic effect for these words was not observed). Why the typical amnesic effect was not obtained for the postdrug words is not clear, but the fact that those words were successfully encoded seemed to provide an unexpected opportunity to test the interference account. Specifically, according to a standard interference account, because the interfering postdrug words were learned well, the presumed interfering force was still in play. As such, no retrograde enhancement should have been observed. Because the typical enhancement of memory for predrug words occurred anyway, it seemed to follow that the interference explanation must be incorrect.

This interpretation makes sense in light of traditional interference theory, according to which interference arises mostly from the subsequent study of similar materials. If the only material that would retroactively interfere with the predrug list consists of words similar to the ones that appeared on that list, then the retrograde enhancement effect observed in this study is hard to explain on the basis of reduced retroactive interference. However, when considered in light of a theory that attributes forgetting to the retroactive effects of mental exertion and memory formation in general, the results do not weigh against an interference interpretation at all. In fact, they support that view.

Subjects in this study were tested nearly two hours after drug administration, and during much of that time they almost surely encoded much less information than they otherwise would have. True, they did manage to encode 12 words during one minute of that two-hour period to the same extent as in the placebo condition, but other evidence reported by Weingartner et al. (1995) clearly demonstrates that the rate of memory formation was greatly reduced for much of the rest of the postdrug period. While still under the influence of the drug, for example, these same subjects studied 21 sentences shortly after taking the recognition test, and their subsequent recall for words in those sentences was markedly impaired. Thus, the drug did induce a state of amnesia (thereby reducing the demands placed on the hippocampus) even though, for one 60-second period, subjects managed to encode a list as well as they ordinarily would have in the absence of the drug.

Similar considerations also apply to an earlier article by Parker et al. (1981), in which they argued that the facilitative effects of alcohol on prior memories are probably not due to interference reduction because, in that study, "...no other formal task was administered to subjects in the intoxicated state, [so] there was no task-related source of interference which alcohol could reduce" (p. 91). However, according to the view espoused here, the interference that matters most is not necessarily task related—it is the interference that accompanies ordinary mental activity and the memory formation associated with that activity (which was undoubtedly reduced by alcohol).

Temporal Properties of Retrograde Facilitation

To summarize, sleep, alcohol, and benzodiazepines all result in retrograde enhancement of memory, and, theoretically, they all do so for the same reason:

The reduced rate of memory formation protects recently formed memories from interference, interference that would otherwise arise because of the demands placed on a limited-resource hippocampal system. Although it has not been shown that a temporal gradient exists for the retrograde enhancement effects of alcohol and benzodiazepines, such a gradient almost surely exists. Whereas a glass of wine might help you to retain a recently encoded prewine conversation, it seems unlikely to enhance all prior memories dating back to childhood to a similar degree. The same arguments apply to the effects of sleep, but in this case the relevant experiments demonstrating the temporal gradient have actually been performed.

As described in Ekstrand (1972), Heine (1914) exposed subjects to nonsense syllables either immediately or two to three hours prior to sleep. A savings test conducted after a retention interval of 24 hours revealed better retention for the group that went to sleep immediately. Ekstrand (1972) reported a similar experiment involving memory for paired-associate words following a 24-hour retention interval in which subjects slept either during the eight hours that followed list presentation or during the eight hours that preceded the recall test. In the immediate sleep condition, 81% of the items were recalled; in the delayed sleep condition, only 66% were recalled. The enhanced performance in the immediate sleep condition presumably arises because, in that condition, memories were protected from interference during the time period when they are the most vulnerable (i.e., shortly after the memories were formed). Note how similar these studies are to the interference studies conducted long ago by Skaggs (1925). Whereas Skaggs manipulated the point of interpolation of mental exertion on a background of mental quietude and found a temporal gradient of interference (with more recent memories being differentially impaired), Heine (1914) and Ekstrand (1972) manipulated the point of interpolation of mental quietude (i.e., sleep) on a background of ordinary mental exertion and found a temporal gradient of retroactive facilitation (with more recent memories being differentially facilitated). The studies were actually conceptually identical (e.g., the immediate sleep condition could be construed as a delayed interference condition), and the results were the same.

NEUROSCIENCE

As already indicated, the standard view in neuroscience holds that new memories that have not yet had a chance to consolidate are more vulnerable to the effects of hippocampal damage than older memories are. As I argued above and as Müller & Pilzecker (1900) argued long ago, new memories are also more vulnerable to the effects of retroactive interference than older memories. This is why, according to my argument, new memories are actually enhanced when subjects subsequently take an amnesia-inducing drug or fall into a state of sleep.

The prevailing view of how memories are initially formed is that the process involves a rapidly formed and relatively long-lasting increase in the probability that postsynaptic neurons in the hippocampus will fire in response to neurotransmitters released from presynaptic neurons. The laboratory analog of this theoretical memory mechanism is long-term potentiation (LTP). LTP is a long-lasting enhancement of synaptic transmission in response to brief, high-frequency stimulation of presynaptic neurons. This artificially induced increase in synaptic efficacy typically lasts only a few days or weeks (but see Abraham et al. 2002, for a case of very long-lasting LTP), so it presumably does not represent the way in which memories are permanently coded. Still, LTP is readily induced in hippocampal neurons, and it is the leading candidate for modeling the neural basis of initial memory formation (Martin et al. 2000). Moreover, the nonspecific retroactive interference story described above plays out almost exactly at the level of LTP, thereby grounding that account with a specific mechanism.

Amnestic Drugs, Sleep, and LTP

Alcohol and benzodiazepines both block the induction of LTP in the hippocampus (Del Cerro et al. 1992, Evans & Viola-McCabe 1996, Givens & McMahon 1995, Roberto et al. 2002, Sinclair & Lo 1986). Moreover, it has also been shown that alcohol does not impair the maintenance of hippocampal LTP induced one hour prior to drug administration (Givens & McMahon 1995). The same is presumably true of benzodiazepines, but this has yet to be empirically demonstrated. Blocking the induction of LTP without impairing the maintenance of previously established LTP is a close neural analog of the effects of alcohol on memory that were reviewed in the previous section. That is, while under the influence of the drug (during which time the induction of hippocampal LTP is impaired), memory formation is impaired by those drugs. At the same time, memories formed prior to drug intake, like LTP effects formed prior to drug intake, are not impaired. In fact, the prior memories are actually enhanced for reasons that will become clear when the effects of LTP induction on previously established LTP are considered in more detail below.

Note that non–rapid eye movement (non-REM) sleep also seems to block the induction of hippocampal LTP (Jones Leonard et al. 1987) without disrupting the maintenance of previously induced LTP (Bramham & Srebo 1989). These experiments, which were performed on sleeping rats, showed that while LTP can be induced during REM sleep (possibly accounting for the fact that we can sometimes remember our dreams), it cannot be induced during non-REM sleep (possibly accounting for the fact that we cannot remember any mental activity that takes place during that stage of sleep). Whereas REM sleep is associated with salient visual imagery (i.e., dreams), non-REM sleep is associated with a considerable amount of mental activity as well (e.g., Pivik & Foulkes 1968). However, memories of that mental activity are rarely formed (i.e., we are completely amnesic for what we think about during non-REM sleep). As a result, during non-REM sleep, prior memories are protected from interference that might otherwise occur.

In light of these considerations, one might imagine that sleep characterized mainly by non-REM sleep (during which LTP cannot be induced and memories cannot be formed) would result in greater retrograde facilitation than sleep characterized mainly by REM sleep (during which LTP can be induced and memories can be formed). An alternative view that was once entertained by the field is that REM sleep is critical to memory formation because it serves to directly enhance the consolidation process (e.g., Fishbein 1996). Ekstrand and colleagues (1972, Yaroush et al. 1971) performed an experiment that was designed to distinguish between these possibilities. These researchers capitalized on the observation that most REM sleep occurs in the second half of the night, whereas most non-REM sleep occurs in the first half. Some subjects in this experiment learned a list, went to sleep immediately, and were awakened four hours later for a test of recall. Others slept for four hours, were awakened to learn a list, slept for another four hours, and then took a recall test. The control (i.e., awake) subjects learned a list during the day and were tested for recall four hours later. The subjects all learned the initial list to the same degree, but the results showed that four hours of mostly non-REM sleep facilitated delayed recall relative to the other two conditions, which did not differ from each other (i.e., REM sleep did not facilitate memory).

These results have been replicated in studies by Plihal & Born (1997, 1999). Curiously enough, these researchers also confirmed earlier work by Karni et al. (1994) showing that REM sleep *does* facilitate the retention of nonhippocampus-dependent procedural memories. Why that might be is somewhat mysterious, but with regard to hippocampus-dependent declarative memories it seems clear that a period of non-REM sleep (during which time the induction of hippocampal LTP is inhibited) has a greater facilitative effect on memory than a similar period of REM sleep. This result fits with the observation that many antidepressant medications, which greatly reduce REM sleep, do not seem to cause memory problems (Vertes & Eastman 2000). In fact, one might even predict that such medications would enhance memory compared to placebo controls over a retention interval that involved a night of sleep (but this prediction has not been tested).

Although the inhibition of LTP induction during non-REM sleep may serve to protect prior memory traces from interference when they are in a fragile physiological state, recent work by McNaughton and his colleagues raises an interesting additional possibility, namely, that when the demands placed on it are reduced, the hippocampus is freed up to actively coordinate memory trace formation in the neocortex. This type of consolidation is conceptually distinct from simply enhancing the physiological stability of the trace. Wilson & McNaughton (1994) found that hippocampal place cells that fired together during a waking experience in rats tended to be *reactivated* together during slow-wave (non-REM) sleep. Hoffman & McNaughton (2002) further showed that coordinated firing activity between different areas of the neocortex is also replayed during quiet wakefulness in macaques. Such reactivation may be a process that emerges whenever the demands placed on the hippocampus are minimized. Indeed, the conditions that appear to protect a fragile memory trace (conditions that are elaborated in the next section) may be a lot like the conditions that set the occasion for the reactivation of previous neural firing patterns (e.g., non-REM sleep, mental quietude). Whether or not this is generally true remains to be determined.

Induction of New LTP Interferes with Previously Induced LTP

Although alcohol, benzodiazepines, and non-REM sleep all block the induction of LTP in the hippocampus, a much more efficient and selective way to inhibit hippocampal LTP is to use an N-methyl-D-aspartate (NMDA) receptor antagonist, such as AP5 or CPP. Morris (1989) showed that AP5 not only prevents the induction of LTP, it also impairs the learning of hippocampus-dependent tasks (i.e., tasks that animals with hippocampal lesions cannot learn). Thus, like alcohol, benzodiazepines, and non-REM sleep, NMDA antagonists inhibit hippocampal LTP and create anterograde amnesia for hippocampus-dependent tasks.

Several of the LTP studies reviewed below rely on NMDA antagonists to investigate the mechanism of retroactive interference. As with psychological studies concerned with the temporal gradient of RI, all of the LTP studies reviewed below involve an initial phase of original learning and a subsequent phase of interfering learning. In some cases, the original learning consists of animals actually learning a behavioral task (e.g., the Morris water maze task), but in other cases the original learning is "virtual" in that it consists of the artificial induction of hippocampal LTP. The virtual learning studies are concerned with the effect of interference on the maintenance of LTP rather than on the maintenance (i.e., retention) of previously formed memories. The same distinction (actual versus virtual) applies to the interfering task. That is, in some cases, interference consists of exposing the animal to an actual behavioral task (e.g., exploring a novel environment), but in other cases it consists of the artificial induction of LTP. Whether interfering learning is actual or virtual, the induction of interfering LTP can be blocked by the use of NMDA antagonists. This should prevent new interfering learning from occurring and should protect original learning (be it actual learning or virtual learning) from impairment that would otherwise occur.

Izquierdo et al. (1999) conducted an animal learning study that was an exact analogue of retroactive interference studies conducted by experimental psychologists. They first trained rats on a task called one-trial step-down inhibitory avoidance (task 1) and subsequently exposed them to a novel environment (task 2) that would serve to interfere with memory for the first task. The avoidance task involves placing the animal on a platform and then delivering a brief shock when it steps down onto a metal grid. Latency to step down from the platform on subsequent test trials is the measure of memory for the training trial (long latency implies good memory). Prior work has shown this to be a hippocampus-dependent task, so it is widely used to investigate declarative memory processes. Exposure to the novel environment (task 2) involved placing the animal in an open field with a pink floor adorned with black-lined squares. After exposure to the task-1 learning trial, the animals were exposed to task 2 either one hour or six hours later, and memory for task 1 was assessed after a 24-hour retention interval. Note that the design of this study is conceptually identical to studies concerned with the temporal point of unrelated interpolated learning, such as those performed by Skaggs (1925). Moreover, a temporal gradient of RI was observed: 24-hour memory of the avoidance task was impaired only when the seemingly unrelated interfering task was presented one hour after learning. This presumably occurred because the memories had not yet had a chance to consolidate when the interfering learning took place. After six hours, the memories were more fully consolidated, so exposure to the novel environment had less of an interfering effect.

Thus, once again, we find evidence for a temporal gradient of retroactive interference. Such a result would be surprising if the traditional reading of the related psychology literature were correct. According to that reading, the temporal point of interpolated (i.e., interfering) learning does not affect the degree of retroactive interference (e.g., Wickelgren 1977). According to my revised reading of that literature, however, it clearly does. Results like those reported by Izquierdo et al. (1999) serve to reinforce that conclusion.

Of particular interest is whether the induction of LTP associated with exposure to the novel environment is responsible for the observed temporally graded retroactive interference. To investigate this, Izquierdo et al. (1999) administered an NMDA antagonist directly into the hippocampus of some of the rats prior to their exposure to the novel environment (which occurred one hour after avoidance learning). The NMDA antagonist prevents the induction of LTP that might be associated with exposure to a novel environment and reduces learning about that environment. With the induction of LTP thus prevented, no retroactive interference effects were observed. That is, memory for the avoidance task was unimpaired by subsequent exposure to the novel environment.

A conceptually similar result was reported by Brun et al. (2001). They showed that memory for a submerged platform in the Morris water maze task was impaired by the subsequent induction of hippocampal LTP by means of high-frequency stimulation delivered through implanted electrodes. In other words, memory for original learning was impaired by virtual interference learning consisting of the induction of LTP. However, if an NMDA receptor antagonist was infused into the hippocampus prior to delivering the high-frequency stimulus (thereby preventing the induction of potentially interfering LTP), no memory impairment was observed. Thus, whether interfering learning was actual or virtual, preventing the induction of LTP during the interference phase of the experiment spared the original learning.

These results immediately suggest a neurophysiological mechanism for temporally graded retroactive interference. Specifically, the induction of LTP during interfering learning impairs recently established LTP associated with original learning, even if the tasks are unrelated. This hypothesis was tested directly by Xu et al. (1998). This experiment was much like the one by Izquierdo et al. (1999) described above except that instead of using an actual task 1, these researchers used a virtual task 1 by artificially inducing hippocampal LTP in freely behaving rats. Once again, they did so by delivering trains of high-frequency stimulation through electrodes implanted into the rats' brains. Exposure to a novel environment (task 2) one hour later completely reversed the previously induced LTP. However, if exposure to the novel environment was delayed for 24 hours after induction of LTP, no effect of that exposure on LTP was observed. Thus, a temporal gradient was observed yet again, and it suggests that recently established LTP is more vulnerable to the disruptive effects of subsequent interference than more remotely established LTP is (presumably because the latter has had time to consolidate). A conceptually similar study performed by Abraham et al. (2002) involved a much more prolonged interference phase and showed that, under such conditions, the LTP temporal gradient can be observed over a period of weeks (instead of hours, as in Xu et al. 1998). In this study, LTP was induced in the hippocampus of rats, and the animals were then housed in their typical "stimulus-poor" home cage environments for two weeks. In this low-interference environment, LTP decayed very gradually. Over the next week, some of these animals were exposed to a complex environment (involving a larger cage, multiple objects, and other animals) for 14 hours per day. Exposure to this environment for several days resulted in complete reversal of the previously induced LTP, whereas LTP in the control animals continued its very gradual decay. By contrast, when exposure to a complex environment was postponed until 90 days after the induction of LTP, no measurable interfering effect was observed.

The next logical experiment was recently reported by Villarreal et al. (2002). Hippocampal LTP was again induced via implanted electrodes (i.e., a virtual learning procedure was used), and the magnitude of LTP was assessed for the next nine days. Some rats received an NMDA receptor antagonist one hour after LTP induction (a treatment that should prevent the further induction of LTP), whereas control rats received a water vehicle. No explicit retroactively interfering task was arranged, so any interference that occurred was presumably due to the normal events in the life of a laboratory rat or to other routine aspects of the experimental procedure (e.g., daily injections of water). The results revealed that LTP decayed back to baseline for the control rats over the next seven days but remained elevated for the experimental subjects. When the NMDA antagonist was no longer administered (after day seven), LTP in the experimental rats also decayed quickly. These results again suggest that previously established LTP falls prey to the interfering effects of subsequently induced LTP.

In an exact analog of the alcohol-induced retrograde enhancement studies reviewed earlier, Villarreal et al. (2002) also trained rats on an eight-arm radial maze and then administered an NMDA receptor antagonist or water vehicle to different subgroups of rats over the next five days. The rats receiving the NMDA antagonist exhibited a retrograde enhancement effect when their memories were tested after six days of treatment. Note how similar this pattern is to the retrograde enhancement effects observed with alcohol and benzodiazepines. Like NMDA receptor antagonists, alcohol and benzodiazepines block the induction of LTP (and induce anterograde amnesia) without compromising previously established LTP. Indeed, these substances protect previously established LTP from the interfering effects of subsequently induced LTP, which may be why retrograde enhancement is observed.

Whereas retrograde enhancement is seen in humans when memory is blocked by alcohol for a matter of hours, in rats the phenomenon may require a much more prolonged phase of memory blockade (perhaps because the rate of interfering memory formation is so low when no interfering task is explicitly arranged).

To summarize, whether original learning is actual or virtual, subsequent interfering learning (whether actual or virtual) creates retroactive interference. The interfering effect is less pronounced the longer the delay between original and interfering learning is (pointing to a role for consolidation), and the effect of interfering learning can be abolished by preventing the induction of LTP using an NMDA antagonist (pointing to the induction of LTP as the source of RI).

CONCLUSION

My attempt to articulate a coherent theory of forgetting was prompted by dissatisfaction with what I derisively referred to as the "atheoretical laundry-list" account of forgetting that pervades the field today. The alternative I propose is that the hippocampus plays an important role in consolidating newly formed memory traces (this is actually the standard view in neuroscience) and that ordinary mental exertion and memory formation interfere with that process, perhaps by drawing on a limited pool of hippocampal resources. The interfering mental activity need not be related to the originally learned material; the formation of memories per se (which, theoretically, involves the induction of hippocampal LTP) disrupts the consolidation of recently formed memories (which, theoretically, involves disrupting the persistence of previously established LTP). Findings from the traditional interference literature, the psychopharmacology literature, and the neuroscience literature converge on this way of thinking.

It is important to emphasize that this theory does not imply that new memories fully overwrite immediately preceding memories. As Morris (1998) observed when commenting on the impressive memory abilities of food-caching birds, "A memory system that could recall only the last item cached, wiping out memory of earlier items, would be unhelpful" (p. 835). But a memory system that creates new memories even at the expense of partially degrading other memories would still be helpful, and that may be the very kind of memory system we have. What the exact variables are that govern the degree to which prior memories are degraded is not known, but one obvious possibility is that the greater and more variable the new learning is, the greater the interfering effect will be. Entering a novel situation that involves unfamiliar activities, strange sights, and unusual sounds may elicit the most hippocampal activity (e.g., Martin 1999, Tulving et al. 1994) and, therefore, the greatest rate of new memory formation. As such, that may be the kind of situation that maximally interferes with the consolidation of previous memories. Indeed, as indicated above, exposure to a novel environment is a potent interfering force in studies involving rats (and that interference decreases the longer ago the original memory was formed).

Throughout this chapter, I have relied on the traditional notion of consolidation according to which new memories are clear but fragile and old ones are faded but robust. Some new evidence suggests that this traditional model may be in need of revision. Nader et al. (2000), for example, reported evidence in support of an old idea (Misanin et al. 1968) that it is recently *activated* memories that are vulnerable to the effects of interference (even if those activated memories had once been consolidated). If this intriguing finding holds up, then the theory advanced here would necessarily apply to recently activated memories instead of just recently formed memories. Dudai (2004) provides a detailed review of the evidence pertaining to the recently revived notion of reconsolidation.

Finally, by articulating this new theory of forgetting, I do not mean to imply that the other elements of the laundry list of factors that might contribute to forgetting are irrelevant. They might very well be relevant to ordinary forgetting even though this has not yet been convincingly established. One such variable that was long ago rejected by experimental psychologists is natural decay. In arguing against decay theory, McGeoch (1932) observed, "No one has ever published experimental evidence that synaptic junctions decrease in intimacy, or anything else, when one forgets" (p. 368). But times have changed in that regard. Bailey & Chen (1989) showed that synaptic varicosities of sensory neurons in aplysia (a simple model system for human neurophysiology) increase in number from approximately 1200 to almost 3000 following a sensitization learning procedure. The number drops off to about 1500 over the next three weeks, which parallels a decrease in the behavioral magnitude of sensitization over the same time period. While this loss might reflect the retroactively interfering forces of (undetected) subsequent learning of some kind, it could instead reflect the natural sequelae of a biologically active neuronal system. And while the sea slug is a comparatively simple system, it is not hard to imagine that similar events unfold in the human brain.

Thus, my point is not that multiple factors are not involved in the process of forgetting. But just because multiple factors are relevant to the story of forgetting, that doesn't mean the field should restrict itself merely to enumerating the possible contributing factors, as it has for some time now. The voluminous body of research on forgetting that has accumulated over the last century tells a much more interesting story than that.

The *Annual Review of Psychology* is online at http://psych.annualreviews.org

LITERATURE CITED

Abraham WC, Logan B, Greenwood JM, Dragunow M. 2002. Induction and experience-dependent consolidation of stable long-term potentiation lasting months in the hippocampus. *J. Neurosci.* 22:9626–34

Anderson JR, Schooler LJ. 1991. Reflections of the environment in memory. *Psychol. Sci.* 2:396–408

Anderson MC, Bjork RA, Bjork EL. 1994. Remembering can cause forgetting: retrieval dynamics in long-term memory. *J. Exp. Psychol.: Learn. Mem. Cogn.* 20:1063–87

Archer JE, Underwood BJ. 1951. Retroactive inhibition of verbal associations as a multiple function of temporal point of interpolation degree of interpolated learning. *J. Exp. Psychol. Appl.* 42:283–90

Bailey CH, Chen M. 1989. Time course of structural changes at identified sensory neuron synapses during long-term sensitization in aplysia. *J. Neurosci.* 9:1774–80

Birnbaum IM, Parker ES, Hartley JT, Noble EP. 1978. Alcohol and memory: retrieval processes. *J. Verbal Learn. Verbal Behav.* 17:325–35

Bramham CR, Srebo B. 1989. Synaptic plasticity in the hippocampus is modulated by behavioral state. *Brain Res.* 493:74–86

Brown AS. 2002. Consolidation theory and retrograde amnesia in humans. *Psychon. Bull. Rev.* 9:403–25

Bruce KR, Pihl RO. 1997. Forget "drinking to forget": enhanced consolidation of emotionally charged memory by alcohol. *Exp. Clin. Psychopharmacol.* 5:242–50

Brun VH, Ytterbø K, Morris RGM, Moser M, Moser EI. 2001. Retrograde amnesia for spatial memory induced by NMDA receptor-mediated long-term potentiation. *J. Neurosci.* 21:356–62

Coenen AML, Van Luijtelaar ELJM. 1997. Effects of benzodiazepines, sleep and sleep deprivation on vigilance and memory. *Acta Neurol. Belg.* 97:123–29

Del Cerro S, Jung M, Lynch L. 1992. Benzodiazepines block long-term potentiation in slices of hippocampus and piriform cortex. *Neuroscience* 49:1–6

Dudai Y. 2004. The neurobiology of consolidations, or, how stable is the engram? *Annu. Rev. Psychol.* 55:51–86

Ebbinghaus H. 1885/1913. *Memory. A Contribution to Experimental Psychology.* New York: Teachers College/Columbia Univ. (Engl. ed.)

Ekstrand BR. 1967. The effect of sleep on memory. *J. Exp. Psychol. Appl.* 75:64–72

Ekstrand BR. 1972. To sleep, perchance to dream (about why we forget). In *Human Memory: Festschrift for Benton J. Underwood*, ed. CP Duncan, L Sechrest, AW Melton, pp. 59–82. New York: Appleton-Century-Crofts

Evans MS, Viola -McCabe KE. 1996. Midazolam inhibits long-term potentiation through modulation of GABA$_A$ receptors. *Neuropharmacology* 35:347–57

Fillmore MT, Kelly TH, Rush CR, Hays L. 2001. Retrograde facilitation of memory by triazolam: effects on automatic processes. *Psychopharmacology* 158:314–21

Fishbein W. 1996. Memory consolidation in REM sleep: making dreams out of chaos. *Sleep Res. Soc. Bull.* 2:55–56

Gabrieli JDE. 1998. Cognitive neuroscience of human memory. *Annu. Rev. Psychol.* 49:87–115

Givens B, McMahon K. 1995. Ethanol suppresses the induction of long-term potentiation in vivo. *Brain Res.* 688:27–33

Heine R. 1914. Über Wiedererkennen und rückwirkende Hemmung. *Z. Psychol. Physiol. Sinnesorgane* 68:161–236

Hewitt GP, Holder M, Laird J. 1996. Retrograde enhancement of human kinesthetic memory by alcohol: consolidation or protection against interference? *Neurobiol. Learn. Mem.* 65:269–77

Hinrichs JV, Ghoneim MM, Mewaldt SP. 1984. Diazepam and memory: retrograde facilitation produced by interference reduction. *Psychopharmacology* 84:158–62

Hoffman KL, McNaughton BL. 2002. Coordinated reactivation of distributed memory traces in primate neocortex. *Science* 297:2070–73

Houston J. 1967. Retroactive inhibition and point of interpolation. *J. Verbal Learn. Verbal Behav.* 6:84–88

Hovland CJ. 1951. Human learning and retention. In *Handbook of Experimental Psychology*, ed. SS Stevens, pp. 613–89. New York: Wiley

Howe T. 1969. Effects of delayed interference on list 1 recall. *J. Exp. Psychol. Appl.* 80:120–24

Izquierdo I, Schröder N, Netto CA, Medina JH. 1999. Novelty causes time-dependent retrograde amnesia for one-trial avoidance in rats through NMDA receptor- and CaMKII-dependent mechanisms in the hippocampus. *Eur. J. Neurosci.* 11:3323–28

Jenkins JB, Dallenbach KM. 1924. Oblivescence during sleep and waking. *Am. J. Psychol.* 35:605–12

Jones Leonard B, McNaughton BL, Barnes CA. 1987. Suppression of hippocampal synaptic activity during slow-wave sleep. *Brain Res.* 425:174–77

Jost A. 1897. Die Assoziationsfestigkeit in ihrer Abhängigkeit von der Verteilung der Wiederholungen [The strength of associations in their dependence on the distribution of repetitions]. *Z. Psychol. Physiol. Sinnesorgane* 16:436–72

Karni A, Tanne D, Rubenstein BS, Askenasy JJM, Sagi D. 1994. Dependence on REM sleep of overnight improvement of a perceptual skill. *Science* 265:679–82

Keppel G. 1968. Retroactive and proactive inhibition. In *Verbal Behavior and General Behavior Theory*, ed. TR Dixon, DL Horton, pp. 172–213. Englewood Cliffs, NJ: Prentice-Hall

Keppel G. 1984. Consolidation and forgetting theory. In *Memory Consolidation: Psychobiology of Cognition*, ed. H Weingartner, ES Parker, pp. 149–61. Hillsdale, NJ: Erlbaum

Lamberty GJ, Beckwith BE, Petros TV. 1990. Posttrial treatment with ethanol enhances recall of prose narratives. *Physiol. Behav.* 48:653–58

Landauer TK. 1974. Consolidation in human memory: retrograde amnestic effects of confusable items in paired-associate learning. *J. Verbal Learn. Verbal Behav.* 13:45–53

Lechner HA, Squire LR, Byrne JH. 1999. 100 years of consolidation—remembering Müller and Pizecker. *Learn. Mem.* 6:77–87

Lisman SA. 1974. Alcoholic "blackout": state dependent learning? *Arch. Gen. Psychiatry* 30:46–53

Lister RG, Eckardt MJ, Weingartner H. 1987. Ethanol intoxication and memory: recent developments and new directions. In *Recent Developments in Alcoholism*, Vol. 5,

ed. M Galanter, pp. 111–27. New York: Plenum

MacLeod MD, Macrae CN. 2001. Gone but not forgotten: the transient nature of retrieval-induced forgetting. *Psychol. Sci.* 121:148–52

Mann RE, Cho-Young J, Vogel-Sprott M. 1984. Retrograde enhancement by alcohol of delayed free recall performance. *Pharmacol. Biochem. Behav.* 20:639–42

Manning CA, Parsons MW, Gold PE. 1992. Anterograde and retrograde enhancement of 24-h memory by glucose in elderly humans. *Behav. Neural Biol.* 58:125–30

Manns JR, Hopkins RO, Squire LR. 2003. Semantic memory and the human hippocampus. *Neuron* 38:127–33

Martin A. 1999. Automatic activation of the medial temporal lobe during encoding: lateralized influences of meaning and novelty. *Hippocampus* 9:62–70

Martin SJ, Grimwood PD, Morris RGM. 2000. Synaptic plasticity and memory: an evaluation of the hypothesis. *Annu. Rev. Neurosci.* 23:649–711

McGaugh JL. 2000. Memory: a century of consolidation. *Science* 287:248–51

McGeoch JA. 1932. Forgetting and the law of disuse. *Psychol. Rev.* 39:352–70

McGeoch JA. 1933. Studies in retroactive inhibition: II. Relationships between temporal point of interpolation, length of interval, and amount of retroactive inhibition. *J. Gen. Psychol.* 9:44–57

McGeoch JA, Nolen ME. 1933. Studies in retroactive inhibition. IV. Temporal point of interpolation and degree of retroactive inhibition. *J. Comp. Psychol.* 15:407–17

Minami H, Dallenbach KM. 1946. The effect of activity upon learning and retention in the cockroach, Periplaneta Americana. *Am. J. Psychol.* 59:1–58

Misanin JR, Miller RR, Lewis DJ. 1968. Retrograde amnesia produced by electroconvulsive shock after reactivation of a consolidated memory trace. *Science* 160:554–55

Morris RGM. 1989. Synaptic plasticity and learning: selective impairment of learning in rats and blockade of long-term potentiation in vivo by the N-methyl-D-aspartate receptor antagonist AP5. *J. Neurosci.* 9:3040–57

Morris RGM. 1998. Down with novelty. *Nature* 394:834–35

Mueller CW, Lisman SA, Spear NE. 1983. Alcohol enhancement of human memory: tests of consolidation and interference hypotheses. *Psychopharmacology* 80:226–30

Müller GE, Pilzecker A. 1900. Experimentelle Beiträge zur Lehre vom Gedächtnis [Experimental contributions to the science of memory]. *Z. Psychol. Ergänz.* 1:1–300

Nadel L, Moscovitch M. 1997. Memory consolidation, retrograde amnesia and the hippocampal complex. *Curr. Opin. Neurobiol.* 7:217–27

Nadel L, Moscovitch M. 2001. The hippocampal complex and long-term memory revisited. *Trends Cogn. Sci.* 5:228–30

Nader K, Schafe GE, LeDoux JE. 2000. Fear memories require protein synthesis in the amygdala for reconsolidation after retrieval. *Nature* 406:722–26

Newton JM, Wickens DD. 1956. Retroactive inhibition as a function of the temporal position of the interpolated learning. *J. Exp. Psychol. Appl.* 51:149–54

Parker ES, Birnbaum IM, Weingartner H, Hartley JT, Stillman RC, Wyatt RJ. 1980. Retrograde enhancement of human memory with alcohol. *Psychopharmacology* 69:219–22

Parker ES, Morihisa JM, Wyatt RJ, Schwartz BL, Weingartner H, Stillman RC. 1981. The alcohol facilitation effect on memory: a dose-response study. *Psychopharmacology* 74:88–92

Plihal W, Born J. 1997. Effects of early and late nocturnal sleep on declarative and procedural memory. *J. Cogn. Neurosci.* 9:534–47

Plihal W, Born J. 1999. Effects of early and late nocturnal sleep on priming and spatial memory. *Psychophysiology* 36:571–82

Pivik T, Foulkes D. 1968. NREM mentation: relation to personality, orientation time, and time of night. *J. Consult. Clin. Psychol.* 32:144–51

Postman L. 1971. Transfer, interference and forgetting. In *Woodworth & Schlosberg's Experimental Psychology*, Volume II: *Learning, Motivation, and Memory*, ed. JW Kling, LA Riggs, pp. 1019–32. New York: Holt, Reinhart & Winston. 3rd ed.

Postman L, Alper T. 1946. Retroactive inhibition as a function of the time interpolation of the inhibitor between learning and recall. *Am. J. Psychol.* 59:439–49

Ribot T. 1881. *Les Maladies de la Memoire (Diseases of Memory)*. New York: Appleton-Century-Crofts

Ribot T. 1882. *Diseases of Memory: An Essay in Positive Psychology*. London: Kegan Paul, Trench

Roberto M, Nelson TE, Ur CL, Gruol DL. 2002. Long-term potentiation in the rat hippocampus is reversibly depressed by chronic intermittent ethanol exposure. *J. Neurophysiol.* 87:2385–97

Robinson ES. 1920. Studies from the psychological laboratory of the University of Chicago: some factors determining the degree of retroactive inhibition. *Psychol. Monogr.* (Whole No. 128) 28:1–57

Rubin DC, Wenzel AE. 1996. One hundred years of forgetting: a quantitative description of retention. *Psychol. Rev.* 103:734–60

Schacter DL. 1992. Understanding implicit memory: a cognitive neuroscience approach. *Am. Psychol.* 47: 559–69

Scoville WB, Milner B. 1957. Loss of recent memory after bilateral hippocampal lesions. *J. Neurol. Neurosurg. Psychiatry* 20:11–21

Sinclair JG, Lo GF. 1986. Ethanol blocks tetanic and calcium-induced long-term potentiation in the hippocampal slice. *Gen. Pharmacol.* 17:231–33

Sisson ED. 1939. Retroactive inhibition: the temporal position of interpolated activity. *J. Exp. Psychol.* 25:228–33

Skaggs EB. 1925. Further studies in retroactive inhibition. *Psychol. Monogr.* (Whole No. 161) 34:1–60

Skaggs EB. 1933. A discussion on the temporal point of interpolation and degree of retroactive inhibition. *J. Comp. Psychol.* 16:411–14

Slamecka NJ. 1966. Differentiation versus unlearning of verbal associations. *J. Exp. Psychol. Appl.* 71:822–28

Squire LR, Clark RE, Knowlton BJ. 2001. Retrograde amnesia. *Hippocampus* 11:50–55

Squire LR, Slater PC, Chace PM. 1975. Retrograde amnesia: temporal gradient in very long-term memory following electroconvulsive therapy. *Science* 187:77–79

Tulving E, Madigan SA. 1970. Memory and verbal learning. *Annu. Rev. Psychol.* 21:437–84

Tulving E, Markowitsch HJ, Kapur S, Habib R, Houle S. 1994. Novelty encoding networks in the human brain: positron emission tomography data. *NeuroReport* 5:2525–28

Underwood BJ. 1957. Interference and forgetting. *Psychol. Rev.* 64:49–60

Underwood BJ. 1983. *Attributes of Memory.* Glenview, IL: Scott, Foresman

Underwood BJ, Ekstrand BR. 1966. An analysis of some shortcomings in the interference theory of forgetting. *Psychol. Rev.* 73:540–49

Underwood BJ, Ekstrand BR. 1967. Studies of distributed practice: XXIV. Differentiation and proactive inhibition. *J. Exp. Psychol. Appl.* 74:574–80

Underwood BJ, Postman L. 1960. Extraexperimental sources of interference in forgetting. *Psychol. Rev.* 67:73–95

Vertes RP, Eastman KE. 2000. The case against memory consolidation in REM sleep. *Behav. Brain Sci.* 23:867–76

Villarreal DM, Do V, Haddad E, Derrick BE. 2002. NMDA receptor antagonists sustain LTP and spatial memory: active processes mediate LTP decay. *Nat. Neurosci.* 5:48–52

Weingartner HJ, Sirocco K, Curran V, Wolkowitz O. 1995. Memory facilitation following the administration of the benzodiazepine triazolam. *Exp. Clin. Psychopharmacol.* 3:298–303

White KG. 2001. Forgetting functions. *Anim. Learn. Behav.* 29:193–207

Wickelgren WA. 1974. Single-trace fragility theory of memory dynamics. *Mem. Cogn.* 2:775–80

Wickelgren WA. 1977. *Learning and Memory.* Englewood Cliffs, NJ: Prentice-Hall

Wilson MA, McNaughton BL. 1994. Reactivation of hippocampal ensemble memories during sleep. *Science* 265:676–79

Wixted JT, Ebbesen E. 1991. On the form of forgetting. *Psychol. Sci.* 2:409–15

Wixted JT, Ebbesen E. 1997. Genuine power curves in forgetting. *Mem. Cogn.* 25:731–39

Xu L, Anwyl R, Rowan MJ. 1998. Spatial exploration induces a persistent reversal of long-term potentiation in rat hippocampus. *Nature* 394:891–94

Yaroush R, Sullivan MJ, Ekstrand BR. 1971. The effect of sleep on memory: II. Differential effect of the first and second half of the night. *J. Exp. Psychol. Appl.* 88:361–66

Annu. Rev. Psychol. 2004. 55:271–304
doi: 10.1146/annurev.psych.55.090902.142005
First published online as a Review in Advance on October 6, 2003

OBJECT PERCEPTION AS BAYESIAN INFERENCE

Daniel Kersten

Department of Psychology, University of Minnesota, Minneapolis, Minnesota 55455;
email: kersten@umn.edu

Pascal Mamassian

Department of Psychology, University of Glasgow, Glasgow G12 8QB, Scotland

Alan Yuille

Departments of Statistics and Psychology, University of California, Los Angeles,
Los Angeles, California 90095-1554

Key Words shape, material, depth, vision, neural, psychophysics, fMRI, computer vision

■ **Abstract** We perceive the shapes and material properties of objects quickly and reliably despite the complexity and objective ambiguities of natural images. Typical images are highly complex because they consist of many objects embedded in background clutter. Moreover, the image features of an object are extremely variable and ambiguous owing to the effects of projection, occlusion, background clutter, and illumination. The very success of everyday vision implies neural mechanisms, yet to be understood, that discount irrelevant information and organize ambiguous or noisy local image features into objects and surfaces. Recent work in Bayesian theories of visual perception has shown how complexity may be managed and ambiguity resolved through the task-dependent, probabilistic integration of prior object knowledge with image features.

CONTENTS

0066-4308/04/0204-0271$14.00

OBJECT PERCEPTION: GEOMETRY AND MATERIAL

Object perception is important for the everyday activities of recognition, planning, and motor action. These tasks require the visual system to obtain geometrical information about the shapes of objects, their spatial layout, and their material properties.

The human visual system is extraordinarily competent at extracting necessary geometrical information. Navigation, judgments of collision, and reaching rely on knowledge of spatial relationships between objects and between the viewer and object surfaces. Shape-based recognition and actions such as grasping require information about the internal shapes and boundaries of objects.

Extracting information about the material that objects are made of is also important for daily visual function. Image features such as color, texture, and shading depend on the material reflectivity and roughness of a surface. Distinguishing different materials is useful for object detection (e.g., texture differences are cues for separating figure from ground) as well as for judging affordances such as edibility (e.g., ripe fruit or not) and graspability (e.g., slippery or not).

Understanding how the brain translates retinal image intensities to useful information about objects is a tough problem on theoretical grounds alone. The difficulty of object perception arises because natural images are both complex and objectively ambiguous. The images received by the eye are complex high-dimensional functions of scene information (Figure 1, see color insert). The complexity of the problem is evident in the primate visual system in which approximately ten million retinal measurements are sent to the brain each second, where they are processed by some billion cortical neurons. The ambiguity of image intensities also poses a major computational challenge to extracting object information. Similar three-dimensional (3-D) geometrical shapes can result in different images, and different shapes can result in very similar images (Figure 1A,B). Similarly, the same material (e.g., polished silver) can give rise to drastically different images depending on the environment, and the same image can be due to quite different materials (Figure 1C,D).

This review treats object perception as a visual inference problem (Helmholtz 1867) and, more specifically, as statistical inference (Knill & Richards 1996, Kersten 1999, Rao et al. 2002a). This approach is particularly attractive because it has been used in computer vision to develop theories and algorithms to extract information from natural images useful for recognition and robot actions.

Computer vision has shown how the problems of complexity and ambiguity can be handled using Bayesian inference, which provides a common framework for modeling artificial and biological vision. In addition, studies of natural images have shown statistical regularities that can be used for designing theories of Bayesian inference. The goal of understanding biological vision also requires using the tools of psychophysics and neurophysiology to investigate how the visual pathways of the brain transform image information into percepts and actions.

In the next section, we provide an overview of object perception as Bayesian inference. In subsequent sections, we review psychophysical (Psychophysics, below), computational (Theoretical and Computational Advances, below), and neurophysiological (Neural Implications, below) results on the nature of the computations and mechanisms that support visual inference. Psychophysically, a major challenge for vision research is to obtain quantitative models of human perceptual performance given natural image input for the various functional tasks of vision. These models should be extensible in the sense that one should be able to build on simple models, rather than having a different model for each set of psychophysical results. Meeting this challenge will require further theoretical advances and Theoretical and Computational Advances (below) highlights recent progress in learning classifiers, probability distributions, and in visual inference. Psychophysics constrains neural models but can only go so far, and neural experiments are required to further determine theories of object perception. Neural Implications (below) describes some of the neural implications of Bayesian theories.

INTRODUCTION TO BAYES

How to Resolve Ambiguity in Object Perception?

The Bayesian framework has its origins in Helmholtz's idea of perception as unconscious inference. Helmholtz realized that retinal images are ambiguous and that prior knowledge was required to account for perception. For example, differently curved cylinders can produce exactly the same retinal image if viewed from the appropriate angles, and the same cylinder can produce very different images if viewed at different angles. Thus, the ambiguous stimulus in Figure 2A could be interpreted as a highly curved cylinder from a high angle of view, a flatter cylinder from a low angle of view, or as a concave cylinder from yet another viewpoint. Helmholtz proposed that the visual system resolves ambiguity through built-in knowledge of the scene and how retinal images are formed and uses this knowledge to automatically and unconsciously infer the properties of objects.

Bayesian statistical decision theory formalizes Helmholtz's idea of perception as inference[1]. Theoretical observers that use Bayesian inference to make optimal

---

[1]Recent reviews include Knill et al. (1996), Yuille & Bülthoff (1996), Kersten & Schrater (2002), Kersten & Yuille (2003), Maloney (2002), Pizlo (2001), and Mamassian et al. (2002).

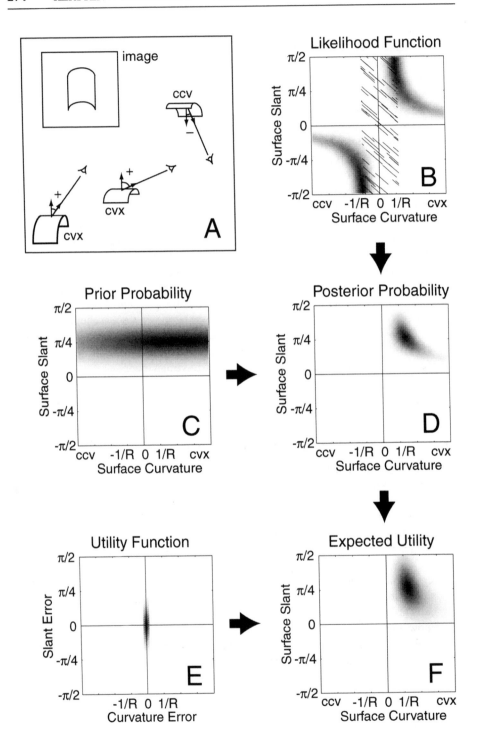

interpretations are called ideal observers. We first consider one type of ideal observer that computes the most probable interpretation given the retinal image stimulus. Technically, this observer is called a maximum a posteriori (MAP) observer. The ideal observer bases its decision on the posterior probability distribution— the probability of each possible true state of the scene given the retinal stimulus. According to Bayes' theorem, the posterior probability is proportional to the product of the prior probability—the probability of each possible state of the scene prior to receiving the stimulus—and the likelihood—the probability of the stimulus given each possible state of the scene. In many applications, prior probability distributions represent knowledge of the regularities of possible object shapes, materials, and illumination, and likelihood distributions represent knowledge of how images are formed through projection onto the retina. Figure 2 illustrates how a symmetric likelihood [a function of the stimulus representing the curvature of the two-dimensional (2-D) line] can lead to an asymmetric posterior owing to a prior toward convex objects. The ideal (MAP) observer then picks the most probable interpretation for that stimulus—i.e., the state of the scene (3-D surface curvature and viewpoint slant) for which the posterior distribution peaks in panel D of Figure 2. An ideal observer does not necessarily get the right answer for each input stimulus, but it does make the best guesses so it gets the best performance averaged over all the stimuli. In this sense, an ideal observer may "see" illusions.

We now take a closer look at three key aspects to Bayesian modeling: the generative model, the task specification, and the inference solution.

THE GENERATIVE MODEL   The generative model, $S \rightarrow I$, specifies how an image description I (e.g., the image intensity values or features extracted from them) is determined by the scene description S (e.g., vector with variables representing surface shape, material reflectivity, illumination direction, and viewpoint). The

---

Figure 2   The ideal observer. (A) The image of a cylinder is consistent with multiple objects and viewpoints, including convex cylinders viewed from above and concave cylinders viewed from below. Therefore, different scene interpretations for this image vary in the estimated surface curvature and slant (the viewing angle). (B) The likelihood represents the compatibility of different scene interpretations with the image (1/R is the curvature in the image). The hatched region represents those surface curvatures that are never compatible with the image, indicating that, for instance, a plane will never project as a curved patch in the image. (C) The prior probability describes an observer preference for convex objects viewed from above. (D) A Bayesian observer then combines likelihood and prior to estimate a posterior probability for each interpretation given the original image. The maximum a posteriori (MAP) is the set of scene parameters for which the posterior is the largest. (E) The utility function represents the costs associated to errors in the estimation of the surface slant and curvature and is dependent on the task. (F) Finally, the posterior probability is convolved with the utility function to give the expected utility associated with each interpretation.

likelihood of the image features, $p(I|S)$, and the prior probability of the scene description, $p(S)$, determine an external generative model. As illustrated later in Figure 5, a strong generative model allows one to draw image samples—the high-dimensional equivalent to throwing a loaded die. The product of the likelihood and prior specifies an ensemble distribution $p(S, I) = p(I|S)p(S)$, which gives a distribution over problem instances (Theoretical and Computational Advances, below). In Bayesian networks, a generative model specifies the causal relationships between random variables (e.g., objects, lighting, and viewpoint) that determine the observable data (e.g., image intensities)[2]. Below, we describe how Bayesian networks can be used to cope with the complexity of problems of visual inference.

THE TASK SPECIFICATION   There is a limitation with the MAP ideal observer described above. Finding the most probable interpretation of the scene does not allow for the fact that some tasks may require more accurate estimates of some aspects of the scene than others. For example, it may be critical to get the exact object shape, but not the exact viewpoint (represented in the utility function in Figure 2E). The task specifies the costs and benefits associated with the different possible errors in the perceptual decision. Generally, an optimal perceptual decision is a function of the task as well as the posterior.

Often, we can simplify the task requirements by splitting S into components (S_1, S_2) that specify which scene properties are important to estimate (S_1, e.g., surface shape) and which confound the measurements and are not worth estimating (S_2, e.g., viewpoint, illumination).

THE INFERENCE SOLUTION   Bayesian perception is an inverse solution, $I \to S_1$, to the generative model, which estimates the variables S_1 given the image I and discounts the confounding variables. Decisions are based on the posterior distribution $p(S|I)$, which is specified by Bayes as $p(I|S)p(S)/p(I)$. The decision may be designed, for example, to choose the scene description for which the posterior is biggest (MAP). But we've noted that other tasks are possible, such as only estimating components of S. In general, an ideal observer convolves the posterior distribution with a utility function (or negative loss function)[3]. The result is the expected utility (or the negative of the expected loss) associated with each possible interpretation of the stimulus. The Bayes ideal observer picks the interpretation that has the maximum expected utility (Figure 2F).

---

[2]When not qualified, we use the term generative model to mean an external model that describes the causal relationship in terms of variables in the scene. Models of inference may also use an internal generative model to test perceptual hypotheses against the incoming data (e.g., image features). We use the term strong generative model to mean one that produces consistent image samples in terms of intensities.
[3]Optimists maximize the utility or gain, whereas pessimists minimize their loss.

How Does Vision Deal with the Complexity of Images?

Recent work (Freeman et al. 2000, Schrater & Kersten 2000, Kersten & Yuille 2003) has shown how specifying generative models in terms of influence graphs (or Bayesian networks) (Pearl 1988), together with a description of visual tasks, allow us to break problems down into categories (see the example in Figure 3A). The idea is to decompose the description of a scene S into n components $S_1, \ldots, S_n$; the image into m features $I_1, \ldots, I_m$; and express the ensemble distribution as $p(S_1, \ldots, S_n; I_1, \ldots, I_m)$. We represent this distribution by a graph where the nodes correspond to the variables $S_1, \ldots, S_n$ and $I_1, \ldots, I_m$, and links are drawn between nodes that directly influence each other. There is a direct correspondence between graphical structure and the factorization (and thus simplification) of the joint probability. In the most complex case, every random variable influences every other one, and the joint probability cannot be factored into simpler parts. In order

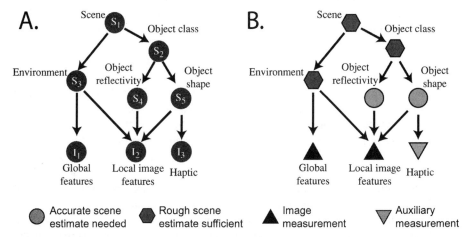

Figure 3   Influence graphs and the visual task. (*A*) An example of an influence graph. Arrows indicate causal links between nodes that represent random variables. The scene class (indoor or outdoor) influences the kind of illumination and background that determine the environment. The scene also determines the kinds of objects one may find (artifactual or not). Object reflectivity (paint or pigment) and shape are influenced by the object class. The model of lighting specified by the environment interacts with reflectivity and shape to determine the image measurements or features. The environment can determine large-scale global features (e.g., overall contrast and color, spatial frequency spectrum) that may be relatively unaffected by smaller-scale objects of interest. Global features can serve to set a context. (*B*) The inference problem depends on the task. The task specifies which variables are important to estimate accurately (*disks*) and which are not (*hexagons*). Triangles represent image measurements or features. For the purpose of later illustration of explaining away, we also distinguish auxiliary features (*upside-down triangles*) that are available or actively sought and which can modulate the probability of object variables that do not directly influence the auxiliary variable. Note that perceptual inference goes against the arrows.

to build models for inference, it is useful to first build quantitative models of image formation—external generative models based on real-world statistics. As we have noted above, the requirements of the task split S into variables that are important to estimate accurately for the task (disks) and those which are not (hexagons) (Figure 3*B*). The consequences of task specification are described in more detail in Discounting and Task Dependence (below).

In the next section, Psychophysics, we review psychophysical results supporting the Bayesian approach to object perception. The discussion is organized around the four simple influence graphs of Figure 4 (see color insert).

PSYCHOPHYSICS

Psychophysical experiments test Bayesian theories of human object perception at several levels. Ideal observers (below) provide the strongest tests because they optimally discount and integrate information to achieve a well-defined goal. But even without an ideal observer model, one can assess the quality of vision's built-in knowledge of regularities in the world.

In Basic Bayes: The Trade-Off Between Feature Reliability and Priors (below), we review the perceptual consequences of knowledge specified by the prior $p(S)$, the likelihood $p(I|S)$, and the trade-off between them. Psychophysical experiments can test theories regarding knowledge specified by $p(S)$. For example, the perception of whether a shape is convex or concave is biased by the assumption that the light source (part of the scene description S) is above the object. Psychophysics can test theories regarding knowledge specified by the likelihood, $p(I|S)$. The likelihood characterizes regularities in the image given object properties S, which include effects of projecting a 3-D object onto a 2-D image. For example, straight lines in three dimensions project to straight lines in the image. Additional image regularities can be obtained by summing over S to get $p(I) = \sum_S p(I|S)p(S)$. These regularities are expected to hold independently of the specific objects in the scene. Image regularities can be divided into geometric (e.g., bounding contours in the image of an object) and photometric descriptions (e.g., image texture in a region).

As illustrated in the examples of Figure 4, vision problems have more structure than basic Bayes. In subsequent sections (Discounting and Task Dependence, Integration of Image Measurements and Cues, and Perceptual Explaining Away), we review psychophysical results pertaining to three additional graph categories, each of which is important for resolving ambiguity: discounting variations to achieve object constancy, integration of image measurements for increased reliability, and perceptual explaining away given competing perceptual hypotheses.

Ideal Observers

Ideal observers provide the strongest psychophysical tests because they are complete models of visual performance based on both the posterior and the task. A Bayesian ideal observer is designed to maximize a performance measure for a visual task (e.g., proportion of correct decisions) and, as a result, serves as a benchmark with which to compare human performance for the same task (Barlow 1962, Green & Swets 1974, Parish & Sperling 1991, Tjan et al. 1995, Pelli et al. 2003). Characterizing the visual information for a task can be critical for proper interpretation of psychophysical results (Eckstein et al. 2000) as well as for the analysis of neural information transmission (Geisler & Albrecht 1995, Oram et al. 1998).

For example, when deciding whether human object recognition uses 3-D shape cues, it is necessary to characterize whether these cues add objectively useful information for the recognition task (independent of whether the task is being performed by a person or by a computer). Liu & Kersten (2003) show that human thresholds for discriminating 3-D asymmetric objects are less than for symmetric objects (the image projections were not symmetric); however, when one compares human performance to the ideal observer for the task, which takes into account the redundancy in symmetric objects, human discrimination is more efficient for symmetric objects.

Because human vision is limited by both the nature of the computations and its physiological hardware, we might expect significant departures from optimality. Nevertheless, Bayesian ideal observer models provide a first approximation to human performance that has been surprisingly effective (cf. Knill 1998, Schrater & Kersten 2002, Legge et al. 2002, Ernst & Banks 2002, Schrater et al. 2000).

A major theoretical challenge for ideal observer analysis of human vision is the requirement for strong generative models so that human observers can be tested with image samples I drawn from $p(I|S)$. We discuss (Basic Bayes: The Trade-Off Between Feature Reliability and Priors, below) results from statistical models of natural image features that constrain, but are not sufficient to specify the likelihood distribution. In Theoretical and Computational Advances (below), we discuss relevant work on machine learning of probability distributions. But we first present a preview of one aspect of the problem.

The need for strong generative models is an extensibility requirement that rules out classes of models for which the samples are image features. The distinction is sometimes subtle. The key point is that images features may either be insufficient to uniquely determine an image or they may sometimes overconstrain it. For example, suppose that a system has learned probability models for airplane parts. Then sampling from these models is highly unlikely to produce an airplane—the samples will be images, but additional constraints are needed to make sure they correspond to airplanes (see Figure 5A). M.C. Escher's pictures and other impossible figures, such as the impossible trident, give examples of images that are not globally consistent. In addition, local feature responses can sometimes overconstrain the image locally. For example, consider the binary image in Figure 5B and suppose our features ΔL are defined to be the difference in image intensity L at neighboring pixels. The nature of binary images puts restrictions on the values that ΔL can take at neighboring pixels. It is impossible, for example, that neighboring ΔLs can both take the value $+1$. So, sampling from these features will not give a consistent image unless we impose additional constraints. Additional consistency conditions are also needed in 2-D images (see Figure 5C) where the local image differences

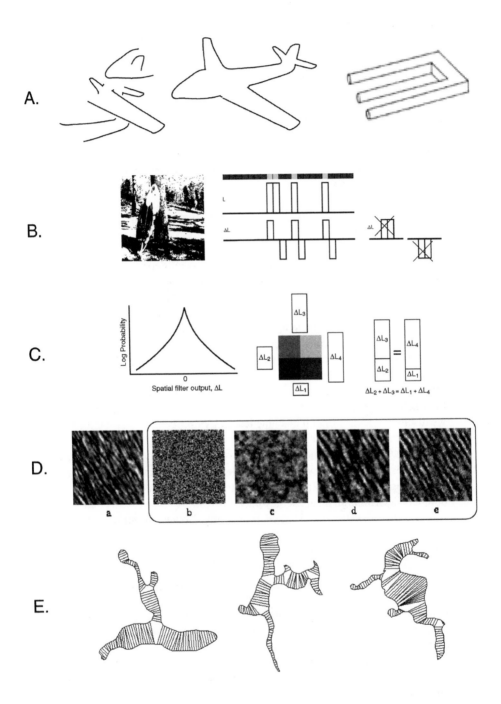

in the horizontal, ΔL_1, ΔL_3, and vertical, ΔL_2, ΔL_4, directions must satisfy the constraint $\Delta L_2 + \Delta L_3 = \Delta L_1 + \Delta L_4$ (this is related to the surface integrability condition that must be imposed on the surface normals of an object to ensure that the surface is consistent).

It is important to realize that strong generative models can be learned from measurements of the statistics of feature responses (discussed more in Theoretical and Computational Advances, below). Work by Zhu, Wu, and Mumford (Zhu et al. 1997, Zhu 1999) shows how statistics on image, or shape, features can be used to obtain strong generative models. Samples from these models are shown in Figure 5D,E.

Basic Bayes: The Trade-Off Between Feature Reliability and Priors

The objective ambiguity of images arises if several different objects could have produced the same image description or image features. In this case, the visual system is forced to guess, but it can make intelligent guesses by biasing its guesses toward typical objects or interpretations (Sinha & Adelson 1993, Mamassian & Goutcher 2001, Weiss et al. 2002) (see Figure 4A). Bayes formula implies that these guesses, and hence perception, are a trade-off between image feature reliability, as embodied by the likelihood $p(I|S)$ and the prior probability $p(S)$. Some perceptions may be more prior driven, and others more data driven. The less reliable the image features (e.g., the more ambiguous), the more the perception is influenced by the prior. This trade-off has been illustrated for a variety of visual phenomena (Bülthoff & Yuille 1991, Mamassian & Landy 2001).

Figure 5   The challenge of building strong generative models. The samples of strong generative models are images that can be used as stimuli for ideal observer analysis of human vision. But models specified by image features may be unable to generate images because the image features may either underconstrain or overconstrain the image. (*A*) A model whose features are airplane parts must impose additional constraints to ensure that the samples form a plane (*left and center panels*). Constraints must prevent an image from being globally inconsistent (*right panel*). (*B*) The nature of binary images (*left panel*) imposes constraints on the feature values (*center panel*) and means that some feature configurations are inconsistent with any image (*right panel*). (*C*) Measurements of natural image statistics (Simoncelli & Olshausen 2001) have shown that the probability distribution of intensity differences between pixels has a characteristic distribution (*left panel*), but to produce natural image samples requires an additional consistency constraint on neighboring filter values (*center and right panels*). (*D*) Samples from a strong generative model learned from image features (Zhu et al. 1997). Panel (*a*) shows the original picture of fur. Panels (*b*)–(*e*) show image samples drawn from several $p(I|fur)s$ with increasing numbers of spatial features and hence increased realism. (*E*) Samples drawn from a generative model for closed curves (Zhu 1999) learned from spatial features.

In particular, Weiss et al. (2002) addressed the aperture problem of motion perception: How to combine locally ambiguous motion measurements into a single global velocity for an object. The authors constructed a Bayesian model whose prior is that motions tend to be slow and which integrates local measurements according to their reliabilities (see Yuille & Grzywacz 1988 for the same prior applied to other motion stimuli). With this model (using a single free parameter), the authors showed that a wide range of motion results in human perception could be accounted for in terms of the trade-off between the prior and the likelihood. The Bayesian models give a simple unified explanation for phenomena that had previously been used to argue for a bag of tricks theory requiring many different mechanisms (Ramachandran 1985).

PRIOR REGULARITIES $p(S)$: OBJECT SHAPE, MATERIAL, AND LIGHTING   Psychophysics can test hypotheses regarding built-in visual knowledge of the prior $p(S)$ independent of projection and rendering. This can be done at a qualitative or quantitative level.

Geometry and shape   Some prior regularities refer to the geometry of objects that humans interact with. For instance, the perception of a solid shape is consistently biased toward convexity rather than concavity (Kanizsa & Gerbino 1976, Hill & Bruce 1993, Mamassian & Landy 1998, Bertamini 2001, Langer & Bülthoff 2001). This convexity prior is robust over a range of object shapes, sizes, and tasks.

More specific tests and ideal observer models will necessitate developing probability models for the high-dimensional spaces of realistic objects. Some of the most highly developed work is on human facial surfaces (cf. Vetter & Troje 1997). Relating image intensity to such measured surface depth statistics has yielded computer vision solutions for face recognition (Atick et al. 1996) and has provided objective prior models for face recognition experiments, suggesting that human vision may represent facial characteristics along principal component dimensions in an opponent fashion (Leopold et al. 2001).

Material   The classical problems of color and lightness constancy are directly tied to the nature of the materials of objects and environmental lighting. However, most past work has implicitly or explicitly assumed a special case: that surfaces are Lambertian (matte). Here, the computer graphics communities have been instrumental in going beyond the Lambertian model by measuring and characterizing the reflectivities of natural smooth homogeneous surfaces in terms of the bidirectional reflectance distribution function (BRDF) (cf. Marschner et al. 2000), with important extensions to more complicated textured surfaces (Dana et al. 1999), including human skin (Jensen et al. 2001). Real images are, of course, intimately tied to the structure of illumination, and below we review psychophysical results on realistic material perception.

Lighting   Studies of human object perception (as well as computer vision) have traditionally assumed simple lighting models, such as a single-point light source with a directionally nonspecific ambient term. One of the best-known examples of a prior is the assumption that light is coming from above. This assumption is particularly useful to disambiguate convex from concave shapes from shading information. The light from above prior is natural when one considers that the sun and most artificial light sources are located above our heads. However, two different studies have now shown that humans prefer the light source to be located above-left rather than straight above (Sun & Perona 1998, Mamassian & Goutcher 2001). A convincing explanation for this leftward bias remains to be advanced.

Apparent motion in depth of an object is strongly influenced by the movement of its cast shadow (Kersten et al. 1997, Mamassian et al. 1998). This result can be interpreted in terms of a stationary light source prior—the visual system is more likely to interpret change in the image as being due to a movement of the object or a change in viewpoint, rather than a movement of the light source.

Do we need more complex lighting models? The answer is surely yes, especially in the context of recent results on the perception of specular surfaces (Fleming et al. 2003) and color given indirect lighting (Bloj et al. 1999), both discussed in Discounting and Task Dependence (below). Dror et al. (2001) have shown that spatial maps of natural illumination (Debevec 1998) show statistical regularities similar to those found in natural images (cf. Simoncelli et al. 2001).

IMAGE REGULARITIES $p(I) = \sum_S p(I|S)p(S)$ Image regularities arise from the similarity between natural scenes. They cover geometric properties, such as the statistics of edges, and photometric properties, such as the distribution of contrast as a function of spatial frequency in the image.

Geometric regularities   Geisler et al. (2001) used spatial filtering to extract local edge fragments from natural images. They measured statistics on the distance between the element centers, the orientation difference between the elements, and the direction of the second element relative to the orientation of first (reference) element. A model derived from the measured statistics and from a simple rule that integrated local contours together could quantitatively predict human contour detection performance. More detailed rules to perceptually organize a chain of dot elements into a subjective curve with a corner or not, or to be split into one versus two groups, have also been given a Bayesian interpretation (Feldman 2001).

Elder & Goldberg (2002) measured statistics of contours from images hand segmented into sets of local tangents. These statistics were used to put probability distributions on three Gestalt principles of perceptual organization: proximity, continuation, and luminance similarity. The authors found that these three grouping cues were independent and that the proximity cue was by far the most powerful. Moreover, the contour likelihood distribution (the probability of a gap length between two tangents of a contour) follows a power law with an exponent very close to that determined psychophysically on dot lattice experiments.

The work of Geisler et al. (2001) deals with distributions on image features, namely edge pairs. To devise a distribution $p(I)$ from which one can draw true contour samples, one needs to also take into account the consistency condition that edge pairs have to lie in an image (see Figure 5A for an airplane analogy). Zhu (1999) describes a procedure that learns a distribution on the image itself, and thus samples drawn from it produce contours (see Figure 5E; Elder & Goldberg 2002).

Photometric regularities   It is now well established that natural scenes have a particular signature in their contrast spatial frequency spectrum in which low spatial frequencies are over-represented relative to high spatial frequencies. This regularity is characterized by a $1/f^\beta$ spectrum, where f is spatial frequency and β is a parameter that can be fit from image measurements (Field 1987, Simoncelli & Olshausen 2001). Human observers are better at discriminating changes in β for Gaussian and natural images when the values of β are near (Knill et al. 1990) or at the value measured from natural images (Parraga et al. 2000), suggesting that the visual system is in some sense tuned to the second-order statistics (i.e., spatial frequency spectrum) of natural images.

The histograms of spatial filter responses (e.g., the simplest filter being differences between neighboring pixel intensities) of natural images also show consistent regularities (Olshausen & Field 2000, Simoncelli & Olshausen 2001). The histograms are non-Gaussian, having a high kurtosis (see first panel in Figure 5C). Zhu & Mumford (1997) have derived a strong generative model they call a generic image prior based on filter histogram statistics.

IMAGE LIKELIHOOD $p(I|S)$ The likelihood characterizes how image regularities result from projection and rendering of objects as a function of view and lighting, and it is related to what is sometimes called the forward optics or computer graphics problem.

Geometrical descriptions   Object perception shows biases consistent with preferred views. Mamassian & Landy (1998) show how the interpretation of a simple line drawing figure changed with rotations of the figure about the line of sight. They modeled their result with a simple Bayesian model that had a prior probability for surface normals pointing upward (Figure 2). This prior can be interpreted as a preference for a viewpoint situated above the scene, which is reasonable when we consider that most of the objects we interact with are below the line of sight.

Why does a vertical line appear longer than the same line when horizontal? Although there have been a number of recent studies of the statistics of image intensities and contours, Howe & Purves (2002) directly compare statistics on the separation between two points in the image with measurements of the causes in the originating 3-D scene. The authors found that the average ratio of the 3-D physical interval to the projected image interval from real-world measurements shows the same pattern as perceived length.

Photometric descriptions   The global spatial frequency amplitude spectrum is an inadequate statistic to capture the structure of specific texture classes. Recent work has shown that wavelet representations provide richer models for category-specific modeling of spatially homogeneous texture regions, such as text, fur, grass, etc. (Portilla & Simoncelli 2000, Zhu et al. 1997). As with the contour case, a future challenge is to develop strong generative models from which one can draw samples of images from $p(I|S)$ (Theoretical and Computational Advances, below). Promising work along these lines is illustrated in Figure 5*D* (Zhu et al. 1997).

WHERE DO THE PRIORS COME FROM?   Without direct input, how does image-independent knowledge of the world get built into the visual system? One pat answer is that the priors are in the genes. Observations of stereotyped periods in the development of human depth perception do in fact suggest a genetic component (Yonas 2003). In another domain, the strikingly rapid development of object concepts in children is still a major mystery that suggests predispositions to certain kinds of grouping rules. Adults, too, are quick to accurately generalize from a relatively small set of positive examples (in many domains, including objects) to a whole category. Tenenbaum (2000; Tenenbaum & Xu 2000, Tenenbaum & Griffiths 2001) provides a Bayesian synthesis of two theories of generalization (similarity-like and rule-like) and provides a computational framework that helps to explain rapid category generalization.

The accurate segmentation of objects such as the kayaks in Figure 1 likely requires high-level prior knowledge regarding the nature of the forms of possible object classes. Certain kinds of priors, such as learning the shapes of specific objects, may develop through what Brady & Kersten (2003) have called opportunistic learning and bootstrapped learning. In opportunistic learning, the visual system seizes the opportunity to learn object structure during those relatively rare occasions when an object is seen under conditions of low ambiguity, such as when motion breaks camouflage of an object in plain view. Bootstrapped learning operates under intermediate or high conditions of ambiguity (e.g., in which none of the training images provide a clear view of an object's boundaries). Then later, the visual system can apply the prior knowledge gained to high (objective) ambiguity situations more typical of everyday vision. The mechanisms of bootstrapped learning are not well understood, although there has been some computer vision work (Weber et al. 2000) (see Theoretical and Computational Advances, below).

General purpose cortical learning mechanisms have been proposed (Dayan et al. 1995, Hinton & Ghahramani 1997); however, it is not clear whether these are workable with complex natural image input. We discuss computer vision methods for learning priors in Theoretical and Computational Advances (below).

Discounting and Task Dependence

How does the visual system enable us to infer the same object despite considerable image variation owing to confounding variables such as viewpoint, illumination, occlusion, and background changes? This is the well-known problem of invariance or object constancy. Objective ambiguity results when variations in a scene property change the image description of an object. As we have seen, both viewpoint and 3-D shape influence the 2-D image.

Suppose the visual task is to determine object shape, but the presence of unknown variables (e.g., viewpoint) confounds the inference. Confounding variables are analogous to noise in classical signal detection theory, but they are more complicated to model and they affect image formation in a highly nonlinear manner. For example, a standard noise model has $I = S + n$, where n is Gaussian noise. Realistic vision noise is better captured by $p(I|S)$, as illustrated in Figure 6B. Here, the problem is making a good guess independent of (or invariant to) the true value of the confounding variable. The task itself can serve to reduce ambiguity by discounting the confounding variable (Freeman 1994, Kersten 1999, Schrater & Kersten 2000, Geisler & Kersten 2002). Discounting irrelevant scene variations (or accounting for object invariance) has received recent attention in the functional magnetic resonance imaging (fMRI) literature, where certain cortical areas show more or less degrees of invariance to size, translation, rotation in depth, or illumination (cf. Grill-Spector et al. 2003).

From the Bayesian perspective, we can model problems with confounding variables by the graph in Figure 4B. We define an ensemble distribution $p(S_1, S_2, I)$, where S_1 is the target (e.g., keys), S_2 is the confounding variable (e.g., pose), and I is the image. Then we discount the confounding variables by integrating them out (or summing over them),

$$p(S_1, I) = \sum_{S_2} p(S_1, S_2, I).$$

Figure 6 Traditional visual noise versus illumination variation. Example of face recognition given confounding variables. The first row and second rows of the top and bottom panels show images of faces s_1 and s_2, respectively. (A) Face recognition is confounded by additive Gaussian contrast noise. Bayesian ideal discriminators for this task are well understood. However, the Gaussian assumption leads to a least squares metric for measuring the similarities between faces. But the similarity between two images of the same face under different lighting can be bigger than the least squares distance between two faces. (B) Face recognition is confounded by illumination variation. This type of uncertainty is more typical of the type of variation encountered during natural visual tasks. The human visual system seems competent at discounting illumination, but Bayesian theories for general illumination variation are more difficult to formulate (cf. Yuille et al. 2001). The columns show different illumination conditions of the two faces. Light direction gradually varies from right (*left-most column*) to left (*right-most column*). In this example, illumination changes are relatively large compared to the illumination-invariant features corresponding to facial identity. The illumination direction changes are ordered for clarity. In actual samples, the illumination direction may not be predictable.

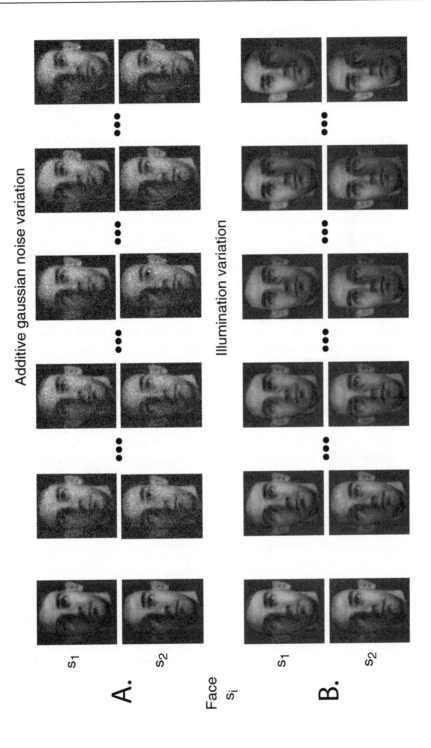

This is equivalent to spreading out the loss function completely in one of the directions (e.g., extending the utility function vertically in Figure 2E). As noted above, the choice of which variables to discount will depend on the task. Viewpoint is a confounding variable that can be discounted if the task is to discriminate objects independent of viewpoint. Illumination is a confounding variable if the task is to recognize or determine the depth of an object, but it is not if the task is to determine the light-source direction. This can be related to notions of utility[4]; discounting a variable is equivalent to treating it as having such low utility that it is not worth estimating (Yuille & Bülthoff 1996) (see Theoretical and Computational Advances, below).

Viewpoint variation   When interpreting 2-D projections of 3-D shapes, the human visual system favors interpretations that assume that the object is being viewed from a general (or generic), rather than accidental, viewpoint (Nakayama & Shimojo 1992, Albert 2000). Freeman (1994) showed that a Bayesian observer that integrates out viewpoint can account for the generic view assumption.

How does human vision recognize 3-D objects as the same despite changes in viewpoint? Shape-based object recognition models range between two extremes—those that predict a strong dependence of recognition performance on viewpoint (e.g., as a function of familiarity with particular views) and those that, as a result of using view-invariant features together with structural descriptions of objects, do not (Poggio & Edelman 1990, Ullman & Basri 1991, Tarr & Bülthoff 1995, Ullman 1996, Biederman 2000, Riesenhuber & Poggio 2002). By comparing human performance to several types of ideal observers that integrate out viewpoint variations, Liu et al. (1995) showed that models that allow rigid rotations in the image plane of independent 2-D templates could not account for human performance in discriminating novel object views. More recent work by Liu & Kersten (1998) showed that the performance of human observers relative to Bayesian affine

---

[4]Bayesian decision theory (see Theoretical and Computational Advances, below) provides a precise language to model the costs of errors determined by the choice of visual task (Yuille & Bülthoff 1996). The cost or risk $R(\alpha; I)$ of guessing α when the image measurement is I is defined as the expected loss (or negative utility):

$$R(\alpha; I) = \sum_S L(\alpha, S) p(S|I),$$

with respect to the posterior probability, $p(S|I)$. The best interpretation of the image can then be made by finding the α that minimizes the risk function. The loss function $L(\alpha, S)$ specifies the cost of guessing α when the scene variable is S. One possible loss function is $-\delta(\alpha - S)$. In this case, the risk becomes $R(\alpha; I) = -p(\alpha|I)$, and then the best strategy is to pick the most likely interpretation. This is MAP estimation and is the optimal strategy for the task requiring an observer to maximize the proportion of correct decisions. A second kind of loss function assumes that costs are constant over all guesses of a variable. This is equivalent to integrating out, summing over, or marginalization of the posterior with respect to that variable.

models (which allow stretching, translations, rotations, and shears in the image) is better for the novel views than for the template views, suggesting that humans have a better means to generalize to novel views than could be accomplished with affine warps. Other related work describes the role of structural knowledge (Liu et al. 1999), the importance of view-frequency (Troje & Kersten 1999), and shape constancy under perspective (Pizlo 1994).

Bayesian task dependence may account for studies where different operationalizations for measuring perceived depth lead to inconsistent, though related, estimates. For instance, the information provided by a single image of an object is insufficient for an observer to infer a unique shape (see Figure 1B). Not surprisingly, these ambiguities will lead different observers to report different depth percepts for the same picture, and the same observer to report different percepts when using different depth probes. Koenderink et al. (2001) show that most of this variability could be accounted for by affine transformations of the perceived depth, in particular, scalings and shears. These affine transformations correspond to looking at the picture from a different viewpoint. The authors call the perceived depth of a surface, once the viewpoint has been discounted, pictorial relief.

Illumination variation   Discounting illumination by integrating it out can reduce ambiguity regarding the shape or depth of an object (Freeman 1994, Yuille et al. 2003, Kersten 1999). Integrating out illumination level or direction has also been used to account for apparent surface color (Brainard & Freeman 1997, Bloj et al. 1999).

Work so far has been for extremely simple lighting, such as a single-point light source. One of the future challenges will be to understand how the visual system discounts the large spatial variations in natural illumination that are particularly apparent in many surfaces typically encountered, such as metal, plastic, and paper (see Figure 1C). Fleming et al. (2003) showed that human observers could match surface reflectance properties more reliably and accurately for more realistic patterns of illumination. They manipulated pixel and wavelet properties of illumination patterns to show that the visual system's built-in assumptions about illumination are of intermediate complexity (e.g., presence of edges and bright light sources) rather than depending on high-level knowledge, such as recognizable objects.

Integration of Image Measurements and Cues

The visual system likely achieves much of its inferential power through sophisticated integration of ambiguous local features. This can be modeled from a Bayesian perspective (Clark & Yuille 1990). For example, a depth discontinuity typically causes more than one type of cue (stereo disparity and motion parallax), and visual inference can exploit this to improve the reliability and accuracy of the depth estimate. Given two conflicting cues to depth, the visual system might get by with a simple averaging of each estimate, even though inaccurate. Or in cases of substantial conflict, it may determine that one measurement is an outlier and should not be integrated with the other measurement (Landy et al. 1995, Bülthoff & Mallot 1988). Ruling out outliers is possible within a single modality (e.g., when integrating disparity and texture gradients in vision) but may not be possible between modalities (e.g., between vision and touch) because in the latter case, single cue information appears to be preserved (Hillis et al. 2002). The visual system is often more sophisticated and combines image measurements weighted according to their reliability (Jacobs 2002, Weiss et al. 2002), which we discuss next.

Figure 4C illustrates the influence graph for cue integration with an example of illumination direction estimation. From a Bayes net perspective, the two cues are conditionally independent given the shared explanation. An important case is when the nodes represent Gaussian variables that are independent when conditioned on the common cause and we have estimates for each cue alone (i.e., $\hat{S}_i$ is the best estimate of S_i from $p(S|I_i)$). Then optimal integration (i.e., the most probable value) of the two estimates takes into account the uncertainty owing to measurement noise (the variance) and is given by the weighted average,

$$\hat{S} = \hat{S}_1 \frac{r_1}{r_1 + r_2} + \hat{S}_2 \frac{r_2}{r_1 + r_2},$$

where r_i, the reliability, is the reciprocal of the variance. This model has been used to study whether the human visual system combines cues optimally (cf. Jacobs 2002 for a review and a discussion of integration in the context of Kalman filtering, which is a special case of Bayesian estimation).

For instance, visual and haptic information about object size are combined and weighted according to the reliability of the source (Ernst & Banks 2002, Gepshtein & Banks 2003). Object size can be perceived both visually and by touch. When the information from vision and touch disagree, vision usually dominates. The authors showed that when one takes into account the reliability of the sensory measurements, information from vision and touch are integrated optimally. Visual dominance occurs when the reliability of the visual estimation is greater than that of the haptic one.

Integration is also important for grouping local image elements likely to belong to the same surface. The human visual system combines spatial frequency and orientation information optimally when detecting the boundary between two regions (Landy & Kojima 2001). Human observers also behave like an optimal observer when integrating information from skew-symmetry and disparity in perceiving the orientation of a planar object (Saunders & Knill 2001). The projection of a symmetric flat object has a distorted or skewed symmetry that provides partial information about the object's orientation in depth. Saunders & Knill show that human observers integrate symmetry information with stereo information weighted according to the reliability of the source.

Prior probabilities can also combine like weighted cues. We discussed above that human observers interpret the shape of an object assuming that both the viewpoint and the light source are above the object (Mamassian et al. 1998, Mamassian & Goutcher 2001). Mamassian & Landy (2001) manipulated the reliability of each of the two constraints by changing the contrast of different parts of the stimuli. For instance, increasing the shading contrast increased the reliability of the light-source prior and biased the observers' percept toward the shape most consistent with the light-source prior alone. Their interpretation of the results was that observers modulated the strength of their priors based on the stimulus contrast. As a consequence, prior constraints behaved just like depth cue integration: Cues with more reliable information have higher weight attributed to their corresponding prior constraint.

Not all kinds of cue integrating are consistent with the simple graph of Figure 4C. Yuille & Bülthoff (1996) have argued that strong coupling of visual cues (Clark & Yuille 1990) is required to model a range of visual phenomena (Bülthoff & Mallot 1988). The graph for explaining away (Figure 4D) provides one useful simple extension to the graphs discussed so far, and we discuss this next.

Perceptual Explaining Away

The key idea behind explaining away is that two alternative perceptual hypotheses can compete to explain the image. From a Bayesian perspective, the competition results from the two (otherwise independent) hypotheses becoming conditionally dependent given the image.

Pearl (1988) was one of the first to emphasize that, in contrast to traditional artificial intelligence expert systems, human reasoning is particularly good at explaining away the effects of alternative hypotheses. In a now classic example, imagine that you emerge from your house in the morning and notice that the grass is wet. Prior probabilities might tell you that it was unlikely due to rain (e.g., you live in Los Angeles), and thus you have probably left the sprinkler on overnight. But then you check the neighbor's lawn and notice that it too is wet. This auxiliary piece of evidence now undercuts the earlier explanation and lowers the probability that you left the sprinkler on. The more probable explanation is that it rained last night, explaining why both lawns are wet. Both the sprinkler and the rain hypothesis directly influence the observation "your lawn is wet," but only the rain hypothesis affects both lawns' being wet.

Human perception is also good at explaining away, but automatically and without conscious thought[5]. In perception, the essential idea is that if two (or more) hypotheses about an object property can explain the same image measurements, then lowering the probability of one of the explanations increases the probability of the other. One can observe explaining away in both material (e.g., lightness and color) and shape perception.

Material   In the Land & McCann (1971) version of the classic Craik-O'Brien Cornsweet illusion, two abutting regions that have the same gradual change of

---

[5]Some related perceptual phenomena Rock described as "perceptual interactions" (Rock 1983).

luminance appear to have different reflectances. Knill & Kersten (1991) found that the illusion is weakened when a curved occluding contour (auxiliary evidence) bounding the regions above and below suggests that the variation of luminance is due to a change in surface orientation (Figure 4D). The lightness gradients are explained away by the gradual surface curvature. Buckley et al. (1994) extended this result when binocular disparities were used to suggest a 3-D surface. These results indicate that some scene attributes (in this case surface curvature) influence the inference of the major scene attributes (material reflectance) that are set by the task.

Another study asked whether human vision could discount the effects of the color of indirect lighting (Bloj et al. 1999). Imagine a concave folded card consisting of a red half facing a white half. With white direct illumination, pinkish light radiates from the white card because of the indirect additional illumination from the red card. Does vision use shape knowledge to discount the red illuminant in order to perceive the true material color, which is white? A change in retinal disparities (an auxiliary measurement) can cause the concave card to appear as convex, without any change in the chromatic content of the stimulus. When the card appears convex, the white card appears more pinkish, as if perception has lost its original explanation for the pinkish tinge in the image and now attributes it to reddish pigment rather than reddish light.

Geometry and shape   Explaining away occurs in discounting the effects of occlusion, and when simple high-level object descriptions override more complex interpretations of line arrangements or moving dots (Lorenceau & Shiffrar 1992, McDermott et al. 2001, Murray et al. 2002). We describe this in more detail in Neural Implications (below).

Explaining away is closely related to previous work on competitive models, where two alternative models compete to explain the same data. It has been argued that this accounts for a range of visual phenomena (Yuille & Bülthoff 1996), including the estimation of material properties (Blake & Bülthoff 1990). This approach has been used successfully in computer vision systems by Tu & Zhu (2002), including recent work (Tu et al. 2003) in which a whole class of generative models, including faces, text, generic shading, and texture models compete and cooperate to explain the entire image (Theoretical and Computational Advances, below). In particular, the generic shading models help detect faces by explaining away shadows and glasses.

Failures to explain away   Visual perception can also unexpectedly fail to explain away. In one simple demonstration, an ambiguous Mach folded card can be interpreted as a concave horizontal edge or a convex vertical edge. A shadow cast over the edge by an object (e.g., pencil) placed in front provides enough information to disambiguate the percept, and yet humans fail to use this information (Mamassian et al. 1998). There has yet to be a good explanation for this failure.

THEORETICAL AND COMPUTATIONAL ADVANCES

Psychophysical and neurophysiological studies of vision necessarily rely on simplifications of both stimuli and tasks. This simplification, however, must be extensible to the visual input experienced during natural perceptual functioning. In the previous sections, several psychophysical studies used models of natural image statistics, as well as models of prior object structure, such as shape. Future advances in understanding perception will increasingly depend on the efficient characterization (and simulation) of realistic images to identify informative image statistics, models of scene properties, and a theoretical understanding of inference for natural perceptual functions. In this section, we discuss relating Bayesian decision theory to current theories of machine learning, learning the probability distributions relevant for vision, and determining algorithms for Bayesian inference.

Bayes Decision Theory and Machine Learning

The Bayesian approach seems completely different from the type of feedforward models required to recognize objects in 150 ms (VanRullen & Thorpe 2001). How does the Bayesian approach relate to alternative models based on neural networks, radial basis functions, or other techniques?

This subsection shows the relationships using concepts from Bayes decision theory (Berger 1985, Yuille & Bülthoff 1996) and machine learning (Vapnik 1998, Evgeniou et al. 2000, Schölkopf & Smola 2002). This relationship also gives a justification for Bayes rule and the intuitions behind it.

We first introduce additional concepts from decision theory: (a) a decision rule $S^* = \alpha(I)$ and (b) a loss function (or negative utility) $L(\alpha(I), S)$, which is the penalty for making the decision $\alpha(I)$ when the true state is S (e.g., a fixed penalty for a misclassification). Suppose we have a set of examples $\{I_i, S_i : i = 1, \ldots, N\}$, then the empirical risk (Vapnik 1998, Schölkopf & Smola 2002) (e.g., the proportions of misclassifications) of the rule $\alpha(I)$ is defined to be

$$R_{emp}(\alpha) = (1/N) \sum_{i=1}^{N} L(\alpha(I_i), S_i). \qquad (1)$$

The best decision rule $\alpha^*(.)$ is selected to minimize $R_{emp}(\alpha)$. For example, the decision rule is chosen to minimize the number of misclassifications. Neural networks and machine learning models select rules to minimize $R_{emp}(\alpha)$ (Vapnik 1998, Evgeniou et al. 2000, Schölkopf & Smola 2002).

Now suppose that the samples $\{S_i, I_i\}$ come from a distribution $p(S, I)$ over the set of problem instances. Then, if we have a sufficient number of samples[6], we can replace the empirical risk by the true risk:

---

[6]The number of samples required is a complicated issue (Vapnik 1998, Schölkopf & Smola 2002).

$$R(\alpha) = \sum_I \sum_S L(\alpha(I), S)p(S, I). \tag{2}$$

Minimizing $R(\alpha)$ leads to a decision rule that depends on the posterior distribution $p(S|I)$ obtained by Bayes rule $p(S|I) = p(I|S)p(S)/p(I)$. To see this, we rewrite Equation 2 as $R(\alpha) = \sum_I p(I)\{\sum_S p(S|I)L(\alpha(I), S)\}$, where we have expressed $p(S, I) = p(S|I)p(I)$. So the best decision $\alpha(I)$ for a specific image I is given by

$$\alpha^*(I) = \arg\min_\alpha \sum_S p(S|I)L(\alpha(I), S), \tag{3}$$

and depends on the posterior distribution $p(S|I)$. Hence, Bayes arises naturally when you start from the risk function specified by Equation 2.

There are two points to be made here. First, the use of the Bayes posterior $p(S|I)$ follows logically from trying to minimize the number of misclassifications in the empirical risk (provided there are a sufficient number of samples). Second, it is possible to have an algorithm, or a network, that computes $\alpha(.)$ and minimizes the Bayes risk but that does not explicitly represent the probability distributions $p(I|S)$ and $p(S)$. For example, Liu et al. (1995) compared the performance of ideal observers for object recognition with networks using radial basis functions (Poggio & Girosi 1990). It is possible that the radial basis networks, given sufficient examples and having sufficient degrees of freedom, are effectively doing Bayesian inference.

Learning Probability Distributions

Recent studies show considerable statistical regularities in natural images and scene properties that help tame the problems of complexity and ambiguity in ways that can be exploited by biological and artificial visual systems. The theoretical difficulties of the Bayesian approach reduce to two issues. First, can we learn the probability distributions $p(I|S)$ and $p(S)$ from real data? Second, can we find algorithms that can compute the best estimators $\alpha^*(.)$? We briefly review the advances in learning distributions $p(I|S)$, $p(S)$, $p(I)$, $p(S|I)$, and decision rules $\alpha(I)$.

The Minimax Entropy theory (Zhu et al. 1997) gives a method for learning probability models for textures $p(I|S)$, where S labels the texture (e.g., cheetah fur). These models are realistic in the sense that stochastic samples from the models appear visually similar to the texture examples that the models were trained on (see Figure 5D). Learning these models is, in principle, similar to determining the mean and variance of a Gaussian distribution from empirical samples (e.g., setting the mean of the Gaussian to be the average of the samples from the Gaussian). The inputs to Minimax Entropy learning are the same histograms of filter responses that other authors have shown as useful for describing textures (Portilla & Simoncelli 2000). The distributions learned by Minimax Entropy are typically non-Gaussian, but lie in a more general class of distributions called exponential models. More advanced models of this type can learn distributions with parameters representing hidden states (Weber et al. 2000).

For certain problems it is also possible to learn the posterior distribution $p(S|I)$ directly, which relates to directly learning a classifier $\alpha(I)$. For example, the AdaBoost learning algorithm (Freund & Schapire 1999) has been applied very successfully to build a decision rule $\alpha(I)$ for classifying between faces (seen from front-on) and nonfaces (Viola & Jones 2001). But the AdaBoost theory shows that the algorithm can also learn the posterior distributions $p(face|I)$ and $p(non face|I)$ (Hastie et al. 2001, Tu et al. 2003). Other workers have learned posterior probabilities $p(edge|\phi(I))$ and $p(not\text{-}edge|\phi(I))$, where $\phi(I)$ are local image features (Konishi et al. 2003). Similarly, Oliva and colleagues have learned a decision rule $\alpha(I)$ to determine the type of scene (urban, mountain, etc.) from feature measurements (Oliva & Schyns 2000, Oliva & Torralba 2001). Fine et al. (2003) used the statistics of the spatio-chromatic structure of natural scenes to segment natural images into regions likely to be part of the same surface. They computed the probability of whether or not two points within an image fall on the same surface given measurements of luminance and color differences.

Visual Inference

It is necessary to have algorithms to perform Bayesian inference after the probability distributions have been learned. The complexity of vision makes it very unlikely that we can directly learn a classifier $\alpha(I)$ to solve all visual tasks. (The brain may be able to do this but we don't know how to). Recently, however, there have been some promising new algorithms for Bayesian inference. Particle filters have been shown to be very useful for tracking objects over time (Isard & Blake 1998). Message passing algorithms, such as belief propagation, have had some success (Freeman et al. 2000). Tu & Zhu (2002) have developed a general purpose algorithm for Bayesian inference known as the Data Driven Markov Chain Monte Carlo (DDMCMC). This algorithm has been very successful at segmenting images when evaluated on datasets with specified ground truth. It works, loosely speaking, by using low level cues to propose high-level models (scene descriptions), which are validated or rejected by generative models. It therefore combines bottom-up and top-down processing in a way suggestive of the feedforward and feedback pathways in the brain, described in the next section. The algorithm has been extended to combine segmentation with the detection and recognition of faces and text (Tu et al. 2003).

NEURAL IMPLICATIONS

What are the neural implications of Bayesian models? The graphical structure of these models often makes it straightforward to map them onto networks and suggests neural implementations. The notion of incorporating prior probabilities in visual inference is frequently associated with top-down biases on decisions. However, some prior probabilities are likely built into the feedforward processes through lateral connections. More dramatically, some types of inverse inference (e.g., to deal with ambiguities of occlusion, rotation in depth, or background clutter) may require an internal generative process that in some sense mirrors aspects of the external generative model used for inference (Grenander 1996, Mumford 1992, Rao & Ballard 1999, Tu & Zhu 2002a, Tu et al. 2003) or for learning (Dayan et al. 1995, Hinton & Ghahramani 1997). There is evidence that descending pathways in cortex may be involved in computations that implement model-based inference using bottom-up and top-down interactions of the sort suggested by the phenomena of perceptual explaining away. In the next two sections, we discuss Bayesian computations in networks with lateral connections and in larger-scale cortical models that combine bottom-up with top-down information.

Network Models with Lateral Connections

One class of Bayesian models can be implemented by parallel networks with local interactions. These include a temporal motion model (Burgi et al. 2000), which was designed to be consistent with neural mechanisms. In this model, the priors and likelihood functions are implemented by synaptic weights. Another promising approach is to model the lateral connections within area MT/V5 to account for the integration and segmentation of image motion (Koechlin et al. 1999).

Anatomical constraints will sometimes bias the processing of information in a way that can be interpreted in terms of prior constraints. For instance, the specific connections of binocular sensitive cells in primary visual cortex will dictate the way the visual system solves the correspondence problem for stereopsis. Some recent psychophysical work suggests that the connections between simple and complex binocular cells implement a preference for small disparities (Read 2002).

There are also proposed neural mechanisms for representing uncertainty in neural populations and thereby give a mechanism for weighted cue combination. The most plausible candidate is population encoding (Pouget et al. 2000, Oram et al. 1998, Sanger 1996).

Combining Bottom-Up and Top-Down Processing

There is a long history to theories of perception and cognition involving top-down feedback or analysis by synthesis (MacKay 1956). The generative aspect of Bayesian models is suggestive of the ascending and descending pathways that connect the visual areas in primates (Bullier 2001, Lamme & Roelfsema 2000, Lee & Mumford 2003, Zipser et al. 1996, Albright & Stoner 2002). The key Bayesian aspect is model-based fitting in which models need to compare their predictions to the image information represented earlier, such as in V1.

A possible role for higher-level visual areas may be to represent hypotheses regarding object properties, represented, for example, in the lateral occipital complex (Lerner et al. 2001, Grill-Spector et al. 2001), which could be used to resolve

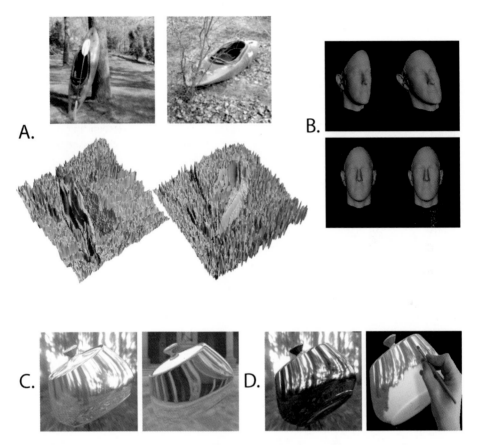

Figure 1 Visual complexity and ambiguity. (*A*) The same object, a kayak, can produce different images. The plots below the images show surface plots of the intensity as a function of position, illustrating the complex variations typical of natural image data that result from a change in view and environment. (*B*) Different shapes (three-quarter views of two different facial surfaces in the *top panel*) can produce the same image (frontal view of the two faces in the *bottom panel*) with an appropriate change of illumination direction. (*C*) The same material can produce different images. A shiny silver pot reflects completely different patterns depending on its illumination environment. (*D*) Different materials can produce the same images. The image of a silver pot could be the result of paint (*right-most panel*). The silver pot renderings were produced by Bruce Hartung using illumination maps made available at: http://www.debevec.org/Probes/ (Debevec 1998).

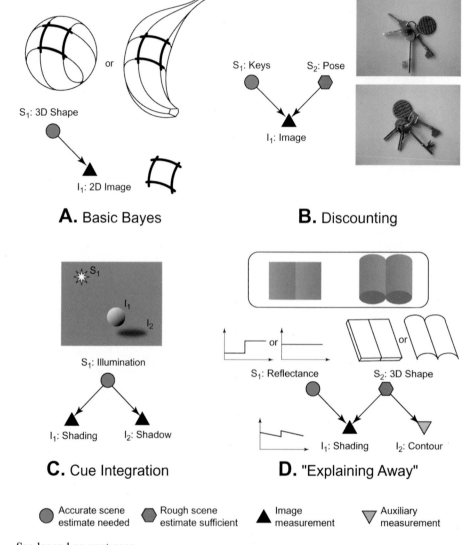

A. Basic Bayes

B. Discounting

C. Cue Integration

D. "Explaining Away"

See legend on next page

Figure 4 Four simple categories of influence graphs. (*A*) Basic Bayes. The four curved line segments are consistent with a spherical and saddle-shaped surface patch (and an infinite family of other 3-D interpretations). Human observers prefer the convex spherical interpretation (Mamassian & Landy 1998). (*B*) Discounting. A given object or object class can give rise to an infinite variety of images because of variations introduced by confounding variables, such as pose, viewpoint, illumination, and background clutter. Robust object recognition requires some degree of object invariance or constancy requiring vision to discount confounding variables, such as pose, illustrated here. There is a one-to-one relationship between graph structure and factorizing the joint probability. If I_i and S_j indicate the ith image and j^{th} object variables, respectively, then $p(\ldots, S_j \ldots, I_i, \ldots)$ is the joint probability. For this graph, $p(S_1, S_2, I) = p(I|S_1, S_2)p(S_1)p(S_2)$. (*C*) Cue integration. A single cause in a scene can give rise to more than one effect in the image. Illumination position affects both the shading on the ball and the relationship between the ball and shadow positions in the image. Both kinds of image measurement can, in principle, be combined to yield a more reliable estimate of illumination direction than either alone, and it is an empirical question to find out if human vision combines such cues, and if so, how optimally. For this graph, $p(S_1, I_1, I_2) = p(I_1|S_1)p(I_2|S_1)p(S_1)$. (*D*) Explaining away. An image measurement (ambiguous horizontal shading gradients) can be caused by a change in reflectance or a change in 3-D shape. A change in the probability of one of them being the true cause of the shading (from an auxiliary contour measurement) can change the probability of the putative cause (from different to same apparent reflectance). For this graph, $p(S_1, S_2, I_1, I_2)$ $= p(I_2|S_2)p(I_1|S_1, S_2)p(S_1)p(S_2)$.

ambiguities in the incoming retinal image measurements represented in V1. These hypotheses could predict incoming data through feedback and be tested by computing a difference signal or residual at the earlier level (Mumford 1992, Rao & Ballard 1999). Thus, low activity at an early level would mean a good fit or explanation of the image measurements. Experimental support for this possibility comes from fMRI data (Murray et al. 2002, Humphrey et al. 1997). Earlier fMRI work by a number of groups has shown that the human lateral occipital complex (LOC) has increased activity during object perception. Murray et al. use fMRI to show that when local visual information is perceptually organized into whole objects, activity in human primary visual cortex (V1) decreases over the same period that activity in higher, lateral occipital areas (LOC) increases. The authors interpret the activity changes in terms of high-level hypotheses that compete to explain away the incoming sensory data.

There are two alternative theoretical possibilities for why early visual activity is reduced. High-level areas may explain away the image and cause the early areas to be completely suppressed—high-level areas tell lower levels to "shut up." Such a mechanism would be consistent with the high metabolic cost of neuronal spikes (Lennie 2003). Alternatively, high-level areas might sharpen the responses of the early areas by reducing activity that is inconsistent with the high level interpretation—high-level areas tell lower levels to "stop gossiping." The second possibility seems more consistent with some single-unit recording experiments (Lee et al. 2002). Lee et al. have shown that cells in V1 and V2 of macaque monkeys respond to the apparently high-level task of detecting stimuli that pop-out owing to shape-from-shading. These responses changed with the animal's behavioral adaptation to contingencies, suggesting dependence on experience and utility.

Lee & Mumford (2003) review a number of neurophysiological studies consistent with a model of the interactions between cortical areas based on particle filter methods, which are non-Gaussian extensions of Kalman filters that use Monte Carlo methods. Their model is consistent with the "stop gossiping" idea. In other work, Yu & Dayan (2002) raise the intriguing possibility that acetylcholine levels may be associated with the certainty of top-down information in visual inference.

Implementation of the Decision Rule

One critical component of the Bayesian model is the consideration of the utility (gain or negative loss in decision theory terminology) associated with each decision. Where and how is this utility encoded? Platt & Glimcher (1999) systematically varied the expectation and utility (juice reward) linked to an eye movement performed by a monkey. The activity of cells in one area of the parietal cortex was modulated by the expected reward and the probability that the eye movement will result in a reward. It will be interesting to see whether similar activity modulations occur within the ventral stream for object recognition decisions.

Gold & Shadlen (Gold & Shadlen 2001) propose neural computations that can account for categorical decisions about sensory stimuli (e.g., whether a field of random dots is moving one way or the other) by accumulating information over time represented by a single quantity representing the logarithm of the likelihood ratio favoring one alternative over another.

CONCLUSIONS

The Bayesian perspective yields a uniform framework for studying object perception. We have reviewed work that highlights several advantages of this perspective. First, Bayesian theories explicitly model uncertainty. This is important in accounting for how the visual system combines large amounts of objectively ambiguous information to yield percepts that are rarely ambiguous. Second, in the context of specific experiments, Bayesian theories are optimal, and thus define ideal observers. Ideal observers characterize visual information for a task and can thus be critical for interpreting psychophysical and neural results. Third, Bayesian methods allow the development of quantitative theories at the information processing level, avoiding premature commitment to specific neural mechanisms. This is closely related to the importance of extensibility in theories. Bayesian models provide for extensions to more complicated problems involving natural images and functional tasks as illustrated in recent advances in computer vision. Fourth, Bayesian theories emphasize the role of the generative model and thus tie naturally to the growing body of work on graphical models and Bayesian networks in other areas, such as language, speech, concepts, and reasoning. The generative models also suggest top-down feedback models of information processing in the cortex.

ACKNOWLEDGMENTS

Supported by NIH RO1 EY11507-001, EY02587, EY12691 and EY013875; NSF SBR-9631682, 0240148, HFSP RG00109/1999-B; and EPSRC GR/R57157/01. We thank Zili Liu for helpful comments.

The *Annual Review of Psychology* is online at http://psych.annualreviews.org

LITERATURE CITED

Albert MK. 2000. The generic viewpoint assumption and Bayesian inference. *Perception* 29:601–8

Albright TD, Stoner GR. 2002. Contextual influences on visual processing. *Annu. Rev. Neurosci.* 25:339–79

Atick JJ, Griffin PA, Redlich AN. 1996. Statistical approach to shape from shading: reconstruction of three-dimensional face surfaces from single two-dimensional images. *Neural Comput.* 8:1321–40

Barlow HB. 1962. A method of determining the overall quantum efficiency of visual discriminations. *J. Physiol.* 160:155–68

Berger J. 1985. *Statistical Decision Theory and Bayesian Analysis.* New York: Springer-Verlag

Bertamini M. 2001. The importance of being

convex: an advantage for convexity when judging position. *Perception* 30:1295–310

Biederman I. 2000. Recognizing depth-rotated objects: a review of recent research and theory. *Spat. Vis.* 13:241–53

Blake A, Bülthoff HH. 1990. Does the brain know the physics of specular reflection? *Nature* 343:165–69

Bloj MG, Kersten D, Hurlbert AC. 1999. Perception of three-dimensional shape influences colour perception through mutual illumination. *Nature* 402:877–79

Brady MJ, Kersten D. 2003. Bootstrapped learning of novel objects. *J. Vis.* 3:413–22

Brainard DH, Freeman WT. 1997. Bayesian color constancy. *J. Opt. Soc. Am. A* 14:1393–411

Buckley D, Frisby JP, Freeman J. 1994. Lightness perception can be affected by surface curvature from stereopsis. *Perception* 23:869–81

Bullier J. 2001. Integrated model of visual processing. *Brain Res. Brain Res. Rev.* 36:96–107

Bülthoff HH, Mallot HA. 1988. Integration of depth modules: stereo and shading. *J. Opt. Soc. Am. A* 5:1749–58

Bülthoff HH, Yuille A. 1991. Bayesian models for seeing surfaces and depth. *Comments Theor. Biol.* 2:283–314

Burgi PY, Yuille AL, Grzywacz NM. 2000. Probabilistic motion estimation based on temporal coherence. *Neural Comput.* 12:1839–67

Clark JJ, Yuille AL. 1990. *Data Fusion for Sensory Information Processing.* Boston: Kluwer Acad.

Dana KJ, van Ginneken B, Nayar SK, Koenderink JJ. 1999. Reflectance and texture of real world surfaces. *ACM Trans. Graph.* 18:1–34

Dayan P, Hinton GE, Neal RM, Zemel RS. 1995. The Helmholtz machine. *Neural Comput.* 7:889–904

Debevec PE. 1998. *Rendering synthetic objects into real scenes: bridging traditional and image-based graphics with global illumina-tion and high dynamic range photography.* Presented at SIGGRAPH

Dror RO, Leung TK, Adelson EH, Willsky AS. 2001. *Statistics of real-world illumination.* Presented at Proc. CVPR, Hawaii

Eckstein MP, Thomas JP, Palmer J, Shimozaki SS. 2000. A signal detection model predicts the effects of set size on visual search accuracy for feature, conjunction, triple conjunction, and disjunction displays. *Percept. Psychophys.* 62:425–51

Elder JH, Goldberg RM. 2002. Ecological statistics of gestalt laws for the perceptual organization of contours. *J. Vis.* 2:324–53

Ernst MO, Banks MS. 2002. Humans integrate visual and haptic information in a statistically optimal fashion. *Nature* 415:429–33

Evgeniou T, Pontil M, Poggio T. 2000. Regularization networks and support vector machines. *Adv. Comput. Math.* 13:1–50

Feldman J. 2001. Bayesian contour integration. *Percept. Psychophys.* 63:1171–82

Field DJ. 1987. Relations between the statistics of natural images and the response properties of cortical cells. *J. Opt. Soc. Am. A* 4:2379–94

Fine I, MacLeod DIA, Boynton GM. 2003. Visual segmentation based on the luminance and chromaticity statistics of natural scenes. Special issue on Bayesian and statistical approaches to vision. *J. Opt. Soc. Am. A* 20:1283–91

Fleming RW, Dror RO, Adelson EH. 2003. Real-world illumination and the perception of surface reflectance properties. *J. Vis.* 3:347–68

Freeman WT. 1994. The generic viewpoint assumption in a framework for visual perception. *Nature* 368:542–45

Freeman WT, Pasztor EC, Carmichael OT. 2000. Learning low-level vision. *Int. J. Comput. Vis.* 40:25–47

Freund Y, Schapire R. 1999. A short introduction to boosting. *J. Jpn. Soc. Artif. Intell.* 14:771–80

Geisler WS, Albrecht DG. 1995. Bayesian analysis of identification performance in monkey visual cortex: nonlinear mechanisms and stimulus certainty. *Vis. Res.* 35:2723–30

Geisler WS, Kersten D. 2002. Illusions, perception and Bayes. *Nat. Neurosci.* 5:508–10

Geisler WS, Perry JS, Super BJ, Gallogly DP. 2001. Edge co-occurrence in natural images predicts contour grouping performance. *Vis. Res.* 41:711–24

Gepshtein S, Banks MS. 2003. Viewing geometry determines how vision and haptics combine in size perception. *Curr. Biol.* 13:483–88

Gold JI, Shadlen MN. 2001. Neural computations that underlie decisions about sensory stimuli. *Trends Cogn. Sci.* 5:10–16

Green DM, Swets JA. 1974. *Signal Detection Theory and Psychophysics.* Huntington, NY: Krieger

Grenander U. 1996. *Elements of Pattern Theory.* Baltimore, MD: Johns Hopkins Univ. Press

Grill-Spector K. 2003. The neural basis of object perception. *Curr. Opin. Neurobiol.* 13: 1–8

Grill-Spector K, Kourtzi Z, Kanwisher N. 2001. The lateral occipital complex and its role in object recognition. *Vis. Res.* 41:1409–22

Hastie T, Tibshirani R, Friedman J. 2001. *The Elements of Statistical Learning.* New York: Springer

Helmholtz H. 1867. *Handbuch der Physiologischen Optik.* Leipzig: Voss. (English tranl. 1924 JPC Southall as *Treatise on Physiological Optics*)

Hill H, Bruce V. 1993. Independent effects of lighting, orientation, and stereopis on the hollow-face illusion. *Perception* 22:887–97

Hillis JM, Ernst MO, Banks MS, Landy MS. 2002. Combining sensory information: mandatory fusion within, but not between, senses. *Science* 298:1627–30

Hinton GE, Ghahramani Z. 1997. Generative models for discovering sparse distributed representations. *Philos. Trans. R. Soc. London Ser. B* 352:(1358):1177–90

Howe CQ, Purves D. 2002. Range image statistics can explain the anomalous perception of length. *Proc. Natl. Acad. Sci. USA* 99:13184–88

Humphrey GK, Goodale MA, Bowen CV, Gati JS, Vilis T, et al. 1997. Differences in perceived shape from shading correlate with activity in early visual areas. *Curr. Biol.* 7:144–47

Isard M, Blake A. 1998. Condensation—conditional density propagation for visual tracking. *Int. J. Comput. Vis.* 29:5–28

Jacobs RA. 2002. What determines visual cue reliability? *Trends Cogn. Sci.* 6:345–50

Jensen HW, Marschner SR, Levoy M, Hanrahan P. 2001. *A practical model for subsurface light transport.* Presented at Computer Graphics (SIGGRAPH)

Kanizsa G, Gerbino W. 1976. Convexity and symmetry in figure-ground organisation. In *Vision and Artifact*, ed. M Henle. New York: Springer

Kersten D. 1999. High-level vision as statistical inference. In *The New Cognitive Neurosciences*, ed. MS Gazzaniga, pp. 353–63. Cambridge, MA: MIT Press. 2nd ed.

Kersten D, Mamassian P, Knill DC. 1997. Moving cast shadows induce apparent motion in depth. *Perception* 26:171–92

Kersten D, Schrater PW. 2002. Pattern inference theory: a probabilistic approach to vision. In *Perception and the Physical World*, ed. R Mausfeld, D Heyer. Chichester: Wiley

Kersten D, Yuille A. 2003. Bayesian models of object perception. *Curr. Opin. Neurobiol.* 13:1–9

Knill DC. 1998. Discrimination of planar surface slant from texture: human and ideal observers compared. *Vis. Res.* 38:1683–711

Knill DC, Field D, Kersten D. 1990. Human discrimination of fractal images. *J. Opt. Soc. Am. A* 7:1113–23

Knill DC, Kersten D. 1991. Apparent surface curvature affects lightness perception. *Nature* 351:228–30

Knill DC, Kersten D, Yuille A. 1996. Introduction: a Bayesian formulation of visual perception. See Knill & Richards 1996, pp. 1–21

Knill DC, Richards W. 1996. *Perception as Bayesian Inference.* Cambridge, UK: Cambridge Univ. Press

Koechlin E, Anton JL, Burnod Y. 1999. Bayesian inference in populations of cortical neurons: a model of motion integration and segmentation in area MT. *Biol. Cybern.* 80:25–44

Koenderink JJ, van Doorn AJ, Kappers AM, Todd JT. 2001. Ambiguity and the 'mental eye' in pictorial relief. *Perception* 30:431–48

Konishi SM, Yuille AL, Coughlan JM, Zhu SC. 2003. Statistical edge detection: learning and evaluating edge cues. *Pattern Anal. Mach. Intell.* 1:37–48

Lamme VA, Roelfsema PR. 2000. The distinct modes of vision offered by feedforward and recurrent processing. *Trends Neurosci.* 23:571–79

Land EH, McCann JJ. 1971. Lightness and the retinex theory. *J. Opt. Soc. Am.* 61:1–11

Landy MS, Kojima H. 2001. Ideal cue combination for localizing texture-defined edges. *J. Opt. Soc. Am. A Opt. Image Sci. Vis.* 18:2307–20

Landy MS, Maloney LT, Johnston EB, Young M. 1995. Measurement and modeling of depth cue combination: in defense of weak fusion. *Vis. Res.* 35:389–412

Langer MS, Bülthoff HH. 2001. A prior for global convexity in local shape-from-shading. *Perception* 30:403–10

Lee TS, Mumford D. 2003. Hierarchical Bayesian inference in the visual cortex. *J. Opt. Soc. Am. A* 20:1434–48

Lee TS, Yang CF, Romero RD, Mumford D. 2002. Neural activity in early visual cortex reflects behavioral experience and higher-order perceptual saliency. *Nat. Neurosci.* 5:589–97

Legge GE, Hooven TA, Klitz TS, Mansfield JS, Tjan BS. 2002. Mr. Chips 2002: new insights from an ideal-observer model of reading. *Vis. Res.* 42:2219–34

Lennie P. 2003. The cost of cortical computation. *Curr. Biol.* 13:493–97

Leopold DA, O'Toole AJ, Vetter T, Blanz V. 2001. Prototype-referenced shape encoding revealed by high-level aftereffects. *Nat. Neurosci.* 4:89–94

Lerner Y, Hendler T, Ben-Bashat D, Harel M,

Malach R. 2001. A hierarchical axis of object processing stages in the human visual cortex. *Cereb. Cortex* 11:287–97

Liu Z, Kersten D. 1998. 2D observers for human 3D object recognition? *Vis. Res.* 38:2507–19

Liu Z, Kersten D. 2003. 3D symmetric shapes are discriminated more efficiently than asymmetric ones. *J. Opt. Soc. Am. A* 20:1331–40

Liu Z, Kersten D, Knill DC. 1999. Stimulus information or internal representation?—A case study in human object recognition. *Vis. Res.* 39:603–12

Liu Z, Knill DC, Kersten D. 1995. Object classification for human and ideal observers. *Vis. Res.* 35:549–68

Lorenceau J, Shiffrar M. 1992. The influence of terminators on motion integration across space. *Vis. Res.* 32:263–73

MacKay DM. 1956. The epistemological problem for automata. In *Automata Studies*, ed. CE Shannon, J McCarthy, pp. 235–50. Princeton: Princeton Univ. Press

Maloney LT. 2002. Statistical decision theory and biological vision. In *Perception and the Physical World*, ed. D Heyer, R Mausfeld, pp. 145–89. Chichester, UK: Wiley

Mamassian P, Goutcher R. 2001. Prior knowledge on the illumination position. *Cognition* 81:B1–9

Mamassian P, Knill DC, Kersten D. 1998. The perception of cast shadows. *Trends Cogn. Sci.* 2:288–95

Mamassian P, Landy MS. 1998. Observer biases in the 3D interpretation of line drawings. *Vis. Res.* 38:2817–32

Mamassian P, Landy MS. 2001. Interaction of visual prior constraints. *Vis. Res.* 41:2653–68

Mamassian P, Landy MS, Maloney LT. 2002. Bayesian modelling of visual perception. See Rao et al. 2002, pp. 13–36

Marschner SR, Westin SH, Lafortune EPF, Torrance KE. 2000. Image-based measurement of the bidirectional reflectance distribution function. *Appl. Opt.* 39:2592–600

McDermott J, Weiss Y, Adelson EH. 2001. Beyond junctions: nonlocal form constraints on motion interpretation. *Perception* 30:905–23

Mumford D. 1992. On the computational architecture of the neocortex. II. The role of cortico-cortical loops. *Biol. Cybern.* 66:241–51

Murray SO, Kersten D, Olshausen BA, Schrater P, Woods DL. 2002. Shape perception reduces activity in human primary visual cortex. *Proc. Natl. Acad. Sci. USA* 99:15164–69

Nakayama K, Shimojo S. 1992. Experiencing and perceiving visual surfaces. *Science* 257:1357–63

Oliva A, Schyns PG. 2000. Diagnostic colors mediate scene recognition. *Cogn. Psychol.* 41:176–210

Oliva A, Torralba A. 2001. Modeling the shape of the scene: a holistic representation of the spatial envelope. *Int. J. Comput. Vis.* 42:145–75

Olshausen BA, Field DJ. 2000. Vision and the coding of natural images. *Am. Sci.* 88:238–45

Oram MW, Foldiak P, Perrett DI, Sengpiel F. 1998. The 'ideal Homunculus': decoding neural population signals. *Trends Neurosci.* 21:259–65

Parish DH, Sperling G. 1991. Object spatial frequencies, retinal spatial frequencies, noise, and the efficiency of letter discrimination. *Vis. Res.* 31:1399–415

Parraga CA, Troscianko T, Tolhurst DJ. 2000. The human visual system is optimised for processing the spatial information in natural visual images. *Curr. Biol.* 10:35–38

Pearl J. 1988. *Probabilistic Reasoning in Intelligent Systems: Networks of Plausible Inference.* San Mateo, CA: Morgan Kaufmann

Pelli DG, Farell B, Moore DC. 2003. The remarkable inefficiency of word recognition. *Nature* 243:752–56

Pizlo Z. 1994. A theory of shape constancy based on perspective invariants. *Vis. Res.* 34:1637–58

Pizlo Z. 2001. Perception viewed as an inverse problem. *Vis. Res.* 41:3145–61

Platt ML, Glimcher PW. 1999. Neural correlates of decision variables in parietal cortex. *Nature* 400:233–38

Poggio T, Edelman S. 1990. A network that learns to recognize three-dimensional objects. *Nature* 343:263–66

Poggio T, Girosi F. 1990. Regularization algorithms for learning that are equivalent to multilayer networks. *Science* 247:978–82

Portilla J, Simoncelli EP. 2000. A parametric texture model based on joint statistics of complex wavelet coefficients. *Int. J. Comput. Vis.* 40:9–71

Pouget A, Dayan P, Zemel R. 2000. Information processing with population codes. *Nat. Rev. Neurosci.* 1:125–32

Ramachandran VS. 1985. The neurobiology of perception. *Perception* 14:97–103

Rao RP, Ballard DH. 1999. Predictive coding in the visual cortex: a functional interpretation of some extra-classical receptive-field effects. *Nat. Neurosci.* 2:79–87

Rao RPN, Olshausen BA, Lewicki MS, eds. 2002. *Probabilistic Models of the Brain: Perception and Neural Function.* Cambridge, MA: MIT Press

Read JCA. 2002. A Bayesian model of stereopsis depth and motion direction discrimination. *Biol. Cybern.* 86:117–36

Riesenhuber M, Poggio T. 2002. Neural mechanisms of object recognition. *Curr. Opin. Neurobiol.* 12:162–68

Rock I. 1983. *The Logic of Perception.* Cambridge, MA: MIT Press

Sanger TD. 1996. Probability density estimation for the interpretation of neural population codes. *J. Neurophysiol.* 76:2790–93

Saunders JA, Knill DC. 2001. Perception of 3D surface orientation from skew symmetry. *Vis. Res.* 41:3163–83

Schölkopf B, Smola AJ. 2002. *Learning with Kernels: Support Vector Machines, Regularization, Optimization, and Beyond.* Cambridge, MA: MIT Press

Schrater PR, Kersten D. 2000. How optimal depth cue integration depends on the task. *Int. J. Comput. Vis.* 40:73–91

Schrater PR, Kersten D. 2002. Vision,

psychophysics, and Bayes. See Rao et al. 2002b, pp. 39–64

Schrater PR, Knill DC, Simoncelli EP. 2000. Mechanisms of visual motion detection. *Nat. Neurosci.* 1:64–68

Simoncelli EP, Olshausen BA. 2001. Natural image statistics and neural representation. *Annu. Rev. Neurosci.* 24:1193–216

Sinha P, Adelson E. 1993. *Recovering reflectance and illumination in a world of painted polyhedra*. Presented at Proc. Int. Conf. Comput. Vis., 4th, Berlin

Sun J, Perona P. 1998. Where is the sun? *Nat. Neurosci.* 1:183–84

Tarr MJ, Bülthoff HH. 1995. Is human object recognition better described by geon structural descriptions or by multiple views? Comment on Biederman and Gerhardstein (1993). *J. Exp. Psychol. Hum. Percept. Perform.* 21:1494–505

Tenenbaum JB. 2000. Bayesian modeling of human concept learning. *Advances in Neural Information Processing Systems*, ed. Solla S, Leen T, Muller KR, 12:59–65. Cambridge, MA: MIT Press

Tenenbaum JB, Griffiths TL. 2001. Generalization, similarity, and Bayesian inference. *Behav. Brain Sci.* 24:629–40; discussion 652–791

Tenenbaum JB, Xu F. 2000. Word learning as Bayesian inference. *Proc. Ann. Conf. Cogn. Sci. Soc., 22nd*, eds. Gleitman LR, Joshi AK. Mahwah, NJ: Lawerence Erlbaum Assoc.

Tjan BS, Braje WL, Legge GE, Kersten D. 1995. Human efficiency for recognizing 3-D objects in luminance noise. *Vis. Res.* 35:3053–69

Troje NF, Kersten D. 1999. Viewpoint dependent recognition of familiar faces. *Perception* 28:483–87

Tu Z, Chen A, Yuille AL, Zhu SC. 2003. Image parsing. *Proc. Int. Conf. Comput. Vis.*, Cannes, France

Tu Z, Zhu S-C. 2002. Image segmentation by data-driven Markov chain Monte Carlo. *IEEE Trans. Pattern Anal. Mach. Intell.* 24:657–73

Ullman S. 1996. *High-Level Vision: Object Recognition and Visual Cognition.* Cambridge, MA: MIT Press

Ullman S, Basri R. 1991. Recognition by linear combination of models. *IEEE Trans. Pattern Anal. Mach. Intell.* 13:992–1006

VanRullen R, Thorpe SJ. 2001. Is it a bird? Is it a plane? Ultra-rapid visual categorisation of natural and artifactual objects. *Perception* 30:655–68

Vapnik VN. 1998. *Statistical Learning Theory.* New York: Wiley

Vetter T, Troje NF. 1997. Separation of texture and shape in images of faces for image coding and synthesis. *J. Opt. Soc. Am. A* 14:2152–61

Viola P, Jones MJ. 2001. Robust real-time object detection. *Proc. IEEE Workshop Stat. Comput. Theor. Vis.*, Vancouver, Can.

Weber M, Welling M, Perona P. 2000. *Unsupervised Learning of Models for Recognition.* Presented at Proc. Eur. Conf. Comp. Vis., 6th, Dublin, Ireland

Weiss Y, Simoncelli EP, Adelson EH. 2002. Motion illusions as optimal percepts. *Nat. Neurosci.* 5:598–604

Yonas A, ed. 2003. Development of space perception. In *Encyclopedia of Cognitive Science*, ed. R Anand, pp. 96–100. London, UK: Macmillan

Yu AJ, Dayan P. 2002. Acetylcholine in cortical inference. *Neural Netw.* 15:719–30

Yuille AL, Bülthoff HH. 1996. Bayesian decision theory and psychophysics. See Knill & Richards 1996, pp. 123–61

Yuille AL, Coughlan JM, Konishi S. 2001. *The KGBR viewpoint-lighting ambiguity and its resolution by generic constraints*. Presented at Proc. Int. Conf. Comput. Vis., Vancouver, Canada

Yuille A, Coughlan JM, Konishi S. 2003. The KGBR viewpoint-lighting ambiguity. *J. Opt. Soc. Am. A Opt. Image Sci. Vis.* 20:24–31

Yuille A, Grzywacz N. 1988. A computational theory for the perception of coherent visual motion. *Nature* 333:71–74

Zhu SC. 1999. Embedding gestalt laws in

Markov random fields. *IEEE Trans. Pattern Anal. Mach. Intell.* 21:1170–87

Zhu SC, Mumford D. 1997. Prior learning and Gibbs reaction-diffusion. *IEEE Trans. PAMI* 19:1236–50

Zhu SC, Wu Y, Mumford D. 1997. Mini-max entropy principle and its applications to texture modeling. *Neural Comput.* 9:1627–60

Zipser K, Lamme VA, Schiller PH. 1996. Contextual modulation in primary visual cortex. *J. Neurosci.* 16:7376–89

Annu. Rev. Psychol. 2004. 55:305–31
doi: 10.1146/annurev.psych.55.090902.141521
Copyright © 2004 by Annual Reviews. All rights reserved
First published online as a Review in Advance on October 27, 2003

DEVELOPMENT IN MIDLIFE

Margie E. Lachman

*Psychology Department, Brandeis University, Waltham, Massachusetts 02454;
email: Lachman@Brandeis.edu*

Key Words   biopsychosocial changes, generativity, health and well-being, middle age, sense of control, work/family balance

■ **Abstract**   The midlife period in the lifespan is characterized by a complex interplay of multiple roles. The goal of this chapter is to summarize research findings on the central themes and salient issues of midlife such as balancing work and family responsibilities in the midst of the physical and psychological changes associated with aging. The field of midlife development is emerging in the context of large demographic shifts in the population. A section on the phenomenology of midlife development presents images and expectations including the seemingly disparate views of midlife as a time of peak functioning and a period of crisis. Conceptual frameworks useful for studying the multiple patterns of change in midlife are presented. Findings demonstrating patterns of gains and losses are reviewed for multiple domains: cognitive functioning, personality and the self, emotions, social relationships, work, and physical health. The need for future research to illuminate and integrate the diverse aspects of midlife is highlighted.

CONTENTS

"Thoroughly unprepared we take the step into the afternoon of life; worse still, we take this step with the false presupposition that our truths and ideals will serve us as hitherto. But, we cannot live the afternoon of life according to the program of life's morning—for what was great in the morning will be little at evening, and what in the morning was true will at evening have become a lie" (Jung 1933, p. 108).

Midlife, the afternoon of life, as Jung (1933) called it in his essay on "The Stages of Life," has become a period of great interest to scholars of the lifespan. To some extent the research findings support Jung's notion that the salient issues and demands of midlife differ from earlier age periods and require adjustments to negotiate the new challenges. Moreover, midlife serves an important preparatory role in the transition to old age, the evening of life. There is, however, much evidence for continuity throughout adulthood in many realms of life, and the consistent self serves as an important resource and foundation for what comes later. What is perhaps most striking is the wide variability in the nature and course of the midlife period. As scholars begin to focus attention more directly on the middle years, it is apparent that to portray midlife is a challenging and complex task because the experiences of middle-aged adults are so diverse and variable. Nevertheless, it is possible to characterize midlife in broad strokes given that a key set of issues and challenges emerges during the middle years. There are some commonalities in the experiences of middle-aged adults even if the specific content and ways of dealing with them are quite diverse. The nature of midlife varies as a function of such factors as gender, cohort, socioeconomic status (SES), race, ethnicity, culture, region of the country, personality, marital status, parental status, employment status, and health status. The goal of this chapter is to present (*a*) a summary of the salient issues and experiences associated with midlife, (*b*) a guide to useful conceptual frameworks for studying development in the middle years, (*c*) an overview of the key research findings about change and stability during midlife in multiple domains of life, and (*d*) possible directions for future research. As we shed more light on midlife and begin to understand some of the regularities and unique challenges, the opportunities to prepare for and enhance the afternoon of life will continue to exceed those available in Jung's time.

The experiences of midlife have some common themes involving both gains and losses (Baltes 1987, Baltes et al. 1999). In describing the middle years, a central task is to identify the alternative pathways to health and well-being (Brim et al. 2004). This requires a focus on multiple trajectories of development and their interplay across major areas of life (Lachman & James 1997, Moen & Wethington 1999). The central issues center around generativity, caring, and concern for others in the work and family spheres (McAdams 2001, McAdams & de St. Aubin 1998), in the context of changes associated with aging in physical and psychological resources. Middle-aged adults are linked to the welfare of others—including children, parents, coworkers, other family members, and friends—and have much to offer society. At the same time, they are addressing their own needs for meaningful work (paid or unpaid), health, and well-being. Midlife is often the time when chronic illness or disease starts to surface, and physical problems such as high blood pressure, high cholesterol, or arthritis pain often take adults by surprise. These physical ailments, although largely treatable with medications or diet, can trigger distress because they signal aging, which is neither desirable nor valued in our culture. On the other hand, the psychological and social changes experienced in midlife are usually associated with positive changes. These may include better emotional regulation (Magai & Halpern 2001), increased wisdom and practical intelligence (Baltes et al. 1999), or a strong sense of mastery (Lachman & Bertrand 2001). The story of midlife is one of complexity, with the juxtaposition of peaks and valleys across the social, psychological, and physical domains. The need to balance multiple roles and manage the conflicts that arise is a reality that is characteristic of middle age, regardless of one's specific lifestyle or circumstances.

THE EMERGING FIELD OF MIDLIFE DEVELOPMENT

Much of the research on midlife has been conducted in the context of other age periods or specialized problems related to work or family. For example, we know a great deal about middle-aged parents from the literature on child development. From this perspective, the focus is on the children and the types of parental styles or interactions that would be most beneficial for the children's optimal development. Studies from the aging literature have focused on middle-aged adults as caregivers for their aging parents. The primary focus is typically on the older adults' welfare, with some recognition of the stresses and overload for the middle-aged adult children as a consequence of the caregiving role.

The population explosion of middle-aged adults and the increased knowledge about this age period have led to the identification of midlife as a segment of the lifespan worthy of study in its own right. The effort to differentiate midlife from other periods of human development also reflects a growing interest in the optimization of aging. If we can identify the roots of aging earlier in adulthood, it may be possible to delay, minimize, or prevent some of the changes in biological, psychological, and social functioning that occur in later life.

We have made progress over the past decade since Brim (1992, p. 171) referred to the middle years as the "last uncharted territory in human development." Despite the increase in research activity on midlife (e.g., Baruch & Brooks-Gunn 1984, Brim et al. 2004, Eichorn et al. 1981, Giele 1982, Helson & Wink 1992, Lachman 2001, Lachman & James 1997, Rossi 1994, Ryff & Seltzer 1996, Willis & Reid 1999), still less is known about this period than about other age periods such as infancy, childhood, adolescence, or old age. It is important to study the middle years, not only because of the large numbers of adults currently in this stage, but also because this period covers a large portion of an individual's lifespan. This period may have been understudied for so long because of assumptions that it is a quiet period with little change, that there is too much diversity and too little regularity to capture the midlife experience, or that middle-aged subjects are difficult to obtain for research because of their busy work and family schedules (Lachman & James 1997). Over the past 10 years there has been a growing effort to collate what we know and to go forward with a systematic examination of this period, usually considered to last between 20 and 40 years (Lachman 2001). It is also important to determine whether the knowledge we have and are gaining about midlife is tied to specific cohorts such as the baby boomers. Longitudinal and panel designs are needed to examine whether the patterns identified are robust and whether they generalize to other cohorts in middle age.

DEMOGRAPHIC TRENDS

The U.S. Census Bureau (2000) report shows there are 73.6 million middle-aged adults, between the ages of 40 and 59, comprising about 26% of the population. Over the past decade, the fastest-growing age segment of the population was the 50- to 54-year age group, with an increase of 55%, and the second-fastest growth was in the 45- to 49-year-old group, which increased 45% (U.S. Census Bureau 2000). This large increase represents the movement of the baby boom cohort into middle age. It is not surprising, given this large bulge in the middle-aged population, that interest in research on the middle years of the lifespan has also increased dramatically during this same decade.

At the same time, those over age 90 are also increasing in vast numbers, as the third-fastest growing group over the past decade (U.S. Census Bureau 2000). These demographic changes have a profound impact on the lives of those in midlife. On the one hand, because of the large cohort size, large numbers of adults are reaching retirement age, which strains health care and social security. Increasingly large numbers of those in midlife have parents who are living longer and entering very old age. The demands and rewards of caregiving and multigenerational living are important aspects of middle-aged adults' lives. While they are raising or launching their own children and negotiating the demands of the workplace, concerns about parents' safety and health permeate many middle-aged lives (Putney & Bengtson 2001). In some cases the parents live nearby or with their children and daily attention may be required. In other cases, when parents live a long distance away, the daily concerns are different but not necessarily less stressful. Many of these demographic changes also have benefits and advantages. For example, many older, retired adults can help to care for the children of middle-aged workers. The large baby boom cohort also wields power and has a good deal of influence over sociopolitical issues.

The Baby Boom Generation

The baby boom generation, those born between 1946 and 1964, is moving through midlife in record numbers. In the year 2000, there were more than 80 million baby boomers ages 35 to 54 in the United States (U.S. Census Bureau 2000). This cohort represents about 30% of the U.S. population.

It is important to place the baby boomers in a sociodemographic context and to consider the implications for their midlife development. A number of factors stemming from the confluence of demographic, historical, and societal changes have created a unique set of circumstances. The most pronounced distinction is that the baby boomers represent an extremely large cohort (Easterlin 1980). Thus, there is more competition for resources and jobs. The effects of history also are important, as was clearly demonstrated by the timing of the Great Depression for cohorts born in the 1920s (Elder 1979). Major historical events such as the Korean and Vietnam wars and the assassinations of John F. Kennedy and Martin Luther King are part of the collective baby boomer experience. The timing and sequencing of individual life events also may have an impact. The baby boom cohort had fewer children at later ages than their parents. Other lifestyle factors such as the increase in number of mothers of young children in the workforce has led to conflict between work and family needs for dual-career couples. More research is needed to investigate the psychosocial implications of these sociodemographic factors.

Some researchers are investigating the extent to which the baby boom generation is different from other cohorts who have already moved or will move through middle age. Carr (2004) compared the experiences of the baby boom with cohorts born earlier (the pre-World War II, silent generation, born 1931–1943) and later (the baby bust generation, born 1965–1970), and examined the implications of macrosocial patterns for microlevel outcomes. She identified cohort differences in occupational and educational attainment, values, and expectations, and examined the impact of historical shifts in access to opportunities, roles, and resources on psychological well-being. Baby bust women had the greatest access to resources that enhance self-esteem, such as higher education, higher-status occupations, and fewer family obstacles to work, which resulted in higher levels of self-acceptance compared to the older cohorts. Yet the women in both the baby bust and baby boom cohorts had lower levels of environmental mastery than women from the silent generation, perhaps because of the increased pressures of balancing work opportunities and family obligations.

The cultural emphasis on youthful appearance and avoiding or minimizing the physical changes associated with aging is characteristic of the baby boom generation. For example, there has been a widespread interest in procedures to maintain a youthful appearance such as plastic surgery and Botox, as well as many types of physical exercise. In part, this emphasis may reflect the baby boomers' strong desire to take control of the aging process (Clark-Plaskie & Lachman 1999, Lachman & Firth 2004). Nevertheless, it is important to acknowledge that the baby boomers are a diverse group culturally and ethnically. Not all baby boomers are physically fit, concerned about their appearance, or feel a strong sense of control over life. Moreover, the cohort spans 18 years, and large differences may exist between the midlife experiences of younger (late) and older (early) groups of baby boomers.

PHENOMENOLOGY OF MIDLIFE

Being in the middle of life may be akin to being in the middle of the term or semester at school, in the middle of the summer, in the middle of a trip or vacation, or in the middle of a book (Lachman & James 1997). When in the middle, it is natural to look back to see what has come before or to evaluate what has been accomplished and to look ahead to determine what comes next or remains to be done. The common experience in the middle is that one has already invested a lot in the enterprise, so one is likely to carefully consider what comes next as the threshold away from the beginning and toward the end is crossed. Not everyone is planful or reflective, so there are likely to be some who do not pause to consider the past and future in midlife. For those who are goal-oriented, midlife is often seen as a time for reflection, but not in the same way as the life review that occurs in later life (Erikson 1963), when time left is presumably shorter and emotional goals are more salient than informational ones (Carstensen et al. 1999, Fredrickson & Carstensen 1990). In later life, achieving ego integrity involves accepting life for what it has been (Erikson 1963). The emphasis in midlife may be on what remains to be done. Although those who have reached midlife are aware that time is advancing, most assume there is still a substantial, but not an infinite, amount of time left. Presumably, there is still just as much time left as has gone by. Of course with life one doesn't know the endpoint, so the timing of the middle is an estimate. Whether one thinks midlife signifies that life is half over or half is still remaining could lead to different outcomes, as optimism research suggests (Isaacowitz et al. 2000). This predicament of being in the middle of life may be an impetus for change but not necessarily a crisis.

In midlife, as in other life periods, one must make choices, and select what to do, how to invest time and resources, and what areas to change (Baltes & Baltes 1990). To the extent that one has some control over outcomes, one also may take responsibility or blame when things do not go well (Lachman & Firth 2004). A serious accident, loss, or illness in midlife often leads to a major restructuring of time and a reassessment of priorities in life (Aldwin & Levenson 2001). Sometimes changes are precipitated by "wake-up calls." Many people know of someone who became sick, developed a chronic illness, or died in middle age, and this can trigger a new appreciation for life. Leisure time typically takes a backseat in midlife, while an increasing amount of time is spent juggling multiple roles and achieving a balance of work and family with personal interests and health needs.

Subjective Age

According to the online Oxford English Dictionary (2000), the word "midlife" first appeared in Funk and Wagnall's Standard Dictionary in 1895. Midlife is defined as "the part of life between youth and old age." The boundaries for midlife are fuzzy, with no clear demarcation. Subjective views of the midlife period show a wide age range (American Board of Family Practice 1990). The most common conception is that midlife begins at 40 and ends at 60 or 65, when old age begins

(Lachman et al. 1994, Lachman & James 1997). Although most surveys report that 40 is the modal entry year and 60 is the modal exit year, there is tremendous variability in the expected timing of midlife (Lachman et al. 1995). Those between ages 40 and 60 are typically considered middle-aged, but there is at least a 10-year range on either end, so that it is not uncommon for some to consider middle age to begin at 30 and end at 75 (Lachman 2001). In a study conducted by the National Council on Aging (2000), nearly half of the respondents ages 65 to 69 considered themselves middle-aged. In fact, one third of Americans in their seventies think of themselves as middle-aged (National Council on Aging 2000). This pattern is similar to findings from a study of Boston-area adults. Half of the men and women between the ages of 60 and 75 considered themselves to be in middle age (ME Lachman, H Maier, R Budner, unpublished manuscript, *Portraits of Middle Age: When and What is Midlife?*).

As Americans live longer and remain healthier for a greater proportion of the lifespan, the upper end of midlife may be stretched further. Middle age does not necessarily signal the middle of the lifespan. It is not realistic to expect a 60-year-old to live to 120. Rather, the upper end of the middle-age period is defined more as a demarcation of when old age sets in. Many people associate the beginning of old age with a decline in physical health (Lutsky 1980). Thus, those who are still relatively well functioning and healthy in their seventies may still consider themselves middle aged. Research shows that the subjective boundaries of midlife vary positively with age (Lachman et al. 1994). The older one is, the later the reported entry and exit years for the midlife period (Lachman & Bertrand 2001). This is tied to the notion of subjective age in which middle-aged adults typically report feeling about ten years younger than they are (Montepare & Lachman 1989). In fact, feeling younger than one's age is associated with greater well-being and health.

Although midlife is a relatively long period, lasting from 20 to 40 years, it has not yet been divided into subperiods akin to the young-old, old-old distinction used to describe later life (Neugarten & Hagestad 1976). Given the expanding period of midlife, it may be useful to think about early and late midlife, as the experiences, roles, and health are likely to be vastly different for those who are 30 to 40 and those who are 50 to 60 and beyond.

Life events such as teenage children leaving home (the empty nest), becoming a grandparent, reaching career goals, or experiencing menopause are typically associated with becoming middle-aged. The timing of entry and exit into midlife may also be tied to social class. Those who are in lower socioeconomic status groups typically report earlier entry and exit years for midlife (Kuper & Marmot 2003). This could be related to social class differences in health (Marmot et al. 1997) or to earlier transitions into life roles such as grandparent (Putney & Bengtson 2001) or retirement (Kim & Moen 2001). In a longitudinal study, those who said that middle age ends earlier than 60 years of age had higher risk for heart disease and other illnesses than those who expected middle age to end after age 70 (Kuper & Marmot 2003).

The use of chronological age as a determinant of midlife may not be ideal because age norms are less stringent for midlife than for periods that occur earlier (e.g., school entry or graduation) and later (e.g., retirement). Many people of the same chronological age are in different life phases with regard to social, family, or work events and responsibilities. For example, at age 40 some adults may have become a parent for the first time, while other 40-year-olds may have grown children and grandchildren, and some may have decided not to have children. Thus, social/family events place people of the same age in very different contexts. If one is either early or late for an event or life transition, or is approaching a developmental deadline (e.g., biological clock), this may have a major impact on one's self-conception and experiences during midlife (Heckhausen 2001, Neugarten 1968).

Images and Expectations

If you ask people of all ages to free-associate to the word "midlife," usually a large percentage will quickly offer the word "crisis." This likely reflects a widespread, cultural stereotype about this period, but not an accurate portrayal, as only a small percentage seems to experience a midlife crisis (Wethington et al. 2004). Middle age, however, is also associated with positive descriptors such as competent, responsible, knowledgeable, and powerful (Lachman et al. 1994). Thus, although midlife is often used as a modifier for crisis, it is also described as an age period with desirable characteristics. There is some empirical support for both of these views, as those in midlife may experience turbulence as well as success (Eichorn et al. 1981).

At one extreme, the notion of midlife as a period of turmoil or crisis (Levinson et al. 1978, Sheehy 1976) is in stark contrast to the view that midlife is the period of peak functioning and responsibility (Neugarten 1968). More than 25 years ago, Neugarten & Datan (1974) commented that opposing views of researchers and clinicians "led to a somewhat unbalanced view of middle age as either plateau or crisis." On the one hand, many researchers believed that midlife is a period of stability and that nothing of great significance occurs until senescence. In contrast, clinicians espoused the view that there are problems and crises in mental health brought on by physical changes and social upheavals during the middle years.

Some well-known conceptualizations of midlife have emerged from clinicians' accounts of their middle-class, middle-aged clients' problems (see Hunter & Sundel 1989). As a result, midlife is often portrayed as a time of crisis and unrest (Farrell & Rosenberg 1981, Jacques 1965, Oldham & Liebert 1989). Subsequent research with more diverse samples has uncovered a more balanced perspective (Baruch & Brooks-Gunn 1984, Brim et al. 2004, Eichorn et al. 1981, Giele 1982, Lachman & James 1997, Rossi 1994, Ryff & Seltzer 1996, Willis & Reid 1999). In contrast to the view from clinical populations, survey-based findings have characterized those in middle age as being on top of their game, "no longer driven, but now the drivers" (Neugarten & Datan 1974). These disparate views can be reconciled if the experiences of midlife are considered from a multidisciplinary, contextual lifespan perspective (Baltes et al. 1999), recognizing the vast range of possibilities for gains and losses and variations by historical period, timing of events in the life course, gender, culture, race, ethnicity, and social class.

RECONCILING THE DISPARATE VIEWS   How can those in midlife be characterized simultaneously as on top of the world and as full of turmoil and crisis? This may be a false dichotomy, as these seemingly disparate views are not incompatible and can be reconciled. The following four perspectives provide useful alternatives for examining the so-called paradox of midlife. By using multivariate methods and longitudinal designs, research can be conducted to verify or investigate these possibilities. One possible view notes that these positions represent two extremes along a continuum, and few people function at either of these endpoints. Rather, most people fall somewhere in the middle, doing fine with neither a peak nor a crisis. A second way to characterize the different portrayals of midlife is that they may not describe the same people but represent individual differences. Midlife is a time of crisis for some people, but for others it may be the peak of their lives. Individual differences in midlife show there are some people who are doing well and others who are not. A third possibility is that there is a sequential relationship between crisis and peak. As Erikson (1963) postulated, it may be necessary or adaptive to experience a crisis or turmoil for growth and development to occur (Avis 1999). The experience of a crisis may allow for subsequent positive development and a peak in performance and status. This would be akin to the changes noted by Marcia (1980) during the transition to adolescence. Those who experienced a crisis prior to resolution of ego identity showed better long-term adjustment than those who formed their identity without a challenge. A fourth possibility is that people may show differential outcomes in various domains of life. Thus, things may be in a state of flux and turmoil in one area of life (e.g., work) while things in another domain (e.g., family) may be going quite smoothly, with a great deal of competence and success. If multiple domains of life are considered, both peaks and valleys, or gains and losses, will be apparent (Baltes et al. 1999). By considering these four alternative conceptions, the portrayal of midlife as both a time of upheaval and a time of mastery is plausible and explicable. To capture these multiple conceptions, research must incorporate multivariate and longitudinal designs to take into account the wide individual variability in the midlife experience. Examination of patterns of change is needed as mean levels may mask the individual variability. Techniques such as cluster analysis allow classification into different typologies, and modeling can be used to illustrate the diverse trajectories of development. Thus, some people in midlife may show a pattern of crisis, whereas others may best be classified as successful, and still others may have a combination of crisis and competence. To examine intraindividual changes and the upward and downward trajectories, or the sequential changes in status, will help further our understanding of midlife development.

Salient Issues in Midlife

Given the increased focus on midlife by researchers, clinicians, other professionals, and laypersons, it is interesting to consider the most prevalent issues faced by those in midlife. Adults typically rate problems for others as more serious than their own problems (Heckhausen & Brim 1997). The use of social downgrading is an effective secondary control strategy and is used especially for areas of life that are expected to be problematic for one's own age group (Heckhausen & Brim 1997). In 12 key life domains rated by a national sample, there were no age differences except in the domain of health, where problems were expected to get worse with age. In the areas of stress, job, and leisure time, problems were expected to decrease after the middle years. In a representative sample of adults in the greater Boston area, participants were asked how frequently they experienced problems in each of 26 different areas of life. The most frequent problems reported by middle-aged adults were related to getting everything done, their memory, energy level, job, and sleep (ME Lachman, H Maier, R Budner, unpublished manuscript).

A national survey conducted by the American Board of Family Practice (1990) found that changes in physical conditions, health, and mental functioning, as well as getting older, were considered the worst aspects of midlife. Respondents expressed concerns especially about increases in chronic illness and being overweight. The desirable aspects reported about midlife reflected feelings of more personal control and freedom. Being settled and having life experience were considered the best things, having financial security, and the freedom and independence that come with grown children were also frequently cited. Improving relationships with family and friends, caring for a frail parent or helping children, and saving for retirement were noted as important goals during midlife (American Board of Family Practice 1990). Thus, there is evidence that the midlife experience includes both gains and losses (Baltes 1987, Neugarten & Datan 1974). The loss of fertility at menopause is sometimes experienced as a gain in sexual freedom (Rossi 1994). Or, the loss of the active parent role when children move out of the home is often accompanied by newfound gains in marital satisfaction and opportunities for exploring new interests, growth, and fulfillment (Ryff & Seltzer 1996).

The Baby Boomers at Midlife, a national survey by the American Association of Retired Persons (AARP) (2002), tracks baby boomers annually and compares them to those who are younger and older. Baby boomers were generally optimistic about the future and expected things to keep getting better. Sixty-four percent of the baby boomers said they were hopeful about the next five years and 80% were satisfied with the way their life is going. The AARP (2002) study found that the optimism levels of the baby boomers resembled those in young adulthood more than those who are in later life. The two areas in which baby boomers felt they were not doing as well as they would like were finances and leisure time. They had expectations that things would get better in both of these areas, but they were less optimistic than other cohorts that they would reach all of their goals. This may be because their goal aspirations are higher than those of older cohorts. Or, perhaps due to the large size of the cohort, baby boomers are more guarded because they know there is more competition for resources and opportunities than in smaller cohorts. Nevertheless, baby boomers were likely to take the blame for their failures to meet their goals, demonstrating a sense of responsibility for the outcomes in their life. Baby boomers said they were worse off than they expected for their health, but that they have a good deal of control over health outcomes. Indeed, many baby boomers do engage in health-promoting behaviors such as exercise (AARP 2002).

Things are reportedly going well in other areas, such as relationships with family and friends, religious or spiritual life, work, and mental health. Friends and family were the areas in which the baby boomers reported the most satisfaction (AARP 2002). They felt squeezed, but not stressed, and were comfortable and confident with their ability to manage family roles (AARP 2001).

The Midlife Crisis

One of the most common expectations of midlife is that there is an inevitable crisis, but the research does not support this (Eichorn et al. 1981). Approximately 26% of the participants over age 40 report having a midlife crisis (ME Lachman, H Maier, R Budner, unpublished manuscript; Wethington et al. 2004), although most of the reported crises occurred before age 40 or after age 50. This raises the question of whether a crisis is unique to midlife (Wethington et al. 2004) or whether it may be cohort specific (Rosenberg et al. 1999).

Jacques (1965) thought the midlife crisis was driven by a fear of impending death. More recent research shows the usual sources of the crises are major life events such as illness or divorce, which are not necessarily only associated with the midlife period (Lachman et al. 1994, Wethington et al. 2004). One third of the time what is described as a midlife crisis is triggered by events such as job loss, financial problems, or illness, which can occur at any time in adulthood (Lachman & Bertrand 2001, Wethington et al. 2004). Personality has been identified as a key factor predisposing some to experience crises at transition points throughout the life course. For example, those who are more neurotic are more likely to have a midlife crisis (Costa & McCrae 1980, Lachman & Bertrand 2001, Whitbourne & Connolly 1999).

Turning points are significant changes in the trajectory of life or an experience or realization that causes someone to reinterpret the past, similar to a midlife crisis (Clausen 1998, Rosenberg et al. 1999). Wethington et al. (2004) examined in what areas of life turning points occurred and whether they clustered in midlife. The most common turning points involved the work domain, usually a change in job or career. They were most likely to occur at midlife for men but earlier for women (Clausen 1990, Moen & Wethington 1999). Entering the thirties may be more disruptive than turning 40 (Wethington et al. 2004), as suggested by Levinson et al.'s (1978) view on the age-30 transition. This is also consistent with the notion of a "quarter-life crisis," occurring for those in their mid twenties and early thirties as they struggle to find satisfaction in work and meaningful relationships (Robbins & Wilner 2001).

CONCEPTUAL FRAMEWORKS

The classic models of midlife are based on Jung's and Erikson's theories (Lachman & James 1997). A major goal of midlife according to Jung (1971) is reflected in the individuation process. Individuation involves the integration or balancing of all aspects of the psyche. Jung's (1971) work set the stage for some of the more recent formulations of midlife. For example, he wrote that the transition to midlife is difficult and must be encountered with a different set of goals than earlier adulthood. Moreover, failure to deal with the psychological and physical changes in middle age could lead to difficulties, akin to a midlife crisis. He also discussed the integration of the feminine (anima) and masculine (animus) aspects of the psyche as part of the individuation process. This integration of sex role characteristics has been investigated extensively (Eichorn et al. 1981, James & Lewkowicz 1997, James et al. 1995, Helson et al. 1995, Neugarten 1968, Parker & Aldwin 1997). To date there is no conclusive evidence as to whether men become more feminine or women become more masculine in midlife. However, there is some indication that agentic qualities emerge for women and communal qualities become more salient for men in the middle years (James et al. 1995). Rather than a replacement of traditional sex roles, they are more likely supplemented with the opposite sex role characteristics.

Stage models of midlife have been popular, beginning with Erikson's (1963) discussion of midlife in the context of the eight stages of the lifespan. Nevertheless, given the irregularity and variability in midlife, it is unlikely that the regular sequences and patterns associated with stages can be useful for depicting the full midlife experience (Brim 1992). According to Erikson, the tasks of middle age rest upon successful resolution of earlier tasks, as portrayed in the epigenetic theory. At each stage there is a crisis, in the sense of a transition or turning point. In midlife, the central theme is generativity versus stagnation. The associated tasks involve concern with producing, nurturing, and guiding the next generation. This includes not only raising offspring but also can apply to transmitting values, mentoring younger workers, or contributing to the world through art or literature. The multifaceted and multidimensional view of generativity in the domains of parenting and societal involvement reflects the critical role that commitment to others plays in the development of well-being in midlife (McAdams 2001, McAdams & de St. Aubin 1998).

Erikson's theories have been applied and extended by other theorists. McAdams (2001) developed a more extensive conception of generativity. Levinson et al. (1978) created a stage theory that includes multiple transitions and stable periods throughout adulthood. Based on studies of the Harvard graduates in the Grant Study and inner city youth, Vaillant (1977, Vaillant & Milofsky 1980) found support for Erikson's stage theory. He also formulated two additional substages for the long midlife period. After intimacy and before the generativity stage, Vaillant suggested, was a time for career consolidation. As a sequel to the generativity stage and before achieving ego integrity, Vaillant (1977) included a substage called "keepers of the meaning," representing the focus on transmission of values to society.

Other work on midlife has been guided by theories of lifespan development and aging (Staudinger & Bluck 2001). It is useful to view midlife in the context of the life course rather than as a disconnected entity. From a lifespan perspective, the dynamic nature of changes in the middle years can be represented as both gains and losses (Baltes 1987, Eichorn et al. 1981). The midlife experience is determined by both biological and cultural/environmental influences. In fact, midlife does not exist as a concept in all cultures (Shweder 1998).

The Selective Optimization with Compensation model (Baltes & Baltes 1990), although developed initially to understand aging, can be applied to the period of midlife. Middle-aged adults are involved in multiple domains of work and social relationships, and often may have conflicting demands. Thus, successful development must entail making choices as well as adapting strategies for optimizing outcomes. Compensation may not come into play as often in midlife as in later life, if there are fewer decrements and unrealized goals. When physical limitations and chronic illness are experienced, however, midlife adults are faced with finding ways to cope or compensate for the losses.

In midlife, there may be some domains in which selection is difficult or not possible. Whereas in later life it may be possible to select positive relationships that offer emotional support (Carstensen et al. 1999, Fredrickson & Carstensen 1990), in midlife there are many required or obligatory roles. It may be necessary for the middle-aged adult to deal with the unpleasant boss, the demanding coworkers, the annoying in-laws, or the ailing parents, whereas it may be more feasible for older adults to reduce or avoid the negative ties. Thus the middle-aged adult may be frequently forced to balance the negative and positive aspects of relationships and other aspects of life. Although this may lead to increased stress, it may also serve as a training ground for emotion regulation in later life (Magai & Halpern 2001).

SELECTED STUDIES OF MIDLIFE

A number of important studies have focused directly on the middle years of the lifespan. One of the earliest studies to focus on midlife was the Kansas City Study of Adult Life, conducted from 1954 to 1964 (Neugarten 1968). This cross-sectional study was notable for integrating the psychological and social aspects of middle age and aging. The results showed personality and situational changes in adulthood and suggested that midlife was a time of peak functioning in psychosocial competence (Neugarten & Datan 1974).

The Bay Area Studies included the Oakland Growth Study and the Berkeley Guidance Study samples (Eichorn et al. 1981). These two cohorts have been studied since their birth in the 1920s, and results provided evidence for both continuity and change in personality and social competence during midlife. The Terman Study followed gifted children from the 1910 birth cohort into middle and old age, and the findings shed light on the personality and behavioral antecedents of adaptive functioning in midlife and longevity (Friedman et al. 1995). A number of other longitudinal studies that began with a focus on child and adolescent development have continued to follow participants into middle age (see Phelps et al. 2002). These long-term studies provide exceptionally rich opportunities to explore the antecedents of successful aging.

A series of relatively small longitudinal studies conducted with college alumni have been helpful in tracing the antecedents of midlife development in several cohorts of well-educated women (Mills College Classes of 1958 and 1969, Radcliffe College class of 1964, Helson & Wink 1992, Helson et al. 1995) and men (Grant Study of Harvard sophomores 1939–42, Vaillant 1977).

The Midlife in the United States (MIDUS) survey was conducted from 1995 to 1996 by the John D. and Catherine T. MacArthur Foundation Research Network on Successful Midlife Development (see Brim et al. 2004). The survey was administered by telephone and mail to a national probability sample of more than 7000 noninstitutionalized adults ranging from 25 to 75 years of age. The major findings from the MIDUS survey are summarized in the volume edited by Brim et al. (2004). This interdisciplinary study allows for integration of psychological, social, and physical aspects of well-being and health, and comparison of middle-aged adults with young and older adults. A major focus of the study was on the factors that influence psychological well-being, physical health, and social responsibility and productivity in the course of midlife development, and the ways in which adults negotiate the challenges of midlife (Brim et al. 2004). A longitudinal follow-up of the MIDUS sample funded by the National Institute on Aging is currently under way. This will provide useful insights into how individuals navigate the middle years and negotiate the transition to old age.

MULTIPLE PATTERNS OF CHANGE

To provide descriptive information about the nature of development in midlife, Lachman et al. (1994) asked adults to rate three age groups (young, middle, and old adults) on multiple dimensions. Across the dimensions there was evidence for the nine possible patterns of change or stability using the three age points (Lachman et al. 1994): (*a*) linear increase, (*b*) linear decrease, (*c*) peak or high point at midlife, (*d*) valley or low point at midlife, (*e*) stability from young to middle age and decline in later life, (*f*) stability from young to middle age and increment in later life, (*g*) decline from young to middle age followed by stability, (*h*) increase from young to middle age followed by stability to old age. A final pattern is characterized by (*i*) no change (stability). These various patterns were representative of the perceptions of change in adulthood across the multiple domains. They illustrate the wide variability and multidirectionality in possible developmental patterns (Staudinger & Bluck 2001). The following discussion of research findings from different life domains further illustrates the variability in patterns and trajectories involving midlife, with evidence for both gains and losses.

Cognitive Functioning

There are mixed patterns of growth and decline in intelligence (Dixon et al. 2001, Miller & Lachman 2000, Sternberg et al. 2001, Willis & Schaie 1999). Most of the work on cognitive aging has compared older adults to young adults, with an assumption that midlife performance falls somewhere in between that of the young and old. If one takes a multidimensional view, it is clear that on some dimensions, the middle aged perform similarly to the young, whereas on other dimensions they resemble those who are older. Results from key longitudinal studies have shown that some aspects of cognitive functioning are maintained or even improved in midlife (Eichorn et al. 1981, Hultsch et al. 1998, Schaie 1996). These include the pragmatic aspects of functioning, such as tacit knowledge (Baltes et al. 1999, Sternberg et al. 2001), that depend on experience. In contrast, aspects of the mechanics of cognition, including speed of processing and working memory, begin to show significant declines in midlife (Baltes et al. 1999). Nevertheless, cognitive changes in midlife occur gradually and do not lead necessarily to disability or functional impairment (Willis & Schaie 1999). Although some aspects of cognitive functioning may show declines, the middle-aged adult typically has the resources and experiences to compensate for them (Miller & Lachman 2000). For example, adults can use higher order skills to compensate for loss of speed in responding. There also are positive generational trends so declines may be less significant in younger cohorts, perhaps due to their higher levels of education (Willis & Schaie 1999).

Those in midlife commonly complain about cognitive declines, especially in memory (Lachman 1991). However, the research on objective change does not support widespread significant declines in memory until later in life. In fact, verbal memory seems to peak in midlife, as does vocabulary, inductive reasoning, and spatial orientation (Willis & Schaie 1999). Characteristics of wisdom often are identified in middle-aged adults, although they seem to be tied more to personality characteristics than to cognitive abilities (Staudinger et al. 1998). The midlife period provides many good opportunities for making intellectual contributions, given the position of the middle aged in the family, in the workplace, and in society.

Personality and the Self

Research on personality in midlife tells two different tales. On the one hand we see strong evidence that personality is set in young adulthood and remains relatively stable throughout the rest of life (Costa & McCrae 1980). This view is based largely on studies of temperamental personality traits, from the Big Five framework: The findings indicate that individual differences in extraversion, neuroticism, openness to experience, agreeableness, and conscientiousness remain stable during the adult years. There is also evidence, however, for changes in personality, especially in dimensions of the self (Markus & Nurius 1986).

Work by Caspi (1987) showed that temperamental qualities are stable with age, and that there is consistency in their effects across multiple domains of life. Thus, midlife behaviors and outcomes in the work and family domain are related to behavioral patterns in childhood and adolescence. For example, shy children delayed key events in adulthood such as marriage and higher education and attained less occupational achievement and stability (Caspi et al. 1989). Gender and SES differences were also apparent. Ill-tempered boys from middle-class backgrounds demonstrated a decline in social status. For women, those who were ill-tempered in childhood were more likely to marry men with low-status jobs in young adulthood and were more likely to be divorced by midlife and rated as poor mothers than their even-tempered counterparts.

Even though longitudinal trait studies show a good deal of consistency, there is some evidence that personality changes during adulthood. Using meta-analysis, Roberts & DelVecchio (2000) found that trait consistency increased in a linear, stepwise manner, until it peaked during midlife, sometime during the fifth decade (ages 50–59). Cross-sectional analyses also show some evidence that personality traits are not completely constant (McCrae & Costa 2003). Based on cross-sectional findings from the MIDUS survey, trait ratings of conscientiousness showed a peak in midlife. Agreeableness showed an upward trajectory with age, and openness and neuroticism showed downward age patterns (Lachman & Bertrand 2001).

Neugarten (1968) reported that the decade of the fifties is an important turning point in personality, with increased introspection and reflection. Sex differences in personality are accentuated during the parenting years in young adulthood and midlife, but the differences are tempered with increasing age (Eichorn et al. 1981, Helson et al. 1995). The self plays an important role in midlife, serving as a resource for negotiating the physical changes and social stresses that may be encountered. No one is immune to the complexities of midlife, yet those who feel a sense of mastery and control are better able to meet the challenges head on and find effective strategies for reducing or dealing with stress (Lachman & Firth 2004). With a well-developed identity and sense of self, most middle-aged adults function well psychologically (Lachman & Bertrand 2001), and are effective at regulating emotions (Magai & Halpern 2001) and coping with changes in many realms (Aldwin & Levenson 2001, Heckhausen 2001).

There is converging evidence that midlife is a time of increased well-being, although the sources of happiness and well-being vary by social class (Markus et al. 2004) and race (Ryff et al. 2004). At the same time, middle-aged adults do experience stress. Almeida & Horn (2004) used daily diaries over a one-week period to examine whether midlife is more stressful than other age periods, and found that both the young and midlife groups had more stressor days and more days with multiple stresses than the older adults. These findings are consistent with other work showing that stress is highest in young adulthood and midlife, and tapers off in later life (Chiriboga 1997). Compared to older adults, younger and midlife adults experienced more frequent overload stressors, especially involving children and financial risk. Younger adults had more work-related events and older adults had more spouse-related events. Midlife adults reported fewer stressors over which they felt no control. In midlife, the sense of control is an important component of health and well-being (Clark-Plaskie & Lachman 1999, Lachman & Weaver 1998b). Some aspects of control show increases with age, whereas in other areas control diminishes. For example, middle-aged adults feel a greater sense of control over their finances than younger adults (Lachman & Weaver 1998a). However, the middle aged reported less control than younger adults over their children.

Aldwin & Levenson (2001) showed a connection between stress and health and highlighted the need for good coping skills in midlife. Midlife adults may encounter stresses in multiple areas of life, such as death of parents or compromised health, yet most middle-aged adults are able to achieve growth and wisdom in the face of these stressors. Indeed, middle-aged adults are able to cope by assimilation (primary control) and accommodation (secondary control; Brandstadter & Renner 1990, Heckhausen 2001, Whitbourne & Connolly 1999). In circumstances in which adults can meet their goals, they are likely to use assimilative strategies, making desired changes to the situation or environment. When there are insurmountable obstacles to their goals, they are able to use accommodative skills, adjusting aspects of the self to resolve discrepancies. Those in midlife also show adaptive coping skills by drawing on their previous life experiences (Aldwin & Levenson 2001). Whether or not midlife is a time in which challenges are more likely to arise compared to other periods, middle-aged adults seem to be better equipped than other age groups to deal with them, as they have developed the skills to moderate the difficulties (Aldwin & Levenson 2001, Chiriboga 1997).

Emotional Development

Research is under way to chart and understand the ways adults negotiate the emotional terrain of the middle years, including parenting growing children and dealing with the aging and death of one's parents. Mroczek (2004) showed with the MIDUS sample that the affect of middle-aged adults is more like that of the young than of the older adults. In fact, older adults report more adaptive emotions, consistent with theories of emotional regulation (Carstensen et al. 1999, Isaacowitz et al. 2000). For positive affect, the middle-aged and young have lower mean levels than older adults. For negative affect, older adults show lower mean levels than middle-aged and younger adults. Variability in affect also showed those in midlife to be more like the young, with greater variability than the old. The relationships between affect and key explanatory variables differed by age period. Marital status and education played an important role in midlife affect. Relationship stress was also salient for middle-aged adults, whereas stress from work was more critical for the young. Physical health was an important factor involved in distress at all ages.

Kessler et al. (2004) showed that the incidence of major depression decreases with age. Differential exposure to stress rather than differential stress reactivity seems to explain the negative relationship between age and major depression. They examined the incidence of depression in relation to status in multiple domains. Marital separation or divorce elevated the risk of depression, although these effects were greater for men. The unemployed had higher depression than the employed and homemakers, but there were no effects of retirement or parental status on depression. There were gender differences in that for men, work and finances had the most important associations with depression, whereas for the women, health and family relationships along with work and finances all contributed to depression.

The psychosocial resources, such as use of downward comparisons and secondary control strategies, at the disposal of the midlife adult may serve as protective factors and help in the adaptation to the losses, impending developmental deadlines (e.g., biological clock), multiple roles, and other challenges associated with midlife (Heckhausen 2001). There is evidence that regulation of emotions is associated with adaptive functioning among middle-aged adults (Lang 2001, Magai & Halpern 2001).

Social Relationships

There is consensus among Americans at midlife that one major component of well-being is positive relations with others, especially parents, spouse, and offspring (Markus et al. 2004). This is consistent with the conclusions from the AARP (2002) study of baby boomers in which family was reported as the most important and satisfying area in their lives. Adults of the so-called sandwich generation, who have young children and older living parents, are not necessarily taking primary responsibility for the care of their parents (Putney & Bengtson 2001). Nevertheless, those who were caring for parents said they were mostly able to cope with the dual responsibilities and felt a "squeeze" but not stress. (AARP 2001).

In addition to psychological and physical changes, middle age often involves a restructuring of social roles (Bumpass & Aquilino 1995), especially in the realms of work (Sterns & Huyck 2001, Kim & Moen 2001) and family (Antonucci et al. 2001, Putney & Bengtson 2001). Midlife adults have a wide range of circumstances involving their children, determined in part by their social class, children's ages, and geographical propinquity (Ryff & Seltzer 1996). Some have young children still in the home, and others have grown children who live on their own or perhaps return to the home after divorce or graduating college. Those who had children in their twenties or early thirties will often become grandparents during the early part of their middle years. Midlife adults also must confront changes in their relationships with their own parents, especially changes due to declining health or death.

One of the harsh realities of middle age is captured in the statistics about the number of living parents. According to the National Survey of Families and Households, as adults enter midlife, 41% have both parents alive, while 77% leave midlife with no parents alive (Bumpass & Aquilino 1995). Behind these figures are the emotional anguish and turmoil associated with parental loss. The experiences of midlife adults are complicated by the mobility of our society, in which adult children are often faced with the long-distance monitoring of parents with failing health and decreased ability to live independently, while dealing with the multiple responsibilities at home and in the workplace (Putney & Bengtson 2001).

Midlife adults may have many interlocking roles (Moen & Wethington 1999). In both the family and work domains, middle-aged adults play an important role in sharing their experience and transmitting their values to the younger generation (McAdams 2001). The middle-aged are involved with the lives of the young and the old. They may be launching children and experiencing the empty nest, adjusting to having grown children return home (boomerang kids), becoming grandparents, giving or receiving financial assistance, taking care of a widowed or sick parent, or getting used to being the oldest generation in the extended family after both parents have passed away (Putney & Bengtson 2001).

Marks et al. (2003) examined how the multiple roles of marital partner, parent, and adult child and varied lifestyles such as cohabitation or remarriage are associated with physical, mental, and social well-being and whether these associations vary by gender and age. They found roles could have different well-being consequences, depending for example on whether or not a parent is in poor health or depending on the age of one's children. Those who were parents had more psychological distress than the child free, but also had greater psychological wellness and generativity, illustrating both gains and losses. In midlife, when one's children become adults, we get a sense of how they have turned out (Keyes & Ryff 1999). Children's outcomes affect parents' evaluations of their own lives and their well-being.

The midlife adult is a major provider of support, but also reaps the benefits of support from others (Antonucci et al. 2001). Social relations with family, friends, and coworkers can provide a major source of satisfaction and contribute to well-being and health in midlife, but also can be a source of stress (Rook 2003, Walen & Lachman 2000). The absence of support or the experience of strain can wreak havoc on middle-aged adults, leading to stress and illness. The most frequent type of daily stressors found in a daily diary study was interpersonal tensions, occurring on almost 24% of the days sampled (Almeida & Horn 2004). There were also gender differences in that women had more stressors from other people and men had more self-focused stressors.

Work

The role of work, whether one works in a full-time career, a part-time job, as a volunteer, or a homemaker, is central during the middle years (Sterns & Huyck 2001). One's identity is in large part defined by one's work. The nature of work can affect one's cognitive capacity and intellectual flexibility (Kohn & Schooler 1978). In the work domain, middle-aged adults may reach their peak in position and earnings. They also may be faced with multiple financial burdens from rent or mortgage, child care, medical bills, home repairs, college tuition, loans to family members, or bills from nursing homes.

The progression of career trajectories during midlife is diverse (Barnett 1997). Some individuals have stable careers, with little mobility, while others move in and out of the labor force, experiencing layoffs and unemployment. The impact of job instability depends on the age of the person or whether or not it occurs in the context of a good job market and economy. Middle-aged adults may experience age discrimination in some job situations, and finding a job in midlife may be difficult because pay demands of older workers are higher than those of younger workers, or technological advances may render the midlife worker's skills outdated or obsolete.

Another phase of the work cycle that often occurs in midlife is the transition to retirement (Kim & Moen 2001). The preretirement phase occurs at different time points, and may be affected by historical variations, timing, planning, adjustment, and resources that are brought to bear on retirement decisions. For some, retirement is a welcome event, and planning can facilitate a better transition. Some may need to postpone retirement when economic conditions change or unexpected circumstances arise (Avolio & Sosik 1999). Middle-aged adults often report they have little time for leisure (AARP 2002). Thus, retirement may be a welcome change, enabling them to have more time to explore interests and to spend with family and friends (Eichorn et al. 1981).

Health and Physical Changes

For middle-aged adults, health is generally good, and most physical changes do not cause disability or alter lifestyles, even if they do raise concerns and lamentations about the woes of getting older (Whitbourne 2001). Some less fortunate are faced with chronic illnesses, disease, or health problems that limit their activities (Spiro 2001). Only 7% of those in their early forties report having a disability (Bumpass & Aquilino 1995). The number of men and women with some form of disability more than doubles by the early fifties (16%), and by the early sixties, 30% have a disability. Thus, for many adults, midlife is characterized by increasing health problems, and this is particularly true for those with low socioeconomic status (Bumpass & Aquilino 1995, Ryff et al. 2004).

Individual differences in the rate of aging are vast and are influenced by such factors as heredity, health habits, and lifestyle. Lifestyle and behaviors in youth and young adulthood can affect health in midlife, and midlife habits affect outcomes in old age. Thus, as many adults recognize, the opportunity to control one's health is enormous (Lachman & Weaver 1998a) because many of the risk factors for chronic illnesses are modifiable, including cigarette smoking, alcohol use, poor diet, excess weight, and physical inactivity (Merrill & Verbrugge 1999). The reported effort devoted to health increases with age and is higher among women than men (Cleary et al. 2004). However, reports of health-related behaviors such as exercise or vitamin use decline with age in general. Thus, with increasing age adults may spend time dealing with chronic conditions, not just on health preventative measures.

Variations in health by socioeconomic status are consistent across age (Marmot et al. 1997), with those lower on the social gradient showing poorer health. Inequality, not lack of material wealth, appears to contribute to ill health. The effects of the gradient are moderated or mediated by factors such as parents' education, work environment, health behavior, social relationships, and sense of control (Marmot et al. 1997). Social support (Ryff et al. 2004) and a strong sense of mastery and control (Lachman & Weaver 1998b) are protective factors for those in lower social classes. Those at the low end of the SES spectrum who have better quality relationships and a greater sense of control are more resilient and show health and well-being comparable to those with higher SES.

Biologically based changes are typically not as dramatic in midlife as in other periods of the lifespan. Some individuals begin to show health declines during the middle years and others pass through midlife with a clean bill of health. Some of the common changes that may emerge in the middle years include back and joint pain, tooth and gum problems, changes in eyesight and other aspects of sensory functioning, and weight gain with related problems such as cardiovascular disease and diabetes (Whitbourne 2001).

One of the major shifts in the middle years occurs in the area of reproduction, especially menopause for women. The median age of the last menstrual period is typically 50–52 years, although there is wide variation in the menopause experience (Avis 1999, Rossi 2004). There is no evidence for a universal experience of distress associated with menopause (Avis 1999). Hot flashes and sweats are related to physiological changes in hormone levels, but their severity varies. Those who have hot flashes and night sweats are more likely to experience depression. Symptoms such as depression, irritability, weight gain, insomnia, and memory loss do not seem to be directly related to menopause. For example, it is possible that the association noted between depression and menopause is based on clinic/patient populations who self-select into treatment (Avis 1999). Attitudes toward menopause and stress can affect symptoms during menopause (Rossi 2004). Cultural differences in the experience of menopause suggest that estrogen is not directly responsible for depression and symptoms. More research is needed to understand to what extent changes in hormones for both men and women do impact musculoskeletal, cardiovascular, and urogenital systems, leading to increases in heart disease, diabetes, hypertension, osteoporosis, urinary incontinence, and autoimmune diseases.

In the 1980s menopause was implicated as a risk factor for osteoporosis and cardiovascular disease (Avis 1999). This led to the medicalization of menopause and the introduction of hormone replacement therapy (HRT). Menopause was seen as a treatable condition that warranted medical intervention (Avis 1999, Rossi 1994). Recently, the benefits of HRT have been questioned, and research evidence suggests that HRT may not only be ineffective for treating heart disease but also may be harmful in increasing the rate of cancer (Petitti 2002).

DIRECTIONS FOR THE FUTURE

Although we have progressed in integrating the various streams of literature that bear on midlife and in incorporating new findings from recent studies, the picture of midlife is still unfolding. Studies using longitudinal and multivariate methods are needed to enable separation of age and cohort effects and to capture the complexity of the period. This will help the field to go beyond what we know for isolated cohorts and for specific domains, to more completely characterize the middle years. Midlife is a period of peak functioning in many domains, including some aspects of cognitive functioning and in the ability to deal with multiple roles and stress. Midlife adults are at the height of assuming responsibility for others and midlife is typically the time of greatest influence and most frequent intergenerational contact. It is a period when rich experiences from multiple domains come into play and the deficits of aging usually have not begun to have a major impact on functioning. Opportunities still exist to make a difference in the quality of one's life and that of others, or to change direction and to reap the benefits of investments in time and effort. Midlife is a period when implementing health-promoting behaviors can help to maintain health and possibly prevent physical problems in later life. It is a time when a sense of control can provide motivation to tackle impending declines in many domains, including health or cognitive functioning (Lachman & Firth 2004, Miller & Lachman 2000). Middle-aged adults often show high levels of mastery gained from successful coping and accumulated experiences of juggling different roles.

Many questions about midlife are unanswered. To make further progress, researchers must recognize the multidisciplinary nature of midlife, and focus on the interplay of biomedical, psychological, and social factors during the middle years. Midlife can provide a window for a glimpse of later life while there is still time to engage in prevention and to influence some aspects of the course of aging. Further studies are needed to supplement the accumulating evidence for ways to take control and compensate for or even postpone aging-related losses that begin during midlife (Lachman & Firth 2004). For example, weight-bearing exercise can prevent or remediate aging-related muscle loss (Whitbourne 2001). Also, engaging in challenging physical and mental activity seems to minimize aging-related cognitive declines (Hultsch et al. 1998). Psychological resources can come into play in adapting to the physical and social losses that occur during midlife. When desired outcomes are not attainable, it is possible to utilize secondary control or accommodative processes for adjustment (Brandstadter & Renner 1990, Heckhausen 2001, Whitbourne & Connolly 1999). Selective optimization processes (Baltes & Baltes 1990, Baltes et al. 1999) can enable the resilient adult to draw on social and psychological resources to compensate for biological decline (Staudinger & Bluck 2001). More research is needed to support the growing knowledge base on midlife development. The well-being of middle-aged adults affects the many others with whom they interact, give care, advise, or influence. Thus, a better understanding of middle age can have far-reaching consequences. These can extend not only to those who are in midlife, but also to those who are younger or older in the family, in the workplace, and in society as a whole.

ACKNOWLEDGMENTS

I would like to acknowledge the generous support from the John D. and Catherine T. MacArthur Foundation Research Network on Successful Midlife Development (Orville Gilbert Brim, Chair) and the National Institute on Aging (grants R01 AG17920-03 and PO1 AG20166-01), which enabled me to write this chapter. I also appreciate the helpful comments on the manuscript from Ron Spiro.

The *Annual Review of Psychology* is online at http://psych.annualreviews.org

LITERATURE CITED

Aldwin CM, Levenson MR. 2001. Stress, coping, and health at midlife: a developmental perspective. See Lachman 2001, pp. 188–214

Almeida D, Horn M. 2004. Is daily life more stressful during middle adulthood? See Brim et al. 2004, pp. 425–51.

Am. Assoc. Retired Persons. 2001. *In The Middle: A Report on Multicultural Boomers Coping with Family and Aging Issues.* Washington, DC: AARP

Am. Assoc. Retired Persons. 2002. *Tracking Study of the Baby Boomers in Midlife.* Washington, DC: AARP

Am. Board Family Practice. 1990. *Perspectives on Middle Age: The Vintage Years.* Princeton, NJ: New World Decisions

Antonucci TC, Akiyama H, Merline A. 2001. Dynamics of social relationships in midlife. See Lachman 2001, pp. 571–98

Avis NE. 1999. Women's health at midlife. See Willis & Reid 1999, pp. 105–47

Avolio BJ, Sosik JJ. 1999. A life-span framework for assessing the impact of work on white-collar workers. See Willis & Reid 1999, pp. 249–74

Baltes PB. 1987. Theoretical propositions of life-span developmental psychology: on the dynamics between growth and decline. *Dev. Psychol.* 23:611–26

Baltes PB, Baltes MM. 1990. Psychological perspectives on successful aging: the model of selective optimization with compensation. In *Successful Aging: Perspectives from the Behavioral Sciences,* ed. PB Baltes, MM Baltes, pp. 1–34. New York: Cambridge Univ. Press

Baltes PB, Staudinger UM, Lindenberger U. 1999. Lifespan psychology: theory and application to intellectual functioning. *Annu. Rev. Psychol.* 50:471–507

Barnett RC. 1997. Gender, employment, and psychological well-being: historical and life course perspectives. See Lachman & James 1997, pp. 325–43

Baruch G, Brooks -Gunn J, eds. 1984. *Women in Midlife.* New York: Plenum

Brandstadter J, Renner G. 1990. Tenacious goal pursuit and flexible goal adjustment. Explication and age-related analysis of assimilative and accommodative strategies of coping. *Psychol. Aging* 5:58–67

Brim OG, ed. 1992. *Ambition: How We Manage Success and Failure Throughout Our Lives.* New York: Basic Books

Brim OG, Ryff CD, Kessler R, eds. 2004. *How Healthy Are We: A National Study of Well-being in Midlife.* Chicago: Univ. Chicago Press

Bumpass LL, Aquilino WS, eds. 1995. *A Social Map of Midlife: Family and Work Over the Middle Life Course.* Vero Beach, FL: MacArthur Found. Res. Netw. Successful Midlife Dev.

Carr D. 2004. Psychological well-being across three cohorts: a response to shifting work-family opportunities and expectations. See Brim et al. 2004, pp. 452–84.

Carstensen LL, Isaacowitz D, Charles ST. 1999. Taking time seriously: a theory of socioemotional selectivity. *Am. Psychol.* 54:165–81

Caspi A. 1987. Personality in the life course. *J. Personal. Soc. Psychol.* 53:1203–13

Caspi A, Bem DJ, Elder GH. 1989. Continuities and consequences of interactional styles across the life course. *J. Personal.* 57:375–406

Chiriboga D. 1997. Crisis, challenge, and stability in the middle years. See Lachman & James 1997, pp. h293–322

Clark-Plaskie M, Lachman ME. 1999. The sense of control in midlife. See Willis & Reid 1999, pp. 181–208

Clausen J. 1998. Life reviews and life stories. In *Methods of Life Course Research: Qualitative and Quantitative Approaches,* ed. JZ Giele, GH Elder, pp. 189–212. Thousand Oaks, CA: Sage

Clausen J. 1990. *Turning Point as a Life Course*

Concept. Presented at Annu. Meet. Am. Sociol. Assoc., Washington, DC

Cleary PD, Zaborski LB, Ayanian MD. 2004. Sex differences in health over the course of midlife. See Brim et al. 2004, pp. 37–63.

Costa PT, McCrae RR. 1980. Still stable after all these years: personality as a key to some issues in adulthood and old age. In *Life-span Development and Behavior*, ed. PB Baltes, OG Brim, pp. 65–102. New York: Academic

Dixon RA, de Frias CM, Maitland SB. 2001. Memory in midlife. See Lachman 2001, pp. 248–78

Easterlin R. 1980. *Birth and Fortune: The Impact of Numbers on Personal Welfare.* New York: Basic Books

Eichorn DH, Clausen JA, Haan N, Honzik MP, Mussen PH, eds. 1981. *Present and Past in Midlife.* New York: Academic

Elder GH. 1979. Historical change in life patterns and personality. In *Life-span Development and Behavior*, ed. PB Baltes, OG Brim, 2:118–59. New York: Academic

Erikson E, ed. 1963. *Childhood and Society.* New York: Norton. 2nd ed.

Farrell MP, Rosenberg SD, eds. 1981. *Men at Midlife.* Boston, MA: Auburn House

Fredrickson BL, Carstensen LL. 1990. Choosing social partners: how old age and anticipated endings make us more selective. *Psychol. Aging* 5:335–47

Friedman HS, Tucker JS, Schwartz JE, Tomlinson-Keasey C, Martin LR, et al. 1995. Psychosocial and behavioral predictors of longevity: the aging and death of the "Termites." *Am. Psychol.* 50:69–78

Giele JZ, ed. 1982. *Women in the Middle Years: Current Knowledge and Directions for Research and Policy.* New York: Wiley

Heckhausen J. 2001. Adaptation and resilience in midlife. See Lachman 2001, pp. 345–91

Heckhausen J, Brim OG. 1997. Perceived problems for self and others: self-protection by social downgrading throughout adulthood. *Psychol. Aging* 12:610–19

Helson R, Stewart AJ, Ostrove J. 1995. Identity in three cohorts of midlife women. *J. Personal. Soc. Psychol.* 69:544–57

Helson R, Wink P. 1992. Personality change in women from the early 40s to the early 50s. *Psychol. Aging* 7:46–55

Hultsch DF, Hertzog C, Dixon RA, eds. 1998. *Memory Change in the Aged.* New York: Cambridge Univ. Press

Hunter S, Sundel M, eds. 1989. *Midlife Myths: Issues, Findings, and Practice Implications.* Newbury Park, CA: Sage

Isaacowitz DM, Charles ST, Carstensen LL. 2000. Emotion and cognition. In *The Handbook of Aging and Cognition*, ed. F Craik, TA Salthouse, pp. 593–631. NJ: Erlbaum

Jacques E. 1965. Death and the mid-life crisis. *Int. J. Psychoanal.* 46:502–14

James JB, Lewkowicz CJ. 1997. Themes of power and affiliation across time. See Lachman & James 1997, pp. 109–43

James JB, Lewkowicz CJ, Libhaber J, Lachman ME. 1995. Rethinking the gender identity crossover hypothesis: a test of a new model. *Sex Roles* 32:185–207

Jung CG, ed. 1933. *Modern Man in Search of a Soul.* New York: Harcourt, Brace & World. 244 pp.

Jung CG, ed. 1971. *The Portable Jung.* New York: Viking

Kessler RC, Gilman SE, Thornton LM, Kendler KS. 2004. Health, well being, and social responsibility in the MIDUS twin and sibling subsamples. See Brim et al. 2004, pp. 124–52.

Keyes CL, Ryff CD. 1999. Psychological well-being in midlife. See Willis & Reid 1999, pp. 161–80

Kim JE, Moen P. 2001. Moving into retirement: preparation and transitions in late midlife. See Lachman 2001, pp. 487–527

Kohn ML, Schooler C. 1978. The reciprocal effects of the substantive complexity of work and intellectual flexibility: a longitudinal assessment. *Am. J. Sociol.* 84:24–52

Kuper H, Marmot M. 2003. Intimations of mortality: perceived age of leaving middle age as a predictor of future health outcomes within the Whitehall II study. *Age Ageing* 32:178–84

Lachman ME. 1991. Perceived control over memory aging: developmental and intervention perspectives. *J. Soc. Issues* 47:159–75

Lachman ME, ed. 2001. *Handbook of Midlife Development.* New York: Wiley

Lachman ME, Bandura M, Weaver SL. 1995. Assessing memory control beliefs: the Memory Controllability Inventory. *Aging Cogn.* 2:67–84

Lachman ME, Bertrand RM. 2001. Personality and the self in midlife. See Lachman 2001, pp. 279–309

Lachman ME, Firth K. 2004. The adaptive value of feeling in control during midlife. See Brim et al. 2004, pp. 320–49.

Lachman ME, James JB, eds. 1997. *Multiple Paths of Midlife Development.* Chicago: Univ. Chicago Press

Lachman ME, Lewkowicz C, Marcus A, Peng Y. 1994. Images of midlife development among young, middle-aged, and older adults. *J. Adult Dev.* 1:201–11

Lachman ME, Weaver SL. 1998a. Sociodemographic variations in the sense of control by domain: findings from the MacArthur study of midlife. *Psychol. Aging* 13:553–62

Lachman ME, Weaver SL. 1998b. The sense of control as a moderator of social class differences in health and well-being. *J. Personal. Soc. Psychol.* 74:763–73

Lang FR. 2001. Regulation of social relationships in later adulthood. *J. Gerontol. B* 56:P321–26

Levinson DJ, Darrow CN, Klein EB, Levinson MH, McKee B, eds. 1978. *The Seasons of a Man's Life.* New York: Knopf

Lutsky NS. 1980. Attitudes toward old age and elderly persons. *Annu. Rev. Gerontol. Geriatr.* 1:287–311

Magai C, Halpern B. 2001. Emotional development during the middle years. See Lachman 2001, pp. 310–44

Marcia JE. 1980. Identity in adolescence. In *Handbook of Adolescent Psychology,* ed. J Adelson, pp. 159–87. New York: Wiley

Marks NF, Bumpass LL, Jun H. 2003. Family roles and well-being during the middle life course. See Brim et al. 2003, pp. 514–49. In press

Markus HR, Nurius P. 1986. Possible selves. *Am. Psychol.* 41:954–69

Markus HR, Ryff CD, Curhan K, Palmersheim K. 2004. In their own words: well-being at midlife among high school and college-educated adults. See Brim et al. 2004, pp. 273–319.

Marmot M, Ryff CD, Bumpass LL, Shipley M. 1997. Social inequalities in health: next questions and converging evidence. *Soc. Sci. Med.* 44:901–10

McAdams DP. 2001. Generativity in midlife. See Lachman 2001, pp. 395–443

McAdams DP, de St . Aubin E, eds. 1998. *Generativity and Adult Development: How and Why We Care for the Next Generation.* Washington, DC: Am. Psychol. Assoc.

McCrae R, Costa PT, eds. 2003. *Personality in Adulthood: A Five Factor Theory Perspective.* New York: Guilford Press. 2nd ed.

Merrill SS, Verbrugge LM. 1999. Health and disease in midlife. See Willis & Reid 1999, pp. 77–103

Miller LS, Lachman ME. 2000. Cognitive performance and the role of health and control beliefs in midlife. *Aging Neuropsychol. Cogn.* 7:69–85

Moen P, Wethington E. 1999. Midlife development in a course context. See Willis & Reid 1999, pp. 3–23

Montepare J, Lachman ME. 1989. "You're only as old as you feel." Self-perceptions of age, fears of aging, and life satisfaction from adolescence to old age. *Psychol. Aging* 4:73–78

Mroczek DK. 2004. Positive and negative affect at midlife. See Brim et al. 2004, pp. 205–26

Natl. Council Aging. (March) 2000. *Myths and Realities 2000 Survey Results.* Washington, DC: NOCA

Neugarten BL, ed. 1968. *Middle Age and Aging: A Reader in Social Psychology.* Chicago: Univ. Chicago Press

Neugarten BL, Datan N. 1974. The middle years. In *The Foundations of Psychiatry,* ed.

S Arieti, pp. 592–608. New York: Basic Books

Neugarten BL, Hagestad G. 1976. Age and the life course. In *Handbook of Aging and the Social Sciences*, ed. R Binstock, E Shanas, pp. 35–55. New York: Van Nostrand-Reinhold

Oldham JM, Liebert RS, eds. 1989. *The Middle Years: New Psychoanalytic Perspectives.* New Haven, CT: Yale Univ. Press

Oxford English Dictionary Online. 2000. London: Oxford Univ. Press

Parker RA, Aldwin CM. 1997. Do aspects of gender identity change from early to middle adulthood? Disentangling age, cohort and period effects. See Lachman & James 1997, pp. 67–107

Petitti DB. 2002. Hormone replacement therapy for prevention: more evidence, more pessimism. *JAMA* 288:99–101

Phelps E, Furstenberg FF Jr, Colby A, eds. 2002. *Looking at Lives: American Longitudinal Studies of the Twentieth Century.* New York: Sage Found.

Putney NM, Bengtson VL. 2001. Families, intergenerational relationships, and kinkeeping in midlife. See Lachman 2001, pp. 528–70

Robbins A, Wilner A, eds. 2001. *Quarterlife Crisis: The Unique Challenges of Life in Your Twenties.* New York: Putnam

Roberts BW, DelVecchio WF. 2000. The rank-order consistency of personality traits from childhood to old age: a quantitative review of longitudinal studies. *Psychol. Bull.* 126:3–25

Rook KS. 2003. Exposure and reactivity to negative social exchanges: a preliminary investigation using daily diary data. *J. Gerontol. B* 58:P100–11

Rosenberg SD, Rosenberg HJ, Farrell MP. 1999. The midlife crisis revisited. See Willis & Reid 1999, pp. 47–73

Rossi AS. 2004. The menopausal transition and aging processes. See Brim et al. 2004, pp. 550–75.

Rossi AS, ed. 1994. *Sexuality Across the Life Course.* Chicago: Univ. Chicago Press

Ryff CD, Keyes C, Hughes D. 2004. Psychological well-being in MIDUS: profiles of ethnic, racial diversity, and life course uniformity. See Brim et al. 2004, pp. 398–424

Ryff CD, Seltzer MG, eds. 1996. *The Parental Experience in Midlife.* Chicago: Univ. Chicago Press

Ryff CD, Singer BH, Palmersheim KA. 2004. Social inequalities in health and well-being: the role of relational and religious protective factors. See Brim et al. 2004, pp. 90–123.

Schaie KW, ed. 1996. *Intellectual Development in Adulthood.* New York: Cambridge Univ. Press

Sheehy G, ed. 1976. *Passages.* New York: Dutton

Shweder R, ed. 1998. *Welcome to Middle Age! And Other Cultural Fictions.* Chicago: Univ. Chicago Press

Spiro A III. 2001. Health in midlife: toward a life-span view. See Lachman 2001, pp. 156–87

Staudinger UM, Bluck S. 2001. A view on midlife development from life-span theory. See Lachman 2001, pp. 3–39

Staudinger UM, Maciel AG, Smith J, Baltes PB. 1998. What predicts wisdom-related performance? A first look at personality, intelligence, and facilitative experiential contexts. *Eur. J. Personal.* 12:1–17

Sternberg RJ, Grigorenko EL, Oh S. 2001. See Lachman 2001, pp. 217–47

Sterns HL, Huyck MH. 2001. The role of work in midlife. See Lachman 2001, pp. 447–86

US Census Bureau. (Nov.) 2000. Resident population estimates of the United States by age and sex. Washington, DC: US Census Bur.

Vaillant GE, ed. 1977. *Adaptation to Life.* Boston, MA: Little Brown

Vaillant GE, Milofsky E. 1980. Natural history of male psychological health: IX. Empirical evidence for Erikson's model of the life cycle. *Am. J. Psychiatry* 137:1348–59

Walen HR, Lachman ME. 2000. Social support and strain from partner, family, and friends: costs and benefits for men and women in adulthood. *J. Soc. Personal Relat.* 17:5–30

Wethington E, Kessler R, Pixley J. 2004. Turning points in adulthood. See Brim et al. 2004, pp. 586–613.

Whitbourne SK. 2001. The physical aging process in midlife: interactions with psychological and sociocultural factors. See Lachman 2001, pp. 109–55

Whitbourne SK, Connolly LA. 1999. The developing self in midlife. See Willis & Reid 1999, pp. 25–46

Willis SL, Reid JD, eds. 1999. *Life in the Middle: Psychological and Social Development in Middle Age.* San Diego: Academic

Willis SL, Schaie KW. 1999. Intellectual functioning in midlife. See Willis & Reid 1999, pp. 233–47

Annu. Rev. Psychol. 2004. 55:333–63
doi: 10.1146/annurev.psych.54.101601.145228
Copyright © 2004 by Annual Reviews. All rights reserved
First published online as a Review in Advance on September 29, 2003

THE INTERGENERATIONAL TRANSFER OF PSYCHOSOCIAL RISK: Mediators of Vulnerability and Resilience

Lisa A. Serbin and Jennifer Karp

Center for Research in Human Development, Department of Psychology, Concordia University, Montreal, Quebec, Canada, H4B 1R6; email: lserbin@vax2.concordia.ca, karpie7@hotmail.com

Key Words   intergenerational processes, transfer of risk, longitudinal studies, parenting, childhood aggression

■ **Abstract**   The recurrence of social, behavioral, and health problems in successive generations of families is a prevalent theme in both the scientific and popular literatures. This review discusses recent conceptual models and findings from longitudinal studies concerning the intergenerational transfer of psychosocial risk, including intergenerational continuity, and the processes whereby a generation of parents may place their offspring at elevated risk for social, behavioral, and health problems. Key findings include the mediational effects of parenting and environmental factors in the transfer of risk. In both girls and boys, childhood aggression and antisocial behavior appear to predict long-term trajectories that place offspring at risk. Sequelae of childhood aggression that may threaten the well-being of offspring include school failure, adolescent risk-taking behavior, early and single parenthood, and family poverty. These childhood and adolescent behavioral styles also predict harsh, aggressive, neglectful, and unstimulating parenting behavior toward offspring. Buffering factors within at-risk families include maternal educational attainment and constructive parenting practices (e.g., emotional warmth, consistent disciplinary practices, and cognitive scaffolding). These findings highlight the potential application and relevance of intergenerational studies for social, educational, and health policy.

CONTENTS

333

INTRODUCTION

During the past century, there has been ongoing concern over the extent to which psychological problems and social dependency seem to recur in the same families over the course of multiple generations (Caspi & Elder 1988, Rutter & Madge 1976). Researchers, practitioners, policy analysts, and the public at large share this concern. The particular focus, in all of these arenas, has been on the personal, social, economic, and health costs of intergenerational patterns of family and individual dysfunction. Mental health problems tend to co-occur with other psychological, social, and health problems, particularly when family resources are limited or impoverished. Accordingly, there is also considerable interest in the environmental and social contexts that are likely to accompany problematic family environments and relationships. Consequently, understanding and studying the circumstances and environments in which families are raised and nurtured, as well as specific patterns of parenting and other aspects of parental functioning, have become topics of broad academic and popular interest.

The processes whereby disadvantaged families place their offspring at risk for continuing negative trajectories are also highly relevant to many current issues in public policy. In the policy arena, a major goal is to disrupt the intergenerational cycles that help to create and sustain a disadvantaged underclass. Internationally, programs aimed at prevention and early intervention for high-risk children have been implemented at many levels within educational, social, and health systems. Nevertheless, there is ongoing debate about the most effective and appropriate targets and methods for early intervention with this vulnerable population of children and families (see Brooks-Gunn 2003 for a recent overview of the results and policy implications of early intervention studies). It has been recognized in recent years that research on intergenerational continuity, focusing on the processes leading to disadvantaged child-rearing conditions within high-risk families, has the potential to inform and guide preventive intervention policies.

In the developmental research domain, there are basic theoretical and conceptual issues involved in studying intergenerational processes. Some of these issues have preoccupied the field of human development for many years. This intersection of basic research and more applied issues presents both conceptual challenges and opportunities for developmental researchers. It is these developments in intergenerational research, currently engaging researchers from a wide range of backgrounds and disciplines, which we present and discuss in this review.

Overview

The proposition that children often resemble their parents is not likely to surprise the readers of this publication. Biological influences of parents on their children (including genetic inheritance and other physical influences such as prenatal maternal health and nutrition) are becoming better understood, with both knowledge and methodology rapidly advancing. We have also learned a great deal in recent decades about the cultural, social, and educational influences of parents on their offspring: environmental factors generally referred to under the broad heading of "parenting and socialization." There are also many other reasons why generations might resemble each other that do not involve a direct "transfer" of characteristics between generations: For example, parents and children may experience common physical, social, and cultural environments, such as inner-city neighborhoods in which overlapping generations of families live (Bradley & Corwyn 2002, Brooks-Gunn et al. 1993, Ingoldsby & Shaw 2002), or historical events that impact several generations, such as long-term geographical displacements following war or famine (Elder 1979, McCord 1995).

Intergenerational similarity is of ongoing interest to researchers because of its relevance to theoretical issues concerning the processes of behavioral development. That is, understanding the reasons why children do, or do not, grow up to resemble their parents with regard to specific characteristics may help us understand the etiology of complex patterns of behavior and cognitive functioning. Understanding the specific processes whereby children living under risk conditions (e.g., family poverty; parental abuse or neglect; and limited parental education, mental health problems, alcoholism, addiction, or criminality) may have either negative or positive outcomes can be very useful in designing preventive intervention programs, or for designing social and educational programs to meet the needs of vulnerable populations.

Reflecting patterns in the general developmental literature, many studies of intergenerational similarity have focused on such widely studied phenomena as social behavior (especially aggression and antisocial behavior) and behavior disorders (especially conduct disorder and criminality). Aspects of parenting and parent-child relations, such as child abuse and patterns of attachment, have also been examined from an intergenerational perspective. Intergenerational studies typically focus on the similarity between generations, as well as attempt to identify the processes that predict outcomes across generations and may explain intergenerational continuity versus discontinuity. Although the issues being addressed by intergenerational research are not necessarily new, recent longitudinal studies have permitted us to approach these issues from new perspectives (Dubow et al. 2003, Patterson 1998, Serbin & Stack 1998). For example, one unique aspect of recent longitudinal, intergenerational studies is that they often permit developmentally appropriate comparisons between generations at comparable stages of development. Another innovative feature of these intergenerational designs is that they typically allow the researcher to predict behavior across the "parental divide" (that is, the transition to parenthood in one or more of the generations included in the sample) and to predict outcomes in the next generation. The mediational role of parenting in the transfer of risk for developmental, health, and social problems has been a central focus of many of these investigations.

An Intergenerational, Longitudinal Approach

The methodology of prospective longitudinal investigations is well established in the field of developmental psychology (Wadsworth 1988). Recent theoretical and methodological advances include an increased focus on tracing differential trajectories for specific risk groups and subgroups within populations, as well as new statistical methodologies that allow us to predict and understand individual patterns of growth. The emergence of the field of developmental psychopathology, in particular, has encouraged the development of new types of prospective longitudinal designs, as we attempt to better understand risk for abnormal development within the complexity of environmental contexts, genetic vulnerability, and patterns of individual growth and change (Rutter & Sroufe 2000).

The Intergenerational Transfer of Risk

The focus of this chapter is on the transfer of risk from parent to child. As used in this context, "risk" is the probabilistic notion that within any population there will be a range of outcomes, both good and bad. In a longitudinal study of risk, it is possible to identify factors that predict, modify, or moderate the probability of specific developmental trajectories toward particular outcomes. Often the focus of these longitudinal studies is on at-risk populations, in which the probability of specific negative outcomes is elevated above population base rates. The theoretical and applied importance of identifying specific risk and protective factors has been widely demonstrated in the developmental literature, with the results of many ongoing studies well known and widely available to the professional and general public (e.g., Furstenberg et al. 1987, Moffitt et al. 2001, and Werner & Smith 1992).

What is unique about the intergenerational approach is the focus on the developmental intersection of two or more generations and their ongoing interaction, affecting the future growth trajectories of all members of the family. In this context, "transfer of risk" refers to a theoretical model or predictive equation in which specific parental characteristics or behaviors increase the probability that similar or related problems will occur in the next generation. Risk factors, although predictive, are not necessarily causal. Beyond identifying intergenerational continuities in the risk for negative outcomes (e.g., an elevated high probability of mental illness in successive generations), the goal of these studies is to understand the processes whereby transfer of risk occurs.

Psychosocial Risk to Offspring

In this review, we focus on intergenerational studies that predict increased risk to offspring that is both specific (i.e., homotypic) and general (i.e., heterotypic). That is, many intergenerational models involve a set of complex predictors (which are often intercorrelated and interactive) and a potential set of complex, interrelated outcomes. For example, the risk to children of parents with histories of problem behavior, including aggression and antisocial behavior, is both specific (for repeating their parents' behavior pattern) and general (in terms of broad elevation of risk for a wide variety of negative outcomes ranging from pediatric injury and illness to school failure, adolescent risk-taking behavior, early parenthood, and problematic patterns of parenting).

Many problematic behavioral patterns, including school dropout, early parenthood, substance abuse, and criminality are associated with low socioeconomic status (SES). Problematic behavioral histories may be both *direct* predictors of poor outcomes in offspring across a variety of middle- and upper-SES, as well as lower-SES, groups, and *indirect* predictors of negative outcomes for offspring, through problematic parental trajectories such as school failure and early parenthood. However, it is important to emphasize that problematic parental behavior and poverty are often closely linked within vulnerable populations. Risk to offspring in such families is predicted by a complex, multifactorial set of predictors (Kraemer et al. 2001), hence the title of the paper: "The Intergenerational Transfer of Psychosocial Risk. . . ."

INTERGENERATIONAL DESIGNS

Cairns et al. (1998) identified three important criteria for designing intergenerational research studies. First, individuals should be observed at roughly the same age (or developmental stage) in two or more successive generations. Second, the longitudinal information should be prospective rather than retrospective. Third, the data should be multilevel, and obtained from multiple measurement sources or domains. We find this to be a useful guide, yet argue that it may be unavoidable for studies to include retrospective information to address certain issues. It is not reconstruction of past events, per se, that is necessarily problematic, but rather the exclusive reliance on individuals' reports of past behavior and events that may lead to recall or retrieval bias.

The intergenerational transfer of risk may be carried out in steps or stages, focusing on distinct aspects of the model and the specific issues being investigated. For example, longitudinal prediction from childhood behavior and experiences to the circumstances of parenthood (e.g., teen parenthood, smoking during and post pregnancy, single parenthood, school drop-out, and family poverty) may be legitimate and interesting targets or intermediate outcome measures in research on the processes of intergenerational transfer of risk. In this type of design, only one generation might be included within a longitudinal analysis, but the issue addressed is highly relevant to the future development of their offspring. Most of the studies included in this review, however, include observations of at least two generations to address issues of the transfer of risk.

In this schematic (Figure 1), the intergenerational stability of risk for a particular behavior or outcome (e.g., childhood behavior problems) is represented by the arrow "a." That is, the relation between the childhood behavior of the parent generation, G1, at Time 1, and the childhood behavior of their offspring, G2, at a later point, Time 3. Arrow "a" represents a statistical prediction from G1 to G2: Depending on the theoretical model, "a" may represent a direct causal path (e.g., a genetically based transfer of risk), or a simple predictive statement (i.e., no direct causal pathway is inferred). Intervening, at Time 2, are the potential mediators of the process. A mediator variable represents the mechanism through which the independent variable is able to influence the dependent variable (Baron & Kenny 1986). As shown in Figure 1, the parenting behavior of the G1 as adults, and the characteristics and context of the G2 child's environment (which may be predicted by the G1's childhood behavior) signify possible mediators. Arrows "b" and "c" represent the relations between the G1 behavior in childhood and the Time 2 mediator, and between the Time 2 mediator and the behavior of the G2 at Time 3, respectively. As we discuss below, evidence supports both continuity (arrow "a") and mediation effects (arrows "b" and "c") within the results of specific studies. Similarly, intergenerational continuity of parenting behavior from G1 to G2 is represented by arrow "d," with possible mediation of this continuity through the childhood behavior and experiences of the G2 (arrows "c" and "e"). Recursive and transactional effects that are not shown in this model (e.g., effect of G2 behavior on G1 parenting) are also suggested by the results of some of the studies described below.

INTERGENERATIONAL PREDICTORS OF PSYCHOSOCIAL RISK

Adolescent Parenthood

Family circumstances at the time of birth are extremely powerful predictors of later outcomes for young children. Adolescent parenthood, in particular, is

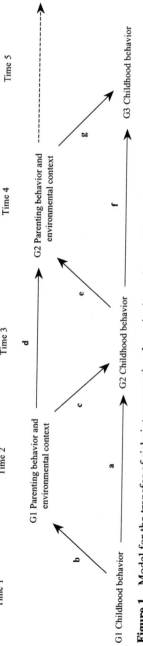

Figure 1   Model for the transfer of risk: intergenerational continuity and potential mediators.

associated with lower socioeconomic status across the subsequent life course of both generations. Early parenthood has been correlated with many forms of future disadvantage, including low parental education, family poverty, single parenthood, low occupational status, and job instability. These socioeconomic and sociodemographic factors are established predictors of risk to young offspring's cognitive, social-emotional, and physical development (Bradley & Corwyn 2002). Like other forms of sociodemographic disadvantage, adolescent parenthood may operate through a variety of mediational pathways, including lowered family access to important social and economic resources, and via the stress induced by exposure to adverse family circumstances. Mediational pathways, including prediction from childhood circumstances and experiences to teen parenthood in the G1, and from teen parenthood of the G1 to negative child outcomes in the G2, have been the focus of several recent longitudinal studies.

Internationally, census data and other national statistics confirm that early parenthood exhibits significant intergenerational continuity (that is, there is an elevated risk of adolescent parenthood in offspring of teen parents). A number of large prospective longitudinal studies, carried out with samples from different countries and cultural backgrounds, have addressed the issues of prediction of early childbearing and its consequences for both parent and child generations. Not surprisingly, the results of these studies show considerable intergenerational continuity in the tendency to have children at an early age. For example, following a sample of 404 African American women from poor Baltimore families and their children over 20 years, from the childhood of the G1 generation into the early adulthood of their children, G2, Furstenberg and his colleagues (Furstenberg et al. 1990) found an elevated risk of teen parenthood in the next generation born to teen mothers, compared with the remainder of the sample (i.e., G2 offspring, born to older parents) and with population norms.

Nevertheless, the majority of children of adolescent mothers did not go on to become teenage parents. In terms of mediators predicting teen parenthood in the G2, those offspring of young G1 mothers who did become teen parents were much more likely to have failed a grade in school, and to be living in poverty, than the G2 offspring who did not repeat the adolescent parenthood of their mothers. A subsequent 30-year outcome study of this sample (Hardy et al. 1998) reported that the daughters of teen mothers had experienced more negative long-term adult outcomes than the daughters of older mothers, in terms of education, financial independence, mental health, and healthy lifestyles. Finally, even for the offspring of teen mothers who avoided early parenthood themselves, having a teenage mother was linked with less positive outcomes in adolescence and early adulthood (e.g., repeating a grade, being arrested) than not having a teenage mother. This finding confirms other reports (e.g., Nagin & Tremblay 1999, 2001) of elevated risk for persistent antisocial behavior in the sons of adolescent mothers.

Consistent are the findings of Manlove in a large prospective study of a nationally representative British sample of 17,733 daughters (G2) of teen mothers (G1), who were consequently at elevated risk for adolescent parenthood (Manlove 1997).

Family SES predicted teenage childbearing in these G2 girls. Further, among the girls from economically disadvantaged families, those with fewer educational supports at home were more likely to have low academic achievement, to receive lower levels of teacher encouragement, and to attend less academically oriented schools: all factors that were in turn linked to a higher risk of teenage childbearing.

In terms of behavioral and social predictors of early childbearing, a number of longitudinal studies have focused on the characteristics and social environments of children during their middle childhood and early adolescent years as predictors of subsequent teen parenthood. In terms of behavioral predictors, several prospective longitudinal studies from diverse countries and communities including Quebec (Serbin et al. 1991a, 1998), rural Iowa (Scaramella et al. 1998), Oregon (Fagot et al. 1998), and New Zealand (Moffitt et al. 2001) confirm that childhood aggression and other forms of externalizing problem behavior appear to predict early parenthood in both girls (Miller-Johnson et al. 1999; Moffitt et al. 2001; Serbin et al. 1991, 1998; Underwood et al. 1996), and boys (Fagot et al. 1998). Unsurprisingly, teen parenthood was also related to prior adolescent delinquency and to risk-taking behavior, including early unprotected sexual activity (Serbin et al. 1991) and smoking (Moffitt et al. 2001). Mediating pathways between early problem behavior and teen parenthood include low levels of academic achievement, school failure, and high school dropout (Furstenberg et al. 1990, Manlove 1997, Serbin et al. 1998).

Several studies have also observed the parenting that the G2 received from their parents, the G1, during childhood and early adolescence, as predictors of adolescent parenthood in the G2 offspring. Observations of G1 parents interacting with G2 offspring (who later became teen parents) as young adolescents reveal negative parenting styles, involving coercive parenting behavior and low levels of supervision and monitoring (Shapiro & Miller 1998). Protective factors that lower the risk of early parenthood include educational achievement (i.e., academic competency, high school completion; Scaramella et al. 1998, Serbin et al. 1998), and supportive parenting styles, including warmth and involvement (Scaramella et al. 1998). Positive encouragement of school-related interests and achievements by parents and teachers (or other adult mentors) has also been identified as protective in several studies (Manlove 1997, Werner 1993).

Physical Health, Growth, and Early Development

One aspect of intergenerational transfer of risk to offspring is through maternal health and health-related behaviors, such as prenatal nutrition (see Chapman & Scott 2001 for a recent review). The importance of prenatal (and even preconception) diet for the physical health of infants is well established, as are the negative effects of smoking, drinking, and substance abuse on infants' physical growth. Equally important intergenerational effects of maternal health may be found for behavioral and cognitive aspects of early development. Some of these processes have been widely recognized and studied (e.g., fetal alcohol syndrome's effects on brain development, behavior, and cognition). Other physical risks to development are only beginning to be explored. For example, the negative effect of prenatal exposure to tobacco on fetal growth has been widely studied (Walsh 1994), but the effects of tobacco exposure on brain development, and consequently its impact on cognitive abilities and behavior, remains to be fully examined. It is likely that the same factors that influence intrauterine physical growth affect the development of the brain, through both biological and environmental pathways (Chapman & Scott 2001).

Currently, longitudinal prospective studies are beginning to address the issues of intergenerational continuity and mediation with regard to health risk behaviors (Wickrama et al. 1999). For example, intergenerational transfer of risk for smoking has been the focus of several recent studies. Wu & Kandel (1995) followed a longitudinal cohort over 19 years, beginning at age 15. Subsequently, they interviewed 201 offspring (aged 9 to 17), along with both parents. They found similarity (current smoking versus nonsmoking) between parents and children. A gender effect was also found: Children's smoking behavior was more closely related to the smoking of their same-gender parent than to the behavior of the other parent, which suggests a gender-related modeling effect. Parents' smoking was related to the quality of parenting: Parents who smoked exhibited less positive parenting than nonsmokers, including parental closeness, supervision, and norm setting. In terms of mediation of intergenerational continuity, G2 smoking patterns were mediated by maternal norm setting.

A subsequent prospective multigenerational study of 214 families, including G1 (grandparents), G2 (parents), and G3 (adolescent offspring), by Chassin et al. (1998) confirms and extends these findings. Intergenerational continuity of smoking behavior was found across the three generations. Again, parenting behaviors were predictive of adolescent smoking, both directly and by raising the likelihood of affiliating with smoking peers. Specifically, lower levels of support and less consistent discipline predicted adolescent smoking. Interestingly, two smoking-specific strategies (discussion and punishment) predicted lower risk of adolescent smoking. These results confirm the likelihood that parental modeling of smoking, discipline strategies such as norm setting, supervision and consistency, positive parenting (closeness, support), and smoking-specific interventions by parents all have the potential to impact adolescent behavior.

With regard to other predictors of physical health across generations, we have looked at long-term predictors of physical health in both mothers and offspring within the Concordia Longitudinal Risk Study of Quebec schoolchildren, initiated in 1976 (Serbin et al. 1991a,b, 1998). In 856 women, for whom complete medical records were available from their mid teens to early adulthood, childhood aggression predicted a variety of negative outcomes related to reproductive health and fertility, including sexually transmitted diseases and other gynecological problems, teen pregnancy, early parenthood, multiparity by early adulthood, and close spacing of births (less than two years apart). Childhood social withdrawal was also predictive of negative reproductive health, including teen pregnancy, multiparity, and close spacing of births. These negative birth circumstances are all documented causes of poor infant health.

Health risk to offspring of the Concordia sample was confirmed in a study of the complete medical records between birth and age four of the 94 children born to adolescent mothers (Serbin et al. 1996). Within this high-risk subsample of offspring, mothers' childhood aggression predicted elevated rates of infections and injuries during the first four years of life, along with higher rates of emergency room visits and hospitalizations. Asthma and respiratory infections accounted for many of these visits, especially among the sons of women with histories of childhood aggression. Beverly Fagot and her colleagues (1998) reported similar negative health and injury patterns in the offspring of aggressive boys from the Oregon Youth Study who had become teen fathers. One mediational mechanism identified in both of these samples is maternal smoking, which was related to parental childhood history of aggression. Other potential mediators suggested by these results are neglect (potentially involving poor nutrition, inadequate hygiene, lack of monitoring, and neglect of household safety precautions such as blocking stairways), and physical abuse by parents. In other words, childhood aggressive behavior seems to predict a negative pattern of parenting, including neglect and possibly family violence, which has an adverse impact on the early health of offspring. Smoking, predicted by childhood aggression in these studies, also seems to mediate the pathway from childhood aggressive behavior to poor early health in offspring.

One additional mediator that may be relevant to early health and growth is young children's cortisol reactivity. Activity of the hypothalamic-pituitary-adrenal (HPA) axis has been related to attentional processes as well as physical health and growth, with direct implications for the effectiveness of immune system response (Gunnar 1998). Children from the Concordia sample have been found to have atypical salivary cortisol response to social stress when observed during a verbal conflict task with their mothers. The children's blunted cortisol response was predicted by mothers' history of aggression, as well as current maternal functioning and parenting style (Granger et al. 1998). Baseline levels of salivary cortisol were correlated between mothers and children, and were predicted, in both generations, by a variety of indices of mothers' distress and by a maternal history of internalizing problems and social withdrawal. These findings, which are currently being replicated and extended, suggest that a neuroendocrine process involving reactivity of the HPA axis may be found to mediate some of the relations between parental behavior, environment, and children's health, as reported above.

In their review article, Chapman & Scott (2001) argue that the health and social policy implications of women's prenatal health for later development of their offspring are widely acknowledged. However, recent studies demonstrating prediction of child outcomes from mothers' health and behavior *prior* to conception suggest that the current policy focus on *prenatal* health, nutrition, and behavior needs to be broadened to include parents' earlier behavioral histories and their health trajectories prior to parenthood. They also encourage the broader use of epidemiological designs, utilizing large community-based (rather than specifically clinical) samples to examine the transfer of health risk between generations. Such epidemiological studies should have considerable relevance to urgent priorities in the areas of health and social policy (Scott et al. 1999).

Parenting

Within most current developmental theories, parenting is viewed as a major factor in the socialization of interpersonal behavior and as an essential element in the early stimulation of cognitive growth. Accordingly, parenting plays a key role as a mediator in most models of the intergenerational transfer of risk for developmental problems and maladaptive behavior that have been proposed. Theories of the origins of parenting behavior suggest that parenting practices are transmitted intergenerationally, with the parenting one receives as a child serving as a model for future parenting behavior in adulthood (Belsky 1984). Two major reviews of the literature related to the intergenerational continuity of parenting have been published in recent years (Putallaz et al. 1998, Van Ijzendoorn 1992). These reviews both conclude that there is generally support for the intergenerational consistency of parenting practices. However, we know relatively little about the causal processes and other contextual factors that influence the development of parenting behavior. Both reviews discuss the necessity of longitudinal studies to address these issues.

Relatively few studies have prospectively examined the relation between the parenting experienced in childhood (i.e., G1 to G2) and subsequent parenting behavior toward the next generation (G2 to G3). Obviously, there is substantial time investment, effort, and cost involved in such studies: It may take 20 to 30 years to make a developmentally appropriate comparison between the parenting behavior of successive generations. Consequently, the majority of "intergenerational" parenting studies in the literature have been carried out by comparing generations at a particular point in time (i.e., using retrospective reports or current intergenerational observations of mothers interacting with grandmothers, etc.), although briefer longitudinal (e.g., prenatal parenting beliefs as predictors of subsequent observations of parents interacting with their young offspring; Belsky et al. 1989) and cross-sectional designs (e.g., comparing parent-child correlations in families who are currently at different points in the life course; Covell et al. 1995) have also been employed. Often, parents' retrospective reports about the parenting that they received as children are compared with their reports of their own current parenting behavior. Not surprisingly, these reports tend to be correlated, but this may be heavily influenced by retrospective and rater biases.

There is considerable evidence of intergenerational consistency with regard to specific aspects of parenting, including attachment relations (Benoit & Parker 1994, Kretchmar & Jacobvitz 2002), harsh parenting practices (Holden & Zambarano 1992; Simons et al. 1991, 1992), and child abuse (Egeland et al. 1988, Hunter & Kilstrom 1979, Kaufman & Zigler 1989, McCloskey & Bailey 2000, Oliver 1993, Rutter 1989, Zeanah & Zeanah 1989). This continuity has generally been attributed by researchers to the social learning of parenting behavior, or to the acquisition of cognitive schemas regarding parenting. Evidence of genetic factors in the continuity of abuse has also been recently reported (Caspi et al. 2002). Mediating processes [e.g., socioeconomic status (SES) and personality characteristics] and various contextual/environmental moderators were also suggested in many of the available studies, although various limitations of the research designs made causal interpretations difficult or impossible to make (Van Ijzendoorn 1992). Also, Putallaz and her colleagues (1998) point out that the roles of temperament and other heritable characteristics, or of genotype-environment interactions, have largely been ignored in this literature to date (although these issues are beginning to be explored; Caspi et al. 2002, Raine 2002).

CONTINUITY OF PARENTING AND PROCESSES OF MEDIATION   In one of the few longitudinal studies to focus primarily on the prediction of positive parenting abilities, Chen & Kaplan (2001) examined the intergenerational transmission of "constructive parenting" (a construct including measures of monitoring, communication, involvement in education, expression of affection, and consistent discipline). In this large-scale study, 2338 young adolescents, recruited from Houston (Texas) public schools at ages 12 to 13, were asked for their perceptions of the parenting they were currently experiencing. They were reassessed in their twenties for measures of intervening variables, and again for measures of parenting in their mid thirties, when their children were ages 6 to 18. The authors report intergenerational continuity of constructive parenting, which was primarily attributable in their equations to role-specific modeling of parenting behaviors. Intergenerational continuity in parenting behavior was partially mediated by the interpersonal relationships of the G2s and their social participation, as reported in their mid twenties. Parent-child similarity was not completely explained by the ongoing personality and social characteristics of the G2s, however, leaving the likelihood of direct transmission of parenting style between generations. Socioeconomic factors and family characteristics (e.g., two-parent family structure), as well as individual characteristics and behaviors of the G2s were also statistically significant predictors of their future parenting.

Many of the recent longitudinal intergenerational studies of parenting have focused on the transfer of negative parenting characteristics and maladaptive behavioral styles. In particular, a series of three-generation, prospective studies of harsh styles of parenting, including severe disciplinary practices, expressed hostility and aggression toward children (Brook et al. 1998, Capaldi et al. 2003b, Conger et al. 2003, Hops et al. 2003, Thornberry et al. 2003a), and child maltreatment (Pears & Capaldi 2001, Zuravin et al. 1996) have recently appeared. Across a variety of risk populations (including rural and inner-city lower-SES families from different regions of the United States and a variety of diverse ethnic and racial groups), there has been consistent support for a direct relation between the negative and maladaptive parenting behavior of G1 (experienced in childhood by G2) and the parenting behavior of G2 in adulthood (as parents toward their own children, G3).

A wide variety of mediating factors have been identified in these studies, although the direct relation between the parenting experienced in childhood and adult parenting behavior is generally supported, even after these mediators are entered into predictive equations. Some identified mediators of harsh and aggressive parenting include the personality traits of the G2 (Brook et al. 1998), and adolescent antisocial and delinquent behavior (Capaldi et al. 2003b, Hops et al. 2003). Reported mediators of child maltreatment include a history of severe sexual abuse of the G2 mothers, and poor attachment relationships between the G2 and the G3 offspring (Zuravin et al. 1996). Parental depression (in the G2) and diagnosis of post-traumatic stress disorder in G2 fathers were also predictive of continuity of abuse (Pears & Capaldi 2001). In terms of buffering factors leading to better outcomes within high-risk families, consistency of discipline in child-rearing practices was identified as a protective factor against the intergenerational continuity of abuse (Pears & Capaldi 2001).

PREDICTING DYSFUNCTIONAL PARENTING AND IMPOVERISHED HOME ENVIRONMENT   As discussed above, most current developmental theories focus on parenting, socialization, and the environment in which children are raised as key elements in the transfer of risk. Beyond the issues of intergenerational continuity and mediation discussed in the previous section, a number of recent studies have examined the prediction of parenting and rearing/environmental conditions from childhood behavior and environmental characteristics, and have included a variety of intervening experiences, such as high school dropout and early parenthood, within their predictive models. In general, these longitudinal studies have found that there are many complex factors predicting problematic parenting behavior and other environmental threats to the development of young offspring, as well as a number of protective factors that may reduce risk within vulnerable populations.

Socioeconomic threats to future successful parenting are well documented in the literature (Bradley & Corwyn 2002). Beyond poverty, adverse family circumstances, and parenting practices in their family of origin, children's behavioral characteristics, their social and academic experiences, and a variety of ongoing environmental/contextual factors have also been linked to parenting outcomes (Chase-Lansdale et al. 1994, Cox et al. 1985, Dunn et al. 2000, Kramer & Baron 1995, Olsen et al. 1999, Simons et al. 1993, Wakschlag et al. 1996). One consistent threat to competent parenting that has now been identified in a number of longitudinal studies is aggression and antisocial behavior during childhood. Behavioral problems identified as risk factors for future parenting problems include adolescent delinquency (Conger et al. 2003, Fagot et al. 1998, Thornberry et al. 2003a), a clinical diagnosis of conduct disorder (Capaldi et al. 2003b, Ehrensaft et al. 2003), and a range of hostile and aggressive social behaviors that may be observed within broader community-based samples (Cairns et al. 1998; Scaramella et al. 1998; Serbin et al. 1991a,b, 1998).

Problematic trajectories have been consistently observed in studies of aggressive girls and boys during the transition to parenthood, across a wide variety of study populations. The pathways from childhood aggression to problematic parenting typically include a number of mediational factors and indirect pathways, including low academic achievement and school failure, early and single parent-hood, low income and poverty status, low levels of perceived social support, and adult mental health problems such as depression and substance abuse. Not surprisingly, high levels of parenting stress and family conflict are also included within these trajectories.

Mediational models and specific trajectories from childhood aggression to parenting have been found to differ for males and females (e.g., single parenthood is more closely associated with poverty, stress, and negative parenting outcomes for mothers and their offspring than for fathers, possibly because single mothers generally have more daily involvement with their children than do single fathers; Serbin et al. 2002, Thornberry et al. 2003a). Findings of specific mediators between childhood aggression and parenting vary somewhat between studies. Certain important elements in these equations, however, especially the role of educational achievement as a buffer against negative parenting outcomes within high-risk samples, are consistently reported across both genders, and across geographically and culturally diverse populations (Cairns et al. 1998; Scaramella et al. 1998; Serbin et al. 1998, 2002; Simons et al. 1991, 1993). In addition to mediational pathways, however, there appears to be a stable and direct trajectory from childhood aggressive and antisocial behavior to hostile and conflictual interpersonal relationships in adulthood, including both harshly punitive and neglectful parenting styles (Capaldi et al. 2003b, Conger et al. 2003, Fagot et al. 1998, Hops et al. 2003, Serbin et al. 1998, Thornberry et al. 2003a), in both males and females.

Another aspect of parenting that has been predicted in intergenerational studies concerns the stimulation of offspring's early cognitive development. In addition to established risk factors such as family of origin SES (i.e., in G1), findings have consistently shown that G2's parental education, ongoing family poverty, lowered levels of social support, family conflict, and subsequently elevated stress levels all impact parents' ability to stimulate the cognitive development of their young children, the G3 (Bradley & Corwyn 2002). The link between these socioeconomic risk factors and the stimulation provided within the physical and social home environment has been established in a variety of studies. However, new findings from intergenerational longitudinal studies demonstrate that childhood behavioral characteristics, in particular aggression and antisocial behavior, add to the risk equation and directly increase the risk for low educational attainment, early parenthood, and adult poverty. In addition to this pathway between G1 childhood aggression and subsequent parenting, childhood behavioral characteristics are also directly predictive of parents' ability to provide cognitive stimulation in the home environment and appropriate levels of scaffolding necessary to help their young children acquire new problem-solving skills (Cairns et al. 1998; Cooperman 1999; Saltaris et al. 2003; Serbin et al. 1991a, 2003).

Aggression and Antisocial Behavior

Aggressive and antisocial behavior has been the subject of many longitudinal studies across the past half century. The stability of childhood aggression into adulthood has been repeatedly demonstrated (Tremblay 2000), as has its relation to adolescent delinquency, adult criminality, and related psychiatric diagnoses such as conduct disorder and antisocial personality disorder (Farrington 1991, Thornberry & Krohn 2003). Until relatively recently, most longitudinal studies of aggressive, antisocial behavior focused primarily on males. Relatively few studies have included samples of aggressive girls. Similarly, in prospective risk studies (e.g., children having a criminal or antisocial parent), high-risk girls have often been excluded from research designs. Within the past decade, however, there has been growing recognition of the importance of early aggressive behavior in girls as a predictor of many negative life outcomes, in addition to the prediction of criminality.

The long-term social and mental health prospects for aggressive girls have consistently been found to be poor across studies of varied populations, and using a variety of measures, classification systems, and operational definitions (Moffitt et al. 2001, Peplar et al. 2003, Putallaz & Bierman 2003, Stack et al. 2003, Underwood 2003, Zoccolillo et al. 1992). Negative adult outcomes of girls' aggression include a variety of mental health and social/occupational problems, including elevated risk for depression, smoking, alcohol and substance-abuse, school failure, early parenthood, low income, single family status, unstable employment history, and conflictual family and social relations. These conditions place the young offspring born to women who are following problematic trajectories at risk for a wide variety of health, psychological, and social problems.

The intergenerational continuity of criminality has been widely established in a large international literature, especially with regard to fathers and sons (McCord 1977, 1995). However, until recently relatively few studies had examined the intergenerational continuity of childhood aggression and antisocial behavior, despite the importance of this pattern for predicting future outcomes and trajectories in children of both sexes. Mediation of intergenerational continuity in childhood aggression is also beginning to be studied within longitudinal studies, along with attempts to include and integrate a widening variety of potential influences and processes within predictive models.

CONTINUITY AND MEDIATION OF CHILDHOOD AGGRESSION   The longitudinal study of childhood aggression by Huesmann and his colleagues (1984, 2003) is one of the best known and most widely cited projects in this literature. It included more than 600 children from age 8 to mid adulthood, plus their parents and children. In this study, intergenerational continuity of aggression was found to be even greater than individual continuity across the life course if successive generations were assessed at approximately the same age (Huesmann et al. 1984). The finding of continuity between generations, especially when assessed in childhood or adolescence, is supported by the results of several other prospective intergenerational studies that have carried out this type of comparison (e.g., Kaplan & Liu 1999, Thornberry et al. 2003a). However, other studies (e.g., Cairns et al. 1998, Cohen et al. 1998, Conger et al. 2003) report minimal intergenerational consistency, or consistency that is entirely mediated by parenting behavior and other intervening events. Intergenerational consistency is less likely to be reported when parents' childhood or adolescent aggression has been used to predict aggressive behavior in considerably younger offspring.

Both consistency and mediators typically vary by gender of parent and child, with fathers and sons usually showing the greatest consistency, and fathers' early antisocial behavior a stronger direct predictor of offspring's aggression than mothers' (e.g., Thornberry 2003a). However, mothers' harsh and aggressive parenting was a significant predictor of offspring's aggression in most of the recent intergenerational studies, with parenting functioning as a mediating factor between the childhood experiences of the mothers and the problem behavior of their offspring (Brook et al. 2002, Conger et al. 2003, Thornberry et al. 2003a). In general, hostile parenting behavior is predictive of aggressive behavior in young offspring.

Several other studies support these conclusions regarding the mediation and prediction of children's antisocial behavior. Over a five-year period, McCord (1991) studied the families of 253 boys aged 5 to 13, from high-risk backgrounds, who were in a preventive treatment program for adolescent delinquency. Criminal fathers in this sample showed a greater likelihood of aggressive and punitive behavior in interacting with their children (and also of being absent from the family). Socialization variables that promoted subsequent crime in the boys included parental conflict and aggression. Conversely, maternal affection and other positive maternal characteristics (e.g., self-confidence) predicted better outcomes within this high-risk sample.

Subsequently, McCord (1999) examined crime and alcoholism across two generations in the Cambridge-Somerville Youth Study. In this report, 214 pairs of fathers and sons were each followed into their fourth decade in age. McCord again found that alcoholic and criminal men were disproportionately likely to be aggressive in their families. They were also found to have fathered sons whose mothers were rated as less competent in their maternal roles. The results of both studies indicated that alcoholism and crime tend to continue in families partially because alcoholic and criminal parents tend to provide poor socializing environments. That is, the mediational role of negative parenting behavior, by both mothers and fathers, is supported by these results. However, both studies indicate mothers' potential to "buffer" high-risk children from negative outcomes, via competent and involved parenting, consistent with the results of other studies.

A recent study by Ehrensaft and colleagues (2003) further confirms both parent-child continuity of antisocial behavior and the mediational effects of parenting. In a short-term (15-month) longitudinal study, 126 African American and Hispanic boys who were at risk for antisocial behavior (defined here as having an older brother with a recent juvenile court conviction) and their families (most families included an unemployed, single parent) were studied. Mothers' history of onset of conduct disorder before age 15 made a direct, incremental contribution to prediction of worsening behavior in these boys over the course of the study. However, maternal diagnosis of conduct disorder at an older age was not predictive of children's behavior. In other words, early onset (before age 15) antisocial behavior in mothers increased the probability of behavioral problems in their sons. However, parenting behavior was also predictive in these results: Lower parental involvement, less monitoring, and higher levels of parent-child conflict were all predictive of worsening behavior problems. These results support the likely contribution of both genetic and socialization factors in predicting antisocial behavior, as well as the mediating role of parenting behavior in the process of intergenerational transfer of risk. They also underscore the potential value of intervention with conduct-disordered adolescent girls as a means of preventing the transfer of risk to another generation.

THE INTERFACE BETWEEN GENETICS AND SOCIALIZATION IN THE PREDICTION OF CHILDHOOD AGGRESSION   It would clearly be informative for intergenerational studies to include detailed examination of both genetic and environmental factors, and their interaction, within the risk equation (Campbell et al. 2000, Caspi et al. 2002, Raine 2002, Rutter 1998, Shaw 2003). One of the few intergenerational studies to date to incorporate a "genetically informed" design into the study of the psychosocial transfer of risk was carried out by Ge and his colleagues (1996). In this study, 45 children aged 12 to 18 years who had been adopted at birth were studied, along with their adoptive parents. The biological parents of 22 of these children had been diagnosed as either having a substance abuse/dependency disorder or antisocial personality disorder. It was found that the biological parents' disorders predicted antisocial/hostile behaviors in their offspring. However, the biological parents' disorders were also associated with the adoptive parents' subsequent parenting behavior.

In particular, adoptive fathers showed significantly higher levels of harsh and inconsistent discipline and lower levels of warmth and nurturance toward adopted children whose biological parents had the highest level of psychiatric disturbance. Ge et al. (1996) concluded that children's antisocial behavior, linked genetically to higher levels of pathology in biological parents, mediated the parenting behavior of their adoptive parents. In a transactional fashion, these children's difficult behavior seemed to have prompted adoptive parents to take on harsher, less affectionate parenting styles, which, in turn, increased their children's risk profile. This study illustrates the potential interactive, recursive, and transactional relation between genetic and environmental risk factors across the course of development.

CHILDHOOD AGGRESSION AS AN INTERGENERATIONAL PREDICTOR OF RISK   From the literature discussed above, it is clear that the long-term trajectories followed by highly aggressive children have negative implications for their future parenting and family functioning, as well as for the outcomes of their children. Risk is transferred to offspring not only in terms of continuity of aggression and other behavior problems, but also in terms of early health and cognitive development. One additional finding that should be mentioned in this context is a report by Capaldi & Clark (1998) that boys showing antisocial behavior in early adolescence are more likely to abuse their future spouses: obviously a factor that increases risk to the young offspring of these families. Assortative mating, with aggressive individuals likely to partner with others who also have conflictual interpersonal styles, has also been reported in several studies (Capaldi & Crosby 1997, Moffitt et al. 2001, Peters 1999). In other words, the offspring are likely to get a "double dose" of maladaptive parenting in such families. Conversely, in terms of protective factors within vulnerable families, several reports have suggested that children at high risk for criminality (e.g., having a parent with history of criminality, substance abuse, or major mental disorder) may be "buffered" from negative outcomes if their parents use an effective style of parenting and discipline.

AGGRESSION AND EDUCATIONAL SUCCESS   The long-term risk profile of childhood aggression and antisocial behavior leading to negative conditions of child rearing is partly mediated by education. That is, educational success and years of education are negatively predicted by childhood aggression, both as a direct effect (aggressive children tend to leave school before graduation) and because of lower academic skills that are typically present from the beginning of the child's school career (e.g., learning problems and lower levels of basic competencies). Aggressive young children who nevertheless acquire competent academic skills and successfully complete high school are far less likely to become young parents, live in poverty, etc. In other words, psychosocial risk can be reduced when an aggressive child does not follow the typical trajectory predicted by their early behavior. This suggests that strong academic support, including early assessment and intervention for academic competencies and learning disabilities, might be an important preventive strategy for these children.

Cognitive Ability and Academic Achievement

The processes discussed in the proceeding sections (e.g., predictors of school dropout, early parenthood, poverty, impoverished home environment, and lowered rates of parental scaffolding of young children's problem-solving attempts) would be expected to place young offspring at risk for early developmental delays and cognitive problems, in addition to behavioral difficulties. Intergenerational continuity with regard to measures of a wide variety of cognitive abilities is well established in the literature. This literature is also known for its many behavior genetic studies, establishing the heritability of IQ (estimates range widely, but most studies provide a substantial heritability quotient), and other types of specific and general problem-solving abilities. Stimulation in the home and parenting have also been explored as predictors of children's cognitive abilities and academic performance. Several recent investigations have explored continuity and prediction with an intergenerational design, from the parents' childhood behavior, performance, and experiences to the subsequent cognitive and academic performance of offspring in childhood.

Cairns et al. (1998) compared the childhood behavior and cognitive development of 57 women, who were followed over a 17-year period, with the social behavior and academic performance of their offspring, who were followed from toddlerhood (age 1 to 2) to early school age. As mentioned in the previous section, aggressive behavior showed little intergenerational continuity in this study, possibly because mothers had been assessed at an older age than their children. However academic competence was predicted intergenerationally. Path models confirmed that family background (SES of G1) was predictive of a "literacy environment" in the homes of the G2 mothers, which in turn predicted academic competency in the G3 offspring. In other words, the effect of G2's childhood environment (SES at Time 1) as an intergenerational predictor of academic competency in their offspring (G3) was mediated by the home and parenting environment at Time 2, when the offspring were toddlers, and prior to the assessment of school achievement in the G3. Similarly, in the Concordia Longitudinal Study, we found that IQ scores of 80 offspring at preschool age were predicted by mothers' childhood aggression. This relation was mediated by current environmental variables, including parenting stress and cognitive stimulation, via quality of the home environment and maternal scaffolding of children's problem solving (Saltaris et al. 2003).

Considering these results, it would be very interesting to design a study that examined heritability of cognitive performance (i.e., utilizing a genetically informed design), measures of childhood aggression and other potentially relevant behavioral characteristics (e.g., attention, task persistence, compliance), as well as potentially relevant mediators (e.g., education, income, parenting, home environment). Some of the genetic continuity in cognitive ability that has been widely reported might be attributable to intergenerational continuity of related childhood behaviors (aggression, attention, etc.). In turn, some of this "behavioral" variability may be mediated by specific environmental influences such as parental scaffolding and quality of the home environment. Several authors have argued the advantages of including both genetic and environmental sources of variance within intergenerational longitudinal models and designs (e.g., Capaldi et al. 2003a, Ge et al. 1996, Rutter 1998, Serbin & Karp 2003).

CONCEPTUAL ISSUES IN INTERGENERATIONAL RESEARCH

In the final section, we highlight several conceptual issues that arose as we prepared this paper, and offer recommendations and suggestions for future intergenerational research projects addressing the transfer of risk from parent to child.

From our perspective, prospective longitudinal intergenerational designs represent a unique methodological approach: a research paradigm that can be adapted to address many types of theoretical and empirical issues. Intergenerational designs can be used to structure both original data collection and secondary analysis of existing data, in order to investigate a wide variety of theoretically based hypotheses and to answer specific research questions.

In many cases available data sets (and the results of previous investigations using those sets) suggest intriguing questions that can be addressed with available information, exploring hypotheses that are highly relevant to current theoretical issues. Alternatively, new data collection can be designed to build onto existing data in a longitudinal study in order to directly address pertinent theoretical issues. In other cases, reconstruction of data, using current conceptual models and modern statistical methods, may provide important information about intergenerational processes.

In many related disciplines (for example, sociology, economics, and epidemiology) there is widespread use of previously collected data sets (Brooks-Gunn et al. 1991). Use of large data banks and research archives is viewed as essential for studying complex phenomena (over which there is rarely the possibility of experimental control) over time. In these disciplines, there is extensive reliance on data sets compiled for multiple (and often unrelated) purposes, such as census data, income tax statistics, or health records. Psychology is now beginning to integrate its basic theoretical and methodological approaches to the study of behavior with the constructs and methods of other disciplines. This is probably the only way we can study complex patterns of behavior and development as they actually happen within the "natural" environment. Working in areas related to mental and physical health, psychologists may need to incorporate models drawn from biologically-based disciplines such as genetics, physiology, neurology, and neuroendocrinology, as well as from the other social and environmental sciences. We need these transdisciplinary models to understand complex issues that are highly relevant to our own disciplinary interests; for example, understanding the health and developmental challenges to children living in poverty.

If psychologists want to benefit from the wealth of data available from archival data and longitudinal studies, they may have to become extremely creative in their adaptation of existing designs to fit new theoretical models. Re-creating measures, for example, from older instruments that are outdated to form constructs that approximate those of current instruments may be necessary. Similarly, combined measures of latent constructs may have to be formed from older measures to accommodate current statistical models and the more powerful programs now available to test theoretical models, such as Linear Structural Relationships (LISREL), Equations (EQS), Structural Equation Model (SEM), or Hierarchical Linear and Nonlinear Modeling (HLM). If a strong theoretical model, or even an implicit model, can be addressed by the data set, this is often worth exploring. As with other types of designs, of course, findings should ideally be replicated in other studies, to examine their generality or specificity across diverse samples, populations, contexts, and historical periods. The strategy of preparing parallel analyses using different longitudinal data sets to test a specific theoretical model is a promising approach to the issue of replication (Capaldi et al. 2003a, Dubow et al. 2003, Thornberry et al. 2003b).

LIMITATIONS OF INTERGENERATIONAL STUDIES OF PSYCHOSOCIAL RISK

Some of the limitations of the intergenerational studies reviewed here can be avoided in future studie. Other limitations (such as the unidirectional nature of time) are probably unavoidable, regardless of new developments in the field.

The Correlational Nature of Longitudinal Research

Even in longitudinal studies where participants are assigned randomly to some type of intervention, the events in peoples' lives, the neighborhoods in which they live, and the various happy and tragic events they experience will be beyond experimental control. These events may occur in an apparently random fashion or systematically, adding noise and potential bias within the predictive equation. We can choose to ignore such unplanned or uncontrolled factors (i.e., treat them as "error" variance) or try to measure and incorporate them as predictive factors or outcomes in our designs. In addition, nonrandom loss of participants is also an important issue that must be addressed within all longitudinal designs, as it may lead to biased results and misleading conclusions (Cotter et al. 2002). Due to the nature of their designs, intergenerational projects including multiple generations will probably have an increased "loading" of these types of variance above studies of single generations. We can try to use statistical controls for some of this variability (e.g., the use of regression analyses, or application of survival analysis techniques). Alternatively, these nonrandom variables may be of conceptual interest within a design, even though individuals have not been randomly assigned to levels of education, income, occupational and marital status, neighborhood, etc.

To confirm whether predictive effects are causal, of course, we will have to rely on future intervention studies, using various experimental, quasi-experimental, or other comparative designs. Sometimes, the results of controlled experimental studies may already have revealed the effects of the predictive factors, such as parenting behavior, which can subsequently be observed within naturalistic longitudinal studies. In this case, the observed phenomena will tell us about the effectiveness and impact of these factors as they actually happen, which may be quite different from the effects seen under controlled experimental conditions.

Specificity of Results to a Specific Sample

As with other longitudinal designs, the results of intergenerational projects are inherently ideographic or specific to the group and events actually sampled. Wars, for example, may be unique in their impact upon a particular generation. WWII had a profoundly different impact upon then draft-age adolescents than did the Vietnam War. Within intergenerational designs, again, the ideographic or specific nature of events and life experiences may be amplified. Probabilities of identical events occurring between successive generations, in multiple families, seem infinitesimal. However, there is certainly a place for the study of ideographic phenomena in many disciplines (e.g., astronomy, history). Often study of unique phenomena goes beyond interesting descriptions: From the study of multiple "unique" cases, general phenomena may appear. As in other areas of psychology, replication of observations in other samples will reveal which developmental phenomena are unique to specific groups or subgroups (in other words, this is partially the study of diversity) and which seem more general or universal.

Incorporating Genetic and Other Biological Processes into Models for Studying the Intergenerational Transfer of Risk

Behavioral similarity between generations is potentially due to both genetic and environmental factors. Without genetic information, we are clearly studying only a piece of the puzzle of intergenerational transfer when we focus on behavior and environment. Use of specific samples that allow behavior genetic models to be incorporated into the design is one solution to this problem (e.g., Ge et al. 1996). New advances in work with physiological, behavioral, or molecular genetic markers may provide opportunities that have not existed in the past to measure the genetic and physiological similarity of parent and child generations (Campbell et al. 2000, Raine 2002, Shaw 2003). Ongoing intergenerational studies may choose to incorporate these new designs and methods into their upcoming data collection. Conceivably, available data can be utilized to construct indices of genetic constructs as this field evolves.

Inconsistencies and Discontinuity of Risk

Although there are many consistencies in the results reported above, there are also inconsistencies. One challenge for researchers is predicting discontinuity of risk, and the processes that may protect some children within vulnerable or at-risk populations. Buffering and protective effects that are consistently reported across studies include parental education and a variety of positive parenting characteristics, including emotional warmth, support, monitoring, and consistency, which appear as mediating factors predicting more positive outcomes for high-risk offspring. Offspring characteristics (e.g., temperament and problem behavior) are often assumed to contribute to ongoing risk profiles within families, although relatively few studies have tested recursive or transactional effects (i.e., of G2 child characteristics on G1 parenting) within their predictive models.

Including "Missing" Parents

Many intergenerational studies have childhood observations of only one of the G1 parents (as the other parent usually was not part of the original sample). Obviously, as children have two biological parents (and potentially more than two individuals raising them), the histories of these individuals ideally should be included in designs which attempt to examine the effects of current parenting and environment while controlling for parental history (Serbin & Stack 1998). In the absence of childhood observations, it may be possible to obtain relevant information from these individuals currently, or from their families or records. In addition to including retrospective information (such as structured, standardized interviews about childhood and family behavioral and health histories), a considerable amount of relevant archival data (e.g., school or health records) may be available about family members who were not part of the original study. In the complete absence of information about the history of one parent, this limitation should clearly be recognized in discussing and interpreting the results of intergenerational studies.

Babies are Not Born According to Researchers' (or Funding Agencies') Schedules

One of the most daunting and difficult issues faced by researchers seeking to carry out intergenerational projects is the difficulty of estimating the number of offspring that will be born to a given sample of parents, or the dates at which children will arrive. This can make for difficulties in designing protocols (including measures appropriate for the developmental level of the children, who may vary widely in age at the time of a study). Alternatively, even if target ages of offspring at the time of assessment are planned and specified within a design (e.g., postpartum, at 12 months, at 36 months, etc.), until children are actually conceived, it will be difficult to specify sample sizes and timetables. Conventional design and projection requirements of funding agencies are typically violated by these projects, and funding may be difficult to obtain and sustain over the years necessary to carry out the project. Creativity is required of both the researcher and the supporting agency in finding practical solutions to these problems.

Implications for Future Intergenerational Studies

It is important to recognize that intergenerational studies have the potential to examine complex models, including genetic and environmental main effects, correlations, and interactions, if the data are available in project archives, or could be collected in the next phase of the study. For example, "pedigree" information could be obtained for grandparents and other relatives via family histories of psychopathology or physical illness. Similarly, it would be possible to collect samples to obtain genetic markers of particular traits from both parents and children. In other words, longitudinal designs are adaptable: We are restricted by the laws of temporal constraint from changing what was done in the past, at the initiation of the study, but not from designing future stages of ongoing projects. If we want to study and understand the complex lives of families over time, then we will have to be extremely creative and flexible, and borrow methods and ideas from many complementary disciplines, to make these projects meaningful.

CONCLUSION

One reason issues of intergenerational transfer of risk are so compelling, beyond their theoretical and empirical centrality within the field of human development, is their potential importance for social, educational, and health policy. Before preventive interventions aimed at improving children's health and well-being can be designed and evaluated, it is essential to identify and evaluate specific predictors of risk and "buffers" promoting resiliency (Institute of Medicine, National Academy of Sciences 1994; Kraemer et al. 2001; Scott et al. 1999). These predictors, if they have the potential for change or implementation, may hold the key to designing effective prevention strategies. Given the critical importance of healthy functioning during early childhood for lifelong development, designing preventive strategies that can be implemented during early childhood, pregnancy, and in some cases, prior to conception, would obviously be ideal. This will require targeting parental functioning and environment for early intervention. Hence, intergenerational studies are potentially important for prevention and policy.

The findings discussed in this chapter may have relevance and utility in addressing urgent social issues. The mediational hypotheses suggested by the findings of intergenerational studies can suggest potential interventions, which could be designed and evaluated using appropriate, controlled experimental methodology. For example, many of the current studies point to maternal education as a key protective element for various aspects of children's development in high-risk families. An obvious follow-up to these results would be an experimental study of the effects of educational support to young mothers (or to girls at risk of high school dropout) on the subsequent development of their children.

Social and economic policy, which has a strong impact on the lives of the most vulnerable young mothers and their families, could also be designed with these findings in mind. For example, sending young single mothers to work may reduce welfare dependency and increase levels of family income. However, unless specific early stimulation and educational supports are included in these programs, requiring mothers to work will not directly address the developmental problems of their children that are related to low levels of maternal education and insufficient early cognitive stimulation. The needs of vulnerable populations of children can only be met once the process of transfer of risk within these families, via parenting and environment, is understood.

In conclusion, intergenerational studies of families have a unique potential to inform us about important conceptual, applied, and policy issues. In particular, recent findings of intergenerational research present new and exciting opportunities to understand the processes of risk and resilience that affect our most vulnerable populations. It is our hope that the results of recent and ongoing intergenerational projects will be closely examined and utilized by researchers and policy analysts alike, in designing effective preventive interventions for at-risk children and their families.

The *Annual Review of Psychology* is online at http://psych.annualreviews.org

LITERATURE CITED

Baron RM, Kenny DA. 1986. The moderator-mediator variable distinction in social psychological research: conceptual, strategic, and statistical considerations. *J. Personal. Soc. Psychol.* 51:1173–82

Belsky J. 1984. The determinants of

parenting: a process model. *Child Dev.* 55:83–96

Belsky J, Youngblade L, Pensky E. 1989. Child-rearing history, marital quality, and maternal affect: intergenerational transmission in a low-risk sample. *Dev. Psychol.* 1:294–304

Benoit D, Parker KCH. 1994. Stability and transmission of attachment across three generations. *Child Dev.* 65:1444–56

Bradley RH, Corwyn RF. 2002. Socioeconomic status and child development. *Annu. Rev. Psychol.* 53:371–99

Brook JS, Tseng L-J, Whiteman M, Cohen P. 1998. A three-generational study: intergenerational continuities and discontinuities and their impact on the toddler's anger. *Genet. Soc. Gen. Psychol. Monogr.* 124:335–51

Brook JS, Whiteman M, Zheng L. 2002. Intergenerational transmission of risks for problem behavior. *J. Abnorm. Child. Psychol.* 30:65–76

Brooks-Gunn J. 2003. *Do you believe in magic? What we can expect from early childhood intervention programs. Soc. Policy Rep. 3–15*, Soc. Res. Child Dev.

Brooks-Gunn J, Duncan GJ, Klebanov PK, Sealand N. 1993. Do neighborhoods influence child and adolescent development? *Am. J. Sociol.* 99:353–95

Brooks-Gunn J, Phelps E, Elder GH. 1991. Studying lives through time: secondary data analyses in developmental psychology. *Dev. Psychol.* 27(6):899–910

Cairns RB, Cairns BD, Xie H, Leung M-C, Hearne S. 1998. Paths across generations: academic competence and aggressive behaviours in young mothers and their children. *Dev. Psychol.* 34:1162–74

Campbell SB, Shaw DS, Gilliom M. 2000. Early externalizing behavior problems: toddlers and preschoolers at risk for later maladjustment. *Dev. Psychopathol.* 12:467–88

Capaldi DM, Clark S. 1998. Prospective family predictors of aggression toward female partners for at-risk young men. *Dev. Psychol.* 34:1175–88

Capaldi DM, Conger RD, Hops H, Thornberry TP. 2003a. Introduction to special section on three-generation studies. *J. Abnorm. Child. Psychol.* 31:123–25

Capaldi DM, Crosby L. 1997. Observed and reported psychological and physical aggression in young, at-risk couples. *Soc. Dev.* 6:184–206

Capaldi DM, Pears KC, Patterson GR, Owen LD. 2003b. Continuity of parenting practices across generations in an at-risk sample: a prospective comparison of direct and mediated associations. *J. Abnorm. Child. Psychol.* 31(2):127–42

Caspi A, Elder GH Jr. 1988. Emergent family patterns: the intergenerational construction of problem behavior and relationships. In *Relationships Within Families: Mutual Influences*, ed. RA Hinde, J Stevenson-Hinde, pp. 218–40. Oxford, UK: Oxford Univ. Press

Caspi A, McClay J, Moffitt TE, Mill J, Martin J, et al. 2002. Role of genotype in the cycle of violence in maltreated children. *Science* 297:851–53

Chapman DA, Scott KG. 2001. The impact of maternal intergenerational risk factors on adverse developmental outcomes. *Dev. Rev.* 21:305–25

Chase-Lansdale PL, Brooks-Gunn J, Zamsky ES. 1994. Young African-American multigenerational families in poverty: quality of mothering and grandmothering. *Child Dev.* 65:373–93

Chassin L, Presson CC, Todd M, Rose JS, Sherman SJ. 1998. Maternal socialization of adolescent smoking: the intergenerational transmission of parenting and smoking. *Dev. Psychol.* 34:1189–201

Chen Z-Y, Kaplan HB. 2001. Intergenerational transmission of constructive parenting. *J. Marriage Fam.* 63:17–31

Cicchetti D, Carlson V, eds. 1989. *Child Maltreatment: Theory and Research on the Causes and Consequences of Child Abuse and Neglect.* New York: Cambridge Univ. Press

Cohen P, Kasen S, Brook JS, Hartmark C. 1998. Behavior patterns of young children and their offspring: a two-generation study. *Dev. Psychol.* 34:1202–8

Conger RD, Neppl T, Kim KJ, Scaramella L. 2003. Angry and aggressive behavior across three generations: a prospective, longitudinal study of parents and children. *J. Abnorm. Child. Psychol.* 31:143–60

Cooperman JM. 1999. *From childhood to parenthood: continuity of risk over time and contextual factors perpetuating the intergenerational transfer of risk.* PhD thesis. Concordia Univ., Montreal, Can.

Cotter RB, Burke JD, Loeber R, Navratil JL. 2002. Innovative retention methods in longitudinal research: a case study of the developmental trends study. *J. Child Fam. Stud.* 11:485–98

Covell K, Grusec JE, King G. 1995. The intergenerational transmission of maternal discipline and standards for behavior. *Soc. Dev.* 4:32–43

Cox MJ, Owen MT, Lewis JM, Riedel C, Scalf-McIver L, Suster A. 1985. Intergenerational influences on the parent-infant relationship in the transition to parenthood. *J. Fam. Issues* 6:543–64

Dubow EF, Huesmann LR, Boxer P. 2003. Theoretical and methodological considerations in cross-generational research on parenting and child aggressive behavior. *J. Abnorm. Child. Psychol.* 31:185–92

Dunn J, Davies LC, O'Connor TG, Sturgess W. 2000. Parents' and partners' life course and family experiences: links with parent-child relationships in different family settings. *J. Child Psychol. Psychiatry* 41:955–68

Egeland B, Jacobvitz D, Sroufe LA. 1988. Breaking the cycle of abuse. *Child Dev.* 59:1080–88

Ehrensaft MK, Wasserman GA, Verdelli L, Greenwald S, Miller LS, Davies M. 2003. Maternal antisocial behavior, parenting practices, and behavior problems in boys at risk for antisocial behavior. *J. Child Fam. Stud.* 12:27–40

Elder GH. 1979. Historical change in life patterns and personality. In *Life-Span Development and Behavior,* ed. PB Bates, OG Brim, 2:117–59. New York: Academic

Fagot BI, Pears KC, Capaldi DM, Crosby L,

Leve CS. 1998. Becoming an adolescent father: precursors and parenting. *Dev. Psychol.* 34:1209–19

Farrington DP. 1991. Childhood aggression and adult violence: early precursors and later-life outcomes. In *The Development and Treatment of Childhood Aggression,* ed. DJ Pepler, KH Rubin, pp. 5–29. Hillsdale, NJ: Erlbaum

Furstenberg FF, Brooks-Gunn J, Morgan SP, eds. 1987. *Adolescent Mothers in Later Life.* New York: Cambridge Univ. Press

Furstenberg FF, Levine JA, Brooks-Gunn J. 1990. The children of teenage mothers: patterns of early childbearing in two generations. *Fam. Plan. Perspect.* 22:54–61

Ge X, Conger RD, Cadoret RJ, Neiderhiser JM, Yates W, et al. 1996. The developmental interface between nature and nurture: a mutual influence model of child antisocial behavior and parent behaviors. *Dev. Psychol.* 32:574–89

Granger DA, Serbin LA, Schwartzman AE, Lehoux P, Cooperman J, Ikeda S. 1998. Children's salivary cortisol, internalizing behaviour problems, and family environment: results from the Concordia Longitudinal Risk Project. *Int. J. Behav. Dev.* 22:707–28

Gunnar MR. 1998. Quality of early care and buffering of neuroendocrine stress reactions: potential effects on the developing human brain. *Prev. Med.* 27:208–11

Hardy JB, Astone NM, Brooks-Gunn J, Shapiro S, Miller TL. 1998. Like mother, like child: intergenerational patterns of age at first birth and associations with childhood and adolescent characteristics and adult outcomes in the second generation. *Dev. Psychol.* 34(6):1220–32

Holden GW, Zambarano RJ. 1992. Passing the rod: similarities between parents and their young children in orientations toward physical punishment. In *Parental Belief Systems: The Psychological Consequences for Children,* ed. JE Sigel, AV McGillicuddy-DeLisi, JJ Goodnow, pp. 143–72. Mahwah, NJ: Erlbaum

Hops H, Davis B, Leve C, Sheeber L. 2003.

Cross-generational transmission of aggressive parent behavior: a prospective, mediational examination. *J. Abnorm. Child. Psychol.* 31:161–69

Huesmann LR, Eron LD, Lefkowitz MM, Walder LO. 1984. Stability of aggression over time and generations. *Dev. Psychol.* 6:1120–34

Huesmann LR, Moise-Titus J, Podolski CL, Eron LD. 2003. Longitudinal relations between children's exposure to TV violence and their aggressive and violent behavior in young adulthood. *Dev. Psychol.* 39(2):201–21

Hunter RS, Kilstrom N. 1979. Breaking the cycle in abusive families. *Am. J. Psychol.* 136:1320–22

Ingoldsby E, Shaw DS. 2002. Neighborhood contextual factors and the onset and progression of early-starting antisocial pathways. *Clin. Child. Fam. Psychol. Rev.* 5:21–55

Inst. Med., Nat. Acad. Sci. 1994. *Reducing Risks for Mental Disorders: Frontiers for Preventive Intervention Research.* Washington, DC: Nat. Acad. Press

Kaplan HB, Liu X. 1999. Explaining transgenerational continuity in antisocial behavior during early adolescence. In *Historical and Geographical Influences on Psychopathology,* ed. P Cohen, C Slomkowski, LN Robins, pp. 163–91. Mahwah, NJ: Erlbaum

Kaufman J, Zigler E. 1989. The intergenerational transmission of child abuse. See Cicchetti & Carlson 1989, pp. 129–50

Kraemer HC, Stice E, Kazdin A, Offord D, Kupfer D. 2001. How do risk factors work together? Mediators, moderators, and independent, overlapping, and proxy risk factors. *Am. J. Psychol.* 158:848–56

Kramer L, Baron LA. 1995. Intergenerational linkages: how experiences with siblings related to the parenting of siblings. *J. Soc. Pers. Relat.* 12:67–87

Kretchmar MD, Jacobvitz DB. 2002. Observing mother-child relationships across generations: boundary patterns, attachment, and the transmission of caregiving. *Fam. Proc.* 41:351–75

Manlove J. 1997. Early motherhood in an intergenerational perspective: the experiences of a British cohort. *J. Marriage Fam.* 59:263–79

McCloskey LA, Bailey JA. 2000. The intergenerational transmission of risk for child sexual abuse. *J. Interpers. Violence* 15:1019–35

McCord J. 1977. A comparative study of two generations of Native Americans. In *Theoretical Concerns in Criminology,* ed. RF Meier, pp. 83–92. Beverly Hills, CA: Sage

McCord J. 1991. The cycle of crime and socialization practices. *J. Crim. Law Criminol.* 82:211–28

McCord J. 1995. Crime in the shadow of history. *Curr. Perspect. Aging Life Cycle* 4:105–18

McCord J. 1999. Alcoholism and crime across generations. *Crim. Behav. Ment. Health* 9:107–17

Miller-Johnson S, Winn D-M, Coie J, Maumary-Gremaud A, Hyman C, et al. 1999. Motherhood during the teen years: a developmental perspective on risk factors for childbearing. *Dev. Psychol.* 11:85–100

Moffitt TE, Caspi A, Rutter M, Silva PA, eds. 2001. *Sex Differences in Antisocial Behavior.* Cambridge, UK: Cambridge Univ. Press

Nagin DS, Tremblay RE. 1999. Trajectories of boys' physical aggression, opposition, and hyperactivity on the path to physically violent and nonviolent juvenile delinquency. *Child Dev.* 70:1181–96

Nagin DS, Tremblay RE. 2001. Parental and early childhood predictors of persistent physical aggression in boys for kindergarten to high school. *Arch. Gen. Psychiatry* 58:389–94

Oliver JE. 1993. Intergenerational transmission of child abuse: rates, research, and clinical implications. *Am. J. Psychiatry* 150:1315–24

Olsen SF, Martin P, Halverson CF. 1999. Personality, marital relationships, and parenting in two generations of mothers. *Int. J. Behav. Dev.* 23:457–76

Patterson GR. 1998. Continuities—a search for causal mechanisms: comment on the special section. *Dev. Psychol.* 34(6):1263–68

Pears KC, Capaldi DM. 2001. Intergenerational transmission of abuse: a two-generational prospective study of an at-risk sample. *Child Abuse Negl.* 25:1439–61

Peplar D, Madsen K, Webster C, Levene K, eds. 2003. *Development and Treatment of Girlhood Aggression.* Hillsdale, NJ: Erlbaum. In press

Pepler DJ, Rubin KH, eds. 1991. *The Development and Treatment of Childhood Aggression.* Hillsdale, NJ: Erlbaum

Peters PL. 1999. *Assortative mating among men and women with histories of aggressive, withdrawn, and aggressive-withdrawn behavior.* PhD thesis. Concordia Univ., Montreal, Can. 190 pp.

Putallaz M, Bierman K, eds. 2003. *Aggression, Antisocial Behavior, and Violence Among Girls: A Developmental Perspective.* New York: Guilford. In press

Putallaz M, Costanzo PR, Grames CL, Sherman DM. 1998. Inter-generational continuities and their influences on children's social development. *Soc. Dev.* 7:389–427

Raine A. 2002. Biosocial studies of antisocial and violent behavior in children and adults: a review. *J. Abnorm. Child Psychol.* 30:311–26

Rutter M. 1989. Intergenerational continuities and discontinuities in serious parenting difficulties. See Cicchetti & Carlson 1989, pp. 317–48

Rutter M. 1998. Some research considerations on intergenerational continuities and discontinuities: comment on the special section. *Dev. Psychol.* 34(6):1269–73

Rutter M, Madge N. 1976. *Cycles of Disadvantage: A Review of Research.* London: Heinemann

Rutter M, Sroufe A. 2000. Developmental psychopathology: concepts and challenges. *Dev. Psychopathol.* 12:265–96

Saltaris C, Serbin LA, Stack DM, Karp JA, Schwartzman AE, Ledingham JE. 2003. Nurturing cognitive competence in preschoolers: a longitudinal study of inter-generational continuity and risk. *Int. J. Behav. Dev.* In press

Scaramella LV, Conger RD, Simons RL, Whitbeck LB. 1998. Predicting risk for pregnancy by late adolescence: a social contextual perspective. *Dev. Psychol.* 34:1233–45

Scott KG, Mason CA, Chapman DA. 1999. The use of epidemiological methodology as a means of influencing public policy. *Child Dev.* 70:1263–72

Serbin LA, Cooperman JM, Peters PL, Lehoux PM, Stack DM, Schwartzman AE. 1998. Intergenerational transfer of psychosocial risk in women with childhood histories of aggression, withdrawal, or aggression and withdrawal. *Dev. Psychol.* 34:1246–62

Serbin LA, Karp J. 2003. Inter-generational studies of parenting and the transfer of risk from parent to child. *Curr. Dir. Psychol. Sci.* 1(2):138–42

Serbin LA, Peters PL, McAffer VJ, Schwartzman AE. 1991a. Childhood aggression and withdrawal as predictors of adolescent pregnancy, early parenthood, and environmental risk for the next generation. *Can. J. Behav. Sci.* 23:318–31

Serbin LA, Peters PL, Schwartzman AE. 1996. Longitudinal study of early childhood injuries and acute illnesses in the offspring of adolescent mothers who were aggressive, withdrawn, or aggressive-withdrawn in childhood. *J. Abnorm. Psychol.* 105:500–7

Serbin LA, Schwartzman AE, Moskowitz DS, Ledingham JE. 1991b. Aggressive, withdrawn, and aggressive/withdrawn children in adolescence: into the next generation. See Pepler & Rubin 1991, pp. 55–69

Serbin LA, Stack DM. 1998. Introduction to the special section: studying intergenerational continuity and the transfer of risk. *Dev. Psychol.* 34(6):1159–61

Serbin LA, Stack DM, DeGenna N, Grunzweig N, Temcheff CE, et al. 2003. When aggressive girls become mothers: problems in parenting, health, and development across two generations. See Putallaz & Bierman 2003. In press

Serbin LA, Stack DM, Schwartzman AE, Cooperman J, Bentley V, et al. 2002. A longitudinal study of aggressive and withdrawn children into adulthood: patterns of parenting and risk to offspring. In *Children of Disordered Parents*, ed. R Peters, R McMahon, pp. 43–69. New York: Kluwer Acad./Plenum

Shapiro S, Miller TL. 1998. Like mother, like child: intergenerational patterns of age at first birth and associations with childhood and adolescent characteristics and adult outcomes in the second generation. *Dev. Psychol.* 34:1220–32

Shaw DS. 2003. Advancing our understanding of intergenerational continuity in antisocial behavior. *J. Abnorm. Child. Psychol.* 31:193–99

Simons RL, Beaman J, Conger RD, Chao W. 1992. Gender differences in the intergenerational transmission of parenting beliefs. *J. Marriage Fam.* 54:823–36

Simons RL, Beaman J, Conger RD, Chao W. 1993. Childhood experience, conceptions of parenting, and attitudes of spouse as determinants of parental behavior. *J. Marriage Fam.* 55:91–106

Simons RL, Whitbeck LB, Conger RD, Chyi-In W. 1991. Intergenerational transmission of harsh parenting. *Dev. Psychol.* 27:159–71

Stack DM, Serbin LA, Schwartzman AE. 2003. Girls' aggression across the life course: long-term outcomes and inter-generational risk. See Peplar et al. 2003. In press

Thornberry TP, Freeman-Gallant A, Lizotte AJ, Krohn MD, Smith CA. 2003a. Linked lives: the intergenerational transmission of antisocial behavior. *J. Abnorm. Child. Psychol.* 31:171–84

Thornberry TP, Hops H, Conger RD, Capaldi DM. 2003b. Replicated findings and future directions for intergenerational studies: closing comments. *J. Abnorm. Child. Psychol.* 31:201–3

Thornberry TP, Krohn MD. 2003. *Taking Stock of Delinquency: An Overview of Findings from Contemporary Longitudinal Studies*. New York: Kluwer Acad./Plenum

Tremblay RE. 2000. The development of aggressive behaviour during childhood: What have we learned in the past century? *Int. J. Behav. Dev.* 24:129–41

Underwood MK. 2003. *Ice and Fire: Anger and Aggression Among Girls*. New York: Guilford. 300 pp.

Underwood MK, Kupersmidt JB, Coie JD. 1996. Childhood peer sociometric status and aggression as predictors of adolescent childbearing. *J. Adolesc. Res.* 6(2):201–23

Van Ijzendoorn MH. 1992. Intergenerational transmission of parenting: a review of studies in nonclinical populations. *Dev. Rev.* 12:76–99

Wadsworth MEJ. 1988. Intergenerational longitudinal research: conceptual and methodological considerations. In *Studies of Psychosocial Risk: The Power of Longitudinal Data*, ed. M Rutter, pp. 255–84. New York: Cambridge Univ. Press

Wakschlag LS, Chase-Lansdale PL, Brooks-Gunn J. 1996. Not just "ghosts in the nursery": contemporaneous intergenerational relationships and parenting in young African-American families. *Child Dev.* 67:2141–47

Walsh RA. 1994. Effects of maternal smoking on adverse pregnancy outcomes: examination of the criteria of causation. *Hum. Biol.* 66:1059–81

Werner EE. 1993. Risk, resilience, and recovery: perspective from the Kauai longitudinal study. *Dev. Psychopathol.* 5:503–15

Werner EE, Smith RS. 1992. *Overcoming the Odds: High Risk Children From Birth to Adulthood*. Ithaca, NY: Cornell Univ. Press

Wickrama KAS, Conger RD, Wallace LE, Elder GH. 1999. The intergenerational transmission of health-risk behaviors: adolescent lifestyles and gender moderating effects. *J. Health Soc. Behav.* 40:258–72

Wu P, Kandel DB. 1995. The roles of mothers and fathers in intergenerational behavioral transmission: the case of smoking and delinquency. In *Drugs, Crime and Other Deviant Adaptations: Longitudinal Studies*, ed. HB Kaplan, pp. 49–81. New York: Plenum

Zeanah CH, Zeanah PD. 1989. Intergenerational transmission of maltreatment: insights from attachment theory and research. *Psychiatry* 52:177–96

Zoccolillo M, Pickles A, Quinton D, Rutter M. 1992. The outcome of childhood conduct disorder: implications for defining adult personality disorder and conduct disorder. *Psychol. Med.* 22:971–86

Zuravin S, McMillen C, DePanfilis D, Risley-Curtiss C. 1996. The intergenerational cycle of child maltreatment: continuity versus discontinuity. *J. Interpers. Violence* 11:315–34

Annu. Rev. Psychol. 2004. 55:365–99
doi: 10.1146/annurev.psych.55.090902.141528
Copyright © 2004 by Annual Reviews. All rights reserved
First published online as a Review in Advance on September 29, 2003

DEVELOPMENT IN THE FAMILY

Ross D. Parke

Department of Psychology, University of California, Riverside, California 92521;
email: ross.parke@ucr.edu

Key Words ethnicity, socialization, siblings, gay-lesbian parents, new reproductive technologies, parenting

■ **Abstract** In this chapter we review theoretical conceptual and empirical advances in family research and the implications for children's development. Three interdependent family subsystems are considered: the parent-child subsystem, the marital subsystem, and the sibling subsystem. Recent work on the family as a unit of analysis is reviewed as well. Several determinants of family socialization strategies are noted, including child and parental characteristics and resources and social capital available to families. Ethnicity is considered by reviewing recent advances in our understanding of African American, Asian American, and Hispanic families. Several new directions in family research are highlighted. These include research on the linkage between families and work, gay and lesbian parenting, the new reproductive technologies, and the effect of parental incarcerations on families. Future trends in family research are noted, including the role of genetics, the biological correlates of family processes, the role of intervention and prevention designs in family research, and the importance of process work on ethnicity-oriented family research.

CONTENTS

0066-4308/04/0204-0365$14.00

THEORETICAL PERSPECTIVES ON THE FAMILY

Several themes are evident in current theoretical approaches to the family. First, systems theory (Sameroff 1994, Thelen & Smith 1994) is the most prominent approach to understanding families (see Cox & Paley 1997 for a review). This approach has transformed the study of the family from a parent-child focus to an emphasis on the family as a social system. To understand fully the nature of family relationships, it is necessary to recognize the interdependence among the roles and functions of all family members.

Second, family members—mothers, fathers, and children—influence each other both directly and indirectly (Minuchin 2002). Examples of fathers' indirect impact include various ways in which fathers modify and mediate mother-child relationships. In turn, women affect their children indirectly through their husbands by modifying both the quantity and the quality of father-child interaction. Children may indirectly influence the husband-wife relationship by altering the behavior of either parent that consequently changes the interaction between spouses.

Third, different units of analysis are necessary in order to understand families. Although the individual level—child, mother, and father—remains a useful and necessary level of analysis, recognition of relationships among family members as units of analysis is necessary. The marital relationship, the mother-child, and the father-child relationship require separate analysis (Parke & O'Neil 1999). Finally, the family as a unit that is independent of the individual or dyads within the family requires recognition (Cook 2001).

A fourth conceptual shift is from unidirectional to transactional models of relationships among family members. There have been various phases in the conceptual thinking in this domain. First, as Kuczynski (2003) outlines, scholars traditionally were guided by unilateral models of parent-child relations. According to this view, the direction of causality was unidirectional, from parent to child. The child's role was relatively passive, the focus was on individuals rather than relationships, and power relations were relatively static. In addition, in this era of thinking, the mother rather than either the father or other members of the family system was the major focus of both theoretical and empirical work.

In the 1960s, with the publication of Bell's classic reformulation (Bell 1968), the field began to recognize the bidirectional nature of the parent-child relationship. This shift occurred in a climate of reevaluation of the competence of the infant and young child; instead of the passive creatures of earlier times, infants and children were viewed as more competent and more active in their own development. In place of the unilateral model, a bilateral model has emerged as the dominant paradigm for guiding research in the parent-child relationship domain (Crouter & Booth 2003, Kuczynski 2003). In contrast to the earlier model, the direction causality is bidirectional, equal agency on the part of parent and child is assumed, interaction within the context of relationships is recognized, and power relations are characterized as "interdependent asymmetry."

At the same time views of the kinds of pathways through which parents can influence their children expanded. Historically, socialization models directed the most attention toward the nature of the parent-child relationship and the types of child-rearing practices that parents employ. The research on the emergence of infant-parent attachment and the classic work on parenting styles exemplify this tradition. More recently, views of parenting and the parent-child relationship have expanded to include parents as active managers of the child's social environment outside the family. In this role, a parent actively regulates the child's access to physical and social resources outside the family (Parke & O'Neil 1999) and serves as a regulator of opportunities for social contact with extrafamilial social partners. Although peer influence increases as children develop (Rogoff 2003), parents continue to play an important regulatory role as gatekeepers and monitors of children's social choices and social contacts, even in adolescence (Mounts 2000). However, researchers recently have recognized that in the managerial domain, as in other parts of the parent-child relationship, children as well as parents play an active and influential role in shaping decisions about children's social opportunities and social contacts (Kerr & Stattin 2003).

Fifth, under the influence of Bronfenbrenner (1979), ecological theory recognition is being given to the embeddedness of families within a variety of other social systems, including both formal and informal support systems as well as the cultures in which they exist (Parke & Kellam 1994). These include a wide range of extrafamilial influences such as extended families, informal community ties such as friends and neighbors, work sites, and social, educational, and medical institutions (Repetti & Wood 1997).

Sixth, developmental considerations are increasingly central to our socialization theories and the importance of considering family relationships from a variety of developmental perspectives is now recognized. Although developmental changes in infant and child perceptual, motor, cognitive, and socioemotional capacities continue to represent the most commonly investigated aspect of development, other aspects of development are viewed as important as well. Under the influence of life course and life span perspectives (Elder 1998, Parke 1988) the importance of examining developmental changes in adults is gaining recognition because parents continue to change and develop during adult years. For example, age at the time of the onset of parenthood can have important implications for how females and males manage their maternal and paternal roles. This involves an exploration of the tasks adults face, such as self-identity, education, and career, and an examination of the relationship between these tasks and the demands of parenting.

Developmental analysis need not be restricted to the level of the individual—either child or parent. Relationships, such as the marital relationship or the mother-infant or father-infant relationship, may follow separate and partially independent developmental courses over childhood (Fincham 1998, Parke 1988). In turn, the mutual impact of different sets of relationships on each other will vary as a function of the nature of the developmental trajectory. Families change their structure (e.g., through the addition of a new child or the loss of a member through death, separation, or divorce) over time, as well as their norms, rules, and strategies. Tracking the family unit itself over development is an important and relatively neglected task (Cook 2001).

A major shift in the last two decades is the challenge to the universality of our family theories. This challenge takes a variety of forms. First, as cross-cultural work in development accumulated, it became evident that generalizations from a single culture (e.g., American) may, in fact, not be valid in other cultural contexts (Gauvain 2001, Rogoff 2003). Second, studies of social class differences in socialization challenged the generality of findings even within one cultural or national context (Hoff et al. 2002). Finally, these were reminders (e.g., Graham 1992) that our efforts to understand cultural and racial diversity in our country was severely limited as revealed by the small percentage of publications focused on minority samples. Currently, there is an increased awareness of the importance of both recognizing and studying variations in families and family socialization strategies in both other cultures (Rogoff 2003) as well as across ethnic groups within our own culture (Parke & Buriel 1998). It is important not only to examine the diversity of familial organization, goals, and strategies across ethnic groups but it is equally critical to explore variations within different ethnic groups. Although there are many similarities across groups and within groups, appreciation of the variations is of central concern.

Another assumption that underlies current theorizing involves the recognition of the impact of secular shifts on families. In recent years, a variety of social changes in American society have had a profound impact on families. These include the decline in fertility and family size, the changes in the timing of the onset of parenthood, the increased participation of women in the workforce, the rise in rates of divorce, and the subsequent increase in the number of single-parent families (Elder 1998, Parke 1996). The ways in which these society-wide changes impact on interaction patterns between parents and children merit examination.

A closely related theme involves the recognition of the importance of the historical period in which the family interaction is taking place. Historical periods provide the social conditions for individual and family transitions. Examples include the 1960s (the Vietnam War era), the 1930s (the Great Depression), and the 1980s (the Farm Belt Depression) (Conger & Elder 1994, Elder & Conger 2000). Across these historical periods, family interaction may, in fact, be quite different due to the peculiar conditions of the particular era. These distinctions among different developmental trajectories, as well as social change and historical period effects, are important because these different forms of change do not always harmonize (Modell & Elder 2002). For example, a family event such as the birth of a child—the transition to parenthood—may have profound effects on a man who has just begun a career, in contrast to the effects on one who has advanced to a stable occupational position. Moreover, individual and family developmental trajectories are embedded within both the social conditions and the values of the historical time in which they exist. The role of parents, as is the case with any social role, is responsive to such fluctuations.

A major shift in the study of families is the renewed interest in the role of biological factors in shaping family functioning. The recent work on genetics has produced not only a more sophisticated understanding of the potential role that genetics can play in the onset of certain behaviors, but in the unfolding of behavior across development. Moreover, Plomin's (1994) reformulation of genetic questions has led to studies of the effects of nonshared family environment on children's development. A second focus is found in studies of hormones and behavior, especially during infancy and adolescence (Gunnar et al. 1997). Third, the increased use of psychophysiological assessments with families represents a further instance of how biological processes are changing socialization studies (Gottman & Katz 1989). Fourth, the resurgence of interest in the use of evolutionary approaches to the study of families is producing new and provocative hypotheses and research directions (Geary & Bjorklund 2000).

Affect is increasingly viewed as a central family process (Gottman et al. 2002). The study of affect has assumed a variety of forms, including the development of emotion regulation (Denham 1998), the development of emotional expression and understanding, and the role of emotion in the enactment of the parenting role (Dix 1991). Cognition is viewed as central to socialization as well. Again the role of cognition comes in many guises, including the child's own cognitive capacities as a determinant of socialization strategies, as well as parents' cognitions, beliefs, and values concerning their parental role as constraints on their socialization practices. Equally important is the recognition of ways in which parents perceive, organize, and understand their children's behaviors and beliefs for appreciating how parent-child relationships are regulated and change (Goodnow 2002). Underlying much of current socialization research is the recognition that cognitive and affective processes are interdependent, mutually influencing each other (Dix 1991).

FAMILY SUBSYSTEMS AND SOCIALIZATION

Consistent with a family systems viewpoint, recent research has focused on a variety of subsystems, including parent-child, marital, and sib-sib systems. In the next several sections we focus on each of these subsystems as contexts for socialization. Finally, we examine recent attempts to conceptualize the family as a unit of analysis.

The Parent-Child Subsystem

In this section we consider the parent-child subsystem and its relation to children's social adaptation. Although it has been common in traditional paradigms to focus on the impact of parent-child interaction, the parent-child relationship, or parental child-rearing styles, according to Parke & O'Neil (1999) this represents only one pathway. In this case, the impact of parent-child interaction is not explicitly to modify or enhance children's relationships with extrafamilial social partners. In addition, this scheme posits that parents may influence their children through a second pathway, namely in their role as direct instructor, educator, or consultant. In this role parents may explicitly set out to educate their children concerning appropriate norms and rules of the culture. This second socialization pathway may take a variety of forms. Parents may serve as coaches, teachers, and supervisors as they provide advice, support, and directions about strategies for managing new social situations or negotiating social challenges. In a third role, parents function as managers of their children's social lives and serve as regulators of opportunities for social contacts and cognitive experiences.

THE PARENT-CHILD RELATIONSHIP   Several recent trends in this heavily researched domain are noteworthy. First, the cast of interactive partners has continued to expand with increased attention devoted to fathers and grandparents as important socializing agents in the family. Careful documentation by Pleck & Masciadrelli (2003) suggests that the average levels of paternal engagement and accessibility have increased in the United States during the last several decades, both in absolute and relative terms (Pleck & Masciadrelli 2003). Moreover, evidence continues to mount that fathers both play distinctive roles in families and have unique effects after controlling for maternal effects (Marsiglio et al. 2000).

A second trend is the increasing focus on coparenting in recognition that mothers and fathers operate as a parenting team and as individual parents (McHale & Rasmussen 1998). This work has identified a variety of forms that coparenting alliances can assume, including "a pattern signifying antagonistic and adult centered or hostile competitive, coparenting dynamics, a pattern marked by significant imbalance or parenting discrepancy in levels of parental engagement with the child and a pattern reflecting cooperation, warmth, cohesion, and child centeredness or high family harmony" (McHale et al. 2002, p. 142). These patterns have been observed across a range of studies with infants, preschoolers, and school-age children and in both European and African American families (Brody et al. 1998, Fivaz-Depeursinge & Corboz-Warnery 1999). Recent work has moved beyond description and revealed links between early coparenting dynamics and later indices of child social adaptation. McHale & Rasmussen (1998) found that hostile-competitive coparenting during infancy was related to aggression, and large parenting discrepancies were related to parent-rated anxiety. Others have found links between problematic family alliances in the first year and insecure mother-child attachments and clinical symptomatology in the preschool years (Fivaz-Depeursinge & Corboz-Warnery 1999, McHale et al. 2002).

Coparenting accounts for unique variance in child measures and clearly needs to be distinguished from traditional parent-child and marital-level processes (McHale et al. 2002). Less is known about the processes that control these various patterns of coparenting but recent work on gatekeeping (Allen & Hawkins 1999, Beitel & Parke 1998) that focuses on ways in which couples facilitate or hinder the involvement of their partners interactions with their children is promising. The similarities and differences of the coparenting relationship in intact and nonintact (divorced, single-parent) families is only poorly understood (Emery et al. 1999). Extensions of theory and empirical work to other family forms [foster parents and birth parents (Erera 1997); parents and grandparents (Smith & Drew 2002); and lesbian parenting partners or these partners and the donor father as coparent (Patterson 2002)] would help define the uniqueness of coparenting forms and processes identified in two-parent intact families.

PARENTS AS ADVISORS, COACHES, AND CONSULTANTS   A large literature supports the role of parents as advisors and coaches as an important pathway through which parents influence their children's development (Mize & Pettit 1997, Ladd & Pettit 2002). Early work with preschool-age (Russell & Finnie 1990) and elementary school–age children (Mize & Pettit 1997) suggested that the quality of parental advice was related positively to children's social competence with peers. This work has been extended to adolescence, where parents shift their advice-giving strategies and try to keep their children from being influenced by peers by talking to them about the future consequences of their behavior. Mounts (2000) found that this "parental guidance" approach was associated with selection of friends with low levels of antisocial behavior and higher levels of academic achievement.

Parents can affect their children's social relationships through monitoring their children's social activities. Poor monitoring is linked to lower academic skills and peer acceptance and higher rates of delinquency and externalizing behavior (Sandstrom & Coie 1999). Although monitoring generally has been viewed as having a parent to child effect, Kerr & Stattin (2000) have reconceptualized this issue as a process that is jointly co-constructed by the parent and child. Monitoring may be a function of the extent to which children share information about their activities and companion choices with their parents; prior research on monitoring could be reinterpreted to suggest that children with poorer social adjustment discussed their activities with parents less than did well-adjusted children.

PARENTS AS PROVIDERS OF SOCIAL OPPORTUNITIES   Parents arrange children's contact with peers by designing children's daily informal and formal activities, which promote or discourage children's peer relationships. Several investigators have examined children's informal play contacts by describing who arranges the contacts, characteristics of the children's playmates, and the relations between these indicators and children's development. Parents who initiated at least one informal play contact had children with a larger range of playmates and more companions with whom children had frequent contact (Kerns et al. 1998).

Although parents' role decreases across middle childhood and adolescence, while children's active role increases, parents and children continue to share responsibility for the initiation and regulation of peer contacts (e.g., Furstenberg et al. 1999, Mounts 2000).

The Marital Subsystem

Considerable evidence indicates that marital functioning is related to children's short-term coping and long-term adjustment. Although the size of the association is not always large, a range of studies link marital discord and conflict to outcomes in children that impair the quality of interpersonal relationships, including antisocial behavior, internalizing and externalizing behavior problems, changes in cognitions, emotions, and physiology in response to exposure to marital conflict, and problematic peer relationships (Cummings et al. 2002). Marital discord may have an indirect influence on children's adjustment that operates through its effect on family functioning and the quality of parenting (Fincham 1998). Factors such as affective changes in the quality of the parent-child relationship, lack of emotional availability, and adoption of less optimal parenting styles have been implicated as potential mechanisms through which marital discord disrupts parenting processes. A second model (Cummings et al. 2002) focuses on the direct effects of witnessed marital conflict on children's outcomes.

In support of the indirect effects model, a meta-analytic review by Erel & Burman (1995) of 68 studies that met a variety of criteria, including independent assessment of marital and parent-child relationships, provided clear support for a positive relationship between the qualities of the parent-child relationship and the marital relationship.

Several hypotheses have been offered to account for these effects, including the spillover hypothesis and the compensatory hypothesis. According to the spillover perspective, mood or behavior in one subsystem transfer to another subsystem (e.g., from marital subsystem to parent-child subsystem). In contrast, the compensatory hypothesis suggests that positive parent-child relationships can be maintained even in the face of marital conflict and can serve as a buffer on children (Erel & Burman 1995). The meta-analysis clearly supports the spillover hypothesis and offers no support for the compensatory concept. In fact, their analysis underscores the difficulty of buffering children from marital conflict and discord. Parents may try to buffer their children by limiting their opportunities to witness marital conflicts and disputes; however, as Erel & Burman suggest, "they cannot shield them from the negative impact that marital discord has on the parent-child relationship" (1995, p. 128).

There is considerable support for the direct effects model as well. More frequent interparental conflict and more intense or violent forms of conflict are particularly disturbing to children and likely to be associated with externalizing and internalizing difficulties (Cummings et al. 2002). Conflict that was child-related in content was more likely than conflict involving other content to be associated with behavior problems in children, such as greater shame, responsibility, self-blame, and fear of been drawn into the conflict. Resolution of conflict, even when the child does not view it, reduces children's negative reactions to exposure to interadult anger and conflict. Exposure to unresolved conflict has been associated with negative affect and poor coping responses in children (Cummings et al. 2002). Conflict is inevitable in most parental relationships and is not detrimental to family relationships and children's functioning under all circumstances. When conflict is expressed constructively, is moderate in degree, is expressed in the context of a warm and supportive family environment, and shows evidence of resolution, children may learn valuable lessons regarding how to negotiate conflict and resolve disagreements (Cummings et al. 2002).

Less well understood are the specific emotional regulatory and cognitive processing mechanisms through which exposure to interparental conflict is carried over into children's understanding of close relationships and their social competence. Several conceptual frameworks have emerged to examine these carryover questions. Using a cognitive-conceptual model, Grych & Fincham (1990) focus on the cognitive and affective meaning that exposure to conflict has for the child. They suggest that children appraise the personal relevance of interadult conflict by using certain dimensions of interparental conflict (e.g., intensity and content of conflict) and contextual factors (e.g., family emotional climate and past history). These appraisals influence the child's coping responses to interparental conflict, including the level of perceived threat to the child, the child's perceived coping efficacy, and causal attributions and ascription of blame made by the child.

In an alternative model, Davies & Cummings (1994) propose that children's emotional security also derives from the quality of the marital relationship. Several interrelated processes account for the impact of emotional security on children's functioning. First, emotional security affects the ability of the children to regulate their own emotions. Second, emotional security influences children's motivation to intervene to regulate the behavior of their parents. Third, emotional security affects the cognitive appraisals and internal representations of family relationships that are made by children. Recently, Davies et al. (2002) provided empirical evidence in support of this viewpoint. In a further variant, Crockenberg & Langrock (2001) have proposed a related model that focused on specific emotions such as anger and sadness witnessed by children during marital conflict. Preliminary support was found for this approach (Crockenberg & Langrock 2001).

Other evidence suggests that chronic, intense marital conflict undermines children's emotional regulatory abilities. Katz & Gottman (1996) found that maritally distressed couples employed a parenting style that was cold, unresponsive, angry, and low in limit setting and structuring. Children who were exposed to this style of parenting exhibited high levels of stress hormones, displayed more anger and noncompliance, and displayed more negative peer interactions. Not all problematic marriages are similar. Some problematic marriages are likely to be characterized by lower levels of openly expressed anger and hostility and higher levels of active withdrawal from interaction. Children in marriages characterized by withdrawal rather than interaction accompanied by anger react differently (Katz & Woodin 2002). Couples who are hostile and detached have the most negative impact on children's adjustment.

The challenge lies in applying these alternative models to future investigations of the links between children's exposure to interparental conflict and their adjustment. Finally, prior work has been largely nondevelopmental or restricted largely to young children. Little is known about the impact of exposure to marital conflict on adolescents, especially on their friendships and close relationships.

The Sibling Subsystem

Sibling relationships have been hypothesized to contribute to children's socialization in a number of significant ways (Dunn 1988, Teti 2002). A social learning framework analogous to the one posited to explain parental contributions to the development of children's social competence (Parke & O'Neil 1999) predicts that through their interactions with siblings, children develop specific interaction patterns and social understanding skills that generalize to relationships with other children. In addition, relationships with siblings also may provide a context in which children can practice the skills and interaction styles that have been learned from parents or others (McCoy et al. 1994). Older siblings function as tutors, managers, or supervisors of their younger brother or sister's behavior during social interactions (Edwards & Whiting 1993) and may function as gatekeepers who extend or limit opportunities to interact with other children outside of the family (Weisner 1993). A second avenue of influence on children's development is their observation of parent interactions with siblings, which parallels the indirect influence that the observation of parent-parent interaction has on children. These interactions have been hypothesized to serve as an important context in which children deal with differential treatment and complex social emotions such as rivalry and jealousy (Volling et al. 2002).

Although experiences with siblings provide a context in which social patterns and social understanding skills may generalize to relationships with peers (Teti 2002), there is only modest evidence of straightforward carryover effects. When associations emerge they may be complicated by birth-order effects and other processes (Dunn 1993). Adding further complexity, recent studies suggest that sibling relationships may play a role in compensating for other problematic relationships by providing an alternative context for experiencing satisfying social relationships and protecting children from adjustment difficulties. East & Rook (1992) found that children who were socially isolated in their peer relationships were buffered from adjustment problems when they reported positive relationships with a favorite sibling. Similarly, Stocker (1994) reported support for the compensatory role of at least one positive relationship (either sibling, friend, or mother) as protection from behavioral conduct difficulties.

Less is known about the reverse effect, namely the impact of friendship on sibling relationships. Kramer & Gottman (1992) examined the role that positive relationships with peers play in children's adaptation to the birth of a new sibling. Children who displayed a more positive interaction style with a best friend and who were better able to manage conflict and negative affect behaved more positively toward their new sibling at both 6 months and 14 months. The authors suggest that management of conflict, a skill that is useful when interacting with siblings, may be more likely to be learned in interactions with peers than in direct interactions with parents.

The challenge for future work is to discover the contexts under which strong, weak, or compensatory connections might be expected between relationship systems as well as the processes through which children's experiences with siblings are translated into peer relationship skills. As Dunn (1993) has argued, friendship involves a mutual and reciprocated relationship with another individual, whereas siblings do not necessarily feel this way about one another. In contrast to sib-sib relationships, friend and peer relationships represent a unique combination of backgrounds, experiences, and temperaments. Further, different role expectations for sib and friend relationships may differentially influence interaction styles. Systematic examination of the moderating and mediating influences of these factors on the associations between sibling and peer relationships would be worthwhile.

The Family as a Level of Analysis

Parent-child, marital, and sibling influences are clearly the most well researched aspects of socialization. However, consideration of these units of analysis alone is insufficient because they fail to recognize the family unit itself as a separate and identifiable level of analysis (Parke & Buriel 1998). Consistent with a systems theory perspective (Sameroff 1994), the properties, functions, and effects of the family unit cannot necessarily be inferred from these smaller units of analysis. Families as units change across development in response to changes in the individual members, life circumstances, and scheduled and unscheduled transitions. Families develop distinct climates (Moos & Moos 1981), styles of responding to events (Reiss 1989), and distinct boundaries (Boss 1999), which, in turn, provide differing socialization contexts for the developing child. Reiss (1989) argues that the family regulates the child's development through a range of processes, including paradigms, myths, stories, and rituals. According to this perspective, the stability and coherence of these processes reside not within individuals, but in the coordinated practices of the entire family. The interaction of the group—beyond the memories of individuals—conserves relationships and regulates and perpetuates many aspects of ongoing family life (Reiss 1989, p. 188).

Myths refer to beliefs that influence family process, provide continuity across generation, and are generally not open to discussion or debate (Sameroff 1994). Reiss (1989) argues that family myths influence mate selection and marital satisfaction. Individuals can set aside destructive family myths by marrying a person with a different and healthier history of family myths. To date, there is little direct evidence of the impact of family myths on children's development.

Family stories have received more attention as vehicles for socialization of young children. Stories are vehicles for the transmission of family values and for teaching family roles. Fiese et al. (1999) report that family of origin experiences may be transmitted across generations through stories and shared memories and in turn, shape contemporary interaction between family members. These investigators have provided a useful framework for studying family stories by focusing on three narrative dimensions, namely, narrative coherence, narrative styles, and relationship beliefs that characterize the form that the content of family stories assume. This report provides promising evidence of the value of this approach for understanding premarital couples (Wamboldt 1999), family dinner interactions (Fiese & Marjinsky 1999), couples with an adopted child (Grotevant et al. 1999), and depressed couples (Dickstein et al. 1999). This approach yielded important insights into child functioning attitudes toward open versus closed adoption, marital satisfaction, and diagnosis of depression (Fiese et al. 1999).

Rituals have been recognized for decades as an important aspect of family life (Fiese et al. 2002), but only in the last decade has the socialization function of rituals become apparent. As Sameroff notes, "Family rituals may range from highly stylized religious observances such as first communion or bar mitzvahs to less articulated daily interaction patterns such as the type of greeting made when someone returns home" (1994, p. 209). Central to the concept of rituals is the fact that they provide meaning to family interactions. Wolin et al. (1988) have identified three types of family rituals: family celebrations (e.g., holidays), or rites of passage (weddings); family traditions (e.g., birthday customs and family vacations); and patterned routines (e.g., dinnertime, bedtime routines, and weekend activities). Methodological progress has recently been marked by the development of a Family Ritual Questionnaire (Fiese et al. 2002). Of importance is the fact that rituals serve a protective function. Fiese et al. (2002) report that families who attach more meaning to their rituals have adolescents who are higher in self-esteem. In sum, rituals are a powerful index of family functioning and may serve as a protective factor for the child. Questions remain about the uniqueness of rituals relative to other forms of family routines or child-rearing practices. Are rituals independent vehicles of socialization or merely a reflection of more central causal influences, such as the quality of parent-child relationship? Finally, the origin of family-level differences is an issue that has received little attention.

DETERMINANTS OF FAMILY SOCIALIZATION STRATEGIES

In this section, a variety of determinants of parenting will be considered. Belsky (1984) proposed a three-domain model of the determinants of parenting, which included personal resources of the parents, characteristics of the child, and contextual sources of stress and support. Some of the work relevant to this model will be reviewed. Recent work on ethnic variations in parenting also will be reviewed in order to expand upon this earlier theoretical scheme.

Child Characteristics

Child characteristics take two forms: universal predispositions that are shared by all children and individual differences in particular characteristics. Over the last several decades, an impressive amount of evidence has documented that infants are biologically prepared for social, cognitive, and perceptual challenges and these prepared responses play a significant role in facilitating children's adaptation to their environment. This evolutionary approach, which was championed early by Bowlby (1973), has continued to receive support (Geary & Bjorkland 2000). Under the influence of recent advances in behavior genetics (e.g., Plomin 1994), there is increasing recognition of the role of individual differences in a wide variety of behavioral characteristics in shaping parental socialization strategies. Perhaps the most well researched determinant of parenting behavior is infant and child temperament (Putnam et al. 2002). Although debates about the relative contributions of genetic and experimental factors to the emergence of individual differences in temperament continue (Putnam et al. 2002), there is no doubt that temperament plays an important role as a determinant of parental socialization tactics. Infants with difficult temperaments elicit more arousal and distress from caregivers than less-difficult infants (Putnam et al. 2002). Children who are more difficult may elicit increasingly coercive strategies from parents (Patterson et al. 1992). On the other hand, fearful children may respond optimally to subtle parental socialization strategies (Kochanska 1997). Other characteristics, in addition to temperament, have been examined, including activity level, social responsiveness, and compliance level. In general, the more-active, less-responsive, and more-noncompliant children elicit more negative parenting and more negative parental arousal and affect (Crouter & Booth 2003). The impacts of these individual differences on parental socialization behavior are not independent of environmental conditions. Crockenberg & Leerkes (2003) showed that the impact of a difficult infant temperament on the parent-infant attachment relationship varied as function of the degree of social support available to the mother, which underscores the potential modifiability of temperament-based influences.

Personal Resources

A variety of studies support the prediction that personal resources—conceptualized as knowledge, ability, and motivation to be a responsible caregiver—alter parenting behaviors (Belsky 1984). Particularly striking are recent studies of how parental psychopathology such as depression will alter parenting behavior (Goodman & Gotlib 2002). A variety of studies have documented that from early infancy onward the patterns of interaction between depressed and nondepressed parents and their offspring are less positive, stimulating, and contingent. Differences are particularly evident when depression is protracted and not merely transient (Campbell et al. 1995). Several studies have found that infants of depressed mothers are more likely to develop insecure attachments. More recent investigations have found links between severe and chronic depression and disorganized attachment behavior

(Lyons-Ruth et al. 2002). Nor are the effects on child-parent attachment restricted to infancy. Teti et al. (1995) found that a similar pattern of insecure attachment was evident among preschool-age children of depressed mothers. Other personal problems such as antisocial personality disorder and schizophrenia, as well as limited education and poverty, contribute to poorer parenting (Cummings et al. 2000). At the same time, positive personal characteristics, such as high intelligence and self-regulation and a transpersonal orientation (i.e., a focus on family, work, and childrearing) are linked with better quality parenting (Pulkkinen et al. 2002). Just as in the case of individual differences in infants and children, recent theorists have argued that some of these individual differences across parents, such as depression and proneness to abuse or coerciveness may, in part, be genetically based. Studies addressing the interplay between genetically based individual differences among infants and parents and environmental factors that enhance or suppress the influence of these characteristics would be valuable.

Families and Social Capital

The concept of social capital considers the relations among people, institutions, and organizations of the community outside the immediate family structure. As described by Coleman (1988), social capital is both the flow of information and the sharing of norms and values that serve to facilitate or constrain the actions of people who interact within the community's social structures (e.g., schools, places of worship, and business enterprises). Children benefit from the presence of norm and value consensus among members of their family and the wider community (Coleman 1988). Monitoring of children is facilitated, as is their socialization through multiple efforts of network members who hold shared family-community norms and values (Elder & Conger 2000). In addition, when one's own family is negligent in fulfilling the socialization role, other adults are available to assume this responsibility.

One important aspect of social capital is the network of social relationships in which families are embedded. Parents' own social networks of other adults, as well as the child members of parental social networks, provide a source of possible play partners for children. Cochran & Niegro (2002) suggested several ways in which these two sets of relationships may be related. First, the child is exposed to a wider or narrower band of possible social interaction partners by exposure to the members of a parent's social network. Second, the extent to which the child has access to the social interactions of his or her parents and members of their social network may determine how well the child acquires a particular style of social interaction. Third, in view of the social support function of social networks, parents in supportive social networks may be more likely to have positive relationships with their children, which in turn may positively affect the child's social adjustment both within and outside the family. Cochran & Niegro (2002) reported that there is overlap between parent and child social networks.

Community networking has implications for youth development. Adolescent boys were found to have better school performance and attendance and more positive social behavior when their social networks included large numbers of nonrelated adults (Cochran & Niegro 2002). In a study by Fletcher et al. (1995), nonrelated adults were found to influence the behavior of adolescents through the emotional support of the adolescents' parents as well as by their modeling of various parenting practices that encouraged and discouraged certain parenting behaviors. Moreover, children of these parents directly influenced the behaviors of their friends in a way that reflected their parents' beliefs and practices. Another way these two networks may be linked was proposed by Coleman (1988), who argued that when both parents and their children are acquainted with other parents and their children, they form network closure. When network closure exists, more shared values and more social control over their offspring are likely, which in turn would be related to better social outcomes. Darling et al. (1995) found that social integration (as indexed by network closure) and value consensus were related to adolescent social and academic outcomes. Adolescents who reported high degree of contact among their parents, their own friends, and their friends' parents were less deviant and higher in academic achievement than their peers who were less socially integrated.

In sum, the social capital in a community can aid parents' socialization of their children through several pathways. First, when parents and children have community ties, more social support is available. Second, parental awareness of community services and their participation in shaping the institutions of the community promote the maintenance of values and norms that influence their children. Third, parental participation with their children enables closer supervision of children and reduces the time children spend with their own peers. The concept of social capital embodies the notion not only that parenting is a community enterprise (Elder & Conger 2000) but also that children as well as adults are active players in the distribution of social capital.

Ethnicity and Development in the Family

There has been a marked increase in interest in how ethnicity shapes development in family contexts. There are at least three reasons for the increased attention to this issue. First, there has been a marked demographic shift in the ethnic composition of families in the United States. In 2002, 31% of the population belonged to a racial or ethnic minority group—a threefold increase over the last half-century (U.S. Census Bureau 2003). Currently 13% of Americans are Hispanic (37 million), 12.7% are African American (36.2 million), 3.9 are Asian American (11 million), and 1% are American Indian or Alaska Natives (2.7 million). Another 4.1% belong to two or more races (4.1 million). In light of these demographic shifts, ethnic groups need to be included in our research projects. A second concern is theoretical. These demographic shifts provide an opportunity to evaluate the generalizability of our assumptions about development within the family. A third reason for this increased focus on ethnicity is policy. As families become increasingly diverse because of new patterns of immigration and acculturation, the need to develop culturally sensitive service programs and policies on behalf of children and families becomes a growing priority. The need for culturally sensitive policy and progress guides is underscored by the disproportionate needs of minority children and families for services. Minorities, especially African American and Hispanic children and adolescents, are at higher risk for a variety of poor outcomes, including academic failure, alcohol and drug use, teen pregnancy, and delinquency (Gonzales et al. 2002). Moreover, rates of poverty are higher among African American and Hispanic families than among European American families (Cauce & Domenech-Rodriguez 2002).

CONCEPTUAL AND METHODOLOGICAL ISSUES   We have made considerable progress in our theoretical conceptualization of cultural variations in children's development. In recent years, the focus on ethnic minority children has shifted away from majority and minority differences in developmental outcomes toward an understanding of the adaptive strategies ethnic minorities develop in response to both majority and minority cultural influences on their development. This new paradigm recognizes the value of within-group analyses involving a single ethnic group as a legitimate research strategy and refocuses attention away from merely documenting group differences to an emphasis on the processes that may account for differences in outcomes for different children in the same group.

A variety of methodological and conceptual barriers have limited our understanding of minority families, including issues of recruitment, retention, measurement of culturally relevant constructs, and coding and interpretation of data. Members of minority groups are often skeptical about participation in scientific studies for a variety of reasons, including the past mistreatment of minorities as research participants. Moreover, in the case of Hispanic or Asian American families, many of whom are recent immigrants—sometimes illegal—there is a healthy wariness of official institutions and distrust of unfamiliar individuals. As a result, many of our minority samples are often biased and unrepresentative. A major challenge is to recruit representative minority samples so that we properly understand the full range of both strengths and weaknesses of different ethnic groups (Parke et al. 2003). Another major issue is the problem of establishing scalar equivalence across different ethnic groups (Knight et al. 2002). Recent work has provided models for establishing scalar equivalence of commonly used questionnaires for assessment of family functioning in Latino families (Knight et al. 2002). Theoretical and statistical advances in scaling, such as Item Response Theory (IRT), can be applied usefully to this issue of cross-group equivalency as well (Flannery et al. 1995). Another issue is "interpretive validity" (Maxwell 1992), or the need to insure that our interpretations of people's behaviors and utterances are consistent with their own understanding of these displays. Gonzales et al. (1996) found that European American raters coded more conflict and more restructiveness in the interactions of African American mother-daughter dyads than did African

American raters. To maintain interpretive validity, care should be taken to match the cultural background of coders with the background of the interactants being rated.

RECENT ADVANCES IN AFRICAN AMERICAN FAMILY RESEARCH   The focus on African American family research has recently shifted from a pathological/disorganizational model to a strength/resilient model (McLoyd et al. 2000). This shift is characterized by (*a*) an examination of African American families within an African American sociocultural context, (*b*) a consideration of the role of grandmothers and other extended family members in child-rearing and child-development activities, and (*c*) an analysis of the presence rather than absence of fathers within the family.

Characteristics of African American extended kin systems noted most frequently in the literature include (*a*) a high degree of geographical propinquity; (*b*) a strong sense of family and familial obligation; (*c*) fluidity of household boundaries, with great willingness to absorb relatives, both real and fictive; (*d*) frequent interaction with relatives; (*e*) frequent extended family get-togethers for special occasions and holidays; and (*f*) a system of mutual aid (Taylor 2000). The influence of the extended family among African Americans is important because of the large number of female-headed households that require child-rearing assistance and economic support (Taylor 2000). The proportion of African American households with elderly heads that have young family members is also high, about one in three families. Although some research suggests that children are better adjusted in grandmother households (Smith & Drew 2002), other research suggests that intergenerational conflict may offset the positive effects of grandmother presence (Moore & Brooks-Gunn 2002).

Until the 1980s, most African American families included two parents; today 45% of all African American children live in two-parent families (U.S. Census Bureau 1999). Despite the fact that nearly half of African Americans live in two-parent families, much of the research on African American families focused either on father absence or their maladaptive responses to familial roles (Gadsen 1999). Now a small but growing body of research is beginning to focus on African American husband-fathers who remain with their families. Pleck & Masciadrelli (2003) note that researchers are beginning to document the high level of involvement among African American husband-fathers in child rearing, family decision-making, and the economic provider role (Yeung et al. 2001). Across several studies African American spouses share equally in the major decisions in the family. Moreover, this work is aiding in shifting the conceptual focus from pathology to an emphasis on strengths and assets of African American families.

A final topic that has received increased attention is the type of discipline used by different ethnic groups. Studies of disciplinary tactics suggest that African American parents are more likely than European American parents to use physical punishment, even after controlling for socioeconomic status (Deater-Deckard & Dodge 1997). However, physical discipline predicted higher levels of externalizing only for European Americans and not for African Americans. Several explanations for these findings have been offered, including the more normative nature of physical punishment and the need to enforce rules in the dangerous environments in which African Americans are more likely to reside (Deater-Deckard & Dodge 1997, McLoyd et al. 2000). Growing up in dangerous neighborhoods brings greater risks for involvement in antisocial behavior that can have serious personal consequences whether one is a victim or a perpetrator. Under these circumstances strict obedience to parental authority is an adaptive strategy that parents may endeavor to maintain through physical discipline (Deater-Deckard & Dodge 1997). This disciplinary method may also serve to impress upon children the importance of following rules in society, and the consequences incurred from breaking those rules when one is a member of an ethnic or racial group that is unfairly stereotyped as violent. Diverse disciplinary methods are used by African American parents. Younger mothers and mothers raising their children alone use more physical discipline. Mothers with less education use more restrictive disciplinary practices, including insensitivity, inflexibility, and inconsistent parental behavior. Mothers who are more involved in organized religion also express more child-oriented disciplinary attitudes (see Gershoff 2002 for review).

RECENT ADVANCES IN ASIAN AMERICAN FAMILY RESEARCH   The Asian American population includes people from 28 Asian countries or ethnic groups (Ishi-Kuntz 2000). It is a very diverse group in terms of languages, cultures, number of generations in the United States, and reasons for immigrating to the United States. The growth of the Asian American population in recent years has been accompanied by shifts in ethnicity and national origin. Before 1970, Japanese Americans were the largest Asian ethnic group, followed by Chinese and Filipinos. By 1990, the three largest Asian groups in the United States were Chinese, Filipino, and Indo-Chinese (Vietnamese, Cambodian, Hmong, and Laotian).

Little empirical research exists on the structure and process of Asian American families, and most research has sampled from Chinese American and Japanese American populations. Often, Asian American families are examined to identify the family characteristics that contribute to children's academic performance. Consequently, there is very little research on the effects of Asian American parents on children's socioemotional development. Typically, Asian American families are seen as patriarchal, with the father maintaining authority and emotional distance from other members (Ishi-Kuntz 2000). Wives are subordinate to their husbands, but in their role as mothers they have considerable authority and autonomy in child rearing. Traditionally, the family exerts control over family members, who are taught to place family needs before individual needs. Children show obedience and loyalty to their parents and, especially in the case of male children, are expected to take care of elderly parents (filial piety). Confucian influences on family life are stronger in some Asian American populations (e.g., Chinese and Vietnamese) than in others (e.g., Japanese) due to differences in immigration patterns and degree of

Westernization of the country of origin. Length of residence in the United States and acculturation also contribute to extensive within-group differences in family structure and roles (Ishi-Kuntz 2000).

Aspects of traditional Asian childrearing practices appear to be continued by Asian American families (Chao & Tseng 2002). Studies tend to be focused primarily upon characteristics of parental control. These studies (Chao 1994, Stewart et al. 1998) have challenged the traditional view of Chinese parents as authoritarian, restrictive, and controlling because these parenting behaviors do not have cross-cultural equivalence for European Americans and Chinese. These child-rearing concepts are rooted in European American culture and are not relevant for describing the socialization styles and goals of Chinese parents. Instead, the style of parenting used by the Chinese American mothers is conceptualized as a type of training performed by parents who are deeply concerned and involved in the lives of their children rather than strict or authoritarian control. Stewart et al. (1998) reported similar findings among Hong Kong Chinese adolescents.

The value of this approach is that it helps resolve paradoxes in the current literature. In studies of ethnicity and achievement, Dornbusch, Steinberg, and their colleagues found that Asian American students rated their parents as more authoritarian than parents from European American or Hispanic groups. Although they scored lower on the optimal parental style of authoritativeness, the Asian students had the highest achievement scores (Steinberg et al. 1992). Work by Chao (1994, 2001) suggests that confusion between authoritarian and training child-rearing concepts among Chinese respondents may account for the paradox. In short, Chinese simply have a different set of child-rearing values and styles that are distinct from the traditional American child-rearing schemes.

RECENT ADVANCES IN HISPANIC FAMILY RESEARCH   Today, Mexican Americans make up the vast majority of Latinos (66%), followed by Central and South Americans, Puerto Ricans, and Cubans. It is estimated that if current immigration trends continue, more than half of the Latino population for the next 50 years will be made up of immigrants and their children (Cauce & Domenech-Rodriguez 2002). Several characteristics distinguish Latino families: (*a*) identification with family, community, and ethnic group; (*b*) personalization of interpersonal relationships and (*c*) Latino Catholic ideology (Cauce & Domenech-Rodriguez 2000).

Latino child-rearing practices encourage the development of a self-identity embedded firmly within the context of the family. Four components of familism have been identified: demographic, structural, normative, and behavioral (Zinn & Wells 2000). Demographic familism reflects the larger family size of Latino families: 3.71 members versus 2.97 for white and 3.31 for African American families (U.S. Census Bureau 2003). In terms of structure, many members of the same family live in the same community and Latinos are less geographically mobile than whites after controlling for social class (Cauce & Domenech-Rodriguez 2002). As in the case of African Americans, there is a high level of cross-generational co-residence arrangements and assistance (Zinn & Wells 2000).

In support of normative familism, Zayas & Rojas-Flores (2002) found that Puerto Rican mothers valued family closeness and respect for authority. Children are expected to be obedient and respectful toward their parents, even after they are grown and functioning as parents themselves. In terms of behavioral familism, Latinos place a great deal of value on living in proximity to relatives (Farr & Wilson-Figueroa 1997). The *familia* network extends further into the community through kinships formed by intermarriage between *familias* and *el compadrazco*, which is the cultural practice of having special friends become godparents of children in baptisms. Adults united through *el compadrazco*, called *compadres* and *comadres*, have mutual obligations to each other similar to those of brothers and sisters. Extended *familia* ties in the community give rise to a sense of identity with one's community.

The family plays an important role in the adaptation of Latinos to life in the United States. During the first ten years following immigration, it is not uncommon for immigrants and their children to live in extended households that include relatives and other nonfamily members (Gonzales et al. 2002). However, as immigrants move out of extended households, they prefer to establish single households in the surrounding area, thus retaining some of the benefits of extended kin and friends, such as social support. The longer immigrants live in the United States, the more their family networks expand. Even as individual family members become acculturated, their local extended family becomes larger. Second- and third-generation Mexican Americans have larger and more integrated extended families than immigrants.

Recent work has focused on the relation between family acculturation and child and adolescent outcomes. Gonzales et al. (2002) found there was substantial support for the links between acculturation and problem behaviors. Problem areas include delinquency and susceptibility to antisocial peers, high rates of alcohol and drug use, increased tobacco use, depressive symptomatology, suicidal ideation, and poorer academic performance. Evidence linking self-esteem and eating disorders with level of acculturation is less clear (Gonzales et al. 2002). Explanations include discrimination and stress due to minority status, decreased acceptance of traditional cultural norms and values, disruptions in family ties, increased intergenerational conflict, and exposure to deviant peer influences (Gonzales et al. 2002).

CONCLUDING PERSPECTIVES ON ETHNICITY AND FAMILIES   At present, and for the foreseeable future, the growth of ethnic minority families will be primarily a result of immigration from Latin America and Asia. Research with families of these groups needs to take into account the acculturation level of parents and children and the effects it has on family processes and child outcomes. Intergenerational differences in acculturation, for example, can create role strains between parents and children that have implications for child-rearing styles, disciplinary practices, and overall parent-child relations. Together with acculturation, recognition of biculturalism as both an adaptation strategy and socialization goal should guide future research. The effects of prejudice and discrimination on ethnic minorities in such areas as social and emotional development, ethnic identity, and achievement motivation deserve much more attention. Language development research should also give greater attention to second language acquisition (usually English) and bilingualism and its relation to cognitive development and school achievement. Much more attention must also be given to the role of ethnic minority fathers, grandparents, and extended family members in the socialization of children. Finally, more observational studies with ethnic minority families should be encouraged.

NEW DIRECTIONS IN FAMILY RESEARCH

Families are dynamic and are continuously confronted by challenges, changes, and opportunities. A number of society-wide changes have produced shifts in family relationships. Fertility rates and family size have decreased, the percentage of women in the workforce has increased, the timing of onset of parenthood has shifted, divorce rates have risen, and the number of single-parent families has increased (Amato 2000, Hetherington & Kelley 2001, Teachman et al. 2000). These social trends provide an opportunity to explore how families adapt and change in response to these shifting circumstances and represent "natural experiments" in family coping and adaptation. Moreover, they challenge our traditional assumptions that families can be studied at a single point in historical time since the historical contexts are constantly shifting. Our task is to establish how socialization processes operate similarly or differently under varying historical circumstances. Several new topics in family research are briefly reviewed to illustrate recent trends in this area of inquiry: the interplay between work and family, gay and lesbian families, the new reproductive technologies, and the impact of parental incarceration on families.

Beyond Maternal Employment: Quality of Mother and Father Employment and Its Impact on Family Socialization

There is an extensive literature on the impact of maternal employment on children's development, marriage, and family role distributions (Harvey 1999). Although there has been an increase in the number of parents who are employed in recent years, many workers experienced increases in work hours, a decrease in job stability, a rise in temporary jobs, and especially among low-wage workers, a decrease in income (Mishel et al. 1999). Because of these changes the theoretical questions have shifted. More recently, instead of examining whether or not one or both parents are employed, researchers have begun to address the issue of the impact of the quality and nature of work on parenting by both mothers and fathers (Perry-Jenkins et al. 2000). Both how much and when parents work matters for children. Not only are heavy parental work schedules associated with negative outcomes for children (Parcel & Menaghan 1994), but work schedules with nonoverlapping hours for husbands and wives negatively affect marital relationships (White & Keith 1990). The related issue of the impact of work quality on families has also received attention. At the same time, job loss and underemployment has serious effects on family life, including marital relationships, parent-child relationships, and child adjustment (Conger & Elder 1994, White & Rogers 2000). As Crouter (1994) noted, there are two types of linkage between family and work. One type of research focuses on work as an "emotional climate" which, in turn, may have carryover effects to the enactment of roles at home settings. A second type of linkage focuses on the skills, attitudes, and perspectives that adults acquire in their work-based socialization as adults and how these variations in job experience alter their behavior in family contexts. In contrast to the short-term perspective of the spillover of emotional climate research, this type of endeavor involves more enduring and long-lasting effects of work on family life.

Work in the first tradition has been conducted by Repetti (1994), who studied the impact of working in a high-stress job (air traffic controller) on subsequent family interaction patterns. She found that the male air traffic controllers were more withdrawn and less angry in marital interactions after high-stress shifts and tended to be behaviorally and emotionally withdrawn during interactions with their children as well. In addition, distressing social experiences at work were associated with higher expressions of anger and greater use of discipline during interaction with the child later in the day. Repetti & Wood (1997) found similar effects for mothers who withdrew from their preschoolers on days when the mothers experienced greater workloads or interpersonal stress on the job. Similarly Crouter et al. (1999) found that parents who reported high work pressure and role overload had more conflicts with their adolescents.

Research in the second tradition of family-work linkage, namely the effects of the nature of men's and women's occupational roles on their parenting behavior, dates back to the classic work of Kohn (1995). Men who experience a high degree of occupational autonomy value independence in their children, reflect on children's intentions when considering discipline, and use reasoning and withdrawal of rewards instead of physical punishment. In contrast, men who are in highly supervised jobs with little autonomy value conformity and obedience, focus on consequences rather than intentions, and use more physical forms of discipline. Several researchers extended this work by focusing on the outcomes of job characteristics for children's development. Cooksey et al. (1997) found that children had fewer behavior problems when their mother's work involved more autonomy working with people and more problem-solving opportunities. Similarly, others found that fathers with greater job complexity and autonomy were less authoritarian (Grimm-Thomas & Perry-Jenkins 1994) and responded with greater warmth to their children and more verbal explanations (Greenberger et al. 1994). However, the process probably operates in both directions: The home experience of parents affects their job performance as well. In fact, arguments at home with a wife or with a child were negatively related to work performance (Frone et al. 1997). These studies underscore the importance of moving beyond employment status per se to a detailed exploration of the nature of work in our studies of family-work linkages.

Gay and Lesbian Couples: How Do Children in Same-Sex Households Fare?

One of the new trends in family research is the exploration of gay and lesbian families and the input of these families on children's development. Recent estimates suggest that there are between one and five million lesbian and gay parents in the United States, with the lower numbers derived from the most conservative assessments on the National Health and Social Life Survey (NHSLS). The higher estimates are based on the more liberal assessments used in the NHSLS and on voter exit polls (Badgett 1998, Patterson & Friel 2000). Regardless of the estimate, it is evident that a larger number of children are growing up in gay or lesbian families.

There are several reasons for scholarly interest in the issue of gay and lesbian parenting. First, a better understanding is needed as a guide to legal and public policy decisions. Evaluation of assumptions concerning the fitness of lesbian and gay individuals to be parents as well as careful evaluation of the impact of same-gender parenting on children are both reasons for this line of inquiry. A further rationale for this work is theoretical, since the recent research on the development of children in gay and lesbian families is another way to assess the uniqueness and necessity of rearing children in homes with both male and female parents. Silverstein has framed this debate in a provocative but helpful way by questioning whether fathers are essential for the successful socialization of children (Silverstein 2002). Similarly, Golombok (2000) has raised the question of whether gender of parent is critical for successful child outcomes or whether a set of gender-neutral characteristics, such as nurturance, protection, and guidance, are more critical ingredients for parental competence. Part of the evidence that is relevant to the debate about the essential father stems from recent work by Patterson (2002) indicating that the development of children raised by lesbian and gay parents is well within normal limits. Work by Flaks et al. (1995) substantiates this picture: Children in heterosexual and lesbian families were not very different in terms of their developmental outcomes.

However, it seems premature to conclude that fathers are replaceable based on this evidence. Studies have relied largely on small samples of highly educated individuals in stable relationships. Furthermore, two other key issues need to be addressed in ongoing work. More needs to be understood about the extent to which role division in lesbian families approximates role division in heterosexual families, and more needs to be understood about the degree to which lesbian couples expose their children to male role models. In the first case, evidence suggests that lesbian couples share household tasks and decision-making responsibilities more equally than do heterosexual couples (Patterson 2002). At the same time, however, lesbian biological mothers viewed their parental role as more salient than either nonbiological lesbian mothers or heterosexual mothers (Hand 1991). Moreover, despite the more egalitarian divisions of household labor in lesbian households, there also exists some traditionality in roles. Biological lesbian mothers are more involved in child care than their partners; nonbiological lesbian mothers spent more time working outside the family (Patterson 2002). This raises the possibility that even in same-gender families, the usual role division concerning child care, which characterizes heterosexual partnerships, may be evident. Whether the nonbiological mothers enact other aspects of more traditional male roles, such as a physical play style, remains to be established. In short, children may be afforded opportunities to experience both maternal and paternal interactive styles in same-gender households.

Although the amount of research on the effects of being reared by two male parents is more limited than the work on two female parents, the available data suggest that the gender identities of children of gay fathers are similar to those of children of heterosexual fathers (Bailey et al. 1995). Moreover, as Bozett (1987) has reported, children develop positive relationships with their gay fathers. One important challenge faced by children of gay parents, however, is their possible stigmatization by others. An issue that requires concerted attention in this debate is the role of social norms and attitudes toward children growing up in same-gender child-rearing unions. Beyond the theoretical plausibility of successful outcomes from this type of child-rearing arrangement, we need to pay more attention to the level of societal acceptance of these family types as a critical factor that can either facilitate or disrupt the successful adaptation of children in these families (Patterson 2002).

As is true of lesbian parents, gay parents are more likely than heterosexual couples to share child-rearing duties evenly (McPherson 1993). More information about the observed and self-reported parenting by gay fathers, such as that provided by Silverstein (2002), is needed, as well as assessments of the effect of these child-rearing arrangements on the children (Patterson 2002). Just as Silverstein (2002) questioned the essential father, these data on the effects of being reared by gay male parents raise a similar question about the essential mother and the extent to which gay couples provide differential exposure to "maternal" or feminine models and opportunities for interaction with a female partner.

This increase in gay and lesbian parents can be profitably viewed as a series of natural experiments that offer the opportunity to explore the validity of our assumptions about the critical ingredients that define successful parenting. Just as the rise in the use of day care due to the rise in women's employment has permitted valuable tests of certain important tenets of attachment theory (Clarke-Stewart & Allhusen 2002), so too should careful studies of same-gender child-rearing arrangements be viewed as opportunities for testing our theories about links between gender and parenting.

The Effects of New Reproductive Technologies on Parenting

In the new millennium the routes to parenthood promise to be increasingly diverse. New reproductive technologies are expanding the ways individuals become parents. Recent changes in childbearing include in vitro fertilization, anonymous and nonanonymous sperm donors, and surrogate mothers. Djerassi (1999) recently argued that just as "technology's gift to women (and men) during the latter half of the twentieth century was contraception, the first 50 years of the new millennium may well be considered the decades of conception" (p. 53).

Various scenarios that may alter our usual ways of conceptualizing families and parenthood are possible (Golombok 2002). Assisted reproductive technology, including in-vitro fertilization, has produced more than 300,000 babies since 1977. Several recent studies have examined the psychological adjustment of children conceived by donor insemination. Although these studies have focused on child outcomes and not on parenting, they nonetheless raise important questions about parent-child relationships in these new technology-assisted families. In Great Britain and the United States the functioning of children born via donor insemination, compared with children in the general population, was similar (Golombok 2002, Patterson 2002) We still have much to learn about the implications for parents or the parent-child relationships of these technology-based conceptions.

Evidence suggests that the sexual orientation of the parents who raise a donor-based child does not make a difference in the child's adjustment. However, we do not know whether important issues such as the disclosure of identity of donors or donor involvement with the family interact with family structural variables (e.g., lesbian or gay versus heterosexual partnerships). Other questions remain as well. Does it make a difference if the identity of the donor is known or unknown? What is the effect of disclosing the nature of the child's conception to the child? What is the effect of disclosing or keeping confidential the identity of the male donor? Does the availability of the male to the child after the birth make a difference in the child's adjustment? Are patterns of parent-child relationships different in couples that have achieved parenthood through in vitro fertilization after a long period of infertility? Do such parents develop closer relationships with their children? Are they overprotective of their offspring? It would also be important to understand how the partner-partner relationship is altered by this sequence leading to parenthood.

A variant on the new assisted reproductive technology is the increased use of surrogate mothers. This innovation raises questions about the effect of this choice on parent-parent, parent-child, and couple-surrogate mother relationships. Again, issues of disclosure arise as in the case of in vitro fertilization. Is there any meaningful developmental effect of the child's learning he or she was born via a surrogate mother? Should the child know the identity of the surrogate mother? What are the implications of contact between the surrogate mother and the child for the child's adjustment? What is the effect of continuing contact between the surrogate mother and the child-rearing family on the parent-parent relationship? Our scientific knowledge about these issues is limited, though there is an accumulating and thoughtful clinical literature that can serve as a guide for research in this area and as a helpful map for practitioners and policy and legal scholars (see Paulson & Sachs 1999).

Other developments may have equal or greater implications for future conceptualization of parenting, namely the development of intracytoplasmic sperm injection (Palermo et al. 1992). This procedure allows the fertilization of a human egg by direct injection of a single sperm under the microscope. This is followed by reintroduction of the fertilized egg back into the woman's uterus. Since 1992, more than 10,000 babies have been born because of this new conception technology (Djerassi 1999). Moreover, this procedure raises issues that future scholars of parenting are going to have to consider. Genetically infertile men could become fathers using this new technology. But other uses are more complex. For example, the sperm of deceased men may be used (through intracytoplasmic sperm injection) to produce a child later. A woman may conceive a child at a much older age, which raises important questions about the effect of timing of the onset of parenthood on parent-child relationships. However, because of the increased longevity of women, a woman in her forties could raise a child at least as long as a 20-year-old woman could in the early 1900s. Our definition of natural and unnatural in regard to the age at which parenting should begin is challenged by these new advances in reproductive technology. Similarly, our definition of parenthood is becoming divorced from biology and instead is a socially constructed category. To understand the effect of these new technological advances on our social understanding of parenting and kinship relations is one of the major issues we will face in this century.

Parental Incarceration and Children

Natural experiments offered by shifts in family structure and organization provide important opportunities for theory testing about family processes. A recent example is the study of the effects of parental incarceration on children (Parke & Clarke-Stewart 2003). This topic provides interesting theoretical and policy perspectives on a variety of issues, including the effects of short-term and long-term parent-child separation and reunion on children and the effects of alternative caregivers on children's adjustment. According to recent estimates (Mumola 2000), nearly 3.6 million parents are under some form of correctional supervision, including parole. These parents have an estimated 2.3 million children (Mumola 2000). The rate of parental incarceration has gone up sharply in the last decade. Gender of the parent is a major factor in incarceration; 90% of incarcerated parents are fathers. However, the number of mothers in prison grew at a faster rate than the number of incarcerated fathers from 1991 to 2000. In addition, there are clear differences in the ethnic make-up of incarcerated parents. In both state and federal prisons, there are more African American parents (47% and 49% in state and federal prisons respectively) than either Hispanic parents (19% and 30%) or white non-Hispanic parents. In terms of age, 58% of children with incarcerated parents are under 10 years of age, with 8 years being the mean age (Mumola 2000).

To understand the impact of parental incarceration, it is important to know the nature of the family living arrangements prior to incarceration. Mothers were more likely than fathers to be living with their children at the time of admission to prison (Mumola 2000). It would be expected that incarceration would carry different meanings and have different consequences for children who do not reside with their parents before incarceration. The extent to which incarceration disrupts the contact patterns between these nonresidential parents and their children, as well as the effects of incarceration on children who were living with their parent at the time of imprisonment, are both issues that merit examination. Another important issue is who looks after the children when parents are incarcerated. For incarcerated fathers, the child's mother is the usual caregiver before the father is arrested, and mothers continue the caregiving responsibility after the father goes to prison. On the other hand, when mothers are put in prison, fathers assume parental responsibility in only about 30% of these cases. Instead, a grandparent becomes the caregiver.

A variety of negative long-term effects of parental incarceration on children have been identified, including poor social-emotional and academic functioning. These effects vary depending on a number of factors. First, incarceration is often preceded by a period of familial instability, poverty, poor parenting, child abuse or neglect, marital discord and conflict, or father absence. A combination of these conditions may have already increased the base rates of children's problem behaviors. Consequently, without measures of the child's environment and behavior prior to incarceration—that is, measures of self-selection factor—it is difficult to attribute the problem behaviors to incarceration per se. Other events also transpire at the time of incarceration that could account for some of the negative effects on children. Relocation and placement with alternative caregivers are both major disruptions in the children's lives, and detrimental to children (Rutter 1987).

Before and during the incarceration, and during the reunion phase after incarceration, different factors are likely to modify children's reactions (Parke & Clarke-Stewart 2003). The most important predictor of how well the child will adjust to the immediate separation is the quality of the parent-child relationship. Two other factors influence children's adjustment during the period of parental incarceration: (a) the nature and quality of the alternative caregiving arrangements and (b) the opportunities to maintain contact with the absent parent. Better child adjustment occurs when there is continuity of care, the quality of care is adequate (Bloom & Steinhart 1993), and there are opportunities to maintain ties with the absent parent (Young & Smith 2000). However, there are many barriers to child visitation, such as correctional system policies, as well as practical barriers (Young & Smith 2000).

Various research gaps exist, including more attention to process issues, more prospective longitudinal studies, and more effort to describe the unique effects of maternal versus paternal incarceration on family functioning. On the policy side, programs to minimize discontinuity for children and to minimize economic hardship need to be developed and evaluated (Parke & Clarke-Stewart 2003).

FUTURE TRENDS

Several issues warrant more attention in future research. First, there are serious measurement obstacles that merit more work, including specifying the role of genetics in family research. The field has progressed beyond the simple environment-gene partitioning argument (Harris 1998) toward a more complex conceptual framework that reframes the debate in terms of gene x environment interactions. According to this view (Reiss 2003), family processes mediate genetic influence in children's outcomes, and the future challenge is to determine how this gene x environment family model plays out across development. Several designs, including cross-fostering studies with nonhuman primates (Suomi 2000), modified sibling designs (Reiss et al. 2000), and prospective adoption designs (Reiss 2003) are promising new approaches for addressing this issue. Second, the measurement of the biological underpinnings of family dynamics is undergoing significant advances but needs to be more carefully measured at various levels of family subsystems. Future work that includes measurement of hormones, for example, not just in individual children, but in parent-child dyads, in marital partners, and in all family members will begin to specify the pervasiveness of observed biological markers at different levels of family structure. Third, more intervention studies are needed to adequately address the perennial "direct of effects" problem in the family research. As Cowan & Cowan (2002) recently argued, intervention studies provide the "gold standard" for testing causal hypotheses. As their review of recent intervention and prevention efforts to modify parenting and marital processes shows, the evidence clearly supports the view that the quality of parent and marital relationships can impact children's adaptation. Moreover, child-based interventions underscore the role of the child as an active agent in shaping parenting and marital processes as well. This body of work underscores the bidirectional nature of family process. In addition to intervention designs, natural experiments continue to be a useful tool for aiding and sorting out causal issues (Rutter 2002). For example, recent work on adopted Romanian children has shown that the length of institutionalization is a major predictor of child later functioning (Rutter et al. 2002). Fourth, more work is needed in cultural variations in families that moves beyond description to detailed delineation of process that accounts for variations in child outcomes in family contexts (Parke 2004). At the same time, specifying when culture matters and when universal assumptions apply is a major challenge for the field (Shweder 2003).

The *Annual Review of Psychology* is online at http://psych.annualreviews.org

LITERATURE CITED

Allen J, Hawkins A. 1999. Maternal gatekeeping: mothers, beliefs and behaviors that inhibit greater father involvement in family work. *J. Marriage Fam.* 61:199–212

Amato PR. 2000. The consequences of divorce for adults and children. *J. Marriage Fam.* 62:1269–87

Badgett MVL. 1998. The economic well being of lesbian, gay and bisexual adults' families. In *Lesbian, Gay and Bisexual Identities in Families: Psychological Perspectives*, ed. CJ Patterson, AR D'Augelli, pp. 179–94. New York: Oxford Univ. Press

Bailey JM, Bobrew D, Wolfe J, Mikach S. 1995. Sexual orientation of adult sons of gay fathers. *Dev. Psychol.* 31:124–29

Beitel A, Parke RD. 1998. Paternal involvement in infancy: the role of maternal and paternal attitudes. *J. Fam. Psychol.* 12:268–88

Bell RQ. 1968. A reinterpretation of the direction of effects in studies of socialization. *Psychol. Rev.* 75:81–95

Belsky J. 1984. The determinants of parenting: a process model. *Child Dev.* 55:83–96

Bloom B, Steinhart D. 1993. *Why Punish the Children? An Appraisal of the Children of Incarcerated Mothers in America.* San Francisco: Natl. Counc. Crime Delinq.

Bornstein M, ed. 2002. *Handbook of Parenting,* Vols. 3, 4, 5. Mahwah, NJ: Erlbaum. 2nd ed.

Boss P. 1999. *Ambiguous Loss.* Cambridge, MA: Harvard Univ. Press

Bowlby J. 1973. *Attachment and Loss:* Vol. 2. *Separation.* New York: Basic Books

Bozett FW. 1987. Children of gay fathers. In *Gay and Lesbian Parents,* ed. FW Bozett, pp. 39–57. New York: Praeger

Brody G, Flor D, Neubaum E. 1998. Coparenting process and child competence among rural African-American families. In *Families, Risk and Competence,* ed. M Lewis, C Feiring, pp. 227–343. Mahwah, NJ: Erlbaum

Bronfenbrenner U. 1979. *The Ecology of Human Development.* Cambridge, MA: Harvard Univ. Press

Campbell SB, Cohn JF, Meyers T. 1995. Depression in first time mothers: mother-infant interaction and depression chronicity. *Dev. Psychol.* 31:349–57

Cauce AM, Domenech-Rodriguez M. 2002. Latino families: myths and realities. See Contreras et al. 2002, pp. 3–25

Chao R. 2001. Extending the research on the consequences of parenting style for Chinese Americans and European Americans. *Child Dev.* 72:1832–43

Chao R, Tseng V. 2002. Parenting of Asians. See Bornstein 2002, 3:49–93

Chao RL. 1994. Beyond parental control and authoritarian parenting style: understanding Chinese parenting through the cultural notion of training. *Child Dev.* 65:1111–19

Clarke-Stewart KA, Allhusen VD. 2002. Non-parental caregiving. See Bornstein 2002, 3:215–52

Cochran M, Niego S. 2002. Parenting and social networks. See Bornstein 2002, 3:393–418

Coleman J. 1988. Social capital in the creation of human capital. *Am. J. Sociol.* 94:95–110

Conger R, Elder G. 1994. *Families in Troubled Times.* New York: Aldine de Gruyter

Contreras JM, Kerns KA, Neal-Barnett AM, eds. 2002. *Latino Children and Families in the United States.* Westport, CT: Praeger

Cook WL. 2001. Interpersonal influence in family systems: a social relations model analysis. *Child Dev.* 72:1179–97

Cooksey EC, Menaghan EG, Jokielek SM. 1997. Life course effects of work and family circumstances on children. *Soc. Forces* 76:637–67

Coulton CJ, Pandey S. 1992. Geographic concentration of poverty risk to children in urban neighborhoods. *Am. Behav. Sci.* 33:238–57

Cowan PA, Cowan CP. 2002. Interventions as tests of family systems theories: marital family relationships in children's development psychopathology. *Dev. Psychopathol.* 14:731–59

Cox MJ, Paley B. 1997. Families as systems. *Annu. Rev. Psychol.* 48:243–67

Crockenberg S, Leerkes E. 2003. Infant negative emotionality, caregiving, and family relationships. See Crouter & Booth 2003, pp. 57–78

Crockenberg SC, Langrock A. 2001. The role of specific emotions in children's responses to interparental conflict: a test of the model. *J. Fam. Psychol.* 15:163–82

Crouter AC. 1994. Processes linking families and work: implications for behavior development in both settings. See Parke & Kellam 1994, pp. 9–28

Crouter AC, Booth A, eds. 2003. *Children's Influence on Family Dynamics.* Mahwah, NJ: Erlbaum

Crouter AC, Bumpus MF, Maguire MC, McHale SM. 1999. Linking parents' work pressure and adolescents' well being: insights into dynamics in dual-earner families. *Dev. Psychol.* 35:1453–61

Cummings EM, Davies PT, Campbell SB. 2000. *Developmental Psychology and Family Process*. New York: Guilford

Cummings EM, Goeke-Morey MC, Graham MA. 2002. Interparental relations as a dimension of parenting. In *Parenting the Child's World*, ed. JG Borkowski, S Landesman-Ramey, M Bristol-Power, pp. 251–64. Mahwah, NJ: Erlbaum

Darling N, Steinberg L, Gringlas B, Dornbusch S. 1995. *Community influences on adolescent achievement and deviance. A test of the functional community hypothesis*. Unpubl. manuscr. Temple Univ., Philadelphia, PA

Davies PT, Cummings EM. 1994. Marital conflict and child adjustment: an emotional security hypothesis. *Psychol. Bull.* 116:387–411

Davies PT, Harold GT, Goeke-Morey MC, Cummings EM. 2002. Child emotional security and interparental conflict. *Monogr. Soc. Res. Child Dev.* Ser. No. 270, 67(3):27–62

Deater-Deckard K, Dodge K. 1997. Externalizing behavior problems and discipline revisited: non-linear effects and variation by culture, context and gender. *Psychol. Inq.* 8:161–75

Demo DH, Allen KR, Fine MA, eds. 2000. *Handbook of Family Diversity*. New York: Oxford

Denham SA. 1998. *Emotional Development in Young Children*. New York: Guilford

Dickstein S, St. Andre M, Sameroff A, Seifer R, Schiller M. 1999. Maternal depression, family functioning and child outcomes: a narrative assessment. *Monogr. Soc. Res. Child Dev.* 64:84–103

Dix T. 1991. The affective organization of parenting: adaptive and maladaptive processes. *Psychol. Bull.* 110:3–25

Djerassi C. 1999. Sex in an age of mechanical reproduction. *Science* 285:53–54

Dunn J. 1988. *The Beginnings of Social Understanding*. Cambridge, MA: Harvard Univ. Press

Dunn J. 1993. *Young Children's Close Relationships*. Newbury Park, CA: Sage

East PL, Rook KS. 1992. Compensatory patterns of support among children's peer relationships: a test using school friends, nonschool friends, and siblings. *Dev. Psychol.* 28:163–72

Edwards CP, Whiting BB. 1993. "Mother, older sibling and me": the overlapping roles of caregivers and companions in the social world of two and three-year-olds in Ngeca, Kenya. In *Parent-Child Play: Descriptions and Implications*, ed. K MacDonald. Albany, NY: SUNY Press

Elder GH. 1998. The life course as developmental theory. *Child Dev.* 69:1–12

Elder GH, Conger RD. 2000. *Children of the Land: Adversity and Success in Rural America*. Chicago: Univ. Chicago Press

Emery RE, Kitzman KM, Waldron M. 1999. Psychological interventions for separated and divorced families. In *Coping with Divorce, Single Parenting and Remarriage: A Risk Resilience Perspective*, ed. EM Hetherington, pp. 323–44. Mahwah, NJ: Erlbaum

Erel O, Burman B. 1995. Interrelatedness of marital relations and parent-child relations: a meta-analytic review. *Psychol. Bull.* 118:108–32

Erera P. 1997. Step- and foster families: a comparison. *Marriage Fam. Rev.* 26:301–15

Farr KA, Wilson-Figueroa M. 1997. Talking about health and health care: experiences and perceptions of Latino women in a farm working community. *Women Health* 25:23–40

Fiese BH, Marjinsky KAT. 1999. Dinnertime stores: connecting family practices with relationship beliefs and child adjustment. *Monogr. Soc. Res. Child Dev.* 64:52–68

Fiese BH, Sameroff AJ, Grotevant HD, Wamboldt FS, Dickstein S, Fravel DL. 1999. The stories that families tell: narrative coherence, narrative interaction and relationship beliefs. *Monogr. Soc. Res. Child Dev.* Ser. No. 257, 64(2):whole issue

Fiese BH, Tomcho JJ, Douglas JM, Josephs K, Poltrock S, Baker T. 2002. A review of 50 years of research on naturally occurring family routines and rituals. *J. Fam. Psychol.* 16:381–90

Fincham F. 1998. Child development and marital relations. *Child Dev.* 69:543–74

Fivaz-Depeursinge E, Corboz-Warnery A. 1999. *The Primary Triangle. A Developmental Systems View of Mothers, Fathers, and Infants.* New York: Basic Books

Flaks DK, Ficher I, Masterpasqua F, Joseph G. 1995. Lesbians choosing motherhood: a comparative study of lesbian and heterosexual parents and their children. *Dev. Psychol.* 29:105–14

Flannery WP, Riese SP, Widaman KF. 1995. An item response theory analysis of the general and academic scales of the Self-Description Questionnaire II. *J. Res. Personal.* 29:168–88

Fletcher AA, Darling NE, Steinberg L, Dornbusch SM. 1995. The company they keep: relation of adolescents' adjustment behavior to their friends' perceptions of authoritative parenting in the social network. *Dev. Psychol.* 31:300–10

Frone MR, Yardley JK, Markel KS. 1997. Developing and testing an integrative model of the work-family interface. *J. Vocat. Behav.* 50:145–67

Furstenberg FF Jr, Cook TD, Eccles J, Elder GH Jr, Sameroff A. 1999. *Managing to Make It: Urban Families and Adolescent Success.* Chicago: Univ. Chicago Press

Gadsen VL. 1999. Black families in intergenerational cultural perspective. In *Parenting and Child Development in "Nontraditional Families,"* ed. EM Lamb, pp. 221–46. Mahwah, NJ: Erlbaum

Gauvain M. 2001. *The Social Context of Cognitive Development.* New York: Guilford

Geary DC, Bjorklund DF. 2000. Evolutionary developmental psychology. *Child Dev.* 71:57–65

Gershoff ET. 2002. Corporal punishment by parents and associated child behaviors experiences: a meta-analytic theoretical review. *Psychol. Bull.* 128:539–79

Golombok S. 2000. *Parenting: What Really Counts?* London, UK: Routledge

Golombok S. 2002. Parenting and contemporary reproductive technologies. See Bornstein 2002, 3:339–62

Gonzales NA, Cauce AM, Mason CA. 1996. Interobserver agreement in the assessment of parental behavior and parent-adolescent conflict: African American mothers, daughters and independent observers. *Child Dev.* 67:1483–98

Gonzales NA, Knight GP, Morgan-Lopez AA, Saenz D, Sirolle A. 2002. Acculturation and the mental health of Latino youths: an integration of critique of the literature. See Contreras et al. 2002, pp. 45–74

Goodman SH, Gotlib IH, eds. 2002. *Children of Depressed Parents.* Washington, DC: Am. Psychol. Assoc.

Goodnow JJ. 2002. Parents' knowledge and expectations: using what we know. See Bornstein 2002, 3:439–60

Gottman JM, Katz LF. 1989. Effects of marital discord on young children's peer interaction and health. *Dev. Psychol.* 25:373–81

Gottman JM, Murray JD, Swanson CC, Tyson R, Swanson KR. 2002. *The Mathematics of Marriage.* Cambridge, MA: MIT Press

Graham S. 1992. Most of the subjects were white and middle class. *Am. Psychol.* 47:766–79

Greenberger E, O'Neil R, Nagel SK. 1994. Linking workplace and home place: relations between the nature of adults' work and their parenting behaviors. *Dev. Psychol.* 30:990–1002

Grimm-Thomas K, Perry-Jenkins M. 1994. All in a day's work: job experiences, self-esteem and fathering in working-class families. *Fam. Relat.* 43:174–81

Grotevant HD, Fravel DL, Gorall D, Piper J. 1999. Narratives of adoptive parents: perspectives from individual and couple interviews. *Monogr. Soc. Res. Child Dev.* 64:69–83

Grych JH, Fincham FD. 1990. Marital conflict and children's adjustment: a cognitive-contextual framework. *Psychol. Bull.* 101:267–90

Gunnar MR, Tout K, deHoan M, Pierce S, Stansburym K. 1997. Temperament, social competence and adrenocorticol activity in preschoolers. *Dev. Psychobiol.* 31:65–85

Hand SI. 1991. *The Lesbian Parenting Couple.* Unpubl. Doc. Diss., The Prof. Sch. Psychol., San Francisco, CA

Harris K. 1998. *The Nurture Assumption.* New York: The Free Press

Harvey E. 1999. Short-term and long-term effects of parental employment on children of the National Longitudinal Survey of Youth. *Dev. Psychol.* 35:445–59

Hetherington EM, Kelley J. 2001. *For Better or for Worse.* New York: Norton

Hoff E, Laursen B, Tardiff T. 2002. Socioeconomic status and parenting. See Bornstein 2002, 3:231–52

Ishi-Kuntz M. 2000. Diversity within Asian-American families. See Demo et al. 2000, pp. 274–92

Katz LF, Gottman J. 1996. Spillover effects of marital conflict. In search of parenting and coparenting mechanisms. See McHale & Cowan 1996, pp. 57–76

Katz LF, Woodin EM. 2002. Hostility, hostile detachment, and conflict engagement in marriages: Effects on child and family functioning. *Child Dev.* 73:636–51

Kerr M, Stattin H. 2003. Parenting of adolescents: action or reaction? In *Children's Influence on Family Dynamics,* ed. AC Crouter, A Booth, pp. 121–51. Mahwah, NJ: Erlbaum

Kerns KA, Cole A, Andrews PB. 1998. Attachment security, parent peer management practices, and peer relationships in preschoolers. *Merrill-Palmer Q.* 44:504–22

Kerr KA, Stattin H. 2000. What parents know, how they know it, and several forms of adolescent adjustment: further support for a reinterpretation of monitoring. *Dev. Psychol.* 36:366–80

Knight G, Tein J, Prost JH, Gonzales NA. 2002. Measurement equivalence and research on Latino children families: the importance of culturally informed theory. See Contreras et al. 2002, pp. 181–202

Kochanska G. 1997. Multiple pathways to conscience for children with different temperaments: from toddlerhood to age 5. *Dev. Psychol.* 33:228–40

Kohn M. 1995. Social structure and personality through time and space. In *Examining Lives in Context: Perspectives on the Ecology of Human Development,* ed. P Moen, GH Elder, K Luscher, pp. 141–68. Washington, DC: Am. Psychol. Assoc.

Kramer L, Gottman JM. 1992. Becoming a sibling with a little help from my friends. *Dev. Psychol.* 28:685–99

Kuczynski L, ed. 2003. *Handbook of Dynamics in Parent-Child Relations.* Thousand Oaks, CA: Sage

Ladd G, Pettit G. 2002. Parenting and peer relationships. See Bornstein 2002, 5:269–309

Lyons-Ruth K, Lyubchik A, Wolfe R, Bronfman E. 2002. Parental depression and child attachment: hostile and helpless profiles of parent and child behavior among families at risk. See Goodman & Gotlib 2002, pp. 89–120

Marsiglio W, Amato P, Day RD, Lamb ME. 2000. Scholarship on fatherhood in the 1990's and beyond. *J. Marriage Fam.* 62:1173–91

Maxwell JA. 1992. Understanding validity in qualitative research. *Harv. Educ. Rev.* 62:279–300

McCoy JK, Brody GH, Stoneman Z. 1994. A longitudinal analysis of sibling relationships as mediators of the link between family processes and youths' best friendships. *Family Relat.* 43:400–8

McLoyd VC, Cauce AM, Takeuchi D, Wilson L. 2000. Marital processes and parental socialization in families of color: a decade review of research. *J. Marriage Fam.* 62:1070–93

McHale J, Lauretti A, Talbot J, Pouquette C. 2002. Retrospect and prospect in the psychological study of coparenting and family group process. See McHale & Grolnick 2002, pp. 127–66

McHale J, Rasmussen J. 1998. Coparental and family group-level dynamics during infancy. Early family predictors of child and family functioning during preschool. *Dev. Psychopathol.* 10:39–58

McHale JP, Cowan PA, eds. 1996. *Understanding How Family-Level Dynamics Affect*

Children's Development. Studies of Two Parent Families (New Direction for Child Development). San Francisco: Jossey-Bass

McHale JP, Grolnick WS, eds. 2002. *Retrospect and Prospect in the Psychological Study of Families.* Mahwah, NJ: Erlbaum

McPherson D. 1993. *Gay parenting couples: parenting arrangements, arrangement satisfaction, and relationship satisfaction.* Unpubl. Doc. Diss., Pac. Grad. Sch. Psychol.

Minuchin P. 2002. Looking toward the horizon: present and future in the study of family systems. See McHale & Grolnick 2002, pp. 259–87

Mishel L, Bernstein J, Schmitt J. 1999. *The State of Working America.* Ithaca, NY: Cornell Univ. Press

Mize J, Pettit GS. 1997. Mothers' social coaching, mother-child relationships style, and children's peer competence: Is the medium the message? *Child Dev.* 68:291–311

Modell J, Elder GH. 2002. Children develop in history: So what's new. In *Child Psychology in Retrospect and Prospect,* ed. WW Hartup, RA Weinberg, pp. 173–206. Mahwah, NJ: Erlbaum

Moore MR, Brooks-Gunn J. 2002. Adolescent parenthood. See Bornstein 2002, 3:173–214

Moos R, Moos BS. 1981. *Family Environment Scale Manual.* Palo Alto, CA: Consult. Psychol. Press

Mounts NS. 2000. Parental management of adolescent peer relationships. What are its effect on friend selection? In *Family and Peers: Linking Two Social Worlds,* ed. KA Kerns, JM Contreras, AM Neal-Barnett, pp. 169–94. Westport, CT: Praeger

Mumola CJ. 2000. Incarcerated parents and their children. *Bureau of Justice Statistics Special Report.* Washington, DC: US Dep. Justice

Palermo G, Joris H, Devorey P, van Steirteghem AC. 1992. Pregnancies after intracytoplasmic injection's songle spermatozoon into an oocyte. *Lancet* 340:17–18

Parcel TL, Menaghan EG. 1994. *Parents' Jobs and Children's Lives.* New York: Aldine de Gruyter

Parke RD. 1988. Families in life-span perspective: a multi-level developmental approach. In *Child Development in Life Span Perspective,* ed. EM Hetherington, RM Lerner, M Perlmutter, pp. 159–90. Hillsdale, NJ: Erlbaum

Parke RD. 1996. *Fatherhood.* Cambridge, MA: Harvard Univ. Press

Parke RD. 2004. SRCD at 70: prospects and promises. *Child Dev.* In press

Parke RD, Buriel R. 1998. Socialization in the family: ethnic and ecological perspectives. In *Handbook of Child Psychology,* W Damon (Ser. ed.), N Eisenberg (Vol. ed.), 3:463–552. New York: Wiley. 5th ed.

Parke RD, Coltrane S, Powers J, Adams M, Fabricius W, et al. 2003. Measurement of father involvement in Mexican-American Families. In *Reconceptualizing and Measuring Father Involvement,* ed. R Day, M Lamb, pp. 17–38. Mahwah, NJ: Erlbaum

Parke RD, Kellam S, eds. 1994. *Exploring Family Relationships with other Social Contexts.* Hillsdale, NJ: Erlbaum

Parke RD, O'Neil R. 1999. Social relationships across contexts: family-peer linkages. In *Minnesota Symposium on Child Psychology,* ed. WA Collins, B Laursen, 30:211–39. Hillsdale, NJ: Erlbaum

Parke RS, Clarke-Stewart KA. 2003. Effects of parental incarceration on children: perspectives, promises and policies. In *From Prison to Home,* ed. J Travis, M Waul, A Solomon, pp. 189–232. Washington, DC: Urban Inst. Press. In press

Patterson C, Friel LV. 2000. Sexual orientation and fertility. In *Infertility in the Modern World: Biosocial Perspectives,* ed. GR Bentley, N Mascie-Taylor. Cambridge, UK: Cambridge Univ. Press

Patterson CJ. 2002. Lesbian and gay parenthood. See Bornstein 2002, 3:317–38

Patterson G, Reid J, Dishion T. 1992. *Antisocial Boys: A Social Learning Approach.* Eugene, OR: Castelia

Paulson RJ, Sachs J. 1999. *Rewinding Your Biological Clock.* New York: Freeman

Perry-Jenkins M, Repetti RL, Crouter AC.

2000. Work and family in the 1990's. *J. Marriage Fam.* 62:981–89

Pleck JH, Masciadrelli BP. 2003. Paternal involvement: levels, sources and consequences. In *The Role of the Father in Child Development*, ed. ME Lamb. New York: Wiley. 4th ed.

Plomin R. 1994. Genetic research and identification of environmental influences. *J. Child Psychol. Psychiatry* 35:817–34

Pulkkinen L, Nurmi J, Kokke K. 2002. Individual differences in personal goals in mid-thirties. In *Paths to Successful Development*, ed. L Pulkkinen, A Caspi, pp. 331–52. New York: Cambridge Univ. Press

Putnam SP, Sanson AV, Rothbart M. 2002. Child temperament and parenting. See Bornstein 2002, 3:255–78

Reiss D. 1989. The represented practicing family: contrasting visions of family continuity. In *Relationship Disturbances in Early Childhood*, ed. AJ Sameroff, RN Emde, pp. 191–220. New York: Basic Books

Reiss D. 2003. Child effects on family systems: behavioral and genetic strategies. See Crouter & Booth 2003, pp. 1–25

Reiss D, Neiderhiser J, Hetherington EM, Plomin R. 2000. *The Relationship Code: Deciphering Genetic and Social Patterns in Adolescent Development*. Cambridge, MA: Harvard Univ. Press

Repetti R, Wood J. 1997. Effects of daily stress at work on mothers' interactions with preschoolers. *J. Fam. Psychol.* 11:90–108

Repetti RL. 1994. Short-term and long-term processes linking perceived job stressors to father-child interactions. *Soc. Dev.* 3:1–15

Rogoff B. 2003. *The Cultural Nature of Human Development*. New York: Oxford

Russell G, Finnie V. 1990. Preschool children's social status and maternal instruction to assist group entry. *Dev. Psychol.* 26:603–11

Rutter M. 1987. Psychosocial resilience and protective mechanisms. *Am. J. Orthopsychiatry* 57:316–31

Rutter M. 2002. Family influences on behavior and development: challenges for the future. See McHale & Grolnick 2002, pp. 321–52

Rutter M, Pickles A, Murray R, Eaves LA. 2002. Testing hypotheses on specific environmental causal effects on behavior. *Psychol. Bull.* 127:291–324

Sameroff AJ. 1994. Developmental systems and family functioning. In *Exploring Family Relationships with Other Social Contexts*, ed. RD Parke, SG Kellam, pp. 199–214. Hillsdale, NJ: Erlbaum

Sandstrom MJ, Coie HD. 1999. A developmental perspective on peer rejection: mechanisms of stability and change. *Child Dev.* 70:955–66

Shweder RA. 2003. *Why Men Barbecue*. Cambridge, MA: Harvard Univ. Press

Silverstein LB. 2002. Fathers and families. See McHale & Grolnick 2002, pp. 35–64

Smith PK, Drew LM. 2002. Grandparenthood. See Bornstein 2002, 3:141–72

Steinberg L, Dornbusch S, Brown B. 1992. Ethnic differences in adolescent achievement: an ecological perspective. *Am. Psychol.* 47:723–29

Stewart SM, Rao N, Bond MH, McBride-Chang C, Fielding R, Kennard BD. 1998. Chinese dimensions of parenting: broadening western predictors and outcomes. *Int. J. Psychol.* 33:345–58

Stocker CM. 1994. Children's perceptions of relationships with siblings, friends, and mothers: compensatory processes and links with adjustment. *J. Child Psychol. Psychiatry* 35:1447–59

Suomi S. 2000. A biobehavioral perspective on developmental psychopathology. In *Handbook of Developmental Psychopathology*, ed. AJ Sameroff, M Lewis, SM Miller, pp. 237–56. New York: Kluwer Acad./Plenum

Taylor RL. 2000. Diversity within African American families. See Demo et al. 2000, pp. 232–51

Teachman JD, Tedrow LM, Crowder KD. 2000. The changing demography of America's families. *J. Marriage Fam.* 62:1234–46

Teti DM. 2002. Retrospect and prospect in the study of sibling relationships. See McHale & Grolnick 2002, pp. 193–224

Teti DM, Gelfand DM, Messinger DS, Isabella

R. 1995. Maternal depression and the quality of early attachment: an examination of infants, preschoolers and their mothers. *Dev. Psychol.* 31:394–405

Thelen E, Smith L. 1994. *A Dynamic Systems Approach to Development.* Cambridge, MA: MIT Press

US Census Bur. 2003. *Population Reports.* Washington, DC: GPO

US Census Bur. 1999. *Population Reports.* Washington, DC: GPO

Volling BL, McElwain NL, Miller AL. 2002. Emotion regulation in context: the jealousy complex between young siblings and its relations with child and family characteristics. *Child Dev.* 73:581–600

Wamboldt FS. 1999. Co-constructing a marriage: analyses of young couples' relationship narratives. *Monogr. Soc. Child Dev.* 64:37–51

Weisner TS. 1993. Overview: sibling similarity and difference in different cultures. In *Siblings in South Asia: Brothers and Sisters in Cultural Context*, ed. CW Nuckolls, pp. 1–17. New York: Guilford

White L, Keith B. 1990. The effect of shift work on the quality and stability of marital relations. *J. Marriage Fam.* 52:453–62

White L, Rogers SL. 2000. Economic circumstances and family outcomes: a review of the 1990's. *J. Marriage Fam.* 62:1035–51

Wolin SJ, Bennett LA, Jacobs FS. 1988. Assessing family rituals. In *Rituals and Family Therapy*, ed. E Imber-Black, J Roberts, R Whiting, pp. 230–56. New York: Norton

Yeung WJ, Sandberg JF, Davis-Kean PE, Hofferth SL. 2001. Children's time with fathers in intact families. *J. Marriage Fam.* 63:136–54

Young DS, Smith CJ. 2000. When moms are incarcerated: the needs of children, mothers, and caregivers. Families in society. *J. Contemp. Hum. Serv.* 81:130–41

Zayas LH, Rojas-Flores L. 2002. Learning from Latino parents: combining etic and emic approaches to designing interventions. See Contreas et al. 2002, pp. 233–54

Zinn MB, Wells B. 2000. Diversity within Latino families: new lessons for family social science. See Demo et al. 2000, pp. 252–73

Annu. Rev. Psychol. 2004. 55:401–30
doi: 10.1146/annurev.psych.55.090902.141950
First published online as a Review in Advance on September 15, 2003

SCHIZOPHRENIA: Etiology and Course

Elaine Walker, Lisa Kestler, Annie Bollini, and Karen M. Hochman

*Department of Psychology and Department of Psychiatry and Behavioral Science,
Emory University, Atlanta, Georgia 30322; email: psyefw@emory.edu,
lkestle@learnlink.emory.edu, abollini@learnlink.emory.edu, khochma@emory.edu*

Key Words   diathesis-stress, genetic, neurodevelopment

■ **Abstract**   Decades of research on schizophrenia have not produced major breakthroughs, but gradual progress has been made in identifying risk factors and clarifying the nature of the etiologic process. This article provides an overview of trends in research findings as well as current assumptions about the interplay between environmental and genetic factors in the etiology of schizophrenia. Based on the cumulative findings, it appears that both genetic and prenatal factors can give rise to constitutional vulnerability. Subsequent neuromaturational processes, especially those that occur during adolescence, and exposure to stressful events can trigger the behavioral expression of this vulnerability.

CONTENTS

0066-4308/04/0204-0401$14.00

INTRODUCTION

Schizophrenia is a complex disorder. From the level of overt behavior, to intracellular processes, it has defied scientific explanation. Up to this point, investigators have not been able to identify a single factor that characterizes all patients with schizophrenia. Despite the challenges, however, many investigators have devoted their professional lives to research on schizophrenia. And, although we have not yet solved the puzzle, the persistent efforts of clinical researchers have put many pieces into place.

The fact that schizophrenia is among the most debilitating of mental illnesses is what compels researchers to continue the search for its causes. Most cases of the disorder are first diagnosed between the ages of 20 and 25, a stage of life when people typically attain independence from parents, develop intimate romantic relationships, and/or begin to pursue work or career goals (DeLisi 1992). The illness can, therefore, have a profound, negative impact on the person's opportunities for attaining social and occupational success, and the consequences can be devastating for the adult life course. Further, the illness knows no boundaries; it occurs in all countries and within all ethnic groups. Across cultures, estimates of the lifetime prevalence of schizophrenia are around 1% (Keith et al. 1991, Kulhara & Chakrabarti 2001, Torrey 1987), although the prognosis may differ among countries (Kulhara & Chakrabarti 2001).

In this article, we provide an up-to-date overview of the status of scientific knowledge and theory about schizophrenia. There is now a clear consensus that schizophrenia is a brain disease. The major pressing questions concern the nature of the etiological process. What are the origins and characteristics of the neural abnormality, and what interactional processes trigger its expression? With reference to these issues, three general themes are emphasized. The first is that the etiology of schizophrenia involves the interplay between brain vulnerabilities and environmental factors. A second theme is that the illness does not emerge from a defect in a specific brain region but rather from the dysfunction of circuits that are comprised of multiple brain regions. The third is that brain maturational processes play a critical role in the etiological process.

We begin with a discussion of history and phenomenology, then proceed to a description of some of the key findings that have shed light on the illness. In conclusion, we offer an integrative framework for conceptualizing the etiologic process.

History and Phenomenology

Historical accounts of behavioral syndromes that parallel schizophrenia appear in records from ancient Mesopotamia, ancient India, ancient Greece and Rome, the Middle Ages, and Europe, from the fifteenth through the seventeenth century (Jeste et al. 1985). However, because psychotic symptoms can be a manifestation of a variety of disorders, it cannot be firmly established that all of these descriptions were comparable to what we now label "schizophrenia." In the mid-to-late nineteenth century, European psychiatrists investigated the etiology, classification, and prognoses of the various types of psychosis. At that time, the most common cause of psychosis was tertiary syphilis, although researchers were unaware that there was any link between psychotic symptoms and syphilis. We now know that the psychological signs of tertiary syphilis frequently overlap with symptoms of what we call schizophrenia. This important discovery served to illustrate how a psychological syndrome can be produced by an infectious agent. It also sensitized researchers to the fact that similar syndromes can result from very different causes, and set the stage for the current assumption that the syndrome we call schizophrenia may have multiple etiologies.

Emil Kraepelin (1856–1926) was the first to differentiate schizophrenia, which he referred to as "dementia praecox" (dementia of the young), from manic-depressive psychosis (for a historical overview, see Howells 1991). He also lumped together "hebephrenia," "paranoia," and "catatonia" (previously thought to be distinct disorders), and classified all of them as subtypes of dementia praecox. Kraepelin based this on their similarities in age of onset and prognosis. He did not believe that any single symptom was diagnostic, but instead based the diagnosis on the total clinical picture, including a degenerative process. If a psychotic patient deteriorated over months and years, the disorder was assumed to be dementia praecox. The assumption that schizophrenia typically has a poor prognosis is still widespread, and research has confirmed that many patients manifest a chronic course that entails lifelong disability (Carpenter & Buchanan 1994). But, as described below, the course varies dramatically among patients, and these differences may reflect distinct etiological processes.

The term schizophrenia was introduced at the beginning of the twentieth century by Eugen Bleuler (1857–1939) (Howells 1991). The word is derived from two Greek words: "schizo," which means to tear or to split, and "phren," which means "the intellect" or "the mind," and was sometimes used to refer to emotional functions. Thus, the word schizophrenia means the splitting or tearing of the mind and emotional stability of the patient. Bleuler classified the symptoms of schizophrenia into fundamental and accessory symptoms (Bleuler 1911). According to Bleuler, the fundamental symptoms are ambivalence, disturbance of association, disturbance of affect, and a preference for fantasy over reality. He postulated that these symptoms are present in all patients, at all stages of the illness, and are diagnostic of schizophrenia. Bleuler's accessory symptoms of schizophrenia included delusions, hallucinations, movement disturbances, somatic symptoms, and manic and melancholic states. He believed that these symptoms often occurred in other illnesses and were not present in all schizophrenia patients. It is also noteworthy that Bleuler's reconceptualization of dementia praecox as "the group of schizophrenias" is reflected in the contemporary view that schizophrenia is a heterogeneous group of disorders with varied etiologies but similar clinical presentations.

The most recent substantive changes in the diagnostic conceptualization of schizophrenia were proposed by Kurt Schneider in the mid 1900s (Schneider 1959). Schneider assumed that certain key symptoms were diagnostic of schizophrenia, and he referred to these as first-rank symptoms. Schneider's first-rank symptoms are types of hallucinations and delusions that characterize the signs of psychosis.

Examples are thought echoing (thoughts are heard out loud), thought broadcasting (belief that others can hear one's thoughts), thought intrusion (feeling that some thoughts originate outside of one's own mind), thought withdrawal (belief that thoughts are taken), and delusional perceptions (a sudden, fixed, false belief about a particular everyday occurrence or perception). When compared to Bleuler's "fundamental" symptoms, Schneider's symptom descriptions were more detailed and specific. Subsequent diagnostic criteria for schizophrenia have been heavily influenced by Schneider's approach.

Beginning in the 1980s, investigators began to emphasize the distinction between "positive" and "negative" symptoms of schizophrenia (Harvey & Walker 1987). The positive symptoms are those that involve an excess of ideas, sensory experiences, or behavior. Hallucinations, delusions, and bizarre behaviors fall in this category. Most of the first-rank symptoms described by Schneider fall into the positive category. Negative symptoms, in contrast, involve a decrease in behavior, such as blunted or flat affect, anhedonia, and lack of motivation. These symptoms were emphasized by Bleuler (1911).

A variety of diagnostic taxonomies for mental disorders proliferated in the middle of the twentieth century, and many believe this had a detrimental effect on research progress. In response, subsequent diagnostic systems were developed with the intent of achieving uniformity and thereby improving diagnostic reliability. Among these were the Feighner or St. Louis diagnostic criteria (Feighner et al. 1972), and the Research Diagnostic Criteria developed by Robert Spitzer and his colleagues (Spitzer et al. 1978). These two approaches had a major impact on the criteria for schizophrenia contained in contemporary diagnostic systems, most notably, the Diagnostic and Statistical Manual of Mental Disorders (DSM).

The DSM is now the most widely used system for diagnosing schizophrenia and other mental disorders. The most recent version of the DSM is the DSM IV-TR (Am. Psychiatric Assoc. 2000). Using DSM IV-TR criteria, schizophrenia can be diagnosed when signs and symptoms of the disorder have been present for six months or more (including prodromal and residual phases). The characteristic symptom criteria for schizophrenia include (a) hallucinations, (b) delusions, (c) disorganized speech (e.g., frequent derailment or incoherence), (d) grossly disorganized or catatonic behavior, and (e) negative symptoms, i.e., affective flattening, alogia, or avolition. At least two or more of these symptoms must be present for at least one month. Only one of the above is necessary if the delusions are bizarre, or if the hallucinated voices consist of a running commentary or of two voices conversing (both of these are derived from Schneider's first-rank symptoms in Table 2). In addition to the clinical symptoms, there must be social/occupational dysfunction. Further, significant mood disorder, such as depression or manic symptoms, must not be present. (This would exclude individuals who meet criteria for major depressive disorder with psychotic symptoms, and bipolar disorder with psychotic symptoms.) Finally, general medical conditions or substance abuse that might lead to psychotic symptoms must be ruled out.

The four subtypes of schizophrenia described in DSM IV are *paranoid, disorganized, catatonic,* and *undifferentiated.* The paranoid type is characterized by a preoccupation with delusions or hallucinations, but there is no disorganized speech, disorganized or catatonic behavior, or flat or inappropriate affect. This is the subtype with the best prognosis. The catatonic type involves a clinical syndrome that is dominated by postural and/or movement abnormalities, mutism, or echolalia. In the disorganized type, all of the following are prominent: disorganized speech, disorganized behavior, and flat or inappropriate affect, but the criteria for the catatonic subtype are not met. This is the subtype with the worst prognosis. Finally, the undifferentiated subtype is diagnosed when the patient does not meet criteria for the previous subtypes, yet does meet the general criteria for schizophrenia. The inclusion of this subtype reminds us that these categories are unlikely to represent distinct diagnostic entities with unique etiologies.

Two other diagnostic categories in the schizophrenia "spectrum" are worth noting. One category, the residual type, is for individuals who have met criteria for schizophrenia in the past, but no longer do. This diagnosis is applied when there is a prominence of negative symptoms, or two or more attenuated "characteristic" symptoms, but no prominent delusions, hallucinations, catatonic symptoms, or disorganized behavior or speech. The other category, schizophreniform disorder, is for individuals whose symptoms do not meet the six-month criterion. This diagnosis is frequently made as a prelude to the diagnosis of schizophrenia, when the patient presents for treatment early in the course of the disorder. Some individuals with this disorder, however, will recover completely and not suffer further episodes of psychosis.

It is important to emphasize that, despite advances in diagnosis, we still do not know the diagnostic boundaries of schizophrenia. Moreover, the boundaries between schizophrenia and mood disorders are obscure. Many individuals who meet criteria for schizophrenia show marked signs of depression. These symptoms are sometimes present before the onset of schizophrenia, and frequently occur in combination with marked psychotic symptoms. As a result, the DSM IV includes a diagnostic category called schizoaffective disorder. This disorder can be conceived of, conceptually, as a hybrid between the mood disorders (bipolar disorder or major depression with psychotic features) and schizophrenia. The two subtypes are the depressive subtype (if the mood disturbance includes only depressive episodes), and the bipolar subtype (where the symptoms of the disorder have included either a manic or a mixed episode). Interestingly, the prognosis for patients with schizoaffective disorder is, on average, somewhere between that of schizophrenia and the mood disorders.

Cognitive and Socioemotional Aspects of Schizophrenia

It is well established that, as a group, schizophrenia patients manifest deficits in virtually all domains of cognitive functioning. Research in this area first focused on higher level processes, such as those tapped by standardized intellectual tests (Aylward et al. 1984) and neuropsychological measures (Goldsamt 1994). More recently investigators have examined basic sensory processing abilities. The results are consistent: schizophrenia patients show performance deficits on cognitive tasks that range from very simple to complex (Green et al. 2000). Further, the cognitive impairments are not merely side effects of treatment, because they are apparent in first-episode, nonmedicated patients.

One of the most basic deficits is in the very earliest stages of sensory information processing. Using a laboratory procedure called backward masking, researchers have shown that schizophrenia patients are slower in the initial processing of visual stimuli (Green et al. 1999). In fact, when brain activity is monitored during the presentation of visual or auditory stimuli, nonmedicated schizophrenia patients show a reduction of activity, relative to normals, in several brain regions, including the thalamus, prefrontal cortex, and parietal lobe (Braus et al. 2002).

Another measure of very basic aspects of information processing is *prepulse inhibition*, a paradigm that indexes the individual's startle responses to repeated sensory stimuli. The startle response, such as an eye blink, is typically inhibited when the startling event is preceded by a prestimulus that is weak and nonstartling; this is called prepulse inhibition. When tested within a few days of their first admission, and before medication, patients manifest a reduction in prepulse inhibition (Perry et al. 2002). Thus they respond to the target sensory stimulus as if it was not preceded by a prestimulus. Again, these findings indicate that some schizophrenia patients have a very basic cognitive impairment that is a consequence of brain dysfunction.

In addition to deficits in the early stages of processing sensory information, schizophrenia patients also manifest impairment in responding to stimuli. This appears to be due to both a deficit in the speed of response selection (Krieger et al. 2001) and the execution of motor responses (Flyckt et al. 2000). Deficits in manual motor speed and coordination are among the most consistently found impairments in schizophrenia (Flashman et al. 1996).

Among the higher level cognitive functions, schizophrenia patients show impairments in verbal and spatial memory, attention, and executive functions, such as abstract reasoning, and planning (Kuperberg & Heckers 2000). The executive functions, subserved by the frontal lobes, have been the focus of intense study because these cognitive abilities are predictive of prognosis (Green et al. 2000).

There are also deficits in thinking about social phenomena. Studies of social-cognitive abilities in schizophrenia patients have consistently shown that patients are impaired in their ability to comprehend and solve social problems (Penn et al. 1997). Deficits in social cognition may be partially due to limitations in more basic cognitive processes, such as memory and reasoning. However, evidence suggests that basic cognitive impairments do not account completely for the more pervasive and persistent social-cognitive deficits observed in schizophrenia.

Blunted and inappropriate affect are among the diagnostic criteria for schizophrenia. It is, therefore, not surprising that patients show abnormalities in the expression of emotion in both their faces and verbal communications; specifically, patients exhibit less intense facial emotion, and fewer positive and more negative expressions (Brozgold et al. 1998, Kring & Neale 1996). Further, patients are less accurate than normal comparison subjects in their ability to label facial expressions of emotion (Penn & Combs 2000, Walker 1981, Walker et al. 1980). Patients with more severe impairments in their abilities to recognize and express emotion also have more problems in social adjustment.

One of the unresolved questions is whether schizophrenia is associated with a decline in cognitive functioning following the clinical onset of the illness. Although earlier research yielded inconsistent results, recent studies indicate that there is a cognitive decline in some patients (Harvey 2001). These findings have implications for our assumptions about the underlying pathological process, and we will return to this issue later when we address the course of schizophrenia.

Cumulative findings from many decades of research on cognitive functions in schizophrenia have shown that the deficits associated with the disorder are not specific to a particular sensory modality, stage of information processing, or cognitive domain (e.g., planning, memory, abstract reasoning). Instead, it appears that the impairments are generalized, although there is some evidence to suggest that certain domains, like working memory, may be more impaired than others (Green et al. 2000). But it is important to keep in mind that the aggregated data on patients obscure substantial individual differences in performance. In the vast majority of studies, there are some patients who perform at or above the average for normals, and others whose level of performance is so low it is outside the range for normals. To date, all cognitive measures, including those tapping the most basic processes, have yielded overlapping distributions for patients and controls. This has been interpreted by some to mean that there is no specific or unique cognitive deficit in schizophrenia. Instead, it may be that cognitive deficits in schizophrenia are nonspecific and secondary consequences of one or more of the etiologic factors that contribute to schizophrenia, such as pre- and perinatal insults. Of course, we cannot rule out the possibility that there is a specific cognitive deficit shared by almost all schizophrenia patients, and we have simply failed to identify it. Perhaps the cognitive deficit is at the level where "cold" cognitive processes interface with emotional processes (Gjerde 1983).

THE ORIGINS OF VULNERABILITY

Early writers on schizophrenia, such as Kraepelin (1913) and Eugen Bleuler (1911), did not offer explicit etiologic theories about the origins of schizophrenia, but they did suggest that there might be a biological basis for at least some cases of the illness. Although theories that emphasized psychosocial determinants gained some credence in the mid 1900s, contemporary theorists assume a biological vulnerability to schizophrenia that is present at birth. Researchers have identified two sources of this vulnerability: genetic factors and prenatal or delivery complications. Both appear to have implications for fetal brain development.

The Genetics of Schizophrenia

One of the most well-established findings in schizophrenia research is that vulnerability to the illness can be inherited (Gottesman 1991). Behavior genetic studies utilizing twin, adoption, and family history methods have all yielded evidence that the risk for schizophrenia is elevated in individuals who have a biological relative with the disorder; the closer the level of genetic relatedness, the greater the likelihood the relative will also suffer from schizophrenia.

In a review of family, twin, and adoption studies conducted from 1916 to 1989, Gottesman (1991) outlined the compelling evidence for the role of genetic factors in schizophrenia. Monozygotic (MZ) twins, who share nearly 100% of their genes, have the highest concordance rate for schizophrenia. Among monozygotic cotwins of patients with schizophrenia, 25% to 50% will develop the illness. Dizygotic (DZ) twins and other siblings share, on average, only about half of their genes. About 10% to 15% of the DZ cotwins of patients are also diagnosed with the illness. Further, as genetic relatedness of the relative to the patient becomes more distant, such as from first-degree (parents, siblings) to second-degree relatives (grandparents, half siblings, aunts, and uncles), the lifetime risk for schizophrenia is reduced.

Adoption studies have provided strong evidence that the tendency for schizophrenia to run in families is primarily due to genetic factors, rather than the environmental influence of being exposed to a mentally ill family member. In a seminal study, Heston (1966) examined the rates of schizophrenia in adoptees with and without a biological parent who was diagnosed with the illness. He found higher rates of schizophrenia, and other mental illnesses, in the biological offspring of parents with schizophrenia, when compared to adoptees with no mental illness in biological parents. Similarly, in a Danish sample, Kety (1988) examined the relatives of adoptees with and without schizophrenia. He found that the biological relatives of adoptees who suffered from schizophrenia had a significantly higher rate of schizophrenia than the adoptive relatives who reared them. Also, the rate of schizophrenia in the biological relatives of adoptees with schizophrenia was higher than in the relatives (biological or adoptive) of healthy adoptees.

But more recent findings from an adoption study indicate that the genetic influences often act in concert with environmental factors. Tienari et al. (1994) conducted an adoption study in Finland, and found that the rate of psychoses and other severe disorders was significantly higher than in the matched control adoptees. However, genetic vulnerability was mainly expressed in association with disruptive adoptive environments, and an elevated rate of schizophrenia was not detected in adoptees reared in healthy family environments. These findings are consistent with the prevailing diathesis-stress models of etiology.

Taken together, the findings from behavioral genetic studies of schizophrenia lead to the conclusion that the disorder involves multiple genes, rather than a single gene (Gottesman 1991). This conclusion is based on several observations, most notably the fact that the pattern of familial transmission does not conform to what would be expected from a single genetic locus, or even a small number of genes. Rather, the genetic liability seems to involve multiple genes acting in concert, or numerous single susceptibility genes acting independently. Consistent with this assumption, attempts to identify a genetic locus that accounts for a significant proportion of cases of schizophrenia have not met with success (Kato et al. 2002). Instead, researchers using molecular genetic techniques have identified an array of genes that seem to account for a very small proportion of cases or of variance in liability. Candidate gene analyses, genome scans, and linkage studies have provided some evidence for the involvement of several specific genes, such as the serotonin type 2a receptor (5-HT2a) gene and the dopamine D3 receptor gene, and several chromosomal regions (i.e., regions on chromosomes 6, 8, 13, and 22) (Badner & Gershon 2002, Mowry & Nancarrow 2001).

One of the most noteworthy genetic discoveries to date is the association between the 22q11 deletion and schizophrenia. The 22q11 deletion occurs in about 0.025% of the general population, and it involves a microdeletion on chromosome 22q11.2 that is often accompanied by physical syndrome that includes structural anomalies of the face, head, and heart. About 25% of individuals with the 22q deletion syndrome meet diagnostic criteria for schizophrenia, but only about 2% of schizophrenia patients have the 22q11 deletion genotype, although the rate of 22q11 deletion may be higher in patients with an earlier onset (Bassett et al. 1998, Karayiorgou et al. 1995).

Findings from molecular genetics also raise questions about the etiologic boundaries between schizophrenia and other psychotic disorders. Early behavioral genetic studies led to the conclusion that there were separable genetic liabilities for schizophrenia and the major affective disorders, namely, bipolar disorder and psychotic depression. But more recent evidence indicates that this is not the case. Using quantitative genetic techniques with large twin samples, researchers have shown that there is significant overlap in the genes that contribute to schizophrenia, schizoaffective disorder, and manic syndromes (Cardno et al. 2002). Other studies have yielded similar results, leading many in the field to conclude that the genetic vulnerability does not conform to the diagnostic boundaries listed in DSM and other taxonomies (e.g., Potash et al. 2001). Rather, it appears that there may be genetic vulnerabilities to psychosis in general, and that the expression of these vulnerabilities can take the form of schizophrenia *or* an affective psychosis, depending on other inherited and acquired risk factors.

Another major issue confronting the field is the relative importance of inherited vulnerability versus external factors that impinge on the developing individual. At this point, researchers are not in a position to estimate the relative magnitude of the inherited and environmental contributors to the etiology of schizophrenia. Moreover, we do not yet know whether genetic vulnerability is present in all cases of schizophrenia. It is possible that some cases of the illness are solely attributable to environmental risk factors. Further, we do not know whether the genetic predisposition to schizophrenia is always expressed, although there is substantive evidence to indicate that it is not. The fact that the concordance rate for schizophrenia in MZ twins is nowhere near 100% suggests that some genetically vulnerable individuals do not develop the illness. It is possible, however, that the genetic liability for schizophrenia sometimes results from a mutation that occurs in only the affected member of discordant MZ pairs. But findings from studies of discordant MZ twins indicate that the rate of schizophrenia is elevated in the offspring of nonaffected cotwins (Gottesman & Bertelsen 1989, Kringlen & Cramer 1989), which suggests that some individuals possess a genetic vulnerability for schizophrenia that they pass on to their offspring despite the fact that they are never diagnosed with the illness. Thus, unexpressed genetic vulnerabilities for schizophrenia may be common in the general population. The presence of unexpressed genetic vulnerability to schizophrenia makes the work of researchers much more difficult. At the same time, the evidence of unexpressed genotypes for schizophrenia leads us to inquire about factors that trigger the expression of illness in vulnerable individuals. This knowledge may, someday, lead to effective preventative interventions.

Prenatal and Postnatal Factors

Events that adversely affect fetal development are now considered to be potential environmental triggers of genetic vulnerability. It is also plausible that they are sufficient, on their own, to produce vulnerability to schizophrenia. There is extensive evidence that obstetrical complications (OCs) have an adverse impact on the developing fetal brain, and numerous studies have shown that schizophrenia patients are more likely to have a history of OCs (Buka et al. 1993, Dalman et al. 1999, McNeil et al. 2000). Included among these are pregnancy problems, such as toxemia and preeclampsia, as well as labor and delivery complications. A review of the OC literature by Cannon (1997) concluded that, among the different types of OCs, labor and delivery complications, which are often associated with hypoxia (fetal oxygen deprivation), were most strongly linked with later schizophrenia. In the National Collaborative Perinatal Project, which involved more than 9000 children followed from birth through adulthood, the odds of schizophrenia increased linearly with an increasing number of hypoxia-related OCs (Cannon et al. 2000, Cannon 1998).

Another prenatal event that has been linked with increased risk for schizophrenia is maternal infection. Researchers have found that the risk rate for schizophrenia is elevated for individuals born shortly after a flu epidemic (Barr et al. 1990, Murray et al. 1992) or after being prenatally exposed to rubella (Brown et al. 2001). The findings from research on viral infection are consistent with reports on the "season-of-birth" effect in schizophrenia. Several studies have found that a disproportionate number of schizophrenic patients are born during the winter months (Bradbury & Miller 1985, Torrey et al. 1997). This timing may reflect seasonal exposure to viral infections, which are most common in late fall and early winter. Thus the fetus would have been exposed to the infection during the second trimester. The second trimester is an important time for brain development, and disruptions during this stage may lead to developmental abnormalities.

Studies of rodents and nonhuman primates have shown that prenatal maternal stress can interfere with fetal brain development, and is associated with elevated glucocorticoid release and hippocampal abnormalities in the offspring (Smythe et al. 1994, Weinstock 1996). Along the same lines, in humans, there is evidence that stressful events during pregnancy are associated with greater risk for schizophrenia and other psychiatric disorders in adult offspring. Researchers have found higher rates of schizophrenia in the offspring of women whose spouses died during their pregnancies (Huttunen 1989) or were exposed to a military invasion during pregnancy (van Os & Selten 1998). It is likely that prenatal stress triggers the release of maternal stress hormones, disturbing fetal neurodevelopment as well as disrupting subsequent functioning of the hypothalamic-pituitary-adrenal axis, which in turn influences behavior and cognition (Welberg & Seckl 2001).

Recent findings indicate that postnatal brain insults can also increase the risk for schizophrenia. There is a substantial body of literature showing that individuals who sustain head injury are at heightened risk for a variety of psychiatric disorders, including schizophrenia. The association between schizophrenia and head injury may be greater for injuries that occur in early childhood. AbdelMalik and colleagues (AbdelMalik et al. 2003) found that head injury before the age of 10 was more common in individuals who developed schizophrenia, and was linked with an earlier onset of illness.

One of the chief questions being pursued by researchers is whether OCs and postnatal brain trauma act independently to increase risk for schizophrenia, or have their effect in conjunction with a genetic vulnerability. It may be that the genetic vulnerability for schizophrenia involves an increased sensitivity to prenatal complications (Cannon 1997, 1998) and/or postnatal brain trauma (AbdelMalik et al. 2003). It is also plausible that prenatal and postnatal brain insults act independently of genetic vulnerabilities, although such effects would likely entail complex interactions among factors (Susser et al. 1999). For example, in order to produce the neurodevelopmental abnormalities that confer risk for schizophrenia, it may be necessary for a specific OC to occur during a critical period of cellular migration and/or in conjunction with other factors such as maternal fever or immune response.

COURSE AND PROGNOSIS

Assuming that genetic and obstetrical factors confer the vulnerability for schizophrenia, the diathesis must be present at birth. Yet, schizophrenia is typically diagnosed in late adolescence or early adulthood, with the average age of diagnosis in males about four years earlier than in females (Riecher-Rossler & Hafner 2000). This raises intriguing questions about the developmental course prior to the clinical onset.

Premorbid Development

There is compelling evidence that signs of schizophrenia are present long before the illness is diagnosed. Most of these signs are subtle, and do not reach the severity of clinical disorder. Nonetheless, when compared to children with healthy adult outcomes, children who later develop schizophrenia manifest deficits in multiple domains. In some of these domains, the deficits are apparent as early as infancy.

In the area of cognitive functioning, children who later develop schizophrenia tend to perform below their healthy siblings and classmates. This is reflected in lower scores on measures of intelligence and achievement, and poorer grades in school (Aylward et al. 1984, Jones et al. 1994). It appears that the magnitude of the deficit becomes more pronounced in adolescence: The standardized achievement test scores of patients with adult-onset schizophrenia drop significantly between ages 13–16 years (Fuller et al. 2002).

Preschizophrenic children also show abnormalities in social behavior. They are less responsive in social situations, show less positive emotion (Walker & Lewine 1990, Walker et al. 1993), and have poorer social adjustment than children with healthy adult outcomes (Done et al. 1994). Further, preschizophrenic children with more serious adjustment problems have more brain and neuropsychological abnormalities after the onset of illness (Walker et al. 1996, Neumann et al. 1996). Studies of the childhood home movies of schizophrenia patients have shown that preschizophrenic children manifest more negative facial expressions of emotion than their siblings as early as the first year of life, indicating that the vulnerability for schizophrenia is subtly manifested in the earliest interpersonal interactions (Walker et al. 1993).

Vulnerability to schizophrenia is also apparent in motor functions. When compared to their siblings with healthy adult outcomes, preschizophrenic children show more delays and abnormalities in motor development, including deficits in the acquisition of early motor milestones such as bimanual manipulation and walking (Walker et al. 1994). Deficits in motor function extend throughout the premorbid period, and persist after the onset of the clinical illness (McNeil & Cantor-Graae 2000). It is important to note that neuromotor abnormalities are not pathognomonic for schizophrenia, in that they are observed in children at risk for a variety of disorders, including learning disabilities. But they are one of several important clues pointing to the involvement of dysfunctional brain circuitry in schizophrenia.

Despite the subtle signs of abnormality that have been identified in children at risk for schizophrenia, most do not manifest diagnosable mental disorders in early and middle childhood. But the picture often changes in adolescence. During postpubescence, many subjects who go on to develop schizophrenia show a pattern of escalating adjustment problems (Walker et al. 1998). This gradual increase in problems includes feelings of depression, social withdrawal, irritability and noncompliance. But this developmental pattern is not unique to schizophrenia; adolescence is also the critical period for the expression of the first signs of mood disorders, substance abuse, and some other behavioral disorders. As a result, researchers view adolescence as a critical period for the emergence of a broad range of psychiatric disorders (Walker 2002).

Among the behavioral risk indicators sometimes observed in preschizophrenic adolescents are subclinical signs of psychotic symptoms. These signs are also the defining features of a DSM Axis II disorder, namely, schizotypal personality disorder (SPD). The diagnostic criteria for SPD include social anxiety or withdrawal, affective abnormalities, eccentric behavior, unusual ideas (e.g., persistent belief in extrasensory phenomena), and unusual sensory experiences (e.g., repeated experiences with confusing noises with peoples' voices, or seeing objects move). Although the individual's unusual ideas and perceptions are not severe or persistent enough to meet criteria for delusions or hallucinations, they are recurring. An extensive body of research demonstrates genetic and developmental links between schizophrenia and SPD. The genetic link between SPD and schizophrenia has been well established through twin and family history studies (Kendler et al. 1995a,b; Raine & Mednick 1995). Recently, several research groups have documented the developmental transition from schizotypal signs to schizophrenia in young adulthood.

Longitudinal studies indicate that 20% to 40% of youth with schizotypal signs eventually show an Axis I schizophrenia spectrum disorder (Miller et al. 2002, Yung et al. 1998). The remainder either show other adjustment problems or a complete remission of symptoms in young adulthood. Given the high rate of progression to schizophrenia, researchers are now attempting to determine whether schizotypal youth who will eventually manifest schizophrenia can be identified prior to the onset of the illness. This is considered a pivotal step in efforts to develop secondary prevention programs.

Recent investigations have revealed that adolescents with SPD manifest some of the same functional abnormalities observed in patients with schizophrenia. For example, SPD youth show motor abnormalities (Walker et al. 1999), cognitive deficits (Diforio et al. 2000), and an increase in cortisol, a stress hormone that is elevated in several psychiatric disorders (Weinstein et al. 1999).

Illness Onset and Course

The onset of the clinical symptoms of schizophrenia can be abrupt or gradual, but it is usually preceded by escalating signs of behavioral dysfunction and subclinical psychotic symptoms, a period referred to as the prodromal phase (Lieberman et al. 2001). Longer untreated psychotic episodes may be harmful for schizophrenia patients and result in a worse course of illness (Davidson & McGlashan 1997). Although some researchers have questioned the validity of this conclusion (Larsen et al. 2001), it has prompted many researchers to focus greater attention on the prodromal period.

Following the clinical onset of schizophrenia, patients vary significantly in their illness course. Some patients experience a full recovery, whereas others show chronic debilitation. It has been estimated that only 20% to 30% of patients are eventually able to lead relatively normal lives, meaning they live independently and/or maintain a job (Cancro 1989). But the majority experience a more debilitating course, with 20% to 30% manifesting continued moderate symptoms, and more than half experiencing significant impairment throughout their adulthood.

Given the chronicity of the illness, it is not surprising that suicide is a leading cause of death among people with schizophrenia (Schwartz & Cohen 2001). Moreover, patients with schizophrenia often suffer from other comorbid conditions. For example, the rate of substance abuse among schizophrenia patients is very high, with as many as 47% in the community and 90% of patients in prison settings meeting criteria for substance abuse or dependence (Regier et al. 1990).

What determines the course of schizophrenia? Male sex, gradual onset, early age of onset, poor premorbid functioning, and family history of schizophrenia are all associated with poorer prognosis (Gottesman 1991). In addition, as would be predicted by the diathesis-stress model, exposure to environmental stressors can exacerbate the course of schizophrenia.

Environmental Stressors

Several lines of research provide support for the hypothesis that stressful events can worsen the course of schizophrenia (for a review, see Norman & Malla 1993). For example, the number of stressful life events increases in the months immediately preceding a schizophrenia relapse (Ventura et al. 1992). Also, patients are more likely to relapse if they live in homes where family members express more negative attitudes and emotion (Butzlaff & Hooley 1998). Given these findings, it is not surprising that intervention programs aimed at reducing stress are beneficial for patients (Norman et al. 2002).

Indirect evidence indicates that stress exposure can also contribute to the onset of symptoms in vulnerable individuals. In a study that examined the interaction between parental psychiatric status and child maltreatment, the offspring of schizophrenic parents manifested significantly greater increases in behavior problems over time if they were also victims of neglect and/or abuse (Walker et al. 1989). Another study showed that high-risk offspring were more likely to develop schizophrenic symptoms if they were raised in institutional settings, rather than by parents or extended family members (Walker et al. 1981). Along the same lines, adopted-away children of biological mothers with schizophrenia are at greater risk for the disorder if their adoptive families are dysfunctional (Tienari et al. 1994) or show "communication deviance" (Wahlberg et al. 1997).

It is well established that stress exposure impacts brain function. This effect is partially mediated by activation of the hypothalamic-pituitary-adrenal (HPA) axis, one of the chief neural systems involved in the biological response to stress. Activation of the HPA axis results in a cascade of neurohormonal events that culminates in the release of cortisol from the adrenal gland. Cortisol has pervasive effects on brain function, and can alter the activity of neurotransmitter systems. When stress hormones are chronically elevated, structural brain changes can occur, such as reductions in hippocampal volume (Lombroso & Sapolsky 1998).

Elevations in cortisol are linked with more severe symptoms and cognitive deficits in schizophrenia (Walder et al. 2000). Walker & Diforio (1997) have reviewed evidence of HPA dysregulation in schizophrenia. In their "neural diathesis-stress model," they describe how heightened cortisol release has the potential to exacerbate schizophrenia symptoms by augmenting dopamine activity. The chronic stress inherent in suffering from a psychotic illness may also contribute to degenerative brain changes.

BRAIN ABNORMALITIES

Structural and Functional Abnormalities

With the advent of neuroimaging techniques in the 1960s, it became possible to document what many had long suspected: that schizophrenia was associated with brain abnormalities. The earliest reports, based on computerized axial tomography, showed that patients had enlarged brain ventricles, especially increased volume of the lateral ventricles (Dennert & Andreasen 1983). As new imaging techniques were developed, these findings were replicated, and additional abnormalities were detected (Henn & Braus 1999). Magnetic resonance imaging (MRI) revealed decreased frontal, temporal, and whole-brain volume (Lawrie & Abukmeil 1998). More fine-grained analyses demonstrated reductions in the size of structures such as the thalamus and hippocampus. In fact, of all the regions studied, the hippocampus is one that has most consistently been identified as distinguishing schizophrenia patients from healthy controls (Schmajuk 2001).

A landmark study of monozygotic twins discordant for schizophrenia was the first to demonstrate that these brain abnormalities were not solely attributable to genetic factors (Suddath et al. 1990). When compared to their healthy identical cotwins, twins with schizophrenia were found to have reduced temporal lobe volumes, with the hippocampal region showing the most dramatic difference between the affected and nonaffected cotwins. Subsequent studies have confirmed smaller brain volumes in affected twins when compared to their healthy identical cotwins (Baare et al. 2001), and thus lend support to the hypothesis that the brain abnormalities may be partially due to factors that interfere with brain development.

Longitudinal studies of brain morphology in schizophrenia have yielded striking evidence of volumetric reductions over time. Decreases in gray matter volume and increases in ventricular size have been documented in the early stages of the illness in patients with young-adult onset (Cahn et al. 2002, DeLisi 1999), and in adolescents with schizophrenia (Rapoport et al. 1999). Although normal adolescents also manifest a developmental reduction in gray matter volume, it is more pronounced in those with schizophrenia. Moreover, adolescents with schizophrenia show volumetric reduction in total cortical and hippocampal volume that is not observed in normal adolescents (Giedd et al. 1999). It appears that brain changes precede the onset of schizophrenia. In a study of individuals with prodromal symptoms, those who subsequently developed schizophrenia showed a decrease in gray matter in the left parahippocampal, fusiform, orbitofrontal and cerebellar cortices, and the cingulate gyrus (Pantelis et al. 2003). Taken together, these findings suggest that abnormal brain changes predate the onset of schizophrenia, and may begin in adolescence.

In addition to structural abnormalities, schizophrenia patients also differ from normals in functional brain characteristics. The most consistent findings from fMRI and PET are reductions in activity in the frontal and temporal regions, especially during the performance of cognitive tasks (Kindermann et al. 1997, Pearlson 1997). Recent findings indicate that reduced brain activity is also observed in the limbic system in schizophrenia patients during the processing of facial emotion (Gur et al. 2002).

While the results of neuroimaging research on schizophrenia are impressive, an important caveat should be kept in mind. Despite the plethora of research findings indicating the presence of gross morphological and functional abnormalities in the brains of schizophrenia patients, no abnormality has been shown to be either specific to schizophrenia or to characterize all patients. Therefore, like the generalized cognitive deficits manifested by patients, the brain abnormalities are viewed as nonspecific indicators of brain dysfunction. In an effort to identify more precisely the origins of the dysfunction, some investigators have looked at the cellular level.

Postmortem studies of the brains of patients have revealed a number of abnormalities in neural density, structure, and interconnections. These include reductions in neuron density, and abnormal neuronal morphology, cytoarchitecture, dendritic arbors and spines, but with no signs of gliosis (Arnold 1999). The absence of gliosis, which typically develops following postnatal brain injury, has led to the conclusion that the cellular abnormalities reflect early developmental abnormalities.

In addition, the widespread nature of the cellular abnormalities observed in schizophrenia have led many researchers to conceptualize the disorder as one that involves malfunction of neural circuits. For example, it has been suggested that schizophrenia may involve abnormal function of "cortico-striatal circuits" that link various regions of the cortex and the limbic system with the striatum (Walker 1994). These circuits involve several neurotransmitter systems, and abnormalities in multiple segments of the circuit could be functionally equivalent with respect to the behavioral disturbance they produce. Further, the brain regions that distinguish these circuits mature at different rates. It is possible that disruption in one or more of the circuits characterized by neuromaturation in adolescence/early adulthood may subserve the onset of symptoms.

Along the same lines, Benes (2000) has suggested that schizophrenia may involve mis-wirings in intrinsic circuits (microcircuitry) within certain brain regions, as well as changes at the level of interconnections between two or more regions within a network (macrocircuitry). Normal postnatal maturational changes, at the level of both macro- and microcircuitry, within the limbic system may then serve as triggers for the onset of schizophrenia during adolescence. Finally, others have suggested that there is a disruption in the cortical-thalamic-cerebellar-cortical circuit that leads to an impairment in synchrony, or coordination of mental processes. Impairment in this basic cognitive process is assumed to produce the diversity of symptoms seen in schizophrenia (Andreasen et al. 1999).

The notion that schizophrenia involves dysfunction of one or more neural circuits, as opposed to a specific brain region, converges with the evidence from other lines of investigation, including phenomenology, cognitive functions, genetics, and the neuroanatomy of schizophrenia. Given that neural circuits involve multiple neurotransmitters and multiple segments, including some that provide inhibitory feedback, their function could be disrupted in numerous ways. Moreover, the disruption of a specific circuit could have relatively broad and nonspecific effects on behaviors.

Neurotransmitters

Brain circuit activity is driven by neurotransmitters. The idea that schizophrenia involves an abnormality in neurotransmission has a long history. Initial neurotransmitter theories focused on epinephrine and norepinephrine. Subsequent approaches have hypothesized that serotonin, glutamate, and/or GABA abnormalities are present in schizophrenia patients. But, compared to other neurotransmitters, dopamine has played a more enduring role in theories about the biochemical basis of schizophrenia.

Dopamine is widely distributed in the brain and is one of the neurotransmitters that enables communication in the circuits that link subcortical with cortical brain regions (Jentsch et al. 2000). Since the 1950s, support for the idea that dopamine might play a central role in schizophrenia has waxed and waned. In the past decade, however, interest in dopamine has resurged, largely because research findings have offered a new perspective.

The initial support for the role of dopamine in schizophrenia was based on two indirect pieces of evidence (Carlsson 1988): (*a*) drugs that reduce dopamine activity also serve to diminish psychotic symptoms, and (*b*) drugs that heighten dopamine activity exacerbate or trigger psychotic episodes. It was eventually discovered that antipsychotic drugs have their effect by blocking dopamine receptors, especially the D2 subtype that is prevalent in subcortical regions of the brain. The newer antipsychotic drugs, or "atypical" antipsychotics, have the advantage of causing fewer motor side effects. Nonetheless, they also act on the dopamine system by blocking various subtypes of dopamine receptors.

Early studies of dopamine in schizophrenia failed to find evidence of excess dopamine or its metabolites in fluids from schizophrenia patients. When investigators examined dopamine receptors, however, they found some evidence of increased densities. Both postmortem and functional MRI studies of patients' brains yielded evidence that the number of dopamine D2 receptors tends to be greater in patients than in normal controls (Kestler et al. 2001). Controversy has surrounded this literature because antipsychotic drugs can change dopamine receptor density. Nonetheless, even studies of never-medicated patients with schizophrenia have shown elevations in dopamine receptors (Kestler et al. 2001).

Other abnormalities in dopamine transmission have also been found. It appears, for example, that dopamine synthesis and release may be augmented in the brains of schizophrenia patients (Lindstrom et al. 1999). When schizophrenia patients and normal controls are given amphetamine, a drug that enhances dopamine release, the patients show more augmented dopamine release (Abi-Dargham et al. 1998, Soares & Innis 1999).

Glutamate is an excitatory neurotransmitter. Glutamatergic neurons are part of the pathways that connect the hippocampus, prefrontal cortex, and thalamus, all regions that have been implicated in the neural circuitry of schizophrenia. Investigators have found evidence of diminished activity at glutamatergic receptors among schizophrenia patients in these brain regions (Carlsson et al. 1999, Goff & Coyle 2001, Tsai & Coyle 2002). One of the chief receptors for glutamate in the brain is the N-methyl-D-aspartic acid (NMDA) subtype of receptor. It has been suggested that these receptors may be abnormal in schizophrenia. Blockade of NMDA receptors produces the symptomatic manifestations of schizophrenia in normal subjects, including negative symptoms and cognitive impairments. For example, administration of NMDA receptor antagonists, such as phencyclidine (PCP) and ketamine, induces a broad range of schizophrenic-like symptomatology in humans, and these findings have contributed to a hypoglutamatergic hypothesis of schizophrenia. Conversely, drugs that indirectly enhance NMDA receptor function can reduce negative symptoms and improve cognitive functioning in schizophrenia patients. It is important to note that the idea of dysfunction of glutamatergic transmission is consistent with the dopamine hypothesis of schizophrenia because there are reciprocal connections between forebrain dopamine projections and systems that use glutamate. Thus dysregulation of one system would be expected to alter neurotransmission in the other.

GABA is an inhibitory neurotransmitter. Some have suggested that its inhibitory effects may be increased in psychotic disorders (Squires & Saederup 1991). On the other hand, the uptake and the release of GABA were reduced in some studies of postmortem brain tissue from schizophrenia patients (Lewis et al. 1999), and there are abnormalities in the interconnections among GABA neurons (Benes & Berretta 2001). More specifically, there is evidence of a loss of cortical GABA interneurons. Current theories about the role of GABA in schizophrenia assume that it is important because cortical processes require an optimal balance between GABA inhibition and glutamatergic excitation.

Other neurotransmitters that have been implicated in schizophrenia include serotonin and noradrenaline (Pralong et al. 2002). However, the evidence to support their role in schizophrenia is more limited.

The true picture of the neurochemical abnormalities in schizophrenia may be more complex than we would like to assume. Neurotransmitter systems interact in intricate ways at multiple levels in the brain's circuitry (Carlsson et al. 2001). Consequently, an alteration in the synthesis, reuptake, receptor density, or receptor affinity for any one of the neurotransmitter systems would be expected to have implications for one or more of the other neurotransmitter systems. Further, because neural circuits involve multiple segments that rely on different transmitters, it is easy to imagine how an abnormality in even one specific subgroup of receptors could result in the dysfunction of all the brain regions by a particular brain circuit.

THE TREATMENT OF SCHIZOPHRENIA

Findings from research on the treatment of schizophrenia have advanced both clinical practice and theories of etiology. Based on the evidence, the contemporary treatment "ideal" is a combination of medication, psychological therapy, and community support. In reality, however, medication is both the first and the *only* treatment received by many patients.

Antipsychotic Medications

The mainstay of contemporary treatment of schizophrenia is antipsychotic medication. Antipsychotic medication can be divided into two major classes. Conventional antipsychotic medications, first introduced in the 1950s, are usually referred to as either "typical" or "first-generation" antipsychotics. (These drugs preceded the release of clozapine (Clozaril) into the North American market in the 1980s.) Chlorpromazine (Thorazine), was the first antipsychotic medication, and the following three decades witnessed the release of various other typical neuroleptics. All of these medications reduce dopamine activity by blocking dopamine receptors, especially the D2 subtype, and these drugs have similar efficacy for the positive symptoms of schizophrenia. They differ from each other, however, in side-effect profiles.

Drug-induced movement abnormalities are the main side effect associated with the typical antipsychotics. There are both early- and late-emerging motor side effects (Sadock & Sadock 2000). Early emerging "extrapyramidal" syndromes include pseudoparkinsonism (clinically similar to Parkinson's disease), dystonic reactions (sudden onset of sustained intense muscle contraction), and akathisia (restlessness).

The most common late-emerging syndrome is tardive dyskinesia (irregular twisting or writhing movements). The cause of these motor side effects is not established, but is assumed to be due to excessive dopamine D2 receptor blockade. The motor symptoms typically decline following the discontinuation of medication.

The side effects caused by the typical antipsychotics have led most clinicians to abandon them in favor of second-generation medications. Nonetheless, they contributed to our understanding of the neurochemistry of schizophrenia, and offered many patients the first opportunity to live outside an institution.

Clozapine and the subsequently introduced antipsychotics are a heterogeneous group of medications that are commonly referred to as the "atypical" or "second-generation" antipsychotics. The atypicals differ significantly from one another in terms of the neurotransmitter receptors that they occupy. However, they all act as dopamine antagonists to some extent, in addition to affecting other neurotransmitter systems, and they have a reduced risk of both the early and late emerging movement disorders (Marder et al. 2002). In addition, clozapine has been shown to be highly effective for treatment-resistant schizophrenia. However, its use is generally confined to the refractory patients because of its potentially serious side-effects (including agranulocytosis), and the requirement for frequent blood monitoring (Alphs & Anand 1999, Naheed & Green 2001). With the exception of clozapine, the atypicals have become the first line in the treatment of schizophrenia and other psychotic disorders. The most commonly prescribed atypical antipsychotics in the United States include Risperdal (risperidone), Zyprexa (olanzapine), Seroquel (quetiapine), and Geodon (ziprasidone).

There are several theories about why the atypical antipsychotics are less likely than the typical neuroleptics to cause extrapyramidal side effects. The potency of the atypicals, which block both dopamine D2 and serotonin 5-HT2A receptors, might be responsible. It has been suggested that reduced serotonergic function in the brain, which can be achieved by blocking the 5-HT2A receptor, reduces extrapyramidal side effects (Richelson 1999). Others have theorized that the unique action of the atypical antipsychotics derives from their low affinity for the dopamine D2 receptor. These drugs, compared to dopamine itself, are loosely bound to, and rapidly released from, the dopamine D2 receptors, whereas the typical antipsychotics bind to the D2 receptors with greater affinity than dopamine (Seeman 2002).

Another new horizon in the treatment of schizophrenia is the future potential to tailor medication to patients' genetic profiles. The new and rapidly developing fields of pharmacogenomics and pharmacogenetics are seeking to uncover the genetic basis of differences in medication response and toxicity. The goal is to be able to individualize therapy based on a patient's genetic makeup (Basile et al. 2002). The field of pharmacogenomics looks at the determinants of drug response at the level of the entire human genome using DNA microarray (DNA chip) analysis, which allows researchers to examine changes in the expression of genes that result from medication (Kawanishi et al. 2000). Pharmacogenetic investigations study DNA sequence variations in candidate genes, which might affect drug response or toxicity (i.e., drug metabolism pathways, receptor gene variants). It is not yet clear whether phenotyping or genotyping will be able to predict an optimal dosage range for a given patient. However, as the technology advances and knowledge is gained, we will continue to move closer to the development of clinically meaningful tests that will be useful for determining the optimal drug, and perhaps also an optimal dosage range for each patient (Basile et al. 2002).

Psychosocial Treatments

When used in conjunction with medication, a variety of psychological therapies have improved prognosis and reduced rates of relapse in schizophrenia. For example, a large body of literature supports the use of family therapy, which includes psychoeducational and behavioral components, in the treatment of schizophrenia (Bustillo et al. 2001). Family therapy has been shown to reduce caregiver burden and improve family members' coping and knowledge about schizophrenia, thus reducing the risk of relapse.

Among the therapies that focus directly on the patient, social skills training seeks to improve functioning by teaching the skills necessary to enhance performance in interpersonal interactions, involvement in leisure activities, and employment. Overall, social skills training has been shown to improve social competence in the laboratory and in the clinic. However, it remains unclear to what extent, if any, this translates into better functioning within the community (Bustillo et al. 2001, Penn & Mueser 1996).

Cognitive behavior therapy (CBT) for schizophrenia draws on the tenets of cognitive therapy (Beck 1976). CBT is used to help psychotic patients deal directly with their symptoms. Specific psychotic symptoms such as hallucinations and delusions are identified for intervention by the patient and therapist (Dickerson 2000). The few published randomized controlled trials of CBT with schizophrenia patients indicate that it is effective in reducing hallucinations and delusions in medication-resistant patients, and as a complement to pharmacotherapy in acute psychosis (Bustillo et al. 2001).

The vulnerability-stress model suggests that specific training in stress management techniques might benefit patients with schizophrenia. A recently published study comparing the outcome of patients randomly assigned to either stress management or a social activities group revealed that the subjects who participated in the stress management program had fewer hospital admissions in the year following treatment (Norman et al. 2002). This effect was most apparent for those who showed a high level of attendance. Thus, stress management training may provide patients with the skills to cope more effectively with acute stressors and reduce the likelihood of symptom exacerbation necessitating hospital admission.

Occupational functioning has been another focus of treatment. The rate of competitive employment for the severely mentally ill has been estimated at less than 20% (Lehman 1995). Vocational rehabilitation programs have a positive influence on work-related activities, but have not been shown to have a substantial impact on patients' abilities to obtain employment independently in the community (Lehman 1995). There is some evidence to suggest that "supported employment programs" produce better results than traditional vocational rehabilitation programs; however, job retention remains a significant problem (Lehman et al. 2002). Also, there is little evidence to support the contention that the employment obtained produces improved self-esteem or quality of life (Bustillo et al. 2001).

Finally, a multifaceted approach to treatment is assertive community treatment (ACT), which was originally developed in the 1970s by researchers in Madison, Wisconsin (Bustillo et al. 2001). This is a comprehensive treatment approach for the seriously mentally ill living in the community. Patients are assigned to a multidisciplinary team (nurse, case manager, general physician, and psychiatrist) that delivers all services to the patient when and where he or she needs them. Services include home delivery of medication, monitoring of physical and mental health status, in vivo social skills training, and frequent contact with family members. The ACT model has been shown to reduce time spent in the hospital, to improve housing stability, and to increase patient and family satisfaction. However, studies have failed to show improvement in social functioning, employment, or other measures of quality of life.

In summary, as mentioned above, evidence that longer duration of untreated psychotic episodes is related with the poorer prognosis has led to more aggressive efforts to provide treatment as soon as possible after the clinical onset. Some even advocate treatment of individuals in the prodromal phase of schizophrenia. Because the atypical antipsychotics have fewer side effects, many believe it is now more reasonable to consider preventive medication for individuals in the prodromal phase. However, researchers have not established reliable criteria for identifying the prodrome, and investigators have raised questions about the long-term consequences of preventive pharmacological and/or psychosocial interventions (Cornblatt et al. 2002). Because treatment with antipsychotic medication, even the atypical antipsychotics, is sometimes associated with serious side effects, there is reason to be cautious about preventive medication until we are able to identify at-risk individuals with greater accuracy (Marder et al. 2002).

SUMMARY AND CONCLUSIONS

In this article we have offered an overview of research findings on the nature and origins of schizophrenia. Progress has been slow, and there is no doubt that investigators have traversed countless blind alleys. Inappropriate paradigms and conceptualizations have been part of the problem. The notion that schizophrenia is a single disease with discrete phenomenological boundaries and a specific cause no longer seems plausible. Rather, the contemporary view assumes that we have not yet clearly defined the boundaries of the disorder, and that the etiologies are diverse, with multiple genetic and environmental contributors. Although this may not strike some as progress, the contemporary view actually reflects the more sophisticated psychobiological perspective that now characterizes scientific thinking about a range of mental and physical illnesses, from depression to cancer.

The picture that has emerged from research on schizophrenia, as well as other psychotic disorders, is best described in an expansion of the diathesis-stress model that has dominated the field for several decades.

Figure 1 illustrates a contemporary version of the diathesis-stress model that encompasses all of the factors that are currently considered to play a significant etiologic role in schizophrenia. This model postulates that constitutional vulnerability to schizophrenia (i.e., the diathesis) can result from both inherited and acquired constitutional factors. The inherited factors are genetically determined characteristics of the brain that influence its structure and function. Acquired vulnerabilities can arise from prenatal events that alter fetal neurodevelopment and

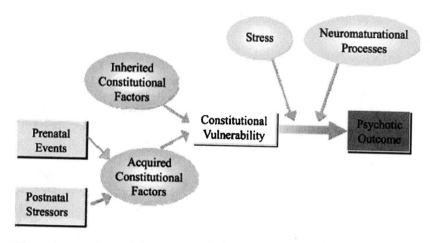

Figure 1   A diathesis-stress model of the etiology of schizophrenia.

postnatal stressors, broadly defined to include brain trauma. Both are assumed to compromise brain structure and function.

Whether the constitutional vulnerability is a consequence of genetic factors, or environmental factors, or a combination of both, the model assumes that vulnerability is, in most cases, congenital. But the assumption that vulnerability is present at birth does not imply that it will be clinically expressed as psychosis at any point in the life span. Rather, we assume that two sets of factors determine the postnatal course of the vulnerable individual.

Adolescent neuromaturation is assumed to be one key element. It is well established that adolescence/early adulthood is a critical period for the expression of the vulnerability for schizophrenia. Rapidly accumulating data indicate that brain changes occur in adolescence and extend into early adulthood (Walker 2002). Thus some aspects(s) of brain maturational processes during the postpubertal period are likely playing an important role in triggering the clinical expression of latent liabilities. It is plausible that the genetic liability for schizophrenia involves an abnormality in genes that govern this maturational process. Alternatively, a latent abnormality in the brain circuitry that matures during this period may be gradually behaviorally expressed during the course of adolescence, culminating in the clinical onset of schizophrenia.

Further, external stress is assumed to influence the expression of the vulnerability. This is a long-standing assumption among theorists, although it is important to qualify this notion. Empirical research has provided evidence that episodes of schizophrenia tend to follow periods of increased life stress (Walker & Diforio 1997). Nonetheless, there is no reliable evidence that schizophrenia patients experience more psychosocial stress during the premorbid period than normals, but rather that they are more sensitive to stress when it occurs. At the biological level, enhanced sensitivity to stress may result from the disruptive effects of stress hormone release on the function of abnormal brain circuitry. This is the essence of the model—it is the interaction between vulnerability and stress that is critical.

In summary, although we have not identified all the pieces of the puzzle, we have made significant progress in moving toward a comprehensive account of the etiology of schizophrenia. In the coming years, we can expect research to yield important information about the precise nature of the brain vulnerabilities associated with schizophrenia, and the mechanisms involved in the interaction of congenital vulnerability with subsequent life stress and neuromaturation.

The *Annual Review of Psychology* is online at http://psych.annualreviews.org

LITERATURE CITED

AbdelMalik P, Husted J, Chow E, Bassett A. 2003. Childhood head injury and expression of schizophrenia in multiply affected families. *Arch. Gen. Psychiatry* 60:231–36

Abi-Dargham A, Gil R, Krystal J, Baldwin RM, Seibyl JP, et al. 1998. Increased striatal dopamine transmission in schizophrenia: confirmation in a second cohort. *Am. J. Psychiatry* 155:761–67

Alphs LD, Anand R. 1999. Clozapine: the commitment to patient safety. *J. Clin. Psychiatry* 60(Suppl. 122):39–42

American Psychiatric Association. 2000. *Diagnostic and Statistical Manual of Mental Disorders*. Washington, DC: Am. Psychiatric Assoc. 886 pp. 4th ed.

Andreasen NC, Nopoulos P, O'Leary DS, Miller DD, Wassink T, Flaum M. 1999. Defining the phenotype of schizophrenia: cognitive dysmetria and its neural mechanisms. *Biol. Psychiatry* 46(7):908–20

Arnold SE. 1999. Neurodevelopmental abnormalities in schizophrenia: insights from neuropathology. *Dev. Psychopathol.* 11(3):439–56

Aylward E, Walker E, Bettes B. 1984. Intelligence in schizophrenia: meta-analysis of the research. *Schizophr. Bull.* 10:430–59

Baare WF, van Oel CJ, Pol H, Schnack HG, Durston S, et al. 2001. Volumes of brain structures in twins discordant for schizophrenia. *Arch. Gen. Psychiatry* 58(1):33–40

Badner JA, Gershon ES. 2002. Meta-analysis of whole-genome linkage scans of bipolar disorder and schizophrenia. *Mol. Psychiatry* 7(4):405–11

Barr CE, Mednick SA, Munk-Jorgensen P. 1990. Exposure to influenza epidemics during gestation and adult schizophrenia: a 40-year study. *Arch. Gen. Psychiatry* 47:869–74

Basile VS, Masellis M, Potkin SG, Kennedy JL. 2002. Pharmacogenomics in schizophrenia: the quest for individualized therapy. *Hum. Mol. Genet.* 11(20):2517–30

Bassett AS, Hodgkinson K, Chow EW, Correia S, Scutt LE, Weksberg R. 1998. 22q11 deletion syndrome in adults with schizophrenia. *Am. J. Med. Genet.* 81(4):328–37

Beck AT. 1976. *Cognitive Therapy and the Emotional Disorders*. New York: Int. Univ. Press

Benes FM. 2000. Emerging principles of altered neural circuitry in schizophrenia. *Brain Res. Brain Res. Rev.* 31(2–3):251–69

Benes FM, Berretta S. 2001. GABAergic interneurons: implications for understanding schizophrenia and bipolar disorder. *Neuropsychopharmacology* 25(1):1–27

Bleuler E. 1911. *Group of Schizophrenias*. Transl. J Zinkin, 1950. New York: Int. Univ. Press (From German)

Bradbury TN, Miller GA. 1985. Season of birth in schizophrenia: a review of evidence, methodology, and etiology. *Psychol. Bull.* 98:569–94

Braus DF, Weber-Fahr W, Tost H, Ruf M, Henn FA. 2002. Sensory information processing in neuroleptic-naive first-episode schizophrenic patients: a functional magnetic resonance imaging study. *Arch. Gen. Psychiatry* 59(8):696–701

Brown AS, Cohen P, Harkavy-Friedman J, Babulas V. 2001. Prenatal rubella, premorbid abnormalities, and adult schizophrenia. *Biol. Psychiatry* 49:473–86

Brozgold AZ, Borod JC, Martin CC, Pick LH, Alpert M, Welkowitz J. 1998. Social functioning and facial emotional expression in neurological and psychiatric disorders. *Appl. Neuropsychol.* 5(1):15–23

Buka SL, Tsuang MT, Lipsitt LP. 1993. Pregnancy/delivery complications and psychiatric diagnosis: a prospective study. *Arch. Gen. Psychiatry* 50:151–56

Bustillo JR, Lauriello J, Horan WP, Keith SJ. 2001. The psychosocial treatment of schizophrenia: an update. *Am. J. Psychiatry* 158(2):163–75

Butzlaff RL, Hooley JM. 1998. Expressed emotion and psychiatric relapse. *Arch. Gen. Psychiatry* 55(6):547–52

Cahn W, Pol HE, Lems EB, van Haren NE, Schnack HG, et al. 2002. Brain volume changes in first-episode schizophrenia: a 1-year follow-up study. *Arch. Gen. Psychiatry* 59(11):1002–10

Cancro R. 1989. Schizophrenia. In *Treatments of Psychiatric Disorders: A Task Force Report of the American Psychiatric Association*, 1–3:1485–606. xliv. Washington, DC: Am. Psychiatric Assoc. 3068 pp.

Cannon TD. 1997. On the nature and mechanisms of obstetric influences in schizophrenia: a review and synthesis of epidemiologic studies. *Int. Rev. Psychiatry* 9(4):387–97

Cannon TD. 1998. Genetic and perinatal influences in the etiology of schizophrenia: a neurodevelopmental model. See Lenzenweger & Dworkin 1998, pp. 67–92

Cannon TD, Rosso IM, Hollister JM, Bearden CE, Sanchez LE, Hadley T. 2000. A prospective cohort study of genetic and perinatal in-

fluences in schizophrenia. *Schizophr. Bull.* 26:351–66

Cardno AG, Rijsdijk FV, Sham PC, Murray RM, McGuffin P. 2002. A twin study of genetic relationships between psychotic symptoms. *Am. J. Psychiatry* 159(4):539–45

Carlsson A. 1988. The current status of the dopamine hypothesis of schizophrenia. *Neuropsychopharmacology* 1(3):179–86

Carlsson A, Hansson LO, Waters N, Carlsson ML. 1999. A glutamatergic deficiency model of schizophrenia. *Br. J. Psychiatry* 37:2–6

Carlsson A, Waters N, Holm-Waters S, Tedroff J, Nilsson M, Carlsson ML. 2001. Interactions between monoamines, glutamate, and GABA in schizophrenia: new evidence. *Annu. Rev. Pharmacol. Toxicol.* 41:237–60

Carpenter WT, Buchanan RW. 1994. Schizophrenia. *N. Engl. J. Med.* 330(10):681–90

Cornblatt B, Lencz T, Obuchowski M. 2002. The schizophrenia prodrome: treatment and high-risk perspectives. *Schizophr. Res.* 54:177–86

Dalman C, Allebeck P, Cullberg J, Grunewald C, Koester M. 1999. Obstetric complications and the risk of schizophrenia: a longitudinal study of a national birth cohort. *Arch. Gen. Psychiatry* 56(3):234–40

Davidson L, McGlashan TH. 1997. The varied outcomes of schizophrenia. *Can. J. Psychiatry* 42:34–43

DeLisi LE. 1992. The significance of age of onset for schizophrenia. *Schizophr. Bull.* 18:209–15

DeLisi LE. 1999. Regional brain volume change over the life-time course of schizophrenia. *J. Psychiatr. Res.* 33(6):535–41

Dennert JW, Andreasen NC. 1983. CT scanning and schizophrenia: a review. *Psychiatr. Dev.* 1(1):105–22

Dickerson FB. 2000. Cognitive behavioral psychotherapy for schizophrenia: a review of recent empirical studies. *Schizophr. Res.* 43: 71–90

Diforio D, Kestler L, Walker E. 2000. Executive functions in adolescents with schizotypal personality disorder. *Schizophr. Res.* 42:125–34

Done DJ, Crow TJ, Johnstone EC, Sacker A. 1994. Childhood antecedents of schizophrenia and affective illness: social adjustment at ages 7 and 11. *Br. Med. J.* 309(6956):699–703

Feighner JP, Robins E, Guze SB. 1972. Diagnostic criteria for use in psychiatric research. *Arch. Gen. Psychiatry* 26:57–63

Flashman L, Flaum M, Gupta S, Andreasen NC. 1996. Soft signs and neuropsychological performance in schizophrenia. *Am. J. Psychiatry* 153(4):526–32

Flyckt L, Wiesel F, Borg J, Edman G, Ansved T, et al. 2000. Neuromuscular and psychomotor abnormalities in patients with schizophrenia and their first-degree relatives. *J. Psychiatr. Res.* 134(4–5):355–64

Fuller R, Nopoulos P, Arndt S, O'Leary D, Ho BC, Andreasen NC. 2002. Longitudinal assessment of premorbid cognitive functioning in patients with schizophrenia through examination of standardized scholastic test performance. *Am. J. Psychiatry* 159(7):1183–89

Giedd JN, Jeffries NO, Blumenthal J, Castellanos FX, Vaituzis AC, et al. 1999. Childhood-onset schizophrenia: progressive brain changes during adolescence. *Biol. Psychiatry* 46(7):892–98

Gjerde PF. 1983. Attentional capacity dysfunction and arousal in schizophrenia. *Psychol. Bull.* 193(1):57–72

Goff DC, Coyle JT. 2001. The emerging role of glutamate in the pathophysiology and treatment of schizophrenia. *Am. J. Psychiatry* 158(9):1367–77

Goldsamt LA. 1994. Neuropsychological findings in schizophrenia. In *The Neuropsychology of Mental Disorders: A Practical Guide*, ed. LF Koziol, CE Stout, pp. 80–93. New York: Thomas. 326 pp.

Gottesman II. 1991. *Psychiatric Genesis: The Origins of Madness*. New York: Freeman. 296 pp.

Gottesman II, Bertelsen A. 1989. Confirming unexpressed genotypes for schizophrenia: risks in the offspring of Fischer's Danish identical and fraternal discordant twins. *Arch. Gen. Psychiatry* 46(10):867–72

Green MF, Kern RS, Braff DL, Mintz J. 2000. Neurocognitive deficits and functional outcome in schizophrenia: Are we measuring the "right stuff"? *Schizophr. Bull.* 26(1):119–36

Green MF, Nuechterlein KH, Breitmeyer B, Mintz J. 1999. Backward masking in unmedicated schizophrenic patients in psychotic remission: possible reflection of aberrant cortical oscillation. *Am. J. Psychiatry* 156(9):1367–73

Gur RE, McGrath C, Chan RM, Schroeder L, Turner T, et al. 2002. An fMRI study of facial emotion processing in patients with schizophrenia. *Am. J. Psychiatry* 159(12):1992–99

Harvey PD. 2001. Cognitive impairment in elderly patients with schizophrenia: age related changes. *Int. J. Geriatr. Psychiatry* 16(Suppl. 1):S78–85

Harvey PD, Walker EF, eds. 1987. *Positive and Negative Symptoms of Psychosis: Description, Research, and Future Directions*. Hillsdale, NJ: Erlbaum. 341 pp.

Henn FA, Braus DF. 1999. Structural neuroimaging in schizophrenia. An integrative view of neuromorphology. *Eur. Arch. Psychiatry Clin. Neurosci.* 249(Suppl. 4):48–56

Heston LL. 1966. Psychiatric disorders in foster home reared children of schizophrenic mothers. *Br. J. Psychiatry* 112:819–25

Howells JG. 1991. *The Concept of Schizophrenia: Historical Perspectives*. Washington, DC: Am. Psychiatric Press. 211 pp.

Huttunen M. 1989. Maternal stress during pregnancy and the behavior of the offspring. In *Early Influences Shaping the Individual*, ed. S Doxiadis, S Stewart, pp. 168–82. NATO Adv. Sci. Inst. Ser.: Life Sci., Vol. 160. New York: Plenum

Jentsch JD, Roth RH, Taylor JR. 2000. Role for dopamine in the behavioral functions of the prefrontal corticostriatal system: implications for mental disorders and psychotropic drug action. *Prog. Brain Res.* 126:433–53

Jeste DV, del Carmen R, Lohr JB, Wyatt RJ. 1985. Did schizophrenia exist before the eighteenth century? *Compr. Psychiatry* 26(6):493–503

Jones P, Rodgers B, Murray R, Marmot M. 1994. Child developmental risk factors for adult schizophrenia in the British 1946 birth cohort. *Lancet* 344:1398–402

Karayiorgou M, Morris MA, Morrow B. 1995. Schizophrenia susceptibility associated with interstitial deletions of chromosome 22q11. *Proc. Natl. Acad. Sci. USA* 92:7612–16

Kato C, Petronis A, Okazaki Y, Tochigi M, Umekage T, Sasaki T. 2002. Molecular genetic studies of schizophrenia: Challenges and insights. *Neurosci. Res.* 43(4):295–304

Kawanishi Y, Tachikawa H, Suzuki T. 2000. Pharmacogenomics and schizophrenia. *Eur. J. Pharmacol.* 410(2–3):227–41

Keith SJ, Regier DA, Rae DS. 1991. Schizophrenic disorders. In *Psychiatric Disorders in America: The Epidemiologic Catchment Area Study*, ed. LN Robins, DA Regier, pp. 33–52. New York: Free Press. 999 pp.

Kendler KS, McGuire M, Gruenberg AM, Walsh D. 1995a. Schizotypal symptoms and signs in the Roscommon Family Study: their factor structure and familial relationship with psychotic and affective disorders. *Arch. Gen. Psychiatry* 52:296–303

Kendler KS, Neale MC, Walsh D. 1995b. Evaluating the spectrum concept of schizophrenia in the Roscommon Family Study. *Am. J. Psychiatry* 152:749–54

Kestler LP, Walker E, Vega EM. 2001. Dopamine receptors in the brains of schizophrenia patients: a meta-analysis of the findings. *Behav. Pharmacol.* 12(5):355–71

Kety SS. 1988. Schizophrenic illness in the families of schizophrenic adoptees: findings from the Danish national sample. *Schizophr. Bull.* 14:217–22

Kindermann SS, Karimi A, Symonds L, Brown GG, Jeste DV. 1997. Review of functional magnetic resonance imaging in schizophrenia. *Schizophr. Res.* 27(2–3):143–56

Kraepelin E. 1913. *Dementia Praecox and Paraphrenia.* Transl. RM Barclay, 1919, in *Psychiatrie* 3(2):48–79. Edinburgh: Livingstone Press. 8th ed. (From German)

Krieger S, Lis S, Gallhofer B. 2001. Cognitive subprocesses and schizophrenia: a reaction-time decomposition. *Acta Psychiatr. Scand. Suppl.* 104(408):18–27

Kring AM, Neale JM. 1996. Do schizophrenic patients show a disjunctive relationship among expressive, experiential, and psychophysiological components of emotion? *J. Abnorm. Psychol.* 105(2):249–57

Kringlen E, Cramer G. 1989. Offspring of monozygotic twins discordant for schizophrenia. *Arch. Gen. Psychiatry* 46:873–77

Kulhara P, Chakrabarti S. 2001. Culture and schizophrenia and other psychotic disorders. *Psychiatr. Clin. North Am.* 24:449–64

Kuperberg G, Heckers S. 2000. Schizophrenia and cognitive function. *Curr. Opin. Neurobiol.* 10(2):205–10

Larsen TK, Friis S, Haahr U, Joa I, Johannessen JO, et al. 2001. Early detection and intervention in first-episode schizophrenia: a critical review. *Acta Psychiatr. Scand.* 103(5):323–34

Lawrie SM, Abukmeil SS. 1998. Brain abnormality in schizophrenia: a systematic and quantitative review of volumetric magnetic resonance imaging studies. *Br. J. Psychiatry* 172:110–20

Lehman AF. 1995. Vocational rehabilitation in schizophrenia. *Schizophr. Bull.* 21(4):645–56

Lehman AF, Goldberg R, Dixon L, McNary S, Postrado L, et al. 2002. Improving employment outcomes for persons with severe mental illnesses. *Arch. Gen. Psychiatry* 59(2):165–72

Lenzenweger M, Dworkin R, eds. 1998. *Origins and Development of Schizophrenia: Advances in Experimental Psychopathology.* Washington, DC: Am. Psychol. Assoc. 557 pp.

Lewis DA, Pierri JN, Volk DW, Melchitzky DS, Woo TU. 1999. Altered GABA neurotransmission and prefrontal cortical dysfunction in schizophrenia. *Biol. Psychiatry* 46(5):616–26

Lieberman JA, Perkins D, Belger A, Chakos M, Jarskog F, et al. 2001. The early stages of schizophrenia: speculations on pathogenesis, pathophysiology, and therapeutic approaches. *Biol. Psychiatry* 50(11):884–97

Lindstrom LH, Gefvert O, Hagberg G, Lundberg T, Bergstrom M, et al. 1999. Increased dopamine synthesis rate in medial prefrontal cortex and striatum in schizophrenia indicated by L-(beta-11C) DOPA and PET. *Biol. Psychiatry* 46(5):681–88

Lombroso PJ, Sapolsky R. 1998. Development of the cerebral cortex: XII. Stress and brain development: I. *J. Am. Acad. Child Adolesc. Psychiatry* 37(12):1337–39

Marder SR, Essock SM, Miller AL, Buchanan RW, Davis JM, et al. 2002. The Mount Sinai conference on the pharmacotherapy of schizophrenia. *Schizophrenia Bull.* 28:(1):5–16

McNeil TF, Cantor-Graae E. 2000. Neuromotor markers of risk for schizophrenia. *Aust. NZ J. Psychiatry* 34(Suppl.):S86–90

McNeil TF, Cantor-Graae E, Weinberger DR. 2000. Relationship of obstetric complications and differences in size of brain structures in monozygotic twin pairs discordant for schizophrenia. *Am. J. Psychiatry* 157(2):203–12

Miller TJ, McGlashan TH, Rosen JL, Somjee L, Markovich PJ, et al. 2002. Prospective diagnosis of the initial prodrome for schizophrenia based on the Structured Interview for Prodromal Syndromes: preliminary evidence of interrater reliability and predictive validity. *Am. J. Psychiatry* 159(5):863–65

Mowry BJ, Nancarrow DJ. 2001. Molecular genetics of schizophrenia. *Clin. Exp. Pharmacol. Physiol.* 28:66–69

Murray RM, Jones PB, O'Callaghan E, Takei N. 1992. Genes, viruses and neurodevelopmental schizophrenia. *J. Psychiatr. Res.* 26:225–35

Naheed M, Green B. 2001. Focus on clozapine. *Curr. Med. Res. Opin.* 17(3):223–29

Neumann C, Walker E, Lewine R, Baum K. 1996. Childhood behavior and adult neuropsychological dysfunction in schizophrenia. *Neuropsychiatry Neuropsychol. Behav. Neurol.* 9:221–29

Norman RM, Malla AK. 1993. Stressful life events and schizophrenia. I: a review of the research. *Br. J. Psychiatry* 162:161–66

Norman RM, Malla AK, McLean RS, McIntosh EM, Neufeld RW, et al. 2002. An evaluation of a stress management program for individuals with schizophrenia. *Schizophr. Res.* 58(2–3):292–303

Pantelis C, Velakoulis D, McGorry PD, Wood SJ, Suckling J, et al. 2003. Neuroanatomical abnormalities before and after onset of psychosis: a cross-sectional and longitudinal MRI comparison. *Lancet* 361(9354):281–88

Pearlson GD. 1997. Superior temporal gyrus and planum temporale in schizophrenia: a selective review. *Prog. Neuropsychopharmacol. Biol. Psychiatry* 21(8):1203–29

Penn DL, Combs D. 2000. Modification of affect perception deficits in schizophrenia. *Schizophr. Res.* 46(2–3):217–29

Penn DL, Corrigan PW, Bentall RP, Racenstein JM, Newman L. 1997. Social cognition in schizophrenia. *Psychol. Bull.* 121(1):114–32

Penn DL, Mueser KT. 1996. Research update on the psychosocial treatment of schizophrenia. *Am. J. Psychiatry* 153(5):607–17

Perry W, Feifel D, Minassian A, Bhattacharjie I, Braff DL. 2002. Information processing deficits in acutely psychotic schizophrenia patients medicated and unmedicated at the time of admission. *Am. J. Psychiatry* 159(8):1375–81

Potash JB, Willour VL, Chiu YF, Simpson SG, MacKinnon DF, et al. 2001. The familial aggregation of psychotic symptoms in bipolar disorder pedigrees. *Am. J. Psychiatry* 158(8):1258–64

Pralong E, Magistretti P, Stoop R. 2002. Cellular perspectives on the glutamate-monoamine interactions in limbic lobe structures and their relevance for some psychiatric disorders. *Prog. Neurobiol.* 67(3):173–202

Raine A, Mednick S, eds. 1995. *Schizotypal Personality Disorder*. New York/London: Cambridge Univ. Press. 510 pp.

Rapoport JL, Giedd JN, Blumenthal J, Hamburger S, Jeffries N, et al. 1999. Progressive cortical change during adolescence in childhood-onset schizophrenia: a longitudinal magnetic resonance imaging study. *Arch. Gen. Psychiatry* 56(7):649–54

Regier DA, Farmer ME, Rae DS, Locke BZ, Keith SJ, et al. 1990. Comorbidity of mental disorders with alcohol and other drug abuse: Results from the Epidemiologic Catchment Area (ECA) study. *JAMA* 264:2511–18

Richelson E. 1999. Receptor pharmacology of neuroleptics: relation to clinical effects. *J. Clin. Psychiatry* 60(Suppl. 10):5–14

Riecher-Rossler A, Hafner H. 2000. Gender aspects in schizophrenia: bridging the border between social and biological psychiatry. *Acta Psychiatr. Scand. Suppl.* 102(407):58–62

Sadock BJ, Sadock VA, eds. 2000. *Kaplan and Sadock's Comprehensive Textbook of Psychiatry*, 1:2265–71. Baltimore, MD: Williams & Wilkins. 3344 pp.

Schmajuk NA. 2001. Hippocampal dysfunction in schizophrenia. *Hippocampus* 11(5):599–613

Schneider K. 1959. *Clinical Psychopathology.* New York/Orlando, FL: Grune & Stratton. 173 pp.

Schwartz RC, Cohen BN. 2001. Risk factors for suicidality among clients with schizophrenia. *J. Counsel. Dev.* 79(3):314–19

Seeman P. 2002. Atypical antipsychotics: mechanism of action. *Can. J. Psychiatry* 47(1):27–38

Smythe JW, McCormick CM, Rochford J, Meaney MJ. 1994. The interaction between prenatal stress and neonatal handling on nociceptive response latencies in male and female rats. *Physiol. Behav.* 55:971–74

Soares JC, Innis RB. 1999. Neurochemical brain imaging investigations of schizophrenia. *Biol. Psychiatry* 46(5):600–15

Spitzer RL, Endicott J, Robins E. 1978. Research Diagnostic Criteria (RDC) for a rationale and reliability. *Arch. Gen. Psychiatry* 35:773–82

Squires RF, Saederup E. 1991. A review of evidence for GABergic redominance/glutamatergic deficit as a common etiological factor in both schizophrenia and

affective psychoses: more support for a continuum hypothesis of "functional" psychosis. *Neurochem. Res.* 16(10):1099–111

Suddath RL, Christison GW, Torrey EF, Casanova MF, Weinberger DR. 1990. Anatomical abnormalities in the brains of monozygotic twins discordant for schizophrenia. *N. Engl. J. Med.* 322(12):789–94

Susser ES, Brown AS, Gorman JM, eds. 1999. *Prenatal Exposures in Schizophrenia: Progress in Psychiatry.* Washington, DC: Am. Psychiatric Press. 275 pp.

Tienari P, Wynne LC, Moring J, Lahti I. 1994. The Finnish adoptive family study of schizophrenia: implications for family research. *Br. J. Psychiatry* 164(Suppl. 23):20–26

Torrey EF. 1987. Prevalence studies in schizophrenia. *Br. J. Psychiatry* 150:598–608

Torrey EF, Miller J, Rawlings R, Yolken RH. 1997. Seasonality of births in schizophrenia and bipolar disorder: a review of the literature. *Schizophr. Res.* 28:1–38

Tsai G, Coyle JT. 2002. Glutamatergic mechanisms in schizophrenia. *Annu. Rev. Pharmacol. Toxicol.* 42:165–79

van Os J, Selten J. 1998. Prenatal exposure to maternal stress and subsequent schizophrenia: the May 1940 invasion of The Netherlands. *Br. J. Psychiatry* 172:324–26

Ventura J, Nuechterlein KH, Hardesty JP, Gitlin M. 1992. Life events and schizophrenic relapse after withdrawal of medication. *Br. J. Psychiatry* 161:615–20

Wahlberg KE, Wynne LC, Oja H, Keskitalo P, Pykalainen L, et al. 1997. Gene-environment interaction in vulnerability to schizophrenia: findings from the Finnish Adoptive Family Study of Schizophrenia. *Am. J. Psychiatry* 154(3):355–62

Walder D, Walker E, Lewine RJ. 2000. The relations among cortisol release, cognitive function and symptom severity in psychotic patients. *Biol. Psychiatry* 48:1121–32

Walker E. 1981. Emotion recognition in disturbed and normal children: a research note.

J. Child Psychol. Psychiatry Allied Discipl. 22(3):263–68

Walker E. 1994. Developmentally moderated expressions of the neuropathology underlying schizophrenia. *Schizophr. Bull.* 20:453–80

Walker E. 2002. Adolescent neurodevelopment and psychopathology. *Curr. Dir. Psychol. Sci.* 11:24–28

Walker E, Baum K, Diforio D. 1998. Developmental changes in the behavioral expression of the vulnerability for schizophrenia. See Lenzenweger & Dworkin 1998, pp. 469–91

Walker E, Cudeck R, Mednick SA, Schulsinger F. 1981. Effects of parental absence and institutionalization on the development of clinical symptoms in high-risk children. *Acta Psychiatr. Scand.* 63(2):95–109

Walker E, Diforio D. 1997. Schizophrenia: a neural diathesis-stress model. *Psychol. Rev.* 104:1–19

Walker E, Downey G, Bergman A. 1989. The effects of parental psychopathology and maltreatment on child behavior: a test of the diathesis-stress model. *Child Dev.* 60(1):15–24

Walker E, Grimes K, Davis D, Smith A. 1993. Childhood precursors of schizophrenia; facial expressions of emotion. *Am. J. Psychiatry* 150:1654–60

Walker E, Lewine RJ. 1990. Prediction of adult-onset schizophrenia from childhood home movies of the patients. *Am. J. Psychiatry* 147:1052–56

Walker E, Lewine RJ, Neumann C. 1996. Childhood behavioral characteristics and adult brain morphology in schizophrenia patients. *Schizophr. Res.* 22:93–101

Walker E, Lewis N, Loewy R, Paylo S. 1999. Motor functions and psychopathology. *Dev. Psychopathol.* 11:509–23

Walker E, Marwit S, Emory E. 1980. A cross-sectional study of emotion recognition in schizophrenics. *J. Abnorm. Psychol.* 89(3):428–36

Walker E, Savoie T, Davis D. 1994. Neuromotor precursors of schizophrenia. *Schizophr. Bull.* 20:441–52

Walker E, Walder D, Reynolds F. 2001. Developmental changes in cortisol secretion in normal and at-risk youth. *Dev. Psychopathol.* 13:719–30

Weinstein D, Diforio D, Schiffman J, Walker E, Bonsall B. 1999. Minor physical anomalies, dermatoglyphic asymmetries and cortisol levels in adolescents with schizotypal personality disorder. *Am. J. Psychiatry* 156:617–23

Weinstock M. 1996. Does prenatal stress impair coping and regulation of hypothalamic-pituitary-adrenal axis? *Neurosci. Biobehav. Rev.* 21:1–10

Welberg LA, Seckl JR. 2001. Prenatal stress, glucocorticoids and the programming of the brain. *J. Neuroendocrinol.* 2:113–28

Yung AR, Phillips LJ, McGorry PD, Hallgren MA, McFarlane CA, et al. 1998. Prediction of psychosis: a step towards indicated prevention of schizophrenia. *Br. J. Psychiatry* 172(Suppl. 33):14–20

Annu. Rev. Psychol. 2004. 55:431–61
doi: 10.1146/annurev.psych.55.090902.142033
First published online as a Review in Advance on October 6, 2003

Clinical Implications of Reinforcement as a Determinant of Substance Use Disorders

Stephen T. Higgins,[1,2] Sarah H. Heil,[1] and Jennifer Plebani Lussier[2]

[1]Department of Psychiatry and [2]Department of Psychology, University of Vermont, Burlington, Vermont 05401; email: stephen.higgins@uvm.edu

Key Words alternative reinforcers, behavioral economics, community reinforcement, contingency management, vouchers

■ **Abstract** Extensive scientific evidence indicates that reinforcement plays an important role in the genesis, maintenance, and recovery from substance use disorders. In this chapter, we review recent clinical research from laboratory, clinic, and naturalistic settings examining the role of reinforcement in substance use disorders. Well-controlled human laboratory studies are reviewed characterizing orderly interactions between the reinforcing effects of drugs and environmental context that have important implications for understanding risk factors for substance use disorders and for the development of efficacious interventions. Recent treatment-outcome studies on voucher-based contingency management and community reinforcement therapy are reviewed demonstrating how reinforcement and related principles can be used to improve outcomes across a wide range of different substance use disorders and populations. Overall, the chapter characterizes a vigorous area of clinical research that has much to contribute to a scientific analysis of substance use disorders.

CONTENTS

0066-4308/04/0204-0431$14.00

INTRODUCTION

One of the most important advances in the scientific analysis of substance use disorders was the discovery that they were subject to the laws of learning and conditioning. That advance came to the forefront in the 1960s and 1970s based on evidence from studies on drug self-administration in laboratory animals and treatment-outcome and laboratory studies conducted with substance abusers (see Bigelow & Silverman 1999).

The reinforcing effect of drugs in laboratory animals was studied as early as the 1940s (Spragg 1940), but two important developments in the 1960s allowed this research area to flourish. First, a technology was developed to deliver intravenous drug injections to awake laboratory animals able to press a lever or emit other responses (Thompson & Schuster 1964, Weeks 1962). This methodology allowed for the administration of rapidly delivered drug injections as behavioral consequences, which is important to effective operant conditioning. The seminal studies demonstrated that animals readily learned an arbitrary response that led to a drug injection (Thompson & Schuster 1964, Weeks 1962). The animals in these studies were made physically dependent through experimenter-administered drug exposure before commencing with the conditioning aspects of the study. Thus, such learning was interpretable as a product of negative reinforcement; that is, behavior strengthened by avoidance of or escape from an aversive state (i.e., the withdrawal syndrome). While demonstrating a role for conditioning in substance use, the information was also congruent with extant theories of substance use disorders that focused on physical dependence and tolerance as central explanatory factors (see Goldberg 1976). Soon thereafter, though, voluntary drug self-administration was established in laboratory animals that were not physically dependent (Deneau et al. 1969). This advance established that abused drugs functioned as unconditioned positive reinforcers in the same manner as food, water, and sex; that is, they increased the future probability of behavior that immediately preceded their delivery. Perhaps most striking was that positive reinforcement was capable of generating in normal laboratory animals the dangerous extremes in drug consumption characteristic of human substance use disorders. For example, monkeys given unconstrained opportunities to self-administer intravenous injections of cocaine consumed the drug to the exclusion of basic sustenance and, barring experimenter intervention, to the point of death (Aigner & Balster 1978, Johanson et al. 1976). The idea that abused drugs promoted repeated drug use by acting as positive reinforcers was not readily interpretable within extant theories of drug dependence and fostered new models of substance use disorders based on psychological principles coupled with those of general pharmacology (Schuster & Thompson 1969).

In the treatment arena, successful clinical trials with alcoholics and other substance abusers demonstrated the efficacy of interventions based explicitly on reinforcement principles (Hunt & Azrin 1973, Miller 1975, Sobell & Sobell 1973, Winett 1973), and clinical-laboratory studies demonstrated that the substance use of even severely dependent individuals was modifiable through the systematic use of reinforcement and punishment (e.g., Bigelow & Liebson 1973, Griffiths et al. 1976). Heated controversies emerged in the area of treatment-outcome research with alcoholics, relating mostly to appropriate treatment goals (complete abstinence versus controlled drinking; see Marlatt 1983). However, the empirical evidence that drug use even among severely dependent individuals was sensitive to reinforcement and punishment contingencies was never refuted.

The overarching importance of these scientific advances was that they situated substance use and related disorders within a body of extant psychological principles and processes that accounted for the continuum of substance use ranging from patterns of infrequent use with few problems to patterns of heavy use and many untoward consequences. Stated in its most parsimonious form the advances established that substance use in all its varieties is governed by the Law of Effect (Thorndike 1898), which is a conclusion that remains valid today. These advances also provided principles and methods for a rigorous experimental analysis of substance use disorders. In the animal laboratory, this scientific framework has maintained a central role in substance use research for the past approximately 40 years. The research has evolved to include sophisticated neuroscience, genetic, and pharmacological methods and concepts (Crabbe 2002, Everitt et al. 2001, Platt et al. 2002), but the central role ascribed to reinforcement in accounting for drug use has remained a constant.

The path of clinical research in substance use disorders has been different. For reasons that appear to be unrelated to any specific study or empirical development, explicit recognition and utilization of reinforcement principles in clinical research on substance abuse waned after the 1970s. That was especially true in the alcohol field where clinical studies on topics related to reinforcement principles largely disappeared. Clinical studies on reinforcement principles continued in the area of illicit drug abuse, although there too the scope of the research was more restricted than might have been expected from the advances discussed above. The influence of psychology's cognitive revolution on clinical research in this area is clear, especially in the areas of alcohol and tobacco research, and was no doubt influential in fostering this alternative path (e.g., Donovan & Marlatt 1980, Gottlieb et al. 1987). Another important contributor was the development of effective pharmacotherapies like methadone for heroin dependence and nicotine replacement products for cigarette smoking, although that is less responsible for trends in the alcohol field where efficacious pharmacotherapies are a more recent development.

Whatever the reasons may have been for the waning of clinical research on reinforcement principles, that trend has corrected itself. A vigorous resurgence of clinical research on reinforcement principles in substance use disorders began in the 1990s and continues today. As will be evident from the research described below, research on cocaine dependence has been influential in this development. In many ways, the recalcitrant nature of cocaine dependence created opportunities for the consideration of alternative views. The repeated failures of many different pharmacological and psychosocial treatments for cocaine dependence made it painfully obvious that no one theoretical camp had a lock on the answers to this problem. When within that context reinforcement-based contingency-management interventions were demonstrated to reliably increase cocaine abstinence in randomized clinical trials, a niche was created for that approach within cocaine and other substance abuse treatment-outcome research (see Higgins & Silverman 1999). Other conceptually related research examining drug reinforcement in the clinical laboratory setting paralleled these developments, including behavioral-economic and other behavioral choice research (see Bickel & Vuchinich 2000). The purpose of this chapter is to review this resurgence of clinical research on reinforcement principles in substance use disorders, including research in laboratory, clinic, and naturalistic settings. Only reports on controlled studies published in peer-reviewed journals since 1990 were included in the review.

CLINICAL RESEARCH ON THE ROLE OF REINFORCEMENT IN SUBSTANCE USE DISORDERS

Much of the research reviewed below can be broadly thought of as examining the influence of environmental context on the reinforcing effects of drugs. The research illustrates two main empirical generalizations about substance use that follow directly from the recognition that abused drugs function as reinforcers. First, drug use is a form of operant behavior that by definition is sensitive to environmental consequences. Second, the degree of control that drugs exert over behavior as reinforcers is malleable and dependent on environmental context. While seemingly simple, we believe the research below will show that understanding the nuances of these empirical generalizations has much to contribute to a scientific analysis of substance use disorders.

Laboratory Settings

DRUG SELF-ADMINISTRATION STUDIES   Experiments examining the influence of alternative, nondrug reinforcers on preference for cocaine use have provided helpful insights into the context-dependent nature of the reinforcing effects of drugs. In an initial experiment on this topic in humans, cocaine users made a series of choices between intranasally administered cocaine and placebo and subsequently between cocaine and varying amounts of money (Higgins et al. 1994a). During sessions comparing cocaine with placebo, subjects exclusively chose cocaine and they consumed all of the drug that was available to them. That outcome demonstrated cocaine's ability to function as a robust reinforcer. In subsequent sessions, subjects made exclusive choices between cocaine and varying amounts of money (Figure 1, *upper panel*). Within that context, choice of cocaine decreased as an orderly graded function of increasing value of the monetary option. That outcome demonstrated the malleability of cocaine's reinforcing effects, which were robust when the alternative was a placebo or little money, but relatively weak as the value of the monetary option increased.

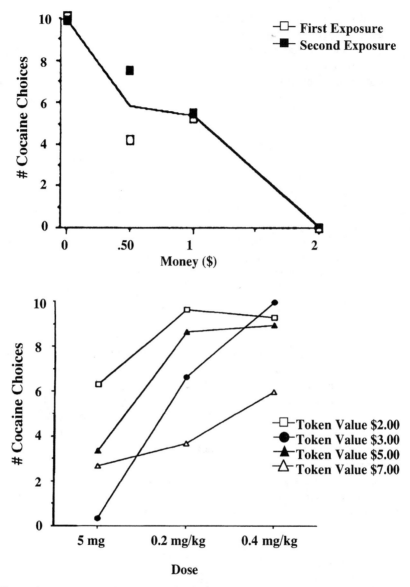

Figure 1 *Upper panel*: Number of cocaine choices as a function of the amount of money offered per choice as an alternative to cocaine. Subjects made a maximum of 10 choices between cocaine and money per session. Each monetary amount was tested twice, with the results from first and second tests shown by separate symbols and the mean of the two tests by the solid line. Reprinted from Higgins et al. 1994a with permission. *Lower panel:* Mean number of cocaine self-administrations per session (maximum = 10) are plotted as a function of cocaine dose for each of four prices of cocaine. Reprinted from Hatsukami et al. 1994 with permission.

This same functional relationship was subsequently demonstrated in studies using smoked and intravenous routes of cocaine administration, larger cocaine doses, and subjects with extensive histories of cocaine abuse and dependence (Donny et al. 2003, Dudish et al. 1996, Foltin & Fischman 1994, Hart et al. 2000, Hatsukami et al. 1994, Walsh et al. 2001). Shown in the lower panel of Figure 1, for example, are results from a study in which crack cocaine users made choices between retaining a token that could later be redeemed for cash or spending the token for an opportunity to smoke cocaine under medical supervision (Hatsukami et al. 1994). Token value ($2, $3, $5, $7) and cocaine dose (5 mg, 0.2 mg/kg, 0.4 mg/kg) were varied across sessions; the 5 mg dose served as a placebo. At the 5-mg dose, the greatest number of cocaine choices occurred at the lowest price ($2) token condition. At the 0.2-mg/kg dose the number of cocaine choices increased across all token prices, but the greatest still occurred at the lowest token price, the fewest at the highest ($7) token price, and intermediate levels at the intermediate ($3 and $5) token prices. When the dose was increased to 0.4 mg/kg, subjects chose almost the maximum number of cocaine administrations available at the $2, $3, and $5 token prices, demonstrating the robust reinforcing effects of that dose of smoked cocaine, but did not do so at the $7 token price. Indeed, the number of choices of the 0.4-mg/kg cocaine dose at the $7 token price was slightly below the number made for the placebo (5 mg) in the $2 token price condition. Similar effects also have been demonstrated with heroin in opiate-dependent subjects (Comer et al. 1997, 1998) and cigarette smoking among nicotine-dependent individuals (Bickel et al. 1995, 1997b; Tidey et al. 1999).

Another contextual factor not underscored by those studies but essential to understanding substance use disorders is the role of temporal delays. In naturalistic settings, individuals often make choices between using drugs in the present versus abstaining and experiencing positive consequences in the future. The following laboratory study with cigarette smokers examined how temporal delays influence the relationships between drug preference and alternative reinforcers (Roll et al. 2000). Regular cigarette smokers who had abstained from recent smoking for several hours made repeated choices between puffs on a cigarette available immediately and money that was available at varying values ($0.10–$2.00/choice) and after varying delays (end of the session, one week, and three weeks). Preference for the drug option decreased as an orderly, increasing function of the value of the monetary alternative consistent with the studies discussed above (larger values produced larger decreases in smoking), but as the delay interval increased, the influence of each of the alternative monetary values decreased significantly (Figure 2). The fundamental point of this study is that temporal delays diminish the ability of alternative, nondrug reinforcers to compete with the immediate reinforcing consequences of drug use.

Other variables also alter the influence of alternative reinforcers on drug self-administration. For example, an alternative source of nicotine enhances the ability of an alternative monetary reinforcer to decrease smoking (Bickel et al. 1997b), and pretreatment with alcohol (Higgins et al. 1996) diminishes the ability of

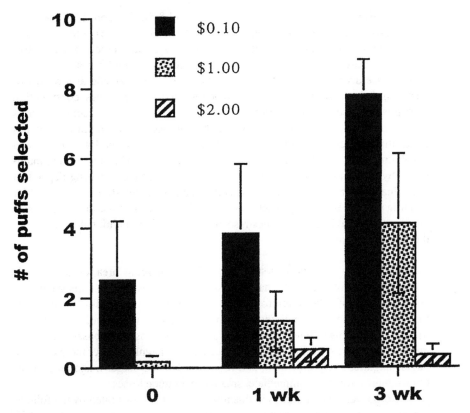

Figure 2   Mean number of choices for cigarette puff versus money in each session (maximum = 10) at one of three monetary values plotted as a function of delay interval between choosing and collecting the monetary option; brackets represent SEMs. Reprinted from Roll et al. 2000 with permission.

monetary reinforcement to decrease preference for cocaine reinforcement. Nondrug reinforcers can influence drug preference in other, less direct ways. For example, when drug use is associated with subsequent increased earnings on a performance task because of experimenter manipulation and not drug-produced enhancement of performance, future preference for drug use increases (see Alessi et al. 2002). Likewise, when drug use is associated with subsequent decreased earnings on the performance task, future preference for drug use decreases. The main point of this research is that not only the direct reinforcing effects of the drug influence the probability of future use, but also environmental consequences that occur while under the influence of the substance.

   The studies reviewed thus far have emphasized the influence of alternative reinforcers on preference for drug reinforcement. However, the relationships demonstrated in these studies can be thought of more generally in terms of constraints on drug use and other available alternatives (Bickel & DeGrandpre 1996). As constraints on drug consumption increase, either in terms of the price or effort required to obtain and use the substance or the quality and magnitude of the alternatives forfeited as a consequence of drug use, drug use decreases. Similarly, as constraints on drug use decrease, either because drugs are readily available at low cost or there is little in the way of alternatives to be forfeited by using drugs, consumption increases. Such sensitivity to price or cost factors is referred to in economic terms as the Law of Demand (Pearce 1986). Behavioral-economics research provides compelling evidence that drug consumption is sensitive to the Law of Demand (Chaloupka et al. 1999). That said, it is also the case that when responding maintained by drug and nondrug reinforcement has been compared in drug-dependent individuals, demand for drug is less sensitive (i.e., more inelastic) than demand for nondrug reinforcement (e.g., Bickel et al. 1997b). In the next section, we review a new area of behavioral-economics research that provides additional insights into these relationships.

DISCOUNTING OF DELAYED CONSEQUENCES   An emerging area of behavioral-economics research suggests that individuals with substance use disorders discount the value of delayed reinforcement and the severity of reinforcement losses to a greater extent than individuals without substance use disorders (Bickel & Marsch 2001). This difference can be summarized as substance abusers showing a greater preference for (a) more immediate, smaller magnitude over more delayed, larger magnitude reinforcement, and (b) more delayed, larger magnitude losses (punishment) over more immediate, smaller magnitude losses.

The procedures and findings in this research area are illustrated by the following study comparing delay discounting in 18 opiate-dependent outpatients and 38 community volunteers matched on age, gender, education, and IQ (Madden et al. 1997). Participants made a series of choices between two hypothetical monetary options or hypothetical drug options (patients only). The use of hypothetical events permitted the investigators to examine monetary amounts, drug doses, and temporal delays that otherwise would not be practically or ethically feasible. Monetary values were tested ranging from $1 to $1000; a similar number of heroin doses were studied in units comparable to the monetary values. Seven delay intervals were tested, ranging from one week to 25 years. Testing began with a choice between the highest values available immediately or following a one-week delay (e.g., $1000 now versus $1000 in one week). As expected, all subjects chose the immediate option. Next, the value of the immediate option was systematically decreased (e.g., $950 now versus $1000 in one week, $900 now versus $1000 in one week, and so on) until subjects indicated preferences across all monetary values, and then the process was repeated but in an ascending order. A record was made of the value at which a subject's preference switched between the immediate and delayed options in the descending and ascending progressions. An average of those two values was used to represent an indifference point where the immediate and delayed options were equivalent. The same series of descending and ascending choices was then repeated using another temporal delay (e.g., $1000 now versus $1000 in one month) until indifference points were established at all delay intervals.

Indifference points for money decreased in both populations as an orderly function of increasing delay interval, and the shapes of the discounting curves were hyperbolic rather than linear (Figure 3, *upper panel*). Delay discounting and the hyperbolic shape of the functions are basic characteristics of operant behavior that are seen in nonhumans and humans alike (Bickel & Marsch 2001). While both groups exhibited hyperbolic discounting, note that the curve of the opiate-dependent group was significantly steeper than the curve in the control group, especially during the initial 60 months. A comparison of discounting curves for heroin and money within the opiate-dependent group showed steep discounting curves for both types of reinforcement, but significantly more so for heroin than money (Figure 3, *lower panel*).

We identified 14 reports of original studies published in peer-reviewed journals characterizing delay discounting in individuals with substance use disorders. The studies reliably demonstrated greater discounting among substance abusers than controls. The results just outlined were replicated in another group of opiate-dependent outpatients using real rather than hypothetical money (K.N. Kirby et al. 1999), thereby supporting the validity of findings with hypothetical events. Other studies in the opiate-dependent population demonstrated that those who were willing to share needles in a vignette discounted money at higher rates than patients who were unwilling to share needles (Odum et al. 2000). Also, drug deprivation increased discounting of money and drugs compared to nondeprived conditions (Giordano et al. 2002).

These observations have been extended to other substance use disorders as well. With regard to alcohol, college students who reported heavy drinking with or without associated problems discounted hypothetical money more than light drinkers (Vuchinich & Simpson 1998), and actively using alcoholics discounted hypothetical money more than abstinent alcoholics and controls, with the abstinent alcoholics scoring intermediate to the other two groups (Petry 2001a).

Current cigarette smokers have been shown to discount hypothetical money more than never-smokers and ex-smokers, with no differences between the latter two groups (Bickel et al. 1999). Greater discounting occurs in smokers versus never-smokers whether the monetary consequences are hypothetical or real (Baker et al. 2003, Mitchell 1999).

Comorbid problems are also associated with increased discounting rates. Substance abusers (mixed group) with a gambling problem (Petry & Casarella 1999) or antisocial personality disorder (Petry 2002) discounted hypothetical money more than substance abusers without those additional problems. Also, gamblers with substance abuse discounted hypothetical money more than gamblers without substance abuse (Petry 2001b). Several of these reports replicated the finding that substance abusers discount delays involving drugs more than those involving money (e.g., Bickel et al. 1999, Petry 2001a).

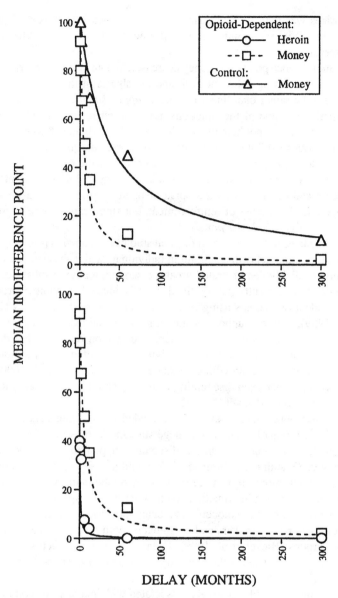

Figure 3 *Upper panel:* Median indifference points between large delayed and small immediate monetary reinforcement are shown as a function of delay duration for opioid-dependent patients and controls as a function of delay interval. *Lower panel:* Median indifference points between large delayed and small immediate monetary and heroin reinforcement for opioid-dependent patients as a function of delay interval. In upper and lower panels, Y axis represents percent choices for the large delayed reinforcer. Reprinted from Madden et al. 1997 with permission.

Whether the greater discounting rates observed among those with substance use disorders represents cause or consequence of the disorders is unknown. The studies showing no difference in discounting between ex-smokers and never-smokers and intermediate levels among abstinent alcoholics compared to active and nonalcoholics could mean that cessation of substance abuse restores discounting closer to normal levels or, alternatively, that recovery from substance use disorders is more likely among those who discount less (Bickel et al. 1999). The findings that substance abusers with antisocial personality disorder or gambling problems had higher discounting rates than substance abusers without those other problems suggest that the measure is capturing a characteristic that extends beyond the substance use disorders. The discounting measure overlaps with scores on impulsivity questionnaires, with modest but significant correlations between them having been noted in most of the above reports. The observation that drug deprivation increases discounting demonstrates that it is not a static phenomenon, as do the observations that drugs and money are discounted differently. This is an emerging area of investigation with many questions remaining to be answered. The studies reviewed provide strong evidence of increased discounting of delayed consequences among individuals with substance use disorders, and they provide potential insights into some reasons why those with more severe dependence or comorbid problems have poorer prognoses. Whether cause or consequence, this characteristic is an important one to consider in efforts to provide a scientific account of substance use disorders, as well as in efforts to treat and prevent them.

INFLUENCE OF ALTERNATIVE REINFORCERS IN NATURALISTIC SETTINGS   An emerging body of research focuses on assessing the influence of naturalistic sources of nondrug reinforcement and substance use disorders. These studies use a questionnaire called the Pleasant Events Schedule (PES), which was initially developed to investigate the role of naturalistic reinforcement density in the study of depression (MacPhillamy & Lewinsohn 1976). The PES is a self-rated behavioral inventory comprised of 320 items that are rated on a three-point scale regarding frequency of occurrence and the enjoyability of the activity during the past 30 days. For activities not engaged in during the past 30 days, subjects rate how enjoyable they anticipate it would have been had they engaged in it. Responses are summarized in 10 scales that were developed both rationally and empirically.

A seminal study using the PES with substance abusers involved a comparison of PES scores from 50 individuals enrolled in treatment for cocaine abuse/dependence and 50 community controls matched on sociodemographics (Van Etten et al. 1998). Cocaine abusers reported a lower frequency of specific types of activities compared to controls, including a lower frequency of nonsocial, introverted, and passive activities. Those differences between the scales remained significant even after controlling for demographics and other potential explanatory variables in multivariate analyses. Cocaine abusers generally did not differ significantly from the comparison group in enjoyability ratings, suggesting that the activities on which they differed in frequency had the potential to be reinforcing in the cocaine abusers had they engaged in them. Within the group of cocaine abusers, cocaine-negative urinalysis results (i.e., abstinence) during a 24-week treatment period were positively correlated with a higher frequency of nonsocial activities even after controlling for the influence of other potential explanatory variables.

The results from this study suggested that it was not the overall frequency of drug-free activities engaged in that differed between cocaine abusers and nonabusers or those with more severe dependence, but the frequency of particular types of activities. Those observations were replicated and extended in a study of binge drinking in 256 college students who completed the PES and other questionnaires regarding recent substance use (Correia et al. 2003). Binge drinkers reported a significantly lower frequency of nonsocial, introverted, and passive outdoor activities than the comparison group.

The PES was used to further examine relationships between substance use and other activities in college students (Correia et al. 1998, 2002) and psychiatric outpatients (Correia & Carey 1999). Subjects in these studies completed the PES twice, once regarding activities they engaged in while under the influence of substances (alcohol and illicit drugs, but excluding nicotine and caffeine) and the other regarding activities engaged in when sober. This permitted the investigators to derive summary measures of frequency and enjoyability ratings for activities engaged in while under the influence of substances (drug-related cross-product) and when sober (drug-free cross-product), and a ratio of the first two measures (drug-related cross-product divided by the sum of the drug-related and drug-free cross-products), resulting in what the investigators termed a reinforcement ratio. This reinforcement ratio was developed to examine predictions from Herrnstein's Matching Law, which is a general law specifying that operant behavior is distributed across multiple sources of reinforcement in proportion to the amount of reinforcement received from each option (Herrnstein 1970). Drug-related cross product and reinforcement ratio were significant predictors of the frequency of substance use in both studies involving college undergraduates (Correia et al. 1998, 2002) and the study in psychiatric outpatients (Correia & Carey 1999).

Considering results across all five studies, they suggest that a relatively low frequency of nonsocial activities and a greater ratio of drug-derived reinforcement as a proportion of all reinforcing activities predict greater substance use in those with substance use disorders as well as in heterogeneous samples of college students. The consistency of these observations across studies, substances, and populations, as well as the connection with a general law of operant conditioning and reinforcement theory, suggests that they may be important to understanding the determinants of substance use in clinic and other naturalistic settings.

EPIDEMIOLOGICAL EVIDENCE

The research reviewed above underscores a robust influence of environmental context on the reinforcing effects of drugs. An obvious question that follows from those observations is whether the epidemiological evidence on prevalence of substance use and related disorders is consistent with the empirical generalizations noted. Certainly, the laboratory studies would predict greater substance use among those with greater constraints on access to alternative, nondrug reinforcers. While surely open to alternative explanations, low socioeconomic status, low educational achievement, and unemployment are reliably associated with increased substance use, abuse, and dependence in the epidemiological literature, consistent with predictions of a reinforcement model.

Consider results from the most recent annual U.S. National Household Survey on Drug Abuse (NHSDA), which is conducted annually and assesses the prevalence of illicit and licit substance use and related disorders among a nationally representative sample of individuals aged 12 years and older (Substance Abuse & Mental Health Services Administration 2002). The survey does not examine socioeconomic status per se, but does examine associations between education and employment status and substance use. Regarding illicit drug use among adults (≥18 years), 4.3% of college graduates reported current use compared to 7.6% of those with less than a high school education. That difference is especially notable considering that lifetime prevalence of illicit drug use is higher in the college graduates (47.2% versus 32.0%). Similar patterns are observed with licit substances. With cigarette smoking, 13.8% of college graduates are current cigarette smokers compared to 33.8% of those with less than a high school education. Alcohol use is a bit more complicated, with 65.2% of college graduates versus 33.4% of those with less than high school being current drinkers. Among current drinkers, though, only 33% of college graduates report recent binge or heavy drinking compared to 66% of those with less than a high school education. If one considers education as a conduit to the monetary wealth necessary to access certain material alternatives and the skills needed to appreciate others (e.g., literature), then the results seem quite consistent with those from the laboratory studies described above.

The NHSDA evidence on associations between employment and substance use parallels that of education, and other epidemiological evidence is also consistent with the NHSDA findings. For example, risk for alcohol, tobacco, and other drug dependence is associated with lower annual income, educational level, and unemployment in the U.S. National Comorbidity Study (Anthony et al. 1994). Epidemiological research from outside of the United States has shown similar relationships between socioeconomic status and risk for substance use disorders (e.g., Poulton et al. 2002).

Treatment Settings

The largest area of investigation in this resurgence of research on reinforcement principles has involved their application to the treatment of substance use disorders. Treatment interventions based on reinforcement principles seek to (*a*) increase availability and reduce constraints on reinforcement derived from healthy alternatives to substance use, (*b*) increase constraints on reinforcement derived from substance use and the substance abusing lifestyle, and (*c*) configure these efforts to accommodate the shortened temporal horizons characteristic of substance use disorders. In this section, we discuss two types of efficacious interventions explicitly designed to accomplish those goals.

Contingency Management

Contingency management (CM) involves the systematic delivery of reinforcing or punishing consequences contingent on the occurrence of a target response, and the withholding of those consequences in the absence of the target response (Higgins & Silverman 1999). The CM intervention that has garnered the most research attention is one in which patients earn vouchers exchangeable for retail items contingent on recent drug abstinence. This treatment approach was initially developed as a novel method to manage cocaine dependence in outpatient settings (Higgins et al. 1991, 1993). A search of the literature from 1991 (publication of first voucher report) through March 2003 identified 55 reports of controlled studies published in peer-reviewed journals where vouchers or related monetary-based CM interventions were used to promote behavior change in persons with substance use disorders (Table 1). As is described in detail below, 85% (47/55) of the reports noted significant changes in at least one of the behaviors targeted by the CM intervention.

REINFORCING ABSTINENCE FROM COCAINE USE   We introduce the voucher intervention by briefly describing the initial randomized trial conducted with it (Higgins et al. 1993). In that study, vouchers were combined with intensive counseling based on the community reinforcement approach (CRA) (see below). The study involved a comparison of CRA plus vouchers versus standard care. The voucher program was implemented around a fixed schedule of urine-toxicology monitoring. Cocaine-negative specimens earned points that were recorded on vouchers and provided to patients. Points began at a low value ($2.50) and increased with each consecutive negative test result. A cocaine-positive result or failure to provide a scheduled specimen reset the voucher value back to the initial low value from which it could escalate again. No money was ever given to patients. Instead, points were used to purchase retail items, with clinic staff making all purchases. Maximum earnings possible across 12 weeks was $997.50 in purchasing power, with average earnings being approximately 60% of maximum.

Thirty-eight cocaine-dependent outpatients were randomized to one of the two treatments. As shown in Figure 4, cocaine abstinence levels in the two treatments were comparable at the start of treatment, but those receiving standard care soon either dropped out of treatment or continued using cocaine, while the majority of those assigned to CRA plus vouchers abstained from cocaine use. These results replicated those from an earlier nonrandomized trial (Higgins et al. 1991), and created considerable interest in dissociating the efficacy of vouchers from CRA. Two

TABLE 1 Voucher-based contingency management studies

Study	N	Gender	Voucher duration (weeks)	Setting	Design	Total possible earnings during voucher intervention	Voucher delivery	Positive outcome ($p \leq .05$)
COCAINE AND OPIATES								
Cocaine								
Higgins et al. 1991	25	M,F	12	DF	1[a,b]	$1038.00	I	Y
Higgins et al. 1993	38	M,F	12	DF	1[b]	$997.50	I	Y
Higgins et al. 1994b	40	M,F	12	DF	1	$997.50	I	Y
Silverman et al. 1996b	37	M[c]	12	M	2	$1155.00	I	Y
Shaner et al. 1997	2	M[c]	8	DF	4	$1000.00	I	Y
Silverman et al. 1998	59	M,F	12	M	2	$1950.00	I	Y
Elk et al. 1998	12	F	≥4	DF	1	≥$296.00	—	N
Kirby et al. 1998	23	M,F	12	DF	3	$420.00(CV1), $570.00(CV2)	I	Y
Silverman et al. 1999	29	M,F	9	M	4	$382.00(CV1), $3480.00(CV2)	I	Y
Higgins et al. 2000	70	M,F	12	DF	2	$997.50	I	Y
Robles et al. 2000	72	M,F	0.29	M	4	$100.00	D	Y
Jones et al. 2001	80	F	1	M	1	$385.00	I	Y
Preston et al. 2001	95	M,F	8	M	3	$554.00	D	Y
Rawson et al. 2002	120	M,F	16	M	1	$1277.50	I	Y
Katz et al. 2002b	40	M,F	1.57	M	4	$400.00	D	Y
Epstein et al. 2003	193	M,F	12	M	2	$1155.00	I	Y
Opiates								
Silverman et al. 1996c	13	M,F	12	M	4	$1155.00	I	Y
Bickel et al. 1997a	39	M,F	23	M	1[b]	$658.38	I	Y
Preston et al. 2000	120	M,F	8	M	2	$554.00	D	Y
Preston et al. 2002	110	M,F	12	M	2[b]	$360.00	D	Y[d]
Robles et al. 2002	48	M,F	22	M	2	$2232.00	I	Y
Cocaine and opiates								
Gruber et al. 2000	52	M,F	4	DF	1[b]	$320.00	I	Y
Jones et al. 2000	25	F	1	M	1	$85.00	I	N

(Continued)

TABLE 1 (Continued)

Study	N	Gender	Voucher duration (weeks)	Setting	Design	Total possible earnings during voucher intervention	Voucher delivery	Positive outcome ($p \leq .05$)
Dallery et al. 2001	15	M,F	9	M	4	$374.40(CV1), $3369.60(CV2)	I	Y
Silverman et al. 2001	40	F	24	M	1[b]	$283.00	I	Y
Katz et al. 2002a	52	M,F	12	DF	1	$1087.50	I	N
Petry & Martin 2002	42	M,F	12	M	1[b]	—	I	Y
Silverman et al. 2002	40	F	78	M	1[b]	$9197.50	I	Y
Polydrug								
Chang et al. 1992	12	F	≥9	M	1[a,b]	≥$135.00	—	N
Carroll et al. 1995	14	F	≥13	M	1[b]	≥$195.00	—	N
Iguchi et al. 1997	103	M,F	12	M	1	$180.00	D	Y[e]
Chutuape et al. 1999	14	M,F	12	M	1[b]	$900.00	D	Y
Piotrowski et al. 1999	102	M,F	17	M	1	$755.00	D	Y
Downey et al. 2000	41	M,F	12	M	2	$997.50	D	N
Carroll et al. 2001	127	M,F	12	M	1	$280.50	I	Y
Carroll et al. 2002	55	M,F	12	M	1	$280.80(CV1), $576.00(CV2)	I	N
Cigarette smoking								
Schmitz et al. 1995	5	M,F	2	M	5	$20.00	I	N
Roll et al. 1996	60	M,F	0.71	NTS	2	$147.50	I	Y
Roll et al. 1998	11	M,F[c]	0.71	NTS	2	$147.50	I	Y
Donatelle et al. 2000	220	F	≥20	DF	1	≥$250.00	D	Y
Roll & Higgins 2000	18	M,F	0.71	NTS	4	$147.00	I	Y
Corby et al. 2000	8	M,F[f]	0.71	NTS	4	$40.00	I	Y
Shoptaw et al. 2002	175	M,F	12	M	1	$447.50	I	Y
Tidey et al. 2002	14	M,F[c]	0.71	NTS	4	$147.50	I	Y
Heil et al. 2003	54	M,F	0.71	NTS	2	$147.50(CV1), $295.00(CV2)	I	Y
Alcohol and marijuana								
Alcohol								
Petry et al. 2000	42	M	8	DF	1	—	I	Y
Marijuana								
Budney et al. 1991	2	M	12	DF	4	$1038.24	I	Y

Study	N	Gender	Setting	Voucher duration	Design	Maximum voucher value	Voucher delivery	Positive outcome
Budney et al. 2000	60	M,F	DF	12	1	$570.00	I	Y
Sigmon et al. 2000	18	M[c]	NTS	5	5	$250.00(CV1), $500.00(CV2), $1000.00(CV3)	I	Y
OTHER TARGETS								
Attendance								
Silverman et al. 1996a	7	M, F	M	6	6	$631.00(CV1)	I	Y
Svikis et al. 1997	142	F	M/DF	1	1	$7.00(CV1), $35.00(CV2), $70.00(CV3)	D	Y
Jones et al. 2000	68	F	DF	1	1	$85.00	I	N
Jones et al. 2001	80	F	M	1	1	$140.00	I	Y
Petry et al. 2001	43	M,F	DF	7	4	—	I	Y
Medication compliance								
Preston et al. 1999	58	M,F	M	12	2	$1155.00	I	Y
Rigsby et al. 2000	55	M,F	M	4	1[b]	$280.00	D	Y
Carroll et al. 2001	127	M,F	M	12	1	$280.50	I	N
Carroll et al. 2002	55	M,F	M	12	1	$280.80(CV1), $576.00(CV2)	I	N
Productivity								
Wong et al. 2003	6	F	M	14	6[b]	—	I	Y

N = sample size, all groups combined. Gender: M = male, F = female. All participants in female-only studies are pregnant and postpartum. Voucher duration = number of weeks voucher intervention was in place. Setting = setting in which study occurred: DF = drug-free clinic, M = medication clinic, NTS = nontreatment setting. Medication clinics breakdown: 79% methadone (n = 27), 9% naltrexone (n = 3), 6% buprenorphine (n = 2), 3% antiretrovirals (n = 1), 3% antipsychotics (n = 1). Design = experimental design: 1 = contingent vouchers versus no voucher control, parallel groups; 2 = contingent vouchers versus noncontingent voucher control, parallel groups; 3 = contingent vouchers, different magnitudes or schedules, parallel groups; 4 = contingent vouchers versus no voucher control, within subject; 5 = contingent vouchers versus noncontingent voucher control, within subject; 6 = contingent vouchers, different magnitudes or schedules, within subject. Total possible earnings during voucher intervention = maximum monetary value that could be earned by the contingent voucher condition. If more than one contingent voucher (CV) schedule was used, total possible earnings of all the schedules equals the amount shown unless otherwise noted [i.e., $420 (CV1), $570 (CV2)]. Voucher delivery: I = immediate (at the same visit that a specimen was provided), D = delayed (at a visit after the specimen was provided). A dash (—) indicates insufficient information to determine. Positive outcome = a significant change was reported for the behavior targeted by the contingency management intervention: Y = yes, N = no.

[a]Nonrandom condition assignment.

[b]The effect of vouchers cannot be dissociated from other interventions.

[c]Mentally ill/schizophrenic.

[d]Based on induction × maintenance phase analyses.

[e]Based on the significant effect of increased treatment plan compliance on urinalysis results.

[f]Adolescents.

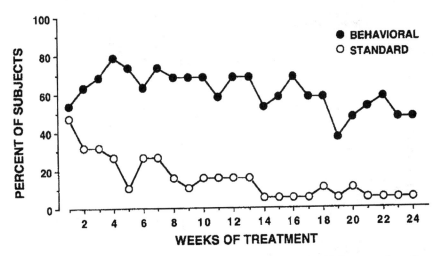

Figure 4 Percent of subjects abstinent from cocaine use in CRA + vouchers (behavioral) and standard (drug abuse counseling) conditions plotted as a function of consecutive treatment weeks. Reprinted from Higgins et al. 1993 with permission.

additional randomized trials by the same group isolated the efficacy of vouchers (Higgins et al. 1994b, 2000), and demonstrated that their effects could be discerned for at least 15 months after the end of the 12-week intervention.

A program of research by Silverman and colleagues replicated and extended those results to cocaine abuse among patients enrolled in methadone-maintenance treatment for opiate dependence (Silverman et al. 1996b, 1998, 1999). Results from the seminal randomized trial by this group comparing contingent voucher-based reinforcement to a noncontingent control condition are shown in Figure 5. Patients in both conditions tested positive for cocaine throughout a five-week baseline. Following implementation of the 12-week voucher intervention, cocaine abstinence increased substantially among those who received them contingent on abstinence, but not those who received them noncontingently. Abstinence decreased in the contingent group during a four-week postintervention period, although a treatment effect remained discernible.

Overall, our literature search identified 16 reports of controlled studies examining the efficacy of voucher-based interventions for increasing cocaine abstinence (Table 1). In 15 of the 16 studies (94%), the investigators reported significant increases in cocaine abstinence. In two trials, the effects of vouchers were not dissociated from CRA (Higgins et al. 1991, 1993), but in each of the other studies, the effects of vouchers on cocaine abstinence were experimentally demonstrated. An important current focus in this area of investigation is the development of less costly voucher models for use in community clinics, about which we say more below.

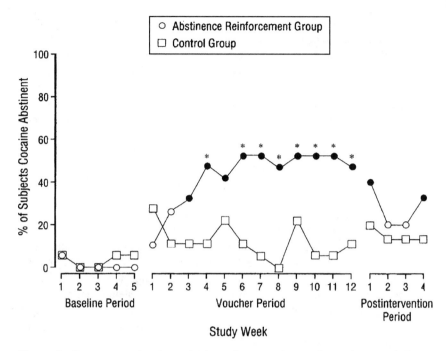

Figure 5 Percentage of patients abstinent from cocaine use in abstinence reinforcement and control groups during 21 consecutive study weeks. Abstinence-based reinforcement was available only during middle voucher period. Reprinted from Silverman et al. 1996b with permission.

REINFORCING OPIATE ABSTINENCE IN OPIATE-DEPENDENT OUTPATIENTS   Ongoing illicit opiate abuse is a problem in a subset of patients enrolled in methadone and buprenorphine (medication comparable to methadone) therapy. In three voucher trials conducted with patients enrolled in methadone-maintenance treatment (Preston et al. 2000, 2002; Silverman et al. 1996c) and two trials conducted with patients undergoing methadone (Robles et al. 2002) or buprenorphine (Bickel et al. 1997a) detoxification, opiate abstinence was significantly increased in the voucher condition (Table 1). In two trials, effects of vouchers were not dissociated from other interventions (Bickel et al. 1997a, Preston et al. 2002), but in each of the others the increases in abstinence were directly attributable to the vouchers.

REINFORCING ABSTINENCE FROM MULTIPLE DRUGS IN OPIATE-DEPENDENT OUT-PATIENTS   We identified 15 reports involving studies on the efficacy of voucher-based contingencies targeting abstinence from two or more substances. Five of the seven (71%) studies targeting abstinence from cocaine and opiates produced positive outcomes. In at least one of the studies with negative outcomes, the reason appeared to be an insufficient magnitude of reinforcement for the amount of behavior change targeted (Jones et al. 2000). That study involved pregnant methadone-maintenance patients who could earn $5/day in vouchers by attending a comprehensive day program and providing cocaine- and opiate-negative urine specimens. Another study involving women from this same comprehensive clinic produced significant increases in cocaine and opiate abstinence, but the women could earn up to $27/day in vouchers by abstaining from cocaine and opiate use and completing a three-hour vocational training session (Silverman et al. 2001). In an interesting innovation, women in the experimental condition in this later study continued to earn vouchers for abstinence and completing vocational tasks for three years, and those in the control group continued to be followed as well (Silverman et al. 2002). Significant increases in cocaine and opiate abstinence were sustained across the three-year period, which is a substantial accomplishment in this population of severely dependent women.

One of the other reports of a positive outcome in this group of studies targeting cocaine and opiate abstinence also merits comment (Petry & Martin 2002). The purpose of this study was to examine whether cocaine and opiate abstinence could be achieved using an overall lower value voucher system. Contingent on submitting cocaine and opiate-negative specimens, patients earned opportunities to make draws from a fishbowl containing slips of paper with values listed on them ranging from no value to $100 by abstaining from cocaine and opiates. Slips of paper that had monetary value were exchanged for retail items kept onsite at the clinic. The cost was kept low by including a larger number of slips with no and low value than slips with high value. Compared to a no-incentive control condition, subjects randomized to the incentive condition achieved significantly longer durations of continuous abstinence from cocaine and opiates during treatment and six months of follow-up. Total value of earnings in the incentive condition was $137 or approximately one fifth of the usual voucher earnings. This creative variation is now undergoing multisite testing in the National Institute on Drug Abuse's Clinical Trials Network.

Among the eight studies targeting simultaneous abstinence from three or more drugs, only four (50%) produced positive outcomes (Table 1). This inverse, graded relationship between the number of drugs targeted by the contingency and the number of trials achieving positive outcomes is not likely a chance phenomenon. There is little question that the value of vouchers is a relevant factor in CM interventions (Dallery et al. 2001, Silverman et al. 1999; but see Carroll et al. 2001). Those studies in which simultaneous abstinence from multiple substances has been achieved involved relatively large voucher values (Silverman et al. 2001, 2002), a combination of incentives for abstinence and compliance with medication to increase abstinence (Carroll et al. 2001), or a creative reinforcement schedule (Petry & Martin 2002, Piotrowski et al. 1999). There is no evidence that the higher rates of success in studies targeting single substances is accounted for by patients substituting other drug use to compensate for giving up the targeted drug.

REINFORCING ABSTINENCE FROM CIGARETTE SMOKING   We identified nine voucher-based CM studies focused on abstinence from cigarette smoking, with eight of the studies reporting positive outcomes (Table 1). Studies in this area can be divided into (*a*) treatment-outcome studies, (*b*) studies conducted with smokers not seeking treatment to assess the feasibility of the approach to a new population or questions about the scheduling of vouchers, and (*c*) studies where CM was used as a tool to examine another topic (e.g., nicotine withdrawal).

An important treatment-outcome study on smoking cessation involved the use of voucher-based contingencies to increase cigarette smoking abstinence during pregnancy and postpartum (Donatelle et al. 2000). There has been a long-standing ceiling in the cessation rates achieved in this population at between 12% and 18%. In the Donatelle et al. trial, 220 pregnant smokers were randomly assigned to receive a smoking-cessation self-help kit only or the kit plus vouchers contingent on biochemically verified smoking abstinence. Those in the voucher condition had a significant other (SO) participate with them as a support person. Costs for the vouchers ($50.00 per monthly test for smokers and $25.00 for SOs) were covered through donations from community businesses and organizations. Smoking cessation rates at end of pregnancy were 32% versus 9% in the voucher and control conditions and 21% versus 6% at the two-month postpartum assessment. The other treatment-outcome trial also produced positive outcomes in a difficult-to-treat subset of smokers, opiate-dependent patients (Shoptaw et al. 2002).

Two of the feasibility studies demonstrated the efficacy of CM for increasing brief smoking abstinence (five days) in schizophrenic cigarette smokers (Roll et al. 1998, Tidey et al. 2002), and a third study did so in adolescent smokers (Corby et al. 2000). Similar brief smoking abstinence studies demonstrated the greater efficacy of the escalating schedule of reinforcement with a rest contingency used in the majority of voucher studies reviewed above compared to a fixed rate of reinforcement (Roll & Higgins 2000, Roll et al. 1996). A final study using the same general approach demonstrated the value of CM as a research tool for investigating nicotine withdrawal in outpatients (Heil et al. 2003). Studies characterizing the nicotine withdrawal syndrome without the use of CM often require participants to reside on a residential research ward to prevent smoking.

REINFORCING ABSTINENCE FROM ALCOHOL OR MARIJUANA USE   The fishbowl procedure described above was first reported as an efficacious intervention for increasing treatment retention and alcohol abstinence in the only voucher-based study on that substance (Petry et al. 2000). Each of the trials examining the efficacy of voucher-based CM for increasing marijuana abstinence produced positive outcomes (Budney et al. 1991, 2000; Sigmon et al. 2000).

REINFORCING OTHER THERAPEUTIC GOALS   In addition to reinforcing abstinence, voucher-based CM has been utilized to enhance medication compliance and other outcomes among individuals with substance use disorders. We identified ten reports; seven of the ten studies (70%) resulted in positive outcomes. Vouchers were efficacious for increased compliance with naltrexone therapy in one trial (Preston et al. 1999) and antiretroviral therapy in another (Rigsby et al. 2000). In two additional trials, voucher-based increases in naltrexone compliance approached statistical (p < 0.10) significance (Carroll et al. 2001, 2002). Other applications have involved increasing clinic attendance among pregnant substance abusers (Svikis et al. 1997), attendance at an HIV drop-in center (Petry et al. 2001), and attendance (Silverman et al. 1996a) and productivity (Wong et al. 2003) at vocational training in methadone-maintenance patients. Other instances of negative outcomes involved clinic attendance in the comprehensive care clinic for pregnant abusers mentioned above, where vouchers appeared to be too low and the schedule too simplistic relative to the therapeutic target (Jones et al. 2000, Svikis et al. 1997).

Community Reinforcement Approach

CRA was first developed for treatment of alcoholism (Hunt & Azrin 1973) and later adapted for use with cocaine-dependent (Higgins et al. 1991) and opiate-dependent (Bickel et al. 1997a) outpatients. CRA seeks to facilitate therapeutic change by manipulating naturalistic reinforcement contingencies. The specific content of CRA varies depending on the clinical population and individual patient needs, but usually has several key components. (*a*) Barriers to treatment engagement such as pending legal matters, homelessness, or other crises are addressed in the initial sessions. (*b*) Unemployed individuals or those with jobs that put them at risk for substance abuse are provided vocational counseling (e.g., Job Club, see Azrin & Besalel 1980). (*c*) Patients are taught how to identify antecedents and consequences of substance abuse, and how to minimize contact with the antecedents of substance use and find healthy substitutes for the positive consequences derived from substance use. (*d*) Behavioral therapy for couples is often provided. (*e*) Individualized skills training is provided to remedy deficits that either interfere with achieving abstinence or increase relapse risk (e.g., drug refusal, social skills, and mood management training). (*f*) Disulfiram therapy is used for those with alcohol problems along with a protocol to monitor and support medication compliance. CRA therapist manuals are available for cocaine (Budney & Higgins 1998) and alcohol (Meyers & Smith 1995) dependence.

CRA has also been adapted for use with SOs of treatment-resistant substance abusers (K.C. Kirby et al. 1999, Meyers et al. 2002, Miller et al. 1999). In those applications, CRA includes education about substance use disorders, information and discussion of the positive consequences of not drinking, assistance with engaging the designated patient and the SO in healthy recreational and social activities, and training in how to manage instances of substance use by the designated patient and how to recommend treatment entry.

We are aware of 11 controlled studies published in peer-reviewed journals since 1990 on the use of CRA, 8 involving treatment of patients with substance use disorders and 3 with SOs of treatment-resistant patients. Six of the trials with patients involved CRA combined with vouchers, five with cocaine-dependent outpatients

(Higgins et al. 1991, 1993, 1994b, 2000, 2003), and one with opiate-dependent outpatients (Bickel et al. 1997a). Each of those trials produced significantly better treatment outcomes than the comparison conditions (drug abuse counseling or CRA without contingent vouchers) (e.g., see Figure 4).

Only one of the CRA plus vouchers trials involved an experimental design that isolated the contribution of CRA to outcome (Higgins et al. 2003). In that trial with 100 cocaine-dependent outpatients, combining CRA with vouchers increased treatment retention, increased cocaine abstinence during treatment but not follow-up, decreased drinking to intoxication during treatment and posttreatment follow-up, and improved employment and other measures of psychosocial functioning during treatment and follow-up compared to vouchers only.

CRA alone was shown to increase opiate abstinence in methadone-maintenance patients (Abbott et al. 1998). As noted above, the original series of studies on CRA were conducted with alcoholics. A more recent study extended the efficacy of CRA to the treatment of homeless alcohol-dependent men and women (Smith et al. 1998). In that study, CRA produced greater reductions in drinking throughout a one-year study period compared to standard care. Each of the three trials examining the efficacy of CRA for assisting SOs facilitate treatment entry in treatment-resistant individuals with substance use disorders have produced positive results (K.C. Kirby et al. 1999, Meyers et al. 2002, Miller et al. 1999).

SUMMARY/CONCLUSIONS

An extensive body of empirical evidence has accumulated over more than 40 years that reinforcement processes play a central role in the genesis, maintenance, and recovery from substance use disorders. In the animal laboratory, there has been a productive program of uninterrupted research examining the influence of reinforcement on various aspects of substance use and related disorders. In the clinical arena, research on the role of reinforcement principles in substance use and related disorders has had a less continuous path, but has again been vigorously and productively pursued during the past decade or so.

Research in the clinical laboratory has outlined relationships between drug use and environmental context that we believe are critical to understanding risk factors for substance use disorders. The research demonstrates that human substance use, even in the most virulent forms such as smoked or intravenous cocaine and heroin use by dependent individuals conforms to predictions of reinforcement theory. Research on the influence of alternative, nondrug reinforcers on drug use, temporal delays and temporal discounting, and molar relations between the reinforcement obtained through substance use as a proportion of overall reinforcement rates offers new insights into how abused substances control human behavior. Additionally, the observations are framed in terms of principles and concepts that have continuity across species and most can be modeled in the animal laboratory. To be sure, there may be some features of substance use disorders that are uniquely human, but probably not the core controlling principles and processes.

The treatment-outcome research reviewed in this chapter outlines how reinforcement principles can be effectively applied to improve clinical outcomes. CM and CRA have been demonstrated to be reliably efficacious across a broad array of different types of substance use disorders and populations, including some of the most treatment-refractory subgroups. This research, particularly the studies with pregnant women, also provides an interesting opportunity for some theoretical considerations. The fact that a pregnant woman would discontinue substance use when offered a voucher for doing so, but not to improve the health of her fetus is perplexing. After all, the vouchers are worth a pittance relative to the value of a healthy baby. Yet, when considered in light of the information covered in this chapter the behavior becomes more understandable. First, consider the fact that the women in question are overwhelmingly of lower socioeconomic status. As such, they likely have relatively fewer healthy sources of alternative reinforcement competing for their behavior compared to women that are more affluent. Second, the benefits to the health of the fetus of quitting substance use are not going to be experienced by the mother in any direct way for several months. Temporal delays weaken the influence of behavioral consequences. Third, the women are drug dependent, which is associated with increased discounting of delayed consequences. Thus, the weakening of delayed consequences is going to be greater than average in these women. Fourth, initial cessation of drug use will increase physical discomfort within several hours or days due to nicotine or other drug withdrawal. Not only does the woman have to forgo substance-produced reinforcement, she also has to make herself physically uncomfortable. Fifth, drug use will result in positive reinforcement within seconds, compounded by similarly rapid-onset relief from withdrawal if in the early stages of a cessation effort. When looked at in this way, rather than perplexing, the efficacy of vouchers seems reasonable and predictable. The vouchers likely provide a bridge of smaller, immediate reinforcers to the larger, delayed reinforcer of a healthy baby, while also changing the ratio of reinforcement derived from drug versus nondrug activities. The fact that reinforcement theory can offer a conceptual framework for understanding a perplexing phenomenon like substance abuse by pregnant women along with a practical intervention for treating the problem is a strong testimonial to the utility of the theory.

In closing, we think this chapter outlines some important recent developments in the area of clinical research on substance use disorders. The research reviewed suggests to us that continuing to examine how reinforcement principles and related processes operate in all aspects of human substance use has much to contribute to a scientific analysis of substance use disorders.

ACKNOWLEDGMENTS

Preparation of this manuscript was supported by research grants DA06113, DA14028, and DA08076, and Training Award DA07242 from the National Institute on Drug Abuse. We thank Warren K. Bickel for comments on the manuscript and Laurianne Verret for assistance in preparing figures and tables.

The *Annual Review of Psychology* is online at http://psych.annualreviews.org

LITERATURE CITED

Abbott PJ, Weller SB, Delaney HD, Moore BA. 1998. Community reinforcement approach in the treatment of opiate addicts. *Am. J. Drug Alcohol Abuse* 24:17–30

Aigner TG, Balster RL. 1978. Choice behavior in rhesus monkeys: cocaine vs. food. *Science* 201:534–35

Alessi SM, Roll JM, Reilly MP, Johanson CE. 2002. Establishment of a diazepam preference in human volunteers following a differential-conditioning history of placebo versus diazepam choice. *Exp. Clin. Psychopharmacol.* 10(2):77–83

Anthony JC, Warner LA, Kessler RC. 1994. Comparative epidemiology of dependence on tobacco, alcohol, controlled substances, and inhalants: basic findings from the National Comorbidity Survey. *Exp. Clin. Psychopharmacol.* 2(3):244–68

Azrin N, Besalel VA. 1980. *Job Club Counselor's Manual.* Baltimore, MD: Univ. Press

Baker F, Johnson MW, Bickel WK. 2003. Delay discounting differs between current and never-smokers across commodities, sign, and magnitudes. *J. Abnorm. Psychol.* 112:382–92

Bickel WK, Amass L, Higgins ST, Badger GJ, Esch RA. 1997a. Effects of adding behavioral treatment to opioid detoxification with buprenorphine. *J. Consult. Clin. Psychol.* 65(5):803–10

Bickel WK, DeGrandpre RJ. 1996. Modeling drug abuse policy in the behavioral economics laboratory. In *Advances in Behavioral Economics,* ed. L Green, J Kagel, 3:69–95. New York: Ablex

Bickel WK, DeGrandpre RJ, Higgins ST. 1995. The behavioral economics of concurrent drug reinforcers: a review and reanalysis of drug self-administration research. *Psychopharmacology* 118:250–59

Bickel WK, Madden GJ, DeGrandpre RJ. 1997b. Modeling the effects of combined behavioral-pharmacological treatment on cigarette smoking: behavioral-economic analyses. *Exp. Clin. Psychopharmacol.* 5:334–43

Bickel WK, Marsch LA. 2001. Toward a behavioral economic understanding of drug dependence: delay discounting processes. *Addiction* 96:73–86

Bickel WK, Odum AL, Madden GJ. 1999. Impulsivity and cigarette smoking: delay discounting in current, never, and ex-smokers. *Psychopharmacology* 146:447–54

Bickel WK, Vuchinich RE, eds. 2000. *Reframing Health Behavior Change With Behavioral Economics.* Mahwah, NJ: Erlbaum. 416 pp.

Bigelow GE, Liebson I. 1973. Behavioral contingencies controlling alcoholics' drinking. *Alcoholism* 9:24–28

Bigelow GE, Silverman K. 1999. Theoretical and empirical foundations of contingency management treatments for drug abuse. See Higgins & Silverman 1999, pp. 15–31

Budney AJ, Higgins ST. 1998. *Treating Cocaine Addiction: A Community Reinforcement Plus Vouchers Approach.* Rockville, MD: NIDA

Budney AJ, Higgins ST, Delaney DD, Kent L, Bickel WK. 1991. Contingent reinforcement of abstinence with individuals abusing cocaine and marijuana. *J. Appl. Behav. Anal.* 24(4):657–65

Budney AJ, Higgins ST, Radonovich KJ, Novy PL. 2000. Adding voucher-based incentives to coping skills and motivational enhancement improves outcomes during treatment for marijuana dependence. *J. Consult. Clin. Psychol.* 68(6):1051–61

Carroll KM, Ball SA, Nich C, O'Connor PG, Eagan DA, et al. 2001. Targeting behavioral therapies to enhance naltrexone treatment of opioid dependence: efficacy of contingency management and significant other involvement. *Arch. Gen. Psychiatry* 58(8):755–61

Carroll KM, Chang G, Behr HM, Clinton

B, Kosten TR. 1995. Improving treatment outcome in pregnant, methadone-maintained women: results from a randomized clinical trial. *Am. J. Addict.* 4:56–59

Carroll KM, Sinha R, Nich C, Babuscio T, Rounsaville BJ. 2002. Contingency management to enhance naltrexone treatment of opioid dependence: a randomized clinical trial of reinforcement magnitude. *Exp. Clin. Psychopharmacol.* 10(1):54–63

Chaloupka FJ, Grossman M, Bickel WK, Saffer H. 1999. Introduction. In *The Economic Analysis of Substance Use and Abuse: An Integration of Economic and Behavioral Economic Research,* ed. FJ Chaloupka, M Grossman, WK Bickel, H Saffer, pp. 1–12. Chicago, IL: Univ. Chicago Press

Chang G, Carroll KM, Behr HM, Kosten TR. 1992. Improving treatment outcome in pregnant opiate-dependent women. *J. Subst. Abuse Treat.* 9(4):327–30

Chutuape MA, Silverman K, Stitzer ML. 1999. Contingent reinforcement sustains post-detoxification abstinence from multiple drugs: a preliminary study with methadone patients. *Drug Alcohol Depend.* 54(1):69–81

Comer SD, Collins ED, Fischman MW. 1997. Choice between money and intranasal heroin in morphine-maintained humans. *Behav. Pharmacol.* 8(8):677–90

Comer SD, Collins ED, Wilson ST, Donovan MR, Foltin RW, Fischman MW. 1998. Effects of an alternative reinforcer on intravenous heroin self-administration by humans. *Eur. J. Pharmacol.* 345(1):13–26

Corby EA, Roll JM, Ledgerwood DM, Schuster CR. 2000. Contingency management interventions for treating the substance abuse of adolescents: a feasibility study. *Exp. Clin. Psychopharmacol.* 8:371–76

Correia CJ, Carey KB. 1999. Applying behavioral theories of choice to substance use in a sample of psychiatric outpatients. *Psychol. Addict. Behav.* 13(3):207–12

Correia CJ, Carey KB, Borsari B. 2002. Measuring substance-free and substance-related reinforcement in the natural environment. *Psychol. Addict. Behav.* 16(1):28–34

Correia CJ, Carey KB, Simons J, Borsari BE. 2003. Relationships between binge drinking and substance-free reinforcement in a sample of college students. A preliminary investigation. *Addict. Behav.* 28(2):361–68

Correia CJ, Simons J, Carey KB, Borsari BE. 1998. Predicting drug use: application of behavioral theories of choice. *Addict. Behav.* 23(5):705–9

Crabbe JC. 2002. Genetic contributions to addiction. *Annu. Rev. Psychol.* 53:435–62

Dallery J, Silverman K, Chutuape MA, Bigelow GE, Stitzer ML. 2001. Voucher-based reinforcement of opiate plus cocaine abstinence in treatment-resistant methadone patients: effects of reinforcer magnitude. *Exp. Clin. Psychopharmacol.* 9(3):317–25

Deneau G, Yanagita T, Seevers MH. 1969. Self-administration of psychoactive substances by the monkey. *Psychopharmacology* 16(1):30–48

Donatelle RJ, Prows SL, Champeau D, Hudson D. 2000. Randomized controlled trial using social support and financial incentives for high risk pregnant smokers: significant other supporter (SOS) program. *Tob. Control* 9(Suppl. III):67–69

Donny EC, Bigelow GE, Walsh SL. 2003. Choosing to take cocaine in the human laboratory: effects of cocaine dose, interchoice interval, and magnitude of alternative reinforcement. *Drug Alcohol Depend.* 69(3):289–301

Donovan DM, Marlatt GA. 1980. Assessment of expectancies and behaviors associated with alcohol consumption. A cognitive-behavioral approach. *J. Stud. Alcohol* 41(11):1153–85

Downey KK, Helmus TC, Schuster CR. 2000. Treatment of heroin-dependent poly-drug abusers with contingency management and buprenorphine maintenance. *Exp. Clin. Psychopharmacol.* 8(2):176–84

Dudish SA, Pentel PR, Hatsukami DK. 1996. Smoked cocaine self-administration in females. *Psychopharmacology* 123(1):79–87

Elk R, Mangus L, Rhoades H, Andres R, Grabowski J. 1998. Cessation of cocaine use during pregnancy: effects of contingency management interventions on maintaining abstinence and complying with prenatal care. *Addict. Behav.* 23(1):57–64

Epstein DH, Hawkins WE, Covi L, Umbricht A, Preston KL. 2003. Cognitive-behavioral therapy plus contingency management for cocaine use: findings during treatment and across 12-month follow-ups. *Psychol. Addict. Behav.* 17(1):73–82

Everitt BJ, Dickinson A, Robbins TW. 2001. The neuropsychological basis of addictive behaviour. *Brain Res. Brain Res. Rev.* 36(2–3):129–38

Foltin RW, Fischman MW. 1994. Effect of buprenorphine on the self-administration of cocaine by humans. *Behav. Pharmacol.* 5(1):79–89

Giordano LA, Bickel WK, Loewenstein G, Jacobs EA, Marsch L, Badger GJ. 2002. Mild opioid deprivation increases the degree that opioid-dependent outpatients discount delayed heroin and money. *Psychopharmacology* 163:174–82

Goldberg SR. 1976. The behavioral analysis of drug addiction. In *Behavioral Pharmacology*, ed. SD Glick, J Goldfarb, pp. 283–316. St. Louis, MO: Mosby

Gottlieb AM, Killen JD, Marlatt GA, Taylor CB. 1987. Psychological and pharmacological influences in cigarette smoking withdrawal: effects of nicotine gum and expectancy on smoking withdrawal symptoms and relapse. *J. Consult. Clin. Psychol.* 55(4):606–8

Griffiths RR, Bigelow GE, Liebson I. 1976. Human sedative self-administration: effects of interingestion interval and dose. *J. Pharmacol. Exp. Ther.* 197(3):488–94

Gruber K, Chutuape MA, Stitzer ML. 2000. Reinforcement-based intensive outpatient treatment for inner-city opiate abusers: a short-term evaluation. *Drug Alcohol Depend.* 57(3):211–23

Hart CL, Haney M, Foltin RW, Fischman MW. 2000. Alternative reinforcers differentially modify cocaine self-administration by humans. *Behav. Pharmacol.* 11(1):87–91

Hatsukami DK, Thompson TN, Pentel PR, Flygare BK, Carroll ME. 1994. Self-administration of smoked cocaine. *Exp. Clin. Psychopharmacol.* 2(2):115–25

Heil SH, Tidey JW, Holmes HW, Badger GJ, Higgins ST. 2003. A contingent payment model of smoking cessation: effects on abstinence and withdrawal. *Nicotine Tob. Res.* 5:205–13

Herrnstein RJ. 1970. On the law of effect. *J. Exp. Anal. Behav.* 13:243–66

Higgins ST, Bickel WK, Hughes JR. 1994a. Influence of an alternative reinforcer on human cocaine self-administration. *Life Sci.* 55:179–87

Higgins ST, Budney AJ, Bickel WK, Foerg FE, Donham R, Badger GJ. 1994b. Incentives improve outcome in outpatient behavioral treatment of cocaine dependence. *Arch. Gen. Psychiatry* 51(7):568–76

Higgins ST, Budney AJ, Bickel WK, Hughes JR, Foerg F, Badger G. 1993. Achieving cocaine abstinence with a behavioral approach. *Am. J. Psychiatry* 150(5):763–69

Higgins ST, Delaney DD, Budney AJ, Bickel WK, Hughes JR, et al. 1991. A behavioral approach to achieving initial cocaine abstinence. *Am. J. Psychiatry* 148(9):1218–24

Higgins ST, Roll JM, Bickel WK. 1996. Alcohol pretreatment increases preference for cocaine over monetary reinforcement. *Psychopharmacology* 123:1–8

Higgins ST, Sigmon SC, Wong CJ, Heil SH, Badger GJ, et al. 2003. Community reinforcement therapy for cocaine-dependent outpatients. *Arch. Gen. Psychiatry.* In press

Higgins ST, Silverman K, eds. 1999. *Motivating Behavior Change Among Illicit Drug Abusers.* Washington, DC: APA

Higgins ST, Wong CJ, Badger GJ, Ogden DE, Dantona RL. 2000. Contingent reinforcement increases cocaine abstinence during outpatient treatment and 1 year of follow-up. *J. Consult. Clin. Psychol.* 68(1):64–72

Hunt GM, Azrin NH. 1973. A community-reinforcement approach to alcoholism. *Behav. Res. Ther.* 11(1):91–104

Iguchi MY, Belding MA, Morral AR, Lamb

RJ, Husband SD. 1997. Reinforcing operants other than abstinence in drug abuse treatment: an effective alternative for reducing drug use. *J. Consult. Clin. Psychol.* 65(3):421–28

Johanson CE, Balster RL, Bonese K. 1976. Self-administration of psychomotor stimulant drugs: the effects of unlimited access. *Pharmacol. Biochem. Behav.* 4(1):45–51

Jones HE, Haug N, Silverman K, Stitzer ML, Svikis D. 2001. The effectiveness of incentives in enhancing treatment attendance and drug abstinence in methadone-maintained pregnant women. *Drug Alcohol Depend.* 61(3):297–306

Jones HE, Haug N, Stitzer ML, Svikis D. 2000. Improving treatment outcomes for pregnant drug-dependent women using low-magnitude voucher incentives. *Addict. Behav.* 25(2):263–67

Katz EC, Chutuape MA, Jones HE, Stitzer ML. 2002a. Voucher reinforcement for heroin and cocaine abstinence in an outpatient drug-free program. *Exp. Clin. Psychopharmacol.* 10(2):136–43

Katz EC, Robles-Sotelo E, Correia CJ, Silverman K, Stitzer ML, Bigelow GE. 2002b. The brief abstinence test: effects of continued incentive availability on cocaine abstinence. *Exp. Clin. Psychopharmacol.* 10(1):10–17

Kirby KC, Marlowe DB, Festinger DS, Garvey KA, La Monaca V. 1999. Community reinforcement training for family and significant others of drug abusers: a unilateral intervention to increase treatment entry of drug users. *Drug Alcohol Depend.* 56(1):85–96

Kirby KC, Marlowe DB, Festinger DS, Lamb RJ, Platt JJ. 1998. Schedule of voucher delivery influences initiation of cocaine abstinence. *J. Consult. Clin. Psychol.* 66(5):761–67

Kirby KN, Petry NM, Bickel WK. 1999. Heroin addicts discount delayed rewards at higher rates than non-drug using controls. *J. Exp. Psychol. Gen.* 128:78–87

MacPhillamy DJ, Lewinsohn PM. 1976. *Manual for the Pleasant Events Schedule.* Eugene: Univ. Oregon

Madden GJ, Petry N, Badger G, Bickel WK. 1997. Impulsive and self-control choices in opioid-dependent subjects and non-drug using controls: drug and monetary rewards. *Exp. Clin. Psychopharmacol.* 5:256–62

Marlatt GA. 1983. The controlled-drinking controversy: a commentary. *Am. Psychol.* 38(10):1097–110

Meyers RJ, Miller WR, Smith JE, Tonigan JS. 2002. A randomized trial of two methods for engaging treatment-refusing drug users through concerned significant others. *J. Consult. Clin. Psychol.* 70(5):1182–85

Meyers RJ, Smith JE. 1995. *Clinical Guide to Alcohol Treatment: The Community Reinforcement Approach.* New York: Guilford. 211 pp.

Miller PM. 1975. A behavioral intervention program for chronic public drunkenness offenders. *Arch. Gen. Psychiatry* 32:915–18

Miller WR, Meyers RJ, Tonigan JS. 1999. Engaging the unmotivated in treatment for alcohol problems: a comparison of three strategies for intervention through family members. *J. Consult. Clin. Psychol.* 67:688–97

Mitchell SH. 1999. Measures of impulsivity in cigarette smokers and non-smokers. *Psychopharmacology* 146:455–64

Odum AL, Madden GJ, Badger GJ, Bickel WK. 2000. Needle sharing in opioid-dependent outpatients: psychological processes underlying risk. *Drug Alcohol Depend.* 60(3):259–66

Pearce DW, ed. 1986. *The MIT Dictionary of Modern Economics.* Cambridge, MA: MIT Press. 3rd ed.

Petry NM. 2001a. Delay discounting of money and alcohol in actively using alcoholics, currently abstinent alcoholics, and controls. *Psychopharmacology* 154(3):243–50

Petry NM. 2001b. Pathological gamblers, with and without substance use disorders, discount delayed rewards at high rates. *J. Abnorm. Psychol.* 110(3):482–87

Petry NM. 2002. Discounting of delayed rewards in substance abusers: relationship to antisocial personality disorder. *Psychopharmacology* 162(4):425–32

Petry NM, Casarella T. 1999. Excessive discounting of delayed rewards in substance abusers with gambling problems. *Drug Alcohol Depend.* 56(1):25–32

Petry NM, Martin B. 2002. Low-cost contingency management for treating cocaine- and opioid-abusing methadone patients. *J. Consult. Clin. Psychol.* 70(2):398–405

Petry NM, Martin B, Cooney JL, Kranzler HR. 2000. Give them prizes, and they will come: contingency management for treatment of alcohol dependence. *J. Consult. Clin. Psychol.* 68(2):250–57

Petry NM, Martin B, Finocche C. 2001. Contingency management in group treatment: a demonstration project in an HIV drop-in center. *J. Subst. Abuse Treat.* 21(2):89–96

Piotrowski NA, Tusel DJ, Sees KL, Reilly PM, Banys P, et al. 1999. Contingency contracting with monetary reinforcers for abstinence from multiple drugs in a methadone program. *Exp. Clin. Psychopharmacol.* 7(4):399–411

Platt DM, Rowlett JK, Spealman RD. 2002. Behavioral effects of cocaine and dopaminergic strategies for preclinical medication development. *Psychopharmacology* 163(3–4):265–82

Poulton R, Caspi A, Milne BJ, Thomson WM, Taylor A, et al. 2002. Association between children's experience of socioeconomic disadvantage and adult health: a life-course study. *Lancet* 360(9346):1640–45

Preston KL, Silverman K, Umbricht A, DeJesus A, Montoya ID, Schuster CR. 1999. Improvement in naltrexone treatment compliance with contingency management. *Drug Alcohol Depend.* 54(2):127–35

Preston KL, Umbricht A, Epstein DH. 2000. Methadone dose increase and abstinence reinforcement for treatment of continued heroin use during methadone maintenance. *Arch. Gen. Psychiatry* 57(4):395–404

Preston KL, Umbricht A, Epstein DH. 2002. Abstinence reinforcement maintenance contingency and one-year follow-up. *Drug Alcohol Depend.* 67(2):125–37

Preston KL, Umbricht A, Wong CJ, Epstein DH. 2001. Shaping cocaine abstinence by successive approximation. *J. Consult. Clin. Psychol.* 69(4):643–54

Rawson RA, Huber A, McCann M, Shoptaw S, Farabee D, et al. 2002. A comparison of contingency management and cognitive-behavioral approaches during methadone maintenance treatment for cocaine dependence. *Arch. Gen. Psychiatry* 59(9):817–24

Rigsby MO, Rosen MI, Beauvis JE, Cramer JA, Rainey PM, et al. 2000. Cue-dose training with monetary reinforcement: pilot study of an antiretroviral adherence intervention. *J. Gen. Intern. Med.* 15:841–47

Robles E, Silverman K, Preston KL, Cone EJ, Katz E, et al. 2000. The brief abstinence test: voucher-based reinforcement of cocaine abstinence. *Drug Alcohol Depend.* 58(1–2):205–12

Robles E, Stitzer ML, Strain EC, Bigelow GE, Silverman K. 2002. Voucher-based reinforcement of opiate abstinence during methadone detoxification. *Drug Alcohol Depend.* 65(2):179–89

Roll JM, Higgins ST. 2000. A within-subject comparison of three different schedules of reinforcement of drug abstinence using cigarette smoking as an exemplar. *Drug Alcohol Depend.* 58:103–9

Roll JM, Higgins ST, Badger GJ. 1996. An experimental comparison of three different schedules of reinforcement of drug abstinence using cigarette smoking as an exemplar. *J. Appl. Behav. Anal.* 29:495–505

Roll JM, Higgins ST, Steingard S, McGinley M. 1998. Use of monetary reinforcement to reduce the cigarette smoking of persons with schizophrenia: a feasibility study. *Exp. Clin. Psychopharmacol.* 6:157–61

Roll JM, Reilly MP, Johanson CE. 2000. The influence of exchange delays on cigarette versus money choice: a laboratory analog of voucher-based reinforcement therapy. *Exp. Clin. Psychopharmacol.* 8(3):366–70

Schmitz JM, Rhoades H, Grabowski J. 1995. Contingent reinforcement for reduced carbon monoxide levels in methadone maintenance patients. *Addict. Behav.* 20(2):171–79

Schuster CR, Thompson T. 1969. Self administration of and behavioral dependence on drugs. *Annu. Rev. Pharmacol.* 9:483–502

Shaner A, Roberts LJ, Eckman TA, Tucker DE, Tsuang JW, et al. 1997. Monetary reinforcement of abstinence from cocaine among mentally ill patients with cocaine dependence. *Psychiatr. Serv.* 48(6):807–10

Shoptaw S, Rotheram-Fuller E, Yang X, Frosch D, Nahom D, et al. 2002. Smoking cessation in methadone maintenance. *Addiction* 97(10):1317–28

Sigmon SC, Steingard S, Badger GJ, Anthony SL, Higgins ST. 2000. Contingent reinforcement of marijuana abstinence among individuals with serious mental illness: a feasibility study. *Exp. Clin. Psychopharmacol.* 8(4):509–17

Silverman K, Chutuape MA, Bigelow GE, Stitzer ML. 1996a. Voucher-based reinforcement of attendance by unemployed methadone patients in a job skills training program. *Drug Alcohol Depend.* 41(3):197–207

Silverman K, Chutuape MA, Bigelow GE, Stitzer ML. 1999. Voucher-based reinforcement of cocaine abstinence in treatment-resistant methadone patients: effects of reinforcement magnitude. *Psychopharmacologia* 146(2):128–38

Silverman K, Higgins ST, Brooner RK, Montoya ID, Cone EJ, et al. 1996b. Sustained cocaine abstinence in methadone maintenance patients through voucher-based reinforcement therapy. *Arch. Gen. Psychiatry* 53(5):409–15

Silverman K, Svikis D, Robles E, Stitzer ML, Bigelow GE. 2001. A reinforcement-based therapeutic workplace for the treatment of drug abuse: six-month abstinence outcomes. *Exp. Clin. Psychopharmacol.* 9(1):14–23

Silverman K, Svikis D, Wong CJ, Hampton J, Stitzer ML, Bigelow GE. 2002. A reinforcement-based therapeutic workplace

for the treatment of drug abuse: three-year abstinence outcomes. *Exp. Clin. Psychopharmacol.* 10(3):228–40

Silverman K, Wong CJ, Higgins ST, Brooner RK, Montoya ID, et al. 1996c. Increasing opiate abstinence through voucher-based reinforcement therapy. *Drug Alcohol Depend.* 41(2):157–65

Silverman K, Wong CJ, Umbricht-Schneiter A, Montoya ID, Schuster CR, Preston KL. 1998. Broad beneficial effects of cocaine abstinence reinforcement among methadone patients. *J. Consult. Clin. Psychol.* 66(5):811–24

Smith JE, Meyers RJ, Delaney HD. 1998. The community reinforcement approach with homeless alcohol-dependent individuals. *J. Consult. Clin. Psychol.* 66:541–48

Sobell MB, Sobell LC. 1973. Alcoholics treated by individualized behavior therapy: one year treatment outcome. *Behav. Res. Ther.* 11(4):599–618

Spragg SDS. 1940. Morphine addiction in chimpanzees. *Comp. Psychol. Monogr.* 15(7):132

Substance Abuse and Mental Health Services Administration. 2002. *Results from the 2001 National Household Survey on Drug Abuse: Volume I. Summary of National Findings.* Off. Appl. Stud., NHSDA Ser. H-17, DHHS Publ. No. SMA 02–3758. Rockville, MD

Svikis DS, Lee JH, Haug NA, Stitzer ML. 1997. Attendance incentives for outpatient treatment: effects in methadone- and nonmethadone-maintained pregnant drug-dependent women. *Drug Alcohol Depend.* 48(1):33–41

Thompson T, Schuster CR. 1964. Morphine self-administration, food-reinforced, and avoidance behaviors in rhesus monkeys. *Psychopharmacology* 5:87–94

Thorndike EL. 1898. Animal intelligence: an experimental study of the associative processes in animals. *Psychol. Rev. Mon. Suppl.* 2:4

Tidey JW, Higgins ST, Bickel WK, Steingard S. 1999. Effects of response requirement and the availability of an alternative reinforcer on cigarette smoking by schizophrenics. *Psychopharmacology* 145:52–60

Tidey JW, O'Neill SC, Higgins ST. 2002. Effects of contingent monetary reinforcement and transdermal nicotine on smoking in schizophrenics. *Exp. Clin. Psychopharmacol.* 10(3):241–47

Van Etten ML, Higgins ST, Budney AJ, Badger GJ. 1998. Comparison of the frequency and enjoyability of pleasant events in cocaine abusers vs. non-abusers using a standardized behavioral inventory. *Addiction* 93(11):1669–80

Vuchinich RE, Simpson CA. 1998. Hyperbolic temporal discounting in social drinkers and problem drinkers. *Exp. Clin. Psychopharmacol.* 6(3):292–305

Walsh SL, Geter-Douglas B, Strain EC,

Bigelow GE. 2001. Enadoline and butorphanol: evaluation of kappa-agonists on cocaine pharmacodynamics and cocaine self-administration in humans. *J. Pharmacol. Exp. Ther.* 299(1):147–58

Weeks JR. 1962. Experimental morphine addiction: methods for autonomic intravenous injects in unrestrained rats. *Science* 138:143–44

Winett RA. 1973. Parameters of deposit contracts in the modification of smoking. *Psychol. Rec.* 23(1):49–60

Wong CJ, Sheppard JM, Dallery J, Bedient G, Robles E, et al. 2003. Effects of reinforcer magnitude on data-entry productivity in chronically unemployed drug abusers participating in a therapeutic workplace. *Exp. Clin. Psychopharmacol.* 11(1):46–55

Annu. Rev. Psychol. 2004. 55:463–91
doi: 10.1146/annurev.psych.55.090902.142054
First published online as a Review in Advance on September 29, 2003

MOTIVATIONAL INFLUENCES ON CIGARETTE SMOKING

Timothy B. Baker,[1] Thomas H. Brandon,[2] and Laurie Chassin[3]

[1]Department of Psychology, University of Wisconsin, and Center for Tobacco Research & Intervention, University of Wisconsin Medical School, Madison, Wisconsin 53711; email: tbb@ctri.medicine.wisc.edu
[2]Department of Psychology and H. Lee Moffitt Cancer Center & Research Institute, University of South Florida, Tampa, Florida 33620; email: brandont@moffitt.usf.edu
[3]Psychology Department, Arizona State University, Tempe, Arizona 85287–1104; email: laurie.chassin@asu.edu

Key Words tobacco, addiction, drug use, nicotine, dependence

■ **Abstract** Cigarette smoking is a leading cause of mortality and morbidity and a particularly common and intractable addictive disorder. Research shows that nicotine is a sine qua non of tobacco addiction and that it produces the hallmark effects of addictive drugs: sensitization, tolerance, physical dependence, and euphoria/elation. Research on the development of smoking reveals that although smoking prevalence has declined from a peak in the mid-1990s, close to 30% of twelfth graders still smoke. Smoking in adolescents is related to development of physical dependence, ethnicity, impulsivity, affective disorder, and peer influences. However, which of these exerts the greatest causal effects is unknown, and their influence no doubt varies across individuals and across development. Once dependence on tobacco smoking is established, evidence suggests that tobacco motivation is strongly influenced by a reduction in withdrawal symptoms, an expectation of stress reduction, and conditioned reinforcement. Nicotine motivation may also be influenced by modulation in stimulus incentive value.

CONTENTS

0066-4308/04/0204-0463$14.00

INTRODUCTION

Cigarette smoking is of great importance. First, it has great societal and clinical importance since it is the leading preventable cause of morbidity and mortality in developed countries (Peto et al. 1992). It is a major cause of cardiac disease, vascular disease, pulmonary disease, and a variety of cancers. Second, cigarette smoking is ubiquitous; about a quarter of all adult Americans smoke cigarettes, and smoking rates are higher in many other countries (CDC Prev. 1999). Finally, cigarette smoking is a prototypic addictive disorder manifesting classic features such as tolerance, withdrawal, and use despite high personal cost. Therefore, if we can discover the causal mechanisms that yield cigarette addiction, this may elucidate causal mechanisms in other addictive disorders.

The present review attempts to provide basic information on the nature of cigarette smoking and its natural history and features. However, the focus of this review is on possible motivational influences on the development and maintenance of smoking. In the first section of this chapter we describe age-related trends in smoking, factors that have been thought to influence its development or uptake, and evidence that youth smoking is associated with a true physical dependence or addiction.

In the second section, we describe the characteristics of heavy, dependent smoking, and review theories and data pertaining to its motivational basis. For instance, we review evidence that dependence on cigarettes might be due to their impact on weight regulation, their cognitive effects, their euphoriant or direct pleasurable effects, their impact on withdrawal symptoms, or their impact on affective reactions to stressors. In reviewing topics in this chapter, we attempt to evaluate the quality of evidence relevant to each topic, identify challenges or constraints that limit inference, and synthesize data with theory.

THE DEVELOPMENT OF TOBACCO SMOKING

Epidemiology of Cigarette Smoking and Tobacco Dependence Among U.S. Youth

PREVALENCE AND TRENDS OVER TIME   National epidemiological data on adolescent tobacco use have been collected using school-based surveys (e.g., Monitoring the Future or MTF, Johnston et al. 2002) and household surveys (e.g., National Household Survey on Drug Abuse or NHSDA, Koppstein 2001). The most recent data suggest that adolescent smoking is fairly common, with 27% of twelfth graders, 18% of tenth graders, and 11% of eighth graders reporting smoking in the past month (Johnston et al. 2002).

This level of smoking prevalence represents a decline from recent peaks in the mid-1990s. Since national surveillance began, there have been significant shifts over time in the prevalence of adolescent smoking. Adolescent smoking increased in the late 1960s (especially among females), peaked in the mid-1970s, and then declined in the late 1970s and 1980s (especially for African Americans; Giovino 1999, Johnston et al. 2002). New increases began in the early 1990s (for both African American and white adolescents) until the mid-1990s, and since then there has been a downturn (Johnston et al. 2002). These dynamic shifts in smoking prevalence are likely driven by complex social forces including changes in the social images of smoking, and changes in price and availability.

Compared to adolescent smoking, much less is known about the epidemiology of adolescent tobacco dependence. "Dependence" is a construct that shares much in common with everyday or prosaic notions of "addiction." Thus, in the Diagnostic and Statistical Manual (DSM) of the American Psychiatric Association (American Psychiatric Association 1994), a diagnosis of dependence requires at least three of seven criteria. These criteria include tolerance and withdrawal, but neither is necessary for the diagnosis. "Tolerance" refers to a decrease in drug effects as a function of repeated use. "Withdrawal" refers to the occurrence of a well-characterized syndrome upon discontinuation of drug use (i.e., falling levels of drug in the body). The other five DSM criteria are that (*a*) the substance is taken in larger amounts or over a longer period of time than was intended, (*b*) the user desires to cut down or control use, or was unable to do so, (*c*) a great deal of time is spent obtaining, using, or recovering from the substance, (*d*) other important activities are compromised due to substance use, and (*e*) use is continued despite knowledge of problematic consequences. Thus, the dependent individual's motivation to use a substance dominates other common motivational tendencies and normal activities.

Dependence per se can be distinguished from "physical dependence": the latter is said to occur when an organism has used sufficient drug so that withdrawal symptoms will be observed should drug use be discontinued or reduced. Thus, physical dependence is a state whose existence is inferred from the observation of withdrawal symptoms once drug use ceases.

In general, adolescent smokers are less likely to be diagnosed with tobacco dependence than are adult smokers (Colby et al. 2000a), although many adolescent smokers consider themselves addicted. Kandel & Chen (2000) used a proxy measure to approximate DSM-IV diagnoses in the NHSDA data. By these criteria, 28.5% of 12- to 17-year-old current smokers (smoking in the past month) would be considered dependent. Dependent adolescents report many of the same symptoms as do dependent adults, including craving, withdrawal, tolerance, and a desire to cut down on smoking (Colby et al. 2000a,b). Compared to adults, adolescents at the same level of self-reported intake were more likely to be diagnosed as dependent, which suggests that adolescents may be especially vulnerable to dependence or sensitive to the effects of nicotine (Kandel & Chen 2000). An important goal of research in this area is the development of valid measures of adolescent tobacco dependence as the extant adult measures may be inappropriate for youths (Colby et al. 2000a,b).

DEMOGRAPHIC CORRELATES   Demographic correlates of smoking suggest possible influences on smoking development. Greater parental education is associated with less likelihood of smoking in offspring (Giovino 1999). In addition, girls appear more influenced by peer smoking than are boys (Hu et al. 1995, Mermelstein 1999). There are large differences in smoking as a function of race/ethnicity, with the highest smoking rates among American Indian/Alaska Native adolescents, followed by whites and then Hispanics, and the lowest rates among Asians and African Americans. These race/ethnicity differences are seen in both school-based and household surveys, so they are not due to differential school attendance (USDHHS 1998), and they are not eliminated when a bioassay is used to validate self-reported smoking (Giovino 1999).

Although studies that sample multiple ethnic groups are still comparatively few and recent, there have been some suggestions that African American and Asian American adolescents report stronger antismoking socialization messages from parents, and that African American parents report feeling particularly empowered to influence their children's smoking (for reviews, see Mermelstein 1999, USDHHS 1998). Perhaps the most replicated race/ethnicity difference is that peer smoking is a relatively weak predictor of adolescent smoking for African American compared to white adolescents (Griesler & Kandel 1998, Mermelstein 1999).

Age Trends and Age-Related Smoking Trajectories

Smoking shows systematic age-related trends, with use peaking at ages 18–25. Retrospective data from the NHSDA suggest that the average age of first use of cigarettes is 15.4 (11–15 in the MTF data), with the average age of daily use being 18 (Koppstein 2001). Retrospective data from the National Comorbidity Study suggest that the onset of nicotine dependence lags at least one year after the onset of daily smoking (Breslau et al. 2001). After the mid-twenties, declines in smoking occur but these declines are modest in comparison to other forms of substance use, perhaps because cigarette smoking is highly addictive, legal, and not immediately performance-impairing (Chassin et al. 2000).

In addition to limitations associated with the retrospective nature of these data, the data are limited in that they describe a single "average" trajectory of age-related changes in smoking, which obscures substantial heterogeneity among subgroups. Recent advances in mixture modeling (Muthen & Muthen 2000) have allowed a small number of longitudinal studies to identify multiple age-related trajectories of smoking behavior (Chassin et al. 2000, Colder et al. 2001, White et al. 2002). These multiple trajectories have included an early-onset group (onset at ages 12–13) that shows a steep rise to heavy smoking; a late-onset group (onset after age 15) that smokes at more moderate levels; an experimenter group that tries smoking in adolescence but does not proceed to daily smoking and is developmentally limited to adolescence; and a group that quits smoking. This approach of distinguishing among smoking trajectories is an important methodological advance because it has the potential to illuminate diverse etiological pathways underlying different trajectories of tobacco use.

Not only is it important to distinguish among multiple developmental trajectories into tobacco dependence but, within any single trajectory, it may be necessary to characterize smoking as a series of stages that have distinct determinants of movement across them (Mayhew et al. 2000). Even if distinct trajectories can be identified among adolescent tobacco users, it is clear that, at least in the United States, chronic tobacco use typically has pediatric origins. This raises the possibility that adolescence is a time when the individual has a heightened vulnerability to tobacco dependence or reward. Such a conjecture is supported by recent animal research showing that adolescent rats acquire nicotine self-administration behaviors much more readily than adults (Belluzzi et al. 2001, Levin et al. 2003). These findings suggest that processes involved in central nervous system development and maturation may play a critical role in the etiology of tobacco use and dependence.

INDIVIDUAL PERSONALITY AND PSYCHOPATHOLOGY   A large literature has linked adolescent tobacco use to intrapersonal characteristics such as temperament, personality, and psychopathology. Perhaps the most replicated finding is that characteristics that reflect behavioral "undercontrol," including sensation seeking and impulsivity (Masse & Tremblay 1997), rebelliousness (Burt et al. 2000), and conduct disorder (McMahon 1999), prospectively predict smoking onset. Adolescents who are "disinhibited" and "deviance prone" are more likely to engage in a variety of correlated "risky" behaviors including smoking and other substance use (Turbin et al. 2000). Less is known about the mechanisms that underlie the relations between these characteristics and tobacco use (McMahon 1999) although adolescents who are "undercontrolled" and impulsive are also more likely to affiliate with substance-using peers (Lynskey et al. 1998). They may also be less likely to consider the long-term negative consequences of smoking, and more likely to smoke as a way to attain adultlike status (Jessor & Jessor 1977).

Another understudied but important question is the relation of comorbidity to adolescent tobacco use (McMahon 1999). For example, the relation between attention deficit hyperactivity disorder (ADHD) and adolescent substance use is generally weakened or eliminated when co-occurring conduct disorder is considered (Flory & Lynam 2003). For cigarette smoking, the data are more conflicting. Although some studies find no correlations between ADHD and smoking in the absence of conduct disorder in clinical (Barkley et al. 1990, Burke et al. 2001) or community samples (Lynskey & Fergusson 1995), other studies have found unique relations between ADHD and smoking above and beyond conduct disorder (Burke et al. 2001, Disney et al. 1999). A link between ADHD and cigarette smoking raises the possibility that smoking can serve to self-medicate attentional deficits among those with ADHD (Flory & Lynam 2003). In support of this hypothesis, Molina & Pelham (2003) recently reported that it is the inattention symptoms of ADHD, as opposed to impulsivity-hyperactivity symptoms, that are most highly associated with later cigarette smoking.

Compared to externalizing characteristics and disorders, the link between internalizing characteristics and disorders and adolescent smoking is less clear and consistent (McMahon 1999). Depressive disorders show unique relations to adolescent smoking, after controlling for other psychiatric disorders both cross-sectionally (Costello et al. 1999) and prospectively (Brown et al. 1996), and early depressive symptoms uniquely and prospectively predict smoking onset (Fleming et al. 2002). However, childhood anxiety disorders do not show those unique relations, and are associated with later smoking onset (Costello et al. 1999). Moreover, harm avoidance in kindergarten is associated with less likelihood of adolescent smoking (Masse & Tremblay 1997). Perhaps anxious children are more concerned with the negative consequences of smoking or rule breaking in general, or are less likely to spend time in peer networks that promote smoking. However, at later ages and stages of smoking, anxiety may motivate heavy smoking and raise risk for the development of nicotine dependence.

Attitudinal/cognitive risk factors   Adolescents form beliefs and attitudes about the effects of smoking before experimenting with it, and these attitudes and beliefs prospectively predict both the onset (Chassin et al. 1984, Conrad et al. 1992) and escalation (Andrews & Duncan 1998) of smoking. However, existing studies of smoking attitudes use explicit measures, which are limited by social desirability biases and people's lack of awareness of their underlying attitudes. Implicit methods for measuring attitudes have recently been developed (Greenwald et al. 1998), but are only now being applied to smoking research (Sherman et al. 2003).

Researchers have questioned whether adolescents are deterred from smoking because of their beliefs in its negative consequences, particularly when these negative consequences may not occur until years after smoking initiation. Not only do individuals generally discount the value of long-term outcomes in health decision-making (Ortendahl & Fries 2002), but adolescents have shown steeper temporal discounting rates than adults (Green et al. 1994). Moreover, many adolescent smokers do not believe there are health risks in "the first few years" (Slovic 2000), and may believe that they will stop smoking before damage is done (Arnett 2000).

There is also some debate about whether adolescents accurately perceive the risks of smoking (Romer & Jamieson 2001). This question is complex, and has produced varying answers depending on factors such as whether risk perceptions are assessed in terms of accuracy of absolute judgments or in terms of risks to people in general versus personalized risk to the self (Millstein & Halpern-Felsher 2002, Weinstein 1999).

Existing evidence suggests that both adolescents and adults show unrealistic optimism about the personalized risks of smoking (Arnett 2000, Weinstein 1999). Thus, it is unclear whether adolescents are any more likely than are adults to underestimate the personalized risks of smoking (Quadrel et al. 1993). The one available longitudinal study found that beliefs in the personalized risks of smoking declined during the middle school years and began to increase in the high school years (above and beyond the effects of smoking behavior; Chassin et al. 2002). Moreover, value on health as an outcome declined during the high school years and did not begin to increase until early adulthood. These data suggest that adolescence is a period of increased cognitive vulnerability to smoking, based both on decreasing perceptions of the personalized risks of smoking and decreasing values on health as an outcome.

Even if adolescents hold strong beliefs in the negative outcomes of smoking, the influence of these beliefs on behavior may be outweighed by the perceived benefits of smoking (Millstein & Halpern-Felsher 2002). One perceived benefit is that it communicates a social image of precocity and adultlike status (Jessor & Jessor 1977). In general, the social image of an adolescent smoker is an ambivalent one, with negative aspects (e.g., unhealthy, foolish) but also images of toughness, sociability, and precocity that may be particularly valued by "deviance-prone" adolescents who are at risk to smoke (Barton et al. 1982). Similarity between self-image and these smoker images have prospectively predicted smoking onset (Aloise-Young et al. 1996).

In addition to expressing a social image of toughness, sociability, and precocity, some adolescents may be influenced by their beliefs that smoking can control body weight. Weight concern, dieting, and the belief that smoking can control body weight have been shown to predict prospectively smoking initiation among adolescent girls, but not boys (Austin & Gortmaker 2001) and these beliefs are held more often by white girls than by African Americans (Klesges et al. 1997). In fact, smoking does suppress body weight (Williamson et al. 1991), which makes this attitude particularly difficult to counter.

In summary, studies of cognitive models of adolescent smoking have supported the influence of beliefs and attitudes, and have been important for antismoking interventions and public policy. However, they have been limited by a reliance on explicit measures of attitudes, they have not yet considered the implications of attitudinal ambivalence, and they have not considered the full complexity of risk perceptions (including a lack of longitudinal studies of age differences). Finally, these cognitive models may be incomplete in that they do not account for the role of affect at the time of decision-making (Loewenstein et al. 2001).

SOCIAL AND CONTEXTUAL INFLUENCES   There has been longstanding research interest in social influences on adolescent smoking (particularly parent and peer influences), which has recently been combined with a focus on macrolevel contextual variables (e.g., neighborhood effects, effects of taxation, advertising, and youth access), which are of interest because of their public policy implications.

Peer smoking is the most consistently identified predictor of adolescent smoking (Conrad et al. 1992, Derzon & Lipsey 1999). The magnitude of self-reported cross-sectional correlations between peer smoking and adolescent smoking is somewhat inflated because it reflects both the actual effects of peer influence as well as the effects of peer selection (i.e., adolescents who smoke seeking out similar others). It also reflects adolescents' biased perceptions that their own behavior is similar to that of their friends. However, significant findings still emerge when peer smoking is tested as a prospective predictor in longitudinal designs (Chassin et al. 2000) and when friends report directly on their own smoking behavior (Urberg et al. 1997). In addition to peer cigarette smoking, affiliation with peers who engage in high levels of other problem behaviors also prospectively predicts smoking initiation (Simons-Morton 2002), as does self-identification with a high-risk social group (Sussman et al. 1994).

Formal social network analysis suggests modest peer influence effects. For example, Ennett & Bauman (1994) identified peer cliques based on patterns of friendship nominations. They found that both selection and peer influence operated to make peer cliques homogenous with regard to smoking, but also that many adolescent smokers were not members of the identified cliques. Moderator variables also suggest that the magnitude of peer influence effects on adolescent smoking varies as a function of gender (stronger effects for females; Hu et al. 1995), ethnicity (strongest effects for white, weakest effects for African Americans; Landrine et al. 1994, Urberg et al. 1997), and parent involvement (weaker effects for those with involved parents; Simons-Morton 2002).

The mechanisms underlying peer influence effects have not been clearly established. Few adolescents report experiences of direct peer "pressure" to smoke (Urberg et al. 1990). Thus, peer influence effects may operate in other ways, such as increasing perceptions that smoking is prevalent and normative (Conrad et al. 1992), communicating a positive social image of smoking, providing access and opportunities for smoking behavior, or providing a means of peer bonding.

In contrast to peer smoking, parent smoking has been less consistently related to adolescent smoking initiation (Conrad et al. 1992) and its effects have been weaker in overall magnitude (Derzon & Lipsey 1999). However, despite its overall low magnitude of effect, parent smoking is a risk factor for adolescent smoking (Derzon & Lipsey 1999). Methodological features of prior studies may have obscured the magnitude of parent smoking effects by failing to (a) directly measure parent smoking, (b) distinguish between biological and custodial parents, and (c) distinguish among different adolescent smoking outcomes. For example, Chassin et al. (2000) found that parent smoking was related to a particular trajectory of smoking characterized by early onset, rapid escalation to heavy levels, and persistence over time. Consistent with these findings, a recent review of twin studies concluded that heritability is stronger for tobacco dependence than for smoking initiation (Sullivan & Kendler 1999). Thus, parent smoking may be an especially powerful risk factor for serious adolescent smoking outcomes. The association between parental and adolescent smoking can reflect multiple pathways of influence, including the effects of heritable individual differences in tobacco effects, heritable personality characteristics, and modeling.

The school environment also provides an important context for smoking acquisition. Adolescents who have conduct problems in school and who have lower levels of academic achievement are more likely to smoke, and low academic achievement and school conduct problems are reciprocally related (Bryant et al. 2000). School climate variables have also been linked to adolescent smoking, such that schools with more permissive norms about smoking, less teacher involvement, and less consistent discipline have higher rates of smoking (e.g., Johnson & Hoffman 2000, Novak & Clayton 2001). School effects may also reflect the broader influence of the neighborhoods in which schools are nested. However, findings have not been convincing in the small number of studies to examine the relation between neighborhood context and adolescent smoking.

Chaloupka (1999) reviewed studies of larger macrolevel social influences and noted several important limitations. Antitobacco social policies such as increased taxation and restrictions on youth access tend to be implemented in communities that also share antismoking norms and values, so that the effects of the policies are hard to disentangle from the effects of these broader community norms. Notwithstanding these limitations, econometric data generally show that adolescent tobacco use is price sensitive (as it is for adults). However, the magnitude of the effect may vary with age, ethnicity, and stage of smoking. For example, infrequent experimentation may be less price sensitive (Emery et al. 2001). Less clear effects have been produced by restrictions on youth access (e.g., merchant interventions, bans on vending machines), and enforcement of youth access policies has been difficult to attain. Finally, adolescent smoking is correlated with self-reported exposure to cigarette advertising (Romer & Jamieson 2002), and epidemiological trends over time show correlations between rises in adolescent smoking and times of cigarette industry advertising campaigns (Pierce & Gilpin 1995). In general, evidence suggests that tobacco advertising can increase smoking onset, and counteradvertising can delay or prevent smoking.

THE MOTIVATIONAL BASIS OF CIGARETTE DEPENDENCE

Transition to Dependent Smoking

Relatively little is known about the transition from youthful experimentation with tobacco to regular, heavy use. It is known that some youthful cigarette smokers do indeed satisfy criteria for tobacco dependence but it also the case that many adolescents do not (Colby et al. 2000a,b). Some evidence suggests that as smokers become more dependent, there is a shift in the motivational basis for their tobacco use. Beginning smokers tend to rate social motives and contextual factors as influential to their smoking; heavy smokers stress the importance of control over negative moods and urges, and the fact that smoking has become "automatic" (Piper et al. 2003). Indeed, one study showed that the best predictor of continued or increased smoking among beginning smokers was reporting that smoking provided good control over negative affect (Wetter et al. 2003). As smoking becomes less linked to external cues, and more linked to internal stimuli such as affect, more and more smokers warrant classification as nicotine dependent (Piper et al. 2003); i.e., they smoke more than they intend, smoking interferes with their lives or harms them, and so on. In the following section we review evidence on processes that may account for dependent cigarette smoking. We address whether nicotine per se is necessary for dependent smoking, whether route of delivery (i.e., smoking) is an important influence on motivation to use nicotine, and which types of nicotine effects are critical, e.g., associative effects and particular actions.

Role of Nicotine

Cigarette smoke contains thousands of constituents, leaving open the possibility that nonnicotine factors significantly influence nicotine reinforcement. Research now clearly indicates that nicotine is essential for prolonged, addictive tobacco use. Nicotine by itself yields the hallmark effects of addictive drugs. It produces tolerance and physical dependence, and acute doses produce elation and pleasure (Corrigall 1999, USDHHS 1988). In addition, pretreatment with nicotine reduces subsequent tobacco self-administration among smokers, even if the pretreatment nicotine is delivered via routes other than smoking (Perkins et al. 1996). This suggests that downward compensation in nicotine self-administration occurs because of the central effects of nicotine, not because of cues produced by the smoking ritual per se. Also, smokers will not self-administer tobacco on a chronic basis if it does not contain nicotine (Caggiula et al. 2001). Although nicotine is essential for the development and maintenance of smoking, once nicotine dependence is established, cues associated with nicotine delivery become highly influential in controlling self-administration behaviors.

PHARMACOKINETICS AND NICOTINE DELIVERY   Although cigarette smoking is highly addictive, other nicotine delivery systems are much less likely to support addictive use. For example, nicotine replacement therapies (NRTs, such as nicotine gum) only rarely sustain self-administration over the long-term (Hughes 1989). This is due, at least in part, to differences in the pharmacokinetics of cigarette smoking versus other nicotine delivery systems. Pharmacokinetics refers to how drug levels vary in body compartments or regions as a function of time.

Nicotine pharmacokinetics depends greatly upon route of administration. When a cigarette is smoked, about 80% of the inhaled nicotine is absorbed in the lungs (Armitage et al. 1975). Absorption is both efficient and extremely rapid because of the large volume of the alveolar surface area and the ready access to the extensive pulmonary capillary beds. In addition, the dissolution of nicotine in the pulmonary beds yields a greater proportion of nonionized nicotine that further promotes its rapid absorption. After absorption in the lungs, nicotine is transported to the brain via arterial blood prior to its passing through the liver or being distributed more widely in venous circulation. Thus, after smoking, nicotine levels may be some 6–10 times higher in arterial versus venous blood (Henningfield et al. 1993). A concentrated bolus of nicotine (mass of nicotine in the blood) reaches the brain some 12–15 seconds after inhalation (Benowitz 1994), where its absorption is rapid because of the high affinity of brain tissue for nicotine (Maziere et al. 1976). Although the absorption of nicotine is rapid, so is its elimination. The terminal elimination half-life of nicotine in the body is about 2 hours, but its distributional half-life in the brain is about 10 minutes. The latter describes the time that it takes a nicotine dose to fall 50% from its peak level in the brain as the nicotine is distributed to other body compartments (Russell 1988). This pattern of rapid rises in nicotine levels in the brain, with rapid distributional tolerance, occurs against a backdrop of trough levels of nicotine that will persist or rise as long as the intercigarette interval is not much greater than 60 minutes (Russell 1988).

Nicotine taken via other routes does not produce this same dramatic sawtooth pattern of effects with respect to brain levels. When taken via buccal absorption or via other routes (even venous infusion), the nicotine bolus is less concentrated, the arrival in the brain is delayed, and there is less of a sawtooth pattern to the nicotine profile across time (Pomerleau & Pomerleau 1992, cf. Frenk & Dar 2000). These differences occur because other routes tend to yield greater initial distribution across body compartments.

Although there is general recognition that rapid onset of drug actions promotes addictive drug use (van Ree et al. 1999), it remains unclear why this is so. Researchers do not really understand which characteristics of drug pharmacodynamics are most determinant of addictiveness. Possible candidates include the concentration of drug in the bolus, the trajectory of the rise time, or the combination of a rapid onset with a rapid offset. The last property might promote high levels of withdrawal plus optimal withdrawal relief. Finally, these pharmacokinetic features might be motivationally significant merely because they reflect a high level of control over drug effects in the brain.

ASSOCIATIVE PROCESSES   Behaviors that once delivered nicotine will persist despite severe degradations in the contingency between nicotine and self-administration behaviors. Thus, repeated nicotine dosing can generate sources of reinforcement that complement, or perhaps supplant, the impact of nicotine itself. That is, self-administration behaviors become somewhat uncoupled from a contingency with nicotine.

Nicotine pretreatment can suppress self-administration, but there is only a weak relation between pretreatment dosage and the dose subsequently self-administered. Among both humans and animals with extensive histories of self-administration, very large pretreatment dosages of nicotine result in rather modest decreases in nicotine self-administration (Benowitz et al. 1998). Such imprecise downward compensation suggests that smoking behavior is reinforced by more than just attaining a particular level of nicotine in the blood.

Other evidence of uncoupling is that although denicotinized cigarettes do not sustain smoking over the long term, over brief periods they do support self-administration, produce pleasure, and reduce craving and withdrawal symptoms (Butschky et al. 1995). Also, although animals will eventually extinguish instrumental responding once it no longer yields nicotine, they are highly resistant to such extinction. Caggiula et al. (2001) report only partial extinction after 17 days of extinction trials. Moreover, cues that were previously paired with nicotine are effective at reinstating self-administration behaviors; more effective, in fact, than nicotine itself (Caggiula et al. 2001).

The causes of uncoupling of nicotine receipt and instrumental behavior are unknown. However, Caggiula et al. (2001) suggest that nicotine may be particularly potent at conferring conditioned reinforcement properties on associated cues. Therefore, organisms may engage in self-administration behaviors because the self-administration behaviors themselves have become reinforcing. Other environmental or social cues might also become rewarding through being paired with nicotine. Of course, the research reviewed above does not reveal the nature of the associative effects that spur self-administration. For instance, nicotine-paired cues could elicit pleasurable/euphoric effects that serve as incentives for further self-administration. Or instead, nicotine could elicit aversive withdrawal effects that set the stage for negative reinforcement.

The evidence reviewed above yields two conclusions: (*a*) Nicotine is essential to the development and long-term maintenance of tobacco self-administration, but (*b*) after extensive self-administration experience, cues associated with nicotine receipt can, by themselves, powerfully affect self-administration behaviors. Thus, although the dependent smoker may smoke to quell or achieve internal states (e.g., to reduce negative moods), external cues powerfully influence self-administration behaviors.

It is clear that pharmacodynamics and associative effects are critically important to the motivation to use nicotine. We now turn to the question of which particular nicotine actions are motivationally significant, and how best to conceptualize nicotine motivational processes.

Motivational Processes

TOLERANCE   As was previously noted, the DSM criteria for diagnosing dependence include the existence of tolerance and physical dependence (the occurrence of a withdrawal syndrome upon discontinuation/reduction of drug use). In the case of tolerance, researchers have reported tolerance to nicotine's tachycardic, euphoriant, and akinetic actions (e.g., Perkins et al. 1994, 2001a). Research also indicates that tolerance is heterogeneous with respect to time course. For example, some tolerance phenomena persist after years of abstinence (Perkins et al. 2001a). Other types are short-lived, such that abstinence of a few hours may restore some cigarette effects (Benowitz 1998). Therefore, even at very high smoking rates, each cigarette may continue to produce pharmacologic effects (e.g., Porchet et al. 1988).

There is some evidence that tolerance plays an important early role in permitting the development of dependent smoking. That is, the youthful smoker must become inured to the toxic and irritating effects of smoking (e.g., nausea) in order for him or her to escalate use to levels that will produce physical dependence (Leventhal & Cleary 1980). However, there is scant evidence that tolerance is an important index of the degree or severity of tobacco dependence among heavy smokers. For instance, Perkins et al. (2002) found little evidence linking tolerance magnitude to withdrawal severity or relapse likelihood among dependent smokers. This suggests that tolerance may be a "low hurdle" in the development of dependence; all dependent smokers are somewhat tolerant to nicotine effects, but tolerance and dependence may not be produced by the same processes. Consequently, tolerance is an insensitive index of dependence.

PHYSICAL DEPENDENCE   Research shows clearly that chronic nicotine exposure results in physical dependence to nicotine; i.e., the tendency to display well-characterized signs of the nicotine withdrawal syndrome. For instance, Malin (2001) has shown that rats exposed to continuous infusion for 7 days of 3- or 9-mg/kg/day nicotine hydrogen tartate (1.05 or 3.15 mg/kg/day expressed as the base), displayed the following abstinence signs: teeth chattering, chewing, gasping, writhing, head shakes, body shakes, tremors, ptosis, and assorted other signs such as spontaneous ejaculation and licking. These signs peaked at about 18–22 hours postcessation. The evidence that these reflect nicotine withdrawal per se is compelling. These signs are temporally tied to drug abstinence; they are linearly related to dose, and they can be precipitated by a competitive nicotine antagonist such as dihydro-∃-erythroidine (e.g., Epping-Jordan et al. 1998, Malin et al. 1998).

One feature of the nicotine withdrawal syndrome may have unique motivational significance. Nicotine withdrawal results in an increase in the threshold required for rewarding brain stimulation (Epping-Jordan et al. 1998). This is seen in the withdrawal syndromes of other drugs and this may account for the anhedonia that tends to accompany withdrawal (Baker et al. 2003). Thus, withdrawal may be aversive not only because negative affect is a principal manifestation, but also because withdrawal decreases the rewarding properties of nonpharmacologic incentives (e.g., social stimuli).

The human nicotine withdrawal syndrome does not comprise the dramatic physical signs that are observed in nicotine research with rats. This may reflect the relatively higher doses given animals (Malin 2001) as well as species differences. However, the nicotine withdrawal syndrome in humans does manifest with a reliable core set of symptoms and signs including dysphoria, anxiety, inability to concentrate, increased appetite, weight gain, sleep disruption, and others (Hughes et al. 1991). Moreover, recent work suggests that the nicotine withdrawal syndrome may persist for months following nicotine abstinence (Piasecki et al. 1998, 2000).

Both animal and human research suggests that the withdrawal syndrome is aversive. For instance, Suzuki et al. (1996) determined that rats would avoid a chamber associated with the nicotine abstinence syndrome precipitated by mecamylamine, a nicotine antagonist. Not only is the syndrome aversive, but nicotine quickly and efficiently alleviates its aversive components. For instance, nicotine administered to withdrawn smokers consistently reduces their self-reports of sadness, anxiety, and anger/irritability (Jorenby et al. 1996, Zinser et al. 1992), and the affective components of withdrawal appear to be most influential in motivating further nicotine self-administration (e.g., Piasecki et al. 2000). Relief of withdrawal-induced negative affect by nicotine has also been reported in animals (Cheeta et al. 2001). These observations, plus the fact that smokers often smoke more, or relapse, in the context of negative affect (Baker et al. 2003), suggest that negative reinforcement through the relief of withdrawal symptoms may play a critical role in sustaining smoking among dependent smokers.

APPETITIVE/EUPHORIANT EFFECTS AND POSITIVE REINFORCEMENT   Like other psychomotor stimulants, nicotine produces subjective sensations that are characterized as a "rush," "elation," or "buzz." These effects are not dependent upon smoking as a delivery system, or upon associative elicitation, since they can follow venous infusion. However, consistent with the material on pharmacokinetics, such subjective effects are more likely to occur with delivery systems that promote rapid rise times of nicotine in the brain.

In research conducted by Garrett & Griffiths (2001), caffeine, cocaine, and nicotine were infused into volunteers who had a history of use of these drugs. Nicotine elicited dose-dependent increases in ratings of "drug effect," "good effect," "like drug," and "high." Moreover, the highest dose of nicotine (3.0 mg/70 kg) was never identified as a placebo, and instead was identified as a stimulant by all subjects. Seven of the nine subjects identified it as cocaine.

Although it is highly likely that nicotine's direct appetitive effects are important to nicotine motivation and addiction, the extent and nature of their influence is unclear. Evidence supporting a role for nicotine's appetitive effects includes the fact that smokers reliably report positive reinforcement as a reason for smoking (e.g., for "pleasurable relaxation," and "stimulation"; Ikard et al. 1969), and they hold expectancies that smoking will enhance positive affect (Copeland et al. 1995). Additionally, a significant proportion of smoking relapse episodes occur when individuals are in positive affect states (Brandon et al. 1990, Shiffman et al. 1996) and positive affect predicts urges to smoke during the course of ongoing smoking (Zinser et al. 1992). Finally, in the laboratory, positive affect imagery elicits stronger urges to smoke than does neutral imagery (Tiffany & Drobes 1990).

Numerous observations, however, suggest that positive reinforcement is not the major motivational influence on dependent smoking. For example, although positive affect imagery does elicit smoking urges, it is less effective than negative affect imagery (Tiffany & Drobes 1990). Also, expectations of negative reinforcement from smoking (e.g., relief of negative affect) predict relapse likelihood, but positive reinforcement expectancies do not. Thus, the latter may have less motivational significance (Copeland et al. 1995, Wetter et al. 1994). Further, relapse is about half as likely to occur during positive affect states than during negative affect states (Brandon et al. 1990, Shiffman et al. 1996). Finally, humans rapidly acquire acute tolerance to nicotine's appetitive actions, so that in the inveterate smoker relatively few cigarettes produce such effects (e.g., Perkins et al. 1994).

SENSITIZATION OF INCENTIVE EFFECTS   According to the Incentive Sensitization Theory (IST; Robinson & Berridge 1993), addictive drugs exert dopaminergic actions in critical mesotelencephalic brain sites. These dopamine actions are thought to imbue drug and drug cues with potent incentive value such that drug use is seductively attractive, even if the organism actually experiences little drug reward. Earlier theories (Wise 1988) held that dopamine determined how rewarding a drug would be. However, based upon a careful review of relevant research, Robinson & Berridge (1993, 2001) concluded that dopamine does not primarily influence drug reward, but instead, it influences expectation or anticipation of reward.

IST explicitly separates the subjective evaluation of drug effects ("liking") from the incentive-motivational effects ("wanting"). According to IST, these two processes are associated with different neuronal systems, and therefore, they are affected differently by drug exposure. Repeated drug use increases the incentive properties of drug cues because of sensitization of mesotelencephalic dopamine systems, but it also simultaneously produces tolerance to drug reward. This could explain why smokers smoke compulsively but often report that they derive scant pleasure from it.

Most support for IST has come from research on addictive drugs other than nicotine (Robinson & Berridge 2001). However, research has suggested striking similarities in motivational influences across different types of addictive drugs (Robinson & Berridge 2001). Therefore, to the extent that IST accounts for other examples of drug dependence, incentive sensitization may also play a role in nicotine dependence. In addition, the tenets of IST are generally consistent with findings from tobacco research (e.g., Carter & Tiffany 1999). For instance, there is clear evidence that nicotine sensitizes the core of the nucleus accumbens so that repeated administration of the same dose produces increased dopamine release (Balfour 2003). In addition, a measure of positive affect and approach motivation (cerebral asymmetry) showed increases when smokers were exposed to smoking cues, but not after they were actually allowed to smoke (Zinser et al. 1999). This suggests that there is more "reward" in the anticipation of smoking than in smoking per se. Finally, there is mounting evidence that nicotine is a potent modulator of the incentive value of cues of reward. Thus, nicotine has the capacity to enhance the incentive value or salience of cues for nonpharmacologic rewards such as a visual reinforcer (Donny et al. 2003).

IST is consistent with many features of dependent smoking. However, more research is needed to establish its relevance. IST is predicated on the notion that addicts derive little pleasure from drug use. This assumption of the model has been little studied in smokers. Little is known regarding the proportion of cigarettes that yield pleasure, the immediacy of the pleasure, and its magnitude—or how cigarettes compare on these dimensions with other reinforcers available to the smoker. In addition, to the extent that nicotine modulates incentive value, researchers should explore how smokers are affected by the increased incentive value of nonpharma-cologic appetitive stimuli once they quit smoking. Does smoking make the whole world "brighter" and more appealing and does quitting make the world more dull and uninteresting? Finally, how do withdrawal and other aversive states affect the incentive value of smoking cues? Is the appeal or salience of such cues largely a function of nicotine deprivation (Baker et al. 2003)? And, if deprivation enhances both incentive salience and nicotine reward, a negative reinforcement model might provide a better explanation for dependence motivation than does IST per se.

NEGATIVE REINFORCEMENT THROUGH REDUCTION OF STRESS AND WITHDRAWAL
Negative affect exerts potent motivational effects on smoking. For instance, smok-ers regularly cite affective control as a principal motive for their tobacco use (e.g., Copeland et al. 1995, Ikard et al. 1969). Numerous studies have found that stress manipulations increase cravings for cigarettes (Payne et al. 1991, Perkins & Grobe 1992) as well as amount and intensity of smoking (e.g., Dobbs et al. 1981, Payne et al. 1991). In addition, expectancies about negative affect reduction are associ-ated with magnitude of nicotine dependence, severity of withdrawal symptoms, and treatment outcome (Copeland et al. 1995, Wetter et al. 1994).

Additional support for the link between smoking and affect is found in population-based studies examining the covariation of smoking with clinical syn-dromes characterized by high negative affectivity, particularly clinical depression. National epidemiological studies in the United States and Australia have found a high degree of comorbidity between depression and smoking (Anda et al. 1990, Degenhardt & Hall 2001). Individuals with a history of major depression are ap-proximately twice as likely as others to be smokers, and smokers are more likely than others to have affective disorders. Such correlational findings do not address the direction of causality, and it is likely that causality between smoking and de-pression is bidirectional, and may reflect a common genetic risk (Kendler et al. 1993).

Finally, postcessation relapse to smoking tends to be precipitated by situations characterized by stress and negative affect (e.g., Brandon et al. 1990). Shiffman et al. (1996) sampled affect and smoking in real-time using palm-top computers. Initial relapse episodes were compared with nonrelapse "temptation" episodes, and with random sampling during nonsmoking. Negative affect differed across the three assessment situations, with the greatest negative affect associated with the relapse episodes, followed by the temptation episodes. Moreover, level of postcessation negative affect is an excellent marker of relapse vulnerability (Kenford et al. 2002; Piasecki et al. 2003a,b).

These strong links between negative affect and measures of smoking motivation and dependence suggest that negative reinforcement plays a critical role in smoking motivation; i.e., smokers smoke to reduce distress (Baker et al. 2003). What is not known is what accounts for this relation. As noted previously, there is compelling evidence that nicotine ameliorates elements of the tobacco withdrawal syndrome including negative affect (Baker et al. 2003, Cheeta et al. 2001). This certainly could account for a relation between negative affect and the motivation to smoke. Moreover, this account is consistent with the fact that negative affect is highly associated with measures of smoking motivation only among abstaining smokers (Sayette et al. 2003, Shiffman et al. 2002, Zinser et al. 1992).

What is not clear is whether nicotine also alleviates the negative affect that arises from stressors. If nicotine reduces negative affect arising from environmental stressors, this would certainly increase the opportunity of smokers to attain negative reinforcement from smoking.

STRESS REDUCTION   A recent authoritative review (Kassel et al. 2003) reveals conflicting evidence as to whether nicotine reduces stress-induced negative affect (SINA) in smokers with little nicotine deprivation (<1.5 h). In theory, smoking-induced reductions in negative affect in these smokers should not be due to withdrawal relief (given the brief deprivation period). Several laboratory studies have reported reductions in SINA (typically anxiety; e.g., Jarvik et al. 1989, Juliano & Brandon 2002, Perkins & Grobe et al. 1992). However, caution is warranted. Even over a brief 1.5-h abstinence period, withdrawal relief may have colored these findings, given the short distributional half-life of nicotine. In addition, nicotine's ability to reduce SINA may depend upon contextual factors. Kassel & Unrod (2000) reported that smoking reduces anxiety in the laboratory setting only when administered concomitantly with a distraction. Nicotine may constrain cognitive workspace such that information about stressors is not processed in the context of distraction. Thus, as has similarly been reported with alcohol (e.g., Steele & Josephs 1988, Curtin et al. 1998) stress reduction may occur via a cognitive mechanism. Finally, there is evidence that smoking is more likely to reduce anxiety before or after a stressful event, rather than affecting reactions during the event (Gilbert 1995, Gilbert et al. 1989, Kassel et al. 2003).

Field research suggests that nicotine can reduce negative affects. For instance, using real-time data collection methods, Jamner and his colleagues (Delfino et al. 2001) found that smoking was followed by decreased anger in both men and women, and decreased sadness in men. However, such reductions in negative affect cannot be attributed to stress reduction per se, as they might instead reflect withdrawal relief.

In contrast to studies suggesting smoking-induced reductions in SINA, others report negative evidence. In one study, smoking did not reduce anticipatory anxiety prior to white noise or a vigilance task stressor (Jarvik et al. 1989). Smoking did reduce anxiety in anticipation of cold pressor and anagram tasks, but posttask anxiety ratings were not, in fact, lower among individuals who smoked. Herbert et al. (2001) reported no reduction in anticipatory anxiety with or without a distraction task. Recently, Britt et al. (2001) showed that when smokers were exposed to a social stressor, smoking reduced the level of withdrawal symptoms, but not anxiety per se. In general, it appears that there are about as many human studies showing little or no relief of SINA as there are studies showing such relief (Kassel et al. 2003).

The studies reviewed above all face significant interpretive challenges. For instance, as noted earlier, it is difficult to disambiguate the stress-reduction versus the withdrawal-reduction effects of nicotine. One strategy used to avoid the prospect of withdrawal coloring results is to examine the effects of nicotine in non-addicted subjects. However, nicotine can produce aversive effects that may mask stress-reducing actions in nicotine-naïve subjects (Foulds et al. 1997). In addition, smokers and nonsmokers tend to differ on the basis of constitutional factors (e.g., personality and psychiatric variables; Breslau 1995), and these differences might influence the degree of stress-reduction obtained from nicotine.

The use of animal models reduces the threat of some of these interpretive challenges. Animal research has shown that nicotine can produce anxiolytic (anxiety reducing) as well as anxiogenic (anxiety causing) effects, with the nature of the effect being determined by dose, the type of anxiety test, the animal's prior experience with nicotine, and the delay between the dose and test (Irvine et al. 2001). Nevertheless, there exists both behavioral (e.g., social interaction under stress; File et al. 1998) and neuropharmacological (e.g., mesoprefrontal dopaminergic response to acute inescapable footshock stress; George et al. 2000) evidence for nicotine-induced anxiolysis. However, animals quickly develop tolerance to the ameliorating effects of nicotine on SINA, but not to withdrawal-induced anxiolysis (Irvine et al. 2001, Szyndler et al. 2001). Thus, the animal data suggest that for chronic users the most available and reliable source of negative affect reduction is withdrawal relief. This conclusion is consistent with much of the human research and with recent theorizing (Baker et al. 2003, Parrott 1999).

EXPECTATIONS OF STRESS REDUCTION   Regardless of whether smoking actually reduces SINA, smokers expect it to do so (Brandon et al. 1999, Copeland et al. 1995, Wetter et al. 1994), and this may influence smoking motivation. For example, a recent study using the "balanced placebo" design (Juliano & Brandon 2002) showed that smokers' experience of smoking-induced anxiety relief depended upon their expectations of such an effect.

It is unknown why smokers have strong expectations that smoking will alleviate SINA. Smoking may indeed alleviate SINA reliably, and research has simply failed to index this sensitively. On other hand, it may be that nicotine's ability to ameliorate withdrawal distress may overshadow, motivationally, its evanescent or inconsistent impact on stress reactivity. Smokers experience some level of withdrawal throughout much of the day, even if smoking ad libitum (see Baker et al. 2003). It is possible that this withdrawal-induced negative affect adds to SINA, and that it is difficult for smokers to distinguish between withdrawal relief and stress relief.

In sum, the bulk of the evidence strongly supports negative reinforcement motives in the maintenance of smoking behavior. Not only is nicotine highly effective in alleviating withdrawal-induced negative affect, but a wide range of research paradigms suggests that expectations of stress relief contribute to the maintenance of adult smoking. What is unclear is the extent to which nicotine is actually effective in reducing affective reactions to external stressors. It may be that smokers assume that smoking ameliorates stress-induced negative affect because it is so effective at reducing withdrawal-induced negative affect (Baker et al. 2003, Parrott 1999).

Acceptance of any conclusions about nicotine's anxiolytic- or stress-reducing effects must be tempered by appreciation of the challenges to research synthesis in this area. Studies differ in terms of stressors, nicotine dose, withdrawal-stress latencies, and measures of affect or stress response. In addition, research in this area is subject to the problems that plague any research on affective phenomena, such as desynchrony across response systems (e.g., Lang 1968) and the fact that affective responses may be unavailable to conscious awareness.

ADDITIONAL MOTIVATIONAL INFLUENCES

Weight regulation   Nicotine delivery via cigarette smoking can certainly produce other effects that influence smoking motivation. For instance, nicotine can reduce body weight, apparently by adjusting body weight set point (Cabanac & Frankham 2002, Schwid et al. 1992). Thus, on average, smokers weigh less than nonsmokers (Williamson et al. 1991), and once people stop smoking they tend to gain weight (Perkins 1993). It is certainly possible that some smokers, particularly women, smoke for weight control motives. Although this is a plausible hypothesis, it is unclear how common this motive is, and the extent to which it is a determinant of smoking maintenance or relapse back to smoking.

Information processing   Smokers report that smoking enhances their cognitive processing (Warburton & Walters 1995), and that abstinence from smoking produces an inability to concentrate (Hughes et al. 1991). In fact, laboratory research supports these assertions. Domino & Kishimoto (2002) showed that nicotine withdrawal disrupted the processing of meaningful stimuli as reflected by P3 event-related potentials, and this effect was reversed by smoking. When withdrawn smokers smoked, it did not produce any frank or net improvements in attentional processing; it only neutralized the deleterious impact of withdrawal. It is clear that smoking restores the information-processing deficits produced by withdrawal. However, the evidence is mixed as to whether and how it enhances information processing in nonwithdrawn individuals.

Despite difficulties in interpreting research on nicotine's impact on cognitive processes (Heishman et al. 1994, Park et al. 2000), some conclusions may be drawn about its effects in nonwithdrawn individuals. First, there is a fairly consistent body of evidence that nicotine enhances alerting (Domino & Kashimoto 2002, Mancuso et al. 2001), i.e., maintaining a state of vigilance such that one is sensitive to stimulus changes (Fan et al. 2002). However, research in nonwithdrawn humans suggests that nicotine does not consistently enhance higher-level attentional processes such as orienting (selection of information from sensory input) or executive control (resolution of conflict regarding response options; e.g.,

Atchley et al. 2002, Griesar et al. 2002, Heishman & Henningfield 2000, Park et al. 2000). [However, nicotine may enhance orienting in schizophrenics (Kumari et al. 2001), and, consequently, contribute to elevated smoking rates in this population.] Moreover, research with humans provides little evidence that nicotine enhances other cognitive faculties such as memory (Heishman et al. 1994). Although some animal research suggests that nicotine may enhance selective attention (Hahn & Stolerman 2002, Hahn et al. 2002), this effect may not occur in humans due to species differences (Park et al. 2000).

In sum, nicotine may directly enhance alertness, and it may produce broader cognitive effects via the alleviation of withdrawal. It is possible that these effects motivate the uptake of smoking or its maintenance. However, if it were discovered that smokers do indeed continue smoking in order to escape or avoid withdrawal-induced cognitive deficits, this would constitute just one particular mechanism via which negative reinforcement affects the maintenance of smoking. At present, there is insufficient information to determine the extent to which smokers maintain smoking or relapse in pursuit of cognitive enhancement.

Although the motivational impact of cognitive enhancement is unknown, cognitive measures are elucidating some of the information-processing substrata of smoking motivation and dependence. Cognitive assays such as the Stroop paradigm and the dot-probe task are revealing that smokers' attention to smoking stimuli is enhanced by withdrawal (Waters & Feyerabend 2000), and enhanced by information that the opportunity to smoke is imminent (Wertz & Sayette 2001). Such cognitive measures may not only offer new methods for assessing the strength of nicotine dependence, but may also suggest stages in motivational processing where tobacco approach behavior may be interrupted effectively.

Motivation: Further Complexities

The above review did not do justice to the complexity of the motivational influences on tobacco smoking. For example, any single smoking episode may be a function of multiple motives that change as function of context and other factors such as cost and the availability of other reinforcers (Carroll & Campbell 2000, Gilbert 1995, Vuchinich & Tucker 1998). Moreover, many smoking episodes may be difficult to attribute to particular motivational influences because smoking may be reflexively primed by subtle or indistinct instigators (Tiffany 1990). In addition, individual differences such as gender may moderate the influence of smoking motivational processes (Gilbert 1995, Perkins et al. 2001b).

CONCLUSIONS

The motivation to smoke cigarettes is multifaceted. No single, monolithic motive accounts for cigarette smoking across individuals and development. The complexity of smoking motivation is reflected by the range of factors associated with the initiation and maintenance of smoking. These factors include stress, genotype, peer and parental relations, personality/temperament, expectancies, and presence of affective symptomatology (Gilbert 1995).

Not only do multiple factors affect cigarette smoking, but their relative impacts appear to vary across the development of addictive smoking. For instance, although peer influences and impression management motives strongly influence the behavior of the neophyte smoker, control of withdrawal symptoms appears to be relatively more influential for heavy-smoking adults.

Our literature review showed that youthful initiation and use is related to a broad array of factors. Such smoking appears to be influenced by family environment, ethnicity, personality, economics, comorbidity, attitudes and beliefs, social networks, and genetics. Although research has now documented the broad range of factors that may contribute to youthful uptake, what is missing is a clear understanding of the relative impacts of these factors, how they "work" together, and which factors are most influential in the progression to tobacco dependence. Moreover, as noted previously, there is evidence that adolescence represents a sensitive period for the development of tobacco use and dependence. It is not known, at present, which factors, in particular, mediate this heightened vulnerability. Research that examines distinct trajectories of smoking progression may elucidate critical risk factors and determinants of dependence. Such research may also be useful for identifying genotypes associated with a vulnerability to dependence.

Despite the heterogeneity in smoking motives, some factors stand out as being influential across the ontogeny of smoking. Multiple sources of evidence point to strong links between negative affect and smoking. For example, preexisting depressive symptoms may set the stage for smoking initiation, and smoking may then further exacerbate depression. Moreover, negative affect appears to be a principal instigator of relapse among smokers trying to abstain.

Although a great deal has been learned about cigarette smoking, many unanswered questions remain. We still do not know enough about nicotine's effects on information processing. For instance, we don't understand why studies yield discrepant results regarding nicotine's attentional effects, and we know little about the motivational significance of nicotine's perceived effects on alertness or attention. Also, we don't yet understand when and how nicotine influences affective and other reactions to stressors. In addition, while we appreciate the strong links between negative affect and smoking motivation, we do not understand the motivational basis of this relation. Does negative affect set the stage for negative reinforcement, or does it merely inflate the incentive value of smoking cues? Similarly, we do not know why negative affective symptoms or certain personality traits create vulnerability to addictive smoking. Is it because they encourage smoking initiation along with a host of other risky behaviors, or do they affect the reinforcing value of nicotine? Along those lines, it remains unclear why the development of addictive smoking is so tightly linked to adolescence. Does central nervous system maturation constitute an optimal neuropharmacologic environment for the acquisition of strong smoking motives?

Certainly, research will ultimately provide answers to these questions, and these questions might be most profitably approached via research that is highly integrative and transdisciplinary. The influences on smoking are diverse, and these influences involve multiple cognitive, biologic, behavioral, and social systems. Relations among these influences may be reciprocal, and each may play a different role in the development of smoking. Such complexity argues for transdisciplinary research efforts that foster a comprehensive and integrated perspective on the development and maintenance of cigarette smoking.

ACKNOWLEDGMENTS

Work on this manuscript was supported by awards P50 CA84724 (TBB), R01 CA80706 and R01 CA94256 (THB), and DA13555 and DA05227 (LC).

The *Annual Review of Psychology* is online at http://psych.annualreviews.org

LITERATURE CITED

Aloise-Young P, Hennigan K, Graham J. 1996. Role of the self-image and smoker stereotype in smoking onset during early adolescence: a longitudinal study. *Health Psychol.* 15:494–97

Am. Psychiatr. Assoc. 1994. *Diagnostic Statistical Manual of Mental Disorders.* Washington, DC: Am. Psychiatr. Assoc. 4th ed.

Anda RF, Williamson DF, Escobedo LG, Mast EE, Giovino GA, Remington PL. 1990. Depression and the dynamics of smoking. A national perspective. *JAMA* 264:1541–45

Andrews J, Duncan S. 1998. The effect of attitude on the development of adolescent cigarette use. *J. Subst. Abuse* 10:1–7

Armitage AK, Dollery CT, George CF, Houseman TH, Lewis PJ, et al. 1975. Absorption and metabolism of nicotine from cigarettes. *Br. Med. J.* 4:313–16

Arnett J. 2000. Optimistic bias in adolescent and adult smokers and nonsmokers. *Addict. Behav.* 25:625–32

Atchley P, Grobe J, Fields LM. 2002. The effect of smoking on sensory and attentional masking. *Percept. Psychophys.* 64:328–36

Austin S, Gortmaker S. 2001. Dieting and smoking initiation in early adolescent girls and boys: a prospective study. *Am. J. Public Health* 91:446–50

Baker TB, Piper ME, McCarthy DE, Majeskie MR, Fiore MC. 2003. Addiction motivation reformulated: an affective processing model of negative reinforcement. *Psychol. Rev.* In press

Balfour DJK. 2003. The psychopharmacology of tobacco dependence. *J. Clin. Psychiatr. Monogr.* 18(1):12–21

Barkley R, Fischer M, Edelbrock C, Smallish L. 1990. The adolescent outcome of hyperactive children diagnosed by research criteria: I. An 8-year prospective follow-up study. *J. Am. Acad. Child Adolesc. Psychiatry* 29:546–57

Barton J, Chassin L, Presson C, Sherman SJ. 1982. Social image factors as motivators of smoking initiation in early and middle adolescents. *Child Dev.* 53:1499511

Belluzzi JD, Young ON, Manzardo AM, Leslie FM. 2001. Adolescent rats acquire nicotine self-administration more rapidly than adults. *Soc. Neurosci.* 27:222.7 (Abstr.)

Benowitz NL. 1994. Acute biological effects of nicotine and its metabolites. In *Effects of Nicotine on Biological Systems II*, ed. PBS Clark, M Quik, F Adlkofer, K Thuran, pp. 9–16. Basel: Birkhäuser Verlag

Benowitz NL. 1998. Nicotine pharmacology and addiction. In *Nicotine Safety and Toxicity*, ed. NL Benowitz, pp. 6–13. New York: Oxford Univ. Press

Benowitz NL, Zevin S, Jacob P. 1998. Suppression of nicotine intake during ad libitum cigarette smoking by high-dose transdermal nicotine. *J. Pharmacol. Exp. Ther.* 287:958–62

Brandon TH, Juliano LM, Copeland AL. 1999. Expectancies for tobacco smoking. In *How Expectancies Shape Experience*, ed. I Kirsch, pp. 263–99. Washington, DC: Am. Psychol. Assoc.

Brandon TH, Tiffany ST, Obremski KM, Baker TB. 1990. Postcessation cigarette use: the process of relapse. *Addict. Behav.* 15:105–14

Breslau N. 1995. Psychiatric comorbidity of smoking and nicotine dependence. *Behav. Genet.* 25:95–101

Breslau N, Johnson E, Hiripi E, Kessler R. 2001. Nicotine dependence in the United States: prevalence, trends, and smoking persistence. *Arch. Gen. Psychiatry* 58:810–16

Britt DM, Cohen LM, Collins FL Jr, Cohen ML. 2001. Cigarette smoking and chewing gum: response to a laboratory-induced stressor. *Health Psychol.* 20:361–68

Brown R, Lewinsohn P, Seeley J, Wagner E. 1996. Cigarette smoking, major depression, and other psychiatric disorders among adolescents. *J. Am. Acad. Child Adolesc. Psychiatry* 35:1602–10

Bryant A, Schulenberg J, Bachman J, O'Malley P, Johnston L. 2000. Understanding the links among school misbehavior, academic achievement, and cigarette use: a national panel study of adolescents. *Prev. Sci.* 1:71–87

Burke J, Loeber R, Lahey B. 2001. Which aspects of ADHD are associated with tobacco use in early adolescence? *J. Child Psychol. Psychiatry* 42:493–502

Burt R, Dinh K, Peterson A, Sarason I. 2000. Predicting adolescent smoking: a prospective study of personality variables. *Prev. Med.* 30:115–25

Butschky MF, Bailey D, Henningfield JE, Pick-

worth WB. 1995. Smoking without nicotine delivery decreases withdrawal in 12-hour abstinent smokers. *Pharmacol. Biochem. Behav.* 50:91–96

Cabanac M, Frankham P. 2002. Evidence that transient nicotine lowers the body weight set point. *Physiol. Behav.* 76:539–42

Caggiula AR, Donny EC, White AR, Chaudhri N, Booth S, et al. 2001. Cue dependency of nicotine self-administration and smoking. *Pharmacol. Biochem. Behav.* 70:515–30

Carroll ME, Campbell UC. 2000. A behavioral economic analysis of the reinforcing effects of drugs: Transition states of addiction. In *Reframing Health Behavior Change with Behavioral Economics*, ed. WK Bickel, RE Vuchinich, pp. 63–87. Mahwah, NJ: Erlbaum

Carter BL, Tiffany ST. 1999. Meta-analysis of cue-reactivity in addiction research. *Addiction* 94:327–40

Cent. Dis. Control Prev. 1999. Cigarette smoking among adults. *Morbid. Mortal. Wkly.* 48:993–96

Chaloupka F. 1999. Macro-social influences: The effects of prices and tobacco-control policies on the demand for tobacco products. *Nicotine Tob. Res.* 1 (Suppl.):77–81

Chassin L, Presson C, Pitts S, Sherman SJ. 2000. The natural history of cigarette smoking from adolescence to adulthood in a midwestern community sample: multiple trajectories and their psychosocial correlates. *Health Psychol.* 19:223–31

Chassin L, Presson C, Rose J, Sherman SJ, Prost J. 2002. Parental smoking cessation and adolescent smoking. *J. Pediatr. Psychol.* 27:485–96

Chassin L, Presson C, Sherman SJ, Corty E, Olshavsky R. 1984. Predicting the onset of cigarette smoking in adolescents: a longitudinal study. *J. Appl. Soc. Psychol.* 14:224–43

Cheeta S, Irvine EE, Kenny PJ, File SE. 2001. The dorsal raphe nucleus is a crucial structure mediating nicotine's anxiolytic effects and the development of tolerance and withdrawal responses. *Psychopharmacology* 155:78–85

Colby S, Tiffany S, Shiffman S, Niaura R. 2000a. Are adolescent smokers dependent on nicotine? A review of the evidence. *Drug Alcohol Depend.* 59(Suppl.):83–95

Colby S, Tiffany S, Shiffman S, Niaura R. 2000b. Measuring nicotine dependence among youth: a review of available approaches and instruments. *Drug Alcohol Depend.* 59(Suppl.):23–39

Colder C, Mehta P, Balanda K, Campbell R, Mayhew K, et al. 2001. Identifying trajectories of adolescent smoking: an application of latent growth mixture modeling. *Health Psychol.* 20:127–35

Conrad K, Flay B, Hill D. 1992. Why children start smoking cigarettes: predictors of onset. *Br. J. Addict.* 87:1711–24

Copeland AL, Brandon TH, Quinn EP. 1995. The Smoking Consequences Questionnaire—Adult: measurement of smoking outcome expectancies of experienced smokers. *Psychol. Assess.* 7:484–94

Corrigall WA. 1999. Nicotine self-administration in animals as a dependence model. *Nicotine Tob. Res.* 1:11–20

Costello E, Erkanli A, Federman E, Angold A. 1999. Development of psychiatric comorbidity with substance abuse in adolescents: effects of timing and sex. *J. Clin. Child Psychol.* 28:298–311

Curtin JJ, Lang AR, Patrick CJ, Stritzke WG. 1998. Alcohol and fear-potentiated startle: the role of competing cognitive demands in the stress-reducing effects of intoxication. *J. Abnorm. Psychol.* 107:547–57

Degenhardt L, Hall W. 2001. The relationship between tobacco use, substance-use disorders and mental health: results from the National Survey of Mental Health and Wellbeing. *Nicotine Tob. Res.* 3:225–34

Delfino RJ, Jamner LD, Whalen CK. 2001. Temporal analysis of the relationship of smoking behavior and urges to mood states in men versus women. *Nicotine Tob. Res.* 3:235–48

Derzon J, Lipsey M. 1999. Predicting tobacco use to age 18: a synthesis of longitudinal research. *Addiction* 94:995–1006

Disney E, Elkins I, McGue M, Iacono W. 1999. Effects of ADHD, conduct disorder, and gender on substance use and abuse in adolescents. *Am. J. Psychiatry* 156:1515–21

Dobbs SD, Strickler DP, Maxwell WA. 1981. The effects of stress and relaxation in the presence of stress on urinary pH and smoking behaviors. *Addict. Behav.* 6:345–53

Domino EF, Kishimoto T. 2002. Tobacco smoking increases gating of irrelevant and enhances attention to relevant tones. *Nicotine Tob. Res.* 4:71–78

Donny EC, Chaudhri N, Caggiula AR, Evans-Martin FF, Booth S, et al. 2003. Operant responding for a visual reinforcer in rats is enhanced by non-contingent nicotine: implications for nicotine self-administration and reinforcement. *Psychopharmacology* 169:68–76

Emery S, White M, Pierce J. 2001. Does cigarette price influence adolescent experimentation? *J. Health Econ.* 20:261–70

Ennett S, Bauman K. 1994. The contribution of influence and selection to adolescent peer group homogeneity: the case of adolescent cigarette smoking. *J. Personal. Soc. Psychol.* 67:653–63

Epping-Jordan MP, Watkins SS, Koob GF, Markou A. 1998. Dramatic decreases in brain reward function during nicotine withdrawal. *Nature* 393:76–79

Fan J, McCandliss BD, Sommer T, Raz A, Posner MI. 2002. Testing the efficiency and independence of attentional networks. *J. Cogn. Neurosci.* 14:340–47

File SE, Kenny PJ, Ouagazzal AM. 1998. Bimodal modulation of anxiety in the social interaction test: role of the dorsal hippocampus. *Behav. Neurosci.* 112:1423–29

Fleming C, Kim H, Harachi T, Catalano R. 2002. Family processes for children in early elementary school as predictors of smoking initiation. *J. Adolesc. Health* 30:184–89

Flory K, Lynam D. 2003. The relation between attention deficit hyperactivity disorder and substance abuse: What role does conduct disorder play? *Clin. Child Fam. Psychol. Rev.* 6:1–16

Foulds J, Stapleton JA, Bell N, Swettenham J, Jarvis MJ, et al. 1997. Mood and physiological effects of subcutaneous nicotine in smokers and never-smokers. *Drug Alcohol Depend.* 44:105–15

Frenk H, Dar R. 2000. *A Critique of Nicotine Addiction.* New York: Kluwer Acad./Plenum

Garrett BE, Griffiths RR. 2001. Intravenous nicotine and caffeine: subjective and physiological effects in cocaine abusers. *J. Pharmacol. Exp. Ther.* 296(2):486–94

George TP, Verrico CD, Xu L, Roth RH. 2000. Effects of repeated nicotine administration and footshock stress on rat mesoprefrontal dopamine systems: evidence of opioid mechanisms. *Neuropsychopharmacology* 23:79–88

Gilbert DG. 1995. *Smoking: Individual Differences, Psychopathology, and Emotion.* Washington, DC: Taylor & Francis

Gilbert DG, Robinson JH, Chamberlin CL, Spielberger DC. 1989. Effects of smoking/nicotine on anxiety, heart rate, and lateralization of EEG during a stressful movie. *Psychophysiology* 26:311–20

Giovino G. 1999. Epidemiology of tobacco use among adolescents. *Nicotine Tob. Res.* 1(Suppl.):31–40

Green L, Fry A, Myerson J. 1994. Discounting of delayed rewards: a life-span comparison. *Psychol. Sci.* 5:33–36

Greenwald A, McGhee D, Schwartz J. 1998. Measuring individual differences in implicit cognition: the implicit association test. *J. Personal. Soc. Psychol.* 74:1464–80

Griesar WS, Zajdel DP, Oken BS. 2002. Nicotine effects on alertness and spatial attention in non-smokers. *Nicotine Tob. Res.* 4:185–94

Griesler P, Kandel DB. 1998. Ethnic differences in correlates of adolescent cigarette smoking. *J. Adolesc. Health* 23:167–80

Hahn B, Shoaib M, Stolerman IP. 2002. Nicotine-induced enhancement of attention in the five-choice serial reaction time task: the influence of task demands. *Psychopharmacology* 162:129–37

Hahn B, Stolerman IP. 2002. Nicotine-induced attentional enhancement in rats: effects of chronic exposure to nicotine. *Neuropsychopharmacology* 27:712–22

Heishman SJ, Henningfield JE. 2000. Tolerance to repeated nicotine administration on performance, subjective, and physiological responses in nonsmokers. *Psychopharmacology* 152:321–33

Heishman SJ, Taylor RC, Henningfield JE. 1994. Nicotine and smoking: a review of effects on human performance. *Exp. Clin. Psychopharmacol.* 2:345–95

Henningfield JE, Stapleton JM, Benowitz NL, Grayson RF, London ED. 1993. Higher levels of nicotine in arterial than in venous blood after cigarette smoking. *Drug Alcohol Depend.* 33:23–29

Herbert M, Foulds J, Fife-Schaw C. 2001. No effect of cigarette smoking on attention or mood in non-depressed smokers. *Addiction* 96:1349–56

Hu FB, Flay BR, Hedeker D, Siddiqui O, Day LE. 1995. The influences of friends' and parental smoking on adolescent smoking behavior: the effects of time and prior smoking. *J. Appl. Soc. Psychol.* 25:2018–47

Hughes JR. 1989. Dependence potential and abuse liability of nicotine replacement therapies. *Biomed. Pharmacother.* 43(1):11–17

Hughes JR, Gust SW, Skoog K, Keenan RM, Fenwick JW. 1991. Symptoms of tobacco withdrawal. A replication and extension. *Arch. Gen. Psychiatry* 48(1):52–59

Ikard FF, Green D, Horn D. 1969. A scale to differentiate between types of smoking as related to management of affect. *Int. J. Addict.* 4:649–59

Irvine EE, Cheeta S, File SE. 2001. Tolerance of nicotine's effects in the elevated plus-maze and increased anxiety during withdrawal. *Pharmacol. Biochem. Behav.* 68:319–25

Jarvik ME, Caskey NH, Rose JE, Herskovic JE, Sadeghpour M. 1989. Anxiolytic effects of smoking associated with four stressors. *Addict Behav.* 14:379–86

Jessor R, Jessor SL. 1977. *Problem Behavior and Psychosocial Development: A Longitudinal Study of Youth.* New York: Academic

Johnson R, Hoffman J. 2000. Adolescent cigarette smoking in US racial/ethnic subgroups: findings from the National

Education Longitudinal Study. *J. Health Soc. Behav.* 41:392–407

Johnston L, O'Malley P, Bachman J, Schulenberg J. 2002. *National Survey Results on Drug Use from the Monitoring the Future Study, 1975–2002*:Volume 1. *Secondary School Students.* Rockville, MD: USDHHS, PHS, NIDA

Jorenby DE, Hatsukami DK, Smith SS, Fiore MC. 1996. Characterization of tobacco withdrawal symptoms: transdermal nicotine reduces hunger and weight gain. *Psychopharmacology* 128:130–38

Juliano LM, Brandon TH. 2002. Effects of nicotine dose, instructional set, and outcome expectancies on the subjective effects of smoking in the presence of a stressor. *J. Abnorm. Psychol.* 111:88–97

Kandel DB, Chen K. 2000. Extent of smoking and nicotine dependence in the US 1991–1993. *Nicotine Tob. Res.* 2:263–75

Kassel JD, Stroud LR, Paronis CA. 2003. Smoking, stress, and negative affect: correlation, causation, and context across stages of smoking. *Psychol. Bull.* 129:270–304

Kassel JD, Unrod M. 2000. Smoking, anxiety, and attention: support for the role of nicotine in attentionally mediated anxiolysis. *J. Abnorm. Psychol.* 109:161–66

Kendler KS, Neale MC, MacLean CJ, Hath AC, Eaves LJ, et al. 1993. Smoking and major depression: a causal analysis. *Arch. Gen. Psychiatry* 50:36–43

Kenford SL, Smith SS, Wetter DW, Jorenby DE, Fiore MC, et al. 2002. Predicting relapse back to smoking: contrasting affective and physical models of dependence. *J. Consult. Clin. Psychol.* 70:216–27

Klesges R, Elliott V, Robinson L. 1997. Chronic dieting and the belief that smoking controls body weight in a biracial population-based adolescent sample. *Tob. Control.* 6:89–94

Koppstein A. 2001. *Tobacco Use in America: Findings from the 1999 National Household Survey on Drug Abuse.* Rockville, MD: USDHHS, SAMHSA, OAS

Kumari V, Soni W, Sharma T. 2001. Influence of cigarette smoking on prepulse inhibition of the acoustic startle response in schizophrenia. *Hum. Psychopharmacol. Clin. Exp.* 10:321–28

Landrine H, Richardson J, Klonoff E, Flay B. 1994. Cultural diversity in the predictors of adolescent cigarette smoking: the relative influence of peers. *J. Behav. Med.* 17:331–35

Lang PJ. 1968. Fear reduction and fear behavior: problems in treating a construct. *In Research in Psychotherapy*, ed. JM Schlien, 3:90–103. Washington, DC: Am. Psychiatr. Assoc.

Leventhal H, Cleary PD. 1980. The smoking problem: a review of the research and theory in behavioral risk modification. *Psychol. Bull.* 88:370–405

Levin ED, Rezvani AH, Montoya D, Rose JE, Swartzwelder HS. 2003. Adolescent-onset nicotine self-administration modeled in female rats. *Psychopharmacology* 169:141–49. DOI: 10.1007/s00213-003-1486-y

Loewenstein G, Weber E, Hsee C, Welch N. 2001. Risk as feelings. *Psychol. Bull.* 127:267–86

Lynskey M, Fergusson D. 1995. Childhood conduct problems, attention deficit behaviors, and adolescent alcohol, tobacco, and illicit drug use. *J. Abnorm. Child Psychol.* 23:281–302

Lynskey M, Fergusson D, Horwood L. 1998. The origins of the correlation between tobacco, alcohol, and cannabis use during adolescence. *J. Child Psychol. Psychiatry* 39:995–1005

Malin DH. 2001. Nicotine dependence studies with a laboratory model. *Pharmacol. Biochem. Behav.* 70:551–59

Malin DH, Lake JR, Upchurch TP, Shenoi M, Rajan N, et al. 1998. Nicotine abstinence syndrome precipitated by the competitive nicotinic antagonist dihydro-beta-erythroidine. *Pharmacol. Biochem. Behav.* 60:609–13

Mancuso G, Lejeune M, Ansseau M. 2001. Cigarette smoking and attention: processing speed or specific effects? *Psychopharmacology* 155:372–78

Masse L, Tremblay R. 1997. Behavior of boys in kindergarten and onset of substance use during adolescence. *Arch. Gen. Psychiatry* 54:62–68

Mayhew K, Flay B, Mott J. 2000. Stages in the development of adolescent smoking. *Drug Alcohol Depend.* 59(Suppl.):61–81

Maziere M, Comar D, Marzano C, Berger G. 1976. Nicotine-11C: synthesis and distribution kinetics in animals. *Eur. J. Nucl. Med.* 1:255–58

McMahon R. 1999. Child and adolescent psychopathology as risk factors for smoking initiation: an overview. *Nicotine Tob. Res.* 1(Suppl.):45–50

Mermelstein R. 1999. Ethnicity, gender, and risk factors for smoking initiation: an overview. *Nicotine Tob. Res.* 1(Suppl.):45–51

Millstein S, Halpern-Felsher B. 2002. Perceptions of risk and vulnerability. *J. Adolesc. Health* 31(Suppl.):1027

Molina BS, Pelham WE Jr. 2003. Childhood predictors of adolescent substance use in a longitudinal study of children with ADHD. *J. Abnorm. Psychol.* 112:497–507

Muthen B, Muthen L. 2000. Integrating person-centered and variable-centered analyses: growth mixture modeling with latent trajectory classes. *Alcohol Clin. Exp. Res.* 24:882–901

Novak S, Clayton R. 2001. The influence of school environment and self-regulation on transitions between stages of cigarette smoking: a multilevel analysis. *Health Psychol.* 20:196–207

Ortendahl M, Fries J. 2002. Time-related issues with application to health gains and losses. *J. Clin. Epidemiol.* 55:843–48

Park S, Knopick C, McGurk S, Meltzer HY. 2000. Nicotine impairs spatial working memory while leaving spatial attention intact. *Neuropsychopharmacology* 22:200–9

Parrott AC. 1999. Does cigarette smoking cause stress? *Am. Psychol.* 54:817–20

Payne TJ, Schare ML, Levis DJ, Colletti G. 1991. Exposure to smoking-relevant cues: effects on desire to smoke and topographical components of smoking behavior. *Addict. Behav.* 16:467–79

Perkins KA. 1993. Weight gain following smoking cessation. *J. Consult. Clin. Psychol.* 61:768–77

Perkins KA, Broge M, Gerlach D, Sanders M, Grobe JE, et al. 2002. Acute nicotine reinforcement, but not chronic tolerance, predicts withdrawal and relapse after quitting smoking. *Health Psychol.* 21:332–39

Perkins KA, D'Amico D, Sanders M, Grobe JE, Wilson A, Stiller RL. 1996. Influence of training dose on nicotine discrimination in humans. *Psychopharmacology* 126(2):132–39

Perkins KA, Gerlach D, Broge M, Sanders M, Grobe JE, et al. 2001a. Quitting smoking produces minimal loss of chronic tolerance to nicotine. *Psychopharmacology* 158:7–17

Perkins KA, Gerlach D, Vender J, Meeker J, Hutchison S. 2001b. Sex differences in the subjective and reinforcing effects of visual and olfactory cigarette smoke stimuli. *Nicotine Tob. Res.* 3:141–50

Perkins KA, Grobe JE. 1992. Increased desire to smoke during acute stress. *Br. J. Addict.* 87:1037–40

Perkins KA, Grobe JE, Fonte C, Goettler J, Caggiula AR, et al. 1994. Chronic and acute tolerance to subjective, behavioral, and cardiovascular effects of nicotine in humans. *J. Pharmacol. Exp. Ther.* 270:628–38

Peto R, Lopez AD, Boreham J, Thun M, Heath C Jr. 1992. Mortality from tobacco in developed countries: indirect estimation from national vital statistics. *Lancet* 339(8804):1268–78

Piasecki TM, Fiore MC, Baker TB. 1998. Profiles in discouragement: two studies of variability in the time course of smoking withdrawal symptoms. *J. Abnorm. Psychol.* 107:238–51

Piasecki TM, Jorenby DE, Smith SS, Fiore MC, Baker TB. 2003a. Smoking withdrawal dynamics: I. Abstinence distress in lapsers and abstainers. *J.Abnorm. Psychol.* 112:3–13

Piasecki TM, Jorenby DE, Smith SS, Fiore MC, Baker TB. 2003b. Smoking withdrawal dynamics: II. Improved tests of withdrawal-relapse relations. *J. Abnorm. Psychol.* 112:14–27

Piasecki TM, Niaura R, Shadel WG, Abrams D, Goldstein M, et al. 2000. Smoking withdrawal dynamics in unaided quitters. *J. Abnorm. Psychol.* 109:74–86

Pierce J, Gilpin E. 1995. A historical analysis of tobacco marketing and the uptake of smoking by youth in the United States: 1890–1977. *Health Psychol.* 14:500–8

Piper ME, Federman EB, Piasecki TM, Bolt DM, Smith SS, et al. 2003. A multiple motives approach to tobacco dependence: the Wisconsin Inventory of Smoking Dependence Motives (WISDM). *J. Consult. Clin. Psychol.* In press

Pomerleau OF, Pomerleau CS, Fagerstroem KO, Henningfield JE, Hughes JR, eds . 1992. *Nicotine Replacement: A Critical Evaluation.* New York: Liss

Porchet HC, Benowitz NL, Sheiner LB. 1988. Pharmacodynamic model of tolerance: application to nicotine. *J. Pharmacol. Exp. Ther.* 244:231–36

Quadrel M, Fischhoff B, Davis W. 1993. Adolescent (in)vulnerability. *Am. Psychol.* 48:102–16

Robinson TE, Berridge KC. 1993. The neural basis of drug craving: an incentive-sensitization theory of addiction. *Brain Res. Rev.* 18:247–91

Robinson TE, Berridge KC. 2001. Incentive-sensitization and addiction. *Addiction* 96:103–14

Romer D, Jamieson P. 2001. Do adolescents appreciate the risks of smoking? Evidence from a national survey. *J. Adolesc. Health* 29:12–21

Romer D, Jamieson P. 2002. Advertising, smoker imagery, and the diffusion of smoking behavior. In *Smoking: Risk Perception and Policy*, ed. P Slovic, pp. 127–58. Thousand Oaks, CA: Sage

Russell MA. 1988. Nicotine replacement: the role of blood nicotine levels, their rate of change, and nicotine tolerance. *Progr. Clin. Biol. Res.* 261:6394

Sayette MA, Martin CS, Hull JG, Wertz JM,

Perrott MA. 2003. Effects of nicotine deprivation on craving response covariation in smokers. *J. Abnorm. Psychol.* 112:110–18

Schwid SR, Hirvonen MD, Keesey RE. 1992. Nicotine effects on body weight: a regulatory perspective. *Am. J. Clin. Nutr.* 55(4):878–84

Sherman SJ, Rose JS, Koch K, Presson CC, Chassin L. 2003. Implicit and explicit attitudes toward cigarette smoking: the effects of context and motivation. *J. Soc. Clin. Psychol.* 22:13–39

Shiffman S, Gwaltney CJ, Balabanis MH, Liu KS, Paty JA, et al. 2002. Immediate antecedents of cigarette smoking: an analysis from ecological momentary assessment. *J. Abnorm. Psychol.* 111:531–45

Shiffman S, Paty JA, Gnys M, Kassel JD, Hickcox M. 1996. First lapses to smoking: within subjects analysis of real time reports. *J. Consult. Clin. Psychol.* 64:366–37

Simons-Morton B. 2002. Prospective analysis of peer and parent influences on smoking initiation among early adolescents. *Prev. Sci.* 3:275–83

Slovic P. 2000. What does it mean to know a cumulative risk? Adolescents' perceptions of short-term and long-term consequences of smoking. *J. Behav. Decis. Mak.* 13:259–66

Steele CM, Josephs RA. 1988. Drinking your troubles away II: an attention-allocation model of alcohol's effect on psychological stress. *J. Abnorm. Psychol.* 97:196–205

Sullivan P, Kendler K. 1999. The genetic epidemiology of smoking. *Nicotine Tob. Res.* 1(Suppl.):51–57

Sussman S, Dent C, McAdams L, Stacy A, Burton D, et al. 1994. Group self-identification and adolescent cigarette smoking: a 1-year prospective study. *J. Abnorm. Psychol.* 103:576–80

Suzuki T, Ise Y, Tsuda M, Maieda J, Misawa M. 1996. Mecamylamine-precipitated nicotine-withdrawal aversion in rats. *Eur. J. Pharmacol.* 314:281–84

Szyndler J, Sienkiewicz-Jarose H, Maciejak L, Siemiatkowski M, Rokicki D, et al. 2001. The anxiolytic-like effect of nicotine undergoes rapid tolerance in a model of contextual fear conditioning in rats. *Pharmacol. Biochem. Behav.* 69:511–18

Tiffany ST. 1990. A cognitive model of drug urges and drug-use behavior: role of automatic and nonautomatic processes. *Psychol. Rev.* 97:147–68

Tiffany ST, Drobes DJ. 1990. Imagery and smoking urges: the manipulation of affective content. *Addict. Behav.* 15:531–39

Turbin M, Jessor R, Costa F. 2000. Adolescent cigarette smoking: health-related behavior or normative transgression? *Prev. Sci.* 1:115–24

Urberg K, Degirmencioglu S, Pilgrim C. 1997. Close friend and group influence on adolescence cigarette smoking and alcohol use. *Dev. Psychol.* 33:834–44

Urberg K, Shyu S, Liang J. 1990. Peer influence in adolescent cigarette smoking. *Addict. Behav.* 15:247–55

US Dep. Health Hum. Serv. 1988. *Health Consequences of Smoking: Nicotine Addiction.* Rep. Surg. Gen. Washington, DC: USDHHS

US Dep. Health Hum. Serv. 1998. *Tobacco Use Among US Racial/Ethnic Minority Groups.* Rep. Surg. Gen. Atlanta, GA: USDHHS/CDC/NCCDPHP/OSH

van Ree JM, Gerrits MA, Vanderschuren LJ. 1999. Opioids, reward and addiction: an encounter of biology, psychology, and medicine. *Pharmacol. Rev.* 51(2):341–96

Vuchinich RE, Tucker JA. 1998. Choice, behavioral economics, and addictive behavior patterns. In *Treating Addictive Behaviors*, ed. R Miller, N Heather, 2:93–104. New York: Plenum

Warburton DM, Walters AC. 1995. Attentional processing. In *Smoking and Human Behavior*, ed. T Ney, A Gale, pp. 223–37. New York: Wiley

Waters AJ, Feyerabend C. 2000. Determinants and effects of attentional bias in smokers. *Psychol. Addict. Behav.* 14:111–20

Weinstein N. 1999. Accuracy of smokers' risk perceptions. *Nicotine Tob Res.* 1(Suppl.): 123–30

Wertz JM, Sayette MA. 2001. Effects of smoking opportunity on attentional bias in smokers. *Psychol. Addict. Behav.* 15:268–71

Wetter DW, Kenford SL, Welsch SK, Smith SS, Fouladi RT, et al. 2003. Smoking behavior among college students: a longitudinal study. *Health Psychol.* In press

Wetter DW, Smith SS, Kenford SL, Jorenby DE, Fiore MC, et al. 1994. Smoking outcome expectancies: factor structure, predictive validity, and discriminant validity. *J. Abnorm. Psychol.* 103:801–11

White HR, Pandina RJ, Chen PH. 2002. Developmental trajectories of cigarette use from early adolescence into young adulthood. *Drug Alcohol Depend.* 65:167–78

Williamson DF, Madans J, Anda RF, Kleinman JC, Giovino GA, Byers T. 1991. Smoking cessation and severity of weight gain in a national cohort. *N. Engl. J. Med.* 324(11):739–45

Wise RA. 1988. The neurobiology of craving: implications for the understanding and treatment of addiction. *J. Abnorm. Psychol.* 97:118–32

Zinser MC, Baker TB, Sherman JE, Cannon DS. 1992. Relation between self-reported affect and drug urges and cravings in continuing and withdrawing smokers. *J. Abnorm. Psychol.* 101:617–29

Zinser MC, Fiore MC, Davidson RJ, Baker TB. 1999. Manipulating smoking motivation: impact on an electrophysiological index of approach motivation. *J. Abnorm. Psychol.* 108(2):2400–54

Annu. Rev. Psychol. 2004. 55:493–518
doi: 10.1146/annurev.psych.55.090902.141954
Copyright © 2004 by Annual Reviews. All rights reserved
First published online as a Review in Advance on October 6, 2003

SELF-KNOWLEDGE: Its Limits, Value, and Potential for Improvement

Timothy D. Wilson and Elizabeth W. Dunn
*University of Virginia, Charlottesville, Virginia 22904-4400;
email: tdw@virginia.edu, edunn@post.harvard.edu*

Key Words   implicit, nonconscious, repression, self-insight, self-perception

■ **Abstract**   Because of personal motives and the architecture of the mind, it may be difficult for people to know themselves. People often attempt to block out unwanted thoughts and feelings through conscious suppression and perhaps through unconscious repression, though whether such attempts are successful is controversial. A more common source of self-knowledge failure is the inaccessibility of much of the mind to consciousness, including mental processes involved in perception, motor learning, personality, attitudes, and self-esteem. Introspection cannot provide a direct pipeline to these mental processes, though some types of introspection may help people construct beneficial personal narratives. Other ways of increasing self-knowledge include looking at ourselves through the eyes of others and observing our own behavior. These approaches can potentially promote self-knowledge, although major obstacles exist. It is not always advantageous to hold self-perceptions that correspond perfectly with reality, but increasing awareness of nonconscious motives and personality is generally beneficial.

CONTENTS

INTRODUCTION

How well do people know themselves? What are the major impediments to self-knowledge? Is it always to people's advantage to try to analyze themselves? Although these are fundamental questions about the nature of the human mind and its ability to know itself, self-knowledge has not been a mainstream topic in psychology. There are many areas of research related to self-knowledge, including the psychoanalytic tradition, personality research in which traits are measured with self-report inventories, and social psychological research on the nature of the self-concept—not to mention the many treatises on self-improvement that occupy substantial shelf space in most bookstores. Self-knowledge has not been a central, organizing topic in empirical psychology, however. There are few courses taught on the topic and few researchers who identify this as the major theme of their research.

One reason for this state of affairs is that investigations of self-knowledge inexorably lead to thorny questions about the limits of consciousness and the nature of the unconscious mental processes, which most psychologists (until recently) have been loath to examine. For many years, research psychologists artfully dodged these difficult issues, developing sophisticated theories of the self and personality with nary a mention of the word "unconscious."

Times have changed. It is difficult to pick up a psychology journal without some reference to nonconscious processing or related terms such as implicit versus explicit processes, automaticity, or procedural versus declarative knowledge. As research on the limits of conscious awareness has exploded, compelling questions about self-knowledge have begun to be asked.

This chapter is divided into three parts. First, we review the most commonly cited reason why people lack self-knowledge, namely motivational factors that lead to repression or suppression. Second, we review nonmotivational systemic reasons why people do not have full access to their mental processes, focusing on research that has found dissociations between implicit and explicit mental processes. Third, we discuss ways in which self-knowledge might be increased and whether this is a worthy goal, focusing on research on introspection and self-perception.

MOTIVATIONAL LIMITS TO SELF-KNOWLEDGE

There are several reasons why people are not an open book to themselves. There might simply be too much information—too many pages to keep in mind at one time. Rather than a simple atlas with a well-marked legend, people may be more like a complex novel with interconnecting story lines, themes, and leitmotivs. Just as literary themes can take extensive analysis (and be open to myriad interpretations), so can it be difficult to unravel the complex themes of the individual psyche. Those unskilled at the art of literary dissection may not succeed in understanding themselves completely.

Perhaps the most common reason cited for failures of self-knowledge is that people are motivated to keep some thoughts and feelings outside of consciousness, usually because they are unpleasant or anxiety provoking. Motivated attempts to avoid unwanted thoughts is one of the central ideas of psychoanalysis, which argues that there is a vast repository of infantile urges that are actively kept out of conscious awareness. Self-knowledge is said to be quite limited, though repression is usually so successful that people do not *know* that it is limited.

Many researchers have attempted to test psychoanalytic ideas under controlled scientific conditions (e.g., McGinnies 1949; for reviews, see Erdelyi 1974, 1985). In recent years there has been renewed interest in the existence of repression, specifically the question of whether people can repress memories of physical and sexual abuse and then recover these memories later in life. A problem in this area of research, however, is that terms such as repression, suppression, and intentional forgetting are used in different ways by different researchers, making it difficult to find common ground. As noted by Erdelyi (1985) this is not a new problem; Freud himself used the term repression in different ways over the course of his career.

Definitions of Repression, Suppression, Intentional Forgetting, and Complete Forgetting

A demonstration of repression, we suggest, would have to meet the following five criteria (cf. Kihlstrom 2002): (*1*) People are motivated to keep thoughts, feelings, or memories outside of awareness; (*2*) the attempt to keep material out of awareness is itself an unconscious process; (*3*) people succeed in removing the undesired material from consciousness; (*4*) the material, once removed from consciousness, still exists in memory and continues to influence people's thoughts, feelings, or behavior; and (*5*) the material is recoverable; i.e., people can become aware of it if the repressive forces are removed (see Table 1).

The term suppression has been used to refer to cases in which people consciously attempt to remove a thought from awareness or prevent themselves from expressing a thought or attitude (e.g., Crandall & Eshleman 2003). We are concerned only with the former meaning of the term, because of its relevance to the issue of self-knowledge. Controlling the expression of a thought does not necessarily limit people's awareness that they have the thought, whereas trying to banish a thought from awareness, if successful, does.

Successful suppression shares all the features of repression except one, namely people's awareness of the attempt to remove something from awareness

TABLE 1   Different ways in which people can lack knowledge of their own feelings, thoughts, and memories

	Successful repression	Successful suppression (intentional forgetting)	Complete forgetting	Unsuccessful suppression	Inaccessibility of the adaptive unconscious
1. Are people motivated to keep material out of awareness?	Yes	Yes	Yes	Yes	No
2. Are people aware of their attempt to keep material out of awareness?	No	Yes	Yes	Yes	N/A
3. Do people succeed in removing the material from awareness?	Yes	Yes	Yes	No	N/A
4. Does the material still exist outside of awareness and influence thoughts, feelings, or behaviors?	Yes	Yes	No	N/A	Yes
5. Is the unconscious material recoverable?	Yes	Yes	N/A	N/A	No

(criterion 2). Repression is, in a sense, an early defense system, whereby material is intercepted and blocked before it reaches consciousness. [As noted by Erdelyi (1985), Freud did not always argue that repression was unconscious, though this criterion is part of the contemporary psychoanalytic meaning of the term.] If these early defenses fail—for example, if anxiety-provoking sexual or aggressive thoughts succeed in reaching consciousness—then suppression is the next line of defense, whereby people deliberately and consciously attempt to eliminate those thoughts. If they succeed in doing so, then the result is the same as with successful repression: The material is kept out of consciousness but continues to influence people's thoughts, feelings, and behavior, and is potentially recoverable (see the third column of Table 1). Similarly, intentional forgetting is the case in which people succeed in removing material from memory (i.e., reducing their ability to recall it), though as will be seen shortly, the material is not completely erased from memory and can be recovered under some circumstances.

Complete forgetting is illustrated in the fourth column of Table 1 and is the theoretical case in which people succeed in removing material from memory completely. The material is erased and is no longer present in memory. The fifth column illustrates the case in which attempts to suppress or forget information fail; people do not succeed in removing the unwanted material from consciousness. Table 1 is meant to bring some definitional order to the use of the terms repression, suppression, intentional forgetting, and the like. Whether there is empirical support for these phenomena is another question.

Empirical Evidence for Repression, Suppression, Intentional Forgetting, and Complete Forgetting

There is no doubt that people often want to keep troubling thoughts or feelings from occupying their conscious minds (criterion 1); 99% of college students reported having attempted to suppress thoughts, in an informal survey conducted by Erdelyi & Goldberg (1979; cited in Erdelyi 1993). Are such conscious attempts at suppression successful? A substantial amount of work by Wegner and colleagues indicates that suppression often fails. Suppression requires substantial mental resources, and if people are under cognitive load it can backfire, increasing the accessibility of the unwanted thought (Wenzlaff & Wegner 2000).

Some recent evidence suggests that suppression can be successful when people are not under cognitive load. Anderson & Green (2001) had participants memorize word pairs (e.g., ordeal-roach) and then presented one of the words with the instruction either to recall and think about or suppress thoughts of the associated word. On a subsequent test, participants showed impaired memory for words that they had previously been asked to suppress, even when offered monetary incentives for accurate recall. Similarly, Macrae et al. (1994) asked participants to avoid stereotypical thinking while writing a passage about a typical day in the life of a male skinhead. Their passages were rated as less stereotypical relative to passages written by control participants who had received no special instructions.

The extent to which suppression is generally successful or unsuccessful continues to be debated (e.g., Crandall & Eshleman 2003, Monteith et al. 1998, Wenzlaff & Wegner 2000). If people do succeed in suppressing or forgetting unwanted thoughts, it is clear that the thoughts are not truly gone. It is, of course, virtually impossible to show that any memory has been completely forgotten because this would involve proving the null hypothesis that no trace of the forgotten material exists in memory (see Table 1, column 4). Research has provided clear evidence for the alternative hypothesis, however, that previously suppressed material can continue to exert an effect (criterion 4).

Wegner and colleagues (1987, Wegner 1994) have shown that attempts to suppress a thought can produce a postsuppression rebound effect, whereby the taboo thought comes to mind with even greater frequency after the suppression episode. Research on intentional forgetting has shown that words people are instructed to forget can influence the word associates people generate in a subsequent "unrelated" study (e.g., Basden et al. 1993, Paz-Caballero & Menor 1999). Similarly, participants in Macrae et al.'s (1994) study who had previously been asked to suppress stereotypic thoughts about skinheads were actually faster to recognize stereotype-relevant words on a lexical decision task, and they chose to maintain greater social distance from a skinhead, relative to controls. Thus, thoughts that people have blocked out of consciousness may still influence them without their awareness.

Under the right conditions, people may be able to regain conscious access to material previously blocked out by their attempts to forget or suppress it (criterion 5). For example, Bjork (1989) and Basden et al. (1993) found that people do well on recognition tests for words they had previously been instructed to forget. Likewise, participants who had previously engaged in suppression wrote highly stereotypical passages about a different male skinhead after the instruction to suppress was relaxed, demonstrating increased accessibility of the stereotypic material (Macrae et al. 1994).

If people can suppress and then recover individual words and stereotypic thoughts, could they also forget and then remember complex personal memories? Most of the controversy in the recovered memory debate centers on this question. There is no doubt that recovered memories can be false, particularly when other people suggest that the events might have occurred (e.g., Loftus 1997, Mazzoni et al. 2001). There is accumulating evidence that such memories can also be true. Schooler (2001), for example, reviewed several case histories in which people remembered instances of being abused, they claimed to have forgotten these events at some point in their lives, and there was independent corroborative evidence of the abuse having occurred. As Schooler (2001) notes, however, these cases do not necessarily meet the criteria necessary to establish repression. People might never have truly forgotten the events, but instead reclassified or redefined them in a way that they confused with having forgotten them. Thus, the most controversial claim about recoverability—that people can forget traumatic events and then remember them years later—has yet to be established definitively.

What about the second criterion for repression, that the attempt to remove unwanted material from one's mind is itself unconscious? Although there is relatively little empirical support for this tenet, which distinguishes repression from the related phenomena included in Table 1, there is suggestive evidence. Some research suggests that if people continue to engage in successful suppression of unwanted material (e.g., prejudiced thoughts), then the process can become automatic through practice (Moskowitz et al. 1999, 2000). That is, exposure to a stimulus (e.g., a member of another race or gender) might trigger inhibition automatically and nonconsciously.

Summary

People are commonly motivated to keep material out of consciousness (criterion 1) and can sometimes do so successfully in the short run (criterion 3), though suppression often fails as a long-term strategy. Suppressed material can potentially influence people without their awareness (criterion 4). The material has been shown to be recoverable under the right circumstances (criterion 5), at least in laboratory studies of relatively innocuous material. It is less clear whether attempts to block unwanted material from the mind can be triggered unconsciously (criterion 2), which is the critical piece separating repression from the other phenomena, though recent research on chronic egalitarian goals suggests that this process can occur automatically. Thus, a patchwork of studies depicts a mental architecture that would allow repression to occur, though no single study has demonstrated all the necessary criteria to establish the existence of repression definitively. To the extent that people are motivated to block out thoughts, feelings, or memories, and succeed in doing so, self-knowledge will obviously suffer.

NONMOTIVATIONAL LIMITS TO SELF-KNOWLEDGE: DISSOCIATION BETWEEN IMPLICIT AND EXPLICIT PROCESSES

A more pervasive limit on self-knowledge, we suggest, is the fact that much of the mind is inaccessible to conscious awareness. Empirical research has increasingly documented the role of nonconscious mental processing (e.g., Kihlstrom 1987, Nisbett & Wilson 1977, Wilson 2002). A new view of unconscious processing has emerged that differs considerably from the Freudian, psychoanalytic version. The mind is viewed as a collection of processing modules that operate efficiently outside of awareness and may have existed before consciousness evolved. These processes are involved in perception, attention, learning, evaluation, emotion, and motivation.

Wilson (2002) referred to these nonconscious processes as the "adaptive unconscious" and specified three main ways in which they differ from the Freudian unconscious. First, mental processes are unconscious because of the architecture of the mind, rather than because of repression or suppression. That is, there are no motivational forces preventing people from knowing their thoughts and feelings; instead, much of the mind is simply inaccessible to consciousness (see the last column of Table 1). Second, the unconscious is much more than the repository of the primitive, infantile drives and desires discussed by Freud. The mind operates quite efficiently by relegating to the unconscious "normal" processes of perception, attention, learning, and judgment. Third, the modern approach makes different assumptions about people's ability to view their unconscious states. Rather than assuming that such states are "recoverable" (see criterion 5 in Table 1), it assumes that a large part of mental functioning is inaccessible to conscious awareness, no matter how much people introspect.

Put differently, modern research on unconscious processes paints a simpler picture than models of repression and suppression. Only one of the criteria necessary to demonstrate repression is applicable, namely criterion 4 (slightly restated), that unconscious processes exist and influence people's thoughts, feelings, or behavior, independent of conscious processes. There is no need to demonstrate people's motives for repression or suppression; the assumption is that a great deal of mental processing is simply inaccessible to conscious scrutiny. Consistent with this assumption, a good deal of independence between nonconscious and conscious processing has been found in many types of psychological functioning.

Implicit Versus Explicit Perception

Few people would claim that they have direct knowledge of how their perceptual systems operate, such as how they perceive depth in their visual fields. People do sometimes make conscious, deliberate judgments about the nature of the physical world, however, such as judging the distance between two points or the incline of a hill when setting out for a hike. Recent research on visual perception has revealed a disconnect between such conscious perceptions and the nonconscious visual system that guides people's behavior.

When walking across uneven terrain, for example, people are quite adept at judging the incline of the ground in front of them and adjusting their gait accordingly. They do so quickly and nonconsciously; people can walk without stumbling while thinking about something else entirely. When asked to make explicit judgments about inclines and distances, however, people make systematic errors, often underestimating distances and overestimating slants (Bhalla & Proffitt 2000, Creem & Proffitt 1999, Proffitt et al. 2003). Further, explicit judgments of distance and slant are easily biased by people's level of fatigue, physical fitness, and health status, whereas implicit judgments (as measured by visually guided action) are not (Bhalla & Proffitt 2000). For example, going for a long run inflates joggers' verbal estimates of a hill's slant, but such fatigue does not affect their ability to accurately adjust a tilt board to match the slant of the hill (Proffitt et al. 1995).

Given that people can assess accurately the steepness of a hill using a tilt board, why do their explicit reports of slant reveal consistent biases? To the extent that conscious visual awareness allows people to plan and modulate their exertion of effort, it may be useful for explicit judgments to reflect one's own physical condition. In contrast, visually guided action must reflect a pure, veridical evaluation if we want to make it up a hill without doing backward somersaults (Bhalla & Proffitt 2000).

Implicit Versus Explicit Motor Learning

But suppose we do want to make a backward somersault. How would our implicit and explicit knowledge allow us to complete this gymnastic feat successfully? Research on motor skill learning suggests that explicit knowledge would guide our somersaults initially, as we imitated a friend or followed a coach's instructions, but that after continued practice implicit knowledge would eventually guide our tumbling (Fitts 1964, Jenkins et al. 1994, Logan 1985). In fact, after extended practice, trying to reassert conscious control over our somersaulting technique might even impair performance (Baumeister 1984, Kimble & Rezabek 1992; see Baumeister & Showers 1986 for a review).

Because implicit knowledge can guide motor skill learning independently of explicit knowledge, amnesiacs can learn complex motor skills, even though they may have no memory of having practiced the skill (Gabrieli 1998). Similarly, normal college students respond faster to stimuli on a computer screen when the positions of the stimuli are determined by a regular, repeating sequence than when the positions are determined randomly, even if they show no awareness or explicit learning of the sequence (Nissen & Bullemer 1987, Willingham & Goedert-Eschmann 1999; but see Shanks & St. John 1994).

Over time, some participants may gain explicit knowledge of the sequence and this knowledge may then guide their behavior, which had previously been guided by implicit knowledge (Willingham 1998). Although the precise relationship between explicit and implicit motor skill learning is unknown, there is some evidence that explicit and implicit learning may be acquired in parallel as one performs a motor task (Willingham & Goedert-Eschmann 1999). Whereas explicit processes allow the gymnast to comply with a coach's demands that she straighten her legs in completing the somersault, implicit processes record this movement, facilitating its future execution.

Implicit Versus Explicit Personality

The study of human personality has been approached from many angles, including psychoanalysis, behaviorism, behavioral genetics, and phenomenology. With the exception of psychoanalysis, few of these approaches have been concerned with nonconscious psychological processes that determine a person's "characteristic behavior and thought," to use Allport's definition of personality (1961, p. 28). In recent years, researchers in diverse areas of personality have begun to investigate the role of implicit personality variables and their relationship to explicit measures.

As in research on perception and motor learning, a striking divergence between implicit and explicit measures has been found (for reviews see Wilson 2002, Wilson et al. 2000). For example, people's chronic motives, such as their needs for achievement, affiliation, and power, have traditionally been measured with the Thematic Apperception Test (TAT), in which people are asked to tell stories about people in photographs, and the content of these stories is systematically coded for the presence of various motives. McClelland et al. (1989) argued that the motives uncovered by this technique are implicit, in that they do not exist at an explicit, conscious level. In fact, explicit, self-report measures of the same motives typically correlate at a very low level with the motives revealed by the TAT (Spangler 1992). Such low correlations, of course, could stem from the fact that one or both measures are low in reliability or validity. McClelland et al. (1989) argued, instead, that the measures tap valid but different motivational constructs. Implicit motives "automatically influence behavior without conscious effort" (pp. 698–699), whereas "self-attributed motives" guide more deliberative, effortful behaviors.

Implicit measures of personality in other domains have also been found to correlate poorly with explicit measures including dependence (Bornstein 1995), attachment (Bartholomew & Shaver 1998, Wilson et al. 2000), and explanatory style (Peterson & Ulrey 1994). Robinson et al. (2003) found substantial independence between self-reported traits (e.g., of extraversion) and a new implicit personality measure, the speed with which people categorize the valence of information (e.g., people's response time on a task in which they classify a word as neutral or negative in meaning). In some studies, implicit and explicit measures of traits (e.g., shyness) do correlate to some degree, but they uniquely predict different kinds of behavior and a dissociation model fits the data well (Asendorpf et al. 2002).

Implicit Versus Explicit Attitudes

Social psychologists traditionally assumed that people have one attitude at a time toward an attitude object and are able to report this attitude. Recently, however, there has been an explosion of research on implicit attitudes (Blair 2002, Brauer et al. 2000, Devine 1989, Dovidio et al. 1997, Fazio & Olson 2003, Greenwald & Banaji 1995, Wilson et al. 2000). One problem with this literature is that a number of different definitions of implicit attitudes have been offered. All share the view that implicit attitudes are automatic responses, but as noted by Bargh (1994), many hybrids of automatic processes vary on the dimensions of conscious access, intentionality, controllability, and effort. Some definitions of implicit attitudes focus on some of these dimensions more than others do. Greenwald & Banaji (1995) emphasized a lack of awareness of the origins of the attitude, such as a failure to recognize that one's positive evaluation results from repeated exposure to an attitude object. Fazio et al. (1995) emphasized the lack of controllability and effort involved in the expression of implicit attitudes, while arguing that the attitude itself is usually conscious (see Fazio & Olson 2003). Gaertner & Dovidio (1986) argue that at least at times, the attitude itself, such as prejudiced feelings, can exist outside of awareness. Wilson et al. (2000) emphasized a lack of awareness of the origin of the attitude and the unintentional and uncontrollable activation of that attitude when the attitude object is encountered, and suggested that awareness of the attitude itself varies according to the type of implicit attitude involved. Brauer et al. (2000) distinguished between two types of implicit prejudice, the extent to which prejudiced attitudes are activated automatically, and the extent to which they are applied when judging members of the target group.

As in the other areas we have reviewed, many studies have found low correlations between explicit and implicit measures of attitudes (e.g., Dovidio et al. 1997, Fazio et al. 1995), though some have found higher degrees of correspondence (e.g., Blair 2002, Nosek et al. 2002). Two main reasons for a lack of correspondence have been discussed (Nosek & Banaji 2002). The first is that people have only one attitude toward an attitude object but are often motivated to distort or disguise that attitude when asked to report how they feel. Implicit measures are viewed as ways to bypass these self-presentational motives because people have less control over their responses on these measures. Fazio et al. (1995), for example, called their implicit priming measure a "bona fide pipeline," reflecting their view that it taps attitudes untainted by self-presentation. According to the self-presentation view implicit and explicit measures will reveal different attitudes in domains in which people are motivated to hide or distort their views (e.g., a prejudiced person who wants to appear unprejudiced), but will reveal the same attitude in domains in which people are willing to report how they really feel (e.g., attitudes toward politics or movies; Greenwald et al. 1998).

The second position argues that there can be a dissociation between implicit and explicit attitudes toward the same attitude object, due to different systems of evaluation. Wilson et al. (2000) endorsed this view in their model of dual attitudes, arguing that neither implicit nor explicit attitudes are "true" or "bona fide," rather, each can exist and direct behavior (albeit different kinds of behavior; see also Dovidio et al. 1997). According to this view, the two systems could in principle evaluate an attitude object in similar ways, resulting in concordance, but often come up with different evaluations, resulting in discordance. In support of the separate systems view, discordance has been found in domains in which self-presentational concerns would seem to be low, such as attitudes toward fruit and bugs (Nosek & Banaji 2002, Wilson et al. 2000).

Implicit Versus Explicit Self-Esteem

In recent years several implicit measures of self-esteem have been developed. As in the other areas we have reviewed, discordance between these measures and explicit measures has often been found. Implicit self-esteem is generally viewed as an efficient evaluation of the self that occurs unintentionally and without awareness, in contrast to explicit self-esteem, which represents a more conscious, deliberative assessment of the self; Greenwald & Banaji (1995, p. 11) defined implicit self-esteem as "the introspectively unidentified (or inaccurately identified) effect of the self-attitude on evaluation of self-associated and self-dissociated objects."

In an early demonstration of this phenomenon, Nuttin (1985) found that people consistently preferred letters that were contained in their own names. Subsequent research has demonstrated that this "name-letter effect" emerges across a variety of cultures and languages and cannot be easily accounted for by alternative explanations, such as mere exposure (Koole & Pelham 2003). Importantly, participants who exhibit the name-letter effect generally do not report having thought about their own names in evaluating the letters, which suggests that this effect occurs without conscious awareness (Koole et al. 2001). This subtle preference for name-letters may influence major life-decisions; people are disproportionately likely to choose careers and home cities whose names resemble their own (e.g., Larry becomes a lawyer in Lawrence; Pelham et al. 2002).

Evidence for implicit self-esteem has also been found using response-time measures designed to assess the degree of association between the self and positive versus negative concepts. On the Implicit Association Test, for example, Greenwald & Farnham (2000) found that participants were much faster to respond when self-relevant items (e.g., their birth month) were paired with pleasant words than when self-relevant items were paired with unpleasant words.

Using a wide range of measures, researchers have consistently observed a dissociation between implicit and explicit self-esteem, with correlations ranging from zero to weakly positive (Bosson 2003, Bosson et al. 2000, Greenwald & Farnham 2000, Jordan et al. 2003, Spalding & Hardin 1999). When, if ever, do implicit and explicit self-esteem correlate with one another? In contrast to the common intuition that we may unearth our deepest, subconscious self-relevant feelings through thoughtful introspection, explicit self-evaluations are more likely to be concordant with implicit self-esteem when motivation and capacity to engage in deliberation are lacking; participants' explicit judgments of whether positive and negative traits described themselves were related to their scores on the name-letter test only when these self-judgments were made quickly or under cognitive load (Koole et al. 2001). Conversely, favoritism for name-letters evaporates when participants are asked to consider their reasons for liking the letters, suggesting that engaging in deliberation steers people away from their immediate, intuitive response in making self-relevant judgments (Koole et al. 2001).

In line with research on the predictive validity of implicit and explicit attitudes more broadly, implicit and explicit measures of self-esteem predict distinct types of behavior. For example, during an interview about their emotional health, participants' self-reported anxiety was related to their explicit self-esteem, whereas their nonverbal anxiety (as rated by the interviewer) was related to implicit self-esteem (Spalding & Hardin 1999).

Summary

Research on such disparate topics as perception, motor learning, personality, attitudes, and self-esteem reveals a frequent discordance between implicit and explicit measures of internal states. There are several reasons why this might be the case, such as people's desire to distort their attitudes on explicit measures due to self-presentational concerns. The discordance has been found even in domains in which self-presentational concerns are low, however. There is substantial evidence that implicit measures often tap mental processes that are nonconscious and inaccessible to introspection (Wilson 2002). Whereas it is relatively unsurprising that people lack conscious access to the mental processes that allow them to judge slant or perform somersaults, the apparent lack of access to one's traits, attitudes, and self-concept is noteworthy. Currently researchers are going beyond demonstrations of discordance and are asking important theoretical questions about the conditions under which discordance will occur (e.g., Nosek 2002) and the consequences of discordance (e.g., Robinson et al. 2003).

INCREASING SELF-KNOWLEDGE

Given the limits to self-knowledge we have reviewed, in what ways can people seek to know themselves better? Is this always a desirable goal? Perhaps the most common way in which people attempt to decipher their feelings, judgments, and motives is introspection.

Introspection

A common metaphor for introspection is that it is like an archaeological dig, whereby people attempt to excavate their hidden mental states. Some aspects of our mental lives are near the surface and easy to examine, whereas others lie under multiple strata and require considerable excavation. Freud, an avid collector of antiquities, was fond of the archeological metaphor, and used it often to describe the process of psychoanalysis, in which considerable digging is often required in order to reveal unconscious wishes and drives.

The more contemporary view is that the vast adaptive unconscious is dissociated from conscious awareness and can never be directly viewed via introspection. Introspection reveals the contents of consciousness, such as at least some of people's current thoughts and feelings. It cannot, however, no matter how deeply people dig, gain direct access to nonconscious mental processes. Instead, people must attempt to infer the nature of these processes, by taking what they know (e.g., their conscious states) and filling in the gaps of what they do not know (their nonconscious states) by constructing a coherent narrative about themselves (McAdams 1993, 2001).

According to this view, introspection is less a matter of unearthing hidden feelings and motives and more a constructive process of inferring what these states might be. Several areas of research on different kinds of introspection can be understood within this framework. With some types of introspection the construction process goes awry and has negative consequences. With others, people succeed in constructing a more coherent narrative than they held before, with beneficial consequences.

EFFECTS OF ANALYZING THE REASONS FOR ONE'S FEELINGS AND ATTITUDES   One kind of introspection that can go awry is thinking about the reasons why we feel the way we do. It might seem like a relatively easy matter to access and report such reasons (e.g., why we like or dislike different models of cars), and that such an analysis would sharpen decision making (e.g., which car we should purchase). There is considerable evidence, however, that people have limited access to the reasons for their evaluations and that the process of generating reasons can have negative consequences. Analyzing reasons has been shown to lower people's satisfaction with their choices (Wilson et al. 1993), lower people's ability to predict their own behavior (Wilson & LaFleur 1995), lower the correlation between people's expressed feelings and their later behavior (Wilson & Dunn 1986, Wilson et al. 1984), lower the correlation between people's evaluations of a product and expert evaluations of it (Wilson & Schooler 1991), and lower the accuracy of sports fans' predictions about the outcome of basketball games (Halberstadt & Levine 1999).

Why does analyzing reasons have these effects? Consistent with the idea that introspection is often a constructive process, people do not have complete access to the actual reasons behind their feelings, attitudes, and judgment and thus generate reasons that are consistent with cultural and personal theories and are accessible in memory (Nisbett & Wilson 1977). But, people do not recognize that the reasons they have just generated are incomplete or inaccurate, and thus assume that their attitude is the one implied by these reasons. Put differently, people construct a new attitude, at least temporarily, that is consistent with the reasons that happen to come to mind, but which might not correspond to their implicit attitudes (Wilson et al. 1989, 1995, 2000).

EFFECTS OF FOCUSING ON ONE'S FEELINGS   Rather than analyzing the reasons for an attitude perhaps people should focus on the nature of the attitude itself. Several studies have purported to find that focusing on how one feels (as opposed to why one feels that way) increases the accessibility of people's feelings and increases the extent to which these feelings predict people's subsequent behavior (e.g., Carver & Scheier 1981, Fazio et al. 1982, Snyder 1982, Wicklund 1982). This kind of self-focus might help sharpen and clarify people's feelings. However, Silvia & Gendolla (2001) reached a different conclusion. They argued that increased self-awareness, induced by focusing one's attention inward, increases people's motivation to act consistently with their attitudes, and does not necessarily increase people's awareness of their feelings.

RUMINATION WHEN DISTRESSED   Another kind of introspection that can be harmful is rumination, whereby people in negative moods repetitively think about how they feel and why they feel that way, without taking action to improve their situation. Research has found that this type of introspection focuses people's attention on negative aspects of their pasts and futures, leads to self-defeating, negative interpretations of their problems, and lowers their ability to find effective solutions to their problems (Lyubomirsky et al. 1998, Nolen-Hoeksema 2000, Ward et al. 2003). One problem with rumination is that it focuses people's attention on negative information about themselves, providing more grist for a pejorative self-narrative.

WRITING ABOUT TRAUMATIC EVENTS   Surely, not all forms of introspection are harmful. Many studies by Pennebaker and colleagues have demonstrated that writing about emotional or traumatic personal experiences has positive effects on health (e.g., Pennebaker et al. 1988), academic performance (e.g., Pennebaker et al. 1990), and job outcomes (Spera et al. 1994; see Pennebaker 1997 for a review). Participants are typically instructed to spend 15 to 30 minutes over three to five days writing about important emotional issues.

Why does this exercise promote physical and mental well-being, while engaging in rumination has negative consequences? Pennebaker's writing exercise may provoke ruminative thoughts initially, but people may gain greater understanding of the problem over the course of writing, thereby reducing intrusive thoughts and worries. Indeed, combining six previous studies, Pennebaker et al. (1997) found that participants who exhibited an increased use of language related to causation (e.g., *infer*) and insight (e.g., *understand*) over the course of writing exhibited greater positive effects of the writing exercise.

In coding transcripts of interviews with recently bereaved gay men, Nolen-Hoeksema et al. (1997) distinguished between thoughts reflecting rumination versus self-analysis. Rumination and self-analysis were negatively correlated, and rumination was associated with more negative outcomes than self-analysis overall. Engaging in more self-analysis was associated with greater well-being in the short term, but also with a relatively slow recovery over the long term.

OTHER KINDS OF INTROSPECTION   Perhaps people can detect their nonconscious dispositions and motives by vividly imaging a future situation and attending to how it would make them feel. Suggestive evidence for this possibility was found in studies by Schultheiss & Brunstein (1999) that examined the relationship between people's implicit and explicit motives. Before being placed in situations that were relevant to people's implicit power motives (e.g., playing a competitive video game), some participants took part in a goal-imagery procedure in which they listened to detailed tape-recorded descriptions of the situations and imagined how they were likely to feel. Compared to control participants, those who did the goal-imagery exercise showed a high correspondence between their implicit and explicit motives, as if they consciously recognized the extent to which the situations were relevant to their implicit motives. The explicit motives of control participants, in contrast, were independent of their implicit motives. Thus, vividly imagining an upcoming situation might allow people to "sample" feelings triggered by their unconscious motives and attitudes.

SUMMARY   The research we have reviewed is consistent with the interpretation that introspection does not provide a direct pipeline to nonconscious mental processes. Instead, it is best thought of as a process whereby people use the contents of consciousness to construct a personal narrative that may or may not correspond to their nonconscious states. Introspection has negative consequences to the extent that it focuses people's attention on unrepresentative data about themselves, and causes people to construct incorrect or incomplete narratives. People who analyze the reasons for their attitudes, for example, often focus on incomplete information and construct new attitudes that are inaccurate. People who ruminate when distressed focus on negative information about themselves and often become more depressed. Introspection can be beneficial if it helps people make sense out of traumatic events that were difficult to explain; by constructing a more meaningful, coherent narrative about the events, people may put the events behind them and achieve more beneficial outcomes.

Other Routes to Self-Knowledge

If introspection is of limited use in accessing one's unconscious states, how can people improve self-knowledge?

SEEING OURSELVES THROUGH THE EYES OF OTHERS   A potential source of self-knowledge is other people. By carefully observing how other people view us, and noticing that their views differ from our own, we could revise our self-narratives accordingly. A description of this process, called symbolic interactionism, has a long tradition in sociology and social psychology, dating to Cooley (1902) and Mead (1934).

This process has the potential to teach us about our nonconscious states, to the extent that other people assess us by observing behaviors that emanate from our nonconscious traits and motives. Some studies, for example, find that (*a*) people often disagree with their peers about their own personality traits; e.g., Mary's view of how agreeable and conscientious she is differs from how agreeable and conscientious her friends think she is; (*b*) peers often agree among themselves about the target's personality, suggesting that they are picking up on something valid; e.g., Mary's friends are likely to agree with each other about how agreeable and conscientious Mary is; and (*c*) in at least some studies, peers' views of the target predict the target's behavior better than the target's self-views; e.g., Mary's friends' judgments of her personality correlate more with Mary's behavior than does Mary's view of her own personality (Kenny 1994, Kolar et al. 1996, Spain et al. 2000).

One interpretation of these findings is that Mary's self-views are based on a self-narrative that does not fully capture her nonconscious personality traits. Her friends might have based their views of Mary on observations of her past behavior that emanated from these nonconscious traits. To the extent that her future behavior emanates from these same traits, her friends will make better predictions than she will. In order to improve the accuracy of her self-narratives, Mary could try to see herself through the eyes of her friends, realize that they view her differently than she views herself, and revise her narrative accordingly.

Several studies, however, call into question people's ability to detect accurately how other people view them, when those views differ from their own (Felson 1993, Kenny & DePaulo 1993, Klonsky et al. 2002, Shrauger & Schoeneman 1979). Rather than taking an objective look at how other people view them and noticing the fact that this view might differ from their own, people often assume that other people see them the way they see themselves (Kenny & DePaulo 1993). Deciphering others' views may also be difficult because people often try to hide their negative assessments, out of politeness or a desire not to hurt someone's feelings. Finally, as with any theory, there is a confirmation bias with self-views, whereby people are more likely to notice and recall instances in which other people seem to share their views than instances in which they do not.

Even if we did recognize that other people viewed us differently than we view ourselves on a particular dimension, it is not always clear who is correct. If Mary realizes that Jason thinks she is undependable, who is to say whether he is more correct than she is? It is possible that Jason is correct, to the extent that his impression is based on careful observations of Mary's past behavior. Surely, however, there are times when people know themselves better than their peers know them.

The extent to which people could better detect how others view them, and decide wisely when it was best to adopt the others' view or maintain their own self-theories, is not clear. Nor is it clear that it is always to people's advantage to adopt others' views, even when they are more accurate (a point we will return to shortly). The obstacles to using others as a route to self-knowledge are likely to be formidable.

INFERRING OUR NONCONSCIOUS STATES FROM OUR BEHAVIOR   If Mary has a faulty view of her own personality, and often acts contrary to this view, there might be a simpler way for her to improve her self-knowledge. Rather than trying to see herself through her friends' eyes, she could observe her own behavior. According to self-perception theory, inferring our internal states from our behavior is a major source of self-knowledge (Bem 1972). To the extent that people's internal states are "weak, ambiguous, or uninterpretable" (Bem 1972, p. 5), people infer these states by observing their behavior and the conditions under which the behavior occurs. If people notice that they are constantly late for appointments, for example, they might rightly infer that they are not as conscientious as they thought. If they see themselves eating a lot of clam dip, and can find no compelling external reason for doing so, they infer that they must like the dip.

Perhaps people can gain knowledge of their nonconscious traits, attitudes, and motives in this manner. To the extent that some of their behavior is driven by these states, people can use these behaviors as a clue to their hidden dispositions. People could discover their nonconscious prejudice toward a minority group, for example, by observing the fact that they avoid contact with members of this group or treat them negatively.

Two nuances to the self-perception process, however, complicate its use as a route to self-knowledge. First, as noted by Wilson (2002), there is an unresolved ambiguity about whether people reveal unconscious states by observing their behavior (which Wilson called self-revelation) or mistakenly infer states that did not exist before (which Wilson called self-fabrication). The self-revelation possibility holds that people had an internal state of which they were not fully aware (e.g., a love of clam dip), which only became conscious when people observed their behavior (eating their fourth portion). Few proponents of self-perception theory have espoused this position, because it would require them to endorse the existence of unconscious attitudes and evaluations—a claim that many theorists were adverse to making. Bem (1972) himself argued that "such claims can edge dangerously close to metaphysics" and "should surely be resisted mightily until all other alternatives, save angels perhaps, have been eliminated" (p. 52).

The self-fabrication possibility holds that people did not previously hold an internal state of which they were unaware, but instead mistakenly inferred the existence of a state that was not actually present. People might mistakenly infer that their fourth portion of clam dip is a sign they love it, when they are really eating so much of it to please their grandmother, who keeps coming around with the hors d'oeuvres tray and telling them that they look too thin. This would be an example of the fundamental attribution error, whereby people underestimate the effects of external factors on their behavior (their hovering grandmother) and misattribute their actions to an internal state (their love of clam dip; see Jones 1990, Ross & Nisbett 1991).

Interestingly, most studies on self-perception theory are examples of self-fabrication and not self-revelation. In the typical study, the experimenter subtly induces people to act in a certain way, such as pressuring people to agree to go a street corner and get signatures on a petition to reduce air pollution. Rather than correctly inferring that they did so because of the experimenter's arm-twisting, people infer that they must feel especially strong about the issue (Kiesler et al. 1969). In other studies, people are induced to attribute their physiological arousal (or signs of it) to the existence of an emotional state such as fear, anger, or sexual attraction (e.g., Schachter & Singer 1962, Zillmann 1978). Valins (1966), for example, asked men to view pictures of scantily clad women while listening to the amplified sound of their heart beating. During some pictures, the men heard their heart rate increase rapidly, and they inferred that these were the pictures that they especially liked. In fact, the sounds they heard were not their heart rates but a prerecording. Thus, the men were induced to infer an internal state (preferences for certain pictures) that had not previously existed.

Most studies on self-perception theory involve self-fabrication, and not self-revelation, because of methodological constraints. In order to demonstrate self-revelation participants would have to be found who had a specific, nonconscious attitude (e.g., a preference for clam dip of which they were unaware), and the conditions under which they inferred the existence of that state studied—a formidable task. It is much easier to induce people to behave in a certain way (e.g., volunteer to collect signatures on a petition) and then get them to mistakenly think this behavior reflects a previously existing internal state (self-fabrication).

It is getting easier to demonstrate self-revelation with the invention of new implicit measures, such as those discussed earlier. As noted, one explanation for the discordance between implicit and explicit measures of attitudes is that people are unaware of the implicit attitude. It may be easier to examine the question of when people will infer the existence of the implicit state, such as having the opportunity to observe their behavior toward the attitude object. Thus, although most research on self-perception theory has examined self-fabrication, self-revelation may also occur.

Such a route to self-knowledge is not easy, because people would need to be relatively certain that the behavior in question is driven by an implicit state and not, for example, by some aspect of the situation (e.g., the hovering grandmother), and be able to put aside their explicit theories about how they feel. As noted above, people often view their internal states through the lens of their self-narratives, which might make it difficult to notice and remember behaviors that are inconsistent with these narratives.

A second nuance to self-perception theory concerns people's awareness of the inference process itself. In order to use the self-perception process as a route to self-knowledge, people would need to do it consciously and deliberately; vowing, for example, to keep closer track of how they act in the presence of minority group members to detect better their level of prejudice. There is considerable evidence, however, that the self-perception process is itself quick and nonconscious. Nisbett & Wilson (1977) reviewed several studies in which people did not seem to be aware of the kinds of inferences they were drawing about their internal states by observing their behavior. In Schachter & Singer's (1962) study of emotion, for example, in which people were given shots of epinephrine and induced (in some conditions) to attribute their subsequent arousal to emotional sources, it is unlikely that people consciously thought, "Gee, I'm feeling kind of revved up; I wonder why? Let's see, it could be that shot, but the experimenter told me it would not have any side effects. Hey, the other participant sure seems angry about this questionnaire we are filling out. Oh, I see, I guess I'm angry too." Instead, people appear to make rapid, nonconscious inferences about their internal states by observing their behavior and the surrounding situation.

Even if the self-perception process often occurs nonconsciously, there is no reason we cannot try to perform it consciously as well. The greatest potential for increasing self-knowledge may lie in reminding ourselves to be better observers of our own behavior and to take the time to examine our actions (e.g., toward minority group members) more carefully. By so doing, people may be able to construct self-narratives that correspond more closely to their adaptive unconscious.

Is It Always Desirable to Improve Self-Knowledge?

Although obtaining self-knowledge seems desirable, there are physical and mental benefits associated with maintaining slight or moderate positive self-illusions, such as believing that one is a little more generous, intelligent, and attractive than suggested by a realistic analysis (Armor & Taylor 1998, Baumeister 1989, Taylor & Brown 1988). People who believe they are better off than they really are may be able to deal with difficult or frightening situations more effectively. HIV-positive men who showed an optimistic bias, in believing that they were relatively unlikely to develop AIDS, were more apt to engage in healthy behaviors (e.g., exercise, safe sex) than their more realistic counterparts (Taylor et al. 1992). Thus, holding inflated views of one's personal characteristics and future prospects may promote positive behavior and successful coping, particularly in situations that might be terrifying or overwhelming if viewed realistically.

Whereas holding positive expectations about one's own capacities and future outcomes may increase motivation, indulging in pure fantasy may undermine motivation (Oettingen 1996). Obese women at a weight loss clinic were asked to estimate how likely they were to achieve their weight loss goals (providing a measure of positive expectations) and to rate their emotional responses to imaginary scenarios such as seeing an old friend after completing the weight loss program (providing a measure of weight-related fantasy). Holding high expectations of future weight loss was positively associated with successful goal attainment, whereas engaging in positive fantasies about having a slim figure was negatively associated with goal attainment; positive expectations may help to lay the groundwork for envisioning and taking steps toward achieving a goal, while fantasizing may impair this process by focusing attention on the outcome rather than the means (Oettingen & Wadden 1991). Positive self-illusions, then, may be valuable to the extent that they remain tied to reality and foster realistic planning. Armor & Taylor (1998) argue that optimism most often takes this beneficial form. For example, people consistently underestimate how long it will take them to complete tasks, displaying optimism, but their estimated times are highly correlated with their actual times, displaying a clear link to reality (Buehler et al. 1994).

Though we acknowledge the benefits of positive illusions, we suggest that accurate self-knowledge is generally a beneficial quality. Often, gaining accurate knowledge does not necessitate puncturing a positive self-balloon. Sometimes people have overly negative views of themselves, and they would be better off recognizing that they have more potential than they think as a public speaker or guitar player. Other times people may not realize which of two positive traits better describes them; they may believe incorrectly that they have more potential as a tennis player than as a musician. In such cases, people's conscious goals and self-views are out of sync with their nonconscious motives and personality, and gaining better knowledge of the nonconscious self should be valuable.

Although research on well-being and self-knowledge is limited, there is some evidence that people are happier when their conscious and nonconscious goals correspond than when they do not. Brunstein et al. (1998) compared people's implicit needs for achievement, power, affiliation, and intimacy, as assessed by the TAT, to explicit, self-report measures of these same motives. On average, people showed little correspondence between their implicit and explicit motives. The people who did, however, reported greater emotional well-being than people whose goals were inconsistent. It may be to people's advantage to develop conscious goals that correspond at least somewhat with the motives of their adaptive unconscious (Schultheiss 2001, Schultheiss & Brunstein 1999).

Similarly, discrepancies between explicit and implicit self-esteem may cause problems, especially the case in which people have high explicit but low implicit self-esteem. Participants who exhibit this dissociation would likely appear anxious during interpersonal interactions while failing to recognize that they were conveying this impression. Due to this lack of awareness, they might be unmotivated to compensate for their anxious appearance, thereby precluding the recruitment of self-presentational strategies (Spalding & Hardin 1999). Indeed, participants who showed an implicit/explicit dissociation of this sort were rated lower in extraversion and were perceived as getting sick more often by their close friends (Bosson 2003). Robinson et al. (2003) found that participants who exhibited a dissociation between implicit and explicit self-esteem reported less pleasant affect than their more congruent counterparts; interestingly, participants who were low in explicit self-esteem were actually happier if they also held low (versus high) implicit self-esteem. Thus, the failure of self-knowledge in this central evaluative domain may have important consequences for interpersonal relationships, social perception, and health.

SUMMARY

Maintaining mild positive illusions can be beneficial, and increasing self-knowledge in these instances is not a desirable goal. Often, however, it is to people's advantage to have at least some awareness of their nonconscious traits, attitudes, and self-concepts. How can people gain such insight? One approach is to reduce attempts to repress or suppress unwanted thoughts.

Although there is piecemeal evidence for the criteria necessary to demonstrate the existence of repression, no study has demonstrated all the criteria simultaneously and it thus remains an elusive phenomenon to nail down empirically. There is better evidence for successful short-term suppression and intentional forgetting, though in neither case are the unwanted thoughts and feelings erased completely, and these efforts might backfire in the long run.

A more common source of self-knowledge failure, we suggest, is the fact that the pervasive adaptive unconscious is inaccessible to consciousness. Introspection is thus of limited use to gain self-knowledge, at least directly. Some forms of introspection are beneficial by helping people construct a coherent personal narrative, even if they do not provide a direct pipeline to unconscious processes. Another approach is to try to see ourselves through the eyes of other people, and if their view differs from ours, consider the possibility that they are correct. The obstacles to this route to self-knowledge, however, are formidable (e.g., recognizing that others hold views different from our own). Making conscious attempts to observe our behavior more carefully, and determine whether it is a reflection of parts of ourselves of which we are unaware, may be easier.

ACKNOWLEDGMENTS

The writing of this chapter was supported by research grant RO1-MH56075 from the National Institute of Mental Health and a National Science Foundation Graduate Fellowship. We thank Jonathan Schooler and Daniel Wegner for their helpful comments on a previous draft.

The *Annual Review of Psychology* is online at http://psych.annualreviews.org

LITERATURE CITED

Allport GW. 1961. *Pattern and Growth in Personality.* New York: Holt, Rinehart & Winston

Anderson MC, Green C. 2001. Suppressing unwanted memories by executive control. *Nature* 410:366–69

Armor DA, Taylor SE. 1998. Situated optimism: specific outcome expectancies and self-regulation. In *Advances in Experimental Social Psychology*, ed. MP Zanna, 30:309–79. San Diego: Academic

Asendorpf JB, Banse R, Muecke D. 2002. Double dissociation between implicit and explicit personality self-concept: the case of shy behavior. *J. Personal. Soc. Psychol.* 83:380–93

Bargh JA. 1994. The four horsemen of automaticity: awareness, intention, efficiency, and control in social cognition. In *Handbook of Social Cognition*, Vol. 1: *Basic Processes;* Vol. 2: *Applications*, ed. RS Wyer Jr, TK Srull, pp. 1–40. Hillsdale, NJ: Erlbaum. 2nd ed.

Bartholomew K, Shaver PR. 1998. Methods of assessing adult attachment: Do they converge? In *Attachment Theory and Close Relationships*, ed. JA Simpson, WS Rholes, pp. 25–45. New York: Guilford

Basden BH, Basden DR, Gargano GJ. 1993. Directed forgetting in implicit and explicit memory tests: a comparison of methods. *J. Exp. Psychol. Learn. Mem. Cogn.* 19:603–16

Baumeister RF. 1984. Choking under pressure: self-consciousness and paradoxical effects of incentives on skillful performance. *J. Personal. Soc. Psychol.* 46:610–20

Baumeister RF. 1989. The optimal margin of illusion. *J. Soc. Clin. Psychol.* 8:176–89

Baumeister RF, Showers CJ. 1986. A review of paradoxical performance effects: choking under pressure in sports and mental tests. *Eur. J. Soc. Psychol.* 16:361–83

Bem DJ. 1972. Self-perception theory. In *Advances in Experimental Social Psychology*, ed. L Berkowitz, 6:1–62. New York: Academic

Bhalla M, Proffitt DR. 2000. Geographical slant perception: dissociation and coordination between explicit awareness and visually guided actions. In *Beyond Dissociation: Interaction Between Dissociated Implicit and Explicit Processing*, ed. Y Rossetti, A Revonsuo, pp. 99–128. Amsterdam: Benjamin

Bjork RA. 1989. Retrieval inhibition as an adaptive mechanism in human memory. In *Varieties of Memory and Consciousness: Essays in Honour of Endel Tulving*, ed. HL Roediger III, FIM Craik, pp. 303–30. Hillsdale, NJ: Erlbaum

Blair IV. 2002. The malleability of automatic stereotypes and prejudice. *Personal. Soc. Psychol. Rev.* 6:242–61

Bornstein RF. 1995. Sex differences in objective and projective dependency tests: a meta-analytic review. *Assessment* 2:319–31

Bosson JK. 2003. Discrepant explicit and implicit self-esteem: relations to self- and friend-ratings of personality and physical health. Unpubl. manuscr., Univ. Texas, Austin

Bosson JK, Swann WB, Pennebaker JW. 2000. Stalking the perfect measure of implicit self-esteem: the blind men and the elephant revisited? *J. Personal. Soc. Psychol.* 79:631–43

Brauer M, Wasel W, Niedenthal P. 2000. Implicit and explicit components of prejudice. *Rev. Gen. Psychol.* 4:79–101

Brunstein JC, Schultheiss OC, Grässmann R. 1998. Personal goals and emotional well-being: the moderating role of motive dispositions. *J. Personal. Soc. Psychol.* 75:494–508

Buehler R, Griffin D, Ross M. 1994. Exploring the "planning fallacy": why people underestimate their task completion times. *J. Personal. Soc. Psychol.* 67:366–81

Carver CS, Scheier MF. 1981. *Attention and Self-Regulation*. New York: Springer

Cooley CH. 1902. *Human Nature and the Social Order.* New York: Scribner's

Crandall CS, Eshleman A. 2003. A justification-suppression model of the expression and experience of prejudice. *Psychol. Bull.* 129:414–46

Creem SH, Proffitt DR. 1999. Separate memories for visual guidance and explicit awareness: the roles of time and place. In *Stratification in Cognition and Consciousness*, ed. BH Challis, BM Velichkovsky, pp. 73–94. Amsterdam: Benjamins

Devine PG. 1989. Automatic controlled processes in prejudice: the role of stereotypes and personal beliefs. In *Attitude Structure and Function*, ed. AR Pratkanis, SJ Breckler, AG Greenwald, pp. 181–212. Hillsdale, NJ: Erlbaum

Dovidio JF, Kawakami K, Johnson C, Johnson B, Howard A. 1997. On the nature of prejudice: automatic and controlled processes. *J. Exp. Soc. Psychol.* 33:510–40

Erdelyi MH. 1974. A new look at the new look: perceptual defense and vigilance. *Psychol. Rev.* 81:1–25

Erdelyi MH. 1985. *Psychoanalysis: Freud's Cognitive Psychology*. New York: Freeman

Erdelyi MH. 1993. Repression: the mechanism and the defense. In *Handbook of Mental Control*, ed. DM Wegner, JW Pennebaker, pp. 126–48. Englewood Cliffs, NJ: Prentice-Hall

Fazio RH, Chen J, McDonel E, Sherman SJ. 1982. Attitude accessibility, attitude-behavior consistency, and the strength of the object-evaluation association. *J. Exp. Soc. Psychol.* 18:339–57

Fazio RH, Jackson JR, Dunton BC, Williams CJ. 1995. Variability in automatic activation as an unobstrusive measure of racial attitudes: a bona fide pipeline? *J. Personal. Soc. Psychol.* 69:1013–27

Fazio RH, Olson MA. 2003. Implicit measures in social cognition research: their meaning and uses. *Annu. Rev. Psychol.* 54:297–327

Felson RB. 1993. The (somewhat) social self: how others affect self-appraisals. In *The Self in Social Perspective*, ed. JM Suls, 4:1–27. Hillsdale, NJ: Erlbaum

Fitts PM. 1964. Perceptual-motor skill learning. In *Categories of Human Learning*, ed. AW Melton, pp. 243–85. New York: Academic

Gabrieli JDE. 1998. Cognitive neuroscience of human memory. *Annu. Rev. Psychol.* 49:87–115

Gaertner SL, Dovidio JF. 1986. The aversive form of racism. In *Prejudice, Discrimination, and Racism*, ed. JF Dovidio, SL Gaertner, pp. 61–89. Orlando: Academic

Greenwald AG, Banaji MR. 1995. Implicit social cognition: attitudes, self-esteem, and stereotypes. *Psychol. Rev.* 102:4–27

Greenwald AG, Farnham SD. 2000. Using the Implicit Association Test to measure self-esteem and self-concept. *J. Personal. Soc. Psychol.* 79:1022–38

Greenwald AG, McGhee DE, Schwartz JLK. 1998. Measuring individual differences in implicit cognition: the implicit association test. *J. Personal. Soc. Psychol.* 74:1464–80

Halberstadt JB, Levine GM. 1999. Effects of reasons analysis on the accuracy of predicting basketball games. *J. Appl. Soc. Psychol.* 29:517–30

Jenkins IH, Brooks DJ, Nixon PD, Frackowiak RSJ, Passingham RE, et al. 1994. Motor sequence learning: a study with positron emission tomography. *J. Neurosci.* 14:3775–90

Jones EE. 1990. *Interpersonal Perception.* New York: Freeman

Jordan CH, Spencer SJ, Zanna MP. 2003. "I love me... I love me not:" implicit self-esteem, explicit self-esteem, and defensiveness. See Spencer et al. 2003, pp. 117–46

Kenny DA. 1994. *Interpersonal Perception: A Social Relations Analysis.* New York: Guilford

Kenny DA, DePaulo BM. 1993. Do people know how others view them? An empirical and theoretical account. *Psychol. Bull.* 114:145–61

Kiesler CA, Nisbett RE, Zanna MP. 1969. On inferring one's beliefs from one's behavior. *J. Personal. Soc. Psychol.* 11:321–27

Kihlstrom JF. 1987. The cognitive unconscious. *Science* 237:1445–52

Kihlstrom JF. 2002. No need for repression. *Trends Cogn. Sci.* 6:502

Kimble CE, Rezabek JS. 1992. Playing games before an audience: social facilitation or choking. *Soc. Behav. Personal.* 20:115–20

Klonsky ED, Oltmanns TF, Turkheimer E. 2002. Informant-reports of personality disorder: relation to self-reports and future research directions. *Clin. Psychol.-Sci. Pract.* 9:300–11

Kolar DW, Funder DC, Colvin CR. 1996. Comparing the accuracy of personality judgments by the self and knowledgeable others. *J. Personal.* 64:311–37

Koole SL, Dijksterhuis A, van Knippenberg A. 2001. What's in a name: implicit self-esteem and the automatic self. *J. Personal. Soc. Psychol.* 80:669–85

Koole SL, Pelham BW. 2003. On the nature of implicit self-esteem: the case of the name letter effect. See Spencer et al. 2003, pp. 93–116

Loftus EF. 1997. Memories for a past that never was. *Curr. Dir. Psychol. Sci.* 6:60–65

Logan GD. 1985. Skill automaticity: relations, implications, and future directions. *Can. J. Psychol.* 39:367–86

Lyubomirsky S, Caldwell ND, Nolen-Hoeksema S. 1998. Effects of ruminative distracting responses to depressed mood on retrieval of autobiographical memories. *J. Personal. Soc. Psychol.* 75:166–77

Macrae CN, Bodenhausen GV, Milne AB, Jetten J. 1994. Out of mind but back in sight: stereotypes on the rebound. *J. Personal. Soc. Psychol.* 67:808–17

Mazzoni GAL, Loftus EF, Kirsch I. 2001. Changing beliefs about implausible autobiographical events: A little plausibility goes a long way. *J. Exp. Psychol. Appl.* 7:51–59

McAdams DP. 1993. *The Stories We Live By: Personal Myths and the Making of the Self.* New York: Morrow

McAdams DP. 2001. The psychology of life stories. *Rev. Gen. Psychol.* 5:100–22

McClelland DC, Koestner R, Weinberger J. 1989. How do self-attributed implicit motives differ? *Psychol. Rev.* 96:690–702

McGinnies E. 1949. Emotionality and perceptual defense. *Psychol. Rev.* 56:244–51

Mead GH. 1934. *Mind, Self, and Society from the Standpoint of a Social Behaviorist.* Chicago: Univ. Chicago Press

Monteith MJ, Spicer CV, Tooman GD. 1998. Consequences of stereotype suppression: stereotypes on AND not on the rebound. *J. Exp. Soc. Psychol.* 34:355–77

Moskowitz GB, Gollwitzer PM, Wasel W, Schaal B. 1999. Preconscious control of stereotype activation through chronic egalitarian goals. *J. Personal. Soc. Psychol.* 77:167–84

Moskowitz GB, Salomon AR, Taylor CM. 2000. Preconsciously controlling stereotyping: Implicitly activated egalitarian goals prevent the activation of stereotypes. *Soc. Cogn.* 18:151–77

Nisbett RE, Wilson TD. 1977. Telling more than we can know: verbal reports on mental processes. *Psychol. Rev.* 84:231–59

Nissen MJ, Bullemer P. 1987. Attentional requirements of learning: evidence from performance measures. *Cogn. Psychol.* 19:1–32

Nolen-Hoeksema S. 2000. The role of rumination in depressive disorders and mixed anxiety/depressive symptoms. *J. Abnorm. Psychol.* 109:504–11

Nolen-Hoeksema S, McBride A, Larson J. 1997. Rumination and psychological distress among bereaved partners. *J. Personal. Soc. Psychol.* 72:855–62

Nosek BA. 2002. *Moderators of the relationship between implicit and explicit attitudes.* Unpubl. PhD diss., Yale Univ.

Nosek BA, Banaji MR. 2002. (At least) two factors moderate the relationship between implicit and explicit attitudes. In *Natura Automatyzmow*, ed. RK Ohme, M Jarymowicz, pp. 49–56. Warszawa: WIP PAN & SWPS

Nosek BA, Banaji MR, Greenwald AG. 2002. Harvesting implicit group attitudes and beliefs from a demonstration web site. *Group Dyn.: Theory Res. Pract.* 6:101–15

Nuttin JM. 1985. Narcissism beyond Gestalt and awareness: the name letter effect. *Eur. J. Soc. Psychol.* 15:353–61

Oettingen G. 1996. Positive fantasy and motivation. In *The Psychology of Action: Linking Cognition and Motivation to Behavior*, ed. PM Gollwitzer, JA Bargh, pp. 226–39. New York: Guilford

Oettingen G, Wadden TA. 1991. Expectation, fantasy, and weight loss: Is the impact of positive thinking always positive? *Cogn. Ther. Res.* 15:167–75

Paz-Caballero MD, Menor J. 1999. ERP correlates of directed forgetting effects in direct and indirect memory tests. *Eur. J. Cogn. Psychol.* 11:239–60

Pelham BW, Mirenberg MC, Jones JT. 2002. Why Susie sells seashells by the seashore: implicit egotism and major life decisions. *J. Personal. Soc. Psychol.* 82:469–87

Pennebaker JW. 1997. *Opening Up: The Healing Power of Expressing Emotions.* New York: Guilford

Pennebaker JW, Colder M, Sharp LK. 1990. Accelerating the coping process. *J. Personal. Soc. Psychol.* 58:528–37

Pennebaker JW, Kiecolt-Glaser JK, Glaser R. 1988. Disclosure of traumas and immune function: health implications for psychotherapy. *J. Consult. Clin. Psychol.* 56:239–45

Pennebaker JW, Mayne TJ, Francis ME. 1997. Linguistic predictors of adaptive bereavement. *J. Personal. Soc. Psychol.* 72: 863–71

Peterson C, Ulrey LM. 1994. Can explanatory style be scored from TAT protocols? *Personal. Soc. Psychol. Bull.* 20:102–6

Proffitt DR, Bhalla M, Gossweiler R, Midgett J. 1995. Perceiving geographical slant. *Psychon. Bull. Rev.* 2:409–28

Proffitt DR, Stefanucci J, Banton T, Epstein W. 2003. The role of effort in perceiving distance. *Psychol. Sci.* 14:106–12

Robinson MD, Vargas PT, Crawford EG. 2003. Putting process into personality, appraisal, and emotion: evaluative processing as a missing link. In *The Psychology of Evaluation: Affective Processes in Cognition and Emotion*, ed. J Musch, KC Klauer, pp. 275–306. Mahwah, NJ: Erlbaum

Ross L, Nisbett RE. 1991. *The Person and the Situation: Perspectives of Social Psychology.* New York: McGraw-Hill

Schachter S, Singer J. 1962. Cognitive, social, and physiological determinants of emotional state. *Psychol. Rev.* 69:379–99

Schooler JW. 2001. Discovering memories of abuse in the light of meta-awareness. *J. Aggress. Maltreat. Trauma* 4:105–36

Schultheiss OC. 2001. An information processing account of implicit motive arousal. In *Advances in Motivation and Achievement*, ed. ML Maehr, P Pintrich, 12:1–41. Greenwich: JAI

Schultheiss OC, Brunstein JC. 1999. Goal imagery: bridging the gap between implicit motives and explicit goals. *J. Personal.* 67:1–38

Shanks DR, St. John MF. 1994. Characteristics of dissociable human learning systems. *Behav. Brain Sci.* 17:367–447

Shrauger JS, Schoeneman TJ. 1979. Symbolic interactionist view of self-concept: through the looking glass darkly. *Psychol. Bull.* 86:549–73

Silvia PJ, Gendolla GHE. 2001. On introspection and self-perception: Does self-focused attention enable accurate self-knowledge? *Rev. Gen. Psychol.* 5:241–69

Snyder M. 1982. When believing means doing:

creating links between attitudes and behavior. See Zanna et al. 1982, pp. 105–30

Spain JS, Eaton LG, Funder DC. 2000. Perspectives on personality: the relative accuracy of self versus others for the prediction of emotion behavior. *J. Personal.* 68:837–67

Spalding LR, Hardin CD. 1999. Unconscious unease and self-handicapping: behavioral consequences of individual differences in implicit and explicit self-esteem. *Psychol. Sci.* 10:535–39

Spangler WD. 1992. Validity of questionnaire and TAT measures of need for achievement: two meta-analyses. *Psychol. Bull.* 112:140–54

Spencer SJ, Fein S, Zanna MP, Olson JM, eds. 2003. *Motivated Social Perception: The Ontario Symposium*, Vol. 9. Mahwah, NJ: Erlbaum

Spera SP, Buhrfeind ED, Pennebaker JW. 1994. Expressive writing and coping with job loss. *Acad. Manag. J.* 37:722–33

Taylor SE, Brown JD. 1988. Illusion and well being: a social-psychological perspective on mental health. *Psychol. Bull.* 116:21–27

Taylor SE, Kemeny ME, Aspinwall LG, Schneider SG, Rodriguez R, et al. 1992. Optimism, coping, psychological distress, and high-risk sexual behavior among men at risk for acquired immunodeficiency syndrome (AIDS). *J. Personal. Soc. Psychol.* 63:460–73

Valins S. 1966. Cognitive effects of false heart-rate feedback. *J. Personal. Soc. Psychol.* 4:400–8

Ward A, Lyubomirsky S, Sousa L, Nolen-Hoeksema S. 2003. Can't quite commit: rumination and uncertainty. *Personal. Soc. Psychol. Bull.* 29:96–107

Wegner DM. 1994. Ironic processes of mental control. *Psychol. Rev.* 101:34–52

Wegner DM, Schneider DJ, Carter SR, White TL. 1987. Paradoxical effects of thought suppression. *J. Personal. Soc. Psychol.* 53:5–13

Wenzlaff RM, Wegner DM. 2000. Thought suppression. *Annu. Rev. Psychol.* 51:59–91

Wicklund RA. 1982. Self-focused attention and

the validity of self-reports. See Zanna et al. 1982, pp. 149–72

Willingham DB. 1998. A neuropsychological theory of motor skill learning. *Psychol. Rev.* 105(3):558–84

Willingham DB, Goedert-Eschmann K. 1999. The relation between implicit and explicit learning: Evidence for parallel development. *Psychol. Sci.* 10:531–34

Wilson TD. 2002. *Strangers to Ourselves: Discovering the Adaptive Unconscious.* Cambridge, MA: Harvard Univ. Press

Wilson TD, Dunn DS. 1986. Effects of introspection on attitude-behavior consistency: analyzing reasons versus focusing on feelings. *J. Exp. Soc. Psychol.* 22:249–63

Wilson TD, Dunn DS, Bybee JA, Hyman DB, Rotondo JA. 1984. Effects of analyzing reasons on attitude-behavior consistency. *J. Personal. Soc. Psychol.* 47:5–16

Wilson TD, Dunn DS, Kraft D, Lisle DJ. 1989. Introspection, attitude change, and attitude-behavior consistency: the disruptive effects of explaining why we feel the way we do. In *Advances in Experimental Social Psychology*, ed. L Berkowitz, 22:287–343. New York: Academic

Wilson TD, Hodges SD, LaFleur SJ. 1995. Effects of introspecting about reasons: inferring attitudes from accessible thoughts. *J. Personal. Soc. Psychol.* 69:16–28

Wilson TD, LaFleur SJ. 1995. Knowing what you'll do: effects of analyzing reasons on self-prediction. *J. Personal. Soc. Psychol.* 68: 21–35

Wilson TD, Lindsey S, Schooler TY. 2000. A model of dual attitudes. *Psychol. Rev.* 107:101–26

Wilson TD, Lisle DJ, Schooler JW, Hodges SD, Klaaren KJ, et al. 1993. Introspecting about reasons can reduce post-choice satisfaction. *Personal. Soc. Psychol. Bull.* 19:331–39

Wilson TD, Schooler JW. 1991. Thinking too much: Introspection can reduce the quality of preferences and decisions. *J. Personal. Soc. Psychol.* 60:181–92

Zanna MP, Higgins ET, Herman CP, eds. 1982. *Consistency in Social Behavior: The Ontario Symposium,* Vol. 2. Hillsdale, NJ: Erlbaum

Zillmann D. 1978. Attribution and misattribution of excitatory reaction. In *New Directions in Attribution Research*, ed. JH Harvey, W Ickes, RF Kidd, 2:335–68. Hillsdale, NJ: Erlbaum

Annu. Rev. Psychol. 2004. 55:519–44
doi: 10.1146/annurev.psych.55.090902.141537
Copyright © 2004 by Annual Reviews. All rights reserved
First published online as a Review in Advance on September 29, 2003

GENDER IN PSYCHOLOGY

Abigail J. Stewart and Christa McDermott

*Psychology Department and Women's Studies Program, University of Michigan,
Ann Arbor, Michigan 48109-1109; email: abbystew@umich.edu, mcdc@umich.edu*

Key Words   sex differences, within-sex differences, social power, intersectionality

■ **Abstract**   Gender is increasingly understood as defining a system of power relations embedded in other power relations. Psychological research on gender—which has most often focused on analysis of sex differences, within-sex variability, and gender roles—has begun to incorporate this new understanding. By drawing on three resources, psychologists can make more rapid progress in understanding gender's significance for psychological processes: social science theories that link the individual and social levels of analysis; constructs (such as identity) that bridge the social and individual levels; and conceptual tools generated in feminist theory, perhaps especially intersectionality. We review these resources, cite active research programs that have employed them, and conclude by offering some practical suggestions about how to incorporate these resources into our research.

CONTENTS

GENDER IN PSYCHOLOGY

Gender is widely recognized to be an important empirical factor (or variable) in understanding many aspects of behavior. In psychology gender is often used empirically, without much consciousness of its social or conceptual significance. In this chapter we focus on the use of gender as an analytic tool in psychology. Of

0066-4308/04/0204-0519$14.00

519

course analytic tools must prove empirically useful (or not), but recognizing the conceptual significance of different ways of using gender in empirical research can, we think, help psychologists identify newer and more powerful ways to use gender to study psychological phenomena. Ordinarily psychologists use gender in empirical research in at least three wholly different ways: to signify sex differences, within-sex variability, and the gender-linked power relations that structure many social institutions and interactions.

First, and perhaps still most often, gender is used to think about ways in which boys and girls or men and women differ. According to this "sex differences approach," psychologists consider how and why average differences in personality, behavior, ability, or performance between the sexes might arise (see, e.g., Block 1984, Buss 1995, Eagly 1994, Levy & Heller 1992, Maccoby & Jacklin 1974, and Maccoby 1998). This approach often appears to assume, or actually does assume, that these differences arise from preexisting "essential" differences between male and female human organisms. In its strongest form, the sex differences approach assumes not only will there be group differences between men and women on key traits but also nonoverlapping distributions. Early on it was noted that few—but some—behavioral differences have nearly nonoverlapping distributions, notably: ejaculation, pregnancy, childbirth, and lactation. These derive directly from demonstrable biological differences between men and women. In most other cases, perceived and demonstrated sex differences on some characteristic or behavior occur with overlapping distributions, sometimes with highly gender-differentiated "tails" of the distribution (e.g., some sex-linked developmental disorders, or extremely high scores in math ability, both of which are disproportionately found in boys). Even in these cases, and more markedly in cases with less differentiated tails on the distribution, there are simply average sex differences with wide and overlapping distributions (Favreau 1993, 1997).

Psychologists have entertained several kinds of hypotheses to account for these, ranging from biological differences (e.g., in behavior-related hormones), differential treatment or socialization (which could, of course, be grounded in biological differences but enhanced by differential treatment), and differential social roles or social situations. All three kinds of explanations are aimed at accounting for overall sex differences, or differences between groups of men and women or girls and boys (see, e.g., Maccoby 1998). They focus, then, on the sharply demarcated differences (in the very few instances of nonoverlapping distributions), or on the aggregate differences in the distributions, or on the gender-differentiated tails. For example, research on gender differences in the rate of depression has explored the potential role of gender-linked hormones, differential socialization toward inhibition, and differential exposure to childhood sexual abuse (see Nolen-Hoeksema et al. 1999).

Some psychologists have noted that in many cases a focus on sex differences ignores the large variance within gender on many characteristics (Martin 1994), and therefore may tend to exaggerate sex differences, or even reinforce or create them in the mind of the public (Hare-Mustin & Marecek 1990, Unger 1989). To avoid such exaggerations, some psychologists have selected particularly "gendered" phenomena (that is, phenomena that are defined by being different, on average, between men and women), and have explored sources of the within-gender variance on those characteristics. Thus, for example, Eccles & Jacobs (1986) noted that both math ability and math performance are "gendered" in that at certain ages boys demonstrate higher average ability and higher performance (see also Eccles et al. 1990). Even at those ages, though, there is enormous variance in math ability and performance among both boys and girls. By examining the factors that predict differential ability and performance within gender they showed that girls' ability and performance scores were predicted by parents' expectations of them. Thus, to the extent that parents form rigid ideas about the math ability and behavior of boys and girls, and act on those ideas, differences between boys and girls are likely to be exaggerated, if not actually created.

Research of this kind can raise further questions about the role of social structure—in addition to social interactions like those between parents or teachers and children—and gender. Some psychologists have suggested that "gender" operates not merely at the level of sex differences, or as the result of social interactions in which beliefs about gender are expressed in actions that actually create confirming evidence for those beliefs, but also in the social structures that define power relationships throughout the culture (Fiske & Stevens 1993, Goodwin & Fiske 2001, Stewart 1998). According to this viewpoint, "gender" describes a set of power relations in which—absent other cues and definitions—maleness signals authority, status, competence, social power and influence, and femaleness signals lack of authority, low status, incompetence, and little power and influence. [This perspective is perfectly compatible with recognition that gender also signals more positive associations with femaleness (e.g., nurturance) and more negative ones with maleness (e.g., violence). From this perspective, the point is that social status and authority are not associated with these characteristics in the same way.]

Psychologists who begin by noticing that gender signifies a set of power relations often focus on how a particular behavior of interest (e.g., leadership, marital conflict, or performance of a task) takes place within social relationships (dyads, organizational hierarchies, broader social structures) that are themselves gendered. For example, a partner may stay in an abusive relationship because she lacks the economic resources to leave. If marital conflict, and perhaps especially violence, takes place in dyads in which one individual has total or relative control of financial and extrafamilial resources, it is important to consider that fact in understanding the factors that maintain both the violence and the relationship. Recognizing the importance of the power structure of the dyad may open up potential avenues for change; shifting some financial and resource power to equalize the balance may actually change the pattern of conflict behavior (White et al. 2001). Equally, scholars who have examined the efficacy of organizational mechanisms for reporting sexual harassment have discovered that those mechanisms rarely produce systematic reporting by women in organizations in which men hold most of the most powerful positions. Fears of retaliation are, under these conditions, quite rational and widely held. Widespread underreporting of these incidents is difficult to understand without an understanding of the gendered power relationships in organizations (Riger 1991).

To summarize, psychologists have found "gender" to be a powerful conceptual tool in at least three ways: (*a*) in sorting individuals into male and female and exploring the ways in which differences in behavior, performance, and characteristics are associated with that individual difference (whether the hypothesized causal mechanism is biological, socialization, or social location); (*b*) in understanding how gender might relate to individual differences among men and among women; and (*c*) in understanding how gender structures social institutions within which men and women operate. These three approaches have generally been viewed as alternatives, and often are pursued in isolation from one another. One of the important recent advances has been an increased inclination to recognize that these three approaches are in fact compatible and can be integrated.

It is fair to say that the first approach (sex differences) is the most well developed within psychology, and the most widely used in the field. At the same time, advances in feminist theory, within interdisciplinary women's studies as well as within psychology, have raised serious questions about the degree to which this approach—by itself—can offer much to our understanding of complex social behavior (see, e.g., Martin 1994, Riger 1992). Some areas of psychology—perhaps especially developmental and clinical psychology—have examined the role of gendered socialization pressures quite thoroughly and with considerable success in adding to our understanding of both average gender differences and the within-gender variance in certain phenomena (e.g., math achievement, emotions, PTSD, and depression; see Brody 1999, Eccles et al. 1990, Fivush & Buckner 2000, Nolen-Hoeksema et al. 1999, Pimlott-Kubiak & Cortina 2004, Powlishta et al. 2001, Zahn-Waxler 2000). Not surprisingly, it has been organizational, social, and community psychology that have been most attuned to the issue of gender in social structure (see, e.g., Gutek & Done 2001, Riger 2000). It is equally unsurprising—given the highly individualistic focus of psychology as a field—that this approach has been least prominent in the exploration of gender in psychology as a whole. We hope, in this chapter, to show how adopting a framework that integrates social structural and individual approaches to understanding gender can provide powerful accounts of particular psychological phenomena. We understand that one factor constraining psychologists in using this kind of framework is the need to identify practical ways to incorporate these different levels of analysis in a single design. We therefore offer some examples of successful strategies for doing so and conclude with some suggestions about how to strengthen our research by using gender more consistently as a conceptual tool.

A Model for Theorizing Gender in Psychology: Linking Social Structure and Personality

An important precondition for using gender as a conceptual tool to full advantage in psychology is having a developed understanding of how to bring factors at different levels of analysis—social structural, individual, and even biological—into a single model. The field of personality theory offers us a remarkably diverse set of models for doing this, but they have been used infrequently in other subfields of psychology and even in empirical personality research. We suspect this is largely due to the isolation of subfields from one another, and propose that these models have wide applicability within psychology (and even in our neighboring disciplines in both the social and biological sciences). There are also, of course, difficulties in operationalizing models at multiple levels; these pose later, and less difficult problems than the absence of adequate, or fully developed, theory.

Psychoanalytic theory offered early ideas about the relationship between the individual and society (Freud 1930/1961). Early critiques of psychoanalytic theory often offered elaborations of the theory designed to address its exclusively intrapsychic and interpersonal focus. Some branches of psychoanalytic theory developed even more extensively the intrapsychic focus (e.g., Klein 1965), while others developed the interpersonal focus (e.g., Sullivan 1953). But a vocal and persistent branch elaborated a "psychosocial" understanding of the individual that incorporated social structure into a model that included attention to individual intrapsychic and interpersonal experiences and their consequences. Erich Fromm (1947) argued, for example, that the dominant economic system in which individuals are embedded shapes personality development. Karen Horney (1939) argued, even more relevantly for thinking about gendered social structure, that women envy not the biological penis, but what it signifies—social power and authority. Many contemporary feminist psychoanalytic theorists have argued for the powerful influence of social structure in creating and constraining the range of emotional and other associations individuals may have to particular social, interpersonal, and individual objects and symbols (Benjamin 1988; Chodorow 1978, 1994; Flax 1990).

During the post-World War II period, a branch of interdisciplinary social science flourished that aimed at studying "culture and personality." Scholars in this tradition focused on understanding how cultural differences—in social structure, practices, and ideology—might shape individual psychology (Honigman 1967, Kluckhohn et al. 1953). Anthropologists including the Kluckhohns and the Whitings (Whiting 1963) exemplified this approach, and examined a range of individual-level behaviors (prosocial behavior, child-rearing practices) in different cultures. Equally, sociologists (Inkeles & Smith 1974; Parsons 1955, 1967) argued that features of the social structure that varied in different contexts (e.g., the gendered differentiation of social roles, the degree of modernization) are consequential for individual personality. Finally, psychologists in this tradition, such as David McClelland, focused on the ways in which transcultural phenomena—like achievement motivation—might nevertheless be predicted by features of the economic system and religion. These approaches required scholars to collect data across different cultures, and to specify direct and indirect connections between the social level and the individual level. For example, McClelland (1967) argued that under capitalism, child-rearing focuses on increasing individual initiative (and hence achievement motivation), but under precapitalist systems it focused on minimizing initiative, while enhancing willingness to submit to authority. In turn, these systematic differences partly account for the relatively higher levels of achievement motivation in capitalist versus precapitalist systems. These theorists began to articulate the specific cultural and societal features that might be pertinent for individual development, and identified mechanisms that might link those features with individual personality development. The approach depended on finding average personality differences across cultures and then linking those differences to differences in social structure.

The culture and personality approach was widely criticized, partly by those who felt that features of the culture or social structure were often identified in a fairly arbitrary way, and by anthropologists who felt that the approach tended to create over-general, even stereotypical images of cultures (Inkeles & Levinson 1954, 1969). Moreover, it depended on viewing different cultures with the same general conceptual categories, an approach in conflict with anthropology's fundamental effort to take different cultures on their own terms, rather than imposing preexisting categories imported from a different culture (Shweder 1991). Nevertheless, psychologists and sociologists have continued to examine links between personality and social structure *within* large, complex cultures like our own. The reasoning here has been that individuals occupy different locations within the social structure, and those different locations are consequential for the development of personality. Sociologist James S. House (1981) and psychologist Carol Ryff (1987) are particularly prominent exponents of these views. Psychologist Joseph Veroff (1983) specified [as did Bronfenbrenner (1986) for developmental psychology] that individual personality must be understood within a variety of social contexts that are increasingly removed from the person (dyad, family, neighborhood or community, and wider society). None of these theorists focused particularly on gender, but all of them provide specific guidance on how to link individual-level phenomena (personality, behavior, attitudes, and performance) with social-level phenomena. One critical tool for making the connection is the concept of identity.

Identity emerged as an important concept in psychology during the same post-war period as culture and personality. Erik Erikson—one of the psychosocial psychoanalytic theorists searching for ways to link the intrapsychic, interpersonal, and social levels of analysis—articulated a relatively broad theory of identity that also provided that link. According to Erikson (1950/1963, 1968), identity is an emergent structure of personality that develops throughout the lifespan but takes on organization and significance in adolescence. He argued that identity is composed of many disparate elements, including one's identification with one's own past experience, with particular characteristics and traits, with ideas and ideologies, and with a defined place (often an occupation, but also other roles, e.g., family and gender) in the social structure. Adolescence is critical to this theory because identity is a self-conscious structure that depends on a certain degree of cognitive understanding of both the self and the social structure; it is also critical because it is a period during which certain kinds of social affirmation (including awarding of degrees, paying of salary, etc.) begin to accrue. These affirmations in turn support some identity developments and preclude others. Erikson's notion of identity is extremely broad and inclusive, which may suggest that one's identity may only have a modest level of coherence derived both from the individual's desire to perceive her/himself as coherent and the social pressures that encourage it. Erikson's "identity" is quite malleable, or subject to continued change over the adult life course, based on both individual experiences and input from the social structure.

Erikson (1968, see also Erikson 1974) viewed identity as gendered in several senses. First, he assumed that identification with a gendered body and with gendered roles was part of identity. Second, he understood that social structures constrained and encouraged identity developments of different sorts in a variety of ways. Finally, he knew that one of these constraints was the operation of gender in heterosexual couples. While feminist psychologists have found many specific observations of Erikson to be grounded in a limited view of gender possibilities (Franz & White 1985, Strouse 1974), the broader theory of identity offers a specific vision of how social structural features are internalized by individuals, and thus how social structure and the individual may be linked. Stewart & Healy (1989) suggested that in fact sociological ideas of generation and individual theories of development such as Erikson's could be integrated—using the concept of identity—to help us examine empirically how and why generations differ. Cole et al. (2001), Helson et al. (1995), and Stewart (2003) have demonstrated how this approach can be used to study changes in gendered phenomena over time.

During the same period when Erikson was developing his personality theory and subsequent scholars were building on it, social psychologists developed a quite separate and significant line of theoretical and empirical understanding of social identity. This approach actually grew out of research on perceptual misestimation (Tajfel 1957), which Tajfel (1981) later generalized to the emotions, values, and stresses attached to group memberships. He showed that these attachments to groups (defined in a variety of ways—by religion, nation, occupation, race, gender, etc.) are consequential for a variety of perceptions and behaviors. Since Tajfel's first powerful observations, many social psychologists have demonstrated that social identities based on group identifications are indeed consequential. Retrospectively this approach can be seen as an elaboration of one element of identity (identification with groups) in Erikson's theory. It offers us a systematic way of understanding how that element of identity operates. It is important to note that social identity theorists define as "groups" some features of the social structure that other theorists would define differently. Thus, some theorists would view "groups" such as occupations, gender, etc., as roles (e.g., Parsons 1955, 1967), while others would view them as social structures (e.g., Gurin et al. 1980). There may be important consequences to these different ways of thinking about these identities (as attached to groups or to social structures), but for many scholars the notion of social identity has offered an approach to linking social structure and individual behavior. More narrowly some psychologists have found connections between social structures and gendered behavior through gender identities.

Gurin and her colleagues (Gurin et al. 1980) noted that social identities could be attached to social strata as well as collections of individual persons. They examined how identification with a social stratum (class, gender, and age) predicted political beliefs (Gurin 1985, 1987). Gurin & Markus (1989) explored how gender consciousness (or identification with a gender stratum) related to other ideas about politics and the family. More recently, Frable (1997) reviewed the literature on a variety of social identities, including gender. She noted an increasing focus in this literature on the development of social identities. Separate developmental models have been offered for the development of racial identities (Cross 1991, 1995; Phinney 1989), feminist identities (Downing & Roush 1985, Downing Hansen 2002, Hyde 2002, Moradi & Mezydlo Subich 2002), and sexual identities (Cass 1979, Diamond & Savin-Williams 2000). These developmental models are designed to articulate the different kinds of origins and pathways that individuals may follow in becoming identified with a particular social stratum. In addition, these models sometimes specify different identity outcomes. Thus, Sellers and his colleagues (Sellers et al. 1998) are interested in the substantively different racial identities (e.g., nationalist, assimilationist) that African Americans may identify with, while Henley and her colleagues are interested in the different kinds of feminist identities (essentialist, liberal, etc.) to which feminists may attach importance (Henley et al. 1998, 2000). These approaches assume that while each social identity may be multidimensional, each serves to define fundamentally or internally represent one's relationship to a collectivity or group (Brewer & Gardner 1996). Thus identity—both in the Eriksonian and the social identity tradition—provides a potential conceptual link between the psychology of the individual and social structures, including gender.

Conceptual Tools for Psychology from Feminist Theory

Although identity provides a critical linking construct, psychologists must work out how to think of gender within each empirical research program. We have seen that in psychology these programs are dominated by notions of gender as sex differences, as within-sex variations, and as social structures. Feminist theorists have offered parallel accounts of gender that allow us to examine gender in terms of the gendered meanings attached to social phenomena, as a social system of power relations embedded in others, and as identities. These accounts in turn have proven useful to some psychological research efforts, and we believe they can enhance others.

Gender as Analytic Tool

First, historian Joan Scott (1988) argued that gender is not merely an empirical "fact" attached to persons or even symbols, but an "analytical tool." That is (among other things), we can use the idea of gender to examine what other categories of analysis may signify—their extra baggage or surplus meaning. For example, we may (in history) think about how particular occupations (such as the military, or medicine or nursing) are gendered, and how that gendering influences public discourse, as well as individuals' possibilities (Anker 1997). When, for example, medical expertise is gendered male (and associated with doctors, as in the contemporary United States), it is viewed as requiring high levels of intellect, training, and authority, but when it is gendered female (and associated with nurses, as in the contemporary United States) it is viewed as requiring high levels of compassion, nurturance, and patience. Opportunities for medical training for women depend on the terms in which the occupation is viewed, as do the salaries for nurses and doctors (see Harden 2001 for a discussion of the very different situation in Russia, where the medical profession is gendered female, and is both low in status and in pay).

In psychology, we can see the use of gender as an analytic tool in research that explores how "traits" may be themselves "gendered"—that is, viewed as strongly associated with masculinity and being male, or femininity and being female. Stewart (1998) argued that the 'big five" personality traits (extraversion, conscientiousness, agreeableness, emotional stability or neuroticism, and openness to experience), introduced as universal descriptors of personality, were "gendered"—that is, associated with masculinity (extraversion or surgency, including dominance) and femininity (particularly agreeableness, but perhaps also neuroticism and conscientiousness), and should be understood in that way. It is equally possible that traits subsumed within these larger traits are also gendered—e.g., "openness to experience" includes aspects of tolerance (probably gendered female), as well as openness to risk-taking (probably gendered male). This notion has been explored from the perspective of sex differences using both meta-analyses (Feingold 1994) and empirical analysis of a large, representative sample (Goldberg et al. 1998).

In a series of studies, Twenge has gone further in using gender as an analytic tool to understand these traits. First, under the assumption that changes in social definitions of gender over time should be represented in changes in average levels of certain individual personality variables, she has examined (Twenge 2001; see also Twenge 1997) changes over time in psychological indicators of assertiveness (which has increased for both men and women in the United States from 1931 to 1993). She notes, though, that the increases for women have been much more substantial than those for men, and now assertiveness produces little sex difference in most studies. In this research Twenge uses gender as an analytic tool, both in the sense of considering the gendered social meanings of particular traits (such as assertiveness) and in the sense of changes in those meanings over time. At the same time she also examines gender in the sense of "sex differences" that is more familiar to most psychologists. There is clearly much more to be done in this area; many of the most familiar personality traits are deeply gendered in their social meanings and symbolism, and psychologists have done little to consider the implications of those meanings within and over time.

Some social psychologists have examined how social behaviors may be gendered in the laboratory. In fact, we can see how certain laboratory paradigms are themselves crucially gendered. For example, many psychologists have argued that mathematics performance is gendered male in our culture (Eccles & Jacobs 1986, Eccles et al. 1990). Claude Steele and his colleagues (Spencer et al. 1999; see also Aronson et al. 1998) actually manipulated the degree to which it was gendered, by telling students that their performance on a laboratory task was diagnostic of sex differences. Doing so differentially affected male and female students' performance, specifically causing female students to perform more poorly.

Finally, many social psychologists have demonstrated that being a solo group representative (a woman, for example) in a group results in being treated as a "token" (Kanter 1977, Spangler et al. 1978, Yoder & Sinnett 1985). In this research, token status was found to be associated with higher levels of stigma [negative stereotyping of the "minority" group by the majority group members (Kanter 1977, Taylor et al. 1978) as well as poorer performance by tokens (Sackett et al. 1991)]. Interestingly, when this paradigm was complicated by considering the usual social status of group members, it turned out that gender was a crucial analytic tool. Thus, Sekaquaptewa & Thompson (2002) have shown that individuals who are "token" or "solo" in a group perform differently depending on their social status in general. Men who are "solo" or "tokens" in otherwise female groups perform as well as the women, while women solos perform less well than the men in their groups. Performance suffers from the combination of circumstances involving both solo status and lower social status, and not from only one of these factors. Only by taking account of the social status associated with being male or being female could this be made clear.

Gender as a Set of Embedded Power Relations

Recognition that gender is critically linked with social status opens up opportunities to think about gender as a set of power relations rather than merely as characteristics or features of individuals. Feminist theorist Catherine MacKinnon (1987) argued, in a powerful essay on "Difference and Dominance," that,

> On the first day that matters, dominance was achieved, probably by force. By the second day, division along the same lines had to be relatively firmly in place. On the third day, differences were demarcated, together with social systems to exaggerate them in perception and in fact, because the systematically differential delivery of benefits and deprivations required making no mistake about who was who. Comparatively speaking, man has been resting ever since. Gender might not even code as difference, might not even mean distinction epistemologically, were it not for its consequences for social power. (p. 40)

Using MacKinnon's reasoning would lead us to conclude that the presence of a female token in an otherwise all-male group introduces a dimension of dominance that can be easily misread as simply "difference." MacKinnon's perspective on gender would lead us to think more carefully about how gendered meanings of social phenomena (including persons) and behavior include relations of dominance. In her early account of the importance of social status in social identity formation, social psychologist Erika Apfelbaum (1979/1999) showed how dominant groups create conditions among subordinates both for obedience or compliance and for the formation of resistant social identities. Equally, Aida Hurtado (1996) has articulated how complex gender, race, and class relations create group identities for white women and women of color, women and men of color, and men of color from different ethnic group backgrounds. Her point in these analyses is to show how different relationships to privilege (often held by white men, but also held by white women, and men of color in varying ways and degrees) complicate the experience of subordination for members of these groups. These analyses build on an understanding of how both gender and racial-ethnic identities are grounded in power relations.

Susan Fiske's (1993) analysis of how gender operates within organizations begins from an understanding of this kind. Fiske argues that in any relationship defined by differential power (like gender), the dominant group (men in this case) can afford to be oblivious to certain kinds of social cues, while the subordinate group (women) cannot. Fiske shows that this means that dominants and subordinates have very different levels and kinds of information about each other; in this sense their asymmetrical power relation drives further asymmetries in their experience and knowledge.

Frable (1990) made a similar kind of argument about the greater effort required of subordinates or "marginals" in social interaction with dominants. She demonstrated that marginality or subordinate status, while associated with greater knowledge or information, also requires considerably greater attention and effort, thus drawing away effort from other areas of performance. This kind of analysis suggests that the performance of dominants and subordinates on tasks for which they are equally qualified might end up being different because of the different number and kind of demands they are facing when they are performing in the context of relationships with each other (see also Frable 1993, 1997).

In a study of patterns and consequences of workplace incivility in the federal courts, Cortina et al. (2002) noted that dominant or subordinate status based on occupation and gender played a role in who instigated and who was the target of uncivil behavior. Incivility directed at female attorneys mostly came from their male peers, as well as from judges of both sexes. Female attorneys were subordinate to both groups, one in terms of gender (in the case of their male peers), the other in terms of occupation (in the case of the judges). Men tended to experience incivility primarily from judges, who were above them in terms of a hierarchy based on occupation status; they did not experience incivility from their fellow female attorneys. Consequently, women were more frequently targets, and experienced more of the severe forms of incivility and almost all of the gendered uncivil acts (in contrast to general incivility).

Examining a more commonplace gendered phenomenon, the objectification of the female body, Fredrickson & Roberts (1997) demonstrated that a particularly gendered everyday experience of power inequity is expressed physically as well as psychologically. Their objectification theory contends that women have learned to see themselves from an outsider's perspective, that of a more powerful male person evaluating a less powerful person as an object. Objectification affects women's perception of their physical selves, creating a habit of monitoring the body and seeing the self as an object. That habit in turn can result in experiences of shame and anxiety and contribute to serious mental health problems such as eating disorders.

In a very different domain, Nolen-Hoeksema and her colleagues (Nolen-Hoeksema et al. 1999) have argued that the observed gender difference in depressive symptoms may well result substantially from several features of women's subordinate social status (along with other factors). These include women's persistent experience of relative social devaluation, as well as their exposure to and fear of violence against them—that is, the very power relations that characterize gender and have been illuminated by Fiske, Frable, and Fredrickson & Roberts.

Multiplicity and Instability of Selves

Postmodern and poststructural theorists have argued that the idea of "identity" is itself a "modernist" notion—one that assumes a stable, coherent individual agent whose behavior flows from an essential core identity or self. They have historicized this idea (noting that this understanding of the self or identity emerged in the Enlightenment and took on increasing force in the twentieth century). Moreover, they point out that if we take full account of the capacity of social processes to construct individuals, we must take seriously the possibility that the presence of this idea in the culture shaped individuals' self-understandings, as well as theorists' notions of persons. These ideas have been recognized by many feminist theorists as potentially threatening to the notion of politicized social identities like "women" (see, e.g., Bordo 1993). Nevertheless, some aspects of these theories have been identified by feminist psychologists as potentially helpful in studying the psychology of gender, among other things (see, e.g., Bohan 2002, Gergen 2001, Hare-Mustin & Marecek 1990).

One particularly valuable use of this kind of theorizing is in an area already rich with activity in psychology: research that has focused on the complexity and situational variability in individuals' selves or identities. While many psychological studies point to some degree or kind of stability and unity of identity, many others have explored the ways in which identities are multiple and overlapping, sometimes conflicting or even mutually contradictory, as well as ways in which identities are salient and visible in some situations and invisible in others. For example, Markus & Nurius (1986) initiated a line of research into "possible selves," arguing that individuals not only have ideas of themselves, but also ideas of the selves they hope to be and of the selves they hope not to become. Moreover, they argue that these different "possible selves"—like "actual" selves—have motivational implications. People strive to become the selves they imagine they could be, and strive to avoid becoming the selves they fear being (see, e.g., Knox et al. 2000). Equally, Linville (1985, 1987) demonstrated that individual differences in self-complexity can be measured, and predict affective reactions to performance feedback, among other outcomes. Many other psychologists have also examined aspects of the organization of selves or identities (see, e.g., Rosenberg & Gara 1985, Woolfolk et al. 1995). In more recent research, Roccas & Brewer (2002) have examined the complexity of social identities and their relationships to tolerance of outgroup members. In a series of studies, Deaux and her colleagues have examined the ways in which identities are negotiated over time and across situations (Deaux & Ethier 1998, Ethier & Deaux 1994). Merely to study these processes is, of course, to recognize that identities are not completely stable and "essential"; rather, they are emergent in social interactions that are sought out and responded to by individual persons.

Finally, considerable empirical attention has recently been paid to the issue of "bicultural identities" among individuals who feel shaped by and loyal to at least two different cultures (LaFromboise et al. 1993). Such individuals are often immigrants from one culture to another, but include second- and third-generation descendents who remain identified with a "home" culture they may have only experienced in a "different" culture. Theorists (e.g., Berry 1988) have articulated alternative types of bicultural identities (e.g., assimilating, accommodating, alternating, etc.), and researchers have explored the prominence of different kinds of bicultural identities in immigrant groups (Smith et al. 2004), as well as the ways in which bicultural persons experience different situations in terms of identity (Hong et al. 2000). Although these researchers do not necessarily focus on gender or feminist identities, and do not explicitly relate their research to feminist theories (see Deaux & Stewart 2001 for an exception), it seems to us (as to Howard 2000) that the developments in these two domains are parallel, compatible, and could usefully inform one another. Explicitly linking them would help psychology to engage more directly in the interdisciplinary dialogue on identity—including gender identity—that is taking place in many fields, both contributing from our empirical knowledge and drawing from the empirical and theoretical resources in other fields (see, e.g., Brubaker & Cooper 2000).

Intersectionality: Theory and Examples

Although multiple and bicultural identities theories can be used to enrich the psychological study of gender, even these theories miss some key aspects of its complexity: the interaction between one's many social identities (i.e., ethnic, class, and gender) and the influences of different social structures on the construction of these identities and relations between members of diverse social groups. Several feminist sociologists (Collins 1994, King 1988), psychologists (Deaux & Stewart 2001, Fine & Weis 1998, Hurtado 1996), critical legal theorists (Crenshaw 1991/1997), and philosophers (Spelman 1988) have advanced intersectionality as a perspective that includes these interactive and structural elements in theories of gender.

Three central tenets of intersectionality are especially useful to the psychological study of gender: (*a*) no social group is homogenous, (*b*) people must be located in terms of social structures that capture the power relations implied by those structures, and (*c*) there are unique, nonadditive effects of identifying with more than one social group. The first idea, the recognition that women (and men) are not a homogenous group, may seem obvious to psychologists, in that one of the purposes of psychological study has been to tease out individual differences. By taking group categories as given, and focusing only on individual-level variance within those groups, however, we avoid attending to how we have constructed these group categories themselves. For example, Hurtado (1996) illustrates how statistical analyses of pay and education parity data misrepresent women of color by assuming to describe "women." By averaging the overall lower pay and education status of women of color (here black, Hispanic, and Native American) with white women's, researchers produce a group average much higher than the average for women of color. A more complex picture continues to emerge when we note that black women have educational attainment at a level comparable to white women's average education level and higher than black men's, yet they are paid less than both of these other groups.

A related line of research shows that women readily acknowledge that women as a group are discriminated against in their place of work, yet tend to deny having ever suffered discrimination, such as pay inequity, personally. This phenomenon is known as denial of personal discrimination. It can be accounted for by cognitive and emotional biases such as a need to justify others' and our own misfortunes in disparate ways, in order to avoid cognitive dissonance (Crosby 1984, Crosby et al. 1993). These processes likely apply to women of all ethnic backgrounds. However, women who experience both gender-based discrimination and discrimination based on ethnicity, face additional interpretive ambiguities. Consider, for example, that African American women, in attempting to make accurate attributions of causality for discrimination experiences, may find it impossible and/or fruitless to identify race or gender as unique sources of those experiences (Essed 1990, Gay & Tate 1998). For this reason, African American women may employ different cognitive coping mechanisms than European American women when dealing with experiences of discrimination, adding another layer of complexity to the causes, perceptions, and effects of discrimination.

By analyzing pay and education parity data in terms of either gender (women versus men) or race (blacks versus whites), the unique pattern of black women's experience is lost along with critical knowledge of how both race and gender "work" to have behavioral consequences. Cole & Stewart (2001) examined how the study of differences such as these can lead to invidious (offensively discriminating) comparisons. Methods that rely on invidious comparisons and seek to legitimate popular stereotypes are "more likely to cause harm and produce distorted and partial findings" (Cole & Stewart 2001, p. 295). In contrast, research that takes into account people's multidimensional experience of the world is more likely to produce new knowledge that presents a complex picture of difference instead of oversimplifying it. Thinking intersectionally encourages us to examine how grouping categories are constructed and to disaggregate them when we must. It does not mean that every dimension of social identity needs to be studied simultaneously, but rather that psychologists must be conscious of the consequences of our analytic strategies.

The second integral part of intersectionality is the notion that people must be understood as located within social structures. Locating a person socially demands consideration of her material reality and the social forces that shape that reality, particularly social disparities and power dynamics. Considering these contexts, we not only find "new" populations overlooked in psychological study but also a fuller picture of the social influences on any person's psychology. Access to power, in particular, is a frequently neglected but strongly influential aspect of social structure. Again turning to the study of discrimination, it should be noted that a critical factor shaping experiences and consequences of discrimination is the victim's access to power. While white women may be excluded from various forms of power, their usually close proximity to white men (as brothers, fathers, lovers, husbands) gives them greater access to the dominant holders of power than a black woman would have who does not regularly interact with white men outside of formal public situations and roles (Hurtado 1996). These unequal relations to privilege create differences, differences that often are, but should not be, attributed to culture or personality.

The third principle, that individuals identify with more than one social group simultaneously and this identification produces unique consequences for the individual, calls for a shift to acknowledging the ways social systems work together to affect gender identities (King 1988). When we stop seeing "race and gender as exclusive or separable categories" we create more complex categories with richer pictures of gender within them (Crenshaw 1991/1997, p. 551). This holds true for all social categories. An individual may share identification with one or more categories with another person, but those identities in combination with the social contexts they do *not* hold in common create a diverse range of experiences, worldviews, and psychological mechanisms for dealing with the world. A professional-class Latina lesbian mother may share the same social categories and hold similar identities to a woman with a demographic background almost mirroring hers but who identifies as straight. However, because of this difference, their gender identities, roles, and interactions with the broader social world are likely to be dissimilar in several crucial ways. Looking specifically at their mothering experiences, they will likely employ different strategies to handle issues of stigma, access to money and credit, transmission of values to their children, and interaction with the legal system. In general, the psychological consequences of everyday interactions will be qualitatively different, despite their shared identity as a mother. For example, the role of co-mother is a unique aspect of lesbian families, creating a new parenting model that Wilson (2001) found emphasizes equality in parental responsibility and caretaking burden in a way that differs from that negotiated in heterosexual couples. Mothering strategies also vary along other social dimensions such as ethnic backgrounds, economic and social classes, or national origins, to name a few.

Patricia Hill Collins (1994) centered her analysis of mothering on women identified with marginalized ethnic groups and observed three themes key to their sense of motherhood not shared by white women: survival, power, and cultural identity. Hill Collins asserts that many Native American, African American, Hispanic, and Asian American mothers need to work to ensure their children's physical survival, structure their mothering patterns based on a dominant group's perception of them as lacking power as mothers, and emphasize development of their children's cultural identity in ways that most white women do not because of their greater social and economic privilege (Collins 1994).

Psychological Studies that Inform Our Study of Gender from an Intersectional Perspective

Gender often acts as a shared attribute that shapes experiences, identities, emotive expressions, and thought processes. But the experience of gender can generate qualitatively different forms of these when gender is experienced in various social and material contexts. Articles in earlier editions of the *Annual Review of Psychology* have explored gender's influence on self-concept and identity and its functioning within the broader social web (Banaji & Prentice 1994, Frable 1997). The studies reviewed revealed many crucial insights into how social structures affect group and individual psychologies. Generally, these studies investigated the impact of one social variable at a time. When looking at more than one social category, researchers kept categories such as gender, class, and ethnicity separated from one another in terms of how they functioned within an individual or group. Recently studies have examined gender, class, ethnicity, race, and sexuality not as separate variables, nor as cumulative, but as intersecting categories that create unique experiences and psychologies that are qualitatively different rather than a mechanical combination of their individual effects.

Although nearly any psychological phenomenon might be fruitfully explored from an intersectional perspective, those strongly influenced by social structures or taking place in the context of social relations are especially likely prospects. On both grounds, violence is an excellent candidate. Fine & Weis (1998) examined the experiences of African American, white, Latina/o, poor and working class women and men. Strikingly, the kinds of violence as well as the psychological effects and methods for dealing with violence varied greatly between and among these groups, depending on several contextual factors. For example, black men experienced violence primarily outside of their homes and reacted to it by patrolling borders around their neighborhoods, dealing with it in the streets. Black women saw the same violence outside and dealt with it by keeping children inside and working to keep violence out of the home. But inside was not necessarily a safe space. Domestic violence was an experience shared by African American women, Latinas, and white women, yet their racial, ethnic, and class identities strongly influenced both their strategies for coping with it and their beliefs about it. For example, African American women and Latinas resisted involving the police with whom they had an ambivalent relationship; they felt the police did not protect them appropriately because of their race/ethnicity.

While these two groups shared similar attitudes and experiences with the police and domestic violence, they dealt with violence at home differently. African American women held the men who perpetrated the violence more responsible. The Latinas interviewed expressed an allegiance to marriage and family that kept them from disrupting the family by leaving violent situations. White working-class women similarly held on to an ideal of a family based on white middle-class values, where the husband acts as provider and protector of the family, despite the incongruity of this model with their lived experiences of family. Within this group, women coped with domestic violence in two distinct ways. "Settled" women opted to maintain secrecy about violence, protecting an ideal of a "good" white family. "Hard-living" women removed themselves from their abusive situation and spoke out about it, usually at great cost to themselves, especially economically. If Fine & Weis had treated the women as a homogenous group dealing with domestic violence (or had treated all ethnic group members as one group ignoring gender), they would have missed the diversity of attitudes and behaviors that characterized these women from different ethnic groups.

Press & Cole (1999) similarly took an intersectional approach when they examined women's attitudes toward abortion, an area where women are frequently divided into two camps—prolife or prochoice. The differences within these groups are thus overlooked because of the emphasis on the differences between them. In focus groups, Press & Cole spoke with prolife and prochoice women from a variety of backgrounds about their attitudes toward abortion and media portrayals of the abortion debate. They found these attitudes were influenced by the women's social and material contexts, though not in a uniform manner. Prolife women expressed similar values and attitudes across classes, while prochoice women's rationales for their support of a woman's right to abortion and value judgments of women who had abortions varied across both class and race. For example, middle-class women used a very individualistic perspective to think about abortion decision making, emphasizing the depth of an individual woman's feelings as the critical justification for her decisions. In contrast, working class women justified decisions in terms of the difficulties that women faced in navigating an authoritative and disempowering health care system on their own behalf.

Identifying with specific social categories not only shapes attitudes but affects behavior as well. Priming an ethnic or gender identity, Shih et al. (1999) found Asian American women's performance on tasks shifted depending on which identity, Asian or female, was more salient. When an Asian identity was made salient, women scored higher on quantitative tests and lower on verbal tests than when their female identity was made salient. In that scenario, the reverse outcomes were produced. By considering individuals' multiple identities, and focusing on how they can play different roles, the researchers uncovered an important aspect of stereotypes that might have been missed if the intersection of ethnicity and gender were ignored.

Examining race, ethnicity, and gender simultaneously does not always produce the same kinds of findings. For example, as noted earlier, Gay & Tate (1998) explored the intersection of ethnicity and race and gender by focusing on the political attitudes of black women. They found that although many black women strongly identify both as "women" and as "blacks," when they are confronted with political situations such as the Million Man March, O.J. Simpson trial, and Clarence Thomas nomination, black women's political attitudes were mostly determined by their racial identity. Landrine et al. (1992) also found that racial identity affected attitudes, including attitudes about gender stereotypes. In their study, white and nonwhite female subjects rated themselves similarly on a measure of personality characteristics associated with stereotypic gender roles. But the groups differed in how they defined the terms. Thus, while a white woman and a nonwhite woman might endorse an item ("passive") at the same level, they were effectively endorsing different items ("am laid back/easygoing" versus "don't say what I really think").

Mary Waters' (1996) research on identity development in adolescents also shows how culture and specifically relations to power from one's position within a culture can determine the very definition and value judgment of a stereotype. She interviewed girls and boys of Caribbean descent, either second generation of immigrants or those who immigrated when they were young. Did they identify as black American, ethnic American or as an immigrant? Class but not gender confounded their choices. Poor and working-class young people identified more often as black or immigrant. Middle-class teens identified more frequently as ethnic. While gender did not influence the choice of these identities, the ramifications of these choices varied greatly along gender lines. Boys' identities were more rigid than girls' identities. Girls were able to move between identities more easily and were less stigmatized by their peers than their male counterparts who faced stricter enforcement of their identities from peers. This study shows there are multiple possibilities for identity development, and not a single one generalizable to all of society or even the entirety of this particular group. Gender, class, immigrant status, parental attitudes, and peer relationships all influenced these teens' identity development.

Most of the research we have discussed has been comparative in nature. It is, though, possible and sometimes necessary to examine a single, carefully defined intersection without a "comparison group." Cortina (2001) developed a measure of workplace sexual harassment for Latinas based broadly on the Sexual Experiences Questionnaire (Fitzgerald et al. 1988), which was itself developed primarily to assess white women's experiences. Cortina included indications of "sexual racism" in the Sexual Experience Questionnaire-Latina, and noted differences in Latinas' interpretations of particular items from the interpretations of Anglo respondents. Espin (1997, 1999) has also focused some of her research on the experience of Latina women in the United States. For example, in one study she examined how a sample of Cuban immigrant lesbians experienced the intersection of ethnicity and sexuality. She explicitly explored the ways in which, on the one hand, their ethnic community encouraged them to be closeted, while, on the other hand, the Anglo lesbian community forced ethnic assimilation. She concluded because of the realities of racism and heterosexism that they have to confront, they are forced to choose for their lives those alternatives that are more tolerable or less costly to them. Some may choose to live in Miami among Cubans, even if that implies "staying in the closet." Others may choose to live in other areas of the country among Anglo lesbians without feeling fully supported in terms of their Cuban identity (Espin 1997, p. 107). In this study, Espin illuminates the diverse experiences of Latina lesbians by focusing on the variation within a single intersection of ethnicity, gender, and sexuality.

How Can Psychologists Use Intersectionality to Improve Research?

It is clear from this review that some psychologists have made productive use of the notion of intersectionality to define critical qualitative differences in the psychologies of certain groups of people in certain social locations. These groups are sometimes simply identified in terms of their social location with respect to two or more social statuses (e.g., white and male, African American and female, female and lesbian, etc.), but often they are defined in terms of their degree of identification with particular social locations. When we attend to this question of identification, it becomes clear that individuals' different identities are more or less salient (though certainly not present or absent), depending on the context or issue. Thus, as we have seen, Gay & Tate (1998) found that for African American women, race is often the most salient identity in the domain of political opinion, while Fine & Weis (1998) found that gender may be most salient in the domain of domestic violence. Both of these studies examined the intersection of race and gender; both also seemed to assume that the women were heterosexual. How do African American lesbians think about and experience violence? Are they as likely as other women to experience violence domestically? Are they more likely to experience it in the public sphere? Thinking intersectionally allows us to ask questions like these, which are important not only because they force us to examine the experiences of previously understudied groups. The questions may also inform us about the assumptions underlying the apparently general and generalizable knowledge we think we have. If, for example, on average women's experience of violence is much more domestic than men's, this may be crucially predicated on the fact that on average women live in households with adult men. That fact—and the importance of that fact to our data and our theories—may only emerge explicitly when we ask questions from an intersectional perspective.

Often it seems that intersectionality requires us to examine all social locations simultaneously—and that degree of complexity is daunting and frequently impractical. We believe that in fact intersectionality requires us to *think about* many different kinds of social locations and identities that might intersect relevantly for the behavior or experience we are studying. But we can and must make choices about which locations and identities may be particularly relevant and/or particularly understudied. In some cases we can make a reasonable judgment that a social location is irrelevant, because it seems logically to be so, and we have empirical evidence that groups based on that location do not differ on the relevant dimension. In many other cases, we have no empirical evidence about the particular location within psychology. In those cases we can benefit from our neighbor disciplines. Anthropologists, sociologists, and historians have often provided rich evidence about the very social locations about which we do not know enough in psychology even to make good first guesses.

We hope that as researchers adopt a perspective informed by intersectionality they will rely more on multiple, especially qualitative, methods. Criticism of mono-method bias in psychological research has a long history. Adopting intersectionality as a research perspective may lead us to more inclusive methodological choices. It may be noteworthy that although research programs implying intersectionality as a perspective have sometimes relied solely on traditional methods in psychology (e.g., experiments and surveys), many have employed mixed methods, or more qualitative approaches. In fact, in research identifying different experiences of high school as a joint function of race and gender, Stewart (2003) makes a specific case for ethnographically informed methods when exploring understudied topics in psychology. Bettie (2000) used the same method to examine high school experiences at the intersections of gender, ethnicity, and social class. It is partly for these reasons that Rabinowitz & Martin (2001) argued that "methodological pluralism is the strategy of choice in addressing the complexity of gender arrangements in our society" (p. 51).

Gender's Diverse Meanings in Psychology

Within mainstream psychology research, gender does not have one meaning. It sometimes signifies sex differences, sometimes intrasex variability, and sometimes gendered social roles and institutions. Locating gender in both individuals and social structures—however persuasive—implies a need for concepts that bridge those levels of analysis.

The notion of identity, both as articulated in Erikson's (1950/1963) comprehensive theory and in Tajfel's (1981) social identity theory, provides a helpful conceptual tool for understanding both how social experiences are inscribed on individual personalities, and how individuals define themselves in relation to social groups, strata, and institutions. Thus we have tried to show that the development of theories of identity in personality and social psychology in fact can serve to enrich and deepen our understanding of gender. In particular, identity theorists have highlighted the importance of social context and point to the need for psychologists to give greater consideration to this influential factor. Similarly, feminist theorists have recognized the significance of social context in individuals' construction and use of gendered identities. Consequently, they have developed some additional conceptual resources that are compatible with the identity theories and with the development of understanding of gender in psychology. These include the use of gender as an analytic tool (rather than a social category), the analysis of gender as a system of power relations embedded in other systems of power relations, and analysis of the multiplicity and instability of identity.

All of these tools can be employed to examine the different psychologies constructed at the intersections of different power relations (gender, race, class, sexuality, and so forth). The challenge for psychology is to incorporate all of these conceptual tools into our research designs and practices. Our goal in this review was to demonstrate that many creative efforts along these lines have already yielded fruit, and to plant the seeds for an even richer harvest.

ACKNOWLEDGMENTS

We are grateful to Jennifer Churchwell, Laura Citrin, Elizabeth R. Cole, Ngaire Donaghue, Andrea Dottolo, Breanne Fahs, Carla Grayson, Jana Haritatos, Kathi Miner-Rubino, Susan Nolen-Hoeksema, Perry Silverschanz, Allison G. Smith, Cynthia Torges, David G. Winter, and Carolyn Zahn-Waxler for helpful suggestions, discussions, and comments on drafts of this manuscript.

The *Annual Review of Psychology* is online at http://psych.annualreviews.org

LITERATURE CITED

Anker R. 1997. Theories of occupational segregation by sex: an overview. *Int. Labour Rev.* 136(3):315–40

Apfelbaum E. 1999 (1979). Relations of domination and movements for liberation: an analysis of power between groups. In *Social Psychology of Intergroup Relations*, ed. WG Austin, S Worchel, pp. 188–204. Belmont, MA: Brooks/Cole

Aronson J, Quinn DM, Spencer SJ. 1998. Stereotype threat and the academic underperformance of minorities and women. See Swim & Stangor 1998, pp. 83–103

Banaji MR, Prentice DA. 1994. The self in social contexts. *Annu. Rev. Psychol.* 45:297–332

Benjamin J. 1988. *The Bonds of Love: Psychoanalysis, Feminism, and the Problem of Domination.* New York: Pantheon

Berry JW. 1988. Acculturation and psychological adaptation: conceptual overview. In *Ethnic Psychology: Research and Practice with Immigrants, Refugees, Native Peoples, Ethnic Groups and Sojourners*, ed. JW Berry,

RC Annis, pp. 41–52. Amsterdam: Swets & Zeitlinger

Bettie J. 2000. Women without class: chicas, cholas, trash, and the presence/absence of class identity. *Signs* 26:1–35

Block J. 1984. *Sex Role Identity and Ego Development.* San Francisco: Jossey-Bass

Bohan J. 2002. Sex differences and/in the self: classic themes, feminist variations, postmodern challenges. *Psychol. Women Q.* 26:74–88

Bordo S. 1993. Feminism, postmodernism, and gender skepticism. In *Unbearable Weight*, pp. 215–43. Berkeley: Univ. Calif. Press

Brewer MB, Gardner W. 1996. Who is this "we"? Levels of collective identity and self representations. *J. Personal. Soc. Psychol.* 71:83–93

Brody L. 1999. *Gender, Emotion and the Family.* Cambridge, MA: Harvard Univ. Press

Bronfenbrenner U. 1986. Ecology of the family as context for human development: research perspectives. *Dev. Psychol.* 22(6):723–42

Brubaker R, Cooper F. 2000. Beyond identity. *Theory Soc.* 29:1–47

Buss D. 1995. Psychological sex differences: origins through natural selection. *Am. Psychol.* 50:164–68

Cass VC. 1979. Homosexuality identity formation: a theoretical model. *J. Homosex.* 4:219–35

Chodorow N. 1978. *The Reproduction of Mothering: Psychoanalysis and the Sociology of Gender.* Berkeley: Univ. Calif. Press

Chodorow N. 1994. *Femininities, Masculinities, Sexualities: Freud and Beyond.* Lexington: Univ. Kentucky Press

Cole E, Stewart AJ. 2001. Invidious comparisons: imagining a psychology of race and gender beyond differences. *Polit. Psychol.* 22:293–308

Cole E, Zucker AN, Duncan LE. 2001. Changing society, changing women (and men). See Unger 2001, pp. 410–24

Collins PH. 1994. Shifting the center: race, class and feminist theorizing about motherhood. In *Representations of Motherhood*, ed. D Bassin, M Honey, MM Kaplan, pp. 56–74. New Haven, CT: Yale

Cortina LM. 2001. Assessing sexual harassment among Latinas: development of an instrument. *Cult. Divers. Ethn. Minor. Psychol.* 7(2):164–81

Cortina LM, Lonsway KA, Magley VJ, Freeman LV, Collinsworth LL, et al. 2002. What's gender got to do with it? Incivility in the federal courts. *Law Soc. Inq.* 27:235–70

Crenshaw K. 1997 (1991). Beyond racism and misogyny: black feminism and 2 Live Crew. In *Women Transforming Politics: An Alternative Reader*, ed. CJ Cohen, KB Jones, JC Tronto, pp. 549–68. New York: NY Univ. Press

Crosby F. 1984. The denial of personal discrimination. *Am. Behav. Sci.* 27:371–86

Crosby F, Cordova DI, Jaskar K. 1993. On the failure to see oneself as disadvantaged: Cognitive and emotional components. In *Group Motivation: Social Psychological Perspectives*, ed. MA Hogg, D Abrams, pp. 87–104. New York: Harvester Wheatsheaf

Cross WE. 1991. *Shades of black.* Philadelphia: Temple Univ. Press

Cross WE. 1995. The psychology of nigrescence: revising the Cross model. In *Handbook of Multicultural Counseling*, ed. JG Ponterotto, JM Casas, LA Suzuki, CM Alexander, pp. 93–122. Thousand Oaks, CA: Sage

Deaux K, Ethier KA. 1998. Negotiating social identity. See Swim & Stangor 1998, pp. 301–23

Deaux K, Stewart AJ. 2001. Framing gendered identities. See Unger 2001, pp. 83–97

Diamond L, Savin-Williams RC. 2000. Explaining diversity in the development of same-sex sexuality among young women. *J. Soc. Issues* 56(2):297–314

Downing NE, Roush KL. 1985. From passive acceptance to active commitment: a model of feminist identity development for women. *Couns. Psychol.* 13:695–709

Downing Hansen N. 2002. Reflections on feminist identity development: implications for theory, measurement, and research. *Couns. Psychol.* 30(1):87–95

Eagly A. 1994. On comparing women and men. *Fem. Psychol.* 4:513–22

Eccles J, Jacobs JE. 1986. Social forces shape math attitudes and performance. *Signs* 11:367–80

Eccles J, Jacobs JE, Harold RD. 1990. Gender role stereotypes, expectancy effects, and parents' socialization of gender differences. *J. Soc. Issues* 46(2):183–201

Erikson EH. 1963 (1950). *Childhood and Society.* New York: Norton. 2nd ed.

Erikson EH. 1968. *Identity: Youth and Crisis.* New York: Norton

Erikson EH. 1974. Once more the inner space: letter to former student. In *Women and Analysis: Dialogues on Psychoanalytic Views of Femininity*, ed. J Strouse, pp. 365–87. New York: Dell

Espin OM. 1997. *Latina Realities: Essays on Healing, Migration, and Sexuality.* Boulder, CO: Westview

Espin OM. 1999. *Women Crossing Boundaries: A Psychology of Immigration and Transformations of Sexuality.* New York: Routledge

Essed P. 1990. *Everyday Racism: Reports from*

Women of Two Cultures. Claremont, CA: Hunter House

Ethier KA, Deaux K. 1994. Negotiating social identity when contexts change: maintaining identification and responding to threat. *J. Personal. Soc. Psychol.* 67(2):243–51

Favreau O. 1993. Do the n's justify the means? Null hypothesis testing applied to sex and other differences. *Can. Psychol.* 34:64–78

Favreau O. 1997. Sex and gender comparisons: Does null hypothesis testing create a false dichotomy? *Fem. Psychol.* 7:63–81

Feingold A. 1994. Gender differences in personality: a meta-analysis. *Psychol. Bull.* 116:429–56

Fine M, Weis L. 1998. *The Unknown City: Lives of Poor and Working-Class Young Adults.* Boston, MA: Beacon

Fiske ST. 1993. Controlling other people: the impact of power on stereotyping. *Am. Psychol.* 48:621–28

Fiske ST, Stevens LE. 1993. What's so special about sex? Gender stereotyping and discrimination. In *Gender Issues in Contemporary Society*, ed. S Oskamp, M Costanzo, pp. 173–96. Thousand Oaks, CA: Sage

Fitzgerald LF, Shullman SL, Bailey N, Richards M, Swecker J, et al. 1988. The incidence and dimensions of sexual harassment in academia and the workplace. *J. Vocat. Behav.* 32:152–75

Fivush R, Buckner JP. 2000. Gender, sadness and depression: the development of emotional focus through gendered discourse. In *Gender and Emotion: Social Psychological Perspectives*, ed. AH Fisher, pp. 232–53. New York: Cambridge Univ. Press

Flax J. 1990. *Thinking Fragments: Psychoanalysis, Feminism, and Postmodernism in the Contemporary West.* Berkeley: Univ. Calif. Press

Frable DES. 1990. Marginal and mindful: deviants in social interactions. *J. Personal. Soc. Psychol.* 59(1):140–49

Frable DES. 1993. Dimensions of marginality: Distinctions among those who are different. *Personal. Soc. Psychol. Bull.* 19(4):370–80

Frable DES. 1997. Gender, racial, ethnic, sexual, and class identities. *Annu. Rev. Psychol.* 48:139–62

Franz C, White KM. 1985. Individuation and attachment in personality development: extending Erikson's theory. *J. Personal.* 53:224–56

Fredrickson BL, Roberts T. 1997. Objectification theory: toward understanding women's lived experiences and mental health risks. *Psychol. Women Q.* 21:173–206

Freud S. 1961 (1930). Civilization and its discontents. In *The Standard Edition of the Complete Psychological Works of Sigmund Freud*, ed. J Strachey, 21:57–145. London: Hogarth

Fromm E. 1947. *Man for Himself.* New York: Holt, Rinehart & Winston

Gay C, Tate K. 1998. Doubly bound: the impact of gender and race on the politics of black women. *Polit. Psychol.* 19:169–84

Gergen M. 2001. *Feminist Reconstructions in Psychology: Narrative, Gender and Performance.* Thousand Oaks, CA: Sage

Goldberg LR, Sweeney D, Merenda PF, Hughes JE. 1998. Demographic variables and personality: the effects of gender, age, education, and ethnic/racial status on self-descriptions of personality attributes. *Personal. Individ. Differ.* 24:393–403

Goodwin SA, Fiske ST. 2001. Power and gender: the double-edged sword of ambivalence. See Unger 2001, pp. 358–66

Gurin P. 1985. Women's gender consciousness. *Public Opin. Q.* 49:143–63

Gurin P. 1987. The political implications of women's statuses. In *Spouse, Parent, Worker: On Gender and Multiple Roles*, ed. FJ Crosby, pp. 167–98. New Haven, CT: Yale Univ. Press

Gurin P, Markus H. 1989. Cognitive consequences of gender identity. In *The Social Identity of Women*, ed. S Skevington, D Baker, pp. 152–72. Newbury Park, CA: Sage

Gurin P, Miller H, Gurin G. 1980. Stratum identification and consciousness. *Soc. Psychol. Q.* 43:30–47

Gutek G, Done RS. 2001. Sexual harassment. See Unger 2001, pp. 367–87

Harden J. 2001. 'Mother Russia' at work. *Eur. J. Women's Stud.* 8(2):181–99

Hare-Mustin R, Marecek J, eds. 1990. *Making a Difference: Psychology and the Construction of Gender.* New Haven, CT: Yale Univ. Press

Helson R, Stewart AJ, Ostrove J. 1995. Identity in three cohorts of women. *J. Personal. Soc. Psychol.* 69:544–57

Henley NM, Meng K, O'Brien D, McCarthy WJ, Sockloskie RJ. 1998. Developing a scale to measure the diversity of feminist attitudes. *Psychol. Women. Q.* 22(3):317–48

Henley NM, Spalding LR, Kosta A. 2000. Development of the short form of the Feminist Perspectives Scale. *Psychol. Women Q.* 24(3):254–56

Hong Y, Morris MW, Chiu C, Chiu V. 2000. Multicultural minds: a dynamic constructivist approach to culture and cognition. *Am. Psychol.* 55(7):709–20

Honigman JJ. 1967. *Personality in Culture.* New York: Harper & Row

Horney K. 1939. *New Ways in Psychoanalysis.* New York: Norton

House JS. 1981. Social structure and personality. In *Social Psychology: Sociological Perspectives,* ed. M Rosenberg, RH Turner, pp. 525–61. New York: Basic Books

Howard J. 2000. Social psychology of identities. *Annu. Rev. Sociol.* 26:367–93

Hurtado A. 1996. *The Color of Privilege: Three Blasphemies on Race and Feminism.* Ann Arbor: Univ. Mich. Press

Hyde JS. 2002. Feminist identity development: the current state of theory, research, and practice. *Couns. Psychol.* 30(1):105–10

Inkeles A, Levinson DJ. 1954. National character: the study of modal personality and sociocultural systems. In *Handbook of Social Psychology,* ed. G Lindzey, 2:977–1020. Reading, MA: Addison-Wesley

Inkeles A, Levinson DJ. 1969. National character. In *Handbook of Social Psychology,* ed. G Lindzey, E Aronson, 4:418–506. Reading, MA: Addison-Wesley. Rev. ed.

Inkeles A, Smith DH. 1974. *Becoming Modern: Individual Change in Six Developing Countries.* Cambridge, MA: Harvard Univ. Press

Kanter RM. 1977. *Men and Women of the Corporation.* New York: Basic Books

King DK. 1988. Multiple jeopardy, multiple consciousness: the context of a black feminist ideology. *Signs* 14:42–72

Klein M. 1965. *Contributions to Psycho-Analysis, 1921–1945.* New York: McGraw-Hill

Kluckhohn C, Murray HA, Schneider DM. 1953. *Personality in Nature, Culture and Society.* New York: Knopf

Knox M, Funk J, Elliott R, Bush EG. 2000. Gender differences in adolescents' possible selves. *Youth Soc.* 31(3):287–309

LaFromboise T, Hardin LKC, Gerton J. 1993. Psychological impact of biculturalism: evidence and theory. *Psychol. Bull.* 114(3):395–412

Landrine H, Klonoff EA, Brown-Collins A. 1992. Cultural diversity and methodology in feminist psychology: critique, proposal, empirical example. *Psychol. Women Q.* 16:145–64

Levy J, Heller W. 1992. Gender differences in human neuropsychological function. In *Sex Differentiation: Handbook of Behavioral Neurobiology,* ed. A Gerall, H Moltz, IL Ward, pp. 245–74. New York: Plenum

Linville PW. 1985. Self-complexity and affective extremity: Don't put all your eggs in one cognitive basket. *Soc. Cogn.* 3:94–120

Linville PW. 1987. Self-complexity as a cognitive buffer against stress-related illness and depression. *J. Personal. Soc. Psychol.* 52:663–76

Maccoby E. 1998. *The Two Sexes: Growing Up Apart, Coming Together.* Cambridge, MA: Belknap

Maccoby E, Jacklin C. 1974. *The Psychology of Sex Differences.* Stanford, CA: Stanford Univ. Press

MacKinnon C. 1987. *Feminism Unmodified: Discourses on Life and Law.* Cambridge, MA: Harvard Univ. Press

Markus H, Nurius P. 1986. Possible selves. *Am. Psychol.* 41:954–69

Martin JR. 1994. Methodological essentialism, false difference, and other dangerous traps. *Signs* 19(3):630–57

McClelland DC. 1967. *The Achieving Society.* New York: Free Press

Moradi B, Mezydlo Subich L. 2002. Feminist identity development measures: comparing the psychometrics of three instruments. *Couns. Psychol.* 30(1):66–86

Nolen-Hoeksema S, Larson J, Grayson C. 1999. Explaining the gender difference in depressive symptoms. *J. Personal. Soc. Psychol.* 77:1061–72

Parsons T. 1955. *Family, Socialization and Interaction Process.* New York: Free Press

Parsons T. 1967. *Sociological Theory and Modern Society.* New York: Free Press

Phinney JS. 1989. Stages of ethnic identity in minority group adolescents. *J. Early Adolesc.* 9:34–49

Pimlott-Kubiak S, Cortina L. 2004. Gender, victimization and outcomes: reconceptualizing risk. *J. Clin. Consult. Psychol.* In press

Powlishta KK, Sen MG, Serbin LA, Poulin-Dubois D, Eichstedt JA. 2001. From infancy through middle childhood: the role of cognitive and social factors in becoming gendered. See Unger 2001, pp. 116–32

Press AL, Cole ER. 1999. *Speaking of Abortion: Television and Authority in the Lives of Women.* Chicago, IL: Univ. Chicago Press

Rabinowitz VC, Martin D. 2001. Choices and consequences: methodological issues in the study of gender. See Unger 2001, pp. 29–52

Riger S. 1991. Gender dilemmas in sexual harassment policies and procedures. *Am. Psychol.* 46:497–505

Riger S. 1992. Epistemological debates, feminist voices: science, social values, and the story of women. *Am. Psychol.* 47:730–40

Riger S. 2000. *Transforming Psychology: Gender in Theory and Practice.* New York: Oxford

Roccas S, Brewer M. 2002. Social identity complexity. *Personal. Soc. Psychol. Rev.* 6(2):88–106

Rosenberg S, Gara MA. 1985. The multiplicity of personal identity. In *Review of Personality and Social Psychology*, ed. P Shaver, 6:87–115. Beverly Hills, CA: Sage

Ryff C. 1987. The place of personality and social structure research in social psychology. *J. Personal. Soc. Psychol.* 53(6):1192–202

Sackett PR, DuBois CLZ, Noe AW. 1991. Tokenism in performance evaluation: the effects of work group representation on male-female and white-black differences in performance ratings. *J. Appl. Psychol.* 76:263–67

Scott J. 1988. *Gender and the Politics of History.* New York: Columbia Univ. Press

Sekaquaptewa D, Thompson M. 2002. The differential effects of solo status on members of high- and low-status groups. *Personal. Soc. Psychol. Bull.* 28(5):694–707

Sellers RM, Smith MM, Shelton JN, Rowley SAJ, Chavous TM. 1998. Multidimensional model of racial identity: a reconceptualization of African American racial identity. *Personal. Soc. Rev.* 2(1):18–39

Shih M, Pittinsky TL, Ambady N. 1999. Stereotype susceptibility: identity salience and shifts in quantitative performance. *Psychol. Sci.* 10:80–83

Shweder RA. 1991. *Thinking through Cultures: Expeditions in Cultural Psychology.* Cambridge, MA: Harvard Univ. Press

Smith AG, Stewart AJ, Winter DG. 2004. Close encounters with the Midwest: forming identity in a bicultural context. *Polit. Psychol.* In press

Spangler E, Gordon MA, Pipkin PM. 1978. Token women: an empirical test of Kanter's hypothesis. *Am. J. Sociol.* 84:160–70

Spelman EV. 1988. *Inessential Woman: Problems of Exclusion in Feminist Thought.* Boston, MA: Beacon

Spencer SJ, Steele CM, Quinn DM. 1999. Stereotype threat and women's math performance. *J. Exp. Soc. Psychol.* 35(1):4–28

Stewart AJ. 1998. Doing personality research: How can feminist theories help? In *The Gender and Psychology Reader*, ed. BM Clinchy, JK Norem, pp. 54–68. New York: NY Univ. Press

Stewart AJ. 2003. Gender, race, and generation in a Midwest high school: using ethnographically-informed methods in psychology. *Psychol. Women Q.* 27:1–11

Stewart AJ, Healy JM. 1989. Linking individual development and social change. *Am. Psychol.* 44:30–42

Strouse J, ed. 1974. *Women and Analysis: Dialogues on Psychoanalytic Views of Femininity.* New York: Dell

Sullivan HS. 1953. *The Interpersonal Theory of Psychiatry.* New York: Norton

Swim JK, Stangor C, eds. 1998. *Prejudice: The Target's Perspective.* San Diego, CA: Academic

Tajfel H. 1957. Value and the perceptual judgment of magnitude. *Psychol. Rev.* 64:192–204

Tajfel H. 1981. *Human Groups and Social Categories.* London: Cambridge Univ. Press

Taylor SE, Fiske ST, Etcoff NL, Ruderman AJ. 1978. Categorical and contextual bases of person memory and stereotyping. *J. Personal. Soc. Psychol.* 36:778–93

Twenge J. 1997. Changes in masculine and feminine traits over time: a meta-analysis. *Sex Roles* 36:305–25

Twenge J. 2001. Changes in women's assertiveness in response to status and roles: a cross-temporal meta-analysis, 1931–1993. *J. Personal. Soc. Psychol.* 81:133–45

Unger RK. 1989. Sex, gender and epistemology. In *Gender and Thought: Psychological Perspectives*, ed. M Crawford, M Gentry, pp. 17–35. New York: Springer-Verlag

Unger RK. 2001. *Handbook of the Psychology of Women and Gender.* New York: Wiley

Veroff J. 1983. Contextual determinants of personality. *Personal. Soc. Psychol. Bull.* 9:331–43

Waters MC. 1996. The intersection of gender, race and ethnicity in identity development of Caribbean American teens. In *Urban Girls: Resisting Stereotypes, Creating Identities*, ed. B Leadbeater, N Way, pp. 65–81. New York: New York Univ. Press

White JW, Donat PLN, Bondurant B. 2001. A developmental examination of violence against girls and women. See Unger 2001, pp. 343–57

Whiting B. 1963. *Six Cultures.* New York: Wiley

Wilson CM. 2001. The creation of motherhood: exploring the experiences of lesbian co-mothers. *J. Fem. Fam. Therapy* 12:21–44

Woolfolk RL, Novalany J, Gara MA, Allen LA, Polino M. 1995. Self-complexity, self-evaluation, and depression: an examination of form and content within the self-schema. *J. Personal. Soc. Psychol.* 68:1108–20

Yoder J, Sinnett J. 1985. Is it all in the numbers? A case study of tokenism. *Psychol. Women Q.* 9:413–18

Zahn-Waxler C. 2000. The development of empathy, guilt, and internalization of distress: implications for gender differences in internalizing and externalizing problems. In *Anxiety, Depression and Emotion*, ed. RJ Davidson, pp. 222–65. New York: Oxford Univ. Press

Annu. Rev. Psychol. 2004. 55:545–71
doi: 10.1146/annurev.psych.55.090902.141550
First published online as a Review in Advance on November 10, 2003

MEDIATED POLITICS AND CITIZENSHIP IN THE TWENTY-FIRST CENTURY

Doris Graber

*Department of Political Science, University of Illinois, Chicago,
Illinois, 60607-7137; email: dgraber@uic.edu*

Key Words media/democracy interface, citizenship models, information processing, learning from news, news media content

■ **Abstract** Since the birth of the nation, concepts about the political duties of citizens have changed drastically to keep pace with growth and development. The information needs have changed as well, as have the institutions that supply this information. In this essay I analyze the interrelation between citizenship in the twenty-first century and the information supply that nourishes it. I focus on studies that explore how political news is shaped to attract public attention and how citizens select it and make sense of it. Evidence from content analyses, focus group data, and intensive interviews supports the conclusion that the news supply is adequate for citizens' civic needs and that they use it judiciously. To accept that conclusion requires abandoning outdated paradigms of citizenship that ignore information-processing capabilities of human beings, the basic motivations that drive the search for political information, and the impact of the ever-increasing complexity of politics.

CONTENTS

0066-4308/04/0204-0545$14.00

INTRODUCTION

Democracy means government controlled by the people. Democracy can be direct, where people actually participate in town meetings or vote on referenda to make rules and laws and provide for their execution. Or democracy can be indirect, where people elect representatives who act as their agents in making and executing laws that govern society. In either case, it is assumed that participants in direct or indirect democracy know enough about the situations with which they are dealing to make intelligent, rational decisions.

How can people acquire such information? In simpler times, when political units were small, democracy could work through face-to-face contacts or written interpersonal communications. Most of the situations with which citizens were dealing involved matters with which they were personally acquainted. In modern democracies, involving millions of people living in widely dispersed locations, democracy via direct or even two-step contacts between citizens is impossible. Most people are no longer in personal contact with their fellow citizens and most of the matters with which governments deal are beyond their personal ken.

Modern journalism developed out of the necessity to professionalize news gathering, news interpretation, and news distribution tasks. When the job became too time consuming and difficult for average people, societies needed specialists who devoted their energies to collecting significant information deemed of interest to their communities and to distribute it cheaply and quickly to interested fellow citizens. The initial distribution venues were printed pages. As technology progressed, electronic transmissions in the form of radio came into vogue. Various forms of television followed.

NEWS MEDIA AND DEMOCRATIC GOVERNANCE

Alexis de Tocqueville was among the first thinkers to hail American news media as a powerful force for the promotion of democracy. In the 1830s, in a chapter on "Liberty of the Press in the United States," he wrote that the press "causes political life to circulate through all the parts" of the vast territory of the United States. Its function is "to detect the secret springs of political designs" and to rally "the interests of the community round certain principles." Besides providing "a means of intercourse between those who hear and address each other without ever coming into immediate contact," the press also serves to promote accountability of public officials by summoning "the leaders of all parties in turn to the bar of public opinion" (Heffner 1984, pp. 94–95).

Similarly, Thomas Jefferson argued in 1787 that liberty in America hinges on a free press. People need "full information of their affairs thro' the channel of the public papers. . . . [W]ere it left to me to decide whether we should have government without newspapers, or newspapers without a government, I should not hesitate a moment to prefer the latter" (Kurland & Lerner 1987). Such great faith in the importance of the press was expressed by a man who had previously complained about ". . .the putrid state into which our newspapers have passed and the malignity, the vulgarity, and mendacious spirit of those who write for them. . ." (Levy 1963, p. 67).

Put into modern language and current social science concepts, what are the functions that news media perform that de Tocqueville and Jefferson deemed so vital for democracies? The French scholar, famous for his keen observational skills, outlines them best (Heffner 1984, Chapter 11): (a) The press is a tool for shared political socialization through which people learn basic values and political orientations to which their society subscribes. Democratic governance requires populations that share a sense of national identity and a consensus about major public actions required to protect the collective welfare. (b) The press collects information about important political events and frames it into news stories that report the salient facts in a context that gives them meaning. (c) The press mobilizes citizens to take action when needed for the public good. (d) The press monitors what government officials are doing and alerts citizens to misbehaviors. Impressive! Modern scholars may disagree about the specifics of each of these functions, but they do not contest that the performance of the press is crucial in a democracy.

In the pages that follow I sample various aspects of recent research that bear on citizens' learning from news stories. I scrutinize the kind of political information that news media offer and note some of the obstacles that make it difficult for mass publics to benefit from news stories.

Important News Media Effects

De Tocqueville's account, of course, is a statement of the potential of the press, rather than an accurate description of the routine performance of the news media. It was based on a number of untested assumptions about what news media could and would cover and what citizens could and would learn from information presented by news media. Many of these assumptions have by now been tested and validated. Social scientists have convincingly demonstrated that people do, indeed, form their impressions about the political world from a succession of stories gleaned from news media (Graber 2001, Kahn & Kenney 2002, Patterson 2002, Zaller 2003). Scholars have also shown that learning is continuous and cumulative because people judge new information from the perspective of previously stored information and use new data to modify and refresh and, occasionally, alter their fund of stored information (Bartels 1993, 1996; Graber 1993; Neuman et al. 1992). These studies refute earlier research on media effects on voting that concluded, based on only a narrow realm of effects, that the media's impact was minimal (Graber 2002b).

News audiences are apt to adopt journalists' interpretations of the meanings and merits of the situations depicted in news stories whenever the information is unfamiliar to them. That makes the media a powerful influence on public opinion (Jeffres 1997, Jensen 1995, Jones 1994, Norris 2000a). However, research has refuted early hypodermic theories about media effects that postulated that news consumers would internalize all news exactly as presented to them (Dalton et al. 1998, Delli Carpini & Keeter 1996, Erbring et al. 1980, Wanta 1997).

The meanings conveyed by news media vary depending on the receivers' existing fund of political knowledge and the societal contexts in which they are situated. Recent research has probed how the various social influences that surround citizens impinge on their learning about politics. Robert Huckfeldt and John Sprague's (1995) detailed study of how people in one community formed their views about the 1984 presidential campaign provides excellent illustrations. Paul Beck and colleagues (2002) extended that work to a national sample. The researchers concluded that newspaper editorial pages are more influential than print news and television, but interpersonal discussions outweigh mass media influence.

The "priming" phenomenon is an especially interesting media effect because it confirms that people do, indeed, absorb information from news stories and use it to guide subsequent thinking. It also confirms the well-documented human preference for "satisficing" rather than "optimizing." To save time and effort, most people tend to make judgments based on limited subsets of the information available to them (Iyengar 1991, Krosnick & Brannon 1993). If schema that have been recently primed by news stories allow them to form opinions, they prefer to probe no further (Anderson 1983).

Iyengar & Kinder's (1987) priming experiments showed that subjects exposed to broadcasts about U.S. military deficiencies, rampant inflation, or pollution of the environment ranked these issues highly among political problems facing the nation. Control groups exposed to broadcasts lacking such stories named other priorities. Similarly, Tewksbury and colleagues (2000) framed a story about large-scale hog farms in five different ways, each representing a particular interest group's perspectives. Readers' evaluations reflected these differences immediately after exposure as well as three weeks later. When news emphasis shifted to different issues, subjects' rankings mirrored the shift (Iyengar 1991, Iyengar & Kinder 1987, Krosnick & McGraw 2002). Moreover, exposure to specific problems primed audiences to evaluate the president's or other politicians' performance in terms of these problems rather than less publicized issues. Evaluations of ordinary people are especially vulnerable to news story priming of stereotypes (Valentino et al. 2002). As one would expect from stimulus generalization theories, the valence assigned to prior problems or stereotypes is then reflected in the subsequent evaluations (Iyengar 1991, Iyengar & Kinder 1987, Krosnick & Brannon 1993).

Other studies show that priming effects differ depending on how well or how poorly informed news consumers are, how interested they are in the news and how amply exposed. Several studies indicate that knowledgeable audience members who have firm, well-grounded political opinions are less susceptible to priming than audience members who know little about issues that dominate the news (Fiske & Taylor 1991, Krosnick & Kinder 1990, Lodge & Stroh 1993, Price & Tewksbury

1997). Other contingencies may alter this. For example, normally prime-resistant news consumers may yield if they trust the media to provide accurate, unbiased information and infer from heavy coverage of an issue that it is, indeed, important and worthy of consideration in their political judgments (Eagly & Chaiken 1993, Miller & Krosnick 2000). Eveland & Shav (2003) investigated the antecedents of trust or distrust of media and identified individual political orientations and conversations within congenial interpersonal networks as important factors.

Many other cues besides priming are embedded in news stories (Barnhurst & Mutz 1997). For instance, the mere fact that a story has received prominent media attention signals that it is important and therefore potentially worthy of consideration when making political judgments. Similarly, audiences pay more heed to stories that appear on the front pages of newspapers, especially with large headlines, or in the opening portions of a newscast because they recognize story placement as a cue to significance.

The finding that many people equate news coverage with significance has led to the heavily researched "agenda-setting" hypothesis. In its starkest iteration, it says that the media rivet people's attention on particular situations although they may fail to influence how people appraise these situations. When interviewers ask people which issues are most important to them or their neighbors, responses tend to reflect the issues featured most amply and prominently in the media they use (Iyengar & Kinder 1987, McCombs & Shaw 1972, Page & Shapiro 1992, Page et al. 1987, Wanta 1997). Numerous studies have tested and confirmed agenda-setting effects through a combination of audience surveys and content analyses of the media these audiences used (Iyengar & Simon 1993, Kerr & Moy 2002, Kim et al. 2002). Some studies have tested agenda-setting for particular issues like the 1990/1991 Persian Gulf crisis, famine in Ethiopia, or equipment failures in nuclear facilities rather than testing the influence of news stories on audiences' overall perception of issue importance (Bosso 1989, Iyengar & Simon 1993, Rubin 1987).

Comparisons of media agendas with public opinion polls and reports about political and social conditions show that agenda setting is most potent for new issues that have not been widely discussed and for issues beyond the realm of personal experience (Weaver et al. 1981). Ader's longitudinal study of agenda setting from 1970 to 1990 for stories discussing environmental pollution provides examples of the opinion-shaping potency of news stories about unfamiliar topics. People's opinions reflected the world created by the news stories, rather than real-world conditions or politicians' pronouncements (Ader 1995, Behr & Iyengar 1985).

While agenda-setting effects are robust, they are subject to the typical context-dependent variations. Personal experiences, conversations with trusted others, and independent reasoning all provide individual consumers with alternatives to media guidance. When these personal factors come into play, they often overpower decision criteria provided by news stories about the rank order of importance of particular issues and, more strongly, the merits of issues. Even front-page news stories that conflict with firmly held audience beliefs lose their agenda-setting potency (Behr & Iyengar 1985, Erbring et al. 1980, Hill 1985). Diana Mutz further refined research on factors that impinge on agenda setting. She examined the "third-person effect" or "cognitive response model"—the impact of knowledge about the views of unknown others. She found that people without strong opinions on an issue do, indeed, find comfort in joining the opinion chorus of the majority (Mutz 1997, 1998). The reverse can happen as well. People who hold strong opinions may become alarmed when they discover that others are strongly opposed. That fear may strengthen their seemingly threatened beliefs (Boniger et al. 1995).

Turning briefly to the press as a tool for shared political socialization: It has indeed served that function in the past. But the process has become increasingly difficult because the U.S. population now represents a much broader array of ethnic and religious traditions and spans a much wider range of socioeconomic and educational experiences. The cultural melting pot has given way to multiculturalism. The many new media that have emerged in recent decades, thanks to advancing technologies, further jeopardize social cohesion. When the news is delivered by thousands of venues that focus on widely diverse issues, the bond of shared information that tied communities together in the past is weakened. Scholars have speculated about the consequences, but few have tested them (Gitlin 1998, Rahn & Rudolph 2001, Turow 1997). The fear is that people will find it increasingly difficult to agree on common political agendas and that norms of tolerance that are so crucial in democracies may weaken (Dahlgren 2001, Sunstein 2001). Rather than participating in nationwide dialog, people may abandon the previously shared public sphere and retreat into a multitude of communication ghettoes (Bennett 1998, Entman & Herbst 2001, Swanson 1997). Public opinion polls show some increases in fragmentation of views in recent decades, though many shared perceptions and values remain intact (Dahlgren 2001, Pew 2000b, Sparks 2001).

Mismatches Between Theorists' Expectations and Reality

There is a huge gap between democratic theorists' expectation and the reality of how much political knowledge the media will transmit and what citizens can and will learn (Bartels 1993, Iyengar & Simon 2000). Journalists have never been motivated or even able to gather all potentially newsworthy information. Neither do they see political education of the public as their primary role (Weaver & Wilhoit 1996). Even top-level political leaders do not receive all information that matters to them, despite their superior access to published and unpublished news accounts and a bevy of employees trained to select and condense information. If political leaders did receive all essential information, they could not absorb all of it because human capacity for processing information is bounded (Graber 2003, Lupia & McCubbins 1998, Simon 1985).

The vast majority of average citizens, contrary to theorists' hopes, survey political news haphazardly, spending less than an hour daily on it. Moreover, they practice "selective attention." They develop choice criteria for following some news stories and ignoring others (Atkin 1985; Chong 2000; Garramone 1985; McGuire 1984, 1999). Selectivity is often subconscious because subjects automatically process information that corresponds to their existing schemas (Bargh 1997, Potter et al. 2002). The results of a summer 2000 Pew poll show that respondents ignored 38% of the news stories about their local community because they seemed neither "important" nor "interesting"; respondents eliminated 46% of the national news stories for these reasons, along with 63% of the stories covering international news (Pew 2000c, Price & Zaller 1993). When one combines these figures with Pew survey data about highly selective attention to a broad array of major news stories, such as accounts about social security and health care reform proposals, the 1990 Bush/Gorbachev summit, or global warming reports—news stories that were ignored by 70% or more of the public—it is obvious that the appetite for important political information is hardly voracious (Pew 2000d).

The record on de Tocqueville's final two points—the role of the press as mobilizer for public action, and the role of the press as watchdog—is similar to what has just been discussed (Cook 1998, Mazzoleni & Schulz 1999). Expectations outrun capacities and motivations. The press does a sporadic job in fostering political action by citizens and in monitoring the behavior of politicians. Its effectiveness is sharply limited because of its eclectic coverage of events, its focus on pleasing rather than educating the public, and the public's frequent unwillingness to pay attention to the news, to take it seriously, and to follow through with active involvement in politics.

THE POLITICAL INFORMATION SUPPLY: QUANTITY, QUALITY, AND PERSUASIVENESS

How rich is the diet of political news that mass media offer to nourish citizenship? Answers to that question come from various disciplinary approaches, many of them in areas of political theory. These range from historical accounts about various features of democracy to empirical and normative studies and formal models. My review covers only studies that assess the media in terms of their usefulness for citizens. I will also assess the practical realities that limit what journalists can provide.

To put into an appropriate perspective the political information supply offered to Americans requires considering the nature of U.S. news media. The large army of vociferous critics of media performance views the media through the rose-colored glasses of an ideal but quite impossible world. These critics expect news media to cover the political issues that the critics deem important, providing a wealth of factual data and contextual information to a presumably news-hungry public. They ignore the fact that most U.S. media are commercial enterprises that must be concerned with attracting the kinds of clienteles and advertisers that allow them to make substantial profits. Considering that audience data consistently show that substantial portions of most audiences flock to entertainment and avoid overly complex news, it is reasonable to present much of the news as "infotainment" (Baum 2002). To mention just one sign of the public's disinterest in complex political accounts: Public television, which wins high praises from media critics, attracts only 2% of the nightly news audience.

The Quantity of News

Given sparse resources and manpower, U.S. media institutions regularly cover only a limited number of prominent institutions, or "beats." On the local level, that might be the mayor's office, the police department, and the schools. Beat coverage is supplemented haphazardly by covering a small number of events breaking elsewhere, and by occasional forays into major investigative reporting. Even if media wanted to cover "all the news that's fit to print," as the front page of the *New York Times* proclaims so deceptively, that is impossible because there simply is too much news to collect and report on a daily basis. In fact, there is not enough time now to report all the news that is currently collected. Audience members, however eager they may be for news and however much of their waking hours they devote to news consumption, cannot absorb most of the news that is readily available to them.

Content analyses show that, contrary to most critics' complaints, a substantial quantity of political news is available in an average week on television nightly newscasts. Viewers tuning in regularly to the half-hour early evening national newscasts on ABC, CBS, and NBC and to a 60-minute CNN newscast once a week can expect to find roughly 61% of the time devoted to news about politics and public policy issues. On average, 18% of that total will be news about foreign affairs, 13% will cover general domestic stories, and another 13% will deal with various social issues. News about the environment will account for approximately 10% of the coverage and 7% will be economic news (Graber 2001). A viewer who watches one half-hour network news broadcast six days a week and adds a CNN broadcast once a week will be exposed to serious political lessons averaging two hours and twenty-four minutes.

In fact, the supply of political information in the twenty-first century is more abundant than ever before when one considers the totality of all offerings available through new technologies, including the Internet. A comparison of news venue availability in 1960 and 2000, conducted by the Federal Communications Commission in ten geographic markets, showed that media outlets, including newspapers, broadcast and cable channels, and satellite television had tripled during that 40-year period (End the Ban on Cross-Ownership 2003, Federal Communications Commission 2002). While there is a great deal of overlap among all these news offerings, there is also a great deal of diversity.

Average citizens' opportunities to observe their government in action have mushroomed. C-SPAN, the Cable Satellite Public Affairs Network, for instance, offers live, gavel-to-gavel coverage of Congress and other public forums featuring public policy discussions. Ordinary Americans can use the Internet for quick and inexpensive exchanges of information with other citizens and with journalists and politicians. These new venues bring a much broader spectrum of political views to the fore and offer new opportunities for citizen participation in politics (Bucy & Gregson 2002, Dahlberg 2001).

As is typical for the dispersion of technical innovations, most people do not yet take full advantage of the rich feast (Bimber 2003). Although roughly two-thirds of all Americans now use the Internet, only one-third—primarily the well educated and economically secure—regularly use it to watch political news offerings (Bimber 2003, Margolis & Resnick 2000, Pew 2000a). This is why most analysts of the news supply discount this superb source of information, arguing that it is primarily a medium for elites. However, it is reasonable to expect demographic disparities to lessen, given the fact that this medium is readily available to average Americans and that by 2010 most Americans will have grown up with it and learned to use it in elementary school. Nonetheless, in line with historical patterns, elites can be expected to remain more interested in politics than mass publics.

The Quality of News

It is impossible to make summary judgments about the quality of the political information supply because there is no agreement among media scholars and no empirical evidence about what constitutes the best mixture of news topics and the degree of attention that should be given to particular topics at various times in the news cycle (Bennett 2002, Patterson 1993, Shoemaker & Reese 1996). The fact that news venues vary greatly in the breadth and depth of news coverage depending on their formats and audiences further mitigates against developing uniform standards. Should quality be judged by the appeal of the news for various demographic groups or should it be judged by standards developed by academics or practitioners? What would be the basis for standards when there is disagreement about what knowledge is essential for effective citizenship? Should economic and technological constraints be factored into evaluations? For example, time and space constraints often force journalists to skimp on useful contextual information for news stories. Such constraints are especially severe for television news that operates on the assumption that mass audiences' attention span to nightly news cannot be stretched beyond 30 minutes. News directors at large media organizations believe, albeit without systematic evidence, that their publics prefer multiple capsule news stories to fewer but lengthier and richer stories. Capsule news stories, which rarely exceed three minutes in length, are often bereft of background information. Journalists hope that key words used in the story will prime audiences to recall relevant information from memory. Although this happens regularly because people supplement news story information with information drawn from memory, should the story nonetheless be faulted for omitting the information (Graber 1993)?

Regardless of which criteria are used, content analyses show that news story quality varies widely among news venues, at different periods in history, and for different topics. Whether judgments about quality are positive or negative depends on the critics' appraisal criteria. For instance, the Project for Excellence in Journalism, a group of experts on television news affiliated with the Columbia University Graduate School of Journalism, uses seven areas of performance to judge the quality of television news (Project for Excellence in Journalism 1997, 1999). The story's focus, range of topics, and local relevance are deemed most crucial. Stories receive excellent ratings if they focus on significant, interesting situations that deal with issues affecting many people in major ways. The range of story topics has to be broad and diverse and salient for various segments of the local community. Other elements that contribute to excellent ratings relate to the authenticity of the story. Top-rated stories are originated by the station and cite many fair, impartial, and knowledgeable sources that represent diverse views. Based on these somewhat elastic criteria, news coverage by 34% of the television stations judged by the Project in 1999 were rated as poor, 34% were rated as fair, and 31% were deemed good or excellent. This shows that even by stringent professional standards, there is a lot of excellent television journalism along with a lot of mediocrity and a more-than-ample supply of horrors.

Besides dealing with the substance of information and the adequacy of documentation, many critics are also concerned with the breadth of orientation on a left-right political spectrum (Alger 1998, McChesney 2000, Schiller 1992). On the whole, the mainstream news media, which rely heavily on mainstream elites as news sources, present a limited centrist political spectrum. This deprives the audience of the opportunity to consider an array of political options that includes the extreme ends of the political spectrum. Whether or not these omissions account for the slim support that perspectives at the extreme ends of the political spectrum receive from the American public remains moot. Americans generally resist radical changes and instead cling to values learned in childhood and thereafter reinforced by their environment (Bartels 1993, Page & Shapiro 1992, Shanahan & Morgan 1999).

The Power to Persuade

Given people's inherent resistance to change and the many personal and societal factors that hamper media agenda setting, it is clear that the news media's power to persuade the public to follow the orientations reflected in news stories is limited (Bartels 1993, Page & Shapiro 1992, Schudson 1995). The quadrennial review of foreign policy opinions gathered by the Chicago Council on Foreign Relations provides numerous illustrations of wide gaps between political elites' well-publicized opinions and the mass public's views (Rielly 1999).

Most news people favor more liberal social policies than favored by much of their audience. The reverse is true for economic policies (Weaver & Wilhoit 1996). News stories tend to reflect journalists' orientation to varying degrees. Discrepancies in political orientations between journalists and mass publics may explain why almost half of the public expresses only limited confidence in the accuracy of the media and why 53% completely or mostly agree that "People who decide what to put on TV news or in the newspapers are out of touch with people like me" (Pew 1998a, 2000c).

Under what circumstances are news stories persuasive? To find answers, John Zaller (2001) developed and tested a model of political persuasion known as *RAS* (receive, accept, sample information). He found that people do, indeed, resist arguments that clash with their political predispositions but only if they recognize the discrepancy. If they do, they rely on their own prior beliefs stored in memory or on other sources that are more believable than news media. Arthur Lupia and Mathew McCubbins studied the conditions under which people are likely to be receptive to political persuasion. They identified trust as crucial. "Without trust there is no persuasion; without persuasion, people cannot learn from others; and without learning from others, it is very difficult for citizens to learn what they need to know" (Lupia 2000; Lupia & McCubbins 2000, p. 48; Popkin & Dimock 2000).

Credibility problems notwithstanding, most citizens think that news media serve their civic needs adequately. They routinely tell pollsters that television news—which is the most widely used medium—provides them with sufficient information to carry out their civic functions. In 2000, 80% of viewers said that they were very or fairly satisfied with television news programs (Pew 2000a). When viewers were asked in 1998, "How good of a job does the evening news do in summing up the events of the day?" 18% gave it an "Excellent" rating and 50% called it "Good," while 21% said it was "Only Fair" and 4% labeled it "Poor." Seven percent gave no ratings (Pew 1998a). The overall impression one receives from tracking the public's appraisals of various aspects of media coverage over the last decade is that the modal response is "Good." It remains an open question how one should merge these positive judgments into a single calculus that combines expressions of mistrust with mixtures of positive and negative appraisals of various media features.

THE USER-FRIENDLINESS OF POLITICAL NEWS

The mere fact that a story appears in a news venue does not assure that it will be noted. In fact, except for prominently displayed news, most stories are ignored. Researchers have discovered that story framing—the perspectives from which a story is told—must be user-friendly to attract audiences. Studies of patterns of attention and inattention show that elements embedded in headlines, initial sentences, and opening broadcast must resonate with people's existing cognitions or emotions (Graber 1993, 2001; McGuire 1984, 1999).

Framing Problems

Frequently, after media significance cues have aroused attention, it flags quickly when audience members discover that their frames for processing this type of subject do not match the frames into which journalists have cast the story. Neuman et al. (1992) compared the frames used by journalists for five news topics with the frames used by audiences and found major disparities. The stories dealt with

South Africa's apartheid problems, defense policy, the 1987 stock market crash, drug abuse, and the AIDS crisis. Journalists preferred conflict-related frames by far for these stories while audiences dwelled on human-interest frames.

Disjunctions between audience frames and news story frames are widespread despite journalists' efforts to stay in tune with their audiences. Such disparities complicate people's efforts to comprehend such stories by matching the information to past learning stored in memory (Graber 1993; Iyengar & Simon 2000; Lupia & McCubbins 1998, 2000). Even when audiences pay attention to stories framed in uncongenial ways, they are likely to forget them quickly because they find it too hard to reinterpret them to match their own mental schema (McGraw et al. 1991, Ottati & Wyer 1990). Mismatches in frames may also prevent people from developing sufficient interest in the story to pay close attention to it.

To be user-friendly, story frames must suggest a link between the thrust of the story and citizens' welfare (Valkenburg et al. 1999). Boniger and colleagues (1995) and Modigliani & Gamson (1979) tried to ascertain which story frames make different types of stories most attractive. Boniger and colleagues tested frames appealing to self-interest, social identification with reference groups, or cherished values in various situations. Modigliani & Gamson tested similar types of frames in situations involving Vietnam, busing, and attitude toward presidential candidates. Nelson et al. (1997) tested how various news frames about a Ku Klux Klan rally affected the audience's level of tolerance for the group. Audiences were more tolerant when the story was framed as a free speech issue than when it was framed as a potential disruption of public order. Such tests indicate that reactions to frames vary depending on the situation. The tests also show that it can be extraordinarily difficult to relate national political debates to the lives of average citizens.

Different frames, if accepted by audiences, lead them to internalize different impressions of the facts and meaning of stories (Brewer 2001). Studies of differential framing therefore support researchers' contentions that news is a constructed product (Altheide 2002, Edelman 1988, Neuman et al. 1992, Wu 2000). Sociologist Philo Wasburn (2002) compared framing when reporters in different countries cover identical events. He noted substantial differences in the presentation of events like the 1982 Falkland war between Great Britain and Argentina, the 1990–1991 Persian Gulf crisis and the 1996 U.S. presidential nomination conventions. Apparently, there are characteristic, culturally linked patterns of news framing—evidence that the pictures of political events presented to audiences hinge very much on the cultural orientation of the story's narrator. Similarly, de Vreese (2002) compared how television newscasts in Britain, Denmark, and the Netherlands framed issues concerning European integration and then assessed the impact of these frames on public opinions in these countries, which varied widely.

Uses and Abuses of Emotional Appeals

Emotional appeals are another important factor in user-friendliness. As great storytellers throughout history have known, stories with which people can identify on a human basis—about emotion-laden issues such as love and hate, greed and generosity, crime and punishment—are exceptionally appealing to audiences. Neuroscience studies show that it is easier to store and retain such stories in memory because emotional arousal releases stimulants into the bloodstream that sensitize perceptions and increases their impact (Damasio 1994, 1999; Gazzaniga 1992, 1998; Goleman 1995).

Nonetheless, many scholars condemn that approach, claiming that emotionally stirred people cannot weigh issues rationally. They point to numerous bad decisions and blame emotional arousal (Petty & Cacioppo 1986a,b). Recent research proves otherwise (Dolan & Holbrook 2001, MacKuen et al. 2001, Marcus & MacKuen 1993, Marcus et al. 2000, Rahn 2000). It shows that emotional arousal, coupled with cognitive resources, is an essential element in many well-reasoned decisions. One example is the likeability heuristic—so named because people are often able to appraise policies and individuals accurately by linking them to previously formed likes and dislikes. For instance, people who like consumer advocate Ralph Nader may carry that liking over to reforms he suggests (Damasio 1999, Johnston 2000, Lodge & Taber 2000, Planalp 1999, Sniderman 2000, Sniderman et al. 1991). Rational analysis would probably have led to the same conclusion.

Audience research indicates that stories with emotional angles capture larger audiences than stories that are bland irrespective of their intrinsic importance (Biocca 1991, Jamieson & Waldman 2003, McQuail 1997). For example, a look at the roster of news stories that captured the most public attention between 1986 and 2002 shows that half of them involved natural or manmade disasters, military events that endangered the lives of Americans, and important pocketbook issues like the price of gasoline. Average citizens can readily identify with these types of issues (Graber 2001, Pew 2003).

While emotion-arousing content can be a welcome incentive to pay attention to news, it can also have adverse consequences. Some audience members may consider it sensationalism and tabloidization, and may become alienated from the media and politics. Failure to vote in elections has been blamed on the negative emotions aroused by cynical news stories because trust in government dips when the public is plied with seemingly credible sensational negative news (Cappella & Jamieson 1997, Rahn & Rudolph 2001). When negative news pervades both print and broadcast media, alienating effects appear to be additive (Cappella & Jamieson 1997).

As is true for other media effects, multiple causes are usually at play. The public's feelings of trust may be driven primarily by political events and politicians' performance, as some scholars contend, rather than by an excessively hostile tone of media coverage of these events. The messenger should not be blamed for the impact of a message covering events beyond the messenger's control (Bishop 2002, Miller & Listhaug 1999, Nye et al. 1997, Pew 1998b). Such reasoning raises the question of whether the nature of events or the stories about them generate public attitudes. Of course, reactions to media stories inevitably reflect reactions to the facts reported in the story intertwined with reactions to the way reporters have framed the story. When one adds reactions stored in a news consumer's memory to the mix, assigning precise weights to each of these factors becomes well nigh impossible.

Research on the effects of cynical news stories illustrates several other typical complications that plague efforts to establish causality (Finkel & Geer 1998). Several studies indicate that the segments of the public who pay most attention to news stories and are most receptive to new information display the highest sense of political efficacy and trust in government (Bennett et al. 1999; Chanley 2002; Norris 2000a,b). That fact casts further doubts about the media's contribution to political alienation. It could exonerate the media or it could indicate that elites are less persuadable than mass publics (McGuire 1999, Zaller 1992). Further doubts spring from evidence that the public continues to consume large amounts of national and international news regularly, despite expressing frustration with run-of-the-mill politics and political news (Key 1965, Kuklinski 2001, Kuklinski et al. 2001, Page & Shapiro 1992, Popkin 1994). Should one then take public expressions of cynicism at face value? They could be artifacts of questions about trust, rather than evidence of deep-seated political malaise. The framing of survey questions, or the mere fact of asking them, may suggest answers (Tourangeau & Smith 1996, Wanke et al. 1995, Zaller & Feldman 1992).

Matching News Presentations to Processing Skills

Many other factors that bear on user-friendliness of news in terms of human information-processing capabilities have received minimal attention from social scientists. The role played by visuals in attracting attention, conveying information, and making it more memorable is a glaring example (Berry & Brosius 1991, Graber 2001, Gregory 1997, Lyn et al. 1985, Messaris 1994). Disincentives for learning from news have attracted minimal research attention, despite their prevalence and profound consequences. For instance, news stories often overwhelm people with more facts and figures and even pictures than they can readily absorb. When journalists present alternative policies, like various health care plans or options for protecting the environment, they provide insufficient guidelines for evaluating these alternatives. Cappella & Jamieson (1997), who studied media coverage of the 1993–1994 healthcare reform debate, report that news stories never classified the 27 different reform proposals introduced in Congress into easily comprehensible categories. To compound the confusion, they labeled the proposals with more than 100 different names.

Complexity levels of print and broadcast statements are often beyond the capacity of audiences with limited education or language skills in the language used by the medium. Stories are routinely written or narrated at an eighth-grade, or even twelfth-grade, comprehension level that ignores the fact that most American adults do not function comfortably above a sixth-grade level. Many stories lack sufficient contextual information to allow average persons to assess their meaning within the larger context of happenings in the political world.

Even more troubling, too many stories are terribly boring, devoid of any dramatic unexpected events that motivate people to pursue the story (Baum 2002, 2003; Brants 1998). As Patterson (2002, p. 164) acknowledges, it is pointless to "increase the supply of useful information without increasing the demand for it. Citizens do not have a fixed amount of attention to give. The more engaging these moments are, the more attention they will pay." Polling data show that pleasurable feelings associated with following the news have declined steadily. In 1995, 54% of respondents in a nationwide polls said that they enjoyed keeping up with the news a lot. By 2000, that had dropped at a steady pace to 45%. Moreover, while younger age groups are pleased by the expansion of news sources, close to half (41%) of senior citizens and citizens with limited education feel overwhelmed by the multitude of choices (Pew 2000a). Often, stories are repetitive because journalists rehash them to cue in readers or viewers who have not yet heard the story. Attentive audiences dislike the repetition. Many stories fail to tell audiences what interests them most—the reasons for particular situations and the likely consequences. They slight the "why's" and "wherefore's" in favor of "who," "what," "where," and "when" questions (Baum 2002, 2003; Graber 1994).

From a neurophysiological perspective, the presentation of many news stories, especially audiovisual ones, suffers because elementary facts of information transmission are ignored. Words and pictures tumble out at a pace that is much too fast for human comprehension (Barry 1997, Gazzaniga 1992). Three-quarters of the television news pictures are on the screen for less than 20 seconds and often shift focus even within that brief time span. Picture and word messages are frequently uncoordinated and even contradictory, forcing audience members to wrestle with the often-impossible task of bringing them into alignment. Stopping points—the miniscule breaks of silence people need to absorb information to which they have just been exposed—are too brief or absent or, worst of all, filled with distracting advertising information. The sequencing of story elements and the jump cuts when the camera switches abruptly from one scene to another are frequently out of sync with human capacities to link disparate story elements together. To put them in sync requires knowing people's expectations about event sequences and telling stories accordingly (Barry 1997, Griffin 1992).

These and many other media shortcomings that have been mentioned here are linked to people's innate information-processing capacities. The human brain is a fantastic instrument for learning, appraising, and judging extraordinarily complex information, but it does have physiologically determined limitations. To make stories about complex political issues comprehensible, these must be respected. Moreover, people have to be motivated to engage in activities that are not inherently pleasurable for most of them—like politics or reading about politics. Social scientists and political practitioners who have routinely ignored these conditions in the past have therefore been unduly surprised by serious failures in political information transmission and political comprehension.

THE DEMAND-SUPPLY EQUATION: ARE CIVIC NEEDS MET?

To what extent does the current supply of political news satisfy the civic needs of average Americans? What and how much do they need to know to be good citizens in a modern democratic society? Answering such questions requires treading on treacherous, minimally researched intellectual terrain—determining the standards by which knowledge requirements for citizenship should be judged (Delli Carpini & Keeter 1996; Graber 2001; Norris 2000a,b; Popkin 1994; Rahn et al. 1994). There is neither a uniform, widely accepted answer nor agreement about who ought to set the ground rules. In fact, there is no agreement about the scope of citizens' roles or about the subject matter and breadth and depth of information that citizens need to master in order to perform citizenship tasks adequately.

The Controversy over Appraisal Criteria

Many theorists and pundits allege that the fully informed, participatory citizen is the ideal model and that the adequacy of media coverage and citizens' knowledge should be assessed from that perspective. Using these standards, and framing survey questions accordingly, they have concluded that most citizens are woefully ignorant and poorly qualified for citizenship duties (Delli Carpini & Keeter 1996, Kuklinski et al. 2000, McGraw & Pinney 1990). They often blame the news media for this state of affairs (Bennett 2003; Delli Carpini & Keeter 1996; Kalb 2001; Kuklinski et al. 2000; Patterson 1993, 2000, 2002). As Thomas Patterson (2000, p. 2) puts it: "[S]oft news and critical journalism are weakening the foundations of democracy by diminishing the public's information about public affairs and its interest in politics." Critics also complain that media fail to discuss long-range political patterns and their likely consequences and that they feature and perpetuate overly dramatized stereotypes rather than offering nuanced comments (Patterson 1993). Postman (1985, p. 141) condemns television news for being "simplistic, nonsubstantive, nonhistorical and noncontextual; that is to say information packaged as entertainment."

More qualitative research tools like focus groups, depth interviews, and experiments yield contrary conclusions, casting doubts on the appropriateness of survey measures to gauge what people actually know and how well they can cope with civic obligations (Iyengar & Simon 2000). Why do these different methodologies yield such disparate results? The answer is that qualitative research probes what people know and allows respondents to discuss the areas of political knowledge with which they are familiar and to frame information in their own way. By contrast, surveys ask for knowledge about topics chosen and framed by researchers, often covering areas of little interest to respondents. Questions usually focus on knowledge of readily measurable details, such as the names and offices of political leaders, the ups and downs of current unemployment or violent crime rates, or procedural facts like the percentage of votes needed to overturn a presidential veto or end a filibuster (Delli Carpini & Keeter 1996). Obviously, answering such questions requires a command of long-forgotten schoolbook knowledge that may have eluded people entirely. The scores provide insights about political sophistication but fail to reveal how well average citizens are equipped to judge the political scene and deal with civic issues.

There are other serious methodological problems with using closed-ended survey questions to assess people's learning from the news. Most researchers fail to ascertain, let alone content-analyze, the media information that, they assume, their subjects encountered. Graber's (2002a) study of news coverage of environmental policies, unemployment rates, and changes in the nation's deficit found that information that interviewers requested in national surveys was largely absent from television newscasts and only sparsely covered by most newspapers. When the information was covered, the framing usually differed substantially from the framing used in interviewers' questions, making it tough for people to answer the questions as posed. Contextually appropriate questions could have yielded far better results.

A major assumption behind survey research—that people retain all information on which their opinions are based—ignores the "on-line processing" phenomenon. As various experimental and observational studies have demonstrated, people process news story information while encountering it but, for the most part, store only the results of the processing, rather than the underlying data (Graber 1993, Lodge et al. 1995). That explains why they often cannot cite the data that underlie their opinions (Graber 1993, Lodge & Stroh 1993). From a research perspective, this means that failure to remember content cannot be equated with snap judgments devoid of an information basis. It also means that the contents of information consumed by subjects must be retrieved from the stimulus messages, rather than the audience's recall. Finally, it means that the key question for democratic citizenship is whether the media offer sufficient attractively packaged information about political issues so that news-hungry citizens can readily acquire a solid basis for their on-line evaluations of the political scene.

The Demands of Modern Citizenship

The crux of the counterargument to the claims of deficient media and ill-informed citizens is that the ideal informed citizen type that is at the center of this debate about media and citizen performance simply does not exist and cannot exist in most advanced industrialized societies, especially in large countries (Graber 2001, Lupia & McCubbins 1998, Neuman et al. 1992, Popkin & Dimock 1999). Sociologist Michael Schudson (1998) has pointed that out in his studies of the changing nature of citizenship. Schudson traced successive stages of citizenship moving from the ideal of the "deferential citizen" in the eighteenth century to the model of the "partisan citizen" prior to World War I and the ideal of the "informed citizen," highly knowledgeable about the intricacies of politics, thereafter. That model held sway until the 1960s when it became increasingly difficult, even for the well educated, to keep abreast of public affairs. According to Schudson's analysis, the informed citizen model now has given way to the more realistic "monitorial citizen" model.

Unlike the fully informed citizens of the prior period, monitorial citizens need not stay fully informed about political developments at all times. They only need to survey the political scene carefully enough to detect major political threats to themselves or their communities. When threats appear, monitorial citizens should consult news stories, party and interest group pronouncements, and the views of trusted individuals (Page & Shapiro 1992, Schudson 1998). Reliance on information shortcuts yields acceptable results (Elkin & Soltan 1999; Mondak 1994; Norris 2000a,b; Popkin & Dimock 1999). For example, when California voters were faced in 1987 with five complex ballot initiatives, some wrestled with the details as required by the informed citizen model to determine which ballot initiative matched their interests best. Others simply ascertained who favored and who opposed each initiative and then sided with their presumed friends. Both sets of voters managed to match their vote to their own welfare with only a slight disadvantage for the group using heuristics (Lupia 1994).

Studies by Ottati & Wyer (1990), Bartels (1996), and Kuklinski & Hurley (1994), among others, also show that monitorial citizens can make sound decisions, although they are somewhat less likely to protect their self-interests. In a Chicago survey, Kuklinski & Hurley found that black citizens who used the race of the message source as a cue for supporting messages were more prone to make choices that conflicted with their stand on the thrust of the message than citizens who studied the actual positions of these sources. The study demonstrates, as do others, that heuristics can mislead—but so can other decision criteria. Precise error rates for various decision approaches do not yet exist, but the evidence suggests that errors made in heuristically guided decisions are random, rather than systematic (Mondak 1993, 1994). Some researchers have tried to estimate to what extent political outcomes might be different if all citizens were well informed. Bartels (1996), for example, argues that there would be fewer Democratic votes and fewer reelections of incumbents during national elections if all voters were well informed. Partisans are apt to disagree about whether that would be good or bad.

Can average Americans who use the readily available news media more or less regularly learn enough to fulfill the duties of monitorial citizens? The research-based answer is yes (Delli Carpini 2000, Lupia 2000, Page 1996, Zaller 2003). Focus group evidence shows that people from all walks of life are far more sophisticated about the political issues that seem important to them than survey-based civics tests indicate (Gamson 2001, Graber 2001). When ordinary people discuss major political issues using their own words and perspectives, even groups that generally score poorly on typical tests—African-Americans, Latinos, and poor people—display political insight and cognitive complexity in addressing major political issues that they regard as matters of concern (Gamson 1992, Tetlock 1993). While their performance is far from the ideal models of the past, it is reasonably adequate for fulfilling major citizen responsibilities such as discussing politics intelligently and voting for candidates and ballot propositions.

The monitorial citizen model stresses that the need for citizen alertness is cyclical—greater in times of crisis and less at other times. Citizen behavior conforms to such cycles. People who normally ignore much of the political news flock to the media in times of crisis. For example, during the six-week period following the 2000 Presidential election, when control of that vital office was at stake, public attention to news skyrocketed. Public opinion poll responses recorded that the public grasped the complex aspects of that situation and judged it intelligently. Similar trends were recorded in the months that followed the terrorist strikes on New York and Washington in 1991 and the events of the war against Iraq in 1993 (Graber 2003).

WHERE DO WE GO FROM HERE?

The record thus far shows that news media are, indeed, important for supplying essential information that enables citizens to perform their civic duties. I have also argued that the quantity and quality of news that various media venues supply collectively is adequate for citizenship needs, especially since it is clear that citizens can perform their political obligations effectively on a low-information diet, supported by an array of well-developed decision shortcuts.

Following in Schudson's (1998) footsteps, I have pleaded that monitorial citizenship is a realistic, politically sound concept. Most scholars in the decision sciences, psychology, economics, and even political science accept the idea that the human capacity for absorbing information is limited (Simon 1995). Many scholars also agree that it is not economically rational for ordinary citizens to invest much effort in collecting political information when expert views from trusted sources are readily available for consideration and adoption (Downs 1957). Consequently, most people are expected to conserve their mental energies most of the time, leaving it to experts to formulate policy options that average people can accept or reject, using simple decision rules.

I have pointed out that many complaints about media and citizen performance are based on assumptions that disregard the characteristics of commercial media systems, fail to acknowledge the transformation of the age of news scarcity into the age of news abundance, ignore the motivations and preferences of most citizens, and pay insufficient heed to the neurophysiological limitations of the human species. Although there is ample research support for all of these findings, they continue to be contested by pundits and scholars clinging to hallowed but outdated paradigms.

While average citizens play important political roles in democracies, the bulk of the burden for political action has always been born by elected and appointed public officials and by citizens with above-average interest in politics whom scholars call "the attentive public." At best, that category comprises no more than 10% of the citizenry (Bennett 1995, Bimber 2001, Devine 1970). Media may play their most important role in supplying the news to the attentive segment of the public that, in turn, routinely relays political information to less-interested fellow citizens. The media's role in informing monitorial citizens may thus be a two-step process. Attentive publics are aroused first by news stories that provide adequate data. Their concerns and recommendations are then transmitted through print and broadcast news stories to less attentive citizens, making it easy for these citizens to form and express sound opinions.

Complex modern societies require intermediaries between citizens and elected and appointed public officials. Relatively small groups of attentive citizens have always served that role along with political parties and interest groups. These proxies relieve the majority of citizens of the burden of continuously monitoring public problems and pondering solutions. Political elites benefit immensely from the new information resources provided by modern technologies, especially the Internet. To the extent that they use this information to formulate better policy choices, and disseminate their views via mass media, the mass public benefits from this information treasure trove, albeit via a two-step transmission process (Bimber 2003). For aficionados of the informed citizen model it may seem heresy to argue that democracy is well served even when most citizens leave most civic tasks, including information collection and policy appraisal, to elites. They should be reminded that direct democracy has never been a constitutional pattern in the United States. Policies and laws have always been made and executed by elites, with most citizens limiting themselves to serving as periodic monitors through electoral mechanisms. The end has been a serviceable, if not ideal, democracy (Dahl 1989).

The *Annual Review of Psychology* is online at http://psych.annualreviews.org

LITERATURE CITED

Ader CR. 1995. A longitudinal study of agenda setting for the issue of environmental pollution. *J. Mass Commun. Q.* 72:300–11

Alger D. 1998. *Megamedia: How Giant Corporations Dominate Mass Media, Distort Competition, and Endanger Democracy.* Lanham, MD: Rowman Littlefield

Altheide DL. 2002. *Creating Fear: News and the Construction of Crisis.* New York: Aldine de Gruyter

Anderson J. 1983. *The Architecture of Cognition.* Cambridge, MA: Harvard Univ. Press

Atkin C. 1985. Information utility and selective exposure to entertainment media. In *Selective Exposure to Communication*, ed. D Zillman, J Bryant, pp. 63–92. Hillsdale, NJ: Erlbaum

Bargh J. 1997. The automaticity of everyday life. In *Advances in Social Cognition*, ed. R Wyer, 10:169–83. Hillsdale, NJ: Erlbaum

Barnhurst KG, Mutz D. 1997. American journalism and the decline of event-centered news. *J. Commun.* 47:27–53

Barry AMS. 1997. *Visual Intelligence: Perception, Image, and Manipulation in Visual Communication.* Albany: State Univ. NY Press

Bartels LM. 1993. Messages received: the political impact of media exposure. *Am. Polit. Sci. Rev.* 87:267–85

Bartels LM. 1996. Uninformed votes: information effects in presidential elections. *Am. J. Polit. Sci.* 40:194–230

Baum MA. 2002. Sex, lies and war: how soft news brings foreign policy to the inattentive public. *Am. Polit. Sci. Rev.* 96:91–109

Baum MA. 2003. *Soft News Goes to War: Public Opinion and American Foreign Policy in the New Media Age.* Princeton, NJ: Princeton Univ. Press

Beck PA, Dalton RJ, Greene S, Huckfeldt R. 2002. The social calculus of voting: interpersonal, media, and organizational influences on presidential choices. *Am. Polit. Sci. Rev.* 96:57–73

Behr RL, Iyengar S. 1985. Television news, real-world cues, and changes in the public agenda. *Public Opin. Q.* 49:38–57

Bennett SE. 1995. Comparing Americans' political information in 1988 and 1992. *J. Polit.* 57:521–32

Bennett SE, Rhine SL, Flickinger RS, Bennett LM. 1999. Videomalaise revisited: reconsidering the relation between the public's view of the media and trust in government. *Harv. Int. J. Press Polit.* 4:8–23

Bennett WL. 1998. The uncivic culture: communication, identity, and the rise of lifestyle politics. *PS: Polit. Sci. Polit.* 31:741–62

Bennett WL. 2002. *News: The Politics of Illusion.* New York: Longman. 5th ed.

Bennett WL, Entman RM, eds. 2001. *Mediated Politics: Communication in the Future of Democracy.* Cambridge, UK: Cambridge Univ. Press

Berry C, Brosius HB. 1991. On the multiple effects of visual format on TV news learning. *Appl. Cogn. Psychol.* 5:519–28

Bimber B. 2001. Information and political engagement in America: the search for effects of information technology at the individual level. *Polit. Res. Q.* 54:53–67

Bimber B. 2003. *Information and American Democracy: Technology in the Evolution of Political Power.* Cambridge, UK: Cambridge Univ. Press

Biocca F, ed. 1991. *Television and Political Advertising: Signs, Codes, and Images.* Hillsdale, NJ: Erlbaum

Bishop G. 2002. Illusion of change. *Public Perspect.* 13:38–41

Boniger DS, Krosnick JA, Berent MK. 1995.

Origins of attitude importance: self-interest, social identification, and value relevance. *J. Personal. Soc. Psychol.* 68:61–80

Bosso CJ. 1989. Setting the agenda: mass media and the discovery of famine in Ethiopia. In *Manipulating Public Opinion*, ed. M Margolis, G Mauser, pp. 153–74. Monterey, CA: Brooks-Cole

Brants K. 1998. Who's afraid of infotainment? *Eur. J. Commun.* 13:315–35

Brewer PR. 2001. Value words and lizard brains: Do citizens deliberate about appeals to their core values? *Polit. Psychol.* 22:45–64

Bucy EP, Gregson KS. 2002. Media participation: a legitimizing mechanism of mass democracy. *New Media Soc.* 3:357–80

Cappella JN, Jamieson KH. 1997. *Spiral of Cynicism: The Press and the Public Good.* New York: Oxford Univ. Press

Chanley VA. 2002. Trust in government in the aftermath of 9/11: determinants and consequences. *Polit. Psychol.* 23:469–83

Chong D. 2000. *Rational Lives: Norms and Values in Politics and Society.* Chicago: Univ. Chicago Press

Cook TE. 1998. *Governing with the News: The News Media as Political Institutions.* Chicago: Univ. Chicago Press

Dahl RA. 1989. *Democracy and Its Critics.* New Haven, CT: Yale Univ. Press

Dahlberg L. 2001. Democracy via cyberspace: mapping the rhetorics and practices of three prominent camps. *New Media Soc.* 2:157–77

Dahlgren P. 2001. The public sphere and the net: structure, space and communication. See Bennett & Entman 2001, pp. 33–55

Dalton RJ, Beck PA, Huckfeldt R, Koetzle W. 1998. A test of media-centered agenda-setting: newspaper content and public interests in a presidential election. *Polit. Commun.* 15:463–81

Damasio AR. 1994. *Descartes' Error: Emotion, Reason, and the Human Brain.* New York: Grosset/Putnam

Damasio AR. 1999. *The Feeling of What Happens: Body Emotion in the Making of Consciousness.* New York: Harcourt

Delli Carpini MX. 2000. In search of the informed citizen. What Americans know about politics and why it matters. *Commun. Rev.* 4:129–64

Delli Carpini MX, Keeter S. 1996. *What Americans Know About Politics and Why it Matters.* New Haven, CT: Yale Univ. Press

Devine DJ. 1970. *The Attentive Public: Polyarchical Democracy.* Chicago: Rand McNally

de Vreese CH. 2002. *Framing Europe: Television News and European Integration.* Amsterdam: Aksant Acad.

Dolan KA, Holbrook TM. 2001. Knowing versus caring: the role of affect and cognition in political perceptions. *Polit. Psychol.* 22:27–44

Downs A. 1957. *An Economic Theory of Democracy.* New York: Harper Row

Eagly AH, Chaiken S. 1993. *The Psychology of Attitudes.* Fort Worth, TX: Harcourt Brace Jovanovich

Edelman M. 1988. *Constructing the Political Spectacle.* Chicago: Univ. Chicago Press

Elkin SL, Soltan KE, eds. 1999. *Citizen Competence and Democratic Institutions.* University Park: Penn. State Univ. Press

End the Ban on Cross-Ownership. 2003. Editorial. *Chicago Tribune,* Mar. 9

Entman RM, Herbst S. 2001. Reframing public opinion as we have known it. See Bennett & Entman 2001, pp. 203–25

Erbring L, Goldenberg E, Miller A. 1980. Front page news and real world cues: a new look at agenda-setting by the media. *Am. J. Polit. Sci.* 24:16–49

Eveland WP, Shah DV. 2003. The impact of individual interpersonal factors on perceived news media bias. *Polit. Psychol.* 24:101–17

Fed. Commun. Comm. 2002. *9th Annu. Rep.* http://www.fcc.gov/mb/csrptpg.html

Finkel SE, Geer J. 1998. A spot check: casting doubt on the demobilizing effect of attack advertising. *Am. J. Polit. Sci.* 42:573–95

Fiske ST, Taylor SE. 1991. *Social Cognition.* New York: McGraw-Hill

Gamson WA. 1992. *Talking Politics.* Cambridge, MA: Cambridge Univ. Press

Gamson WA. 2001. Promoting political engagement. See Bennett & Entman 2001, pp. 56–74

Garramone GM. 1985. Motivation and political information-processing: Extending the gratification approach. In *Mass Media and Political Thought,* ed. S Kraus, R Perloff, pp. 201–22. Beverly Hills, CA: Sage

Gazzaniga MS. 1992. *Nature's Mind: The Biological Roots of Thinking, Emotions, Sexuality, Language and Intelligence.* Harmondsworth: Penguin

Gazzaniga MS. 1998. *The Mind's Past.* Berkeley: Univ. Calif. Press

Gitlin T. 1998. Public spheres or public sphericules? In *Media, Ritual and Identity,* ed. J Curran, T Liebes, pp. 168–74. London: Routledge

Goleman D. 1995. *Emotional Intelligence.* New York: Bantam Books

Graber DA. 1993. *Processing the News: How People Tame the Information Tide.* Lanham, MD: Univ. Press Am.

Graber DA. 1994. Why voters fail information tests: Can the hurdles be overcome? *Polit. Commun.* 11:331–46

Graber DA. 2001. *Processing Politics: Learning from Television in the Internet Age.* Chicago: Univ. Chicago Press

Graber DA. 2002a. *Is democracy doomed if citizens are misinformed and ignorant? A practical politics perspective.* Presented at Annu. Meet. Midwest Polit. Sci. Assoc., 60th, Chicago

Graber DA. 2002b. *Mass Media and American Politics.* Washington, DC: CQ Press. 6th ed.

Graber DA. 2003. Framing politics for mass consumption. In *Political Psychology as a Perspective on Politics. Advances in Political Psychology,* Vol. 1, ed. M Hermann pp. 31–58. London: Elsevier

Gregory RL. 1997. *Eye Brain: The Psychology of Seeing.* Princeton, NJ: Princeton Univ. Press. 5th ed.

Griffin M. 1992. Looking at TV news: strategies for research. *Communication* 13:121–41

Heffner RD, ed. 1984. *Alexis de Tocqueville,*

Democracy in America, Vol. 1. New York: Penguin

Hill DB. 1985. Viewer characteristics and agenda setting by television news. *Public Opin. Q.* 49:340–50

Huckfeldt R, Sprague J. 1995. *Citizens, Politics, and Social Communication.* New York: Cambridge Univ. Press

Iyengar S. 1991. *Is Anyone Responsible? How Television Frames Political Issues.* Chicago: Univ. Chicago Press

Iyengar S, Kinder DR. 1987. *News that Matters: Television and American Opinion.* Chicago: Univ. Chicago Press

Iyengar S, McGuire WJ, eds. 1993. *Explorations in Political Psychology.* Durham, NC: Duke Univ. Press

Iyengar S, Simon AF. 1993. News coverage of the Gulf Crisis and public opinion: a study of agenda-setting, priming and framing. *Commun. Res.* 20:365–83

Iyengar S, Simon AF. 2000. New perspectives and evidence on political communication campaign effects. *Annu. Rev. Psychol.* 51:149–69

Jamieson KH, Waldman P. 2003. *The Press Effect: Politicians, Journalists, and the Stories that Shape the Political World.* New York: Oxford Univ. Press

Jeffres LW. 1997. *Mass Media Effects.* Prospect Heights, IL: Waveland. 2nd ed.

Jensen KB. 1995. *The Social Semiotics of Mass Communication.* Thousand Oaks, CA: Sage

Johnston VS. 2000. *Why We Feel: The Science of Human Emotions.* Cambridge, MA: Perseus Books

Jones BD. 1994. *Reconceiving Decision-Making in Democratic Politics.* Chicago: Univ. Chicago Press

Kahn KF, Kenney PJ. 2002. The slant of the news: how editorial endorsements influence campaign coverage and citizens' views of candidates. *Am. Polit. Sci. Rev.* 96:381–94

Kalb M. 2001. *One Scandalous Story: Clinton, Lewinski, and Thirteen Days that Tarnished American Journalism.* New York: Free Press

Kerr PA, Moy P. 2002. Newspaper coverage of fundamentalist Christians, 1980–2000. *Journalism Mass Commun. Q.* 79:7–25

Key VO Jr., with the assistance of Cummings MC Jr. 1965. *The Responsible Electorate.* Cambridge, MA: Harvard Univ. Press

Kim SH, Scheufele DA, Shanahan J. 2002. Think about it this way: attribute agenda-setting function of the press and the public's evaluation of a local issue. *Journalism Mass Commun. Q.* 79:54–72

Krosnick JA, Brannon LA. 1993. The impact of the Gulf War on the ingredients of presidential evaluations: multidimensional effects of political involvement. *Am. Polit. Sci. Rev.* 87:963–75

Krosnick JA, Kinder DR. 1990. Altering the foundations of support for the president through priming. *Am. Polit. Sci. Rev.* 84:497–512

Krosnick JA, McGraw KM. 2002. Psychological political science versus political psychology true to its name: a plea for balance. In *Political Psychology*, ed. KR Monroe, pp. 79–94. Mahwah, NJ: Erlbaum

Kuklinski JH, ed. 2001. *Citizens and Politics: Perspectives from Political Psychology.* Cambridge, UK: Cambridge Univ. Press

Kuklinski JH, Hurley NL. 1994. On hearing and interpreting political messages: a cautionary tale of citizen cue-taking. *J. Polit.* 56:729–51

Kuklinski JH, Quirk PJ, Jerit J, Rich RF. 2001. The political environment and citizen decision making: information, motivation, and policy tradeoffs. *Am. J. Polit. Sci.* 45:410–24

Kuklinski JH, Quirk PJ, Jerit J, Schwieder D, Rich RF. 2000. Misinformation and the currency of democratic citizenship. *J. Polit.* 62:790–815

Kurland PB, Lerner R, eds. 1987. *The Founders' Constitution*, Vol. 5, Amend. I, Doc. 8. http://press-pubs.uchicago.edu/founders/documents/amendI_speechs8.html

Levy LW. 1963. *Jefferson and Civil Liberties: The Darker Side.* Cambridge, MA: Harvard Univ. Press

Lodge M, Steenbergen MR, Brau S. 1995. The responsive voter: campaign information and the dynamics of candidate evaluation. *Am. Polit. Sci. Rev.* 89:309–26

Lodge M, Stroh P. 1993. Inside the mental voting booth: an impression-driven process model of candidate evaluation. See Iyengar & McGuire 1993, pp. 225–63

Lodge M, Taber C. 2000. Three steps toward a theory of motivated political reasoning. See Lupia et al. 2000, pp. 183–213

Lupia A. 1994. Shortcuts versus encyclopedias: information and voting behavior in California insurance reform elections. *Am. Polit. Sci. Rev.* 88:63–78

Lupia A. 2000. Who can persuade whom? How simple cues affect political attitudes. In *Thinking About Political Psychology*, ed. JH Kuklinski, Part II. New York: Cambridge Univ. Press

Lupia A, McCubbins MD. 1998. *The Democratic Dilemma: Can Citizens Learn What They Need to Know?* New York: Cambridge Univ. Press

Lupia A, McCubbins MD. 2000. The institutional foundations of political competence: how citizens learn what they need to know. See Lupia et al. 2000, pp. 47–66

Lupia A, McCubbins MD, Popkin SL, eds. 2000. *Elements of Reason: Cognition, Choice, and the Bounds of Rationality.* Cambridge, UK: Cambridge Univ. Press

Lyn M, Shavitt S, Ostrom T. 1985. Effects of pictures on the organization and recall of social information. *J. Personal. Soc. Psychol.* 49:1160–68

MacKuen M, Marcus GE, Neuman WR, Keele L, Wolak J. 2001. *Emotional framing, information search, and the operation of affective intelligence in matters of public policy.* Presented at Annu. Meet. Midwest Polit. Sci. Assoc., 59th, Chicago

Marcus GE, MacKuen M. 1993. Anxiety, enthusiasm, and the vote: the emotional underpinnings of learning and involvement during presidential campaigns. *Am. Polit. Sci. Rev.* 87:672–85

Marcus GE, Neuman WR, MacKuen M. 2000. *Affective Intelligence and Political Judgment.* Chicago: Univ. Chicago Press

Margolis M, Resnick D. 2000. *Politics as Usual: The Cyberspace Revolution.* Thousand Oaks, CA: Sage

Mazzoleni G, Schulz W. 1999. 'Mediatization' of politics: a challenge for democracy? *Polit. Commun.* 16:247–61

McChesney RW. 2000. *Rich Media, Poor Democracy: Communication Politics in Dubious Times.* New York: The New Press

McCombs ME, Shaw DR. 1972. The agenda-setting function of the mass media. *Public Opin. Q.* 36:176–87

McGraw KM, Pinney N. 1990. The effects of general domain specific expertise on memory and judgment. *Soc. Cogn.* 8:9–30

McGraw KM, Pinney N, Newmann DS. 1991. Memory for political actors: contrasting the use of semantic and evaluative organizational strategies. *Polit. Behav.* 12:41–58

McGuire WJ. 1984. Search for the self: going beyond self-esteem and the reactive self. In *Personality and the Prediction of Behavior*, ed. RA Zucker, J Aronoff, AI Rabin, pp. 73–120. New York: Academic

McGuire WJ. 1999. *Constructing Social Psychology: Creative and Critical Processes.* Cambridge, UK: Cambridge Univ. Press

McQuail D. 1997. *Audience Analysis.* Thousand Oaks, CA: Sage

Messaris P. 1994. *Visual Literacy: Image, Mind, and Reality.* Boulder, CO: Westview

Miller A, Listhaug O. 1999. Political performance and institutional trust. In *Critical Citizens: Global Support for Democratic Government*, ed. P Norris, pp. 204–16. New York: Oxford Univ. Press

Miller JM, Krosnick JA. 2000. News media impact on the ingredients of Presidential evaluations: Politically knowledgeable citizens are guided by a trusted source. *Am. J. Polit. Sci.* 44:301–15

Modigliani A, Gamson WA. 1979. Thinking about politics. *Polit. Behav.* 1:5–30

Mondak JJ. 1993. Public opinion and heuristic processing of source cues. *Polit. Behav.* 15:167–92

Mondak JJ. 1994. Cognitive heuristics, heuristic processing, and efficiency in political decision-making. In *Research in Micropolitics: New Directions in Political Psychology*, ed. MX Delli Carpini, L Huddy, RY Shapiro, 4:117–42. Greenwich CT: JAI

Mutz DC. 1997. Mechanism of momentum: Does thinking it make it so? *J. Polit.* 59:104–25

Mutz DC. 1998. *Impersonal Influence: How Perceptions of Mass Collectives Affect Political Attitudes*. New York: Cambridge Univ. Press

Nelson T, Clawson RA, Oxley ZM. 1997. Media framing of a civil liberties conflict and its effect on tolerance. *Am. Polit. Sci. Rev.* 91:567–83

Neuman WR, Just MP, Crigler AN. 1992. *Common Knowledge: News and the Construction of Political Meaning*. Chicago: Univ. Chicago Press

Norris P. 2000a. *A Virtuous Circle: Political Communications in Postindustrial Societies*. Cambridge, UK: Cambridge Univ. Press

Norris P. 2000b. The impact of television on civic malaise. In *Disaffected Democracies: What's Troubling the Trilateral Countries?* ed. SJ Pharr, RD Putnam, pp. 231–51. Princeton, NJ: Princeton Univ. Press

Nye JS Jr, Zelikow PD, King PD. 1997. *Why People Don't Trust Government*. Cambridge, MA: Harvard Univ. Press

Ottati VC, Wyer RS. 1990. The cognitive mediators of political choice: toward a comprehensive model of political information processing. In *Information and Democratic Processes*, ed. JA Ferejohn, JH Kuklinski, pp. 186–216. Urbana: Univ. Ill. Press

Page BI. 1996. *Who Deliberates: Mass Media in Modern Democracy*. Chicago: Univ. Chicago Press

Page BI, Shapiro RY. 1992. *The Rational Public: Fifty Years of Trends in American Policy Preferences*. Chicago: Univ. Chicago Press

Page BI, Shapiro RY, Dempsey GR. 1987. What moves public opinion? *Am. Polit. Sci. Rev.* 81:22–43

Patterson TE. 1993. *Out of Order*. New York: Knopf

Patterson TE. 2000. *Doing Well and Doing Good: How Soft News and Critical Journalism Are Shrinking the News Audience and Weakening Democracy—and What News Outlets Can Do About It*. Cambridge, MA: Joan Shorenstein Cent. Press, Polit. Public Policy

Patterson TE. 2002. *The Vanishing Voter: Public Involvement in an Age of Uncertainty*. New York: Knopf

Petty RE, Cacioppo JT. 1986a. The elaboration likelihood model of persuasion. In *Advances in Experimental and Social Psychology*, ed. L Berkowitz, 19:123–205. Orlando, FL: Academic

Petty RE, Cacioppo JT. 1986b. *Communication and Persuasion: Central and Peripheral Routes to Attitude Change*. New York: Springer

Pew Res. Cent. People Press. 1998a. *Media Consumption Questionnaire*. http://www.people-press.org/med98que.htm

Pew Res. Cent. People Press. 1998b. *American News Habits*. http://www.people-press.org/med98rpt.htm

Pew Res. Cent. People Press. 2000a. *Attitudes Toward the News: Internet Sapping Broadcast News Audience*. http://people-press.org/reports/print.php3?PageID=206

Pew Res. Cent. People Press. 2000b. *Media Report*. http://www.people-press.org/med00rpt.htm

Pew Res. Cent. People Press. 2000c. *Questionnaire: Internet Sapping Broadcast News Audience*. http://people-press.org/reports/print.php3?PageID=210

Pew Res. Cent. People Press. 2000d. *Data Archive*. http://www.people-press.org/database00.htm

Pew Res. Cent. People Press. 2000e. *Media Credibility: Internet Sapping Broadcast News Audience*. http://people-press.org/reports/print.php3?PageID=207

Pew Res. Cent. People Press. 2003. *Public Attentiveness to News Stories: 1986–2002*. http://people-press.org/nii/

Planalp S. 1999. *Communicating Emotion: Social, Moral and Cultural Processes*. New York: Cambridge Univ. Press

Popkin SL. 1994. *The Reasoning Voter: Communication and Persuasion in Presidential Campaigns.* Chicago: Univ. Chicago Press. 2nd ed.

Popkin SL, Dimock MA. 1999. Political knowledge and citizen competence. In *Citizen Competence and Democratic Institutions*, ed. SL Elkin, KE Soltan, pp. 117–46. University Park: Penn. State Univ. Press

Popkin SL, Dimock MA. 2000. Knowledge, trust, and international reasoning. See Lupia et al. 2000, pp. 214–38

Postman N. 1985. *Amusing Ourselves to Death: Public Discourse in the Age of Show Business.* New York: Penguin

Potter WK, Pashupati K, Pekurny RG, Hoffman E, Davis K. 2002. Perceptions of television: a schema explanation. *Media Psychol.* 4:27–50

Price V, Tewksbury D. 1997. News values and public opinion: a theoretical account of media priming and framing. In *Progress in the Communication Sciences*, ed. GA Barnett, FJ Boster, pp. 173–212. Greenwich, CT: Ablex

Price V, Zaller J. 1993. Who gets the news? Alternative measures of news reception and their implications for research. *Public Opin. Q.* 57:133–64

Proj. Excell. Journal. 1997, 1999. *Projects-1997/1999.* http://www.journalism.org

Rahn WM. 2000. Affect as reason: the role of public mood in political reasoning. See Lupia et al. 2000, pp. 130–50

Rahn WM, Krosnick JA, Breuning M. 1994. Rationalization and derivation processes in survey studies of political candidate evaluation. *Am. J. Polit. Sci.* 38:582–600

Rahn WM, Rudolph TJ. 2001. National identities and the future of democracy. See Bennett & Entman 2001, pp. 453–67

Rielly JE. 1999. *American Public Opinion and U.S. Foreign Policy, 1999.* http://www.ccfr.org/publications/opinion/opinion.html

Rubin DM. 1987. How the news media reported on Three Mile Island and Chernobyl. *J. Commun.* 37:42–57

Schiller HI. 1992. *Mass Communication and American Empire.* Boulder, CO: Westview

Schudson M. 1995. *The Power of News.* Cambridge, MA: Harvard Univ. Press

Schudson M. 1998. *The Good Citizen: A History of American Public Life.* New York: Free Press

Shanahan J, Morgan M. 1999. *Television and its Viewers: Cultivation Theory and Research.* Cambridge, MA: Cambridge Univ. Press

Shoemaker PJ, Reese SD. 1996. *Mediating the Message: Theories of Influences on Mass Media Content.* White Plains, NY: Longman

Simon HA. 1985. Human nature in politics: the dialogue of psychology with political science. *Am. Polit. Sci. Rev.* 79:203–304

Simon HA. 1995. Rationality in political behavior. *Polit. Psychol.* 16:45–61

Sniderman PM. 2000. Taking sides: a fixed choice theory of political reasoning. See Lupia et al. 2000, pp. 67–84

Sniderman PM, Brody RA, Tetlock PE. 1991. *Reasoning Choice: Explorations in Political Psychology.* Cambridge, UK: Cambridge Univ. Press

Sparks C. 2001. The Internet and the global sphere. See Bennett & Entman 2001, pp. 75–95

Sunstein C. 2001. *Republic.com.* Princeton, NJ: Princeton Univ. Press

Swanson DL. 1997. The political-media complex at 50: putting the 1996 presidential election in context. *Am. Behav. Sci.* 40:1264–82

Tetlock PE. 1993. Cognitive structural analysis of political rhetoric: methodological and theoretical issues. See Iyengar & McGuire 1993, pp. 380–405

Tewksbury D, Jones J, Peske MW, Raymond A, Vig W. 2000. The interaction of news advocate frames: manipulating audience perceptions on a local public policy issue. *Journalism Mass Commun. Q.* 77:804–29

Tourangeau R, Smith TW. 1996. Asking sensitive questions: the impact of data collection mode, question format, and question context. *Public Opin. Q.* 60:181–227

Turow J. 1997. *Breaking up America:*

Advertising and the New Media World. Chicago: Univ. Chicago Press

Valentino NA, Hutchings VL, White IK. 2002. Cues that matter: how political ads prime racial attitudes. *Am. J. Polit. Sci.* 96:75–90

Valkenburg PM, Semetko H, de Vreese CH. 1999. The effect of news frames on readers' thoughts and recall. *Commun. Res.* 26:550–69

Wanke M, Schwarz N, Noelle-Neumann E. 1995. Asking comparative questions: the impact of the direction of the comparison. *Public Opin. Q.* 59:347–52

Wanta W. 1997. *The Public and the National Agenda.* Mahwah, NJ: Erlbaum

Wasburn PC. 2002. *The Social Construction of International News: We're talking About Them, They're Talking About Us.* Westport, CT: Praeger

Weaver DH, Graber DA, McCombs ME, Eyal CH. 1981. *Media Agenda-Setting in a Pres-idential Election: Issues, Images, and Interest.* New York: Praeger

Weaver DH, Wilhoit GC. 1996. *The American Journalist in the 1990's: U.S. News People at the End of an Era.* Mahwah, NJ: Erlbaum

Wu HD. 2000. Systemic determinants of international news coverage: a comparison of 38 countries. *J. Commun.* 50:110–30

Zaller J. 1992. *The Nature and Origins of Mass Opinions.* Cambridge, UK: Cambridge Univ. Press

Zaller J. 2001. Monica Lewinsky and the mainsprings of American politics. See Bennett & Entman 2001, pp. 252–78

Zaller J. 2003. A new standard of news quality: burglar alarms for the monitorial citizen. *Polit. Commun.* 20:109–30

Zaller J, Feldman S. 1992. A simple theory of the survey response: answering questions v. revealing preferences. *Am. J. Polit. Sci.* 36:579–616

Annu. Rev. Psychol. 2004. 55:573–90
doi: 10.1146/annurev.psych.55.090902.141922
First published online as a Review in Advance on July 11, 2003

THE INTERNET AND SOCIAL LIFE

John A. Bargh and Katelyn Y. A. McKenna

*New York University, New York, New York 10003; email: john.bargh@nyu.edu,
kym1@nyu.edu*

Key Words   communication, groups, relationships, depression, loneliness

■ **Abstract**   The Internet is the latest in a series of technological breakthroughs in
interpersonal communication, following the telegraph, telephone, radio, and television.
It combines innovative features of its predecessors, such as bridging great distances
and reaching a mass audience. However, the Internet has novel features as well, most
critically the relative anonymity afforded to users and the provision of group venues in
which to meet others with similar interests and values. We place the Internet in its historical context, and then examine the effects of Internet use on the user's psychological
well-being, the formation and maintenance of personal relationships, group memberships and social identity, the workplace, and community involvement. The evidence
suggests that while these effects are largely dependent on the particular goals that users
bring to the interaction—such as self-expression, affiliation, or competition—they also
interact in important ways with the unique qualities of the Internet communication
situation.

CONTENTS

INTRODUCTION

It is interactive: Like the telephone and the telegraph (and unlike radio or television), people can overcome great distances to communicate with others almost
instantaneously. It is a mass medium: Like radio and television (and unlike the
telephone or telegraph), content and advertising can reach millions of people at
the same time. It has been vilified as a powerful new tool for the devil, awash in

pornography, causing users to be addicted to hours each day of "surfing"—hours during which they are away from their family and friends, resulting in depression and loneliness for the individual user, and further weakening neighborhood and community ties. It has been hailed by two U.S. presidents as the ultimate weapon in the battle against totalitarianism and tyranny, and credited by Federal Reserve Board Chairman Alan Greenspan with creating a "new economy." It was denounced by the head of the Miss France committee as "an uncontrolled medium where rumormongers, pedophiles, prostitutes, and criminals could go about their business with impunity" after it facilitated the worldwide spread of rumors that the reigning Miss France was, in fact, a man (Reuters 2001). "I'm terrified by this type of media," she said.

"It," of course, is the Internet. Although some welcome it as a panacea while others fear it as a curse, all would agree that it is quite capable of transforming society. Hard-nosed and dispassionate observers have recently concluded that the Internet and its related technologies

> "...will change almost every aspect of our lives—private, social, cultural, economic and political ... because [they] deal with the very essence of human society: communication between people. Earlier technologies, from printing to the telegraph ... have wrought big changes over time. But the social changes over the coming decades are likely to be much more extensive, and to happen much faster, than any in the past, because the technologies driving them are continuing to develop at a breakneck pace. More importantly, they look as if together they will be as pervasive and ubiquitous as electricity." (Manasian 2003, p. 4)

The Internet is fast becoming a natural, background part of everyday life. In 2002, more than 600 million people worldwide had access to it (Manasian 2003). Children now grow up with the Internet; they and future generations will take it for granted just as they now do television and the telephone (Turow & Kavanaugh 2003). In California, 13-year-olds use their home computer as essentially another telephone to chat and exchange "instant messages" with their school friends (Gross et al. 2002). Toronto suburbanites use it as another means of contacting friends and family, especially when distance makes in-person and telephone communication difficult (Hampton & Wellman 2001). And people routinely turn to the Internet to quickly find needed information, such as about health conditions and remedies, as well as weather forecasts, sports scores, and stock prices.

This is not to say that Internet technology has now penetrated the entire planet to a similar extent. For example, in 2001 only 1 in 250 people in Africa was an Internet user, compared with a world average of 1 in 35, and 1 in 3 for North America and Europe. But the trend is clearly for ever-greater availability: The coming wireless technology (see Geer 2000, p. 11) will enable people in developing countries, who lag behind the rest of the world in hardwired infrastructure, to leapfrog technological stages and so come on-line much sooner than they would otherwise have been able to—much as eastern Europe in the 1990s, lacking extensive hardwire telephone infrastructure, leapfrogged directly to cell phones (Markoff 2002, *Economist* 2003a).

The main reason people use the Internet is to communicate with other people over e-mail—and the principal reason why people send e-mail messages to others is to maintain interpersonal relationships (Hampton & Wellman 2001, Howard et al. 2001, McKenna & Bargh 2000, Stafford et al. 1999). As Kang (2000, p. 1150) put it, "the 'killer application' of the internet turns out to be other human beings." But this was not so obvious to the early investors in the Internet—in the 1990s telecom companies invested (and lost) billions of dollars in interactive television and in delivering movies and video over the Internet. (Interestingly, the original supposed "killer app" of the telephone also was to broadcast content such as music, news, and stock prices—and its use in this manner persisted in Europe up to World War II.)

No one today disputes that the Internet is likely to have a significant impact on social life; but there remains substantial disagreement as to the nature and value of this impact. Several scholars have contended that Internet communication is an impoverished and sterile form of social exchange compared to traditional face-to-face interactions, and will therefore produce negative outcomes (loneliness and depression) for its users as well as weaken neighborhood and community ties. Media reporting of the effects of Internet use over the years has consistently emphasized this negative view (see McKenna & Bargh 2000) to the point that, as a result, a substantial minority of (mainly older) adults refuses to use the Internet at all (Hafner 2003). Others believe that the Internet affords a new and different avenue of social interaction that enables groups and relationships to form that otherwise would not be able to, thereby increasing and enhancing social connectivity. In this review, we examine the evidence bearing on these questions, both from contemporary research as well as the historical record.

THE INTERNET IN HISTORICAL CONTEXT

The Internet is but the latest in a series of technological advances that have changed the world in fundamental ways. In order to gauge the coming impact of the Internet on everyday life, and to help separate reality from hyperbole in that regard, it is instructive to review how people initially reacted to and then made use of those earlier technological breakthroughs.

First, each new technological advance in communications of the past 200 years—the telegraph, telephone, radio, motion pictures, television, and most recently the Internet—was met with concerns about its potential to weaken community ties (Katz et al. 2001, p. 406). The *telegraph*, by eliminating physical distance as an obstacle to communication between individuals, had a profound effect on life in the nineteenth century (Standage 1998). The world of 1830 was still very much the local one it had always been: No message could travel faster than a human being could travel (that is, by hand, horse, or ship). All this changed in two decades because of Samuel Morse's telegraph. Suddenly, a message from

London to New York could be sent and received in just minutes (Spar 2001, p. 60), and people could learn of events in distant parts of the world within hours or days instead of weeks or months. There was great enthusiasm: The connection of Europe and America in 1858 through the transatlantic cable was hailed as "the event of the century" and was met with incredible fanfare. Books proclaimed that soon the entire globe would be wired together and that this would create world peace. According to one newspaper editorial, "it is impossible that old prejudices and hostilities should longer exist, while such an instrument has been created for the exchange of thought between all the nations of the earth" (Standage 1998, pp. 82–83). At the same time, however, governments feared the potential of such immediate communication between individual citizens. Tsar Nicholas I of Russia, for example, banned the telegraph as an "instrument of subversion" (Spar 2001, p. 31). Similar raptures and fears have often been expressed, in our time, about the Internet as well.

The closest parallel to today's Internet users were the telegraph operators, an "on-line" community numbering in the thousands who spent their working lives communicating with each other over the wires but who rarely met face to face. They tended to use low-traffic periods to communicate with each other, sharing stories, news, and gossip. Many of these working relationships blossomed into romances and even marriages. For example, Thomas Edison, who began his career as a telegraph operator, proposed to his wife Mina over the telegraph (Standage 1998, pp. 129–142). And today, worldwide, people send each other more than a billion text messages each day from their mobile phones (*Economist* 2003b), in a form of communication conceptually indistinguishable from the old telegraph.

The telephone—invented accidentally by Alexander Graham Bell in the 1880s while he was working on a multichannel telegraph—transformed the telegraph into a point-to-point communication device anyone could use, not only a handful of trained operators working in code. The effect was to increase regular contact between family, friends, and business associates, especially those who lived too far away to be visited easily in person, and this had the overall effect of strengthening local ties (Matei & Ball-Rokeach 2001). Nevertheless, concerns continued to be raised that the telephone would harm the family, hurt relationships, and isolate people—magazines of the time featured articles such as "Does the telephone break up home life and the old practice of visiting friends?" (Fischer 1992).

The next breakthrough, radio, fared no differently. Like the wireless Internet emerging today, radio freed communication from the restriction of hard-wired connections, and was especially valuable where wires could not go, such as for ship-to-shore and ship-to-ship communication. However, its broadcast capability of reaching many people at once—thousands, even millions—was a frightening prospect for governments of the time. When Marconi got off the ship in England to demonstrate his new invention to the British, customs officials smashed his prototype radio as soon as he crossed the border, "fearing that it would inspire violence and revolution" (Spar 2001, p. 7). Eventually, however, radio brought the world into everyone's living room and so eliminated distance as a factor in news dissemination like never before. And indeed, it did soon prove to be a powerful propaganda tool for dictators and democratically elected leaders alike.

But television had the greatest actual (as opposed to feared) impact on community life, because individuals and families could stay at home for their evening entertainment instead of going to the theater or to the local pub or social club. Sociologist Robert Putnam (2000) has documented the dramatic decrease in community involvement (such as memberships in fraternal organizations and bowling leagues) since the introduction of television in the 1950s (see also DiMaggio et al. 2001). This negative effect of television viewing on the individual's degree of involvement in other, especially community, activities has been the basis for contemporary worries that Internet use might displace time formerly spent with family and friends (e.g., Nie & Erbring 2000).

The Internet combines, for the first time in history, many of these breakthrough features in a single communication medium. Like the telegraph and telephone, it can be used for person-to-person communication (e.g., e-mail, text messages); like radio and television, it can operate as a mass medium. And it can serve as a fabulous global library as well—fully 73% of American college students now use the Internet more than their university library for researching term papers (Jones 2002). As DiMaggio et al. (2001, p. 327) note, the variety of functions that the Internet can serve for the individual user makes it "unprecedentedly malleable" to the user's current needs and purposes.

However, the Internet is not merely the Swiss army knife of communications media. It has other critical differences from previously available communication media and settings (see, e.g., McKenna & Bargh 2000), and two of these differences especially have been the focus of most psychological and human-computer interaction research on the Internet. First, it is possible to be relatively anonymous on the Internet, especially when participating in electronic group venues such as chat rooms or newsgroups. This turns out to have important consequences for relationship development and group participation. Second, computer-mediated communication (CMC) is not conducted face-to-face but in the absence of non-verbal features of communication such as tone of voice, facial expressions, and potentially influential interpersonal features such as physical attractiveness, skin color, gender, and so on. Much of the extant computer science and communications research has explored how the absence of these features affects the process and outcome of social interactions.

EFFECTS ON INTERPERSONAL INTERACTION

A good example of that approach is Sproull & Kiesler's (1985) "filter model" of CMC, which focuses on the technological or engineering features of e-mail and other forms of computer-based communications. According to this perspective, CMC limits the "bandwidth" of social communication, compared to traditional face-to-face communication settings (or to telephone interaction, which at least occurs in real time and includes important nonverbal features of speech). Sproull & Kiesler (1985) considered CMC to be an impoverished communication experience, with the reduction of available social cues resulting in a greater sense or feeling of anonymity. This in turn is said to have a deindividuating effect on the individuals involved, producing behavior that is more self-centered and less socially regulated than usual. This reduced-information model of Internet communication assumes further that the reduction of social cues, compared to richer face-to-face situations, must necessarily have negative effects on social interaction (i.e., a weaker, relatively impoverished social interaction). Note also that this engineering or bandwidth model assumes that the "channel" effects of Internet communication are the same for all users and across all contexts—in other words, it predicts a main effect of communication channel.

Spears et al. (2002) contrasted the engineering model with the "social science" perspective on the Internet, which assumes instead that personal goals and needs are the sole determinant of its effects. [In the domain of communications research, Blumler & Katz's (1974) "uses and gratifications" theory is an influential version of this approach.] According to this viewpoint, the particular purposes of the individuals within the communication setting determine the outcome of the interaction, regardless of the particular features of the communication channel in which the interaction takes place.

The third and most recent approach has been to focus on the interaction between features of the Internet communication setting and the particular goals and needs of the communicators, as well as the social context of the interaction setting (see Bargh 2002, McKenna & Bargh 2000, Spears et al. 2002). According to this perspective, the special qualities of Internet social interaction do have an impact on the interaction and its outcomes, but this effect can be quite different depending on the social context. With these three guiding models in mind, we turn to a review of the relevant research.

In the Workplace

In the 1980s—before the Internet per se even existed—Sara Kiesler and her colleagues (e.g., Kiesler et al. 1984) pioneered research on the interpersonal effects of e-mail communication within organizations and the workplace. Consistent with their "limited bandwidth" model, one conclusion from their studies was that the deindividuating nature of CMC produced an increase in aggressive and hostile exchanges between communication partners and a reduction in the usual inhibitions that operate when interacting with one's superiors. However, subsequent meta-analytic reviews of the CMC literature on this point by Walther et al. (1994) and Postmes & Spears (1998) concluded that there was no overall main effect of CMC to produce greater hostility and aggressiveness among communicants. Walther et al. (1994) concluded that insults, name calling, and swearing in CMC were "over-reported activities," and a study by Straus (1997) comparing 36 CMC and 36 face-to-face three-person work groups similarly concluded that "the incidence of personal attacks in groups in either communication mode was exceedingly small and was not associated with cohesiveness or satisfaction, suggesting further that the impact of this behavior was trivial" (p. 255).

From the perspective of social identity theory, Spears and colleagues (e.g., Reicher et al. 1995, Spears et al. 2002) have argued that CMC is not so much deindividuating as it is depersonalizing—that the decreased salience of personal accountability and identity makes group-level social identities all the more important, so that the real effect of CMC is to increase conformity to those local group norms. Thus, whether the depersonalizing effect of CMC leads to more negative or more positive behavior relative to face-to-face interactions is said to depend on the particular content of those group norms (Postmes & Spears 1998).

Two recent surveys of U.S. college students are relevant here: Cummings et al. (2002, p. 104) found that e-mail was considered as useful as face-to-face interactions for getting work done and building school-related relationships; in the Jones (2002) nationwide survey, 60% of college students reported that the Internet (mainly e-mail) had been beneficial to their relationships with classmates, compared with just 4% who believed it had had a negative impact on those relationships.

An important use of CMC in the corporate world and elsewhere has been to conduct negotiations between parties who are separated by physical distance (see Carnevale & Probst 1997). Thompson and her colleagues (see Thompson & Nadler 2002 for a review) have conducted extensive research on the process and outcomes of such negotiations, compared to those of traditional face-to-face negotiations, and have noted several pitfalls and traps to watch out for. The main problem with such "e-gotiation," according to these researchers, is the implicit assumptions people have concerning time delays in hearing back from their adversaries as well as about the motivations of those adversaries. For example, people tend to assume that the other party to the negotiation reads and is aware of the content of the e-mail message one just sent to them as soon as that message is sent—thus any delays in hearing back are attributed to stalling or intentional disrespect by the other party. These findings of greater distrust over CMC compared to face-to-face negotiations are the opposite of what is found in the domain of relationship formation on the Internet (see next section), and therefore serve as an instructive example of how the interpersonal effects of the Internet vary as a function of the social context.

Thompson and colleagues also report an intervention that seems to ameliorate the negative, distrust-evoking nature of electronic negotiation: having the two parties talk on the telephone prior to the start of the negotiations (Thompson & Nadler 2002). Other studies also point to the transforming nature of telephone interaction, as if the telephone were a bridge between the "virtual" and the "real." The Cummings et al. (2002) survey comparing on-line (Internet) with off-line modes of communication grouped the telephone together with face-to-face as off-line, and found that international bankers and college students alike considered off-line communication more beneficial to establishing close social (as opposed to work) relationships. Nie & Erbring (2000) similarly considered interacting over the telephone to be "real" whereas Internet interaction was not; hence substituting e-mail for telephone contact was described as a "loss of contact with the social environment." And in the survey by McKenna et al. (2002, Study 1; see next section) on close relationship formation among Internet newsgroup members, all of those who eventually moved their Internet relationships to "real life" (face-to-face) had first interacted with their partner on the telephone—no one went directly from the Internet to a face-to-face meeting without first talking on the phone.

Personal (Close) Relationships

EFFECTS OF INTERNET USE ON EXISTING RELATIONSHIPS   On no issue has research on the social effects of the Internet been more contentious than as to its effect on close relationships, such as those with family and friends. Two studies that received considerable media attention were the HomeNet project by Kraut et al. (1998) and the large-scale survey reported by Nie & Erbring (2000; also Nie 2001). Both reports concluded that Internet use led to negative outcomes for the individual user, such as increases in depression and loneliness, and neglect of existing close relationships. However, nearly all other relevant studies and surveys—including a follow up of the HomeNet sample by Kraut and his colleagues—reached the opposite conclusion.

Kraut et al. (1998) followed a convenience sample of Pittsburgh residents and their families who as of the mid 1990s did not yet have a computer in the home. The researchers gave these families a computer and Internet access, and then found after a two-year period a reliable but small increase in reported depression and loneliness as a function of the amount of Internet use. However, a later follow-up study of the same sample (Kraut et al. 2002) revealed that these negative effects had disappeared, and instead across nearly all measures of individual adjustment and involvement with family, friends, and community, greater Internet use was associated with positive psychological and social outcomes. For example, the more hours the average respondent spent on the Internet, the more (not less) time he or she also spent face-to-face with family and friends.

In their press release, Nie & Erbring (2000) reported data from a U.S. nationwide survey of approximately 4000 people, and concluded from those data that heavy Internet use resulted in less time spent with one's family and friends. On the surface, this would seem to contradict the Kraut et al. (2002) conclusions (and those of the studies reviewed below), but a closer look at the actual findings removes the apparent contradiction. These reveal that over 95% of Nie & Erbring's (2000) total sample did not report spending any less time with family and friends because of their Internet use; moreover, even among the heaviest users, 88% reported no change in time spent with close others.

Several other national surveys have found either that Internet users are no less likely than nonusers to visit or call friends on the phone, or that Internet users actually have the larger social networks (DiMaggio et al. 2001, p. 316). Howard et al. (2001) concluded from their large random-sample survey "the Internet allows people to stay in touch with family and friends and, in many cases, extend their social networks. A sizeable majority of those who send e-mail messages to relatives say it increases the level of communication between family members . . . these survey results suggest that on-line tools are more likely to extend social contact than detract from it" (p. 399). Wellman et al. (2001) similarly concluded from their review that heavy users of the Internet do not use e-mail as a substitute for face-to-face and telephone contact, but instead use it to help maintain longer distance relationships (Wellman et al. 2001, p. 450).

Nie (2001) has responded to his critics by arguing that time is a limited commodity, so that the hours spent on the Internet must come at a cost to other activities. "We would expect that all those spending more than the average of 10 hours a week on the Internet would report substantially fewer hours socializing with family members, friends, and neighbors. It is simply a matter of time" (p. 425). However, in the Nie & Erbring (2000) results, the real and substantial decrease associated with heavy Internet use was in watching television and reading newspapers, not in social interaction with friends and family.

RELATIONSHIP FORMATION ON THE INTERNET   In the original study in this research domain, Parks & Floyd (1995) administered a questionnaire concerning friendship formation to people participating in Internet newsgroups (electronic bulletin boards devoted to special interest topics). Results showed that on-line relationships are highly similar to those developed in person, in terms of their breadth, depth, and quality. In another study, McKenna et al. (2002) surveyed nearly 600 members of randomly selected popular newsgroups devoted to various topics such as politics, fashion, health, astronomy, history, and computer languages. A substantial proportion of respondents reported having formed a close relationship with someone they had met originally on the Internet; in addition, more than 50% of these participants had moved an Internet relationship to the "real-life" or face-to-face realm. Many of these on-line relationships had become quite close—22% of respondents reported that they had either married, become engaged to, or were living with someone they initially met on the Internet. In addition, a two-year follow up of these respondents showed that these close relationships were just as stable over time as were traditional relationships (e.g., Attridge et al. 1995, Hill et al. 1976).

Follow-up laboratory experiments by McKenna et al. (2002) and Bargh et al. (2002) focused on the underlying reasons for the formation of close relationships on the Internet. In these studies, pairs of previously unacquainted male and female college students met each other for the first time either in an Internet chat room or face-to-face. Those who met first on the Internet liked each other more than those who met first face-to-face—even when, unbeknownst to the participants, it was the same partner both times (McKenna et al. 2002). Moreover, the studies revealed that (a) people were better able to express their "true" selves (those self-aspects they felt were important but which they were usually unable to present in public) to their partner over the Internet than when face-to-face, and (b) when Internet partners liked each other, they tended (more than did the face-to-face group) to project qualities of their ideal friends onto each other (Bargh et al. 2002). The authors argued that both of these phenomena contribute to close relationship formation over the Internet. For example, related research on long-distance relationships (Rohlfing 1995, Stafford & Reske 1990) finds that tendencies to idealize one's often-absent partner causes long-distance couples to report higher relationship satisfaction compared with geographically close relationships (see also Murray et al. 1996).

The relative anonymity of the Internet can also contribute to close relationship formation through reducing the risks inherent in self-disclosure. Because self-disclosure contributes to a sense of intimacy, making self-disclosure easier should facilitate relationship formation. In this regard Internet communication resembles the "strangers on a train" phenomenon described by Rubin (1975; also Derlega & Chaikin 1977). As Kang (2000, p. 1161) noted, "Cyberspace makes talking with strangers easier. The fundamental point of many cyber-realms, such as chat rooms, is to make new acquaintances. By contrast, in most urban settings, few environments encourage us to walk up to strangers and start chatting. In many cities, doing so would amount to a physical threat."

Overall, then, the evidence suggests that rather than being an isolating, personally and socially maladaptive activity, communicating with others over the Internet not only helps to maintain close ties with one's family and friends, but also, if the individual is so inclined, facilitates the formation of close and meaningful new relationships within a relatively safe environment.

Group Membership and Social Support

One of the novel aspects of the Internet for social life is the wide variety of special interest newsgroups available; there are tens of thousands of newsgroups devoted to everything from Indian cooking to dinosaurs to raincoat fetishes. There are also e-mail "listservs" in which group members can post messages to all other members, and of course websites specializing in about every topic imaginable. These virtual groups can be fertile territory for the formation of friendships and even close relationships because of the shared interests and values of the members (see McKenna et al. 2002)—perceptions of similarity and shared beliefs (in addition to the shared strong topical interests) are known to contribute to attraction between individuals (Byrne 1971). And especially for important aspects of one's identity for which there is no equivalent off-line group, membership and participation in a relevant virtual group can become a central (and very real) part of one's social life. Two main types of virtual group membership that fit this bill have been studied thus far: those devoted to stigmatized social identities, and those chartered explicitly to provide social support for debilitating or life-threatening illnesses.

STIGMATIZED IDENTITIES   McKenna & Bargh (1998) reasoned that people with stigmatized social identities (see Frable 1993, Jones et al. 1984), such as homosexuality or fringe political beliefs, should be motivated to join and participate in Internet groups devoted to that identity, because of the relative anonymity and thus safety of Internet (compared to face-to-face) participation and the scarcity of such groups in "real life." Moreover, because it is their only venue in which to share and discuss this aspect of their identity, membership in the group should be quite important to these people, and so the norms of such groups should exert a stronger than usual influence over members' behavior. This prediction was confirmed by an archival and observational study of the frequency with which stigmatized-group members posted messages to (i.e., participated in) the group: Unlike in other Internet groups, participation increased when there was positive feedback from the other group members and decreased following negative feedback (McKenna & Bargh 1998, Study 1).

Moreover, according to Deaux's (1993) model of social identity, members of stigmatized-identity Internet groups should, because of the importance of that identity to them, incorporate their virtual-group membership into their self-concepts. If so, we would expect members of these groups to want to make this new and important aspect of identity a social reality (Gollwitzer 1986) by sharing it with significant others. Structural modeling analyses of survey responses were consistent with these predictions, across two replications focusing on quite different types of stigmatized social identities, thereby demonstrating the self-transformational power of participation in Internet groups. The average respondent was in his or her mid 30s, so that many respondents, directly because of their Internet group participation, had "come out" to their family and friends about this stigmatized aspect of themselves for the first time in their lives.

Such results support the view that membership and participation in Internet groups can have powerful effects on one's self and identity. Note here also that, as Spears et al. (2002) have argued, group processes and effects unfold over the Internet in much the same way as they do in traditional venues. Predictions about on-line group behavior and its consequences were generated from theories (social identity theory, self-completion theory) that were developed based on research on off-line, face-to-face groups.

ON-LINE SUPPORT   In harmony with these conclusions, Davison et al. (2000) studied the provision and seeking of social support on-line by those with grave illnesses, and found that people used Internet support groups particularly for embarrassing, stigmatized illnesses such as AIDS and prostate cancer (and also, understandably, for those illnesses that limit mobility such as multiple sclerosis). The authors point out that because of the anxiety and uncertainty they are feeling, patients are highly motivated by social comparison needs to seek out others with the same illness (p. 213), but prefer to do this on-line when the illness is an embarrassing, disfiguring, or otherwise stigmatized one, because of the anonymity afforded by Internet groups (p. 215).

This is not to say that on-line social support groups are only helpful for stigmatized illnesses, only that they are especially valuable to those sufferers. McKay et al. (2002), for example, found that diabetes self-management and peer support over the Internet led to just as much improvement in physiologic, behavioral, and mental health—especially in dietary control—as did conventional diabetes management. And Wright (2000) showed that among older adults using SeniorNet and other on-line support websites for the elderly, greater participation in the on-line community was correlated with lower perceived life stress. Just as with the need to express important aspects of one's identity, then, people will be especially likely to turn to Internet groups when embarrassment or lack of mobility makes participation in traditional group settings problematic.

IMPLICATIONS FOR RACISM AND PREJUDICE   Certainly, being a member of a minority or ethnic social group constitutes a stigma in many social situations (e.g., Crocker & Major 1989). Racial, gender, or age-related features are easily identifiable (e.g., Brewer 1988) and therefore not easily concealable within traditional venues. However, they are much more concealable over the Internet. Accordingly, Kang (2000) has argued that one potential social benefit of the Internet is to disrupt the reflexive operation of racial stereotypes, as racial anonymity is much easier to maintain on-line than off-line. For example, studies have found that African Americans and Hispanics pay more than do white consumers for the same car, but these price differences disappear if the car is instead purchased on-line (Scott Morton et al. 2003). However, the continuing racial divide on the Internet (DiMaggio et al. 2001, Hoffman & Novak 1998), in terms of the lower proportion of minority versus majority group members who have on-line access, can only attenuate the impact of any such positive, race-blind interpersonal effects on society.

Yet racism itself is socially stigmatized—especially when it comes to extreme forms such as advocacy of white supremacy and racial violence (see McKenna & Bargh 1998, Study 3). Thus the cloak of relative anonymity afforded by the Internet can also be used as a cover for racial hate groups, especially for those members who are concerned about public disapproval of their beliefs; hence today there are more than 3000 websites containing racial hatred, agendas for violence, and even bomb-making instructions (Lee & Leets 2002). Glaser et al. (2002) infiltrated such a group and provide telling examples of the support and encouragement given by group members to each other to act on their hatreds. All things considered, then, we don't know yet whether the overall effect of the Internet will be a positive or a negative one where racial and ethnic divisions are concerned.

Community Involvement

As noted above, Nie & Erbring (2000) argued that the Internet was creating a "lonely crowd" in cyberspace, because Internet use "necessarily" takes time away from family and friends. However, the evidence very consistently points in the opposite direction concerning the effect of Internet use on off-line community involvement. A random national survey by Katz et al. (2001) showed that the more time Internet users spent on-line, the more likely they were to belong to off-line religious, leisure, and community organizations, compared to nonusers (p. 412). Use of the Internet also was not associated with different levels of awareness of and knowledge about one's neighbors (p. 414).

In the Gross et al. (2002) study of California teenagers (described above), even the regular Internet users in their sample continued to spend most of their after-school time on traditional activities, many of which involved peer interaction (participating in clubs or sports, hanging out with friends). A 1998 survey of nearly 40,000 visitors to the National Geographic website similarly found that heavy Internet use was associated with greater levels of participation in voluntary organizations and politics (Wellman et al 2001, p. 436). Finally, Kavanaugh & Patterson (2001) concluded from the Blacksburg (Virginia) Electronic Village study "the longer people are on the Internet, the more likely they are to use the Internet to engage in social-capital-building activities" (p. 507). Thus, contrary to some well-publicized claims, Internet use does not appear to weaken the fabric of neighborhoods and communities.

THE MODERATING ROLE OF TRUST

In important ways, using the Internet involves a leap of faith. We type in our credit card numbers and other personal information in order to make purchases over the Internet and trust that this information will not be used in unauthorized or fraudulent ways. We write frank and confidential messages to our close colleagues and friends and trust that they won't circulate these messages to others. We trust anonymous fellow chat room and newsgroup members with our private thoughts and dreams, and because of the intimacy such self-disclosure creates, come to trust them enough to give them our phone numbers.

Or we don't.

Just as in close relationships (Wieselquist et al. 1999), whether we are motivated to trust or not to trust our interaction partners or website operators is an important moderator of how we respond to the "limited bandwidth" and relative lack of information over the Internet, compared to traditional social interaction and business transaction settings. As we have seen, negotiators over the Internet react to the lack of information and cues they have regarding their opponents by assuming the worst, and so interpret ambiguous data such as delays in e-mail responses as evidence of sinister motives (Thompson & Nadler 2002). Yet after initial liking is established while meeting a new acquaintance over the Internet, people tend next to idealize that person—that is, assuming the best about them (McKenna et al. 2002). The difference between the two situations is not the Internet, because its characteristics as a communication channel are the same in both cases; the difference is in the social contexts and the different interpersonal motivations and goals that are associated with the two contexts.

Trust turns out even to moderate differences in the rate of Internet adoption across countries. Keser et al. (2002) correlated data on Internet adoption rates (proportion of homes with Internet access) with answers to a question on the World Values Survey: "Can people generally be trusted, or is it that you can't be too careful in dealing with people?" The degree of trust within a country, indexed by the percentage of respondents who gave the former instead of the latter answer to the values question, explained nearly two-thirds of the national differences in Internet adoption rate, and this relation holds after other possibly relevant variables, such as number of computers in the country, are statistically controlled.

This is why "spam"—unsolicited junk e-mail with usually fake return addresses and often fraudulent claims—is a real threat to the social life of the Internet: It threatens to undermine that important sense of trust for many people (Gleick 2003). Today, spam constitutes nearly half of all e-mail traffic, turning the most common activity on the Internet into an annoyance and chore as users must sort through and delete the unwanted mail from their inboxes (*Economist* 2003c). Fortunately, government and corporations appear finally to be recognizing the problem and taking action to reduce and regulate junk e-mail (Hansell 2003). Here again, the Internet appears to be following in the footsteps of its technological predecessors, which also saw their utility threatened early on by unregulated, self-interested use. For example, amateur radio enthusiasts filled the public airwaves with chatter in the early twentieth century, thus making them unlistenable for the home audience, before governments finally stepped in to regulate the new medium (Spar 2001). The spam problem and its attempted resolution illustrates that it is not a matter of *whether* governments will attempt to regulate and police the Internet, but of *how* and *how much* they will do so.

CONCLUSIONS

People are not passively affected by technology, but actively shape its use and influence (Fischer 1992, Hughes & Hans 2001). The Internet has unique, even transformational qualities as a communication channel, including relative anonymity and the ability to easily link with others who have similar interests, values, and beliefs. Research has found that the relative anonymity aspect encourages self-expression, and the relative absence of physical and nonverbal interaction cues (e.g., attractiveness) facilitates the formation of relationships on other, deeper bases such as shared values and beliefs. At the same time, however, these "limited bandwidth" features of Internet communication also tend to leave a lot unsaid and unspecified, and open to inference and interpretation. Not surprisingly, then, one's own desires and goals regarding the people with whom one interacts has been found to make a dramatic difference in the assumptions and attributions one makes within that informational void.

Despite past media headlines to the contrary, the Internet does not make its users depressed or lonely, and it does not seem to be a threat to community life—quite the opposite, in fact. If anything, the Internet, mainly through e-mail, has facilitated communication and thus close ties between family and friends, especially those too far away to visit in person on a regular basis. The Internet can be fertile territory for the formation of new relationships as well, especially those based on shared values and interests as opposed to attractiveness and physical appearance as is the norm in the off-line world (see Hatfield & Sprecher 1986). And in any event, when these Internet-formed relationships get close enough (i.e., when sufficient trust has been established), people tend to bring them into their "real world"—that is, the traditional face-to-face and telephone interaction sphere. This means nearly all of the typical person's close friends will be in touch with them in "real life"—on the phone or in person—and not so much over the Internet, which gives the lie to the media stereotype of the Internet as drawing people away from their "real-life" friends.

Still, the advent of the Internet is likely to produce dramatic changes in our daily lives. For example, together with high-speed computing and encryption technology it already plays a significant role in crime and terrorism by enabling private communication across any distance without being detected (Ballard et al. 2002, p. 1010). And we quite rightly have been warned that repressive regimes may harness the Internet and all of the data banks that connect to it to increase their power over the population (Manasian 2003, p. 23; Shapiro 1999). A step in this direction is the 2001 "Patriot Act," (enacted in the United States following the September 11 attacks) which called for the technology to monitor the content of Internet traffic to be built into the Internet's very infrastructure. However, these important issues concerning the Internet lie outside of our purview in this chapter.

We emphasize, in closing, one potentially great benefit of the Internet for social-psychological research and theorizing: by providing a contrasting alternative to the usual face-to-face interaction environment. As Lea & Spears (1995) and O'Sullivan (1996) have noted, studying how relationships form and are maintained on the Internet brings into focus the implicit assumptions and biases of our traditional (face-to-face) relationship and communication research literatures (see Cathcart & Gumpert 1983)—most especially the assumptions that face-to-face interactions, physical proximity, and nonverbal communication are necessary and essential to the processes of relating to each other effectively. By providing an alternative interaction setting in which interactions and relationships play by somewhat different rules, and have somewhat different outcomes, the Internet sheds light on those aspects of face-to-face interaction that we may have missed all along. Tyler (2002), for example, reacting to the research findings on Internet interaction, wonders whether it is the presence of physical features that makes face-to-face interaction what it is, or is it instead the immediacy of responses (compared to e-mail)? That's a question we never knew to ask before.

Our review has revealed many cases and situations in which social interaction over the Internet is preferred and leads to better outcomes than in traditional interaction venues, as well as those in which it doesn't. As the Internet becomes ever more a part of our daily lives, the trick for us will be to know the difference. But it is reassuring that the evidence thus far shows people to be adapting pretty well to the brave new wired (and soon to be wireless) social world.

ACKNOWLEDGMENTS

Preparation of this chapter was supported in part by Grant MH60747 from the National Institute of Mental Health and by the Center for Advanced Study in the Behavioral Sciences, Stanford, CA. We thank Russell Spears, Tom Postmes, and Susan Fiske for their comments and suggestions on an earlier draft.

The *Annual Review of Psychology* is online at http://psych.annualreviews.org

LITERATURE CITED

Attridge M, Berscheid E, Simpson JA. 1995. Predicting relationship stability from both partners versus one. *J. Personal. Soc. Psychol.* 69:254–68

Ballard JD, Nornik JG, McKenzie D. 2002. Technological facilitation of terrorism: definitional, legal, and policy issues. *Am. Behav. Sci.* 45:989–1016

Bargh JA. 2002. Beyond simple truths: the human-Internet interaction. *J. Soc. Issues* 58(1):1–8

Bargh JA, McKenna KYA, Fitzsimons GM. 2002. Can you see the real me? Activation and expression of the 'true self' on the Internet. *J. Soc. Issues* 58(1):33–48

Blumler J, Katz E. 1974. *The Uses of Mass Communication.* Thousand Oaks, CA: Sage

Brewer MB. 1988. A dual process model of impression formation. In *Advances in Social Cognition*, ed. TK Srull, RS Wyer Jr., 1:1–36. Hillsdale, NJ: Erlbaum

Byrne D. 1971. *The Attraction Paradigm.* New York: Academic

Carnevale PJ, Probst TM. 1997. Conflict on the Internet. In *Culture of the Internet*, ed. S Kiesler, pp. 233–55. Mahwah, NJ: Erlbaum

Cathcart R, Gumpert G. 1983. Mediated interpersonal communication: toward a new typology. *Q. J. Speech* 69:267–77

Crocker J, Major B. 1989. Social stigma and self-esteem: the self-protective properties of stigma. *Psychol. Rev.* 96:608–30

Cummings JN, Butler B, Kraut R. 2002. The quality of online social relationships. *Commun. ACM* 45(July):103–8

Davison KP, Pennebaker JW, Dickerson SS. 2000. Who talks? The social psychology of illness support groups. *Am. Psychol.* 55:205–17

Deaux K. 1993. Reconstructing social identity. *Personal. Soc. Psychol. Bull.* 19:4–12

Derlega VJ, Chaikin AL. 1977. Privacy and self-disclosure in social relationships. *J. Soc. Issues* 33(3):102–15

DiMaggio P, Hargittai E, Neuman WR, Robinson JP. 2001. Social implications of the internet. *Annu. Rev. Sociol.* 27:307–36

Economist. 2003a. Mar. 29:58

Economist. 2003b. Apr. 5:58

Economist. 2003c. Apr. 26:58

Fischer C. 1992. *America Calling: A Social History of the Telephone to 1940.* Berkeley: Univ. Calif. Press

Frable DES. 1993. Being and feeling unique: statistical deviance and psychological marginality. *J. Personal.* 61:85–110

Geer S. 2000. *Pocket Internet.* London: Profile Books

Glaser J, Dixit J, Green DP. 2002. Studying hate crime with the Internet: What makes racists advocate racial violence? *J. Soc. Issues* 58(1):177–93

Gleick J. 2003. Tangled up in spam. *New York Times Mag.*, Feb. 9, p.42

Gollwitzer PM. 1986. Striving for specific identities: the social reality of self-symbolizing. In *Public Self and Private Self*, ed. R Baumeister, pp. 143–59. New York: Springer

Gross EF, Juvonen J, Gable SL. 2002. Internet use and well-being in adolescence. *J. Soc. Issues* 58(1):75–90

Hafner K. 2003. Eluding the web's snare. *New York Times*, April 17:G1

Hampton K, Wellman B. 2001. Long distance community in the network society. *Am. Behav. Sci.* 45:476–95

Hansell S. 2003. Spam sent by fraud is made a felony under Virginia law. *New York Times*, April 30, p. C1

Hatfield E, Sprecher S. 1986. *Mirror, Mirror: The Importance of Looks in Everyday Life.* Albany: State Univ. NY Press

Hill CT, Rubin Z, Peplau LA. 1976. Breakups before marriage: the end of 103 affairs. *J. Soc. Issues* 32:147–68

Hoffman DL, Novak TP. 1998. Bridging the racial divide on the Internet. *Science* 280:390–91

Howard PEN, Rainie L, Jones S. 2001. Days and nights on the Internet. *Am. Behav. Sci.* 45: 383–404

Hughes R Jr., Hans JD. 2001. Computers, the internet, and families: a review of the role new technology plays in family life. *J. Fam. Issues* 22:778–92

Jones EE, Farina A, Hastorf AH, Markus H, Miller DT, et al. 1984. *Social Stigma: The Psychology of Marked Relationships*. San Francisco: Freeman

Jones S. 2002. *The Internet Goes to College*. Washington, DC: Pew Internet/Am. Life Proj. http://www.pewinternet.org

Kang J. 2000. Cyber-race. *Harv. Law Rev.* 113:1130–1208

Katz JE, Rice RE, Aspden P. 2001. The Internet, 1995–2000. *Am. Behav. Sci.* 45:405–19

Kavanaugh AL, Patterson CJ. 2001. The impact of community computer networks on social capital and community involvement. *Am. Behav. Sci.* 45:496–509

Keser C, Leland J, Shachat J, Huang H. 2002. *Trust, the Internet, and the Digital Divide. IBM Res. Rep. RC22511*, Yorktown Heights, NY

Kiesler S, Siegel J, McGuire T. 1984. Social psychological aspects of computer-mediated communication. *Am. Psychol.* 39:1129–34

Kraut R, Kiesler S, Boneva B, Cummings J, Helgeson V, et al. 2002. Internet paradox revisited. *J. Soc. Issues* 58(1):49–74

Kraut R, Patterson M, Lundmark V, Kiesler S, Mukopadhyay T, et al. 1998. Internet paradox: a social technology that reduces social involvement and psychological well-being? *Am. Psychol.* 53:1017–31

Lea M, Spears R. 1995. Love at first byte? Building personal relationships over computer networks. In *Understudied Relationships: Off the Beaten Track*, ed. JT Wood, S Duck, pp. 197–233. Thousand Oaks, CA: Sage

Lee E, Leets L. 2002. Persuasive storytelling by hate groups online. *Am. Behav. Sci.* 45:927–57

Manasian D. 2003. Digital dilemmas: a survey of the Internet society. *Economist*, Jan. 25:1–26

Markoff J. 2002. High-speed wireless internet network is planned. *New York Times*, Dec. 26, p. C1

Matei S, Ball-Rokeach SJ. 2001. Real and virtual social ties. *Am. Behav. Sci.* 45:550–64

McKay HG, Glasgow RE, Feil EG, Boles SM, Barrera M. 2002. Internet-based diabetes self-management and support initial outcomes from the diabetes network project. *Rehabil. Psychol.* 47:31–48

McKenna KYA, Bargh JA. 1998. Coming out in the age of the Internet: identity 'demarginalization' through virtual group participation. *J. Personal. Soc. Psychol.* 75:681–94

McKenna KYA, Bargh JA. 2000. Plan 9 from cyberspace: the implications of the Internet for personality and social psychology. *Personal. Soc. Psychol. Bull.* 4:57–75

McKenna KYA, Green AS, Gleason MJ. 2002. Relationship formation on the Internet: What's the big attraction? *J. Soc. Issues* 58(1):9–31

Murray SL, Holmes JG, Griffin DW. 1996. The self-fulfilling nature of positive illusions in relationships: Love is blind, but prescient. *J. Personal. Soc. Psychol.* 71:1155–80

Nie NH. 2001. Sociability, interpersonal relations, and the Internet: reconciling conflicting findings. *Am. Behav. Sci.* 45:420–35

Nie NH, Erbring L. 2000. *Internet and Society: A Preliminary Report*. Stanford Inst. Quant. Study Soc., Stanford, CA

O'Sullivan PB. 1996. *A match made in cyberspace: interpersonal communication theory and interpersonal communication technology*. Annu. Meet. Intern. Commun. Assoc., Chicago

Parks MR, Floyd K. 1995. Making friends in cyberspace. *J. Commun.* 46:80–97

Postmes T, Spears R. 1998. Deindividuation and anti-normative behavior: a meta-analysis. *Psychol. Bull.* 123:238–59

Putnam RD. 2000. *Bowling Alone*. New York: Simon & Schuster

Reicher S, Spears R, Postmes T. 1995. A social identity model of deindividuation phenomena. *Eur. Rev. Soc. Psychol.* 6: 161–98

Reuters. 2001. Miss France not a man. Apr. 27

Rohlfing ME. 1995. Doesn't anybody stay in one place anymore? An exploration of the understudied phenomenon of long-distance relationships. In *Understudied Relationships: Off the Beaten Track*, ed. JT Wood, S Duck, pp. 173–96. Thousand Oaks, CA: Sage

Rubin Z. 1975. Disclosing oneself to a stranger: reciprocity and its limits. *J. Exp. Soc. Psychol.* 11:233–60

Scott Morton F, Zettelmeyer F, Silva-Risso J. 2003. Consumer information and discrimination: Does the Internet affect the pricing of new cars to women and minorities? *Quant. Mark. Econ.* 1:65–92

Shapiro AL. 1999. Think again: the Internet. *Foreign Policy* 115:14–27

Spar DL. 2001. *Ruling the Waves: Cycles of Discovery, Chaos, and Wealth from the Compass to the Internet.* New York: Harcourt

Spears R, Postmes T, Lea M, Wolbert A. 2002. When are net effects gross products? The power of influence and the influence of power in computer-mediated communication. *J. Soc. Issues* 58(1):91–107

Sproull L, Kiesler S. 1985. Reducing social context cues: electronic mail in organizational communication. *Manag. Sci.* 11:1492–512

Stafford L, Kline SL, Dimmick J. 1999. Home e-mail: relational maintenance and gratification opportunities. *J. Broadcast. Electron. Media* 43:659–69

Stafford L, Reske JR. 1990. Idealization and communication in long-distance premarital relationships. *Fam. Relat.* 39:274–79

Standage T. 1998. *The Victorian Internet.* New York: Berkley Books

Straus SG. 1997. Technology, group process, and group outcomes: testing the connections in computer-mediated and face-to-face groups. *Hum.-Comput. Interact.* 12:227–66

Thompson L, Nadler J. 2002. Negotiating via information technology: theory and application. *J. Soc. Issues* 58(1):109–24

Turow J, Kavanaugh AL, eds. 2003. *The Wired Homestead.* Cambridge, MA: MIT Press

Tyler TR. 2002. Is the Internet changing social life? It seems the more things change, the more they stay the same. *J. Soc. Issues* 58(1):195–205

Walther JB, Anderson JF, Park DW. 1994. Interpersonal effects in computer-mediated interaction: a meta-analysis of social and antisocial communication. *Commun. Res.* 21:460–87

Wellman B, Haase AQ, Witte J, Hampton K. 2001. Does the Internet increase, decrease, or supplement social capital? *Am. Behav. Sci.* 45:436–55

Wieselquist J, Rusbult CE, Foster CA, Agnew CR. 1999. Commitment, pro-relationship behavior, and trust in close relationships. *J. Personal. Soc. Psychol.* 77:942–66

Wright K. 2000. Computer-mediated social support, older adults, and coping. *J. Commun.* 50(3):100–18

Annu. Rev. Psychol. 2004. 55:591–621
doi: 10.1146/annurev.psych.55.090902.142015
First published online as a Review in Advance on July 11, 2003

SOCIAL INFLUENCE: Compliance and Conformity

Robert B. Cialdini and Noah J. Goldstein

*Department of Psychology, Arizona State University, Tempe, Arizona 85287-1104;
email: Robert.Cialdini@asu.edu, Noah.Goldstein@asu.edu*

Key Words   obedience, norms, foot-in-the-door, door-in-the-face, motivation

■ **Abstract**   This review covers recent developments in the social influence literature, focusing primarily on compliance and conformity research published between 1997 and 2002. The principles and processes underlying a target's susceptibility to outside influences are considered in light of three goals fundamental to rewarding human functioning. Specifically, targets are motivated to form accurate perceptions of reality and react accordingly, to develop and preserve meaningful social relationships, and to maintain a favorable self-concept. Consistent with the current movement in compliance and conformity research, this review emphasizes the ways in which these goals interact with external forces to engender social influence processes that are subtle, indirect, and outside of awareness.

CONTENTS

INTRODUCTION

The study of social influence is renowned for its demonstration and explication of dramatic psychological phenomena that often occur in direct response to overt social forces. Some of the most memorable images from the field's history depict participants struggling to comprehend their circumstances and to respond in accordance with their private judgments in the face of external pressures to do otherwise. These images include a middle-aged gentleman nearly brought to hysterics by a stranger in a lab coat, as exhibited in Milgram's (1974) work on obedience to authority. They also include that bespectacled and rather befuddled young man

0066-4308/04/0204-0591$14.00   **591**

in Asch's (1956) line-judgment conformity experiments, whose perceptions pitted the likelihood of an incorrect consensus against the likelihood of an incorrect eyeglass prescription. In these classic illustrations, the targets of influence were confronted with explicit social forces that were well within conscious awareness. In contrast, Freedman & Fraser's (1966) seminal investigation of the foot-in-the-door technique, an example of compliance gaining without overt pressure, revealed the subtler aspects of social influence. Although all three lines of research have been prominent in stimulating decades of insightful inquiries into the nature of compliance and conformity, scholars in recent years have been inclined to explore topics more in line with the latter approach; that is, researchers have tended to concentrate their efforts on examining social influence processes that are subtle, indirect, and nonconscious.

The social-cognitive movement has also reverberated throughout contemporary influence research, as investigators attempt to uncover the ways in which targets' implicit and explicit goals affect information processing and decision-making in influence contexts. As an organizational framework, this chapter focuses on the extent to which three central motivations—to be accurate, to affiliate, and to maintain a positive self-concept (see also Cialdini & Trost 1998, Wood 2000)—drive targets' cognitions and behaviors in the areas of compliance and conformity. We place a special emphasis on scholarly work published between 1997 and 2002.

COMPLIANCE

Compliance refers to a particular kind of response—acquiescence—to a particular kind of communication—a request. The request may be explicit, as in the direct solicitation of funds in a door-to-door campaign for charitable donations, or it may be implicit, as in a political advertisement that touts the qualities of a candidate without directly asking for a vote. But in all cases, the target recognizes that he or she is being urged to respond in a desired way.

Goal of Accuracy

Stated simply, people are motivated to achieve their goals in the most effective and rewarding manner possible. A person's desire to respond appropriately to a dynamic social situation demands an accurate perception of reality. The need to correctly interpret and react to incoming information is of paramount importance, particularly to targets of compliance-gaining attempts. One inaccurate perception, cognition, or behavior could mean the difference between getting a bargain and being duped. A great deal of recent compliance research has investigated how targets of various influence techniques process information and respond to requests as they attempt to gain an accurate construal of the situation and respond accordingly.

AFFECT AND AROUSAL   Much of the compliance research on arousal and affective states has focused on the effect of discrete emotions on targets' cognitions as well as on the eventual outcome of the influence attempt. After receiving a request, targets use their feelings as cues for effective responding. For example, Whatley et al. (1999) differentiated between the emotions and related goals associated with public and private compliance in response to a favor. They posited that individuals avoid or alleviate feelings of shame and fear via public compliance, and guilt and pity via private compliance. Several other researchers have also focused on the impact of targets' actual or anticipated guilt on compliance (e.g., Boster et al. 1999; O'Keefe & Figgé 1997, 1999; Rind 1997; Tusing & Dillard 2000). In addition, investigators have explored the influence of mere arousal, finding that the simple arousal elicited by performing an interesting task enhances the likelihood of compliance with a request (Rind 1997, Rind & Strohmetz 2001).

Searching for a broader perspective on the role of affect in compliance scenarios, Forgas (1998a) argued that the conditions under which affect mediates the processing of and responses to requests can be explained by the affect infusion model (AIM; Forgas 1995). The AIM contends that a target's mood will permeate the processing of a request to the extent that the processing is effortful and exhaustive (Forgas 1995, 1998a). That is, an individual's affective state is likely to be integrated into the processing of the request in situations that call for constructive elaboration of "the available stimulus information, require the activation and use of previous knowledge structures, and result in the creation of new knowledge from the combination of stored information and new stimulus details" (Forgas 2001, p. 152). Forgas (1998a) suggested that the processing of a request will be more sensitive to mood if the appeal is unconventional (requiring more substantive processing), and rather impervious to mood if it is conventional. Combined with other findings demonstrating the role of the AIM in influencing the communication and bargaining strategies employed by compliance requesters (Forgas 1999) and negotiators (Forgas 1998b), the evidence as a whole appears to validate the notion that mood effects in compliance scenarios are mediated by both the targets' and requesters' levels of information processing.

The AIM, like many other theories of affect and cognition, focuses on processes that occur while an individual is experiencing a transient emotion or set of emotions. Dolinski & Nawrat (1998) established the success of a technique designed to increase compliance immediately after a particularly arousing mood has subsided. In one demonstration of their fear-then-relief procedure, a card matching the general appearance of a parking ticket was placed either under a windshield wiper (commonly where parking tickets are found) or on a door of illegally parked cars in Poland. The cards placed on the door were advertisements (No Anxiety), whereas the windshield wiper cards were either fake parking tickets (Anxiety) or advertisements (Anxiety-then-Relief). Drivers who experienced apprehension followed by assuagement were more likely to comply with a request than those who continued to be anxious or those never made anxious in the first place. The authors suggested that fear-then-relief participants behaved in a relatively mindless manner, caused by a diversion of resources to cognitions and counterfactuals regarding the fear-provoking event.

THAT'S-NOT-ALL TECHNIQUE   As in the fear-then-relief procedure, targets in compliance situations are often burdened with the task of correctly comprehending, evaluating, and responding to requests in a relatively short time, and therefore lack the luxury of entirely deliberate and rational decision-making. One strategy commonly employed by sales professionals that takes advantage of people's limited abilities to make well-reasoned judgments is the that's-not-all technique (TNA; Burger 1986). Influence agents utilize this technique by presenting a target with an initial request, followed by an almost immediate sweetening of the deal—either by reducing the cost or by increasing the benefits of compliance—before the message recipient has an opportunity to respond. Although obligations to reciprocate the solicitor's generosity have been shown to be at least partially responsible for the effect in some situations, Burger advanced a second, broader explanation for the phenomenon based on the contrast between the two requests and shifting anchor points (see Burger 1986).

Researchers have recently resumed the pursuit of understanding the processes that mediate the technique's efficacy, seeking to clarify the psychological mechanisms at work through an exploration of the tactic's limitations. For example, Burger and colleagues (1999) demonstrated that the procedure could backfire when the original request is too costly or demanding. Although the evidence is indirect, the authors suggest that both these and earlier (Burger 1986) findings are congruent with the theory that the initial request modifies the anchor point individuals use when deciding how to respond to the more attractive request. Thus, by first elevating a prospective customer's anchor point, the salesperson increases the likelihood that the better deal will fall into a range of acceptance that is based on this higher anchor point (Burger 1986, Burger et al. 1999). In the case of an unreasonably large initial request, the excessively high anchor value may be perceived as completely out of the range of acceptance, leading to immediate rejection even before the solicitor has a chance to revise the request (Burger et al. 1999).

Pollock et al. (1998) suggested an alternative account for the original TNA findings. They contended that TNA procedures succeed because potential customers mindlessly act on counterfactuals that create the appearance of a bargain. These authors reported results consistent with the position that the success of the TNA tactic is at least partially due to individuals' mindless consideration of the deal. However, their research did not provide a direct test of their account against the modified anchor point explanation, and the Pollock et al. mechanism alone does not explicitly predict the boomerang effect found by Burger et al. (1999).

RESISTANCE   Following the work of Pollock et al. (1998), some researchers have placed the that's-not-all tactic among a class of influence strategies referred to as disrupt-then-reframe techniques (DTR; Davis & Knowles 1999, Knowles & Linn 2003). The DTR technique operates by disrupting an individual's understanding of and resistance to an influence attempt and reframing the persuasive message or request so that the individual is left more vulnerable to the proposition (Davis &

Knowles 1999). The procedure is thought to work by disturbing the evaluation stage of Gilbert's (1991) two-stage model for message and situation comprehension (Knowles & Linn 2003). In the initial demonstration of the strategy, Davis & Knowles (1999) went door-to-door selling holiday cards for $3. In addition to a control condition ("They're three dollars"), the sales pitch included a disruptive element ("They're three hundred pennies"), a reframing element ("It's a bargain"), or various permutations of these possibilities. The researchers found increased compliance relative to the control only in the disrupt-followed-by-reframe condition ("They're three hundred pennies... that's three dollars. It's a bargain."), suggesting that a target's general, high-order representation of the event ("I am being solicited") must be disturbed before the issue can be reframed ("It's a bargain") for the target. Knowles and colleagues suggest that the that's-not-all technique is a special case of DTR in which the revision of the original request serves as the disruption; the reframing ("It's a bargain") is implicit rather than explicit (Davis & Knowles 1999, Knowles & Linn 2003).

The disrupt-then-reframe tactic enhances the likelihood of compliance by suppressing the target's resistance processes rather than by directly bolstering the desirability of request fulfillment. Knowles & Linn (2003) argue that forces drawing targets away from compliance (omega forces) in any given circumstance may be of a qualitatively different nature than those driving them toward compliance (alpha forces). Investigations of the processes associated with alpha strategies of influence are ubiquitous in the literature (see Cialdini 2001), whereas omega strategies have been quite underserved (Knowles & Linn 2003, Sagarin et al. 2002). Researchers do not yet fully understand how these processes function together in influence settings. Thus, the area is likely to draw considerable attention in the future.

AUTHORITY AND OBEDIENCE   Individuals are frequently rewarded for behaving in accordance with the opinions, advice, and directives of authority figures. Authorities may achieve their influence via several distinct routes, first articulated by French & Raven (1959) in their seminal work on the bases of social power. Although the universe of power bases has been challenged, modified, and updated considerably over the years (see Koslowsky & Schwarzwald 2001), the distinction between authority based on one's expertise and authority derived from one's relative position in a hierarchy has remained relevant in differentiating mere compliance from what is commonly referred to as obedience. In more recent analyses of the many forms of influence at the disposal of authorities and other agents, researchers have categorized strategies employing expert power in a class called *soft tactics* and approaches utilizing hierarchy-based legitimate power in a class known as *harsh tactics* (Koslowsky et al. 2001, Raven et al. 1998). More generally, soft influences originate from factors within the influence agent (e.g., credibility), whereas the power of harsh influences is derived externally by means of an existing social structure (cf. Koslowsky & Schwarzwald 2001).

Several studies have examined the use of authority and power within organizational settings. For example, supervisors' usage of primarily soft strategies has been found to correlate positively with subordinates' job satisfaction ratings, whereas there are indications that the reverse may be true when predominantly harsh tactics are employed (Koslowsky et al. 2001, Raven et al. 1998). Authorities who demonstrate consideration for their subordinates' needs—as opposed to those who exploit power differences—are also likely to engender a more favorable compliance rate (Schwarzwald et al. 2001). Moreover, because the level of volition associated with compliance is a function of the quality of the treatment subordinates receive (Tyler 1997), authorities stand to benefit greatly by treating subordinates with fairness and respect. However, it should be noted that the success of an authority's use of nonforceful measures may actually be augmented by the additional use of forceful means, so long as the attitudinal compliance brought about by the nonforceful influence attempt is not undermined (Emans et al. 2003). In support of this notion, Emans et al. (2003) showed that supervisors whose compliance-gaining repertoires included the use of both forceful and nonforceful techniques were most likely to elicit compliance with their requests.

Most organizations would cease to operate efficiently if deference to authority were not one of the prevailing norms. Yet, the norm is so well entrenched in organizational cultures that orders are regularly carried out by subordinates with little regard for potential deleterious ethical consequences of such acts (Ashford & Anand 2003, Brief et al. 2001, Darley 2001). Personnel managers, for instance, may discriminate based on race when instructed to do so by an authority figure (Brief et al. 1995), particularly those who are high in Right-Wing Authoritarianism (Petersen & Dietz 2000).

One illustration of destructive organizational obedience frequently cited by social psychologists is the systematic murder of millions of innocent people during the Holocaust. Over the years, it has been common practice for researchers, teachers, and textbook authors to refer to Stanley Milgram's (1974) groundbreaking work on obedience to authority as demonstrative of the principles and processes underlying the behaviors of seemingly ordinary German citizens (Miller 1995). A number of scholars have argued that such portrayals misrepresent the true nature of perpetrator behaviors in the Holocaust. They point to numerous differences between the obedience demonstrated in the Milgram experiments and the wanton and deliberate cruelty practiced by many concentration camp executioners. For example, whereas it is clear that Milgram's participants were emotionally and attitudinally in opposition to the orders they were given, many of the Holocaust atrocities were committed willingly and often quite sadistically (Berkowitz 1999, Goldhagen 1996). Others have stressed that, unlike Nazi order-givers, the experimenter in the Milgram studies possessed not only legitimate authority, but expert authority as well (Blass 1999, Darley 1995, Lutsky 1995; but see Elms 1995). Although the movement to redress this growing concern is gaining considerable momentum, Milgram's experiments in particular (e.g., Miller 1995), and social psychology in general (see Darley et al. 2001, Newman & Erber 2002), still provide much insight into the production and perpetuation of obedience-related malfeasance within hierarchically based organizations.

It is noteworthy that few studies of obedience to authority both utilize experimental designs and employ behavioral dependent measures. This trend is likely the result of ethical constraints placed on researchers working with human subjects (Elms 1995). One somewhat feasible alternative to ethically questionable obedience experiments is active role-playing (Meeus & Raaijmakers 1995). This method is characterized by physically placing role-players in the position of a would-be participant, and asking them to demonstrate how they believe a genuine participant would act if the circumstances were real.

The Milgram studies revealed the potentially harmful consequences of an illegitimate authority posing as a legitimate authority. Similarly, previous research has shown that we are also susceptible to those feigning expertise, largely due to our use of heuristics (see Cialdini 2001) and our perceptions of invulnerability to such duplicitous manipulations (Sagarin et al. 2002). Sagarin et al. (2002) found that the most effective treatment for instilling resistance to ads containing spurious experts was one that demonstrated participants' vulnerability to the ads, followed by simple rules for identifying fraudulent experts.

SOCIAL NORMS   In addition to authorities, individuals often look to social norms to gain an accurate understanding of and effectively respond to social situations, especially during times of uncertainty (Cialdini 2001). Social norms have been found to influence a range of behaviors in a myriad of domains, including recycling (Schultz 1999), littering (Kallgren et al. 2000), and tax evasion (cf. Kahan 1997). Cialdini and colleagues (e.g., Cialdini et al. 1991) have argued that a close examination of the seemingly inconsistent literature on norms and their impact on behavior yields a meaningful distinction between norms that inform us about what is typically approved/disapproved (injunctive norms) and those that inform us about what is typically done (descriptive norms). The impact of these social norms on both subtle behavior-shaping and more overt compliance-gaining will be determined by the extent to which each of the norms is focal (Kallgren et al. 2000) and the degree to which the different types of norms are in alignment (Cialdini 2003).

Investigators have corroborated the findings of earlier research that relevant norms direct behavior only when they are in focus. This is true not only for norms outside of the self, but for personal norms as well; for example, the strength of individuals' personal norms against littering predicted littering behaviors only when these individuals focused attention on themselves rather than on external stimuli (Kallgren et al. 2000). Taken together, the results suggest that one's actions are relatively unaffected by normative information—even one's own—unless the information is highlighted prominently in consciousness.

Given that relevant norms must be salient in order to elicit the proper norm-congruent behavior, individuals attempting to persuade others to engage in a particular behavior face the dual challenge of making the norm salient not only immediately following message reception, but in the future as well. Cialdini and associates (R.B. Cialdini, D.W. Barrett, R. Bator, L. Demaine, B.J. Sagarin, K.L.v. Rhoads, & P.L. Winter, paper in preparation) maintain that the long-term efficacy of persuasive communications such as public service announcements is threatened because normative information becomes less accessible over time. They hypothesized and experimentally confirmed that linking an injunctive normative message to a functional mnemonic cue would increase norm accessibility later by activation of the norm upon perception of the same or a similar cue.

Goal of Affiliation

Humans are fundamentally motivated to create and maintain meaningful social relationships with others. For example, implicit in the concept of injunctive norms is the idea that if we engage in behaviors of which others approve, others will approve of us, too. Accordingly, we use approval and liking cues to help build, maintain, and measure the intimacy of our relationships with others. We also move closer to achieving these affiliation-oriented goals when we abide by norms of social exchange with others, such as the norm of reciprocity.

LIKING   One of the clearest implications of our desire to affiliate with others is that the more we like and approve of them, the more likely we are to take actions to cultivate close relationships with them. This may be accomplished via a number of means, including responding affirmatively to requests for help. Indeed, the social influence literature is rife with demonstrations of the positive relationship between our fondness for a person and the likelihood of compliance with his or her request (Cialdini & Trost 1998). For example, physical attractiveness, a predictor of interpersonal liking, has been demonstrated to influence responding in a number of domains, ranging from tip earnings (Lynn & Simons 2000) to the likelihood of being asked for identification in bars (McCall 1997).

Researchers have focused recently on the extent to which heuristics—which generally provide accurate shortcuts for effective decision-making—lead individuals to respond to strangers in ways that belie the absence of a truly meaningful relationship between them. Because we so often rely on the heuristic rule that the more we like someone with whom we have an existing relationship, the greater should be our willingness to comply with the request, we tend to use the rule automatically and unwittingly when the request comes from strangers, as well (Burger et al. 2001). This is even more likely the case under the burdens of a heavy cognitive load, such as when the request is made face-to-face and is unexpected. Burger et al. (2001) found that simply being exposed to a person even for a brief period without any interaction substantially increased compliance with that person's request. In addition, greater perceived similarity—another cue for potential friend- or acquaintanceship—has been demonstrated to lead to enhanced compliance, even when the apparent similarities are based on superficial matches such as shared names, birthdays, and even fingerprint types (Burger et al. 2001,

2003). Some caution is warranted in generalizing these results to both genders, however, because nearly all of the participants were female. Because of the tendency of females to be more relationship-oriented than males (Cross & Madson 1997), there is reason to believe that these effects may be stronger among women than men.

Dolinski et al. (2001) also argued that certain situational cues activate heuristics that lead us to treat strangers as if they were friends or acquaintances. The authors contend that scripts for dealing with strangers or with friends and acquaintances are activated by the particular mode of communication in which we are engaged. Specifically, we tend to associate monologues with strangers and dialogues with closer relationships. In a series of studies, Dolinski and his colleagues showed that simply engaging people in a short, trivial dialogue prior to making the target request was sufficient to elevate compliance relative to a monologue condition ("Hi. I hope you are fine today"). Although the findings suggest that dialogue engagement can be an effective component of an influence agent's request, topics of high involvement are likely to be processed more actively and responded to more deliberately than those of low involvement, allowing for the possibility of a backfire effect (Dolinski et al. 2001).

Impression management through ingratiation is another means by which individuals utilize the liking principle for maximal influence. Research has demonstrated that even subtle forms of ingratiation, such as remembering a person's name (Howard et al. 1995, 1997), can potentially shape that person's response to a request. A great deal of the previous ingratiation research, in large part focusing on the effects of flattery, made use of an experimental paradigm in which targets' and observers' judgments of the ingratiator could be compared (Gordon 1996, Vonk 2002). Investigators have found that targets of ingratiation tend to view the ingratiator more positively than do onlookers (Gordon 1996). The traditional explanation for the target-observer difference has been that the target is motivated to accept the obsequious comments as genuine praise in order to serve his or her self-esteem. Observers, on the other hand, can analyze the behavior more critically (e.g., account for possible ulterior motives) because their feelings of self-worth are not on the line (Vonk 2002). Once the target has uncritically accepted the ingratiator's intentions as wholly good-natured, greater affinity for the adulator follows and leads to increased compliance. Although principles of self-enhancement and liking are doubtless components of the link between compliments and compliance, the norm of reciprocation may be another. In some cases, the recipient of a laudatory remark may comply out of a sense of indebtedness and obligation to the ingratiator, a hypothesis that remains open to empirical study.

RECIPROCATION   The norm of reciprocation—the rule that obliges us to repay others for what we have received from them—is one of the strongest and most pervasive social forces in all human cultures (Gouldner 1960). It helps us build trust with others and pushes us toward equity in our relationships (Kelln & Ellard 1999). The rule tends to operate most reliably in public domains, but is so deeply ingrained in most individuals via socialization that it powerfully directs behavior in private settings as well (Whatley et al. 1999). The influence of obligations to reciprocate has also been shown in commercial exchanges. For example, numerous studies have demonstrated the ability of service workers to harness the potency of the norm to boost their tip earnings (e.g., Rind & Strohmetz 1999, Strohmetz et al. 2002; see also Cialdini & Goldstein 2002).

DOOR-IN-THE-FACE TECHNIQUE   The norm of reciprocity has also been used to explain the effectiveness of the door-in-the-face technique (DITF; Cialdini et al. 1975). Briefly, one employs the strategy by preceding the request for a truly desired action with a more extreme request that is likely to get rejected. Cialdini et al. (1975) explained the phenomenon in terms of reciprocal concessions, arguing that the target feels a normative obligation to reciprocate the influence agent's concession with a concession of his or her own; specifically, this is accomplished by moving from a position of noncompliance to one of compliance. Accordingly, the success of the strategy hinges on the target's perception that the requester has made a legitimate concession (Cialdini et al. 1975). Researchers have repeatedly found that this rejection-then-moderation procedure produces a significant increase in compliance with the target request (Cialdini & Trost 1998; for meta-analyses, see O'Keefe & Hale 1998, 2001).

The reciprocal concessions explanation of the DITF phenomenon had been challenged periodically over the years (e.g., Dillard et al. 1984, Fern et al. 1986), but it seems there has been a recent resurgence of attempts to account for the data with alternative theories. Some researchers have pointed to meta-analytic findings that the size of the concession is not a significant predictor of compliance in the DITF paradigm (see Fern et al. 1986; O'Keefe & Hale 1998, 2001), which suggests that this violates one of the core predictions laid out by a reciprocal concessions model (O'Keefe & Figgé 1997, 1999; O'Keefe 1999; Tusing & Dillard 2000). However, according to the original explanation put forth by Cialdini et al. (1975; see also Hale & Laliker 1999), because the target's choice is a dichotomous one—yes or no—the reciprocal concessions account predicts that any retreat sizeable enough to be perceived as a genuine concession will activate the mechanism for a concession in return. Thus, once a certain threshold is met and the target interprets the requester's move as an authentic concession, increasing the difference between the sizes of the requests would have little effect on the outcome. O'Keefe (1999) argued against this explanation, positing that the existence of systematic variation in participants' personal thresholds would suggest that meta-analyses surveying a large number of studies should record at least somewhat of an advantage for DITF conditions employing larger concessions. Even if this were the case, however, most individual studies (and the meta-analyses that summarize them) have not been equipped to measure directly one key feature of the reciprocal concessions explanation: that is, whether participants perceived a genuine concession in the move to the second request.

The emphasis on authenticity of the concession is not limited only to the target's perception that the second request is truly less demanding than the initial request;

authenticity also refers to the target's beliefs regarding the requester's motives. That is, individuals in a DITF scenario will be less likely to fall victim to the technique when they have reason to suspect that the requester is employing a sales device (Mowen & Cialdini 1980). Some authors (O'Keefe & Figgé 1997, Tusing & Dillard 2000) have argued that the reciprocal concessions explanation does not speak to findings that the DITF strategy tends to be more effective when the requests are prosocial in nature (Dillard et al. 1984; O'Keefe & Hale 1998, 2001). However, the foregoing analysis suggests that targets will be more likely to question the influence agent's motives, to perceive the apparent concession as illegitimate, and consequently, to refuse to comply when the request involves noncharitable causes. These assertions are consistent with the reciprocal concessions approach to the DITF.

Several investigators have also claimed that the originally proposed model is not supported because it is silent with respect to the effect of delay between requests (Dillard et al. 1984, Dolinski et al. 2001). Yet, the reciprocal concessions explanation does indeed predict that a greater time lapse between requests will lead to a less successful outcome, a finding reported in meta-analyses (see O'Keefe & Hale 1998, 2001). Longer delays may reduce the perception that the second request is a genuine concession, either by increasing the likelihood that the target will infer an ulterior motive on the part of the requester, or by making the smaller request seem more like a separate request rather than a concession (see Mowen & Cialdini 1980). Furthermore, contrary to the assertions of Dolinski et al. (2001), there is some evidence that the obligation individuals feel stemming from the norm of reciprocity does in fact diminish over time, at least for small favors between strangers (e.g., Burger et al. 1997). Thus, targets should feel less compelled to reciprocate a concession—even when made in earnest—with a concession of their own as the time between the two requests grows longer.

O'Keefe & Figgé (1997, 1999; see also Tusing & Dillard 2000) proposed an alternative account for the DITF effect based on guilt. They contend that targets feel guilty after rejecting the initial request, and seek to mollify this negative affect by agreeing to fulfill the subsequent request. Millar (2002) demonstrated the potential power of guilt in DITF exchanges by manipulating the degree to which guilty feelings were induced by the rejection of the larger request and reduced by the acceptance of the smaller request. The author found superior compliance rates in the condition characterized by high guilt induction and high guilt reduction. Yet, if individuals are primarily motivated to live up to the standards made salient to them once they have refused the initial appeal and to reduce feelings of guilt, one would expect that compliance with the second request would be equally effective at fulfilling these goals irrespective of the person making the second request (Dolinski et al. 2001). However, the evidence clearly demonstrates that the DITF technique ceases to be effective when a different person makes the second request (Cialdini et al. 1975; O'Keefe & Hale 1998, 2001), a finding that substantially weakens the social responsibility/guilt reduction explanation.

Dolinski et al. (2001) posited their own account of the DITF, suggesting that mere dialogue involvement may be responsible for the technique's success.

According to the dialogue involvement model, simply engaging in the initial exchange should promote a target's willingness to comply with the influence agent's subsequent request. This explanation, however, is not supported by research revealing that the strategy is no longer successful when the second request is the same size as the first (e.g., Cialdini et al. 1975).

Taken as a whole, it appears that recently proposed explanations for the DITF effect are not fully consistent with the available data. This is not to say that multiple factors never operate in DITF exchanges, nor is it likely that the compulsion to reciprocate a genuine concession is the driving force behind the strategy's efficacy in every case. Rather, it is probable that potential mediators such as self-presentation, perceptual contrast, dialogue involvement, social responsibility, and guilt reduction may function at some level in DITF scenarios. However, the data provided by the extant literature still appear to favor a reciprocal concessions-based account as one of the leading mechanisms underlying observed DITF effects.

Goal of Maintaining a Positive Self-Concept

People have a strong need to enhance their self-concepts by behaving consistently with their actions, statements, commitments, beliefs, and self-ascribed traits (Cialdini & Trost 1998). This notion provides the basis for much of the recent research on compliance, particularly with regard to the role of self-perception processes.

FOOT-IN-THE-DOOR TECHNIQUE   One compliance strategy designed to take advantage of people's basic desire for consistency is the foot-in-the-door technique (FITD; Freedman & Fraser 1966). The procedure involves first asking a target individual to comply with a small request, typically one that is minimally invasive so that the target is almost certain to respond affirmatively. After securing compliance, either the initial requester or an associate of the requester makes a larger, often related request. The strategy is considered effective when the demanding task's compliance rates are superior for those who received the initial request as compared to those who received no earlier request. Freedman & Fraser (1966) speculated that a major process underlying the FITD effect is one akin to self-perception (Bem 1972). That is, after agreeing to the initial request, targets ascribe traits to themselves reflecting their recent actions, and this change in self-view helps direct future compliance. There has been much debate regarding the mediators of the effect.

Although researchers have argued that self-perception cannot account for all of the FITD findings (see Dillard et al. 1984), the explanation has received much empirical support, albeit often of an indirect nature (for a meta-analysis, see Burger 1999). For example, Burger & Guadagno (2003) found indirect support for self-perception as a mediator of the FITD effect in their investigation of self-concept clarity. Self-concept clarity is an individual difference measure that gauges the extent to which a person's self-concept is, among other things, accessible (cf. Burger & Guadagno 2003; see also Campbell et al. 1996). Based on the finding that it is easier to manipulate the self-views of those whose self-concepts are more readily accessible (R.E. Guadagno & J.M. Burger, paper in preparation), Burger & Guadagno (2003) predicted that only those with clearer self-concepts would succumb to FITD; the results generally supported the hypothesis and were congruent with a self-perception account of FITD effects. Burger's meta-analysis (1999) of 30 years of FITD investigations yielded a number of other findings consistent with a self-perception explanation. Among them are that targets are more likely to comply with the second request when the initial appeal is behaviorally fulfilled (or at least attempted; see Dolinski 2000), and less likely to comply when the first request is so large that nearly everyone refuses.

Gorassini & Olson (1995) have challenged the assertion that self-perception processes could fully account for the efficacy of the FITD tactic. They noted that because nearly all of the previous research on the topic failed to measure changes in self-perception directly, valid conclusions regarding self-perception as a mediator could not be drawn. In an experiment using private compliance as the dependent variable—a measure more sensitive to mediation by self-perception processes than public compliance—the researchers found that increases in participants' perceptions of their own helpfulness following fulfillment of an initial request did not lead to increased compliance with a second request. Employing somewhat more sensitive and reliable measures of self-perception change, Burger & Caldwell (2003) conducted a conceptually similar study, and found that participants' compliance rates were in fact mediated by one dimension of a self-rated helpfulness scale administered immediately after the initial compliance. One possible explanation for these discrepant outcomes is that situational variables within each set of experiments may have motivated participants to be consistent with their own trait attributions to different extents; individual differences may have played a role as well.

Cialdini et al. (1995) argued that dispositional tendencies toward consistent responding might moderate the degree to which individuals behave in line with predictions made by consistency theories; they developed the Preference for Consistency (PFC) scale to measure such a construct. The researchers showed that only those who scored high on the PFC scale complied in accordance with consistency-based theories, including FITD. They concluded that individuals high in PFC are more consistent than those low in PFC in that they are more likely to determine their reactions to novel stimuli by relating the incoming information to already established information, such as pre-existing attitudes, prior behaviors, and commitments. Guadagno et al. (2001) found that focusing low-PFC participants on their prior helpfulness actually reduced the likelihood of their compliance on the subsequent request. The authors suggest that those low in PFC may have exhibited the backfire effect because they have a greater desire to act inconsistently with previous behaviors, specifically when those prior actions have been made salient.

Together, these findings both bolster the notion of self-perception as a mediator of the FITD effect and suggest its potential limitations (Guadagno et al. 2001). The results of these studies indicate that simply engaging in self-perception processes may not be sufficient to produce the FITD effect; rather, one must also have the motivation to be consistent with this self-view (Cialdini et al. 1995, Gorassini & Olson 1995, Guadagno et al. 2001).

Since the technique's initial demonstration, the archetypical foot-in-the-door study has involved observing an individual's response to a truly desired request after the person not only attempts, but also successfully completes, an initial task. However, Dolinski (2000) demonstrated that the self-inference process could operate to produce a significant FITD effect even in situations in which one's earnest attempt to fulfill a request fails. He concluded that the focus of our self-inferences is on the processes associated with the compliance attempt itself, rather than on the outcome of that attempt.

It is also noteworthy that Dolinski (2000) found that both those who succeeded and those who failed to accomplish the initial favor tended to rate themselves as more submissive, but not more altruistic, than controls when surveyed later. This is inconsistent with the results of Gorassini & Olson (1995), in which an increase in self-rated helpfulness, but no parallel increase in self-rated submissiveness, was found in a strong FITD manipulation versus a control condition. Furthermore, Burger & Caldwell (2003) found that enhanced compliance was related to the Providing Support dimension of participants' self-rated helpfulness scores, and not those related to Volunteering or Feeling Compassion. Although the disparities in self-rating scores across these three studies are less than comparable because of their measurement as well as methodological differences, it nonetheless underscores the fact that researchers have yet to uncover the exact nature of the self-inferences that lead individuals to comply with a subsequent request. Future consideration should be given to the investigation of the extent to which individuals are focusing on each of three domains—their general dispositions, their actions, or their attitudes toward relevant issues (Burger & Caldwell 2003)—when undergoing self-perception processes in compliance situations.

Of course, self-perception and consistency motives may not be the only processes mediating FITD, nor may they even be the strongest (Burger & Caldwell 2003). Burger (1999) identified several other variables that had bearing on the size and direction of FITD effects, such as conformity, attributions, and commitments. In addition, certain factors may cause boomerang effects. For instance, resistance is especially likely if the same person makes both requests with little or no delay in between, presumably because the norm of reciprocity dictates that after the target agrees to a request, it would be out of turn for the influence agent to make a new one (Burger 1999, Chartrand et al. 1999). It is quite possible, for example, that Gorassini & Olson (1995) found no increase in private compliance in the FITD condition—despite an increase in self-rated helpfulness—because the same individual (i.e., the experimenter) made both requests within a relatively short period of time, thereby instigating norm-based resistance to compliance with the second request.

CONSISTENCY AND COMMITMENT   Individuals are driven to be consistent not only with their trait self-attributions, but with their previous behaviors and commitments as well. The extent to which one's commitments are made actively is one powerful determinant of the likelihood of request compliance (Cialdini & Trost 1998). For example, Cioffi & Garner (1996) solicited volunteers for an AIDS awareness project by asking participants to indicate their decisions on a form in either an active or passive manner. Irrespective of their choice, participants who made an active rather than a passive choice took a more extreme position toward their decision (even weeks later) and were more likely to show up if they had agreed to volunteer. In support of a self-perception analysis of active commitments, the authors found that more effortful displays of one's choice spurred individuals to attribute their decisions to their traits, attitudes, and tendencies (as opposed to self-presentational concerns) to a much greater extent than those who made passive commitments.

Public commitments also tend to be more persistent than private commitments (Cialdini & Trost 1998). Car salespeople regularly utilize strategies, such as the low-ball technique, that take advantage of our motivation to act consistently with our prior public commitments. An influence agent employing this tactic first offers an acceptable deal to the target. Once a target's commitment to the proposal has been secured, the cost of carrying out the deal is substantially increased (Cialdini et al. 1978). In the case of car sales, the technique is successful because prospective buyers face their own commitments to the requester and perhaps to themselves when deciding whether or not to accept the modified deal. The success of the low-ball technique has been demonstrated among equal-status laypeople in nonconsumer domains as well (e.g., Guégen et al. 2002). Burger & Cornelius (2003) revealed that the public nature of the commitment is the keystone of the low-ball technique's efficacy. They found that relative to a control request, a low-ball procedure eliciting a public commitment demonstrated enhanced compliance, whereas compliance rates declined when the requester made no attempt to obtain a public commitment before revealing the true cost of request fulfillment.

A core assumption regarding the success of consistency-based compliance techniques is that targets act consistently with their self-views and prior commitments in order to serve the ultimate motivation of maintaining or enhancing their self-esteem. It stands to reason, then, that individuals whose cultures place less of an emphasis on self-concept positivity and related maintenance and enhancement goals (such as Japan; for a review, see Heine et al. 1999) may be less susceptible to tactics that exploit these motivations. Furthermore, the importance and meaning of self-consistency as a general notion varies considerably among different cultures. For example, in cultures characterized by greater levels of interdependence, people are more likely to view their actions as being driven by their roles and others' expectations rather than by internal attributes (cf. Heine & Lehman 1997). In a demonstration of this principle, Cialdini et al. (1999) examined in two cultures the degree to which compliance decisions are steered by the desire to act in accordance with one's prior responses to comparable requests. They found that consistency needs had a greater influence on participants in an individualistic country (the United States) than in a collectivistic country (Poland); it is notable, however, that these differences were in large part due to participants' personal individualistic-collectivistic orientations. Because much of the field's knowledge of compliance is primarily based on North American participants, future research in this area is necessary to redress this imbalance.

CONFORMITY

Conformity refers to the act of changing one's behavior to match the responses of others. Nearly half a century ago, Deutsch & Gerard (1955) distinguished between informational and normative conformity motivations, the former based on the desire to form an accurate interpretation of reality and behave correctly, and the latter based on the goal of obtaining social approval from others. The extant literature has upheld the conceptual independence of each of these motivational factors (see Cialdini & Trost 1998), although the two are interrelated and often difficult to disentangle theoretically as well as empirically (David & Turner 2001). In addition, both accuracy- and affiliation-oriented goals act in service of a third underlying motive to maintain one's self-concept, both via self-esteem protection as well as self-categorization processes.

Goal of Accuracy

Research on accuracy as a central motivation for conformity has examined the phenomenon in some diverse and relatively unexplored domains. Investigators, for example, have demonstrated that individuals may conform to information supplied by a group of confederates when reconstructing their memories for stimuli (Meade & Roediger 2002, Walther et al. 2002, Wright et al. 2000). As another example, Castelli et al. (2001) explored the types of people we look to for valid information under uncertainty. They showed that participants were more likely to conform to (and implicitly view as more accurate) the objective estimates of a confederate who earlier used stereotype-consistent (versus stereotype-inconsistent) traits to describe an outgroup member, even though they publicly expressed little faith in the confederate's judgments.

Quinn & Schlenker (2002) proposed that a strong accuracy goal could counteract the normative pressures individuals face when making a decision for which they are accountable (i.e., must be prepared to explain their decision) to a set of people whose views on the issue are known. The dominant response of individuals in this situation is to conform to the audience's position (Lerner & Tetlock 1999, Pennington & Schlenker 1999), a consequence that often stems from the desire to gain the approval of the people to whom the individuals are answerable (Quinn & Schlenker 2002). The authors theorized that because being accountable for one's actions tends to highlight the importance of the task (Lerner & Tetlock 1999) and amplify the salience of one's goals irrespective of the orientations of those goals (Schlenker & Weigold 1989), only those primed with a motivation to make accurate decisions and who were held accountable for their judgments would resist pressures to conform to the audience's known but flawed decision. The results confirmed the hypothesis. Although participants in this study were accountable to only a single individual, it does suggest conditions characterized by accountability and salient accuracy goals may create the most suitable environment for the promotion of independent decision-making, even in cases in which the individual is accountable to an entire group of people and the consensus for an opposing position is high.

PERCEIVED CONSENSUS   How we react to beliefs held by others is often contingent on our perceptions of the level of consensus for those beliefs. Social psychologists have continued to investigate how individuals differentially process messages associated with numerical majorities and minorities and to explore the extent to which normative and informational influences govern motivations to conform to each type of source. The two most prominent theories, Moscovici's (1980) conversion theory and Mackie's (1987) objective consensus approach, differ in their interpretation of the influences exerted by majorities and minorities in terms of cognitive and motivational processes. Simply put, conversion theory suggests that majority influence is normative, whereas the objective consensus account views it as informational.

Recently, Erb et al. (2002) addressed this apparent incompatibility by considering individuals' prior attitudes toward the relevant influence topic. The researchers found that when the target's previously formed opinion is strongly opposed to the message being conveyed, the recipient's motivation to avoid deviance from the majority group will hamper message elaboration (unless a target's self-interest is specifically threatened) (Martin & Hewstone 2001) and instead focus the individual on the normative concerns of fitting in, a process consistent with conversion theory. On the other hand, when recipients hold moderately opposing attitudes toward the message topic, they are more receptive to the position endorsed by the majority, and therefore more likely to engage in extensive processing of the message and see the group with the numerically superior advantage as representing an objective consensus; this finding is congruent with Mackie's (1987) account. When both the source and the issue were of low relevance to targets holding no prior attitudes on the subject, the targets applied little cognitive effort to process the message, often using an accuracy heuristic favoring the majority (Erb et al. 1998).

Although the topic has been eliciting greater attention in recent years, the effects of perceived consensus on individuals' intergroup attitudes and behaviors, such as prejudice, stereotyping, and discrimination, has been a relatively underserved area of conformity research (Crandall et al. 2002, Stangor et al. 2001). Crandall et al. (2002) advocated a return to a social normative approach to study the phenomenon, finding an almost perfect correlation between individuals' likelihood of expressing or tolerating prejudice and their perceptions of the extent to which most others approve of those behaviors. Sechrist & Stangor (2001) found that higher prejudiced participants sat at a greater distance from an African American confederate than did those lower prejudiced participants; most interesting, however, was the finding that this difference was heightened when the participants learned that their attitudes were shared by a clear majority of other individuals.

Presumably, normative influences were the primary motivational forces operating in the aforementioned studies, indicating to the participants the kinds of beliefs that are generally accepted and encouraged by the majority. However, the perception of a consensus among group members' intergroup attitudes and behaviors is certain to exert an informational influence as well. Consistent with this suggestion, researchers have demonstrated that confidence in the accuracy of one's intergroup beliefs over time is a positively related function of the perceived level of consensus (cf. Stangor et al. 2001). Other researchers (e.g., Schaller & Latané 1996) have examined the consensually shared nature of stereotypes in more dynamic environments. Kenrick et al. (2002) suggest that the kinds of stereotypes that are most communicable (and therefore most likely to be shared) are those that provide accurate, functional information relevant to vital social motivations such as self-protection.

DYNAMICAL SYSTEMS   Much like the majority of social psychological research, traditional investigations of conformity phenomena have been dominated by static social influence environments described by relatively microlevel theories (Vallacher et al. 2003). Recent years, however, have been marked by an increased emphasis on the processes that drive conformity in more fluid, complex systems and on the group-level consequences of dynamic behavior and belief shifts over time. Based on the more unidimensional social impact theory (SIT; Latané 1981), Latané developed dynamic social impact theory (DSIT; 1996) to explain the higher-order processes that emerge over time from local-level conformity within multiple-person assemblages of varying sizes, functions, complexities, and levels of interpersonal interaction. One of the central postulates on which the theory is founded is that, all else being equal, an individual occupying a given social space will be more likely to conform to the attitudes, beliefs, and behavioral propensities exhibited by the local numerical majority than by either the local numerical minority (for exceptions, see Nowak & Vallacher 2001) or less proximate persons. Influence at the local levels may be informational, normative, or both. The model predicts four core forms of self-organization emerging within the aggregate: (*a*) clustering of attitudes (or opinions, behavioral tendencies, etc.) in social space; (*b*) a reduction in diversity via a consolidation of attitudes; (*c*) correlations across attitudes possessed by cluster members; and (*d*) continuing diversity (i.e., lack of complete convergence) of attitudes. Regarding this last point, clusters of individuals sharing the minority attitude rarely dissolve because each member of that cluster is surrounded by a local numerical majority of individuals holding that same minority attitude; that is, as a general rule, the self-reinforcing nature of clusters tends to perpetuate their existence once they are formed.

Computer simulations, the most common methodology utilized to assess the validity of the theory's assertions, have provided much support for DSIT and related dynamical systems theories (Nowak & Vallacher 1998). Experimental, archival, and field study data also confirm the predictions laid out by these models (Bourgeois 2002). Dynamical systems theories have also successfully modeled large-scale societal transitions, such as the economic and political transformations that occurred in Poland after the fall of Communism (Nowak & Vallacher 2001). Recent efforts to integrate dynamical systems and evolutionary psychological perspectives have also proved fruitful in understanding the emergence of both universal as well as culture-specific functional social norms (Kenrick et al. 2002), an area that will likely be of burgeoning interest to social psychologists in the future.

AUTOMATIC ACTIVATION   Up to this point, we have reported on conformity research in which the motivation to conform to others is initiated, at least to some degree, within the target's awareness. Conformity may also be the product of the less mindful activation of accuracy- or affiliation-oriented goals, providing an adaptive shortcut that maximizes the likelihood of effective action with minimal expense to one's cognitive resources (Chartrand & Bargh 1999). Epley & Gilovich (1999) demonstrated that individuals primed with words conceptually related to conformity were more likely than those primed with neutral words to adhere to subjective evaluations made by a group of confederates. Participants primed with nonconformity terms, however, were no more likely to deviate from the confederates' responses than those primed with neutral terms. Yet, in a theoretically similar experiment, Pendry & Carrick (2001) found that participants primed with a nonconformist association (skinhead punk) or a conformist association (accountant) were respectively less or more likely to conform to others' objective judgments relative to a control; but the effects of the nonconformist prime were stronger. The observed asymmetries in priming effects both within and between the two studies suggests that future investigations into the automatic activation of conformity-related goals should give careful consideration to participants' semantic interpretations of the stimuli used to represent intended priming constructs.

Goal of Affiliation

BEHAVIORAL MIMICRY   Interest has resurged in a conformity phenomenon known as behavioral mimicry, which appears to operate completely outside of conscious awareness. Also dubbed the chameleon effect, the term describes behavior matching of postures, facial expressions, vocal characteristics, and mannerisms that occurs between two or more individuals (Chartrand & Bargh 1999).

Chartrand & Bargh (1999) found that participants nonconsciously conformed their facial expressions and mannerisms to closely mirror a confederate's gestures. In addition, individuals exposed to an interaction partner who mimicked their behaviors increased their affinity for that person, which suggests that the process is functional in building rapport and promoting the development of social relationships (Chartrand & Bargh 1999; see also Hess et al. 1999). The authors argued that the mediating mechanism responsible for the effect is the perception-behavior link (see Dijksterhuis & Bargh 2001). That is, individuals' perceptual representations of others' behaviors nonconsciously and directly activate mannerism-specific behavioral representations that manifest themselves in the individuals' mimicking actions. Thus, behavior matching is more likely to occur in circumstances that enhance a would-be imitator's attentional focus on others (Gump & Kulik 1997) and less likely to occur in situations that diminish external focus (Sanchez-Burks 2002) or specifically motivate internal focus (Johnston 2002).

Although the evidence suggests that the direct link from perception to behavior operates irrespective of the motivation to affiliate (Chartrand & Bargh 1999), Lakin & Chartrand (2003) reasoned that the effects of behavioral mimicry might be amplified in circumstances in which that goal was activated. The researchers triggered individuals' affiliation goals via either explicit (expected interaction) or implicit (priming) methods. They found that regardless of whether the participants were consciously aware of these goals, those motivated to affiliate mimicked the behaviors of a confederate to a greater extent than those in the control condition. Furthermore, a second study revealed that the chameleon effect and its subsequent impact on rapport building were augmented when participants' nonconscious goals to affiliate were first thwarted. Thus, it appears likely that relationship-oriented objectives do play a part in many of our everyday experiences with behavioral mimicry. Lakin & Chartrand (2003) proposed that ephemeral affiliation desires briefly strengthen the perception-behavior link because of increased attention to relevant environmental stimuli, an explanation that can be extended to more chronic affiliative goals as well (Chartrand & Bargh 1999).

GAINING SOCIAL APPROVAL   Unlike the subtleties characteristic of behavioral mimicry, individuals often engage in more conscious and deliberate attempts to gain the social approval of others, to build rewarding relationships with them, and in the process, to enhance their self-esteem. Conformity offers such an opportunity, although the extent to which the phenomenon is not only socially prescribed, but also normatively embraced, differs across cultures. In a meta-analysis of conformity studies employing Asch-like line judgment tasks, Bond & Smith (1996) showed that residents of collectivist countries were more inclined to conform to the estimates of a group of confederates than were residents of individualistic countries. Similarly, Cialdini et al. (1999) found that when considering whether to comply with a request, participants were more likely in a collectivistic country (Poland) than in an individualistic country (the United States) to base their decisions on the actions of their peers. Kim & Markus (1999) argued that cultures assign very different meanings to the concepts of conformity and nonconformity; specifically, nonconformity represents deviance in East Asian cultures but uniqueness in Western cultures. The authors demonstrated that the culturally assigned meanings attached to these concepts are evident in each culture's respective magazine ads, and manifested themselves in participants' preferences and choices for objects. For example, when asked to make a selection out of an array containing pens of two colors—one color in the majority and the other color in the minority—East Asians tended to pick the pen characterized by the majority color, whereas Americans were inclined to choose the pen marked by the less common color.

Researchers have also continued to investigate the extent to which affiliation and self-image enhancement goals are activated and strengthened when an individual's self-esteem is threatened by the prospect (or actual occurrence) of not fitting in with the group. Tafarodi et al. (2002) argued that racial minorities who possess bicultural identities and who are oriented toward personal cultural integration with or assimilation by the host culture carry with them the burden of knowing that their physical appearance may designate them for social exclusion by the majority. They reported that Chinese Canadian participants were more likely to conform their subjective judgments of artwork to those made by European Canadians (but not other Chinese Canadians) only after viewing their own reflections in a mirror; the data suggest normative motives, in particular, had been activated. Williams et al. (2000) demonstrated the potent influence of overt social exclusion over the Internet, a domain whose inherent anonymity suggests the negative effects of ostracism might be attenuated. Despite the potentially mitigating role of privacy, the authors nonetheless found that participants who were ignored in a virtual ball toss game were more likely to report lower self-esteem and a greater need for belongingness, and conformed more to the judgments of a completely different group in a later task. It is also clear that individuals need not suffer rejection nor ridicule from others firsthand in order to actively (but not necessarily consciously) pursue goals related to social approval and self-esteem via conformity. For example, in one study, participants who watched a videotape in which a person humorously ridiculed another were more inclined than those who viewed other scenes (i.e., no humorous ridicule or a person engaging in humorous self-ridicule) to match their opinions to those of other ostensible participants (Janes & Olson 2000). Taken together, these results suggest that even when not directly, personally, or publicly the target of others' disapproval, individuals may be driven to conform to restore their sense of belonging and their self-esteem.

Goal of Maintaining a Positive Self-Concept

As we have already described, people are frequently motivated to conform to others' beliefs and behaviors in order to enhance, protect, or repair their self-esteems. Following this logic, one way to combat conformity behavior might be to affirm individuals' self-concepts. Accordingly, one study revealed that individuals who focused on a fundamental foundation of their self-worth, such as a self-attribute, were less likely to conform later to others' opinions than were control condition participants or those who focused on an external source of self-esteem, such as an achievement (Arndt et al. 2002).

Deviating from the attitudes and actions of others at times may also act in service of these self-esteem-related goals by helping to provide individuals with a sense of uniqueness and personal identity (Blanton & Christie 2003, Kim & Markus 1999, Nail et al. 2000). Yet, individuals also maintain positive self-assessments by identifying with and conforming to valued groups (Brewer & Roccas 2001, Pool et al. 1998). This latter point provides the basis for the self-categorization perspective on majority and minority influence, as well as recent research on deindividuation effects on conformity.

MAJORITY AND MINORITY INFLUENCE   The extent to which one identifies with a message source—be it a majority or a minority—is a significant factor in determining the information processing strategies one employs as well as the outcome of an influence attempt (David & Turner 2001). One view of majority and minority influence that appears to be garnering increasing interest and support is the self-categorization perspective (Turner 1985). Self-categorization theory holds that the conventional distinction between informational and normative influence creates a false dichotomy because the two processes are interrelated in most cases; normativeness implies accuracy, and vice versa (David & Turner 2001). The theory posits that individuals categorize themselves at varying degrees of abstraction, and use their social identities to reduce uncertainty when faced with prospective group conflict. In support of self-categorization considerations, the classic effects of majority and minority influence have been found only in situations in which the source is an ingroup member. When they are outgroup members, irrespective of source status, participants tend to engage in no attitude change (Alvaro & Crano 1997) or to move their opinions in the direction opposite of the advocated position (David & Turner 1996).

David & Turner (1999) argued that when an ingroup minority attempts to persuade a target, the message recipient becomes pressured to provide a direct and public response within a short period. The situational forces that characterize the interaction highlight for the target the divergence between the ingroup majority position, which connotes correctness, and the argument advanced by the ingroup minority. When the immediacy and public nature of the circumstances is no longer pressing, and the salience of that prior conflict wanes, the target's frame of reference expands to incorporate the outgroup, leading the target to perceive the ingroup minority as similar to the self. The target is then more likely to manifest these perspective changes (and the subsequent influence of the ingroup minority) on delayed, private, and less direct measures. Several studies yielded indirect evidence consistent with their account (David & Turner 1999).

Also based on the notion that targets often share a common identity with the minority group, Alvaro & Crano (1997) suggested that an ingroup minority provokes indirect change—that is, change in a target's attitude toward matters related to the focal issue, but not toward the focal issue itself—because the message recipient (*a*) elaborately processes the information because of its distinctive source, (*b*) wishes to avoid identification with the source, (*c*) is motivated not to denigrate the source or counterargue the message in the name of ingroup solidarity, and (*d*) experiences an imbalance in the system of beliefs surrounding his or her focal attitude. The target works within these constraints to resolve the destabilization of the relevant cognitive constellation by changing his or her attitude on interrelated issues rather than on the focal issue, which reduces tension by restoring stability to the belief structure (Alvaro & Crano 1997). Crano & Chen (1998) proposed that this shift in related attitudes would provoke a further cognitive imbalance between the newly changed related attitudes and the unmoved focal attitude; this cognitive incongruence would be redressed over time by eventually changing one's focal attitude to comport with the recently shifted attitudes. Crano and colleagues (Alvaro

& Crano 1997, Crano & Chen 1998) found strong correlational support for these hypotheses.

DEINDIVIDUATION EFFECTS   Self-categorization theory has also been offered as an explanation for conformity-related deindividuation phenomena in the form of the Social Identity model for Deindividuation Effects (SIDE; Reicher et al. 1995). The SIDE model distinguishes itself from classical deindividuation accounts in that "responsiveness to a group norm is not a mindless or irrational process reflecting a reduced sense of self . . . but may be a conscious and rational process relating to a meaningful sense of identity" (Spears et al. 2001, p. 336). In support of the predictions laid out by the SIDE model, a meta-analysis conducted by Postmes & Spears (1998) revealed that rather than engage in antinormative activities, individuals subjected to deindividuation procedures instead conformed their behaviors to local, situation-specific norms defined by the group identity.

Computer-mediated communication, a context capable of creating anonymity and physical isolation, has been the favored paradigm for investigating the SIDE model (Spears et al. 2001). Using this setting, Postmes et al. (2001) showed that members of anonymous groups unwittingly primed with a particular group norm were more likely to follow (and socially transmit) that norm than were members of identifiable groups, an effect mediated by their identification with the group. It is noteworthy, however, that these behaviors are related to cognitive processes rather than strategic motives, in which self-presentational concerns would be paramount. Thus, the differential effects of anonymity and identifiability may be reversed—that is, identifiable individuals may be more likely to adhere to group norms than anonymous individuals—when group members face social sanctions for norm deviance (Sassenberg & Postmes 2002).

Visually anonymous groups have also been found to engage in greater group-related self-categorization, which serves to augment affiliative factors such as group attraction both directly and indirectly (Lea et al. 2001; but see Sassenberg & Postmes 2002). In further support of the SIDE account, common-identity groups (in which members perceive a common social identity with the entire group) exhibit greater group salience and are more likely to induce conformity to group norms than are common-bond groups (characterized by bonds between individual group members) when members are anonymous (Sassenberg 2002); some evidence suggests that the opposite may be true when members are identifiable (Spears et al. 2001).

CONCLUSION

In our review of the current literature, we emphasized three core motivations that provide the bases for targets' responses to influence attempts: accuracy, affiliation, and the maintenance of a positive self-concept. For clarity and ease of treatment, we associated each social influence–related phenomenon with whichever goal appeared to be the principal driving force underlying the occurrence of that phenomenon. However, it should be noted that targets' behaviors often serve multiple goals. For example, self-categorization theory holds that conforming to valued ingroup members may fulfill all three goals. We also examined the extent to which targets were mindful of the activation of these goals and of external influences in general, finding that recent research has tended to favor social influence processes that are subtle, indirect, heuristic-based, and outside of awareness. This is consistent with the recent movement in social psychology toward the demonstration of nonconscious goal activation and automaticity in everyday life (e.g., Bargh & Chartrand 1999). We expect this trend will persist in future years.

It is noteworthy that although this review has focused almost exclusively on recent developments in the areas of compliance and conformity, many of the field's classic investigations are relevant in today's research, albeit in different forms. A great deal of empirical work continues to explore the mediators and moderators of traditional compliance tactics, such as the foot-in-the-door and the door-in-the-face techniques. The early work on conformity conducted by Asch (1956) and Deutsch & Gerard (1955) has made a lasting contribution to our understanding of how multiple goals operate in social influence settings. And Milgram's (1974) research on obedience to authority continues to spur debate on several levels, including interpretation of the original results, questions of external validity, ethical concerns, and issues relating to the presentation of the material to others.

Although social influence research appears to be firmly embedded in its historical roots, it has not remained stagnant. Investigators have employed new methodologies to clarify the mechanisms operating in traditional phenomena, proposed integrative theories and models of social influence (see Nail et al. 2000, MacDonald et al. 2003, Vallacher et al. 2003), and begun to examine relatively unexplored topics, such as resistance-related influence strategies, dynamical systems, and cross-cultural research. In sum, the evidence suggests that scholarly work in compliance and conformity research will be a source of clarification, innovation, and lively deliberation for years to come.

ACKNOWLEDGMENTS

Preparation of this chapter was supported by a National Science Foundation Graduate Research Fellowship provided to the second author. We gratefully acknowledge Jenessa Shapiro, Jon Maner, and Christopher Wilbur for their very valuable comments on an earlier version of the manuscript.

The *Annual Review of Psychology* is online at http://psych.annualreviews.org

LITERATURE CITED

Alvaro EM, Crano WD. 1997. Indirect minority influence: evidence for leniency in source evaluation and counterargumentation. *J. Personal. Soc. Psychol.* 72:949–64

Arndt J, Schimel J, Greenberg J, Pyszczynski T. 2002. The intrinsic self and defensiveness: evidence that activating the intrinsic self reduces self-handicapping and conformity. *Personal. Soc. Psychol. Bull.* 28:671–83

Asch SE. 1956. Studies of independence and conformity: a minority of one against a unanimous majority. *Psychol. Monogr.* 70:(9) Whole No. 416

Ashford BE, Anand V. 2003. The normalization of corruption in organizations. In *Research in Organizational Behavior*, ed. BM Staw, RM Kramer, Vol. 25. Greenwich, CT: JAI. In press

Bargh JA, Chartrand TL. 1999. The unbearable automaticity of being. *Am. Psychol.* 54:462–79

Bem DJ. 1972. Self-perception theory. In *Advances in Experimental Social Psychology*, ed. L Berkowitz, 6:1–62. New York: Academic

Berkowitz L. 1999. Evil is more than banal: situationism and the concept of evil. *Personal. Soc. Psychol. Rev.* 3:246–53

Blanton H, Christie C. 2003. Deviance regulation: a theory of identity and action. *Rev. Gen. Psychol.* 7:115–49

Blass T. 1999. The Milgram paradigm after 35 years: some things we now know about obedience to authority. *J. Appl. Soc. Psychol.* 29:955–78

Bond R, Smith PB. 1996. Culture and conformity: a meta-analysis of studies using Asch's (1952, 1956) line judgment task. *Psychol. Bull.* 119:111–37

Boster FJ, Mitchell MM, Lapinski MK, Cooper H, Orrego VO, Rienke R. 1999. The impact of guilt and type of compliance-gaining message on compliance. *Commun. Monogr.* 66:168–77

Bourgeois MJ. 2002. Heritability of attitudes constrains dynamic social impact. *Personal. Soc. Psychol. Bull.* 28:1063–72

Brewer MB, Roccas S. 2001. Individual values, social identity, and optimal distinctiveness. In *Individual, Self, Relational Self, Collective Self*, ed. C Sedikides, MB Brewer, pp. 219–37. Philadelphia, PA: Psychology Press

Brief AP, Buttram RT, Dukerich JM. 2001. Collective corruption in the corporate world: toward a process model. In *Groups at Work: Advances in Theory and Research*, ed. ME Turner, pp. 471–99. Hillsdale, NJ: Erlbaum

Brief AP, Buttram RT, Elliot JD, Reizenstein RM, McCline RL. 1995. Releasing the beast: a study of compliance with orders to use race as a selection criterion. *J. Soc. Issues* 51:177–94

Burger JM. 1986. Increasing compliance by improving the deal: the that's-not-all technique. *J. Personal. Soc. Psychol.* 51:277–83

Burger JM. 1999. The foot-in-the-door compliance procedure: a multiple-process analysis and review. *Personal. Soc. Psychol. Rev.* 3:303–25

Burger JM, Caldwell DF. 2003. The effects of monetary incentives and labeling on the foot-in-the-door effect: evidence for a self-perception process. *Basic Appl. Soc. Psychol.* 25:235–41

Burger JM, Cornelius T. 2003. Raising the price of agreement: public commitment and the low-ball compliance procedure. *J. Appl. Soc. Psychol.* In press

Burger JM, Guadagno RE. 2003. Self-concept clarity and the foot-in-the-door procedure. *Basic Appl. Soc. Psychol.* 25:79–86

Burger JM, Horita M, Kinoshita L, Roberts K, Vera C. 1997. Effects of time on the norm reciprocity. *Basic Appl. Soc. Psychol.* 19:91–100

Burger JM, Messian N, Patel S, del Prado A, Anderson C. 2003. What a coincidence! The effects of incidental similarity on compliance. *Personal. Soc. Psychol. Bull.* In press

Burger JM, Reed M, DeCesare K, Rauner S, Rozolios J. 1999. The effect of initial request size on compliance: more about the that's-not-all technique. *Basic Appl. Soc. Psychol.* 21:243–49

Burger JM, Soroka S, Gonzago K, Murphy E, Somervell E. 2001. The effect of fleeting attraction on compliance to requests. *Personal. Soc. Psychol. Bull.* 27:1578–86

Campbell JD, Trapnell PD, Heine SJ, Katz IM, Lavellee LF, Lehman DR. 1996. Self-concept clarity: measurement, personality correlates, and cultural boundaries. *J. Personal. Soc. Psychol.* 59:538–49

Castelli L, Vanzetto K, Sherman SJ, Arcuri L. 2001. The explicit and implicit perception of in-group members who use stereotypes: blatant rejection but subtle conformity. *J. Exp. Soc. Psychol.* 37:419–26

Chartrand TL, Bargh JA. 1999. The chameleon effect: the perception-behavior link and social interaction. *J. Personal. Soc. Psychol.* 76: 893–910

Chartrand TL, Pinckert S, Burger JM. 1999. When manipulation backfires: the effects of time delay and requester on the foot-in-the-door technique. *J. Appl. Soc. Psychol.* 29: 211–21

Cialdini RB. 2001. *Influence: Science and Practice.* Boston, MA: Allyn & Bacon. 4th ed.

Cialdini RB. 2003. Crafting normative messages to protect the environment. *Curr. Dir. Psychol. Sci.* 12:105–9

Cialdini RB, Cacioppo JT, Bassett R, Miller JA. 1978. Low-ball procedure for producing compliance: commitment then cost. *J. Personal. Soc. Psychol.* 36:463–76

Cialdini RB, Goldstein NJ. 2002. The science and practice of persuasion. *Cornell Hotel Restaur. Adm. Q.* 43:40–50

Cialdini RB, Kallgren CA, Reno RR. 1991. A focus theory of normative conduct: a theoretical refinement and reevaluation of the role of norms in human behavior. In *Advances in Experimental Social Psychology,* ed. MP Zanna, 24:201–34. San Diego, CA: Academic

Cialdini RB, Trost MR. 1998. Social influence: social norms, conformity, and compliance. In *The Handbook of Social Psychology,* ed. DT Gilbert, ST Fiske, G Lindzey, 2:151–92. Boston: McGraw-Hill. 4th ed.

Cialdini RB, Trost MR, Newsom JT. 1995. Preference for consistency: the development of a valid measure and the discovery of surprising behavioral implications. *J. Personal. Soc. Psychol.* 69:318–28

Cialdini RB, Vincent JE, Lewis SK, Catalan J, Wheeler D, Darby BL. 1975. Reciprocal concessions procedure for inducing compliance: the door-in-the-face technique. *J. Personal. Soc. Psychol.* 31:206–15

Cialdini RB, Wosinska W, Barrett DW, But-

ner J, Gornik-Durose M. 1999. Compliance with a request in two cultures: the differential influence of social proof and commitment/consistency on collectivists and individualists. *Personal. Soc. Psychol. Bull.* 25:1242–53

Cioffi D, Garner R. 1996. On doing the decision: effects of active versus passive choice on commitment and self-perception. *Personal. Soc. Psychol. Bull.* 22:133–44

Crandall CS, Eshleman A, O'Brien L. 2002. Social norms and the expression and suppression of prejudice: the struggle for internalization. *J. Personal. Soc. Psychol.* 82:359–78

Crano WD, Chen X. 1998. The leniency contract and persistence of majority and minority influence. *J. Personal. Soc. Psychol.* 74:1437–50

Cross SE, Madson L. 1997. Models of the self: self-construals and gender. *Psychol. Bull.* 122:5–37

Darley JM. 1995. Constructive and destructive obedience: a taxonomy of principal-agent relationships. *J. Soc. Issues* 51:125–54

Darley JM. 2001. The dynamics of authority in organization. See Darley et al. 2001, pp. 37–52

Darley JM, Messick DM, Tyler TR, eds. 2001. *Social Influences on Ethical Behavior in Organizations.* Mahwah, NJ/London: Erlbaum

David B, Turner JC. 1996. Studies in self-categorization and minority conversion: Is being a member of the outgroup an advantage? *Br. J. Soc. Psychol.* 35:179–200

David B, Turner JC. 1999. Studies in self-categorization and minority conversion: the ingroup minority in intragroup and intergroup contexts. *Br. J. Soc. Psychol.* 38:115–34

David B, Turner JC. 2001. Majority and minority influence: a single process self-categorization analysis. In *Group Consensus and Minority Influence: Implications for Innovation,* ed. CKW De Dreu, NK De Vries, pp. 91–121. Malden, MA: Blackwell

Davis BP, Knowles ES. 1999. A disrupt-then-reframe technique of social influence. *J. Personal. Soc. Psychol.* 76:192–99

Deutsch M, Gerard HB. 1955. A study of normative and informative social influences upon individual judgment. *J. Abnorm. Soc. Psychol.* 51:629–36

Dijksterhuis A, Bargh JA. 2001. The perception-behavior expressway: automatic effects of social perception on social behavior. In *Advances in Experimental Social Psychology*, ed. MP Zanna, 33:1–40. San Diego, CA: Academic

Dillard JP, Hunter JE, Burgoon M. 1984. Sequential-request persuasive strategies: meta-analysis of foot-in-the-door and door-in-the-face. *Hum. Commun. Res.* 10:461–88

Dolinski D. 2000. On inferring one's beliefs from one's attempt and consequences for subsequent compliance. *J. Personal. Soc. Psychol.* 78:260–72

Dolinski D, Nawrat M. 1998. "Fear-then-relief" procedure for producing compliance: beware when the danger is over. *J. Exp. Soc. Psychol.* 34:27–50

Dolinski D, Nawrat M, Rudak I. 2001. Dialogue involvement as a social influence technique. *Personal. Soc. Psychol. Bull.* 27:1395–406

Elms AC. 1995. Obedience in retrospect. *J. Soc. Issues* 51:21–32

Emans BJM, Munduate L, Klaver E, van de Vliert E. 2003. Constructive consequences of leaders' forcing influence styles. *Appl. Psychol.: Int. Rev.* 52:36–54

Epley N, Gilovich T. 1999. Just going along: nonconscious priming and conformity to social pressure. *J. Exp. Soc. Psychol.* 35:578–89

Erb HP, Bohner G, Rank S, Einwiller S. 2002. Processing minority and majority communications: the role of conflict with prior attitudes. *Personal. Soc. Psychol. Bull.* 28:1172–82

Erb HP, Bohner G, Schmalzle K, Rank S. 1998. Beyond conflict and discrepancy: cognitive bias in minority and majority influence. *Personal. Soc. Psychol. Bull.* 24:620–33

Fern EF, Monroe KB, Ramon AA. 1986. Effectiveness of multiple request strategies: a synthesis of research results. *J. Mark. Res.* 23:144–52

Forgas JP. 1995. Mood and judgment: the affect infusion model (AIM). *Psychol. Bull.* 117:39–66

Forgas JP. 1998a. Asking nicely? The effects of mood on responding to more or less polite requests. *Personal. Soc. Psychol. Bull.* 24:173–85

Forgas JP. 1998b. On feeling good and getting your way: mood effects on negotiation strategies and outcomes. *J. Personal. Soc. Psychol.* 74:565–77

Forgas JP. 1999. Feeling and speaking: mood effects on verbal communication strategies. *Personal. Soc. Psychol. Bull.* 25:850–63

Forgas JP. 2001. On being moody but influential: the role of affect in social influence strategies. See Forgas & Williams 2001, pp. 147–66

Forgas JP, Williams KD, eds. 2001. *Social Influence: Direct and Indirect Processes*. Philadelphia/Hove, UK: Psychology Press

Freedman JL, Fraser SC. 1966. Compliance without pressure: the foot-in-the-door technique. *J. Personal. Soc. Psychol.* 4:195–202

French J, Raven B. 1959. The bases of social power. In *Studies in Social Power*, ed. D Cartwright, pp. 150–67. Ann Arbor, MI: Inst. Soc. Res.

Gilbert DT. 1991. How mental systems believe. *Am. Psychol.* 46:107–19

Goldhagen DJ. 1996. *Hitler's Willing Executioners: Ordinary Germans and the Holocaust*. New York: Knopf

Gorassini DR, Olson JM. 1995. Does self-perception change explain the foot-in-the-door effect? *J. Personal. Soc. Psychol.* 69:91–105

Gordon RA. 1996. Impact of ingratiation on judgments and evaluations: a meta-analytic investigation. *J. Personal. Soc. Psychol.* 71:54–70

Gouldner AW. 1960. The norm of reciprocity: a preliminary statement. *Am. Sociol. Rev.* 25:161–78

Guadagno RE, Asher T, Demaine LJ, Cialdini RB. 2001. When saying yes leads to saying no: preference for consistency and the reverse foot-in-the-door effect. *Personal. Soc. Psychol. Bull.* 27:859–67

Guéguen N, Pascual A, Dagot L. 2002. Lowball and compliance to a request: an application in a field setting. *Psychol. Rep.* 91:81–84

Gump BB, Kulik JA. 1997. Stress, affiliation, and emotional contagion. *J. Personal. Soc. Psychol.* 72:305–19

Hale JL, Laliker M. 1999. Explaining the door-in-the-face: Is it really time to abandon reciprocal concessions? *Commun. Stud.* 50:203–10

Heine SJ, Lehman DR. 1997. Culture, dissonance, and self-affirmation. *Personal. Soc. Psychol. Bull.* 23:389–400

Heine SJ, Lehman DR, Markus HR, Kitayama S. 1999. Is there a universal need for positive self-regard? *Psychol. Rev.* 106:766–94

Hess U, Philippot P, Blairy S. 1999. Mimicry: fact and fiction. In *The Social Context of Nonverbal Behavior*, ed. P Philippot, RS Feldman, EJ Coates, pp. 213–41. Cambridge, UK/New York: Cambridge Univ. Press

Howard DJ, Gengler CE, Jain A. 1995. What's in a name? A complimentary means of persuasion. *J. Consum. Res.* 22:200–11

Howard DJ, Gengler CE, Jain A. 1997. The name remembrance effect: a test of alternative explanations. *J. Soc. Behav. Personal.* 12:801–10

Janes LM, Olson JM. 2000. Jeer pressure: the behavioral effects of observing ridicule of others. *Personal. Soc. Psychol. Bull.* 26:474–85

Johnston L. 2002. Behavioral mimicry and stigmatization. *Soc. Cogn.* 20:18–35

Kahan D. 1997. Social influence, social meaning, and deterrence. *VA. Law Rev.* 83:349–95

Kallgren CA, Reno RR, Cialdini RB. 2000. A focus theory of normative conduct: when norms do and do not affect behavior. *Personal. Soc. Psychol. Bull.* 26:1002–12

Kelln BRC, Ellard JH. 1999. An equity theory analysis of the impact of forgiveness and retribution on transgressor compliance. *Personal. Soc. Psychol. Bull.* 25:864–72

Kenrick DT, Maner JK, Butner J, Li NP, Becker

DV, Schaller M. 2002. Dynamical evolutionary psychology: mapping the domains of the new interactionist paradigm. *Personal. Soc. Psychol. Rev.* 6:347–56

Kim HS, Markus HR. 1999. Deviance or uniqueness, harmony or conformity? A cultural analysis. *J. Personal. Soc. Psychol.* 77:785–800

Knowles ES, Linn JA. 2003. Approach-avoidance model of persuasion: alpha and omega strategies for change. In *Resistance and Persuasion*, ed. ES Knowles, JA Linn. Mahwah, NJ: Erlbaum. In press

Koslowsky M, Schwarzwald J. 2001. The power interaction model: theory, methodology, and empirical applications. In *The Use and Abuse of Power: Multiple Perspectives on the Causes of Corruption*, ed. AY Lee-Chai, JA Bargh, pp. 195–214. Philadelphia, PA: Psychology Press

Koslowsky M, Schwarzwald J, Ashuri S. 2001. On the relationship between subordinates' compliance to power sources and organisational attitudes. *Appl. Psychol.: Int. Rev.* 50:455–76

Lakin JL, Chartrand TL. 2003. Using nonconscious behavioral mimicry to create affiliation and rapport. *Psychol. Sci.* 14:334–39

Latané B. 1981. The psychology of social impact. *Am. Psychol.* 36:343–56

Latané B. 1996. Dynamic social impact: the creation of culture by communication. *J. Commun.* 46:13–25

Lea M, Spears R, de Groot D. 2001. Knowing me, knowing you: anonymity effects on social identity processes within groups. *Personal. Soc. Psychol. Bull.* 27:526–37

Lerner JS, Tetlock PE. 1999. Accounting for the effects of accountability. *Psychol. Bull.* 125:255–75

Lutsky N. 1995. When is "obedience" obedience? Conceptual and historical commentary. *J. Soc. Issues* 51:55–66

Lynn M, Simons T. 2000. Predictors of male and female servers' average tip earnings. *J. Appl. Soc. Psychol.* 30:241–52

MacDonald G, Nail PR, Levy DA. 2003. Expanding the scope of the social response context model. *Basic Appl. Soc. Psychol.* In press

Mackie DM. 1987. Systematic and nonsystematic processing of majority and minority persuasive communications. *J. Personal. Soc. Psychol.* 53:41–52

Martin R, Hewstone M. 2001. Determinants and consequences of cognitive processes in majority and minority influence. See Forgas & Williams 2001, pp. 315–30

McCall M. 1997. Physical attractiveness and access to alcohol: What is beautiful does not get carded. *J. Appl. Soc. Psychol.* 27:453–62

Meade ML, Roediger HL III. 2002. Explorations in the social contagion of memory. *Mem. Cogn.* 30:995–1009

Meeus WHJ, Raaijmakers QAW. 1995. Obedience in modern society: the Utrecht studies. *J. Soc. Issues* 51:155–76

Milgram S. 1974. *Obedience to Authority.* New York: Harper & Row

Millar M. 2002. Effects of a guilt induction and guilt reduction on door in the face. *Commun. Res.* 29:666–80

Miller AG. 1995. Constructions of the obedience experiments: a focus upon domains of relevance. *J. Soc. Issues* 51:33–54

Moscovici S. 1980. Toward a theory of conversion behavior. In *Advances in Experimental Social Psychology*, ed. L Berkowitz, 13:209–39. New York: Academic

Mowen JC, Cialdini RB. 1980. On implementing the door-in-the-face compliance technique in a business context. *J. Mark. Res.* 17:253–58

Nail PR, MacDonald G, Levy DA. 2000. Proposal of a four-dimensional model of social response. *Psychol. Bull.* 126:454–70

Newman LS, Erber R, eds. 2002. *Understanding Genocide: The Social Psychology of the Holocaust.* Oxford/New York: Oxford Univ. Press

Nowak A, Vallacher RR. 1998. *Dynamical Social Psychology.* New York: Guilford

Nowak A, Vallacher RR. 2001. Societal transition: toward a dynamical model of social change. In *The Practice of Social Influence in Multiple Cultures*, ed. W Wosinska, RB

Cialdini, DW Barrett, J Reykowski, pp. 151–71. Mahwah, NJ: Erlbaum

O'Keefe DJ. 1999. Three reasons for doubting the adequacy of the reciprocal concessions explanation of door-in-the-face effects. *Commun. Stud.* 50:211–20

O'Keefe DJ, Figgé M. 1997. A guilt-based explanation of the door-in-the-face influence strategy. *Hum. Commun. Res.* 24:64–81

O'Keefe DJ, Figgé M. 1999. Guilt and expected guilt in the door-in-the-face technique. *Commun. Monogr.* 66:312–24

O'Keefe DJ, Hale SL. 1998. The door-in-the-face influence strategy: a random-effects meta-analytic review. In *Communication Yearbook*, ed. ME Roloff, 21:1–33. Thousand Oaks, CA: Sage

O'Keefe DJ, Hale SL. 2001. An odds-ratio-based meta-analysis of research on the door-in-the-face influence strategy. *Commun. Rep.* 14:31–38

Pendry L, Carrick R. 2001. Doing what the mob do: priming effects on conformity. *Eur. J. Soc. Psychol.* 31:83–92

Pennington J, Schlenker BR. 1999. Accountability for consequential decisions: justifying ethical judgments to audiences. *Personal. Soc. Psychol. Bull.* 25:1067–81

Petersen LE, Dietz J. 2000. Social discrimination in a personnel selection context: the effects of an authority's instruction to discriminate and followers' authoritarianism. *J. Appl. Soc. Psychol.* 30:206–20

Pollock CL, Smith SD, Knowles ES, Bruce HJ. 1998. Mindfulness limits compliance with the that's-not-all technique. *Personal. Soc. Psychol. Bull.* 24:1153–57

Pool GJ, Wood W, Leck K. 1998. The self-esteem motive in social influence: agreement with valued majorities and disagreement with derogated minorities. *J. Personal. Soc. Psychol.* 75:967–75

Postmes T, Spears R. 1998. Deindividuation and anti-normative behavior: a meta-analysis. *Psychol. Bull.* 123:238–59

Postmes T, Spears R, Sakhel K, De Groot D. 2001. Social influence in computer-mediated communication: the effects of anonymity on group behavior. *Personal. Soc. Psychol. Bull.* 27:1243–54

Quinn A, Schlenker BR. 2002. Can accountability produce independence? Goals as determinants of the impact of accountability on conformity. *Personal. Soc. Psychol. Bull.* 28:472–83

Raven BH, Schwarzwald J, Koslowsky M. 1998. Conceptualizing and measuring a power/interaction model of interpersonal influence. *J. Appl. Soc. Psychol.* 28:307–22

Reicher SD, Spears R, Postmes T. 1995. A social identity model of deindividuation phenomena. *Eur. Rev. Soc. Psychol.* 6:161–98

Rind B. 1997. Effects of interest arousal on compliance with a request for help. *Basic Appl. Soc. Psychol.* 19:49–59

Rind B, Strohmetz D. 1999. Effect on restaurant tipping of a helpful message written on the back of customer's checks. *J. Appl. Soc. Psychol.* 29:139–44

Rind B, Strohmetz D. 2001. Effect on restaurant tipping of presenting customers with an interesting task and of reciprocity. *J. Appl. Soc. Psychol.* 31:1379–84

Sagarin BJ, Cialdini RB, Rice WE, Serna SB. 2002. Dispelling the illusion of invulnerability: the motivations and mechanisms of resistance to persuasion. *J. Personal. Soc. Psychol.* 83:526–41

Sanchez-Burks J. 2002. Protestant relational ideology and (in)attention to relational cues in work settings. *J. Personal. Soc. Psychol.* 83:919–29

Sassenberg K. 2002. Common bond and common identity groups on the internet: attachment and normative behavior in on-topic and off-topic chats. *Group Dynam.: Theory Res. Pract.* 6:27–37

Sassenberg K, Postmes T. 2002. Cognitive and strategic processes in small groups: effects of anonymity of the self and anonymity of the group on social influence. *Br. J. Soc. Psychol.* 41:463–80

Schaller M, Latané B. 1996. Dynamic social impact and the evolution of social representations: a natural history of stereotypes. *J. Commun.* 46:64–77

Schlenker BR, Weigold MF. 1989. Self-identification and accountability. In *Impression Management in the Organization*, ed. RA Giacalone, P Rosenfeld, pp. 21–43. Hillsdale, NJ: Erlbaum

Schultz PW. 1999. Changing behavior with normative feedback interventions: a field experiment on curbside recycling. *Basic Appl. Soc. Psychol.* 21:25–36

Schwarzwald J, Koslowsky M, Agassi V. 2001. Captain's leadership type and police officers' compliance to power bases. *Eur. J. Work Organ. Psychol.* 10:273–90

Sechrist GB, Stangor C. 2001. Perceived consensus influences intergroup behavior and stereotype accessibility. *J. Personal. Soc. Psychol.* 80:645–54

Spears R, Postmes T, Lea M, Watt SE. 2001. A SIDE view of social influence. See Forgas & Williams 2001, pp. 331–50

Stangor C, Sechrist GB, Jost JT. 2001. Social influence and intergroup beliefs: the role of perceived social consensus. See Forgas & Williams 2001, pp. 235–52

Strohmetz DB, Rind B, Fisher R, Lynn M. 2002. Sweetening the till: the use of candy to increase restaurant tipping. *J. Appl. Soc. Psychol.* 32:300–9

Tafarodi RW, Kanf SJ, Milne AB. 2002. When different becomes similar: compensatory conformity in bicultural visible minorities. *Personal. Soc. Psychol. Bull.* 28:1131–42

Turner JC. 1985. Social categorization and the self-concept: a social cognitive theory of group behavior. In *Advances in Group Processes*, ed. EJ Lawler, 2:77–122. Greenwich, CT: JAI

Tusing KJ, Dillard JP. 2000. The psychological reality of the door-in-the-face: it's helping, not bargaining. *J. Lang. Soc. Psychol.* 19:5–25

Tyler TR. 1997. The psychology of legitimacy. *Personal. Soc. Psychol. Rev.* 1:323–44

Vallacher RR, Nowak A, Miller ME. 2003.

Social influence. In *Comprehensive Handbook of Psychology: Personality and Social Psychology*, ed. MJ Lerner, T Millon, 5:383–417. New York: Wiley

Vonk R. 2002. Self-serving interpretations of flattery: why ingratiation works. *J. Personal. Soc. Psychol.* 82:515–26

Walther E, Bless H, Strack F, Rackstraw P, Wagner D, Werth L. 2002. Conformity effects in memory as a function of group size, dissenters and uncertainty. *Appl. Cogn. Psychol.* 16:793–810

Whatley MA, Webster MJ, Smith RH, Rhodes A. 1999. The effect of a favor on public and private compliance: How internalized is the norm of reciprocity? *Basic Appl. Soc. Psychol.* 21:251–59

Williams KP, Cheung CKT, Choi W. 2000. Cyberostricism: effects of being ignored over the internet. *J. Personal. Soc. Psychol.* 79:748–62

Wood W. 2000. Attitude change: persuasion and social influence. *Annu. Rev. Psychol.* 51:539–70

Wright DB, Self G, Justice C. 2000. Memory conformity: exploring misinformation effects when presented by another person. *Br. J. Psychol.* 91:189–202

Annu. Rev. Psychol. 2004. 55:623–55
doi: 10.1146/annurev.psych.55.090902.142009
Copyright © 2004 by Annual Reviews. All rights reserved
First published online as a Review in Advance on October 27, 2003

GROUP PERFORMANCE AND DECISION MAKING

Norbert L. Kerr
Department of Psychology, Michigan State University, East Lansing, Michigan 48823;
email: kerr@msu.edu

R. Scott Tindale
Department of Psychology, Loyola University Chicago, Chicago, Illinois 60626;
email: rtindal@luc.edu

Key Words   group motivation, process losses, process gains, group information processing, shared cognitions

■ **Abstract**   Theory and research on small group performance and decision making is reviewed. Recent trends in group performance research have found that process gains as well as losses are possible, and both are frequently explained by situational and procedural contexts that differentially affect motivation and resource coordination. Research has continued on classic topics (e.g., brainstorming, group goal setting, stress, and group performance) and relatively new areas (e.g., collective induction). Group decision making research has focused on preference combination for continuous response distributions and group information processing. New approaches (e.g., group-level signal detection) and traditional topics (e.g., groupthink) are discussed. New directions, such as nonlinear dynamic systems, evolutionary adaptation, and technological advances, should keep small group research vigorous well into the future.

CONTENTS

INTRODUCTION

Many *Annual Review* chapters begin like acts of confession—Father/reader, it has been one week/five years since my/the last confession/review of this literature. In the present case, it has been more than a dozen years since the topics of this chapter—group performance and decision making—were last surveyed in the pages of the *Annual Review of Psychology* by Levine & Moreland (1990). As in most confessions, we have omitted many fascinating matters and many of the omissions are intentional. The latter include several of the group-relevant topics that were also omitted in Levine & Moreland's chapter—large group (e.g., crowd, mob, organizational) behavior (see Wilpert 1995, Bond & Smith 1996); intergroup relations (see Hewstone et al. 2002, Pettigrew 1998); special types of groups (e.g., therapy groups, children's groups)—as well as a few of the topics that they did cover—viz. group structure, group composition, and conflict in groups. With respect to the latter topic, we are interested in one aspect of conflict within groups—how group members resolve opinion or preference conflicts in consensus-seeking groups—but are not concerned with several other related aspects, such as conflict arising from interdependence among group members (e.g., as in social dilemmas, bargaining, negotiation, and coalition formation; see recent reviews of several of these topics by Komorita & Parks 1995, Carnevale & Pruitt 1992, Bazerman et al. 2000) or general processes of social influence (cf. Wood 2000).

We also largely omit coverage of two other topics—leadership and team performance. Work on these topics has been (or soon will be) reviewed in *Annual Review* chapters (e.g., Chemers 2000; Goethals, manuscript in preparation; Guzzo & Dickson 1996). The distinction between performance teams (the focus of the latter review) and performance groups (the focus of the present review) is, we confess, a fuzzy one. Team research tends to focus on relatively longer-term groups with multiple task responsibilities, often functioning within an organization. Team research tends to have a relatively applied research focus and to be conducted in more applied subdisciplines (e.g., I/O psychology, management). Small group performance research, on the other hand, tends to be basic research conducted by social psychologists, and is usually studied experimentally in ad-hoc laboratory groups. However, there are many exceptions to these general rules. In our judgment, the distinction is a rather artificial one that reflects more about subdisciplinary territoriality than about fundamental differences in focus or objectives. We offer the present review both to summarize the past dozen years' activity on the "small groups" side of the border (with occasional glimpses of work that spans the border) and to contribute to more intellectual border traffic.

We focus on groups performing tasks and/or making decisions. Our primary interest is in the group's output or product (e.g., solution, decision) and the processes whereby the group achieves that product. The chapter has two main sections. The first focuses on recent research (defined here as appearing since 1989, the period following Levine & Moreland's review) on group performance at a variety of response-creation or response-sequencing tasks, including production, problem-solving, and creativity tasks. The second section focuses on the topic of group decision making, i.e., collective response selection. Much of the work in these areas has been focused on a particular topic, question, or contrast. In our review, we concentrate on those topics which have received sustained research attention and/or on which some tangible progress has been made.

GROUP PERFORMANCE

Group Process Losses and Gains

Much of the work to be reviewed here explicitly or implicitly utilizes one or more baseline models that predict the group's product under certain process assumptions (Steiner 1972, Davis 1969). The best-known and most widely utilized example is Steiner's (1972) potential productivity baseline—the group's optimal level of performance under the assumption of some idealized coordination/combination of member resources. Absent some such baseline, it will often be difficult to meaningfully characterize whether groups are achieving, exceeding, or falling short of any reasonable expected level of performance. With such a baseline, one can test and refine one's theoretical assumptions.

The ubiquitous finding across many decades of research (e.g., see Steiner 1972, Hill 1982) is that groups usually fall short of reasonable potential productivity baselines—in Steiner's terminology, they exhibit process losses. The theoretical and empirical analyses of such process losses have shed considerable light on group dynamics. Some more recent work, though, has sought to identify informative exceptions to this rule—that is, to identify tasks and performance contexts in which groups might reach or even exceed their apparent potential. One such potential productivity baseline is the performance level of the group's most capable member. A few studies have reported performance groups attaining this criterion (Laughlin et al. 1995, 1998b, 2003). And, a very few studies (Laughlin et al. 2002, Michaelsen et al. 1989, Tindale & Sheffey 2002, Sniezek & Henry 1989) have reported the elusive process gain or "assembly bonus effect"—group performance that is better than the performance of any individual or any combination of individual member efforts. Such claims need to be examined very carefully. Such effects are usually modest, and it is easy to underestimate the potential of the group and consequently to overstate the group's level of achievement (cf. Tindale & Larson 1992a,b).

It may sometimes be hard for scholars to agree on just what a group's true potential is; it is far less difficult and probably ultimately more productive to document work conditions or interventions that improve group performance (and thus, help groups approach or possibly exceed any plausible potential productivity baseline). So, for example, giving group members task-relevant information that simplifies or reframes their task can enhance group performance (Laughlin et al.

1999, 2003). Several recent meta-analyses indicate that more cohesive groups (and their individual members) tend generally to be more productive (Evans & Dion 1991, Gully et al. 1995, Mullen & Copper 1994, Oliver et al. 1999), although it appears that group norms must favor high productivity (Langfred 1998), group members must be committed to performance goals (Podsakoff et al. 1997), and task requirements further moderate the relationship (Craig & Kelly 1999, Zaccaro 1991). Moreover, at least part of the robust association between cohesiveness and group performance may stem from good performance enhancing the group's cohesiveness (Mullen & Copper 1994).

Because failure to identify and utilize the resources of capable group members is a clear source of group process loss, considerable useful work has been devoted to analyzing and assisting groups' efforts to identify their best members. At least for some tasks, groups can recognize member expertise (i.e., they can do better than chance; Henry 1993). Some of the cues that underlie perceived expertise have been identified (e.g., loquacity, use of reason to influence, member confidence and dominance; Littlepage & Mueller 1997, Littlepage et al. 1995). And some work conditions that improve groups' recognition of expertise have also been discovered (e.g., larger groups, Littlepage & Silbiger 1992; explicit instructions to share task information or to try to identify the most capable group member, Henry 1995, Henry et al. 2002; receiving regular performance outcome feedback, Henry et al. 1996; prior experience working together, Littlepage et al. 1997, Goodman & Shah 1992). Moreland and his colleagues (e.g., Moreland 1999, Moreland & Argote 2003) have analyzed the problem in terms of the creation of a transactive memory, mutual awareness of "who knows what." They have shown that one effective way to develop such transactive memory is by being trained as a group (e.g., Liang et al. 1995), where it appears to be the opportunity to learn about one another's competencies, and not other confounding aspects of group training (e.g., stronger group identification, better opportunities to communicate with one another, enhanced task motivation) that is crucial (Moreland & Myaskovsky 2000).

There has been growing interest in whether "electronic groups"—where intermember communication is managed electronically rather than in face-to-face interaction—might have certain performance advantages. Clearly, such groups permit more flexible (e.g., geographically distributed; nonsimultaneous) forms of intragroup communication, and (at least in principle) ready access to in- and out-group resources. In addition, electronic groups can foster stronger group identification (Lea et al. 2001) and adherence to group norms (Spears et al. 1990; although see Douglas & McGarty 2001). However, several studies show either no performance advantage for such electronic group performance settings (e.g., Straus & McGrath 1994) or some disadvantage, especially when the group's task requires close coordination of member efforts or members are unfamiliar with the electronic technology (Hollingshead et al. 1993, Straus & McGrath 1994). Likewise, giving group members access to electronic databases containing group member capability information has generally not boosted group effectiveness (Moreland 1999). One striking exception to this generally disappointing picture is the facilitative effect of computerized brainstorming, to be discussed below.

Group Brainstorming

The productive use of potential productivity baselines is nicely illustrated by recent work on group brainstorming, a method of collective idea generation popularized by Osborn (1957). Such groups are instructed to generate as many ideas as possible, to avoid criticism of any ideas, and to strive to combine and improve on others' ideas. Both Osborn and most members of brainstorming groups (cf. Paulus et al. 1993) believe that such groups routinely outperform equal-sized sets of non-interacting individuals (the nominal group baseline). However, several decades of research have shown that nominal groups usually outperform such brainstorming groups (e.g., Mullen et al. 1991). Older (i.e., pre-1989) research indicated that this was, in large part, due to "production blocking"—the inability for more than one group member to talk (and, perhaps, think) at a time (Diehl & Stroebe 1987). More recent work has refined, extended, and challenged these conclusions.

The negative impact of production blocking seems not to stem from simple interference with memory or from the unpredictability of speaking turns (Diehl & Stroebe 1991). Rather, it appears that the usual melee of group discussion tends to interfere with our ability to get a productive train of thought started, or can effectively "derail" an ongoing train of thought (Nijstad 2000). Such work illustrates a broader shift of attention away from the suboptimality of performance groups and toward a distinctive and novel brand of "social cognition"—viz. the effects of group contexts upon cognition (Levine et al. 1993, Hinsz et al. 1997, Larson & Christensen 1993). In addition to production blocking, at least two other processes have been implicated in process loss in brainstorming groups: an unwillingness to contribute ideas because of evaluation apprehension, and a convergence via social comparison on a relatively low standard for performance in face-to-face groups (Camacho 1995, Larey & Paulus 1995, Paulus & Dzindolet 1993, Paulus et al. 1996, Roy et al. 1996).

Others have utilized this knowledge about the sources of process loss in brainstorming groups to develop improvements on traditional group brainstorming. For example, training a facilitator to minimize production blocking and evaluation apprehension can reduce or even eliminate the usually observed process loss (Offner et al. 1996, Oxley et al. 1996). Alternative framing of a problem can help prevent the "derailment" caused by production blocking in unstructured group discussion (e.g., sequential consideration of relevant subtasks) and improve group (and individual) performance (Coskun et al. 2000). Most noteworthy has been the work on electronic brainstorming where computer software allows isolated individuals to type in their ideas without interruption (i.e., no production blocking; Gallupe et al. 1994), to be anonymous (low evaluation apprehension; Cooper et al. 1998), and yet to be able to see copies of other group members' ideas on the screen whenever they like. Such computerized brainstorming groups have been found not only to perform as well as nominal groups (e.g., Gallupe et al. 1991) but, when fairly large (n > 9), even to outperform them (Dennis & Valacich 1993, 1994; Valacich et al. 1994). The latter result seems not to stem from the relatively higher likelihood of very large groups coming up with rare, "off-the-wall" ideas (Connolly et al. 1993), but rather—in line with Osborne's original claims for group brainstorming—from the stimulating effect of exposure to others' ideas, a suggestion that (*a*) has been supported in several recent studies (Leggett-Dugosh et al. 2000, Nijstad et al. 2003, Paulus & Yang 2000; although also see Ziegler et al. 2000) and (*b*) all else being equal, encourages heterogeneity/diversity in idea-generating groups (Schruijer & Mostert 1997, Stroebe & Diehl 1994).

Group Motivation Losses and Gains

Levine & Moreland's (1990) review appeared after an active period of research that documented and explained reduced levels of motivation among members of task performing groups relative to comparable individual performers. Such effects have been referred to as group motivation losses (Steiner 1972) or as social loafing (Latané et al. 1979). Older research identified a number of distinct psychological mechanisms underlying such effects (e.g., reduced risks of evaluation; opportunities to free ride on other group members' efforts; and an unwillingness to do the work that a capable, free-riding partner could be doing) as well as a number of moderating variables (e.g., high task interest or involvement tends to attenuate these effects; B.N. Smith et al. 2001). More recent work has identified additional moderating variables, either through new original research or via meta-analysis. Karau & Williams' (1993) meta-analysis established, for example, that social loafing effects are stronger for males and for groups from Western cultures. Because such cultural differences are often attributed to stable differences in a more general individualist-collectivist personality disposition, it is not surprising that social loafing appears to be relatively stronger among individualists (Erez & Somech 1996, Wagner 1995) or those who see themselves as better than others (Charbonnier et al. 1998, Huguet et al. 1999). Social loafing is attenuated by high group cohesion (Everett et al. 1992, Karau & Hart 1998, Karau & Williams 1997, Worchel et al. 1998) or anticipated punishment for poor performance (Miles & Greenberg 1993). Likewise, conditions that increase the cost of effortful task performance (e.g., fatigue; Hoeksema van Orden et al. 1998, Anshel 1995) or reduce one's sense of responsibility to the group (Kerr & Stanfel 1993) tend to increase social loafing.

Paralleling this empirical work has been valuable theoretical work designed to integrate and organize this large literature. Several scholars (Karau & Williams 1993, Shepperd 1993) have independently argued that expectancy-value theories provide a useful theoretical framework. Such models also suggest that there may be group situations in which the instrumentality of one's task efforts and/or the value attached to effort-mediated outcomes might be higher than for comparable individual performers. This observation prompted a search for group motivation gains—where group members exert greater task effort than comparable individual performers. At least two such phenomena have been demonstrated empirically. The first, social compensation, occurs when "...individuals increase their efforts on collective tasks to compensate for the anticipated poor performance of other group members" (Karau & Williams 1997, p. 158). These effects have been obtained (Williams & Karau 1991, Karau & Williams 1997, Hart et al. 2001) under conditions that much other research would suggest are ideal for inducing social loafing—conditions of low identifiability and high risk that one may have to shoulder an inequitably large share of the group's work. There is, though, one key difference—group success must be extremely important to the more capable group member. Loafing will occur if the group task is not very important (Williams & Karau 1991, Exp. 3). Given the strong opposing forces encouraging both reduced and enhanced effort, this phenomenon appears to be easily disrupted—e.g., by how partner effort is communicated (Hart et al. 2001, Williams & Karau 1991). It is observed with low-cohesiveness groups, but oddly, not with more highly cohesive groups (Karau & Williams 1997, Exp. 2). Clearly, more research is needed to establish the robustness and boundary conditions of the social compensation effect.

The other recently documented motivation gain effect is the Köhler effect. It occurs when less-capable members of groups working at conjunctive tasks (i.e., where the poorest performance defines the group score) increase their effort. After this effect's discovery in the 1920s (Köhler 1926), it was forgotten until fairly recently (Witte 1989). However, in the last decade, the overall motivation gain effect has been replicated several times (Hertel et al. 2000a,b, 2003), as has the moderating effect of member ability discrepancy—viz. lower gains for small or very large discrepancies in partner ability [originally observed by Köhler (1926)] (Messé et al. 2002; Stroebe et al. 1996, Exp. 1)—and of partner sex (Lount et al. 2000). The psychological causes of the effect have yet to be clearly established. There is some evidence that the indispensability of the less-capable member's contribution to the group's performance (or, to that member's evaluation within the group) is crucial (Hertel et al. 2000a, Exp. 2) and that the effect may be due (at least in part) to a social comparison process that either affects the goals members set (Stroebe et al. 1996) and/or induces intragroup competition (Stroebe et al. 1996, Exp. 2, 3). The latter possibility is bolstered by work demonstrating the potential of intergroup competition for enhancing group member task motivation (Erev et al. 1993).

Group Goal Setting

There has long been interest in the process and effects of group goal setting on both group performance and member attitudes (e.g., satisfaction). Much of this work (e.g., Yammarino & Naughton 1992, Durham et al. 1997, Johnson et al. 1997, Ludwig & Geller 1997) seeks to demonstrate that group performance, member performance, and/or member satisfaction are enhanced by collective agreement on a challenging goal (versus "do your best," self-set, assigned, or no-goal control conditions). Generally, productivity and satisfaction do tend to be higher when groups collectively set challenging performance goals (O'Leary-Kelly et al. 1994, Wegge 2000); however, these facilitative effects are neither highly consistent nor very strong (Locke et al. 1997, Larey & Paulus 1995). Much of the recent work in this area has focused on exploring when and why group goal setting has its effects. For example, Latham et al. (1994) found that participative group goal setting (PGGS) can enhance performance via enhancing the group's task knowledge. Other work (Wegge & Kleinbeck 1996, Wegge 2000) implicates anxiety reduction as a key mediator of the PGGS-performance relationship. Another group-level construct, collective efficacy (Bandura 1997), mediates the goal setting–performance relationship (Prussia & Kinicki 1996); as shared feelings of capability increase in a group, groups tend to set higher goals for themselves and perform better. Elsewhere, Roberson et al. (1999) show that group members' sense of procedural fairness can mediate the PGGS-satisfaction relationship. Participative goal setting appears to be a complex process with several mediating mechanisms; it remains a theoretical and empirical challenge to provide a systematic and comprehensive account of this process (cf. Wegge 2000, Weldon & Weingart 1993). Work that explores the group goal-setting process itself (e.g., Hinsz 1991, 1992, 1995; Mesch et al. 1994) should contribute to such an account.

Stress and Group Performance

Groups are routinely called upon to perform under highly stressful conditions. A tempting, intuitive guess is that increasing stress (e.g., time pressure, poor work environments, complex tasks, etc.) would generally degrade group performance. The reality seems to be much more complex. The older literature on the effects of stress on individual performance (see Kaplan et al. 1993, or Karau & Kelly 1992, for reviews) suggested a number of regularities—stress tends to increase the performance quantity with an accompanying decline in quality, to narrow attention onto more vital task features, and to prompt more simplified, heuristic information processing. For the most part, these regularities have been replicated in both earlier (for reviews, see Brown & Miller 2000, and Kelly & Karau 1993) and more recent research on performance groups. Karau & Kelly (1992) and De Grada et al. (1999) show that increasing time pressure leads to greater task focus within performance groups. Within certain limits, groups seem able to adapt to higher levels of stress (Brown & Miller 2000, Hollenbeck et al. 1997, Volpe et al. 1996); however, if such stress grows sufficiently high, group performance will eventually be degraded (Adelman et al. 2003, Entin & Serfaty 1999, Urban et al. 1996). As the Yerkes-Dodson Law would suggest, sometimes increases in stress (from low to moderate levels) can actually enhance aspects of group performance (Karau & Kelly 1992). Attempts have also been made to both describe how performance groups allocate their limited resources (e.g., time; Littlepage & Poole 1993) and to identify ideal group performance strategies for combating the process losses arising from stressful working conditions (Haertel & Haertel 1997, Littlepage & Karau 1997).

Kelly and her colleagues have continued to build on their older work on the effects of one particular source of stress—time pressure—on collective performance. That older work (see Kelly 1988) suggested that the pace and quality of a group's work could be set or "entrained" by initial time limits on group performance. Hence, groups given lax initial time limits can be entrained to work slowly and carefully at a creativity task, so that if they are later required to work under stressful, stringent time limits, they will work more slowly but with higher quality than groups entrained under more stringent time limits (Kelly & Karau 1993). However, in other work (Kelly et al. 1990), it has been shown that this pattern depends upon how group members attribute any initial difficulty with the task.

A related, promising line of theory and research has been proposed by Kruglanski and his colleagues (e.g., Kruglanski et al. 2002). This research extends earlier work on the effects of "need for closure" (i.e., the desire for definite, nonambiguous solutions) among individuals to the group level. Kruglanski argues that stressful group work conditions tend to increase this need, which has a number of consequences for information exchange and utilization. Groups under stress should (and do; see Kruglanski et al. 1993) exhibit a stronger desire for uniformity of opinion/preference. Unless group members already have very strongly held preferences (in which case the "freezing" that is a common result of enhanced need for closure can lead to a reduced readiness to yield to others), such uniformity can be achieved through stronger attempts to influence opinion deviates and/or a greater readiness to yield to others. Both processes should encourage centralization of power/influence in a few influential group members (e.g., leaders), manifest by greater conversational and power asymmetry in the group (De Grada et al. 1999) and communication patterns centralized on the more powerful members (Pierro et al. 2003; although see Brown & Miller 2000). Once a clear group position or solution has been achieved, a heightened need for closure also should (and does; see Kruglanski & Webster 1991) prompt (*a*) stronger tendencies for group members to support that position, and (*b*) pressures to accept those that conform and reject those that deviate from that position. In summary, Kruglanski has shown that stressful conditions tend to result in a "closing of the group mind"—an aversion to unpopular options, an acceptance of autocratic leadership and extant group norms. The validity of these arguments is bolstered by empirical demonstrations of similar effects due to varying need for closure in groups via group composition (De Grada et al. 1999, Kruglanski & Webster 1991).

Collective Induction

Laughlin and his colleagues (e.g., Laughlin 1996, 1999; Laughlin & Hollingshead 1995) have undertaken a programmatic line of research on collective induction, groups inferring some general principle or rule from concrete empirical manifestations of that principle. In a typical collective induction experiment, participants (individuals or groups) are first given an exemplar of some to-be-discovered rule involving standard playing cards. They are then asked to choose a new card, are told whether the new card fits the rule, and then are asked to generate a hypothesis about what the rule might be. They then continue the process of card selection, feedback, and hypothesizing for several rounds until a final hypothesis is solicited.

Laughlin (1996, 1999) has proposed a set of postulates that both summarizes this program of research and constitutes a theory of how groups perform induction (and conceptually similar) problems. Several of these postulates (e.g., the distinction between intellective and judgmental tasks; criteria for solution demonstrability) are based on older research (preceding the time span covered in this review). However, several reflect more recent work. For example, a few common ways in which groups resolve preference disagreement among their members have been identified (Postulate 1) and each has been formalized using a particular social combination model or scheme (Postulate 2; Davis 1973) (e.g., random selection among alternatives = equiprobability decision scheme; voting = majority/plurality decision scheme; demonstration = truth-wins decision schemes). A few simple combination rules nicely organize the data for a large number of experiments (Laughlin 1988, 1992; Laughlin & McGlynn 1986; Laughlin & Shupe 1996; Laughlin et al. 1991, 1997, 1998a)—if more than one plausible hypothesis is proposed, group choice is restricted to that set of hypotheses (Postulate 7); if a majority favors a hypothesis, it will be the group's choice, but if there is no such majority, the group will use turn taking to make a choice (Postulate 8); absent a majority preference, a group with H viable hypotheses in hand will settle on a new, emergent hypothesis with a small but finite probability [estimated to be $1/(H + 1)$] (Postulate 8). From these, it follows that the unique correct hypothesis is very likely to be discovered by the group if and only if it is proposed by some group member on some trial—at least under the conditions modeled in this paradigm (errorless feedback, multiple trials); groups seem to be fairly effective in retaining correct and winnowing out incorrect hypotheses. Several studies (e.g., Karau & Williams 1997; Laughlin & Bonner 1999; Laughlin et al. 1995, 1998b) suggest that induction is facilitated more by additional evidence than by additional hypotheses (Postulate 11). It is well known that individuals tend to prefer confirmatory to disconfirmatory tests; this seems also to describe group induction. Moreover, in the Laughlin paradigm, with many plausible hypotheses evident initially, such a confirmatory strategy can also be shown (see Laughlin et al. 1997, 1998b) to be relatively more effective (Postulate 12). Finally, groups have been shown to perform near the level of the best in a like-sized set of individual performers, but only if the groups are given sufficient information and time (Postulate 10; Laughlin et al. 1995, 1998a); if time or information is sparse, groups will do less well (e.g., Laughlin et al. 1991).

GROUP DECISION MAKING

Group decision-making research in the 1960s and 1970s typically emphasized the processes involved in moving from a diverse set of individual positions or preferences to agreement on a consensus choice for the group. Stemming largely from early work by social choice theorists (Arrow 1963, Black 1958), psychologists attempted to define formal models to describe the influence functions that led to consensus. Early models by Lorge & Solomon (1955), Smoke & Zajonc (1962), Steiner (1966, 1972), and others culminated in social decision scheme theory (Davis 1973) and its various offshoots (Kerr 1981, Penrod & Hastie 1981, Stasser & Davis 1981). The key topics of inquiry during that time involved jury decision-making (Hastie et al. 1983, Stasser et al. 1982, Tindale & Davis 1983), and group polarization or choice shift (Myers & Lamm 1976, Stasser et al. 1989).

These topics are still receiving attention on both theoretical and empirical levels. However, the dominant paradigm behind recent group decision-making research has focused on information rather than on preferences (Brauner & Scholl 2000, Hinsz et al. 1997, Kameda et al. 2002, Larson & Christiansen 1993). Stasser & Titus's (1985) now classic finding that groups were less-than-optimal users of information and often would ignore information that was not widely shared among the members presented a counterintuitive finding and a new paradigm for studying a variety of aspects of group decision-making and social influence. The "shared versus unshared information" paradigm has been replicated and expanded in a variety of interesting directions and become a mainstay of group research during the 1990s. Thus, much of our discussion focuses on information processing in and by groups trying to reach consensus on a given decision alternative.

Combining Preferences

Recent work on preference combination in groups has addressed continuous rather than discrete decision alternatives. Davis (1996) proposed his Social Judgment Scheme (SJS) model for groups as an extension of his earlier work on discrete-alternative consensus processes (i.e., Social Decision Schemes or SDS theory; Davis 1973). The SJS model is a weighted linear combination of member preferences where the weights are an exponential function of the distances between a given member's preference and all other members' preferences. (See Davis 1996 or Kameda et al. 2002 for a more complete description of the model.) The weight given to any member decreases exponentially as an increasing function of the discrepancy of that member's preference from the other members of the group. Thus, members whose preferences are similar to one another receive larger weights and members whose preferences deviate from most other members receive very little weight. Although formulated recently, the model has fared well in empirical tests (Davis 1996, Davis et al. 1993).

Crott et al. (1991) developed a model based on Black's (1958) work with single-peaked preference curves. Black showed that the median position among the group members dominates (in the game theoretic sense) any other possible position along the continuum, assuming member preference distributions are single peaked. Crott et al. (1991) found that a median model provided a good fit to group decision data from three different decision tasks. Davis et al. (1997) also found support for a median-based model using a civil-trial mock-jury task.

Both Davis's (1996) SJS model and Crott et al.'s (1991) median model are conceptually similar to majority/plurality models, which tend to well describe group consensus processes with discrete decision alternatives. As argued by Kameda et al. (2002; see also Tindale & Kameda 2000), like majority models, they show the influence of "social sharedness" at the preference level. The idea of social sharedness is that things that are shared among the group members tend to have an inordinate impact on the group response. For majority/plurality models, the alternative that shows the response option with the most sharedness tends to win or be chosen by the group. Both the Crott et al. (1991) median model and Davis's (1996) SJS model also emphasize the degree of preference sharing. The SJS model emphasizes shared preferences explicitly by giving more weight to those members whose preferences are similar (i.e., close to one another on the response dimension). It is easiest to see the sharedness aspect of the median model by comparing it to a model based on the mean when there is a skewed distribution of member responses. Extremely discrepant members in the tail of the distribution will have little impact on the median relative to the impact they would have on the mean. Thus, the median represents the most common or shared position even in skewed preference distributions. Recent work by Hinsz (1999) has argued that which members should be most influential in the group may also depend on the group's task or context. He has formulated a variety of models that differ as a function of the weights given to members based on their position along a judgmental continuum (e.g., most central member, most extreme member, etc.).

Another question that received attention in the past decade is whether groups attenuate or exacerbate individual decision biases (Kerr et al. 1996, Tindale 1993). Although groups tend to outperform individuals in many domains, groups also can fall prey to the same heuristic-based biases found at the individual level (Argote et al. 1990, Smith et al. 1998, Tindale et al. 1996, Whyte 1993). Tindale (1993) showed that a simple majority decision process can lead to either attenuation or exacerbation of a particular bias depending on how prevalent the bias is at the individual level. Kerr et al. (1996), using an SDS framework, showed that the question is far more complicated than it first appears. Using computer simulations, they showed that whether groups will be more, less, or equally as biased as individuals depends on (a) the type of bias, (b) the type of group decision process, (c) the strength of the bias, and (d) the individual preference distribution in the group. They also showed that not only could unbiased group decision processes exacerbate individual biases at the group level, but that biases may also influence the group decision processes (cf. Tindale et al. 1996). Recent empirical work inspired by the Kerr et al. framework has been generally supportive (Kerr et al. 1999).

Just as group decision-making research in general has been extended to continuous response distributions, research on jury decision making in particular has followed suit (see Tindale et al. 2001). Rather than focusing on criminal trials and categorical (guilty, not guilty) responses, recent work has focused on civil trials and the amount of compensation awarded to plaintiffs. Although earlier work showed juries in a relatively favorable light as mechanisms for administering justice (Hastie et al. 1983), more recent findings on civil trials have suggested less sanguine conclusions. Work by Horowitz and his colleagues (Horowitz et al. 1996) has shown that jurors in civil trials often misinterpret jury instructions, mistakenly recall evidence, and fail to distinguish between different plaintiffs in a multiplaintiff case. In terms of damage allocations, juries are easily influenced by anchors provided during the trial (e.g., amount requested by the plaintiff; Hinsz & Indahl 1995). Sunstein et al. (2002) showed that although juries were consistent (i.e., showed high interjury reliability) in their judgments of negligence, their ability to follow judges' instructions regarding punitive damages was extremely poor. Juries were actually less consistent than individual jurors in punitive damage award judgments, often showing huge differences in awards across different juries and typically awarding punitive damages in cases where they were not warranted. Finding ways to alleviate such problems may be at the forefront of jury research in the near future.

Combining Preferences with Limited (or No) Discussion

The aforementioned models all deal with processes associated with how groups reach consensus through discussion. However, a number of lines of research have developed where discussion is either limited or nonexistent, and where the decision is made either by a single source or by a statistical algorithm. One of these lines of research involves "judge-advisor systems" (Budescu & Rantilla 2000, Sniezek 1992, Sniezek & Buckley 1995). In many decision settings, multiple people may provide advice to a decision maker, but the final decision is in the hands of a single person. Thus, a number of researchers have begun to assess how much influence the "advisors" have on the final decision of the "judges." The general finding is that advisors influence judges, but judges give their own positions more weight (Harvey et al. 2000, Yaniv & Kleinberger 2000). They also give more weight to advisors whose preferences are similar to their own (Harvey et al. 2000). These findings are similar to those for decision-making groups where shared preferences are likely to prevail, but postgroup individual preferences tend to move back toward each individual's initial position (Hinsz et al. 1997, Tindale & Kameda 2000). There is also evidence that judges are sensitive to the accuracy of the advice they receive. Advisors who have been correct in the past or who have more information at their disposal are given more weight than advisors with less-accurate records (Budescu et al. 2003). However, the best predictor of an advisor's influence is the advisor's level of confidence (Kuhn & Sniezek 1996, Van Swol & Sniezek 2002).

Overall, it appears that forecasters would be better off letting their judgments be generated by simple linear models, such as averages, than by using their own intuitive weighting schemes (Ariely et al. 2000, Johnson et al. 2001). Much as individual decision makers are not able to optimally use information at their disposal, it appears that groups rarely combine their individual preferences in an optimal way. Ariely et al. (2000) showed that, assuming pairwise conditional independence and random individual error distributions, the average of J probability estimates

($J =$ the number of estimators) will always be better than any of the component individual estimates and that as J increases, the average will tend toward perfect calibration diagnosticity (accurate representation of the true state of affairs), even when information provided to the various estimators is less than optimal. In addition, Johnson et al. (2001) empirically showed the accuracy of the average probability estimate to be robust over a number of conditions, even when individual estimates were not independent. Thus, decision makers' tendency to weight their own opinions heavier than those of their advisors may often be a suboptimal strategy.

Sorkin et al. (2001) approached the notion of optimal preference combination using a signal detection approach. Their model defines ideal group performance by using the individual members' sensitivity parameters (d') to set weights for combining the member preferences. Then, depending on the group's criterion, the model predicts when the group should choose one response over another (e.g., guilt versus innocence). The model can also be used to specify other types of decision rules, such as majority wins (Sorkin et al. 1998). One of the more interesting findings from both their empirical and simulation work is that majority processes tend to maximize group performance in situations where ideal weighting schemes are not possible (i.e., the members don't know each other's accuracy scores or d' values). In addition, simple majorities work better than more stringent criteria (e.g., two-thirds majorities, unanimity, etc.). Kameda & Hastie (1999) have also found that majority processes tend to produce high levels of decision performance with very little cost in terms of cognitive effort. They speculate that majority norms may have evolved in many cultures because of their adaptive properties.

Combining or Sharing Cognitions

Hinsz et al. (1997) argued that group research has shifted to an *information*-processing paradigm, and this is certainly true in the area of group decision making. Based on the groundbreaking work by Stasser & Titus (1985) on the dominant role of shared versus unshared information and the "hidden profile" procedure, numerous studies have explored the role of information distribution and exchange in group decision making. The initial finding—that groups focus on and discuss shared information at the expense of unshared information, thus leading to their failure to uncover hidden profiles—has been well replicated (see Wittenbaum & Stasser 1996). Research uncovering how and why the effect exists, and the contextual factors that moderate its strength, have proved fruitful ground for research.

Gigone & Hastie (1993, 1996) replicated the original Stasser & Titus (1985) findings using a multi-cue judgment task, and varied whether the cues were shared or unshared among the group members. Consistent with the Stasser & Titus (1985) findings, shared cues were more important for predicting group judgments than were unshared cues, with importance generally being a linear function of the degree of sharedness. Interestingly, cues that were actually brought up during discussion did not increase in weight as a function of their being mentioned.

In addition, the effects of the cues on group judgments were totally mediated by the member preferences. Thus, at least in this context, the distribution of information in the group (i.e., information or cognitive sharedness) influenced group judgments only indirectly through member preferences (i.e., preference sharedness). A more recent study (Winquist & Larson 1998) found that pooled (discussed) unshared information did impact positively on group decision quality when groups were given a sufficient amount of time to reach consensus.

Four basic processes seem to underlie the bias toward shared information. First, a simple information-sampling model (e.g., Stasser & Titus 1985) correctly predicts that shared information is more likely to be discussed, especially early in the discussion. Second, especially in hidden profile situations, premature closure may also play a role (Karau & Kelly 1992, Kelly & Karau 1998, Kruglanski & Webster 1996). The need to reach consensus in a situation where most of the members already share the same preference could lead to reduced information exchange and early consensus. Majority processes are quite consistent with this idea (Kameda et al. 2002). Third, it appears that people prefer to both receive and present information that is shared (Wittenbaum et al. 1999). People are perceived as more competent, knowledgeable, and credible when they share information that others already know. Finally, Brodbeck et al. (2002) and Greitemeyer & Schulz-Hardt (2003) show that group members do not like to change their initial preferences once formed. Thus, hidden profiles, which lead to biased individual preferences, can also lead members to misinterpret new information that is inconsistent with their already formed preferences.

More recent studies have documented a variety of moderators of this phenomenon (F.C. Brodbeck, R. Kerschreiter, A. Mojzisch, & S. Schulz-Hardt, unpublished manuscript). First, Larson et al. (1994) have shown that unshared information becomes more prevalent in group discussion over time. Thus, extending the discussion time of groups should improve the chance that unshared information is brought up during discussion. Placing all of the unshared information (assuming this information has implications for the decision quality) in the hands of at least one group member has also been shown to increase its effect on the final group decision (Stasser & Stewart 1998, McLeod et al. 1997). Work by Sawyer (1997) and Sheffey et al. (1989) has shown that allowing group members to have access to informational records (rather than relying on memory) during discussion can attenuate hidden profile effects. There is some evidence that training group members to explore more information can aid in information exchange (Larson et al. 1994; Wittenbaum 1998, 2000). Sometimes a group leader can aid in information sharing as well (Larson et al. 1996), as can having at least one group member who is an advocate for the alternative favored by unshared information (Brodbeck et al. 2002). Assigning group members to be responsible for certain categories of information and making sure that knowledge of who knows what is shared among the group members (like a transactive memory system; Wegner 1987, Stewart & Stasser 1995) has improved performance in hidden profile situations, as has convincing group members that there exists a unique correct solution to its decision task (Stasser & Stewart 1992). Increasing the amount of preference diversity (Brodbeck et al. 2002) or having members rank order alternatives (Hollingshead 1996) can also improve information sharing and decision quality. Finally, there is recent evidence that splitting the decision task into two components—information search first, followed by integration and decision—helps to insure that all relevant information is aired and used in the group decision (F.C. Brodbeck, R. Kerschreiter, A. Mojzisch, & S. Schulz-Hardt, unpublished manuscript).

Cognitive Centrality of Group Members

Recent work by Kameda et al. (1997) extended the idea of knowledge sharing to look at the influence members have within the group as a function of how much information they share with others. Using a social network framework, Kameda et al. devised a model to represent the degree to which any given member was "cognitively central" in the group. The greater the degree of overlap between the information held by a given member and the information held by other members on average, the greater the degree of centrality for that member. Both when cognitive centrality was measured (Study 1) and manipulated (Study 2), groups were more likely than not to choose the preference held by the most cognitively central member even when that member held the minority view. Kameda et al. (1997) argue that the enhanced social power accrues from perceptions of expertise for the cognitively central member in the focal knowledge domain, which fits nicely with Wittenbaum et al.'s (1999) findings concerning perceived competence as a consequence of mentioning shared information. However, Sargis & Larson (2002) found that cognitively peripheral members (those holding more unique information) can be influential when their information is perceived as important for the task. In addition, Spoor et al. (2002) found that females in mixed gender groups were less influential when they were cognitively central (compared to when they were more peripheral). Thus, considerably more research on this topic is needed before a clear understanding of the role of cognitive centrality in group decision making can be achieved.

Shared Task Representations and Mental Models

Specific pieces or types of information are not the only cognitive elements that group members can share (Tindale & Kameda 2000). Laughlin (1980, 1999) has argued that one of the reasons groups are better problem solvers than are individuals is that they may share a conceptual system of ideas that allows them to realize when a proposed solution is correct within that system, the first element of his notion of demonstrability (Laughlin & Ellis 1986). Tindale et al. (1996) referred to such shared conceptual systems as "shared task representations" and have argued that they can influence both group processes and outcomes. In essence, Tindale et al. argue that decision alternatives that fit within or are supported by the shared representation are easier to defend, and thus more likely to be chosen by the group. Thus, majorities or minorities favoring the alternative consistent with the shared representation will be more powerful within the group (relative to comparably large majorities/minorities favoring other alternatives).

Tindale et al. (1996) argue the group problem solving work by Laughlin (1980) and the work on the "leniency bias" in mock jury decision making (Davis 1980, MacCoun & Kerr 1988, Tindale & Davis 1983) are both instances of shared representation effects. More recently, Tindale et al. (1996) have shown that shared decision biases or heuristics can produce similar deviations from symmetric majority processes. For example, Tindale et al. (1993) found that groups given the "loss" framing of the standard "Asian disease" problem (Tversky & Kahneman 1981) would choose the riskier alternative even when a majority of the members favored the less risky alternative.

Recent research has shown that shared representations potentially operate in two different ways to affect group decisions. First, Smith et al. (1998), using a "sunk cost" problem, found that sunk cost arguments were persuasive, even if only a minority of members mentioned them as reasons for their decisions. Second, Tindale et al. (1998), examine videotaped group discussions of conjunction problems (cf. Tindale et al. 1993a) and showed that groups rarely discussed strategies, but rather simply exchanged information concerning their individual judgments, and quite often (greater than 60% of the time) simply chose a single member's undefended judgment. When this occurred, they were more likely to endorse the judgment of an incorrect member for conjunction problems that typically led to errors, but more likely to endorse the judgment of a correct member for conjunction problems that typically did not lead to errors. Thus, as long as a given individual preference is plausible within the shared representation, the group members may find it acceptable without thorough debate.

Shared task representations might best be conceptualized as a component of mental models that are shared among the group members (Cannon-Bowers et al. 1993, Helmreich 1997, Hinsz 1995). Although mental models can be shared without member awareness, shared meta-knowledge of the model (i.e., knowledge of what other members know and their role within the system) should aid groups in using the model effectively. Cannon-Bowers et al. (1993) have distinguished between models of the task and models of the group itself (i.e., what group members are likely to do or know—e.g., transactive memory) and have argued that both are important. Although research is still rather sparse, most findings to date support the idea that groups function better (made better choices, worked more efficiently, etc.) when they share the same ideas as to what the task is and the roles that the various members play (Mathieu et al. 2000). Although shared mental models may develop over time, they can also be instantiated effectively through training (Helmreich 1997, Marks et al. 2000).

Group Decision Making Procedures

Although group information processing and continuous response distributions have been particularly active topics for group research over the past decade, a number of other topics/issues have received attention as well. Continuing the traditions from social choice theory, agenda or procedural issues are still being actively explored (see Kameda et al. 2002). Davis and his colleagues (Davis et al. 1993, 1997) have continued to examine the role of straw polls, voting orders, group size, etc., in civil mock juries. They have found that polling a jury early can lead to quicker decisions, but may increase the likelihood of a hung jury. And similar to earlier findings with mock criminal juries (Davis et al. 1989), early poll responses can influence those voting later in the sequence.

Kameda (1996, 1991; Kameda & Sugimori 1993, 1995) has studied the implications of different voting procedures, including some not typically seen in Western cultures. For example, Kameda (1996) compared *nemawashi*—an informal consensus seeking technique that involves a leader contacting each group member individually and offering inducements for compliance—to a variety of other consensus generating procedures (mean, median, relative power, etc.). Interestingly, *nemawashi* faired relatively poorly except in relation to dictatorial decision procedures. Kameda (1991) also showed that breaking apart a decision into component parts can change the types of decisions groups will reach. Even if two of three members of a group are against some policy in total, if they disagree on which parts of the overall proposal they do not like, voting on separate components can lead to the group endorsing the overall proposal. In addition, Kameda & Sugimori (1995) showed that minority positions within a group become more likely to be chosen if the overall group is broken into subgroups and subgroups are allowed to make decisions before subgroup decisions are combined.

Groupthink

Another topic of longstanding interest that has continued to receive research attention is groupthink—Janis's (1972, 1982) delineation of a set of conditions and processes that can lead to disastrous outcomes for decision making groups. Although the historical illustrations and logic of groupthink remain compelling (e.g., see the special issue of *Organizational Behavior and Human Decision Processes,* Vol. 7, 1998) and are often cited in textbooks on groups, the research support for the theory has been quite mixed. It appears that both good and poor decision outcomes can occur because of and in spite of many of the conditions hypothesized to trigger groupthink. For example, the work on hidden profiles (Wittenbaum & Stasser 1996) and shared task representations (Tindale et al. 1996) shows that groups can make disappointingly poor decisions without being highly cohesive, having strong and directive leaders, or feeling a sense of urgency. Conversely, there is evidence that strong, directive leaders can sometimes enhance performance (Peterson et al. 1998), as can cohesiveness (though only under some circumstances, Mullen et al. 1994). Probably the main contribution of the theory in the long run will be the provocative research that it spawned, research that has shown us that constructs that typically are seen as positive aspects of groups (cohesiveness, collective efficacy, etc.) do not invariably lead to improved group outcomes (Mullen et al. 1994, Whyte 1998).

CONCLUDING THOUGHTS

We began this chapter by likening it to a confession. Like a confession, its aim has been to look back at what has been done and to look forward to how things might be done better. With these aims in mind, we conclude by describing some patterns that have characterized the last decade plus of research on small group performance and decision making, and by offering a few prescriptions for future research.

General interest in group processes has waxed and waned in psychology. Moreland et al. (1994) analyzed such trends and found that after nearly three decades of declining publication rates, there has since the late 1980s been a steady rise in publications on groups. However, they also show that little if any of that increase stemmed from work on intragroup processes (our present focus). Rather, the recent growth in group research can largely be attributed to the study of individual cognition about groups (e.g., stereotype formation, perceived group homogeneity) and to approaches popular in European social psychological circles with clear relevance to groups, but with a clear interpersonal (e.g., minority influence) or intergroup (e.g., social identity theory) focus. For those interested in intragroup processes, per se, this could be viewed as a half-empty glass. On the other hand, as this chapter and more-quantitative analyses (Moreland et al. 1994, Hogg & Moreland 1995) demonstrate, research on intragroup processes continues to represent a substantial and fairly constant share of the whole group research enterprise. Filling the glass must await progress in linking knowledge at these different levels of analysis. So far the strongest efforts have been made to apply individual-level cognitive and information processing models to the analysis of group processes, but attempts are also being made for similar applications from or to more interpersonal (e.g., Kerr 2001a) and intergroup (e.g., Haslam 2001, Wildschut et al. 2002) level models.

One theme that runs through both the recent performance and decision making literatures is that a single basic processes in groups can lead to both good versus poor performance, depending on the context in which that processes is enabled. For example, both motivation losses and gains can largely be explained using the notion of instrumentality in an expectancy-value framework (Karau & Williams 1993; Kerr 2001b). Something similar can be seen in decision-making groups. A simply majority processes tends to allow groups to perform better than individuals (reach more optimal solutions, make fewer errors, etc.) typically because most individuals will more often favor the correct or better alternative. However, a bias or heuristic at the individual level which tends toward a less optimal strategy will lead the same majority process in the group to result in poorer decisions relative to individuals working alone. Whereas earlier work attempted to explain good vs poor performance with different types of group processes, much of the more recent work has shown how the same processes can lead to both types of outcomes.

Considerable interest and attention is being paid in contemporary psychology (e.g., Snyder & Lopez 2002) to "positive psychology," which emphasizes adaptive human functioning (in contrast to a more traditional focus on human error, suboptimality, or pathology). A traditional focus in small group performance research has been on group suboptimality—groups tend to do perform better than individuals, but not as well as they could. But a theme that runs through much of the more recent work is that basic group processes can result in performance that meets or even exceeds reasonable expectations. In many instances, groups are satisficing entities–often it's not that groups cannot perform near their upper limits, it's that they simply don't need to. If a simple combination of member judgments tends to produce reasonably accurate probabilistic estimates, the additional effort necessary to make the combination "as accurate as it can possibly be" may often not be worth it. If a simply majority is more-often-than-not correct, then the additional effort necessary to figure out when they might be wrong may be inefficient (Kameda & Hastie 1999). Many group norms may have developed because they work most of the time and require little processing effort. The dominance of shared information may also reflect group satisficing. If all of the members of a group know something, it probably does have more validity than something that is only known by one member. Ideas that are shared among the group members will dominate because they require no additional justification–new ideas presented by only one person will need further elaboration and will only be influential to the degree that they appear to be important. Thus, much of the work discussed under the rubric of "social sharedness" (e.g., Kameda et al. 2002, Tindale & Kameda 2000) can be seen as demonstrating the satisficing nature of groups. Such considerations should encourage us to take a broader view of group effectiveness, considering such matters as how efficient various group processes are and how certain group processes that contribute to ineffectiveness in one context might be quite useful heuristics in many (or even most) other contexts.

A common criticism of much small-group research is that it oversimplifies an obviously complex set of processes. Much of the past work on small group decision-making has tended to focus on linear, antecedent-consequence type relations with manipulations of independent variables (e.g., group size, task type) causing changes in dependent variables (e.g., group choice, implicit decision scheme). Although this approach has taught us much about group decision-making, its very nature focuses attention on one or a few variables while ignoring virtually all others. There is general agreement that groups are certainly more complex than most of our theories and methods would suggest. The difficulty has and continues to be, "how can this complexity best be analyzed and understood?" It is worth noting a few fairly recent and promising ways of addressing such questions.

- One is Arrow, McGrath & Berdahl's (2000) ambitious attempt to develop a complex systems theory of small group formation, coordination, development, and adaptation. This theory has yet to receive much research attention (though see Berdahl 1998, 1999).

- A second is the use of dynamic systems approaches (e.g., Vallacher & Nowak 1994) to the study of group processes, best illustrated by research on dynamic social impact theory (Nowak et al. 1990, Latané & Bourgeois 2001). A number of very interesting findings have emerged from the simulation and empirical work utilizing this theory (e.g., many social influence processes produce spatial clusters where everyone holds similar opinions; such clustering depends on the structure of available communication channels; Latané & L'Herrou 1999).

- A third is the use of evolutionary principles and models to explore the adaptiveness of various forms of group decision making. For example, some scholars have argued that the popularity of majority-rules based on shared preferences may stem from their adaptive value. Such decision processes can effectively constrain self-interested behavior to the advantage of group (and species) fitness (Henrich & Boyd 1998; Kameda et al. 2002) and provide "fast and frugal" heuristics in diverse and complex decision environments (Kameda & Hastie 1999, Sorkin et al. 2001).

- A fourth utilizes the tools of modern information technology to pose questions that might never arise in the usual contexts of face-to-face groups. Research discussed earlier (e.g., on computerized brainstorming and electronic groups) as well as other fascinating new topics (e.g., using virtual reality to create and analyze group processes; Blascovich 2001) illustrates this exciting new approach to the study of groups (McGrath & Berdahl 1998).

We end our review (like a confession) with an appeal for absolution—from the scholars whose relevant work we may have missed or mischaracterized, and from you, the reader, who may have been misled by our errors of omission or commission. Please have mercy on us, contrite suboptimal scholars. Our penance will be to read carefully all the missed or misunderstood papers that are certain to be brought to our attention.

ACKNOWLEDGMENTS

The first author thanks NSF (BCS 9974664) and the Centre for the Study of Group Processes, University of Kent, for their support during the sabbatical leave when this chapter was written. The second author also thanks NSF (SES 0136332).

The *Annual Review of Psychology* is online at http://psych.annualreviews.org

LITERATURE CITED

Adelman L, Miller SL, Henderson D, Schoelles M. 2003. Using Brunswikian theory and a longitudinal design to study how hierarchical teams adapt to increasing levels of time pressure. *Acta Psychol.* 112(2):181–206

Anshel MH. 1995. Examining social loafing among elite female rowers as a function of task duration and mood. *J. Sport Behav.* 18(1):39–49

Argote L, Devadas R, Melone N. 1991. The base-rate fallacy: contrasting processes and outcomes of group and individual judgments. *Organ. Behav. Hum. Decis. Process.* 46:296–310

Ariely D, Au WT, Bender RH, Budescu DV, Dietz CB, et al. 2000. The effects of averaging subjective probability estimates between and within judges. *J. Exp. Psychol.: Applied* 6:130–47

Arrow H, McGrath JE, Berdahl JL. 2000. *Small Groups as Complex Systems: Formation, Coordination, Development, and Adaptation.* Thousand Oaks, CA: Sage

Arrow KJ. 1963. *Social Choice and Individual Values.* New Haven, CT: Yale Univ. Press. 2nd ed.

Bandura A. 1997. *Self-Efficacy: The Exercise of Control.* New York: Freeman. 500 pp.

Bazerman MH, Curhan JR, Moore DA, Valley KL. 2000. Negotiation. *Annu. Rev. Psychol.* 51:279–314

Berdahl JL. 1998. The dynamics of composition and socialization in small groups: insights gained from developing a computational model. In *Composition: Research on Managing Groups and Teams*, ed. DH Gruenfeld, pp. 209–27. Stamford, CT: JAI

Berdahl JL. 1999. *Power, perceptions, and performance in small groups: insights gained from a computational model.* Univ. Ill., Urbana-Champaign. Unpubl. doctoral diss.

Black D. 1958. *The Theory of Committees and Elections.* London: Cambridge Univ. Press

Blascovich J. 2001. Immersive virtual environmental technology as a tool in psychological science. *Psychol. Sci. Agenda* 14(6):8–9

Bond MH, Smith PB. 1996. Cross-cultural social and organizational psychology. *Annu. Rev. Psychol.* 47:205–35

Brauner E, Scholl W. 2000. The information processing approach as a perspective for group research. *Group Process. Intergroup Relat.* 3:115–22

Brodbeck FC, Kerschreiter R, Mojzisch A, Frey D, Schulz-Hardt S. 2002. The dissemination of critical, unshared information in decision-making groups: the effects of prediscussion dissent. *Eur. J. Soc. Psychol.* 32:35–56

Brown TM, Miller CE. 2000. Communication networks in task-performing groups: effects of task complexity, time pressure, and interpersonal dominance. *Small Group Res.* 31(2):131–57

Budescu DV, Rantilla AK. 2000. Confidence in aggregation of expert opinions. *Acta Psychol.* 104:371–98

Budescu DV, Rantilla AK, Yu HT, Krelitz TM. 2003. The effects of asymmetry among advisors on the aggregation of their opinions. *Organ. Behav. Hum. Decis. Process.* 90(1):178–94

Cannon-Bowers JA, Salas E, Converse SA. 1993. Shared mental models in team decision making. In *Individual and Group Decision Making*, ed. NJ Castellan Jr., pp. 221–46. Hillsdale, NJ: Erlbaum

Carnevale PJ, Pruitt DG. 1992. Negotiation and mediation. *Annu. Rev. Psychol.* 43:531–82

Charbonnier E, Huguet P, Brauer M, Montiel JM. 1998. Social loafing and self-beliefs: People's collective effort depends on the extent to which they distinguish themselves as better than others. *Soc. Behav. Personal.* 26(4):329–40

Chemers MM. 2000. Leadership research and theory: a functional integration. *Group Dyn.* 4(1):27–43

Connolly T, Routhieaux RL, Schneider SK. 1993. On the effectiveness of group brainstorming: test of one underlying cognitive mechanism. *Small Group Res.* 24(4):490–503

Cooper WH, Gallupe RB, Pollard S, Cadsby J. 1998. Some liberating effects of anonymous electronic brainstorming. *Small Group Res.* 29(2):147–78

Coskun H, Paulus PB, Brown V, Sherwood JJ. 2000. Cognitive stimulation and problem presentation in idea-generating groups. *Group Dyn.* 4(4):307–29

Craig TY, Kelly JR. 1999. Group cohesiveness and creative performance. *Group Dyn.* 3(4):243–56

Crott HW, Szilvas K, Zuber JA. 1991. Group decision, choice shift, and polarization in consulting, political and local political scenarios: an experimental investigation. *Organ. Behav. Hum. Decis. Process.* 49:22–41

Davis JH. 1969. *Group Performance.* Reading, MA: Addison-Wesley

Davis JH. 1973. Group decision and social interaction: a theory of social decision schemes. *Psychol. Rev.* 80:97–125

Davis JH. 1980. Group decision and procedural justice. In *Progress in Social Psychology*, ed. M Fishbein, 157–229. Hillsdale, NJ: Erlbaum

Davis JH. 1996. Group decision making and quantitative judgments: a consensus model. In *Understanding Group Behavior: Consensual Action by Small Groups*, ed. E Witte, JH Davis, 1:35–59. Mahwah, NJ: Erlbaum

Davis JH, Au W, Hulbert L, Chen X, Zarnoth P. 1997. Effect of group size and procedural influence on consensual judgment of quantity: the example of damage awards on mock civil juries. *J. Personal. Soc. Psychol.* 73:703–18

Davis JH, Kameda T, Parks C, Stasson, M. 1989. Some social mechanics of group decision making: the distribution of opinion, polling sequence, and implications for consensus. *J. Personal. Soc. Psychol.* 57(6):1000–12

Davis JH, Stasson MF, Parks CD, Hulbert L, Kameda T, et al. 1993. Quantitative decisions by groups and individuals: voting procedures and monetary awards by mock civil juries. *J. Exp. Soc. Psychol.* 29:326–46

De Grada E, Kruglanski AW, Mannetti L, Pierro A. 1999. Motivated cognition and group interaction: Need for closure affects the contents and processes of collective negotiations. *J. Exp. Soc. Psychol.* 35(4):346–65

Dennis AR, Valacich JS. 1993. Computer brainstorms: More heads are better than one. *J. Appl. Psychol.* 78(4):531–37

Dennis AR, Valacich JS. 1994. Group, subgroup, and nominal group idea generation: new rules for new media? *J. Manag.* 20(4):723–36

Diehl M, Stroebe W. 1987. Productivity loss in brainstorming groups: toward the solution of a riddle. *J. Personal. Soc. Psychol.* 53(3):497–509

Diehl M, Stroebe W. 1991. Productivity loss in idea-generating groups: tracking down the blocking effect. *J. Personal. Soc. Psychol.* 61(3):392–403

Douglas KM, McGarty C. 2001. Identifiability and self-preservation: computer-mediated communication and intergroup interaction. *Br. J. Soc. Psychol.* 40:399–416

Durham CC, Knight D, Locke EA. 1997. Effects of leader role, team-set goal difficulty, efficacy, and tactics on team effectiveness. *Organ. Behav. Hum. Decis. Process.* 72(2):203–31

Entin EE, Serfaty D. 1999. Adaptive team coordination. *Hum. Factors* 41:312–25

Erev I, Bornstein G, Galili R. 1993. Constructive intragroup competition as a solution to the free rider problem: a field experiment. *J. Exp. Soc. Psychol.* 29:463–78

Erez M, Somech A. 1996. Is group productivity loss the rule or the exception? Effects of culture and group-based motivation. *Acad. Manag. J.* 39(6):1513–37

Evans CR, Dion KL. 1991. Group cohesion and performance: a meta-analysis. *Small Group Res.* 22(2):175–86

Everett JJ, Smith RE, Williams KD. 1992. Effects of team cohesion and identifiability on social loafing in relay swimming performance. *Int. J. Sport Psychol.* 23:311–24

Gallupe RB, Bastianutti LM, Cooper WH. 1991. Unblocking brainstorms. *J. Appl. Psychol.* 76(1):137–42

Gallupe RB, Cooper WH, Grise ML, Bastianutti LM. 1994. Blocking electronic brainstorms. *J. Appl. Psychol.* 79(1):77–86

Gigone D, Hastie R. 1993. The common knowledge effect: information sharing and group judgment. *J. Personal. Soc. Psychol.* 65:959–74

Gigone D, Hastie R. 1996. The impact of information on group judgment: a model and computer simulation. In *Understanding Group Behavior: Consensual Action by Small Groups*, Vol. 1, ed. E Witte, JH Davis, pp. 221–51. Mahwah, NJ: Erlbaum

Goodman PS, Shah S. 1992. Familiarity and work group outcomes. In *Group Process and Productivity*, ed. S Worchel, W Wood, JA Simpson, pp. 276–98. Newbury Park, CA: Sage

Greitemeyer T, Schulz-Hardt S. 2003. Preference-consistent evaluation of information in the hidden profile paradigm: beyond group-level explanations for the dominance of shared information in group decisions. *J. Personal. Soc. Psychol.* 84(2):322–39

Gully SM, Devine DJ, Whitney DJ. 1995. A meta-analysis of cohesion and performance: effects of levels of analysis and task interdependence. *Small Group Res.* 26(4):497–520

Guzzo RA, Dickson MW. 1996. Teams in organizations: recent research on performance and effectiveness. *Annu. Rev. Psychol.* 47:307–38

Haertel CEJ, Haertel GF. 1997. SHAPE-assisted intuitive decision making and problem solving: Information-processing-based training for conditions of cognitive busyness. *Group Dyn: Theory Res. Pract.* 1:187–99

Hart JW, Bridgett DJ, Karau SJ. 2001. Coworker ability and effort as determinants of individual effort on a collective task. *Group Dyn.* 5(3):181–90

Harvey N, Harries C, Fischer I. 2000. Using advice and assessing its quality. *Organ. Behav. Hum. Decis. Process.* 81:252–73

Haslam SA. 2001. *Psychology in Organizations: The Social Identity Approach*. London: Sage

Hastie R, Penrod SD, Pennington N. 1983. *Inside the Jury*. Cambridge, MA: Harvard Univ. Press

Helmreich RL. 1997. Managing human error in aviation. *Sci. Amer.* 276:62–67

Henrich J, Boyd R. 1998. The evolution of conformist transmission and the emergence of between-group differences. *Evol. Hum. Behav.* 19:215–41

Henry RA. 1993. Group judgment accuracy: reliability and validity of post discussion confidence judgments. *Organ. Behav. Hum. Decis. Process.* 56(1):11–27

Henry RA. 1995. Improving group judgment accuracy: information sharing and determining the best member. *Organ. Behav. Hum. Decis. Process.* 62(2):190–97

Henry RA, Kmet J, Desrosiers E, Landa A. 2002. Examining the impact of interpersonal cohesiveness on group accuracy interventions: the importance of matching versus buffering. *Organ. Behav. Hum. Decis. Process.* 87(1):25–43

Henry RA, Strickland OJ, Yorges SL, Ladd D. 1996. Helping groups determine their most accurate member: the role of outcome feedback. *J. Appl. Soc. Psychol.* 26(13):1153–70

Hertel G, Deter C, Konradt U. 2003. Motivation gains in computer-mediated work groups. *J. Appl. Soc. Psychol.* In press

Hertel G, Kerr NL, Messé LA. 2000a. Motivation gains in groups: paradigmatic and theoretical advances on the Koehler effect. *J. Personal. Soc. Psychol.* 79:580–601

Hertel G, Kerr NL, Scheffler M, Geister S, Messé LA. 2000b. Exploring the Koehler motivation gain effect: impression management and spontaneous goal setting. *Z. Sozialpsychol.* 31(4):204–20

Hewstone M, Rubin M, Willis H. 2002. Intergroup bias. *Annu. Rev. Psychol.* 53:575–604

Hill GW. 1982. Group versus individual performance: Are N + 1 heads better than one? *Psychol. Bull.* 91:517–39

Hinsz VB. 1991. Individual versus group decision making: social comparison in goals for individual task performance. *J. Appl. Soc. Psychol.* 21(12):987–1003

Hinsz VB. 1992. Social influences on the goal choices of group members. *J. Appl. Soc. Psychol.* 22(16):1297–17

Hinsz VB. 1995. Goal setting by groups performing an additive task: a comparison with individual goal setting. *J. Appl. Soc. Psychol.* 25(11):965–90

Hinsz VB. 1999. Group decision making with responses of a quantitative nature: the theory of social decision schemes for quantities. *Organ. Behav. Hum. Decis. Process.* 80:28–49

Hinsz VB, Indahl KE. 1995. Assimilation to anchors for damage awards in a mock civil trial. *J. Appl. Soc. Psychol.* 25:991–1026

Hinsz VB, Tindale RS, Vollrath DA. 1997. The emerging conceptualization of groups as information processes. *Psychol. Bull.* 121(1):43–64

Hoeksema van Orden CYD, Gaillard AWK, Buunk BP. 1998. Social loafing under fatigue. *J. Personal. Soc. Psychol.* 75:1179–90

Hogg MA, Moreland RL. 1995. European and American influences on small groups research. Presented at Soc. Exper. Soc. Psychol. meet., Washington, DC

Hollenbeck JR, Sego DJ, Ilgen DR, Major DA, Hedlund J, Phillips J. 1997. Team judgment-making accuracy under difficult conditions: construct validation of potential manipulations using the TIDE 2 simulation. In *Team Performance Assessment and Measurement: Theory, Methods, and Applications*, ed. T Brannick, E Salas, C Prince, pp. 111–36. Malwah, NJ: Erlbaum

Hollingshead AB, McGrath JE, O'Connor KM. 1993. Group task performance and communication technology: a longitudinal study of computer-mediated versus fact-to-face work groups. *Small Group Res.* 24(3):307–33

Hollingshead AB. 1996. The rank-order effect in group decision making. *Organ. Behav. Hum. Decis. Process.* 68:181–93

Horowitz IA, FosterLee L, Brolly I. 1996. Effects of trial complexity on decision making. *J. Appl. Psychol.* 81:757–68

Huguet P, Charbonnier E, Montiel JM. 1999. Productivity loss in performance groups: People who see themselves as average do not engage in social loafing. *Group Dyn.* 3(2):118–31

Janis I. 1972. *Victims of Groupthink.* Boston, MA: Houghton Mifflin

Janis I. 1982. *Groupthink: Psychological Studies of Policy Decisions and Fiascoes.* Boston, MA: Houghton Mifflin. 2nd ed.

Johnson TR, Budescu DV, Wallsten TS. 2001. Averaging probability judgments: Monte Carlo analyses of asymptotic diagnostic value. *J. Behav. Dec. Mak.* 14:123–40

Johnson SR, Ostrow AC, Perna FM, Etzel EF. 1997. The effects of group versus individual goal setting on bowling performance. *Sport Psychol.* 11(2):190–200

Kameda T. 1991. Procedural influence in small-group decision making: deliberation style and assigned decision rule. *J. Personal. Soc. Psychol.* 61:245–56

Kameda T. 1996. Procedural influence in consensus formation: evaluating group decision making from a social choice perspective. In *Understanding Group Behavior: Consensual Action by Small Groups*, Vol. 1, ed. E Witte, JH Davis, pp. 137–61. Mahwah, NJ: Erlbaum

Kameda T, Hastie R. 1999. *Social sharedness and adaptation: adaptive group decision heuristics.* Presented at 17th Subj. Probabil., Util., Decis.-Mak. Conf., Mannheim, Ger.

Kameda T, Ohtsubo Y, Takezawa M. 1997. Centrality in socio-cognitive network and social influence: an illustration in a group decision making context. *J. Personal. Soc. Psychol.* 73:296–309

Kameda T, Sugimori S. 1993. Psychological entrapment in group decision-making: an assigned decision rule and a groupthink phenomenon. *J. Personal. Soc. Psychol.* 65:282–92

Kameda T, Sugimori S. 1995. Procedural influence in two-step group decision making: power of local majorities in consensus formation. *J. Personal. Soc. Psychol.* 69:865–76

Kameda T, Takezawa M, Tindale RS, Smith CM. 2002. Social sharing and risk reduction: exploring a computational algorithm for the psychology of windfall gains. *Evol. Hum. Behav.* 23(1):11–33

Kaplan MF, Wanshula LT, Zanna MP. 1993. Time pressure and information integration in social judgment: the effect of need for structure. In *Time Pressure and Stress in Human Judgement and Decision Making*, ed. O Svenson, J Maule, pp. 255–67. New York: Plenum

Karau SJ, Hart JR. 1998. Group cohesiveness and social loafing: effects of a social interaction manipulation on individual motivation within groups. *US: Educ. Publ. Found.* 2(3):185–91

Karau SJ, Kelly JR. 1992. The effects of time scarcity and time abundance on group performance quality and interaction process. *J. Exp. Soc. Psychol.* 28(6):542–71

Karau SJ, Williams KD. 1993. Social loafing: a meta-analytic review and theoretical integration. *J. Personal. Soc. Psychol.* 65:681–706

Karau SJ, Williams KD. 1997. The effects of group cohesiveness on social loafing and social compensation. *US: Educ. Publ. Found.* 1(2):156–68

Kelly JR. 1988. Entrainment in individual and group behavior. In *The Social Psychology of Time: New Perspectives*, ed. JE McGrath, pp. 89–110. Newbury Park, CA: Sage

Kelly JR, Futoran GC, McGrath JE. 1990. Capacity and capability: seven studies of entrainment of task performance rates. *Small Group Res.* 21(3):283–314

Kelly JR, Karau SJ. 1993. Entrainment of creativity in small groups. *Small Group Res.* 24(2):179–98

Kelly JR, Karau SJ. 1999. Group decision making: the effects of initial preferences and time pressure. *Personal Soc. Psychol. Bull.* 25:1342–54

Kerr NL. 1981. Social transition schemes: charting the group's road to agreement. *J. Personal. Soc. Psychol.* 41:684–702

Kerr NL. 2001a. Is it what one says or how one says it? Style vs. substance from an SDS perspective. In *Group Consensus and Minority Influence: Implications for Innovation*, ed. C DeDreu, NK De Vries, pp. 201–28. Malden, MA: Blackwell

Kerr NL. 2001b. Motivation gains in performance groups: aspects and prospects. In *The Social Mind: Cognitive and Motivational Aspects of Interpersonal Behavior*, ed. JP Forgas, KD Williams, pp. 350–70. New York: Cambridge Univ. Press

Kerr NL, MacCoun R, Kramer GP. 1996. Bias in judgment: comparing individuals and groups. *Psychol. Rev.* 103:687–719

Kerr NL, Niedermeier KE, Kaplan MF. 1999. Bias in jurors vs bias in juries: new evidence from the SDS perspective. *Organ.*

Behav. Hum. Decis. Process. 80(1):70–86

Kerr NL, Stanfel JA. 1993. Role schemata and member motivation in task groups. *Personal. Soc. Psychol. Bull.* 19(4):432–42

Köhler O. 1926. Kraftleistungen bei Einzel- und Gruppenabeit [Physical peformance in individual and group situations]. *Ind. Psychotech.* 4:209–26

Komorita SS, Parks CD. 1995. Interpersonal relations: mixed-motive interaction. *Annu. Rev. Psychol.* 46:183–207

Kruglanski AW, Shah JY, Pierro A, Mannetti L, Livi S, Kosic A. 2002. *The closing of the "group mind" and the emergence of groupcentrism*. Presented at Soc. Exp. Soc. Psychol., Columbus, OH

Kruglanski AW, Webster DM. 1991. Group members' reactions to opinion deviates and conformists at varying degrees of proximity to decision deadline and of environmental noise. *J. Personal. Soc. Psychol.* 61(2):212–25

Kruglanski AW, Webster DM. 1996. Motivated closing of the mind: "seizing" and "freezing." *Psychol. Rev.* 103(2):263–83

Kruglanski AW, Webster DM, Klem A. 1993. Motivated resistance and openness to persuasion in the presence or absence of prior information. *J. Personal. Soc. Psychol.* 65(5):861–76

Kuhn LM, Sniezek JA. 1996. Confidence and uncertainty in judgmental forecasting: differential effects of scenario presentation. *J. Behav. Decis. Mak.* 9:231–47

Langfred CW. 1998. Is group cohesiveness a double-edged sword? An investigation of the effects of cohesiveness on performance. *Small Group Res.* 29(1):124–43

Larey TS, Paulus PB. 1995. Social comparison goal setting in brainstorming groups. *J. Appl. Soc. Psychol.* 26(18):1579–96

Larson JR, Christensen C. 1993. Groups as problem-solving units: toward a new meaning of social cognition. *Br. J. Soc. Psychol.* 32(1):5–30

Larson JR, Christensen C, Abbott AS, Franz TM. 1996. Diagnosing groups: charting the flow of information in medical decision-making teams. *J. Personal. Soc. Psychol.* 71(2):315–30

Larson JR Jr, Foster-Fishman PG, Keys CB. 1994. Discussion of shared and unshared information in decision-making groups. *J. Personal. Soc. Psychol.* 67:446–61

Latané B, Bourgeois MJ. 2001. Successfully simulating dynamic social impact: three levels of prediction. In *Social Influence: Direct and Indirect Processes. The Sydney Symposium of Social Psychology*, ed. JP Forgas, KD Williams, pp. 61–76. Phildelphia, PA: Psychology Press

Latané B, L'Herrou T. 1999. Spatial clustering in the conformity game: dynamic social impact in electronic groups. *J. Personal. Soc. Psychol.* 70(6):1218–30

Latané B, Williams K, Harkins S. 1979. Many hands make light the work: the causes and consequences of social loafing. *J. Personal. Soc. Psychol.* 37:822–32

Latham GP, Winter DC, Locke EA. 1994. Cognitive and motivational effects of participation: a mediator study. *J. Organ. Behav.* 15(1):49–63

Laughlin PR. 1980. Social combination processes of cooperative, problem-solving groups on verbal intellective tasks. In *Progress in Social Psychology*, Vol. 1, ed. M Fishbein, pp. 127–55. Hillsdale, NJ: Erlbaum

Laughlin PR. 1988. Collective induction: group performance, social combination processes, and mutual majority and minority influence. *J. Personal. Soc. Psychol.* 54:254–67

Laughlin PR. 1992. Performance and influence in simultaneous collective and individual induction. *Organ. Behav. Hum. Decis. Process.* 51:447–70

Laughlin PR. 1996. Group decision making and collective induction. In *Understanding Group Behavior: Vol. 1. Consensual Action by Small Groups*, ed. J Davis, E Witte, pp. 61–80. Mahwah, NJ: Erlbaum

Laughlin PR. 1999. Collective induction: twelve postulates. *Organ. Behav. Hum. Decis. Process.* 80(1):50–69

Laughlin PR, Bonner BL. 1999. Collective induction: effects of multiple hypotheses and multiple evidence in two problem domains. *J. Personal. Soc. Psychol.* 77(6):1163–72

Laughlin PR, Bonner BL, Altermatt TW. 1998a. Collective versus individual induction with single versus multiple hypotheses. *J. Personal. Soc. Psychol.* 75:1481–89

Laughlin PR, Bonner BL, Miner AG. 2002. Groups perform better than the best individuals on Letters-to-Numbers problems. *Organ. Behav. Hum. Decis. Process.* 88(2):605–20

Laughlin PR, Bonner BL, Miner AG, Carnevale PJ. 1999. Frames of reference in quantity estimations by groups and individuals. *Organ. Behav. Hum. Decis. Process.* 80(2):103–17

Laughlin PR, Chandler JS, Shupe EI, Magley VJ, Hulbert LG. 1995. Generality of a theory of collective induction: face-to-face and computer-mediated interaction, amount of potential information, and group versus member choice of evidence. *Organ. Behav. Hum. Decis. Process.* 63:98–111

Laughlin PR, Ellis AL. 1986. Demonstrability and social combination processes on mathematical intellective tasks. *J. Exp. Soc. Psychol.* 22:177–89

Laughlin PR, Gonzalez CM, Sommer D. 2003. Quantity estimations by groups and individuals: effects of known domain boundaries. *Group Dyn.* 7(1):55–63

Laughlin PR, Hollingshead AB. 1995. A theory of collective induction. *Organ. Behav. Hum. Decis. Process.* 61:94–107

Laughlin PR, Magley VJ, Shupe EI. 1997. Positive and negative hypothesis testing by cooperative groups. *Organ. Behav. Hum. Decis. Process.* 69:265–75

Laughlin PR, McGlynn RP. 1986. Collective induction: mutual group and individual influence by exchange of hypotheses and evidence. *J. Exp. Soc. Psychol.* 22:567–89

Laughlin PR, Shupe EI. 1996. Intergroup collective induction. *Organ. Behav. Hum. Decis. Process.* 68:44–57

Laughlin PR, Shupe EI, Magley VJ. 1998b. Effectiveness of positive hypothesis testing for cooperative groups. *Organ. Behav. Hum. Decis. Process.* 73:27–38

Laughlin PR, VanderStoep SW, Hollingshead AB. 1991. Collective versus individual induction: recognition of truth, rejection of error, and collective information processing. *J. Personal. Soc. Psychol.* 61:50–67

Lea M, Spears R, deGroot D. 2001. Knowing me, knowing you: anonymity effects on social identity processes within groups. *Personal. Soc. Psychol. Bull.* 27:526–37

Leggett-Dugosh K, Paulus PB, Roland EJ, Yang HC. 2000. Cognitive stimulation in brainstorming. *J. Personal. Soc. Psychol.* 79(5):722–35

Levine JM, Moreland RL. 1990. Progress in small group research. *Annu. Rev. Psychol.* 41:585–634

Levine JM, Resnick L, Higgins T. 1993. Social foundations of cognition. *Annu. Rev. Psychol.* 44:585–612

Liang DW, Moreland RL, Argote L. 1995. Group versus individual training and group performance: the mediating factor of transactive memory. *Personal. Soc. Psychol. Bull.* 21(4):384–93

Littlepage G, Robison W, Reddington K. 1997. Effects of task experience and group experience on group performance, member ability, and recognition of expertise. *Organ. Behav. Hum. Decis. Process.* 69(2):133–47

Littlepage GE, Karau SJ. 1997. Utility and limitations of the SHAPE-assisted intuitive decision-making procedure. *Group Dyn.* 1(3):200–7

Littlepage GE, Mueller AL. 1997. Recognition and utilization of expertise in problem-solving groups: expert characteristics and behavior. *Group Dyn.* 1(4):324–28

Littlepage GE, Poole JR. 1993. Time allocation in decision making groups. *J. Soc. Behav. Personal.* 8(4):663–72

Littlepage GE, Schmidt GW, Whisler EW, Frost AG. 1995. An input-process-output analysis of influence and performance in problem-solving groups. *J. Personal. Soc. Psychol.* 69(5):877–89

Littlepage GE, Silbiger H. 1992. Recognition

of expertise in decision-making groups: effects of group size and participation patterns. *Small Group Res.* 23(3):344–55

Locke EA, Alavi M, Wagner JA III. 1997. Participation in decision making: an information exchange perspective. In *Research in Personnel and Human Resources Management*, 15:293–331. Stamford, CT: JAI. 383 pp.

Lorge I, Solomon H. 1955. Two models of group behavior in the solution of eureka-type problems. *Psychometrica* 20:139–48

Lount R, Messé LA, Kerr NL. 2000. Trying harder for different reasons: conjunctivity and sex composition as bases for motivation gains in performing groups. *Z. Sozialpsychol.* 31:221–30

Ludwig TD, Geller ES. 1997. Assigned versus participative goal setting and response generalization: managing injury control among professional pizza deliverers. *J. Appl. Psychol.* 82(2):253–61

MacCoun R, Kerr NL. 1988. Asymmetric influence in mock jury deliberations: juror's bias for leniency. *J. Personal. Soc. Psychol.* 54:21–33

Marks MA, Zaccaro SJ, Mathieu JE. 2000. Performance implications of leader briefings and team-interaction training for team adaptation to novel environments. *J. Appl. Psychol.* 85:971–86

Mathieu JE, Heffner TS, Goodwin GF, Salas E, Cannon-Bowers JA. 2000. The influence of shared mental models on team process and performance. *J. Appl. Psychol.* 85:273–83

McGrath JE, Berdahl JL. 1998. Groups, technology, and time: use of computers for collaborative work. In *Theory and Research on Small Groups. Social Psychological Applications to Social Issues*, Vol. 4, ed. RS Tindale, L Heath, pp. 205–28. New York: Plenum

McLeod PL, Baron RS, Weighner MM, Yoon K. 1997. The eyes have it: minority influence in face-to-face and computer-mediated group discussion. *J. Appl. Psychol.* 82:706–18

Mesch DJ, Farh JL, Podsakoff PM. 1994. Effects of feedback sign on group goal setting, strategies, and performance. *Group Organ. Manag.* 19(3):309–33

Messé LA, Hertel G, Kerr NL, Lount RB Jr, Park ES. 2002. Knowledge of partner's ability as a moderator of group motivation gains: an exploration of the Koehler discrepancy effect. *J. Personal. Soc. Psychol.* 82(6):935–46

Michaelsen LK, Watson WE, Black RH. 1989. A realistic test of individual versus group consensus decision making. *J. Appl. Psychol.* 74:834–39

Miles JA, Greenberg J. 1993. Using punishment threats to attenuate social loafing effects among swimmers. *Organ. Behav. Hum. Decis. Process.* 56:246–65

Moreland RL. 1999. Transactive memory. In *Learning Who Knows What in Work Groups and Organizations*, ed. L Thompson, J Levine, pp. 3–31. Mahwah, NJ: Erlbaum. 364 pp.

Moreland RL, Argote L. 2003. Transactive memory in dynamic organizations. In *Understanding the Dynamic Organization*, ed. R Peterson, E Mannix, pp. 135–62. Mahwah, NJ: Erlbaum

Moreland RL, Hogg MA, Hains SC. 1994. Back to the future: social psychological research on groups. *J. Exp. Soc. Psychol.* 30(6):527–55

Moreland RL, Myaskovsky L. 2000. Exploring the performance benefits of group training: transactive memory or improved communication? *Organ. Behav. Hum. Decis. Process.* 82(1):117–33

Mullen B, Anthony T, Salas E, Driskell JE. 1994. Group cohesiveness and quality of decision making. *Small Group Res.* 25:189–204

Mullen B, Copper C. 1994. The relation between group cohesiveness and performance: an integration. *Psychol. Bull.* 115(2):210–27

Mullen B, Johnson C, Salas E. 1991. Productivity loss in brainstorming groups: a meta-analytic integration. *Basic Appl. Soc. Psychol.* 12(1):3–23

Myers DG, Lamm H. 1976. The group polarization phenomenon. *Psychol. Bull.* 83(4):602–27

Nijstad BA. 2000. *How the group affects the mind: effects of communication in idea gen-*
erating groups. Utrecht Univ. Unpubl. doctoral diss.

Nijstad BA, Stroebe W, Lodewijkx HFM. 2003. Cognitive stimulation and interference in groups. Exposure effects in an idea generation task. *J. Exp. Soc. Psychol.* In press

Nowak A, Szamrej J, Latane B. 1990. From private attitude to public opinion: a dynamic theory of social impact. *Psychol. Rev.* 97(3):362–76

Offner AK, Kramer TJ, Winter JP. 1996. The effects of facilitation, recording, and pauses on group brainstorming. *Small Group Res.* 27(2):283–98

Oliver LW, Harman J, Hoover E, Hayes SM, Pandhi NA. 1999. A quantitative integration of the military cohesion literature. *Mil. Psychol.* 11(1):57–83

O'Leary-Kelly AM, Martocchio JJ, Frink DD. 1994. A review of the influence of group goals on performance. *Acad. Manag. J.* 37:1285–301

Osborn AF. 1957. *Applied Imagination.* New York: Scribner

Oxley NL, Dzindolet MT, Paulus P. 1996. The effects of facilitators on the performance of brainstorming groups. *J. Soc. Behav. Personal.* 11(4):633–46

Paulus PB, Dzindolet MT. 1993. Social influence processes in group brainstorming. *J. Personal. Soc. Psychol.* 64:575–86

Paulus PB, Dzindolet MT, Poletes GW, Camacho LM. 1993. Perception of performance in group brainstorming: the illusion of group productivity. *Personal. Soc. Psychol. Bull.* 19:78–79

Paulus PB, Larey TS, Putman VL, Leggett KL, Roland EJ. 1996. Social influence processes in computer brainstorming. *Basic Appl. Soc. Psychol.* 18(1):3–14

Paulus PB, Yang HC. 2000. Idea generation in groups: a basis for creativity in organizations. *Organ. Behav. Hum. Decis. Process.* 82(1):76–87

Penrod SD, Hastie R. 1981. A computer simulation of jury decision making. *Psychol. Rev.* 87:133–59

Peterson RS, Owen PD, Tetlock PE, Fan ET,

Martorana P. 1998. Group dynamics in top management teams: groupthink, vigilance, and alternative models of organizational failure and success. *Organ. Behav. Hum. Decis. Process.* 73:272–305

Pettigrew TF. 1998. Intergroup contact theory. *Annu. Rev. Psychol.* 49:65–85

Pierro A, Mannetti L, De Grada E, Livi S, Kruglanski AW. 2003. Autocracy bias in informal groups under need for closure. *Personal. Soc. Psychol. Bull.* 29(3):405–17

Podsakoff PM, MacKenzie SB, Ahearne M. 1997. Moderating effects of goal acceptance on the relationship between group cohesiveness and productivity. *J. Appl. Psychol.* 82(6):374–83

Prussia GE, Kinicki AJ. 1996. A motivational investigation of group effectiveness using social-cognitive theory. *J. Appl. Psychol.* 81:187–98

Roberson QM, Moye NA, Locke EA. 1999. Identifying a missing link between participation and satisfaction: the mediating role of procedural justice perceptions. *J. Appl. Psychol.* 84(4):585–93

Roy MC, Gauvin S, Limayem M. 1996. Electronic group brainstorming: the role of feedback on productivity. *Small Group Res.* 27(2):215–47

Sargis EG, Larson JR. 2002. Informational centrality and member participation during group decision making. *Group Process. Intergroup Relat.* 5(4):333–47

Sawyer JE. 1997. *Information sharing and integration in multifunctional decision-making groups.* Presented at Annu. Meet. Soc. Judgm. Decis. Making, Philadelphia, PA

Schruijer SGL, Mostert I. 1997. Creativity and sex composition: an experimental illustration. *Eur. J. Work Organ. Psychol.* 6(2):175–82

Sheffey S, Tindale RS, Scott LA. 1989. *Information sharing and group decision-making.* Presented at Midwest. Psychol. Assoc., Chicago, IL

Shepperd JA. 1993. Productivity loss in performance groups: a motivation analysis. *Psychol. Bull.* 113:67–81

Smith BN, Kerr NA, Markus MJ, Stasson MF. 2001. Individual differences in social loafing: need for cognition as a motivator in collective performance. *Group Dyn.* 5(2):150–58

Smith CM, Tindale RS, Anderson EM. 2001. The impact of shared representations on minority influence in freely interacting groups. In *Group Consensus and Minority Influence: Implications for Innovation,* ed. C DeDreu, NK DeVries, pp. 183–200. Malden, MA: Blackwell

Smith CM, Tindale RS, Steiner L. 1998. Investment decisions by individuals and groups in "Sunk Coast" situations: the potential impact of shared representations. *Group Process. Intergroup Relat.* 2:175–89

Smoke W, Zajonc RB. 1962. On the reliability of group judgments and decisions. In *Mathematical Methods in Small Group Processes,* ed. J Crisswell, H Solomon, P Suppes, pp. 322–33. Stanford, CA: Stanford Univ. Press

Sniezek JA. 1992. Groups under uncertainty: an examination of confidence in group decision making. *Organ. Behav. Hum. Decis. Process.* 62:159–74

Sniezek JA, Buckley T. 1995. Cueing and cognitive conflict in judge-advisor decision making. *Organ. Behav. Hum. Decis. Process.* 62:159–74

Sniezek JA, Henry RA. 1989. Accuracy and confidence in group judgment. *Organ. Behav. Hum. Decis. Process.* 43(1):1–28

Snyder CR, Lopez SJ. 2002. *Handbook of Positive Psychology.* London: Oxford Univ. Press

Sorkin RD, Hays C, West R. 2001. Signal-detection analysis of group decision making. *Psychol. Rev.* 108:183–203

Sorkin RD, West R, Robinson DE. 1998. Group performance depends on the majority rule. *Psychol. Sci.* 9:456–63

Spears R, Lea M, Lee S. 1990. Deindividuation and group polarization in computer-mediated communication. *British J. Soc. Psychol.* 29(2):121–34

Spoor J, Craig T, Kelly J. 2002. *Cognitive centrality and group gender compostion.* Poster presented at Annu. Meet. Soc. Personal. Soc. Psychol., Savannah, GA

Stasser G, Davis JH. 1981. Group decision making and social influence: a social interaction sequence model. *Psychol. Rev.* 88:523–52

Stasser G, Kerr NL, Bray RN. 1982. The social psychology of jury deliberation: structure, process, and product. In *The Psychology of the Courtroom*, ed. NL Kerr, RN Bray, pp. 221–56. New York: Academic

Stasser G, Kerr NL, Davis JH. 1989. Influence processes and consensus models in decision-making groups. In *Psychology of Group Influence*, ed. P Paulus, pp. 279–326. Hillsdale, NJ: Erlbaum

Stasser G, Stewart DD. 1992. Discovery of hidden profiles by decision-making groups: solving a problem vs. making a judgment. *J. Personal. Soc. Psychol.* 63:426–34

Stasser G, Titus W. 1985. Pooling of unshared information in group decision making: biased information sampling during discussion. *J. Personal. Soc. Psychol.* 48:1467–78

Steiner ID. 1966. Models for inferring relationships between group size and potential group productivity. *Behav. Sci.* 11:273–83

Steiner ID. 1972. *Group Process and Productivity*. New York: Academic

Stewart DD, Stasser G. 1995. Expert role assignment and information sampling during collective recall and decision making. *J. Personal. Soc. Psychol.* 69:619–28

Stewart DD, Stasser G. 1998. The sampling of critical, unshared information in decision-making groups. *Eur. J. Soc. Psychol.* 28:95–113

Straus MA, McGrath JE. 1994. Does the medium matter? The interaction of task type and technology on group performance and member reactions. *J. Appl. Psychol.* 79(1):87–97

Stroebe W, Diehl M. 1994. In *European Review of Social Psychology*, ed. W Stroebe, M Hewstone, pp. 271–303. New York: Wiley

Stroebe W, Diehl M, Abakoumkin G. 1996. Social compensation and the Köhler Effect: toward a theoretical explanation of motivation gains in group productivity. In *Understanding Group Behavior: Consensual Action by Small Groups*, ed. E Witte, J Davis, 2:37–65. Mahwah, NJ: Erlbaum

Sunstein CR, Hastie R, Payne JW, Schkade DA, Viscusi WK. 2002. *Punitive Damages: How Juries Decide*. Chicago: Univ. Chicago Press

Tindale RS. 1993. Decision errors made by individuals and groups. In *Individual and Group Decision Making: Current Issues*, ed. N Castellan Jr., pp. 109–24. Hillsdale, NJ: Erlbaum

Tindale RS, Anderson EM, Smith CM, Steiner L, Filkins J. 1998. *Further explorations of conjunction errors by individuals and groups.* Presented at Br. Psychol. Soc. Soc. Psychol. Sect. Conf., Centerbury, UK

Tindale RS, Davis JH. 1983. Group decision making and jury verdicts. In *Small Groups and Social Interaction*, Vol. 2, ed. H Blumberg, AP Hare, V Kent, MF Davies, pp. 9–38. Chichester, UK: Wiley

Tindale RS, Filkins J, Thomas LS, Smith CM. 1993a. *An attempt to reduce conjunctive errors in decision-making groups.* Presented at Annu. Meet. Soc. Judgm. Decis. Making, Washington, DC

Tindale RS, Kameda T. 2000. "Social sharedness" as a unifying theme for information processing in groups. *Group Process. Intergroup Relat.* 3:123–40

Tindale RS, Larson JR Jr. 1992a. Assembly bonus effect or typical group performance: a comment on Michaelsen, Watson, & Black (1989). *J. Appl. Psychol.* 77:102–5

Tindale RS, Larson JR Jr. 1992b. It's not how you frame the question, it's how you interpret the results. *J. Appl. Psychol.* 77:109–10

Tindale RS, Nadler J, Krebel A, Davis JH. 2001. Procedural mechanisms and jury behavior. In *Blackwell Handbook in Social Psychology: Group Processes*, ed. MA Hogg, RS Tindale, pp. 574–602. Oxford, UK: Blackwell

Tindale RS, Sheffey S. 2002. Shared information, cognitive load, and group memory. *Group Process. Intergroup Relat.* 5(1):5–18

Tindale RS, Sheffey S, Filkins J. 1990. *Conjunction errors by individuals and groups.* Presented at Annu. Meet. Soc. Judgm. Decis. Making, New Orleans, LA

Tindale RS, Sheffey S, Scott LA. 1993b. Framing and group decision-making: Do cognitive changes parallel preference changes? *Organ. Behav. Hum. Decis. Process.* 55:470–85

Tindale RS, Smith CM, Thomas LS, Filkins J, Sheffey S. 1996. Shared representations and asymmetric social influence processes in small groups. In *Understanding Group Behavior: Consensual Action by Small Groups,* ed. E Witte, JH David, 1:81–103. Mahwah, NJ: Erlbaum

Tversky A, Kahneman D. 1981. The framing of decisions and the psychology of choice. *Science* 211:453–58

Urban JM, Weaver JL, Bowers CA, Rhodenizer L. 1996. Effects of workload and structure on team processes and performance: implications for complex team decision making. *Hum. Factors* 38(2):300–10

Valacich JS, Dennis AR, Connolly T. 1994. Idea generation in computer-based groups: a new ending to an old story. *Organ. Behav. Hum. Decis. Process.* 7(3):448–67

Vallacher RR, Nowak NA, eds. 1994. *Dynamical Systems in Social Psychology.* San Diego, CA: Academic

Van Swol LM, Sniezek JA. 2002. *Trust me, I'm an expert*: trust and confidence and acceptance of expert advice. Presented at 8th Conf. Behav. Decis. Res. Manag. (BDRAM), Chicago

Volpe CE, Cannon-Bowers JA, Salas E, Spector PE. 1996. The impact of cross-training on team functioning: an empirical investigation. *Hum. Factors* 38(1):87–100

Wagner JA. 1995. Studies in individualism collectivism: effects on cooperation in groups. *Acad. Manag. J.* 38(1):152–72

Wegge J. 2000. Participation in group goal setting: some novel findings and a comprehensive model as a new ending to an old story. *Appl. Psychol.: An Int. Rev.* 49(3):498–516

Wegge J, Kleinbeck U. 1996. Goal setting and

group performance: impact of achievement and affiliation motives, participation in goal setting, and task interdependence of group members. In *Advances in Motivation,* ed. T Gjesme, R Nygard, pp. 145–77. Oslo: Scand. Univ. Press

Wegner DM. 1987. Transactive memory: a contemporary analysis of the group mind. In *Theories of Group Behavior,* ed. B Mullen, Goethals, pp. 185–208. New York: Springer

Weldon E, Weingart LR. 1993. Group goals and group performance. *Br. J. Soc. Psychol.* 32(4):307–34

Whyte G. 1993. Escalating commitment in individual and group decision making: a prospect theory approach. *Organ. Behav. Hum. Decis. Process.* 54(3):430–55

Whyte G. 1998. Recasting Janis's groupthink model: the key role of collective efficacy in decision fiascoes. *Organ. Behav. Hum. Decis. Process.* 73:185–209

Wildschut T, Insko CA, Gaertner L. 2002. Intragroup social influence and intergroup competition. *J. Personal. Soc. Psychol.* 82(6):975–92

Williams KD, Karau SJ. 1991. Social loafing and social compensation: the effects of expectations of co-worker performance. *J. Personal. Soc. Psychol.* 61:570–81

Wilpert B. 1995. Organizational behavior. *Annu. Rev. Psychol.* 46:59–90

Winquist JR, Larson JR. 1998. Information pooling: when it impacts group decision making. *J. Personal. Soc. Psychol.* 74:371–77

Witte EH. 1989. Koehler rediscovered: the anti-Ringelmann effect. *Eur. J. Soc. Psychol.* 19(2):147–54

Wittenbaum GM. 1998. Information sampling in decision-making groups: the impact of members' task-relevant status. *Small Group Res.* 29(1):57–84

Wittenbaum GM. 2000. The bias toward discussing shared information: Why are high-status group members immune? *Commun. Res.* 27(3):379–401

Wittenbaum GM, Hubbell AP, Zuckerman C. 1999. Mutual enhancement: toward an understanding of collective preference for shared information. *J. Personal. Soc. Psychol.* 77:967–78

Wittenbaum GM, Stasser G. 1996. Management of information in small groups. In *What's Social about Social Cognition*, ed. JL Nye, AM Brower, pp. 967–78. Thousand Oaks, CA: Sage

Wood W. 2000. Attitude change: persuasion and social influence. *Annu. Rev. Psychol.* 51:539–70

Worchel S, Rothgerber H, Day EA, Hart D, Butemeyer J. 1998. Social identity and individual productivity within groups. *Br. J. Soc. Psychol.* 37:389–413

Yammarino FJ, Naughton TJ. 1992. Individualized and group-based views of participation in decision making. *Group Organ. Manag.* 17(4):398–413

Yaniv I, Kleinberger E. 2000. Advice taking in decision-making: egocentric discounting and reputation formation. *Organ. Behav. Hum. Decis. Process.* 83:260–81

Zaccaro SJ. 1991. Nonequivalent associations between forms of cohesiveness and group-related outcomes: evidence for multidimensionality. *J. Soc. Psychol.* 131(3):387–99

Ziegler R, Diehl M, Zijlstra G. 2000. Idea production in nominal and virtual groups: Does computer-mediated communication improve group brainstorming? *Group Process. Intergroup Relat.* 3(2):141–58

Annu. Rev. Psychol. 2004. 55:657–87
doi: 10.1146/annurev.psych.55.090902.141502

CREATIVITY

Mark A. Runco

*Psychology Department, California State University, Fullerton, California 92834;
email: runco@fullerton.edu*

Key Words   divergent thinking, ideation, originality, flexibility, domains of
performance, implicit theories, problem finding

■ **Abstract**   Creativity has clear benefits for individuals and society as a whole.
Not surprisingly, a great deal of research has focused on creativity, especially in the
past 20 years. This chapter reviews the creativity research, first looking to the relevant
traits, capacities, influences, and products, and then within disciplinary perspectives on
creativity (e.g., biological, cognitive, developmental, organizational). Great headway is
being made in creativity research, but more dialogue between perspectives is suggested.
New and important areas of research are highlighted, and the various costs and benefits
of creativity are discussed.

CONTENTS

0066-4308/04/0204-0657$14.00

INTRODUCTION

The world is becoming more and more complex. Modern conveniences abound, and technology seems to have touched everything from cooking to mass production, from communication to driving. In some ways life today is easier than ever before. In other ways, it is more difficult. Although we may now use a cellular phone to keep track of family members and to synchronize our appointments, we must also master cell phone operation—and update the requisite skills each time we buy a new cell phone. We must also develop new skills to operate our televisions, ovens, automobiles, and computers. Perhaps it would be most accurate to say that we have more opportunities than ever before, but more demands are placed upon us as well.

This complexity is increasing and will continue to do so. The information boom is not slowing down, and technological advances are occurring more often. Such changes reflect cultural evolution, which is unlike biological evolution in its rapidity. Although there is some debate about this (Gould 2002), biological evolution seems to take a great deal of time; changes are not maintained until they have been selected for generations and generations. Cultural evolution, on the other hand, can be seen in changes that occur from one generation to the next. This is Lamarckian, in contrast to Darwinian, evolution (Wilson 1978). It is fast and part of the reason life today is so complicated and complex.

All of this implies that creativity is more important now than ever before. This is because creativity is a useful and effective response to evolutionary changes. In addition to what may be its most obvious function, namely as part of the problem-solving process (Mumford et al. 1991, Runco 1994, Torrance 1971, Wallas 1926), creative ideation allows the individual to remain flexible (Flach 1990; Runco 1986, 1994). Creativity is usually tied to original behavior, and indeed, originality is necessary for creativity, but it is not sufficient. Creativity is a syndrome or complex (Albert & Runco 1989, MacKinnon 1983/1960, Mumford & Gustafson 1988), and flexibility is an important part of it. The flexibility of creative persons is what gives them the capacity to cope with the advances, opportunities, technologies, and changes that are a part of our current day-to-day lives.

This view of creativity implies that it is reactive; and surely, it often is a reaction to problems or challenges. Yet creativity is also one of the engines of cultural evolution. As Paulus & Nijstad (2003) described it, innovation is a vital process today, and that innovation requires change. In their words, "the basis for such change comes down to the stimulating effects of new ideas. . . . Creativity is therefore often defined as the development of original ideas that are useful or influential." In this perspective, creativity is not only a reaction to but also a contribution to change and evolution. Creativity thus underlies problem solving and problem finding; it plays a role in reactions (e.g., adaptations and solutions) but it is also often proactive.

Bruner (1962) claimed that we must encourage the creativity of our children and students as preparation for the future, given that the future is more difficult than ever before to define. Given the "greying of America," it will come as no surprise that more and more research is exploring life span creativity. The research reviewed in this chapter suggests that creativity facilitates late-life adaptations and growth (Cohen 1989; Cohen-Shalev 1986, 1989; Dudek & Hall 1991; Gott 1992, 1993; Helson 1990; Hogg 1993; Lindauer 1992, 1993; Runco & Charles 1997; Zausner 1999). This is especially true of the flexibility allowed by creativity, because older adults tend to rely on routines and, unless intentionally creative, become inflexible (Rubenson & Runco 1995). Creativity contributes to both physical and psychological health (Eisenman 1991, Mraz & Runco 1994, Pennebaker et al. 1997, Runco & Richards 1997) and to optimal human functioning (Bloom 2001).

Creativity is not, however, just a concern and target for individuals. Its benefits are just as clear for society and culture (Simonton 1991). As noted above, creativity plays an important role in technological advance, in the social and behavioral sciences, and in the humanities and arts (Dudek 2003). Because of its role in innovation and entrepreneurship, creativity has become one of the key concerns of organizations and businesses. The organizational perspective and research is reviewed below. Before turning to specific perspectives on creativity, it will be useful to put this chapter into context with the field of creative studies.

BACKGROUND AND CONTEXT

Although a number of excellent studies of creative talents and creative persons were published before 1950 [see Albert & Runco (1986) or Runco (1999a) for histories of the field], a great deal of credit is given to J.P. Guilford (1950). His presidential address to the American Psychological Association was titled "Creativity," and his argument at that time, and his subsequent empirical efforts, went a long way toward convincing individuals of the possibility of being scientific about creativity. Guilford also argued convincingly that creativity was a vital "natural resource." This may be a good example of zeitgeist ("the spirit of the times"), for Guilford's arguments were entirely compatible with the assumptions and needs of the 1950s. Many other examples of zeitgeist have been reported in the creativity literature (Shlain 1999, Simonton 1984).

The present chapter is in part an update to the review of Barron & Harrington (1981). Many significant advances have occurred since they published their chapter in the *Annual Review of Psychology*, and a number of new directions of study have opened. These new directions (and resulting new issues) are covered below. They imply that this chapter is not simply an extension of the fine work of Barron & Harrington (1981). Consider in this regard the fact that Barron & Harrington (1981) devoted most of their review to (*a*) creativity in relation to intelligence, and (*b*) creativity and personality (the title of their chapter was "Creativity, Intelligence, and Personality"). These emphases—intelligence and personality—are given much less attention in the current literature, and thus in this chapter. The relationship between creativity and intelligence has been researched since 1981. Runco & Albert (1987), for instance, reported that the threshold theory (wherein a minimum level of intelligence is a prerequisite for creative performance) is only found with certain measures of creativity. And there is research on creativity and personality, which is reviewed later in this chapter. Yet, neither of these emphases is as central to the field as they were in 1981. At that point, there was still a concern that creativity was simply an expression of general intelligence and not a distinctive capacity (Getzels & Jackson 1962, Wallach & Kogan 1965, Wallach & Wing 1969). That view is no longer prevalent. The topic is still being investigated, but these investigations are no longer motivated by the need for discriminant validity (the distinctiveness mentioned just above). Personality is also being studied, but many other influences on creative work have been identified. Some of these are tied to the individual's potentials, dispositions, abilities, and capacities, and some are tied to the environment and social context. The creative personality, indeed the creative person, is only one focus for contemporary research.

The literature on creativity is quite diverse. It can be organized in several ways. In this review I first use a scheme proposed by Rhodes (1961/1987) that distinguished between the creative person, process, product, and press. (Press research may be the least intuitively obvious label in this list. It refers to pressures on creativity. Examples are given below.) This framework takes us quite a distance into the creativity research, but leaves a number of gaps. For that reason, I then review research reflecting different disciplinary assumptions. I review the behavioral perspective on creativity, research on the biology of creativity, then clinical, cognitive, developmental, economic, educational, historiometric, organizational, psychometric, and social research. These approaches overlap a great deal, and an interdisciplinary perspective is best, but the disciplinary scheme does help round out this review. Because several important topics do not fit neatly into either the alliterative or the disciplinary categorization schemes, I end this chapter by covering explicit theories of creativity and key issues in the field. It is interesting to compare the issues that are receiving the most attention today with those of 20–25 years ago.

This chapter will be a success to the degree that it convinces readers that creativity is more important now than ever before. Consider the breadth of the research reviewed here. This breadth demonstrates the numerous and diverse applications of creativity and is suggestive of its importance. Creativity is useful; it can be applied each day to many aspects of our lives. In fact, as noted above, it can help us keep up with the challenges of modern life. This is part of the take-home message of this chapter: Creativity does not just play a role in the arts, invention, and innovation; it also is a part of our everyday lives (Runco & Richards 1997). The benefits of creativity are numerous, especially if its duality, suggested earlier, is acknowledged. Creativity is not just a kind of problem solving and a reaction, but can also be proactive. This duality is apparent in the review of the different perspectives on creativity below.

PERSON, PRODUCT, PRESS, AND PROCESS

Probably the most often-used structure for creative studies is that suggested by Rhodes (1961/1987). It is an alliterative scheme that divides creative studies (and findings) into the following categories: person, process, press, and product. The person category includes research on personal characteristics. These may reflect personality, for example, and there has been copious research on the traits that characterize creative persons. Barron & Harrington (1981) summarized the research to that point as indicating that creative individuals have a "high valuation of aesthetic qualities in experience, broad interests, attraction to complexity, high energy, independence of judgment, autonomy, intuition, self-confidence, ability to resolve antinomies or to accommodate apparently opposite or conflicting traits in one's self concept, and finally, a firm sense of self as 'creative'" (p. 453). The concept of "domains" (e.g., art versus science) is very relevant here, however, for there may be differences in the traits that allow creative performances in different fields.

Personality research frequently includes intrinsic motivation as a core characteristic of creative persons. In actuality, motivation may be tied to states and drives as much as to personality, but it does make sense that creative persons tend to follow intrinsic interests, and that tasks that are intrinsically motivated tend to be free from the evaluations and constraints that can inhibit creativity (Amabile 2003, Stohs 1992). Certainly, creative efforts are sometimes extrinsically motivated (Rubenson & Runco 1992, 1995). Amabile (2003) demonstrated experimentally how certain kinds of extrinsic factors (e.g., evaluation) could inhibit creative thinking.

Process research may be less personal and more behavioral. Csikszentmihalyi (2003), for example, presented a systems theory in which creative ideas originate with an individual, may then influence a particular field (e.g., experts and curators and others devoted to one interest or area), and may eventually even have an impact on the more general domain. This description is in some ways parallel to descriptions of historical processes, such as dialectical materialism, wherein changes occur only after periods representing one perspective (or "thesis"), a movement to the opposite extreme (an "antithesis"), and finally a synthesis. This is, however, just a parallel, and dialectical materialism is usually used to describe something over a longer period (and perhaps more general than "an idea"). Experimental demonstrations of important processes have also been reported. Associative processes, for example, seem to be involved in divergent thinking and problem solving, at least when the problem at hand is open-ended (e.g., Martindale & Hasenfus 1978, Runco 1991a). More is said about these processes in the Cognitive Research section below.

The concept of "press" was proposed by Harry Murray (1938) and is used in the creativity literature to describe pressures on the creative process or on creative persons. Rhodes (1961/1987, p. 220) stated that "press refers to the relationship of human beings and their environment." Press influences may be general, and perhaps operate through implicit valuation and tradition (as would be the case for cultural, organizational, or familial presses), or more specific (as would be the case in interpersonal exchanges or environmental settings). Much of the research on press focuses on social dynamics. Press is not, however, entirely social nor even a part of objective experience. Murray (1938) distinguished between alpha and beta pressures. The former pressures reflect the more objective aspects of press, and the latter the individual's interpretation of some contextual pressure. These are significantly different, but the differences are not always acknowledged (cf. Mraz & Runco 1994).

Amabile & Gryskiewicz (1989) and later Witt & Beorkrem (1989) identified the following "situational influences on creativity": freedom, autonomy, good role models and resources (including time), encouragement specifically for originality, freedom from criticism, and "norms in which innovation is prized and failure not fatal" (Witt & Beorkrem, pp. 31–32). Some influences can also inhibit creativity. These include a lack of respect (specifically for originality), red tape, constraint, lack of autonomy and resources, inappropriate norms, project management, feedback, time pressure, competition, and unrealistic expectations. These do not necessarily inhibit creativity; they are potential inhibitors. Recall the alpha and beta presses identified by Murray (1938), one being objective and one being subjective. Competition is a good example of how these may differ, for competition may both stimulate and inhibit creative work (Watson 1968); its impact depends on the individual's interpretation. The same may hold true for resources, at least in the sense that creative insights may sometimes absolutely require resources, but sometimes result from paucity ("Necessity is the mother of invention").

Time is indeed an important resource. Mednick (1962), for example, suggested that original ideas are remote and well removed from the original problem or initial idea. This remoteness requires time; it takes time to move from idea to idea to idea, and to find (eventually) the "remote associate." A number of empirical studies have confirmed Mednick's (1962) predictions. Time is also important for incubation, though here it is time away from a task rather than devoted to it. Many notable creative achievements (e.g., Darwin's theory of evolution) seem to have required sustained efforts (Gruber 1988). A creative insight is not a quick "aha!" but instead is protracted (Gruber 1981a, Wallace 1991). This conclusion can be easily applied to many aspects of everyday life; people should take their time if they want a creative idea or solution. Similarly, students and employees should be given sufficient time if they are expected to do creative work.

The role of press in the creative process also can be seen in the research on family background. Most work in this area seems to focus on family structure, in contrast to family process. The relevant structural variables include birth order, family size and number of siblings, and age gap (or interval). Much of this research parallels studies of giftedness (Albert 1980), and those focused on IQ and academic aptitude (e.g., Zajonc & Markus 1975). Sulloway (1996), for instance, presented data showing that middle children are the most rebellious, and are therefore potentially creative (also see Gaynor & Runco 1992, Runco & Bahleda 1987). Albert & Runco (1989) reported that the autonomy within a family, not just the number of siblings or family structure, could dramatically influence creativity. Very likely, family structure has an impact on development and creativity because it determines family processes. Larger families have more-authoritarian parents, just to name one example of how structure can determine process.

Some recent research suggests that certain environmental designs for schools are conducive to creativity (Hasirci & Demirkan 2003). Although it would be best to design an environment on an individual-by-individual basis (and take an individual's idiosyncrasies and interpretations into account), all other things being equal, environments should allow independent work, be stimulating but not distracting, and allow easy access to resources. These findings align well with those in the organizational setting (Amabile 2003, Witt & Beorkrem 1989).

The product approach to creativity focuses on outcomes and those things that result from the creative process. The assumption here is that studies of products (e.g., publications, paintings, poems, designs) are highly objective, and therefore amenable to the scientific method. Products can be counted, for example, and sometimes it is just the quantity of one's efforts that is measured. The value of this approach is supported by the amazing productivity of Piaget, Picasso, and other luminaries (Simonton 1984). The problem with this approach is that it often informs us only about productivity and not about creativity. Also, it can be quite misleading because what it takes to be productive may differ from what it takes to be creative. An individual can be productive without being original; and originality is the most widely acknowledged requisite for creativity. In methodological terms, productivity and creativity are correlated but not synonymous.

Rarely is the product approach used with noneminent individuals (cf. O'Quin & Bessemer 1989). Usually it directs an investigation to eminent persons. After all, eminent individuals tend to be the most productive. They are also unambiguously creative. There is no doubt about their talent. The problem is that inferences are necessary to identify the influences on their productivity. Further, generalizations to noneminent populations may not be warranted. Gardner (1993) reported that that the eminent creators he studied (e.g., Picasso, Freud, and T.S. Elliot) were in some ways childlike and tended to promote themselves, but these tendencies may not apply to everyday creativity or to the creative efforts of children and other noneminent persons.

DISCIPLINARY EMPHASES

Quite a bit of research does not fit easily into the categories above (person, product, process, and press). For that reason it is necessary to employ a more detailed framework. A disciplinary framework—organized by behavioral, biological, clinical, cognitive, developmental, historiometric, organizational, psychometric, and social perspectives—works well and is summarized below. There is overlap with the person, product, process, and press categories, but without the disciplinary survey, some research would be overlooked. The more notable examples of overlap are highlighted in the concluding section below.

The Behavioral Perspective

It is not easy to apply the behavioral perspective to creativity. This is because creativity does not lend itself easily to overt behaviors (Epstein 2003). Yet, there are behavioral correlates of creativity, such as insight and novelty (Epstein 2003, Runco 1994, Stokes 1999). Epstein, for example, reported a number of studies that suggest that insight results from "the spontaneous integration of previously learned responses." He used reinforcement to teach a series of discrete behaviors and then placed the research participants in a setting where they could solve a problem by integrating the discrete behaviors into one series or solution. This research does not really inform us about where the integration occurs, nor if insights in the natural environment are also a reflection of this kind of spontaneous integration, but it does demonstrate that the probability of insights can be increased through experience. It is impressive that subhuman species, including porpoises (Pryor et al. 1969) and pigeons (Epstein 2003), can be taught to demonstrate insightful behaviors.

The Biology of Creativity

The complex nature of creativity seems to have inhibited certain areas of research, including that subsumed under the biological label. In fact, some of the research in this area does not pinpoint creativity but instead involves related behaviors and aptitudes. Sperry's (1964) well-known research on the hemispheres of the brain exemplifies this. His work is often applied to art and creativity (e.g., Edwards 1989), but in fact the original studies of individuals who received commissurotomies (the corpus callosum, connecting the two hemispheres, was surgically bisected to inhibit seizures) referred to skills more aligned with simultaneous and sequential processing than with originality and the other components of creativity. Perhaps the most significant flaw in the various theories of right-brain creativity is that creativity actually requires the capacities from both hemispheres. Creativity is not always or entirely intuitive, for example, nor even radically original. Creativity instead reflects originality and appropriateness, intuition and logic. It requires both hemispheres. As Katz (1997) put it, "Creative activity cannot be localized as a special function unique to one of the cerebral hemispheres. Rather, productive thought involves the integration and coordination of processes subserved by both hemispheres."

Hoppe & Kyle (1991) and TenHouten (1994) studied Sperry's patients and described how they lacked this kind of integrated thought. Hoppe & Kyle suggested that the problem was alexithemia, a lack of emotionality and affect. They found clear evidence of this in the language of the patients, and in the lack of affect-laden interpretations of experience. The patients described things rather than their reactions to things. They also "showed a relatively impoverished fantasy life."

Shlain (1999) tied hemispheric communication—a "shuttle back and forth, intertwining the warp and woof of right and left, space and time, art and physics" (p. 742)—to self-reflection and zeitgeist. Both of these in turn are involved in creativity. It can't be emphasized too strongly that creativity is best viewed as a whole-brain (rather than right-brain) process.

Various investigations have focused on EEGs. Hoppe & Kyle (1991), for instance, employing the commissurotomy patients, found that there was little activity in the right temporal area (T4) when individuals were listening to music or viewing a movie that was highly emotional. The left hemisphere was also relatively inactive. This included Broca's and Wernickes' areas (F3, T3). One interpretation of this is that "inner speech" is lacking (Hoppe & Kyle 1991). Meanwhile, there was a high level of activity in P3, the left parietal area. Consistent with the proposal outlined above, concerning emotionality, Hoppe & Kyle reported high coherence between the right frontal (F4) and the P3 areas. This was taken to be indicative of "a possible interhemispheric aspect of inhibition of expression." Control subjects had coherence between the F4 and T3 areas, which implied "a possible mechanism facilitating the transformation of the effective understanding in the right hemisphere into verbal expression of the lower left hemisphere."

Martindale & Hasenfus (1978) suggested that EEG activity would vary in different stages of the creative process. They relied on the stages outlined by Wallas (1926), which have shown their usefulness through years and in some very recent work. (For a review of stage theories, see Runco 1994.) Martindale & Hasenfus measured EEGs at the right posterior temporal area and found more alphas during the inspiration stage than in the elaboration stage, at least in notably creative individuals. Martindale & Hasenfus (1978) also proposed that low cortical arousal would allow defocused attention, which would in turn facilitate the associations that provide original insights.

Einstein's Brain

Diamond et al. (1985) apparently held the perspective that we can learn about creativity by studying unambiguous cases, in particular eminent individuals. This approach makes a number of assumptions, including the assumption about generalizing from one or few cases to other persons, but it is a commonly used approach (see also Davis et al. 2003, Gruber 1988, Rothenberg 1990, Runco 1998a, Wallace 1991). Diamond et al. examined the brain of Albert Einstein. They reported that, in area 39 of the left hemisphere, there was a significantly smaller mean ratio of neuron to glial cells than in control scientists. No differences were found in three other areas of the brain or in the right hemisphere. Diamond et al. felt this implied that Einstein's cortex may have had an unusual "metabolic need," and they discussed the role of the cortex in associative thinking and "conceptual power." Mednick (1962) and many others (e.g., Mendelsohn 1976) have described how associative processes can contribute to creative thinking and problem solving.

Before leaving the biological and neuropsychological research, it is worth noting that more and more theorists are calling for investigations of the prefrontal lobes and their role in creativity. Arieti (1976) mentioned the prefrontal lobes in his theory of creativity; he was one of the first researchers to argue that a "magic synthesis" occurs when the entire brain (rather than one hemisphere) is involved. Elliott (1986) also pointed to the prefrontal lobes, as did Norlander (2000). The latter cited evidence from cerebral regional blood flow, but studies of the hypofrontality of schizophrenic patients show them to lack the integrations necessary for meaningful thinking. Perhaps hypotheses about prefrontal lobes will soon be accurately tested with newer methodologies. Already inferences about creativity and the brain may be drawn from magnetic imaging of musicians (Albert et al. 1995). These methodologies will allow us to move beyond the research that relied on weaker inferences, such as those resulting from studies of head trauma.

Clinical Research

In the introduction to this chapter, I suggested that creativity studies have changed since Barron & Harrington (1981) reviewed the field in an earlier *Annual Review of Psychology* chapter. I suggested that less attention is being given to the relationships between creativity and intelligence and personality than in 1981. On the other hand, several issues were included in that 1981 review that are receiving more attention than ever before. Some of these are clinical issues, including what was once called "the mad genius controversy" (Becker 1978).

Most of the research on this topic involves the affective disorders, and in particular the bipolar disorders (Andreasen 1997, Hershman & Lieb 1998, Jamison 1997, Richards 1990). Yet a number of investigations have recently looked specifically at schizophrenia and creativity (Sass & Schuldberg 2001), and Eysenck (1999) suggested that creativity was related to psychosis. This relationship was, however, apparent only in the components of the creative process, and not in the creative person. In other words, creative people were not necessarily psychotic, but they have the same cognitive tendency as psychotic persons. Eysenck felt this cognitive tendency involved overinclusive thinking.

Other disorders with ties to creativity include alcoholism (Noble et al. 1993, Rothenberg 1990, Runco et al. 1990b), suicide (Lester 1999, Mraz & Runco 1994), and stress (Carson & Runco 1999, Mraz & Runco 1994). Rothenberg (1990), for example, interviewed Nobel prize-winning author John Cheever, a self-reported alcoholic.

Looking in the direction of health (rather than disorder), creativity has been associated with self-actualization (Maslow 1971, Rogers 1970, Runco et al. 1990a), and longevity (Kaun 1991; Lindauer 1992, 1993; Runco & Charles 1997). Aging and creativity are discussed below (in the Developmental Research section); for now, only the domain differences in longevity are noted. Writing and poetry, for example, seem to be the domains in which creative persons have the shortest life expectancy.

One clear strength of research in this general area is the emphasis on the difference between objective and subjective experience. Recall here that in some areas of research objective experience is taken to apply uniformly to everyone; interpretations are ignored. The same mistake was made in the early research on stress (Holmes & Rahe 1967), when stressors were identified and stress was tied to objective experiences and assessed with event scales. Stress is now viewed as a matter of interpretation, and assessments now focus on perceived stress rather than entirely on objective events. Indeed, a general premise of the clinical research is to acknowledge the discrepancy between the objective world and subjective experience (see Smith 1999, Smith et al. 1989). This potential discrepancy is important for all of psychology, but especially important for research on creativity, for it can often be understood only by taking into account subjective processes.

Cognitive Research

The cognitive research on creativity is quite diverse. Basic cognitive processes that have been studied include memory (Pollert et al. 1969), attention (Martindale & Greenough 1973), and knowledge (Mumford et al. 1991, Rubenson & Runco 1995). Cognitive research has also focused on tactics, strategies, metacognition (Adams 1980, Root-Bernstein 1988, Runco 1999c), and intellectual skills (e.g., divergent thinking). The former tend to be nomethetic studies and the latter idiographic.

Attention Deployment

Attention deployment seems to be particularly important for creative thinking. Wallach (1970), for example, suggested that wide attention deployment facilitates the discovery of remote and original ideas. He felt that someone who is capable of broad attention deployment will have "a broader range of stimulus information … a broader range of memory traces … a greater sensitivity to the utilizing of incidental cues," with "more diffuse or extensive deployment of attention in the reception of information, in its retrieval, or both" (pp. 1248–1249). Along similar lines, Martindale & Greenough (1973) looked to defocused attention, which they felt occurred during periods of low cortical arousal and led to a large number of associations.

Very different evidence is also available wherein attention is focused and creative insights suffer. Smith et al. (1990), for example, suggested that evaluation and pressure often lead directly to anxiety and divided attention, and that this undermines creative thinking because attention is directed to a stressor rather than to the task or problem at hand. Smith et al. acknowledged that there is probably a threshold, below which creative thinking is unaltered (see also Toplyn & McGuire 1990).

Knowledge plays a role in creative cognition—two roles, in fact. Declarative and factual knowledge may supply the individual with options when he or she is solving problems, but at the same time can inhibit creative thinking if the individual looks only to established knowledge. Indeed, experts are often inflexible, and thus overlook original options, precisely because they rely so heavily on established knowledge (Hayes 1978, Simon & Chase 1973). The second role of knowledge involves tactics, for these rely on procedural knowledge. Without a doubt, tactics are often used to solve important problems (Root-Bernstein 1988, Runco 1999a). Tactics are among the most teachable aspects of creative thinking.

The flexibility mentioned above is often studied via divergent thinking tests. These are open-ended assessments (unlike traditional tests, which have one correct or conventional answer) and are scored for fluency (the number of ideas or solutions given), originality (the unusualness or uniqueness of the ideas given), and flexibility (the variety or diversity of the ideas). These tests were widely criticized, but they do seem to have psychometric qualities that parallel IQ tests and other accepted measures and are often used. They should be viewed as providing an estimate of the potential for creative thinking, however, for they are only predictors.

Torrance (1974) suggested that an elaboration score be used, at least with certain divergent thinking tests, and several new scoring techniques have been proposed since the original *Annual Review of Psychology* chapter on creativity was published in 1981. Runco & Charles (1993), for instance, suggested that the appropriateness of ideas could be taken into account. This is important because creativity is usually defined as a combination of originality and appropriateness (or fit). Runco & Mraz (1992) suggested that more accurate scores could be calculated from ideational pools. The idea here is that a set, or pool, of ideas provides more information than does an examination of single ideas. Qualitative scores have been used by Khandwalla (1994) and Dudek & Verreault (1989).

Other key cognitive aspects of creativity have been reviewed, including conceptualization (Mumford et al. 1989), imagination (Singer 1999), incubation (Smith & Dodds 1999), insight (Sternberg & Davidson 1999), intuition (Policastro 1999), Janusian processes (i.e., the ability to consider two very different perspectives simultaneously) (Rothenberg 1999), logic (Johnson-Laird 1999), metaphors (Gibbs 1999), mindfulness (Moldoveanu & Langer 1999), misjudgment (Runco 1999d), perceptgenesis (i.e., the role of perception in cognition) (Smith 1999), perspective (Runco 1999e), and synaesthesia (Domino 1989). Quantum theory, chaos theory, and nonlinear dynamics have also recently been used to explain creative thinking (Goswami 1999, Richards 1990, Zausner 1998).

Developmental Research

Various developmental stages have been identified in the empirical research. These never apply universally, but some do seem to apply to large numbers of children and adolescents. Torrance (1968), for example, found a fourth-grade slump in creative thinking, and Raina (1997) found evidence of the same outside of the United States. This slump is widely cited, but importantly, seems to describe approximately 50% of the population—by no means is it universal. Smith (1990) suggested that another slump occurs somewhat later, in preadolescence. Harrington et al.

(1987), Johnson (1985), and Jaquish & Ripple (1981) also investigated creativity during adolescence. A great deal of attention has been devoted to creativity during adulthood (Gott 1992, 1993; Helson 1990; Hogg 1993; Jaquish & Ripple 1981, 1984–85; Kaun 1991; Lindauer 1992, 1993; McCrae et al. 1987; Mumford et al. 1989; Simonton 1984). This probably reflects the more general trend in all of the social and behavioral sciences and the demographic trend (i.e., the "greying of America"). A number of early studies on creativity during adulthood are still important (e.g., Lehman 1962, 1966).

Research suggests that creative potential may be tied to family background. Birth order, family size and number of siblings, age gap, and family tendencies and values may each play some role (Albert & Runco 1989, Gaynor & Runco 1992, Sulloway 1996). Perhaps most impressive in predictive power are the findings of birth order, and of the frequency with which middle-born children develop into adults who maintain the potential for rebelliousness and nonconformity (Sulloway 1996). Apparently, the dynamics of growing up with an older sibling, especially one of the same sex, drives the middle-born child to find his or her own niche, and this is often in some unconventional direction. Rebellion and nonconformity do not guarantee creative work, but many creative individuals have rebelled and resisted convention.

Sex differences can be explained in terms of family background (and the transmission of social roles), though biology is a strong influence as well. Sex differences are not always found in assessments of creativity, though historical analyses do uncover differences that may reflect bias and favoritism. There does seem to be a benefit in being raised in a psychologically androgynous fashion (Harrington et al. 1983) rather than as a stereotypical male or female. The androgynous individual may have more options available when solving problems, rather than just options that are stereotypically masculine or feminine, and he or she may be more flexible than the stereotyped male or female.

Early family experiences may help explain differences between boys and girls (Baer 2003, Tegano & Moran 1989), but it is also now clear that sex differences also reflect life span discrepancies between men and women (Helson 1990, Reis 1999, Walberg & Stariha 1992). Reis described how the developmental and career paths of women are more diverse than those of men. She also concluded that relationships play a larger role in women's creative efforts than in men's creative efforts. In her view, women face unique barriers and need to make more of a conscious effort to devote themselves to creativity than do men. Helson's (1990) findings complement this view, and her data are the result of a well-designed longitudinal study of women from Mills College.

Economic Factors and Theories

The economic basis of creativity has been investigated. Dudek et al. (1993), for example, felt that socioeconomic status (SES) contributed to creative thinking during an individual's developmental years, with higher SES being beneficial to creativity. Though "necessity is the mother of invention," the alternative—that some necessities are common in lower SES levels and stimulate creative thinking—has not been supported empirically, at least not directly. Indirect support comes from findings of high divergent thinking in families with a large number of children (Runco & Bahleda 1987), given that family size and SES are inversely related.

Most of the economic work on creativity does not look to SES but instead draws on economic theory. Walberg & Stariha (1992), for example, argued that creativity, learning, and achievements are forms of human capital. Rubenson & Runco (1992) developed the "psychoeconomic theory" that led to descriptions of optimal groups for creative work and descriptions of the costs (psychic and objective) of creative efforts. The value and limitations of this model were described in the articles following the 1992 paper and in several articles in the 1991 *Creativity Research Journal* (Rubenson 1991; Runco 1991b,c; Sternberg & Lubart 1991). Most of the economic predictions have yet to be tested empirically.

Educational Research

This may be one of the most important areas for research because there are serious concerns about the impact of education on creativity. It is possible, for example, that the expectations placed on young children to conform in the classroom (sitting quietly in rows of desks, thinking about topics chosen by the teacher) lead to the fourth-grade slump (Runco 1999a, Torrance 1968). Biological changes may explain this, given that children's nervous systems seem to become sensitive to conventions (Gardner 1982), but some of that drop in originality may also reflect the pressures to conform that characterize many educational settings. Clearly, most tests given in the schools require primarily convergent thinking (there is only one correct or conventional answer) and relegate divergent thinking (where an individual can think about original options).

One problem is that individuals and organizations are more likely to invest in traditional educational skills (e.g., literacy) than in creative skills. Rubenson & Runco (1992) outlined the reasons for this; the basic idea is that creativity is a riskier investment, with less-certain payoffs, than literacy and other skills tied to traditional education. This same idea might apply to organization decisions as well: An employer may be more likely to hire an applicant who has a degree from an accredited educational institution than an applicant who has invested as much time in a creativity enhancement program. One reason for this is that the former has clearer benefits to offer the organization. The ideal arrangement would be for the educational system to integrate creative skills into the curriculum. Headway is being made in this regard (Runco 1992).

Quite a bit of research is relevant to education and creativity, even if it was not conducted in a classroom. For example, researchers have examined the impact of test directions (and instructions) on divergent thinking and creative problem solving (Harrington 1975, Reiter-Palmon et al. 1997, Runco 1986, Chand & Runco 1992), and frequently these instructions could easily be adapted to the educational setting.

Dudek et al. examined the divergent thinking of 1445 elementary school students. They reported significant differences among schools and suggested that these were tied to differences in SES. This is consistent with other investigations of SES (Dhillon & Mehra 1987, Lichtenwalner & Maxwell 1969, Srivastava 1982). Dudek et al. also found significant differences between classrooms within schools and suggested that the immediate classroom environment has an impact on divergent thinking. The finding replicates what Wallach & Kogan (1965) reported in their classic study of creative thinking. They too emphasized the immediate classroom environment and felt that creativity is inhibited by several common classroom conditions and instructions (e.g., testlike activities) and released when activities are presented in permissive and gamelike fashion. The teachers themselves are potential models for children (Graham et al. 1989, Runco 1992) and their expectations may be very influential (Runco 1984, 1989). Interestingly, creativity may contribute to the effectiveness of a teacher. In this case, it is not teachers as influence but creativity as influence on teaching.

Historical and Historiometric Research

Creativity has been defined in various ways throughout history (Boorstin 1992, Dudek 2003). This is readily apparent in the biographical analyses cited throughout this chapter (see also Davis et al. 2003). Albert & Runco (1999) presented a history of creativity research. Boorstin (1992) took a wider view, and a more traditionally historical perspective, in his lengthy volume on "the creators." He was more interested in creative persons than creativity, and thus did not deal in depth with historical changes in the concept of creativity. Dudek (2003) examined conceptual changes in depth, but she looked mostly to art.

Historiometric research is very relevant to the present psychological perspective of creativity. Simonton (1984) defined the historiometry as "a scientific discipline in which nomothetic hypotheses about human behavior are tested by applying quantitative analyses to data concerning historical individuals." Although the data are archival and nonexperimental, the analytic methods are extremely powerful and often able to control or test the influence of the most likely biases in this kind of data. Simonton's (1984, 1988) methods are innovative and powerful, and have generated a large number of convincing findings. Simonton has, for example, presented data on the impact of zeitgeist, war, and role models (also see Simonton 2003).

Organizational Perspectives

Earlier in this chapter, I reviewed the *Creative Work Environment Inventory* and the research of Amabile (2003) and Witt & Beorkrem (1989). I used these works as an example of research on the creative press, but that research was specifically intended to forward knowledge about creativity in organizations. In that sense, it fits into the present section of this chapter as well. Recall here that resources and autonomy seem to be relevant to organizational creativity. Note also the parallel with educational and even home settings. Those same factors are relevant to any social context, at least if creativity is a concern (see Albert & Runco 1989, Houtz 2003).

Runco (1995) examined an organization that was itself designed to produce creativity. The employees—and participants in his research—were artists. He administered the adjective check list (ACL; Gough & Heilbrun 1980) and found large discrepancies between the self-descriptions of the artists and their descriptions of an "ideal artist." Even more telling was the correlation between job satisfaction and creativity scores from the ACL: The most creative artists were the least satisfied by their jobs. It appeared that "time and resources" (one scale from the measure of organizational climate) were the biggest concern of the artists.

Extensive reviews of the literature on organizational innovativeness have been prepared by Service (2003) and Rickards & deCock (2003).

Psychometric Research

The psychometric approach assumes that creative potential can be captured in paper-and-pencil tests. It further assumes that creative potential is widely distributed. This follows from the fact that students and other noneminent persons typically participate in psychometric studies. No psychometric investigations were found with eminent participants taking the tests. The focus of psychometric studies is validation and the establishment of reliability. Validation takes many forms, including discriminant validation (e.g., the empirical separation of creativity from IQ and traditional expressions of intelligence) and predictive validation (e.g., finding how strongly the creativity test is associated with some measure of real-world performance). Reliability often involves comparisons of judges' ratings (Runco 1989) but sometimes is based on the internal consistency of the items within the test (Nunnally 1978).

The revised semantic scale (O'Quin & Bessemer 1989) and the work environment inventory (Witt & Beorkrem 1989) demonstrate psychometric research in this area. Much more commonly used are the divergent thinking tests (Guilford 1968, Torrance 1974). A number of new scoring techniques and divergent thinking tasks have been developed in the past 20 years (Runco 1999a). These too are the subjects of numerous psychometric investigations. Attitude measures (Basadur, 1994), consensual assessment (Amabile 2003), and socially valid measures (Sing 2003) are also receiving increased amounts of attention. One claim is that attitudes are the most sensitive to enhancement of all aspects of the creativity complex. Lifetime achievement can now be assessed (Richards et al. 1988) as well. The creative personality scale (CPS; Gough & Heilbrun 1980) has been available for more than 20 years, but new scales from the ACL have been developed fairly recently (Domino 2003).

Social Research

A number of works have explicitly tied social processes to creativity (Albert 1983, Amabile 2003, Paulus & Nijstad 2003, Simonton 2003, Montuori & Purser 1999). The typical rationale is that too much attention was given to individual characteristics (e.g., personality, ability) in the early research on creativity, and that social processes are very influential. These may occur within the family (Albert 1980, Albert & Runco 1989), the educational setting (Dudek et al. 1994), or the organizational setting (Basadur 1994, Rickards & deCock 2003, Runco 1995, Runco & Basadur 1993).

Brainstorming research exemplifies the social research on creativity. This is a group technique for solving problems (Parnes & Meadow 1959, Osborn 1953), the key features of which are to (*a*) postpone judgment; (*b*) focus on quantity, not quality (i.e., the number of ideas, not the probability of their success); and (*c*) hitchhike or piggyback (extend the line of thought suggested by someone else in the group). Rickards & deCock (2003) reviewed the extensive research on brainstorming and concluded that it is somewhat ineffective, at least in terms of creative problem solving. Often, individuals who work alone generate more and better ideas than groups. This is often explained in terms of social loafing. Granted, there may be benefits to brainstorming (e.g., team building) that justify its use, even if it is not the best way to find high-quality solutions to problems.

Other examples of social research on creativity are given in the discussions of culture, organization, and research on families. The organizational research reviewed above suggests that certain kinds of evaluations (e.g., criticism from a supervisor) can inhibit creative thinking, and that resources (including other people) are often necessary for creative work.

CURRENT TRENDS IN THE FIELD

The categories of research (i.e., person, product, process, and press, and the disciplinary categories) reviewed above suggest that in many ways creativity research has broadened its scope in the past 20 years. It is now more of an interdisciplinary effort than ever before, and new techniques, topics, and applications are apparent in the research. The journals mentioned by Barron & Harrington in their 1981 *Annual Review of Psychology* article included *Intelligence*, the *Journal of Creative Behavior*, and the *Gifted Child Quarterly*; at the time this chapter was written, the *Creativity Research Journal* was 15 years old. In 1999 the *Encyclopedia of Creativity* was published, and Sternberg (1999) and Runco (1998b, 2003a, 2003b) later published handbooks on creativity. The field is also more focused, and more selective. It is not easy to pinpoint exactly how it is selective, however. It is not, for example, simply more rigorous and scientific. If that were the case, there would be fewer qualitative, nonexperimental, and quasi-experimental efforts; instead, there are more (Dudek & Verreault 1989, Khandwalla 1994, Murdock & Moore 2003). The selection that has occurred within the field may be best viewed as topical, and perhaps due to the current zeitgeist. Certain topics clearly are not receiving the attention they did 20 years ago. Several empirical efforts have identified the topics that are receiving attention in the current creativity research. One such empirical effort involves implicit and explicit theories.

Implicit and Explicit Theories of Creativity

Runco et al. (1997) surveyed 143 individuals who were actively involved in the field of creative studies (e.g., doing research). They were given a survey that asked them to judge and rank the importance of various topics and issues for future research. They were also asked to judge the importance of various developmental influences and traits for creative achievement. Results indicated that the topics rated as most important for future research were "actual creative behaviors," motivation and drive, imagery, imagination, and creative products. Some generality of these findings is suggested by the lack of group differences: Respondents who had taught creativity courses did not differ from those who had not, nor did individuals who had published a book or article differ significant from those who had not published. (Most respondents had in fact published something on creativity, but some had merely submitted work or inquired about submitting a manuscript. This latitude insured that the sample was moderately heterogeneous.) Also notable was that "behaviors reflecting motivation" were viewed as the most critical for creative achievement. This was followed in the ratings by problem finding (skill) and behaviors reflecting "adaptive cognition" (p. 43). The last of these reflects the kind of creativity mentioned in the introduction to this chapter; it includes flexibility and is creativity of the reactive problem-solving sort.

Here is the entire list of topics included in the survey, presented with the highly rated (and thus viewed as important for future research) topics listed first, and the topics viewed as unimportant listed at the end: Creative Behavior, Motivation or Drive, Imagery, Imagination, Creative Products, Metacognitive Processes, Divergent Thinking, Social Influences, Problem Solving, Cognitive Processes, Intuition, Developmental Processes, Emotion and Affect, Education, Incubation, Mental Health, Personality, Environmental Influences, Giftedness, Potential, Art/Artists, Cross-Cultural Differences, Humor, Science, Enhancement, Leadership, Intelligence, Free Will, Testing and Measurement, Brainstorming, Gender Differences, Neurobiology, Business/Management, Mental Illness, Therapy, and Psychic or Futuristic Phenomena.

Runco & Bahleda (1987) used a similar methodology to study artists' implicit theories of creativity. They found significant differences between judgments of artistic and scientific creativity. Artists said they felt that scientific creativity was "thorough" and "patient," and that artistic creativity involved emotions, imagination, and expressiveness. Artists' views are very interesting, but it is important to recognize that generalizability is low. Different groups seem to have quite different implicit theories of creativity. Teachers (Runco 1984, Runco et al. 1992), parents (Johnson et al. 2003, Runco 1989), children (Miller & Sawyers 1989), and the general population (Sternberg 1981) have each been investigated. Differences include parents' emphasis on motivational and intellectual characteristics, and teachers' emphasis on interpersonal behaviors.

Trend Analyses

Another useful approach for identifying trends in the field involves analysis of the published literature. Feist & Runco (1993), for instance, examined research published in the *Journal of Creative Behavior* between 1969 and 1989. They found a decrease in the attention being given to personality, and an increase in social research and educational studies of creativity. They also examined *Psychological Abstracts* for the 1980s and discovered that approximately 0.01% of the abstracts involved creativity. This reflected a substantial increase, for Guilford (1950) reported that only 0.002% of the publications from 1920 to 1950 were devoted to creativity. According to Feist & Runco (1993), approximately 9000 works on creativity were published between 1960 and 1991. Feist & Runco reported indications of an increase in educational and social research. They also found indications of a decrease in research on the creative personality. These observations are based on one outlet (i.e., the *Journal of Creative Behavior*), and on publications between 1969 and 1989. As the reviews of social, educational, and personality research reviewed earlier in this chapter show, exceptions to the reported increases and decreases are easy to find.

TOPICS OF CONTINUED OR DISCONTINUED INTEREST

Problem Finding

A more casual observation (not based on data of any sort) suggests that a few topics that were being studied 20 years ago (and more) have recently received an increased amount of attention. Barron & Harrington (1981), for instance, reviewed the research on problem finding, which was at that point in early stages. Csikszentmihalyi & Getzels (1971) published their classic study on the problem finding of artists before that 1981 review, but a great deal of research has been devoted to problem finding since then. Csikszentmihalyi (2003), for example, reported an 18-year follow-up of that first 1976 study. This follow-up demonstrated that the problem-finding skills of artists were effective in predicting the quality of their work, even 18 years later. The problem finding of children has been investigated (Okuda et al. 1991, Wakefield 1985), as has the problem finding of college students (Chand & Runco 1992) and artists (Kay 1991). Jay & Perkins (1997) reviewed the research to that point, and Runco (1994) edited *Problem Finding, Problem Solving, and Creativity*, which contains contributions from a number of investigators and gives a good overview of the progress in this area. Very importantly, it appears that we can and should distinguish between problem identification (just noticing that there is a problem at hand) and problem definition and redefinition (making a problem operational and workable). It may no longer be sufficient to refer to "problem finding" in a general sense.

Evolutionary Theories of Creativity

Evolutionary theories of creativity are much more common today than 20 years ago. These use evolutionary principles to describe the creative process, and sometimes describe the role of creativity in evolution. Campbell's (1960) paper is the seminal work in the former, but in the past 20 years Albert (2003), Lumsden & Findlay (1988), and Simonton (1998) have extended it. Here creativity may contribute to the variation that is one of two critical aspects of evolution (at least in the Darwinian sense, with selection being the other critical aspect). Creative ideas are often deviant and new, and as such broaden the range of options and the variation.

The variations supplied by creative efforts do not always benefit fitness and adaptiveness. Indeed, the "dark side of creativity" has given us weapons of mass destruction and other evil inventions and techniques (McLaren 1993). Admittedly, some of these unfortunate inventions and techniques are unplanned and the result of other, possibly beneficial, innovations. All too often, an advance is offered, but some of the implications are detrimental (McLaren 1993).

Creativity in the Moral Domain

The antithesis of the dark side, creative morality, is receiving even more attention (Gruber 1993). This area may have been overlooked previously because of the potential oxymoron: Morality often implies agreement among persons or groups, and even a kind of conformity (to mores, rules, and traditions), while creativity is tied to individualism and originality. Yet, as Gruber pointed out, moral leaders are often highly creative. In addition, creativity in the moral domain is greatly needed: Many problems (e.g., energy, ecology, and equality) are serious and need to be approached from a creative perspective (Stein 1993). Some of the best work on creativity in the moral domain has involved case study research. I turn now to that approach to creative studies.

Case Studies

A large number of case studies have been reported in the past 20 years. These often utilize new methodologies (see Davis et al. 2003). The following have been examined in the creativity literature: Piaget (Gruber 1999); John Cheever (Rothenberg 1990), Paul Klee, Pablo Picasso, and Lautrec (Pariser 1991); Dorothy Richardson (Wallace 1991); Rabindranath Tagore (Raina 1997); Shakespeare (Simonton 1999); Anne Sexton (Sanguinetti & Kavaler-Adler 1999); George Bernard Shaw (Tahir 1999); Beethoven (Hershman & Lieb 1998); William James (Osowski 1989); Einstein (Miller & Sawyers 1989); Piaget (Gruber 1999); Sylvia Plath (Lester 1999, Runco 1998b); the Wright brothers (Jakab 1999); the Brontë sisters (VanTassel-Baska 1999); Lewis Carroll (Morrison 1999); Paul Cezanne (Machotka 1999); Charles Darwin (Gruber 1981b, Keegan 1999); Georgia O'Keefe (Zausner 1999); Virginia Woolf (Ippolito 1999); and William Wordsworth (Jeffrey 1999). Gardner (1993) threw a wider net and in one volume explored the lives of Freud, Einstein, Picasso, Stravinsky, T.S. Eliot, Martha Graham, and Gandhi. Davis et al. (2003) provided an overview of many other case studies and discussed the pros and cons of the relevant methodologies.

Sometimes investigations focus on unambiguously creative persons but look to large samples (rather than single cases). Ludwig (1995), for example, published a careful and detailed analysis of more than 1100 eminent persons, and Sulloway

(1996) similarly investigated nearly the same number of creative revolutionaries. Their book titles are both quite apt: Ludwig gave a number of examples of *The Price of Greatness*, and Sulloway found that middle-born children often develop into nonconformists and as such are *Born to Rebel*. This work is fascinating but is archival and therefore has the limitations of nonexperimental ex post facto research.

CONCLUSIONS

Most of the research reviewed above implies that creativity is beneficial. Creativity facilitates and enhances problem solving, adaptability, self-expression, and health. The potential costs for creativity should also be acknowledged. Its association with the various disorders implies this (Eysenck 1999, Richards 1990, Schuldberg 1997), by the profile of "ideal students," which emphasizes conventional rather than creative behavior (Torrance 1968), and by the madness and eccentricity that have long been attributed to creative geniuses (Becker 1978, Ludwig 1995). In fact, because it is so strongly tied to originality, and original behavior is always contrary to norms, all creativity is a kind of deviance. No wonder there is frequent stigma attached to creativity (Eisenman 1991, Plucker & Runco 1999, Rubenson & Runco 1992, Runco 1999d).

The creativity research is best understood by considering various perspectives (e.g., person, process, product, or press). The research on creativity is itself helpful in this regard, for it demonstrates that insights are often inhibited by "functional fixity" or "fixedness" (Ward & Smith 2003), and this kind of fixity can be avoided through flexibility (Adams 1980, Wicker 1985). Individuals who study and apply creativity should maintain a flexible approach and avoid relying too heavily on one perspective. Consider how misleading it would be to rely on the press perspective of creativity. This perspective might help with the objective and contextual factors involved in some settings, but if personality or process work is ignored because it belongs in another theoretical category (i.e., the person or process categories), a realistic view will never be achieved. To be realistic, both press and person factors need to be recognized. To be realistic, the situation must be studied, as well as the individual and his or her interpretation of that context. An interdisciplinary perspective on creativity should keep investigators out of theoretical ruts (Isaksen et al. 1994). This chapter suggests that this kind of interdisciplinarity might draw from a very wide range of perspectives, including the biological, cognitive, developmental, and the others summarized above.

Another important example of interplay between approaches involves the clinical and cognitive perspectives. Recall here that creativity is often associated with mood disorders (Richards 1990) and psychosis (Eysenck 1999). These mood disorders may be associated with creativity because of mood per se, or indirectly, via cognitive tendencies that result from particular moods or mood swings. Eysenck (1999), for example, suggested that psychotic individuals have a tendency to rely on overinclusive thinking. They do not use the conventional conceptual boundaries. This leads them to ideas that are not at all realistic, which in turn leads to psychotic behavior (and behavior that implies they are out of touch with reality). Yet according to Eysenck, overinclusive thought also allows creative persons to find original insights. Schuldberg (1997) similarly described cognitive tendencies that characterize clinical populations but are associated with creative insights.

Creativity is expressed in different ways in different domains. Evidence for domain differences in the creative personality, the creative product, the creative process, and the creative press is available (Solomon et al. 1999, Milgram & Milgram 1976, Plucker 2000, Runco 1986). Mathematical creativity differs from artistic creativity, then, and each of these differs from the creativity that characterizes interpersonal, organizational, athletic, or political creativity. Many different domains have been proposed and explored (Plucker 2000, Runco & Pritzker 1999), but the concept of domains must be acknowledged because most of what has been uncovered about creativity is domain specific. Clarifying these differences is one of the most important impetuses in the literature.

Early research on creativity examined artists (e.g., Patrick 1935, 1937) and architects (Barron 1972), but at this point the concept of domains was implicit: Those studying creativity focused on particular domains, but not much was said about the number and significance of domain differences. Gardner (1983) was explicit about the need to recognize domains and itemized seven of them: musical, mathematical, verbal-symbolic, bodily kinesthetic, spatial, interpersonal, and intrapersonal. He later added "the naturalist" (see Solomon et al. 1999). In very brief terms, the naturalist is sensitive to flora and fauna. Recall here that moral creativity has received recent attention (Gruber 1993). Recall also that creativity is now viewed as something that can be found and used in an "everyday" domain (Runco & Richards 1997). This has become a popular domain for research, in part because it acknowledges the creativity that is an aspect of coping and day-to-day problem solving, and because it allows us to consider the potentials of children. Everyday creativity does not require high-level achievement or expertise, so children can (and do) demonstrate it. Everyday creativity may also be a part of mundane problem solving (Cohen & Ambrose 1999). The more recent research has also explored what might be called subdomains. Poets seem to differ from novelists, for example, and both may differ from playwrights and writers of situation comedies (Pritzker 1999). Designers (Sawyers & Canestaro 1989), performing artists (Nemiro 1997), and fine artists seem to differ in their thought patterns and cognitive styles (Domino 1989).

The recognition of different domains, such as the naturalist, makes it relatively easy to understand culture differences in creativity. In Western culture, many creative achievements (and educational programs) focus on verbal and mathematical domains, but in other cultures, traditions may value the naturalist, or perhaps performances in spatial or other nonverbal domains. Differences apparently reflect the degree of dogma (or latitude) and locus of control within a culture (Aviram & Milgram 1977), as well as attitudes and values (Johnson et al. 2003) and expectations (Dudek et al. 1993). Cultural similarities have been reported as well. Raina (1984), for example, found that children in India, like their counterparts in the United States, frequently experience a fourth-grade slump in original thinking. This apparently characterizes approximately 45% to 60% of the fourth-grade population of students (Torrance 1968). Importantly, 11% and 38% of the students involved in the original longitudinal study showed improvements during the same period. Not all fourth-grade children slump—far from it—and some actually improve their creative thinking.

The take-home message I promised in the beginning of this chapter concerned the increasingly diverse applications of creativity. At this point, the role of creativity in both basic research and applied research should be apparent, as should the potential role of creativity outside of research—as applied to the natural environment. The various domains listed above confirm that creativity is applied widely, as does the duality of creativity mentioned in the first section of this chapter and exemplified throughout the literature. Creativity drives innovation and evolution, providing original ideas and options, but it is also a reaction to the challenges of life. It sometimes helps when solving problems, but also sometimes allows problems to be avoided. It is both reactive and proactive (Heinzen 1994).

When Barron & Harrington (1981) wrote the previous chapter on this topic for the *Annual Review of Psychology*, many investigators seemed to be unconvinced about the separation of creativity from traditional intelligence. Since that time the separation seems to have been widely accepted. Now the research is mostly directed at the correlates, benefits, and conditions of creativity. The research has become extremely diversified, which is why there are numerous different perspectives and a large number of applications of experimental findings. Sadly, investigations of correlates of creativity do not necessarily take us any closer to understanding the actual mechanisms that underlie creative capacities (Jay & Perkins 1997; Runco 1995, 1996). Another concern is that some experimental findings may apply to a correlate of creativity and not to creativity per se. Recall here that Sperry's (1964) research was on hemispheric specialization, not on creativity; the behavioral research examined novelty and insight, not creativity; the product approach to creativity focuses on productivity, not creativity. It is almost as if we have gone too far. When Barron & Harrington (1981) published the first *Annual Review of Psychology* review of creativity, the primary question was: Is creativity distinct from traditional intelligence? Apparently, the distinctiveness of creativity is rarely questioned. Research is connecting creativity with these other things (productivity, novelty, adaptability, and so on), but perhaps we should again ask about its distinctive nature instead. Granted, to be objective markers of covert processes are necessary, but it is possible that the field has spread the conceptual umbrella too far.

We do know much more about what creativity is and is not. We know, for example, that originality is necessary but not sufficient for creativity, and that creativity is associated with certain forms of psychopathology, but does not guarantee it. Creativity is not a kind of psychopathology! Creative persons are sometimes quite healthy, physically and mentally (Runco & Richards 1997), and may even be self-actualized. Some clinicians take this to be the epitome of mental health (Maslow 1971, Rogers 1970). Creativity can facilitate problem solving, yet here again there are signs of separation. Not all creativity involves problem solving, and not all problem solving requires creativity. We know much more about creativity than we did in 1981, but this includes the knowledge that plenty of research has yet to be conducted.

The *Annual Review of Psychology* is online at http://psych.annualreviews.org

LITERATURE CITED

Adams J. 1980. *Conceptual Blockbusting*. New York: Norton

Albert RS. 1980. Family position and the attainment of eminence: a study of special family positions and special family experiences. *Gifted Child Q.* 24:87–95

Albert RS, ed. 1983. *Genius and Eminence: A Social Psychology of Creativity and Exceptional Achievement*. Oxford: Pergamon

Albert RS. 2003. The achievement of eminence as an evolutionary strategy. See Runco 2003b. In press

Albert RS, Runco MA. 1986. The achievement of eminence: a model of exceptionally gifted boys and their families. In *Conceptions of Giftedness*, ed. R Sternberg, JE Davidson, pp. 332–57. New York: Cambridge Univ. Press

Albert RS, Runco MA. 1989. Independence and cognitive ability in gifted and exceptionally gifted boys. *J. Youth Adolesc.* 18:221–30

Albert RS, Runco MA. 1999. The history of creativity research. In *Handbook of Human Creativity*, ed. RS Sternberg, pp. 16–31. New York: Cambridge Univ. Press

Albert T, Pantey C, Wiendruch C, Rockstroh B, Taub E. 1995. Increased cortical representation of the fingers of the left hand in string players. *Science* 270(13):305–7

Amabile TM. 2003. Within you, without you: towards a social psychology of creativity, and beyond. See Runco & Albert 2003. In press

Amabile TM, Gryskiewicz ND. 1989. The Creative Environment Work Scales: Work Environment Inventory. *Creat. Res. J.* 2:231–54

Andreasen NC. 1997. Creativity and mental illness: prevalence rates in writers and their first-degree relatives. See Runco & Richards 1997, pp. 7–18

Arieti S. 1976. *The Magic Synthesis*. New York: Basic Books

Aviram A, Milgram RM. 1977. Dogmatism, locus of control, and creativity in children educated in the Soviet Union, the United States, and Israel. *Psychol. Rep.* 40:27–34

Baer J. 2003. Sex differences. See Runco 2003b. In press

Barron F. 1972. *Artists in the Making*. New York: Seminar Press

Barron F, Harrington D. 1981. Creativity, intelligence, and personality. *Annu. Rev. Psychol.* 32:439–76

Basadur M. 1994. Managing creativity in organizations. In *Problem Finding, Problem Solving, and Creativity*, ed. MA Runco, pp. 237–68. Norwood, NJ: Ablex

Becker G. 1978. *The Mad Genius Controversy*. Newbury Park: Sage

Bloom M, ed. 2001. *Promoting Creativity Across the Lifespan*. Washington, DC: Child Welf. League Am.

Boorstin DJ. 1992. *The Creators: A History of the Heroes of the Imagination*. New York: Random House

Bruner J. 1962. The conditions of creativity. In *On Knowing: Essays for the Left Hand*, ed. J Bruner. Cambridge, MA: Harvard Univ. Press

Campbell D. 1960. Blind variation and selective retention in creative thought as in other knowledge processes. *Psychol. Rev.* 67:380–400

Carson DK, Runco MA. 1999. Creative problem solving and problem finding in young adults: interconnections with stress, hassles, and coping abilities. *J. Creat. Behav.* 33:167–90

Chand I, Runco MA. 1992. Problem finding skills as components in the creative process. *Personal. Individ. Differ.* 14:155–62

Cohen LM. 1989. A continuum of adaptive creative behaviors. *Creat. Res. J.* 2:169–83

Cohen LM, Ambrose D. 1999. Adaptation and creativity. See Runco & Pritzker 1999, pp. 9–22

Cohen-Shalev A. 1986. Artistic creativity across the adult life span: an alternative approach. *Interchange* 17:1–16

Cohen-Shalev A. 1989. Old age style: developmental changes in creative production from a life-span perspective. *J. Aging Stud.* 3:21–37

Csikszentmihalyi M. 2003. The domain of creativity. See Runco & Albert 2003. In press

Csikszentmihalyi M, Getzels JW. 1971. Discovery-oriented behavior and the originality of creative products: a study with artists. *J. Personal. Soc. Psychol.* 19:47–52

Davis S, Keegan R, Gruber HE. 2003. Creativity as purposeful work: the evolving systems view. See Runco 2003a. In press

Dhillon PK, Mehra D. 1987. The influence of social class and sex on primary school children's creative thinking. *Asian J. Psychol. Educ.* 19:1–10

Diamond M, Scheibel A, Murphy G, Harvey T. 1985. On the brain of a scientist: Albert Einstein. *Exp. Neurol.* 88:198–204

Domino G. 1989. Synesthesia and creativity in fine arts students: an empirical look. *Creat. Res. J.* 2:17–29

Domino G. 2003. Assessment of creativity on the ACL: an empirical comparison of four scales. *Creat. Res. J.* In press

Dudek SZ. 2003. Art and aesthetics. See Runco 2003b. In press

Dudek SZ, Hall W. 1991. Personality consistency: eminent architects 25 years later. *Creat. Res. J.* 4:213–32

Dudek SZ, Strobel MG, Runco MA. 1993. Cumulative and proximal influences of the social environment on creative potential. *J. Genet. Psychol.* 154:487–99

Dudek SZ, Verreault R. 1989. The creative thinking and ego functioning of children. *Creat. Res. J.* 2:64–86

Edwards B. 1989. *Drawing on the Right Side of the Brain*. Los Angeles: Tarcher

Eisenman R. 1991. Creativity: Is it disruptive? *Creat. Child Adult Q.* 16:223–37

Elliott PC. 1986. Right (or left) brain cognition, wrong metaphor for creative behavior: It is prefrontal lobe volition that makes the (human/humane) difference in release of creative potential. *J. Creat. Behav.* 20:202–14

Epstein R. 2003. Generativity theory as a theory of creativity. See Runco & Albert 2003. In press

Eysenck HJ. 1999. Personality and creativity. In *Creativity Research Handbook*, ed. MA Runco. Cresskill, NJ: Hampton Press

Feist GJ, Runco MA. 1993. Trends in the creativity literature: an analysis of research in the *Journal of Creative Behavior* (1967–1989). *Creat. Res. J.* 6:271–86

Flach F. 1990. Disorders of the pathways involved in the creative process. *Creat. Res. J.* 3:158–65

Gardner H. 1982. *Art, Mind, and Brain*. New York: Basic Books

Gardner H. 1983. *Frames of Mind*. New York: Basic Books

Gardner H. 1993. *Creative Minds*. New York: Basic Books

Gaynor JLR, Runco MA. 1992. Family size, birth order, age-interval, and the creativity of children. *J. Creat. Behav.* 26:108–18

Getzels J, Jackson P. 1962. *Creativity and Intelligence: Explorations with Gifted Students*. New York: Wiley

Gibbs R. 1999. Metaphors. See Runco & Pritzker 1999, pp. 209–20

Goswami A. 1999. Quantum theory of creativity. See Runco & Pritzker 1999, pp. 491–500

Gott K. 1992. Enhancing creativity in older adults. *J. Creat. Behav.* 26:40–49

Gott K. 1993. Creativity and life satisfaction of older adults. *Educ. Gerontol.* 19:241–50

Gough HG, Heilbrun AB. 1980. *The Adjective Check List Manual.* Palo Alto, CA: Consulting Psychol. Press

Gould SJ. 2002. *The Structure of Evolutionary Theory.* Cambridge, MA: Harvard Univ. Press

Graham BC, Sawyers JK, DeBord KB. 1989. Teachers creativity, playfulness, and style of interaction with children. *Creat. Res. J.* 2:41–50

Gruber HE. 1981a. On the relation between 'a ha' experiences and the construction of ideas. *Hist. Sci.* 19:41–59

Gruber HE. 1981b. *Darwin on Man: A Psychological Study of Scientific Creativity.* Univ. Chicago Press. 2nd ed.

Gruber HE. 1988. The evolving systems approach to creative work. *Creat. Res. J.* 1:27–51

Gruber HE. 1993. Creativity in the moral domain: ought implies can implies create. *Creat. Res. J.* 6:3–16

Gruber HE. 1999. Jean Piaget. See Runco & Pritzker 1999, pp. 381–86

Guilford JP. 1950. Creativity. *Am. Psychol.* 5:444–54

Guilford JP. 1968. *Creativity, Intelligence, and Their Educational Implications.* San Diego: EDITS/Robert Knapp

Harrington DM. 1975. Effects of explicit instructions to "be creative" on the psychological meaning of divergent thinking test scores. *J. Personal.* 43:434–54

Harrington DM, Block J, Block JH. 1983. Predicting creativity in preadolescence from divergent thinking in early childhood. *J. Personal. Soc. Psychol.* 45:609–23

Hasirci D, Demirkan H. 2003. Creativity in learning environments: the case of two sixth grade art rooms. *J. Creat. Behav.* 37:17–41

Hayes JR. 1978. *Cognitive Psychology.* Homewood, IL: Dorsey

Heinzen T. 1994. Situational affect: proactive and reactive creativity. See Shaw & Runco 1994, pp. 127–46

Helson R. 1990. Creativity in women: inner and outer views over time. *Theories of Creativity,* eds. MA Runco, RS Albert, pp. 46–58. Newbury Park, CA: Sage

Hershman DJ, Lieb J. 1998. *Manic Depression and Creativity.* Amherst, NY: Prometheus Books

Hogg J. 1993. Creative, personal, and social engagement in the later years: realization through leisure. *Ir. J. Psychol.* 14:204–18

Holmes TH, Rahe RH. 1967. The Social Readjustment Rating Scale. *J. Psychom. Res.* 11:213–18

Hoppe K, Kyle N. 1991. Dual brain, creativity, and health. *Creat. Res. J.* 3:150–57

Houtz J, ed. 2003. *An Educational Psychology of Creativity.* Cresskill, NJ: Hampton Press

Isaksen SG, Murdock MC, Firestien R, Treffinger DJ, eds. 1994. *Understanding and Recognizing Creativity.* Norwood, NJ: Ablex

Jakab PL. 1999. Wilbur and Orville Wright. See Runco & Pritzker 1999, pp. 721–26

Jamison K. 1997. Mood disorders and patterns of creativity in British writers and artists. See Runco & Richards 1997, pp. 19–32

Jaquish GA, Ripple RE. 1981. Cognitive creative abilities and self-esteem across the adult life-span. *Hum. Dev.* 24:110–19

Jaquish GA, Ripple RE. 1984–1985. A life-span developmental cross-cultural study of divergent thinking abilities. *Int. J. Hum. Dev.* 20:1–11

Jay E, Perkins D. 1997. Problem finding: the search for mechanism. In *Creativity Research Handbook,* Vol. 1, ed. MA Runco, pp. 257–93. Cresskill, NJ: Hampton Press

Jeffrey L. 1999. William Wordsworth. See Runco & Pritzker 1999, pp. 715–20

Johnson D, Runco MA, Raina MK. 2003. Parents' and teachers' implicit theories of children's creativity: a cross-cultural perspective. *Creat. Res. J.* 14:427–38

Johnson LD. 1985. Creative thinking potential: another example of U-shaped development? *Creat. Child Adult Q.* 10:146–59

Johnson-Laird P. 1999. Logic and reasoning. See Runco & Pritzker 1999, pp. 155–61

Katz A. 1997. Creativity in the cerebral hemispheres. In *Creativity Research Handbook*, ed. MA Runco, pp. 203–26. Cresskill, NJ: Hampton Press

Kaun DE. 1991. Writers die young: the impact of work and leisure on longevity. *J. Econ. Psychol.* 12:381–99

Kay S. 1991. The figural problem finding and problem solving of professional and semiprofessional artists and nonartists. *Creat. Res. J.* 4:233–52

Keegan R. 1999. Charles Darwin. See Runco & Pritzker 1999, pp. 493–500

Khandwalla PN. 1993. An exploratory study of divergent thinking through protocol analysis. *Creat. Res. J.* 6:241–60

Kogan N. 1974. Creativity and sex differences. *J. Creat. Behav.* 8:1–13

Lehman HC. 1962. The creative production rates of present versus past generations of scientists. *J. Gerontol.* 17:409–17

Lehman HC. 1966. The psychologist's most creative years. *Psychology.* 21:363–69

Lester D. 1999. Sylvia Plath. See Runco & Pritzker 1999, pp. 387–92

Lichtenwalner JS, Maxwell JW. 1969. The relationship of birth order and socioeconomic status to the creativity of preschool children. *Child Dev.* 40:1241–47

Lindauer MS. 1992. Creativity in aging artists: contributions from the humanities to the psychology of old age. *Creat. Res. J.* 5:211–31

Lindauer MS. 1993. The span of creativity among long-lived historical artists. *Creat. Res. J.* 6:221–39

Ludwig A. 1988. Method and madness in the arts and sciences. *Creat. Res. J.* 11:93–101

Ludwig A. 1995. *The Price of Greatness.* New York: Guilford

Lumsden CJ, Findlay CS. 1988. Evolution of the creative mind. *Creat. Res. J.* 1:75–91

Machotka P. 1999. Paul Cezanne. See Runco & Pritzker 1999, pp. 251–58

MacKinnon D. 1983 (1960). The highly effective individual. See Albert 1983, pp. 114–27

Martindale C, Greenough J. 1973. The differential effect of increased arousal on creative and intellectual performance. *J. Genet. Psychol.* 123:329–35

Martindale C, Hasenfus N. 1978. EEG differences as a function of creativity, stage of the creative process, and effort to be original. *Biol. Psychol.* 6:157–67

Maslow AH. 1971. *The Farther Reaches of Human Nature.* New York: Viking Press

McCrae RR, Arenberg D, Costa PT Jr. 1987. Declines in divergent thinking with age: cross-sectional, longitudinal, and cross-sequential analyses. *Psychol. Aging.* 2:130–37

McLaren R. 1993. The dark side of creativity. *Creat. Res. J.* 6:137–44

Mednick SA. 1962. The associative basis for the creative process. *Psychol. Rev.* 69:200–32

Mendelsohn GA. 1976. Associative and attentional processes in creative performance. *J. Personal.* 44:341–69

Milgram RM, Milgram N. 1976. Creative thinking and creative performance in Israeli students. *J. Educ. Psychol.* 68:255–58

Miller HB, Sawyers JK. 1989. A comparison of self and teachers' ratings of creativity in fifth grade children. *Creat. Child Adult Q.* 14:179–85, 229–38

Moldoveanu MC, Langer E. 1999. Mindfulness. See Runco & Pritzker 1999, pp. 221–34

Montuori A, Purser R, eds. 1999. *Social Creativity*, Vols. 1, 2. Cresskill, NJ: Hampton Press

Morrison D. 1999. Lewis Carroll. See Runco & Pritzker 1999, pp. 245–50

Mraz W, Runco MA. 1994. Suicide ideation and creative problem solving. *Suicide Life Threat. Behav.* 24:38–47

Mumford MD, Gustafson SB. 1988. Creativity syndrome: integration, application, and innovation. *Psychol. Bull.* 103:27–43

Mumford MD, Mobley MI, Uhlman CE, Reiter-Palmon R, Doares LM. 1991. Process analytic models of creative capacities. *Creat. Res. J.* 4:91–122

Mumford MD, Olsen KA, James LR. 1989. Age-related changes in the likelihood of major contributions. *Int. Aging Hum. Dev.* 29:9–32

Murdock M, Moore M. 2003. Creativity and qualitative research. In *Creativity Research Handbook*, Vol. 2, ed. MA Runco. Cresskill, NJ: Hampton Press. In press

Murray HA. 1938. *Explorations in Personality*. New York: Oxford Univ. Press

Nemiro J. 1997. Interpretive artists: a qualitative study of the creativity of actors. *Creat. Res. J.* 10:229–39

Noble EP, Runco MA, Ozkaragoz TZ. 1993. Creativity in alcoholic and nonalcoholic families. *Alcohol* 10:317–22

Norlander T. 2000. Conceptual convergence in creativity: incubation and brain disease state. *Creat. Res. J.* 13:329–33

Norlander T, Gustafson R. 1997. Effects of alcohol on picture drawing during the verification phase of the creative process. *Creat. Res. J.* 10:355–62

Nunnally JC. 1978. *Psychometric Theory*. New York: McGraw-Hill. 2nd ed.

Okuda SM, Runco MA, Berger DE. 1991. Creativity and the finding and solving of real-world problems. *J. Psychoeduc. Assess.* 9:45–53

O'Quin K, Bessemer S. 1989. The development, reliability, and validity of the revised creative product semantic scale. *Creat. Res. J.* 2:268–78

Osborn A. 1953. *Applied Imagination*. New York: Scribner's

Osowski JV. 1989. Ensembles of metaphor in the psychology of William James. In *Creative People at Work*, ed. DB Wallace, H Gruber, pp. 127–46. New York: Oxford Univ. Press

Pariser D. 1991. Normal and unusual aspects of juvenile artistic development in Klee, Lautrec, and Picasso. *Creat. Res. J.* 4:51–65

Parnes S, Meadow A. 1959. Effects of brainstorming instruction on creative problem solving of trained and untrained subjects. *J. Educ. Psychol.* 50:171–76

Patrick C. 1935. Creative thought in poets. *Arch. Psychol.* 26:1–74

Patrick C. 1937. Creative thought in artists. *J. Psychol.* 4:35–73

Paulus PP, Nijstad BA, eds. 2003. *Group Creativity*. New York: Oxford Univ. Press. In press

Pennebaker JW, Kiecolt-Glaser JK, Glaser R. 1997. Disclosure of trauma and immune functioning: health implications for psychotherapy. See Runco & Richards 1997, pp. 287–302

Plucker J. 2000. Beware of hasty, simple conclusions: the case for content generality of creativity. *Creat. Res. J.* 11:179–182

Plucker J, Runco MA. 1999. Deviance. See Runco & Pritzker 1999, pp. 541–45

Policastro E. 1999. Intuition. See Runco & Pritzker 1999, pp. 89–94

Pollert LH, Feldhusen JF, Van Mondfrans AP, Treffinger DJ. 1969. Role of memory in divergent thinking. *Psychol. Rep.* 25:151–56

Pritzker S. 1999. Writing and creativity. See Runco & Pritzker 1999, pp. 727–37

Pryor KW, Haag R, O'Reilly J. 1969. The creative porpoise: training for novel behavior. *J. Exp. Anal. Behav.* 12:653–61

Raina MK. 1984. *Social and Cultural Change and Changes in Creative Functioning in Children*. New Delhi: Natl. Counc. Educ. Res. Training

Raina MK. 1997. Most dear to all the Muses: mapping Tagorean networks of enterprize. *Creat. Res. J.* 10:153–73

Reis SM. 1999. Women and creativity. See Runco & Pritzker 1999, pp. 699–708

Reiter-Palmon R, Mumford MD, Boes JO, Runco MA. 1997. Problem construction and creativity: the role of ability, cue consistency, and active processing. *Creat. Res. J.* 9:9–23

Rhodes M. 1961/1987. An analysis of creativity. In *Frontiers of Creativity Research: Beyond the Basics*, ed. SG Isaksen, pp. 216–22. Buffalo, NY: Bearly

Richards R. 1990. Everyday creativity, eminent creativity, and health: afterview for CRJ issues on creativity and health. *Creat. Res. J.* 3:300–26

Richards R, Kinney DK, Benet M, Merzel APC. 1988. Assessing everyday creativity: characteristics of the Lifetime Creativity Scales and validation with three large samples. *J. Personal. Soc. Psychol.* 54:476–85

Rickards T, deCock C. 2003. Understanding organizational creativity: toward a multi-paradigmatic approach. See Runco 2003a. In press

Rogers C. 1970. Toward a theory of creativity. In *Creativity*, ed. PE Vernon, pp. 137–51. New York: Penguin

Root-Bernstein R. 1988. *Discovering*. Cambridge Univ. Press

Rothenberg A. 1990. Creativity, mental health, and alcoholism. *Creat. Res. J.* 3:179–201

Rothenberg A. 1999. Janusian process. See Runco & Pritzker 1999, pp. 103–8

Rubenson DE. 1991. Creativity, economics, and baseball. *Creat. Res. J.* 4:205–8

Rubenson DL, Runco MA. 1992. The psycho-economic approach to creativity. *New Ideas Psychol.* 10:131–47

Rubenson DL, Runco MA. 1995. The psycho-economic view of creative work in groups and organizations. *Creativ. Innovat. Manag.* 4:232–41

Runco MA. 1984. Teachers' judgments of creativity and social validation of divergent thinking tests. *Percept. Mot. Skills* 59:711–17

Runco MA. 1986. Flexibility and originality in children's divergent thinking. *J. Psychol.* 120:345–52

Runco MA. 1989. Parents' and teachers' ratings of the creativity of children. *J. Soc. Behav. Personal.* 4:73–83

Runco MA. 1991a. *Divergent Thinking*. Norwood, NJ: Ablex

Runco MA. 1991b. On economic theories of creativity [comment]. *Creat. Res. J.* 4:198–200

Runco MA. 1991c. On investment and creativity: a response to Sternberg and Lubart [comment]. *Creat. Res. J.* 4:202–5

Runco MA. 1992. *Creativity as an Educational Objective for Disadvantaged Students.* Storrs, CT: Natl. Res. Cent. Gift. Talent.

Runco MA. 1994. Creativity and its discontents. See Shaw & Runco 1994, pp. 102–23

Runco MA. 1995. The creativity and job satisfaction of artists in organizations. *Empiric. Stud. Arts* 13:39–45

Runco MA. 1996. Personal creativity: definition and developmental issues. *New Dir. Child Dev.* 72(Summer):3–30

Runco MA, ed. 1998a. *Creativity Research Handbook*, Vol. 1. Cresskill, NJ: Hampton Press

Runco MA. 1998b. Suicide and creativity: the case of Sylvia Plath. *Death Stud.* 22:637–54

Runco MA. 1999a. Chronology of significant events in the history of creativity research. See Runco & Pritzker 1999

Runco MA. 1999b. Self-actualization and creativity. See Runco & Pritzker 1999, pp. 533–36

Runco MA. 1999c. Time for creativity. See Runco & Pritzker 1999, pp. 659–63

Runco MA. 1999d. Misjudgment. See Runco & Pritzker 1999, pp. 235–40

Runco MA. 1999e. Perspective. See Runco & Pritzker 1999, pp. 373–76

Runco MA, ed. 2003a. *Creativity Research Handbook*, Vol. 2. Cresskill, NJ: Hampton Press. In press

Runco MA, ed. 2003b. *Creativity Research Handbook*, Vol. 3. Cresskill, NJ: Hampton Press. In press

Runco MA, Albert RS. 1987. The threshold hypothesis regarding creativity and intelligence: an empirical test with gifted and nongifted children. *Creat. Child Adult Q.* 11:212–18

Runco MA, Bahleda MD. 1987. Implicit theories of artistic, scientific, and everyday creativity. *J. Creat. Behav.* 20:93–98

Runco MA, Basadur M. 1993. Assessing ideational and evaluative skills and creative styles and attitudes. *Creat. Innovat. Manag.* 2:166–73

Runco MA, Charles R. 1993. Judgments of originality and appropriateness as predictors of creativity. *Personal. Individ. Differ.* 15:537–46

Runco MA, Charles R. 1997. Developmental trends in creativity. In *Creativity Research Handbook*, ed. MA Runco. Cresskill, NJ: Hampton Press

Runco MA, Ebersole P, Mraz W. 1990. Self

actualization and creativity. *J. Soc. Behav. Personal.* 6:161–67

Runco MA, Johnson D, Bear P. 1992. Parents' and teachers' implicit theories of children's creativity. *Child Stud. J.* 23:91–113

Runco MA, Mraz W. 1992. Scoring divergent thinking tests using total ideational output and a creativity index. *Educ. Psychol. Meas.* 52:213–21

Runco MA, Nemiro J, Walberg H. 1997. Personal explicit theories of creativity. *J. Creat. Behav.* 31:43–59

Runco MA, Noble EP, Luptak Y. 1990. Agreement between mothers and sons on ratings of creative activity. *Educ. Psychol. Meas.* 50:673–80

Runco MA, Pritzker SR, eds. 1999. *Encyclopedia of Creativity.* San Diego, CA: Academic

Runco MA, Richards R, eds. 1997. *Eminent Creativity, Everyday Creativity, and Health.* Norwood, NJ: Ablex

Sanguinetti C, Kavaler-Adler S. 1999. Anne Sexton. See Runco & Pritzker 1999, pp. 551–58

Sass LA, Schuldberg D. 2001. Introduction to the special issue: creativity and the schizophrenia spectrum. *Creat. Res. J.* 13(1):1–4

Sawyers JE, Canastero N. 1989. Creativity and achievement in design coursework. *Creat. Res. J.* 2:125–33

Schuldberg D. 1997. Schizotypal and hypomanic traits, creativity, and psychological health. See Runco & Richards 1997, pp. 157–72

Service R. 2003. Organizational innovativeness: a comprehensive review and models. In *Creativity Research Handbook,* Vol. 2, ed. MA Runco. Cresskill, NJ: Hampton Press

Shaw MP, Runco MA, eds. 1994. *Creativity and Affect.* Norwood, NJ: Ablex

Shlain L. 1999. Zeitgeist. See Runco & Pritzker 1999, pp. 737–43

Simon HA, Chase W. 1973. Skill in chess. *Am. Sci.* 61:394–403

Simonton DK. 1984. *Genius, Creativity, and Leadership.* Cambridge, MA: Harvard Univ. Press

Simonton DK. 1988. *Scientific Genius.* New York: Cambridge Univ. Press

Simonton DK. 1991. Political pathology and societal creativity. *Creat. Res. J.* 3:85–99

Simonton DK. 1999. William Shakespeare. See Runco & Pritzker 1999, pp. 559–64

Simonton DK. 2003. See Runco & Albert 2003. In press

Sing L. 2003. *Creat. Res. J.* In press

Singer JL. 1999. Imagination. See Runco & Pritzker 1999, pp. 13–26

Smith GJW. 1999. Perceptgenesis. See Runco & Pritzker 1999, pp. 347–54

Smith GJW, Carlsson I, Andersson G. 1989. Creativity and subliminal manipulations of projected self-images. *Creat. Res. J.* 2:1–16

Smith KLR, Michael WB, Hocevar D. 1990. Performance on creativity measures with examination-taking instructions intended to induce high or low levels of test anxiety. *Creat. Res. J.* 3:265–80

Smith SM, Dodds R. 1999. Incubation. See Runco & Pritzker 1999, pp. 39–44

Solomon B, Powell K, Gardner H. 1999. Multiple intelligences. See Runco & Pritzker 1999, pp. 273–83

Sperry RW. 1964. The great cerebral commissure. *Sci. Amer.* 210:42–52

Srivastava B. 1982. A study of creative abilities in relation to socioeconomic status and culture. *Perspect. Psychol. Res.* 5:37–40

Stein M. 1993. Moral issues facing intermediaries between creators and the public. *Creat. Res. J.* 6:197–200

Sternberg RJ. 1981. Implicit theories of intelligence, creativity, and wisdom. *J. Personal. Soc. Psychol.* 49:607–27

Sternberg RJ, Davidson JE. 1999. Insight. See Runco & Pritzker 1999, pp. 57–70

Sternberg RJ, Lubart T. 1991. Short selling investment theories of creativity? A reply to Runco. *Creat. Res. J.* 4:202–5

Sternberg RS, ed. 1999. *Handbook of Human Creativity.* New York: Cambridge Univ. Press

Stohs JH. 1992. Intrinsic motivation and

sustained art activity among male fine and applied artists. *Creat. Res. J.* 5:245–52

Stokes P. 1999. Novelty. See Runco & Pritzker 1999, pp. 297–304

Sulloway F. 1996. *Born to Rebel.* New York: Pantheon

Tahir L. 1999. George Bernard Shaw. See Runco & Pritzker 1999, pp. 565–70

Tegano DW, Moran JD III. 1989. Sex differences in the original thinking of preschool and elementary school children. *Creat. Res. J.* 2:102–10

TenHouten W. 1994. See Shaw & Runco 1994

Toplyn G, McGuire W. 1990. The differential effect of noise on creative task performance. *Creat. Res. J.* 4:337–48

Torrance EP. 1968. A longitudinal examination of the fourth-grade slump in creativity. *Gifted Child Q.* 12:195–99

Torrance EP. 1971. Are the Torrance tests of creative thinking biased against or in favor of "disadvantaged" groups? *Gifted Child Q.* 15:75–80

Torrance EP. 1974. *Torrance Tests of Creative Thinking: Norms and Technical Manual.* Bensenville, IL: Scholastic Test. Serv.

VanTassel-Baska J. 1999. Bronte sisters. See Runco & Pritzker 1999, pp. 229–34

Wakefield JF. 1985. Towards creativity: problem finding in a divergent-thinking exercise. *Child Study J.* 15:265–70

Walberg HJ, Stariha WE. 1992. Productive human capital: learning, creativity, and eminence. *Creat. Res. J.* 5:323–40

Wallace DB. 1991. The genesis and microgenesis of sudden insight in the creation of literature. *Creat. Res. J.* 4:41–50

Wallach MA. 1970. Creativity. *Carmichael's Handbook of Child Psychology*, ed. P Mussen, pp. 1211–72. New York: Wiley

Wallach MA, Kogan N. 1965. *Modes of Thinking in Young Children.* New York: Holt, Rinehart & Winston

Wallach MA, Wing C. 1969. *The Talented Student.* New York: Holt, Rinehart & Winston

Wallas G. 1926. *The Art of Thought.* New York: Harcourt Brace Jovanovich

Ward T, Smith S. 2003. See Runco 2003b. In press

Watson JD. 1968. *The Double Helix.* New York: Atheneum

Wicker A. 1985. Getting out of our conceptual ruts. *Am. Psychol.* 40:1094–103

Wilson EO. 1978. *On Human Nature.* Cambridge, MA: Harvard Univ. Press

Witt LA, Beorkrem M. 1989. Climate for creative productivity as a predictor of research usefulness and organizational effectiveness in an R&D organization. *Creat. Res. J.* 2:30–40

Zajonc RB, Markus GB. 1975. Birth order and intellectual development. *Psychol. Rev.* 82:74–88

Zausner T. 1998. When walls become doorways: creativity, chaos theory, and physical illness. *Creat. Res. J.* 11:21–32

Zausner T. 1999. Georgia O'Keeffe. See Runco & Pritzker 1999, pp. 305–10

Annu. Rev. Psychol. 2004. 55:689–714
doi: 10.1146/annurev.psych.55.090902.141927
First published online as a Review in Advance on October 20, 2003

PSYCHOLOGY AND CULTURE

Darrin R. Lehman,[1] Chi-yue Chiu,[2] and Mark Schaller[3]

[1]*Department of Psychology, University of British Columbia, Vancouver, British Columbia, V6T 1Z4 Canada; email: darrin.lehman@ubc.ca*
[2]*Department of Psychology, University of Illinois, Champaign-Urbana, Champaign, Illinois 61801; email: cychiu@s.psych.uiuc.edu*
[3]*Department of Psychology, University of British Columbia, Vancouver, British Columbia, V6T 1Z4 Canada; email: schaller@psych.ubc.ca*

Key Words   cross-cultural differences in social cognition, cultural emergence

■ **Abstract**   Psychological processes influence culture. Culture influences psychological processes. Individual thoughts and actions influence cultural norms and practices as they evolve over time, and these cultural norms and practices influence the thoughts and actions of individuals. Large bodies of literature support these conclusions within the context of research on evolutionary processes, epistemic needs, interpersonal communication, attention, perception, attributional thinking, self-regulation, human agency, self-worth, and contextual activation of cultural paradigms. Cross-cultural research has greatly enriched psychology, and key issues for continued growth and maturation of the field of cultural psychology are articulated.

CONTENTS

0066-4308/04/0204-0689$14.00

INTRODUCTION

The relations between psychology and culture are multifaceted and dynamic, so inquiry into cultural psychology takes many distinct forms. Much recent research in cultural psychology focuses on cross-cultural comparisons. The past several years have witnessed an explosion of research on differences between East Asians and European North Americans in such areas as perception, thinking, and self-concept (e.g., Heine et al. 1999, Masuda & Nisbett 2001, Nisbett et al. 2001). Other recent research focuses on the situation-specific activation of cultural schemata (e.g., Hong et al. 2000). Still other lines of recent work focus on the psychological processes that contribute to origins of cultures and persistence of cultural information. This latter research, for example, reveals how distinct cultural populations emerge as the consequence of interpersonal communication and social influence (e.g., Harton & Bourgeois 2004). Each of these avenues of research contributes to our understanding of *psychology and culture*, yet oddly up until now they have not been considered together.

GOALS OF THIS REVIEW

With these observations in mind, we have three major goals for this review. One goal is to provide a faithful, albeit selective, review of recent research in cultural psychology. We had to omit considerable detail on topics that have already been reviewed thoroughly in other recently published papers, of which there are many, especially on cross-cultural differences (e.g., Choi et al. 1999, Diener et al. 2003, Fiske et al. 1998, Heine et al. 1999, Nisbett & Norenzayan 2002, Nisbett et al. 2001, Triandis & Suh 2002). We devote more space to topics that have not been so thoroughly reviewed as of late.

A second goal is to consider together two substantial bodies of research in cultural psychology that typically have been treated as entirely independent literatures: Research on the ways in which psychological processes influence culture, and research on the ways in which culture influences psychological processes.

Third, this chapter is meant to provide more than a summary of empirical findings; rather, we aim to illuminate deeper insights that emerge when these many different findings—addressing many different kinds of questions—are considered in aggregate. We highlight conceptual connections between superficially dissimilar phenomena, attempt to resolve apparent inconsistencies and outstanding debates, and identify important directions for future research within the vast area of cultural psychology.

PSYCHOLOGICAL FOUNDATIONS OF CULTURE

Virtually every definition of culture (e.g., Hofstede 1980, Mead 1955) suggests that it represents a coalescence of discrete behavioral norms and cognitions shared by individuals within some definable population that are distinct from those shared within other populations. These normative beliefs and behaviors provide resources for realizing individual and collective goals, and so are often institutionalized in a variety of formal and informal ways. Moreover, there exist means for transmitting beliefs and behaviors to new members of the cultural population, so that the norms defining a culture may persist over very long periods of time.

Given this tacit definition of culture, psychological perspectives can yield novel answers to fundamental questions about the origins and persistence of culture: How do beliefs and behaviors become normative; that is, widely shared within populations? How do different types of norms coalesce to the point that a recognizable "culture" emerges? Why do cultural norms have certain content rather than other content? Why are some normative beliefs and behaviors successfully transmitted to new cultural members whereas others fail to persist over time? A body of theory and research is emerging that addresses these questions by focusing on cognitive processes and interpersonal behavior.

Evolutionary Perspectives on Culture

From an evolutionary perspective, solitude is dangerous; mutually supportive collective behavior is beneficial, both for survival and sexual reproduction. Thus, it makes sense to assume that humans have an evolved tendency toward the establishment of shared beliefs, behaviors, and normative structures that help hold social collectives together (Campbell 1982). Cultural norms—common beliefs, expectations, and practices—may also have conferred adaptive advantages by facilitating efficient coordination of activities necessary for survival, sexual reproduction, and the successful rearing of children to mating age. Consequently, several theoretical analyses suggest that culture emerged as an extraordinary and highly flexible sort of evolutionary adaptation (Barkow et al. 1992).

This evolutionary perspective also implicates constraints operating on the cultural norms that are and are not likely to emerge. Some beliefs and behaviors are better than others at solving adaptive problems, and these are the beliefs and behaviors that are likely to become and remain culturally normative. Examples are provided by recent analyses of specific kinds of cultural norms, including norms governing sexual behavior, communal sharing, and morality (Kameda et al. 2003, Kenrick et al. 2003, Pinker 2002). For instance, Krebs & Janicki (2004) articulated how evolutionary processes may have shaped culturally shared conceptions of morality pertaining to a broad set of behavioral domains, including obedience, reciprocity, interpersonal helping, social responsibility, and group solidarity. An important implication of this perspective is the assertion that, although culture may be socially constructed, there are fundamental biologically based constraints on the construction process: Some specific kinds of beliefs and behaviors are especially likely to be normative across human populations, whereas others are extraordinarily unlikely ever to be popular.

Psychological Needs and the Creation of Culture

Other conceptual approaches focus on specific psychological needs and their consequences for the creation of cultural norms. One perspective is offered by Terror

Management Theory, which posits that culture emerged, in part, to serve as a psychological buffer against the existential anxiety that results from the awareness of our own mortality (Greenberg et al. 1997, Solomon et al. 2004). Culture acts as such a buffer because many specific beliefs and behaviors that define cultural worldviews offer symbolic immortality (e.g., religious beliefs that provide for some sort of life after death, and ritualized practices of naming one's children after oneself so that one's name lives on). Culture also provides a buffer against anxiety by providing a set of values and normative standards against which an individual may be judged a worthwhile, socially acceptable person. The goal is to feel that one is a valuable member of a meaningful culture, which in turn evokes a feeling of symbolic immortality that mitigates the fear of finitude. This line of reasoning leads to two broad hypotheses. One hypothesis is that feelings of self-worth buffer against existential anxiety. Consistent with this hypothesis, events that temporarily enhance self-esteem also reduce anxiety responses to death-related thoughts and imagery (Greenberg et al. 1993, Harmon-Jones et al. 1997). The other hypothesis is that awareness of one's own mortality leads to enhanced attempts to defend one's own cultural worldview. Dozens of studies have supported this hypothesis in myriad ways. For instance, mortality salience increases derogation of alternative cultural worldviews, punishment of individuals who violate cultural rules, rewards to those who uphold cultural values, and unwillingness to desecrate iconic cultural symbols (Florian & Mikulincer 1997, Greenberg et al. 1995, Rosenblatt et al. 1989). More broadly, this theory offers a psychologically functional explanation for the remarkable persistence of extant cultural norms and values, including those that objectively appear to be trivial or even self-defeating.

Another approach suggests that culture arises in part from an epistemic need for verifiable knowledge, and for certainty and confidence in our perceptions of the world around us. The creation of a shared reality—a common set of beliefs, expectations, and rules for interpreting the world—helps fulfill this need to validate one's own construction of reality (Hardin & Higgins 1996). Classic research on norm formation is consistent with this perspective (Sherif 1936). Also consistent with this approach is recent research revealing that attitudes are more likely to be activated into working memory under conditions in which those attitudes are consistent with perceived cultural norms (Sechrist & Stangor 2001), and that recalled information is often assimilated toward shared cultural representations (Harris et al. 1992, Lau et al. 2001a). More direct evidence supporting the role of epistemic needs in the creation and maintenance of culture has emerged from research in which individuals' needs for epistemic "closure" are measured or manipulated. Under conditions in which needs for closure are heightened, individuals are more likely to conform with perceived norms, are more likely to reject deviants from social groups, and are quicker to achieve consensus—all evidence that the need for epistemic certainty contributes to the formation and persistence of culture (Kruglanski & Webster 1991; Kruglanski et al. 1993; Richter & Kruglanski 1999, 2004).

The terror management and epistemic perspectives are well supported by empirical evidence, and identify conceptually complementary processes that help explain why cultures emerge at all. Understandably, however, neither approach addresses questions about why *some* cultural norms are more likely than others to arise.

Interpersonal Communication and the Creation of Culture

A very different perspective on the origins of culture implies that cultures—and the specific norms that define these cultures—emerge as unintended byproducts of interpersonal interaction. Dynamic Social Impact Theory provides one particularly well-defined model of cultural origins (Latané 1996). This model considers the consequences of persuasion processes within a dynamical systems framework, and reveals that the defining features of culture—the coalescence of distinctive shared beliefs and norms within a population—can arise simply as a consequence of interpersonal communication (Harton & Bourgeois 2004, Latané 1996, Latané & Bourgeois 2001). Because social influence attends any act of communication, and because individuals communicate more regularly with others who are closer to them in geographic or social space, a dynamic process is set in motion in which neighboring individuals mutually influence each other on a wide variety of beliefs and behaviors. In addition, people differ in their ability to influence others. As people communicate with their neighbors and others in close proximity, some will be more convincing and will persuade more people to agree with them. Over time, this mutual influence process leads to the emergence of different "clusters" of beliefs and behaviors. These different beliefs and behaviors tend to become increasingly correlated over time as well: Beliefs and behavioral practices that are initially unrelated tend to coalesce so that people in one cluster share a particular set of norms, whereas those in another cluster share a different set of norms. Furthermore, through majority influence, diversity in beliefs, values, and practices within a cluster will diminish. However, clustering also protects minorities from majority influence, thus ensuring continued diversity. This analysis has been supported in carefully controlled laboratory studies that track the emergence of rudimentary cultures over time (Latané & L'Herrou 1996), and also in longitudinal studies of real-world populations over time (Bourgeois & Bowen 2001, Guimond & Palmer 1985). The cultural processes predicted by the theory have been observed in a wide variety of beliefs and behaviors, ranging from attitudes toward mathematicians to alcohol use (Harton & Bourgeois 2004).

Some constraints on the emergence of culture are implied by Dynamic Social Impact Theory. The dynamic process and its specific outcomes vary as a function of the number and proximity of individuals within any given population, as well as their potency as sources of social influence (Latané 1996). In addition, the operation of these processes is hypothesized to occur more readily among beliefs and behaviors that are more highly prone to social influence. Consistent with this analysis, attitudes that are highly heritable—and so are less amenable to social influence (for examples and empirical elaboration, see Tesser 1993)—are less likely to coalesce into distinct cultural clusters (Bourgeois 2002).

If indeed culture emerges and evolves as the byproduct of interpersonal communication, then the specific contents of cultures are likely to be influenced by individual-level processes that govern the contents of communication. Beliefs and behaviors that are more "communicable," for whatever reason, are more likely to become culturally normative and to remain that way (Heath et al. 2001, Schaller 2001, Schaller et al. 2002, Sperber 1984). The contents of communication are constrained by many different psychological considerations, and these considerations therefore can exert indirect consequences on culture. For instance, the specific contents of socially shared stereotypes are influenced by concerns ranging from impression management to social identity, and these cultural-level consequences appear largely unintended—an indirect by-product of the more direct influences on interpersonal communication (Haslam et al. 1998, Ruscher 1998, Schaller & Conway 1999).

Complementarity of Different Perspectives on the Origins of Culture

The processes specified by these different conceptual approaches to culture are logically independent and complementary. Several recent lines of research reveal points of integration between these different perspectives. Of particular note are studies revealing how psychological needs—including needs based on evolutionary pressures—may influence communication processes.

Evolutionary considerations suggest that individuals may be especially likely to communicate information that has affective content relevant to survival and reproduction; consequently, knowledge structures that are highly evocative of these affective states may be especially likely to become culturally shared (Kenrick et al. 2002). Research on contemporary "urban legends" is consistent with this analysis: Legends that elicit greater disgust are more likely to be communicated and to become part of popular culture (Heath et al. 2001).

Epistemic needs—such as needs for cognitive efficiency and closure—also exert important influences on the kinds of information that individuals attempt to communicate, and so constrain the specific contents of emergent cultural norms and whether they persist over time (Crandall & Schaller 2004, Kashima 2000b, McIntyre et al. 2003, Thompson et al. 2000). In addition, epistemic needs influence individuals' understanding of and memory for communicated information (Richter & Kruglanski 2004). This in turn affects the persistence of various cultural norms. Individuals more easily recall information that is sufficiently novel to merit attention, but is not so unusual as to wholly violate existing perceptions of reality (Cohen 2001). This process places important constraints on the nature of religious mythologies and other "magical" belief systems that evolve over time within a culture (Barret & Nyhof 2001, Norenzayan & Atran 2004). Constraints on memory processes also influence the persistence of other cultural artifacts that depend on an oral tradition, such as ballads and children's counting-out rhymes (Rubin 1995).

CULTURAL FOUNDATIONS OF PSYCHOLOGY

Just as psychological processes exert fundamental influences on culture, so too culture exerts fundamental influences on basic psychological processes. Most inquiries into cross-cultural psychological differences are informed by the concept of cultural schemas or paradigms, which consist of a set of socially shared practices, norms, values, and other mental events that are loosely organized around some common theme (Shore 1996, Triandis 1989). These cultural paradigms guide the construction of meaning across many domains of social life. Among the most heavily researched cultural paradigms in psychology are those that have focused on two overlapping conceptual distinctions: the distinction between independent and interdependent self-concept (Markus & Kitayama 1991), and the distinction between individualism and collectivism (Triandis 1989). There is increasing consensus among cultural researchers that these and other cultural paradigms help individuals and groups solve complex problems of social coordination (Cohen 2001, Fiske 2000, Kashima 1999, Sperber 1996). Culture represents an inescapably fundamental element in individuals' physical and social environments, and so—through the mechanisms of cultural learning—has enduring consequences on individuals' thoughts, feelings, and behaviors (Boesch & Tomasello 1998, Carpenter et al. 1998, Fiske 2000).

Clearly a cultural paradigm is not the same as any demographically defined regional group or ethnocultural population (Kashima 2000a, Triandis 1989). Nevertheless, the underlying influence of complex cultural paradigms often is manifested in meaningful between-group differences in shared cognitions, behaviors, and normative practices (Han & Shavitt 1994, Kashima & Kashima 1998, Kim & Markus 1999, Peng & Nisbett 1999, Rothbaum & Tsang 1998). Consequently, within much psychological research, regional or ethnocultural groups often are used as proxies for cultural paradigms. Such studies test hypotheses about differences in basic psychological processes between demographically defined groups. The vast majority of such research, and what we focus on in this review, concerns comparisons between East Asians and European North Americans. The aim is neither to dichotomize the world nor to claim that these cultures represent the rest of the world. Rather, it is to articulate two divergent systems of co-construction of culture and psychology. At the outset, however, it is important to note that we recognize that there is significant variability both across the various East Asian and European North American cultures, and within cultures.

Attending, Perceiving, Thinking, and Attributing

Adaptive learning requires both attunement to environmental information that is diagnostic of specific outcomes, and detection of covariation between environmental events and adaptive response patterns. Solution of such complex problems requires coordination of attention. Nisbett and his colleagues (2001) suggested that as the ecological and symbolic environment coevolved, East Asians developed an intellectual tradition emphasizing holistic, dialectical information processing. This intellectual tradition is categorically different from the European North American intellectual tradition, which privileges an analytical, linear thinking style. East Asians therefore should be especially attentive to object-context relations, good at detecting covariation of events, believe in change instead of consistent trends, have high tolerance of seemingly incompatible cognitions, and prefer to rely on holistic impressions rather than formal logic to solve problems.

Consistent with these notions, East Asians have better memory for objects-in-context than European North Americans (Masuda & Nisbett 2001), are more field dependent (Ji et al. 2000), are more confident in their ability to detect covariation (Ji et al. 2000), have stronger expectations that outcome or behavioral trends will reverse in the future (Ji et al. 2001), are more likely to attribute incompatible traits or values to the self (Choi & Choi 2002), are less surprised by counterintuitive behaviors or counterintuitive research findings (Choi & Nisbett 2000), have a greater tendency to consider arguments from both sides and to compromise in conflict situations (Peng & Nisbett 1999), are more influenced by exemplar typicality when asked to make rule-based categorization and categorical inferences (Norenzayan et al. 2002), and are more willing to accept deductive inferences when the premises are believable (Norenzayan et al. 2002).

Compared to East Asians, European North Americans are more likely to attribute situationally induced events to the actor's dispositions (Choi & Nisbett 1998, Miyamoto & Kitayama 2002), and attribute the causes of social events to the actor's internal factors (Morris & Peng 1994, Zarate et al. 2001). In addition, they are less aware of the influence of the situation on behavior (Morris & Peng 1994), and they make stronger predictions of trait-relevant behavior based on previous trait-relevant behavior (Norenzayan et al. 2002). By comparison, East Asians are more affected by information about situational constraints when predicting trait-relevant behavior in a particular situation (Norenzayan et al. 2002).

The two groups also differ in how they use information to make social inferences. Specifically, East Asians exclude less directly relevant information than European North Americans when they make causal inferences (Choi et al. 2003). And East Asians rely more on relational information (i.e., the target's interpersonal network, or community memberships) than individuating information in making social predictions, whereas European North Americans exhibit the reverse pattern (Gelfand et al. 2000).

Interestingly, in many of these studies (e.g., Choi & Nisbett 1998, Ji et al. 2000, Miyamoto & Kitayama 2002, Norenzayan et al. 2002) East Asians' responses deviate from those of European North Americans only when the relevance of the East Asian intellectual paradigm is made salient (e.g., when the contradictions between holistic and analytical reasoning are made salient, when the research participants are not given control over the test procedures, when the situational constraints on behavior are highlighted, or when the stimulus behavior is not diagnostic of personal dispositions). This "salience" effect suggests that although East Asians are also capable of analytical and person-focused reasoning, they apply the culturally encouraged way of thinking once the relevance or applicability of the East Asian intellectual paradigm is made salient in the particular context. Of course, European North Americans are also capable of thinking more holistically and relationally, although, interestingly, empirical demonstrations of this are currently lacking.

Constructing Selfhood

CONSTRUCTION OF SELF-CONCEPTS   Cultural paradigms play a constitutive role in the evolution of the self. Geertz (1966) argued that culture not only provides a model of self, it is a model for self. That is, not only does culture define what the self is, it also prescribes how people should manage their self in everyday life. In anthropological discourse, the "Western" self, characterized as self-contained and autonomous, is generally taken as a point of departure. Non-Western conceptions of selves are defined by the negation of these qualities (Sokefeld 1999). Similar rhetoric has dominated psychological analyses of the self as a cultural construction. The focus of psychological inquiry has been on how the interdependent cultural paradigm provides an alternative construction of self from that which is derived within the independent cultural paradigm. Research on people's spontaneous self-descriptions has revealed consistent group differences: East Asians generally mention more interdependent or group-related self-statements, whereas European North Americans generally mention more independent self-statements (Rhee et al. 1995, Wang 2001).

SELF-REGULATION   Solution of complex social problems also requires social consensus on how individuals should behave in a society. An important cultural coordination device for self-regulation is the shared ideal type of human development in the culture. Tweed & Lehman (2002) described the ideal types of a learned person in the Socratic tradition (which grows out of an independent cultural paradigm) and the Confucian intellectual tradition (which grows out of an interdependent cultural paradigm). An ideal Socratic learner is an active learner who pursues knowledge for its own sake, values self-generated knowledge, and engages in self-directed learning through dialogic exchanges. By contrast, ideal Confucian learners view knowledge pursuit as a route to self-improvement. Learning is achieved through applying the self, and constantly reflecting and meditating on traditional wisdom (see also Kim 2002, Li 2002). An ideal Socratic learner derives self-respect from the actualization of one's potentials for independent learning, whereas an ideal Confucian learner derives self-respect from moral self-transformation and from pursuits of prosocial goals.

Ideal types of a learned person are rooted in cultural models of human development. Within an independent cultural paradigm, the goals of personal development are self-direction (Iyengar & Lepper 1999), pursuits of personal excellence, and actualization of inner potentials. These goals focus on the attainment of positive outcomes. Research has shown that European North Americans perceive success-foregone events to be more important than failure-avoidance events (Lee et al. 2000), attribute successes to internal causes more often than to external causes (Hallahan et al. 1997), feel that success situations have more influence on self-esteem than do failure situations (Kitayama et al. 1997), and find success feedback to be more motivating than failure feedback (Heine et al. 2001).

Within an interdependent cultural paradigm, the goal of personal development is to transcend the bounded individual self through cultivating concerns for the collective good. This cultural orientation prescribes devaluation of one's distinctive personal strengths that are unrelated to or would even hinder actualization of collective goals, and valuation of personal qualities that would facilitate actualization of these goals. The emphasis on devaluation of distinctive personal strengths may create a propensity toward self-criticism (Heine et al. 2000) and a strong motivation to avoid failures that would reflect badly on the group. Consistent with these ideas, East Asians pursue more avoidance goals than do European North Americans (Elliot et al. 2001), perceive failure-avoidance events to be more important than success-foregone events (Lee et al. 2000), think that failures would decrease their self-esteem more than successes would increase their self-esteem (Kitayama et al. 1997), and find failure feedback to be more motivating than success feedback (Heine et al. 2001). In addition, East Asians believe that although others are more likely than them to encounter positive events, they are less likely than others to encounter negative events (Chang et al. 2001, Heine & Lehman 1995).

Many entrenched egocentric biases in self-appraisals found among European North Americans may be related to the high accessibility of the independent cultural paradigm in the West. Such biases include self-enhancement (viewing one's personal attributes as better than they really are), unrealistic optimism (perceiving the self as more invulnerable and more likely to experience positive events than it really is), and self-affirmation (justifying one's personal choices). These biases are much less evident in East Asians (Chang et al. 2001; Heine & Lehman 1995, 1997a,b; Hetts et al. 1999; Kurman 2001). East Asians also use more negative and fewer positive self-descriptions than do European North Americans, particularly when they describe themselves in front of an authority figure (Kanagawa et al. 2001), and they are more modest when describing their achievement (Akimoto & Sanbonmatsu 1999). In some studies, East Asians even exhibit a significant self-criticism bias (Heine et al. 2000, Hetts et al. 1999) or unrealistic pessimism (Heine & Lehman 1995). In addition, they are less likely to view criticism or negative feedback as a self-threat. In response to failure feedback, East Asians do not defend their self-esteem by derogating strong performers (Brockner & Chen 1996), and persist more than European North Americans (Heine et al. 2001).

CULTURAL CONSTRUCTION OF AGENCY   It would be a mistake to conclude that East Asians do not value agency. Human agency consists of personal but also collective or group agency (Bandura 2002). Agentic blends of personal and group agency may vary across cultural paradigms. For example, European North Americans tend to privilege personal agency, whereas East Asians tend to privilege group agency (Chiu et al. 2000, Menon et al. 1999). Markus & Kitayama (2002) refer to these as disjoint and conjoint models of agency, respectively. The former, which originates in the independent self, is agency that is separate or distinct from the actions of others. The latter, which originates in the interdependent self, is agency that in important ways is impelled by others, in relationship and interaction with those others.

Despite cultural variations in the relative primacy of personal (disjoint) and group (conjoint) agency, these two modes of agency may coexist in people, and are not antithetical to each other (Bandura 2002). For example, European North Americans can exercise their personal agency through pursuing their self-chosen activities, or group agency through pursuing a self-identified collective choice (Iyengar & Lepper 1999).

CULTURAL TRADEOFF   Self-enhancement serves a self-esteem function. With a weaker self-enhancement tendency and a stronger self-criticism tendency, East Asians often report lower levels of self-esteem than do those from independent cultures (Campbell et al. 1996, Heine & Lehman 2004). However, this does not imply that self-worth is not important to those from interdependent cultures (Kitayama & Karasawa 1997), but rather that self-worth is built on a different psychological foundation. And some recent research reveals that East Asians hold positive and sometimes unrealistically positive views of the self when they appraise themselves on dimensions that are central to the cultural definition of the self (e.g., communal traits, collectivistic attributes; Brown & Kobayashi 2002; Kurman 2001; but see Heine & Lehman 1999). Thus, for people from interdependent cultures, lower self-esteem may be compensated for by positive feelings of being a valued member of the group, and of being psychologically connected to group members.

SOURCES OF SELF-WORTH AND LIFE SATISFACTION   Different cultural paradigms suggest different ideas of what constitutes a good life, and prescribe different routes to self-worth. For East Asians, self-worth is established on the social standing of one's group, as well as the group's appraisal of the self. Compared to European North Americans, East Asians are more likely to perceive group failures as ego-threatening, although they are less likely to perceive personal failures as ego-threatening (Chen et al. 1998). Feedback on group performance, which has little impact on self-evaluations by European North Americans, significantly affects self-evaluations by East Asians (Earley et al. 1999).

Similarly, factors related to personal agency (self-esteem, identity consistency, personal freedom, and pursuit and attainment of individual goals) and personal affect are better predictors of life satisfaction for European North Americans than for East Asians, whereas factors related to feelings of connectedness (pursuit and attainment of interdependent goals, and quality of interpersonal relationships) are better predictors of life satisfaction for East Asians than for European North Americans (Diener & Diener 1995, Kwan et al. 1997, Oishi & Diener 2001, Oishi et al. 1999, Schimmack et al. 2002b, Suh 2002, Suh et al. 1998). In addition, events involving personal influence are more cognitively accessible to European North Americans, whereas events involving adjustment are more cognitively accessible to East Asians. Finally, influence events that are accessible to European North Americans tend to evoke feelings of efficacy, whereas adjustment events that are accessible to East Asians tend to evoke feelings of relatedness (Morling et al. 2002).

Connecting to the Social World

Joint activities invariably involve social coordination, and culture's influence on these activities is pronounced. For example, East Asians are more likely to take the perspective of the interaction partner than are European North Americans, who in turn are more likely to project their own perspectives onto their interaction partner (Cohen & Gunz 2002). In interpersonal communication, East Asians are more attuned to the relational context, and more sensitive to the presence of a common ground of knowledge in the communication context, than are European North Americans (Haberstroh et al. 2002).

Consistent with the finding that those from collectivistic cultures are more sensitive to the relational context than are those from individualistic cultures, group opinions, concerns for in-group benefits, and group harmony play a more important role than personal attitudes and preferences in social interactions for East Asians, and the reverse is true for European North Americans. For example, compared to European North Americans, East Asians find commercial advertisements that appeal to in-group benefits, harmony, and family integrity more persuasive, and those that appeal to personal preferences and benefits less persuasive (Han & Shavitt 1994). East Asians tend to make choices that will enhance in-group benefits, and will be popular in the group. By contrast, European North Americans tend to make competitive choices, and choices that highlight their personal distinctiveness and individuality (Aaker & Schmitt 2001, Domino & Regmi 1992, Kim & Markus 1999). In resolving conflicts, East Asians prefer mediational or accommodating strategies that minimize interpersonal animosity, whereas European North Americans prefer direct, confrontational strategies (Briley et al. 2000, Derlega et al. 2002, Ohbuschi et al. 1999).

Cultures also provide guidelines on how to regulate children's behavior and how to integrate children into the cultural world. European North American mothers expect earlier attainment of independence in children than East Asian mothers (Stewart et al. 1999; see also comparative work on cosleeping, Shweder et al. 1995), who in contrast place greater emphasis on regulation of children's social demeanors (Schulze et al. 2001). For example, Japanese teachers are more likely to direct communication to the group than are European North American teachers, who in turn are more likely to direct communication to individual students (Hamilton et al. 1991).

CONTEXTUAL ACTIVATION AND CULTURAL FRAME SWITCHING

One of our overarching points is that contrastive cultural paradigms are available to regional or ethnocultural groups. Evidence from several lines of research supports this idea. First, as noted, group differences are accentuated when the relevance or applicability of cultural paradigms are highlighted in the judgment or behavioral context, and attenuated when the paradigm's relevance is obscure (Choi & Nisbett 1998, Hong et al. 2003, Ji et al. 2000, Kanagawa et al. 2001, Miyamoto & Kitayama 2002, Norenzayan et al. 2002). These findings make plain that culture does not rigidly determine the responses of its group members. Instead, culture provides interpretive perspectives for making sense of reality.

Aside from the cultural paradigm's applicability, its epistemic value in a particular situation also affects how likely it is to be adopted in the situation. A particular cultural paradigm is likely to be adopted when it offers a consensually validated, conventionalized solution to a problem, and when the problem solver lacks the capability, motivation, or resources to consider alternative solutions. Consistent with this idea, the likelihood of following a cultural paradigm in judgment and decision making increases when people need to recruit culturally validated reasons to justify their decisions (Briley et al. 2000), have a high need for cognitive closure (Chiu et al. 2000, Morris & Fu 2001), are cognitively busy (Knowles et al. 2001), or need to make judgments under time pressure (Chiu et al. 2000).

In addition, people often express or affirm their ethnocultural identities by engaging in practices prescribed by the dominant cultural paradigm in their ethnocultural group. Not surprisingly, culture's influences on behavior are particularly pronounced in ethnocultural groups when ethnocultural identities are accessible (Rhee et al. 1995), or when there is strong identification with the group (Jetten et al. 2002).

Second, people often follow different cultural paradigms in different contexts. For example, European North American students mention more group attributes and fewer idiocentric attributes when their collective self is primed than when their private self is primed. This finding reveals that both independent and interdependent self-construals are available to European North Americans, and contextual priming can bring to the forefront one or the other of these self-construals (Gardner et al. 1999, Trafimow et al. 1991).

Susanna Harrington, a multicultural informant of South American origin in Sparrow's (2000) study, said, "I think of myself not as a unified cultural being but as a communion of different cultural beings. Due to the fact that I have spent time in different cultural environments I have developed several cultural identities that diverge and converge according to the need of the moment" (p. 190). This notion of flexibility in cultural frame switching may help explain a consistent finding regarding immigration, ethnic identity, and psychological well-being: Immigrants with both a strong ethnic identity and a strong national identity tend to exhibit the best psychological adaptation (Phinney et al. 2001).

Experiences of cultural frame switching are familiar to groups with multiple cultural identities. Hong and her colleagues (Hong et al. 1997, 2000, 2003) have captured cultural frame switching experiences in their research by priming bicultural individuals (i.e., Hong Kong Chinese, Chinese Americans) with either Chinese cultural icons (e.g., the Chinese dragon) or American cultural icons (e.g., Mickey Mouse). Bicultural individuals made more external or group attributions and fewer individual dispositional attributions when they were primed with Chinese cultural icons than when they were primed with American cultural icons. Analogous cultural priming effects have been found in other studies using different bicultural samples (e.g., Chinese Canadians, multicultural Hawaiians, and Dutch-Greek bicultural children; Bhawuk & Brislin 1992, Lehman et al. 2004, Ross et al. 2002, Verkuyten & Pouliasi 2002), and a variety of cultural primes (e.g., language, experimenter's cultural identity, and salience of ethnocultural identity; Gardner et al. 1999, Hong et al. 2001, Ross et al. 2002, Trafimow et al. 1997, Verkuyten & Pouliasi 2002) on various dependent measures (e.g., endorsement of cultural values, moral decisions, spontaneous self-concept, memory for object context, and self-esteem; Briley & Wyer 2001, Gardner et al. 1999, Hong et al. 2001, Lehman et al. 2004, Ross et al. 2002, Verkuyten & Pouliasi 2002).

The findings from cultural frame switching research are consistent with the idea that cultural paradigms are consensually validated interpretive tools (DiMaggio 1997). Individuals with extensive multicultural experiences may have more tools in their toolbox than do monocultural individuals (Tweed & Lehman 2002, Yamada & Singelis 1999). How multicultural individuals choose among the multiple tools available to them depends on how they manage their multiple cultural identities. As noted, cultural paradigms serve important identity expression functions. Some bicultural individuals view their dual cultural identities as oppositional, whereas others see them as independent or complementary (Benet-Martinez et al. 2002, Tsai et al. 2000). Among bicultural minorities, some seek to assimilate into the majority group by aligning their values with those in the majority group (Tafarodi et al. 2002), whereas others seek to affirm their ethnocultural identity by adhering to the dominant values in their ethnocultural group and by distancing themselves from the majority group (Kosmitzki 1996). Variations in how dual identities are managed are related to bicultural individuals' responses to cultural priming. Those who view their dual identities as independent or complementary tend to assimilate their responses to those expected from the primed cultural paradigms. Those who view their dual identities as oppositional and those who seek to affirm their ethnocultural identities may respond reactively to the cultural primes, and exhibit responses that are contrastive to the responses expected from the primed cultural paradigms (Benet-Martinez et al. 2002, Bond & Cheung 1984).

The above analysis points to what we refer to as the paradox of group differences and cultural influence. When culture is reduced to a fixed response pattern in a regional or ethnocultural group, the absence of predicted group differences poses a threat to the explanatory utility of culture (Briley & Wyer 2001). In a recent review of group differences in individualism and collectivism, Oyserman et al.

(2002) found that those from individualistic cultures do not always have higher scores on measures of individualism and lower scores on measures of collectivism than do those from collectivistic cultures. On the face of it, this seems to threaten the construct validity of individualism and collectivism.

The threat is more apparent than real when we separate individualism and collectivism as cultural paradigms from group averages on value measures of individualism and collectivism. Psychological influences of culture are much more contextualized and dynamic than a model of culture as fixed response patterns in groups would anticipate (Briley & Wyer 2001, Fiske 2002, Hong & Chiu 2001). Paradoxically, the explanatory utility of cultural paradigms is most apparent when the predicted group differences emerge in a concrete situation only when cultural paradigms are relevant and useful in that situation, and disappear when they are not. Thus, the absence of group differences in some circumstances might highlight the explanatory utility of culture, instead of undermining it. A critical test of the theoretical utility of a cultural account of psychological processes is whether we can predict the specific circumstances under which group differences will emerge based on known principles of cultural knowledge application.

In response to Oyserman et al.'s (2002) observations, some cultural psychologists, instead of abandoning individualism and collectivism, have called for more dynamic, nuanced analyses of cultural processes (Kitayama 2002). Others have sought to identify the specific context within which predicted group differences in individualism and collectivism should arise. An emerging finding is that coherent group differences are likely to be observed when cultural differences are made salient by placing contrastive cultural paradigms in juxtaposition, such as when Japanese and European North Americans are asked to use each other as a reference group to calibrate their self-ratings (Heine et al. 2002), or when individualism scores and collectivism scores are pitted against each other (Schimmack et al. 2002a).

DYNAMIC INTERPLAY BETWEEN PSYCHOLOGY AND CULTURE

Psychological processes influence culture. Culture influences psychological processes. Individual thoughts and acts influence cultural norms and practices as they evolve over time, and these cultural paradigms influence the future thoughts and actions of individuals, which then influence the persistence and change of culture over time. And so on. By methodological necessity, most psychological research focuses on fixed slices of this inherently dynamic process, and culture often is conceptualized in static terms, thus reinforcing stereotypical images of a certain culture. To understand more fully the relations between psychology and culture, however, it is necessary to focus more explicitly on this dynamic interaction. Several lines of research illustrate promising strategies for doing so. One strategy is to examine the effects of existing cultural paradigms on those communication processes that are so central to the ongoing evolution of cultures. The existing cultural popularity of any piece of knowledge influences the manner in which that knowledge is communicated, which in turn constrains future representation of that knowledge at both the cognitive and cultural levels (Chiu et al. 1998, 1999; Lau et al. 2001b). This constraint on communication and culture itself differs across cultures. For example, individuals from interdependent cultures are more attentive to the development of common ground in communication (Haberstroh et al. 2002). A complementary strategy is to apply the logical and methodological tools of dynamical systems theory to examine the longitudinal consequences of interpersonal interaction on both individual- and cultural-level outcomes (Kameda et al. 2003, Kashima et al. 2000, Kenrick et al. 2003, Latané 1996). As these tools and research strategies are applied in increasingly sophisticated ways, we should be able to describe more fully the complex set of processes that bind psychology and culture together.

FUTURE DIRECTIONS

Much recent research has demonstrated the strength of culture in influencing the perceptions, construals, thoughts, feelings, and behaviors of its members. Culture promotes, encourages, and sustains ways of being, and in turn these then seem natural and ubiquitous. This makes clear the pitfalls of interpreting any given culturally based practice without first considering its relation to the cultural context. Nothing transpires in a cultural vacuum.

Findings from the burgeoning field of cultural psychology are significantly enhancing the generativity of psychological theorizing. Not only are we discovering fascinating differences between people from distinct cultures, we are gaining deeper understandings of the psychological processes that support behaviors of many kinds. It is becoming fashionable in empirical work to "unpack" culture, and thus to attempt to gain a better handle on why, precisely, the cultural differences exist. More developmental research is sorely needed within cultural psychology in order to increase understanding of culturally based psychological processes, and how such processes take shape as children are socialized and develop into adulthood. There is also a need for inquiry into a broader array of cultural paradigms, as well as inquiry into additional variables that can serve as proxies for wellmined paradigms. Markus' recent work (e.g., Markus et al. 2003) comparing high school–educated and college-educated groups is a noteworthy example of the latter. Finally, as is true with many areas of psychology, cross-cultural research would benefit from having a greater percentage of studies being conducted with people other than college sophomores (Sears 1986).

Cultural psychology no doubt soon will move beyond the east-west comparisons that have become so commonplace. Broader coverage of world cultures will take the field in new and exciting directions. Yet learning about different cultures and different ways of being is tough going. For many social-personality psychologists who do not engage in cross-cultural research it has been difficult enough to be convinced that those who grow up participating in East Asian cultures can be so different from those who grow up participating in European North American cultures. The notion that one may have to go through this learning process again and again with still different cultures can be unsettling. Yet if the goal of psychology is to better understand *people*, and the ways they think, feel, and behave, we see no reason to be closed to this process.

Given globalization, increasingly cultural psychology will focus on how new members learn a culture. And this connects with one of the more interesting issues in the field concerning public versus private culture. In what ways is culture external and in what ways is it internal? Can culture reasonably be reduced to individual psychology? Or can culture be studied only from a distance? How does culture get into the heads of individuals? Analyses such as Sperber's (1996), of internalization of cultural representations ("culture in mind"), exemplify an important channel for future research.

Consideration of how societies adapt to multiculturalism, how citizens are educated about cross-cultural differences, ways that people learn flexible cultural styles (Tweed & Lehman 2002), and intercultural relations and conflict (Eidelson & Eidelson 2003) will become more and more important in the coming years. In a similar vein, understanding religion and religion's influence on psychology (Atran & Norenzayan 2004) will take on greater importance, as will a better appreciation for cultural change and its affect on people.

The field of cultural psychology will also be well served by research that focuses more fully on the dynamic relations between psychology and culture. We have discussed research on the psychological foundations of culture as well as research on the cultural foundations of psychology, but we have done little more than merely juxtapose these two fertile lines of inquiry. There remains a need to integrate these different lines of research, conceptually as well as empirically. An explicitly dynamical approach (e.g., Vallacher et al. 2002), abetted by sophisticated research methods that allow the tracking of dynamic bidirectional influences over time, will be of considerable utility in forging this sort of integration.

More generally, it will be important to develop a deeper understanding of the complex connections between cross-cultural differences and psychological universals. The integration of cultural psychology with evolutionary psychology presents itself as one particularly exciting opportunity. Depending on the particular level of analysis that one focuses on, one can perceive differences or similarities between any two populations. Since the field of cultural psychology took off in the mid-1990s, considerable resources have been devoted to the documentation and understanding of cross-cultural differences, many of which operate at very basic levels of attention, perception, and cognition. Still, there remains a powerful desire among many research psychologists to demonstrate ways in which ostensible cross-cultural differences may in fact be manifestations of deeper psychological similarities in motivation and cognition. Sometimes different actions by different peoples may indeed reflect similar underlying psychological processes. However, even when people from different cultures appear to be psychologically "the same," there may be fundamental cross-cultural differences in the deep meanings of the motivations, cognitions, emotions, and behaviors. That is, the entire dynamic—both content *and* process—may differ. In the rush to document the existence of psychic universals unaffected by cultural context, the very heart of the psychological process may be fundamentally misunderstood. This reflects an essential tension that accompanies any investigation into the intersection of the study of culture (which typically assumes meaningful cross-cultural differences) and the study of psychology (which typically assumes fundamental human universals). It remains for future research in cultural psychology to confront this tension, and to find ways of resolving it so that we may more fully comprehend the important relations between human culture and human psychology.

ACKNOWLEDGMENTS

We thank Emma Buchtel, Lynne Cooper, Dov Cohen, Ed Diener, Steve Heine, Li-jun Ji, Heejung Kim, Anna Lehman, Ara Norenzayan, Shige Oishi, and Harry Triandis for helpful comments on an earlier version of this chapter.

The *Annual Review of Psychology* is online at http://psych.annualreviews.org

LITERATURE CITED

Aaker J, Schmitt B. 2001. Culture-dependent assimilation and differentiation of the self: preferences for consumption symbols in the United States and China. *J. Cross-Cult. Psychol.* 32:561–76

Akimoto SA, Sanbonmatsu DM. 1999. Differences in self-effacing behavior between European and Japanese Americans: effect on competence evaluation. *J. Cross-Cult. Psychol.* 30:159–77

Atran S, Norenzayan A. 2004. Religion's evolutionary landscape: counterintuition, commitment, compassion, communion. *Brain Beh. Sci.* In press

Bandura A. 2002. Social cognitive theory in cultural context. *Appl. Psychol: An Int. Rev.* 51:269–90

Barkow JH, Cosmides L, Tooby J. 1992. *The Adapted Mind: Evolutionary Psychology and the Generation of Culture.* New York: Oxford Univ. Press

Barret JL, Nyhof MA. 2001. Spreading nonnatural concepts: the role of intuitive conceptual structures in memory and transmission of cultural materials. *J. Cogn. Cult.* 1:69–100

Benet-Martinez V, Leu J, Lee F, Morris MW. 2002. Negotiating biculturalism: cultural frame switching in biculturals with oppositional versus compatible cultural identities. *J. Cross-Cult. Psychol.* 33:492–516

Bhawuk DPS, Brislin R. 1992. The measurement of intercultural sensitivity using the concepts of individualism and collectivism. *Int. J. Intercult. Relat.* 16:413–36

Boesch C, Tomasello M. 1998. Chimpanzee and human cultures. *Curr. Anthropol.* 39:591–614

Bond MH, Cheung M-K. 1984. Experimenter's language choice and ethnic affirmation by Chinese trilinguals in Hong Kong. *Int. J. Intercult. Relat.* 8:347–56

Bourgeois MJ. 2002. Heritability of attitudes constrains dynamic social impact. *Personal. Soc. Psychol. Bull.* 28:1063–72

Bourgeois MJ, Bowen AM. 2001. Self-organization of alcohol-related attitudes and beliefs in a campus housing complex: an initial investigation. *Health Psychol.* 20:434–37

Briley DA, Morris MW, Simonson I. 2000.

Reasons as carriers of culture: dynamic versus dispositional models of cultural influence on decision-making. *J. Consum. Res.* 27:157–78

Briley DA, Wyer RS Jr. 2001. Transitory determinants of values and decisions: the utility (or nonutility) of individualism and collectivism in understanding cultural differences. *Soc. Cogn.* 19:197–227

Brockner J, Chen Y-R. 1996. The moderating roles of self-esteem and self-construal in reaction to a threat to the self: evidence from the People's Republic of China and the United States. *J. Personal. Soc. Psychol.* 71:603–15

Brown JD, Kobayashi C. 2002. Self-enhancement in Japan and America. *Asian J. Soc. Psychol.* 5:145–68

Campbell DT. 1982. Legal and primary-group social controls. *J. Soc. Biol. Struct.* 5:431–38

Campbell JD, Trapnell PD, Heine SJ, Katz IM, Lavallee LF, Lehman DR. 1996. Self-concept clarity: measurement, personality correlates, and cultural boundaries. *J. Personal. Soc. Psychol.* 70:141–56

Carpenter M, Nagell K, Tomasello M. 1998. Social cognition, joint attention, and communicative competence from 9 to 15 months of age. *Monogr. Soc. Res. Child Dev.* 63:1–174

Chang EC, Asakawa K, Sanna LJ. 2001. Cultural variations in optimistic and pessimistic bias: Do Easterners really expect the worst and Westerners really expect the best when predicting future life events? *J. Personal. Soc. Psychol.* 81:476–91

Chen Y-R, Brockner J, Katz T. 1998. Toward an explanation of cultural differences in ingroup favoritism: the role of individual versus collective primacy. *J. Personal. Soc. Psychol.* 75:1490–502

Chiu C-y, Krauss RM, Lau IY-m. 1998. Some cognitive consequences of communication. In *Social and Cognitive Psychological Approaches to Interpersonal Communication*, ed. SR Fussell, RJ Kreuz, pp. 127–43. Hillsdale, NJ: Erlbaum

Chiu C-y, Krauss RM, Lee S-l. 1999. Communication and social cognition: a post-Whorfian approach. In *Progress in Asian Social Psychology*, ed. T Sugiman, M Karasawa, J Liu, C Ward, 2:127–43. Map-ku, Korea: Kyoyook-Kwahak-Sa

Chiu C-y, Morris MW, Hong Y-y, Menon T. 2000. Motivated cultural cognition: the impact of implicit cultural theories on dispositional attribution varies as a function of need for closure. *J. Personal. Soc. Psychol.* 78:247–59

Choi I, Choi Y. 2002. Culture and self-concept flexibility. *Personal. Soc. Psychol. Bull.* 28:1508–17

Choi I, Dalal R, Kim-Prieto C, Park H. 2003. Culture and judgment of causal relevance. *J. Personal. Soc. Psychol.* 84:46–59

Choi I, Nisbett RE. 1998. Situational salience and cultural differences in the correspondence bias and actor-observer bias. *Personal. Soc. Psychol. Bull.* 24:949–60

Choi I, Nisbett RE. 2000. Cultural psychology of surprise: holistic theories and recognition of contradiction. *J. Personal. Soc. Psychol.* 79:890–905

Choi I, Nisbett RE, Norenzayan A. 1999. Causal attribution across cultures: variation and universality. *Psychol. Bull.* 125:47–63

Cohen D. 2001. Cultural variation: considerations and implications. *Psychol. Bull.* 127:451–71

Cohen D, Gunz A. 2002. As seen by the other . . .: perspectives on the self in the memories and emotional perceptions of Easterners and Westerners. *Psychol. Sci.* 13:55–59

Crandall CS, Schaller M. 2004. Scientists and science: how individuals' goals shape cultural norms. See Schaller & Crandall 2004, pp. 200–23

Derlega VJ, Cukur CS, Kuang JCY, Forsyth DR. 2002. Interdependent construal of self and the endorsement of conflict resolution strategies in interpersonal, intergroup, and international disputes. *J. Cross-Cult. Psychol.* 33:610–25

Diener E, Diener M. 1995. Cross-cultural correlates of life satisfaction and self-esteem. *J. Personal. Soc. Psychol.* 68:653–63

Diener E, Oishi S, Lucas RE. 2003. Personality, culture, and subjective well-being: emotional and cognitive evaluations of life. *Annu. Rev. Psychol.* 54:403–25

DiMaggio P. 1997. Culture and cognition. *Annu. Rev. Sociol.* 23:263–87

Domino G, Regmi MP. 1992. Cooperation and competition in Chinese and American children. *J. Cross-Cult. Psychol.* 23:456–67

Earley PC, Gibson CB, Chen CC. 1999. "How did I do?" versus "How did we do?": cultural contrasts of performance feedback use and self-efficacy. *J. Cross-Cult. Psychol.* 30:594–619

Eidelson RJ, Eidelson JI. 2003. Dangerous ideas: five beliefs that propel groups toward conflict. *Am. Psychol.* 58:182–92

Elliot AJ, Chirkov VI, Kim Y, Sheldon KM. 2001. A cross-cultural analysis of avoidance (relative to approach) personal goals. *Psychol. Sci.* 12:505–10

Fiske AP. 2000. Complementarity theory: why human social capacities evolved to require cultural complements. *Personal. Soc. Psychol. Rev.* 4:76–94

Fiske AP. 2002. Using individualism-collectivism to compare cultures—A critique of the validity and measurement of the constructs: comments on Oyserman et al. (2002). *Psychol. Bull.* 128:78–88

Fiske AP, Kitayama S, Markus HR, Nisbett RE. 1998. The cultural matrix of social psychology. In *The Handbook of Social Psychology*, ed. D Gilbert, S Fiske, G Lindzey, pp. 915–81. San Francisco: McGraw-Hill

Florian V, Mikulincer M. 1997. Fear of death and the judgment of social transgressions: a multidimensional test of terror management theory. *J. Personal. Soc. Psychol.* 73:369–80

Gardner WL, Gabriel S, Lee A. 1999. "I" value freedom, but "we" value relationships: self-construal priming mirrors cultural differences in judgment. *Psychol. Sci.* 10:321–26

Geertz C. 1966. Religion as a cultural system. In *Anthropological Approaches to Religion*, ed. M Banton, pp. 1–46. London: Tavistock

Gelfand MJ, Spurlock D, Sniezek JA, Shao L. 2000. Culture and social prediction: the role of information in enhancing confidence in social predictions in the United States and China. *J. Cross-Cult. Psychol.* 31:498–516

Greenberg J, Pyszczynski T, Solomon S, Pinel E, Simon L, Jordan K. 1993. Effects of self-esteem on vulnerability-denying defensive distortions: further evidence of an anxiety-buffering function of self-esteem. *J. Exp. Soc. Psychol.* 29:229–51

Greenberg J, Simon L, Porteus J, Pyszczynski T, Solomon S. 1995. Evidence of a terror management function of cultural icons: the effects of mortality salience on the inappropriate use of cherished cultural symbols. *Personal. Soc. Psychol. Bull.* 21:221–28

Greenberg J, Solomon S, Pyszczynski T. 1997. Terror management theory of self-esteem and cultural worldviews: empirical assessments and conceptual refinements. In *Advances in Experimental Social Psychology*, ed. M Zanna, 29:61–139. New York: Academic

Guimond S, Palmer DL. 1985. The political socialization of commerce and social science students: epistemic authority and attitude change. *J. Appl. Soc. Psychol.* 26:1985–2013

Haberstroh S, Oyserman D, Schwarz N, Kuhen U, Ji L-j. 2002. Is the interdependent self more sensitive to question context than the independent self? Self-construal and the observation of conversational norms. *J. Exp. Soc. Psychol.* 38:323–29

Hallahan M, Lee F, Herzog T. 1997. It's not just whether you win or lose, it's also where you play the game: a naturalistic, cross-cultural examination of the positivity bias. *J. Cross-Cult. Psychol.* 28:768–78

Hamilton VL, Blumenfeld PC, Akoh H, Miuram K. 1991. Group and gender in Japanese and American elementary classrooms. *J. Cross-Cult. Psychol.* 22:317–46

Han S-P, Shavitt S. 1994. Persuasion and culture: advertising appeals in individualistic and collectivistic societies. *J. Exp. Soc. Psychol.* 30:326–50

Hardin CD, Higgins ET. 1996. Shared reality: how social verification makes the subjective objective. In *Handbook of Motivation and*

Cognition: Foundations of Social Behavior, ed. RM Sorrentino, ET Higgins, pp. 28–84. Chichester: Wiley

Harmon-Jones E, Simon L, Greenberg J, Pyszczynski T, Solomon S, McGregor H. 1997. Terror management theory and self-esteem: evidence that increased self-esteem reduces mortality salience effects. *J. Personal. Soc. Psychol.* 72:24–36

Harris RJ, Schoen LM, Hensley D. 1992. A cross-cultural study of story memory. *J. Cross-Cult. Psychol.* 23:133–47

Harton HC, Bourgeois MJ. 2004. Cultural elements emerge from dynamic social impact. See Schaller & Crandall 2004, pp. 41–75

Haslam SA, Turner JC, Oakes PJ, Reynolds KJ, Eggins RA, et al. 1998. When do stereotypes become really consensual? Investigating the group-based dynamics of the consensualization process. *Eur. J. Soc. Psychol.* 28:755–76

Heath C, Bell C, Sternberg E. 2001. Emotional selection in memes: the case of urban legends. *J. Personal. Soc. Psychol.* 81:1028–41

Heine SJ, Kitayama S, Lehman DR, Takata T, Ide E, et al. 2001. Divergent consequences of success and failure in Japan and North America: an investigation of self-improving motivations and malleable selves. *J. Personal. Soc. Psychol.* 81:599–615

Heine SJ, Lehman DR. 1995. Cultural variation in unrealistic optimism: Does the West feel more invulnerable than the East? *J. Personal. Soc. Psychol.* 68:595–607

Heine SJ, Lehman DR. 1997a. The cultural construction of self-enhancement: an examination of group-serving bias. *J. Personal. Soc. Psychol.* 72:1268–83

Heine SJ, Lehman DR. 1997b. Culture, dissonance, and self-affirmation. *Personal. Soc. Psychol. Bull.* 23:389–400

Heine SJ, Lehman DR. 1999. Culture, self-discrepancies, and self-satisfaction. *Personal. Soc. Psychol. Bull.* 25:915–25

Heine SJ, Lehman DR. 2004. Move the body, change the self: acculturative effects on self-concept. See Schaller & Crandall 2004, pp. 305–31

Heine SJ, Lehman DR, Markus HR, Kitayama S. 1999. Is there a universal need for positive self-regard? *Psychol. Rev.* 106:766–94

Heine SJ, Lehman DR, Peng K, Greenholtz J. 2002. What's wrong with cross-cultural comparisons of subjective Likert scales? The reference-group effect. *J. Personal. Soc. Psychol.* 82:903–18

Heine SJ, Takata T, Lehman DR. 2000. Beyond self-presentation: evidence for self-criticism among Japanese. *Personal. Soc. Psychol. Bull.* 26:71–78

Hetts JJ, Sakuma M, Pelham BW. 1999. Two roads to positive self-regard: implicit and explicit self-evaluation and culture. *J. Exp. Soc. Psychol.* 35:512–59

Hofstede G. 1980. *Culture's Consequences: International Differences in Work-Related Values*. Beverly Hills, CA: Sage

Hong Y-Y, Benet-Martinez V, Chiu C-y, Morris MW. 2003. Boundaries of cultural influence: construct activation as a mechanism for cultural differences in social perception. *J. Cross-Cult. Psychol.* 34:453–64

Hong Y-Y, Chiu C-y. 2001. Toward a paradigm shift: from cross-cultural differences in social-cognition to social-cognitive mediation of cultural differences. *Soc. Cogn.* 19:181–96

Hong Y-Y, Chiu C-y, Kung TM. 1997. Bringing culture out in front: effects of cultural meaning system activation on social cognition. In *Progress in Asian Social Psychology*, ed. K Leung, Y Kashima, U Kim, S Yamaguchi, 1:135–46. Singapore: Wiley

Hong Y-Y, Ip G, Chiu C-y, Morris MW, Menon T. 2001. Cultural identity and dynamic construction of the self: collective duties and individual rights in Chinese and American cultures. *Soc. Cogn.* 19:251–69

Hong Y-Y, Morris MW, Chiu C-y, Benet-Martinez V. 2000. Multicultural minds: a dynamic constructivist approach to culture and cognition. *Am. Psychol.* 55:709–20

Iyengar SS, Lepper MR. 1999. Rethinking the value of choice: a cultural perspective on intrinsic motivation. *J. Personal. Soc. Psychol.* 76:349–66

Jetten J, Postmes T, Mcauliffe B. 2002. "We're

all individuals": group norms of individualism and collectivism, levels of identification and identity threat. *Eur. J. Soc. Psychol.* 32:189–207

Ji L-j, Nisbett RE, Su Y. 2001. Culture, change, and prediction. *Psychol. Sci.* 12:450–56

Ji L-j, Peng K, Nibsett RE. 2000. Culture, control, and perception of relationships in the environment. *J. Personal. Soc. Psychol.* 78:943–55

Kameda T, Takezawa M, Hastie R. 2003. The logic of social sharing: an evolutionary game analysis of adaptive norm development. *Personal. Soc. Psychol. Rev.* 7:2–19

Kanagawa C, Cross SE, Markus HR. 2001. "Who am I?" The cultural psychology of the conceptual self. *Personal. Soc. Psychol. Bull.* 27:90–103

Kashima ES, Kashima Y. 1998. Culture and language: the case of cultural dimensions and personal pronoun use. *J. Cross-Cult. Psychol.* 29:461–86

Kashima Y. 1999. Culture, groups, and coordination problems. *Psychol. Beitrage* 41:237–51

Kashima Y. 2000a. Conceptions of culture and person for psychology. *J. Cross-Cult. Psychol.* 31:14–32

Kashima Y. 2000b. Maintaining cultural stereotypes in the serial reproduction of narratives. *Personal. Soc. Psychol. Bull.* 26:594–604

Kashima Y, Woolcock J, Kashima ES. 2000. Group impressions as dynamic configurations: the tensor product model of group impression formation and change. *Psychol. Rev.* 107:914–42

Kenrick DT, Li NP, Butner J. 2003. Dynamical evolutionary psychology: individual decision rules and emergent social norms. *Psychol. Rev.* 110:3–28

Kenrick DT, Maner JK, Butner J, Li NP, Becker DV, Schaller M. 2002. Dynamical evolutionary psychology: mapping the domains of the new interactionist paradigm. *Personal. Soc. Psychol. Rev.* 6:356–67

Kim HS. 2002. We talk, therefore we think? A cultural analysis of the effect of talking on thinking. *J. Personal. Soc. Psychol.* 83:828–42

Kim HS, Markus HR. 1999. Deviance or uniqueness, harmony or conformity? A cultural analysis. *J. Personal. Soc. Psychol.* 77:785–800

Kitayama S. 2002. Culture and basic psychological processes—toward a system view of culture: comment on Oyserman et al. (2002). *Psychol. Bull.* 128:89–96

Kitayama S, Karasawa M. 1997. Implicit self-esteem in Japan: name letters and birthday numbers. *Personal. Soc. Psychol. Bull.* 23:736–42

Kitayama S, Markus HR, Matsumoto H, Norasakkunkit V. 1997. Individual and collective processes in the construction of the self: self-enhancement in the United States and self-criticism in Japan. *J. Personal. Soc. Psychol.* 72:1245–67

Knowles ED, Morris MW, Chiu C-y, Hong Y-Y. 2001. Culture and process of person perception: evidence for automaticity among East Asians in correcting for situational influences on behavior. *Personal. Soc. Psychol. Bull.* 27:1344–56

Kosmitzki C. 1996. The reaffirmation of cultural identity in cross-cultural encounters. *Personal. Soc. Psychol. Bull.* 22:238–48

Krebs D, Janicki M. 2004. Biological foundations of moral norms. See Schaller & Crandall 2004, pp. 125–48

Kruglanski AW, Webster DM. 1991. Group members' reactions to opinion deviates and conformists at varying degrees of proximity to decision deadline and of environmental noise. *J. Personal. Soc. Psychol.* 61:212–25

Kruglanski AW, Webster DM, Klem A. 1993. Motivated resistance and openness to persuasion in the presence or absence of prior information. *J. Personal. Soc. Psychol.* 65:861–76

Kurman J. 2001. Self-enhancement: Is it restricted to individualistic cultures? *Personal. Soc. Psychol. Bull.* 27:1705–16

Kwan VSY, Bond MH, Singelis TM. 1997. Pancultural explanations for life satisfaction: adding relationship harmony to self-esteem. *J. Personal. Soc. Psychol.* 73:1038–51

Latané B. 1996. Dynamic social impact: the creation of culture by communication. *J. Commun.* 6:13–25

Latané B, Bourgeois MJ. 2001. Successfully simulating dynamic social impact: three levels of prediction. In *Social Influence: Direct and Indirect Processes: The Sydney Symposium on Social Psychology*, ed. J Forgas, K Williams, pp. 61–76. Philadelphia, PA: Psychol. Press

Latané B, L'Herrou T. 1996. Spatial clustering in the conformity game: dynamic social impact in electronic groups. *J. Personal. Soc. Psychol.* 70:1218–30

Lau IY-m, Chiu C-y, Hong Y-Y. 2001a. I know what you know: assumptions about others' knowledge and their effects on message construction. *Soc. Cogn.* 19:587–600

Lau IY-m, Chiu C-y, Lee S-l. 2001b. Communication and shared reality: implications for the psychological foundations of culture. *Soc. Cogn.* 19:350–71

Lee AY, Aaker JL, Gardner WL. 2000. The pleasure and pains of distinct self-construals: the role of interdependence in regulatory focus. *J. Personal. Soc. Psychol.* 78:1122–34

Lehman DR, Hamamura T, Akieda N. 2004. *Contextual Memory is Influenced by Self-Construal Priming, But Only for Bi-Culturals*. Vancouver, Can.: Univ. BC. Unpubl. manuscr.

Li J. 2002. A cultural model of learning: Chinese "heart and mind for wanting to learn." *J. Cross-Cult. Psychol.* 33:248–69

Markus HR, Kitayama S. 1991. Culture and self: implications for cognition, emotion, and motivation. *Psychol. Rev.* 98:224–53

Markus HR, Kitayama S. 2002. Models of agency: sociocultural diversity in the construction of action. In *The 49th Annu. Neb. Symp. Motivation: Cross-Cultural Differences in Perspectives on Self*, ed. V Murphy-Berman, J Berman. Lincoln: Univ. Neb. Press

Markus HR, Ryff CD, Barnett K, Palmersheim K. 2003. In their own words: well-being at midlife among high school and college-educated adults. In *A Portrait of Midlife in the United States*, ed. CD Ryff, RC Kessler. Chicago: Univ. Chicago Press

Masuda T, Nisbett RE. 2001. Attending holistically versus analytically: comparing the context sensitivity of Japanese and Americans. *J. Personal. Soc. Psychol.* 81:922–34

McIntyre A, Lyons A, Clark A, Kashima Y. 2004. The microgenesis of culture: serial reproduction as an experimental simulation of cultural dynamics. See Schaller & Crandall 2004, pp. 227–58

Mead M. 1955. *Cultural Patterns and Technical Change*. New York: Mentor Books

Menon T, Morris MW, Chiu C-y, Hong Y-Y. 1999. Culture and the construal of agency: attribution to individual versus group dispositions. *J. Personal. Soc. Psychol.* 76:701–17

Miyamoto Y, Kitayama S. 2002. Cultural variation in correspondence bias: the critical role of attitude diagnosticity of socially constrained behavior. *J. Personal. Soc. Psychol.* 83:1239–48

Morling B, Kitayama S, Miyamoto Y. 2002. Cultural practices emphasize influence in the United States and adjustment in Japan. *Personal. Soc. Psychol. Bull.* 28:311–23

Morris MW, Fu H-Y. 2001. How does culture influence conflict resolution? A dynamic constructivist analysis. *Soc. Cogn.* 19:324–49

Morris MW, Peng K. 1994. Culture and cause: American and Chinese attributions for social and physical events. *J. Personal. Soc. Psychol.* 67:949–71

Nisbett RE, Norenzayan A. 2002. Culture and cognition. In *Stevens' Handbook of Experimental Psychology: Cognition*, ed. H Pashler, DL Medin, 2:561–97. New York: Wiley. 3rd ed.

Nisbett RE, Peng K, Choi I, Norenzayan A. 2001. Culture and systems of thought: holistic versus analytic cognition. *Psychol. Rev.* 108:291–310

Norenzayan A, Atran S. 2004. Cognitive and emotional processes in the cultural transmission of natural and nonnatural beliefs. See Schaller & Crandall 2004, pp. 149–69

Norenzayan A, Choi I, Nisbett RE. 2002. Cultural similarities and differences in social inference: evidence from behavioral predictions and lay theories of behavior. *Personal. Soc. Psychol. Bull.* 28:109–20

Ohbuschi K-I, Fukushima O, Tedeschi JT. 1999. Cultural values in conflict management: goal orientation, goal attainment, and tactical decision. *J. Cross-Cult. Psychol.* 30:51–71

Oishi S, Diener EF. 2001. Goals, culture, and subjective well-being. *Personal. Soc. Psychol. Bull.* 27:1674–82

Oishi S, Diener EF, Lucas RE, Suh EM. 1999. Cross-cultural variations in predictors of life satisfaction: perspectives from needs and values. *Personal. Soc. Psychol. Bull.* 25:980–90

Oyserman D, Coon HM, Kemmelmeier M. 2002. Rethinking individualism and collectivism: evaluation of theoretical assumptions and meta-analyses. *Psychol. Bull.* 128:3–72

Peng K, Nisbett RE. 1999. Culture, dialectics, and reasoning about contradiction. *Am. Psychol.* 54:741–54

Phinney JS, Horenczyk G, Liebkind K, Vedder P. 2001. Ethnic identity, immigration, and well-being: an interactional perspective. *J. Soc. Issues* 57:493–510

Pinker S. 2002. *The Blank Slate: The Modern Denial of Human Nature.* New York: Viking

Rhee E, Uleman JS, Lee HK, Roman RJ. 1995. Spontaneous self-descriptions and ethnic identities in individualistic and collectivistic cultures. *J. Personal. Soc. Psychol.* 69:142–52

Richter L, Kruglanski AW. 1999. Motivated search for common ground: need for closure effects on audience design in interpersonal communication. *Personal. Soc. Psychol. Bull.* 25:1101–14

Richter L, Kruglanski AW. 2004. Motivated closed mindedness and the emergence of culture. See Schaller & Crandall 2004, pp. 101–21

Rosenblatt A, Greenberg J, Solomon S,

Pyszczynski T, Lyon D. 1989. Evidence of terror management theory: I. The effects of mortality salience on reactions to those who violate or uphold cultural values. *J. Personal. Soc. Psychol.* 57:681–90

Ross M, Xun WQE, Wilson AE. 2002. Language and the bicultural self. *Personal. Soc. Psychol. Bull.* 28:1040–50

Rothbaum F, Tsang BY-P. 1998. Lovesongs in the United States and China on the nature of romantic love. *J. Cross-Cult. Psychol.* 29:306–19

Rubin DC. 1995. *Memory in Oral Traditions: The Cognitive Psychology of Epic, Ballads, and Counting-out Rhymes.* New York: Oxford Univ. Press

Ruscher JB. 1998. Prejudice and stereotyping in everyday communication. In *Advances in Experimental Social Psychology*, ed. M Zanna, 30:241–307. New York: Academic

Schaller M. 2001. Unintended influence: social-evolutionary processes in the construction and change of culturally-shared beliefs. In *Social Influence: Direct and Indirect Processes*, ed. JP Forgas, KD Williams, pp. 77–93. Philadelphia, PA: Psychol. Press

Schaller M, Conway LG. 1999. Influence of impression-management goals on the emerging contents of group stereotypes: support for a social-evolutionary process. *Personal. Soc. Psychol. Bull.* 25:819–33

Schaller M, Conway LG, Tanchuk TL. 2002. Selective pressures on the once and future contents of ethnic stereotypes: effects of the communicability of traits. *J. Personal. Soc. Psychol.* 82:861–77

Schaller M, Crandall CS, eds. 2004. *The Psychological Foundations of Culture.* Hillsdale, NJ: Erlbaum

Schimmack U, Oishi S, Diener EF. 2002a. *Individualism: A Valid and Important Dimension of Cultural Differences.* Urbana-Champaign: Univ. Ill.

Schimmack U, Radhakrishnan P, Oishi S, Dzokoto V. 2002b. Culture, personality, and subjective well-being: integrating process models of life satisfaction. *J. Personal. Soc. Psychol.* 82:582–93

Schulze PA, Harwood RL, Merich A. 2001. Feeding practices and expectations among middle-class Anglo and Puerto Rican mothers of 12-month-old infants. *J. Cross-Cult. Psychol.* 32:397–406

Sears DO. 1986. College sophomores in the laboratory: influences of a narrow database on social psychology's view of human nature. *J. Personal. Soc. Psychol.* 51:515–30

Sechrist GB, Stangor C. 2001. Perceived consensus influences intragroup behavior and stereotype accessibility. *J. Personal. Soc. Psychol.* 80:645–54

Sherif M. 1936. *The Psychology of Social Norms.* New York: Harper

Shore B. 1996. *Culture in Mind: Cognition, Culture, and the Problem of Meaning.* New York: Oxford Univ. Press

Shweder R, Jensen LA, Goldstein WM. 1995. Who sleeps by whom revisited: a method for extracting moral goods implicit in practice. In *Cultural Practices as Contexts for Development*, ed. JJ Goodnow, PJ Miller, F Kessel, pp. 21–40. San Francisco: Jossey-Bass

Sokefeld M. 1999. Debating self, identity, and culture in anthropology. *Curr. Anthropol.* 40:417–47

Solomon S, Greenberg J, Schimel J, Arndt J, Pyszczynski T. 2004. Human awareness of mortality and the evolution of culture. See Schaller & Crandall 2004, pp. 15–40

Sparrow LM. 2000. Beyond multicultural man: complexities of identity. *Int. J. Intercult. Relat.* 24:173–201

Sperber D. 1984. The epidemiology of beliefs. In *The Social Psychological Study of Widespread Beliefs*, ed. C Fraser, G Gaskell, pp. 25–44. Oxford UK: Clarendon

Sperber D. 1996. *Explaining Culture: A Naturalistic Approach.* Oxford: Blackwell

Stewart SM, Bond MH, Deeds O, Chung SF. 1999. Intergenerational patterns of values and autonomy expectations in cultures of relatedness and separateness. *J. Cross-Cult. Psychol.* 30:575–93

Suh EM. 2002. Culture, identity consistency, and subjective well-being. *J. Personal. Soc. Psychol.* 83:1378–91

Suh EM, Diener EF, Oishi S, Triandis HC. 1998. The shifting basis of life satisfaction judgments across cultures: emotions versus norms. *J. Personal. Soc. Psychol.* 74:482–93

Tafarodi RW, Kang S-J, Milne AB. 2002. When different becomes similar: compensatory conformity in bicultural visible minorities. *Personal. Soc. Psychol. Bull.* 28:1131–42

Tesser A. 1993. The importance of heritability in psychological research: the case of attitudes. *Psychol. Rev.* 100:129–42

Thompson MS, Judd CM, Park B. 2000. The consequences of communicating social stereotypes. *J. Exp. Soc. Psychol.* 36:567–99

Trafimow D, Silverman ES, Fan RM-T, Law JSF. 1997. The effects of language and priming on the relative accessibility of the private self and the collective self. *J. Cross-Cult. Psychol.* 28:107–23

Trafimow D, Triandis HC, Goto SG. 1991. Some tests of the distinction between the private self and the collective self. *J. Personal. Soc. Psychol.* 60:649–55

Triandis HC. 1989. The self and social behavior in differing cultural contexts. *Psychol. Rev.* 96:506–20

Triandis HC, Suh EM. 2002. Cultural influences on personality. *Annu. Rev. Psychol.* 53:133–60

Tsai JL, Ying Y-W, Lee PA. 2000. The meaning of being Chinese and being American: variation among Chinese American young adults. *J. Cross-Cult. Psychol.* 31:302–32

Tweed RG, Lehman DR. 2002. Learning considered within a cultural context: Confucian and Socratic approaches. *Am. Psychol.* 57:89–99

Vallacher RR, Read SJ, Nowak A. 2002. The dynamical perspective in personality and social psychology. *Personal. Soc. Psychol. Rev.* 6:264–73

Verkuyten M, Pouliasi K. 2002. Biculturalism among older children: cultural frame switching, attributions, self-identification, and attitudes. *J. Cross-Cult. Psychol.* 33:596–609

Wang Q. 2001. Culture effects on adults' earliest childhood recollection and self-description: implications for the relation between memory and the self. *J. Personal. Soc. Psychol.* 81:220–33

Yamada A, Singelis TM. 1999. Biculturalism and self-construal. *Int. J. Intercult. Relat.* 23:697–709

Zarate MA, Uleman JS, Voils CI. 2001. Effects of culture and processing goals on the activation and binding of trait concepts. *Soc. Cogn.* 19:295–323

Annu. Rev. Psychol. 2004. 55:715–44
doi: 10.1146/annurev.psych.55.082602.133124
Copyright © 2004 by Annual Reviews. All rights reserved
First published online as a Review in Advance on September 22, 2003

TEACHING OF SUBJECT MATTER

Richard E. Mayer

Department of Psychology, University of California, Santa Barbara,
California 93106-9660; email: mayer@psych.ucsb.edu

Key Words   educational psychology, cognitive psychology, learning, instruction, reading

■ **Abstract**   Psychology of subject matter refers to the scientific study of learning and instruction within school subjects. The growing research literature on teaching and learning of school subjects represents one of educational psychology's most productive accomplishments of the past two decades. The purpose of this chapter is to examine representative advances in the psychology of subject matter, including how people learn to read words, comprehend printed passages, write compositions, solve arithmetic word problems, and understand how scientific systems work. The introduction provides a historical overview of how to promote transfer and is followed by reviews of representative research in learning and teaching of reading fluency, reading comprehension, writing, mathematics, and science.

CONTENTS

INTRODUCTION

Psychology of subject matter refers to the scientific study of learning and instruction within specific school subjects such as reading, writing, mathematics, science, and history (Bruer 1993, Mayer 1999, Shulman & Quinlan 1996). The growing research literature on teaching and learning of school subjects represents one of educational psychology's most productive accomplishments of the past two decades (Mayer 2001a). The continuing development of psychologies of subject matter is consistent with trends in cognitive science, including the focus on learning as (*a*) a change in knowledge rather than solely as a change in behavior, and (*b*) as a domain-specific rather than domain-general activity (Bruer 1993).

Advances in the psychology of subject matter have contributed to the creation of an educationally relevant science of learning and instruction (Bransford et al. 1999, Lambert & McCombs 1998, Mayer 1999, Phye 1997). Importantly, research on the psychology of subject matter shows the benefits of building a science of instruction that is contextualized in school subjects rather than presented as general context-free principles. A review of research on teaching of subject matter contributes to theory (by focusing on knowledge representation and cognitive processing in specific domains), to methodology (by focusing on cognitive task analyses of realistic tasks), and to practice (by identifying effective instructional procedures).

The purpose of this chapter is to examine some representative advances in the psychology of subject matter, including how people learn to read words, comprehend printed passages, write compositions, solve arithmetic word problems, and understand how scientific systems work. The introduction provides a historical overview of how to promote transfer and is followed by reviews of representative research in learning and teaching of reading fluency, reading comprehension, writing, mathematics, and science.

Three Views of How to Promote Transfer

How can we help people learn so that they will be able to transfer what they have learned to new situations? Transfer occurs when a learner applies what was learned to new situations. Transfer is often cited as the major goal of education, and the concept of transfer is at the heart of the science of instruction (Bruer 1993, Mayer 2002, Mayer & Wittrock 1996, Shulman & Quinlan 1996). For more than 100 years, psychologists have sought to understand how best to promote transfer (Haskell 2001, Mayer 2002, Singley & Anderson 1989), resulting in three major views of transfer: general transfer, specific transfer, and specific transfer of general knowledge.

General transfer refers to the idea that it is possible to improve the mind in general. For example, as the twentieth century began, the dominant theory of transfer was the doctrine of formal discipline, namely, the idea that certain school subjects such as Latin and geometry would produce "proper habits of mind" that could improve learning across all tasks. However, when educational psychologists subjected the doctrine of formal discipline to careful empirical study in the early 1900s, no evidence for general transfer was found (Thorndike 1913, Thorndike & Woodworth 1901).

Specific transfer refers to the idea that previous learning helps on a new task only if the new task requires exactly the same behavior as was learned. This is the theory of transfer that Thorndike and others offered—under the name "transfer by identical elements"—as an alternative to the failed doctrine of formal discipline. More recently, Singley & Anderson (1989, p. 51) have proposed that skills can be presented as production systems in which "productions, once learned, can serve as the identical elements of Thorndike's theory." Thus, transfer occurs to the extent that productions required in a previously learned skill are the same as those required in a to-be-learned skill.

Thorndike's theory of transfer by identical elements, and the updated versions still in use today, have been challenged not on the grounds that specific transfer theory is incorrect but rather that it is incomplete. In the early 1900s, Judd (1908) demonstrated learning a general principle about light refraction could promote transfer of how to shoot at underwater targets at various depths. Similarly, Wertheimer (1959) demonstrated that learning a general principle about the structure of parallelograms enabled students to transfer their learning of how to compute the area of a parallelogram to unusual shapes. Instead of specific transfer of specific responses, these researchers proposed what can be called specific transfer of general knowledge—the idea that students can apply a general principle or conception to new tasks that require the same principle or conception. This specific-transfer-of-general-knowledge approach underlines advances in cognitive strategy instruction (Pressley 1990) as well as the teaching of subject matter.

Like Goldilocks's search for a place to rest, psychology's search for a theory of transfer has taken it to three places—first to general transfer theories which were too soft, then to specific transfer theories which were too hard, and finally to a hybrid theory of specific transfer of general knowledge which seems to be just right. Thus psychology enters the new millennium equipped with a potentially powerful conception of transfer, and one that drives the successful new field of psychology of subject matter. In particular, the search for what to teach has moved from general habits to specific responses, and finally to general principles and conceptions that apply to a particular domain. For example, in arithmetic instead of teaching Latin or geometry as a way to discipline the mind (i.e., general transfer), or solely memorizing arithmetic facts or procedures (i.e., specific transfer), instruction includes a focus on underlying concepts such as a mental number line that helps students understand a wide array of addition and subtraction problems (i.e., specific transfer of general knowledge).

Cognitive task analysis is the primary tool of researchers in the field of psychology of subject matter. The goal is to identify the cognitive processes and knowledge required to accomplish basic academic tasks. Once the underlying processes, conceptions, principles, or strategies have been pinpointed, the goal of instruction is to insure they develop in the minds of learners. In the remainer of this chapter, several representative academic tasks and the cognitive processes underlying them are examined.

TEACHING OF READING FLUENCY: THE TASK OF READING A PRINTED WORD

Learning to read is generally recognized as the single most important task for students in the primary grades. Although interest in learning to read has a long history dating back to the seminal work of Huey (1908/1968), the pace and fruitfulness of reading research has blossomed in the past two decades. In this section I explore the issue of how a person accomplishes the task of reading a printed word. In short, what does someone need to know in order to read a printed word? The starting point in answering this question is to conduct a cognitive task analysis—that is, a description of the cognitive processes that a person would need to go through in order to accomplish the task. I review research on three component processes in word reading as shown in Table 1—being aware of sound units in words (i.e., phonological awareness), translating printed words into spoken words (i.e., decoding), and determining the meaning of words (i.e., meaning access).

TABLE 1 Component processes in reading a word

Name	Definition
Being aware of sound units	Recognizing, producing, and manipulating phonemes
Decoding words	Converting a printed word into sound
Accessing word meaning	Finding a mental representation of the word's meaning in one's memory

Being Aware of Sound Units: Insuring Phonological Awareness

The English language consists of approximately 42 sound units ranging from /a/ as in "say" to /z/ as in "zoo." *Phonological awareness* refers to the processes of recognizing, producing, and manipulating the sound units of a language. Examples of phonological awareness include segmentation—that is, given a spoken word such as "cat," the student can produce the three constituent sounds /c/, /a/, and /t/—and blending—that is, given some spoken sounds such as /n/, /i/, and /s/ the student can combine them into a spoken word, "nice." Other examples include deletion of the first phoneme (for the spoken word "top" say it without the /t/), deletion of the last phoneme (for the spoken word "same" say it without the /m/), substitution of the first phoneme (for the spoken word "ball" change the beginning sound from /b/ to /k/), and substitution of the last phoneme (for the spoken word "park" change the last sound from /k/ into /t/). In sum, as a first step in word reading, students need to know that words are composed of sound units (or phonemes), and students need to be able to hear, produce, and manipulate them.

Children tend to develop phonological awareness through the primary grades. This observation can be called the phonological development hypothesis, which has been examined in a variety of studies. One way to test this hypothesis is to conduct cross-sectional studies of the phonological awareness performance of students at various ages. For example, when children were asked to segment spoken words into constituent phonemes, almost none of the four-year-olds succeeded whereas most of the six-year-olds did (Liberman et al. 1974). Similarly, when children were asked to segment spoken words in constituent syllables, approximately half of the four-year-olds succeeded whereas almost all six-year-olds did (Liberman et al. 1974).

Another way to test the phonological development hypothesis is to conduct longitudinal studies, examining the phonological awareness performance of students at various points in their childhood. For example, Juel et al. (1986) gave a battery of phonological awareness tests to a group of children at several points across their primary grades, including segmentation, blending, deletion of first phoneme, deletion of last phoneme, substitution of first phoneme, and substitution of last phoneme. Upon entering first grade, they averaged 35% correct on the phonological awareness tests, and by the end of first grade they averaged 73% correct. Upon entering second grade, they averaged 83% correct, and by the end of second grade they averaged 86% correct.

Phonological awareness is a prerequisite to learning to read. This statement can be called the phonological awareness hypothesis, which has been tested in numerous studies. One way of testing the phonological awareness hypothesis is to compare the phonological awareness performance of good and poor readers. For example, Bradley & Bryant (1978) found that younger good readers performed better than older poor readers on tests of phonological awareness such as identifying which of four words lacked a sound contained in the other four words (e.g., answering that "rag" is the odd word among "sun, sea, sock, rag"). Similarly, students who have difficulty learning to read tend to lack phonological awareness (Stanovich 1991).

A second way of testing the phonological awareness hypothesis is to conduct longitudinal studies comparing a child's phonological awareness early in schooling with the child's reading performance several years later. For example, Bradley & Bryant (1985) found a strong correlation ($r = 0.5$) between the scores of four- and five-year-olds on a phonological awareness test with their scores on a standardized test of reading achievement given three years later. In a similar study, children's phonological awareness scores taken at the beginning of first grade correlated strongly with their scores on pronouncing printed words ($r = 0.5$) or writing spoken words ($r = 0.6$) at the end of second grade (Juel et al. 1986).

In a review of longitudinal studies testing the phonological awareness hypothesis, Wagner & Torgesen (1987) reported 20 cases in which children's performance on tests of phonological awareness at an early age correlated strongly with their performance on tests of reading achievement at a later age, even when the effects of cognitive ability were controlled. Consistent with the phonological awareness hypothesis, Wagner & Torgesen (1987, p. 202) concluded that "phonological awareness and reading are related independent of general cognitive ability."

A third way of testing the phonological awareness hypothesis is to determine whether instruction in phonological awareness helps students learn to read. For example, some five- and six-year-olds received phonological awareness training in 40 ten-minute sessions spread over a two-year period (Bradley & Bryant 1985, 1991). In a typical training session, the child was given a picture of a bus and then asked to pick out the picture starting with the same sound from a group of pictures. Other students (control group), received 40 ten-minute sessions involving the same words but without phonological tasks. When tested at the end of the two-year instructional period, students who had received phonological awareness training scored nearly one year ahead of control students on a standardized test of reaching achievement. When tested five years later, the trained group still scored higher than the control group on reading achievement.

In another study, some kindergarteners received 28 twenty-minute sessions on phonological awareness over a seven-week period whereas other kindergarteners (control group) received no phonological awareness training beyond regular classroom activities (Bradley & Bryant 1985). Although both groups scored about the same on a pretest of phonological awareness, the trained group showed a large gain on a posttest of phonological awareness compared to almost no gain for the control group. Importantly, by the end of the school year 35% of the phonological awareness trained group were classified as readers, compared to 7% of the control group.

Other researchers have also found that providing direct instruction in phonological awareness (sometimes called phonemic awareness) can help improve later reading achievement (Bus & van IJzendoorn 1999, Ehri et al. 2001). For example, in a review of 36 published studies, Bus & van IJzendoorn (1999, p. 411) found consistent evidence that "phonological training reliably enhances phonological and reading skills." Similarly, in a review of 52 published studies, Ehri et al. (2001, p. 260) found consistent evidence that "phonemic awareness instruction is effective... in helping children acquire phonemic awareness and in facilitating transfer of phonemic awareness skills to reading."

The study of phonological awareness represents one of the landmark success stories in the annals of psychologies of subject matter. Within the past 20 years, researchers have succeeded in identifying phonological awareness as a prerequisite skill for learning to read. Goswami & Bryant (1992, p. 49) summarize the story as follows:

> There can be little doubt that phonological awareness plays an important role in reading. The results of a large number of studies amply demonstrate a strong (and consistent) relationship between children's ability to disentangle and to assemble the sounds of words and their progress in learning to read.... There is also evidence that successful training in phonological awareness helps children learn to read.... However, it is only the first step.

What happens if students do not build sufficient phonological awareness skills within their first few years of primary school? Stanovich (1986, p. 364) describes a "causal chain of escalating negative effects" in which students with poor phonological skills have reduced opportunities to develop automaticity in decoding, which in turn causes them to have to pay more attention to the process of word decoding, leaving less capacity for comprehending what they are reading. Thus, they wind up with a more limited vocabulary and knowledge base, both of which are needed for reading comprehension. Phonological awareness training—even as little as 5 to 18 hours of direct instruction—attempts to break this chain and give students a chance to become proficient readers.

Decoding Words: Building Automatic Phonics Processing

The English language consists of 26 letters that, in various ways, are related to 42 sounds. *Decoding* refers to the process of converting a printed word into a sound. Thus, decoding consists of pronouncing printed words but does not necessarily involve knowing what the words mean. Examples include giving a student a printed word (such as "CAT") and asking the student to read it aloud (such as saying "cat") or giving the student a printed pseudoword (such as "BLUD") and asking the student to read it aloud (such as saying "blood").

Development of automatic decoding processing (i.e., being able to decode words without using conscious mental effort) is a prerequisite for success in reading. This can be called the decoding hypothesis, and is based on the idea that attentional capacity is limited. When it must be used to decode words, it cannot be used to make sense of the material. Consistent with the decoding hypothesis, third- and fifth-grade students who scored high on a standardized test of reading comprehension were much faster in pronouncing pseudowords or unfamiliar words than were students who scored low on reading comprehension (Perfetti & Hogaboam 1975).

A second way of testing the decoding hypothesis is to teach students how to decode so the decoding process becomes automatic. For example, asking students to read and reread a passage aloud until they make no errors (i.e., the method of *repeated reading*) is a useful way to build decoding automaticity (Dowhower 1994, Koskinen & Blum 1986, Samuels 1979). Overall, the "preponderance of research shows that children need to develop fast and automatic word decoding processes before they can become proficient in reading comprehension" (Mayer 2003). Even in learning a second language, decoding skill in one's native language is a major predictor of decoding skill in one's second language, which in turn is a major predictor of reading comprehension in one's second language (Meschyan & Hernandez 2002).

Perhaps the most contentious debate in the field of reading instruction concerns whether to use a phonics or a whole-word approach for teaching students how to decode words (Adams 1990; Chall 1983, 2000; Pressley 1998). In the phonics approach, children learn to produce the sounds for individual letters or letter groups and to blend those sounds together to form a word. In the whole-word approach, children learn to pronounce a word as a single unit, which can be called sight-reading. Fortunately, the "great debate" has been subjected to a great amount of careful research, and the results clearly show that some instruction in phonics is needed for the development of reading achievement (Adams 1990; Chall 1983, 2000; Pressley 1998). Almost all observers call for a balanced approach that includes aspects of phonics and whole-word instruction (Pressley 1998).

The study of decoding represents another success story in the annals of psychologies of subject matter. Within the past 20 years, researchers have reached consensus that balanced instruction including phonics promotes decoding automaticity, which is needed for success in reading.

Accessing Word Meaning: Fostering a Rich Vocabulary

The third component process in word reading is *meaning access*, which refers to finding a mental representation of the meaning of a word in one's memory. Meaning access depends on having a rich vocabulary, such as knowing that "cat" refers to a four-legged furry creature that purrs.

Less-skilled readers are more likely to rely on the sentence context when reading a word than are more-skilled readers (West & Stanovich 1978). In short, skilled readers have automatized their meaning access processing so that when they read a word they effortlessly know what it means without having to use context cues to figure it out. When meaning access does not require attentional capacity, readers can use all of their attention for making sense of the passage.

The *vocabulary hypothesis* is that having a strong vocabulary—which allows readers to access word meaning effortlessly—promotes performance on tests of reading comprehension. In support of this hypothesis, Anderson & Freebody (1981) reported that children who have better vocabularies perform better on tests of reading comprehension, and Meschyan & Hernandez (2002) report a high correlation between vocabulary test score and reading comprehension test score. Similarly, students perform better on tests of reading comprehension when unfamiliar words are replaced with more familiar synonyms (Marks et al. 1974).

It is estimated that young readers need to increase their vocabularies by at least 2000 words per year (Nagy & Scott 2000). What is the best way to promote a rich vocabulary—that is, fast and effortless word recognition? On the one hand, direct instruction involves teaching the definitions of a core set of words, whereas on the other hand immersion involves asking students to engage in many literate activities such as reading. Direct instruction is most effective when students are encouraged to use the words in familiar contexts and improves reading comprehension only in passages that include the newly learned words (Beck et al. 1982, Stahl & Fairbanks 1986). Yet, according to Nagy & Herman (1987), it is not possible for students to achieve the full vocabulary growth they need each year solely via direct instruction, so immersion is the only reasonable alternative. According to this view, students must learn the bulk of new vocabulary words through reading, listening to, or producing prose. Less research has been conducted on vocabulary learning than on processes in the foregoing sections, so continued work is needed.

TEACHING OF READING COMPREHENSION: THE TASK OF COMPREHENDING A PASSAGE

The previous section focused on learning to read (reading fluency); this section focuses on reading to learn (reading comprehension). Reading comprehension is the process of making sense out of a text passage, that is, building a meaningful mental representation of the text. This process of active learning occurs when a reader (*a*) selects relevant information from a text passage, (*b*) organizes the incoming material into a coherent mental representation, and (*c*) integrates the incoming material with existing knowledge. What does someone need to know in order to understand a passage, that is, engage in active learning? Four cognitive processes are involved in reading comprehension: using prior knowledge (which involves the process of integrating), using prose structure (which involves the processes of selecting and organizing), making inferences (which involves the processes of integrating and organizing), and using metacognitive knowledge (which involves the monitoring of cognitive processing). These processes are summarized in Table 2.

Using Prior Knowledge: Teaching Readers to Integrate Knowledge

The reader's prior knowledge—including his or her storehouse of schemas—constitutes the single most important factor underlying individual differences in reading comprehension. According to schema theory, reading comprehension is a process of assimilating presented information to existing knowledge, so the

TABLE 2   Component processes in comprehending a passage

Name	Definition
Using prior knowledge	Activating and assimilating to existing schemas
Using prose structure	Distinguishing important and unimportant material Organizing material into a coherent structure
Making inferences	Adding appropriate inferences to the material
Using metacognitive knowledge	Determining whether the passage makes sense

outcome of learning depends both on what was presented and the reader's existing knowledge. Thus, in order to make sense of a passage, a reader must possess and use relevant schemas.

For example, in Bartlett's (1932) classic study, students who recalled an unfamiliar folk story they had read tended to leave out many details (leveling), embellish particularly distinctive details (sharpening), and reorganize the story on the basis of a theme such as a war battle or hunting accident (rationalization). According to Bartlett, students dropped all references to a spirit world because these did not fit their existing schemas and students reorganized the story so it would fit with an existing schema. Classic cognitive studies have confirmed that students perform more poorly on reading comprehension tests when they lack appropriate prior knowledge (Bransford & Johnson 1972) and that different material is learned depending on the prior knowledge used by the reader (Pichert & Anderson 1977).

In spite of their skill in reading fluency, young readers often lack appropriate schemas to understand prose (Gernsbacher 1990). For example, American elementary school children had difficulty in reading about the history of the French and Indian War (Beck et al. 1991). However, when the passage was reframed as a conflict in which both France and England claimed the same piece of land, students could use a familiar schema (i.e., a fight between two sides that both want the same thing) to make sense of the passage. Students learned much more from the passage if they read the reframed version (Beck et al. 1991) or received some equivalent background information before reading the original passage (McKeown et al. 1992). A major theme of research on prior knowledge is that reading material should be appropriate for the interests and experience of the reader.

Using Prose Structure: Teaching Readers to Select and Organize Knowledge

The second process in Table 2 is the ability to use prose structure (e.g., the hierarchical organization of ideas), including recognizing the difference between important ideas and minor details. Beginning readers often lack sensitivity to prose structure. When asked to read and recall material from a text passage, younger readers and less-skilled readers tend to remember important and unimportant information equally well whereas older and more-skilled readers tend to remember important information better than unimportant information (Brown & Smiley 1977, Taylor 1980). Similarly, older readers and more-skilled readers spend more time reading sentences with topic shifts—usually the first sentence in a passage or section—than do younger or less-skilled readers (Gernsbacher 1990, Hyona 1994).

Can readers be taught to use prose structure during reading? One technique is to teach students how to outline or summarize passages. For example, Chmielewski & Dansereau (1998) taught some students how to outline a passage as a concept map—consisting of nodes and links—whereas other students received no training. On a subsequent reading task in which no note taking was allowed, the mapping group performed much better on a retention test than did the control group. Similarly, Cook & Mayer (1988) taught students how to outline textbook paragraphs based on prose structures such as classification (e.g., breaks material into categories as in a hierarchy), sequence (e.g., describes a step-by-step process as in a flow chart), and comparison (e.g., compares two or more things along several dimensions as in a matrix). Students who received structure training performed better on understanding new text passages than did control students. Finally, students who were told to take notes by filling in a compare/contrast matrix learned more from a lecture than students who were told to take conventional notes (Kiewra et al. 1991). Overall, less-skilled readers benefit from direct instruction in how to organize incoming material.

Making Inferences: Teaching Readers to Integrate and Organize Knowledge

The third process in Table 2 is inference-making. Weaver & Kintsch (1991) estimate that readers may need to make as many as a dozen inferences to understand a sentence in a passage. Although researchers recognize that "the ability to make inferences is a cornerstone of reading competence" (Winne et al. 1993, p. 53), young readers are notoriously poor at making inferences during reading (Oakhill & Yuill 1996). For example, kindergarteners are less likely than are fourth graders to make inferences while listening to sentences, such as inferring that a key was used for the sentence, "Our neighbors unlocked the door" (Paris & Lindauer 1976). Similarly, in reading a story about a boy reaching for a heavy cookie jar that was on a high shelf just as the door opened, older readers were more likely than younger readers to infer that the boy was caught in the act of doing something he was not supposed to do (Paris & Upton 1976).

Can students be taught to make appropriate inferences while reading? In a series of classroom studies, practice in making inferences about text passages spread over five weeks improved the reading comprehension of second graders and poor-reading fourth graders but not good-reading fourth graders (Hansen 1981, Hansen & Pearson 1983). In a similar study, primary grade children received seven 30-minute training sessions on inference making such as generating questions that could be answered by a text (Oakhill & Yuill 1996). For poor readers, the trained group showed an improvement in reading comprehension as compared to a control group, but for good readers the training had no effect. Finally, Winne et al. (1993) provided nine sessions of inference training to poor comprehenders in grades 4 through 6, including asking students to answer inference questions about a passage and then providing correct answers. The trained group showed improvements in reading as compared to other groups. Overall, there is encouraging evidence that students can learn to improve their inference-making skills.

Using Metacognitive Knowledge: Teaching Readers to Monitor Processing

The final process listed in Table 2 is using metacognitive knowledge, that is, knowledge of one's cognitive processing. The most important metacognitive process in reading is comprehension monitoring—the process of recognizing when a passage does not make sense—but elementary school children are not good at it. Markman (1979) found that elementary school children in grades 3, 5, and 6 did not recognize inconsistencies in passages, such as that "there is no light at the bottom of the ocean" and "fish that live at the bottom of the ocean can see the color of their food." Similarly, most third graders did not recognize inconsistencies in a passage such as statements about a strainer that "water passes through the holes and the spaghetti stays in the strainer" and "the spaghetti passed through the holes in the strainer into the bowl and the water stayed in the strainer" (Vosniadou et al. 1988).

Can students be taught to monitor their comprehension? There is encouraging evidence that students can learn to improve their comprehension monitoring skills. For example, Rubman & Waters (2000) asked students to represent a passage by placing figures on a magnetic board or to simply read the passage. Low-skill third and sixth graders in the storyboard construction group were much more likely to recognize inconsistencies than those in the read-only group, and weaker effects were found for the high-skill third and sixth graders. Similarly, Markman & Gorin (1981) found that 8- and 10-year-olds were better able to recognize inconsistencies in a passage after being shown examples in other passages. In addition, third graders who received examples as well as direct instruction in how to use comprehension-monitoring strategies performed particularly well on recognizing inconsistencies in passages as compared to nontrained students (Elliot-Faust & Pressley 1986).

TEACHING OF WRITING: THE TASK OF WRITING A COMPOSITION

What are the cognitive processes involved in writing a composition? In order to answer this question, Hayes & Flower (1980) asked students to think aloud as they wrote an essay on a topic such as "How I spent my summer vacation." In analyzing the writers' thinking-aloud protocols, Hayes & Flower identified three cognitive processes in writing: planning, in which the writer remembers or finds relevant information, decides how to organize it, and sets goals for how to communicate

TABLE 3   Component processes in writing a composition

Name	Definition
Planning	Remembering or finding relevant information, deciding how to organize it, and setting goals for communicating with the audience
Translating	Producing printed text on paper or screen
Reviewing	Detecting and correcting errors in the text

with the audience; translating, in which the writer produces text; and reviewing, in which the writer detects and corrects errors in the text. This analysis is similar to others (Gould 1980, Kellogg 1994), including a revised model by Hayes (1996), and is summarized in Table 3.

Planning: Teaching Writers to Find, Organize, and Adapt Material

A major cognitive process in writing an essay is planning, which includes the subprocesses of generating (i.e., recalling relevant information from one's memory or locating relevant information from external sources), organizing (i.e., figuring out how to organize the material in a coherent way), and goal setting (i.e., evaluating the material against criteria such as appropriateness for the audience).

Gould (1980) found that adults who were asked to write a short business letter spent about two thirds of their time in pauses—generally after long clauses or sentences—which suggests that most of the time was spent in local planning. In Gould's study the writers did not show long pauses before they started—indicating a lack of global planning—and did not spend much time revising what they had written. Matsuhashi (1982) obtained similar results in watching high school students write essays. Apparently, when the task is very simple or the writers are inexperienced, there is not much global planning.

Bereiter & Scardamalia (1987) identified a developmental trend in planning activities for writing in which children entering elementary school don't generate many ideas, older elementary school children generate many ideas but fail to organize or evaluate them (i.e., knowledge telling), and older high school students generate a lot of ideas that they also evaluate and organize (i.e., knowledge transforming).

Can students be taught to engage in prewriting activities that foster appropriate planning processes? Kellogg (1994) asked college students to write an essay on a given issue. Before starting to write the essay, they were told to write as many ideas as they could think of (generating group), to write a list of important ideas (listing group), to produce a hierarchical outline (outline group), or were given no instructions (no prewriting activity group). Students in the outline group produced higher quality essays than students in any of the other groups. When students are instructed to engage in planning processes—including generating, evaluating, and organizing ideas—they write better essays.

Another way to foster the planning process is to ask students to write about familiar topics. For example, Caccamise (1987) reported that students produced more ideas when planning to write about a familiar topic than an unfamiliar one. Overall, students need to have access to material that they have organized and thought about.

Translating: Helping Writers Overcome Cognitive Load

In the process of translating, the writer carries out the writing plan by producing written text. Writers tend to alternate between cognitive processes such as planning and translating, by generating a plan, writing a little bit, then checking the plan, and so on (Hayes & Flower 1980).

Translating demands conscious attention. According to Nystrand (1982), the written text should be legible, grammatical, meaningful, coherent, and appropriate for the intended audience. If writers focus their attention on lower level aspects of translating—such as writing legible and grammatical sentences—they may not have sufficient remaining attentional capacity to handle higher level aspects of translating—such as writing an essay that makes sense and influences the reader. One way to remove low-level constraints on translating is to allow students to dictate an essay. For example, fourth- and sixth-grade students who were asked to dictate an essay generated more words and slightly better essays than students who were asked to write an essay by hand (Bereiter & Scardamalia 1987). Consistent with the constraint removal idea, Read (1981) has shown that even six-year-olds can writing interesting stories when they are told to not worry about spelling, punctuation, or grammar.

In a related study, students were asked to write a preliminary draft followed by a final draft (Glynn et al. 1982). Students who were told to write a polished preliminary draft (i.e., paying attention to spelling, punctuation, and grammar) generated lower quality final drafts than did students who were told to write unpolished preliminary drafts (i.e., not paying attention to spelling, punctuation, and grammar). Apparently, students in the unpolished draft group could devote more attention to writing a powerful essay because they did not have to focus their attention on low-level aspects of translating.

Using a word processor may be another way to remove low-level constraints on translating. For example, students generated higher quality essays when they used a word processor than when they wrote in longhand, but only if they were experienced in using the word processor (Kellogg & Mueller 1993). In a review, Bangert-Drowns (1993) found that the advantage for word processors was greater for younger writers who were experienced with using word processors. However, for more experienced writers, the quality of essays was generally equivalent with word processors or pens (Bangert-Drowns 1993, Kellogg 1994). Apparently, when the output device (handwriting or word processing) requires undue attention and the writing task itself is demanding, the quality of the final product can suffer.

Reviewing: Helping Writers Detect and Correct Errors

Reviewing refers to detecting errors in a written text and correcting them. When asked to write an essay, college freshmen spent less than 10% of their time on reading or revising what they wrote (Pianko 1979). Similarly, when asked to write a one-page business letter, managers also spent less than 10% of their time reading or revising what they wrote (Gould 1980). Most of the corrections students make are surface and mechanical revisions rather than improvements in the organization or effectiveness of the text (Fitzgerald 1987). Even when middle school students are required to revise their essays, they fail to detect most of their mechanical syntax errors (e.g., subject-verb disagreement) and referent errors (e.g., misuse of a pronoun) and fail to correct most of the errors they detect (Bartlett 1982). Overall, there is clear and compelling evidence that students could benefit from training in how to revise their essays.

Revision training focuses on helping students become more effective in the reviewing process. McCutchen et al. (1997, McCutchen 2000) reported that seventh graders were more successful in correcting errors in meaning from an essay on a familiar topic (e.g., Christopher Columbus) than an unfamiliar topic (e.g., Margaret Mead). When the teacher highlighted sentences with mechanical errors, seventh graders focused more on mechanical errors and less on errors in meaning. Apparently, young writers are easily distracted from the task of detecting and correcting errors in meaning.

In an exemplary study, Fitzgerald & Markman (1987) gave sixth graders a series of thirteen 45-minute sessions on how to make additions, deletions, substitutions, and rearrangements in compositions (i.e., revision training). On a subsequent writing assignment, students who had received direct instruction in these revision activities made more revisions and produced higher quality written products than did untrained sixth-grade students who spent an equivalent amount of time reading fine literature.

TEACHING OF MATHEMATICS: THE TASK OF SOLVING A WORD PROBLEM

What does someone need to know in order to solve an arithmetic word problem such as: "At Lucky, butter costs 65 cents per stick. Butter at Vons costs 2 cents less per stick than butter at Lucky. If you need to buy 4 sticks of butter, how much will you pay at Vons?" Table 4 lists four cognitive processes in mathematical problem solving: translating, integrating, planning, and executing (Mayer 1992).

Problem Translating: Teaching Students to Represent Sentences

In translating, the problem solver converts each sentence into an internal mental representation. This process requires linguistic knowledge (such as knowing that Vons and Lucky are proper nouns) and factual knowledge (such as knowing that

TABLE 4   Component processes in solving an arithmetic word problem

Name	Definition
Translating	Converting each sentence into an internal mental representation
Integrating	Building a coherent mental representation of the problem situation
Planning/monitoring	Devising a solution plan and keeping track of how well it works
Executing	Carrying out a solution plan

there are 100 cents in a dollar). For example, the first sentence can be mentally represented as "Lucky $= 0.65$," the second sentence as "Vons $=$ Lucky $- 0.02$," and the third as "Total Cost $= 4 \times$ Vons." Research shows that people have a particularly difficult time in translating relational statements, that is, sentences that express a quantitative relation between two variables (such as the second sentence). For example, when primary grade children were asked to listen to and repeat back a problem such as "Joe has three marbles. Tom has five more marbles than Joe. How many marbles does Tom have?" they sometimes recalled the problem as "Joe has three marbles. Tom has five marbles. How many marbles does Tom have?" (Riley et al. 1982). Similar results were found when college students were asked to read and recall a list of eight word problems (Mayer 1982). When college students were asked to write an equation to represent relational sentences such as "There are six times as many students as professors at this university," they wrote the wrong equation (e.g., $6S = P$) about one third of the time (Soloway et al. 1982). Hegarty et al. (1995) found that poor problem solvers were particularly prone to errors in remembering relational statements as compared to successful problem solvers.

These results demonstrate that students need instruction in how to represent the sentences in word problems, particularly relational sentences. In an exemplary training study, college students who had difficulty in solving word problems received two 30-minute training sessions in how to represent the sentences in word problems on a number line (Lewis 1989). As a result, their error rates on solving word problems fell dramatically as compared to students who had not received the training. In a school-based study, middle school students participated in a 20-day prealgebra unit that emphasized translating relational sentences into tables, graphs, equations, and their own words (Brenner et al. 1997). Students who participated showed larger gains in solving word problems than did students who received conventional instruction.

Problem Integrating: Teaching Students to Use Problem Schemas

A sentence-by-sentence translation of each sentence in a word problem is a good first step, but the ultimate goal in understanding a problem is to build a situation model—that is, a mental representation of the situation being described in the problem (Kintsch & Greeno 1985, Mayer & Hegarty 1996, Nathan et al. 1992). Problem integrating occurs when a problem solver builds a mental representation of the situation described in the problem. The process of integrating requires that the problem solver select relevant information from the problem statement, organize it into a coherent representation, and make necessary inferences (Mayer 1992). Integrating depends on schematic knowledge—that is, knowledge of problem types (such as knowing that the butter problem is a total cost problem in which total cost = unit cost × number of units).

When high school students were asked to sort word problems into categories, they showed high levels of agreement and were quite fast in their decisions (Hinsley et al. 1977). Overall, 18 categories were created, such as distance-rate-time problems, work problems, and area problems, which suggests that the students had developed schemas for common types of word problems. In a related study, Mayer (1981) identified approximately 100 types of word problems in some commonly used middle-school mathematics textbooks, including varieties of the categories found by Hinsley et al. (1977). When students were asked to read and then recall a list of eight word problems, they made more errors in recalling rare problem types (i.e., those appearing infrequently in textbooks) than common problem types (i.e., those appearing frequently in textbooks) (Mayer 1982).

Experts and novices differ in the way they sort word problems. For example, Quilici & Mayer (1996) found that students who lacked experience in statistics tended to sort statistics word problems based on cover story (such as grouping all problems about rainfall) whereas students who had taken several statistics courses tended to sort statistics word problems based on the type of statistical test involved (such as grouping all t-test problems). Similarly, seventh graders who are poor problem solvers tend to sort problems on the basis of the cover story (such as putting together all problems about money) whereas good problem solvers tend to sort problems on the basis of the underlying mathematical structure (Silver 1981).

Successful and unsuccessful problem solvers tend to engage in different cognitive processes while reading word problems (Lewis & Mayer 1987, Verschaffel et al. 1992). Unsuccessful problem solvers tend to focus on the numbers in the problem and to use the keywords in the problem to determine what operation to apply (e.g., "less than" primes subtraction). For example, in the following problem the keyword "less than" primes the incorrect arithmetic operation of subtracting 2 from 65: "At Lucky, butter costs 65 cents per stick. This is 2 cents less per stick than butter at Vons. If you need to buy 4 sticks of butter, how much will you pay at Vons?" Unsuccessful problem solvers are more likely to give the incorrect answer, $(0.65 - 0.02) \times 4 = 2.52$, for this version of the problem, but they tend to give the correct answer for a version in which the keyword primes the correct arithmetic operation (e.g., "At Lucky, butter costs 65 cents per stick. Butter at Vons costs 2 cents less per stick than butter at Lucky. If you need to buy 4 sticks of butter, how much will you pay at Vons?"). In contrast, successful problem solvers give the correct answer for both versions of the problem (Hegarty et al. 1995, Mayer & Hegarty 1996, Verschaffel et al. 1992). Eye movement studies (Hegarty et al. 1995) show that unsuccessful problem solvers spend more time looking at the numbers and keywords (e.g., 65, 2, less than, 4, how much) in a word problem whereas successful problem solvers spend more time looking at the variable names (e.g., Lucky, Vons). The unsuccessful problem solvers appear to be engaging in a process of number grabbing or direct translation whereas the successful problem solvers appear to be building a situation model (Mayer & Hegarty 1996). Consistent with this distinction, Low & Over (1989) found that problem solving scores correlated highly with students' scores on detecting missing or irrelevant information in word problems.

There appears to be a developmental trend in which students create more differentiated problem schemas as they gain more experience. For example, kindergarteners seem to know cause/change problems ("Pete has two marbles. Tim gives him three more marbles. How many marbles does Pete have now?"), but as children gain more experience over the next few years, they distinguish other types, such as combination problems ("Pete has two marbles. Tim has three marbles. How many do they have altogether?") and comparison problems ("Pete has two marbles. Tim has three more marbles than Pete. How many marbles does Tim have?") (Riley et al. 1982).

Students can learn to build situation models, that is, coherent representations of the situation described in the problem. For example, Low (1989) taught students to detect whether word problems contained irrelevant information, needed additional information, or neither—a task that requires students to build a coherent situation model of the problem. Students who received training showed large improvements in their word problem solving performance as compared to students who received no instruction. In another training study, students who received training in how to use a computer program to represent a word problem as an on-screen animation performed better on a subsequent word problem solving test than did students who practiced solving word problems (Nathan et al. 1992). In short, students benefit from training aimed at helping them learn to translate a word problem into a situation model.

Solution Planning and Monitoring: Teaching Students to Devise Solution Plans

The third cognitive process in Table 4 is planning and monitoring, in which the student devises a solution plan and keeps track of how well it works during problem solving. Planning is based on strategic knowledge, that is, general strategies such as finding a related problem, restating the problem in a different way, and breaking the problem into subgoals (Mayer 1992, Schoenfeld 1985). When students receive instruction and practice in how to carry out planning strategies such as these, they perform better on a subsequent word problem-solving test than subjects who simply practice solving the problems (Schoenfeld 1985).

Worked-out examples are step-by-step descriptions of how to solve example problems and are commonly found in mathematics textbooks (Mayer et al. 1995).

Reed (1999) has shown that students need support in how to use worked-out examples, including verbal explanations for each step and instructions for when to use a particular worked-out example. Catrambone (1995) has shown that students benefit when each subgoal is explicitly labeled and explained in worked-out examples.

Students' attitudes can influence their problem-solving strategies. Some students believe that word problems are solved by applying meaningless procedures, which can be stated as follows: "Ordinary students cannot expect to understand mathematics; they expect simply to memorize it and apply what they have learned mechanically and without understanding" (Schoenfeld, 1992, p. 359). For example, many third-grade students believe that "all story problems can be solved by applying the operations suggested by the key words present in the story, e.g., in all suggests addition, left suggests subtraction, share suggests division" (Lester et al. 1989, p. 84). A recent national survey of U.S. mathematics students revealed that 54% of the fourth graders and 40% of the eighth graders thought that the bulk of mathematics learning consists of memorizing rules (Silver & Kenney 2000).

Verschaffel et al. (2000) have shown how mathematics students from all over the world often solve math word problems by manipulating symbols without understanding what they are doing. They seek to carry out an arithmetic computation without trying to make sense of the problem, a strategy that Schoenfeld (1991, p. 316) calls "suspension of sense-making." In contrast, a key to successful problem solving is the development of what can be called a "productive disposition," that is, an "inclination to see mathematics as sensible, useful, and worthwhile, coupled with a belief in diligence and one's self-efficacy" (Kilpatrick et al. 2001, p. 5).

Students can learn productive planning strategies by working on realistic math problems in authentic settings. For example, in the Jasper project, students view a video that describes an adventure story in which some decisions need to be made based on mathematical computations (Bransford et al. 1996, Van Haneghan et al. 1992). Students who received practice in developing strategies for solving the Jasper problems showed larger gains in solving word problems than did matched students who received regular classroom instruction.

Solution Execution: Teaching Students to Carry Out Procedures

The fourth process in Table 4 is solution-executing, that is, carrying out a solution procedure. Solution executing requires procedural knowledge, that is, algorithms such as how to add, subtract, multiply, and divide (Mayer 1992).

Fuson (1992) has described how children's skill in solving simple addition problems (such as $2 + 4 = 6$) develops from counting-all procedures (such as counting 1, 2, pause, 3, 4, 5, 6), to counting-on procedures (such as starting with 2 and then counting on 3, 4, 5, 6), to derived facts procedures (such as "I can take 1 from the 4 and give it to the 2, and I know 3 plus 3 is 6"), to known facts (such as memorizing that 2 plus 4 is 6). For example, Groen & Parkman (1972) used a reaction-time paradigm to find that most first graders use a counting-on procedure for simple addition. Siegler & Jenkins (1989) have shown that primary-grade children have a variety of procedures available for simple addition problems and select the one that best fits any particular problem. Brown & Burton (1978) found that students' errors in solving three-column subtraction problems occur because students are correctly applying an incorrect procedure—a procedure that has one or more bugs (incorrect steps) in it.

Students can learn procedures as a meaningless sequence of steps. To help them understand what they are doing, students need to see how procedures are related to concrete situations and concepts. For example, concrete manipulatives are concrete objects used to represent steps in arithmetic procedures, such as using sticks bundled by tens (English 1997, Resnick & Ford 1981). In a research review, Hiebert & Carpenter (1992, p. 70) concluded "the effectiveness of concrete materials in classrooms have yielded mixed results." More recently, Moreno & Mayer (1999) found that children's learning of addition and subtraction of signed numbers was improved when they played with an educational game that represented the steps visually as a bunny moving along a number line. Schwartz et al. (1996) found similar improvements in students' skills on addition and subtraction of signed numbers when they practiced using a computer-based image of a train of various lengths along a number line.

Case and his colleagues (Case & Okamoto 1996; Griffin et al. 1994, 1995) have shown that skill in applying arithmetic procedures (such as solving the problem $2 + 4 = 6$) is linked to the child's conceptual understanding of a mental number line (as measured by telling which of two numbers is larger, moving a token along a number line for a specified count, and so on). For example, about 50% of the students in Case's studies entered school without adequate knowledge of a mental number line. When students were given 40 short lessons involving explicit instruction in using a mental number line (such as moving a token along a path for a specified number of steps in a board game), they showed a great improvement both in their ability to a use a mental number line (which can be called number sense) and in their ability to learn arithmetic. In a review, Bruer (1993, p. 90) concludes "for mathematics to be meaningful, conceptual knowledge and procedural skills have to be interrelated in instruction."

TEACHING OF SCIENCE: THE TASK OF UNDERSTANDING HOW THINGS WORK

What are the cognitive processes involved in scientific reasoning? According to the traditional view, science learning involves adding knowledge to memory. In contrast, according to the conceptual change view, science learning involves changing one's mental model of how something works (Limon & Mason 2002, Posner et al. 1982). A mental model is a cognitive representation of the functional parts of a system and the cause-and-effect relations showing how a change in the state of one part affects a change in the next one (Gentner & Stevens 1983, Halsford 1993, Mayer

TABLE 5   Component processes in understanding how a scientific system works

Name	Definition
Recognizing an anomaly	Realizing that one's mental model is flawed
Creating a new model	Mentally constructing a new mental model
Using a new model	Using a mental model to test hypotheses in research

1992). Three important steps in conceptual change are: (*a*) recognizing an anomaly (i.e., realizing that one's current mental model is not able to explain the observable facts), (*b*) constructing a new model (i.e., creating a model that is able to explain the observable facts), and (*c*) using a new model (i.e., making and testing predictions of the model in new situations). These three processes are summarized in Table 5.

Recognizing an Anomaly: Teaching by Confronting Misconceptions

The first step in conceptual change is to recognize that one's conception of how something works does not square with the available data. In short, rather than starting as blank slates, people enter the science classroom with mental models of how the world works, and often their mental models are incorrect. For example, many people harbor misconceptions (or preconceptions) about the laws of motion, such as predicting that a ball shot through a curved tube will continue to curve once it exits from the tube (McCloskey et al. 1980), an object traveling at a constant speed over a cliff will continue moving horizontally and then fall straight down (Kaiser et al. 1985, McCloskey 1983), or that a ball dropped by a running person will fall straight down (McCloskey 1983). In short, many people believe in impetus theory—the idea that an object moves only when a force is acting on it—although school-taught Newtonian theory is that an object continues moving unless a force acts on it.

Can students be taught to recognize their misconceptions? Clement (1982) found that a conventional course in physics did little to eliminate students' misconceptions. However, Chi (2000) asked some students to engage in self-explanations as they read a text on how the human heart works—that is, they explained the text aloud as they read it. Most students began with a flawed mental model of the heart that Chi calls the single-loop model, i.e., the idea that the arteries carry blood from the heart to the body (where oxygen is collected and waste is deposited) and veins carry blood from the body to the heart (where it is cleaned and reoxygenated). Students who engaged in self-explanations were more likely to recognize that their mental model conflicted with the information presented in the text, such as "the right side pumps blood to the lungs and the left side pumps blood to other parts of the body."

In a classroom study, fifth and sixth graders were asked to make predictions, then take measurements, and explain why the measurements conflicted with their predictions (Vosniadou et al. 2001). For example, after trying to pull a heavy table that they could not move, students concluded that no force was acting on the table—consistent with impetus theory. However, when they used a dynamometer, they measured a considerable force being exerted on the table by their pulling. In the ensuing classroom discussion, students had to reconcile the conflicting information that an object can be nonmoving and still have a force exerted on it. Students who participated in these kinds of cognitive conflict episodes showed greater improvements in solving physics problems than did nontrained students. Overall, research on recognizing misconceptions shows that "cognitive conflict seems to be the starting point in the process of conceptual change" (Limon 2001, p. 373).

Constructing a New Model: Teaching by Providing a Concrete Analogy

Once learners recognize that their models are flawed, the next step is to build a new model (as shown in the second process in Table 5). According to the Posner et al. (1982) the new model should be intelligible (i.e., the learner understands it), plausible (i.e., the learner can reconcile the model with the available data and other knowledge), and fruitful (i.e., the learner can use the model in new situations). Gentner (1989) proposed that students understand how a new system works by relating it to a familiar system. For example, Gentner & Gentner (1983) found that some students understand an electrical circuit is like a water-flow system in which the wires are like pipes, the electrons are like water, the battery is like a pump, and the resistor is like a constriction in a pipe.

One way to foster the process of model construction in students is to provide concrete representations of the model. For example, adding pictorial models to textbook passages or animated models to online narration helps students understand how various systems work, such as brakes, pumps, lungs, and lightning storms (Mayer 1989, 2001). In a focused set of studies, students learned Newton's laws of motion by playing various video games in which a ball could be "kicked" in any direction using a joystick (White 1993, White & Frederiksen 1998). In the microworld called ThinkerTools, the balls behaved in line with the laws of motion, and students were asked to discuss the validity of various possible ways to describe the laws. Students who participated in the ThinkerTools microworld for daily 45-minute sessions over a two-month period showed fewer misconceptions about the physics of motion than did control students. Overall, experience with familiar, concrete models can help students replace their incorrect mental models.

Using a New Model: Teaching Students How to Test Hypotheses

The third process in conceptual change is using a new model to make predictions in a new situation (as listed in the third line of Table 5). There is consistent evidence that high school students have substantial difficulty in two important aspects of scientific reasoning—generating theories and interpreting data. For example, Klahr (2000) asked students to figure out what the RPT button did on a programmable toy vehicle called BigTrack. They could press any sequence of buttons on the control panel and then see what the vehicle did. Most children only considered one theory, ignored conflicting results, and just kept testing the same theory repeatedly. In a computer-based simulation of a biology experiment (Dunbar 1993), most students began with a theory and ran experiments intended to confirm the theory (i.e., they engaged in confirmation bias). When the resulting data conflicted with their theory, most students tended to ignore the results and they continued to seek to confirm their theory. Kuhn et al. (1988) found that students were unable to judge whether a piece of data refuted a theory. Other researchers have shown that most high school students do not systematically test hypotheses in a way consistent with Piaget's formal operations, which is the level of thinking required for scientific reasoning (Karplus et al. 1979, Lawson & Snitgen 1982).

What can be done to improve students' skill in testing hypotheses? When Lawson & Snitgen (1982) provided direct instruction in how to test hypotheses for biological theories, students showed substantial improvements in their scores on tests of scientific thinking. In an exemplary study (Carey et al. 1989), seventh graders participated in a three-week science unit focusing on scientific thinking, including intensive investigations on topics such as "Why do yeast, flour, sugar, salt, and warm water produce a gas?" Students who participated showed substantial improvements in their beliefs about science and scientific research. Overall, there is growing evidence that scientific reasoning can be taught (Halpern 1992, Linn & Hsi 2000).

CONCLUSION

This chapter provides an overview of recent advances in the psychology of subject matter. The first step is to clearly define a subject matter domain (such as reading fluency, reading comprehension, writing, mathematics, or science) and within the domain clearly specify a target task (such as reading a word aloud, comprehending a paragraph, writing an essay, solving an arithmetic word problem, or understanding how something works). The next step is to conduct a cognitive task analysis, specifying the major cognitive processes required to accomplish the task (such as listed in Tables 1 through 5). Finally, research is needed to determine how people learn each of the needed cognitive processes, including how to help them learn.

Although the grand learning theories of the early twentieth century have faded away (Mayer 2001b), researchers have made progress in understanding how people learn in specific subject areas (Mayer 2002). Research on the psychology of subject matter is a prime example of the shift from domain-general cognitive theories to domain-specific cognitive theories. Research on the psychology of subject matter also exemplifies a shift in research methods for studying how people perform on decontextualized sterile laboratory tasks to how people perform on contextualized realistic tasks. Finally, research on the psychology of subject matter represents one of educational psychology's greatest success stories. In short, research on how people learn subject matter has yielded progress in understanding human learning and cognition.

In closing, I share Shulman & Quinlan's (1996, p. 420–421) recent assessment of the field: "As we approach the 21st century, we can anticipate the return of the psychology of school subjects to its former centrality in educational psychology." However, unlike earlier attempts to study the teaching of school subjects, psychology comes equipped with techniques for analyzing and describing the knowledge underlying academic performance (Anderson et al. 2001).

AUTHOR NOTE

For an expanded review of this material, see Mayer 2003.

The *Annual Review of Psychology* is online at http://psych.annualreviews.org

LITERATURE CITED

Adams MJ. 1990. *Beginning to Read.* Cambridge, MA: MIT Press

Anderson LW, Krathwohl DR, Airasian PW, Cruickshank KA, Mayer RE, et al. 2001. *A Taxonomy for Learning, Teaching, and Assessing.* New York: Longman

Anderson RG, Freebody P. 1981. Vocabulary knowledge. In *Comprehension and Teaching: Research Reviews*, ed. JT Guthrie, pp. 77–117. Newark, DE: Int. Read. Assoc.

Bangert-Drowns RL. 1993. The word processor as an instructional tool: a meta-analysis of word processing in writing instruction. *Rev. Educ. Res.* 63:69–93

Bartlett EJ. 1982. Learning to revise: Some component processes. See Nystrand 1982

Bartlett FC. 1932. *Remembering.* Cambridge, UK: Cambridge Univ. Press

Beck IL, McKeown MG, Sinatra GM, Loxterman JA. 1991. Revising social studies text from a text-processing perspective: Evidence of improved comprehensibility. *Read. Res. Q.* 26:251–76

Beck IL, Perfetti CA, McKeown MG. 1982. Effects of long-term vocabulary instruction on lexical access and reading comprehension. *J. Educ. Psychol.* 74:506–21

Bereiter C, Scardamalia M. 1987. *The Psychology of Written Composition.* Hillsdale, NJ: Erlbaum

Bradley L, Bryant P. 1978. Difficulties in auditory organization as a possible cause of reading backwardness. *Nature* 271:746–47

Bradley L, Bryant P. 1985. *Rhyme and Reason in Reading and Spelling.* Ann Arbor, MI: Univ. Mich. Press

Bradley L, Bryant P. 1991. Phonological skills before and after learning to read. In *Phonological Processes in Literacy*, ed. SA Brady, DP Shankweiler, pp. 37–45. Hillsdale, NJ: Erlbaum

Bransford JD, Brown AL, Cocking RR, eds. 1999. *How People Learn.* Washington, DC: Natl. Acad. Press

Bransford JD, Johnson MK. 1972. Contextual prerequisites for understanding: some investigations of comprehension and recall. *J. Verbal Learn. Verbal Behav.* 11:717–26

Bransford JD, Zech L, Schwartz D, Barron B, Vye N, Cognition & Technol. Group at

Vanderbilt. 1996. Fostering mathematical understanding in middle school students: lessons from research. In *The Nature of Mathematical Thinking*, ed. RJ Sternberg, T Ben-Zeev, pp. 203–50. Mahwah, NJ: Erlbaum

Brenner ME, Mayer RE, Moseley B, Brar T, Duran R, et al. 1997. Learning by understanding: the role of multiple representations in learning algebra. *Am. Educ. Res. J.* 34:663–89

Brown AL, Smiley SS. 1977. Rating the importance of structural units of prose passages: a problem of metacognitive development. *Child Dev.* 49:1076–88

Brown JS, Burton RR. 1978. Diagnostic models for procedural bugs in basic mathematical skills. *Cogn. Sci.* 2:155–92

Bruer JT. 1993. *Schools for Thought: A Science of Learning in the Classroom.* Cambridge, MA: MIT Press

Bus AG, van IJzendoorn MH. 1999. Phonological awareness and early reading: a meta-analysis of experimental studies. *J. Educ. Psychol.* 91:403–14

Caccamise DJ. 1987. Idea generation in writing. In *Writing in Real Time*, ed. A Matsushashi, pp. 224–53. Norwood, NJ: Ablex

Carey S, Evans R, Honda M, Jay E, Unger C. 1989. "An experiment is when you try it and see if it works": a study of grade 7 students' understanding of the construction of scientific knowledge. *Int. J. Sci. Educ.* 11:514–29

Case R, Okamoto Y. 1996. The role of central conceptual structures in the development of children's thought. *Monogr. Soc. Res. Child Dev.* 6:(11 & 2, Ser. No. 246)

Catrambone R. 1995. Aiding subgoal learning: effects on transfer. *J. Educ. Psychol.* 87:5–17

Chall JS. 1983. *Learning to Read: The Great Debate.* New York: McGraw-Hill

Chall JS. 2000. *The Academic Achievement Challenge.* New York: Guilford

Chi MTH. 2000. Self-explaining: the dual processes of generating inference and repairing mental models. In *Advances in Instructional Psychology:* Volume 5. *Educational Design and Cognitive Science,* ed. R Glaser, pp. 161–238. Mahwah, NJ: Erlbaum

Chmielewski TL, Dansereau D. 1998. Enhancing the recall of text: Knowledge mapping training promotes implicit transfer. *J. Educ. Psychol.* 90:407–13

Clement J. 1982. Students' preconceptions in elementary mechanics. *Am. J. Phys.* 50: 66–71

Cook LK, Mayer RE. 1988. Teaching readers about the structure of scientific text. *J. Educ. Psychol.* 80:448–56

Dowhower SL. 1994. Repeated reading revisited: research into practice. *Read. Writ. Q.* 10:343–58

Dunbar K. 1993. Concept discovery in a scientific domain. *Cogn. Sci.* 17:397–434

Ehri LC, Nunes SR, Simone R, Willows DM, Schuster BV, et al. 2001. Phonemic awareness instruction helps children learn to read: evidence from the National Reading Panel's meta-analysis. *Read. Res. Q.* 36:250–87

Elliot-Faust DJ, Pressley M. 1986. How to teach comparison processing to increase children's short- and long-term listening comprehension monitoring. *J. Educ. Psychol.* 78:27–33

English LD. 1997. *Mathematical Reasoning: Analogies, Metaphors, and Images.* Mahwah, NJ: Erlbaum

Fitzgerald J. 1987. Research on revision in writing. *Rev. Educ. Res.* 57:481–506

Fitzgerald J, Markman LR. 1987. Teaching children about revision in writing. *Cogn. Instr.* 41:3–24

Fuson KC. 1992. Research on whole number addition and subtraction. See Grouws 1992, pp. 243–75

Gentner D. 1989. The mechanism of analogical learning. In *Similarity and Analogical Reasoning,* ed. S Vosniadou, A Ortony, pp. 199–241. New York/London: Cambridge Univ. Press

Gentner D, Gentner DR. 1983. Flowing waters or teaming crowds: mental models of electricity. See Gentner & Stevens 1983, pp. 99–130

Gentner D, Stevens AL. 1983. *Mental Models.* Hillsdale, NJ: Erlbaum

Gernsbacher MA. 1990. *Language Comprehension as Structure Building.* Hillsdale, NJ: Erlbaum

Glynn SM, Britton BK, Muth D, Dogan N. 1982. Writing and revising persuasive documents: cognitive demands. *J. Educ. Psychol.* 74:557–67

Goswami U, Bryant P. 1992. Rhyme, analogy, and children's reading. In *Reading Acquisition*, ed. PB Gough, LC Ehri, R Treiman, pp. 49–63. Hillsdale, NJ: Erlbaum

Gould JD. 1980. Experiments on composing letters: some facts, some myths, and some observations. In *Cognitive Processes in Writing*, ed. LW Gregg, ER Steinberg, pp. 97–127. Hillsdale, NJ: Erlbaum

Griffin SA, Case R, Capodilupo S. 1995. Teaching for understanding: the importance of central conceptual structures in the elementary school mathematics curriculum. In *Teaching for Transfer: Fostering Generalization of Learning*, ed. A McKeough, J Lupart, A Marini, pp. 123–52. Hillsdale, NJ: Erlbaum

Griffin SA, Case R, Siegler RS. 1994. Rightstart: providing the central conceptual prerequisites for first formal learning of arithmetic to students at risk for school failure. In *Classroom Lessons: Integrating Cognitive Theory and Classroom Practice,*ed. K McGilly, pp. 125–49. Cambridge, MA: MIT Press

Groen GJ, Parkman JM. 1972. A chronometric analysis of simple addition. *Psychol. Rev.* 97:329–43

Grouws DA, ed. 1992. *Handbook of Research on Mathematics Teaching and Learning.* New York: Macmillan

Halpern DF, ed. 1992. *Enhancing Thinking Skills in the Sciences and Mathematics.* Hillsdale, NJ: Erlbaum

Halsford GS. 1993. *Children's Understanding: The Development of Mental Models.* Hillsdale, NJ: Erlbaum

Hansen J. 1981. The effects of inference training and practice on young children's comprehension. *Read. Res. Q.* 16:391–417

Hansen J, Pearson PD. 1983. An instructional study: improving the inferential comprehension of good and poor fourth-grade readers. *J. Educ. Psychol.* 75:821–29

Haskell RE. 2001. *Transfer of Learning.* San Diego, CA: Academic

Hayes JR. 1996. A new framework for understanding cognition and affect in writing. In *The Science of Writing*, ed. C W Levy, S Ramsdell, pp. 1–28. Mahwah, NJ: Erlbaum

Hayes JR, Flower LS. 1980. Identifying the organization of writing processes. In *Cognitive Processes in Writing*, ed. LW Gregg, ER Steinberg, pp. 3–30. Hillsdale, NJ: Erlbaum

Hegarty M, Mayer RE, Monk C. 1995. Comprehension of arithmetic word problems: a comparison of successful and unsuccessful problem solvers. *J. Educ. Psychol.* 87:18–32

Hiebert J, Carpenter TP. 1992. Learning and teaching with understanding. See Grouws 1992, pp. 65–97

Hinsley D, Hayes JR, Simon HA. 1977. From words to equations. In *Cognitive Processes in Comprehension*, ed. M Just, P Carpenter, pp. 89–106. Hillsdale, NJ: Erlbaum

Huey EB. 1968 (1908). *The Psychology and Pedagogy of Reading.* Cambridge, MA: MIT Press

Hyona J. 1994. Processing of topic shifts by adults and children. *Read. Res. Q.* 29:76–90

Judd CH. 1908. The relation of special training and general intelligence. *Educ. Rev.* 36:28–42

Juel C, Griffin PL, Gough PB. 1986. Acquisition of literacy: a longitudinal study of children in first and second grade. *J. Educ. Psychol.* 78:243–55

Kaiser MK, Profitt DR, McCloskey M. 1985. The development of beliefs about falling objects. *Percept. Psychophys.* 38:533–39

Karplus R, Karplus E, Formisano M, Paulsen A. 1979. Proportional reasoning and control of variables in seven countries. In *Cognitive Process Instruction*, ed. J Lochhead, J Clement, pp. 47–104. Hillsdale, NJ: Erlbaum

Kellogg RT. 1994. *The Psychology of Writing.* London/New York: Oxford Univ. Press

Kellogg RT, Mueller S. 1993. Performance

amplification and process restructuring in computer-based writing. *Int. J. Man-Mach. Stud.* 39:33–49

Kiewra K, DuBois N, Christian D, McShane A, Meyerhoffer M, Roskelley D. 1991. Note-taking functions and techniques. *J. Educ. Psychol.* 83:240–45

Kilpatrick J, Swafford J, Findell B. 2001. *Adding It Up: Helping Children Learn Mathematics.* Washington, DC: Natl. Acad. Press

Kintsch W, Greeno JG. 1985. Understanding and solving word problems. *Psychol. Rev.* 92:109–29

Klahr D. 2000. *Exploring Science.* Cambridge, MA: MIT Press

Koskinen PS, Blum IH. 1986. Paired repeated reading: a classroom strategy for developing fluent reading. *Read. Teach.* 40:70–75

Kuhn D, Amsel E, O'Loughlin M. 1988. *The Development of Scientific Thinking Skills.* San Diego: Academic

Lambert NM, McCombs BL. 1998. *How Students Learn.* Washington, DC: Am. Psychol. Assoc.

Lawson AE, Snitgen DA. 1982. Teaching formal reasoning in a college biology course for preservice teachers. *J. Res. Sci. Teach.* 19:233–48

Lester FK, Garofalo J, Kroll DL. 1989. Self-confidence, interest, beliefs, and metacognition: key influences on problem-solving behavior. In *Affect and Mathematical Problem Solving,* ed. DB McLeod, VM Adams, pp. 75–88. New York: Springer-Verlag

Lewis AB. 1989. Training students to represent arithmetic word problems. *J. Educ. Psychol.* 81:521–31

Lewis AB, Mayer RE. 1987. Students' misconception of relational statements in arithmetic word problems. *J. Educ. Psychol.* 79:363–71

Liberman IY, Shankweiler D, Fischer FW, Carter B. 1974. Explicit syllable and phoneme segmentation in the young child. *J. Exp. Child Psychol.* 18:201–12

Limon M. 2001. On cognitive conflict as an instructional strategy for conceptual change: a critical appraisal. *Learn. Instr.* 11:357–80

Limon M, Mason L, eds. 2002. *Reframing the Process of Conceptual Change.* Dordrecht, Netherlands: Kluwer Acad.

Linn MC, Hsi S. 2000. *Computers, Teachers, Peers.* Hillsdale, NJ: Erlbaum

Low R, Over R. 1989. Detection of missing and irrelevant information within algebraic story problems. *Br. J. Educ. Psychol.* 59:296–305

Markman EM. 1979. Realizing that you don't understand: elementary school children's awareness of inconsistencies. *Child Dev.* 50:643–55

Markman EM, Gorin L. 1981. Children's ability to adjust their standards for evaluating comprehension. *J. Educ. Psychol.* 73:320–25

Marks CB, Doctorow MJ, Wittrock MC. 1974. Word frequency in reading comprehension. *J. Educ. Res.* 67:259–62

Matsuhashi A. 1982. Explorations in real-time production of written discourse. See Nystrand 1982, pp. 269–90

Mayer RE. 1981. Frequency norms and structural analysis of algebra story problems into families, categories, and templates. *Instr. Sci.* 10:135–75

Mayer RE. 1982. Memory for algebra story problems. *J. Educ. Psychol.* 74:199–216

Mayer RE. 1989. Models for understanding. *Rev. Educ. Res.* 59:43–64

Mayer RE. 1992. *Thinking, Problem Solving, Cognition.* New York: Freeman. 2nd ed.

Mayer RE. 1999. *The Promise of Educational Psychology:* Volume 1. *Learning in the Content Areas.* Upper Saddle River, NJ: Prentice Hall

Mayer RE. 2001a. What good is educational psychology? *Educ. Psychol.* 36:83–88

Mayer RE. 2001b. Changing conceptions of learning: a century of progress in the scientific study of education. In *Education Across a Century: The Centennial Volume. One Hundredth Yearbook of the National Society for the Study of Education,* ed. L Corno, pp. 34–75. Chicago: Univ. Chicago Press

Mayer RE. 2001c. *Multimedia Learning.* New York: Cambridge Univ. Press

Mayer RE. 2002. *The Promise of Educational Psychology:* Volume 2. *Teaching for*

Meaningful Learning. Upper Saddle River, NJ: Prentice Hall

Mayer RE. 2003. *Learning and Instruction.* Upper Saddle River, NJ: Prentice Hall

Mayer RE, Hegarty M. 1996. The process of understanding mathematics problems. In *The Nature of Mathematical Thinking,* ed. RJ Sternberg, T Ben-Zeev, pp. 29–54. Mahwah, NJ: Erlbaum

Mayer RE, Sims V, Tajika H. 1995. A comparison of how textbooks teach mathematical problem solving in Japan and the United States. *Am. Educ. Res. J.* 32:443–60

Mayer RE, Wittrock MC. 1996. Problem-solving transfer. In *Handbook of Educational Psychology,* ed. DC Berliner, RC Calfee, pp. 47–62. New York: Macmillan

McCloskey M. 1983. Intuitive physics. *Sci. Am.* 2484:122–30

McCloskey M, Caramazza A, Green B. 1980. Curvilinear motion in the absence of external forces: native beliefs about the motion of objects. *Science* 210(4474):1139–41

McCutchen D. 2000. Knowledge, processing, and working memory: implications for a theory of writing. *Educ. Psychol.* 35:13–23

McCutchen D, Francis M, Kerr S. 1997. Revising for meaning: effects of knowledge and strategy. *J. Educ. Psychol.* 89:667–76

McKeown MG, Beck IL, Sinatra GM, Loxterman JA. 1992. The contribution of prior knowledge and coherent text to comprehension. *Read. Res. Q.* 27:79–93

Meschyan G, Hernandez A. 2002. Is native-language decoding skill related to second-language learning? *J. Educ. Psychol.,* 94:14–22

Moreno R, Mayer RE. 1999. Multimedia supported metaphors for meaning making in mathematics. *Cogn. Instr.* 17:215–48

Nagy WE, Herman PA. 1987. Breadth and depth of vocabulary knowledge: implications for acquisition and instruction. In *The Nature of Vocabulary Acquisition,* ed. M McKeown, M Curtis, pp. 19–35. Hillsdale, NJ: Erlbaum

Nagy WE, Scott JA. 2000. Vocabulary processes. In *Handbook of Reading Research,* ed. ML Kamil, PB Rosenthal, PD Pearson, R Barr, 3:269–84. Mahwah, NJ: Erlbaum

Nathan MJ, Kintsch W, Young E. 1992. A theory of algebra word problem comprehension and its implications for the design of learning environments. *Cogn. Instr.* 9:329–89

Nystrand M, ed. 1982. *What Writers Know.* New York: Academic

Oakhill J, Yuill N. 1996. Higher order factors in comprehension disability: processes and remediation. In *Reading Comprehension Difficulties,* ed. C Cornoldi, J Oakhill, pp. 69–92. Mahwah, NJ: Erlbaum

Paris SG, Lindauer BK. 1976. The role of inference in children's comprehension and memory for sentences. *Cogn. Psychol.* 8:217–27

Paris SG, Upton LR. 1976. Children's memory for inferential relationships in prose. *Child Dev.* 47:660–68

Perfetti CA, Hogaboam T. 1975. The relationship between single word decoding and reading comprehension skill. *J. Educ. Psychol.* 67:461–69

Phye GD, ed. 1997. *Handbook of Academic Learning.* San Diego: Academic

Pianko S. 1979. A description of the composing process of college freshman writers. *Res. Teach. Engl.* 13:5–22

Pichert J, Anderson RC. 1977. Taking different perspectives on a story. *J. Educ. Psychol.* 69:309–15

Posner GJ, Strike KA, Hewson PW, Gertzog WA. 1982. Accommodation of scientific conception: toward a theory of conceptual change. *Sci. Educ.* 66:211–27

Pressley M. 1990. *Cognitive Strategy Instruction That Really Improves Children's Academic Performance.* Cambridge, MA: Brookline Books

Pressley M. 1998. *Reading Instruction That Really Works.* New York: Guilford

Quilici JH, Mayer RE. 1996. Role of examples in how students learn to categorize statistics word problems. *J. Educ. Psychol.* 88:144–61

Read C. 1981. Writing is not the inverse of reading for young children. In *Writing: The*

Nature, Development and Teaching of Written Communication. Volume 2: Writing: Process, Development and Communication, ed. CH Frederiksen, JF Dominic. Hillsdale, NJ: Erlbaum

Reed SK. 1999. *Word Problems.* Mahwah, NJ: Erlbaum

Resnick LB, Ford WW. 1981. *The Psychology of Mathematics for Instruction.* Hillsdale, NJ: Erlbaum

Riley M, Greeno JG, Heller J. 1982. The development of children's problem solving ability in arithmetic. In *The Development of Mathematical Thinking,* ed. H Ginsburg, pp. 153–96. New York: Academic

Rubman CN, Waters HS. 2000. A, B seeing: the role of constructive processes in children's comprehension monitoring. *J. Educ. Psychol.* 92:503–14

Samuels SJ. 1979. The method of repeated readings. *Read. Teach.* 32:403–8

Schoenfeld AH. 1985. *Mathematical Problem Solving.* Orlando, FL: Academic

Schoenfeld AH. 1991. On mathematics and sense making: an informal attack on the unfortunate divorce of formal and informal mathematics. In *Informal Reasoning and Education,* ed. JF Voss, DN Perkins, JW Segal, pp. 311–43. Hillsdale, NJ: Erlbaum

Schoenfeld AH. 1992. Learning to think mathematically: problem solving, metacognition, and sense making in mathematics. See Grouws 1992, pp. 334–70

Schwartz BB, Nathan MJ, Resnick LB. 1996. Acquisition of meaning for arithmetic structures with Planner. In *International Perspectives on the Design of Technology-supported Learning Environments,* ed. S Vosniadou, E De Corte, R Glaser, H Mandl, pp. 61–80. Hillsdale, NJ: Erlbaum

Shulman LS, Quinlan KM. 1996. The comparative psychology of school subjects. In *Handbook of Educational Psychology,* ed. DC Berliner, RC Calfee, pp. 399–422. New York: Macmillan

Siegler RS, Jenkins E. 1989. *How Children Discover New Strategies.* Hillsdale, NJ: Erlbaum

Silver E. 1981. Recall of mathematical problem information: solving related problems. *J. Res. Math. Educ.* 12:54–64

Silver EA, Kenney PA. 2000. Results from the seventh mathematics assessment of the National Assessment of Educational Progress. Reston, VA: Natl. Council Teach. Math.

Singley MK, Anderson JR. 1989. *The Transfer of Cognitive Skill.* Cambridge, MA: Harvard Univ. Press

Soloway E, Lochhead J, Clement J. 1982. Does computer programming enhance problem solving ability? Some positive evidence on algebra word problems. In *Computer Literacy,* ed. RJ Seidel, RE Anderson, B Hunter, pp. 171–86. New York: Academic

Stahl SA, Fairbanks MM. 1986. The effect of vocabulary instruction: a model-based meta-analysis. *Rev. Educ. Res.* 56:72–110

Stanovich KE. 1986. Mathews effects in reading: some consequences of individual differences in the acquisition of literacy. *Read. Res. Q.* 21:360–407

Stanovich KE. 1991. Discrepancy definitions of reading disability: Has intelligence led us astray? *Read. Res. Q.* 26:7–29

Taylor BM. 1980. Children's memory for expository text after reading. *Read. Res. Q.* 15:399-411

Taylor BM, Beach RW. 1984. The effects of text structure instruction on middle-grade students' comprehension and production of expository text. *Read. Res. Q.* 19:134–46

Thorndike EL. 1913. *Educational Psychology.* New York: Columbia Univ. Press

Thorndike EL, Woodworth RS. 1901. The influence of improvement in one mental function upon the efficiency of other functions. *Psychol. Rev.* 8:247–61

Van Haneghan J, Barron L, Young M, Williams S, Vye N, Bransford J. 1992. The Jasper series: an experiment with new ways to enhance mathematical thinking. See Halpern 1992, pp. 15–38

Verschaffel L, De Corte E, Pauwels A. 1992. Solving compare problems: an eye movement test of Lewis and Mayer's consistency hypothesis. *J. Educ. Psychol.* 84:85–94

Verschaffel L, Greer B, De Corte E. 2000. *Making Sense of Word Problems*. Lisse, Netherlands: Swets & Zeitlinger

Vosniadou S, Ionnides C, Dimitrakopoulou A, Papademetriou E. 2001. Designing learning environments to promote conceptual change in science. *Learn. Instr.* 11:381–419

Vosniadou S, Pearson PD, Rogers T. 1988. What causes children's failures to detect inconsistencies in text? Representation versus comparison difficulties. *J. Educ. Psychol.* 80:27–39

Wagner RK, Torgesen JK. 1987. The nature of phonological processing and its causal role in the acquisition of reading skills. *Psychol. Bull.* 101:192–212

Weaver CA, Kintsch W. 1991. Expository text. In *Handbook of Reading Research, Vol. 2*, ed. R Barr, ML Kamil, PB Mosenthal, PD Pearson, pp. 230–45. Hillsdale, NJ: Erlbaum

Wertheimer M. 1959. *Productive Thinking*. New York: Harper & Row

West RF, Stanovich KE. 1978. Automatic contextual facilitation in readers of three ages. *Child Dev.* 49:717–27

White B. 1993. ThinkerTools: causal models, conceptual change, and science education. *Cogn. Instr.* 10:1–100

White B, Frederiksen JR. 1998. Inquiry, modeling, and metacognition: making science accessible to all students. *Cogn. Instr.* 16:3–118

Winne PH, Graham L, Prock L. 1993. A model of poor reader's text-based inferencing: effects of explanatory feedback. *Read. Res. Q.* 28:53–66

Annu. Rev. Psychol. 2004. 55:745–74
doi: 10.1146/annurev.psych.55.090902.141456
First published online as a Review in Advance on November 3, 2003

COPING: Pitfalls and Promise

Susan Folkman and Judith Tedlie Moskowitz

*Osher Center for Integrative Medicine, University of California, San Francisco,
California 94143-1726; email: folkman@ocim.ucsf.edu, moskj@ocim.ucsf.edu*

Key Words coping critique, coping measurement, positive emotion, coping
effectiveness, coping and meaning

■ **Abstract** Coping, defined as the thoughts and behaviors used to manage the internal and external demands of situations that are appraised as stressful, has been a focus of research in the social sciences for more than three decades. The dramatic proliferation of coping research has spawned healthy debate and criticism and offered insight into the question of why some individuals fare better than others do when encountering stress in their lives. We briefly review the history of contemporary coping research with adults. We discuss three primary challenges for coping researchers (measurement, nomenclature, and effectiveness), and highlight recent developments in coping theory and research that hold promise for the field, including previously unaddressed aspects of coping, new measurement approaches, and focus on positive affective outcomes.

CONTENTS

0066-4308/04/0204-0745$14.00

INTRODUCTION

The past 35 years have seen a dramatic proliferation of coping research across social and behavioral science, medicine, public health, and nursing. Research ranges from small-sample qualitative studies to large-scale population-based studies, with content ranging from the exploration of abstract theoretical relationships to applied studies in clinical settings. Many investigators undertook this research with the hope that the concept of coping might help explain why some individuals fare better than others do when encountering stress in their lives. Many other concepts, such as culture, developmental history, or personality, can also help explain these individual differences, but coping is unlike these other concepts in that it lends itself to cognitive-behavioral intervention. As such, its allure is not only as an explanatory concept regarding variability in response to stress, but also as a portal for interventions.

Background

A large proportion of contemporary coping research can be traced back to the publication of Richard Lazarus's 1966 book, *Psychological Stress and the Coping Process*. Previously, most research on coping had been couched in the framework of ego-psychology and the concept of defense, as exemplified by the work of Haan (1969), Menninger (1963), and Vaillant (1977). This research was often concerned with pathology and depended on the evaluation of unconscious processes. In his book, Lazarus presented a contextual approach to stress and coping that helped set a new course. Lazarus's formulation expanded the boundaries of coping beyond defense and an emphasis on pathology to include a wider range of cognitive and behavioral responses that ordinary people use to manage distress and address the problems of daily life causing the distress. Lazarus's theory placed great emphasis on the role of cognitive appraisal in shaping the quality of the individual's emotional response to a troubled person-environment relationship and to the ways in which the person coped with the appraised relationship. His cognitively oriented theory of stress and coping occurred within the context of the "cognitive revolution" and its intense interest in the relation between cognition and emotion (e.g., Mandler 1975, Simon 1967) and information processing under conditions of stress (e.g., Horowitz 1976, Janis & Mann 1977, Leventhalet al. 1980). This historical context undoubtedly helped create the fertile environment in which Lazarus's theory of stress and coping took root.

Coping as a distinct field of psychological inquiry emerged during the 1970s and 1980s. By 1974 publications included a major book edited by Coelho, Hamburg, & Adams titled *Coping and Adaptation*, as well as scholarly books on coping with illness (Antonovsky 1979, Moos & Tsu 1977) and coping with childhood and adolescence (Murphy & Moriarty 1976). Lazarus & Folkman (Folkman & Lazarus 1980, Lazarus & Folkman 1984) defined coping as thoughts and behaviors that people use to manage the internal and external demands of situations that are appraised as stressful. This definition became widely accepted (Tennen et al. 2000) and tools with which to measure these coping thoughts and behaviors were developed (e.g., Billings & Moos 1981, Folkman & Lazarus 1980, Pearlin & Schooler 1978). By the early 1980s, reports of empirical studies of coping began to appear in growing numbers. Since then many new measures have been developed and tens of thousands of studies have been published (Somerfield & McCrae 2000). Major books on coping were published, including *Stress, Coping, and Development* (Aldwin 1994) and *The Handbook of Coping* (Zeidner & Endler 1996). Although defense-focused research continued throughout this period within psychology (e.g., Vaillant 2000, Cramer 2000), cognitive approaches prevailed.

The Contextual, Cognitive Model of Coping

Coping is a process that unfolds in the context of a situation or condition that is appraised as personally significant and as taxing or exceeding the individual's resources for coping (Lazarus & Folkman 1984). The coping process is initiated in response to the individual's appraisal that important goals have been harmed, lost, or threatened. These appraisals are characterized by negative emotions that are often intense. Coping responses are thus initiated in an emotional environment, and often one of the first coping tasks is to down-regulate negative emotions that are stressful in and of themselves and may be interfering with instrumental forms of coping. Emotions continue to be integral to the coping process throughout a stressful encounter as an outcome of coping, as a response to new information, and as a result of reappraisals of the status of the encounter. If the encounter has a successful resolution, positive emotions will predominate; if the resolution is unclear or unfavorable, negative emotions will predominate. To date, emphasis has been given to negative emotions in the stress process. However, new research about the role of positive emotions in the stress process and the role of coping in generating and sustaining these emotions has been prompted by recent evidence that positive and negative emotions co-occur throughout the stress process.

What Have We Learned?

In the years since the early 1980s, we have learned that coping is a complex, multidimensional process that is sensitive both to the environment, and its demands and resources, and to personality dispositions that influence the appraisal of stress and resources for coping. We have found that coping is strongly associated with the regulation of emotion, especially distress, throughout the stress process. We have found that certain kinds of escapist coping strategies are consistently associated with poor mental health outcomes, while other kinds of coping— such as the seeking of social support or instrumental, problem-focused forms of coping—are sometimes associated with negative outcomes, sometimes with positive ones, and sometimes with neither, usually depending on characteristics of the appraised stressful encounter. We have learned about the development of coping over the life span. And we have learned that coping skills can be taught through cognitive-behavioral therapies.

Despite the substantial gains that have been made in understanding coping per se, we seem only to have scratched the surface of understanding the ways in which coping actually affects psychological, physiological, and behavioral outcomes both in the short- and the longer-term. The discovery task is not simple. Coping is not a stand-alone phenomenon. It is embedded in a complex, dynamic stress process that involves the person, the environment, and the relationship between them.

Our goals in this chapter are twofold: first, to review central issues in coping research, and second, to review recent developments in coping theory and research that hold promise for the field. The literature on coping is vast, and we found it necessary to limit our review in several ways. We focus on coping research that is consistent with the cognitive, contextual approach as opposed to trait approaches or approaches based primarily on defense processes. We also focus on research with adults as opposed to children, and on populations that are not impaired by severe psychopathology.

CHALLENGING ISSUES

Numerous articles have been published that contain forceful criticisms of coping research, especially methodology (for review, see Somerfield & McCrae 2000). In this section we discuss three major issues that are widely debated in the coping literature: measurement, nomenclature, and the determination of effectiveness.

Measurement

The widespread interest in a contextual approach to stress and coping of the 1970s and 1980s motivated the development of new measures to assess coping in specific stressful situations. For the most part, the first generation of these new coping measures took the form of a checklist of thoughts and behaviors that people use to manage stressful events. Respondents were usually asked to provide a retrospective report of how they coped with a specific stressful event or they were asked to respond to vignettes that portrayed stressful situations. Answers were scored Yes/No or on Likert scales. Examples of inventories intended to be applicable in general populations include the Ways of Coping (Folkman & Lazarus 1980, 1988); the COPE (Carver et al. 1989); Coping Response's Inventory (Moos 1993); the Coping Strategy Indicator (Amirkhan 1990); and the Coping Inventory for Stressful Situations (Endler & Parker 1990; see Schwarzer & Schwarzer 1996 for a comprehensive review of coping measures).

These inventories are helpful in that they allow multidimensional descriptions of situation-specific coping thoughts and behaviors that people can self-report (Stone et al. 1992). Nevertheless, the inventory approach has many limitations, including:

- potentially burdensome length (Stone & Neale 1984)
- inadequate sampling of coping inherent in checklist approaches and response keys that are difficult to interpret (Stone et al. 1992)
- variations in the recall period (Porter & Stone 1996)
- changes in meaning of a given coping strategy depending on when it occurs (e.g., logical analysis before the problem would be constructive thinking, afterward it could be rumination)
- unreliability of recall (Coyne & Gottlieb 1996), and
- confounding of items with their outcomes (Stanton et al. 1994).

The most prominent of all the criticisms of the checklist approach concerns the problem of retrospective report and the accuracy of recall about specific thoughts and behaviors that were used one week or one month earlier. Stone & Neale (1984) developed the Daily Coping Inventory, a measure of daily coping efforts, to remedy the problem of recall. Instead of asking subjects to recall their most stressful event retrospectively across one week, two weeks, or a month, as most inventories request, subjects are asked to think about the most bothersome event that occurred that day. A study by Ptacek et al. (1994) provided support for shortening the recall period to one day. They compared brief daily coping reports completed by college students over seven days with retrospective reports of coping over the same period. Correlations between daily coping measures (averaged across days) and the retrospective measures ranged from 0.47 to 0.58.

Stone and his colleagues subsequently developed momentary coping assessments using ecological momentary assessment techniques (Stone et al. 1998) in a study that compared the "real-time" approach of the momentary assessments with one- and two-day retrospectively reported coping. Approximately 30% of the participants failed to retrospectively report items they had reported on the momentary assessments, and conversely, approximately 30% of the participants retrospectively reported items that were not reported on the momentary assessments.

Momentary and retrospective accounts yield different information about coping. Approaches with short recall are especially useful in intraindividual designs to study the relationship between changes in coping and changes in proximal outcomes such as mood or illness symptoms (Tennen et al. 2000). Some suggest that intraindividual designs are by far the preferred way to understand how coping affects physical and emotional well-being (Lazarus 2000). The momentary assessment procedure, however, has its own shortcomings. As Stone et al. (1998) point out, their subjects were asked repeatedly to recall their coping efforts, which may have resulted in some coping not being reported, perhaps because participants thought they already had reported it. Further, the momentary focus may result in reports of very concrete, discrete events, thereby missing ongoing problems or more abstract, complex problems. The momentary assessments might also elicit literal reports of specific thoughts and actions, and miss the broader conceptualizations of coping that are better perceived with the benefit of some retrospection, such as those that involve finding meaning. Conversely, retrospective accounts may be more subject to distortion associated with participants' efforts to create a coherent narrative of what happened or to find meaning in the event. Stone et al. point out that retrospective accounts may actually be better predictors of future outcomes than the momentary assessments. One explanation for this may be that what participants report as coping has become the "true story" for them and thus predicts future actions.

Narrative approaches provide an interesting alternative to checklist approaches. A great deal can be learned by asking people to provide narratives about stressful events, including what happened, the emotions they experienced, and what they thought and did as the situation unfolded. Narrative approaches are helpful in understanding what the person is coping with, which is especially important when the stressful event is not a specific event named by the investigator, such as coping with exams, or a particular health-related procedure, such as an endoscopy. For example, Folkman et al. (1994) analyzed the narratives of the caregiving partners of men with acquired immunodeficiency syndrome (AIDS) who had been asked to report the most stressful event related to caregiving. Within the general category of caregiving, narratives revealed many different sources of stress, including adjusting to illness progression, the shifting of responsibilities from the caregiver to the patient, unexpected improvement in the patient's health, and role conflict. These insights were helpful in understanding the caregivers' perspectives regarding what they were actually coping with in their daily lives.

Narrative approaches are also useful for uncovering ways of coping that are not included on inventories. In their analysis of narratives provided by caregivers of people with dementia, for example, Gottlieb & Gignac (1996) identified ways of coping not included on most inventories, such as ways of making meaning (normalizing experiences and feelings, "reading" cognitions and internal states of the care recipient) and vigilance (continuous watchfulness). Moskowitz & Wrubel (2000) analyzed 246 stressful event narratives in a sample of 20 human immuno-deficiency virus positive (HIV+) men who each had up to 13 interviews over a two-year period. They coded the narratives for coping thoughts and behaviors and tried to match them to the eight categories of coping contained in the Ways of Coping (Folkman & Lazarus 1988). Moskowitz & Wrubel identified coping processes not included on the Ways of Coping inventory, such as offering support, mentally preparing for what was coming, and venting emotion through crying or writing.

Moskowitz & Wrubel also examined the overlap between a quantitative measure (the Ways of Coping, Folkman & Lazarus 1988) and their narrative analysis. First they examined the extent to which the eight kinds of coping measured by the Ways of Coping appeared spontaneously in the narratives and found the proportion of matches ranging from 8% to 42%. They then looked in the opposite direction and found that spontaneous accounts of the eight kinds of coping that appeared in the narratives were matched by reports on the Ways of Coping much more consistently, the proportion of matches ranging from 57% to 100%. These findings suggest that narrative and quantitative approaches overlap, but are not equivalent.

There is no gold standard for the measurement of coping. Momentary accounts address the problem of bias due to recall, but they may underrepresent the complexity of coping over time and the complexity of what people actually cope with. Retrospective accounts address the problems of complexity, but introduce the effects of coping processes that take place in the interim. Retrospective accounts, in a sense, may be telling us what the person is doing now to cope with what happened then, as well as what the person did then to cope with what happened then. Some might call this "error" or "noise." We consider it another aspect of coping. Finally, narrative methods generate ways of coping that are not contained in checklists. However, without the prompting of a checklist, people may overlook some of the ways they coped.

The measurement of coping is probably as much art as it is science. The art comes in selecting the approach that is most appropriate and useful to the researcher's question. Sometimes the best solution may involve several approaches. A narrative approach with a small sample can be very useful in defining the domains of stressors that are relevant for the study population. This information can then be used to define a limited range of stressors to be used with a quantitative measure. This approach is also useful for uncovering ways of coping that are not included on standard coping inventories Momentary and retrospective accounts provide different perspectives on coping. One or the other may be preferable, depending on whether the outcome of interest is proximal (such as mood), a behavioral outcome (such as resolution of interpersonal conflict or performance on a test), or more distal (such as recovery from surgery or recurrence of mental or physical illness).

Coping Nomenclature: Conceptual and Empirical Approaches

Coping inventories usually contain several dozen specific thoughts and behaviors. If one counted the unique items on all inventories there would probably be hundreds. A challenge for coping researchers is to find a common nomenclature for these diverse coping strategies so that findings across studies can be discussed meaningfully.

Researchers have generally clustered coping responses rationally, using theory-based categories; empirically, using factor analysis; or through a blend of both rational and empirical techniques. One of the earlier nomenclatures, proposed by Folkman & Lazarus (1980), used a rational approach to distinguish two major theory-based functions of coping: problem-focused coping, which involves addressing the problem causing distress, and emotion-focused coping, which is aimed at ameliorating the negative emotions associated with the problem. Some examples of problem-focused coping are making a plan of action or concentrating on the next step. Examples of emotion-focused coping are engaging in distracting activities, using alcohol or drugs, or seeking emotional support.

The theoretical distinction between problem-focused and emotion-focused coping provides a useful way of talking about many kinds of coping in broad brushstrokes and it is used extensively in the coping literature. Other conceptualizations of coping functions often fit these categories. For example, Billings & Moos (1981) proposed a three-factor conceptualization of coping consisting of Active Cognitive (e.g., tried to see the positive side; considered several alternatives) and Active Behavioral (e.g., talked with a friend, tried to find out more about the situation), which are problem-focused coping, and Avoidance (e.g., tried to reduce tension by eating more, got busy with other things to avoid thinking about the problem), which is a form of emotion-focused coping.

Several investigators found that the problem-focused and emotion-focused distinction was a good starting point, but they identified meaning-focused coping as a different type of coping in which cognitive strategies are used to manage the meaning of a situation. Pearlin & Schooler (1978), for example, included the responses of positive comparisons or selective ignoring in this category. Park & Folkman (1997) also proposed a meaning-making factor as a useful way to think about coping efforts in which the person draws on values, beliefs, and goals to modify the meaning of a stressful transaction, especially in cases of chronic stress that may not be amenable to problem-focused efforts. Gottlieb & Gignac (1996) found that meaning-making coping, including making causal attributions and searching for meaning in adversity, was caregivers' most frequently reported way of coping with demented care recipients' behavior.

Empirically derived categories of coping usually include the three theoretically derived factors mentioned above—problem-focused coping, emotion-focused coping, and meaning-focused coping—but also often include a social factor. In developing the Coping Strategy Indicator, Amirkhan (1990) started with 161 coping responses. Principal-factor analysis produced a three-factor solution of Problem-Solving, Seeking Support, and Avoidance that provided a good fit to the data. Zautra et al. (1996) compared several empirical structures of coping based on an 11-subscale dispositional version of the COPE inventory (Carver et al. 1989) in a sample of 169 recently divorced women. A four-factor solution that reflected the now-familiar pattern of problem-focused, emotion-focused, social coping, and meaning-focused coping provided an adequate fit to the data: Active (active, restraint, planning), Avoidance (denial, drugs, mental disengagement), Support (seeking instrumental support, seeking emotional support), and Positive Cognitive Restructuring (positive reinterpretation, humor, acceptance).

Although nomenclature such as problem-focused, emotion-focused, social coping, and meaning-focused coping helps the synthesis of findings across studies, it also runs the risk of masking important differences within categories. For example, distancing, which is a form of coping in which the person recognizes a problem but deliberately makes efforts to put it out of his or her mind, and escape-avoidance, which is more of an escapist flight that can include behaviors such as drinking, are both avoidant forms of coping that are usually grouped together under "emotion-focused coping." Distancing, however, is often adaptive when nothing can be done, such as when waiting for the outcome of a test, whereas escape-avoidance is usually a maladaptive way of coping with the same kind of situation.

Sometimes this kind of distinction is important to retain. If sample size allows, statistical techniques such as structural equation modeling can be used to examine unique effects of individual coping responses even though they are grouped into larger latent factors (Hull et al. 1991).

A second set of issues related to the grouping of coping responses concerns the evaluation of the psychometric qualities of coping scales based on the groupings. Usually we expect measures of psychological constructs to have high levels of internal consistency, with alphas typically above 0.85 or 0.90. This standard is not necessarily appropriate for coping scales. Billings & Moos summarized this problem more than 20 years ago: "...typical psychometric estimates of internal consistency may have limited applicability in assessing the psychometric adequacy of measures of coping ... an upper limit may be placed on internal consistency coefficients by the fact that the use of one coping response may be sufficient to reduce stress and thus lessen the need to use other responses from either the same or other categories of coping" (Billings & Moos 1981, p. 145).

Another psychometric issue has to do with the expectation that a multifactorial scale should have factors that are independent of one another. Conceptually and empirically, however, distinct kinds of coping seem to travel together. Problem-focused coping, for example, is usually used in tandem with positive reappraisal or meaning-focused coping. This partnership suggests that these two forms of coping facilitate each other. Looking for the positive in a grim situation, for example, may encourage the person to engage in problem-focused coping. Conversely, effective problem-focused coping can lead to a positive reappraisal of the individual's competence (or luck), or it may lead to an appreciation of another person's contribution to the solution. To insist that coping factors be uncorrelated in order to achieve a psychometric purity by, for example, eliminating items that correlate across factors, may actually result in a reduction of the validity of the measure.

Coping Effectiveness

An important motivation for studying coping is the belief that within a given culture certain ways of coping are more and less effective in promoting emotional well-being and addressing problems causing distress, and that such information can be used to design interventions to help people cope more effectively with the stress in their lives. Despite the reasonableness of this expectation, the issue of determining coping effectiveness remains one of the most perplexing in coping research (Somerfield & McCrae 2000).

The contextual approach to coping that guides much of coping research states explicitly that coping processes are not inherently good or bad (Lazarus & Folkman 1984). Instead, the adaptive qualities of coping processes need to be evaluated in the specific stressful context in which they occur. A given coping process may be effective in one situation but not in another, depending, for example, on the extent to which the situation is controllable. Further, the context is dynamic, so that what might be considered effective coping at the outset of a stressful situation may be deemed ineffective later on. Thus, in preparing for an examination, it is adaptive to engage in problem-focused coping prior to the exam and in distancing while waiting for the results (Folkman & Lazarus 1985). Conversely, when dealing with a major loss, such as the death of a spouse, it may be adaptive initially to engage in some palliative coping to deal with the loss and then later, after emotional equilibrium is returning, to engage in more instrumental coping to deal with future plans (Stroebe & Schut 2001).

The evaluation of coping in a contextual model requires a two-pronged approach. First, appropriate outcomes must be selected. Second, attention must be given to the quality of the fit between coping and the demands of the situation.

OUTCOMES   Broadly viewed, outcomes refer to the status of diverse goals that are personally significant to the individual or that are selected by the researcher on an a priori basis for their relevance to the question at hand. Several investigators have identified coping goals that are fairly generic, such as solving the problem and feeling better (Cummings et al. 1994, McCrae & Costa 1986), or problem-solving, managing emotional distress, protecting self-esteem, and managing social interactions (Laux & Weber 1991). Zeidner & Saklofske (1996) name eight goals: resolution of the conflict or stressful situation, reduction of physiological and biochemical reactions, reduction of psychological distress, normative social functioning; return to prestress activities, well-being of self and others affected by the situation, maintaining positive self-esteem, and perceived effectiveness.

These lists are helpful, but they mask important complexities. First, some outcomes tend to be proximal and are probably influenced by momentary coping (e.g., biochemical reactions) and others are more distal and are probably influenced by coping over time (e.g., normative social functioning, return to prestress activities). These distinctions actually make it useful to consider both distal and proximal outcomes in the same study so that we can learn more about how coping works both in the short- and long-term. Menaghan (1982), for example, used distress as an indicator of emotional well-being in the near term and numbers of life problems as an indicator of longer-term effectiveness.

Second, coping responses that are effective with respect to one outcome may have a negative impact on another (Folkman 1992, Zeidner & Saklofske 1996). In a study of physicians' mistakes, for example, Wu et al. (1993) found that physicians who coped by accepting responsibility for the mistake made constructive changes in their practice (problem-solving), but also experienced more distress.

A third point has to do with an assumption that a successful goal outcome involves mastery or resolution. Zeidner & Saklofske (1996, p. 158) for example, state that adaptive coping "should lead to a permanent problem resolution with no additional conflict or residual outcomes while maintaining a positive emotional state." This approach does a disservice to the chronic, inherently unresolvable situations and conditions that characterize the stress most people are most troubled by such as chronic illness, caregiving, unemployment, and bereavement, and which are the most challenging in terms of coping (Mattlin et al. 1990). Gignac & Gottlieb

(1997) make the interesting observation that research on coping effectiveness is virtually nonexistent in the area of chronic stress.

A fourth issue has to do with who evaluates the status of the goal. Is it an observer or is it the person doing the coping? A number of investigators (e.g., Aldwin & Revenson 1987, Gignac & Gottlieb 1996, Ntoumanis & Biddle 1998) ask participants to appraise the efficacy of their own coping efforts. In their study of caregivers of patients with dementia, for example, Gignac & Gottlieb (1996), assessed caregivers' appraisals of their coping efficacy in response to the symptom of their family member's dementia they found most upsetting. Importantly, these efficacy appraisals were made in terms of progress toward goal outcomes identified in qualitative analysis of interview data (a problem-solving/instrumental goal, the maintenance of self-esteem, the regulation of emotional and physiological arousal, the development of greater self-understanding, and the preservation of harmonious relations with relatives) rather than in terms of mastery or resolution. Observer ratings of coping efficacy are used less frequently, and usually in relation to behavioral outcomes such as performance on an exam (Carver & Scheier 1994, Folkman & Lazarus 1985) or on a laboratory-based task (Aspinwall & Richter 1999), or to biological outcomes, such as immune markers of HIV disease progression (e.g., Ironson et al. 2002).

COPING-ENVIRONMENT FIT   A full account of coping effectiveness must consider characteristics of the context and the fit between those characteristics and various types of coping. Several approaches have been taken to characterize situations. One is to classify stressful situations in terms of what they are about in objective terms, such as illness, death, or children (Billings & Moos 1981, Mattlin et al. 1990). This approach ignores psychological dimensions that are theoretically relevant to a contextual approach to coping. The approach in which the investigator characterizes situations as a threat, loss, or challenge (McCrae 1984) is closer to the contextual theory in that it uses dimensions to classify situations that reflect different kinds of stress and that suggest different coping approaches (e.g., approach versus avoidance; problem versus emotion-focused). However, the classification is made by someone who may not share the individual's history, dispositions, or goals, all of which are relevant to the appraisal of threat, loss, and challenge.

The approach to characterizing the context most consistent with a contextual formulation is to obtain the individual's own appraisal of the situation, event, or condition in relation to a theoretically relevant dimension. The most frequently assessed dimension is the opportunity for personal control, or the appraisal of control or changeability. The fit between the appraisal of controllability and coping is sometimes referred to as the goodness of fit (Conway & Terry 1992, Folkman 1984, Zeidner & Saklofske 1996). Theoretically, appraisals of control call for greater proportions of active, instrumental problem-focused forms of coping, and appraisals of lack of control call for more active or passive emotion-focused coping. Presumably, people who choose coping strategies that fit the appraised controllability of a task will have better outcomes than people who do not. There is mixed support for this hypothesis. In a study of hemodialysis patients and adherence, Christensen et al. (1995) found that coping involving planful problem solving was associated with more favorable adherence when the stressor involved a relatively controllable aspect of the hemodialysis context. For stressors that were less controllable, emotional self-control, a form of emotion-focused coping, was associated with more favorable adherence. Terry & Hynes (1998) made distinctions among problem- and emotion-focused kinds of coping in a study of women coping with a medical procedure, in vitro fertilization, which they considered uncontrollable. Direct attempts to manage the problem were related to poorer adjustment, which supported the goodness-of-fit hypothesis. They also found that emotion-focused approach to coping was better related to adjustment. Escape, another form of emotion-focused coping, was not. Park et al. (2001) found support for the fit between problem-focused coping and controllability in a sample of HIV+ men, but the evidence for a fit between emotion-focused coping and lack of control was less strong. Conversely, Macrodimitris & Endler (2001) found evidence for a fit between lower perceived control and high emotion-oriented coping for the psychological adjustment of people with type 2 diabetes, but did not find evidence for the fit between higher perceived control and instrumental coping.

People's ability to modify their coping according to the situational demands is sometimes referred to as coping flexibility, which involves the systematic use of a variety of strategies across different situations rather than the more rigid application of a few coping strategies (Lester et al. 1994). Flexibility has been measured in three different ways: through a card sorting procedure in which the individual places cards containing descriptions of coping into categories that range from "most like me" to "least like me" (Schwartz & Daltroy 1991), by counting the number of coping options selected from a coping inventory for each of several scenarios (Lester et al. 1994), and by examining the flexibility of appraisals of controllability and the flexibility of coping in relation to the appraisal (Cheng 2001). The study by Lester et al. suggested coping flexibility using the card sort method and the inventory count method is associated with greater well-being. Cheng tested her hypotheses about appraisal in a laboratory study and found that the results predicted flexible appraisal processes in a real-life setting. However, Cheng did not relate flexibility to relevant outcomes.

Theoretically, the concept of goodness of fit and the related notion of coping flexibility make sense. The studies to date suggest, however, that these concepts need to be tested with more refined categories of coping. It also may be necessary to take into account additional situational characteristics, such as whether or not it involves a goal of such significance that it cannot be easily relinquished (Carver & Scheier 1998, Stein et al. 1997).

NEW DEVELOPMENTS

Coping research is itself dynamic and new directions are emerging that are helping the field move forward, including future-oriented proactive coping, a dual-process model of coping, social aspects of coping, and three new directions that are tied closely to emerging emotion research: emotion-approach coping, emotion-regulation, and positive emotion and coping.

Future-Oriented Proactive Coping

Although the concept of threat—anticipated harm or loss—is central to cognitive theories of stress, most studies of coping focus on how people cope with events that occurred in the past or that are occurring in the present. One of the new developments in coping has to do with ways people cope in advance to prevent or mute the impact of events that are potential stressors, such as a pending lay-off, a medical procedure that has been scheduled, or having to deal with the results of a test that is scheduled in the near future (Aspinwall & Taylor 1997).

Aspinwall & Taylor (1997) refer to these responses to potential stressors as "proactive coping." Their model defines five interrelated components of the proactive coping process: (a) the importance of building a reserve of resources (including temporal, financial, and social resources) that can be used to prevent or offset future net losses (see also Hobfoll 1989), (b) recognition of potential stressors, (c) initial appraisals of potential stressors, (d) preliminary coping efforts, (e) and the elicitation and use of feedback about the success of one's efforts (Aspinwall 2003).

Schwarzer & Knoll (2003) distinguish among reactive coping, which alludes to harm or loss experienced in the past; anticipatory coping, which refers to efforts to deal with a critical event that is certain or fairly certain to occur in the near future (e.g., preparing for an exam); preventive coping, which foreshadows an uncertain threat potential in the distant future (e.g., beginning an exercise program to prevent an age-related medical condition such as osteoporosis); and proactive coping, which involves upcoming challenges that are potentially self-promoting. According to Schwarzer & Knoll the proactive person creates opportunities for growth, and though like Aspinwall & Taylor (1997), they emphasize the importance of accumulating resources, the purpose of these resources is to enable the individual to move toward positively valanced goals that are challenging and associated with personal growth.

Future-oriented coping, including anticipatory, preventive, and proactive coping, deserves attention. This type of coping may be a particularly good candidate for inclusion in cognitive-behavioral or psychoeducational interventions. Measures need to be developed that tap coping methods that are distinctly future-oriented so we can learn how people manage to reduce the potential adverse impact of future events and maximize opportunities for benefit.

Dual Process Model of Coping

In general, we are not highlighting models of coping that are condition-specific in this review, but we have chosen to discuss Stroebe & Schut's (1999, 2001) Dual Process Model of Coping (DPM) because it illustrates a theoretically based cognitive model of coping designed for an important context that has broad relevance in the social, behavioral, and health sciences, namely, bereavement.

The DPM specifies a dynamic process of coping whereby the bereaved person oscillates between two orientations: loss and restoration. Loss-oriented coping includes grief work, breaking bonds and thinking of the deceased person in a different place, and denying and avoiding changes associated with restoration. Restoration-oriented coping includes attending to secondary stressors that come about as a consequence of the bereavement, such as changing identity and role from "wife" to "widow," or mastering new skills and responsibilities that had previously been the provenance of the deceased. Each of these orientations can be thought of as a set of related goals. Importantly, the DPM defines adaptive coping as involving oscillation between loss- and future-orientations, between approach and avoidant coping, and between positive and negative reappraisals. Thus, the DPM specifies the major adaptive tasks associated with bereavement, specific cognitive processes associated with each adaptive task, and describes what "effective" coping might look like in this context. Several studies have tested various aspects of the model, and findings suggest that the DPM, with its characteristic pattern of oscillation, is helpful in explaining adjustment to bereavement (for review see M.S. Stroebe, H. Schut, & W. Stroebe, under review).

Social Aspects of Coping

Although most models of coping view the individual as embedded in a social context, the literature on coping is dominated by individualistic approaches that generally give short shrift to social aspects. Themes of personal control, personal agency, and direct action are central to most theories of coping (e.g., Lazarus & Folkman 1984, Pearlin & Schooler 1978), all of which reflect the emphasis on the individual. Dunahoo et al. (1998) have described these individualistic approaches as "Lone Ranger, 'man against the elements' perspective," but as they point out, "Even the Lone Ranger had Tonto" (p. 137).

Recent discussions of social aspects of coping include the impact of individual coping on social relationships and vice versa (e.g., Berghuis & Stanton 2002, Coyne & Smith 1991, DeLongis & O'Brien 1990, O'Brien & DeLongis 1997) and the notion of communal, prosocial coping (e.g., Wells et al. 1997).

INDIVIDUAL COPING AND SOCIAL RELATIONSHIPS   O'Brien & DeLongis (1997) summarize some of the main issues related to the coping of couples. Their review indicates that strategies that may be beneficial to the individual's well-being are not necessarily beneficial to the individual's spouse, and vice versa. Further, an individual's strategies that may be beneficial to the spouse may be hurtful to the individual. For example, Coyne & Smith (1991) studied coping strategies intended to buffer or protect another person from stress. In a study of myocardial infarction patients, they found that the use of such strategies by wives resulted in improved self-efficacy for the husbands, but diminished self-efficacy for the wives.

Berghuis & Stanton (2002) evaluated infertile couples' coping with a failed attempt to inseminate. They found that the individual's level of distress was influenced both by the individual and the spouse. The pattern of findings suggests that women and men tend to experience each other's coping strategies differently. Women, for example, benefited from their male partner's problem-focused coping, but the converse was not true, and avoidance by female partners contributed to distress in men, but the converse was not true.

COMMUNAL COPING   As a counterpoise to the emphasis on individualistic coping, Hobfoll and his colleagues have developed a multiaxial coping model that takes both individualistic and communal perspectives into account. It includes a prosocial-antisocial dimension and a passive-active dimension (Wells et al. 1997). The communal perspective is contained in the prosocial-antisocial dimension and refers to coping responses that are influenced by and in reaction to the social context. Thus, a person may delay or not engage in a direct action to solve a problem if that action is perceived as causing distress to another member of the social environment. Communal coping can be prosocial (e.g., "Join together with others to deal with the situation together," "Think carefully about how others feel before deciding what to do"), or antisocial (e.g., "Assert your dominance quickly," "Be firm, hold your ground") (Monnier et al. 1998). In a series of studies, Hobfoll and his colleagues found that active prosocial coping was associated with better emotional outcomes (Wells et al. 1997), and that women use more prosocial and men use more antisocial coping (Dunahoo et al. 1998).

Religious Coping

Religious coping received little attention until relatively recently. Now it has become one of the most fertile areas for theoretical consideration and empirical research. The interest in religious coping is spurred in part by evidence that religion plays an important role in the entire stress process, ranging from its influence on the ways in which people appraise events (Park & Cohen 1993) to its influence on the ways in which they respond psychologically and physically to those events over the long term (Seybold & Hill 2001). But people also use religion specifically to help cope with the immediate demands of stressful events, especially to help find the strength to endure and to find purpose and meaning in circumstances that can challenge the most fundamental beliefs.

The recent interest in religious coping has been fueled by increasing evidence that religious involvement affects mental and physical health (Seybold & Hill 2001). Religious involvement is not synonymous with religious coping. Religious involvement can be a part of an individual's life independent of stress in that person's life. However, some people do become involved with religion as a way of coping with stress. Further, studies by Holland et al. (1999) and Baider et al. (1999) show a relationship between a measure of religious and spiritual beliefs and practices and active forms of coping.

Kenneth Pargament (1997) has articulated complicated conceptual issues inherent in the study of religious coping in his seminal book, *The Psychology of Religion and Coping*, and in subsequent publications. One issue is the need to distinguish religious coping from religious dispositions and psychological and religious outcomes (Smith et al. 2000) that parallel similar issues in the conceptualization and measurement of coping more generally (cf. Lazarus & Folkman 1984, Stanton et al. 1994). A second issue is the need to define methods of religious coping that are distinct from methods of secular coping. Pargament et al. (1988), for example, defined three such methods: the self-directing approach, in which people rely on their God-given resources in coping; the deferring approach, in which people passively defer the responsibility for problem solving to God; and the collaborative approach, in which people work together with God as partners in the problem-solving process (preprint, ms pp. 6–7). A third issue has to do with the potential confounding between religious and nonreligious coping. Religious methods of gaining control, for example, could be just a reflection of a basic nonreligious desire for control. A fourth issue has to do with the fuzzy boundaries between concepts of religiosity and spirituality (Zinnbauer et al. 1997). Many diverse points of view are expressed in the literature on this issue. Spirituality can exist outside the boundaries of formal religion, but spirituality is also a part of religion. In this section, when we refer to religious coping, we also include spiritual coping, such as efforts to find meaning and purpose, or efforts to connect with a higher order or divine being that may or may not be religious.

Until the late 1990s, most measures of religious coping relied on just one or two items that asked about religious involvement, religiosity, or prayer. For example, one of the earliest coping measures, the Ways of Coping (Folkman & Lazarus 1980, 1988), has just one item that is clearly religious, "I prayed." The COPE (Carver et al. 1989), another widely used measure of coping, has a religious coping subscale that consists of four items: "I seek God's help," "I put my trust in God," "I try to find comfort in my religion," and "I prayed."

In the late 1990s, Pargament and his colleagues developed the RCOPE, an important contribution to the measurement of religious coping (Pargament et al. 2000). The RCOPE is designed to assess five religious coping functions: (*a*) finding meaning in the face of suffering and baffling life experiences, (*b*) providing an avenue to achieve a sense of mastery and control, (*c*) finding comfort and reducing apprehension by connecting with a force that goes beyond the individual, (*d*) fostering social solidarity and identity, and (*e*) assisting people in giving up old objects of value and finding new sources of significance. Specific religious coping methods were defined for each of these religious functions, and subscales were created. In other work, Pargament and his colleagues grouped religious coping methods into positive and negative patterns (Pargament et al. 1998). Positive religious coping methods are an expression of "a sense of spirituality, a secure relationship with God, a belief that there is meaning to be found in life, and a sense of spiritual connectedness with others" (Pargament et al., p. 712). Benevolent religious reappraisals, collaborative religious coping, and seeking spiritual support are examples of coping methods that fall within this category. Negative religious coping is an expression of "a less secure relationship with God, a tenuous and ominous view of the world, and a religious struggle in the search for significance" (Pargament et al., p. 712). It includes punitive religious reappraisals, demonic religious reappraisals, reappraisals of God's powers, and spiritual discontent.

Pargament et al. (2001) conducted one of the few studies to examine religious coping (as opposed to religious involvement) as a predictor of mortality. The study produced mixed findings. The authors used items from the RCOPE (Pargament et al. 2000) to measure positive religious coping and religious struggle in a two-year longitudinal study of 596 hospitalized persons 55 years of age or older. They found that religious struggle items (e.g., "Wondered whether God had abandoned me," "Questioned God's love for me"), but not positive religious coping, predicted mortality after controlling for demographic, physical health, and mental health variables. The authors point out that their study was the first empirical study to identify religious variables that increase the risk of mortality. Their study shows the importance of using measures of religious coping that include methods that are potentially maladaptive as well as those that are potentially adaptive.

Emotional Approach Coping

In the majority of studies of coping and adjustment, emotion-focused coping has been associated with higher levels of distress. Stanton and colleagues (Stanton et al. 1994, Stanton et al. 2000, Stanton et al. 2002) suggest that this is due to several flaws in the way emotion-focused coping is usually measured and analyzed. First, emotion-focused coping can include many different types of coping depending on the study. Second, emotion-focused items that indicate approach (e.g., "I get upset and am really aware of it") and items that reflect avoidance of emotions (e.g., "I try not to think about it") are often combined into a single scale when, in fact, their effects may be very different and they may actually be inversely correlated. Third, many of the emotion-focused items on the most commonly used coping scales are confounded with distress (e.g., "I get upset and let my emotions out," "I become very tense") and therefore the correlations with distress outcomes are likely to be inflated. Stanton and colleagues set out to address these issues by developing a scale to assess coping through emotional approach that was uncontaminated by distress and focused only on emotional approach types of coping.

Coping through emotional approach involves actively processing and expressing emotion (Stanton et al. 1994, Stanton et al. 2000). The emotional approach scale consists of two subscales: emotional processing (e.g., "I realize that my feelings are valid and important," "I take time to figure out what I'm really feeling") and emotional expression (e.g., "I feel free to express my emotions," "I let my feelings come out freely") (Stanton et al. 2000). The subscales have acceptable reliability and validity and are relatively distinct from other forms of coping (Stanton et al. 2000).

In one of their earlier studies, Stanton et al. (1994) demonstrated that emotional approach coping (which combined expression and processing items) was associated with decreased depression and hostility and increased life satisfaction over a one-month period for women but increased depression and decreased life satisfaction for men. In a subsequent set of studies in which emotional processing and expression were analyzed as separate subscales, neither was associated with depression but emotional expression was associated with life satisfaction for both men and women. In addition, emotional processing and emotional expression were associated with hope in women (but not in men). In a study of women with stage I or II breast cancer (Stanton et al. 2000), coping with cancer through emotional expression was associated with improved perceptions of health, decreased distress, fewer medical visits, and increased vigor at a three-month follow up. Coping through emotional processing, however, was associated with increases in distress over the three-month study period. Stanton et al. (2000) suggest that although emotional processing appears to be adaptive in the shorter term, if it continues over the longer term may become ruminative and therefore less beneficial in terms of adjustment.

Work by Nolen-Hoeksema and her colleagues supports this possibility. Rumination, the tendency to passively and repeatedly focus on negative emotions and the possible consequences of those negative emotions, is associated with increased symptoms of depression and anxiety and onset of major depressive episodes (Nolen-Hoeksema 2000, Nolen-Hoeksema & Davis 1999, Nolen-Hoeksema et al. 1999). Future work on emotional approach coping should explore the point at which emotional approach coping may become rumination.

Emotion Regulation

Emotion regulation is the process "by which individuals influence which emotions they have, when they have them, and how they experience and express these emotions. Emotion regulatory processes may be automatic or controlled, conscious or unconscious, and may have their effects at one or more points in the emotion generative process" (Gross 1998b, p. 275). To the extent that coping is aimed at ameliorating negative emotions or promoting positive emotions, it falls under the rubric of emotion regulation. However, emotion regulation also includes nonconscious processes that, according to our definition, do not fall under the purview of coping. In addition, since the coping process is prompted by negative emotion, it happens after the occurrence of emotion in the stress process, not prior, as with some forms of emotion regulation (but see our discussion of proactive and anticipatory coping). Eisenberg et al. (1997) classify both coping and emotion regulation under the larger category of self-regulation and note that coping involves the regulatory processes that occur in stressful contexts. Finally, although problem-focused coping is initiated by the occurrence of a negative emotion, problem-focused forms of coping do not fall under the category of emotion regulation in the sense that they are aimed at changing the source of the stress and, therefore, can be seen as nonemotional actions (Gross 1998b).

Eisenberg et al. (1997) identify two types of emotion regulation: one that involves regulating the internal feeling states and associated physiological processes (what they label emotion regulation) and the second that involves regulating the behavioral concomitants of emotion (labeled emotion-related behavior regulation). Gross (1998b) distinguishes two general classes of emotion regulation depending on where they occur in the emotion-generating process. Antecedent-focused regulation includes situation selection, situation modification, attentional deployment, and cognitive change. Response-focused regulation includes response modulation.

In a series of lab studies (e.g., Butler et al. 2003; Gross 1998a; Gross & John 2003b; Gross & Levenson 1993, 1997). Gross and colleagues have compared reappraisal, an antecedent-focused form of regulation to suppression, a response-focused form of regulation. They found that reappraisal and suppression have different affective, cognitive, social, and physiological consequences (see Gross & John 2003b for a review). For example, compared to participants in a control condition who were instructed to simply watch a distressing film clip, participants who were told to inhibit their emotional expression while watching the clip (the suppression condition) had poorer recall for details of the clip in an unexpected test at the end of the session (Richards & Gross 2000). In a second study, one group of participants was instructed to reappraise a set of emotionally evocative slides by viewing them as medical professionals would. When compared to the suppression group, which was instructed to suppress their emotional expression in response to the slides, the reappraisal group had better performance on a subsequent test in which they were asked to write down information associated with each slide as the slides were viewed again (Richards & Gross 2000).

Gross & John (2003a) developed the Emotion Regulation Questionnaire, a measure of individual differences in the tendency to reappraise or suppress. When compared to those who report using less suppression, those individuals who report using higher levels of suppression also reported having poorer memory for conversations and performed more poorly when asked to recall events they had reported in a daily diary a week earlier. Reappraisal was not related to either form of memory test.

Butler et al. 2003 examined the social consequences of reappraisal and suppression by having unacquainted female dyads watch an upsetting film, then discuss their reactions. One of the pair was given a secret instruction to suppress, reappraise, or interact naturally with the other member of the pair. Interestingly, the partners of the suppressors had greater increases in blood pressure than the partners of the reappraisers or those who acted naturally. It appears that interacting with a partner who suppresses emotional reactions is stressful for the person with whom he or she is interacting.

The work on emotion regulation adds to the coping literature by providing an in-depth look at the effects of some forms of emotion-focused types of coping. The forms of emotion regulation that Gross and colleagues are studying in the lab can be considered emotion-focused coping because they are elicited in response to the depiction of disturbing, stressful events that the individual is unable to control or change. One challenge for future work in this area is to delineate the extent to which these lab studies generalize to more applied stressful contexts. For example, when receiving frightening news such as the diagnosis of cancer, would suppressing one's emotional reaction lead to poorer recall for the information from the physician than immediate reappraisal of the news?

Coping and Positive Emotion

An exciting new development in the field of coping has to do with the growing awareness of the presence of positive emotion in the stress process (Bonanno & Keltner 1997, Folkman 1997, Folkman & Moskowitz 2000). This awareness has been fueled by growing interest in positive emotion more generally among emotion researchers (e.g., Danner et al. 2001; Fredrickson & Joiner 2002; Fredrickson & Levenson 1998; Fredrickson et al. 2000; Haidt 2000; Harker & Keltner 2001; Isen 1993, 2002) and a trend in psychology in general to focus on positive traits and concepts (e.g., Aspinwall & Clark 2003, Major et al. 1998, O'Leary & Ickovics 1995, Seligman & Csikszentmihalyi 2000). Interest in positive emotion in the stress process has opened a new avenue for coping research.

A number of studies have documented that positive emotion can occur with relatively high frequency, even in the most dire stressful context, and can occur during periods when depression and distress are significantly elevated. Silver & Wortman (1987; as reported in Wortman 1987), assessed positive and negative emotions in a sample of people who had severe spinal cord injuries and a sample of parents who had lost a child to sudden infant death syndrome. In both samples, despite the severity of the loss and the high levels of negative emotions reported, positive emotions occurred with surprising frequency. In the sample of people with spinal cord injury, happiness was reported more frequently than negative emotions by the third week after injury. In a sample of parents who lost a child to sudden infant death syndrome, positive and negative emotions were reported with approximately the same frequency three weeks after the child's death, and by three months positive emotions were reported more frequently than negative emotions.

Westbrook & Viney (1982) interviewed a sample of patients who were hospitalized with a chronic or disabling illness and a comparison group of healthy adults regarding their "life at the moment, the good things and the bad; what it's like for you" (p. 901). As expected, when compared to the control group, patients' responses revealed significantly more anxiety, depression, anger, and helplessness. However, their responses also showed significantly *more* positive feelings than did the responses of the comparison group. Viney et al. (1989) also found co-occurrence of positive and negative emotions in a sample of chronically ill men. Although the negative emotions of anxiety, depression, and helplessness were more frequent in the chronically ill groups when compared to a healthy control group, the positive emotion of enjoyment was also more frequent in the ill groups.

A similar co-occurrence of positive and negative emotion was found in a sample of caregiving partners of men with AIDS. Although the depression scores of the caregivers in the study were in the range that would classify them as at risk for clinical depression, when asked to report how often they experienced various positive and negative emotions in the previous week, the participants reported experiencing positive emotion as least as frequently as they experienced negative emotion, with the exception of the time immediately surrounding the death of the partner (Folkman 1997). Three years after the death of the partner, although the mean depression score of the bereaved caregivers was still significantly higher than the general population mean, positive emotions were reported significantly more frequently than negative emotions in the past week (Moskowitz et al. 2003).

The co-occurrence of positive and negative emotion has important implications for coping. On the one hand, if positive and negative emotions are simply bipolar opposites, then coping that reduces distress should simultaneously increase positive emotion, and vice versa. On the other, the co-occurrence phenomenon suggests there may be a degree of independence, in which case different kinds of coping may be associated with the regulation of positive and negative affect.

There is mounting evidence that although some coping strategies affect both positive and negative emotion, a number of strategies are related to just one or the other. Stone et al. (1995) examined the association of distraction, situation redefinition, direct action, catharsis, acceptance, seeking social support, relaxation, and religion with positive and negative affect as reported in end-of-day diaries. They found that relaxation and direct action were uniquely associated with positive affect, whereas distraction and acceptance were also associated with lower levels of negative affect.

Carver & Scheier (1994) studied the associations of coping with positive and negative emotion over the course of an exam. None of the coping responses measured prior to the exam was associated with positive challenge or benefit emotions during the postexam, pregrade period. However, use of problem-focused coping and positive reframing after the exam predicted challenge emotions (e.g., excited, eager) after the grades were announced.

Prospective data from a study of 110 caregiving partners of men with AIDS assessed bimonthly pre- and postbereavement indicated problem-focused coping and positive reappraisal were consistently associated with increases in positive affect, but only inconsistently related to decreases in negative affect (Moskowitz et al. 1996).

Analyses of narrative data from the AIDS caregiver study indicated that other types of coping, not captured by traditional checklist measures of coping, are likely to be related to positive emotion in the context of ongoing stress (Folkman 1997). At the conclusion of the interview, participants were asked to describe a positive meaningful event about "something that you did, or something that happened to you that made you feel good and that was meaningful to you and helped you get through the day."

This question was posed to 1794 participants, and 99.5% were able to report a positive meaningful event. In an in-depth analysis of 215 events reported by 36 participants, Folkman et al. (1997) found that the events often concerned something other than caregiving or bereavement (the subject of the focal stressors) and instead were associated with other roles that participants had (e.g., coworker, family member). In addition, they often concerned what on the surface appeared to be comparatively minor events (e.g., a beautiful sunset, a kind word from a friend, a good grade on a test). These findings suggested that under enduring stressful conditions such as caregiving or bereavement, people consciously seek out positive meaningful events or infuse ordinary events with positive meaning to increase their positive affect, which in turn provides respite from distress and thereby helps replenish resources and sustain further coping.

COPING, THE SEARCH FOR MEANING, AND POSITIVE EMOTION   One of the central tasks in coping with severe stress is to integrate the occurrence of the stressor with one's beliefs about the world and the self (Janoff-Bulman 1989, 1999; Park & Folkman 1997). A common theme in the coping processes related to positive emotion is their link to the individual's important values, beliefs, and goals that comprise the individual's sense of meaning (Folkman 1997).

Positive reappraisal, for example, involves a reinterpretation of the event in terms of benefits to one's values, beliefs, and goals. Problem-focused coping, when effective, is associated with feelings of mastery and control, goals that are generally valued in Western culture. Positive meaningful events are linked to positive emotion precisely because they reaffirm what one values and help one to focus on those values while coping with the ongoing stressful event.

PERCEIVING BENEFIT AS A COPING STRATEGY   Individuals who have experienced a severe stressful event such as a tornado or hurricane, being diagnosed with cancer, or losing a loved one to AIDS, often report that something positive has come out of the experience, such as closer relationships with family and friends, reprioritizing of goals, and greater appreciation of life. These benefits and personal changes have been called stress-related growth (Park et al. 1996), post-traumatic growth (Tedeschi et al. 1998), and benefit finding (Affleck & Tennen 1996, Tennen & Affleck 2002).

The perception of growth after a stressful experience is generally examined as an outcome. Efforts have been made to study the process by which persons experiencing stress arrive at the conclusion that they have experienced benefits from the stress. Park et al. (1996) examined stress-related growth in response to a recent stressful event in a sample of college students. The coping responses of acceptance ("I get used to the idea that it happened," "I accept the reality of the fact that it happened") and positive reinterpretation ("I look for something good in what is happening," "I learn something from the experience") were cross-sectionally related to stress-related growth.

Another approach links cognitive processing and the discovery of meaning. In a qualitative analysis of the bereavement narratives of HIV+ gay men who had lost a close friend or partner to AIDS, Bower et al. (1998) studied the association of cognitive processing and finding meaning with the decline of CD4 cells (T-helper cells that are attacked by the HIV virus) and mortality. Cognitive processing was defined as "deliberate, effortful, or long-lasting thinking about the death" (p. 980), which could be considered a form of coping with the friend's death. Statements coded as cognitive processing included "I keep thinking about what lessons are for me, what can I learn," "I'm muddling through my own feeling of . . . what could have been, what was, and what is, and . . . I'm more thinking of my future." Discovery of meaning was defined as a "major shift in values, priorities, or perspectives in response to the loss" (p. 980). Statements classified as discovery of meaning included "In one way I suppose that his passing influenced me to believe more strongly about the quality of life and living life in a satisfying way as much as possible," "I certainly appreciated more the friends that I have and became much closer with them," and "I would say that (his) death lit up my faith."

Sixty-five percent of the sample was classified as having engaged in cognitive processing about the death and 40% of the sample reported finding meaning in their bereavement. Cognitive processing was significantly associated with finding meaning, and although the majority of participants who found meaning were classified as high in cognitive processing, less than half of the participants who did not find meaning were classified as high in cognitive processing. Furthermore, participants classified as finding meaning had a less-rapid decrease in CD4 count compared to participants who did not find meaning. Discovery of meaning was also associated with lower risk of mortality.

Tennen and Affleck (Affleck & Tennen 1996; Tennen & Affleck 1999, 2002) examined a slightly different question. They studied a coping response called benefit reminding, which they define as effortful cognitions in which the individual reminds himself or herself of the possible benefits stemming from the stressful experience. The assumption is that benefit reminding can only be used as a coping strategy by those who have already found some benefit or perceived some positive consequences from the stressor. Thus, rather than being a coping strategy that precedes finding meaning or perceiving benefits in response to stress, benefit reminding is conceptualized as a form of coping that follows the perception of benefits. In a study of women with fibromyalgia, an illness associated with chronic pain, Tennen & Affleck (1999) demonstrated that benefit reminding was uniquely associated with pleasant mood. Their data, which included daily ratings of pain, mood, and coping, demonstrated that although benefit reminding was as prevalent on high-pain days as on lower-pain days, benefit reminding was significantly associated with increased pleasant mood (e.g., happy, cheerful) but not necessarily decreased negative mood. "Thus, on days when these chronic pain sufferers made greater efforts to remind themselves of the benefits that have come from their illness, they were especially more likely to experience pleasurable mood, regardless of how intense their pain was on these days" (p. 297).

The emerging interest in positive emotions in the stress process and coping processes associated with them is one of the most exciting developments in coping theory and research. What is needed is a clearer delineation of the interplay between positive and negative emotions and research to identify coping processes associated with positive emotions during both acute and chronic stress.

CONCLUSIONS

Thirty-five years ago, when coping research was just emerging, the concept of coping was still somewhat akin to a black box in the stress process. Over subsequent years, we have begun to see what's inside the black box. Throughout this period, there has also been extensive and sometimes contentious debate about the merits of coping research. Healthy debate and thoughtful criticism are signs that a field is maturing. At the same time, new methodologies and new ways of thinking about coping are emerging. Despite the complexities inherent in the study of coping, the area continues to hold great promise for explaining who thrives under stress and who does not, and it continues to hold great promise for informing effective interventions to help people better handle both acute and chronic stress.

The *Annual Review of Psychology* is online at http://psych.annualreviews.org

LITERATURE CITED

Affleck G, Tennen H. 1996. Construing benefits from adversity: adaptational significance and dispositional underpinnings. *J. Personal.* 64:899–922

Aldwin CM. 1994. *Stress, Coping, and Development: An Integrative Perspective.* New York: Guilford

Aldwin CM, Revenson TA. 1987. Does coping help? A reexamination of the relation between coping and mental health. *J. Personal. Soc. Psychol.* 53:337–48

Amirkhan JH. 1990. A factor analytically derived measure of coping: the coping strategy indicator. *J. Personal. Soc. Psychol.* 59:1066–74

Antonovsky A. 1979. *Health Stress and Coping.* San Francisco, CA: Jossey-Bass

Aspinwall LG. 2003. Proactive coping, wellbeing, and health. In *The International Encyclopedia of the Social and Behavioral Sciences,* ed. NJ Smelser, PB Baltes. Oxford: Elsevier. In press

Aspinwall LG, Clark A. 2003. Taking positive changes seriously: toward a positive psychology of cancer survivorship and resilience. *Cancer.* In press

Aspinwall LG, Richter L. 1999. Optimism and self-mastery predict more rapid disengagement from unsolvable tasks in the presence of alternatives. *Motiv. Emot.* 23(3):221–45

Aspinwall LG, Taylor SE. 1997. A stitch in time: self-regulation and proactive coping. *Psychol. Bull.* 121:417–36

Baider L, Russak SM, Perry S, Kash K, Gronert M, et al. 1999. The role of religious and spiritual beliefs in coping with malignant melanoma: an Israeli sample. *Psychooncology* 8:27–35

Berghuis JP, Stanton AL. 2002. Adjustment to a dyadic stressor: a longitudinal study of coping and depressive symptoms in infertile couples over an insemination attempt. *J. Consult. Clin. Psychol.* 70(2):433–38

Billings AG, Moos RH. 1981. The role of coping responses and social resources in attenuating the stress of life events. *J. Behav. Med.* 4:139–57

Bonanno GA, Keltner D. 1997. Facial expressions of emotion and the course of conjugal bereavement. *J. Abnorm. Psychol.* 106:126–37

Bower JE, Kemeny ME, Taylor SE, Fahey JL. 1998. Cognitive processing discovery of meaning CD4 decline and AIDS-related mortality among bereaved HIV-seropositive men. *J. Consult. Clin. Psychol.* 66(6):979–86

Butler EA, Egloff B, Wilhelm FH, Smith NC,

Gross JJ. 2003. The social consequences of emotion regulation. *Emotion* 3:48–67

Carpenter BN, ed. 1992. *Personal Coping: Theory, Research, and Application.* Westport, CT: Praeger/Greenwood

Carver CS, Scheier MF. 1994. Situational coping and coping dispositions in a stressful transaction. *J. Personal. Soc. Psychol.* 66:184–95

Carver CS, Scheier MF. 1998. *On the Self-Regulation of Behavior.* London: Cambridge Univ. Press

Carver CS, Scheier MF, Weintraub JK. 1989. Assessing coping strategies: a theoretically based approach. *J. Personal. Soc. Psychol.* 56:267–83

Cheng C. 2001. Assessing coping flexibility in real-life and laboratory settings: a multimethod approach. *J. Personal. Soc. Psychol.* 80(5):814–33

Christensen AJ, Benotch EG, Wiebe JS, Lawton WJ. 1995. Coping with treatment-related stress: effects on patient adherence in hemodialysis. *J. Consult. Clin. Psychol.* 63:454–59

Coelho GV, Hamburg DA, Adams JE, eds. 1974. *Coping and Adaptation.* New York: Basic Books

Conway VJ, Terry DJ. 1992. Appraised controllability as a moderator of the effectiveness of different coping strategies: a test of the goodness of fit hypothesis. *Aust. J. Psychol.* 44:1–7

Coyne JC, Gottlieb BH. 1996. The mismeasure of coping by checklist. *J. Personal.* 64:959–91

Coyne JC, Smith DA. 1991. Couples coping with a myocardial infarction: a contextual perspective on wives' distress. *J. Personal. Soc. Psychol.* 61(3):404–12

Cramer P. 2000. Defense mechanisms in psychology today: further processes for adaptation. *Am. Psychol.* 55(6):637–46

Cummings EM, Davies PT, Simpson KS. 1994. Marital conflict gender and children's appraisals and coping efficacy as mediators of child adjustment. *J. Fam. Psychol.* 8(2):141–49

Danner DD, Snowdon DA, Friesen WV. 2001. Positive emotions in early life and longevity: findings from the nun study. *J. Personal. Soc. Psychol.* 80:804–13

DeLongis A, O'Brien T. 1990. An interpersonal framework for stress and coping: an application to the families of Alzheimer's patients. In *Stress and Coping in Later-life Families,* eds. MAP Stephens, JH Crowther, SE Hobfoll, DL Tennenbaum, pp. 221–39. Washington, DC: Hemisphere

Dunahoo CL, Hobfoll SE, Monnier J, Hulsizer MR, Johnson R. 1998. There's more than rugged individualism in coping. Part 1: Even the Lone Ranger had Tonto. *Anxiety, Stress, Coping: An Int. J.* 11(2):137–65

Eisenberg N, Fabes RA, Guthrie IK. 1997. Coping with stress: the roles of regulation and development. In *Handbook of Children's Coping: Linking Theory and Intervention,* ed. SA Wolchik, IN Sandler, pp. 41–70. New York: Plenum

Endler NS, Parker JDA. 1990. Multidimensional Assessment of coping: a critical evaluation. *J. Personal. Soc. Psychol.* 58:844–54

Folkman S. 1984. Personal control and stress and coping processes: a theoretical analysis. *J. Personal. Soc. Psychol.* 46:839–52

Folkman S. 1992. Making the case for coping. See Carpenter 1992, pp. 31–46

Folkman S. 1997. Positive psychological states and coping with severe stress. *Soc. Sci. Med.* 45:1207–21

Folkman S, Chesney MA, Christopher-Richards A. 1994. Stress and coping in caregiving partners of men with AIDS. *Psychiatr. Clin. N. Am.* 17:35–53

Folkman S, Lazarus RS. 1980. An analysis of coping in a middle-aged community sample. *J. Health Soc. Behav.* 21:219–39

Folkman S, Lazarus RS. 1985. If it changes it must be a process: study of emotion and coping during three stages of a college examination. *J. Personal. Soc. Psychol.* 48:150–70

Folkman S, Lazarus RS. 1988. *Ways of Coping Questionnaire.* Palo Alto, CA: Consult. Psychol. Press

Folkman S, Moskowitz JT. 2000. Positive affect and the other side of coping. *Am. Psychol.* 55:647–54

Folkman S, Moskowitz JT, Ozer EM, Park CL. 1997. Positive meaningful events and coping in the context of HIV/AIDS. See Gottlieb 1997, pp. 293–314

Fredrickson BL, Joiner T. 2002. Positive emotions trigger upward spirals toward emotional well-being. *Psychol. Sci.* 13(2):172–75

Fredrickson BL, Levenson RW. 1998. Positive emotions speed recovery from the cardiovascular sequelae of negative emotions. *Cogn. Emot.* 12:191–220

Fredrickson BL, Mancuso RA, Branigan C, Tugade MM. 2000. The undoing effect of positive emotions. *Motiv. Emot.* 24:237–58

Gignac MAM, Gottlieb BH. 1996. Caregivers' appraisals of efficacy in coping with dementia. *Psychol. Aging* 11(2):214–25

Gignac MAM, Gottlieb BH. 1997. Changes in coping with chronic stress: the role of caregivers' appraisals of coping efficacy. See Gottlieb 1997, pp. 245–67

Gottlieb BH, ed. 1997. *Coping with Chronic Stress. Plenum Series on Stress and Coping.* New York: Plenum

Gottlieb BH, Gignac MAM. 1996. Content and domain specificity of coping among family caregivers of persons with dementia. *J. Aging Stud.* 10(2):137–55

Gross JJ. 1998a. Antecedent- and response-focused emotion regulation: divergent consequences for experience expression and physiology. *J. Personal. Soc. Psychol.* 74: 224–37

Gross JJ. 1998b. The emerging field of emotion regulation: an integrative review. *Rev. Gen. Psychol.* 2:271–99

Gross JJ, John OP. 2003a. Wise emotion regulation. In *The Wisdom of Feelings: Psychological Processes in Emotional Intelligence*, ed. LF Barrett, P Salovey, pp. 297–319. New York: Guilford

Gross JJ, John OP. 2003b. Individual differences in emotion regulation processes: affective and social consequences. *J. Personal. Soc. Psychol.* 85:348–62

Gross JJ, Levenson RW. 1993. Emotional suppression: physiology self-report and expressive behavior. *J. Personal. Soc. Psychol.* 64: 970–86

Gross JJ, Levenson RW. 1997. Hiding feelings: the acute effects of inhibiting negative and positive emotion. *J. Abnorm. Psychol.* 106:95–103

Haan N. 1969. A tripartite model of ego functioning: values and clinical research applications. *J. Nerv. Ment. Dis.* 148:14–30

Haidt J. 2000. The positive emotion of elevation. *Prev. Treat.* 3. Article 3. http://journals.apa.org/prevention/volume3/pre0030003c.html

Harker L, Keltner D. 2001. Expressions of positive emotion in women's college yearbook pictures and their relationship to personality and life outcomes across adulthood. *J. Personal. Soc. Psychol.* 80:112–24

Hobfoll SE. 1989. Conservation of resources: a new attempt at conceptualizing stress. *Am. Psychol.* 44:513–24

Holland JC, Passik S, Kash KM, Russak SM, Gronert MK, et al. 1999. The role of religious and spiritual beliefs in coping with malignant melanoma. *Psychooncology* 8:14–26

Horowitz M. 1976. *Stress Response Syndromes.* New York: Jason Aronson

Hull JG, Lehn DA, Tedlie JC. 1991. A general approach to testing multifaceted personality constructs. *J. Personal. Soc. Psychol.* 61(6):932–45

Ironson G, Solomon GF, Balbin EG, O'Cleirigh C, George A, et al. 2002. The Ironson-Woods Spirituality/Religiousness Index is associated with long survival health behaviors, less distress and low cortisol in people with HIV/AIDS. *Ann. Behav. Med.* 24(1):34–48

Isen AM. 1993. Positive affect and decision making. In *Handbook of Emotions*, ed. M Lewis, JM Haviland, pp. 417–35. New York: Guilford

Isen AM. 2002. A role for neuropsychology in understanding the facilitating influence of positive affect on social behavior and cognitive processes. See Snyder & Lopez 2002, pp. 528–40

Janis I, Mann L. 1977. *Decision Making*. New York: Free Press

Janoff-Bulman R. 1989. Assumptive worlds and the stress of traumatic events: applications of the schema construct. *Soc. Cogn.* 7:113–36

Janoff-Bulman R. 1999. Rebuilding shattered assumptions after traumatic life events: coping processes and outcomes. See Snyder 1999, pp. 305–23

Laux L, Weber H. 1991. Presentation of self in coping with anger and anxiety: an intentional approach. *Anxiety Res.* 3(4):233–55

Lazarus RS. 1966. *Psychological Stress and the Coping Process*. New York: McGraw-Hill

Lazarus RS. 2000. Toward better research on stress and coping. *Am. Psychol.* 55(6):665–73

Lazarus RS, Folkman S. 1984. *Stress Appraisal and Coping*. New York: Springer

Lester N, Smart L, Baum A. 1994. Measuring coping flexibility. *Psychol. Health* 9(6):409–24

Leventhal H, Meyer D, Nerenz D. 1980. The commonsense representation of illness danger. In *Contributions to Medical Psychology*, ed. S Rachman, 2:7–30. Oxford: Pergamon

Macrodimitris SD, Endler NS. 2001. Coping control and adjustment in Type 2 diabetes. *Health Psychol.* 20:208–16

Major B, Richards C, Cooper ML, Cozzarelli C, Zubek J. 1998. Personal resilience, cognitive appraisals and coping: an integrative model of adjustment to abortion. *J. Personal. Soc. Psychol.* 74:735–52

Mandler G. 1975. *Mind and Emotion*. New York: Wiley

Mattlin JA, Wethnington E, Kessler RC. 1990. Situational determinants of coping and coping effectiveness. *J. Health Soc. Behav.* 31:103–22

McCrae RR. 1984. Situational determinants of coping responses: Loss threat and challenge. *J. Personal. Soc. Psychol.* 76:117–22

McCrae RR, Costa PT. 1986. Personality coping and coping effectiveness in an adult sample. *J. Personal.* 54:385–405

Menaghan E. 1982. Measuring coping effectiveness: a panel analysis of marital problems and coping efforts. *J. Health Soc. Behav.* 23(3):220–34

Menninger K. 1963. *The Vital Balance: The Life Process in Mental Health and Illness*. New York: Viking

Monnier J, Hobfoll SE, Dunahoo CL, Hulsizer MR, Johnson R. 1998. There's more than rugged individualism in coping. Part 2: Construct validity and further model testing. *Anxiety, Stress, Coping: An Int. J.* 11(3):247–72

Moos RH. 1993. *Coping Responses Inventory*. Odessa, FL: Psychol. Assess. Resourc.

Moos RH, Tsu VD. 1977. The crisis of physical illness; an overview. In *Coping with Physical Illness*, ed. RH Moos, pp. 1–22. New York: Plenum

Moskowitz JT, Folkman S, Acree M. 2003. Do positive psychological states shed light on recovery from bereavement? Findings from a 3-year longitudinal study. *Death Stud.* 27:471–500

Moskowitz JT, Folkman S, Collette L, Vittinghoff E. 1996. Coping and mood during AIDS-related caregiving and bereavement. *Ann. Behav. Med.* 18(1):49–57

Moskowitz JT, Wrubel J. 2000. *Apples and oranges: using qualitative and quantitative approaches to coping assessment*. Presented at Am. Psychol. Soc., Miami, FL

Murphy LB, Moriarty AE. 1976. *Vulnerability, Coping and Growth*. New Haven, CT: Yale Univ. Press

Nolen-Hoeksema S. 2000. The role of rumination in depressive disorders and mixed anxiety/depressive symptoms. *J. Abnorm. Psychol.* 109(3):504–11

Nolen-Hoeksema S, Davis CG. 1999. "Thanks for sharing that": ruminators and their social support networks. *J. Personal. Soc. Psychol.* 77:801–14

Nolen-Hoeksema S, Larson J, Grayson C. 1999. Explaining the gender difference in depressive symptoms. *J. Personal. Soc. Psychol.* 77:1061–77

Ntoumanis M, Biddle SJH. 1998. The relationship of coping and its perceived effectiveness to positive and negative affect in sport. *Personal. Indiv. Differ.* 24:773–88

O'Brien TB, DeLongis A. 1997. Coping with chronic stress: an interpersonal perspective. See Gottlieb 1997, pp. 161–90

O'Leary VE, Ickovics JR. 1995. Resilience and thriving in response to challenge: an opportunity for a paradigm shift in women's health. *Women's Health* 1:121–42

Pargament KI. 1997. *The Psychology of Religion and Coping.* New York: Guilford

Pargament KI, Kennell J, Hathaway W, Grevengoed N, Newman J, Jones W. 1988. Religion and the problem-solving process: three styles of coping. *J. Sci. Study Relig.* 27(1):90–104

Pargament KI, Koenig HG, Perez LM. 2000. The many methods of religious coping: development and initial validation of the RCOPE. *J. Clin. Psychol.* 56(4):519–43

Pargament KI, Koenig HG, Tarakeshwar N, Hahn J. 2001. Religious struggle as predictor of mortality among medically ill elderly patients. *Arch. Intern. Med.* 161:1881–85

Pargament KI, Smith BW, Koenig HG, Perez L. 1998. Patterns of positive and negative religious coping with major life stressors. *J. Sci. Study Relig.* 37(4):710–24

Park CL, Cohen LH. 1993. Religious and nonreligious coping with the death of a friend. *Cogn. Ther. Res.* 17(6):561–77

Park CL, Cohen LH, Murch RL. 1996. Assessment and prediction of stress-related growth. *J. Personal.* 64(1):71–105

Park CL, Folkman S. 1997. Meaning in the context of stress and coping. *Rev. Gen. Psychol.* 1:115–44

Park CL, Folkman S, Bostrom A. 2001. Appraisals of controllability and coping in caregivers and HIV+ men: testing the goodness-of-fit hypothesis. *J. Consult. Clin. Psychol.* 69(3):481–88

Pearlin LI, Schooler C. 1978. The structure of coping. *J. Health Soc. Behav.* 9:3–21

Porter LS, Stone AA. 1996. An approach to assessing daily coping. See Zeidner & Endler 1996, pp. 133–50

Ptacek JT, Smith RE, Espe K, Raffety B. 1994. Limited correspondence between daily coping reports and retrospective coping recall. *Psychol. Assess.* 6:41–49

Richards JM, Gross JJ. 2000. Emotion regulation and memory: the cognitive costs of keeping one's cool. *J. Personal. Soc. Psychol.* 79:410–24

Schwartz CE, Daltroy LH. 1991. *Measuring coping flexibility: development of the Flex measure.* Presented at Annu. Meet. Soc. Behav. Med.. Washington, DC

Schwarzer R, Knoll N. 2003. Positive coping: mastering demands and searching for meaning. In *Comprehensive Handbook of Psychology*, Vol. 9, ed. AM Nezu, CM Nezu, PA Geller. New York: Wiley. In press

Schwarzer R, Schwarzer C. 1996. A critical survey of coping instruments. See Zeidner & Endler 1996, pp. 107–32

Seligman MEP, Csikszentmihalyi M. 2000. Positive psychology: an introduction. *Am. Psychol.* 55:5–14

Seybold KS, Hill PC. 2001. The role of religion and spirituality in mental and physical health. *Curr. Direct. Psychol. Sci.* 10(1):21–24

Silver R, Wortman CB. 1987. The role of positive emotions in the coping process. Unpublished manuscript. Univ. Waterloo, Waterloo, Ontario, Can.

Simon HA. 1967. Motivational and emotional controls of cognition. *Psychol. Rev.* 74:29–39

Smith BW, Pargament KI, Brant C, Oliver JM. 2000. Noah revisited: religious coping by church members and the impact of the 1993 Midwest flood. *J. Community Psychol. Spec. Iss.: Spiritual Relig. Community Psychol.* 28(2):169–86

Snyder CR, ed. 1999. *Coping: The Psychology of What Works.* New York: Oxford Univ. Press

Snyder CR, Lopez SJ, eds. 2002. *Handbook of Positive Psychology.* London: Oxford Univ. Press

Somerfield MR, McCrae RR. 2000. Stress and coping research: methodological challenges, theoretical advances, and clinical applications. *Am. Psychol.* 55(6):620–25

Stanton AL, Danoff-Burg S, Cameron CL, Ellis AP. 1994. Coping through emotional approach: problems of conceptualization and confounding. *J. Personal. Soc. Psychol.* 66: 350–62

Stanton AL, Danoff-Burg S, Cameron CL, Bishop M, Collins CA, et al. 2000. Emotionally expressive coping predicts psychological and physical adjustment to breast cancer. *J. Consult. Clin. Psychol.* 68(5):875–82

Stanton AL, Kirk SB, Cameron CL, Danoff-Burg S. 2000. Coping through emotional approach: scale construction and validation. *J. Personal. Soc. Psychol.* 78:1150–69

Stanton AL, Parsa A, Austenfeld JL. 2002. The adaptive potential of coping through emotional approach. See Snyder & Lopez 2002, pp. 148–58

Stein N, Folkman S, Trabasso T, Richards TA. 1997. Appraisal and goal processes as predictors of psychological well-being in bereaved caregivers. *J. Personal. Soc. Psychol.* 72:872–84

Stone AA, Kennedy-Moore E, Neale JM. 1995. Association between daily coping and end-of-day mood. *Health Psychol.* 14:341–49

Stone AA, Kennedy-Moore E, Newman MG, Greenberg M, Neale JM. 1992. Conceptual and methodological issues in current coping assessments. See Carpenter 1992, pp. 15–29

Stone AA, Neale JM. 1984. New measure of daily coping: development and preliminary results. *J. Personal. Soc. Psychol.* 46(4):892–906

Stone AA, Schwartz JE, Neale JM, Shiffman S, Marco CA, et al. 1998. A comparison of coping assessed by ecological momentary assessment and retrospective recall. *J. Personal. Soc. Psychol.* 74(6):1670–80

Stroebe MS, Schut H. 1999. The dual process model of coping with bereavement: rationale and description. *Death Stud.* 23:197–224

Stroebe MS, Schut H. 2001. Meaning making in the dual process model of coping with bereavement. In *Meaning Reconstruction, the Experience of Loss*, ed. RA Neimeyer, pp. 55–73. Washington, DC: Am. Psychol. Assoc.

Tedeschi RG, Park CL, Calhoun LG, eds. 1998. *Posttraumatic Growth: Positive Changes in the Aftermath of Crisis.* Mahwah, NJ: Erlbaum

Tennen H, Affleck G. 1999. Finding benefits in adversity. See Snyder 1999, pp. 279–304

Tennen H, Affleck G. 2002. Benefit-finding and benefit-reminding. See Snyder & Lopez 2002, pp. 584–97

Tennen H, Affleck G, Armeli S, Carney MA. 2000. A daily process approach to coping: linking theory research and practice. *Am. Psychol.* 55(6):626–36

Terry DJ, Hynes GJ. 1998. Adjustment to a low-control situation: reexamining the role of coping responses. *J. Personal. Soc. Psychol.* 74(4):1078–92

Vaillant GE. 1977. *Adaption to Life.* Boston, MA: Little, Brown

Vaillant GE. 2000. Adaptive mental mechanisms: their role in a positive psychology. *Am. Psychol.* 55:89–98

Viney LL, Henry R, Walker BM, Crooks L. 1989. The emotional reactions of HIV antibody positive men. *Br. J. Med. Psychol.* 62(2):153–61

Wells JD, Hobfoll SE, Lavin J. 1997. Resource loss, resource gain, and communal coping during pregnancy among women with multiple roles. *Psychol. Women Q.* 21(4):645–62

Westbrook MT, Viney LL. 1982. Psychological reactions to the onset of chronic illness. *Soc. Sci. Med.* 16:899–905

Wortman CB. 1987. Coping with irrevocable loss. In *Cataclysms, Crises and Catastrophes: Psychology in Action*, ed. GR Van den Bos, BK Bryant, pp. 189–235. Washington, DC: Am. Psychol. Assoc.

Wu A, Folkman S, McPhee S, Lo B. 1993. Do house officers learn from their mistakes? *JAMA* 265:2089–94

Zautra AJ, Sheets VL, Sandler IN. 1996. An examination of the construct validity of coping dispositions for a sample of recently divorced mothers. *Psychol. Assess.* 8:256–64

Zeidner M, Endler NS. 1996. *Handbook of Coping.* New York: Wiley

Zeidner M, Saklofske D. 1996. Adaptive and maladaptive coping. See Zeidner & Endler 1996, pp. 505–31

Zinnbauer BJ, Pargament KI, Cole B, Rye MS, Butter EM, et al. 1997. Religion and spirituality: unfuzzying the fuzzy. *J. Sci. Study Relig.* 36(4):549–64

Annu. Rev. Psychol. 2004. 55:775–801
doi: 10.1146/annurev.psych.55.090902.142040
Copyright © 2004 by Annual Reviews. All rights reserved
First published online as a Review in Advance on July 11, 2003

Survey Research and Societal Change

Roger Tourangeau

Joint Program in Survey Methodology, University of Maryland, and Survey Research Center, University of Michigan, College Park, Maryland 20742;
email: RTourang@survey.umd.edu

Key Words   response rates, modes of data collection, telephone sampling, Web surveys

■ **Abstract**   Surveys reflect societal change in a way that few other research tools do. Over the past two decades, three developments have transformed surveys. First, survey organizations have adopted new methods for selecting telephone samples; these new methods were made possible by the creation of large databases that include all listed telephone numbers in the United States. A second development has been the widespread decline in response rates for all types of surveys. In the face of this problem, survey researchers have developed new theories of nonresponse that build on the persuasion literature in social psychology. Finally, surveys have adopted many new methods of data collection; the new modes reflect technological developments in computing and the emergence of the Internet. Research has spawned several theories that examine how characteristics of the data collection method shape the answers obtained. Rapid change in survey methods is likely to continue in the coming years.

CONTENTS

0066-4308/04/0204-0775$14.00   **775**

INTRODUCTION

Perhaps no other research tool used by social scientists is as sensitive to social and technological change as the sample survey. Surveys are themselves part of the fabric of contemporary life—survey research is a multibillion dollar industry in the United States, surveys provide critical information to decision-makers in government and business, and polls and their results are widely discussed by the general public (which often seems to overstate and resent their influence)—but surveys rest on a delicate and complicated relationship between those who conduct surveys and those who take part in them. Virtually all surveys in the United States are voluntary (with some notable exceptions, such as the census of the population conducted every 10 years and the American Community Survey done continuously by the Bureau of the Census), and long-term trends in the social climate (such as changes in the level of civic engagement) can affect how successful surveys are in reaching potential respondents and in persuading them to take part. Because of the size, complexity, and expense of major surveys, which can involve tens of thousands of participants and exceed $100 million in cost, they almost inevitably come to reflect social and technological changes.

In fact, survey practice is a kind of bellwether of social and technological change. For example, the widespread diffusion of telephones throughout American society led to the widespread adoption of telephone interviewing by survey organizations in the 1960s and 1970s; similarly, the development of desktop and laptop computing led directly to the development of computer-assisted telephone interviewing (CATI) and computer-assisted personal interviewing (CAPI), respectively. In CATI and CAPI surveys, each question appears on the screen of the interviewer's computer and the interviewer directly keys in the answer. CATI became popular in the mid 1970s and, with the advent of lightweight laptops, CAPI caught on in the 1980s and 1990s. Virtually all major federal surveys now use some form of computer-assisted data collection (see Couper & Nicholls 1998 for an excellent summary of these developments). Advances in computing and telephone technology have led to such advances in survey methods as e-mail, Web, and interactive voice response (IVR) surveys, in which a computer plays recorded questions over the telephone.

Survey methodology is affected by subtler societal shifts as well. For example, Singer and her colleagues (Singer 2003, Singer et al. 1993) have documented changes in public attitudes toward privacy and confidentiality—views about whether surveys are an invasion of privacy and whether federal agencies pool data among themselves or share them with other organizations—and demonstrated their impact on willingness to take part in the decennial census. Most survey researchers see the rise of telemarketing, along with the various countermeasures people now take to screen out telemarketers and other unwanted callers, as an important factor contributing to the decline in survey response rates over the last decade. Concerns about crime may have contributed to shifts in residential patterns, including the rise of gated communities, which make it much harder for survey organizations to carry out face-to-face interviewing. According to one estimate, more than eight million Americans now live in gated communities and nearly 40% of newly built residential developments are gated (Blakely & Snyder 1997). Add to this the growing number of people living in locked urban apartment buildings, assisted-living communities, or other settings that shield residents from unwanted visitors, and it's apparent that it's a lot harder to reach potential respondents than it used to be.

These long-term societal trends are reflected in many ways in surveys. One consequence that we'll examine in detail is the general decline in survey response rates, the proportion of eligible persons selected for survey samples who end up providing data. With some federal surveys in the United States, the problem of rising nonresponse rates is somewhat masked because the interviewers make an increased number of callbacks and, as a result, contact almost every sample case. Even in these surveys, though, the refusal rates (the proportion of respondents who refuse to take part among those that are contacted) are rising (Atrostic et al. 2001). In addition, the number of contact attempts needed to reach potential respondents is increasing, and as a result, survey costs are rising. Any cost savings that can be traced to the computerization of surveys has either been negligible (as some have argued) or swamped by other sources of increased cost, such as rapid rises in data collection costs. The double bind of higher costs and lower response rates has fueled new theories to deepen our understanding of nonresponse and its implications for the accuracy of survey estimates. In addition, survey statisticians have developed new, more cost-efficient methods of selecting samples for telephone surveys.

This review focuses on three recent developments in survey methodology—new methods for telephone sampling, new theories about the sources and consequences of nonresponse, and new modes of data collection. All three developments have had major impact on surveys, all have occurred within the last 15 years or so, and all of them reflect much broader movements within American society. This review thus updates Groves's *Annual Reviews* chapter on telephone surveys (1990) and Dillman's on mail surveys (1991). It has a somewhat different focus from two other recent *Annual Reviews* chapters related to survey research, both of which focus on questionnaire design and other measurement issues (Krosnick 1999, Presser & Schaeffer 2003).

METHODS OF TELEPHONE SAMPLING

Telephone surveys became a relatively popular method of data collection once most of the U.S. population could be reached by telephone. As late as 1963, some 20% of U.S. households still did not have telephones (Thornberry & Massey 1988); currently, about 96% of American households have a telephone. (A basic social unit for survey researchers is the household, a group of people who share the same residence. Households may include just one person, a family, or a set of unrelated individuals.) Another key requirement for the widespread adoption of telephone interviewing was a reasonably efficient method for selecting telephone samples. This problem is more difficult than it may seem at first blush and wasn't completely solved until 1978, when a former Census Bureau statistician, Joseph Waksberg, documented the statistical properties of a method of sampling that was soon adopted throughout the industry (Waksberg 1978). The method Waksberg explored had been previously proposed by Warren Mitofsky, a statistician working at CBS, and the technique they developed is generally referred to as the Mitofsky-Waksberg method.

The Mitofsky-Waksberg Method

Telephone samplers face two related problems. On the one hand, a high percentage of all residential telephone numbers (currently about 30%) are unlisted; thus, sampling from telephone directories can produce samples that do not accurately represent the telephone population, let alone the entire household population. (In the jargon of survey research, such samples are said to suffer from *undercoverage*.) The exclusion of unlisted numbers from telephone samples might not be such a serious problem, but those with unlisted telephone numbers differ systematically from those with listed numbers. To cite one surprising difference, they tend to have lower incomes than households with listed numbers (American Statistical Association 1999). As a result, statistics from telephone surveys would be seriously biased if unlisted numbers were omitted from the samples. This potential for large biases means that directory samples are unacceptable for most federal and academic surveys. On the other hand, most of the possible numbers that can be generated from a list of active area codes and three-digit prefixes (or exchanges) are not, in fact, residential telephone numbers. Only about one quarter of the possible numbers formed by adding random endings to active area code/prefix combinations yield working residential numbers. This method of sampling, known as full random-digit dialing (full RDD), includes both listed and unlisted numbers, but it's quite inefficient. Fully three fourths of the sample numbers will never yield interviews, even after repeated callbacks, because they are not working residential numbers (WRNs). Not all unassigned numbers can be readily distinguished from working numbers; when dialed, the number simply rings. Thus, the presence of these hard-to-identify nonworking numbers can markedly drive up the cost of conducting telephone surveys.

The Mitofsky-Waksberg method takes advantage of the fact that telephone companies tend to hand out telephone numbers in sequence rather than randomly. As a result, once a number is found to be a WRN, nearby numbers are likely to be WRNs, too. The Mitofsky-Waksberg method starts with a full RDD sample of primary numbers. A randomly generated four-digit suffix is added to an active area code/prefix combination. (For example, the number 3198 would be appended to the 301 314 combination, yielding a 10-digit number that is potentially a working telephone number.) When a primary number turns out to be a WRN, additional numbers are generated from the same "100-bank." A 100-bank consists of all the potential telephone numbers that share their first eight digits (e.g., the numbers from 301 314-3100 to 301 314-3199 make up one bank). Roughly 65% of these secondary numbers turn out to be WRNs. Thus, the Mitofsky-Waksberg method represented a big improvement in efficiency over full RDD; depending on the number of secondary selections per working primary number, the overall proportion of WRNs in the sample can more than double to 50% or better.

Waksberg showed that this two-stage method of selecting phone numbers yielded an equal-probability sample of all WRNs (not just the listed ones) and had other desirable statistical properties as well. Consider the sampling probabilities. Waksberg showed that the probability that any given WRN (the jth WRN from bank i) falls into the sample depends on the number of primary numbers selected (a), the number of WRNs in that 100-banks (M_i), and the number of secondary numbers that are selected from each bank:

$$\Pr(WRN_{ij}) = \frac{a}{A} \frac{M_i}{100} \frac{k}{M_i}$$

$$= \frac{ak}{100A}.$$

The first term (a/A) is the probability of selecting a bank, the second is the probability that that bank will be retained in the sample (that is, it is the probability that a randomly generated primary number from the bank will be a WRN), and the final term is the fraction of the WRNs from the bank that are selected into the sample, given that the bank was retained. (A total of k WRNs is selected from each bank, including the primary number and $k - 1$ secondary numbers.)

Despite its elegant theoretical properties, the Mitofsky-Waksberg method has its operational difficulties. For instance, it is not always obvious whether a primary number is a WRN or not; in addition, the design may require more selections from a bank than it has WRNs (that is, k may be greater than M_i). As a result, researchers have continued to search for better methods to select telephone samples.

List-Assisted Telephone Sampling

A breakthrough occurred in 1993, when Casady & Lepkowski published an important paper on what are now called list-assisted designs (Casady & Lepkowski 1993; see also Lepkowski 1988). By the 1990s, it was possible to scan in (and deduplicate) information from all the telephone directories in the United States. Using the resulting database, one could determine whether any 100-bank of possible phone numbers included any residential listings. The Mitofsky-Waksberg method works in part because it screens out empty banks—banks with no WRNs at all. (These empty banks will always be associated with primary numbers that turn out not to be WRNs.) Casady and Lepkowski examined the designs possible when banks are classified at the outset according to the number of residential listings they contain. In particular, they examined a design in which banks are stratified into two groups—those with at least one residential listing and those with no residential listings ("zero banks"). Some banks with no residential listings contain residential numbers that either are not yet listed or are unlisted, but the "hit rate" is quite low in the zero banks. In fact, Brick et al. (1995) estimate that only 1.4% of the numbers in zero banks are WRNs. This implies that roughly 70 numbers have to be generated and dialed to find a single WRN. Clearly, the costs per completed case are going to be considerably higher in the stratum consisting of the zero banks than in the other stratum, where more than 50% of the numbers are WRNs.

The problem of how to distribute sample cases across strata with varying costs per case is a classical sampling problem, and Casady & Lepkowski (1993) worked out the optimal solution for sampling from zero and nonzero banks. Under most reasonable assumptions, only a small percentage of the completed cases will come from the zero banks. As a result, excluding the zero banks entirely would have little impact on the statistics from the survey. In addition, according to Brick and his colleagues (Brick et al. 1995), only about 3.5% of all telephone households are in zero banks. Moreover, the households in this stratum don't differ much from households associated with banks with one or more residential listings, with one exception—households in zero banks are more likely to have moved recently. (The zero banks with WRNs may often be newly opened banks with residential numbers that have been assigned recently. Thus, they would overrepresent recent movers who are receiving previously unassigned phone numbers.) Based on the theoretical results presented by Casady and Lepkowski and the empirical results of Brick and his colleagues, most survey researchers have switched from the Mitofsky-Waksberg method of telephone sampling to the "truncated" design, in which all of the selections come from banks of telephone numbers with at least one residential listing. From a statistical vantage point, the truncated design had the additional advantage that it yields a simple random sample of WRNs, whereas the two-stage Waksberg-Mitofsky design clustered the sample in banks. This clustering reduces the precision of the estimates from the survey. The adoption of the list-assisted design was doubtless hastened by the fact that Waksberg was himself a coauthor on one of the key papers and seemed to be giving his blessing to the new method.

List-assisted telephone sampling was made possible by technological changes that permitted commercial firms to create and manipulate giant databases—in this case, databases containing information on some 75 million U.S. households. Theoretical and empirical results demonstrated that the method was quite efficient and could be made even more efficient if the sampling process simply ignored numbers in the zero banks. Of course, the minimal bias associated with the omission of the zero banks is itself the outcome of a social process, one that could change in the coming years.

These developments might have ushered in a golden age for telephone surveys if it weren't for two offsetting trends. First, telephone surveys' coverage of the U.S. household population may have peaked. By 1980, 93% of U.S. households had a telephone (Thornberry & Massey 1988) and the percentage has crept up only slightly since then to the current level of about 96%. The trend now may be downward, with a small but growing proportion of the U.S. population having cellular telephone service only. Although in principle these cell-only subscribers could be included in telephone samples, as long as the recipient of a call on a cell phone incurs charges for the call, it is unlikely in practice that cell-only households will be represented in telephone surveys. The rapidly increasing popularity of cell phones in the United States—currently, there are about 40 cell phones per 100 persons in the United States (International Telecommunications Union 2001)—thus represents a long-term threat to the representativeness of telephone survey samples. This is already a problem in several European countries, where the proportion of cell-only households exceeds that of the United States. A more immediate threat comes from a second set of developments—the array of technologies now available to help people screen out unwanted calls. By 1995, the majority of U.S. households had answering machines and roughly 40% reported they used them to screen their calls (Tuckel & O'Neill 1995; see also Oldendick & Link 1994, who report the results from a study of South Carolina residents). There is little doubt that both of these proportions are rising. Although answering machines are the most popular technology for call screening, caller ID and call blocking are becoming more widespread as well (Link & Oldendick 1999, Tuckel & O'Neill 1996). By 1996, about 10% of all households nationally had caller ID. The use of these various devices to fend off unwanted calls is widely seen as contributing to the falling response rates afflicting surveys in the United States and throughout the Western world; these trends in response rates are the next topic we take up.

DECLINING RESPONSE RATES

The challenge presented by falling response rates is perhaps the greatest threat survey researchers have faced in the past 10 years, and an entire conference was devoted to the topic in 1999 (Groves et al. 2002). The threat posed by falling response rates has provoked two main responses among survey researchers. One approach has been to explore the reasons for nonresponse more deeply than before, partly with a view toward developing new methods for boosting response rates; the other approach has been to examine the consequences of nonresponse. Survey researchers have also tried to bridge these two approaches by developing better theories linking the causes of nonresponse to their likely impact on survey statistics.

Causes of Nonresponse

Traditionally, survey researchers have distinguished among various types of nonresponse. For example, in a panel survey (in which attempts are made to interview respondents multiple times), some respondents may move and the researchers may be unable to track them to their new location; other respondents may tire of participating and drop out. Groves & Couper (1998) argue that it is generally useful to distinguish among three main forms of nonresponse—nonresponse due to noncontact, nonresponse due to the refusal to cooperate, and nonresponse due to inability to participate (e.g., inability to complete an interview in English). The trends in response rates seem to reflect increasing difficulty on all three fronts.

Consider first the mounting difficulties of contacting potential respondents. As we have already noted, for telephone surveys, caller ID, call blocking, and answering machines have created formidable and widespread barriers to contact (Link & Oldendick 1999; Oldendick & Link 1994; Tuckel & O'Neill 1995, 1996). These technologies have caught on quickly—the majority of American households now have answering machines, caller ID, or both, and substantial numbers of households use them to screen out unwanted calls. Many survey professionals report anecdotally that telephone response rates have plummeted over the last decade or so. Although the published evidence for this dramatic downturn is not so clear, Steeh and her colleagues (Steeh et al. 2001) show that it takes an increasing number of attempts to reach households selected for the University of Michigan's Survey of Consumer Attitudes (SCA) and the Georgia State Poll. The average number of call attempts per interview for the SCA peaked at approximately 12 in 1999, the last year Steeh and her colleagues examined; in the mid 1990s, the figure was close to six calls. Similarly, although the evidence is largely anecdotal, many survey researchers believe it is also much more difficult than it used to be to contact potential respondents in face-to-face surveys; as noted above, far more people now live in gated communities, institutions, locked apartment buildings, or other settings that shield residents from unwanted visitors than lived in such settings 10 or 15 years ago. Other long-term social trends, including greater participation by women in the labor force and the rise of single-person households, have also contributed to the increased difficulty in reaching people at home.

The second major form of nonresponse is refusal to take part in the survey. Steeh and her coworkers (2001) argue that any recent fall in telephone response rates probably reflects greater difficulty in contacting telephone households rather than higher rates of refusal to participate, but the opposite seems to be the case for face-to-face surveys. Nonresponse due to refusal to take part in surveys seems to be rising for household surveys all over the developed world (Groves & Couper 1998, de Leeuw & de Heer 2002). With some federal surveys in the United States, which place a premium on high response rates, the problem of rising nonresponse rates is somewhat obscured because the interviewers try harder, making more callbacks and taking other measures to maintain response rates. Even in these surveys, though, the refusal rates appear to be rising (see, for example, Atrostic et al. 2001), driving up the overall nonresponse rates. Figure 1 displays the overall nonresponse rates and refusal rates for two major federal surveys—the Consumer Expenditure Survey (CES) and the National Health Interview Survey (NHIS). Both showing increasing overall nonresponse rates and, in both cases, the overall increase mainly reflects a rise in the rate of refusals. The NHIS data also suggest that noncontact may be increasing in that survey.

Researchers have cited many possible causes for this increased reluctance to take part in surveys, including the decline in the level of civic engagement (Putnam 1995; see also Groves et al. 2000), reduced amounts of free time (although see Robinson & Godbey 1997, who argue that Americans actually have more free time

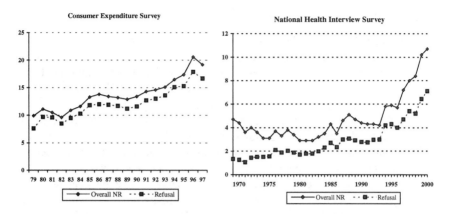

Figure 1   The overall nonresponse and refusal rates for the Consumer Expenditure Survey (*left*) and the National Health Interview Survey (*right*). Adapted from Groves & Couper 1998.

than they used to), increased concern about privacy and confidentiality (Singer et al. 1993), rising hostility toward telemarketers, and even the possibility of identity theft. Whatever the reason for the change, refusal rates definitely seem to be rising for household surveys.

Long-term shifts in the demographic makeup of the U.S. population— specifically, the rising percentage of foreign-born and elderly Americans—are the basis for additional concerns about survey nonresponse. These concerns focus on the final form of nonresponse distinguished by Groves & Couper (1998), sample persons who are unable to provide data. In 2002, 11.5% of the U.S. population was foreign-born; according to Long Form data from Census 2000, 8.1% of the population over age five reported that they speak English less than "very well." Many surveys now field both Spanish and English questionnaires, but only two thirds of those who are less than completely fluent in English are Spanish speakers. Similarly, the rising proportion of the population over 65 years of age suggests that an increasing percentage of sample persons will be unable to complete interviews because they have hearing problems or other physical infirmities that prevent them from participating. Surveys are likely to rely more on "proxy" reporters to provide information that sampled persons are unable to provide for themselves.

Rising rates of nonresponse reflect mounting difficulties in reaching people, persuading them to take part, and making it possible for them to complete an interview. The problem affects both telephone and in-person surveys, but it's probably worse for telephone surveys—currently, very few telephone surveys achieve response rates higher than 60% (whereas some face-to-face surveys still achieve 90% response rates). For longitudinal surveys, panel attrition—losses due to nonresponse in the second or later waves of the survey—compound the effects of nonresponse in the first wave, especially in surveys that make no attempt to include initial nonrespondents in later rounds.

Maintaining Response Rates

Survey efforts to maintain response rates have centered on methods to improve rates of contacting sample households and to lower rates of refusal. It has been known for quite some time that the key to making contact is repeated callbacks. This is true for mail (Heberlein & Baumgartner 1978, Dillman 1991), telephone (Weeks et al. 1980, 1987), and face-to-face surveys (RM Groves, DA Wissoker, L Greene, ME McNeeley, DA Montemarano, unpublished manuscript, 2001). At some level, the process of making contact with sample households is quite simple— it's just matter of overcoming barriers to access and reaching the household when someone's home. The determinants of when and how often people are at home may be complicated, but there's not much survey researchers can do about those dynamics and their efforts have focused on finding more efficient call-scheduling algorithms (e.g., Weeks et al. 1980, 1987) or on overcoming barriers to access (e.g., by leaving messages on answering machines; Tuckel & Schulman 2000, Xu et al. 1993). Given enough time and effort, it is possible to reach nearly everyone in the sample, but this can be costly and will be difficult to sustain in the long run.

And once survey interviewers reach people, they may still find it difficult to persuade them to take part. Perhaps the most common method that surveys have used to counter stiffening resistance to participation has been to offer incentives. In mail surveys, a small payment (e.g., $2) sent with the questionnaire is often an effective means of boosting response rates (Church 1993, Fox et al. 1988, Yu & Cooper 1983). Church's (1993) meta-analysis comes to three main conclusions about incentives in mail surveys: (*a*) Prepaid incentives are more effective for increasing response rates than incentives that are contingent on completion of the questionnaire; (*b*) monetary incentives are more effective than nonmonetary gifts; and (*c*) bigger incentives are more effective than smaller ones (although a large incentive can have diminished impact relative to smaller ones if it seems suspiciously large; James & Bolstein 1992). Church finds an average increase in response rates of 19 percentage points in mail surveys that provide monetary incentives up front. These three same generalizations about the timing, form, and amount of incentives seem to hold for telephone and face-to-face surveys as well, according to a recent meta-analysis by Singer and her colleagues (Singer et al. 1999). Overall, though, incentives appear to have less impact in telephone and face-to-face surveys than in mail surveys, with "lower percentage point gains per dollar expended" (Singer 2002, p. 165). Although most surveys offer respondents cash or checks, survey researchers have examined a variety of methods for providing incentives, including entering the names of survey participants in sweepstakes for relatively large monetary amounts or making charitable donations in their name. The track record of these alternative payment vehicles is mixed at best (Singer 2002, Warriner et al. 1996).

There are three main theories about how incentives work in surveys. The first is that incentives create a sense of obligation on the part of sample members, perhaps by triggering the norm of reciprocity or by inducing sample members to view the request as part of a larger social exchange between themselves and the institutions that sponsor and carry out surveys (Dillman 1978, Goyder 1987). This first set of theories may help explain why small, prepaid incentives are so effective. Still, when surveys are long or impose especially onerous demands on respondents (such as the need to provide biological specimens), much larger incentives are common, and respondents probably see the incentives in economic terms, as compensation for their time and trouble. This view might be labeled the economic theory of incentives. The final theory suggests that incentives provide a reason for participating in the survey among those who would not otherwise have a motive to take part (Groves et al. 2000); they may lack sufficient interest in the survey topic, liking for the interviewer, or feeling of civic duty to take part, but the money gives them a reason to complete the survey. The main empirical consequence of this final theory is that incentives will have the largest impact within subgroups of the population that would ordinarily be least likely to cooperate.

The other major approach to improving response rates has focused on the interviewer's approach to sample members, including the messages they leave on answering machines in telephone surveys. The findings suggest that scripted messages and introductions have relatively little effect on cooperation (Baumgartner 1990, Daves 1990, Tuckel & Schulman 2000, Xu et al. 1993), although Xu and colleagues did find that leaving a message improved the chances of making contact with sample households. By contrast, customizing the introductions to the concerns or interests of the sample person does seem to improve cooperation (Dillman et al. 1976, Groves & McGonagle 2001, Morton-Williams 1993).

Consequences of Nonresponse

Survey statisticians assess the impact of nonresponse in terms of its effects on the variance and bias of estimates derived from survey data. The impact of nonresponse on the variance mainly reflects the reduced sample sizes that result from nonresponse. For means and proportions, the impact of nonresponse on the bias depends on both the nonresponse rate and the difference between respondents and nonrespondents:

$$Bias = E(p_n)(\bar{Y}_r - \bar{Y}_n) \tag{1}$$

in which $E(p_n)$ is the expected nonresponse rate, $\bar{Y}_r$ is the mean for the respondents, and $\bar{Y}_n$, the mean for the nonrespondents. (Like other survey statistics, the nonresponse rate is subject to sampling error and fluctuates from sample to sample.) For example, imagine a political poll trying to predict the proportion of voters supporting a particular candidate. If the proportion is the same among respondents and nonrespondents, then the bias will be zero; in such cases, nonresponse is effectively just another stage of random sampling.

Equation 1 assumes that nonresponse is deterministic—that is, given a fixed survey design, everyone in the target population will either always be a respondent or always be a nonrespondent. Lessler & Kalsbeek (1992) give a more general expression for the bias in a mean or proportion, based on the more realistic assumption that nonresponse may be probabilistic:

$$Bias = Cov(r_i, Y_i) - E(p_n)\bar{Y}. \tag{2}$$

Equation 2 shows that the bias mainly reflects the covariance between the probability of becoming a respondent (r_i) and the values of the substantive variable of interest (Y_i); the final term is the product of the overall mean $(\bar{Y})$ and the expected nonresponse rate. The bias formulas are more complicated for analytic statistics like subgroup differences or regression coefficients.

Equations 1 and 2 imply that when there is no relation between the phenomenon of interest (say, political attitudes) and the probability of becoming a respondent in the survey—that is, no difference between the respondents and nonrespondents on the variables of interest—there won't be any bias in the survey estimates.

Three recent studies, one with a randomized experimental design, show that this condition may often be met in surveys. All three studies demonstrate little or no relationship between nonresponse rates and nonresponse bias (Curtin et al. 2000, Keeter et al. 2000, Merkle & Edelman 2002). Although each of these studies has its limitations, taken together they present a strong case that larger nonresponse rates don't necessarily signal larger biases. The study by Keeter and his colleagues used a randomized experiment that varied the length of the field period and the number of callbacks in a telephone survey; the two experimental groups differed markedly in response rates (60.6% versus 36.0%), but only 14 of the 91 variables they examined showed significant substantive differences and most of these were quite small. Merkle & Edelman (2002) tracked response rates and overall error in exit polls at sample precincts across four elections. The results indicate virtually no correlation between the two. They argue that the factors that produce nonresponse in exit polls (e.g., whether local election officials allow interviewers to stand near the entrance to the polling place) are completely unrelated to the variable of interest, vote choice. Curtin and his colleagues (2000) looked at the Index of Consumer Sentiment from the Survey of Consumer Attitudes. Using detailed call records data, they were able to simulate the impact of ending efforts to interview sample cases after, say, 5 or 10 callbacks. Again, there were small effects from these large (simulated) changes in the data collection protocol.

These results do not indicate that nonresponse is never a problem, but they do suggest that when the variables of interest are unrelated to the factors that produce nonresponse (as in the exit polls), falling response rates may not be a major worry. Still, it is an article of faith among survey researchers that high response rates are better than low ones, and there is widespread concern that at some point survey results will be rendered wildly inaccurate because of mounting nonresponse. After all, the *Literary Digest* polls that were based on large but unrepresentative samples did just fine in predicting the outcomes of the presidential elections from 1916 through 1932. It wasn't until 1936 (when the *Literary Digest* predicted that Landon would defeat Roosevelt with 57 percent of the vote) that its flaws became spectacularly apparent. The continuing concern that nonresponse will introduce similar errors into contemporary surveys has motivated theoretical and empirical efforts to determine when nonresponse will seriously bias survey estimates.

Theories of Nonresponse

Robert Groves and his colleagues have been leaders in this effort. Groves & Couper (1998), for example, focus on the process by which sample persons decide whether to take part in face-to-face surveys. These decisions are made quite quickly in the brief encounters during which interviewers attempt to persuade the members of the sample to complete an interview; sample persons process the interviewer's presentation of the survey request using the same heuristics they apply to other persuasive messages on not particularly involving topics (Chaiken 1980, Cialdini 1984, Petty & Cacioppo 1984). Successful interviewers tend to avert a refusal long enough to learn something about the concerns of the sample member and to tailor their presentation of the survey to address those concerns. They highlight whatever features of the survey (its topic or sponsorship) are likely to appeal to the sample person or they explicitly counter any sources of reluctance to participate. According to Groves and Couper, maintaining the interaction and crafting tailored appeals are crucial skills for interviews, skills that can be trained (Groves & McGonagle 2001).

Groves et al. (2000) present a more detailed theory of survey participation, the "leverage-salience theory." According to this theory, different persons assign different values to the different features of the survey highlighted in the survey request (e.g., the topic of the survey, its sponsorship, what the data will be used for, how long the interview might take). Some sample persons may positively value a particular attribute of the survey; others may value the same attribute negatively. These values are the "leverages" of the survey's features for a given person. When the survey is presented to sample members, one of more of its attributes is made salient to them either during the interaction with an interviewer or in the advance letter sent to sample members ahead of time. These momentary saliences determine which attributes persons consider in deciding whether to cooperate; the characteristics of the sample persons help determine the values they place on the salient attributes. Depending on which features of the survey are made salient to them and how they value these features, the sample person may yield to or resist the request to take part.

In an experiment, Groves et al. (2000) examined one feature of the survey request (whether an incentive was offered) and one characteristic of the sample persons (their level of civic engagement) and found the predicted interaction between the two. Among those high on civic engagement, the inherent features of the survey were enough to produce a high level of cooperation and the incentive had little further impact. By contrast, among those with low levels of civic engagement, cooperation was quite low unless a monetary incentive was offered.

NEW MODES OF DATA COLLECTION

Perhaps the most striking change in survey research over the last 25 years or so has been the increasing use of computer-assisted methods for collecting survey data. Traditionally, surveys have relied on three main methods of data collection—face-to-face interviews (in which interviewers contact the respondents in person, typically at their homes, read them the questions, and record their answers), telephone interviews (in which interviewers contact respondents by telephone, read the questions to them, and record their answers), and mail surveys (in which the survey researchers mail a paper questionnaire to the respondents, who fill it out it and return it by mail). Each of these methods has been revolutionized by the widespread adoption of computer technologies.

The traditional modes of data collection in fact consist of packages of features, which can on occasion be uncoupled. For example, the traditional mail survey usually involved the selection of the sample from a list (e.g., of the employees at a company), delivery of the questionnaire and other survey materials by mail, use of a paper questionnaire, and follow-up with nonrespondents via further mailings (Dillman 1978, 1991). But this bundling of features isn't necessary. Some survey organizations have had interviewers deliver paper questionnaires in person for the respondents to complete and return to the interviewer (e.g., Aquilino 1994). This combination of features tended to achieve the high response rates associated with face-to-face interviewing and the increased levels of reporting of sensitive information associated with self-administered questionnaires. Another variation involves mailing electronic questionnaires to the respondents on diskettes, a method referred to as disk-by-mail. This permits the programming of complicated "skip patterns" that allow respondents to navigate easily through complex questionnaires; most self-administered paper questionnaires avoid complex skip instructions ("If yes, go to Section D") because respondents often have trouble following them (Redline & Dillman 2002). Many surveys, including the decennial census, also use mixed mode strategies; Census 2000 started with a mail questionnaire in most areas, with in-person follow-up visits for those who didn't mail back their completed census forms in time.

The arrival of a variety of computer-assisted methods for collecting survey data has not only transformed the traditional trio of face-to-face, telephone, and mail surveys but has also created a number of hybrid modes. We focus here on the three methods that are gradually supplanting the traditional methods.

First Phase of the Computer Revolution

The switch from traditional paper questionnaires to computer-assisted methods took place in two phases. The computer-assisted methods introduced during the first phase represented only a modest change from the traditional paper-based methods. For example, computer-assisted telephone interviewing (CATI) was first introduced at Chilton Research Services in 1971 and gradually displaced paper-and-pencil telephone interviews during the 1970s (Fink 1983), but most survey respondents were probably unaware of the change. Instead of reading the questions and recording the answers on a paper questionnaire, interviewers read the questions from a computer screen and entered the answers electronically; once computers got fast enough, there was no reason the respondents would have noticed any difference. And the scientific evaluations of the switch from paper telephone interviews to CATI suggest that the impact of this phase of the computer revolution on telephone surveys was modest at best. Experimental comparisons of the two methods found small gains in survey cost, timeliness, and data quality from computerization (Bergman et al. 1994, Catlin & Ingram 1988, Groves & Mathiowetz 1984). The data quality improvements from CATI mostly take the form of lower rates of missing data (because computers are less prone to inadvertently skipping items than interviewers are). In addition, it was now possible to administer more complicated questionnaires via telephone than before because the computer can follow complex routing instructions more readily than unassisted interviewers can.

Once personal computers became light enough (and their batteries would permit a long enough period of operation without needing to be charged), a parallel shift occurred in face-to-face surveys—computer-assisted personal interviewing (CAPI) began displacing paper-and-pencil interviewing beginning in the late 1980s and throughout the 1990s. Although this change may have been more apparent to the respondents—they could see the interviewer's laptop—the switch from paper to CAPI didn't seem to have much more of an effect on costs, response rates, the composition of the samples, or the answers the respondents gave than the switch to CATI had (Baker et al. 1995, Martin et al. 1993, Tourangeau et al. 1997).

Mail surveys were the least affected by this first wave of technological change. Some large mail surveys, including the decennial census, adopted optical character recognition and other advanced technologies for scanning the data in (Blom & Lyberg 1998). Occasionally, surveys sent electronic rather than paper questionnaires either on a diskette via regular mail (Downes-Le Guin & Soo Hoo 1994, Olson & Schneiderman 1995) or via e-mail (Couper et al. 1999, Kiesler & Sproull 1986, Saris & Pijper 1986, Schaefer & Dillman 1998). For the most part, though, mail surveys were (and are) still done on paper.

The second phase of the computerization of the data collection process brought about a more revolutionary change—a move away from interviewer administration and toward direct administration of the questions by the computer. This change has had a larger impact on the costs and results of the surveys.

Face-to-Face Interviewing

Face-to-face surveys have had several major advantages over other modes of data collection. They generally achieve higher response rates than telephone or mail surveys; they can incorporate a variety of response aids (such as calendars that help delimit the time period the questions cover or "show cards" that list the answer options for a question) that would be difficult or impossible to use in other modes; unlike mail surveys, they don't require the respondents to be able to read; and, of course, they feature an interviewer who is on hand to assist the respondents, for example, by answering their questions (though, in many cases, interviewers are trained to give neutral but uninformative answers to respondent queries).

The big drawback to face-to-face interviews is the interviewer. One problem is sheer variability across interviewers, which can be a major source of error in surveys (Groves 1989, chapter 8). In addition, a large body of evidence suggests that respondents may be reluctant to disclose sensitive information to an interviewer. Several important national studies collect information on illicit drug use, risky sexual behaviors, and other potentially embarrassing topics, and respondents' reluctance to be truthful about such subjects in face-to-face interviews is a clear limitation of this method of data collection. This problem is not limited to face-to-face interviewing, but affects telephone interviews as well. Some studies find higher levels of reporting sensitive information in face-to-face than in telephone interviews (Holbrook et al. 2003, Johnson et al. 1989; see also de Leeuw & van der Zouwen's 1988 meta-analysis), but others find the opposite (Hochstim 1967, McQueen 1989), and at least one study reports mixed results in an experimental comparison of the two modes (Aquilino 1994). The advantage of self-administration over either method of interviewer administration is much clearer: Self-administration increases reporting of behaviors that are known to be underreported in surveys (for example, abortions; see Lessler & O'Reilly 1997, Mott 1985) and decreases reports about behaviors that are known to be overreported (e.g., attendance at religious services; Presser & Stinson 1998). Moreover, it reduces the discrepancy between men and women in the average number of opposite-sex sex partners they report by lowering the average number reported by men and increasing the average reported by women (Tourangeau & Smith 1996). That men consistently report more opposite-sex sex partners than women do has long been an embarrassment for surveys on sexual behavior (Smith 1992); in the aggregate, the totals for the two sexes should match because men and women are reporting on the same pairings.

So interviewers are both a blessing and a curse. The ideal would be a method of data collection that combines the advantages of face-to-face interviewing with the benefits of self-administration. A first approximation to this ideal was achieved by having the interviewers bring a portable cassette player to the respondents; the cassette played a recording of the questions to the respondents, who provided their answers on an answer sheet that they then sealed in an envelope (Cynamon & Camburn 1992). This methodology retained most of the advantages of face-to-face interviewing (such as high response rates) but minimized the role of the interviewer in eliciting sensitive information. The drawback was that the method didn't allow for complicated routing patterns; everyone had to listen to and answer all the questions.

As the power and speed of laptop computers continued to increase, it became feasible to have the computer administer the questions, presenting the text of the questions (and the answer categories) on-screen and simultaneously playing a recording of them to the respondents via earphones. The respondents entered their answers using the keypad of the computer. The interviewer was there to set up the computer and to answer questions, but was completely unaware of the respondents' answers. This new method—known as audio computer-assisted self-interviewing (audio-CASI)—was developed independently by researchers at the University of Michigan (Johnston & Walton 1995) and the Research Triangle Institute (O'Reilly et al. 1994). It combined all the flexibility and capabilities of computer-assisted interviewing (automated routing, built-in checks for out-of-range values, and so on) with the privacy of self-administration. In addition, as O'Reilly and his colleagues demonstrated, it worked for respondents with limited reading skills.

A series of experimental comparisons has demonstrated the advantages of audio-CASI for the collection of sensitive information over both face-to-face interviews (Epstein et al. 2001, Newman et al. 2002, Tourangeau & Smith 1996) and paper self-administered questionnaires (Lessler et al. 1994, 2000; O'Reilly et al. 1994; Turner et al. 1998). Respondents are more willing to admit to symptoms of emotional distress (Newman et al. 2002), episodes of anxiety and depression (Epstein et al. 2001), illicit drug use (Lessler et al. 2000), and abortions (Lessler et al. 1994) under audio-CASI than under other methods of data collection. In addition, men report fewer sexual partners and women report more when audio-CASI is used than under CAPI (Tourangeau & Smith 1996).

Apart from its other virtues, audio-CASI represents the ultimate in standardized interviewing. The questions are read exactly as worded by experienced interviewers (or, in some cases, actors); mispronunciations, hesitations, and other mistakes are left on the cutting room floor. Every respondent receives precisely the same stimulus, delivered in the best possible way. As a result, computer-assisted self-administration appears to eliminate variation across interviewers as a source of error (Tourangeau et al. 1997).

Telephone Interviewing

The telephone analogue to audio-CASI was developed at roughly the same time as the face-to-face version. This method of data collection has been referred to as interactive voice response (IVR), touchtone data entry (TDE), or telephone audio-CASI. We refer to it as IVR, the term used at most market research firms. The various labels refer to the same methodology, in which a computer plays a recording of the questions over the telephone to the respondents, who indicate their answers by pressing the keys on the handset or, more recently, by saying them out loud. IVR systems are now a fixture of contemporary life and are widely used for routine transactions (e.g., for catalog sales, airline reservations, and banking). The initial survey application of the method was to collect data from businesses (Harrell & Clayton 1991, Phipps & Tupek 1990, Werking et al. 1988). Later, surveys of the general population adopted IVR as well (Appel et al. 1992, Blyth 1997, Frankovic 1994, Gribble et al. 2000, Turner et al. 1996). IVR is particularly popular among market researchers, especially for brief interviews. Just as audio-CASI has begun to supplant earlier methods for gathering information in face-to-face settings, IVR may gradually displace other forms of data collection by telephone.

Experimental comparisons indicate that IVR has advantages over interviewer-administered telephone surveys similar to the advantages of audio-CASI over interviewer-administered face-to-face surveys. IVR elicits higher levels of reporting of sensitive information, such as drug use (Gribble et al. 2000) or risky sexual behaviors (Turner et al. 1996), than other forms of telephone interviewing; in addition, IVR respondents in customer satisfaction surveys are more willing to complain about the service they've received (Tourangeau et al. 2002).

IVR is used in surveys in two different ways. In recruit-and-switch IVR surveys, telephone interviewers contact the respondents, recruit them to take part, and then switch them into the IVR system. In inbound IVR, respondents dial directly into the system themselves. Both variants are prone to the low response rates that characterize telephone surveys more generally. In addition, though, IVR interviews are subject to a form of nonresponse—breaking off—that is relatively rare in surveys with a live interviewer. With the recruit-and-switch version of IVR, many sample cases opt out of the interview during the switch to IVR; with both versions, many cases quit partway through the IVR questions. In one survey, Tourangeau and his colleagues (2002) observed a break-off rate of more than 30%; Cooley et al. (2000) report a rate of 24% in another study. A key factor seems to be the length of the IVR interview; without an interviewer, there are few inducements to finishing the questions and few barriers to quitting. This form of nonresponse adds to the bias from total nonresponse in IVR surveys—that is, it increases the value of $E(p_n)$ in Equation 1.

Web Surveys

Profound as the changes are that audio-CASI and IVR have produced, they pale in comparison to the dramatic changes brought on by the emergence of Web surveys. Roughly 60% of the adult population of the United States now has access to the Internet either at home or at work. Web surveys are the third generation of computerized counterparts to mail questionnaires (after disk-by-mail and e-mail surveys), and, like audio-CASI and IVR surveys, they combine the advantages of computerization and self-administration.

Web surveys have their own unique benefits as well. They eliminate the need for interviewers, sharply reducing the cost of data collection as compared to telephone and face-to-face interviews (though not necessarily compared to mail surveys). In addition, Web questionnaires can incorporate rich visual content (still images, diagrams, video clips) that would be difficult or impossible to deliver in a telephone or a mail survey. Given this marriage of low cost and high capabilities, it is hardly surprising that the growth in Web surveys has been explosive. Despite serious concerns about coverage and nonresponse in Web surveys (Couper 2001), the commercial research sector has rapidly embraced the Web for faster and cheaper data collection, and almost daily there are reports of new surveys being conducted over the Internet.

Still, the sampling problems in Web surveys are formidable. A substantial proportion of the population still does not have Internet access and those who have access differ substantially from those who don't, a difference that some observers have called a "digital divide" (National Telecommunications and Information Administration 2000). Even if the coverage problem weren't so severe, it would still be extremely difficult to sample Internet users because there is no centralized list of households or persons with Internet access. With dwellings and telephone numbers, there are well-established methods for creating sampling frames and for selecting samples that give complete or nearly complete coverage of the population of interest. With Web surveys, there are no comparable methods yet.

The most ambitious attempt to date to create a representative sample for Web surveys has been carried out by Knowledge Networks, a firm that has created a large panel of households designed to represent the U.S. population. (CentERdata has created a similar but smaller panel in the Netherlands.) Knowledge Networks recruits panel members on an ongoing basis using RDD telephone surveys; recruits get WebTV units and free Internet access in exchange for their participation in the panel. In principle, this strategy might yield a representative sample, but several practical problems complicate matters. On its face, the panel provides the same population coverage as any list-assisted telephone sample, omitting approximately 7% or 8% of the household population. But the sample omits additional portions of the population because some areas do not have WebTV; these coverage losses involve about another 7% of the household population. Even worse, sample members have multiple opportunities to avoid participating in the panel. Some households were never contacted for the initial telephone survey or refused to complete that interview; others completed the initial telephone interview but refused to take part in the panel. Still others said they would join the panel, but wouldn't permit the installation of WebTV, and, for any given survey, some panel participants are unwilling or unavailable to complete the Web questionnaire. The cumulative response rate taking into account nonresponse at these various stages is generally between 20% and 30% (Dennis 2001). Thus, although the panel may have started out as a reasonably representative sample of the general population, the added coverage losses resulting from the need for access to WebTV and cumulative effect of nonresponse over the multiple stages of recruitment and data collection yield samples of uncertain representativeness.

Web surveys also raise some new measurement issues. Two rival approaches for the design of Web questionnaires have already evolved—the static (or scrollable) and dynamic (or interactive) approaches. Web surveys descended from mail questionnaires and computer-assisted interviewing and these distinct pedigrees have led to the different design camps. Dillman (2000) (see also Dillman et al. 1998) is the leading advocate of the static approach, which argues for designing Web surveys as electronic versions of mail questionnaires. Web questionnaires embodying this approach typically consist of a single HTML form, with the respondents scrolling through the instrument much as they would page through a paper questionnaire. The questionnaire does not automate the skip instructions or carry out checks for inconsistent or out-of-range answers. Until the respondent presses the "submit" button at the end of the survey, he or she can back up and change answers at will. Web surveys that follow the computer-assisted interviewing tradition are more interactive in nature. One or more questions are presented on a screen, and responses are transmitted to the server after every question or set of questions. This permits automated skips, range and error checks, and all the other capabilities of CATI or CAPI instruments. Respondents can page back through earlier answers, or the programming can prevent this. Similarly, respondents can be permitted to skip an item or be forced to provide a response to every question.

Norman and his colleagues (Norman et al. 2001) report an experimental comparison of static and dynamic versions of the same questionnaire. Their results suggest that the static version, which permits rapid scrolling through the questionnaire, might be best for some tasks (e.g., entering data from existing records), but the dynamic version might be best for others. But exploration of the issue of the relative merits of each design approach has barely begun.

Web surveys often feature "user-friendly" interfaces to attract potential respondents and maintain their interest long enough to complete the questions. The danger is that seemingly irrelevant features of the interface may affect how respondents answer the questions. Nass and his colleagues (Fogg & Nass 1997, Nass et al. 1996, Reeves & Nass 1996) have investigated reactions to computer interfaces that featured recorded voices or line drawings of faces (see also Walker et al. 1994). They argue that computers can trigger reactions from users like those evoked by other people; people sometimes seem to treat computers as if they were social actors rather than as inanimate tools. To the extent that people respond to computers as if they had human characteristics, adding a variety of humanizing cues may offset the benefits of computer-assisted self-administration for items on sensitive topics. Tourangeau et al. (2003) explicitly examined this possibility in a series of experiments that varied the characteristics of the interface in Web and IVR surveys. For example, they compared Web surveys that included pictures of and text messages from either a male or a female investigator; similarly, they varied whether an IVR survey used a male or female voice to record the questions. They found little support for the "social interface" hypothesis; respondents gave the same number of socially desirable answers regardless of the "gender" of the interface or the other humanizing characteristics it had. Still, they did find some impact of the interface on responses to a battery of attitude items on sex roles; the answers were, on average, tilted in a profeminist direction when the interface showed pictures of a female investigator or administered the questions in women's voice than when it displayed a male investigator or used a male voice. Because Web surveys make it easy to add animation, visual images, and other potential humanizing cues, interface designs for Web surveys are likely to remain a lively topic for research.

Theories of Mode Effects

Tourangeau & Smith (1996) (see also Tourangeau et al. 2001) argue that respondents give different answers to the same questions under different modes of data collection largely because of underlying differences in three key variables—the degree of privacy the method affords, the legitimacy it confers, and the cognitive burdens it imposes on the respondents. For example, they argue that audio-CASI is a relatively effective method for eliciting sensitive information mainly because it creates a strong sense of privacy (since the interviewer is unaware of the respondent's answers). In addition, because an interviewer is still present, he or she can provide the respondent with various tokens of the legitimacy of surveys, such as photo ID badges and letters from senior federal officials endorsing the survey. Finally, audio-CASI reduces the burden on working memory by presenting questions both aurally and visually; respondents can review the question text (and answer options) and set their own pace through the questionnaire. By contrast, telephone surveys are less likely to be viewed as private (unless an IVR system administers the questions). Because the questions are only presented aurally, long questions or long lists of answer options may tax the limits of working memory, and the interviewer may hurry the respondents. And respondents may be skeptical about the legitimacy of telephone surveys, confusing them with telemarketing calls (van Leeuwen & de Leeuw 1999). Some results by Moon (1998) suggest that Web respondents may also be concerned about the privacy of their answers; she found that respondents were more likely to give socially desirable answers when they thought a computer across the country was administering the questions than when they thought the computer in front of them was.

Holbrook et al. (2003) emphasize somewhat different variables. They argue that telephone surveys encourage respondents to use satisficing strategies to get through the interview, producing data that are worse than those from face-to-face interviews. Satisficing may take a number of forms in surveys, including nondifferentiation (giving similar responses to every item), selecting the "no opinion" or "don't know" options, or acquiescence (Krosnick 1991, 1999). This difference between telephone and face-to-face surveys may reflect the greater cognitive burden of telephone interviews, lower respondent motivation in that setting, respondent distraction during the interview, or a reduced sense of accountability.

CONCLUSION

Surveys will doubtless continue to evolve rapidly in response to broad movements in the larger society. Like most large-scale human endeavors, surveys are swept up in the tides of technological and social change; most survey innovations are adopted long before there is research evidence from methodological studies regarding their value. Given the proliferation of new modes of data collection, survey researchers are likely to continue to carry out comparisons between modes for some time to come. Several major research programs are already examining the design features of Web surveys as such surveys continue their explosive growth. Another major issue for Web surveys is whether the results can be adjusted statistically to compensate for the poor coverage of the total population and the low response rates characteristic of Web surveys (Couper 2001).

One other lively research area worth noting involves the character of the interaction that goes on in survey interviews. Some researchers have questioned whether standardization has gone too far in surveys (Suchman & Jordan 1990). Traditionally, interviewers are trained to avoid biasing respondents (Fowler & Mangione 1990), but critics have argued that this means that they don't offer respondents much in the way of help or clarification. In the face of these criticisms, some researchers have taken a closer look at the interactions that actually take place in face-to-face interviews (Maynard & Schaeffer 2002, Schaeffer & Maynard 1996). Others have experimented with alternatives (dubbed conversational interviews) to the traditional method of standardization (Conrad & Schober 2000, Schober & Conrad 1997). Survey respondents clearly bring with them interpretive habits developed over a lifetime of everyday conversations (Schwarz 1996). Because of the huge cost associated with using interviewers to administer surveys, there is little doubt that researchers will continue to investigate how to make them more effective at collecting survey data.

Survey costs have been a major consideration in all three of the trends discussed here. The possibility of reduced cost was probably the main motivation for the move to list-assisted telephone sampling. Rising costs also impose serious constraints on efforts to maintain survey response rates. And the promise of greatly reduced costs is perhaps the strongest argument in favor of Web surveys. Along with rapid technological change, concerns about the cost of surveys are likely to remain primary forces behind the search for new and better methods to conduct surveys.

ACKNOWLEDGMENT

I am very grateful to Stanley Presser and Mick Couper for their very helpful and encouraging comments on an earlier draft of this chapter.

The *Annual Review of Psychology* is online at http://psych.annualreviews.org

LITERATURE CITED

Am. Stat. Assoc. 1999. *More about telephone surveys*. Alexandria, VA: Sect. Surv. Res. Methods, Am. Stat. Assoc.

Appel MV, Tortora RD, Sigman R. 1992. Direct data entry using Touch-Tone and voice recognition technology for the M3 survey. *Res. Rep. Ser. No. RR-92/01, Bur. Census, Stat. Res. Div.*

Aquilino WS. 1994. Interview mode effects in surveys of drug and alcohol use. *Public Opin. Q.* 58:210–40

Atrostic BK, Bates N, Burt G, Silberstein A. 2001. Nonresponse in U.S. government household surveys: consistent measures, recent trends, and new insights. *J. Off. Stat.* 17: 209–26

Baker RP, Bradburn NM, Johnson R. 1995. Computer-assisted personal interviewing: an experimental evaluation of data quality and survey costs. *J. Off. Stat.* 11:415–34

Baumgartner RM. 1990. *Telephone answering machines and completion rates for telephone surveys*. Presented at Ann. Meet. Am. Assoc. Public Opin. Res., May 17–20, Lancaster, PA

Bergman LR, Kristiansson KE, Olofsson A, Säfström M. 1994. Decentralised CATI versus paper and pencil interviewing: effects on the results of the Swedish labor force surveys. *J. Off. Stat.* 10:181–95

Blakely EJ, Snyder MG. 1997. *Fortress America: Gated Communities in the United States*. Washington, DC: Brookings Inst. Press

Blom E, Lyberg L. 1998. Scanning and optical character recognition in survey organizations. In *Computer Assisted Survey Information Collection*, ed. MP Couper, RP Baker, J Bethlehem, CZ Clark, J Martin, et al., pp. 499–520. New York: Wiley

Blyth WG. 1997. Developing a speech recognition application for survey research. In *Survey Measurement and Process Quality*, ed. L Lyberg, P Biemer, M Collins, E de Leeuw, C Dippo, et al., pp. 249–66. New York: Wiley

Brick JM, Waksberg J, Kulp D, Starer A. 1995. Bias in list-assisted telephone surveys. *Public Opin. Q.* 59:218–35

Casady RJ, Lepkowski JM. 1993. Stratified telephone survey designs. *Surv. Method.* 19: 103–13

Catlin O, Ingram S. 1988. The effects of CATI on costs and data quality: a comparison of CATI and paper methods in centralized interviewing. See Groves et al. 1988, pp. 437–50

Chaiken S. 1980. Heuristic versus systematic information processing and the use of source versus message cues in persuasion. *J. Personal. Soc. Psychol.* 39:752–66

Church AH. 1993. Estimating the effects of incentives on mail survey response rates: a meta-analysis. *Public Opin. Q.* 57:62–79

Cialdini RB. 1984. *Influence: The New Psychology of Modern Persuasion*. New York: Quill

Conrad FG, Schober MF. 2000. Clarifying question meaning in a household telephone survey. *Public Opin. Q.* 64:1–28

Cooley PC, Miller HG, Gribble JN, Turner CF. 2000. Automating telephone surveys: using T-ACASI to obtain data on sensitive topics. *Comput. Hum. Behav.* 16:1–11

Couper MP. 2001. Web surveys: a review of issues and approaches. *Public Opin. Q.* 64:464–94

Couper MP, Blair J, Triplett T. 1999. A comparison of mail and e-mail for a survey of employees in federal statistical agencies. *J. Off. Stat.* 15:39–56

Couper MP, Nicholls W II. 1998. The history and development of computer-assisted survey information collection methods. In *Computer-Assisted Survey Information Collection*, ed. MP Couper, RP Baker, J Bethlehem, CZ Clark, J Martin, et al., pp. 1–22. New York: Wiley

Curtin R, Presser S, Singer E. 2000. The effects of response rate changes on the Index of Consumer Sentiment. *Public Opin. Q.* 64:413–28

Cynamon M, Camburn D. 1992. *Employing a new technique to ask questions on sensitive topics.* Presented at Ann. Meet. Natl. Field Dir. Conf., May 17–20, Ft. Lauderdale, FL

Daves R. 1990. *You know what to do at the beep, but do survey researchers?* Presented at Midwest Assoc. Public Opin. Res., Chicago IL

de Leeuw E, de Heer W. 2002. Trends in household survey nonresponse: a longitudinal and international comparison. See Groves et al. 2002, pp. 41–54

de Leeuw E, van der Zouwen J. 1988. Data quality in telephone and face to face surveys: a comparative meta-analysis. See Groves et al. 1988, pp. 283–99

Dennis JM. 2001. *Response timing and coverage of non-Internet households: data quality in an Internet-enabled panel.* Presented at Ann. Meet. Am. Assoc. Public Opin. Res., May 17–20, Montreal

Dillman DA. 1978. *Mail and Telephone Surveys.* New York: Wiley

Dillman DA. 1991. The design and administration of mail surveys. *Annu. Rev. Sociol.* 17: 225–49

Dillman DA. 2000. *Mail and Internet Surveys: The Tailored Design Method.* New York: Wiley

Dillman DA, Gallegos JG, Frey JH. 1976. Reducing refusal rates for telephone interviews. *Public Opin. Q.* 40:66–78

Dillman DA, Tortora RD, Conradt J, Bowker D. 1998. *Influence of plain vs. fancy design on response rates for web surveys.* Presented at Jt. Stat. Meet., Aug. 9–13, Dallas

Downes-Le Guin T, Soo Hoo B. 1994. *Disk-by-mail data collection for professional populations.* Presented at Annu. Meet. Am. Assoc. Public Opin., May 12–15, Danvers, MA

Epstein JF, Barker PR, Kroutil LA. 2001. Mode effects in self-reported mental health data. *Public Opin. Q.* 65:529–49

Fink JC. 1983. CATI's first decade: the Chilton experience. *Soc. Methods Res.* 12:153–68

Fogg BJ, Nass C. 1997. Silicon sycophants: The effects of computers that flatter. *Int. J. Hum. Comput. Stud.* 46:551–61

Fowler FJ, Mangione TW. 1990. *Standardized Survey Interviewing: Minimizing Interviewer Error.* Newbury Park, CA: Sage

Fox RJ, Crask MR, Kim J. 1988. Mail survey response rates: a meta-analysis of selected techniques for inducing response. *Public Opin. Q.* 52:467–91

Frankovic KA. 1994. *Interactive polling and Americans' comfort level with technology.* Presented at Annu. Meet. Am. Assoc. Public Opin., May 12–15, Danvers, MA

Goyder J. 1987. *The Silent Majority: Nonrespondents on Sample Surveys.* Boulder, CO: Westview

Gribble JN, Miller HG, Cooley PC, Catania JA, Pollack L, et al. 2000. The impact of T-ACASI interviewing on reporting drug use among men who have sex with men. *Subst. Use Misuse* 80:869–90

Groves RM. 1989. *Survey Costs and Survey Errors.* New York: Wiley

Groves RM. 1990. Theories and methods of telephone surveys. *Annu. Rev. Sociol.* 16:221–40

Groves RM, Biemer P, Lyberg L, Massey J, Nicholls W, Waksberg J, eds. 1988. *Telephone Survey Methodology.* New York: Wiley

Groves RM, Couper MP. 1998. *Nonresponse in Household Surveys.* New York: Wiley

Groves RM, Dillman DA, Eltinge JL, Little RJA, eds. 2002. *Survey Nonresponse.* New York: Wiley

Groves RM, Mathiowetz N. 1984. Computer assisted telephone interviewing: effects on interviewers and respondents. *Public Opin. Q.* 48:356–69

Groves RM, McGonagle K. 2001. A theory-guided interviewer training protocol regarding survey participation. *J. Off. Stat.* 17:249–66

Groves RM, Singer E, Corning A. 2000. Leverage-salience theory of survey partici-

pation: description and an illustration. *Public Opin. Q.* 64:299–308

Harrell L, Clayton R. 1991. *A voice recognition technology in survey data collection: results of the first field tests.* Presented at Natl. Field Technol. Conf., May 11–16, San Diego

Heberlein TA, Baumgartner R. 1978. Factors affecting response rates to mailed questionnaires: a quantitative analysis of the published literature. *Am. Sociol. Rev.* 43:447–62

Hochstim J. 1967. A critical comparison of three strategies of collecting data from households. *J. Am. Stat. Assoc.* 62:976–89

Holbrook AL, Green MC, Krosnick JA. 2003. Telephone versus face-to-face interviewing of national probability samples with long questionnaires: comparisons of respondent satisficing and social desirability response bias. *Public Opin. Q.* 6:79–125

Int. Telecommun. Union. 2001. *ITU Yearbook of Statistics.* Geneva

James JM, Bolstein R. 1992. Large monetary incentives and their effect on mail survey response rates. *Public Opin. Q.* 56:442–53

Johnson T, Hougland J, Clayton R. 1989. Obtaining reports of sensitive behaviors: a comparison of substance use reports from telephone and face-to-face interviews. *Soc. Sci. Q.* 70:174–83

Johnston J, Walton C. 1995. Reducing response effects for sensitive questions: a computer-assisted self interview with audio. *Soc. Sci. Comput. Rev.* 13:304–19

Keeter S, Kohut A, Miller C, Groves R, Presser S. 2000. Consequences of reducing nonresponse in a large national telephone survey. *Public Opin. Q.* 64:125–48

Kiesler S, Sproull L. 1986. Response effects in the electronic survey. *Public Opin. Q.* 50:402–13

Krosnick JA. 1991. Response strategies for coping with the cognitive demands of attitude measures in surveys. *Appl. Cogn. Psychol.* 5:213–36

Krosnick JA. 1999. Survey research. *Annu. Rev. Psychol.* 50:537–67

Lepkowski JM. 1988. Telephone sampling

methods in the United States. See Groves et al. 1988, pp. 73–98

Lessler JT, Caspar RA, Penne MA, Barker PR. 2000. Developing computer-assisted interviewing (CAI) for the National Household Survey on Drug Abuse. *J. Drug Issues* 30:19–34

Lessler JT, Kalsbeek W. 1992. *Nonsampling Error in Surveys*. New York: Wiley

Lessler JT, O'Reilly JM. 1997. Mode of interview and reporting of sensitive issues: design and implementation of audio computer-assisted self-interviewing. In *The Validity of Self-Reported Drug Use: Improving the Accuracy of Survey Estimates*, ed. L Harrison, A Hughes, pp. 366–82. Rockville, MD: Natl. Inst. Drug Abuse

Lessler JT, Weeks MF, O'Reilly JM. 1994. Results from the National Survey of Family Growth Cycle V Pretest. In *1994 Proc. Sect. Surv. Methods Res.*, pp. 64–70. Alexandria, VA: Am. Stat. Assoc.

Link MW, Oldendick RW. 1999. Call screening: Is it really a problem for survey research? *Public Opin. Q.* 63:577–89

Martin J, O'Muircheartaigh C, Curtice J. 1993. The use of CAPI for attitude surveys: an experimental comparison with traditional methods. *J. Off. Stat.* 9:641–61

Maynard DW, Schaeffer NC. 2002. Standardization and its discontents: standardization, interaction, and the survey interview. In *Standardization and Tacit Knowledge: Interaction and Practice in the Survey Interview*, ed. DW Maynard, H Houtkoop-Steenstra, NC Schaeffer, J van der Zouwen, pp. 3–47. New York: Wiley

McQueen DV. 1989. Comparison of results of personal interview and telephone surveys of behavior related to risk of AIDS: advantages of telephone techniques. In *Conf. Proc.: Health Surv. Res. Methods*, pp. 247–52. Washington, DC: Dep. Health Hum. Serv. Publ. No. (PHS) 89-3447

Merkle D, Edelman M. 2002. Nonresponse in exit polls: a comprehensive analysis. See Groves et al. 2002, pp. 243–58

Moon Y. 1998. Impression management in computer-based interviews: the effects of input modality, output modality, and distance. *Public Opin. Q.* 62:610–22

Morton-Williams J. 1993. *Interviewer Approaches*. Aldershot: Dartmouth

Mott F. 1985. *Evaluation of fertility data and preliminary analytic results from the 1983 survey of the National Longitudinal Surveys of Work Experience of Youth*. Rep. Natl. Inst. Child Health Hum. Dev. Cent. Hum. Resourc. Res.

Nass C, Fogg BJ, Moon Y. 1996. Can computers be teammates? *Int. J. Hum.-Comput. Stud.* 45:669–78

Natl. Telecommun. Inf. Adm. 2000. *Falling Through the Net: Toward Digital Inclusion*. Washington, DC: US Dep. Commer.

Newman JC, Des Jarlais DC, Turner CF, Gribble J, Cooley P, Paone D. 2002. The differential effects of face-to-face and computer interview modes. *Am. J. Public Health* 92:294–97

Norman KL, Friedman Z, Norman K, Stevenson R. 2001. Navigational issues in the design of online self-administered questionnaires. *Behav. Inf. Technol.* 20:37–45

Oldendick RW, Link MW. 1994. The answering machine generation. *Public Opin. Q.* 58:264–73

Olson L, Schneiderman M. 1995. *Physicians' participation in a disk-by-mail survey*. Presented at Ann. Meet. Am. Assoc. Public Opin. Res., May 18–21, Ft. Lauderdale, FL

O'Reilly J, Hubbard M, Lessler J, Biemer P, Turner C. 1994. Audio and video computer assisted self-interviewing: preliminary tests of new technology for data collection. *J. Off. Stat.* 10:197–214

Petty RE, Cacioppo JT. 1984. The effects of involvement on responses to argument quality and quantity: central and peripheral routes to persuasion. *J. Personal. Soc. Psychol.* 46:69–81

Phipps P, Tupek A. 1990. *Assessing measurement errors in a touchtone recognition survey*. Presented at Int. Conf. Meas. Errors Surv., Nov., Tucson, AZ

Presser S, Schaeffer NC. 2003. The science of

asking questions. *Annu. Rev. Sociol.* 29:65–88

Presser S, Stinson L. 1998. Data collection mode and social desirability bias in self-reported religious attendance. *Am. Sociol. Rev.* 63:137–45

Putnam RD. 1995. *Bowling Alone: The Collapse and Revival of American Community.* New York: Simon & Schuster

Redline CD, Dillman DA. 2002. The influence of alternative visual designs on respondents' performance with branching instructions in self-administered questionnaires. See Groves et al. 2002, pp. 179–93

Reeves B, Nass C. 1996. *The Media Equation: How People Treat Computers, Television, and New Media Like Real People and Places.* Cambridge, MA: CSLI/Cambridge Univ. Press

Robinson JP, Godbey G. 1997. *Time for Life: The Surprising Ways Americans Use their Time.* University Park: Penn. State Univ. Press

Saris W, Pijper M. 1986. Computer assisted interviewing using home computers. *Eur. Res.* 14:144–50

Schaefer DR, Dillman DA. 1998. Development of a standard e-mail methodology: results of an experiment. *Public Opin. Q.* 62:378–97

Schaeffer NC, Maynard DW. 1996. From paradigm to prototype and back again: interactive aspects of "cognitive processing" in survey interviews. In *Answering Questions: Methodology for Determining Cognitive and Communicative Processes in Survey Research,* ed. N Schwarz, S Sudman, pp. 65–88. San Francisco: Jossey-Bass

Schober MF, Conrad FG. 1997. Does conversational interviewing reduce survey measurement error? *Public Opin. Q.* 60:576–602

Schwarz N. 1996. *Cognition and Communication: Judgmental Biases, Research Methods, and the Logic of Conversation.* Mahwah, NJ: Erlbaum

Singer E. 2002. The use of incentives to reduce nonresponse in household surveys. See Groves et al. 2002, pp. 163–78

Singer E. 2003. Exploring the meaning of consent: participation in research and beliefs about risks and benefits. *J. Off. Stat.* In press

Singer E, Mathiowetz N, Couper M. 1993. The impact of privacy and confidentiality concerns on survey participation: the case of the 1990 U.S. Census. *Public Opin. Q.* 57:465–82

Singer E, Van Hoewyk J, Gebler N. 1999. The effect of incentives on response rates in interviewer-mediated surveys. *J. Off. Stat.* 15:217–30

Smith TW. 1992. Discrepancies between men and women in reporting number of sexual partners: a summary from four countries. *Soc. Biol.* 39:203–11

Steeh C, Kirgis N, Cannon B, DeWitt J. 2001. Are they really as bad as they seem? Nonresponse rates at the end of the twentieth century. *J. Off. Stat.* 17:227–47

Suchman L, Jordan B. 1990. Interactional troubles in face-to-face survey interviews. *J. Am. Stat. Assoc.* 85:232–41

Thornberry O, Massey J. 1988. Trends in United States telephone coverage across time and subgroups. See Groves et al. 1988, pp. 41–54

Tourangeau R, Couper MP, Steiger DM. 2003. Humanizing self-administered surveys: experiments on social presence in Web and IVR surveys. *Comput. Hum. Behav.* 19:1–24

Tourangeau R, Rasinski K, Jobe J, Smith TW, Pratt W. 1997. Sources of error in a survey of sexual behavior. *J. Off. Stat.* 13:341–65

Tourangeau R, Rips LJ, Rasinski K. 2001. *The Psychology of Survey Response.* New York: Cambridge Univ. Press

Tourangeau R, Steiger DM, Wilson D. 2002. Self-administered questions by telephone: evaluating interactive voice response. *Public Opin. Q.* 66:265–78

Tourangeau R, Smith TW. 1996. Asking sensitive questions: the impact of data collection mode, question format, and question context. *Public Opin. Q.* 60:275–304

Tuckel P, O'Neill H. 1995. A profile of telephone answering machine owners and screeners. *1995 Proc. Sect. Surv. Res.*

Methods, pp. 1157–62. Alexandria, VA: Am. Stat. Assoc.

Tuckel P, O'Neill H. 1996. New technology and nonresponse bias in RDD surveys. *1996 Proc. Sect. Surv. Res. Methods*, pp. 889–94. Alexandria, VA: Am. Stat. Assoc.

Tuckel P, Schulman M. 2000. The impact of leaving different answering machine messages on nonresponse rates in a nationwide RDD survey. *2000 Proc. Sect. Surv. Res. Methods*, pp. 901–6. Alexandria, VA: Am. Stat. Assoc.

Turner CF, Ku L, Rogers SM, Lindberg LD, Plec JH, Sonenstein FL. 1998. Adolescent sexual behavior, drug use, and violence: increased reporting with computer survey technology. *Science* 280:867–73

Turner CF, Miller HG, Smith TK, Cooley PC, Rogers SM. 1996. Telephone audio computer-assisted self-interviewing (T-ACASI) and survey measurement of sensitive behaviors: preliminary results. In *Survey and Statistical Computing 1996*, ed. R Banks, J Fairgrieve, L Gerrard, T Orchard, C Payne, A Westlake, pp. 121–30. Chesham, Bucks, UK: Assoc. Stat. Comput.

van Leeuwen R, de Leeuw E. 1999. *I'm not selling anything: experiments in telephone introductions.* Presented at Int. Conf. Surv. Nonresponse, Oct. 28–31, Portland, OR

Waksberg J. 1978. Sampling methods for random digit dialing. *J. Am. Stat. Assoc.* 73:40–46

Walker J, Sproull L, Subramani R. 1994. Using a human face in an interface. In *Proc. Conf. Hum. Factors Comput.*, pp. 85–99. Boston: ACM

Warriner K, Goyder J, Gjertsen H, Hohner P, McSpurren K. 1996. *Charities, no, lotteries, no, cash, yes: main effects and interactions in a Canadian incentives experiment.* Presented at 4th Int. Soc. Sci. Methodol. Conf., Univ. Essex, Colchester, UK

Weeks MF, Jones BL, Folsom RE, Benrud CH. 1980. Optimal times to contact sample households. *Public Opin. Q.* 44:101–14

Weeks MF, Kulka RA, Pierson SA. 1987. Optimal call scheduling for a telephone survey. *Public Opin. Q.* 51:540–49

Werking G, Tupek A, Clayton R. 1988. CATI and touchtone self-response applications for establishment surveys. *J. Off. Stat.* 4:349–62

Xu M, Bates BJ, Schweitzer JC. 1993. The impact of messages on survey participation in answering machine households. *Public Opin. Q.* 57:232–37

Yu J, Cooper H. 1983. A quantitative review of research design effects on response rates to aquestionnaires. *J. Mark. Res.* 20:36–44

Annu. Rev. Psychol. 2004. 55:803–32
doi: 10.1146/annurev.psych.55.090902.141601
First published online as a Review in Advance on October 6, 2003

HUMAN RESEARCH AND DATA COLLECTION VIA THE INTERNET

Michael H. Birnbaum

Department of Psychology, California State University, Fullerton,
California 92834–6846; email: mbirnbaum@fullerton.edu

Key Words   anonymity, browser-based research, CGI, computers in psychology, computer programming, experimental dropouts, experimenter bias, HTML, HTML forms, Internet research, Java, JavaScript, methodology, missing data, on-line research, Perl, survey, Web experiment, WWW

■ **Abstract**   Advantages and disadvantages of Web and lab research are reviewed. Via the World Wide Web, one can efficiently recruit large, heterogeneous samples quickly, recruit specialized samples (people with rare characteristics), and standardize procedures, making studies easy to replicate. Alternative programming techniques (procedures for data collection) are compared, including client-side as opposed to server-side programming. Web studies have methodological problems; for example, higher rates of drop out and of repeated participation. Web studies must be thoroughly analyzed and tested before launching on-line. Many studies compared data obtained in Web versus lab. These two methods usually reach the same conclusions; however, there are significant differences between college students tested in the lab and people recruited and tested via the Internet. Reasons that Web researchers are enthusiastic about the potential of the new methods are discussed.

CONTENTS

0066-4308/04/0204-0803$14.00

INTRODUCTION

In the last decade, a new protocol for sending information on the World Wide Web (WWW), hypertext transfer protocol (HTTP), created a new way to conduct psychological research. This new technique allows researchers to collect data from participants all over the world 24 hours a day and seven days per week. Surveys and experiments can be delivered quickly to anyone connected to the Web and data can be saved automatically in electronic form, reducing costs in lab space, dedicated equipment, paper, mailing costs, and labor. Once an experiment or survey is properly programmed, data can be stored in a form ready for analysis, saving costs of data coding and entry that used to be an expensive and time-consuming part of the research process.

Computer Developments that Set the Stage

By early 1995, a number of changes were under way that created the conditions for a new approach to psychological research:

- Computer hardware and software improved; it became less expensive to own computers and easier to operate them.
- The number of individuals who owned or had access to personal computers, email, and the WWW was increasing exponentially.
- More and more valuable content was being added to the WWW.
- Speed of connections to the Internet were improving and browsers, the programs that display WWW content, were now able to handle more complex media and programming languages of Java and JavaScript (initially called "LiveScript").
- Hypertext markup language (HTML) 2 supported the technique of forms.

The new standard of HTML 2, introduced in late 1994, supported forms, which allowed a person viewing a Web page to easily send data back to a designated server, which could process, code, filter, and save data electronically. This technique made it possible for a person, even without an email account, to be able to participate in a survey from an Internet-connected computer (e.g., in a public library or campus computer facility) even if that computer was not configured to send email.

Within a few months, psychologists began using this technique to collect data in surveys and experiments. A number of these "pioneers" contributed chapters to Birnbaum's (2000b) edited book, which included a chapter by Musch & Reips (2000) that summarized the (short) history of psychological experiments (not surveys) on the WWW [see also Musch (2000)].

Musch & Reips (2000) noted that the first psychological experiments (with manipulated variables) conducted via the Web were those of Welch & Krantz (1996) and Krantz et al. (1997). Krantz (1998) maintains a Web site, "Psychological Research on the Net," (http://psych.hanover.edu/research/exponnet.html) that lists experiments currently running on the Internet. The site had 35 links to on-line studies on June 17, 1998. By May 11, 1999, there were 65 links, and on May 10, 2003, there were 150 links, including 45 to projects in social psychology and 30 to studies of cognitive psychology.

Several of these links lead to multiple experiments. For example, Jonathan Baron (http://www.psych.upenn.edu/~baron/qs.html) has been running about 50 studies per year from his site. The PsychExps site at Ole Miss (http://psychexps. olemiss.edu/) listed 33 lab and research studies on May 10, 2003, most of which were in cognitive psychology. Similarly, the student research project site at my Decision Research Center of Fullerton (http://psych.fullerton.edu/mbirnbaum/ decisions/thanks.htm) listed 21 studies on that same date. Ulf-Dietrich Reips's Web Experimental Psychology Lab (http://www.psychologie.unizh.ch/genpsy/Ulf/Lab/ WebExpPsyLab.html), which began operations in 1995, had links to 16 active studies in English and 12 in German plus about 80 in its archive on this same date in 2003. The Web Experiment List (http://genpsylab-wexlist.unizh.ch/) listed 166 studies in 2003. Although not all studies are listed in these sites (and some items are duplicates), the numbers give an indication of the rapid expansion of this method of doing research. A few hours visiting the links would convey to the reader a general impression of the kinds of studies being done this way.

Although any given work may have more than one focus, I divide my review in three distinct topic areas, according to my judgment of a work's main thrust. These three areas are (*a*) Techniques that describe or analyze "how-to" issues. For example, how can we randomly assign participants to between-subjects conditions? (*b*) Web methodology, which deals with internal and external validity of Internet research. For example, what are the threats to internal and external validity if people drop out of Web-based experiments, and what are the considerations of using particular techniques to reduce such dropouts? (*c*) Web versus lab comparisons, which includes findings specific to the Internet and comparisons of Web and lab studies of the same phenomena. For example, do experiments in decision making that are conducted via the Web yield the same conclusions as those done in the lab? In what ways do results obtained in Web and lab differ?

A fourth major area of research involves social psychology of the Internet, which deals with the Internet as a new social situation or communication medium. For example, do people exhibit different social behaviors on-line and in person? This topic is the focus of a separate review (Bargh & McKenna 2004) and will not be covered here except in relation to methodological issues in Web research.

TECHNIQUES

Many books and articles describe techniques that can be useful for conducting research via the WWW. Items that are primarily commercial and directed to the general audience (e.g., books on HTML, JavaScript, Java, Perl, etc.) are not summarized here, but those that are specifically directed to psychological researchers are discussed.

Getting Started: HTML Forms

Probably the easiest way to get started with the techniques of Web-based research is to make a survey or experiment using one of the free programs (e.g., Birnbaum 1998) to create the Web page for a simple survey or factorial experiment. These programs are available from the following URL: http://psych.fullerton.edu/mbirnbaum/programs/.

SurveyWiz and FactorWiz are Web pages that make Web pages for collecting data via the WWW. Within each Web page is a list of instructions for use (see also Birnbaum 2000c, 2001a). Creating a Web form with SurveyWiz is as simple as typing the questions and pushing buttons for the type of input device desired. The program supports text boxes, which are boxes into which a participant can respond by typing a number or short answer. SurveyWiz and FactorWizRB also support radio buttons, which allow the user to click along a rating scale.

The most fundamental technique of Web-based research is HTML, the formatting language used to compose Web pages. A Web page (a document) can contain formatted text, links to other information on the Web, pictures, graphics, animations, and other media such as sounds or video. Many software products are available to create Web pages, including free ones such as Birnbaum's (2000c) FactorWiz, WEXTOR by Reips & Neuhaus (2002), Schmidt's (1997b) WWW Survey Assistant, and White & Hammer's (2000) Quiz-o-matic (which makes self-scoring quizzes). Despite the availability of free and commercial software to make Web pages, a Web researcher needs to have a basic understanding of the "tags" (commands) of HTML. There are many free tutorials available on the WWW for learning HTML, as well as many commercial books on the subject.

The only introductory text in English on Web research is Birnbaum's (2001a), intended for behavioral researchers who are new to Web research. It includes a brief introduction to HTML, including the technique of forms (Chapters 2–5), spreadsheet and statistical software useful in Web research (Chapters 6, 7, and 12–15), an introduction to JavaScript (Chapters 17–19), and a brief introduction to advanced topics such as Java, Authorware, and other methods (Chapter 20). Several chapters cover psychological content with examples of how to program the experiments, explanations of the examples, and instructions on how to analyze the data. A compact disk (CD) accompanies the book with many programming examples, experiments that are ready to run, and data for those experiments. There are also chapters on methodology, recruiting, and ethics of Web studies. Materials for using this book with both undergraduate and graduate students are available from the following URL: http://psych.fullerton.edu/mbirnbaum/psych466/.

Books by Janetzko (1999) and Janetzko et al. (2002) also include much useful information on how to execute psychology experiments via the WWW. The latter is an edited book with useful treatments of methodology and statistics, as well as many interesting examples of experiments written by authors of the chapters, ready to run from the accompanying CD. Unfortunately, these works are available only in German at this time.

It is worth mentioning that psychologists in German-speaking nations took to Web research very quickly. The first edition of *Internet für Psychologen* (Batinic 2000) appeared in 1997, and the *German On-line Research Society* began its annual meetings that year (Batinic et al. 1999). Within two years, the society invited papers in English as well as German (e.g., Birnbaum 1999c), and recently, much of their work has become available in English (Batinic et al. 2002, Reips 2001b, Reips & Bosnjak 2001).

Client-Side Programming

The "server" is the computer that stores Web pages and delivers ("serves") them to people who send requests to view them. The "browsers," programs that request and display Web pages, or the computers that run programs to contact the server, are known as the clients. Client-side programs run on the participant's computer rather than on the server. They are often implemented by a "plug-in," an extra software component that helps Web browsers run such programs. Modern Web browsers, such as Internet Explorer, Netscape Navigator, and Mozilla (among others), come with JavaScript and Java installed, which are the two most popular languages for client-side programming. These languages are "free," in that neither programmer nor participant needs to buy anything.

Authorware programs, which also run on the client computer, are executed by means of the Authorware Player, a plug-in that can be downloaded free; however, the Authorware program (used to create experiments, demonstrations, or other content) is expensive.

JavaScript is a programming language that has many uses in Web-based research (Birnbaum 2001a). JavaScript programs can be included as source code in a Web page, and the program loads and runs on the client (i.e., the participant's) machine. By running on the client computer, the program does not burden the server or network with computation and communication delays, which might slow down interactions within an experiment. Including source code in the Web page makes it easy for other researchers to study the programs used and to build upon them. Commercial programmers do not want people to be able to copy and reuse their work, but academic scientists thrive when knowledge is available for inspection, criticism, and modification.

A potential problem with running a program on the client's computer is that one relies on the participant to have the proper software installed and running.

If a person did not have a compatible browser with the proper plug-ins, then client-side programs would not work for that user. Indeed, many users turned off JavaScript and Java when these programs first became available, fearing security gaps. Today, such fears have mostly been allayed by good experiences with the programs and concerns have been outweighed by the value they provide. Although one now expects to find JavaScript and Java on most users' machines, it is still the case that most users would need to make a special effort to download and install certain plug-ins such as the Authorware player, even though such plug-ins are free.

JavaScript is the focus of several works demonstrating its usefulness in psychological research. Baron & Siepmann (2000) show how it can be used to control questionnaire studies, with materials randomized for each participant. Birnbaum & Wakcher (2002) illustrate how to use JavaScript to control a probability learning study (Birnbaum 2002). They also provide a link to a brief tutorial with references to useful resources, at the following URL: http://psych.fullerton.edu/mbirnbaum/brmic/. Lange (1999) shows how JavaScript can be used to accomplish some interesting and useful effects in her on-line museum of perception, and Schmidt (2001) reviews its use in delivering animations on the Web.

Java is a very powerful programming language (which should not be confused with JavaScript). Java can be used to make both stand-alone programs and applets (small programs) that can be precompiled and sent as byte codes along with a Web page, in much the same way that images are sent and incorporated in a page's display. The browser then uses its Java engine to execute the programs on the client computer. For discussions of this approach, with many excellent applications to cognitive psychology experiments, see Francis et al. (2000) and Stevenson et al. (1999). McClelland's (2000) on-line book, *Seeing Statistics*, has a number of Java applets that allow one to "see" and manipulate graphical displays to get a better understanding of fundamental statistical ideas (available at http://www.seeingstatistics.com/).

Instruction on Java by McClelland is available from the Advanced Training Institutes in Social Psychology (ATISP) site: http://ati.fullerton.edu/.

An advantage of Java is the power provided by a fully object-oriented language, with superior control of graphics. In computer programming, an "object" can be conceived as a block of code that is abstract enough that it can be specialized in new ways or generalized for new purposes that were not part of its original design. An object can combine the roles of functions and data structures. A key to programming in the language is to learn how to create objects that will have the greatest generality, can be used as building blocks, and can be reused in new ways. These concepts can be difficult to master, but once a person has learned the language, it opens up many possibilities for controlling graphics and measuring events (such as the position of the mouse) that represent behaviors of the participant. The language of Java is still in flux, so programmers have had to revise their programs to preserve compatibility as new versions of the language were introduced (Francis et al. 2000).

Authorware is a commercial program that can be used to do many of the same tasks as can be accomplished by Java. A possible advantage of Authorware is that it is not as difficult to learn as a programming language. One can create experiments (or other interactive media, such as tutorials) by means of a graphical user interface on which icons representing loops, decisions, and other high-level operations can be placed on a flow-line. Authorware can be used to create cognitive psychology experiments, with accurate control of stimulus timing and measurement of response times (McGraw et al. 2000a,b; Williams et al. 1999). The PsychExps site at Ole Miss is a powerful, virtual laboratory in cognitive psychology, in which investigators from many institutions use the site to run new experiments and lab demonstrations of classic experiments. Instructional material on the Authorware approach is available from the ATISP Web site and from the PsychExps Web site: http://psychexps.olemiss.edu/.

The goal of client-side programming (in JavaScript, Java, Authorware, etc.) is that the program should run equally well on any client's system and browser. However, this ideal has yet to be fully achieved, and one must test any new program with the major systems (Mac, Windows, etc.), major browsers (Internet Explorer, Netscape Navigator, Mozilla, etc.), and various versions of those browsers. Because languages such as Java and JavaScript are still young and developing, a programmer needs to be flexible and energetic to maintain code that will stay compatible with new forms of these languages.

Server-Side Programming

By using a server-side common gateway interface (CGI) program, one can at least guarantee that all users will be able to run the experiment. A server-side program runs on the server, so it does not require the participant to have any special hardware or software (beyond the basic ability to read HTML Web pages).

Schwarz & Reips (2001) compared the use of JavaScript against CGI in a Web experiment and found more and more attrition (more dropouts) in the JavaScript condition compared to the CGI condition, as users worked through the experiment. When their research was conducted, many Web users lacked compatible JavaScript or had it turned off in their browsers. In addition, Internet Explorer's version of JavaScript was "buggy" and not completely consistent with Navigator's. Schwarz & Reips did not find any significant effects of this variable, however, on their theoretical conclusions in a study of the hindsight bias.

Today, so many Web sites depend on JavaScript that it would be frustrating to spend much time on the Web without it. I suspect that if the Schwarz & Reips study were repeated today, there would be less of a difference in attrition between these two ways of controlling an experiment, assuming both were equally well programmed.

Perl is a "free" and open language that can be downloaded and used without charge. It is probably the most widely used language for server-side, CGI programming. Many Web sites are devoted to this language. Schwartz (1998) presents a brief tutorial on Perl. Instructional material by Schmidt (2000) on server-side programming, with links to useful resources, can be retrieved from the Web site from the ATISP site.

Many different ways are often available to accomplish the same task in computer programming, including programming for the Web. But the pros and cons of different methods should be considered in selecting the "best" way to handle a given situation. Take, for example, the problem of random assignment to between-subjects conditions. This can be accomplished by a CGI script running on the server, which means that it will work for all users but may slow down the experiment as the participant waits for a response from the server. When participants wait for a response from the server, they may think that the experiment "froze up" and quit the experiment. Alternately, a client-side program, such as a JavaScript routine, can handle random assignment to conditions; in this case it frees the server, but it may not work for all users. Finally, random assignment can be handled by very simple HTML, which ensures it works and works quickly for the greatest number of participants.

A simple solution for random assignment via HTML is to create a page with a list of months and ask the participant to click the month of his or her birth. Each month would be linked to one of the conditions of the study. For example, January might be assigned to Condition 1, February to Condition 2, March to Condition 1, etc. During the course of the study, the association of birth months to conditions can be counterbalanced to allow a check for any horoscope effects and to equalize the probability of assignment to conditions. Birnbaum (1999a) used this approach.

Another variation of this HTML technique would be to ask the user to click on the last digit of some form of ID, such as driver's license number, Social Security number, etc., with different digits linked to different conditions. The assignment of digits to conditions can be counterbalanced (in a Latin Square, for example) over time.

When choosing such a random device, it is important to be clear that the outcomes can still be random even when outcomes may not be equally probable. For example, there are more odd birthdays (date within the month) than even ones, so if people were assigned to two conditions by odd or even birthdays, one expects slightly more than half of participants to end up in the odd condition. Counterbalancing the assignment equalizes the numbers in the two groups as well as making possible a test of whether being born on an odd- or even-numbered birthday makes a difference for the behavior under examination.

A simple JavaScript program can also handle random assignment to conditions; for example, see Birnbaum (2001a, Chapter 17). Birnbaum's example script can be easily modified for any number of conditions. In the script, a random number is selected using the pseudo random number generator of JavaScript. In case the user does not have JavaScript installed, the Web page reverts to the HTML birthday method. Other client-side methods to handle random assignment include Java (Francis et al. 2000) and Authorware (McGraw et al. 2000b), among others.

For descriptions of how assignment can be accomplished by means of server-side CGI scripts, see Morrow & McKee (1998) and Schmidt (2000). A CGI script in Perl to handle random assignment to conditions, written by William Schmidt, is available from http://psych.fullerton.edu/mbirnbaum/programs/PERL_script2. htm.

Another task that can be accomplished in many ways on the Web is animation. For a study of different ways of creating animations on the Web, see the article by Schmidt (2001), which reviews the pros and cons of animated graphics interchange formats (gifs), movies, Flash animations, Java, and JavaScript.

Although certain tasks can be done well on either the server or the participant's computer, other tasks can or should only be done on the server. For example, the routine to save the data must be run on the server. A simple script for sorting and saving data by William Schmidt is available from the above-listed ATISP site. Other cases where server-side programming should be used (rather than client-side programming) include password control of access to files and scoring of on-line tests when there may be an incentive to cheat. Any task where security is an issue should only be run on the server. Schmidt (2000) describes many other examples of server-side programming.

Run Your Own Server

Schmidt et al. (1997) describe the advantages of operating your own server (see also Reips 1997). At the ATISP site (http://ati.fullerton.edu), Schmidt explains how to download and install the free Apache Web server on a PC, which includes the free distribution of Perl. All that is required is a desktop computer attached to the Internet and the free software. The system works best with a fixed Internet protocol (IP) address, but Schmidt notes there are even ways to work around that limitation. With a Mac running operating system (OS) X, Apache and Perl come preinstalled and can be easily turned on, as described by Reips, in the following URL: http://ati.fullerton.edu/ureips/all_you_need/index.html.

Many campus computing centers restrict what a professor or student can do on the campus network (there are legitimate security concerns of allowing students to add CGIs to a university server, for example). In response to concerns for security, some campus centers may arbitrarily put excessive restrictions on what a professor can do. To overcome such restrictions and to provide maximal control, many Web experimenters now run their own Web servers, and some have even moved their research off campus to be hosted by commercial Internet providers, where they enjoy greater freedom.

Stimulus Delivery

As computer hardware and software improve, it becomes easier and easier to deliver visual and auditory stimuli via the WWW. But there are limitations on what can be delivered and the precision of the stimulus delivered (Krantz 2001). A potential problem is that different users have different computers, systems, browsers, monitors, and speakers, so the actual stimulus received may differ quite a bit from what the experimenter intended. The stimuli received may vary from person to person. Fortunately, perception obeys constancy properties that help make many such variations irrelevant to the results (Krantz 2001); people quickly adapt to fixed background conditions (such as brightness setting on a monitor), so that such variables, which change from person to person, have little effect. Nevertheless, such lack of control must be taken into consideration.

Even something as simple as how a browser and system displays different colors cannot be taken for granted. There were supposed to be 216 so-called Web-safe colors that would be displayed the same by all browsers (Birnbaum 2001a), but even these are not produced exactly the same by Internet Explorer and Netscape Navigator. For more information on color see the following sites:

http://seurat.art.udel.edu/Site/Cookbook.html

http://hotwired.lycos.com/webmonkey/00/37/index2a.html?tw=design

http://www.visibone.com/

http://www.websitetips.com/color/

Questions have also been raised involving the accurate control and measurement of temporal intervals on the participant's computer. Despite problems with stimulus control and response measurement, a number of classic perceptual and cognitive experiments have been successfully implemented on the Web. These Web studies appear to work quite well, despite imperfections introduced by the Web medium (Eichstaedt 2001, 2002; Gordon & Rosenblum 2001; Hecht et al. 1999; Horswill & Coster 2001; Krantz 2001; Lange 1999; Laugwitz 2001; Ruppertsberg et al. 2001; Schmidt 2001; Stevenson et al. 1999; Van Veen et al. 1998).

When the participant has to wait for a large visual or auditory file to download before it can be presented, he or she might get bored and quit the experiment. In recent years, attention has been devoted to speeding up transmission on the WWW by compressing pictures, graphics, and sounds, and finding ways to display a stimulus before the file has completely downloaded. One familiar method for sending graphics is to send a "progressive" file that presents a grainy but complete version of the final picture quickly and then improves the image as the details are received and interpreted (Krantz 2001).

The mp3 standard for auditory files has made it possible to send relatively small files of music or speech that sound quite good. Additional information with links to on-line resources are in Birnbaum (2001a, Chapter 14) and Krantz (2001).

By means of streaming media, it is possible to send video movies with sound in (almost) real time, once a buffer is filled. The idea of streaming media is that the first part of a file can begin to play while the rest of the file is still being downloaded. For information on QuickTime and free streaming servers, see http://www.apple.com/quicktime/.

If one has a good connection to the Web and the proper plug-ins, one can even watch "live" television via the Web. For example, with the Windows Media Player, one can view the educational, Annenberg/CPB channel from the following URL: http://www.learner.org/channel/channel.html.

With the Flash Player and RealPlayer plug-ins, one can view the German television channel, *Deutsche Welle*, and receive "live" broadcasts from the following URL: http://www.dw-world.de.

At the time of this writing, these technique are of good enough quality for psychological research only with computers that have fast connections to the Internet and which have the proper plug-ins installed (e.g., QuickTime, RealPlayer, Windows Media Player, etc.). However, it is likely that by the time this chapter is published, most people with Internet access will have the appropriate connection and software needed to display experiments with streaming video, making such research practical to conduct via the Web.

METHODOLOGY

Web methods help solve some old problems of lab research with undergraduates, but they create new problems that require special solutions. A number of works discuss advantages and possible drawbacks of Web-based research (Bandilla 2002; Birnbaum 1999b, 2001a, 2003; Dillman 2000; Dillman & Bowker 2001; Hewson et al. 1996; Petit 1999; Piper 1998; Reips 1997, 2000, 2001a; 2002b; Schiano 1997; Schmidt 1997a; Smith & Leigh 1997).

Perhaps the three most important advantages of Web research over lab research with the undergraduate "subject pool" are as follows: On the Web one can achieve large samples, making statistical tests very powerful and model fitting very clean. With clean data the "signal" of systematic deviations can be easily distinguished from "noise." Second, Web studies permit generalization from college students to a wider variety of participants. Third, one can recruit specialized types of participants via the WWW that would be quite rare to find among students. At the same time, studies conducted via the WWW have several potential problems and disadvantages. These methodological pros and cons are reviewed in the next sections, including methods to address some of the potential problems introduced by Web research.

Multiple Submissions

In lab research it has rarely been considered a problem that a participant might serve twice in an experiment and thus reduce the effective degrees of freedom. However, in Web research, the possibility of multiple submissions has received considerable attention (Birnbaum 2000b, 2001a,b, 2004; Reips 2000, 2001a, 2002b; Schmidt 1997a, 2000). Table 1 summarizes methods intended to prevent multiple submissions or to detect them so that they can be removed from the data.

Each method is based on a particular theory of why a person might want to submit multiple sets of data. The first idea is that people may think that if it is good

TABLE 1   Avoiding or detecting multiple submissions

Method	Tactic
Instructions	Tell people to participate only once
Remove incentives	Rewards not available for those who participate more than once
Replace incentive	Provide alternative site for repeated play
Use identifiers	Common gateway interface (CGI) script allows only one submission; option: replace previous data or refusal to accept new
Use identifiers	Filter data to remove repeats
Use Internet protocol (IP), email address	Check for repeated IP addresses
Passwords	Allow participation by password only
Cookies	Check cookie for previous participation
CGI scripts	CGI checks for referring page and other features
Log file analysis	Can detect patterns of requests
Subsample follow up	Contact participants to verify ID
Check for identical data records	Filter identical or nearly identical records

to participate, it would be better to participate many times. So the first method is simply to ask people not to participate more than once.

The next methods are to remove or replace incentives to participate more than once. For example, if each participant is given a payment or a chance at a prize, there is an incentive to collect multiple payments or improve one's chances to win the prize. Instructions could then state that each person can be paid only once or receive no more than one chance at the prize. If the study is interesting (e.g., a video game or intellectual challenge), one could provide a separate site where those who want to continue to play with the materials can do so without adding to the regular data file.

Identifiers, such as student numbers, phone numbers, email addresses, mailing address, demographics, or names, can be used to identify each record of data. It is an easy matter to sort by such identifiers to detect multiple submissions from the same person.

In some research, it might be intended that each person should participate repeatedly to see how behavior changes with practice. Each person might be asked how many times he or she had already done the task. Date and time stamps on each record can be used to identify the temporal spacing in which submissions were received.

The Internet protocol (IP) address can be used to spot multiple submissions. The IP is a number such as 137.151.68.63, which represents a computer on the campus of California State University, Fullerton. Although IP addresses do not uniquely identify a person, when two submissions arrive in a short period from the same IP, they likely represent multiple submissions from the same person. A conservative procedure is to remove records coming from the same or similar IP addresses even if they are separated in time (Reips 2000). A similar IP is an address with all but the number after the last dot the same; for example, 137.151.68.63 and 137.151.68.15 are two different computers on my home campus. Reips found, even in the days of mostly fixed IP addresses, that this conservative procedure of deleting any submissions from similar IPs would have almost no impact on the data set.

Of course, when data are collected in labs, one should expect the same IP address to come up again and again as different participants are tested on the same machine. Another complication is that IP addresses are now mostly "dynamic," which means that two different users from an Internet service provider might receive the same IP on different days, because the Internet service provider (e.g., AOL) will assign IP addresses to users as they come and go. This also means that the same user might come to a study from two different IP addresses on two occasions. Therefore, it is useful to obtain additional identifiers, such as the last four digits of a Social Security number or driver's license number, or an email address.

Instead of checking data for multiple submissions and removing them, it is possible to program the server to refuse to accept multiple submissions from the same ID (IP or other identifier). A CGI script could be used to check the identifiers and refuse to save subsequent submissions by the same ID, if this were deemed necessary.

One can use passwords to identify each participant and use a CGI script to monitor admission to the study, or one can place passwords in the data file to identify each record of data. Cookies (data stored on the participant's computer) can also be used to keep track of how many times a person at that computer has participated. However, this procedure would not prevent a person from participating from different computers or from erasing the cookie, which some people do as a general protection of their privacy.

CGI scripts can be used to check for the referring page that sent the data. The referring page is the WWW document that sent data to the CGI. One can find not only what uniform resource locator (URL) (i.e., Web page) called the CGI (sent data), but one can also detect what URL referred the participant to that Web page.

It is good policy to check the referring page (that sent the data), as a general security measure. If that page is not located on the home server (the server that housed the study), it might mean that a hacker is sending data from some other site. One can also glean valuable information from an analysis of the server's log file, which keeps track of requests and submissions of files and data. See also Breinholt & Krueger (1999) and Reips (2001a, 2002b). Reips has written software that can be used to analyze log files in order to determine where in a study the participant might have dropped out, for example. He also advises that Web experimenters keep log files for possible reanalysis by other investigators.

Reips (2000, 2001b) suggests following up a subsample of participants to check their identities, should this issue become a concern. For example, in a study in which each participant has a chance at a prize and provides an email address to be contacted in case they win, one might check a subsample of those addresses to verify the identities of those people.

One can also search for identical data records. If a study is long enough, it is unlikely that two records would be the same unless the same person submitted data twice. Should one find a number of identical submissions in a short time interval, they are likely multiple copies.

Although the issue of multiple submissions is one of the first questions that Web experimenters are asked, Web researchers are of the consensus that this issue has not been a real problem (Birnbaum 2000b, 2001b; Musch & Reips 2000). In my experience, I find that multiple submissions are rare and easy to detect. They typically occur when a participant scrolls to the bottom of the questionnaire, clicks the submit button, reads the "thank you" page, and uses the "back" button on the browser to return to the study. The person may then add a comment or change a response, and click the submit button to navigate forward again. Such cases are easy to spot and filter from the data, because they come in sequentially with the same IP, the same email address, and for the most part, the same data in a short period.

In a careful analysis of 1000 data records, I found only one case in which the same person sent data on two different occasions. One woman participated exactly twice, months apart, and interestingly, agreed on 19 of her 20 decisions (Birnbaum 2001b). In the days of mostly fixed IPs, Reips (1997) analyzed 880 records and found only four submissions from the same or similar IP addresses. Reips's procedure is conservative since it might eliminate two different students who both participated from the same campus.

A researcher should have a clear prior policy on whether to retain the new data or the old, in case data have changed between submissions. In my decision-making research, I always take the last submission, since I want the person's last, best, most considered decision. However, in some areas of research (perhaps where debriefing might alter a person's response), one might have a policy to take only the first set of data and delete any subsequent ones that might have been affected by debriefing. Reips's LogAnalyzer program (http://genpsylab-logcrunsh.unizh.ch/) allows one to choose either first or last submissions for its analysis.

Dropouts in Between-Subjects Research

A serious threat to internal validity of a between-subjects experiment occurs when there are dropouts, people who begin a study and quit before completing it. Even when there are equal dropout rates in experimental and control groups, dropouts can cause the observed results to show the opposite of the true effects (Birnbaum 2003, Birnbaum & Mellers 1989). For example, a harmful treatment might look helpful.

Consider a workshop intended to help students prepare for the SAT. Suppose participants are randomly assigned to a control group or treatment group who receive the program. Suppose this workshop actually lowers scores on the SAT, but also includes a practice test with advice not to take the real SAT exam if you did poorly on the practice exam. Such a program increases the correlation between performance on the test and likelihood of taking the test (as opposed to dropping out). Such an intervention could easily look helpful (because those who dropped out were those who would have achieved low scores), even though the treatment itself lowers the average SAT. Birnbaum & Mellers (1989) presented numerical examples illustrating how in a true experiment, with equal dropout in both experimental and treatment groups, the harmful treatment can produce a higher mean level of performance among those who do not drop out. Thus, dropouts can make a true experiment give false results.

Web-based research has been found to have larger dropout rates than lab studies. In the lab, other people are present, so a person would have to explain that he or she would like to quit the study and leave early. Web participants are free of any such possible social pressure or embarrassment. They simply click a button to quit a study and do something else (Birnbaum 2003). Knapp & Heidingsfelder (2001) and Frick et al. (2001) discuss the issue and describe procedures intended to reduce dropouts. See also O'Neil & Penrod (2001).

The "high-hurdle" and "warm-up" techniques of Reips (2000, 2002b) are intended to cause those who would drop out of a study to do so before the random assignment to conditions. In the high-hurdle technique, one asks for personal information early and includes a page that loads slowly, in order to encourage impatient or resistant people to drop out early, leaving cooperative participants behind. By asking for identifying information early, it may help those quit early who would be loath to provide the information later, and it may create more social pressure among those who do provide the information to stick it out to the end of the study. Frick et al. (2001) presented an empirical application of this approach. If the method works as theorized, then the method exchanges a threat to external validity (How do results with self-selected cooperative people generalize to others?) for the threat to internal validity (Do different people drop out of the treatment and control groups?).

Bosnjak (2001) and Bosnjak & Batinic (2002) consider the related issues of why people may not wish to "drop in" to participate in surveys or to answer all items. Welker (2001) notes that one of the reasons that surveys sent via regular mail have higher response rates than surveys sent by email is that not everyone reads his or her email. In a study with a fixed population of people with email accounts, a random sample of 900 was selected to receive invitations to a survey by email. It was found that the overall response rate was only 14%; however, for this sample of 900, 330 never read their email during the two months of the survey. When these nonreaders were taken into account, the response rate was figured to be 22%, which is higher, but still rather low.

Self-selection of participants means that results of any survey may not be accurate as a description of the population to which inference may be desired. By repeated reminders and combinations of electronic and postal mailings, it is possible to increase response rates (Dillman 2000). Tourangeau (2004) documents a trend in survey research: The refusal rates and nonresponse rates to surveys of all types has doubled in the last decade; that review includes discussion of surveys by mail, email, phone, and Internet.

Recruiting Participants Via the Web

The Web can be used not only to test participants, but also to recruit them. Indeed, four types of studies should be distinguished, composed of the four combinations of recruitment method (Web or other) and testing method (Web or lab). By recruiting from the Web, it is possible to easily obtain large sample sizes; one can obtain samples that are heterogeneous with respect to age, education, income, social class, and nationality; and it is possible to reach people with special or rare characteristics. One might recruit people with rare characteristics via the Web and then test them in the lab. Or one might recruit people from the local "subject" pool and test them in the lab. Similarly, one might recruit and test in the Web or one might recruit from the "subject pool" and test via the WWW. Examples of these four types of studies are discussed in Birnbaum (2003).

Birnbaum (2001a, Chapter 21) and Reips (2000, 2001a,b) review a number of different techniques for recruiting participants via the WWW. One method is passive: Let people find the study via search engines or links. One can register an experiment with search engines that still accept "suggest a site" and wait for participants to find the study on the Web.

A study of sexual behavior (suggested to *Yahoo!*) was initiated in 1995 at Fullerton, which recruited entirely by this passive method. In the next four years, the study was completed by more than 10,000 participants who completed a questionnaire of more than 400 items (Bailey et al. 2000). During the course of that study, several other Web sites placed links to the study, which illustrates the point that even though one may choose a method of recruitment, that method does not completely control recruitment. It seems likely that it makes a difference if a study is linked in a site for incest victims as opposed to one for swingers. The people who place the links are being "helpful," but they may influence how people come to find the study. Information concerning the link that sent a person to the site can be recorded, and data can be analyzed separately according to what link referred each person to the study, but the lack of complete control over recruiting should be clear from this example.

Another method of recruitment is to announce a study via email. However, it is bad manners to send unsolicited email messages to people who don't want to receive them (Birnbaum 2003, Hewson et al. 1996), so it is recommended that one should *not* send any request that might be seen as "spam" (electronic "junk" mail) to all members of a mailing list. Such spam may generate "flames" (angry messages) to the entire list, which could injure one's reputation and be counterproductive. Instead, one should seek cooperation of a relevant organization with an Internet presence. If the organization vouches that the researcher is a serious scientist and that the research would be of interest or benefit to its members, the organization can provide good help and save the researcher from going down in "flames."

Pam Drake, a former graduate assistant of mine, wanted to recruit elderly people interested in genealogy. She contacted a relevant on-line genealogy organization, which agreed to back her research by sending a request to participate to its members. Within a week, she had more than 4000 data records from her targeted group, and she had received many friendly messages of encouragement and support. Other ways that an organization could help would be by listing a link to your study in its Web site, posting a message to an electronic bulletin board, or including information about the study in its newsletter.

One can also recruit by requesting a link in sites that list on-line psychology studies, such as the sites maintained by Krantz (1998) and by Reips (1995), mentioned above. There are also sites that list free things on the Web. If your experiment yields an estimate of one's IQ, for example (Wilhelm & McKnight 2002), it could be described as a free IQ test. Many "self-discovery" sites would be happy to list a link to ability or personality tests that provide feedback.

Banners, or advertising links placed in Web sites, might also be used. These are usually commercial announcements, so one runs the risk of looking like "free enterprise," which usually means there's a catch (i.e., not free). Some scientists have explored this method and estimated that less than 1% of those who view the banner will click the link. Because this method has expense associated with it, it may not be cost-effective; nevertheless, there may be some situations in which one might want to test the sort of people who would click such links placed at certain special sites (Buchanan 2000).

For example, in personality testing, a person might want to study visitors to body-piercing sites, to see if their personalities differ systematically from those who visit "traditional family values" sites. The multiple-site entry technique (Reips 2000, 2002b) uses different methods to recruit different types of people to sites that contain the same basic content, to see if the data collected at the different sites are systematically correlated with the recruitment method. As a check on the recruitment method, one can ask the participants to indicate the group with which they more closely identify.

Many personality taxonomies have been developed based on paper-and-pencil analyses of data from college students. Because college students are homogeneous on several variables (age, education, etc.) it is reasonable that correlates of such variables would not emerge in factor-analytic studies of personality. Because Web studies reach more heterogeneous participants, recruitment via the Web has advantages over traditional studies of undergraduate personality (Buchanan 2000, 2001; Buchanan & Smith 1999a,b; Hertel et al. 2002; Mueller et al. 2000; Pasveer & Ellard 1998). McKenna & Bargh (2000), Schillewaert et al. (1998), and Reips (2000, 2002b) discuss the multiple-site entry method, which has good potential for establishing criterion groups that can be used to develop and validate personality tests.

The Internet is a convenient medium for cross-cultural or international research as well. Here the criterion groups are nationalities or cultures. Once an experiment is running on the Web, participants from anywhere in the world can access it. An investigator can form collaborations with scientists in other nations who can recruit to the same site from different strata of their populations. It is then easy to compare data from participants recruited similarly in different nations. Studies by Pagani & Lombardi (2000) and Pohl et al. (2002) illustrate this technique. It would be quite useful in an area where one wishes to compare data across cultures to investigate evolutionary theories of human behavior (such as jealousy, as in Voracek et al. 2001).

One method of regulating the selection of participants tested via the Web is to recruit an on-line panel (Baron & Siepmann 2000, Göritz et al. 2002). Such a panel consists of a group of people who have been preselected on some basis (e.g., for representative distributions of gender, age, education level, etc.) to be members of a panel that will be used repeatedly, much like the families used for Nielson television ratings.

Sampling Bias and Stratified Analysis

It would be a mistake to treat data recruited from the Web as if they represented a sample of some stable population of "Web users." The list of people with access to the Internet is expanding every day, and no method yet devised has been shown to reach those users in a random fashion. By using different techniques, many different substrata of Web users might be reached, but there is no guarantee that any particular method of recruitment would yield a sample representative of some particular population.

One approach to this problem in experimental research is to analyze the research question separately within each substratum of a heterogeneous sample. With large numbers of participants in Web studies, it becomes possible to separate the data by age, education, gender, and other demographic variables and to analyze the data separately in each slice. If the same conclusions are reached in each subsample, one begins to believe that the results have generality to other groups besides college sophomores (Birnbaum 1999b).

When the purpose of the research is to estimate a population parameter from a Web sample, however, then neither college sophomores nor self-selected Web participants should be considered as random samples of any particular population. Those who take lower division psychology courses are not a random sample of college students, let alone of some wider population. Those who enroll in psychology are more likely to be female and less likely to be engineers than the campus average. Those who are recruited via the Web are on average older than college students, have greater mean education, and greater variance in age and education than do college students.

As an example of research intended to estimate a population parameter, one might want to forecast the results of an election by a survey of potential voters. For this purpose, neither college undergraduates, nor self-selected samples (such as are easy to recruit via the Web) are appropriate. In this case, participants are said to be self-selected because they decide whether to participate and whether to drop in or drop out. For more discussion of problems of self-selection, see Birnbaum (1999b, 2000b, 2001a, 2003), Bandilla (2002), Brenner (2002), Bosnjak & Batinic (2002), Corkrey & Parkinson (2002), Dillman (2000), Dillman & Bowker (2001), Musch et al. (2001), Reips (2000, 2002c), and Stanton (1998).

For an example of a survey of a sample randomly selected for invitation from a particular membership list of Internet users, see Lukawetz (2002). Lukawetz found that those who used the Internet less frequently were less likely to respond to the survey and more likely to respond late. Thus, even when a population can be defined, there is evidence that self-selected volunteers are not a random sample of that group.

The problem with self-selection is that the results may not generalize from the self-selected sample to some larger population. For example, a survey of political opinions recruited from a Web site for gun owners might yield a different conclusion with respect to people's opinions of political candidates than a survey recruited from a Web site devoted to environmental issues. Even if the same survey materials were used, neither group would be likely to forecast the outcome of the next election.

The most famous case of misuse of data from a self-selected sample is the *Literary Digest's* erroneous prediction that Alf Landon would defeat Franklin D. Roosevelt for the presidency in 1936. Even though the sample size was very large, the readers of this magazine who self-selected to mail in the survey were much more likely to favor Republican candidates than was the average voter (Huff 1954).

Response Bias

The input devices used to accept responses can influence how a participant would respond. In fact, some input devices should be avoided completely. For example, the check box should not be used because it allows only two responses: yes or no (Birnbaum 2001a). If a box is unchecked, does that mean that the participant responded "no" or does it mean the person did not respond to the item? One should allow at least three responses (yes, no, and no response) and sometimes even four (yes, no, no answer, and refuse to answer) for a "yes-no" question.

The pull-down selection list is a very complicated answering device. The user must click on the device to see a list of alternative answers. The user must then scroll through the choices to select an answer. As in a "yes-no" item, there should be no preselected answer, or people who skip the item will be recorded as having made that answer. The preselected choice should be coded as a nonresponse and given a label such as "choose from this list." The distance and direction of each possible response from the preselected choice may influence the results.

For example, suppose we want to determine in what category a person's monthly income falls. Suppose the default choice is listed as $0, and many levels are listed between $0 and $200 per month. It is likely that this procedure would yield lower estimates of monthly income than if the default were more than $1 million per month, if there were many levels between $1 million and $10,000 per month, and where one must scroll down past many options to see lower ranges of income.

The size of a text box for a numerical answer may also influence the response. For example, consider the question, "How many traffic accidents have you had?" A size $= 1$ input text box (which suggests to the participant that a 1-digit number is expected) would likely produce smaller numbers than a size $= 3$ box (which signals that a 3-digit number might be expected). Birnbaum (2001a, Chapter 5) described an experiment on the value of the St. Petersburg gamble in which significantly different averages were obtained by different lists of values in a pull-down list and these results were in turn different from the mean obtained with a large text box. See Dillman & Bowker (2001) and Reips (2002a,d) for further discussion of how changes in arrangements or display as well as other surface features might alter the results one obtains.

Experimenter Bias

When an experimenter or her assistant knows the research hypothesis, receives responses from the participant, and then enters the data for analysis, small biases can enter the data file in many ways. The experimenter might give additional undocumented instructions, might provide subtle reinforcing cues, might repeat a question as if expecting a different answer, and might miscode or mistype the data in the expected direction. An error in the expected direction might not be noticed, but an error in the unpredicted direction might be caught. A possible advantage of Web studies is that these many sources of experimenter biases can be standardized and documented so that other scientists can repeat the experiment exactly. By eliminating the lab assistant, some of the sources of bias are eliminated.

The potential drawback is that if the participant has a question about the instructions, there is no lab assistant to explain or clarify the task. This means that every aspect of an experiment, including the wording of instructions, must be carefully thought out before launching an experiment on the Internet. Furthermore, one must take into consideration the variety of people around the world who may have very different interpretations of the instructions.

PILOT TESTING IN THE LAB

As noted earlier, it is possible to have several thousand people complete a Web study in a few days, so before launching a study, it must be thoroughly checked. It would be a kind of vandalism of scientific resources to waste people's time completing a flawed research instrument. Such checking should involve at least three main parts.

First, decide if the data analysis will answer the question addressed by the research. Those who design a study without planning the analysis usually fail to devise an experiment that answers the original question (Birnbaum 2001a, 2003).

Second, check the programming of the study, including coding of the data. I have found surveys on-line in which the same code value was used for missing data as for one of the legitimate answers. In one case, if a person were from India or if he or she did not respond, the coded value was the same, 99. Fortunately, this problem was caught before much data had been collected.

I find many problems that my students fail to notice because they do not check their work carefully. I have seen students make mistakes in code such that when the participant answers the second question, the answer to the first is replaced. Click a radio button to Question 3, and the one for Question 2 goes out. Part of the checking process should include sending test data to make absolutely sure that each button and each response field is functioning properly and that the experimenter knows where the data go in the file. One should also view the experiment using several types of computers, monitors, browsers, and versions of those browsers to preview the different experiences that participants will have with these variations.

This second part of pilot testing should include testing some naive participants in the lab, and interviewing them to make sure that they understood the instructions. Data from this lab test should be analyzed to make sure that the method of analysis works and is error free. It is often when analyzing data that students notice that they have made a coding error in their programming. Based on the pilot study, any improvements should be made and then rechecked before the study is put on-line.

As a third part of the pretest, participants in the lab test should also be closely observed, as some interesting things may be discovered. One of my students placed a response device above the material on which the response was to be made. Watching people, I saw that some participants answered before they scrolled down to see the material to which they were supposed to be responding.

In another student project, participants were instructed to take out some coins and toss them, in a variation of the random response technique (Musch et al. 2001). For example, consider the question of whether a person used an illegal drug in the past 24 hours. The random response technique, if it works, allows the researcher to estimate the proportion of people who used the drug, without knowing for any individual whether he or she used the drug. Participants were instructed to toss two coins, and if they got two heads, they were to respond "yes" and if they got two tails, they were to respond "no;" however, if they got a heads and tails or tails and heads, they were to respond with the truth. Thus, a "yes" or "no" does not indicate for any person if it came from the coins or from the truth. But the researcher can subtract off 25% heads and 25% tails and multiply by two to get the correct answer. For example, if 30% of the overall sample said "yes," it means that 10% of the truth-tellers said "yes." This is a very clever method, if it works as planned.

Out of 15 participants pretested in the lab, however, only one student actually took out any coins, and that one asked first if she should actually do what the instructions said to do. Had this study been placed on the Web, the experimenter never would have known what the participants were doing (or in this case, not doing). The solution in this case was to add additional instructions, and to add questions asking the participants if they did, indeed, use coins or not, and if not, why not. Even after the instructions emphasized the importance of following the instructions, about half of undergraduates tested conceded that they did not, in fact, use the coins, giving reasons such as "lazy" or "I had nothing to hide" as explanations for not following the instructions.

Lists of other tests to perform and standards to check before launching a study on the Web are given by Birnbaum (2001a, Chapters 12 and 21) and Gräf (2002). Reips (2002b,d) also provides lists of standards and "dos and don'ts" that one should consider before launching one's study. These lists will likely continue to expand as more is learned about on-line research.

WEB VERSUS LAB

Once an experiment is running on the Web, it is a simple matter to replicate the experiment in the lab. A number of studies compared data obtained in the lab against data obtained via the Web, to see if the two ways of conducting research reach the same conclusions (Birnbaum 1999b, 2001a; Horswill & Coster 2001; Krantz & Dalal 2000; Krantz et al. 1997; Musch & Klauer 2002; Reips 2002b,c; Van Veen et al. 1998; Voracek et al. 2001).

Krantz & Dalal (2000) reviewed nine studies comparing Web and lab versions and concluded that results from the two methods yielded surprising agreement. Subsequent studies have generally conformed to this result. However, that conclusion should not be taken to mean that there would be no significant difference between subjects recruited from the Web and college students, nor does it mean that no significant effect of different types of monitors and browsers should be expected.

Those working with cognitive psychology experiments take it for granted that if they program their experiments properly, the same basic results should be observed (Stevenson et al. 1999, Williams et al. 1999). Indeed, such Web experiments consistently replicate classic results, even when the independent and dependent variables involve manipulation or measurement of brief time intervals, which are thought to be less precisely controlled or measured via the Web (Eichstaedt 2002, Francis et al. 2000, McGraw et al. 2000b).

However, the thesis that the same conclusions might be reached in lab and Web research does not mean that Web and lab studies will not yield significantly different results. Birnbaum (1999b), for example, set out to recruit a special population of participants—people with advanced education in decision-making. He found that people holding doctorates who have read a scientific work on decision theory are significantly less likely to violate stochastic dominance than undergraduates who have not studied decision-making. With undergraduates, 68% said they would prefer to play a gamble with a 0.85 probability to win $96, a 0.05 probability to win $90, and a 0.10 probability to win $12 rather than a gamble with a 0.90 probability to win $96, 0.05 to win $14, and 0.05 to win $12, even though the second gamble dominates the first. The 95 people with doctorates and who had read on decision-making had 50% violations on this choice, which is still very high but significantly lower than the rate observed with undergraduates.

Significant correlations were also found with gender: Female undergraduates violated stochastic dominance more often than male undergraduates. Indeed, the undergraduate sample in Birnbaum's (1999b) "lab" study was 73% female, whereas the participants recruited from the Web had only 56% females. However, the conclusions with respect to models of decision-making were no different in these groups, even though the rates of violation were significantly different in demographic categories.

Birnbaum (1999b, 2000a, 2001b; Birnbaum & Martin 2003) conducted a series of Web experiments with thousands of participants, indicating that cumulative prospect theory (Tversky & Kahneman 1992) is not descriptive of risky decision-making. Five new paradoxes have been devised that yield contradictions to this theory. Cumulative prospect theory implies that people's judgments should satisfy stochastic dominance, coalescing, lower cumulative independence, upper cumulative independence, and upper tail independence. However, data from thousands of participants tested in the lab and via the Web show that these properties are systematically and significantly violated. Web experiments have now tested a variety of techniques for displaying the risky gambles, and the results continue to hold up with thousands of participants. In addition, violations of restricted branch independence and of distribution independence are opposite the pattern predicted by cumulative prospect theory's weighting function.

This series of experiments would have taken decades to accomplish had the studies been run by the techniques used in lab research. This advantage in efficiency is the probably the greatest advantage of Web research over previous methods of research and will be the primary motivation of those who switch to this new method. In these tests of decision-making properties, tests with undergraduates in classrooms and in labs also yield the same conclusions as those from the Web.

Web studies, by having larger samples, usually have greater power than lab studies, despite greater noise due to technical variations (hardware, systems, and browsers) and demographic diversity in Web samples. Data quality can be defined by variable error, constant error, reliability, or validity. Comparisons of power and of certain measures of quality have found cases where Web data are higher in quality by one or another of these definitions than are comparable lab data, though not always (Birnbaum 1999b, 2000a; Reips 2002c; Tuten et al. 2002).

Many Web researchers are convinced that data obtained via the Web can be "better" than those obtained from students (Baron & Siepmann 2000, Musch & Reips 2000, Reips 2000), despite the obvious advantage that the lab offers for control. Based on what has been done, however, I don't think it appropriate to argue yet that Web data are better than lab data, because the relevant comparisons have not been completed and the Web-versus-lab variable is not really a single independent variable. For example, those recruited via the WWW have been older, better educated, and perhaps more motivated that the usual undergraduate sample tested in the lab.

Part of the difference may occur because the average participant in early Web studies had more education than did the typical undergraduate in the lab. Perhaps more highly educated participants are also higher in intelligence, or better at reading and following directions. Birnbaum (1999b), who intended to recruit highly educated participants, found that only 2% of females who have earned a doctorate violated transparent dominance (a rational property of decision making) while tested via the WWW. In contrast, 14% of female undergraduates tested in the lab violated the same property. Is this difference due to being tested in the lab versus on-line, or is it due to the difference in education or its unmeasured correlates? For comparison, 12% of females tested via the Web with some college (but no degree) violated the same property. So, if we consider conformity to transparent dominance as an index of data quality, the Web data would indeed be judged higher in quality, but most of the apparent difference might be explainable by the confounded effects of education or other correlates of the method of recruitment.

Part of the belief that Web data are better than lab data may also be because many participants in early Web studies participated as volunteers out of interest, whereas students often participate as one way to complete an assignment (Reips 2000). Many Web experimenters have been pleasantly surprised (as I was) to receive many messages from Web participants expressing interest and encouragement in the research. It makes one think that Web participants are more motivated than college students and perhaps take the tasks more seriously. Interestingly, the confidence that Web experimenters have in their data runs contrary to the impression held by some that on the Web people are more likely to misrepresent themselves.

Bargh & McKenna (2004) reviewed research on the social psychology of the Internet. Social psychologists theorize that the Internet creates new social situations. There is a great deal of theorizing backed by a little data that people may behave differently, perhaps taking on a new identity via the Web, where they might feel anonymous (Joinson 1999, Sassenberg & Kreutz 2002), compared to how they would respond in person. It has also been argued to the contrary, that people might be more honest with a computer than with a human interviewer on sensitive matters, such as details of one's sex life (Bailey et al. 2000). This new and growing literature has already been reviewed in several books (Döring 2002a, Gackenbach 1998, Joinson 2002, Suler 1996, Wallace 2001). If people do behave differently, it might mean that research conducted via the WWW would reach systematically different conclusions from those obtained in the lab.

Kraut et al. (1998) suggested that spending a lot of time on the Internet might interfere with one's social life with real people, and might lead to depression. Brenner (2002) provides a skeptical review of the topic of "Internet addiction," a term referring to pathologically excessive use of the Internet to the detriment of one's real life. Döring (2002b) reviews studies of cyber romance, noting that these relationships are quite common and real. Janetzko (2002) reviews the topic of dialog and interview "bots," computer programs that emulate the behavior of humans. Perhaps one day these bots will be perfected and we will have an Internet sequel to the tale of Pygmalion. Perhaps people will fall in love with a computer program. For more on the social psychology of the Internet, see the review by Bargh & McKenna (2004).

SUMMARY AND CONCLUSIONS

Even if people do not love the computers themselves, it is clear that many psychologists have indeed become enamored of the possibilities provided by these new methods for conducting psychological research via the WWW.

In the short time since Web experimentation has become possible, a great deal has been learned about the techniques, methodology, and results of Web studies. Programs and instructional materials are now available to make it relatively easy for a new investigator in this field to be able to implement simple studies to run via the WWW. Investigators who have begun research using these techniques have for the most part judged the method to be successful and plan to continue research of this type. Although some methodological problems have emerged in Web-based research because of the lack of control in Web studies, many investigators consider the advantages in experimental power, low cost, and convenience of testing via the Web to outweigh its disadvantages. Experience with studies done via the Web and in the lab indicates that if Web studies are properly designed, one can replicate lab results in many fields of psychology. Significant differences between results of lab studies with undergraduates and Web studies of people recruited via the Web have been reported, but these may be due to the differences in people tested rather than the method.

ACKNOWLEDGMENTS

This work was supported by National Science Foundation Grants SBR-94,10572, SES 99-86,436, and BCS-01,29453. I thank Ulf-Dietrich Reips for many helpful comments and suggestions on a previous draft of the manuscript.

The *Annual Review of Psychology* is online at http://psych.annualreviews.org

LITERATURE CITED

Bailey RD, Foote WE, Throckmorton B. 2000. Human sexual behavior: a comparison of college and Internet surveys. See Birnbaum 2000b, pp. 141–68

Bandilla W. 2002. Web surveys—an appropriate mode of data collection for the social sciences? See Batinic et al. 2002, pp. 1–6

Bargh JA, McKenna KYA. 2004. The Internet and social life. *Annu. Rev. Psychol.* 55:573–90

Baron J, Siepmann M. 2000. Techniques for creating and using web questionnaires in research and teaching. See Birnbaum 2000b, pp. 235–65

Batinic B, ed. 2000. *Internet für Psychologen.* Göttingen, Ger.: Hogrefe

Batinic B, Reips U-D, Bosnjak M, eds. 2002. *Online Social Sciences.* Göttingen, Ger.: Hogrefe & Huber

Batinic B, Werner A, Gräf L, Bandilla W,

eds. 1999. *Online Research: Methoden, Anwendungen, Ergebnisse.* Göttingen, Ger.: Hogrefe

Birnbaum M. 1998. *SurveyWiz and FactorWiz.* http://psych.fullerton.edu/mbirnbaum/programs/

Birnbaum MH. 1999a. How to show that 9 > 221: collect judgments in a between-subjects design. *Psychol. Methods* 4:243–49

Birnbaum MH. 1999b. Testing critical properties of decision making on the Internet. *Psychol. Sci.* 10:399–407

Birnbaum MH. 1999c. *WWW Research and Decision Making.* Keynote address to German Online Res. Soc. Meet., Nürnberg, Ger.

Birnbaum MH. 2000a. Decision making in the lab and on the Web. See Birnbaum 2000b, pp. 3–34

Birnbaum MH, ed. 2000b. *Psychological Experiments on the Internet.* San Diego: Academic

Birnbaum MH. 2000c. SurveyWiz and FactorWiz: JavaScript Web pages that make HTML forms for research on the Internet. *Behav. Res. Methods Instrum. Comput.* 32:339–46

Birnbaum MH. 2001a. *Introduction to Behavioral Research on the Internet.* Upper Saddle River, NJ: Prentice Hall

Birnbaum MH. 2001b. A Web-based program of research on decision making. See Reips & Bosnjak 2001, pp. 23–55

Birnbaum MH. 2002. Wahrscheinlichkeitslernen. In *Das Experimental-psychologische Praktikum im Labor und WWW*, ed. D Janetzko, M Hildebrand, HA Meyer, pp. 141–51. Göttingen, Ger.: Hogrefe

Birnbaum MH. 2004. Methodological and ethical issues in conducting social psychology research via the Internet. In *Handbook of Methods in Social Psychology*, ed. C Sansone, CC Morf, AT Panter, pp. 359–82. Thousand Oaks, CA: Sage

Birnbaum MH, Martin T. 2003. Generalization across people, procedures, and predictions: violations of stochastic dominance and coalescing. In *Emerging Perspectives on Decision Research*, ed. SL Schneider,

J Shanteau, pp. 84–107. New York: Cambridge Univ. Press

Birnbaum MH, Mellers BA. 1989. Mediated models for the analysis of confounded variables and self-selected samples. *J. Educ. Stat.* 14:146–58

Birnbaum MH, Wakcher SV. 2002. Web-based experiments controlled by JavaScript: an example from probability learning. *Behav. Res. Methods Instrum. Comput.* 34:189–99

Bosnjak M. 2001. Participation in nonrestricted Web surveys: A typology and explanatory model for item non-response. See Reips & Bosnjak 2001, pp. 193–207

Bosnjak M, Batinic B. 2002. Understanding the willingness to participate in online surveys—the case of e-mail questionnaires. See Batinic et al. 2002, pp. 81–92

Breinholt G, Krueger H. 1999. A tutorial on creating logfiles for event-driven applications. *Behav. Res. Methods Instrum. Comput.* 31:410–15

Brenner V. 2002. Generalizability issues in Internet-based survey research: implications for the Internet addiction controversy. See Batinic et al. 2002, pp. 93–113

Buchanan T. 2000. Potential of the Internet for personality research. See Birnbaum 2000b, pp. 121–40

Buchanan T. 2001. Online personality assessment. See Reips & Bosnjak 2001, pp. 57–74

Buchanan T, Smith JL. 1999a. Research on the Internet: validation of a World Wide Web mediated personality scale. *Behav. Res. Methods Instrum. Comput.* 31:565–71

Buchanan T, Smith JL. 1999b. Using the Internet for psychological research: personality testing on the World-Wide Web. *Br. J. Psychol.* 90:125–44

Corkrey R, Parkinson L. 2002. A comparison of four computer-based telephone interviewing methods: getting answers to sensitive questions. *Behav. Res. Methods Instrum. Comput.* 34:354–63

Dillman DA. 2000. *Mail and Internet Surveys: The Tailored Design Method.* New York: Wiley

Dillman DA, Bowker DK. 2001. The Web questionnaire challenge to survey methodologists. See Reips & Bosnjak 2001, pp. 159–78

Döring N. 2002a. *Sozialpsychologie des Internet*. Göttingen, Ger.: Hogrefe

Döring N. 2002b. Studying online love and cyber romance. See Batinic et al. 2002, pp. 333–56

Eichstaedt J. 2001. An inaccurate timing filter for reaction time measurement by JAVA applets implementing Internet-based experiments. *Behav. Res. Methods Instrum. Comput.* 33:179–86

Eichstaedt J. 2002. Measuring differences in preactivation on the Internet: the content category superiority effect. *Exp. Psychol.* 49:283–91

Francis G, Neath I, Surprenant AM. 2000. The cognitive psychology online laboratory. See Birnbaum 2000b, pp. 267–83

Frick A, Bächtiger MT, Reips U-D. 2001. Financial incentives, personal information, and drop-out in online studies. See Reips & Bosnjak 2001, pp. 209–19

Gackenbach J, ed. 1998. *Psychology and the Internet: Intrapersonal, Interpersonal, and Transpersonal Implications*. San Diego: Academic

Gordon MS, Rosenblum LD. 2001. Audiovisual speech Web-lab: an Internet teaching and research laboratory. *Behav. Res. Methods Instrum. Comput.* 33:267–69

Göritz A, Reinhold N, Batinic B. 2002. Online panels. See Batinic et al. 2002, pp. 27–47

Gräf L. 2002. Assessing Internet questionnaires: the online pretest lab. See Batinic et al. 2002, pp. 49–68

Hecht H, Oesker M, Kaiser A, Civelek H, Stecker T. 1999. A perception experiment with time-critical graphics animation on the World Wide Web. *Behav. Res. Methods Instrum. Comput.* 31:439–45

Hertel G, Naumann S, Konradt U, Batinic B. 2002. Personality assessment via Internet: comparing Online and paper-and-pencil questionnaires. See Batinic et al. 2002, pp. 115–33

Hewson CM, Laurent D, Vogel CM. 1996. Proper methodologies for psychological and sociological studies conducted via the Internet. *Behav. Res. Methods Instrum. Comput.* 28:186–91

Horswill MS, Coster ME. 2001. User-controlled photographic animations, photograph-based questions, and questionnaires: three Internet-based instruments for measuring drivers' risk-taking behavior. *Behav. Res. Methods Instrum. Comput.* 33:46–58

Huff D. 1954. *How to Lie with Statistics*. New York: Norton

Janetzko D. 1999. *Statistische Anwendungen im Internet*. Munich: Addison-Wesley

Janetzko D. 2002. Artificial dialogues—dialogue and interview bots for the World Wide Web. See Batinic et al. 2002, pp. 357–64

Janetzko D, Meyer HA, Hildebrand M, eds. 2002. *Das Experimental-psychologische Praktikum im Labor und WWW [A practical course on psychological experimenting in the laboratory and WWW]*. Göttingen, Ger.: Hogrefe

Joinson AN. 1999. Social desirability, anonymity, and Internet-based questionnaires. *Behav. Res. Methods Instrum. Comput.* 31:433–38

Joinson AN. 2002. *Understanding the Psychology of Internet Behaviour: Virtual Worlds, Real Lives*. Basingstoke, Hampshire, UK: Palgrave Macmillian

Knapp F, Heidingsfelder M. 2001. Drop-out analysis: effects of the survey design. See Reips & Bosnjak 2001, pp. 221–30

Krantz JH. 1998. *Psychological Research on the Net*. http://psych.hanover.edu/research/exponnet.html

Krantz JH. 2001. Stimulus delivery on the Web: What can be presented when calibration isn't possible? See Reips & Bosnjak 2001, pp. 113–30

Krantz JH, Ballard J, Scher J. 1997. Comparing the results of laboratory and world-wide web samples on the determinants of female attractiveness. *Behav.*

Res. Methods Instrum. Comput. 29:264–69

Krantz JH, Dalal R. 2000. Validity of Web-based psychological research. See Birnbaum 2000b, pp. 35–60

Kraut R, Patterson M, Lundmark V, Kiesler S, Mukopadhyay T, Scherlis W. 1998. Internet paradox: a social technology that reduces social involvement and psychological well-being? *Am. Psychol.* 53:1017–31

Lange M. 1999. Museum of perception and cognition website: using JavaScript to increase interactivity in web-based presentations. *Behav. Res. Methods Instrum. Comput.* 31:34–45

Laugwitz B. 2001. A Web-experiment on colour harmony principles applied to computer user interface design. See Reips & Bosnjak 2001, pp. 131–45

Lukawetz G. 2002. Empirically quantifying unit-nonresponse-errors in online surveys and suggestions for computational correction methods. See Batinic et al. 2002, pp. 403–15

McClelland G. 2000. *Seeing Statistics.* Florence, KY: Duxbury Press

McGraw KO, Tew MD, Williams JE. 2000a. The integrity of Web-based experiments: Can you trust the data? *Psychol. Sci.* 11:502–6

McGraw KO, Tew MD, Williams JE. 2000b. PsychExps: an on-line psychology laboratory. See Birnbaum 2000b, pp. 219–33

McKenna KYA, Bargh JA. 2000. Plan 9 from cyberspace: the implications of the Internet for personality and social psychology. *Personal. Soc. Psychol. Rev.* 4:57–75

Morrow RH, McKee AJ. 1998. CGI scripts: a strategy for between-subjects experimental group assignment on the World-Wide Web. *Behav. Res. Methods Instrum. Comput.* 30:306–8

Mueller JH, Jacobsen DM, Schwarzer R. 2000. What are computing experiences good for: a case study in on-line research. See Birnbaum 2000b, pp. 195–216

Musch J. 2000. Die Geschichte des Netzes: Ein historischer Abriss. See Batinic 2000, pp. 15–37

Musch J, Broeder A, Klauer KC. 2001. Improving survey research on the World-Wide Web using the randomized response technique. See Reips & Bosnjak 2001, pp. 179–92

Musch J, Klauer KC. 2002. Psychological experimenting on the World Wide Web: investigating context effects in syllogistic reasoning. See Batinic et al. 2002, pp. 181–212

Musch J, Reips U-D. 2000. A brief history of Web experimenting. See Birnbaum 2000b, pp. 61–87

O'Neil KM, Penrod SD. 2001. Methodological variables in Web-based research that may affect results: sample type, monetary incentives, and personal information. *Behav. Res. Methods Instrum. Comput.* 33:226–33

Pagani D, Lombardi L. 2000. An intercultural examination of facial features communicating surprise. See Birnbaum 2000b, pp. 169–94

Pasveer KA, Ellard JH. 1998. The making of a personality inventory: help from the WWW. *Behav. Res. Methods Instrum. Comput.* 30:309–13

Piper AI. 1998. Conducting social science laboratory experiments on the World Wide Web. *Libr. Inf. Sci. Res.* 20:5–21

Pohl RF, Bender M, Lachmann G. 2002. Hindsight bias around the world. *Exp. Psychol.* 49:270–82

Reips U-D. 1995. *Web Experimental Psychology Lab.* http://www.psychologie.unizh.ch/genpsy/Ulf/Lab/WebExpPsyLab.html

Reips U-D. 1997. Das psychologische Experimentieren im Internet. In *Internet für Psychologen*, ed. B Batinic, pp. 245–65. Göttingen, Ger.: Hogrefe

Reips U-D. 2000. The Web experiment method: advantages, disadvantages, and solutions. See Birnbaum 2000b, pp. 89–117

Reips U-D. 2001a. Merging field and institution: running a Web laboratory. See Reips & Bosnjak 2001, pp. 1–22

Reips U-D. 2001b. The Web experimental psychology lab: five years of data collection on the Internet. *Behav. Res. Methods Instrum. Comput.* 33:201–11

Reips U-D. 2002a. Context effects in Web surveys. See Batinic et al. 2002, pp. 69–79

Reips U-D. 2002b. Standards for Internet experimenting. *Exp. Psychol.* 49:243–56

Reips U-D. 2002c. Theory and techniques of conducting Web experiments. See Batinic et al. 2002, pp. 219–49

Reips U-D. 2002d. Internet-based psychological experimenting: five dos and five don'ts. *Soc. Sci. Comput. Rev.* 20:241–49

Reips U-D, Bosnjak M, eds. 2001. *Dimensions of Internet Science.* Lengerich, Ger.: Pabst Sci.

Reips U-D, Neuhaus C. 2002. WEXTOR: a Web-based tool for generating and visualizing experimental designs and procedures. *Behav. Res. Methods Instrum. Comput.* 34:234–40

Ruppertsberg AI, Givaty G, Van Veen HAHC, Bülthoff H. 2001. Games as research tools for visual perception over the Internet. See Reips & Bosnjak 2001, pp. 147–58

Sassenberg K, Kreutz S. 2002. Online research and anonymity. See Batinic et al. 2002, pp. 213–27

Schiano DJ. 1997. Convergent methodologies in cyber-psychology: a case study. *Behav. Res. Methods Instrum. Comput.* 29:270–73

Schillewaert N, Langerak F, Duhamel T. 1998. Non-probability sampling for WWW surveys: a comparison of methods. *J. Mark. Res. Soc.* 40:307–22

Schmidt WC. 1997a. World-Wide Web survey research: benefits, potential problems, and solutions. *Behav. Res. Methods Instrum. Comput.* 29:274–79

Schmidt WC. 1997b. World-Wide Web survey research made easy with WWW Survey Assistant. *Behav. Res. Methods Instrum. Comput.* 29:303–4

Schmidt WC. 2000. The server-side of psychology web experiments. See Birnbaum 2000b, pp. 285–310

Schmidt WC. 2001. Presentation accuracy of Web animation methods. *Behav. Res. Methods Instrum. Comput.* 33:187–200

Schmidt WC, Hoffman R, MacDonald J. 1997. Operate your own World-Wide Web server. *Behav. Res. Methods Instrum. Comput.* 29:189–93

Schwartz A. 1998. Tutorial: PERL, a psychologically efficient reformatting language. *Behav. Res. Methods Instrum. Comput.* 30:605–9

Schwarz S, Reips U-D. 2001. CGI versus JavaScript: a Web experiment on the reversed hindsight bias. See Reips & Bosnjak 2001, pp. 75–90

Smith MA, Leigh B. 1997. Virtual subjects: using the Internet as an alternative source of subjects and research environment. *Behav. Res. Methods Instrum. Comput.* 29:496–505

Stanton JM. 1998. An empirical assessment of data collection using the Internet. *Pers. Psychol.* 51:709–25

Stevenson AK, Francis G, Kim H. 1999. Java experiments for introductory cognitive psychology courses. *Behav. Res. Methods Instrum. Comput.* 31:99–106

Suler J. 1996/2003. *The Psychology of Cyberspace.* http://www.rider.edu/~suler/psycyber/psycyber.html

Tourangeau R. 2004. Survey research and societal change. *Annu. Rev. Psychol.* 55:775–801

Tuten TL, Urban DJ, Bosnjak M. 2002. Internet surveys and data quality: a review. See Batinic et al. 2002, pp. 7–26

Tversky A, Kahneman D. 1992. Advances in prospect theory: cumulative representation of uncertainty. *J. Risk Uncertain.* 5:297–323

Van Veen HAHC, Bülthoff HH, Givaty G. 1998. Psychophysics tests on the Internet: an evaluation. *Perception* S27:179

Voracek M, Stieger S, Gindl A. 2001. Online replication of evolutionary psychological evidence: sex differences in sexual jealousy in imagined scenarios of mate's sexual versus emotional infidelity. See Reips & Bosnjak 2001, pp. 91–112

Wallace PM. 2001. *The Psychology of the Internet.* Cambridge, UK: Cambridge Univ. Press

Welch N, Krantz JH. 1996. The World-Wide Web as a medium for psychoacoustical demonstrations and experiments: experience and results. *Behav. Res. Methods Instrum. Comput.* 28:192–96

Welker M. 2001. E-mail surveys: non-response figures reflected. See Reips & Bosnjak 2001, pp. 231–38

White RJ, Hammer CA. 2000. Quiz-o-matic: a free Web-based tool for construction of self-scoring on-line quizzes. *Behav. Res. Methods Instrum. Comput.* 32:250–53

Wilhelm O, McKnight PE. 2002. Ability and achievement testing on the World Wide Web. See Batinic et al. 2002, pp. 151–80

Williams JE, McGraw KO, Tew MD. 1999. Undergraduate labs and computers: the case for PsychExps. *Behav. Res. Methods Instrum. Comput.* 31:287–91

AUTHOR INDEX

SUBJECT INDEX

A

Abandonment anxiety
  integrative science of the
  person and, 14
Abortion
  gender in psychology and,
  535
Abuses
  mediated politics and
  citizenship in the
  twenty-first century,
  556–58
Academic achievement
  intergenerational transfer
  of psychosocial risk and,
  351–52
Accommodation
  culture and psychology,
  700
Acculturation
  development in the family
  and, 384
  immigrant family
  development
  in the family and,
  384
Acetylcholine
  hypocretin and,
  130–31
Achievement motivation
  gender in psychology and,
  523–24
Acoustic signal
  speech perception and,
  149–73
Action potentials
  bridging brain and
  behavior, 30
Actions
  developmental psychology
  and functional

neuroimaging, 87, 90, 93,
  97, 99, 102, 104, 108,
  110, 115–16
Activation factor
  neurobiology of
  consolidations and, 58–59
Acute stress
  coping and, 745–68
Adaptation
  creativity and, 673, 676
  culture and psychology,
  701
  development in the family
  and, 384
  group performance and
  decision making, 623, 643
  integrative science of the
  person and, 10, 18
  teaching of subject matter
  and, 727–28
Addiction
  motivational influences on
  smoking, 463–84
Additive Gaussian noise
  variation
  object perception as
  Bayesian inference and,
  287–88
Adenylate cyclase
  neurobiology of
  consolidations and,
  58–59
Adjective check list
  creativity and, 671
Adolescents
  creativity and, 667
  development in the family
  and, 383
  developmental psychology
  and functional
  neuroimaging, 108

gender in psychology and,
  524
  intergenerational transfer
  of psychosocial risk and,
  333, 338, 340–41
  motivational influences on
  smoking, 464–66
  schizophrenia and, 401–24
Advisors
  parents as
  development in the
  family and, 365, 371
Affect
  coping and, 745–68
  culture and psychology,
  694
  integrative science of the
  person and, 14–16
  social influence and,
  592–94
Affect infusion model
  social influence and, 593
Affiliation
  Internet and social life,
  572–85
  social influence and, 591,
  598–602, 606, 609–11,
  613
Affirmation
  social
  gender in psychology
  and, 524–25
African Americans
  development in the family
  and, 381–83, 390
  gender in psychology and,
  526, 532, 534–35, 537
  mediated politics and
  citizenship in the
  twenty-first century, 562
  social influence and, 607

877

Cumulative Indexes

CONTRIBUTING AUTHORS, VOLUMES 45–55

CHAPTER TITLES, VOLUMES 45–55

Clinical and Counseling Psychology: Specialized Modes of Therapy

Cognitive Processes

Community Psychology

Genetics of Behavior
See BIOLOGICAL PSYCHOLOGY

Gerontology (Maturity and Aging)
See DEVELOPMENTAL PSYCHOLOGY

Health Psychology

Industrial Psychology

Learning and Memory

Psychopharmacology
See BIOLOGICAL PSYCHOLOGY

Research Methodology

Sleep
See BIOLOGICAL PSYCHOLOGY

Social Psychology

Social Psychology: Attitude Structure

Social Psychology: Collective Social

BARGAINING, NEGOTIATION, CONFLICT, SOCIAL JUSTICE

Special Topics

Special Topics in Psychopathology: Language and Communication

Timely Topics

Vision